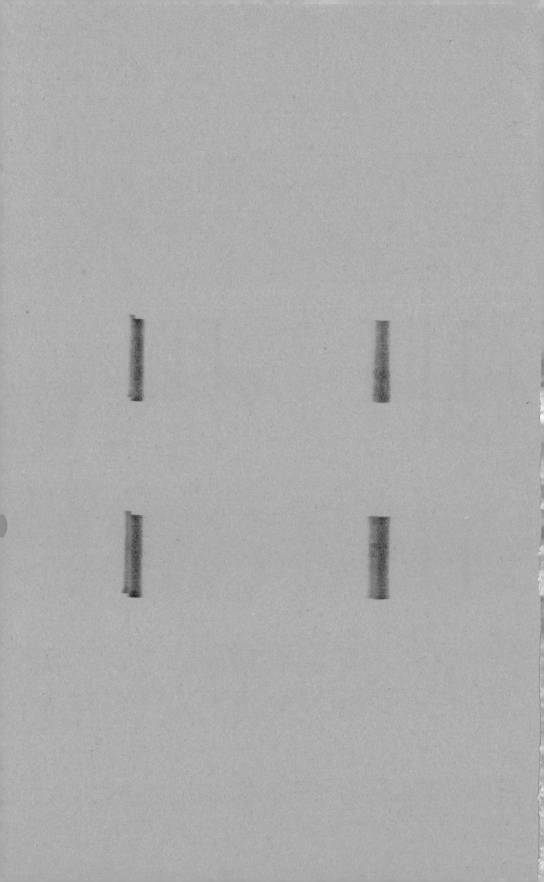

# WHY YOU LIKE IT

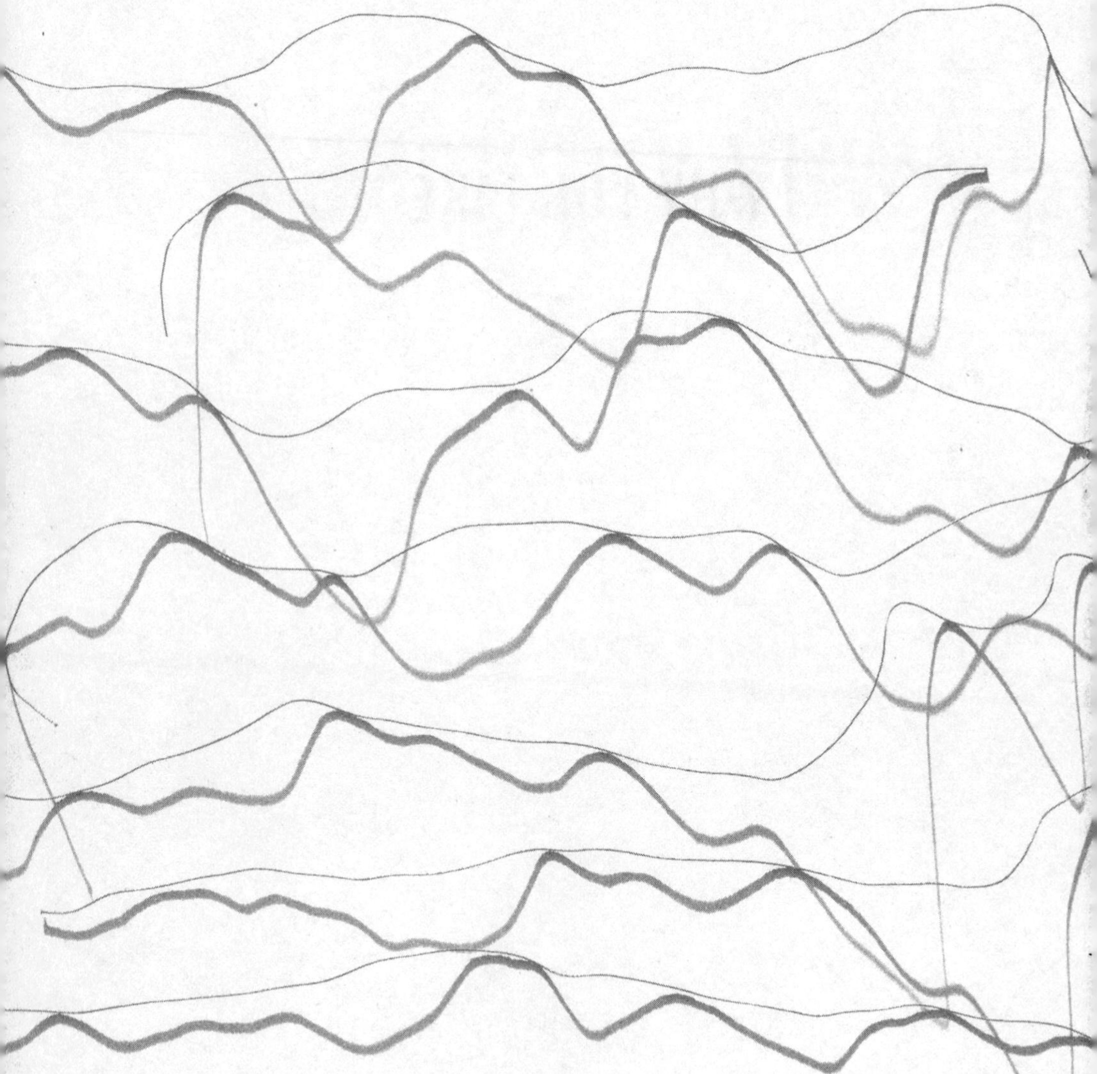

# WHY YOU LIKE IT

•••

*The Science and*
*Culture of Musical Taste*

NOLAN GASSER

FLATIRON
BOOKS
NEW YORK

## NOTE

Frequent reference is made in this book to the companion website:

http://www.WhyYouLikeIt.com

All information on the website, whether or not related to this book, is the property of the author. Flatiron Books has no relation to, or responsibility for, the WhyYouLikeIt website or any of its content.



www.flatironbooks.com

Designed by Susan Walsh

Frontispiece art by Susan Walsh

Figures courtesy of the author

The Library of Congress Cataloging-in-Publication Data is available upon request.

ISBN 978-1-250-05719-8 (hardcover)
ISBN 978-1-250-05720-4 (ebook)

Our books may be purchased in bulk for promotional, educational, or business use. Please contact your local bookseller or the Macmillan Corporate and Premium Sales Department at 1-800-221-7945, extension 5442, or by email at MacmillanSpecialMarkets@macmillan.com.

First Edition: April 2019

10 9 8 7 6 5 4 3 2 1

*For Lynn, Camille, and Preston*

# CONTENTS

# PREFACE

When I was twenty-three, my buddy Glenn Georgieff and I sold all of our belongings and flew to Paris, where I spent the next two years studying composition, playing jazz, and searching for answers to questions I hadn't quite yet formulated. By the end of the first year, we'd built up a pretty good circle of friends, mainly other expats but also a few *bons Parisiens*. During one of our regular dinner *soirées*, one of our French friends stood up, a few glasses of Beaujolais in, and proposed a game where she would go around the room and align each person with a literary genre that matched their personality. To Glenn, at that moment an aspiring novelist with bohemian tendencies, she tagged "*un roman*" (a novel); to another, a rather quirky and colorful girl in our company, she assigned a haiku. She then turned to me and stared a while; finally she said, "I've got it: you're . . . an encyclopedia."

In truth, I felt a bit insulted: As the one active artist in the bunch, shouldn't I be aligned with something more romantic, more aesthetic—I don't know, maybe a sonnet, or an epic poem? And while I still think I got shortchanged in my literary *nom de guerre*, I must admit that there was—and is—truth there. Beyond my creative aspirations, I have always been prone to want to see the bigger picture, the story behind the story, the history that gives rise to the present reality. And so, as clichéd as it sounds, this book is literally decades in the making—a chance for me to be encyclopedic for a change, to wax comprehensive about the topic that has defined me since I first plucked out "Three Blind Mice" on the piano by ear, at the age of four: music.

In the years since Paris, I've managed to successfully formulate a good many of the questions I couldn't quite articulate in my youth. I've even managed to find a few satisfying answers—about music, if not about life in general. This book offers the most comprehensive evidence to this former claim: my best attempt to explain not just what music is, but why it matters to us.

Enabling my audacity to tell this story have been a few facts along the way. The first is my lifelong commitment to music education—formally via a bachelor's degree in piano and composition, a master's degree in composition, and a PhD in musicology; and informally via perpetual self-study in myriad music-intersecting disciplines: history, philosophy, physics, neuroscience, sociology, and psychology.

The second source of this audacity is my similarly eclectic approach as a composer and pianist—working across multiple styles, or "species," as I'll soon label them, from practically my earliest attempts. Even today, most of my compositional and performance efforts will inevitably involve mixing a bit of this style and a bit of that style, in search of some fresh musical expression.

The third and perhaps most consequential source in enabling this book is the good fortune I gained in 2000—when I was tapped to be the chief musicologist for a tech start-up: the company now called Pandora. Never would I have predicted in 2000 that this company, and its "Music Genome Project"—of which I am the architect—would become so widely utilized by music lovers throughout the US and beyond, and so influential in the digital music revolution of the early 2000s. This fortuitous opportunity has no doubt given me the bona fides to write a book about musical taste. But more practically, my work at Pandora enabled me to dig into all realms of music more deeply than I would have otherwise; it forced me to approach musical analysis and musicology in ways I hadn't previously; and it allowed me to confront headlong a profound mystery I hadn't even considered before: What is musical taste and where does it come from?

Indeed, I liken this book to a "mystery novel"—a musical whodunit: only at the end will you truly know the whys and wherefores of your musical taste.

*Why You Like It* is indeed about musical taste, but it also touches upon many other subjects that skirt along its edges. As I like to say, discussing musical taste gives me the opportunity to talk about music in general, since every dimension of music—its history, theory, practice, aesthetics, science, culture, psychology, etc.—impacts what music we like and why we like it. While this presents terrific opportunities for an "encyclopedic" guy like me, it also poses serious challenges—not least the daunting need to synthesize and explain *everything* related to music. This accounts for the wide scope of topics tackled in this book, for better or worse. Yet, to the degree that I've succeeded in my efforts, this broad approach affords a potentially rich bounty to lay nonmusician readers of this book: to not only better understand their musical taste, but also to heighten—even change—how they listen to, and think about, music. This is the case, moreover, whether your tastes are limited to the boundaries of pop, rock, jazz, hip hop, electronica, world music, or classical—or whether, like me, they transcend multiple musical domains.

This book is first and foremost aimed at the "average" music lover, not the trained musician. To be fair, it skews a bit toward those with a modicum of musical background—having taken piano lessons as a child, for example. It should also be noted that this book cites the names of lots and lots of musicians and composers—from every era and genre. While in many cases these names will be accompanied by a brief contextual description, in many others they will not—namely, when the person is particularly prominent within the genre in question. If you encounter a stand-alone name you are unfamiliar with, do not panic: you are instead kindly invited to look it up on Wikipedia, etc.; after all, learning more about famous musicians should be a welcome goal of anyone exploring musical taste.

However, rest assured that prior music training is not a prerequisite. Nor is this book aimed at academics or professionals in the fields of anthropology, physics, neuroscience, sociology, or psychology—although some broad awareness in one or more of these fields won't hurt. At the same time, it is my sincere hope that professional musicians, as well as academics in science, sociology, or psychology, will gain something of value from this book: I know I did in researching and writing it.

There is, of course, a rich tradition of technical books about music written by musicians—including composers—aimed at lay readers. Standing in the wake of related efforts by giants like Leonard Bernstein (*The Joy of Music*, *The Unanswered Question: Six Talks at Harvard*), Aaron Copland (*What to Listen for in Music*), and Virgil Thomson (*The Art of Judging Music*)—not to mention celebrated academics like Dan Levitin, Elizabeth Hellmuth Margulis, and David Huron—I am humbled and a bit petrified. I've done my best to learn from their superb models in combining technical discussions with clear examples, personal stories, and humor.

My apprehension at not living up to the high bar of my models, however, has been superseded by my passion to share this story of music and musical taste with those willing to pick up this book. For years, indeed, I would tell friends and strangers alike: "Someday I'm going to write a big book about music." Remarkably, that someday actually happened.

# INTRODUCTION

## *In the Ear of the Beholder*

In reviewing a highly anticipated concert by the New York Philharmonic, a prominent New York music critic wrote the following:

> [This] music is the dreariest kind of rubbish. Does anybody for a moment doubt that [the composer] would not write such chaotic, meaningless, cacophonous, ungrammatical stuff, if he could invent a melody?

To whom is this offended music critic referring: Arnold Schoenberg—the father of atonal and 12-tone music? Karlheinz Stockhausen—the pioneer of post-WWII avant-garde classical music? John Cage—the guru of 1950s experimental music? Frank Zappa—the iconoclast of rock and classical sound collage? . . . Actually, would you believe the critic was talking about Claude Debussy—the venerated composer of "Clair de lune"? Those familiar with Nicolas Slonimsky's *Lexicon of Musical Invective*, his entertaining anthology of critical assaults on the music of the "Great Masters," will recognize that such vicious attacks of the past are commonly aimed at composers and works held today as the most critically acclaimed and widely beloved. In this case, the "dean" of New York music critics, Henry Krehbiel, was excoriating Debussy's orchestral tone poem *La Mer* in its American premiere in March 1907. Slonimsky's *Lexicon* is packed with such juicy epithets that today make us shake our heads in bemusement: Beethoven's symphonies are called "hideous," "injurious," and "barbarous"; music by Brahms labeled "wanton," "tiresome," and "intolerable"—by no less than George Bernard Shaw; Mahler's works called "grotesque," "simplistic," and "ponderous."[1]

Beyond the comfort that these now "blasphemous" rebukes offer a contemporary composer who receives a stinging review, they likewise display the general human tendency to recoil from the new and unfamiliar: "Music is an art-in-progress," Slonimsky writes, and what today is considered bizarre and unacceptable often becomes a prized model tomorrow. This is true, of course, not only of classical works of the nineteenth and twentieth centuries, but extends back to Plato in his rails against the depravity of young kithara players in the fourth century BCE,[2] and forward to a steady dismissal of virtually every musical movement of the past hundred years, from jazz to rock to hip hop and beyond; even the Beatles were deemed "a catastrophe, a preposterous farrago of Valentine-card romantic sentiments" by *Newsweek* magazine in 1964.[3]

The takeaway in all this, however, is not just that critics often get it wrong, though they do; nor is it merely that time has a way of relegating initial critical assessments as comically shortsighted, though it often does. Another key point here is that opinions on music vary widely—that for myriad reasons, one person's favorite is another's rubbish. It may be that on his deathbed in 1923, Krehbiel regretted his rash assessment of *La Mer* and now held it as a masterpiece, or that the *Newsweek* Beatle-disparager later became the first on his block to buy *Sgt. Pepper*—though we'll likely never know in these cases; it actually *is* true, however, that Shaw later disavowed his attacks on Brahms, calling them "my only mistake."[4]

But though it may—and often does—change over time, at any one moment, each of us has our own intensely personal and deeply felt musical taste. Indeed, there are many today—including those with advanced musical training—who dislike listening to Beethoven (too melodramatic) or Brahms (too dour) or Mahler (too sentimental), even if they can intellectually concede their genius and historical importance. Mark Twain's witty gem that "Wagner's music is better than it sounds" can probably apply to most of us in our preferred musical diet: "Yeah, I know jazz is cool, but I just don't get it." "Sure, everyone loves Bruce Springsteen, but I never liked his songs." "My friends all love house music, but I find it annoying" . . . I can hear you fill in your own version as I type this. The truth is that it's really only "great music" if it's "great" to you; otherwise it's like that movie that everyone raves about, but which you found weak: you might not be surprised it won an Oscar, but you wouldn't want to watch it again.

Without doubt, music has great power over us, and very few have ever been heard to utter the words "I hate music." The music we love is a significant part of who we are, and the passion we feel toward our favorite songs, singers, bands, and composers is rivaled only by what we offer to our family and closest friends—if that! But why is this so? Why do we love some musical styles and dislike others? What does the music we love reveal about our personality? How can we discover more music that fits our musical profile? And why do some songs send shivers down our spine or put a spring in our step, while others leave us cold or put us in a foul mood?

These are a few of the tantalizing questions regarding the sources, nature, and implications of our own, personal musical taste that I will be tackling in this book. In the pages that follow, I will attempt to provide a framework through which we can begin to understand why we like the music we do. I will pursue this by relating music to a wide array of associated topics—mathematics, physics, neuroscience, biology, evolution, culture, sociology, and psychology—as well as delving into the technical aspects of the music itself. This may all seem a daunting exercise, for both writer and reader, but such is necessary if we hope to properly understand our musical taste, our musical "being."

At the very least, this book will offer a colorful and eclectic exploration into the rich diversity of music and its surprisingly deep connections to the world around and within us. Beyond merely eliciting interesting information, however, it also, I hope, will explain how gaining a better understanding of our musical taste is a key to living a healthier and more productive life. Let's get started!

## What Is Musical Taste?

Before launching too deeply into the whys and wherefores of your musical taste, it will be useful to define exactly what is meant by the expression, at least in the context of this book. On a surface level, one's "musical taste" refers to the music that aligns with one's personal preferences—and hence the commonly used term "musical preferences" as a more formal equivalent, particularly in academic literature. We tend to listen to music that we like, that moves us positively on an emotional and/or intellectual level, and that generally makes us feel good, more than we do music that has the opposite effect—or so we hope. And yet a good percentage of our musical interactions are hardly so straightforward, or so directly tied to our conscious intentions.

According to research by the social psychologists Matthias Mehl and James Pennebaker, the average person listens to music about 14 percent of their waking lives—about the same as spent watching television, and about half as much as engaged in conversation.[5] Assuming eight hours of sleep, that's two and a half hours a day, each and every day—or over fifteen hours a week; for most of us, moreover, this number is drastically lower than our reality. Not all of this music, of course, is material we consciously select, or even enjoy, and thus our musical "barometer" is constantly challenged and in need of calibration.

For example:

You start your day going to spin class at the gym and sweat to DJ mixes of hip hop and pop tunes by Lil John, the Black Eyed Peas, Taylor Swift, and Michael Jackson; you drive to work and flip between radio stations playing classic rock by the Eagles, Steely Dan, and Lynyrd Skynyrd, and "alt-rock" songs by Panic! at the Disco, the Killers, and Imagine Dragons; the lobby at work pipes in old-school R&B tunes by Al Green, Otis Redding, and Aretha Franklin; a run to the supermarket yields "standards" by Frank Sinatra, Michael Bublé, and Etta James; and a dinner gathering with friends at an Italian restaurant provides a soundtrack of old standbys by Louis Prima, Luciano Pavarotti, and Dean Martin. Only then do you return home and put on a CD or digital playlist of *your* choice—perhaps Tchaikovsky or Maroon 5 or Fela Kuti—before retiring for the night.

The hypothetical scenario above underscores the fact that for most of us, the music we listen to each day is a complex amalgam of voluntary and involuntary encounters, and is aligned with the many diverse contexts and circumstances of our daily lives: practical (motivation at the gym), functional (getting to work), environmental (at the grocery store), social (at the restaurant), and leisure (choosing a CD at home), among others. As such, our "musical taste" is continually being engaged and queried as we pursue our day-to-day routines and responsibilities, whether we're consciously aware of it or not. This in turn affords us an opportunity: to bolster our sensitivity to and critical awareness of the music we hear, to engage more deliberately with the listening experience, and to enhance the scope and clarity by which we define the music we like and don't like. These are in fact among the chief goals of this book—for at least some of the time, and to at least some degree more than is currently the case. Put another way, the goal of this book is not only to inform the nature of your musical taste, but also to provide you with the tools to enhance it.

## Good versus Bad Taste

It should be noted, however, that the sense in which the expression "musical taste" is discussed here stands in contrast to another common understanding—where the notion of "taste" is subsumed under the domain of aesthetics and carries with it a more absolute and objective connotation. In this regard, one's "taste"—musical and otherwise—is viewed as a reflection of one's sophistication, culture, and breeding, as well as one's ability to perceive the subtleties of beauty and morality within an art object.

This belief that "true" works of art possess *objective* qualities that a moral, educated individual can perceive and ought to uphold has roots in Plato's *Republic*, but found particular enthusiasm in the eighteenth century, notably in the writings of Kant and Hume. The latter's highly influential "On the Standard of Taste" (1757) argued that although opinions toward artworks may be subjective, the works themselves reveal the degree to which they do or don't meet the standards of being truly praiseworthy. These standards are based on a set of "rules" that are grounded in moral judgments. Given, however, that the average person is drawn only to "the grosser and more palpable qualities of the object," it is up to a "true" critic to identify a worthy work of art. Hume admits individual and cultural preferences, but insists that only with adequate experience and practice can anyone develop "good" taste.[6]

To cite a specific application of this perspective to music, the influential nineteenth-century British periodical *The Musical World* published an article entitled "On Musical Taste" in 1838. Here the anonymous writer, relying on presumably objective grounds, deigns to reveal to us the identity of the "greatest" of all composers. The "best music," he writes, "is composed with a view of exciting in our minds the noblest emotions"—namely those "connected with the adoration of the Supreme Being. Tried by this test, Handel is the greatest of composers."[7]

That the empirical "truth" regarding the quality of a given composer can be precisely determined—in this case, that of the Baroque master George Frideric Handel—seems beyond question in this writer's mind. The only variable, then, is the degree to which an individual listener has successfully cultivated the "taste" required to judge the art of music, and thus distinguish "gold from tinsel."[8]

Although such absolutist claims of a single standard of taste have yielded in our own time to more broad-minded beliefs about subjective artistic judgment, conceptual descendants of Hume survive in the still common notion of "good" versus "bad" taste, and of "high" versus "low" art. In intellectual thought, such discussions have generally moved from philosophy to sociology and psychology, where taste is deemed a product of one's social class, education, and wealth—and can unduly influence how we perceive others as well as ourselves. Much more on this, as pertains to music, will be discussed in Interlude F.

And while I myself would unapologetically assert a higher artistic value for some musical works over others—J. S. Bach's *St. Matthew Passion* over Psy's "Gangnam Style," to cite an extreme case—I would also quickly admit that such a judgment is ultimately a matter of *my* opinion. That this opinion would be shared by a large—perhaps overwhelming and historically based—number of other people makes it common wisdom, but it does not make it "true" in some objective, empirical sense; undoubtedly, there are those—among the billion-plus who watched the video—who would assign the contemporary K-pop dance song, with its infectious riffs and upbeat grooves, a higher aesthetic value than the eighteenth-century German sacred oratorio, with its ornate obbligatos and lilting arias—even if I'd want to yell at them.

By contrast, one *can* usually claim some objective distinction between one musical work and another when it comes to artistic craft, technical sophistication, or formal scope, etc. That is, a three-and-a-half-minute pop song for one singer and four-piece band using repeating patterns of three or four chords is clearly *less* sophisticated than a two-and-a-half-*hour*-long work for orchestra, chorus, and soloists divided into multiple movements using complex, ever-changing harmonies and dazzling displays of counterpoint (multiple voice parts moving simultaneously). On this front, Bach would beat Psy hands down. But impressive craft is by no means a guarantor of aesthetic value.

In the end, however, such arguments are extraneous to the discussion of this book. The "truth" is that each of us at any given moment likes some musical works and dislikes others, and telling the person who loves "Gangnam Style" that he has "bad taste" will probably only piss him off—and not get him to change his opinion. More useful is for each of us to better understand the nature of our own current preferences, including the musical elements that underlie them, in order to continually enhance and expand our musical universe—perhaps even to the point of liking the *St. Matthew Passion*, though perhaps not.

My own hesitation to pass any "elitist" judgment on someone else's aesthetic sensibility, regardless of how convinced I am of mine, is surely an outgrowth of my egalitarian American roots, and this nation's long-standing emphasis on freedom of opinion and expression. A case in point is a mid-nineteenth-century passage from the *Spirit of the Times* newspaper (New York, 1854), where an author going by the name of "Vale" defends against those who decry "there is no musical taste in America" by noting: "With music, as with taste, there is no standard. It is something better felt than described. The best is unwritten, but lies 'scored' deep in the hearts of all breathing creatures."[9]

Vale's claim is surely derived from the ancient Latin idiom "*De gustibus non est disputandum*" (In matters of taste, there can be no disputes), implying that everyone's taste is in the end subjective, and thus arguing "right" or "wrong" is futile. This doesn't mean that we don't or even that we shouldn't debate, but rather that such arguments are unlikely to sway another's opinion. The better discussion is an internal one: What is my current musical taste, and what am I going to do about it?

## The Definition

With all that as prelude, I am now ready to present my definition of "musical taste," formulated expressly for this book. To wit:

> **Musical taste** is the full mix of musical and cultural dimensions—from the macro level of genre, style, and era to the micro level of distinct musicological attributes—that at any given moment and in any particular configuration correspond to an individual's liking and appreciation.

This is admittedly a bit dense, so let's break it down a bit to provide more clarity.

By "the full mix of musical and cultural dimensions," I mean *every* conceivable element or parameter of a song or work that gives it its identity.* These

* I readily acknowledge that the term "**song**" is commonly used (e.g., by Pandora, Spotify, Apple, etc.) to indicate *any* piece of music, whether sung or not. However, I'd prefer to adhere to a stricter usage: that a song is a short *vocal* work, whether folk, pop, classical, etc. As such, the term is, to my mind, inappro-

include, on the one hand, the surface or *metadata* (data about data) elements—genre, style, era, artist, album, sales, chart history, etc.—that provide contextual information but say nothing precisely about how the music actually sounds. On the other hand, there are the distinct *musicological* elements of sound, melody, harmony, rhythm, etc., that can only be fully derived by analysis, and which often defy or at least challenge expectations of genre, style, and the like. Both sides of the equation—and all those in between—factor into what defines and determines one's musical taste.

Next, our definition of musical taste does not assume or advocate for a single, uniform, unyielding musical taste for any individual, but rather recognizes that what is deemed a "great" or "perfect" song at one moment—e.g., at the gym—may be deemed "bad" or "wrong" at another—e.g., at a dinner party or at home before bedtime. In part this is due to the appropriateness of the musical content for that time, place, or function, but it may also be a product of the way our ears and our brains interpret or experience the music at that moment for any number of reasons—where what was pleasing at 10 a.m. that morning is suddenly annoying at 9 p.m. At the same time, our definition acknowledges that our musical taste is by no means static throughout our lifetime: much of what we loved as kids may by adulthood seem banal; certainly, much of the music we love in our thirties or forties would have been deemed boring or unintelligible during our teen years, etc. Indeed, by virtue of our development, our experience, our education, and our attitudes, our musical taste is constantly evolving and changing—as well it should.

Finally, the reasons why we gravitate toward, or away from, a particular song or work are complex, and may stem from "any configuration" of its identity—whether on the "macro" or "micro" levels. That is, our preference for a given song may arise from its broad associations with a favorite genre, subgenre, era, etc.—e.g., "I love 1950s Afro-Cuban jazz"; or from a purely musicological element that transcends genre—e.g., "I love dense vocal arrangements." To be sure, musical preferences will often arise through a common mix of macro and micro factors—e.g., Afro-Cuban jazz and active, syncopated Latin percussion; Broadway and dense vocal arrangements, etc.—but not always. One may generally dislike hip hop, for example, but enjoy a specific hip hop song that has an attractive chorus melody or instrumental riff, just as one may generally like reggae but dislike a specific reggae song by virtue of its offensive lyrics or "trite" melody. It is for such reasons that a key argument of this book is that we often do ourselves a disservice by reducing our conception of music to broad genre labels like "rock,"

---

priately applied to a purely *instrumental* composition (a Chopin nocturne, a Miles Davis track, etc.) or to vocal music whose scope extends beyond the modest connotation of a "song" (an opera, etc.). To those latter, therefore, I'll adopt the word "work," as generic as it may be. Indeed, at times I'll need to use both terms together, as "songs and works"—which I prefer to the occasionally used, though equally generic, term "musics."

"jazz," "classical," etc., despite their convenience.

It goes without saying that a song that matches our musical taste is one that we like. But the definition of "musical taste" in this book seeks a deeper reality, namely that there is something within the music itself that inspires a degree of appreciation—a response, even if unconsciously registered, of recognition and admiration. As will be discussed in the chapters ahead, music operates vibrantly on an emotional level within us, but there cannot be true preference if there is not also a practical, technical, and intellectual dimension that registers favorably to our ears and brain—whether or not a listener could articulate or define it. That is, if you are to truly understand "why you like it," you also need to know—at least to some degree—*what* you like and *why* you might appreciate it.

## The Road Ahead

As suggested above, this book attempts to take a 360-degree view of musical taste, incorporating insights gained from science, sociology, and psychology, as well as from music history, music theory, and musicology. In doing so, however, I've adopted a somewhat unorthodox sequence and structure for this book.

At the broadest level, the contents of the book can be divided into two categories: purely musical and "extramusical"—meaning disciplines (science, sociology, psychology, etc.) that likewise have application beyond music. Rather than present these categories separately and in sequence, however, I've opted to intersect them: generally two purely musical chapters per one extramusical chapter. This pattern will enable the reader to see the "mystery novel" of their musical taste unfold gradually through both musical and extramusical topics—which makes sense, since these two categories play such complementary roles in defining it.

In devising the precise sequence of this integration, moreover, I recognized an elegant and successive logic that was initially unanticipated. The details of this logic will be best understood in the course of reading, but I can preview it here by summarizing the actual sequence of chapters and "interludes"—as I call those chapters dedicated to the extramusical topics.

Given the disposition of chapters and interludes, the book proceeds in eight parts:

*Part One, "A Gift of the Gods,"* begins with two chapters that introduce the musicological basis of your musical taste—meaning the details of the musical discourse that can be identified through trained analysis and careful listening—whether or not you, the listener, can "hear" them in action. After providing a brief orientation on how this exploration will unfold (Chapter 2), we'll get officially started with a breakdown of the first of five musical parameters: melody (Chapter

3). We'll then be ready for our first extramusical discussion (Interlude A)—that introduces the very origins of our musicality and musical taste, and tackles the prickly question of whether or not music was an adaptive trait in our evolution.

*Part Two, "Bar Bands in Andromeda,"* continues the step-by-step exploration of music analysis with discussions on harmony (Chapter 4) and rhythm (Chapter 5). These, especially the account on harmony, will then provide a useful backdrop to our second extramusical topic (Interlude B)—which reviews the well-established and intimate links between what we experience as music and some fundamental realities of mathematics and physics.

*Part Three, "Unity and Heterogeneity,"* concludes the analytical portion of our purely musical chapters, with discussions on the parameters of form (Chapter 6) and sound (Chapter 7). With our musicological survey complete, we'll be ready to tackle the most involved extramusical discussion (Interlude C)—an overview of the currently exploding field of musical neuroscience, revealing how the ear and brain come to apply meaning to sound stimuli, including the miraculous neurological processes underlying music listening.

*Part Four, "Musical Metaphors,"* utilizes the knowledge gained in the musicological survey chapters to begin exploring actual musical taste. We begin by employing the metaphor of the "musical genotype"—based on seven fictional music lovers, each with a penchant for a distinct realm, or "species," of music. An introduction to the genotype concept (Chapter 8) is followed by our first exemplar, aligned with pop music (Chapter 9). The commonplace use of repetition and patterns in the pop "species" segues nicely into the last of our science-based extramusical discussions (Interlude D), on cell biology: specifically, the interlude will explore how our insatiable love for repetition—the endlessly repeating riffs and chord patterns of pop music, for example—finds metaphoric reflection in the very way our cells divide and grow. Together, these four science-based interludes will give you, the reader, a greater sense of not only why musical works carry the properties they do, but also why *your* musical taste is—relatively speaking—pretty close to everyone else's.

*Part Five, "Parlez-vous Gamelan?,"* starts with the introduction of two more genotypes, dedicated to rock (Chapter 10) and jazz (Chapter 11) music, respectively. Following these is the first of two extramusical discussions aligned to sociology (Interlude E)—here exploring how our native culture can claim credit for the music we naturally gravitate to, in terms of the "normative" aspects of our musical discourse and language, in ways both obvious and subtle.

*Part Six, "Questioning the Omnivore,"* delves into the two most socially distinct genotypes, those aligned with hip hop (Chapter 12) and electronica (Chapter 13). These in turn provide a perfect segue to the second sociology-based extramusical discussion (Interlude F)—which tackles the opposite side of the cultural coin of Interlude E by exploring the more constricting aspect of musical subculture (or intraculture, as we'll call it), where musical taste becomes personal identity, and musicological nuance becomes an extension of character and group allegiance.

*Part Seven, "Who Are You, Anyway?,"* completes our survey of the seven genotypes with the two most complex exemplars, those devoted to world music (Chapter 14) and classical music (Chapter 15). These sophisticated accounts will prepare the reader for the final extramusical discussion (Interlude G)—which in fact pursues that final mile of our musical taste: our individual psychology. Here we explore the nature of musical emotion, and the relationship between our personality, our listening habits, and our musical taste.

*Part Eight, "Your Hit Parade,"* brings our "mystery novel" to a close with two discussions: Chapter 16 wraps up the genotype theme by providing some clues on how these fictional accounts relate to you and your "hit parade." Having gained, through all the preceding chapters, an understanding of the sources, nature, origins, and implications of your musical taste, a concluding Epilogue offers reflections and prescriptions on how such understanding can be put to optimal use—so that you may truly "live with music" and benefit in myriad ways by *activating* and *empowering* your musical taste.

In previewing the order and disposition of this book, you may have recognized another advantage: preventing the reader from being overloaded by too much consecutive musical or extramusical material. That is, sixteen consecutive chapters on music theory, history, and musicology could well get a bit intense, especially for those with no or limited musical training; having a periodic break with extramusical interludes should thus cleanse the mental palate, while simultaneously expanding consciousness about our musical taste. Similarly, reading seven chapters in a row that explore the intersections of music and anthropology, math, physics, neuroscience, cell biology, sociology, subcultural studies, and psychology—without explicitly discussing the music itself—might become challenging, if not frustrating. The interactive back-and-forth thus offers the best of both worlds, thematically and attention-wise.

Talking about musical taste is no simple matter, but given that we all partake of its effects on a daily basis, it is perhaps worthwhile to get a bit ambitious about it.

Before diving into this ambitious agenda, though, I will first offer a bit of the bona fides whereby I can claim myself worthy to be your guide through this varied terrain: a behind-the-scenes historic tour of the initial music operation at the company now known as Pandora Radio—gained from my perspective as its chief musicologist, and the architect of the Music Genome Project (Chapter 1). The history of Pandora is admittedly a bit of a story within a story, and not fundamental to our exploration of musical taste—meaning that you could skip it and not be handicapped in grasping the book's main themes. Yet, given the broad interest in the company and its place in our culture, and especially its relevance for how this book and many of my ideas for it came into being, it seemed a reasonable place to get things started.

As an aside, you should note that this book also benefits from a robust online supplement—a companion website (www.WhyYouLikeIt.com). The WYLI website contains a bounty of reference material, exclusively prepared audio samples, links, playlists, etc. Each audio link on the website is associated with a specific passage in the book, with the ebook version containing embedded links within the text. In addition, the WYLI website contains periodic "expert" supplements to the main text—at times explicitly referenced, at times not—that expand even beyond the more "standard" clarifications and bibliographic citations found in the book's footnotes and endnotes. In short, you will have no shortage of good reasons to visit the WYLI website again and again.

*one*

# THE RISE AND REBIRTH OF THE SAVAGE BEAST

• • •

## The Rise

In February 2000, I was up to my eyeballs in academic articles, preparing myself for the dreaded qualifying exams required to proceed unfettered into the dissertation phase of a PhD program. I was in my sixth year at Stanford University in the doctoral program in musicology, and had long before chosen my emphasis—polyphonic music of the Renaissance—and had even written a few chapters of my dissertation, a study on the relationship between sacred music and Marian devotion in Renaissance Milan (a fitting topic for a nice Jewish boy).

Then, in the midst of my ever-increasing anxiety, an email appeared in my in-box: "Wanted: Music analyst for a new music technology company."

Vaguely intrigued, I replied with my rough credentials to the anonymous sender:

> Doctoral student in musicology at Stanford; professional pianist and composer, versed in all styles of classical and popular music . . .

Fast-forward a month or so, and I found myself sitting down with Tim Westergren, one of three founders of a company later called Pandora Radio. Our meeting took place at the Coffee House on the Stanford campus, where Tim had been an undergraduate years before, earning a BA in political science, though likewise taking a few music courses. We discussed the current chaos in the music industry, the stranglehold that the major labels had on breaking and selling artists, and the potential of a database technology to codify musicological information. Several months prior, Tim had in fact held his own pivotal conversation with an old Stanford classmate, Jon Kraft—and, importantly, with Jon's longtime friend, Will Glaser. From it would ensue the birth of a company, Savage Beast Technologies.[10]

## Thorny Problems & Prescient Solutions

How that initial conversation, in November 1999, between Tim, Will, and Jon gave rise to a revolutionary music technology enterprise, then, requires a bit of backstory—most especially, on two of the three founders: Tim, the company's catalyst, who would become its public face; and Will, the behind-the-scenes product inventor and technologist who could turn it into a reality.[11]

Tim Westergren's unlikely involvement in the birth of a tech start-up was—like so many historic endeavors before and since—built out of frustration and failure. He had been playing blues and rock piano since childhood, and in the years following his graduation from Stanford in 1988 had tried, unsuccessfully, to launch a series of acoustic-rock bands, as songwriter and pianist—most notably YellowWood Junction, once named San Francisco's "most promising un-signed band."[12] Disillusioned by the road and the tribulations of the record business, by 1995 he switched to producing records, composing commercial jingles, and scoring independent movies—including the 1999 experimental drama *The Last Best Sunday.*

It was in this latter capacity that Tim gained a few key insights that would prove critical. Typically, a film director will try to coax a composer to a "cue" in a particular way by providing an existing sample recording (called a temp track) and adding commentary like "more relaxed" or "more scary" or "less sentimental," etc. As a film composer myself, I can say that this is generally a helpful technique—providing the composer with guidance toward the director's vision, while likewise inviting him to create something original. Yet, Tim made an entirely different observation: How, he wondered in some frustration, does music actually evoke such emotions as "relaxed," "scary," and "sentimental"? How does rhythm or harmony or instrumentation influence the experience of these attitudes? And—importantly—was there any way to develop a technology that could help connect them all?

In fateful serendipity, while these fanciful ideas were swimming in his head, Tim read an article in the *New York Times*—"What's a Record Exec to Do with Aimee Mann?" (July 11, 1999)—about the professional struggles of this celebrated but increasingly marginalized adult alternative singer-songwriter.[13] The article noted the complex shifts in purchase habits and demographics taking place at this pivotal Y2K moment, brought on already by the distraction of the Internet and the high production value of music videos on MTV and VH1: "Young people today don't feel the need to own the music they listen to," the article concludes. The result was a music industry increasingly fixated on big-selling hit makers like Britney Spears, Christina Aguilera, Ricky Martin, and the Backstreet Boys—with diminishing patience for distinctive, "artsy" figures like Aimee Mann.

But the article likewise places Mann's struggles at her own feet. After a few hits in the 1980s with the new wave band 'Til Tuesday (notably "Voices Carry"), Mann launched a solo career in 1993, gaining critical, though not much commercial, success; in the process, she fought with one label after another: "She's the model of an artist who has been chewed up and spit out by the music business . . . But Aimee herself is a pain. She's not a good people person. She's never really allowed herself to be close to anyone at any record label," stated Dick Wingate, who originally signed 'Til Tuesday to Epic Records.[14] Things reached a climax just as the article was penned, when her current label, Interscope Records, led by famed producer Jimmy Iovine, refused to release the album she'd been working on for three years because it had no "single," and unless Aimee wanted to be a "star," there was just no point—this despite the fact that her previous two albums had sold over 225,000 copies.

Reading this, Tim surely saw a tragic tale of a gifted but misunderstood artist who struggled to gain access to her own considerable fan base simply because she didn't "play the game," and instead had the audacity to strive for artistic excellence. As the article states, "The riddle of Mann's existence is that she wants respect from an industry that only rewards respect—and artistic freedom—to those who make it a lot of money." Doubtless too Tim saw a bit of himself in Mann's story, and his many years seeking recognition from an industry that was incapable of and uninterested in offering it to him. Together with his earlier musings on the mysterious sources of one's reaction to music, this spotlight on the plight of talented musicians to reach an audience went a long way in spawning the notion of a potential new enterprise.

But the article doesn't simply end with Mann's rejection; instead it closes on an upbeat and rather prescient note. Mann was able to buy back her master recordings from Interscope and release the album on her own label, SuperEgo, calling it *Bachelor No. 2*. Even more impactful on Tim's thinking was news that Mann had been contacted by Dick Wingate, now an executive at Liquid Audio, inviting her to sell the album's tracks directly to consumers as downloads; just a few months earlier, Liquid Audio had offered its first digital downloads via Amazon.com, which by 1999 had made online shopping more commonplace. Wingate states confidently, "This technology should encourage disenfranchised artists like Aimee . . . to distribute their music the moment it's done. . . . Artists want to communicate directly with their fans." Similar sites, such as MP3.com, were likewise gaining traction in the marketplace, leading Jonathan Van Meter, the author of the *New York Times* article, to conclude: "The paradigm is shifting."

One can imagine a proverbial *flash* going off in Tim's head as these disparate ideas coalesced: the prospect of a technology to help demystify music; the imperative to help struggling or "disenfranchised" artists connect with fans; and a growing paradigm shift in the music business brought on by digital technology. The time was certainly ripe for something innovative in the "music technology" space: Napster, the enfant terrible of the digital music era, had launched its peer-to-peer MP3 file-sharing service in June 1999—at once turning a generation on to the art of downloading music from the Internet and marking the individual song, as opposed to the album, the primary focus of the musical experience.[15] These were indeed the "Wild West" days in the music business.

The idea of launching a tech company to tackle arcane problems like music-fan matchmaking was by no means radical for folks living in the Bay Area in late 1999—when the dot-com bubble was still inflating. Not knowing how exactly to go about it, however, Tim turned to his former Stanford pal, Jon Kraft—who years before had sold a company he founded, the Stanford Technology Group, to Ascential Software. Jon, in turn, thought of his friend—and former housemate in Menlo Park—Will Glaser. Jon's hunch to tap Will, it turns out, was spot-on.

In contrast to Tim, Will grew up in an environment where tackling thorny science-based problems with disruptive business-based solutions was practically routine. His father, Donald A. Glaser, was a professor of physics and molecular biology at UC Berkeley, who in 1960 won the Nobel Prize in Physics.[16] Will had clearly inherited his dad's outsized ambition—such as when he became the first undergraduate at Cornell University to complete a triple major: in computer science, mathematics, and physics, graduating in 1988. Rather than pursue an academic career like his father, however, Will early on set out to tackle the business world. After working as an engineer at a few tech firms in the Bay Area, he founded his own in 1995, Hydra Systems—which built PC-based computers that could also run Apple software, something otherwise impossible at the time. He sold the company in 1997, at which point he became an in-demand tech consultant.

Indeed, both Jon and Will were active consultants in late 1999, relishing the good money and the lack of responsibility that otherwise came with running a company. Still, when Will received Jon's invitation to meet his friend Tim for a drink to discuss a potential business venture, Will accepted. Tim made his pitch: that the two of them help him start a company to solve the "music industry problem" by moving beyond genre to explore what truly defined each individual's taste. Will was skeptical, and yet the three continued the conversation at Will's San Francisco apartment. It was there that Tim offered an astute observation while reviewing Will's CD collection: seeing albums by Eric Clapton and the Rolling Stones, Tim opined that Will probably did not much like the guitarist Jeff Beck, as unlike Clapton and Keith Richards, Beck was inclined to complex, virtuosic solos; Tim continued: "I bet you also like Mark Knopfler of Dire Straits, as he fits that more melodic Clapton/Richards mold." Will was now impressed, and more importantly, was prompted to pull out his trusty "Blue Binder"—his repository of random technology and innovation ideas that in moments of inspiration entered his mind, enough to warrant a quick summary, and perhaps a few mathematical calculations to suggest the prospect of further development. Most entries would never find their way into the real world, but with Tim's "trick," Will was reminded of an idea he had back in 1995. He called it the "Blockbuster Video Algorithm," which mused on how one might solve the common problem of how to recommend a video to someone based simply on aspects of the film. In essence, Will wanted to teach the computer to "comprehend" the myriad subtleties that underlie human preference toward a complex art form, in this case film: he spent days on the idea, developing the required mathematics, and forging the basis of a recommendation algorithm. And indeed, with some modifications, this "Binder" entry—an early notion of "Machine Learning"—in time became the approach upon which Tim, Will, and Jon built their new company.

Taking a big breath, that is, Will and Jon agreed to forego the luxury of their consulting careers to form this new music-based enterprise that Tim was advocating. Jon would handle the business duties, while Will would run technology and product development. Tim, with no tech or business background, would oversee marketing and, of course, music—though, fortunately for me, he would soon require help on the latter front. Jon dubbed the company Savage Beast Technologies (after a commonly misquoted line from William Congreve's 1697 play, *The Mourning Bride*: "Music has charms to soothe a savage breast"), powered by a technology that Will would, in short order, christen the Music Genome Project.

## What's in a Name? Part 1

It is a true blessing of my professional life that the technology I helped to develop, the Music Genome Project (MGP), is rather famous—even among those who aren't technologically savvy. This is, however, an uncommon occurrence. While tech-based companies and products frequently become household names, the proprietary technologies that power them rarely do: Who has heard of Graph Search (Facebook), or PageRank (Google), or eBox (eBay) outside of a few technophiles and those who work at these firms?[17] But things were always different with Savage Beast—as they still are with its latter-day namesake, Pandora Radio. From the beginning, the very soul of the company was entwined with the name of its technology—one with the added gravitas of being associated with perhaps the greatest scientific achievements of modern times: the Human Genome Project.

First conceived in the mid-1980s, the Human Genome Project was officially launched in 1990 with the aim of determining the DNA sequence of the entire human genome—and of mapping every individual gene of our species.[18] As such, the expression "genome project" was in the air, so to speak, so it is thus not a surprise that Will—whose father had long been engaged, academically and commercially, in the field of molecular biology—would suggest it for his and Tim's fledgling company. After all, the goal of the technology was to "break down" music in a way that resembled how biologists "broke down" DNA—plus it sounded good.

As the architect of the music analysis protocol at Savage Beast, I would come to find great inspiration in its metaphoric association with the biological "genome" construct: that our complete and complex *individual* identity as humans could be defined by the distinctive "expression" that each of us registers upon the *universal* set of twenty-thousand-plus genes we all share.[19]

## Let the Games Begin

But such complex musings were still a ways off during that first encounter with Tim at the Stanford Coffee House in March 2000. Tim impressed me with his earnest passion for building a business based largely on music analysis, and I managed to do likewise with my displayed facility on a broad range of musical topics. Importantly, our conversation also had a strong moral component: perhaps it was possible, we dreamed in enthusiastic accord, that an intelligent, database-driven engine recommending music to average music lovers could break the stranglehold of the labels and "save" the music industry—why not? Tim, again, was an experienced musician, yet being largely self-taught, he needed someone with a thorough background in music analysis and a wide palette of musical knowledge to build out the Music Genome Project and help run the new company's music operation.

The company "office" at this point was a rented studio apartment in Will's building, in the Potrero Hill district of San Francisco, where a few days later I met Will and Jon, as well as three recent hires—a secretary, Adriana Ulloa, and two brilliant engineers, Jeff Stearns and Eric Bieschke, who would help Will design the software that underpins the technology. It was in this cramped space that Tim and Will unveiled to me the prototype of the Music Genome—an enhanced Excel spreadsheet with about fifty musical "genes" analyzing about seven hundred and fifty songs; the genes were, in truth, a bit naïve: tempo—fast to slow; harmony—major or minor; danceable—low to high, plus a bunch of instruments. "This is what we'd want you to help us develop," Tim explained with a wry smile. Glancing over the spreadsheet, I immediately knew this would be fun, and was entirely doable—though how exactly I couldn't say. I reminded Tim of the one hurdle I had to overcome before I could join his endeavor: a five-week trip to Milan to conduct research for my dissertation, starting in three days. "Not a problem," Tim said. "You can work on it while you're in Italy." The next day, while driving to pick up my passport, I got a call from Jon: "We'd like to offer you the job of vice president of music." While quietly wondering to myself who exactly the "president" of music might be, I took a deep breath at this exciting but unexpected shift in my career path, and simply said, "I'll take it."

Over the next five weeks, I tried to balance the demands of conducting intensive academic research at the Biblioteca Sforzesca, revamping the prototype of the Music Genome, and spending leisure time with my wife, Lynn, and our then four-year-old daughter, Camille. With ample intake of cappuccinos, Chianti, and pizza, it wasn't all that difficult. Indeed, after walking through the winding, ancient streets of Milan, or past the breathtaking grandeur of Il Duomo, I may never have been more inspired or more equipped to contemplate the prospects of a "genomic" approach to music analysis.

As was made clear to me before I left California, Savage Beast Technologies was a profit-driven company, and so our initial work focused on the only sector of the musical marketplace that really "mattered": pop and rock—and related genres like country, R&B, folk, etc. It would be several years, in fact, before the MGP would be applied to the symphonies of Haydn or the ballets of Stravinsky, let alone the motets of the early sixteenth century; for now, it was aimed at the dance-pop of Abba and the rock anthems of Bruce Springsteen. And that was fine by me—since not only was I too raised on rock and roll, but I also had confidence that the rigors of hardcore analytical musicology were perfectly equipped to tackle a standardized approach to dissecting pop music. I just had to figure out how.

I'll review in fuller detail how exactly I merged my musical background and training with my incipient role as "architect" of the MGP in the next chapter, but suffice it to say here that upon my return to the US in early May, Tim's original prototype of fifty genes had blossomed into a "Version 0.5" consisting of nearly 150 genes; the larger number enabled a more granular approach to music analysis, devising genes that could capture the contour of a melody, the diatonic or chromatic profile of a chord progression, the intensity of a rhythm's syncopation, and so forth. Meanwhile, there were changes afoot in the business profile of Savage Beast. During my Italian excursion, Jon had managed to complete their "angel" round of funding—$1.5 million—from a variety of sources, including $250K from famed "seed stage" venture capitalist and founder of Garage.com, Guy Kawasaki, alongside investments from various friends and acquaintances. With this fresh funding and a wave of optimism, the founders sublet a small office in the Civic Center district of San Francisco, and hired a few new engineers, as well as a gifted visual designer, Dan Lythcott-Haims, who would be responsible for the company's internal and external (user-experience) design over the next ten years. In short order, this music start-up was open for business!

## Finding My Way

Those early days were fairly surreal, especially for me, as I'd never actually worked in an office before. On my second or third day, Jon buoyantly led our first all-hands meeting, where he made a confident pronouncement: "I am about to begin raising a Series B round of $3 million so we can really grow; I expect that we'll be able to close this round within three months." That didn't happen. Money was still flowing in the Valley—with the NASDAQ reaching its peak in early March 2000—but the storm clouds were definitely gathering. After years of stock overvaluation and ubiquitous venture capital, the investment door was about to shut, and tight. Our timing probably could not have been worse. Happily, we were all fairly oblivious as to how dire things were about to get. This was no doubt a good thing—just as I rolled up my sleeves to create a relatively novel entity: a corporate music department responsible for everything from content acquisition to a complex music analysis operation to the dissemination of coded music into the Music Genome database.

During that same week, Tim and I began our work together on the MGP. My many expansions were happily received with hearty enthusiasm. At the same time, Tim was always keen to pose tough questions and offer constructive feedback. Indeed, throughout my tenure at Savage Beast/Pandora, Tim and I maintained a constructive working relationship and close friendship. What he may have lacked in formal music training, he made up for with natural musical instincts, which were always laser-focused on the practical objectives of the MGP on behalf of our commercial enterprise—something I could lose sight of when trying to most accurately analyze music using a genomic approach.

## The Main Genome

There was much to do on the music front. We first needed to finalize the new Pop/Rock Genome, which henceforth became known as the "Main Genome," even as we built out the others. A philosophy for constructing a musical genome gradually emerged in my mind: what we were trying to capture was not only the musicological *essence* of songs, but also the human *experience* of listening to them. This led me, on the one hand, to devise genes that could collectively capture the full scope of the musical parameters (melodic construction, harmonic activity, use of instruments, etc.) at work in a song and, on the other, to devise genes that summarized *how* those parameters impacted the listener. This latter, for example, led me to devise a category of genes I called "Compositional Dominance"—that is, quantifying which parameters were most "dominant" in the listening experience. After a few weeks of nonstop analysis, we were at last ready to hail the arrival of the first "complete" genome.

of analysts and a steady stream of relevant songs to analyze. It was at this point that my role as head of the music operation really took off, and where Tim began to migrate away from a daily involvement in the analysis process and more toward the broader array of business concerns that would quickly consume his attention. To begin generating a team of music analysts, I wrote up the following ad and placed it at various college music departments, community centers, music stores, recording studios, and rehearsal spaces:

> Attention Bay Area Musicians!! The perfect "gig" awaits you! We are a new and dynamic Music Internet Company based in San Francisco, and we invite you to join our growing team: get paid to listen to music, earn good money, enjoy a flexible schedule, and improve your understanding of Popular music. Sound good? Then call us . . . but only if you possess considerable knowledge of Popular music, have experience as a performing musician, and have a solid grounding in music theory.

Within days the phone began ringing from eager musicians of all stripes. At first, the interview process was done ad hoc, as I grilled applicants on their background and experience with music analysis and pop repertoire, getting an intuitive feel for whether they'd be qualified or not. By late May we had a small but enthusiastic team of analysts, all Bay Area musicians active in the pop/rock space: Vince Littleton, Bob Coons, Brian McCarthy, Allison Lovejoy, and Bill Cutler. It was indeed the "perfect gig," providing a steady daytime paycheck earned while expanding one's musical knowledge, all the while keeping evenings free—when the *actual* gigs were. Such was the case in mid-2000, as it continues to be today, with the rare analyst position filling within days of being posted.

CDs were likewise chosen initially in a rather ad hoc fashion: we'd go to the nearby Tower Records and pick up handfuls of "classic" and new releases in the various subgenres spread across the pop/rock species. We also began a protocol that would continue to this day: to analyze not every song on a CD, but rather only a selected "editorial" set—hits, of course, but also other tracks deemed noteworthy for one reason or another. There was a strange, palpable excitement in reaching for a great CD or artist to analyze for the first time; a friendly competition would ensue for various favorites—forcing us to implement a policy not to "horde" CDs, but to pick a new one only when the previous one was analyzed. All analyses were done on paper and run through the same algorithm that Will, with weightings assistance from Tim and me, had finalized. Within a month, the number of songs analyzed using my newly designed Genome had topped fo hundred.

These early efforts of our fledgling music department, however, also exp the need for a more formalized protocol. Specifically, prompted by fee from the engineers, I recognized two immediate needs: the first was a set

The next order of business was to test the ability of the "matching engin now utilizing my newly updated Genome, to accurately align songs together i a way that made sense musically. You can analyze songs down to the minutest o details, but if you can't utilize the resulting data to connect songs in a compelling, satisfying way, then what's the point? And this is where Will's algorithm, dating back to the "Blue Binder," was on full display: using an Excel spreadsheet he developed whereby Tim and I could experiment, we forged a "weighting vector" that became the default for the genome and its matching engine, prior to any personalizing input. I cannot claim to understand the full nature of the algorithm behind the MGP, but I do know that the weightings that I helped to assign are a big part of how that default matching-learning process works.[20] The rationale behind these assignments involved creating a balance between high-level musicological attributes (such as tempo, meter, stylistic conventions, instrumentation, etc.) and more "local," experiential aspects (such as vocal timbre, an instrumental solo, a chromatic chord progression, etc.)—that, plus a lot of experimentation.

The details of those early matches and weighting tweaks are fairly blurry now, but there's one seminal test of our algorithm that still sticks in my mind—from mid-May 2000: the source song was "Eleanor Rigby" by the Beatles; the top match that came up in our spreadsheet was "New York Mining Disaster 1941" by the Bee Gees. Both of these songs had been analyzed months earlier, the Beatles song by me and the Bee Gees song by Tim. At first, we both looked at the displayed match and said, "Shit—this doesn't work." Seeing a Bee Gees song as the top recommendation, we had immediately gone in our minds to their most popular era, circa 1977—*Saturday Night Fever*—which we had also analyzed. How could a disco song match the wistful elegance of "Eleanor Rigby"? we asked ourselves. But then we played the two songs back to back, and to our amazement, it was a beautiful and fitting match! "New York Mining Disaster 1941" was not a disco song, but a Bee Gees ballad of ten years prior: a brooding song in a minor key with a sad, narrative lyric, stepwise modal melody, and rich vocal harmonies. That is, all of its most pronounced musicological characteristics were akin to those found in "Eleanor Rigby"; the Bee Gees song even featured a solo cello toward the end—akin to the string quartet that accompanies the Beatles song. From this we learned two valuable things: (1) don't assume you know a song just from the name of the artist, and (2) this Music Genome Project *does* work!

## How to Build a Music Operation

Feeling pretty good about the underlying technology, we were now primed to ratchet up the production; creating decent matches from a set of seven hundred and fifty songs was nice, but a thriving business it did not make. Both to ensure ever-improved matches and to create a market-viable database, we needed a team definitions for each individual gene, as well as for the larger groupings ("chromosomes," if you will) to which each gene belonged; the second was a more codified scoring system—whereby every point on our ten-point scale was imbued with a very precise meaning, and not just a gradual and potentially vague position on a sliding scale. Formalizing these elements would go a long way in ensuring a normalized and consistent approach among analysts to scoring each gene. Once put together, this would constitute the first in a series of genome-specific Music Genome Project Manuals—that still serve in the training and support of Pandora music analysts. An early sketch of the manual's "pre-amble," dated May 17, 2000, reads:

> The intention of the Song Analysis process is to capture the fundamental musical and textual characteristics of songs, using criteria that are common across all genres and styles of popular music. The vast majority of the categories are designed to be as objective as possible, so as to avoid introducing too much subjective variation among Analysts. The more consistent the data, the more effective the information will be, not only in understanding interrelationships of music, but also in developing a sense of an individual listener's musical preferences.

As the operation grew, I likewise recognized another need: a more methodical way to obtain CDs—perhaps even to get them for free. For this, I turned to one of our analysts, Bill Cutler—a talented guitarist-songwriter with local roots going back to the Haight-Ashbury days (having worked with Jerry Garcia, Bob Weir, and members of Jefferson Airplane), continually active in various rock styles as both a songwriter and producer; surely he would know someone. And indeed he did: in mid-June, Bill introduced me to one of the more colorful characters who ever worked at Savage Beast, Lou Bramy. Lou was a raw, occasionally testy guy, a longtime music—as well as Vietnam War—veteran, who had worked as the A&R director for Atlantic Records, among other radio and record company posts. Lou had literally grown up in the record-distribution business, as his dad, Al Bramy, was a pioneer in the field—all but writing the book on the flow of records from labels to retailers, such as Tower Records, from the early 1960s. Lou seemed to know *everyone* in the music business, and was able to introduce Savage Beast to the power brokers in the industry. He joined the company informally in September 2000, formally in January 2001, later becoming senior VP of business development. Lou was creative and tireless in his desire to make the company relevant, and the two of us became quite close. He was also, however, not someone whose bad side you wanted to be on—as the founders would soon find out.

## A New Swinging Genome

Things seemed to be going terrifically well. The company was expanding in the music, engineering, and business divisions—such that by late June we were bursting out of our San Francisco office. In early July, Jon announced to everyone that we were moving—to Oakland! This was a bit of a disappointment to me personally, living as I did in San Francisco—but there were perks as well: for the first time in my life, I had my own office!

The team of music analysts kept growing, now vetted by a written music exam; by September 2000 we had some twenty analysts, including two new recruits—Steve Hogan and Michelle Alexander—who some eighteen years later are still with the company, today in senior positions in the music operation! With this much analysis going on, it became necessary to create some formalized training and quality-assurance protocols, starting with a two-week analysis tutorial program and progressing to various data-cleanup procedures via a division of authority between regular and "senior" analysts. The Main Genome Manual was gradually taking shape, and analysis was transitioning from a handwritten approach to a computer-based interface: the MGPi (Music Genome Project interface) that Will and the engineering team developed, in coordination with the music team, to overcome the problems associated with hand-coded song analyses. Revenue-generating business too was starting to develop, with a few tepid clients—including Tower Records—for an online version of our recommendation engine, thematically dubbed "Music Hunter," in keeping with our Savage Beast theme.

Then, in October 2000, our first big deal: an invitation from the online division of Barnes & Noble to develop a comprehensive music-discovery application dedicated . . . to jazz! Wait, what? We've been busting our butt on pop and rock for the past six months, and they want an app for jazz—which, by the way, constitutes at most 3 percent of the CD market? . . . Why, of course we'll do it! In fact, the project—an interactive "Jazz Discovery" application—was a blessing from the standpoint of the Savage Beast music department, not least in allowing me to develop a second genome, one dedicated to a musical species that is, on the whole, rather more complex than its pop/rock counterpart. Designing a Jazz Genome gave me an opportunity to act on the insights I'd been gaining over the past six months about the overall musical "genomic process"—how to better get at the "truth" behind the music through the nuances of its musicology and listening experience.

There was also great personal excitement at the prospect: I've been playing jazz intently since my teenage years; in fact, my personal progression with the realm largely followed its historical evolution—from ragtime to Dixieland to swing to bebop to cool to fusion; this is not all of jazz, of course, but a pretty good swath, and I was well aware of the key luminaries and most of its minor heroes—as well as the principal ingredients of the musical language in its various guises. Still, it seemed wise to up the ante and convene a small "advisory panel"—a set of gifted and experienced jazz musicians and friends—to help me brainstorm about the requisite genes for this rich, now century-old tradition: alto saxophonist John Handy, vibes player Roger Glenn, guitarist Ray Obiedo, and pianist Marcus Silva, along with consultations from various jazz singers. After a handful of sessions, probably more valuable for the priceless anecdotes we shared than for their genomic insights, I'd gathered what I needed and could begin my "architectural" process.

Cue seven months of frenetic work: nonstop CD listening and study; constant gene additions, deletions, and edits; jazz analyst hires and training sessions; visual design templates; CD acquisitions and a flurry of analysis; manual design; database and UI adjustments—till at last, on May 30, 2001, the bn.com Jazz Discovery app was officially launched. As stated in the press release, this was an interactive web-based app "to introduce people to Jazz and give Jazz enthusiasts sophisticated tools to navigate through the music." We had handpicked hundreds of jazz songs in every genre and era, focusing on all primary jazz instruments, and featuring dozens of major jazz artists and seminal works. Users with any level of jazz background could enter the app by simply clicking on a link devoted to a jazz style, instrument, or mood, or via an historical timeline defined by era and artist. With every click, users received an instant set of recommendations of albums to purchase on the B&N site that genomically matched their source selection.

It was a jazz geek's dream, and had allowed me to indulge in my fondness for organizing repertoire. The new, underlying Jazz Genome was also a monumental step forward in our overall genomic methodology: nearly twice as many genes as pop/rock, with a far greater ability to capture the often sophisticated nuances of the melodic, harmonic, rhythmic, and formal aspects of this wide-ranging repertoire—from the 1920s two-beat "trad" of Louis Armstrong to the quasi-classical orchestrations of Gil Evans to the wild abstractions of Ornette Coleman, to name but a few. Significantly, the Jazz Genome likewise allowed for a detailed inquiry into the nature, style, and varied approaches of improvisation—the sine qua non of jazz, and a key element that underlies one's personal taste in the music; more on this in the coming chapters. Finally, during this extensive R&D period, we developed a number of other techniques to identify the roots of musical perception and preference. Most important were the so-called "Focus Traits"—catchy expressions like "Sultry Vocals," "Virtuoso Trumpet Solo," and "Wild Harmonies"—that were triggered by distinct clusters of genes; these not only assisted the matching engine, but also enabled us to better relay the rationales of our recommendations to the listener.

To be sure, there were still considerable holes in the analyzed repertoire at the launch of Jazz Discovery (about two thousand tracks), which could deliver an occasional odd recommendation, but in general it worked quite well for the content found on the app. However, this lack of broad coverage in jazz—as with other genres—would pose a consumer-facing problem until we could develop strategies for overcoming it, not least by analyzing more content, but also via other techniques developed in the months after launch. Still, Barnes & Noble was a happy client, and already discussing future genre "discovery" apps—which never happened. Reviews were positive—for example, the *Los Angeles Times* (June 15, 2001) stated, "It is fun to rove through Jazz Discovery's byzantine passages and intersections. More than that, the site has the potential to serve as a powerful educational tool."[21] We were, for the first time, getting "out there" in a major way, and feeling pretty good about ourselves.

## The Storm Clouds Gather

But while Jazz Discovery was good for the Savage Beast music department and the MGP's development, as well as for the company's sense of pride and confidence in our growing identity as the preeminent purveyor of music recommendation, it did virtually nothing for our bottom line: earning us a mere $20,000 for seven months of work! Little wonder that a crisis was in the works.

Awareness among employees that the company was facing financial challenges had started to surface as far back as February 2001, when employees were first asked to accept a salary "deferral," to be paid back a month later. Facing a veritable brick wall of resistance from the investment community, Jon and Will were forced to dig into their own pockets with modest "bridge loans" to the company. As early as October 2000, I too had tried to stir the investment pot—and in fact introduced Jon to two friends in the field who would later come to play big roles in the company's future: Peter Gotcher and Gene D'Ovidio. But for the time being, money was really going in just one direction: out.

A more serious alarm was sounded starting in June 2001, when a sporadic series of temporary deferrals was replaced with actual pay cuts—which did not sit well with the music analysts. In October 2001, after living with this downturn for three months, the analysts gathered together, and in the spirit of union-like solidarity drafted a letter to Tim expressing their frustration with an increasingly untenable situation: "We feel," they declared, "we are running more on faith than facts."

Sadly, there was not much the founders could do. The pay cuts stood, accompanied by full-salary deferrals for months at a time. Keeping morale high in the music department was not easy, and we ultimately lost a few good analysts. Other parts of the operation also suffered: at times, we literally ran out of CDs, forcing us to assign the analysts to return to albums already "editorialized"—meaning that they now had to analyze *every* song on the album, even the crappy ones. In

June 2002, Jon Kraft resigned as CEO; this was not a huge surprise, given that he had all along been commuting from Los Angeles, and in the preceding months had been showing up less and less. Tim took over marketing and customer development, while Will subsumed control of operations and finances. Finally, later in the same month, an unexpected bit of good news—a bridge loan for $650,000; this enabled Tim and Will to pay back a portion of deferred salaries, though with over $1 million owed to employees, it was but a Band-Aid. Patience was fraying, and annoyance boiling to anger: Tim and Will were arguing about strategy, and I even got into rows with Ms. Ulloa, now director of music operations (replaced by Steve Hogan in September 2002). Savage Beast, once riding high, was now singing the blues.

## The Beat Goes On

And yet, even during these difficult months, we made good progress in fulfilling the mission of the Music Genome Project. Work on the Jazz Genome and the Jazz Discovery app had by necessity brought an ever more standardized process to the music operation in all facets—from hiring to training to repertoire selection to CD acquisition to analysis to quality control to the user-facing display of our recommendations, etc. It was gradually becoming a well-oiled machine: Lou Bramy had worked his magic with various major labels and distributors to get advance copies of new releases, and discounts on "catalogue" (that is, older) content, if not free catalogue—as with the Blue Note label.

Indeed, throughout the latter part of 2001 and throughout 2002, Lou was increasingly driving business development, and finding creative ways to market the output of the MGP—most especially via his closest business connection, Tower Records. Given the nominal development fees being paid by partners, and the even smaller licensing fees being garnered from online versions of the MGP, an alternative strategy was needed—which led to the development of a new business arena for the company: music kiosks. Through a series of complex partnerships—with Tower Records, *CMJ* (the *College Music Journal*), the kiosk manufacturer NCR, and others—Lou initiated the deals, and worked with Tim and Will to develop a strategy to place Savage Beast–powered kiosks in music retailers around the country. Under the august label Music Discovery Network, the goal was to enable patrons of Tower, and eventually other retailers, to navigate from familiar to unfamiliar but related repertoire: songs could be heard without opening a CD's packaging, enabling patrons to know if it—and other, related CDs—were worth buying. We received a monthly licensing fee from each Tower store that carried our kiosks.

Our business courtship with Tower Records actually dated back to April 2001. Its kickoff was the Music Discovery app for Tower's online music store—a simpler version of Jazz Discovery, dedicated to pop and rock, and based on a select group of Focus Traits ("Funky Beat," "Storytelling Lyrics," "Loud and Distorted," etc.). As such, the music kiosk offering was a fairly logical progression. The Music Discovery Network (MDN) was launched in November 2001, initially in three Tower stores. As with Jazz Discovery, this was a major, company-wide undertaking, involving a great deal of design, development, testing, and kiosk integration—plus, of course, lots of music analysis.

## The Beast Gets Shady

Beyond keeping up with new releases, the MDN project required the addition of songs aligned with the *CMJ*—selected from their famed weekly charts. These were largely independent releases in various rock and pop styles and generally posed no problem for the analysis team. But a few did: for while the Pop/Rock Genome nominally allowed for the inclusion of "urban" genres like hip hop, rap, and electronic dance music, it was in truth ill-equipped to properly distinguish between the many diverse approaches to rhythm, syncopation, vocal delivery, and especially lyrical content found in these styles. I was well aware of this analytical limitation prior to the MDN project, and in fact had begun tepidly working on a Rap/Electronica Genome as far back as December of 2000, just before the Jazz Discovery deal was initiated. With the latter now complete and launched, a proper R&D process could likewise begin for rap and dance music, in March 2001.

Hip hop and electronica, however, were not exactly genres I knew intimately. I thus immediately recognized that beyond doing a great deal of self-study, I would need some professional help—especially for hip hop. But rather than form another advisory panel, I was able to rely on a single expert, Davey D—a renowned hip hop historian and DJ—who likewise lived and worked in Oakland. In our many sessions, Davey would bring armfuls of CDs and recount the early days of hip hop, in New York as well as in Oakland; the varied evolution in hip hop style and production; the fierce distinction and rivalry between East and West Coast rap; the culture and lifestyle of the rap stars, from Chuck D to N.W.A to Tupac to Jay-Z to Eminem, who was huge at the time, to Nelly, etc. Occasionally Davey D would bring along a local rapper or two, and we'd discuss various rapping and rap-writing techniques, as well as issues surrounding beat construction, production, etc. Armed with my primer background, I then began poring through dozens and dozens of rap and hip hop tracks, identifying the means to capture the minute elements that would distinguish two rap tracks that on the surface, or to the uninitiated, would sound the same: the speed of the rap delivery, the level of vocal pitch fluctuation, the degree of shouting, the clarity of enunciation, the attitude of the rapper, the prominence of the backbeat, the metric subdivision, the sound of the kick drum, the language use and topic of the lyrics, the level of profanity or violent references, etc., etc.

In many ways, my experience here underscored the kinds of musical/cultural presumptions that can forge and potentially delimit our musical taste, as well as the potential evolution in appreciation and understanding that can arise through open-minded exposure. I confess that I had little interest or patience for rap music prior to starting work on the Rap/Electronica Genome—it was not music I was well experienced with, nor that I understood very well; it was, in short, not "my" music. But through exposure and engaged listening, I came to recognize the wealth of creativity—musically and lyrically—possible in the music, and came to find new favorites: Public Enemy, Twista, and Eminem.

Simultaneous to the development of the hip hop side of the Rap/Electronica Genome, I did a similar deep dive into the dance/electronica side of things—likewise a realm with which I was not terribly familiar. As the musical materials were not quite so specialized and culturally rooted as rap, I was able to devise the genes unique to the dance realm without an outside expert—relying only on my intense self-study and the development I was able to garner through our analyst study sessions, which were now becoming standard in genome development. The goal here too was to be able to distinguish between songs within the various "subgenres"—house, techno, trance, trip hop, drum and bass, etc.—that to a novice would sound identical. Primarily this meant delineating the often very complex rhythmic structure—beat-pattern definition and length, rhythmic density, number of distinct patterns, level of metric discernibility, etc.—as well as the often dense and complex "soundscape" created by various synthesizers and acoustic-manipulation techniques. As with rap—and even more so—I came to discover a wealth of music in the electronica family that met my own musical taste that I never knew before: Kraftwerk, Chemical Brothers, Fatboy Slim, Talvin Singh, etc.

Initially, these two urban species were to be analyzed via the same genome (Rap/Electronica), but for various reasons—as much administrative as musical—we decided to divide them into two, a Rap Genome and a Dance Genome, each containing around 320 genes. Analysis of both realms started by early May, and though we didn't need to hire new analysts with a specific hip hop or dance background, as we had with jazz, we did need to hire expert "song selectors" for rap (including Davey D). They who not only selected the songs, but likewise catalogued some of the cultural "metadata" info that was key to a rap fan's understanding of the music beyond the purely musical discourse—such as a track's level of market exposure, "street cred," street-viewed lyrical caliber, label and producer stature, etc.

## Our Last Best Hope

The upshot of all this was that by November 2001 we had sufficient material to confidently launch the Music Discovery Network and its proposed army of kiosks, able to offer compelling recommendations for in-store fans of most prominent musical genres and styles: Pop, Rock, Heavy Metal, Punk, R&B, Gospel, Blues, Americana, Folk, Country, Bluegrass, Jazz, Hip Hop, Rap, Disco, and Electronica, among others. While the actual number of songs analyzed was not incredible—around 250,000 songs at that time—we had at last developed techniques to "aggregate" artist and album content, to help ensure that a consumer's "seed" song would not return an error; once identified, however, it would inevitably direct the user to recommendations based on our actual analyses.

In the weeks leading up to the MDN launch, Lou—along with Tim, Will, and others at the company, notably Patrick Dominguez, our marketing director and a close ally of Lou's—had been working furiously to maximize its market and industry exposure. There was, in fact, something poetic about Lou's driving presence at Savage Beast, and in particular in the alliance he orchestrated with Tower Records: forty years earlier, his dad, Al, had revolutionized the field of record distribution primarily through his relationship with Tower; now, Lou was attempting to help revolutionize digital distribution by again forging key ties with Tower, via the MDN. Alas, it was not meant to be either for Lou or for Tower Records—which would be out of business by fall 2006.

Response to the MDN was limited, but generally quite good, and indeed helped in the long march toward pulling ahead of the many competitors we faced in the music recommendation space—MoodLogic,[22] MusicBuddha,[23] Mubu,[24] Cantametrix,[25] MongoMusic,[26] MusicGenome,[27] among others—none of which, I would hasten to add, are still in existence. A lengthy article in *New Media Music* (October 14, 2001), just prior to the launch of the MDN, for example, wrote in part:

> As the searcher interacts with the Savage Beast system, using the focus traits and buying or downloading songs, the system adapts to that user's musical preferences, creating a "taste portrait" that deepens with each visit. Adding it all up, the damn thing works amazingly well.[28]

## The Tipping Point

Throughout 2002, the MDN—both online and via the kiosks—became a prime focus of our business, as well as, indeed, our music analysis operation. We also attempted to expand its reach by establishing a "Network" for independent and unsigned artists—a harbinger to the type of promotion that would later underlie Pandora's appeal. Another tepid strategy was the creation of a high-profile advisory board. Lou was again a key force behind this, bringing on folks like jazz producer Orrin Keepnews, veteran record executives Joe Smith and Ron Goldstein, famed rock journalist Ben Fong-Torres, and Tower Record exec Stan Goman. I too made a contribution to the board in the person of rocker Steve Miller—with whose band I was playing and recording periodically at the time.

And yet the tide was too firmly against any real chance that the MDN or an A-list advisory board might "save" Savage Beast. By the fall, we were in many ways simply going through the motions, and everyone expected the ax to fall at any moment. On November 3, 2002, an all-hands meeting announced that once again salaries would be deferred—indefinitely. By this time I had two kids, with my son, Preston, just over a year old. My wife, Lynn, had been terrifically patient over these past two years, but enough was enough: with no shortage of sadness, the next day I walked into Tim's office and announced my resignation—temporary, it turned out. Ever the gentleman, Tim accepted it with graciousness: "I totally understand, Professor, and hope we can bring you back when we've managed to get over this hump." Lou Bramy, Patrick Dominguez, and several analysts left at or around the same time as me, leaving the music operation largely in a state of suspended animation.

In the months that followed, Tim and Will continued to find some business opportunities for Savage Beast—namely, a licensing deal with AOL Music and a kiosk trial with Best Buy—but neither brought in much revenue. My personal adjustment to this employment transition was fairly smooth: I increased the time spent working with the online classical music service Classical Archives—with whom I'd been engaging sporadically since June 2002, now becoming its half-time artistic director;[29] the remainder of my time was spent performing and composing—which after a long hiatus once more became a prime focus of my musical identity.

Throughout the summer of 2003, however, Lou began to express an increasingly tense preoccupation with Savage Beast, his anger growing with regard to his—and other employees'—deferred wages. It turns out that deferring wages while an employee continues to work normal hours is actually against California labor laws. As such, Lou and a few other former employees were gearing up to present a lawsuit to Savage Beast, and Lou now wanted me—and Pat—to join their ranks. I was then owed something like $80,000—not an inconsequential amount of money for my young family. However, out of loyalty to Tim—plus my own stubborn belief that what we had developed at Savage Beast still had potential to transform the music industry—I declined Lou's invitation; I'm glad I did.

But all of this must truly have shaken both Tim and Will to their cores, and one can imagine them seriously contemplating: "Should we call it quits?"[30]

## Changing of the Guard

Of course, neither Tim nor Will did quit—not yet, anyway. Instead they pushed forward with their mission to present the Music Genome Project to the world. The odds were certainly stacked against them—crushing personal and business debt, lawsuits, maxed-out credit cards, endless investor rejection, paltry business revenue—but they had an arrow in their quiver that was able to overcome them all: persistence! In early 2004, in allegedly their 349th pitch, they somehow managed to convince Larry Marcus of Walden Venture Capital to lead a Series B round (the same round Jon Kraft had promised in 2000) of $9 million. This infusion of cash would grant the company nothing short of a new lease on life. I take a slight bit of credit in securing the new funding, as Marcus—a musician himself—was introduced to the company by Gene D'Ovidio, who years before I had brought to the company's attention. With the arrival of Marcus and his sizable investment, the need—and opportunity—for some significant changes was quickly articulated: for one, the company needed to hire a new CEO; and, more importantly, it should reevaluate its current business model. Could any business make money by putting kiosks in record stores?

I first came to know all the drama unfolding through 2004, when, like most other present and past employees, I was informed late in the year that my deferred salary would finally be paid back—in full! Tim called to give me a cursory summary of things, but then added, "So, Professor, how'd you like to come back and finish building us a World Music Genome?" The answer was a no-brainer: hell, yes! On January 6, 2005, I was back at the office, now as an "independent contractor," yet bearing the august title of chief musicologist.

On my first day back, I immediately saw that a number of changes had transpired since my departure two years earlier: first, the rather odd office space configuration the company had been inhabiting in previous years was now replaced by a large single space, indeed a complete floor. More dramatically, we had a new CEO, Joe Kennedy; a new COO, Etienne Handman; and a new CTO, Tom Conrad—who Will had hired as VP of engineering months before announcing his own exit from the company in January 2005. Larry Marcus had lobbied hard for Joe's appointment in July 2004, particularly as the deals with AOL and Best Buy fell apart; the board consented. It was, in fact, a brilliant move. Joe was an experienced executive with an MBA from Harvard Business School and a background in computer science, as well being an enthusiastic amateur musician. Prior to joining Savage Beast, Joe was president and CEO of E-Loan, taking that office shortly after the company went public. Joe in turn brought on Etienne, who had been E-Loan's chief information officer.

## The Beast Takes on the World

The notion of building out a genome dedicated to "world music"—that is, the huge expanse of music created by musicians outside of North America or England, in styles beyond the traditional "Western" genres subsumed by popular, jazz, and art music—had, in fact, begun in earnest well before my departure in 2003. As the profile of the Music Discovery Network expanded in the first half of 2001, we felt the need to extend our catalogue. Tim thus gave me a green light to begin the R&D process toward building a World Music Genome. As it turned out, my training as a musicologist had completely bypassed any direct relationship with world music: Stanford had no ethnomusicology department, or even classes, and the area had not markedly attracted my attention. I certainly enjoyed a number of non-Western musical approaches, notably Indian, but from a purely "lay" standpoint. I thus embarked on a fascinating journey of musical discovery for myself—for which I'll ever be grateful.

My preliminary research began in July 2001, when I began compiling an enormous document with information about musical practices around the world. After weeks of nonstop listening, reading, and note taking, I was ready to begin constructing V.01 of the World Music Genome. After another month of continual tweaking and improving, I was ready to assemble a team of analysts to start rigorously putting varied repertoire through the genomic test. Finally, by late October, having arrived at V.95, we were ready to start interfacing with the engineers to put the algorithmic properties onto the genome, and then begin analysis. But just then, I received a note from Tim: "Right now it doesn't make sense to go through the process of freezing and handing off the World Genome . . . Given our limited analyst pool, and in the context of everything else, it makes sense to hold on." What was estimated to be a few months, of course, turned into years—until, that is, the company had emerged from the brink.

As such, when I returned to work in early 2005, I could simply pick up from where I'd left off three and a half years earlier. Thanks to the company's new fiscal health, we were able to purchase every decent-selling "world music" CD from the previous ten years, along with hundreds of CDs representing styles and musical cultures that had little or no market exposure in the US. After a bit of renewed R&D on my end, and a slate of sessions with some newly hired analysts, the World Music Genome was at last ready for the engineers—as well as for official analyst training.

The genome clocked in at over 375 genes and was able to astutely define the musicological and experiential attributes of everything from Brazilian samba to Indian ragas, from Celtic jigs to Bulgarian women's chorus, and from Tuvan throat singing to Mexican mariachi, etc., etc. In particular, the genome had to be able to capture the dramatic diversity in vocal delivery and melodic characteristics, the intense rhythmic complexity found in numerous cultures, and the explosion of instruments and instrumental timbres. Key too was the experiential element—especially for Western ears: To what degree, for example, would a melodic or vocal style appear unusual, odd, or downright alien to an "average" American listener? With the World Music Genome, there is no doubt that we had arrived at our most sophisticated construct to date. Along the way, I had discovered previously foreign styles and artists that have become personal favorites: Nubian singer–oud player Hamza El Din, Cape Verdean songstress Cesária Évoria, Pakistani sacred singer Nusrat Fateh Ali Khan, the Afro Celt Sound System, Senegalese singer Youssou N'Dour, and the Klezmatics, to name but a few.

By June, we had completed all the gene weightings, and by July had entered the many Focus Traits—with such colorful designations as "Wild Vocal Technique," "Droning Tones," "Quirky World Track," and "Extreme Joy"—into the MGPi. By August 2005, therefore, the World Music Genome was up and running—with music by Shakira, Iz, Bob Marley, the Gispy Kings, Ravi Shankar, the Chieftains, and their less well-known international brethren being analyzed and ready to spur recommendations to eager fans of world music. The question was, however, where were people going to find them?

## The Rebirth

As noted, around the time of Joe's arrival at Savage Beast, the hard-won deals with AOL Music and Best Buy were slowly fizzling, demonstrating once and for all that a licensing approach to the Music Genome Project—whether online or in stores—was not viable for the long term. For what it's worth, I had long been saying to Tim, "We've got to figure out a way to get this technology *directly* into the hands of music lovers!" I'm sure I wasn't alone in such a pronouncement. Okay, but how do you do that? Unbeknownst to me at the time, the founders had in fact early on toyed with a bold idea for how the MGP might be employed: Internet radio; but with the company's limited seed funding and the wary business climate of the time, such a business-to-consumer approach was deemed impossible. Now, however, with Marcus' substantial investment, this idea resurfaced and was bravely embraced by the new leadership: the company had found its future.

Internet radio—that is, streaming audio across the Internet in a way that cannot be recorded or directly manipulated by the listener (not "on demand")—had been around in some form since 1993.[31] As its underlying technology improved, the incipient services of Internet radio were able to offer higher quality streams to a greater number of listeners. In September 2001, the service Live365 launched, providing a wide variety of music stations, in over 260 "genres." Most tech-savvy people had at least heard of Internet radio in 2005, myself included, but its prospects of supporting a thriving business were less than obvious.

The inaugural radio product at Savage Beast was dubbed, not surprisingly, "theBeast.fm." The person taking the lead in our shift to radio was Etienne Handman, our COO, who conferred with me regularly on its development; Etienne, in fact, had been a classically trained trumpeter, and we got along very well. As part of his duties, he had to learn the FCC's arcane rules governing webcasting: no more than three songs by the same artist during any given three-hour period, etc.; he then needed to figure out how to make "playlists" using our Safari interface, starting from a given song or artist "seed." On April 15, he gave me access to test-drive two "radio stations"—one for Bob Dylan, the other for the Police. I was told to listen and to take note of songs that "didn't make sense," while likewise ignoring the occasional "weird thing," such as a song repeating twice in a row. After much tweaking, by late May 2005, the company was, in Joe's words, "racing forward to launch the new product." There was a growing consensus, however, that "theBeast.fm" was too wonky a name; but what, then, should we call it?

## What's in a Name? Part 2

In the same email sent about our "racing forward," Joe noted that one of the last open questions regarding our new radio service was indeed its name. There had been several names used during the development phase, not only theBeast.fm, but also one that Joe himself had suggested, writing it down once on the back of a copy of *Billboard* magazine: Pandora. The reaction of most everyone was negative, as one immediately thought of Pandora's box: the Greek myth wherein Zeus punishes humanity—following Prometheus' theft of the secret of fire—by sending this first human woman to earth with a jar (not a box, in fact) that she defiantly opens, thereby releasing every ill into the world: envy, sickness, hatred, disease, etc. How could we name our new wonderful service after this debacle?

Tim was especially hopeful that I'd come up with a good candidate and came to my office to ask me personally: "Surely, there's a name you can think of?" Not wanting to let Tim down, I proceeded to rack my brain for options. Being the music geek that I am, I could only think of names that were musical in nature, and specifically that might suggest the power of the MGP. After dismissing obvious genre-based terms like Nocturne or Aria (both of which were taken anyway), I moved on to other mythological names with musical reference, such as Apollo (the Greek god of music) and Orpheus (the greatest musician of Greek mythology), neither of which moved Tim much. Going even deeper, I then arrived at a name that in many ways was absolutely perfect: an historical *and* mythological character, representing the ultimate synthesis of music and science—just like the MGP; a name that holds to this day the greatest respect among both musicians and mathematicians: Pythagoras!

The problem, however, is that I neglected to follow the first rule Joe had established in his call for suggestions: "It should be easy to spell." Ah, yes—that's a problem, since neither musicians nor mathematicians can readily spell Pythagoras, let alone the general public! As it turned out, though, no one else was able to come up with a better name than Pandora, which by contrast is hard to misspell. It was also pointed out that after all those bad things came pouring out of Pandora's jar, there was one more item left: hope. With that, the protesting ceased.

As such, the name Pandora was "locked," and plans were initiated to roll out the beta test for friends and family starting on July 17. The feedback was very positive, but also very instructive on the experience, and for adding new features—such as a running history of songs heard on each station and the ability to share stations, rate songs, buy songs, among much else. After five weeks and thousands of test users, Pandora was officially launched to the public on September 1, 2005—complete with the now-famed "thumbs-up" and "thumbs-down" options, whereby the database would gradually learn a listener's personal preferences with regard to Focus Traits and individual genes. Initially, the service was to be called "Pandora Radio powered by Savage Beast Technologies," but it soon became clear that a better solution would be to actually match the product to the company name. Pandora.com, owned by a "cyber-squatter," was easily bought, and sometime around July 25, it became the chief URL, and soon the official name of the company. After more than five tumultuous years of trial and error, inspiration and disappointment, growth and near-death, we had finally found a platform to showcase our beloved MGP: with Pandora, the Beast was truly reborn.

## A Battle for the Final Genome

My official last day working on the World Music Genome was August 11, 2005—halfway through the Pandora beta test. In the thirteen years since, my involvement with the company has been generally sporadic, if not less. A critical task in the first few years following launch was to participate, as the chief musicologist/architect of the MGP, in the near nonstop media inquiries, speaking with journalists to discuss Pandora and its underlying music technology.[32]

The most meaningful contribution I've made to the company since 2005, however, was the completion of the sixth and final music genome, dedicated to classical music. There is some irony to the fact that the musical species that granted me the bona fides to design the MGP in the first place became the last one to be treated to its own genome. But as it's money, and not art, that makes the world go round, it's little surprise. Talk of designing a Classical Genome began almost immediately upon completion of the World Music Genome, though it wasn't until June 2006 that I heard anything concrete; prior to that, the engineering team "just didn't have the available bandwidth."

When Etienne finally came back with a "green light," however, it was not what I expected: to my dismay, the vision was to make the Classical Genome "a hybrid combination of existing metadata, light analysis, and curated listener tagging": he imagined at most sixty genes to distinguish, say, one movement of a Beethoven sonata from another. What??! I immediately expressed concern, and asked for a meeting with the powers that be to make an opposing case. The rationale for this truncated version was simply that "classical music is but a tiny percentage of music sales" (estimated at 2 to 3 percent), and thus not worth a huge investment in time or resources. Yet, after many conversations over the next three months, I was happily able to convince Tim, Tom, Joe, and Etienne that, despite its small sales impact, this species of music was a vital and cherished aspect of our culture, and deserved the same comprehensive approach—from genome R&D to analyst hiring and training to weightings to Focus Traits, etc.—that we'd used on the others. Whew!

As with World Music, preliminary work on a Classical Genome had actually begun during the early Savage Beast days—going back to mid-August 2001, again during the long rollout toward the MDN release, and just a month after beginning to sketch out the World Music Genome. By late September, I had conducted enough self-review and gene sketches to produce a V.01, which over the next few months evolved to a V.4, with plans to put an analyst team together to test repertoire—when, thanks again to our financial woes, Tim closed the spigot: no new genomes.

Fast-forward to late 2006: the spigot was reopened. I could get back to work on the Classical Genome! Although I didn't need to start from scratch, things were not quite as well developed here as they had been with the World Music Genome. I was able to complete a fair bit of the remaining work on the Classical Genome R&D from home—including determining the gene weightings, defining the Focus Traits, and completing the mammoth eighty-two-page Classical Genome Manual. But some work required visits to the Pandora offices, including for dozens of intensive sessions vetting the new genome with a team of classical analysts headed by Michelle Alexander, the one remaining pop/rock analyst with a classical background.

Then there was the critical task of building out a proper classical "library." Selecting the albums to represent and populate a genome had been a critical issue with every species, of course, but with classical it was a distinct type of challenge: whereas for other genomes we would seek out big sellers, artists and CDs, and suitable representatives of less-known styles and genres, for classical it was all about selecting the "definitive" recording of each key work—at least at first. That is, for classical, it was less about the individual performances of, say, a Mozart piano concerto (e.g., Alfred Brendel versus Rudolf Serkin, etc.) or a Bruckner symphony (e.g., the Vienna versus Berlin Philharmonics, etc.) than it was about the work "itself." Two renditions of a Bob Dylan or Cole Porter song need to be analyzed as two separate entities by virtue of the very different approaches generally taken by the artists, but when two violinists record the Tchaikovsky Violin Concerto in D, the differences are—on a "genomic" level—rather insignificant. The melodies, harmonies, rhythm, forms, instrumentation, and so forth do not change (or shouldn't) from one rendition to another; rather the differences are "interpretive," and difficult for anyone but the most skilled music critics to articulate in a clearly quantifiable fashion. The upshot is that each classical work was generally analyzed but once, though some "performance practice" genes would allow a distinction between, say, a Bach concerto performed by a modern versus "period" orchestra.

The solution, therefore, was to create a list of critical works and "definitive" performances to get us started—which I completed by September 2007 through an exhaustive survey of the *Penguin Guide to Classical Recordings*, among other resources. Analysis had begun prior to this, following the completion of the weight vector in June, though work on the Focus Traits did not conclude until January 2008.

It was, safe to say, a major effort. The Classical Genome contains over 350 genes and is indeed the genome of which I'm most proud—perhaps, admittedly, because it was the last. Beyond its ability to distinguish between the radical shifts in musical language and praxis ranging from a Gregorian chant created in the fifth century to an aleatoric (chance-based) work written last Tuesday, and everything in between, it is able to capture the experiential dimension to a fair degree; I was able to achieve this in part by turning to the wonderful lexicon of Italian expression terms—"*cantabile*" (lyrical), "*maestoso*" (majestic), "*agitato*" (tense), "*doloroso*" (sorrowful), etc.—that can be applied remarkably well to repertoire written well outside the eighteenth and nineteenth centuries. With over 1,500 years of music creation, spread across dozens of countries around the world (principally in Europe, of course), the classical repertoire is a massively rich and varied triumph of human inventiveness, and I am thus so grateful that I was able to tackle it on a genomic level for the benefit of Pandora listeners; it will also give us ample opportunity for discussion in the chapters ahead.

## And the Rest Is History

The Classical Genome effort was capped with a unique public event: a "Classical Launch Party" at the Regency theater in San Francisco on November 13, 2007. It was a comic theatrical representation of how Pandora works—featuring me conducting a twenty-four-piece orchestra, with six vocalists, performing works by Vivaldi, Corelli, Bach, Mozart, Haydn, Stravinsky, and others, as Tim, playing the role of a classical novice, discovers Pandora Classical for the first time. It was a riot, and was ecstatically received by the five-hundred-plus Pandora fans lucky enough to get tickets. It was also a small symbol of just how far we'd come in these past seven years. Pandora was fast becoming a household name, with by then over nine million registered users.

Indeed, it is safe to say that no one, not even Tim and Will, could have predicted the astronomical success Pandora would have in the US marketplace. Today, regardless of where I travel in the US, it is now seemingly an exception that I meet someone who doesn't know—and regularly use—Pandora. There are many secrets to its success. Among the most critical early on were the "town hall meetings" that Tim began hosting in 2006—traveling from city to city across the US, meeting with the growing ranks of Pandora enthusiasts at schools, community centers, and theaters to discuss the service and receive feedback; these informal sessions, numbering over five hundred, did much to endear Tim and the company to everyday music lovers.

The most important marketing vehicle for the service, however, was certainly the iPhone—and later its Android counterparts—able to carry Pandora as a mobile app, starting in 2007. In his interview on the *Charlie Rose* show in July 2010, Tim noted that "it is impossible to overstate" the importance of the iPhone in Pandora's success.[33] The relationship with Apple was largely reciprocal, in fact, as the Pandora app helped Apple to sell lots of phones—as Tim shared with *Fortune* magazine in June 2010.[34] The numbers of Pandora registered users in the US just kept growing and growing—reaching 250 million by 2014—out of 300 million citizens! Helpful too were the successful efforts to integrate Pandora into countless other products, including mobile devices, web services like Facebook, home electronics, and especially car entertainment systems—today integrated into over twenty-five different manufacturers. Tim's notion of "Pandora everywhere," first introduced in a blog post in May 2007, has in fact largely come true—it can be heard in restaurants, stores, gyms, and elevators, beyond people's earbuds, headphones, speakers, and cars. As of March 2018, Pandora has seventy-eight million active listeners, spending over a billion collective listening hours per month, and representing over 9 percent of all radio listening in the US—ranking as the number one radio "station" in fourteen of the top fifteen US markets; not bad for a company that nearly died more than once.

It has not been all smooth sailing since Pandora launched in 2005, however, by any means. The high royalty rates that began vexing Live365 in 2002 likewise started to plague Pandora almost from the very start. It reached a crisis point in spring 2007, when the Copyright Royalty Board (a federal panel made up of three judges appointed by the Librarian of Congress), under pressure from SoundExchange, the record industry's collection arm, made a surprise announcement regarding new royalty rates for the period 2006–10: services like Pandora would be charged per song, per listener, at a rate considerably higher than had existed previously; the results would be catastrophic, costing over 70 percent of revenue, and by all accounts would force the business to close.[35] No stranger to near-death experiences, Tim sprang into action, as did everyone at the firm, building alliances in the industry to create a "SaveNetRadio" campaign, lobbying Congress and mobilizing the huge audience of Pandora users to write their representatives. Even I did my part, urging a few friends in Congress to take steps to help resolve the matter. Over the next eighteen months, a series of high-stakes negotiations, angry exchanges, proposed bills, and congressional votes finally led to a solution—the passing of the Webcaster Settlement Act (H.R. 7084), granting the ability for SoundExchange and Internet radio providers to negotiate directly for a rate that both sides could live with. It is no exaggeration to say that on September 30, 2008, Pandora was saved—again!

The intervening years have continued to provide Pandora with its share of challenges. In part this has come from the nonstop arrival of competitors in the Internet radio space—or "Pandora killers" as the media has affectionately called them: Spotify Radio, iHeartRadio, Songza, Beats Music, Rdio (bought by Pandora in 2015), and Apple Radio, among others. The launch of each has been heralded with predictions of once and for all crushing Pandora's dominance—which, given the company's continued high market share (currently over 70 percent), has yet to happen. More than anything, it is hard to be a "first mover" in any space, as Pandora clearly was in the personalized radio space; it becomes increasingly dangerous, therefore, not only to ignore competitors, but also to lag behind consumer trends.

Yet the greatest challenge Pandora has ever faced, historically as today, is the royalty issue—and the seriously onerous rates it must pay out to record companies via SoundExchange, currently at over 50 percent of total revenue.[36] It is due to royalties, moreover, that Pandora remains a US-only service.*

Admittedly, the music royalty debate is a hugely complex and controversial topic, and will not be litigated here.[37] But it is certainly true that Pandora and Tim personally have received a fair bit of harsh criticism, not only from industry folks but also from a number of musicians—from Burt Bacharach to Pink Floyd—accusing them of trying to cheat artists.[38] Knowing Tim as I do, and his deep commitment to supporting a "musicians' middle class," it was painful for me to witness such attacks. At the same time, no one needs to pity Tim or Pandora; the success of the service and its enormous user base enabled Pandora to go public in 2011—something that once seemed impossible.

Indeed, the whole story is for me almost hard to believe. In March 2011, prior to the IPO, I was at the Consumer Electronics Show in Las Vegas when a Silicon Valley VC asked me, "So, how does it feel to have created something that a hundred million people love?" "Pretty darn good," I responded, "pretty darn good." I've often said that I'm possibly the luckiest musicologist in the world—

* The service was available in Australia and New Zealand in 2012 through 2017, having to pull out due to rising royalties.

or close to it. Of course, I have no illusions about my role in bringing Pandora to the world; such would never have happened without the collective efforts of Tim, Will, Jon, Joe, Tom, Etienne, Jeff, Dan, scores of talented music analysts, engineers, and other employees—not to mention the wisdom of investors like Larry Marcus and my friend Peter Gotcher (who participated in a $12 million round in 2005 and who until May 2017 sat on the company's board of directors). At the same time, I know I played a valuable role, as the chief musicologist (now emeritus) of this unlikely paradigm-shifting company.

Again, I have no current role in the company, and thus no direct responsibility for the ways—positive and negative—that Pandora Radio functions for users, nor for its many shifts in leadership and services over the past year. These shifts include, most dramatically, Tim Westergren's surprising departure as CEO in June 2017—replaced two months later by Roger Lynch, founding CEO of Sling TV; significantly, they also include the long-overdue, in my view, launch of an on-demand service—Pandora Premium—to compete directly with services like Spotify. And perhaps most consequential, these shifts include the announcement in September 2018 that its former rival Sirius/XM will buy Pandora for $3.5 billion (following an earlier investment of $480 million in 2017), in a deal to close in spring 2019. Undoubtedly, many more changes will arise by the time this book sees the light of day.

Yet, so long as Pandora exists, the Music Genome Project will continue its role in generating the service's playlists—since, as noted, all the genomes, entrance exams, manuals, and other documents I spearheaded are still being used by Pandora music analysts. At the same time, as Pandora's "head of research" Oscar Celma recently fleshed out for me, playlist generation now includes all the "Big Data" gathered via the billions of thumbs-up and thumbs-down pushed by users over the years, as well as myriad other methods embodied as complex algorithms, human curators, and machine learning.[39] As a regular user myself, I have both my criticisms (e.g., frequent frustration at the hegemony of "hits" played on the pop- and rock-oriented stations) and suggestions (e.g., I'd love the ability to create "transgenome" stations, where a seed in rock would yield a genomically aligned song in jazz or classical, and vice versa). And if perchance they were to embrace the latter idea, perhaps they'll also bring me back to help direct it, to make sure it's done right! For the moment, though, all signs seem to suggest that Pandora will continue to survive and thrive long into the future.

part one

# A GIFT OF THE GODS

*two*

# UNDER THE MUSICAL HOOD: AN ORIENTATION

## A Gift of the Gods

It seemingly speaks to music's inherent cultural prestige that the very word derives from the Greek "*mousikē,*" referring to works or products of all nine Muses. The Muses, of course, are mythological goddesses, patronesses of all the arts and sciences, embodying the inspiration and source of knowledge within these fields. Initially the Greek term referred to any product aligned with the Muses' broad sphere of influence, but gradually it came to be limited to the aural art we now understand by the word "music"—and its unusually large number of cognates throughout Europe and beyond. This broad, quasi-universal correlation to *mousikē* might suggest a tacit conception of music as holding preeminence among the arts. In any event, it does reinforce the prominence that music holds in the lives of people throughout the world, and supports an intuition that our connection to music extends beyond mere pleasure to something deeper both within and without us—as will be argued later in this book.

Much like spoken language, the human expression of music is a complex reflection of the individual culture that produces it. In each case, a culture emphasizes, manipulates, and suppresses musical elements in ways that collectively give rise to its varied yet distinctive musicological and "musico-experiential" identity. American folk songs sound and feel different from traditional Chinese or Ghanaian or Indian or Celtic folk songs by virtue of the different ways that their creators and performers manipulate the musical elements that underlie them. This extends beyond mere differences in spoken language to concrete musical differences. The specific approaches taken with regard to melody, rhythm, and instrumentation, for example, will vary between these folk styles, with each element playing its role in defining that musicological/experiential identity. It is the task of **musicology** as a discipline—and music analysis as a technique—to articulate this identity from an empirical and technical standpoint. And it was to musicology and music analysis that I first turned when tasked with the job of redefining the Music Genome Project.

Indeed, within days of signing on to my new role at Pandora, I had my first *aha* moment in how to revamp the MGP: I decided to adapt and adopt a tool commonly used in undergraduate "music appreciation" courses—that I had first employed as a TA, and then as an adjunct professor at Stanford. It was a nifty acronym first devised by musicologist Jan LaRue in his *Guidelines for Style Analysis*: **SHMRF** (pronounced "schmurf"), standing for Sound-Harmony-Melody-Rhythm-Form.[40] These are certainly not all the subdivisions of musical discourse, as LaRue himself admitted, but within them they cover a great deal of ground. More importantly, they got me thinking of musical genes as being grouped in a clean musicological manner.

The one top-level parameter that was decidedly absent in LaRue's acronym—at least from the standpoint of our need to analyze pop and rock songs—was lyrics or, more broadly, text. I thus took the liberty of adding a "T" to the end of LaRue's neologism, creating **SHMRFT** ("schmurft"). In fact, I would generally introduce newly hired music analysts to Savage Beast by explaining that their job was to "schmurft" the songs they were assigned. Other musical categories were eventually added to the "genomic" protocol as well, of course, which quickly made the acronym unpronounceable.

## An Unwinding of Parameters

As it is the primary goal of this book to describe the sources and nature of our musical taste, a key task is to unwind the elements or parameters of one of its main ingredients: the music itself. The following five chapters—minus the extra-musical interludes—are thus dedicated to taking you "under the musical hood," introducing you to the principal musical parameters active in the songs you hear, both through definitions and via examples in a wide variety of styles and approaches.

This task comes with a warning: we will herewith enter the harrowing field of **music theory**—*Lasciate ogni speranza, voi ch'entrate!* ("Abandon all hope ye who enter"—from Dante's *Inferno*). Okay, it's not that bad, but it is admittedly a dense and potentially dry field that has been known to periodically cause eyes, and brains, to glaze over. So why go there—and why not merely provide a short summary condensed into a single, brief chapter? Well, first, there's so much important information to convey about each parameter that deciding what to leave out would be a challenge. Next, I increasingly recognized that in this book I had a real opportunity to explain the depth, richness, and complexities of music to an audience of music lovers who for whatever reasons lacked grounding in them.

Lastly, and most convincingly, I realized that I would otherwise be continually explaining musical nuance after musical nuance when later trying to relate a song or work to an individual's musical taste and listening experience. How could I conclude that a listener seems to gravitate to music that features "chromatic harmony, syncopated rhythms, and dense counterpoint" without clearly defining "chromatic," "harmony," "syncopated," and "counterpoint"? Doing so each time would provide a jumbled account of musicological elements, not to mention considerably slow down the discussion. Better to provide a thorough and disciplined account of each parameter up front. The reader can then refer back to the theoretical discussion in the music theory chapters, aided by the glossary at the end of the book, as need be.

This, at any rate, is the rationale I'm providing for the detailed discussion about to begin. It comes with a firm awareness that there is already a large corpus of books out there on music theory for nonmusicians.[41] You are heartily encouraged to explore them—after you've finished this book, of course. Indeed, there is admittedly much that is missing or shortchanged in this discussion of music theory, as is inevitably the case for a subject that literally has no bottom.

Yet this discussion has a few advantages over others—at least for a book aimed at musical taste. For one, explanations of musical concepts are here offered with the listening experience of nonmusicians chiefly in mind. That is why I occasionally offer an historical account of how a particular music theory approach or concept evolved over time—as a means to better understand *why* the music sounds as it does. As musicologist J. Peter Burkholder put it, "Music theory is better when it is historically conscious."[42] Further, this discussion takes a rather eclectic approach to explaining each concept. That is, to the degree that makes sense, each parameter is explained via its application to *multiple* musical **genres** or "**species**"—classical, jazz, pop/rock, world, hip hop, etc. By contrast, most music theory books relate the concepts exclusively to the Western classical music repertory, despite the fact that most listeners today spend much of their time elsewhere.

As this is primarily a book for nonmusicians, my goal is to keep highly technical or arcane jargon to a minimum. I will not always succeed, alas, as avoiding the arcane can be near impossible when the subject matter is music theory. Definitions of musical terms and concepts will be limited to what is deemed necessary to gain a suitable understanding of one's musical taste. When the urge to get more highly technical overcomes me, I will relegate the more complex material to an endnote (with yet more detail occasionally placed on the WYLI website)—which can be skimmed or ignored without losing the basic meaning. Helping out, as noted, will be a glossary of musical terms—defining those terms and expressions placed in **bold** in the text. Experienced musicians, on the other hand, may find the musical discussions in these chapters fairly rudimentary, and thus are invited to skim these chapters.

As a further aid to our discussion, I have opted to include a good number of score excerpts (that is, passages of music notation, or "sheet music," written in **treble clef**, **octave treble clef**, and **bass clef** only) in the main body of the text. As noted, all of these excerpts are aligned with audio samples found in the audio supplement portion of the WYLI website. If you have never read sheet music before, don't worry—the ability to read these excerpts is not required to understand the music theory concepts being discussed. As such, you need only glance at them. At the same time, even if it's just lines, dots, and squiggles to you, I encourage you to linger over them, especially while listening to the audio samples, as much information can be discerned from the graphic nature of musical notation.

Finally, in unwinding the parameters of music theory, my approach will deviate ever so slightly from the path laid out in LaRue's SHMRF acronym noted earlier. Instead of starting with sound, our discussion will begin with melody; it will then proceed to harmony, rhythm, form, and finally sound (creating the rather unfortunate acronym of **MHRFS**). Regardless, I promise that this discussion of music theory won't hurt too much. More importantly, going to a dinner party will never be the same again!

*three*

# MELODY: THE FACE OF MUSIC

As promised in the past chapter, we start our music theory primer not with sound, but rather with melody. There are, I admit, many good reasons to start with sound: without sound there is no melody. The generation of sound leads to musical pitch from which melodies are born—so why not start there? Perhaps it's unjustified, but my fear was that launching straight into the prickly nature of sound waves, frequencies, and overtones would rekindle frightful memories of high school physics exams just as we were getting started. Believe me, we'll have plenty of opportunities to explore the more brain-teasing concepts of music theory, including the nature of sound—no need to scare anyone away by opening with the thorniest topic.

For a book dedicated to understanding the nature of the music you love, better, I thought, to start with the much more intuitive parameter of melody. Indeed, for many—and in many musical cases—melody is the most prominent parameter we experience. It is certainly the most basic means by which we communicate music to one another. And no one has ever requested to play a game of "Name That Overtone."

At any rate, it is with melody that we begin, and with it we introduce our first in a series of anthropomorphic similes: a melody may be likened to . . . a human face. Like a face, each melody is unique, with its own character, sharing traits with those related to it and those not. Human faces, despite having only a small number of discrete elements—eyes, nose, mouth, ears, eyebrows, cheeks, chin—come in infinite variety, and yet we are able to recognize individual ones we've seen before, even in passing. This ability, known as face perception, is a key element of our neurological mechanism, and is active from infancy.[43]

Similarly, melodies draw on a limited number of primary elements—at most twelve discrete tones in the Western tradition, through usually far fewer. Yet we somehow can recognize as distinct those we've heard before, even just once. As with faces, this musical ability begins early, with infants as young as two months old able to discriminate one short melody from another.[44] The simile can be taken too far, certainly, but is useful in the recognition that just as we attach a strong, individual identity to a face, so too do individual melodies have the power to create within us strong and emotionally charged identities—and just as seeing the face of a loved one can make us happy, so too can hearing a well-loved melody.

## Melody and Lyrics, Part 1: Spoiler Alert

Before we get going, I'm afraid I need to shake things up with a spoiler alert:

*This book doesn't much focus on lyrics, or in fact on any text set to music.*

"What?!" I can hear the complaints now. "But lyrics are the most important part of a song—how can you expect to explain musical taste without factoring in the text?" It is true that for many listeners, lyrics are the most impactful part of a song. Yet for other listeners, lyrics or text are experienced as a secondary, at times generic consideration compared to the musical content, even if in your native tongue. I'm often one of the latter, I confess. Tim Westergren used to say that some folks are "lyrics people" and some are "music people." Obviously, many are both, and can be swayed more by the music or the lyrics depending on the song or the individual hearing. In one controlled study led by the music therapist Valerie Stratton, the use of sad lyrics impacted listeners above and beyond the nature of the melody, suggesting an inherently greater power of lyrics over mood.[45] Maybe.

Regardless, lyrics will not be my focus here. It may instead be assumed that most songs and vocal works discussed in this book reasonably reflect the lyrics or text they set in one or more ways: sentiment, topic, scansion (poetic meter and rhythm), sound, etc. Naturally, varied composers will handle this interaction differently, depending on their skill level, ambition, priorities, etc. For example, a songwriter may intentionally contrast the mood of the lyrics with an opposing musical style out of a sense of irony. Or an opera composer may intentionally set an aria in a way that contradicts its normal, spoken declamation.

Obviously, lyrics and texts set to music can vary drastically in subject matter, mood, attitude, form, meter, scansion, literary ambition, use of vulgarity, etc. Taking all of these factors into account not only would enter us deeply into the complex realm of poetics, but also would impossibly lengthen this book. It is true that the Music Genome Project takes into consideration several of these elements in forming its matches (remember the *T* in "SHMRFT") but as I'm here concerned with the factors that underlie our *musical* taste, they will by and large be ignored. Sorry.

Okay, back to our regularly scheduled program. . . .

## The Basics of Melody

What is a **melody**? Well, from a technical standpoint, a melody is set of **pitches**—also called **notes** or **tones**—arranged in a particular sequence in musical time. This flow of pitches can proceed in a manner that is strictly rhythmic or free, or both. The distance between one pitch and the next is called an **interval**, which can be small or large. The distance between the lowest and the highest pitch within a complete melody, on the other hand, is referred to as its **range**—or, more technically, its **ambitus**. As a general rule, melodies rarely have ranges much larger than an octave and a quarter, which is in line with what most individuals can sing.

Within a melody, there are usually distinct sections, or **phrases**, of varying length, much as a paragraph is divided into distinct clauses and sentences. Unlike in a paragraph, however, it is not unusual for the same melodic phrase to repeat one or more times (sometimes many more times) within an overall melody. These repetitions can be in immediate succession, or separated by contrasting material, or both. The parallelism between melodies and paragraphs, moreover, underscores the natural affinity that exists between music and human speech in general.

The basic elements of melody mentioned so far are shown in Figure 3.1—using a familiar nursery rhyme, "Old MacDonald," with which we'll likewise introduce the other parameters:

**Figure 3.1: "Old MacDonald"—basic melodic elements**

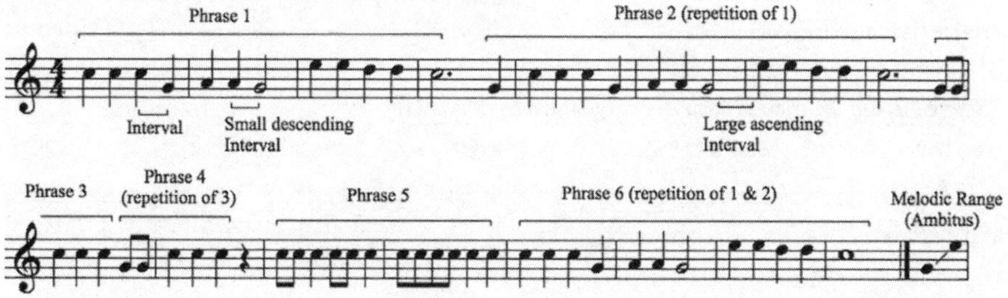


Diving a bit deeper, we can understand intervals (the distance between notes) by picturing a piano keyboard (Figure 3.2). Starting on the pitch marked C, a melody may proceed immediately up or down to a *different* pitch, or it may repeat the *same* pitch again, whereby it's called a **unison**. If it does move up or down, the interval is given both a number—from a 2nd to an **octave** (eight notes away); and a quality or "flavor"—either **major**, **minor**, or **perfect**, as follows:

**Figure 3.2: Piano keyboard octave—intervals (partial)**

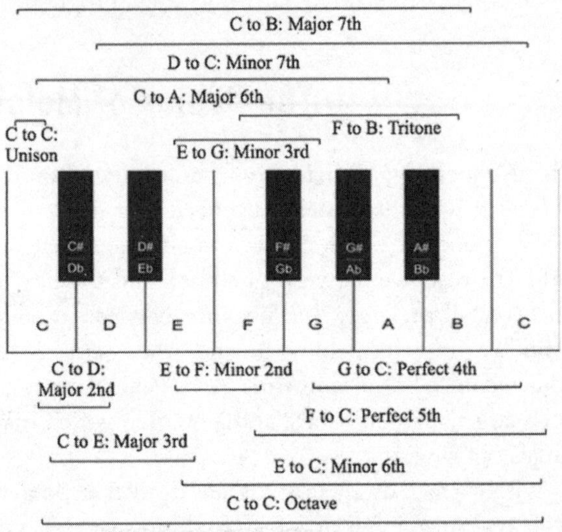


Of course, an interval also can exceed an octave—practically from a 9th (an octave plus a 2nd) to a 13th (an octave plus a 6th)—though rarely beyond this in the context of an actual melody, whether sung or played on an instrument.

Each interval type has its own character within a melody. Of course, this character depends on its context and placement as the melody proceeds, as well as its interaction with rhythm, harmony, or sound. Speaking generally, though, smaller intervals (unison, 2nd, 3rd) carry a rather smooth, effortless affect as they move up or down, while larger leaps (6th, 7th, octave, etc.) appear more angular or dramatic to the ear. The midsized perfect 4th and perfect 5th often carry a strong, solid, even majestic quality—as in the opening notes of the *Star Wars* main theme (Figure 3.3):

**Figure 3.3: *Star Wars* main theme—strong intervals (4ths, 5ths)**

The **tritone** (a distance of three consecutive major 2nds, also called an augmented 4th or diminished 5th), on the other hand, is a bit of a strange beast. It has a rather colorful place in music history: famously it was called *diabolus in musica* ("the devil in music") from at least the ninth century, due to its perceived harsh sound. This censure, however, was more directed at the tritone as a harmonic (simultaneously sounding) interval than as a melodic (consecutively sounding) one. Yet its use as a melodic interval was likewise avoided, undoubtedly because it's actually hard to sing. However, a few famous examples have surfaced more recently—notably the opening of "Maria" from *West Side Story* (Figure 3.4). Devil be gone!

**Figure 3.4: "Maria" (from *West Side Story*)—use of melodic tritone**

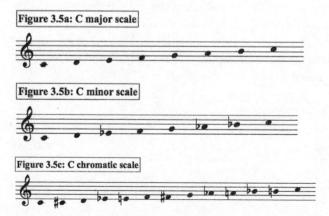

Again, speaking generally, major intervals have a brighter sound, while minor intervals have a darker sound. We'll discuss why an interval would be deemed "perfect" (or "imperfect") in Interlude B.

When musicians speak of the distance of a minor 2nd (C–D♭), the term **half step** is commonly used, whereas a major 2nd (C–D) is called a **whole step** (or whole tone)—that is, made up of two consecutive half steps (C–C♯, C♯–D). The sequence of half steps and whole steps from one pitch to the same pitch an octave higher (e.g., C–C') in turn creates a **scale**. There are many different types of scales, the most common in the West being the **major**, **minor**, and **chromatic**. Major and minor scales are called **diatonic** (literally "proceeding by tones"), signifying that they are seven-note scales comprising a smooth, alternating pattern of whole and half steps—like playing just the white keys of the piano from C to C' (major scale) or from A to A' (minor scale). The chromatic scale, by contrast, comprises exclusively half steps. These three common scales are shown in Figures 3.5 a–c:

**Figure 3.5a: C major scale**

**Figure 3.5b: C minor scale**

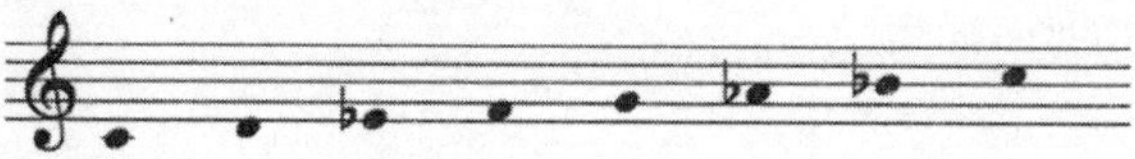

**Figure 3.5c: C chromatic scale**

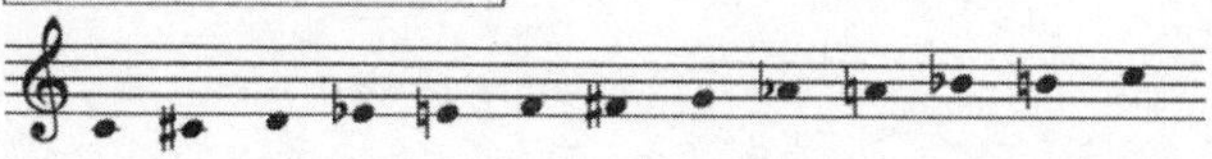

It is probably safe to say that a good many melodies in your "hit parade" are composed primarily or exclusively of notes within either a major or minor scale—perhaps with a few occasional chromatic intervals thrown in for spice.

Okay, how are we doing? Not too overwhelmed, I hope. Believe me: if at any time in these music theory discussions (Chapters 3–7) you start to feel that way, please don't fret. Perhaps reread the passage, but regardless, know that it is not essential that you grasp every aspect of any given concept being introduced. There will be many other opportunities to get closer to that goal. With each mention, moreover, you will gain an ever-clearer understanding of the theory underlying the music you love.

## The Melodic Building Blocks

Scales—or "**modes**," as they are sometimes called—are a fundamental component of musical theory and music analysis. Beyond the major, minor, and chromatic scales, there are many other, often exotic variants used within both Western and non-Western traditions. Indeed, the specific pitch structure of the scales used in a given culture or style is a key factor in defining its overall musical identity. Not all scales are structured as consecutively stepwise, by the way, but may include periodic interval leaps of a minor 3rd or larger.

The most famous and universal of these scale variants is a class known as **pentatonic scales** (five notes per octave), comprising a mix of stepwise (major or minor 2nds) and skipped (major or minor 3rds) intervals. There are myriad variations in the distribution of the scale's five intervals as used by different cultures around the world. At the same time, many geographically remote cultures share a similar or even identical structure in their pentatonic scales; an example is the **major pentatonic scale**—heard, for example, by playing the black notes on the piano starting on G♭ (Figure 3.6, here starting on C)—found in Celtic, West African, Chinese, Mongolian, Southeast Asian, and ancient Greek music, among others.[46] How a single scale came to gain such universality speaks not only to the history of early human migration and cultural exchange, but also to a basic element of human physiology (e.g., reflecting natural emotional sounds like cries), as we'll discuss in Interlude A.

**Figure 3.6: Major pentatonic scale—starting on C**

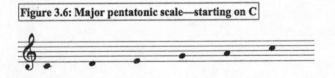

A common variant of the major pentatonic scale is, not surprisingly, the **minor pentatonic scale**—heard, for example, by playing the black notes on the piano starting on E♭ (Figure 3.7, here starting on C); this is similarly widespread, found in cultures as remote as Scottish, Andean, and Japanese, etc. Importantly, the minor pentatonic scale has its own variant—or "offspring," if you will. It should be familiar to most Anglo-American ears, as it is found in a great deal of popular music as the **blues scale** (Figure 3.8). As will be noticed, it is identical to the minor pentatonic except for an extra note between the third and fourth degrees (a tritone above the first note). This is a "blue note," which helps give blues and rock songs their distinct and "edgy" attitude.

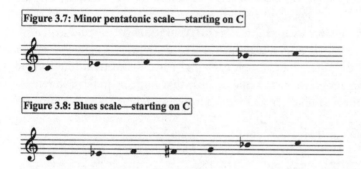

**Figure 3.7: Minor pentatonic scale—starting on C**

**Figure 3.8: Blues scale—starting on C**

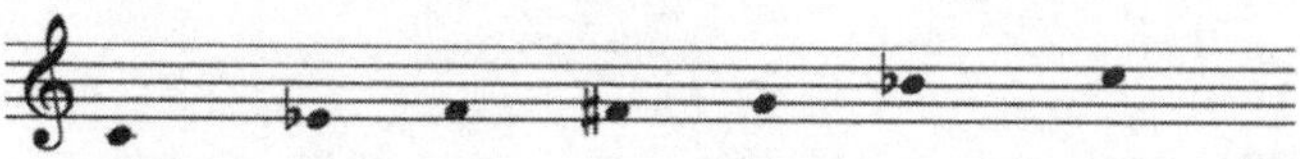

But while scales form the "building blocks" of melodies, they are not themselves melodies. It is, to be sure, possible that a given melody may present a complete (or near-complete) ascending or descending scale in one or more of its phrases—as in the closing phrases of "Do-Re-Mi" from *The Sound of Music*, (Figure 3.9).

**Figure 3.9: "Do-Re-Mi" (from *The Sound of Music*)—partial ascending scales**

So: a nee-dle pul-ling thread.
La: a note to fol-low so.
Ti: a drink with jam and bread.

But such cases are rare. Most melodies will present at most a few ascending or descending half or whole steps in a scale-like succession before then repeating a note or skipping up or down by a larger interval.

The number of possible permutations using all of these intervallic and directional options is virtually infinite, in turn enabling a virtually infinite number of potential melodies—especially when rhythm is added to the mix. A few calculations have been attempted to place some finite bounds to these possible melodies—resulting in some pretty incomprehensible numbers.* In short, we won't be running out of melody prospects any time soon.

## Intervallic Examples

Beyond the few melodic excerpts given above, I next present a good number more, with a brief commentary attached to each, along with a few more musicological concepts introduced along the way. These examples are not meant to form some sort of "representational sample" of melodies or melody types or to suggest any "universal rules" of melodic construction. Rather, they embody an eclectic sample of excerpts from (generally) well-known songs and works in various styles that illustrate some *commonly used* features and techniques of melodic structure.

As noted above, small intervals—and especially stepwise major and minor 2nds—present to the listener a smooth, easy, and natural affect, and indeed are easiest to both sing and play. It thus makes sense that most melodies will rely on 2nds and 3rds as their primary or dominant intervals. Here are some examples:

**Figure 3.10: "London Bridge Is Falling Down" (traditional)—melodic 2nds**

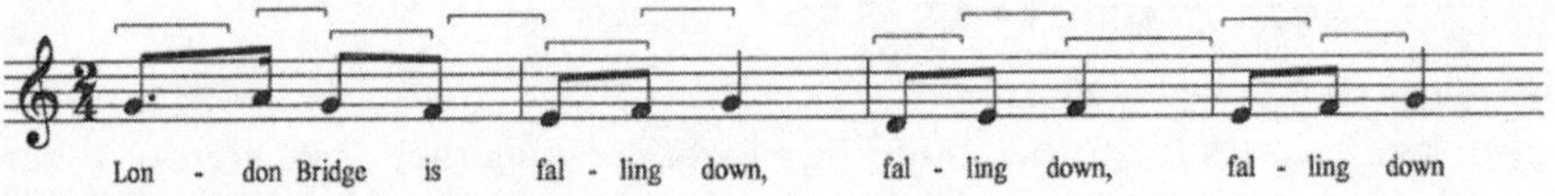


**Figure 3.11: The Doors, "People Are Strange"—mix of melodic 2nds and 3rds**

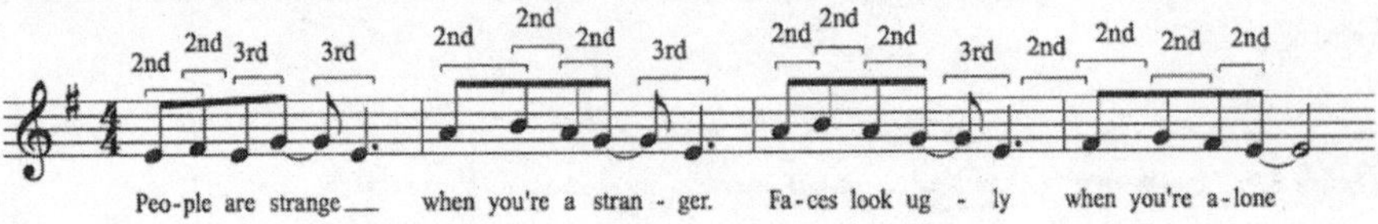


**Figure 3.12: J. S. Bach, *Goldberg Variations*, Aria (mm. 1–4)—melodic 2nds, with leap between phrases**

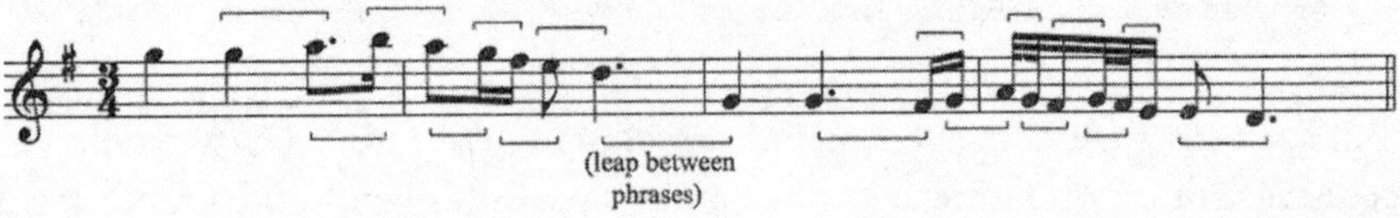


In all of these examples, stepwise motion is the dominant intervallic tendency, with occasional leaps of a 3rd or greater to provide contrast or emphasis,

* As an example, a blogger named "ferrouslepidoptera" calculated the possibilities of a thirty-two-note melody using any intervallic combination, with six potential rhythmic values, and came to a whopping 123,511,210,975,209,861,511,554,928,715,787,036 possible melodies!

particularly between phrases. This is markedly the case with the Bach Aria, where leaps between one phrase and the next create a dramatic level of contrast and distinction that is, in fact, fairly uncommon.

Many melodies are more decidedly built upon a string of small leaps—most especially of 3rds or 4ths—as in these examples:

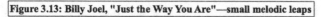

**Figure 3.13: Billy Joel, "Just the Way You Are"—small melodic leaps**

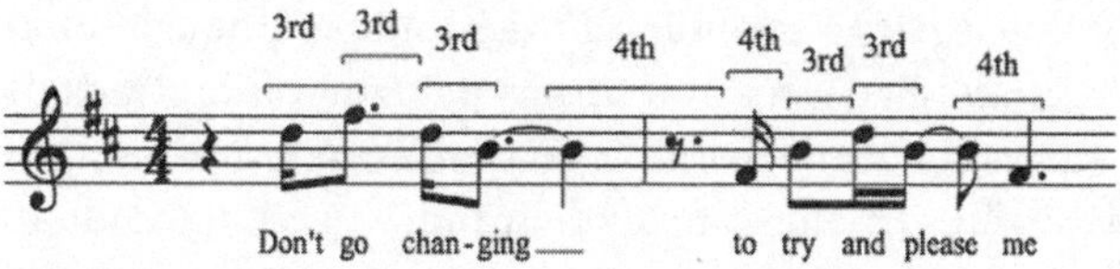


**Figure 3.14: Hozier, "Take Me to Church" (chorus)—small melodic leaps**

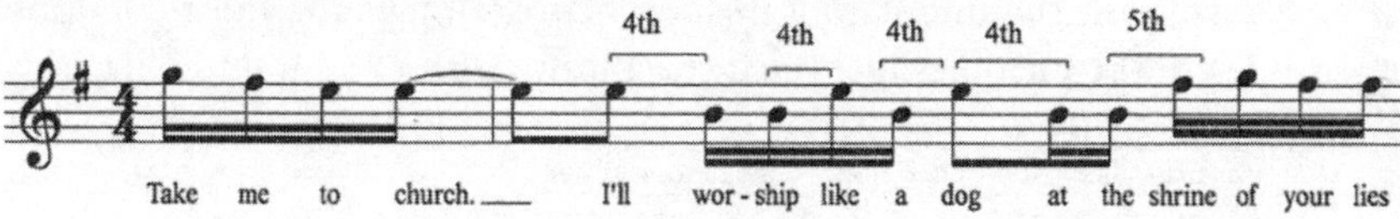


However, when leaps of a 3rd or 4th are employed as the primary intervallic tendency in a melody, they are inevitably followed by unisons or stepwise intervals—providing a welcome relief to both performers and listeners (see examples above).

Some songs and works, by contrast, create their identity by emphasizing even larger intervals (6ths, 7ths, octaves) within a single phrase, not uncommonly at the beginning of the song or work, to establish focus or drama—as in these examples:

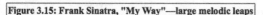

**Figure 3.15: Frank Sinatra, "My Way"—large melodic leaps**

**Figure 3.16: Cole Porter, "I Love You"—large melodic leaps**

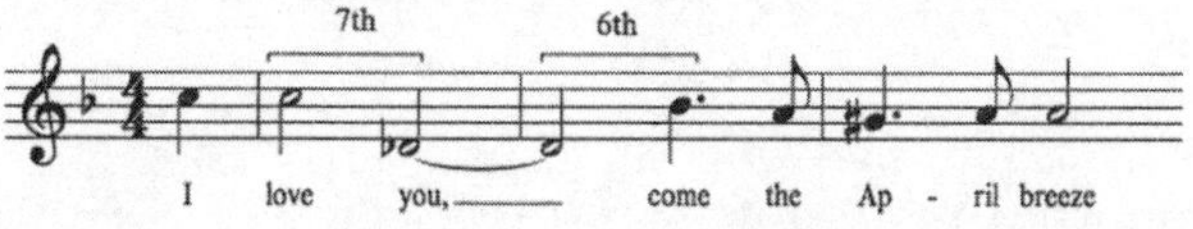


**Figure 3.17: Harold Arlen, "Somewhere over the Rainbow"—large melodic leaps**

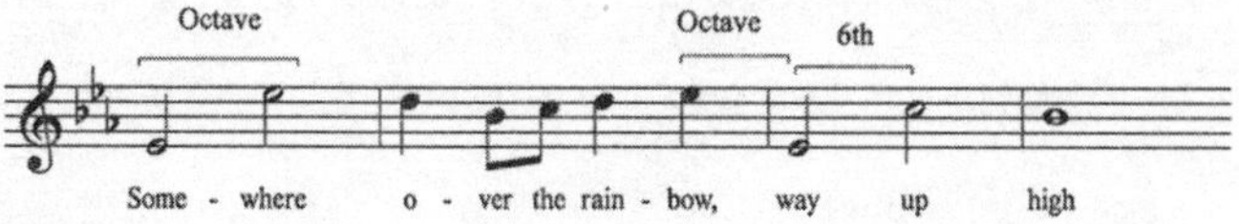

Again, leaps are commonly followed by stepwise motion, particularly in vocal music.

## The Shape's the Thing

The word "**contour**" is commonly used in musicology to describe the overall shape or pattern of melodies—such as ascending or descending. The ethnomusicologist Bruno Nettl has established a set of terms to describe various melodic contours used commonly throughout the world: beyond the two just mentioned, Nettl introduced "undulating" (a balanced mix of ascending and descending), "pendulum" (swinging back to two melodic areas via large leaps), "arc" (ascent followed by slow descent), etc.[47] Most of the examples cited above follow one of these contours, with the undulating melody being perhaps the most common. Here are a few more melodies identified specifically with each of these shapes:

**Figure 3.18: Leonard Cohen, "Hallelujah"—ascending contour**

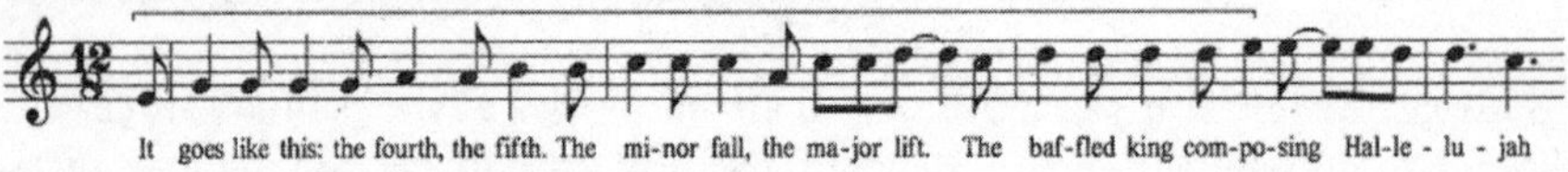
It goes like this: the fourth, the fifth. The mi-nor fall, the ma-jor lift. The baf-fled king com-po-sing Hal-le - lu - jah

**Figure 3.19: Duke Ellington, "Don't Get Around Much Anymore"—descending contour**

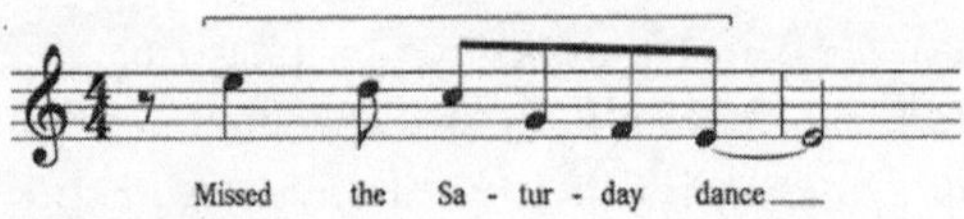
Missed the Sa - tur - day dance

**Figure 3.20: The Beatles, "Yesterday"—undulating contour**

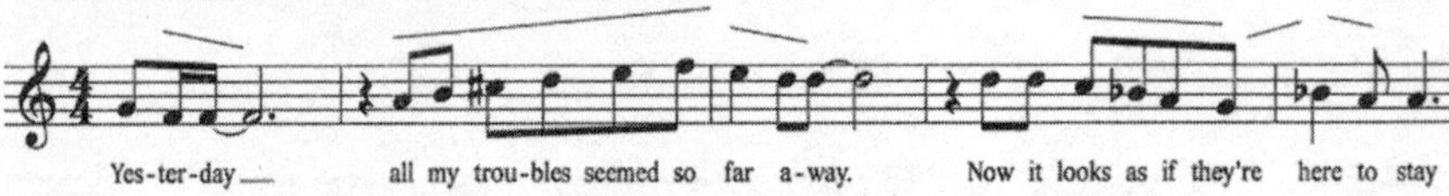
Yes-ter-day all my trou-bles seemed so far a-way. Now it looks as if they're here to stay

**Figure 3.21: Nirvana, "Lithium" (verse)—pendulum contour**

I'm so hap-py 'cause to - day I've found my friends in my head

**Figure 3.22: George Gershwin, "Someone to Watch Over Me" (refrain)—arc contour**

There's a some-bo-dy I'm long-ing to see, I hope that he turns out to be some-one who

Another common contour, moreover, is a static, or "monotone," melody—where the repetition of a single pitch is the dominant intervallic tendency. This approach is assuredly quite ancient, especially aligned with rituals of one kind or another—as an intermediate step between speaking and singing.[48] Its use in the West extends back to the early church, used to recite the Book of Psalms (Figure 3.23), and is found periodically in opera recitative (sung speech) and other classical era approaches for dramatic effect—as in Schubert's song "Death and the Maiden," capturing the inanimate lethargy of death (Figure 3.24). While a periodic facet of Western popular music during the 1950–'80s, as in Bob Dylan's "Subterranean Homesick Blues" (Figure 3.25), the monotonic approach to melody has returned to some level of prominence with the rise of hip hop and rap music. While rap lyrics are ostensibly delivered as an unpitched "declamation," many rappers—e.g., Snoop Dogg, Dr. Dre, Eric B. & Rakim, etc.—will latch on to a single pitch (often aligned with the root of the harmony) and stick to it more or less as a kind of anchor, as in Snoop Dogg's "Gin & Juice" (Figure 3.26).

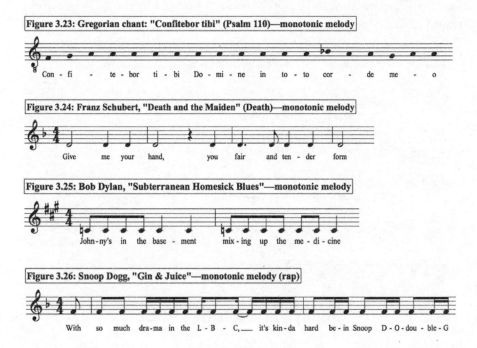

**Figure 3.23: Gregorian chant: "Confitebor tibi" (Psalm 110)—monotonic melody**

Con - fi - te - bor ti - bi Do - mi - ne in to - to cor - de me - o

**Figure 3.24: Franz Schubert, "Death and the Maiden" (Death)—monotonic melody**

Give me your hand, you fair and ten - der form

**Figure 3.25: Bob Dylan, "Subterranean Homesick Blues"—monotonic melody**

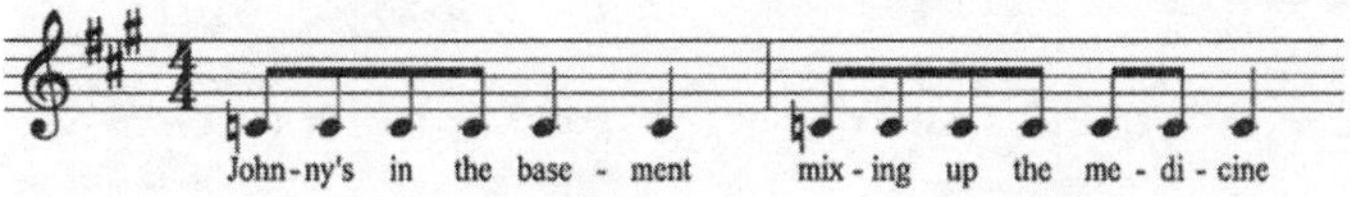
John-ny's in the base - ment mix - ing up the me - di - cine

**Figure 3.26: Snoop Dogg, "Gin & Juice"—monotonic melody (rap)**

With so much dra-ma in the L - B - C, it's kin-da hard be - in Snoop D - O - dou - ble - G

## Phrase by Phrase

As indicated previously, complete melodies are generally divided into smaller phrases. The relationship between the phrases—how they flow from one to another—is a key factor in the melody's identity and our experience of it. At times the phrases are quite clearly delineated, while in other cases the precise division can be a source of some ambiguity. We'll touch more on this when discussing form in Chapter 6. Likewise the length of phrases can vary considerably, from a few notes to dozens or more—as demonstrated in the examples above.

Importantly, the relationship between phrases is often rather formal in nature—via exact or varied repetition (Figures 3.27 and 3.29) or via a common technique known as a **sequence** (Figures 3.28 and 3.29). A sequence is defined as "the more or less exact repetition of a passage at a higher or lower level of pitch."[49] The sequence may be considered a type of melodic "archetype," as it is used in melodies of nearly every culture and style. The rationale is simply that sequences enable a clear and identifiable narrative by delivering two or more (rarely more than three) related phrases consecutively—providing both similarity and distinction. They have a particular power to grab the ear's attention and help focus the mind on the flow of musical content. Certain periods have embraced sequences more emphatically than others—notably the **Baroque era** (1600–1750) of classical music and our own era of popular music. Here are a mix of songs and works featuring both phrase repetition and sequence:

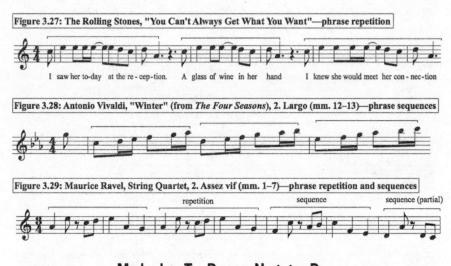

**Figure 3.27: The Rolling Stones, "You Can't Always Get What You Want"—phrase repetition**

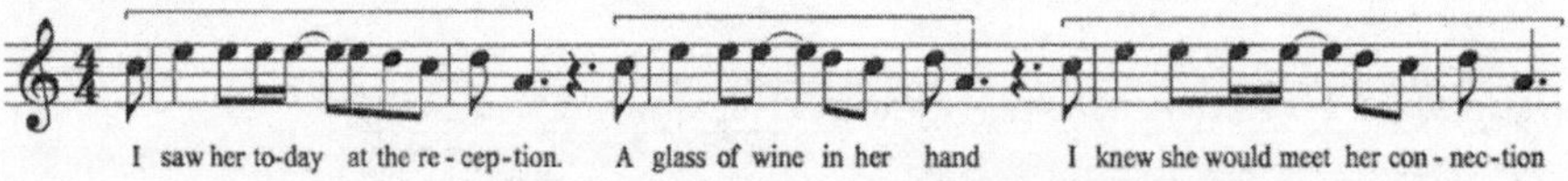
I saw her to-day at the re-cep-tion.
A glass of wine in her hand
I knew she would meet her con-nec-tion

**Figure 3.28: Antonio Vivaldi, "Winter" (from *The Four Seasons*), 2. Largo (mm. 12–13)—phrase sequences**

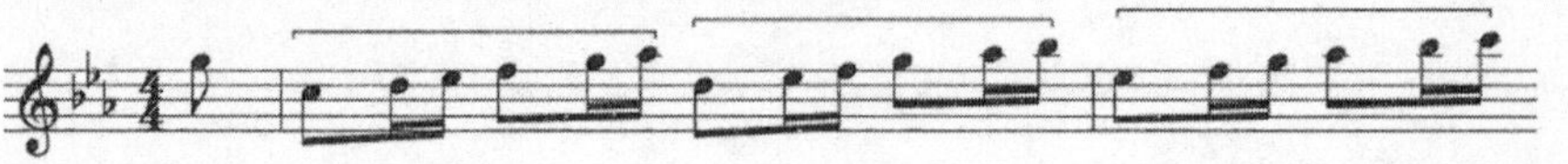

**Figure 3.29: Maurice Ravel, String Quartet, 2. Assez vif (mm. 1–7)—phrase repetition and sequences**

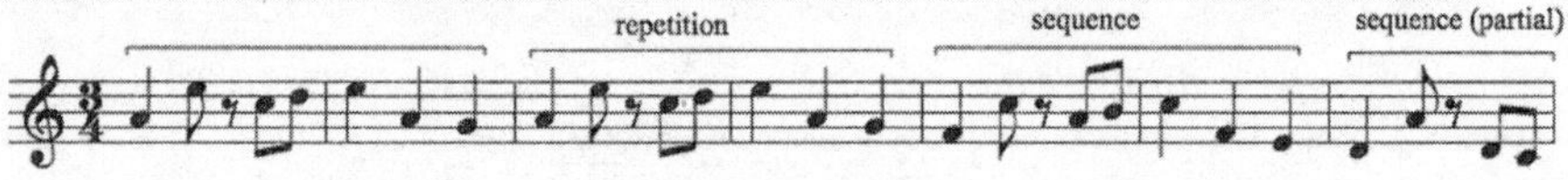
repetition
sequence
sequence (partial)

## Melody: To Be or Not to Be

Throughout this discussion so far on melody, we've bypassed one key question: When is a consecutive flow of pitches not a "melody," but rather something else? This can be a difficult question, as in some cases a melodic phrase to one listener is but a fragment or pattern to another.

Musicology, in fact, has a number of terms for incomplete or quasi-melodic ideas—that in some cases take on a structural or defining quality in a song or work. Chief among these is the **ostinato** (from the Italian meaning "obstinate")—described as the "repetition of a musical pattern many times in succession while other musical elements are generally changing."[50] Ostinatos have been used throughout music history and survive in modern music in the guise of **riffs**—which account for some of the most memorable and beloved musical elements in rock and pop music. A riff is that infectious repeating pattern—such as at the start of "Satisfaction" by the Rolling Stones or "Sunshine of Your Love" by Cream—that inevitably inspires someone in the room, perhaps you, to flamboyantly pull out the air guitar.

Another common term for a quasi-melody is **motive** (or **motif**), defined by the *Grove Dictionary of Music*—the musicologist's bible—as "a short musical idea . . . regarded as the shortest subdivision of a **theme** or phrase that still maintains its identity as an idea."[51] Within classical music, composers—most famously nineteenth-century figures like Beethoven and Wagner—have used short motives as structural or compositional devices to lend greater cohesion to their works. Here are a few examples of these structural "quasi-melodic" ideas:

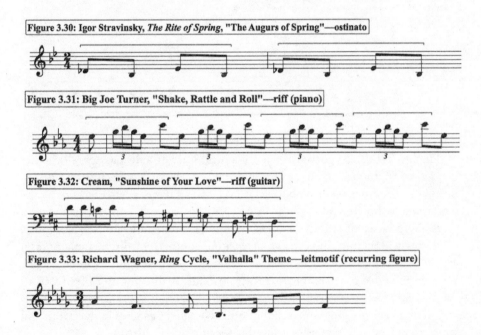

**Figure 3.30: Igor Stravinsky, *The Rite of Spring*, "The Augurs of Spring"—ostinato**

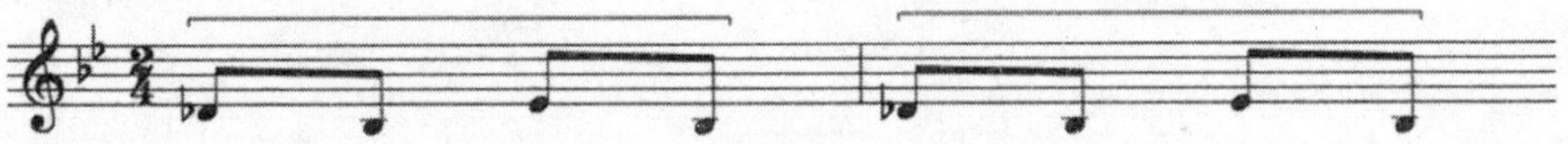

**Figure 3.31: Big Joe Turner, "Shake, Rattle and Roll"—riff (piano)**

**Figure 3.32: Cream, "Sunshine of Your Love"—riff (guitar)**

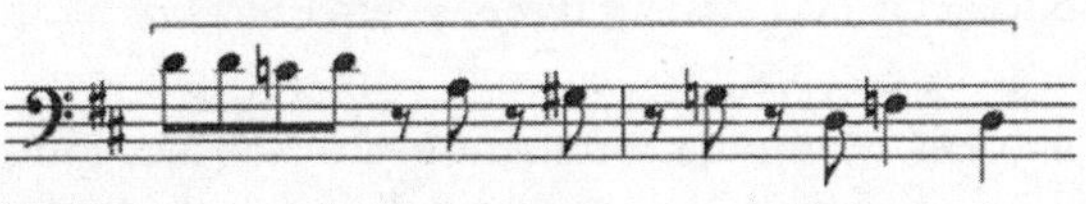

**Figure 3.33: Richard Wagner, *Ring* Cycle, "Valhalla" Theme—leitmotif (recurring figure)**

At times, of course, we can more definitely say that a particular series of pitches is *not* a melody, even if it can be called "musical" in some way or another. What do we mean? Think of a simple bass pattern in a rock song whose sole purpose is to support the song harmonically and rhythmically (Figure 3.34), or perhaps a slow-moving sequence of pitches that largely fill out the harmony within a choral setting (Figure 3.35). These may be "pretty" or "rhythmic" within the larger texture, but on their own they elicit little narrative—that is, melodic—interest or definition. A slightly more complex case would be an "inner" line within a **contrapuntal** context—meaning where multiple "melodic" lines proceed simultaneously: the "inner" series of pitches may support other melodies above or below it, but by itself does not constitute a clear melody (see Figure 3.36).

**Figure 3.34: Ed Sheeran, "Perfect" (verse 3)—nonmelodic bass line**

**Figure 3.35: W. A. Mozart, "Ave verum corpus"—nonmelodic accompaniment (below)**

**Figure 3.36: Alexander Borodin, String Quartet No. 2, 3. Notturno (mm. 24–27)—nonmelodic counterpoint (below)**

Finally, in this category will fall a good number of **solo** passages—whether in jazz, rock, bluegrass, or any style/genre that incorporates **improvisation**. By nature, improvisation embodies a level of spontaneity on the part of the performer—who, theoretically at least, creates a "melody" on the spot over a preestablished set of chords or other harmonic foundation. To be sure, gifted musicians will at times be capable of creating some decidedly melodic phrases within their solo, particularly when it is previously worked out to some degree. Yet even the most gifted improvisers—from Louis Armstrong to Miles Davis to Slash—will present material in their improvised solo passages that may have lots of soul or sass or fire, but which cannot quite be called melodies in the traditional sense. Here are some examples using this specific set of artists:

**Figure 3.37: Louis Armstrong, "West End Blues"—trumpet solo (opening cadenza)**

Figure 3.38: Miles Davis, "All Blues"—trumpet solo (start)

Figure 3.39: Slash, "Sweet Child o' Mine"—guitar solo (start)

## Melodies around the World

Next, we must take note of the many, diverse melodic types found in practices and styles outside the West. Indeed, in most non-Western cultures, melody—as paired with rhythm—takes on an especially heightened focus in a song or work's overall musical identity. This is especially true given the common lack of an established, indigenous system of vertical harmony (chords) in many cultures or traditions. In such an environment, melodic definition, subtlety, and performance techniques have given rise to some very distinct sounds and approaches.

Specifically, melodies can vary from culture to culture in the nature of their scales, modes, and **tuning**—the systems by which the notes of scales and modes are defined. This includes pitch relationships that are outside the traditional set of twelve intervals described above—that is, **microtones** (smaller than a minor 2nd), as well as various exotic scales that may sound odd to inexperienced Western ears. "Ethnic" melodies also utilize forms of melodic **ornamentation** and embellishment typically absent in the West. These include a huge array of effects and techniques—such as slides, multiphonics (two pitches simultaneously), overtone singing, humming, clicking, throat singing, etc. Indeed, all of us in the West owe it to ourselves to become acquainted with the rich and diverse canvas of ethnic melodies and melodic approaches—starting with those examples available on the WYLI website.

The link between melodic practice and cultural identity is itself a fascinating topic. Much research and speculation on this relationship has been developed over the years, famously via Alan Lomax's *Cantometrics* publications in the 1960s, relating melodic characteristics to the cultural and social practices of the purveyors.[52] We'll have further opportunity to explore non-Western musical practices and their link to culture in the pages ahead. But for the moment, here are examples of melodies in the five folk traditions mentioned in Chapter 2:

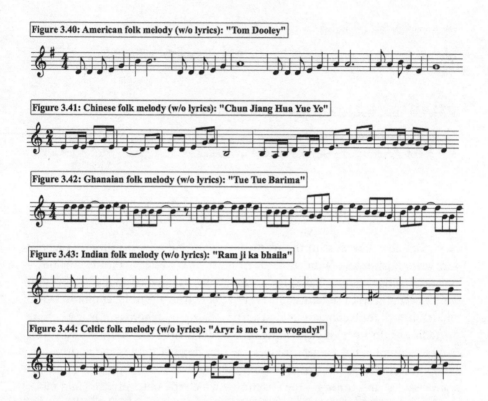

Figure 3.40: American folk melody (w/o lyrics): "Tom Dooley"

Figure 3.41: Chinese folk melody (w/o lyrics): "Chun Jiang Hua Yue Ye"

Figure 3.42: Ghanaian folk melody (w/o lyrics): "Tue Tue Barima"

Figure 3.43: Indian folk melody (w/o lyrics): "Ram ji ka bhaila"

Figure 3.44: Celtic folk melody (w/o lyrics): "Aryr is me 'r mo wogadyl"

It is true that the sounds and experiences of each of these folk styles are quite distinct from one another. And yet most of the melodic characteristics we've reviewed in this chapter will find resonance in them all: a common reliance on stepwise motion, with occasional skips or leaps; a generally clear division of a larger melody into distinct phrases; a discernible overall contour; the use of motive-like patterns; occasional sequences, etc. Amid the diversity, there is surely an element of universality in the ways humans create melody.

## Melody and Lyrics, Part 2: Text Setting

Although, as confessed above, the issue of lyrics is largely bypassed in this book, there are few facets of the music-text dynamic that do squarely fall within the realm of musicology, and thus warrant brief description here. These include two contrasting ways in which a melody sets a text, in terms of the number of notes per syllable. The first is **syllabic**, and is rather intuitive—where each note is aligned with a single syllable, as in these examples:

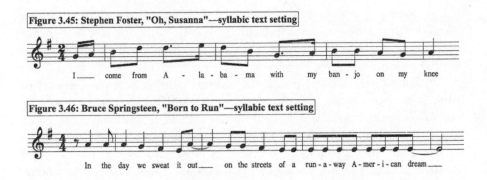

**Figure 3.45: Stephen Foster, "Oh, Susanna"—syllabic text setting**

I___ come from A - la - ba - ma with my ban - jo on my knee

**Figure 3.46: Bruce Springsteen, "Born to Run"—syllabic text setting**

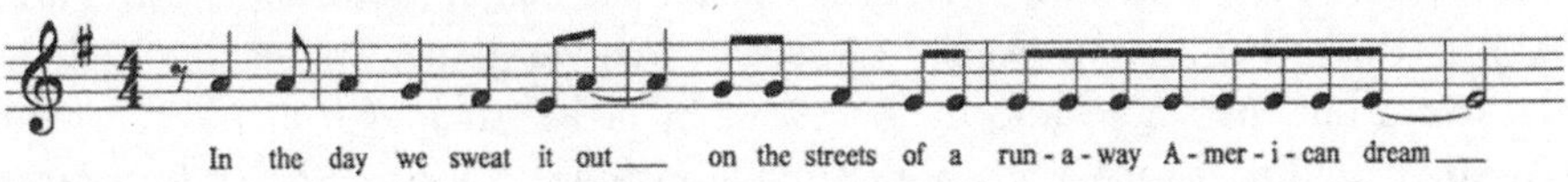
In the day we sweat it out___ on the streets of a run - a - way A - mer - i - can dream___

As the Stephen Foster example above (Figure 3.45) shows, even a predominantly syllabic song will have an occasional syllable that is given a second or third note. These are normally just a step away (minor or major 2nd) from the initial note, and are generally heard as an effortless expressive gesture. A vast majority of the vocal music you hear, regardless of style, falls fully or predominantly into the syllabic category. This is not a surprise, of course, as the syllabic approach reflects the inherently discursive or persuasive intent of most vocal music. Too many notes per syllable, and it can be hard to understand what is being sung.

And yet there is a contrasting approach, which goes by the twenty-five-cent name of **melismatic**. The word "melisma" is of ancient Greek origin, and simply means "song" or "melody." But it has come to be associated with any melodic passage in which a single syllable is set to several notes—at least five, and up to ten or more. A classic example is on the first syllable of "Gloria" in the Christmas carol "Angels We Have Heard on High" (Figure 3.47):

**Figure 3.47: "Angels We Have Heard on High"—melismatic text setting**

Glo - - - - - - - ri - a

Use of this florid approach stems back to the ancient world, not only in ancient Greece, but also in the Hebrew "*te'amim*" (cantillation) tradition, among many others, and may have been associated with intently meditative worship.[53] The technique later blossomed within Gregorian chants, and was sometimes referred to as a "jubilus"—a term first used by St. Augustine to signify the spiritual joy he felt when singing many notes to a single syllable.[54]

Today, a melisma refers to any context in which this technique is used. Notable cases in the Western classical tradition include Notre-Dame organum of the eleventh and twelfth centuries, the French chanson of the fourteenth century, and the Baroque cantata or oratorio of the seventeenth and eighteenth centuries, to name a few. Melismatic singing is likewise quite common in numerous non-Western traditions, most especially in Arabic, North African, and Indian vocal music. If the vocal melisma is your thing, these would all be styles and traditions worth exploring.

Within Western popular music, the melisma is a common vocal gesture in African-American genres like the blues, gospel, and R&B. It was initially an outgrowth of the "moan" of slavery-era forms such as the spiritual and the field holler. The melisma went from the black church via gospel singers like Mahalia Jackson to mainstream radio in the 1960s by artists such as Jackie Wilson and Aretha Franklin. It then saw a big resurgence in the 1990s and 2000s by a number of virtuosic, indeed "acrobatic," female singers in the R&B and pop realm—including Mariah Carey, Christina Aguilera, Whitney Houston, and Beyoncé. This oft-criticized trend has begun to fade in recent years, with artists like Kesha and Katy Perry opting, as the *New York Times* put it, "for a less daunting technical virtuosity."[55] Turn on Top 40 radio or TV talent shows like *The Voice*, however, and you'll hear that the melisma is still alive and well. Here are a few examples from across styles and centuries:

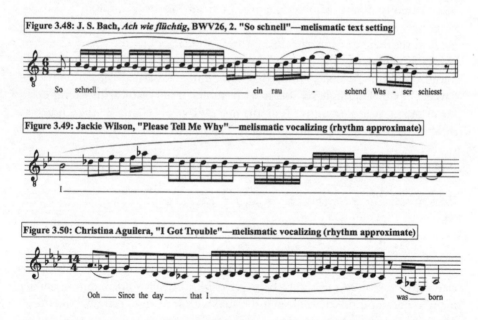

**Figure 3.48: J. S. Bach, *Ach wie flüchtig*, BWV26, 2. "So schnell"—melismatic text setting**

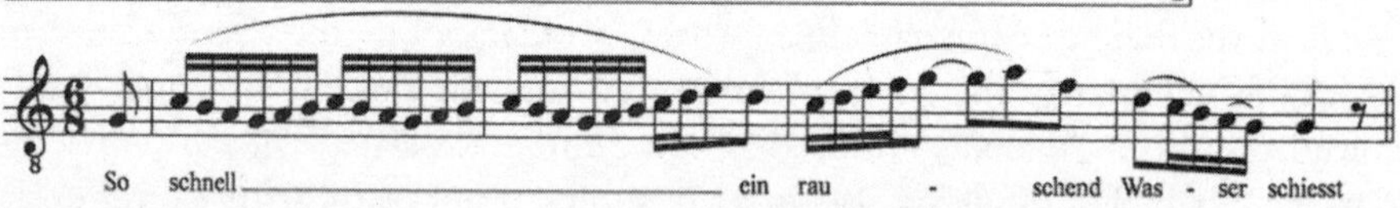
So schnell ein rau - schend Was - ser schiesst

**Figure 3.49: Jackie Wilson, "Please Tell Me Why"—melismatic vocalizing (rhythm approximate)**

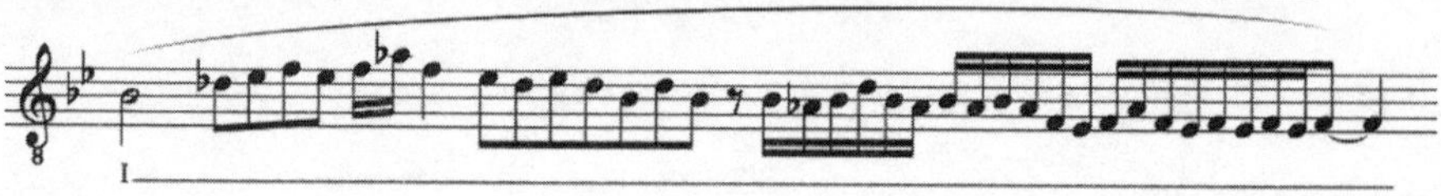
I

**Figure 3.50: Christina Aguilera, "I Got Trouble"—melismatic vocalizing (rhythm approximate)**

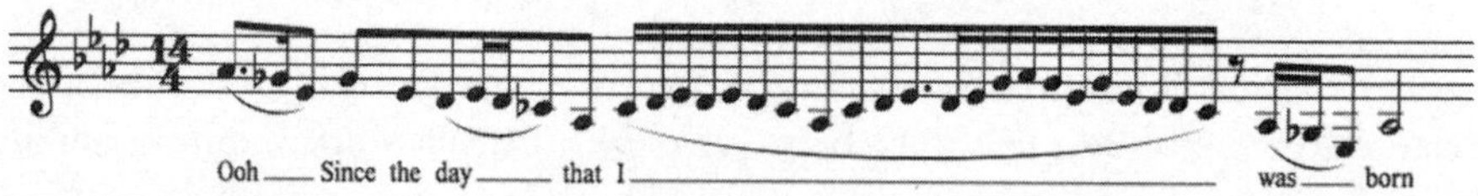
Ooh Since the day that I was born

Of course, a good many vocal works in a good many styles fall between the extremes of syllabic and melismatic. Technically, this is sometimes called "**neumatic**." However, you'll be hard-pressed to find a practicing musician who uses this word.* Here are two examples of this in-between approach:

---

* The expression comes from the term "neume"—the class of notational signs used for Gregorian

**Figure 3.51: Gaetano Donizetti, "Vieni! la mia vendetta" (from *Lucrezia Borgia*)—neumatic text setting**

Vie - ni! la mia ven - det - ta È me - di - ta - ta e pron - ta

**Figure 3.52: John Legend, "All of Me"—neumatic text setting**

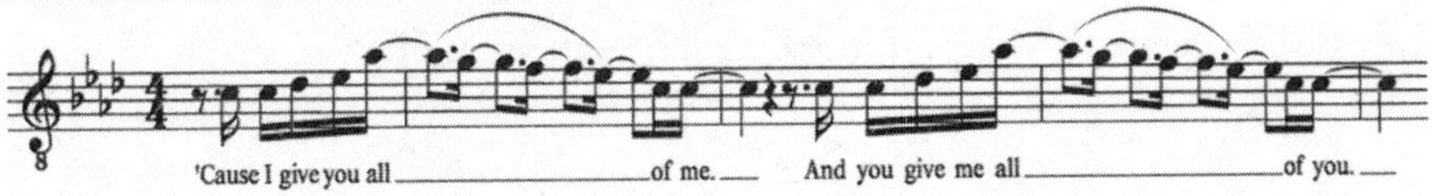
'Cause I give you all of me. And you give me all of you.

Finally, there is a particular musicological device that touches on the link between musical content and the actual *meaning* of the text. I'm not speaking of the music reflecting the mood or subject matter of the lyrics as a whole—what the Germans call *Tonmalerei* (tone painting). As noted above, it is to be assumed that most composers will accomplish this reflection to some degree or another—for example, matching a sad lyric with a slow tempo, minor chords, and small intervals; or a cheerful lyric with a fast tempo, major chords, and intervallic leaps, etc. Those are terribly simplistic examples, of course. But in fact they speak to the challenge of articulating the many ways in which a composer can possibly reflect lyrical content.

Instead, I'm talking about a very limited and specific technique of depicting the semantic meaning of a word or phrase (whether explicit or implicit) with a targeted musical response—or, as it's usually termed in English, **word painting**. This has a long and rich tradition in Western music, embodying the link between music and the esteemed field of rhetoric.[56] Stereotypical examples include "rising" or "falling" words depicted via an ascending or descending melody; "hurrying" or "fleeing" words depicted with a flurry of fast notes; and number words depicted by a matching number of voices, such as "one" or "two" depicted by a solo or duet, etc.

Such "pictorial" cases of word painting became standard fare during the Renaissance, and especially in the sixteenth-century secular genre of the madrigal (Figure 3.53). It continued heartily through the Baroque era, famously in Handel's *Messiah* (Figure 3.54), and in a good many opera arias and songs during the eighteenth and nineteenth centuries (Figure 3.55). Its use in folk and popular music is comparatively limited, though a good number of instances exist—especially when the lyrics include words like "up," "rise," "higher," "down," "fall," "lower," "fast," "slow," and the like (see Figure 3.56).

Word painting can indeed be trite, and has received its fair share of criticism

---

chants from the ninth century; the "neumatic" style specifically refers to the neume form that contains two to four notes written together, to be sung to a single syllable.

from music theorists through the ages. But it also can be realized with great subtlety and creativity, in turn delighting those sensitive or attentive enough to recognize it. It is thus worth "keeping an ear out" for word painting in your favorite vocal works—assuming you can understand the words. Here are a few examples:

**Figure 3.53: Thomas Weelkes, "As Vesta was" (madrigal)—word painting**

same a - scend - - - - ing

**Figure 3.54: G. F. Handel, "Ev'ry valley shall be exalted" (from *Messiah*)—word painting**

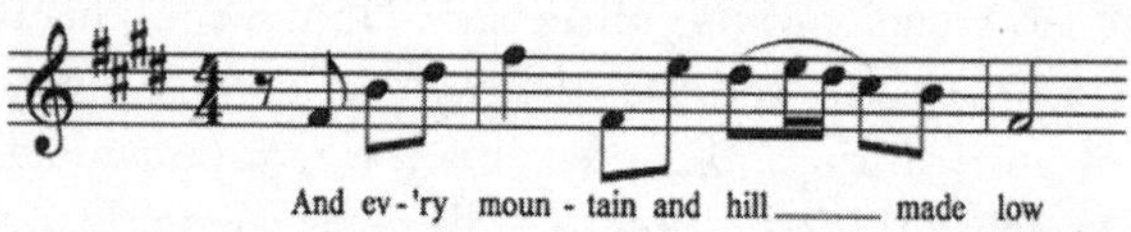
And ev - 'ry moun - tain and hill ___ made low

**Figure 3.55: "Swing Low, Sweet Chariot" (spiritual)—word painting**

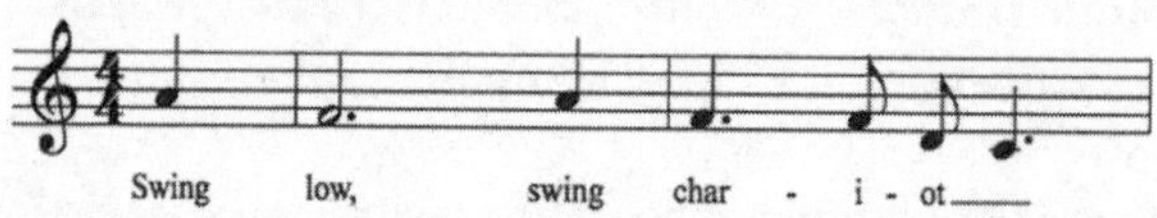
Swing low, swing char - i - ot ___

**Figure 3.56: Muse, "Falling Away with You"—word painting**

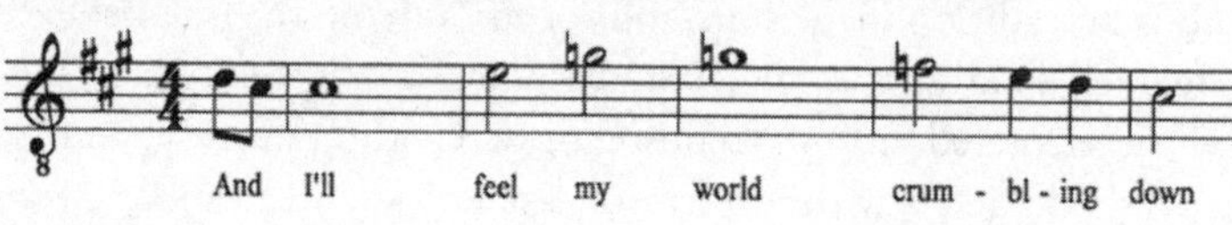
And I'll feel my world crum - bl - ing down

In sum, the "face" of melody comes in many shapes, forms, and aesthetic dispositions. Like those of people, the similarities can be as striking as the differences. And remember that it can be as delightful to encounter a new face or a new melody as reencountering those we've long known and loved.

Here are a few suggested exercises to test your awareness and listening *engagement* with melody:

1. Next time you hear any well-known song: Can you track the flow of rising and falling intervals in the main melody? Can you identify small, stepwise intervals? What about big leaps (6th, 7th, octaves)? What about strong 4ths and 5ths—or perhaps a "devilish" tritone?
2. Next time you hear any familiar melody: Try to track the different

phrases. Is it easy to distinguish when one phrase ends and another begins? Do you hear phrase repetition? How much does repetition define the melody as a whole?

3. Next time you hear a classical melody by Bach, Mozart, Haydn, or Beethoven: Do you hear the outlines of scale patterns? Can you identify passages that specifically outline complete or partial major, minor, or chromatic scales?
4. Next time you hear a folk or pop song you know: Follow the contour of the melody. Is it mainly ascending or descending, or both? To what degree is the melody monotonic?
5. Next time you hear a classic rock song: Can you identify a short, repeating riff (ostinato)? How much does it seem to define the song? What about melodic sequences? Can you identify them, and how prominently are they used?

The next musical parameter to be discussed will be harmony, in Chapter 4. But before we get there, let's transition our minds from the technical dimensions of music analysis to the extramusical sources of our musical taste. That part of our journey begins in Interlude A, with a discussion on the anthropological roots of our collective, human taste for music.

# Interlude A

## *The Evolution of Musical Taste: Music and Anthropology*

### A Doctrine of "Universal" Affection

This book is grounded on a premise: we all love music. To be sure, we may all love different music. . . . You may love the songs of Adele, or you may hate that pop drivel; you may dig the hard bop of Wes Montgomery, or you just may not "get" jazz; you may respect the rhymes of Lil Wayne, or the monotony of rap may drive you mad; you may adore Bartók, or you may find modern classical music ugly. . . . No two people share the same exact taste in music, but everyone loves it.

Well, okay, not everyone. In fact, a not insignificant portion of the population (around 4 percent) suffers from a condition known as amusia—or, as it is commonly known, tone deafness. Amusia can arise as a "natural" genetic variation or by means of a devastating accident, and has an equally wide range of symptoms.[57] On the mild end, amusia can lead to mere apathy toward music. A more pronounced case may affect one's ability to correctly perceive pitch, rhythm, or sound. At its most severe, amusia can lead to severe disdain toward music. In *Musicophilia*, Oliver Sacks chronicles a number of cases, ranging from a cantor who would occasionally sing notes horribly out of tune without noticing, to a woman for whom music could sound like "pots and pans thrown on the floor."[58] Not all sufferers of amusia, moreover, dislike music—though anyone who cannot "properly" perceive the parameters of music would arguably have a diminished reason to love it.

And yet, like all rare physiological deficiencies caused by either genetics or misfortune, amusics are the exceptions that prove the rule. Barring a neurological anomaly, that is, chances are quite high that any given person on the planet will love music of one kind or another. Either that, or they're just no fun at parties! We'll thus stick to our aforementioned premise: we all love music.[59]

And if this strikes you as a reasonable conclusion, you are not alone. Indeed, the assertion that music is a "universal language" has become fairly commonplace. Among the earliest iterations of the axiom is by the American poet Henry Wadsworth Longfellow, who while traveling across Europe in 1835 reflected,

"Music is the universal language of mankind—poetry their universal pastime and delight."[60] Musicians themselves, not surprisingly, are eager to concur: Peter Gabriel, Alicia Keys, and West African singer-songwriter Angelique Kidjo have each uttered a similar phrase in the past few years—citing music's ability "to unify audiences in peace and love," as Keys told the *New York Times* in 2013.[61] Philosophers, psychologists, and sociologists have similarly seized upon this "kumbaya" notion of music's universality—as the language whereby we can share our highest values across cultures. As the philosopher Kathleen Higgins recently wrote, music can be "a significant means of cross-cultural communication . . . a vehicle for recognizing—and directly experiencing—our common humanity."[62]

This uplifting sentiment, however, is a bit naïve on its surface, and so is worth unpacking a bit. To assert that music is universally loved, for example, should not imply that music is a single, universal language understood uniformly by all peoples around the world.[63]

Indeed, there have been a good many critics of Longfellow's idealistic notion of music as a "universal language." George Bernard Shaw, for example, upon hearing Grieg's *Peer Gynt* Suite performed in quick succession by two regional English orchestras, quipped: "Though music be a 'universal language,' it is spoken with all sorts of accents."[64] Leonard Meyer, a musicologist we'll meet frequently in this book, echoed Shaw's assertion in 1956, declaring: "Music is *not* a universal language: the languages and dialects of music are many."[65] Ethnomusicologist Bruno Nettl was even more assertive—cautioning against a Western ethnocentric orientation of musical "universalism" in favor of celebrating those elements that make each musical culture unique. To be sure, Nettl does not deny the existence of some universal musical elements or concepts that can unite diverse cultures—particularly as compared to spoken language: "Music is not the universal language," he writes, "but musics are not as mutually unintelligible as languages."[66]

We'll be addressing several topics ensuing from the question of musical universals in the pages ahead, but it may here be useful to recount one striking example—stemming from the field of neuroscience. In a 2001 study, twenty subjects were administered an EEG (electroencephalogram) whereby the neuroelectrical activity of their brains was observed while carrying out three distinct activities: listening to a movement of a cello suite by J. S. Bach, listening to a recording of a spoken short story, and carrying out a spatial imagination task with no sound. The researchers observed that *uniquely* while listening to music, different and physically remote areas of the brain produced a *universal* and homogenous scaling—that is, "a synchronization of neurons in distributed populations"—via the so-called "gamma band," or patterns of neural oscillations at frequencies of 25 to 100 Hz. In other words, when listening to music—as opposed to listening to spoken language or just thinking abstractly—remote areas of the brain of *each subject* were somehow "universally" correlated and synchronized as a normal part of this cognitive function.[67]

Okay, this by itself doesn't prove that we all love music, but it does begin to reveal that there is something distinct and potent about the act of listening to music.

A better substantiation of our universal love of music is the simple fact that virtually every society on earth produces it and uses it as a primary means to define itself—or as the influential cultural anthropologist-ethnomusicologist Alan P. Merriam put it, "Every society has occasions signaled by music which draw its members together and reminds them of their unity."[68] A key takeaway here is not just that every society makes music, but that every *member* of the society participates in that music making—whether as a performer or as a listener. Indeed, we must be careful not to get caught up in the distinctly Western distinction between musical "experts" and the rest of us when it comes to "being musical." As neuroscientist Isabelle Peretz notes, "There is increasing evidence that humans share a predisposition for music, especially when the focus is perception [listening] rather than production [performance]. To recognize a melody and move to the beat of music are trivial skills for most humans and, at the same time, fundamental to our musicality."[69]

All of this suggests something involuntary and pleasurable about our engagement with music—why else would it be so universally embraced? To be sure, the sounds and discourses that pass as music in one culture may well strike members of another culture as odd or even unpleasant, but such does not negate the fact that musical "utterances," to use Nettl's term, are embraced or "loved" everywhere and by virtually everyone. We'll tackle some of those cultural distinctions in Interlude E, but for the moment, let's rest our case: we all love music. All right, but why?

## The First Shredders

A good place to start is to query where music came from in the first place: Have we as a species always been musical? If not, when and how did we start making music? And, for that matter, why? Of course, there were no tape recorders or iPhones at the dawn of *Homo sapiens sapiens*—some 200,000 years ago. Indeed, hard evidence of even the most dubious variety goes back no further than 100,000 years ago, with definitive proof less than half that ancient. As such, there is an abundance of mystery involved in considering the "origins" of music, leading in turn to a great deal of speculation and often heated scholarly debate. How fun is that!

Archaeomusicology—the intersection of archeology and ethnomusicology—arose in the 1970s with the express goal of uncovering and testing musical artifacts of ancient and prehistoric societies. Although some scholars would point to a "whistle," found in the Haua Fteah cave in Libya, made of a phalanx bone of a bison around 100,000 years ago as the "oldest surviving instrument,"[70] considerably more attention has gone to another candidate: the Divje Babe "flute," derived from the left femur of a juvenile cave bear, dated to 60,000 years ago. The "flute" was discovered in 1995 by Ivan Turk in a Middle Paleolithic cave in Slovenia that is associated with both Neanderthal and Cro-Magnon activity. Dozens of tests on the "flute" have led to competing theories on whether its holes were a product of human manipulation or carnivore bites—with strong evidence for the former.[71]

More definitively man-made, on the other hand, are a set of flutes and pipes dating to around 40,000 years ago—most famously a pipe made from a wing bone of a griffon vulture found in the Hohle Fels cave near Ulm, Germany. Replicas have revealed the pipe capable of sounding diatonic scales, even playing such "modern" tunes as "Amazing Grace" and the main theme from J. S. Bach's *Art of the Fugue*.[72] Significantly, the Hohle Fels pipe was found alongside other artifacts, such as a female figurine, suggesting an aesthetically engaged society rich in music and art.

So what does this all mean? First, to set some context, we humans may have origins back 200,000 years, but it was only around 125,000 years ago that we first ventured out of our cradle in East Africa; this attempt, however, was a flop. Apparently, our earliest ancestors were not yet sufficiently clever to displace the much stronger, though denser Neanderthals; thus, they retreated. Then, around 75,000 years ago, they reattempted the migration, and this time, somehow much savvier, they succeeded. *Homo sapiens* (anatomically modern humans) reached South Asia by 50,000 years ago and Europe by around 43,000 years ago, in each case gradually replacing the Neanderthals, who fell to extinction by around 30,000 years ago—contributing a bit to our DNA in the process through interbreeding.[73]

We thus can see that, at a minimum, instrumental music was present among our ancestors just as we were settling into Europe 40,000 years ago—and potentially common early in our second, successful migration, either by us or our Neanderthal "cousins" 60,000 years ago. The Haua Fteah "whistle" would then put a musical time stamp closer to the first abortive migration effort 100,000 years ago. And, of course, these are just the musical artifacts that survive! Archaeomusicologists tend to focus on bone or mammoth ivory flutes because they are easier to identify than whistles or percussion-like instruments such as the bullroarer—a wooden slat spun around by a string, creating a sound like a howling wolf. Further, we can only imagine how many instruments of equal or greater antiquity are forever lost to us if originally made of perishable materials like wood, hide, reeds, or shells. In short, we most assuredly have been making use of musical instruments, if not "shredding," since quite early in our career as human beings.

## The First Crooners

It is prevailing scholarly wisdom, moreover, that even before we humans made musical sounds with external instruments, we likely made them with our main internal one—our voice. Choral and solo singing is even more ubiquitous today than is instrumental music throughout the world, and there is a general consensus that singing—along with human-generated percussion such as clapping—represents the original mode of musical expression.

Among the more colorful, if controversial, theories related to our early singing life was offered by the paleoanthropologist Steven Mithen in his 2005 book, *The Singing Neanderthals*. Although not a musician himself (he actually admits to being tone-deaf), Mithen was drawn to explore the subject in an effort to reconcile recent findings in the hominid fossil record with the current understanding of how humans came to acquire advanced cognitive functioning, notably language.[74]

Pivotal for Mithen was the recognition that Neanderthals and other premodern humans possessed vocal anatomy similar to ours: if we can sing, so could they. From this, he developed the theory that before our ancestors acquired either language or music, per se, they utilized a kind of *protolinguistic* mode to communicate both information and emotion. He gave it the nifty acronym "Hmmmmm" (yes, five *m*'s): holistic, manipulative, multi-modal, musical, and mimetic. This communication mode, Mithen argued, comprised "holistic" phrases utilizing pitch variation, rhythm, and timbre, as well as gestures, animal sounds, even dance. Each vocal gesture, that is, was a music-like "unit that had to be learned, uttered and understood as a single acoustic sequence."[75] Mithen dates the rise of the Hmmmmm mode as far back as *Homo ergaster* (1.9 million years ago), from where it split into the distinct modes of music and language in *Homo sapiens* some 200,000 years ago.

Mithen's theory has, not surprisingly, seen its share of critics. Take one of his proposed vocalizations, by a hominid 500,000 years ago, supposedly signifying: "Go and hunt the hare I saw five minutes ago behind the stone at the top of the hill." All this from rhythmic grunts, pitch shifts, gestures, and dance moves? According to linguist Maggie Tallerman, such semantic complexity far exceeds the capacity of a prelinguistic mind; his theory, she says, is "lovely, but wrong."[76] The cognitive neuroscientist Philip Lieberman is even more blunt: after citing Mithen's deficits in recent ape-language research, he calls his theory "speculation embellished by fanciful stories."[77]

While the particulars of Mithen's Hmmmmm theory—including the stunning idea that our ancestors relied on perfect pitch to communicate their holistic phrases[78]—are today viewed with skepticism at best, his broader proposition remains tantalizing to many scholars: before we spoke, we sang. Mithen was in fact not the first to make this claim, with similar assertions traced back to Plato, Charles Darwin, and the eighteenth-century philosopher-composer Jean-Jacques Rousseau, among others.[79] Rousseau, for example, imagined the "first language" as consisting only of vowels, crooning, and yowling: "Since sounds, accent, and number, which are from nature, would leave little to articulation . . . it would be sung rather than spoken."[80] More recently, the anthropologist Iain Morley has corroborated Mithen's claim that premodern humans could sing—discerning the requisite vocal anatomy as well as corresponding neurological structures dating back to *Homo heidelbergensis*, 400,000 years ago—in turn concurring that a protomusicality paved the way for language.[81]

And yet even this more modest proposal—that *some* form of music paved the way for the rise of language—has its detractors. The neuroscientist Aniruddh Patel, for example, has spent a lifetime studying the intersection of language and music and, while acknowledging the allure of such a theory, finds it entirely without empirical basis.[82] Whether or not music provided an entrée to semantic, spoken language, however, there is little debate that musical vocalization—singing—is a natural human impulse, or at least an innate human capability, and must have constituted our earliest mode of musical expression. A prime body of evidence behind this belief is the intrinsic musicality of infants, who show an innate preference for singing over speech, and who naturally demonstrate the skill to recognize and discriminate among musical elements such as pitch, rhythm, and timbre.

## The First Tune

All of this leads us back to the broader mystery of the origins of music: When, how, and why did it begin? In fact, we've already touched a bit upon the *when*—likely back to our earliest days as a species, if not considerably earlier; and the *how*—probably with our singing voice before we took up constructing instruments. So what else can we say about the beginnings of music—from whence our musical taste arose in the first place?

First, a brief step back, for implicit in this question is another one—surprisingly, perhaps, yet to be posed: What exactly do we mean by "music"? Lucky us, defining this word is almost as controversial as asking where it came from.

Starting at the generic end, we have *Merriam-Webster*'s definition:

> The science or art of ordering tones or sounds in succession, in combination, and in temporal relationships to produce a composition having unity and continuity.[83]

For a vast majority of the "musical" exemplars heard and produced by folks around the world, this definition is adequate and comprehensive—as sterile as it may be. A song by Kenny Chesney, an opera by Janáček, a free improv by Ornette Coleman, a chant sung by Tibetan monks, and millions of other examples one could cite are indeed products of fixed and/or improvised pitches, rhythms, sounds, and silences progressing temporally from a moment of initiation to one of completion.

However, a good many musicians and scholars have felt compelled to offer new definitions of music that widen its scope—and account for previously unfamiliar sounds, techniques, and listening experiences. Several of these definitions have come in response to works within the Western avant-garde tradition since 1950—epitomized perhaps by John Cage's *4'33"*, where a pianist sits on stage for four and a half minutes without ever touching the keyboard. Other definitions reveal a broader, non-Eurocentric openness to the huge variety of "musical" approaches one can find around the world: an African talking drum, a Tuvan throat singer, etc.

The result is a profusion of idiosyncratic, at times abstract, definitions of music—by composers, musicologists, and musically minded psychologists and neuroscientists. Some intriguing ones include "organized sound," by composer Edgard Varèse; "an ordered arrangement of sounds and silences whose meaning is presentative rather than denotative," by musicologist Thomas Clifton; and—deep breath—"intentionally created, non-linguistic, acoustical events, structured in time and produced in social contexts," by musical neuroscientist Eckart Altenmüller, among others.[84]

On the other end of the spectrum, it is useful to consider that a good many languages—those of the Navaho and the Hausa tribe in central Africa, among others—have no separate word for music at all, or divide different types into distinct words, or else combine it with other artistic or social endeavors that we in the West may not even consider related. As Bruno Nettl notes, "The concept of music is not universally present or everywhere the same. Even within one society a particular sound may be regarded as musical in one context and as non-musical in another."[85]

The point for our present discussion is not that we ourselves need to pick a single definition of music and stick with it, but rather that we have to be open-minded as to what our Middle or Upper Paleolithic ancestors might have conceived of as music when it first appeared. It might well have been something quite different from our own conception today—just as today what members of one culture call music, those of another might call language, sound, or even noise. Indeed, the same may be said for members within the *same* culture, as we'll discuss in later chapters!

Okay, so keeping this flexible, multidimensional "definition" firmly in mind, let's try to imagine music's first manifestation: How did it come about? How was it used? Why was it perpetuated beyond its initial inception? What happened next?

Well, here's what almost certainly *did not* happen:

At some far distant "before there was music" moment, one of our cave-dwelling ancestors, in a solitary burst of extraordinary inspiration, stood up and belted out the first "tune," to the astonishment and delight of his cavemates—from whence the practice quickly went stunningly viral throughout the hominid population.

Such a fanciful notion, in fact, is not unlike a good many ancient myths on the origins of music, where it is often defined as a gift to man from the all-powerful and benevolent gods at some auspicious moment in the unknowable past. Of course, true innovation, like the emergence of music, rarely happens in a moment of epiphanic singularity—or divine gift giving. Instead it is a process, both mysterious and multimodal. As the anthropologist H. G. Barnett explained, cultural innovations don't arise from scratch, but instead forge together two or more elements already in existence into something new: "If we may use a biological analogy, an innovation is like a genetic cross or hybrid; it is totally different from either of its parents, but it resembles both of them in some respects."[86] Moreover, innovation does not generally emerge from a single individual but rather, as psychologist Keith Sawyer notes, "from a complex social and organizational system."[87]

Our hominid ancestors might not have produced semantically infused Hmmmmm vocalizations before they began giving singing concerts at the cave hearth, but they most certainly were making protomusical vocalizations to one another: sustained and pitched signaling calls, rhythmic grunts, mimicked animal sounds, cooing and sweet tones to woo a mate or lull a child to sleep, etc. Gradually, it seems likely, such unconscious vocalizations morphed into something explicit and deliberate: tones and rhythms became intentionally manipulated for their own sake and effect. Before they knew it, our forebears had crossed the innovative threshold from unconscious protomusical vocalization to conscious music—probably without even recognizing they had done so. As the new practice became more willfully embraced, rehearsed, and shared among clans, our ancestors—with their larger brains, cognitive fluidity, and powers of self-awareness—began to bring to it greater form and dimensionality. The innovation took root among the broader population, and the first "musical cultures" arose—each one responding, as Nettl suggests, to its own distinct social, psychological, and aesthetic needs.[88]

The raw materials of the new practice were all around our forebears—including the foundations of musical pitch/tonal hierarchies discussed in Chapter 3. Many writers point to the ubiquity of animal sounds—chimp and ape cries, and especially birdsong. Darwin, notably, focused great attention on the latter in his *Descent of Man* as a prime vehicle of sexual selection: "The true song . . . of most birds . . . are chiefly uttered during the breeding-season, and serve as a charm, or merely a call-note, to the other sex."[89] This sexual power of birdsong—as well as the mating sounds of various primates—was then defined by Darwin as a prime source for the prelinguistic origins of music, as well as its vital role in human mate selection: "It seems probable that the progenitors of man, either males or females or both sexes, before acquiring power of expressing their mutual love in articulate language, endeavored to charm each other with musical tones and rhythms."[90] Similarly, the ubiquity of rhythm in the natural world—in the patterns of woodpeckers and croaking frogs, the staccato fall of raindrops, the steady flow of water in streams or breaking waves—would lend limitless inspiration for free or patterned metric manipulation in early human songs. Finally, those proto-musical vocalizations—the sustained pitches to signal danger or pass information, the sweet tones of courtship and "motherese" (lullaby-like speech)—were already present in the throats of our ancestors, merely awaiting the innovative will to forge them into song.

All it took to create that "first tune," therefore, was the mental leap—probably originating a thousand times at once—to produce and recognize this new aural entity as no longer mere communicative sound but rather something else: music. And once present, so it remained with them, to be embraced and cultivated down to our own time. But why was this the case? Why was this new entity so nurtured and sustained, and not simply discarded or dismissed as an interesting yet peripheral exercise—like any number of sound effects we humans can generate? What uses or rationales did music serve to warrant such an enduring response?

Many, in fact, are the answers given by scholars from a myriad of disciplines—above and beyond music's supposed Darwinian role in mate selection. Among the most frequently cited include its use to accompany religious rituals, as a more appropriate and effective way to communicate with the gods or to connect with the divine or supernatural realm. To be sure, this is a practice alive and well in our own time: a good many religions today incorporate singing or chanting (musical speech) into their liturgy, finding it to be "more pleasing to God" than mere speaking. Other oft-cited uses for music include remembering and better transmitting stories or myths; accompanying ritualistic movement and dance; enhancing cooperative identity and group cohesion; and promoting individual emotional well-being, not least via soothing songs and lullabies. Less commonly articulated though intriguing rationales include music's use to protect territory or to scare enemy invaders—perhaps using loud singing with percussion accompaniment.[91]

Of course, we have no idea how frequently music was used in any of these capacities by our ancient ancestors, or during which precise phases of our hominid past—let alone what it may have sounded like for this or that purpose. What we can say, however, is that by at least the time of the Hohle Fels flute, our hunter-gatherer ancestors possessed the skill, craftsmanship, time, and motivation to construct a highly musical flute—presumably to be used in some kind of collective ritual. This era of the Upper Paleolithic (50,000 to 40,000 years ago), in fact, is considered by many anthropologists as a watershed "moment" in our development, when we shifted from being mere "anatomically modern" to "behaviorally modern" humans—via such cognitive and cultural milestones as abstract and symbolic thinking, burials, and of course the consistent use of music and the figurative arts. Associated with these external developments, moreover, is the presumed arrival of an inner emotional life not unlike that which we possess today. That is to say, a flute performance taking place in a cave 40,000 years ago held the same broad potential to push the emotional buttons within our forebears as one taking place in a concert hall last Tuesday might have within us.

## The Big, Fat Music-Evolution Debate

Thinking about the origins of music, and the long-ago phases during which our ancestors might have shifted from generating protomusical vocalizations to actually making music, raises yet another thorny question: Does our ability to create and cultivate music—and thus ultimately to forge an individual musical taste—suggest an *innate* biological aptitude to do so? Or, to put it more pointedly: Is music an adaptive trait shaped by natural selection? Well, get ready: for however contentious the previously discussed musical questions may be, they pale in comparison to this one—where there are nearly as many theoretical models as there are theorists positing them! Everyone loves a good debate, of course, and for many of the scholars involved, this is their Ali-Frazier.

In order to properly set the scene, however, let's make sure we understand the arguments. What they do *not* concern is the casual or colloquial notion that we may or may not have "evolved" to become musical beings; that much is certain. Instead, it is a more formal question: whether the human genotype became fixed in its current state—via adaptive mutation over millions of years—explicitly and directly by virtue of our music-making capacities. Those supporting this notion that we humans possess a "music-specific genotype" are commonly identified as "*adaptationists*"; those in dissent are predictably called "*nonadaptationists*." Of course, their individual arguments are never quite as straightforward as all that.

Charles Darwin, as suggested earlier, placed a sizable opening bid for the adaptationist camp in his *Descent of Man*. The "song" basis of sexual selection densely articulated by Darwin for birds and apes was likewise used to justify a similar claim made for mankind. Like modern apes, Darwin argued, our forebears used singing to attract mates; this in turn suggested to him a strong case "that the vocal organs were primarily used and *perfected* in relation to the propagation of the species."[92] Music, in other words, was largely used for purposes of sexual selection, and as such, our species *evolved* over the millennia to find ever more effective ways to use it on behalf of our successful propagation—that is, our survival.

A mere decade later, however, the influential philosopher and psychologist William James countered Darwin with an equally unequivocal bid for the nonadaptationist position. This is a bit surprising, since James was in most ways a devoted adherent to Darwin's ideas, applying them creatively to his own philosophical and psychological theories. Yet in his *Principles of Psychology* (1890) he takes direct aim at music as a target of natural selection, suggesting instead that musical passions, like other aesthetically derived emotions, are mere "accidents" of our instincts. For James, our love of music—as with all the arts—did not evolve independently for some practical utility to our species, but rather entered the mind "by the back stairs"; it is not unlike our response to a rocky boat ride—where the queasiness we feel is but an "accidental" (nonevolved) product of the way our nervous system inherently operates: "Sea-sickness, the love of music, of the various intoxicants, nay, the entire aesthetic life of man, shall have to trace to this accidental origin."[93] In short, music played no role in our survival.

And so it lay for more than a century: two titans of nineteenth-century thought issuing conflicting accounts of why we love music, with relatively little reverberation.[94]

Then, in 1997, a new round began—and this time the table would soon be overrun. Initially at a conference at MIT and then in his book *How the Mind Works*, cognitive scientist Steven Pinker doubled down on James' nonadaptationist view, though with a far sharper tongue: "As far as biological cause and effect are concerned, music is useless." Ouch! He continues, more colorfully: "Music appears to be a pure pleasure technology, a cocktail of recreational drugs that we ingest through the ear to stimulate a mass of pleasure circuits at once."[95]

For Pinker, music may be pleasurable, but it did not, as James might say, evolve for utility's sake; instead it simply "borrows the mental machinery" of other skills, not least language, whose prosody (the shifting patterns of pitch and rhythm in speech) it mimics and heightens. So, why then is music itself so important to us? To this Pinker responds with what has surely become his most famous expression: "I suspect that music is auditory cheesecake, an exquisite confection crafted to tickle the sensitive spots of . . . our [adaptive] mental faculties."[96] His use of cheesecake was not flip, as earlier he used the metaphor when describing the dubious adaptive value of all sensorial pleasure:

> We enjoy strawberry cheesecake, but not because we evolved a taste for it. We evolved circuits that gave us trickles of enjoyment from the sweet taste of ripe fruit, the creamy mouth feel of fats and oils from nuts and meat, and the coolness of fresh water. Cheesecake packs a sensual wallop unlike anything in the natural world because it is a brew of megadoses of agreeable stimuli which we concocted for the express purpose of pressing our pleasure buttons. Pornography is another pleasure technology.[97]

Okay, then. Music is like pornography and fattening cheesecake, not to mention biologically useless. In my view, the prolific response—on all sides—to the adaptationist question over the past two decades has arisen as much in response to Pinker's inflammatory word choice as to the substance of his argument. Reducing a primary and beloved aspect of human life around the world to useless cheesecake did much to mobilize the troops so inclined to mount a counterattack. Musicologist Ian Cross, for example, had Pinker clearly in mind when he exclaimed, with clear laden emotion: "What music is for *some* at present is not what music is for others, was for our predecessors, or could be for our children."[98]

Among the counterarguments to Pinker's nonadaptationist position, we may first mention that of Steven Mithen, for whom the Hmmmmm mode represents a fundamental adaptive trait in humans, as the precursor to language: "The evolutionary history of 'Hmmmmm' ensured that the human mind evolved to enjoy melody and rhythm, which were critical features of communication before becoming usurped by language."[99] Leaving Mithen's speculative theory aside, however, others in the modern adaptational camp have relied on one of three well-reasoned arguments: sexual selection, social cohesion, and mother-infant bonding.

The *sexual selection* argument is made forcefully by evolutionary psychologist Geoffrey Miller, an expert in the broader field of sexual selection in human evolution. Miller embraces Darwin's view of music as a vehicle of sexual courtship, updating the famed naturalist's reliance on animal analogies with a modern awareness of mate selection and evolutionary anthropology. Miller readily concedes James' and Pinker's point that music provides no direct utility to survival, such as finding food or avoiding predators; its evolutionary purpose, therefore, must relate to its reproductive benefits—as an "indicator" for sexual selection: "to advertise reproductively important things like age, health, fertility, status, and general fitness."[100] To physical fitness, moreover, Miller adds "creativity indicators"—signaling that a prospective mate "can keep them entertained over long-term relationships, so they don't get bored and incur the maladaptive costs of separation and searching again."[101] As a clearly provocative example, he cites rock guitarist Jimi Hendrix—who, despite self-destructing at age twenty-seven, had sex with hundreds of women and fathered at least three children. To this troubling stereotype of the philandering rocker, one could easily add figures like Mick Jagger and Gene Simmons, as well as nineteenth-century classical virtuosos Franz Liszt and Niccolò Paganini, both famed for their many youthful sexual conquests.[102] How such misogynistic behavior explains the copious musical output by women—not to mention celibate monks and middle-aged composers—is left unsaid.

The *group cohesion* argument avoids these real-world oversights by focusing on the universal "groupishness" of music making, using the term of musicologist Steven Brown. As opposed to sexual selection, Brown contends that music's survival advantages "come about from its ability to promote group-wide cooperation, coordination, cohesion, and catharsis, and this operates to increase both the absolute and relative fitness of groups."[103] In this theory, music arose in tandem with the broad evolution of rituals among our ancestors, acting specifically as a "reward system" to promote and reinforce group welfare—as well as warfare. Getting even more nuanced, musicologist Ian Cross credits music's adaptive ability to forge group cohesion to its lack of any specific meaning—its "floating intentionality," as he calls it. Unlike language, Cross argues, music is not bound to specific semantic meaning; instead, communal music leads to a "semantic indeterminacy" that in turn brings about a "shared intentionality" within a group: where language may easily lead to conflict, music naturally promotes a sense of affiliation and cooperation.[104]

Incidentally, both Brown and Cross ground their group cohesion theories on a key musical phenomenon, one that we'll revisit often in this book: **entrainment**—the uniquely human ability for a group of individuals to lock into a regular, periodic pulse: to collectively count "1, 2, 3, 4" in time with the music, for example. Entrainment all but guarantees cooperativity, shared action, and shared intention—even as individual interpretations of the music may diverge. As such, Cross theorizes that music's entrainment capability is a kind of evolutionary "missing link," developed in our early hominid lineage, whereby we improved our very capacity for collaboration and for culture in general.

A third key argument among the adaptationists involves the innate musicality of infants, and especially the intimate *mother-infant bond* enabled via music. The most prominent advocate of this argument is psychologist Sandra Trehub, who in a series of studies on six- to ten-month-olds has demonstrated the remarkable "processing predisposition" for music among infants. From her experiments, Trehub has documented musical skills "that are evident in infancy, well before they have obvious utility"—and thus "can be considered predispositions."[105] These include an uncanny ability to recognize variations in melody, the musical parameter we just reviewed (Chapter 3), including altered pitches within a consistent melodic contour, and recognition of "out-of-tune" notes within major or minor scales.

Even more impressive are Trehub's observations with regard to the universality of mother-infant music, whether so-called motherese or actual infant-directed songs—both of which are "common to all cultures and historical periods."[106] Importantly, Trehub has noted its striking musicological uniformity: higher pitch centers, slower tempos, and more emotive vocal quality than other types of singing—as well as melodic material that is structurally simple and highly repetitive. Similarly universal is the response given by the infants themselves to these forms of musical exchange—granting longer attention and displaying lower arousal/anxiety levels. Together, these factors suggest to Trehub that music, and especially mother's song, is an adaptive trait that may have "enhanced infant survival in difficult ancestral conditions."[107]

## The Debate Thickens: Enter the Neuroscientists

So concludes our summary of the three dominant social science arguments in favor of the adaptationist camp—sexual selection, group cohesion, and the mother-infant bond. However, the anthropologists, psychologists, and musicologists mentioned above are not the only ones at the poker table. We must also acknowledge the savvy players using *neurobiological evidence* to argue their side of the debate—providing a mild preview to what we'll explore in greater depth in Interlude C.

Chief among the neuroscientists supporting the adaptationist position are Isabelle Peretz and Dan Levitin—one of the most popular authors writing on the subject of music and the brain. Levitin in fact dedicates the final chapter of his celebrated book *This Is Your Brain on Music* to the question of musical evolution (entitled "The Music Instinct," a not-so-subtle rejoinder to Pinker's 1994 book *The Language Instinct*). Citing the palpable level of brain activity associated with music processing and the specialized brain structures and dedicated memory systems used therein, Levitin feels emboldened to flatly support the adaptationist position: "Music's evolution origins are established."[108]

Peretz likewise leans in the adaptationist direction, though hedges her bet a bit. The main question she ponders is whether a clear distinction can be drawn between how we process music as opposed to language, or more to the point: Does the human brain possess mechanisms devoted specifically to music processing, or by contrast, does this feat involve merely co-opting the "general purpose" processing of language? Supporting a separate music-processing "module," as she calls it, is our ability to "tonally encode pitch" (tonal coding)—that is, to tell one note from another.[109] She specifically cites a case study of a patient who after an accident could recognize the lyrics and speech intonation of a familiar song, but not its hummed melody. To Peretz, this illustrates "exceptional isolation of musical modules in the developing brain," which in turn "argues against the view that all of music processing components are the result of general abilities or language abilities."[110]

As noted, though, Peretz hedges her bet: while she sees these neurobiological findings as "compatible" with an adaptive function of music, she admits that the evidence is not "compelling." To wit, we turn next to another celebrated neuroscientist, Aniruddh Patel, who posed these same questions just to reach an opposite conclusion. In his exhaustive study, *Music, Language, and the Brain*, Patel likewise devotes an extended chapter to the topic of musical evolution—wherein he considers whether music might be more an "exaptation" (a co-opted trait, like feathers on birds) than an adaptation targeted by natural selection.[111] Applying a rigorous methodology (involving a "null hypothesis" approach: assume a negative assessment unless proven otherwise), Patel vows to accept the adaptationist position *only* if he can confirm three factors: music processing is domain specific (not involving the co-opting of language processing), is found innately in humans, and applies only to humans—collectively demonstrating that indeed it was targeted specifically by natural selection for *our* survival.

I'll spare you the details of his involved ten-part methodology and instead provide the summary: he first applies his null-hypothesis approach to language, which overrides its initial negative assumption, and thereby passes the adaptive test with flying colors.[112] Music, you'll gather, does not fare as well. To Peretz' "tonal coding" argument, for example, Patel argues that this skill arrives more slowly than does language acquisition, and further can be argued as relying on the same neuronal networks in the brain as those encoding speech prosody—via what he calls a "shared syntactic integration resource."[113] In sum, Patel's overall conclusion is that music, as opposed to language, does not override the null hypothesis, or, as he puts it: "Based on current evidence, music does not seem to be a biological adaptation."[114]

And yet this should not suggest that Patel is ready to high-five Pinker in the "cheesecake" debate. In fact, he forcefully labels this a false dichotomy, claiming that music "belongs in a different category." Music, he argues, is an ideal example of a "transformative technology"—not unlike fire, written language, aircraft, and the Internet—that once invented becomes "intimately integrated into the fabric of our life."[115] We may be able to survive without it, as Pinker suggests, but once it's invented and incorporated, there is no going back. Over the years, Patel has continued to develop his "transformative technology of the mind" theory (or TTM), which suggests that music cognition is ultimately rooted in other brain functions, especially language and general auditory use—even though, unlike these others, it can lead to the development of specialized brain regions and functionality, such as for tonal encoding and beat-based entrainment.[116]

And indeed, Patel's TTM is just one of several "neither/nor" arguments out there that eschew the dichotomy between the adaptationist and Pinkeresque nonadaptationist positions. The two most well-known are the "*theory of mind*" and the "*mixed origins of music*" theory—each of which proposes how music may have initially come to hold such a vital place in human life without requiring music-specific "modules" in the brain. The former, introduced by psychologists David Premack and Guy Woodruff in 1978, emphasizes the role of empathy or "perspective taking," as Levitin calls it, in our development and evolution: music plays a key role in engendering empathy, they argue, via its profound ability—as in rituals—to communicate and elicit emotion in others and in ourselves.[117] The latter, developed by neuroscientist Eckart Altenmüller in 2013, attributes the rise of music to its potent ability to elicit strong or "chill" emotions within us; music-derived chills may have initially developed to help with auditory perception or memory consolidation, but were later valued for general "aesthetic" feelings of well-being, to forget the hardships of life during the Ice Age, for example.[118]

## The Bets Are In: Now My Two Cents

Okay, so what do we make of all this? Was music adaptive or not? Well, with so many theories out there—of which we've reviewed but a small portion—I'm admittedly a bit cautious about offering a definitive opinion.

That said, my tendency is to likewise adopt a somewhat middle-of-the-road approach—though more a "both/and" than a "neither/nor" position. Specifically, my belief is that while *music* may not be an adaptive trait, our inherent *musicality* is. Again, I don't believe that music—however it might be conceived—was consciously invented one fine spring day by one of our uniquely gifted ancestors after a long day at the hunt. Instead, that which came to be "music"—an intentionally devised vehicle using pitch and/or pulsed rhythm—was only acknowledged and cultivated as such *after* its constituent elements had been unconsciously used, perceived, and appreciated. Our innate ability to "encode" musical pitch may indeed be neurobiologically associated with language acquisition and/or our ability to locate sounds within an environment via "auditory scene analysis"—as psychologist Laurel Trainor suggests; likewise our ability to generate a steady musical beat (entrainment) may be aligned with general "vocal learning" or using sounds to communicate—as Patel has suggested. And yet, these functions are *preeminent mechanisms of our musicality*, and thus, regardless of their indebtedness to these other functions, are assuredly an adaptive part of our evolutionary history.

Imagine one day in a cave—perhaps 40,000, or 100,000, or even 200,000 years ago—a group of hunter-gatherers is sitting around a roaring fire when one of them half consciously delivers a pitched vocalization in a steady pulse; as the internalized beat persists, in a moment of spontaneous creativity, he suddenly makes the pitch rise and then fall in a proto-artful way. Among those listening, some feel the sudden pleasure of a shiver down the spine, and eagerly encourage the presenter to "do it again." Or imagine a mother in these bygone years carrying an infant in her arm while foraging for berries; as the child cries and fidgets, the mother intuitively vocalizes a patterned sequence of tones—not just sound but "creative sound," capturing the infant's attention and soothing him back to sleep.

Are these moments music? I'd say no, but they certainly are musical. None of those things—the pitched and patterned vocalization, the steady beat, the chills, or the moderating arousal level—would have happened if those neurobiological mechanisms or domain-specific "modules" were not all already in place, undoubtedly a product of much earlier adaptation.

Similarly adaptive, importantly, is the very creative impulse that would have inspired our ancient vocalizers to turn sound into something more. As Michael Gazzaniga, the "father" of cognitive neuroscience, wrote in relation to our inherent love of art and beauty and our ability to create fiction: "What people find beautiful is not arbitrary or random but has evolved over millions of years of hominid sensory, perceptual, and cognitive development . . . something that has allowed us to engage in pretense [fiction, separate from reality]."[119]

The Israeli historian Yuval Harari has also seized upon our innovative use of fiction in his provocative book *Sapiens* as the key means by which we were able to successfully migrate out of Africa for the second time, around 70,000 years ago. He labels this shift the "Cognitive Revolution," generated by "accidental genetic mutations [that] changed the inner wirings of the brains of Sapiens"; this enabled us to conceive fiction, in turn allowing us "not merely to imagine things, but to do so collectively." That, Harari argues, made all the difference in how we were able to make it successfully out of Africa, and ultimately conquer the planet.[120] Creativity is so adaptive, Harari suggests, it may be the main reason we're still here.

This creative impulse, itself a component of the "theory of mind" noted above, is not only innovative and beneficial, but also attractive. Hearing our ancient cave vocalizer turn a creative "musical" phrase would have made him or her more attractive to a potential mate, increasing the chances that those musicality-inclined genes would be passed on, as Miller argued. Levitin concurs: "Humans who just happened to find creativity attractive may have hitched their creative wagons to musicians and artists, and—unbeknownst to them at the time—conferred a survival advantage to their offspring."[121] Similarly, the infant calmed and attracted by his mother's creative vocalization would, years later, carry forth that same tradition, along with the genes that reinforce it. Our innate, adapted musicality, bolstered by our creative impulse, thus forged an attractive and beneficial skill set among our ancient forebears that ensured its survival unto the present day.

Meanwhile, back at the cave, our precocious vocalizer may indeed try to "do it again"—perhaps with success, perhaps not. In either event, over the ensuing decades, centuries, and millennia, those vocalizations, imbued with innate creative drive, would take shape and evolve to where, at some point, they would be recognized—by them and likely us—as music, as art. In this scenario, however, music is not an adaptive trait, but a product of cultural evolution, an "exaptation" of innate musically sensitive modules and the creative instinct. Once developed, true "music" would be exploited for its profound abilities to better attract mates, form strong group bonds, elicit and share emotion, and assist in general cognitive development—as well as enhance or "recycle" domain-specific neurological modules evolved from earlier times. Perhaps, indeed, this consciously created musical art arose in conjunction with Harari's "Cognitive Revolution"—where it was employed to better clothe, remember, and emotionally consolidate the "fiction" created by our ancient pioneers on their way out of Africa.

In sum, my two cents, again, is that although music is nonadaptive, musicality *is* adaptive; and since musicality begets music, we might say that music is indirectly adaptive. In fact, I am not alone in this dual perspective, as suggested in a recent set of essays led by Peretz, Trehub, and others.[122] A key goal of these researchers is to establish a "multicomponent perspective" of musicality—linking the developmental, cognitive, and neurological mechanisms that underlie it. This includes using the techniques of comparative biology to trace the origins of musicality—perhaps back to a distant species (shared with primates or birds) from whom we evolved our own variety.

Is this perspective correct? Of course, we'll never know for certain. However, once informed of the various arguments, it is really of little consequence whether music was targeted by natural selection (to use Patel's phraseology) or not. We'll never know, for example, whether language in fact preceded music or whether some sort of "musilanguage" (as Steven Brown calls it) preceded them both—which is a mystery at the heart of so many of the theories just discussed. Perhaps someday we'll discover a uniquely musical gene that will prove music's successful selection within our DNA—but I wouldn't hold my breath. And yet, from what we've now learned, it does seem clear that we *Homo sapiens* are indeed hardwired to be musical creatures, whether naturally selected or not.

And with that, we can return to the question asked many pages ago: Have we as a species always been musical? In a word, yes. Why didn't I just say that in the first place and forgo all that technical detail about this or that evolutionary theory? Well, for one, it's sort of interesting. But most importantly, in so doing, we've introduced many key concepts involved in understanding not only music and its place in our lives, but also the elements and rationale underlying our musical taste.

You may rightly note that we have *not really* answered the question posed at the start of this interlude: We all love music, but why? Saying that we love music because we've "always" loved music is a tautology in the extreme, so we must try to do better—and we will in the interludes ahead. But first, let's return to the chapters dedicated to the actual music itself, starting with our next parameter: harmony.

part two

# BAR BANDS IN ANDROMEDA

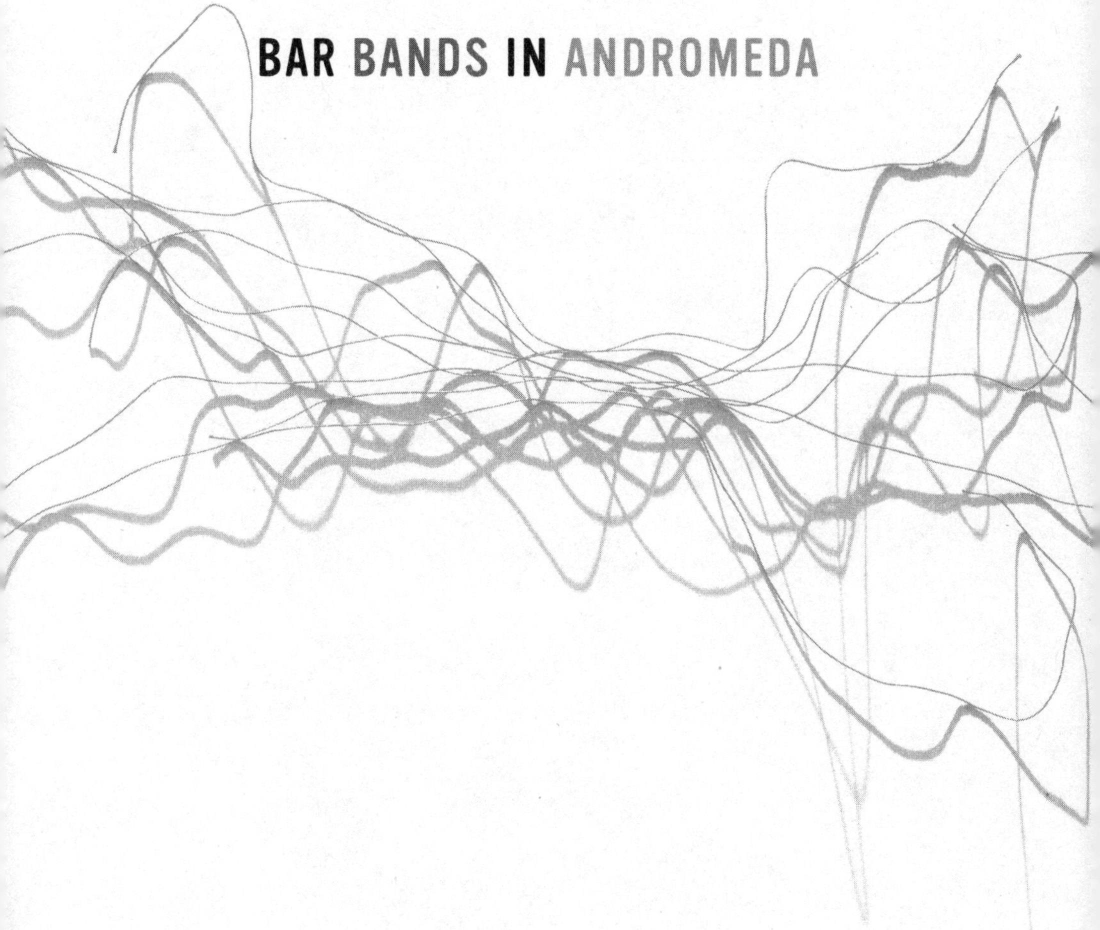

*four*

# HARMONY: THE INTERNAL BODY OF MUSIC

•••

Of all the terms associated with the key musical parameters, "harmony" is unique in its broad and invariably positive usage in nonmusical contexts as well. When people, governments, or ideas are "in harmony"—in agreement or accord—it is a good thing; situations that are "harmonious" are pleasant and desirable. The term is rooted in the Greek noun "*harmonía*" (agreement, joint) and verb "*harmozo*" (to join together), and even in ancient Greece carried a variety of meanings, both musical and metaphysical—such as by Plato in his dialogue *Timaeus*: "The body of heaven is visible, but the soul is invisible, and partakes of reason and harmony."[123]

In ancient Greek music theory, the term "*harmonía*" and its variants held various speculative and technical meanings, not least being the combining or juxtaposing of tones in a specific and orderly manner, as in the melodic intervals and scales discussed in Chapter 3.[124] This diverse and somewhat abstract meaning of "harmony" continued through the Middle Ages and Renaissance. Since the nineteenth century, however, the term has taken on a different and more limited connotation: as the *vertical* or simultaneous sounding of two or more pitches—in other words, **chords**. This includes not just how chords are formed and defined, but also how they *function* in sequence, as a **chord progression**. It is in this musical context that "harmony" is most commonly understood today, and likewise how we'll use it here.[125]

I've aligned harmony with the "internal body" in our anthropomorphic exercise. Why? Well, for most people not trained in music, harmony is the element of the listening experience not generally perceived with clear external definition, as melody is, for example. Harmony is something that occurs "inside" the musical discourse, and yet its presence nonetheless lends the music its coherence and narrative movement. An average, untrained listener might be hard-pressed to define the specific nature of a song's underlying chords or chord progressions, but those details undoubtedly influence and shape the listening experience.

In a similar way, most of us untrained in medicine would be hard-pressed to define the specifics of another person's musculoskeletal system, organ function, or even general health just by looking at them. And yet our awareness and overall conception of that person is undeniably affected by these internal workings. And just as greater awareness of how those internal body elements function can provide increased understanding and appreciation of the person we're encountering, so too can greater awareness of the internal harmonic elements improve our appreciation and enjoyment of the song we're hearing. Okay, I'll admit it's a strange simile, but that doesn't mean there's not some logic there.

Moving on. As noted above, our modern conception of harmony is strongly aligned with the *simultaneous* sounding of two or more notes—as a harmonic interval, like a major 3rd; or a chord, like a major chord (Figure 4.1):

**Figure 4.1: Major 3rd and major chord (F major)**

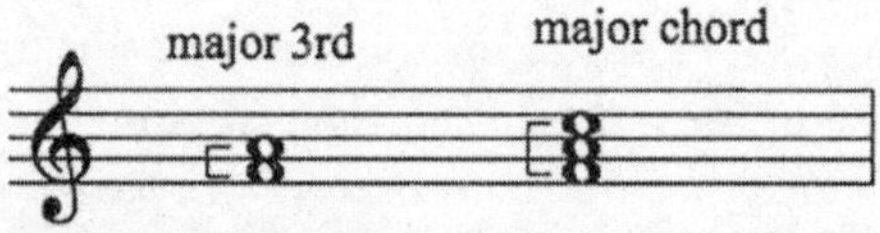


But the study and manifestation of **harmony** extends well beyond the appearance of intervals and chords. Admittedly, harmony is a huge topic and can be challenging for nonmusicians, but given how impactful it is on our individual musical taste, I believe it's worth wading through some of its more technical descriptions.

## The Basics of Harmony

Let's begin by returning to our introductory nursery rhyme, "Old MacDonald," now seen from the standpoint of harmony. The melody we examined in Chapter 3 is here defined via a set of chords, in this case a steady alternation of three strong-sounding triads (three-note chords): C major, F major, and G major (Figure 4.2):

**Figure 4.2: "Old MacDonald"—basic harmonic elements: major triads**

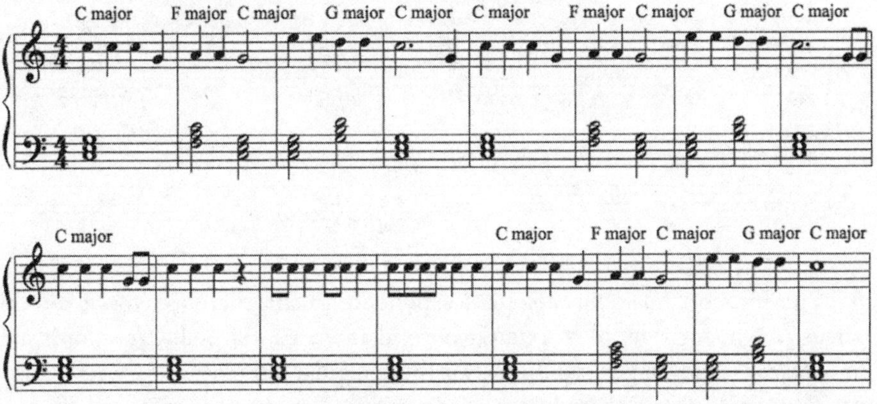


A simple melody is thus similarly accompanied by a simple approach to harmony: the alternation of three major chords. And yet underlying even this simple example is a set of rich and sophisticated harmonic concepts.

One basic concept is the distinction between **consonance** and **dissonance**. On the surface, this connotes a difference between a "pleasant" and an "unpleasant" sound, respectively. There is no doubt a subjective, psychological aspect to this division, but there is also a scientific one, involving the ratios derived from two pitches sounding simultaneously (as frequencies, or periodic vibrations of sound waves) which we'll explore in Interlude B. It is not surprising, therefore, that the relative distinctions between and within these two categories have varied over time.

In present-day music theory, however, the distinction between consonant and dissonant intervals is clear and precise. Of the thirteen intervals possible within a full octave, eight are consonant, five are dissonant. The consonant intervals are themselves divided into two subcategories: "**perfect**" and "**imperfect**"; the rationale for these rather judgmental adjectives stems back to ancient Greece, and is grounded in numerical ratios—as, again, we'll discuss in detail in Interlude B. For the moment, though, we can simply note that the perfect consonances are the unison, 4th, 5th, and octave; imperfect consonances are the minor 3rd, major 3rd, minor 6th, and major 6th. Dissonant intervals include the tritone, minor 2nd, major 2nd, minor 7th, and major 7th. These are spelled out in the figure on the next page (Figure 4.3):

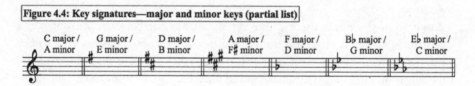

**Figure 4.3: Vertical intervals—perfect consonances (PC), imperfect consonances (IC), and dissonances (D)**

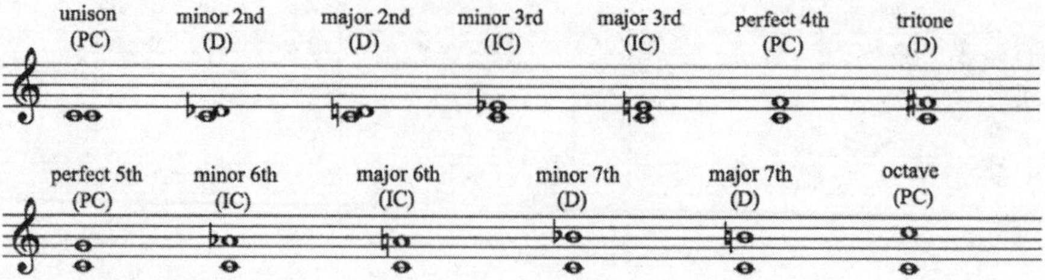


Our emotional and physiological experience of this dichotomy—of smooth versus rough, for example—extends beyond intervals, naturally, to chords and musical sonorities in general. In fact, it is the regular alternation between consonance and dissonance that gives music its motion, energy, and spice.

Before pursuing more on this matter, let's review a few other basic dimensions of harmony. Another primary concept is that of a **key**, which in turn is related to an associated scale. Simply put, a key is the adherence of a song, work, or musical passage to one of the major or minor scales (e.g., C major, F major, B♭ minor, F♯ minor, etc.), and is generally the basis for which the passage or work begins and ends. In music notation, this key/scale relationship is indicated by a **key signature**, displayed as a grouping of one or more **sharps** (♯) or **flats** (♭)*—or the absence of either in the case of C major and A minor—at the start of each staff (Figure 4.4):

**Figure 4.4: Key signatures—major and minor keys (partial list)**

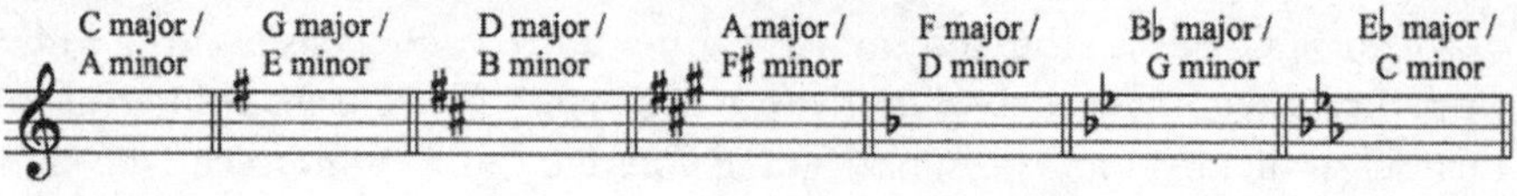


Commonly, a song or work—or section thereof—is established as being "in" a particular key, which in turn delimits to some degree the tones that populate or dominate the passage, as well as the chords that support those tones. This already demonstrates the interrelationship between melody and harmony—or as the esteemed music theorist Carl Dahlhaus put it, "Harmony comprises not only the ('vertical') structure of chords but also their ('horizontal') movement."[126]

Chords themselves come in a variety of "flavors," each a composite of two or more intervals—usually 3rds—stacked on top of one another. There are six

* To these two common notation symbols must be added the natural sign (♮), which either cancels the preceding sharp or flat, or indicates that the note is neither sharp nor flat—as in the white keys of the piano; collectively these symbols are called "accidentals."

primary chord types, which collectively dominate a vast majority of the musical works that most of us hear on any given day: major, minor, diminished, augmented, dominant 7th, and diminished 7th (Figure 4.5):

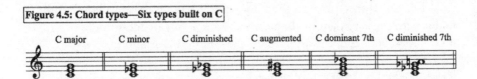

**Figure 4.5: Chord types—Six types built on C**

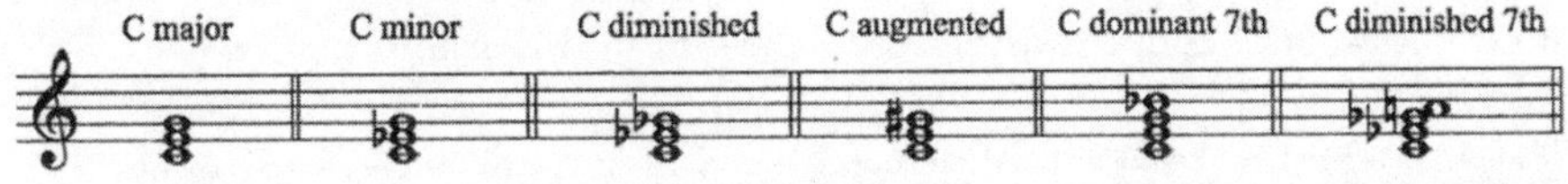


The first four are known as **triads**—that is, made up of three notes, arranged as two stacked 3rds; of these, the **major and minor chords** are by far more commonly employed. The final two chords are examples of **7th chords**, of which there are other varieties as well.† The major or minor scale aligned with the key of the passage provides the available notes of the "diatonic" (of the scale) chords, while any chords using pitches outside the scale are considered "chromatic" (Figures 4.6 a and b):

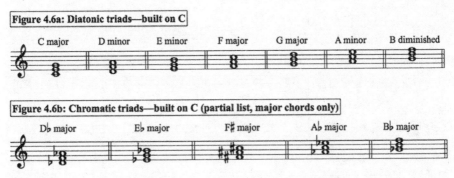

**Figure 4.6a: Diatonic triads—built on C**

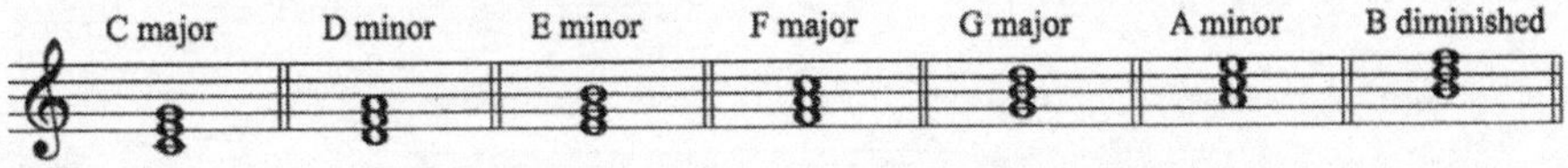


**Figure 4.6b: Chromatic triads—built on C (partial list, major chords only)**

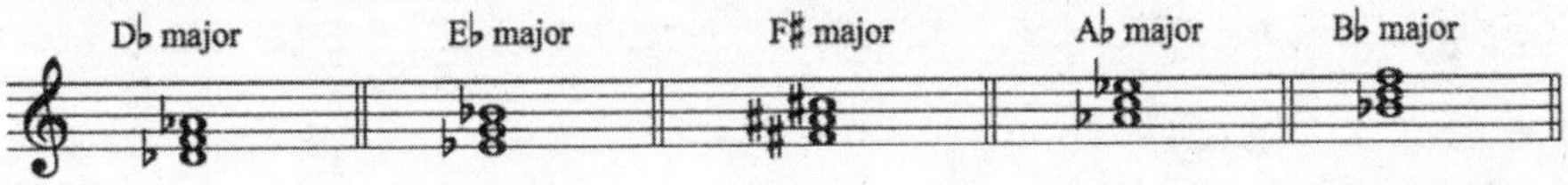


The overall *governing system* of keys and scales, of diatonic versus chromatic chords, and of the functional expectations of individual chords and chord progressions within a given key is called **tonality**—and it has reigned over most of Western music since the mid-seventeenth century. And though tonality provides the framework for how a composer or a performer is likely to utilize chords and chord progressions within a key, the actual level of diversity and potential complexity of chordal activity is so vast that the framework can be hard, if not impossible, to fully define.

† As presented in Figure 4.5 (and commonly among music examples throughout the book), the triads and other chords are arranged with the chord note—or "**root**"—on the bottom; logically, therefore, such chords are said to be in "**root position**" (*C*–E–G for a C major chord), whereas they are said to be in "**inversion**" when the order of the notes of the chord is rearranged. So, for example, when the third is on the bottom (E–G–*C* for a C major chord), the chord is said to be in "first inversion"; when the fifth is on the bottom (G–*C*–E for a C major chord), it is said it to be in "second inversion," etc.

## Tonality and the Movement of Diatonic Chords

To help gain a bit of clarity, however, let's turn to a few musical examples. On one end of the tonal spectrum is a simple harmonic passage, where all the chords fall in line with the key's diatonic framework—that is, major and/or minor chords all built on the pitches of the associated scale—as in this example:

**Figure 4.7: Bob Dylan, "Blowin' in the Wind" (transposed to C major, partial lyrics)—diatonic chords**

The logic that drives the selection and flow of chords in this example stems not only from the dictates of Dylan's melody and his personal harmonic sensibility, but also from the narrative potential of the chords themselves. Chords in sequence have a sort of life of their own, and though there are a great number of possibilities in how one chord can follow another, there are also innumerable conventions and expectations that arise from tradition and from the sounds of the chords themselves.

Among those conventions is how chords help bring a melodic phrase to a partial or complete stop, called a **cadence.**[127] A musical cadence can be likened to punctuation in a written paragraph: a comma (pause), a semicolon (tentative stop), a period (full stop), etc. Throughout the history of Western music, composers and theorists have documented the need to articulate musical punctuation: a pause or break in the musical narrative.

The manner in which musical punctuation is defined has evolved considerably over the centuries. In the Middle Ages and Renaissance, a cadence—a pause or stop—primarily involved the coming together of two consecutive intervals: namely, from a 3rd to a unison, or from a 6th to an octave (Figure 4.8):

**Figure 4.8: Intervallic cadences—3rd to unison; 6th to octave**

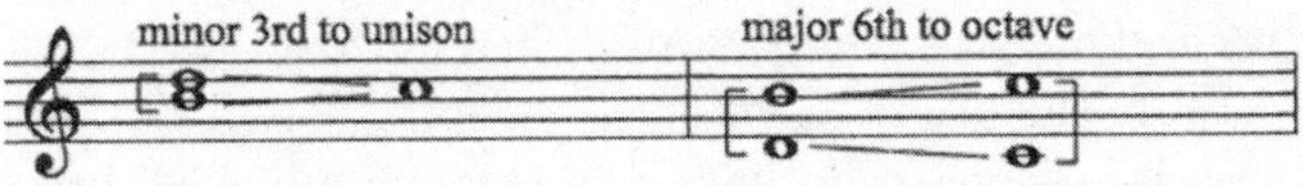


With the establishment of the system of tonality, however, during the so-called "**common practice period**" (roughly 1650 to 1900), a cadence was defined not so much as a sequence of two consecutive intervals but rather as a progression of chords. There are numerous types of chordal cadences, with the most common being the **authentic** (V–I),* **plagal** (IV–I), and **half cadence** (ending on V).

The Roman numerals indicated above, incidentally, simply represent the degrees of the diatonic scale upon which the chord is built—from I (1) to VII (7). It is a common tool of harmonic analysis to use Roman numerals to identify the degrees of the scale and the triads built upon them, with major chords represented with uppercase numerals and minor chords with lowercase numerals (I = major, i = minor, etc.). Each degree, moreover, has its own designation—as follows:

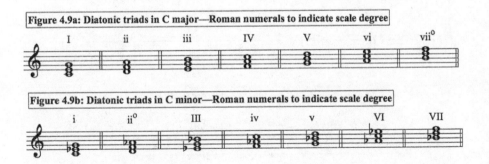

**Figure 4.9a: Diatonic triads in C major—Roman numerals to indicate scale degree**

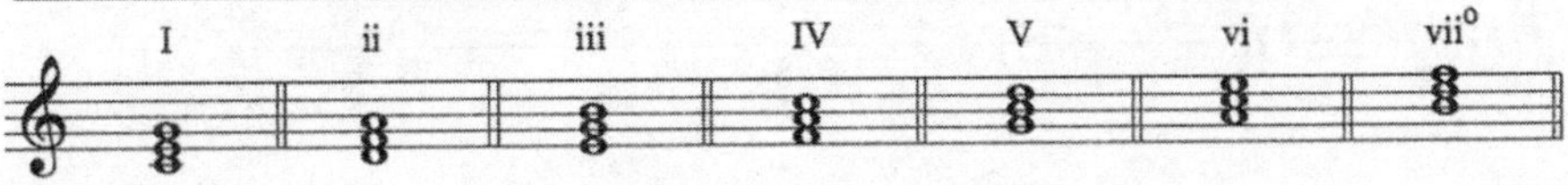


**Figure 4.9b: Diatonic triads in C minor—Roman numerals to indicate scale degree**

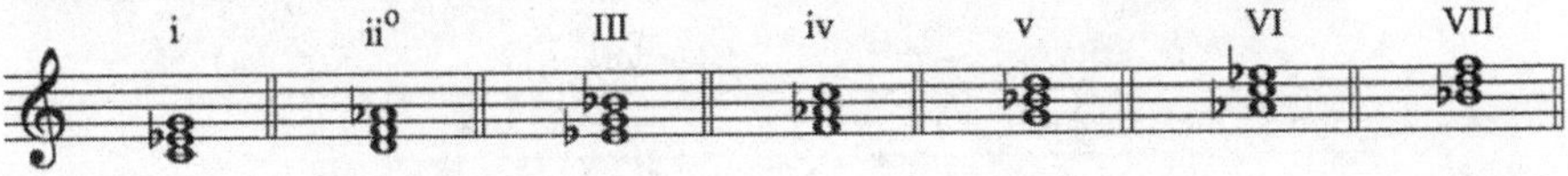


You don't need to worry about most of these designations, but three are important: the **tonic** (I), **dominant** (V), and **subdominant** (IV).[128] These are the chords that define a key: the tonic is the "home" chord; the dominant and, to

---

* An "authentic" cadence is likewise called a "perfect" cadence, with the former term more common among American musicians and writers.

a slightly lesser degree, the subdominant are the "close-to-home" chords, so to speak—that is, they help to establish and reinforce the identity of the tonic as the "home" or key-defining chord. This is no truer than at a cadence, the moment of harmonic punctuation.

Both the authentic (V–I, or V–i if going to a minor tonic) and plagal (IV–I) cadences bring a musical passage to a close or *resolution*—like a period. Of the two, the authentic cadence is harmonically stronger and considerably more common: it likely appears dozens of times in most every song you hear. Common as well is that the V chord in an authentic cadence is not a simple triad, but rather a dominant 7th chord—designated V7—where its seventh degree resolves to the third degree of the tonic chord (e.g., from F to E, when moving from G7 to C major—see Figure 4.10b). The plagal cadence is sometimes labeled the "Amen cadence," so called because it appears at the end of many traditional Christian hymns and gospel songs; compared to the authentic cadence, the plagal cadence has a softer, somewhat solemn quality. Finally, a half cadence (ending on the V chord) brings a passage to a midpoint pause—although the energy of the music halts, the need is still felt to continue, and to eventually "resolve" with a more conclusive authentic or plagal cadence.

The half and authentic cadence (here as V7 to I) are both demonstrated "in action" in Figures 4.10a–b—using portions of the Bob Dylan song from Figure 4.7.

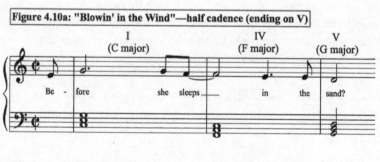

**Figure 4.10a: "Blowin' in the Wind"—half cadence (ending on V)**

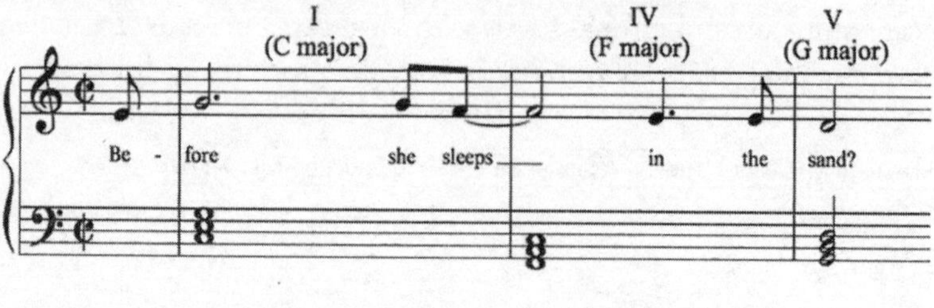


**Figure 4.10b: "Blowin' in the Wind"—authentic cadence (ending V7–I)**

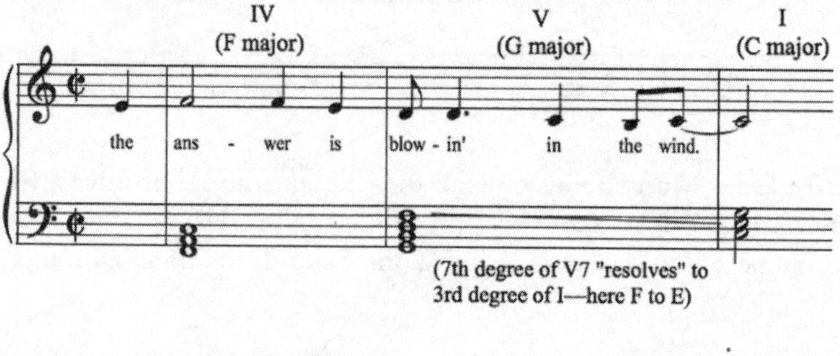

Another very common type of cadence in the Western tradition is the **deceptive** (or interrupted) **cadence**, which, as the name suggests, has the ability to *deceive* the listener's ear. It does this by preparing your ear to hear an authentic cadence, but instead of going to the tonic (C major in the key of C), it moves to another chord—usually the vi chord (A minor in the key of C) or the IV chord (F major in the key of C). This catches the listener's attention (consciously or not), with a sort of aural surprise or tease—and thus its use (or lack thereof) can play a role in defining your musical taste. The classical tradition has tons of examples of deceptive cadences, but so too does the pop and rock repertoire—as seen in these examples:

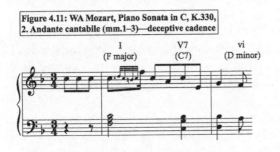

**Figure 4.11: WA Mozart, Piano Sonata in C, K.330, 2. Andante cantabile (mm.1–3)—deceptive cadence**

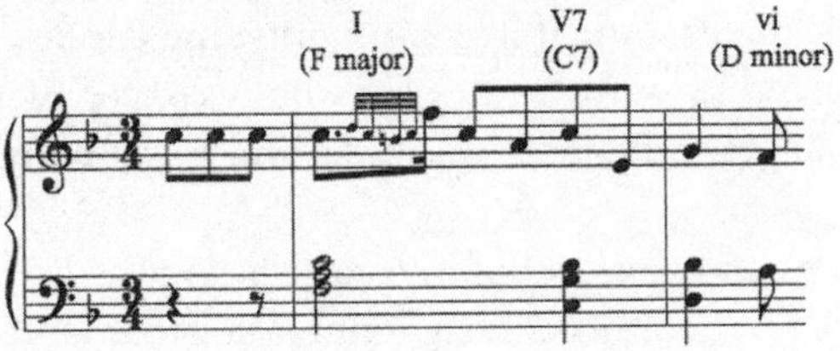

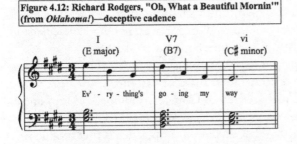

**Figure 4.12: Richard Rodgers, "Oh, What a Beautiful Mornin'" (from *Oklahoma!*)—deceptive cadence**

**Figure 4.13: The Beatles, "Ob-La-Di, Ob-La-Da"—deceptive cadence**

## Modulation and Harmonic Momentum

Given the impulse of so much music—though by no means all, as we'll see—to drive forward with an element of energy or momentum, it's not surprising that a song or work's harmony commonly moves from the "home" (tonic) key to another, "foreign" key. This process of harmonic shift is called **modulation**, and likely occurs in a good majority of the songs or works you hear, to some degree or another. A modulation can be quite temporary or more structural and long-lasting in nature; it can be to an adjacent key (e.g., the V or IV) or to a more remote one (e.g., the iii, VI, ♭VII, etc.); it can be effected smoothly and subtly or suddenly.

To understand what we mean by an *adjacent* or a *remote* key, it will be helpful to introduce you to a staple of music theory, even if it's a bit thorny: the **Circle of 5ths**. Having a rudimentary understanding of this somewhat wonky concept will help you understand why some changes in key sound simple, and some sound complex.

Keys are related not only to scales and chords, but also to each other—both closely and remotely. Each major key (e.g., C major) has a minor key that is "related" to it, such that it's actually called the "**relative minor**"—A minor in the case of C major. The relationship exists because both the C major and A minor scales have the exact same key signature (no sharps or flats). Two other quick examples: G minor is the relative minor to B♭ major because both have 2 flats; F♯ minor is the relative minor to A major, since both have 3 sharps.

Further, a major/minor pair of keys is harmonically *adjacent* to another major/minor pair if it has just one more or less sharp or flat: thus C major/A minor (no sharps or flats) is most closely related to G major/E minor (1 sharp) and F major/D minor (1 flat), but more *remotely* related to D major/B minor (2 sharps) and B♭ major/G minor (2 flats). What this means in practice is that modulating from D major (2 sharps) to A major (3 sharps), or from F minor (4 flats) to B♭ minor (5 flats) is relatively "easy" and straightforward, whereas modulating from E major (4 sharps) to B♭ major (2 flats) is quite complex and "drastic." From a listener's perspective, therefore, we may not even notice the modulation from D major to A major, whereas the shift from E major to B♭ major will likely sound a bit "tweaky." At any rate, this whole construct—which you certainly don't need to memorize—is commonly displayed as an actual circle, as in the figure on the next page (Figure 4.14).

**Figure 4.14: The Circle of 5ths—major keys: upper case; relative minor keys: lower case**

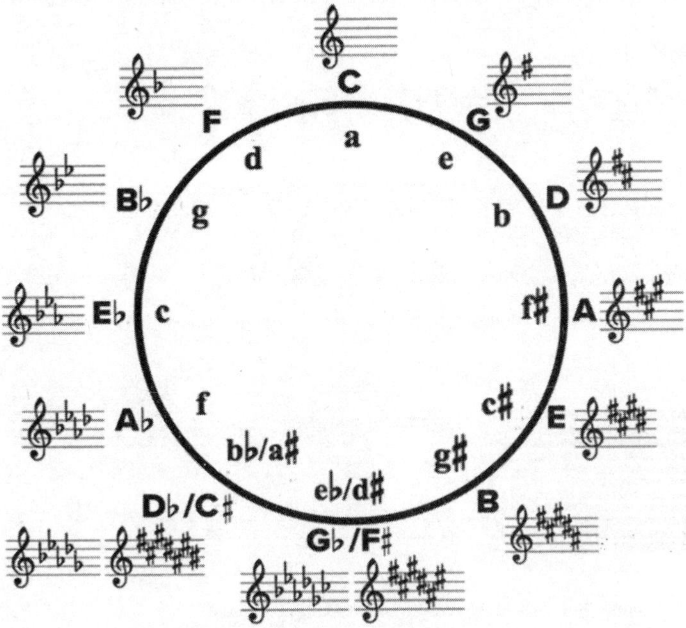


In most styles of Western music, a modulation away from the tonic will commonly be followed by an eventual return to it, perhaps by way of numerous other short- or long-term modulations. It is like taking a journey away from home to a foreign destination, then returning home by way of several brief layovers. There is thus a palpable element of tension-release in this process—where modulation *away* from the tonic creates tension that can only be released via a modulation *back* to the tonic.

Indeed, the history of classical music since the mid-seventeenth century is in many ways dominated by the broad narrative thrust of establishing a **home key** (e.g., C major), moving to a foreign key (e.g., G major, the dominant), and then returning back again. This is the foundation of many standard forms—most notably the sonata form (see Chapter 6), which composer Arnold Schoenberg likened to a "living organism," specifically by virtue of its "organic" processes of development and narrative logic.[129] But it likewise undergirds a good percentage of works in popular and jazz genres as well. We'll explore the historical, psychological, and even neurological implications of harmonic modulation later, but for now here are a few musical examples:

**Figure 4.15: Domenico Scarlatti, Sonata in G, K. 431—adjacent modulation**

**Figure 4.16: George Gershwin, "'S Wonderful"—remote modulation**

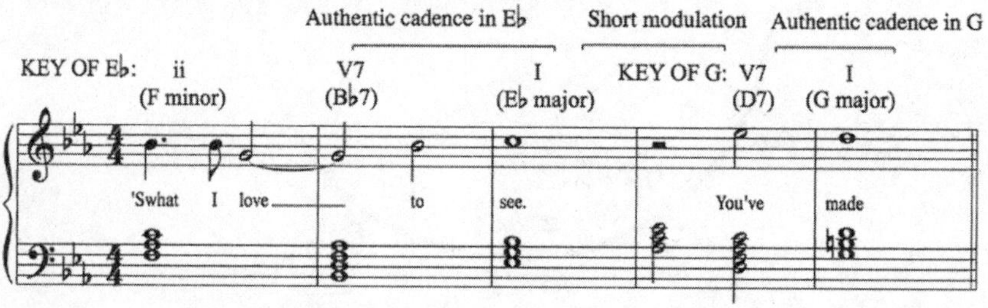


**Figure 4.17: Talking Heads, "And She Was"—very remote modulation**

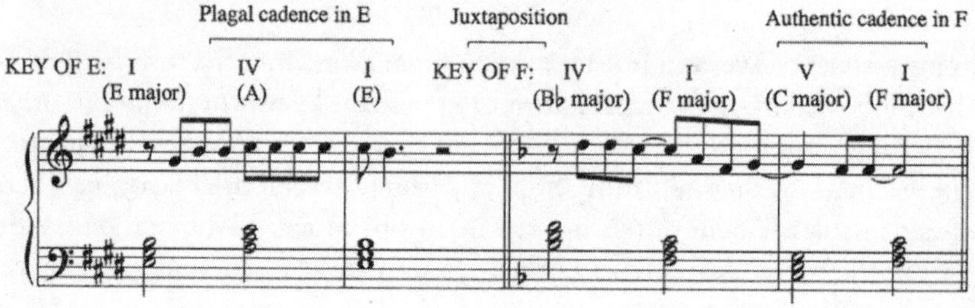


These examples not only exemplify the frequent use of modulation in various styles (classical, jazz, and rock), but also display three rather different means of affecting a modulation (see notes on the examples above). The Scarlatti example illustrates an *adjacent* modulation, between two keys that are one step away on the Circle of 5ths: from G major (1 sharp) to D major (2 sharps), effected gradually over several measures. The Gershwin example illustrates a *remote* modulation, between two keys that are four steps apart on the Circle of 5ths: from E♭ major (3 flats) to G major (1 sharp), effected by a short, one-measure transition. The Talking Heads example then illustrates a *very remote* modulation, between two keys that are five steps away on the Circle of 5ths: from E major (4 sharps) to F major (1 flat), effected by a sudden juxtaposition. While these are just three examples chosen at random, they underscore the vast harmonic diversity and creativity that musicians of all stripes can employ, and that we as listeners can experience just by turning on the radio.

## The Pattern Effect

Among the most effective ways in which harmony can impact our listening experience is via repeating patterns. To be sure, a chord progression can carry great forward momentum and narrative thrust, but it can also generate a sense of equilibrium, steadiness, and "groove" by repeating a pattern of chords over and again. The hypnotic potential of a repeating or oscillating harmonic pattern has surely been recognized and exploited by musicians since two notes first sounded together, and has manifested itself in countless ways ever since. Not surprisingly, the nature of a repeating chord progression can vary considerably—in design, length, complexity, and listening effect. The simplest **chord pattern** in fact is an oscillating two-chord pattern, such as that which harmonically supports the repeating melodic phrase of the Rolling Stones song displayed in Figure 3.27—presented here with the melody and chord symbols above only.

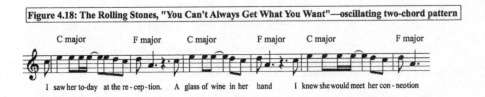

**Figure 4.18: The Rolling Stones, "You Can't Always Get What You Want"—oscillating two-chord pattern**

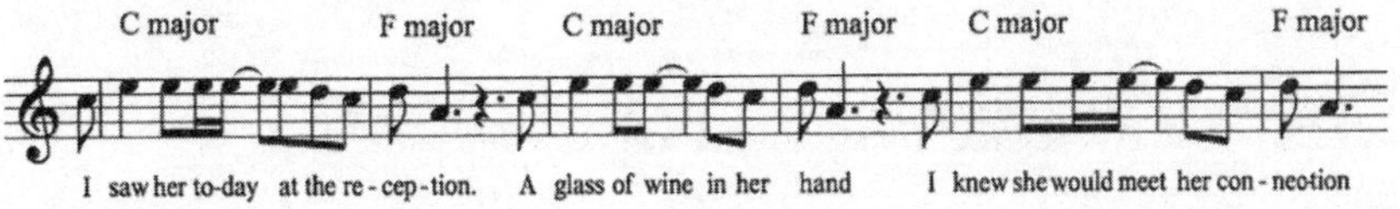
C major
F major
C major
F major
C major
F major
I saw her to-day at the re-cep-tion. A glass of wine in her hand I knew she would meet her con-nection

The insistent back-and-forth between C major and F major (the diatonic I and IV chords) creates a state of harmonic ease and relaxation, like rocking back and forth on a swing. This is in many ways the source of the "groove" in this song that its fans find so appealing (see more examples in Chapter 10). At the same time, the static repetition carries with it an expectation that a change may eventually come—as it indeed does numerous measures later, at the chorus lyric "But if you try sometime," which provides the listener with a satisfying release and forward motion.

More common than a two-chord oscillation, however, are various repeating patterns of three or more chords, able to create at once a level of forward momentum and harmonic equilibrium. Classical, jazz, popular, and world music styles have all embraced many of these patterns, with certain repeating harmonic progressions gaining broad cultural currency and adoption—as is particularly the case with the I–V–vi–IV example shown in Figure 4.22. Here are a few such examples of common chord progressions:

**Figure 4.19: La folia (Baroque era)—common bass (chord) cycle**

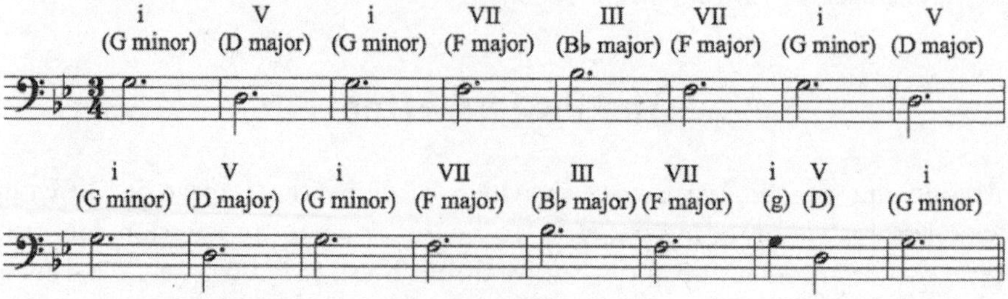


**Figure 4.20: 12-bar blues (in C major)—repeating chord progression**

**Figure 4.21: I–VI–II–V ("rhythm changes")—jazz-era common chord pattern**

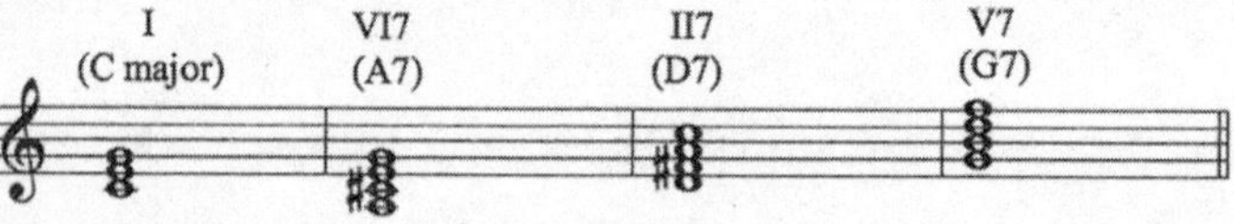


**Figure 4.22: I–V–vi–IV—pop/rock/country/reggae common chord pattern**

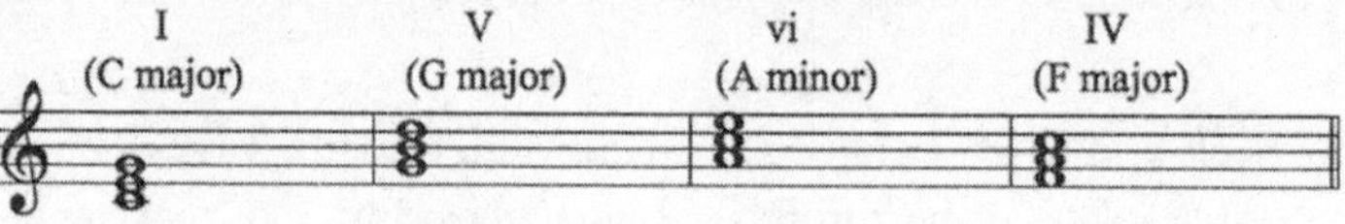


This may seem an impressive list, but in truth it represents only a small portion of the many commonly used chord progressions. Further, there are countless more repeating chord progressions used in songs and works that don't gain wide adoption. The progressions can repeat twice before moving on to something else, or repeat more intently as a kind of loop—thereby creating a greater degree of that hypnotic potential discussed above. Here are two examples representing these two extremes—the first, a classical work that repeats a four-chord progression only twice before moving on; the second, a rock tune that repeats the same three-chord progression for the entire song:

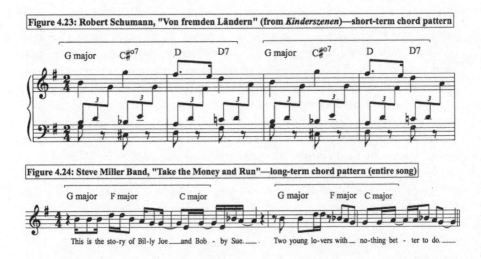

**Figure 4.23: Robert Schumann, "Von fremden Ländern" (from *Kinderszenen*)—short-term chord pattern**

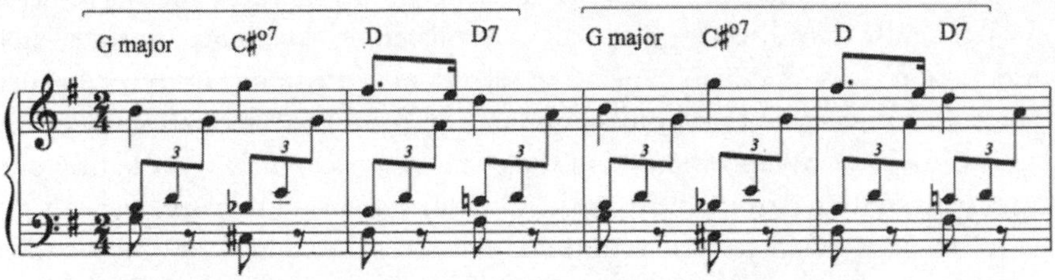


**Figure 4.24: Steve Miller Band, "Take the Money and Run"—long-term chord pattern (entire song)**

Further, the greater the length of the repeating chord progression, the more it moves from being a purely harmonic phenomenon to being a formal one as well. For instance, the 12-bar blues, as well as the classical pattern in Figure 4.19, are not only chord progressions but also musical forms—basically types of the variation form (see Chapter 6).[130] This is not just a technical distinction, moreover, since a chord progression's greater length gives rise to a different kind of listening experience—generally less hypnotic, more broadly narrative. In any event, as an *engaged* listener, you should be on the lookout for repeating chord progressions in the songs you hear: they're everywhere. Composers, especially in commercial genres, use them all the time, because they work. And they probably play a big role in why you like many of the songs you do.

## The Tricky Side of Harmony

Thus far in our harmony primer, we have talked a fair bit about chords, and how they function within major and minor keys. We've discussed the structure of major and minor triads, as well as dominant 7th chords, and their typical use and behavior within relatively simple, diatonic scenarios. While this basic review is sufficient for a fair bit of music within the commercial or popular realm, there are many songs, genres, and styles where this is rather inadequate. The truth is that harmony frequently gets "tricky" even within pop, rock, and other commercial forms of Western music—not to mention jazz, classical, and many world music traditions.

As broaching this tricky side of harmony runs the risk of overwhelming the lay reader, it would be easy—perhaps even wise—for me to bypass them altogether here. But, if you haven't noticed, I tend not to heed such warnings.

Instead, I believe I'd be derelict in my duties if I didn't at least attempt to distill some of the key concepts of "advanced harmony" to the nonmusician—given how frequently they directly impact all of our listening experience. Further, their introduction is also a valuable means to relay some core trends in music history. That said: please note that your command of these concepts is by no means required to move beyond them, and thus you are welcome to skim lightly over them, or even to bypass them altogether, if your eyes begin to glaze over.

To maximize clarity, we'll introduce "advanced harmony" by way of three broad topics: extended chords, chromaticism, and atonality.

We begin with **extended chords**. As noted earlier, the common variety or "flavor" of chords (see Figure 4.5) comprises stacked 3rds, either as triads (1–3–5) in the case of major, minor, diminished, and augmented chords; or with an added 7th (1–3–5–7) in the case of dominant and diminished 7th chords. In many instances, however, other notes are included as additions to, or replacements of, these stacked 3rds—a 2nd, 4th, tritone, 6th, 9th, etc. These additional notes, often part of a moving melody over a sustained chord, help to enrich the sound—and in some cases can even obscure the nature of the basic chord. When sounding at the same time as the "chord" tones, these extra notes are called, logically, "**nonchord tones**." Often, however, they occur *between* two chord tones, where they are, again logically, called "**passing tones**." Examples of these two common scenarios appear below:

**Figure 4.25: Irving Berlin, "Cheek to Cheek"—use of nonchord tones (NC)**

**Figure 4.26: Drake, "Passionfruit"—use of passing tones (PT)**

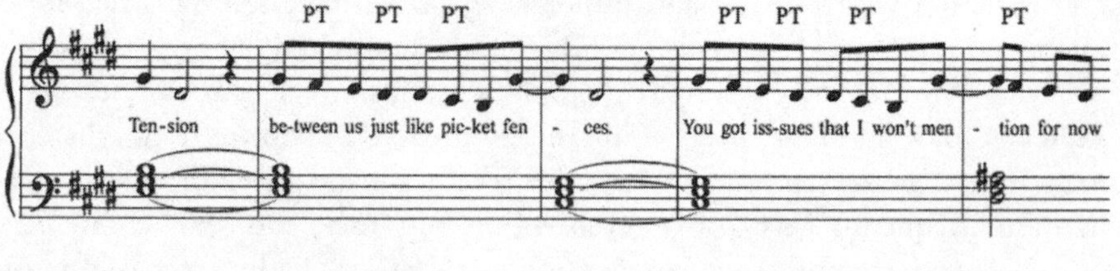


Another very common manifestation of extended chords is the stacking of additional 3rds (or 4ths) on top of a dominant 7th chord, in order to make new "altered" or complex chords. Common extended dominant 7th chords, as well as other common extended chords, are shown below (Figures 4.27 a and b):

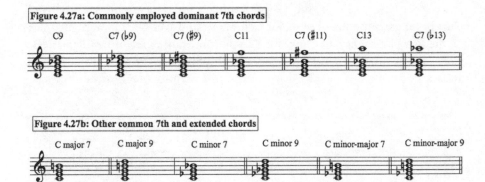

**Figure 4.27a: Commonly employed dominant 7th chords**

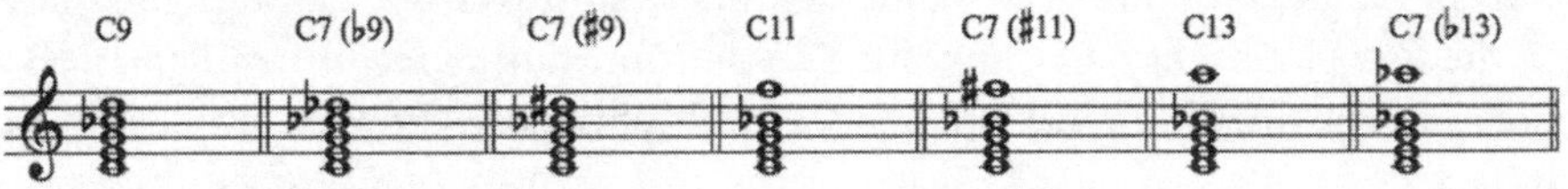


**Figure 4.27b: Other common 7th and extended chords**

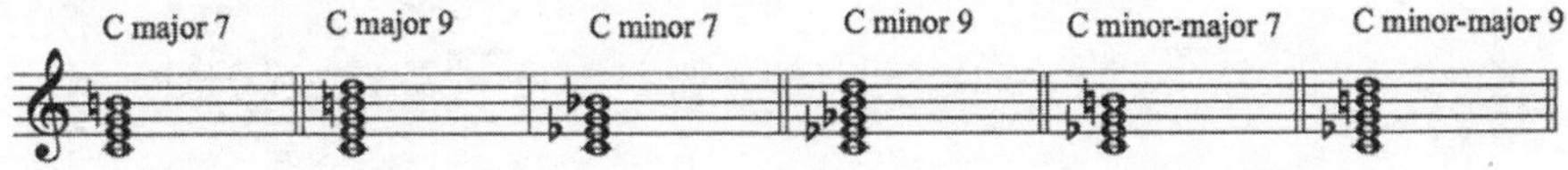


The conscious use of these altered or complex 7th chords began via the gradual expansion of tonality through the latter nineteenth century, and especially in the works of the **Impressionist** school of composers in France during the 1880s and '90s, notably Claude Debussy, Maurice Ravel, and Erik Satie. What we now call major or minor 7th and 9th chords, as well as dominant 9th, 11th, and 13th chords, were exploited both for their "exotic" sound quality and as a means to expand tonality without breaking from it—as seen in these examples:

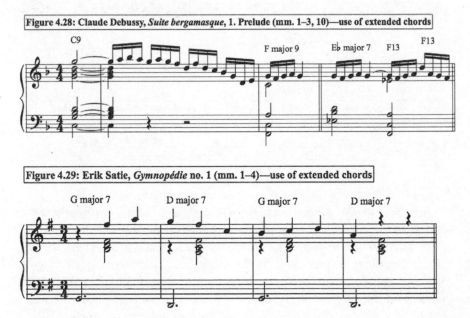

**Figure 4.28: Claude Debussy, *Suite bergamasque*, 1. Prelude (mm. 1–3, 10)—use of extended chords**

**Figure 4.29: Erik Satie, *Gymnopédie* no. 1 (mm. 1–4)—use of extended chords**

Importantly, these "exotic" chords were then gradually adopted into the incipient language of jazz, from the 1920s, and have remained an essential element in that species ever since. Indeed, the use of complex chords—especially those built on the dominant 7th chord—is a sort of sine qua non of jazz, particularly since the 1940s. The rich and "exotic" sounds created by expanded or "altered" 7th chords are undoubtedly a major factor in what drives a jazz lover *to* the music in the first place. They are thus also a likely contributing factor in what drives a non-jazz fan *away* from it. Here is an example of the use of these complex chords in jazz:

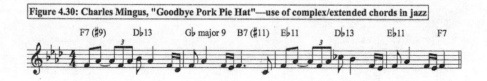

**Figure 4.30: Charles Mingus, "Goodbye Pork Pie Hat"—use of complex/extended chords in jazz**

Extended chords have likewise entered into other more "popular" styles, including pop, rock, R&B, and Broadway—though generally limited to the simpler 7th and 9th chords, as in these examples:

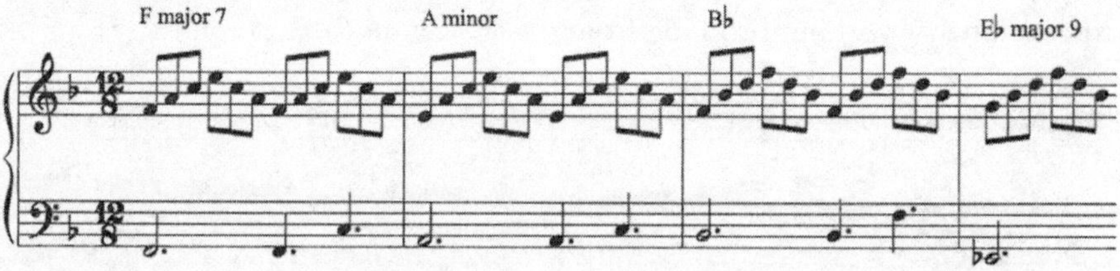

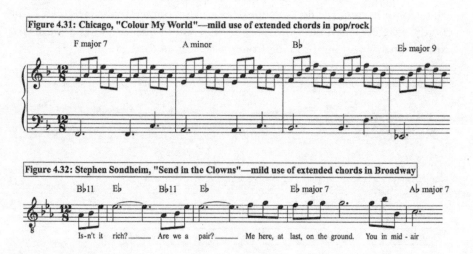

**Figure 4.31: Chicago, "Colour My World"—mild use of extended chords in pop/rock**

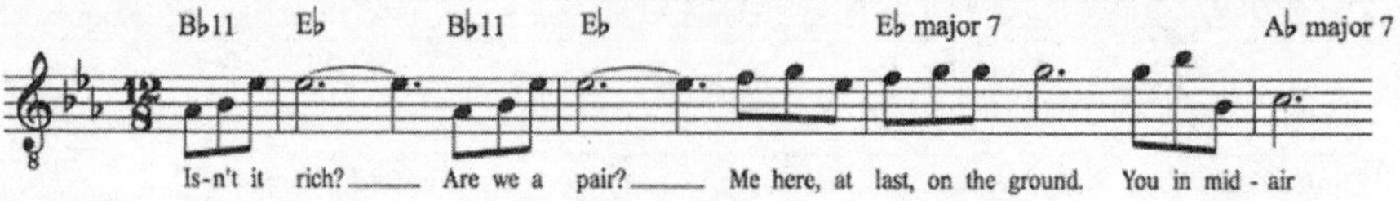


**Figure 4.32: Stephen Sondheim, "Send in the Clowns"—mild use of extended chords in Broadway**

Next, we move to the second topic of advanced harmony: **chromaticism**. In contrast to the circumscribed application of "extended chords," "chromaticism" is a more general term that describes any use of harmony that extends beyond simple, diatonic principles. As such, the mere use of fancy extended or "altered" *chords* may constitute chromaticism. More commonly, though, the term suggests the use of chord *progressions* that use chords outside the purely diatonic realm, or that involve a modulation between two keys quite far apart on the Circle of 5ths (see Figures 4.16 and 4.17). And while these definitions of chromaticism might suggest they first began after the rise of tonality in the mid-seventeenth century, there are a few pronounced usages in earlier periods—notably in the so-called "ars subtilior" (subtler art) chansons of the late fourteenth century; and famously in the repertoire of Italian madrigals from the late sixteenth century, by composers such as Carlo Gesualdo (Figure 4.33). Thus, if you like sophisticated harmony, you might want to check out these "tricky" harmonies of the Middle Ages and Renaissance era:

**Figure 4.33: Carlo Gesualdo, "Resta di darmi noia" (1611)—rare chromaticism in Renaissance (esp. at * )**

(text: "Stop tormenting me")

Historical anomalies aside, though, chromaticism is more emphatically the purview of the latter stages of the "common practice period"—during the **Romantic era** (c. 1800–1900)—when it became a tool in the broader aim to heighten emotional expressiveness.[131] Starting with Beethoven and increasingly through composers like Schubert, Schumann, and Chopin, use of nondiatonic chord progressions (direct chord movement, remote modulations, etc.) and other forms of chromaticism became a powerful means to increase expression and drive narrative intensity in ways that a simpler diatonic approach could not. A pivotal shift came in the works of Richard Wagner, who in many ways broke open the potential of chromaticism to attain hyperintense emotion, while at the same time helping to strain the very definitions of tonality. Here are two examples of nineteenth-century chromaticism:

**Figure 4.34: Frédéric Chopin, Mazurka in F♯ Minor, Op. 6, no. 1 (mm. 5–9)—chromaticism in 19th c. classical (esp. at * )**

**Figure 4.35: Richard Wagner, *Tristan und Isolde*, Prelude (mm. 1–8)—chromaticism in 19th c. classical (esp. at *, including the Tristan chord)**

The potential of chromaticism unveiled by nineteenth-century classical composers had tremendous consequences for subsequent music making, not only in the classical realm, but in other styles as well—most especially jazz and rock, and to some degree Broadway. In many ways, jazz and rock began as reactions against the increasing complexity of the species that preceded them (classical and jazz, respectively). That is, both jazz and rock began with a relatively simple (diatonic) harmonic orientation. But, as often happens as artistic movements mature and evolve, these styles gradually found ways to embrace the more complex prospects of chromaticism. In jazz, this began with bebop and post-bop styles in the 1950s and '60s, where the relatively simple original chords of "standards" were made chromatic via "substitutions" and reharmonizations—practices alive and well in jazz today. In rock, chromaticism saw its heyday in the late 1960s and '70s, most notably during the "art rock" era. Here are examples in both jazz and rock:

**Figure 4.36: John Coltrane, "Giant Steps"—chromaticism in jazz**

**Figure 4.37: The Beatles, "Sexy Sadie"—chromaticism in rock**

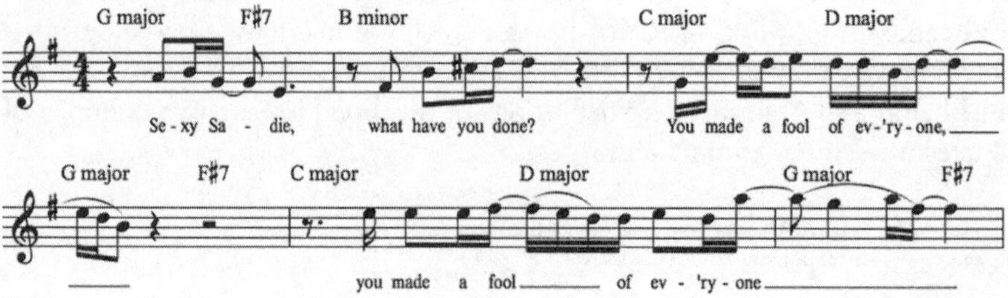


This should not suggest, however, that most rock music today embraces a strongly chromatic harmonic approach—quite the contrary, as the vast majority of rock songs released today are decidedly diatonic and often rather simple (e.g., with a limited number of chords placed in repeating patterns)—but there are exceptions, as in some "alt-rock" bands, such as the Muse song "Butterflies and Hurricanes," which we'll discuss in detail in Chapter 10. And again, your personal reaction to any of these songs, favorable or unfavorable, will in many ways arise from your response to the level of chromaticism employed in them.

Moving on to our third "tricky" topic: the harmonic experimentation that took place in the second half of the nineteenth century—embodied famously in Wagner's "Tristan chord" (Figure 4.35)—not only demonstrated the new vistas open to composers writing in the tonal idiom, but also began to threaten its harmonic hegemony. Through the remaining decades of the nineteenth century, classical composers like Liszt, Mahler, Strauss, Mussorgsky, and those of the Impressionist school increased the use of chromaticism, as well as extended chords, to a point where saying that a passage was "in" a key became difficult, if not impossible. By the dawn of the twentieth century, it became clear that a nontonal—or "**atonal**"—orientation was possible. Indeed, to some, such as Mahler's disciple Arnold Schoenberg, a move into atonal harmony was historically inevitable.[132]

Over the next several decades, forward-minded composers such as Schoenberg, Stravinsky, Bartók, and Berg embraced the challenge of exploring an atonal landscape via a wide array of complex harmonic devices—many of which are complex enough to make even trained musicians cry "Mommy!" They include fancy-sounding approaches like nonchordal constructs, **polychordal** or polytonal techniques, 12-tone or "serial" harmony, parallel harmony, nondiatonic scales or modes, etc.[133] Here is an example:

**Figure 4.38: Arnold Schoenberg, Drei Klavierstücke, Op. 11, no. 1 (mm. 1–5)—atonal harmony in early 20th c.**

The employment of such "wild" and often quite dissonant approaches likewise helped bring about a schism of sorts between "classical" composers and audiences, something still with us today. Indeed, you might be one of those who doesn't like or "get" modern classical music that uses these types of harmonic approaches, and much prefer to seek the diatonic shelter of simpler popular styles. Again, it was the increased complexity of classical works in the 1910s and '20s, and the resulting schism, that opened the door to other, more "accessible" styles (ragtime, jazz, blues, etc.). Through the mid-twentieth century, avant-garde composers—such as Boulez, Stockhausen, Ligeti, and Penderecki—only expanded the complexity of harmony via things like **clusters** (a group of adjacent half and whole steps sounding simultaneously) and greater overt dissonance. Here are two examples:

Figure 4.39: Pierre Boulez, *Twelve Notations*, 2. Très vif—overt dissonance in mid-20th century

Figure 4.40: Bernard Herrmann, "Shower Scene" (from *Psycho*)—overt dissonance in mid-20th century

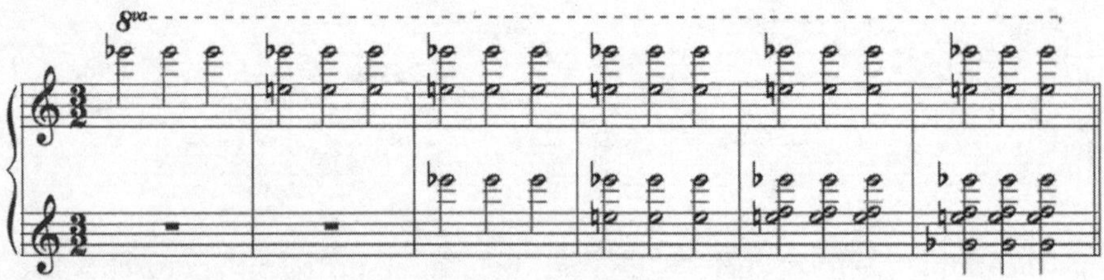

Not surprisingly, the audience for works of this nature is relatively small.

This is not to say, however, that every classical composer after 1920 took up the atonal path. Some composers of the 1930s and '40s, such as Copland, Prokofiev, and Vaughan Williams, maintained a more tonal or at least consonant approach to harmony in many of their works, as seen in this example:

Figure 4.41: Sergei Prokofiev, *Peter and the Wolf* (mm. 1–4)—tonal harmony in 20th c. classical

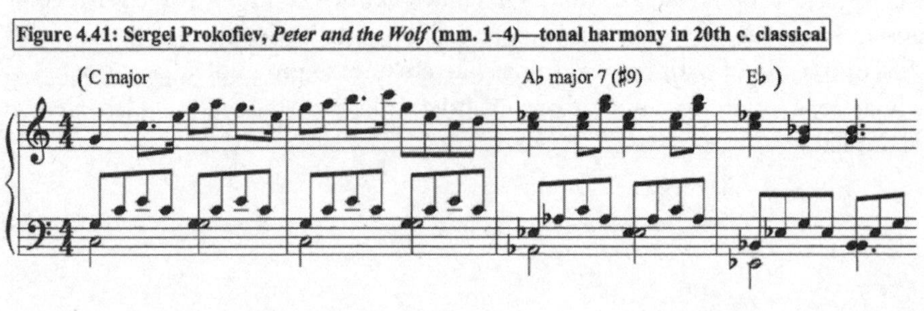


Beginning in the 1970s, moreover, composers like Philip Glass and Steve Reich made a more overt rebellion again the harmonic complexity of the preceding decades via a "minimalist" approach. This style commonly features sustained passages (sometimes considerably so) of very simple diatonic chord progressions, even mere simple triads, as seen in this example:

Today, "classical" composers—myself included—can avail themselves of the full array of harmonic options, from simple (diatonic) to highly complex (chromatic, atonal, etc.), which can be both a blessing and a challenge.

It is likewise not surprising that these ultracomplex approaches to harmony have found little embrace within other, more popular genres, including jazz and rock. Of course, there are exceptions—such as the "free jazz" movement led by Ornette Coleman and late-stage John Coltrane, as well as the "progressive" rock of Frank Zappa and the British band Gentle Giant. But these exceptions largely prove the rule: popular music is meant to please the audience, and too much harmonic complexity makes that hard to do. As we'll explore shortly in Interlude B, the roots of this common aversion to hypercomplex harmony lies partly in science—by virtue of the inherent acoustic properties (frequencies, overtones, etc.) that arise via dissonant intervals, and our relatively negative physiological response to them compared to consonant intervals.

At the same time, as will be discussed in Interludes E and F, science is not alone in this dynamic—whether our general reaction to complex harmony is favorable or unfavorable. Cultural learning plays a key role as well. In fact, the rise of harmonic complexity via classical composers in the twentieth century did much to more broadly "open the ears" of both composers and audiences in a variety of popular styles as well. This explains the tolerance, even embrace, of dissonance in small, controlled doses—as in the periodic clusters in the jazz recordings of Thelonious Monk and Wynton Marsalis; the occasional nontonal or dissonant moments in songs by Jimi Hendrix, the Police, and the Foo Fighters; as well as myriad atonal passages within contemporary film scores, especially when the tension level is high.

In short, the public at large is far more tolerant of harmonic complexity than it was, say, fifty or a hundred years ago, which is not to say, however, that it's "anything goes" for everyone.

## Modes, Drones, and Stasis

We conclude our "intro" to harmony with a brief look at an aspect quite in contrast to the one just reviewed: the use of diatonic modes, sustained drones, and harmonic stasis. These might even be called the "simpler" side of harmony. And although its usage has important roots in early—that is pre-seventeenth-century—music history, it is alive and well in much of the music produced and listened to today. Indeed, I'd be willing to bet that much of your favorite music makes use of these harmonic elements to a partial or substantial degree.

Let's back up a bit. The system of tonality is built on the movement and functionality of chords and chord progressions within and between keys. Prior to its rise in the mid-seventeenth century, however, another system guided composers in the way notes were placed together in simultaneous sounding: the **church modes.** We've mentioned modes already in our discussion of melody, as another term for scale. Indeed, the church modes are a set of stepwise, diatonic scales, with roots in ancient Greek and Middle Eastern modal traditions.[134] Their history and theory is complex and not germane to our discussion, but it is useful to note here that by the late ninth century a system of eight modes was established as the codifying framework for the vast repertoire of Christian plainsong known as Gregorian chant.[135] Although there were eight octave modes, they were paired, such that there were only four "tonics"—or *finals* as they are properly called (Figure 4.43):

**Figure 4.43: Eight Church modes (o = mode final)**

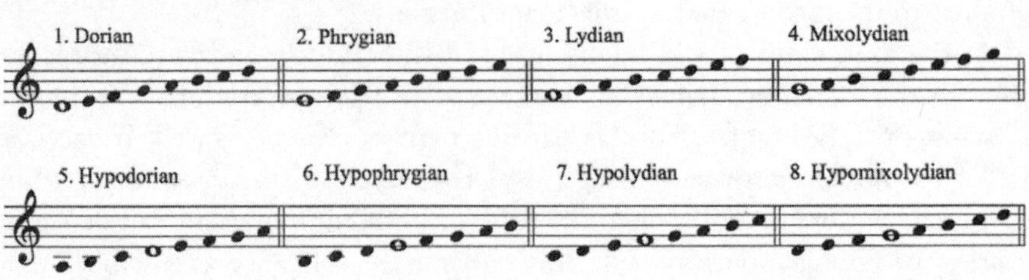


The church modes were initially a purely melodic consideration—a set of eight "scales" governing the creation of monophonic (single-line) melodies, such as Gregorian chants. Yet as polyphony (multi-line music) became widespread, from the eleventh century, the church modes likewise became a factor in governing harmonic activity. That is, they were also used to define how the individual moving lines should come together to form acceptable vertical intervals—and especially at cadences. This was the case even as polyphony became ever more sophisticated during the latter Middle Ages and Renaissance, often featuring four or more voices moving at once.

It is important to remember that during this time "chords" as distinct conceptual entities did not yet exist. That is, composers of the Middle Ages and Renaissance conceived of their music *not* as a progression from one vertical (harmonic) moment to another, but rather as a combined flow of independent horizontal (melodic) lines moving together in a complementary and "harmonious" manner—obeying the rules of counterpoint to produce a pleasing, collective musical narrative. This is not to say, however, that we today cannot locate "chords" within this music, especially in works from the early Renaissance (early 15th c.) onward; it's just that they can only anachronistically be called "chords." And indeed, if we today analyze Renaissance music, we *can* regularly locate major and minor triads, as well as various common chord progressions, within the contrapuntal (multimelody) texture. It's just that these vertical sonorities, again, were not consciously created entities, but rather a happy by-product of the individual contrapuntal lines sounding together, based on rules of consonance, dissonance, and "**voice leading**"—meaning the conventions employed by composers to write smooth-sounding melodies.

Undoubtedly, the Renaissance composers of motets, Masses, **chansons**, and madrigals—the key genres of the fifteenth and sixteenth centuries—intuited that these sonorities had a distinct aural essence and a pleasing quality, even if they didn't know what to call them. Undoubtedly too their audiences experienced these "chordal" soundings with increased cognition and appreciation.

And indeed, from the mid-sixteenth century, the tide began to turn more decidedly toward a new "harmonic" orientation and the ultimate rise of the twenty-four major and minor keys of tonality.[136] Again, this is a complex story we need not recount here. But the transition can be seen in many ways as a gradual catching up of what composers—and audiences—were already experiencing: that harmony as a distinct construct of vertical-sounding "chords" was in need of recognition and cultivation. In short, placing emphasis on chords as a driving force in composition made for some very pleasing and taste-inspiring music. The transition of modality to tonality—a long and tortured story through much of the seventeenth century—is not only about the rise of chords, of course, but they certainly played a key role (no pun intended).

Incidentally, this distinction in harmonic usage between the Middle Ages and the Baroque era (early 17th c.) is also a principal reason why much "early" music can sound so exotic to our ears today—where despite a largely diatonic orientation (the exception of Figure 4.33 notwithstanding), the familiar flow of chords and well-formed chord progressions is generally absent. It is my hope, however, that despite—or, better, because of—these distinctions, those unfamiliar with this music will take the time to explore the splendors of medieval and Renaissance polyphony, such as that by Guillaume de Machaut, Guillaume Dufay, Josquin des Prés, Roland de Lassus, and Palestrina—the latter three attaining a climax of beauty that (in this writer's viewpoint, anyway) has scarcely been matched since.

The harmonic application of **modality**, however, is not limited to the polyphonic works of the Middle Ages and Renaissance. Most especially, it manifests itself by the use of a **drone**—that is, a sustained "droning" pitch sounding throughout a work or section, while one or more melodies appear above or below.

Drones are an ancient musical phenomenon, and may well represent a kind of musical "archetype" with primitive origins.[137] As a deliberate technique, the drone developed especially in Asia before being adopted in the West, largely as an instrumental effect to support a vocal melody; its appearance in Europe was likely quite early in the Middle Ages, though as an improvised accompaniment, it was rarely written down. The wide popularity of drones as accompaniment to individual melodies throughout the Middle Ages, however, is demonstrated through common depictions of instruments that are particularly suited to this function—such as bagpipes or the hurdy-gurdy. Its use is likewise demonstrated in the extended drone-like passages in the polyphonic vocal works in the late twelfth and early thirteenth centuries—namely, in the organum of the Notre-Dame school (see Figure 4.44):

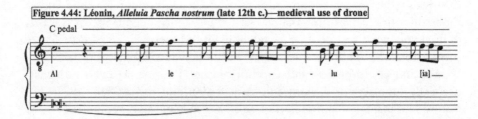

**Figure 4.44: Léonin, *Alleluia Pascha nostrum* (late 12th c.)—medieval use of drone**

The drone is particularly palpable as a harmonic phenomenon by virtue of its hypnotic experiential quality—one of stillness or stasis, an anchoring sustain that colors and enriches the melodic narrative usually flowing above it. As the South African musicologist Peter Van der Merwe put it, a drone is like a "frozen chord," shaping any melody it accompanies "even in the absence of further harmony."[138] Indeed, the "drone effect" has gained favor in myriad styles and musical approaches all around the world—from the tanpura (plucked string instrument) drones of Indian ragas to the trumpet drones of Tibetan chants to Scottish bagpipe music, and beyond. We'll have more to say about drones when discussing texture in Chapter 7.

Likewise in the West the drone—also known as a **pedal point**—has made its way into our everyday listening experience in myriad ways.*[139] This includes countless "static" passages found in classical, jazz, folk, rock, and various "experimental" styles. Indeed, several popular genres and subgenres are all but defined

* The terms "drone" and "pedal point" (or "pedal") will often be used interchangeably in this book.

by their frequent use of drones—including ambient (electronica) and new age music. Here are a few examples of drones/pedal points in various styles:

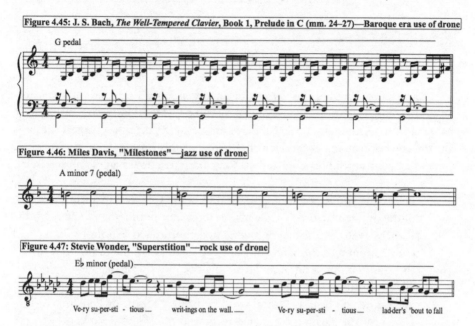

**Figure 4.45: J. S. Bach, *The Well-Tempered Clavier*, Book 1, Prelude in C (mm. 24–27)—Baroque era use of drone**

**Figure 4.46: Miles Davis, "Milestones"—jazz use of drone**

**Figure 4.47: Stevie Wonder, "Superstition"—rock use of drone**

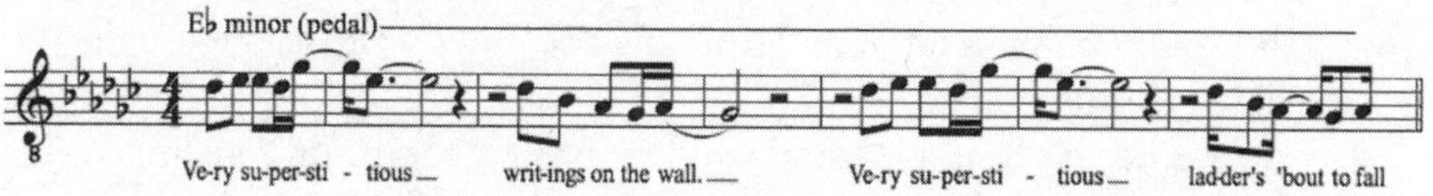


Finally, we may note that the examples by Miles Davis and Stevie Wonder above illustrate not only drones, but also the use of modes or modality in a modern, chord-based context. This is commonly referred to as "modal jazz" or "modal rock." In such cases, the experience of "stasis" is achieved by limiting the chords to those arising diatonically from a single mode. The most prominent modes used in this regard are the Mixolydian and Dorian modes (see Figure 4.43)—both of which are staples of blues and blues-based rock, and their steady reliance on dominant 7th chords (see Figure 4.20). "Modal" songs in the jazz and rock styles are often based on a single chord or, just as commonly, shift back and forth between two or three chords. When two or more chords are used, however, they are not conceived in a tonal—that is functional or key-based—relationship to one another, but rather simply to the mode or modes that underlie them. Here are two famous examples:

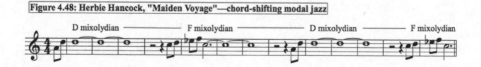

**Figure 4.48: Herbie Hancock, "Maiden Voyage"—chord-shifting modal jazz**

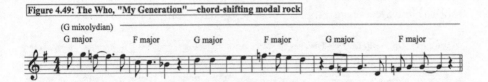

Figure 4.49: The Who, "My Generation"—chord-shifting modal rock

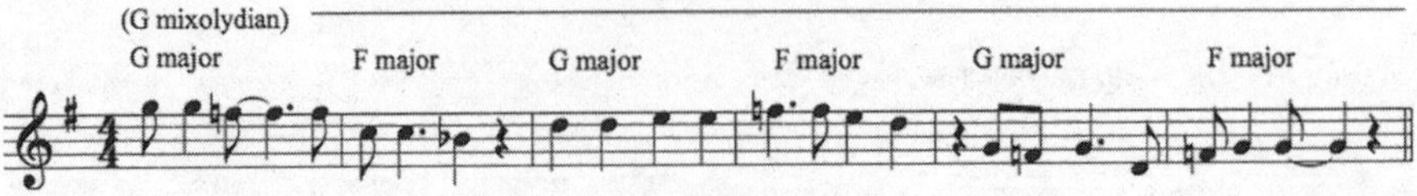


Okay, I know that I've pushed my luck about as far as I can and thus will stop here. Hopefully I didn't lose you—or not too much. If so, don't worry: again, we'll have many opportunities to review these harmony concepts in the chapters ahead—and thereby help you understand how harmony potently impacts your musical taste.

To test your new knowledge of harmony, here are a few suggested exercises:

1. Next time you hear a folk, pop, or rock song: Can you identify some of the different chord types—major, minor, or dominant 7th chords? Perhaps even diminished or augmented chords? Do major or minor chords seem to dominate? And can you distinguish the tonic from the dominant or subdominant, or identify other scale degrees upon which chords sound?
2. Next time you hear a classical work by Bach, Mozart, or Haydn: Listen for the harmonic cadence at the end of phrases. Can you make out the prevalence of authentic cadences? Do you hear a half cadence, or a plagal cadence? What about a deceptive cadence? If so, what was its effect on you?
3. Next time you hear a more complex rock or jazz song: Can you identify a modulation from the home key to another key center? If so, did the change appear smooth or abrupt?
4. Next time you hear a "groove-oriented" rock or R&B song: Can you identify a repeating pattern of chords? How many chords are in the pattern? How does the pattern impact the listening experience?
5. Next time you hear any less mainstream music, whether classical, jazz, or something else: Can you hear how the harmony defines the experience of the music? Can you identify complex approaches to harmony, whether extended chords, chromaticism, or even atonality? What about drones? Do you like this music? Can you articulate the role that the harmony in the music plays in your response to it?

*five*

# RHYTHM: THE MOVEMENT OF MUSIC

If a song's harmonic nature will commonly elude an untrained listener, such is generally not the case with its underlying rhythmic identity. Turn on the radio or put on a CD of music in any style, and chances are you'll be able to accurately feel the "groove" and tap your foot to the beat of the music, or recognize that a discernible rhythm is vague or lacking. This is probably even true of that cousin of yours who, you insist, has "absolutely no sense of rhythm!"

More so than harmony or even melody, rhythm is something we all intuitively understand, as it echoes the flow of our daily lives: the pace of our walking, the beating of our heart, the practical ways we divide our day; indeed, rhythm is connected to our innate drive to define time and its passage, to organize the interactions we have with the world around us. Rhythm, as the arts philosopher Susanne Langer wrote, is "the most elementary means of abstracting motion from the work it actually performs."[140] That is to say, we are hard-pressed to experience any interaction we have with the world around us—including the listening to of music—apart from the rhythmic "abstraction" we impart to it.

Rhythm is often aligned in casual discussions to our heartbeat, and in fact many are the studies that show how the variable beating of our hearts can be impacted by musical rhythm.[141] But as an anthropological simile related to our experience of listening to music, it is lacking. A fast "death metal" song may be symbolically akin to a rapid heart rate, but the intense drama of a slow-moving passage by Shostakovich or a horror movie film score may not be so well reflected by a quiet, steady pulse. A more fitting simile, it seems, is actual bodily movement—the intensity and motion of hands, legs, head, and torso, moving lightly or emphatically, with graceful regularity or spastic spurts, or hardly at all. The analogy to dance here is obvious, of course, and is not unwelcome: beyond being a "sister art" to music, dance is likely the anthropological foundation upon which all cultures generate a musical style.[142]

Further, the simile has an historical precedent, namely with the pedagogical method known as "eurythmics," developed in the 1910s by Swiss composer and educator Émile Jaques-Dalcroze, as a means to teach and experience music through movement and dance.[143]

At any rate, we will here unwind the musical parameter of rhythm as it relates to our listening experience. To be sure, rhythm as an overall aesthetic topic can be quite complex, given its multilayered intersection with our psychological and physiological perceptions of time, from foreground to background phenomena. Rest assured that we will touch only lightly upon such aesthetic complexities, as our predominant experience of rhythm, and its influence on our musical taste, takes place at or just below the musical surface. Even still, however, you'll need to pay close attention while reading this chapter—for despite the intuition we all have for *feeling* rhythm, *explaining* it is at times easier said than done.

## The Basics of Rhythm

In the broadest sense, musical rhythm involves the measurement, description, and organization of musical duration or "temporality," at every level and in any manner. Practically, it concerns the duration of notes (pitched or unpitched) and their movement as defined by a "regulated succession of strong and weak elements."[144] This movement can be regular, or not so much; it can be consistent, or not so much; it can give rise to a discernible beat or tempo, or not so much. Understood in this way, every piece of music has a rhythmic identity, even if you can't dance to it.

The primary element of rhythm is the **beat** (or **pulse** or **tactus**), technically defined as the "temporal unit of a composition."[145] This is the element to which you tap your foot, clap your hands, snap your fingers, or sway your body while listening (or dancing) to a song with a pronounced and alluring rhythm. It is also that element you identify as moving the music forward at a steady pace even if not demonstrably inviting you to move along with it.

In either event, beats are commonly perceived as being connected together in a pattern or grouping of strong (stressed) and weak (unstressed) units, usually in groups of two, three, or four. This grouping is called a **meter**. A song's meter (such as 4/4, 3/4, 6/8, etc.) provides a level of expectancy as the music flows whereby we can predict when the next strong beat will likely occur, and when it will likely not.

The pacing of beats within a meter in turn gives rise to the song's **tempo**—defined as the speed at which the music is performed.[146] A song is deemed slow, moderate, or fast based on the distance between its successive beats, often measured via clock time as "**beats per minute**," or **bpm**. Most music lies within a preferred range of 60 to 150 bpm, outside of which our cognitive capacity to track the beat becomes increasingly compromised.

In practice, the interrelation between beat, meter, and tempo can get pretty complex. This is in part due to the subjective rhythmic perceptions of each individual listener, and in part due to the technical conventions of rhythmic notation and performance. To demonstrate what I mean by this, let's take a look at our go-to nursery rhyme, "Old MacDonald" (Figure 5.1):

**Figure 5.1: "Old MacDonald"—basic rhythmic info**

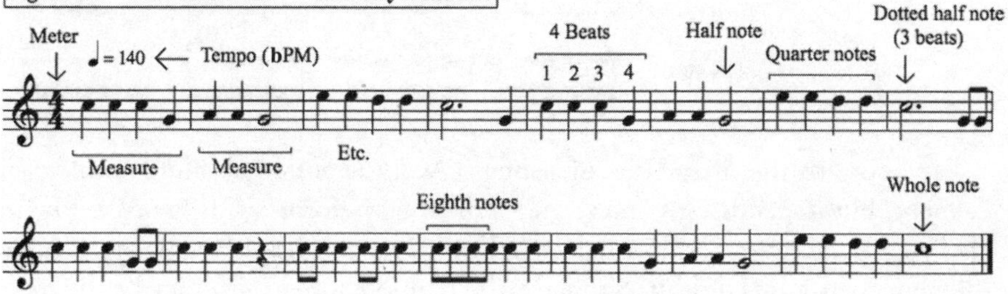


The song is here notated as being in the meter of 4/4—meaning that each **measure** or **bar** (the grouping of beats divided by a vertical bar line) contains four **quarter notes** (♩).* The tempo in turn is defined as the speed of the successive quarter notes, in this case where quarter notes are to be sung at 140 beats per minute (♩ = 140).

And though you may indeed tap your foot at the speed of the quarter note, it is also possible (if not likely) that you would naturally tap your foot at the pacing of two quarter notes, or the **half note** (𝅗𝅥); you might even clap your hands at the level of the full measure—at the pacing of four quarter notes, or the **whole note** (𝅝). Indeed, if you were feeling particularly energized, you might even move both feet at the pacing of half a quarter note, or the **eighth note** (♪); such might especially be the case if the song were sung twice as slow (♩ = 70).

A map of simple note-value subdivisions, demonstrating the simple arithmetical relationship between the values, is shown in Figure 5.2:

* To clarify meter designations a bit, the top number always indicates the *number* of beats per measure, while the bottom number indicates the *note value* equal to one beat, based on its arithmetical relation to a whole note; that is: 1 = whole note; 2 = half note; 4 = quarter note; 8 = eighth note; 16 = sixteenth note; 32 = thirty-second note, etc. To cite a few examples: 3/1 = three beats per measure, where a whole note gets one beat; 2/2 = two beats per measure, where a half note gets one beat; 5/8 = five beats per measure, where an eighth note gets one beat, and so forth.

**Figure 5.2: Simple rhythmic subdivisions—whole note to sixteenth notes**

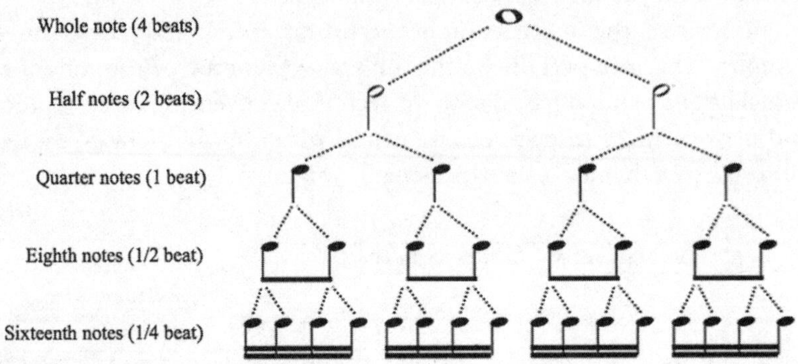


The point is that the "beat" of a song or work is not an absolute ontological element, but depends on context and individual perception. It is not *wrong* to clap your hands at either the quarter, half, whole, or eighth note—it may just be different than how I'd do it. Similarly, the tempo you perceive may be different from mine, since we're basing it on different note values. These differences can even suggest different meters—not just 4/4, but also 2/4, or even 2/2. As I said, it can get pretty complex.

Of course, in many cases the placement of the "principal" beat will be less prone to subjective variability, especially when being experienced within a group context, like a concert—which inherently promotes uniformity in rhythmic perception.

As noted in Interlude A, the ability of a group to collectively sync to a single rhythmic beat when listening to music is known as entrainment—which neuroscientists like Ani Patel have labeled as a "fundamental cognitive skill," perhaps pointing to an evolutionary role for musical awareness.[147] Yet, though we may all track the same beat marker, we can also be well aware of the wider gamut of hierarchical relationships—above and below that same beat level—as being "commensurate" within a larger or smaller grouping structure.[148] Indeed, it is this potentially multilayered perception and definition within a single song that helps make rhythm such a fundamental component in impacting our musical taste.

## Common-Variety Meters

Given the human propensity to synchronize via the process of entrainment, it is not surprising that a good portion of the world's music making involves high-level rhythmic identities that are decidedly simple and straightforward. Practically speaking, this amounts to clear rhythmic divisions into groups of two, three, or four—or, in music-speak, into meters like 2/4, 3/4, or 4/4 (also marked as **c** for "common time"). Music written in these three meters collectively accounts for a good majority of what most of us hear on a regular basis, especially in the West. The notational figures themselves are known as **time signatures**. In these instances, the quarter note receives one beat, with two, three, or four beats per measure, respectively (Figure 5.3):

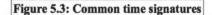

**Figure 5.3: Common time signatures**

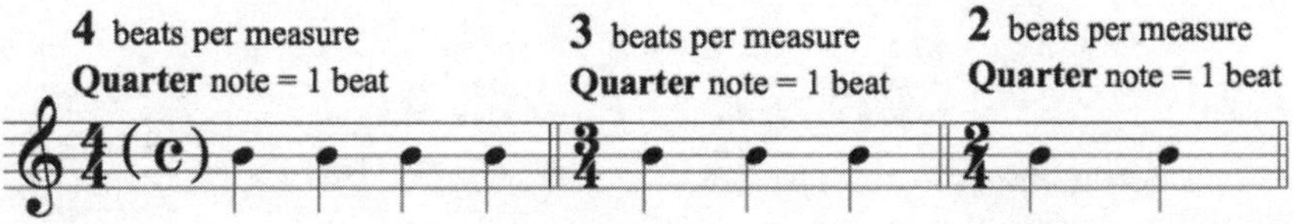


A basic distinction here is between a **duple** (2/4, 4/4) and **triple** (3/4) meter. Both duple and triple are quite common metric orientations, though since the Baroque era, duple meter has gained a notable upper hand among songs, works, and movements in most Western styles. This may in fact reflect a slight biological predisposition: while studies have shown infants as young as seven months able to infer both duple and triple meter from rhythmic patterns, greater discernment (e.g., the ability to recognize metric inconsistency) has been demonstrated with duple meter.[149] At any rate, the trend toward duple has grown especially within popular music of the past century or so, where the music is often closely aligned with youth dancing. By some estimates, for example, 90 percent of rock music is in 4/4, though to my knowledge no one has conducted a proper survey.[150]

In perhaps their most generic forms, duple meter is represented by the military march,* while triple is embodied in the waltz (Figures 5.4 and 5.5):

**Figure 5.4: John Philip Sousa, "The Stars and Stripes Forever"—duple meter march**

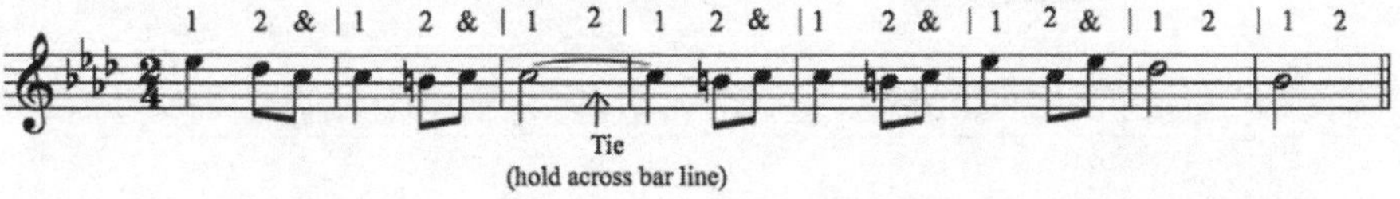


**Figure 5.5: Johann Strauss Jr., "Blue Danube" Waltz—triple meter waltz**

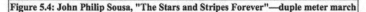

* In its original form, the Sousa example was written in so-called "cut time" (sometimes "alla breve"), notated with the meter symbol ¢. Technically it is equal to 2/2: two beats per measure, with the half note getting one beat; it is common not only in marches but in early jazz songs.

To reinforce the distinction, here are two examples drawn from a more contemporary repertoire:

**Figure 5.6: Meghan Trainor, "All about That Bass"—duple meter pop song**

**Figure 5.7: Kelly Clarkson, "Breakaway"—triple meter pop song**

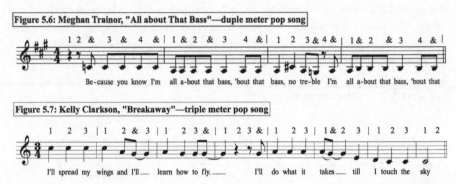

The examples above, moreover, allow us to introduce a subtle yet vital distinction in how meters are defined—between a "simple" and "compound" orientation. The four examples above are all **simple**—meaning that *each beat* is divided into *two equal parts*: that is, one quarter note is divided into two equal eighth notes (counted "1-and, 2-and," etc.). Thus 2/4 and 4/4 are simple duple meters; 3/4 is a simple triple meter.

But there is another common metric orientation: **compound**—meaning that *each beat* is divided into *three equal parts*: that is, one dotted quarter note is divided into three equal eighth notes. As with the simple cases, compound meters can be either duple or triple: 6/8 and 12/8 are **compound duple** meters; 9/8 is a **compound triple** meter. Illustrative examples of these are as follows:

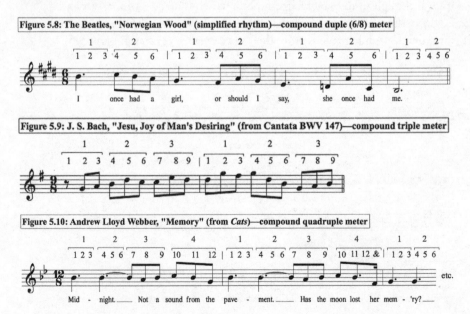

**Figure 5.8: The Beatles, "Norwegian Wood" (simplified rhythm)—compound duple (6/8) meter**

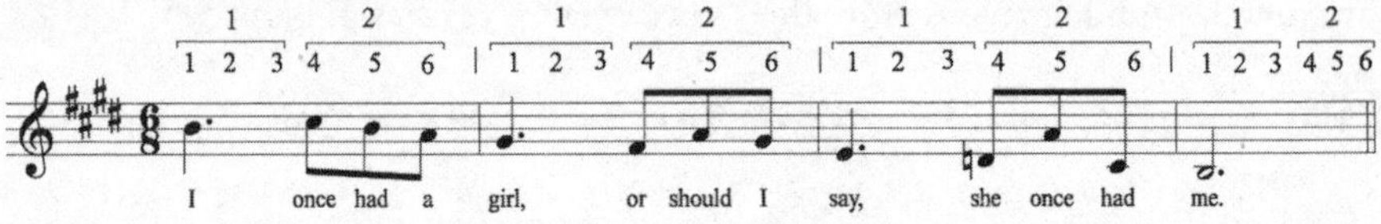


**Figure 5.9: J. S. Bach, "Jesu, Joy of Man's Desiring" (from Cantata BWV 147)—compound triple meter**

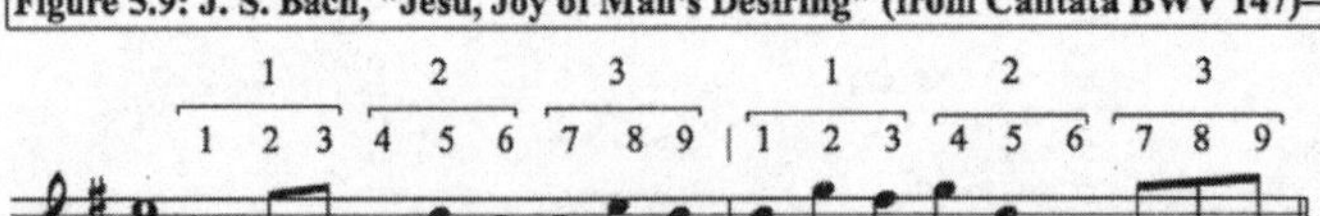


**Figure 5.10: Andrew Lloyd Webber, "Memory" (from *Cats*)—compound quadruple meter**

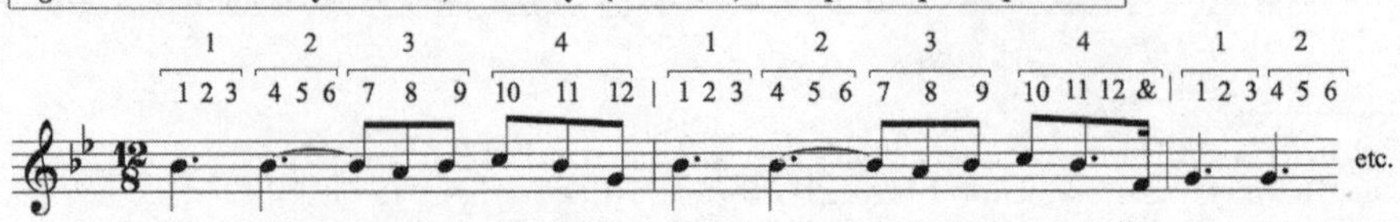

In compound meters, the surface of the music presents a rather lilting "triple" orientation—where one can easily count "1-2-3, 1-2-3," etc., as the music proceeds. At the same time, each of these groupings of three are in turn arranged into a "higher" grouping of beats—either two (6/8), three (9/8), or four (12/8) per measure. This underscores the inherent multilayered rhythmic definition active in so much of the music we hear, where a complementary—duple or triple—orientation takes place at both the beat *and* the measure level. These three multilayered groupings are demonstrated in Figure 5.11:

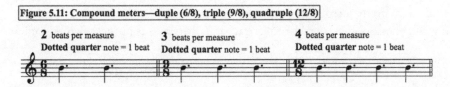

**Figure 5.11: Compound meters—duple (6/8), triple (9/8), quadruple (12/8)**

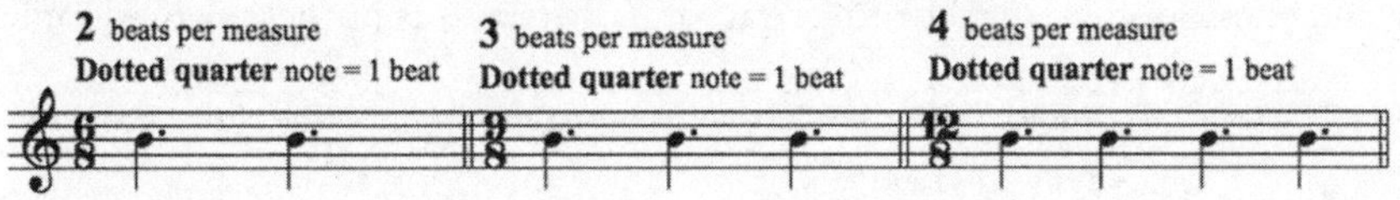


Incidentally, this exposes an inherent ambiguity in the way we hear triple-based meter, and the potential tension between our aural perceptions and the manner in which the music may be notated. That is, the division of a single beat into three equal parts may be written in different ways; here are two common ones: (1) in 6/8 meter (compound duple), a dotted quarter is divided into three equal eighth notes; and (2) in 4/4 meter (simple duple) a quarter note is divided into three eighth note **triplets** (see Figures 5.12 a and b). Triplets (notated with a small 3 above the notes) are sometimes called a "borrowed division," placing three notes in the normal place of two, and are pedagogically pronounced "tri-po-let" or "tri-pa-let."

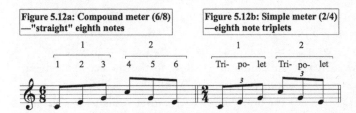

**Figure 5.12a: Compound meter (6/8) —"straight" eighth notes**

**Figure 5.12b: Simple meter (2/4) —eighth note triplets**

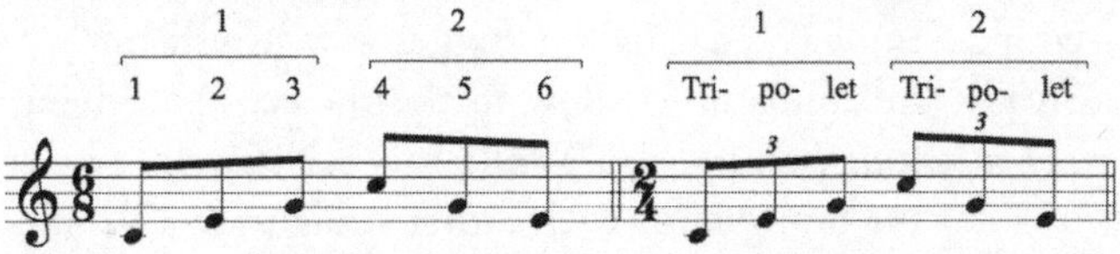


In short, the nuanced elements of rhythm and meter have a potentially powerful impact on our musical experience, and thus on our musical taste. Being on the lookout for their individual and combined subtleties, therefore, will help you locate your metric "sweet spots."

## The Devil's in the Details

Now that we've introduced the basic rhythmic elements of beat, tempo, and meter, we can begin to explore some of the ways in which rhythm actually manifests itself in a concrete, experiential way. In essence, identifying the meter, beat structure, and tempo of a song or work is like providing instructions to an improv troupe—they provide a road map of sorts to the actors, but don't actually define how they'll carry out the scene; or, as musicologist Joseph Kerman put it, "Meter is background; rhythm is foreground."[151] That is, the meter (and tempo) provides a framework against which the rhythm interacts, at times aligning, and at times conflicting, in turn forging the details that give the music's temporal experience its variety, its excitement, and its energy.

In some cases, the rhythmic activity of the music aligns rather cleanly in accordance with the predictable expectations of its meter, in terms of beat positioning and stress, not least on the first beat, or *downbeat*—as in these two examples:

**Figure 5.13: Gioacchino Rossini, *William Tell* Overture (opening phrase)—predictable rhythmic accents**

**Figure 5.14: Jerry Bock, "Sunrise, Sunset" from *Fiddler on the Roof* (verse)—predictable rhythmic accents**

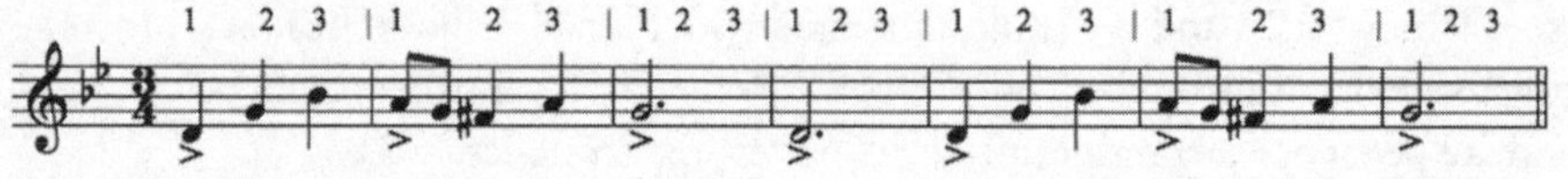


Here, the musical emphases or **accents** (notated musically as >) fall on the meter's "strong" beats: on beats 1 and 2 in 2/4 meter (Rossini); on beat 1 only in 3/4 meter (*Fiddler*)—with de-emphasized activity falling unobtrusively on "weak beats." This creates a steady and undisrupted flow to the music, like driving a car down a smooth road at a consistent speed. While this can certainly be engaging and fulfilling, it is not uncommon for even rather straightforward music to at times interject rhythmic activity that defies those predictable expectations; indeed, both of the above-quoted works will subsequently partake in such behavior, as displayed here:

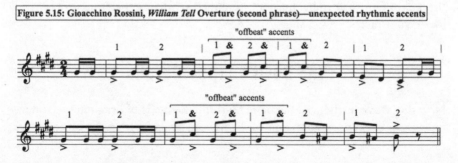

**Figure 5.15: Gioacchino Rossini, *William Tell* Overture (second phrase)—unexpected rhythmic accents**

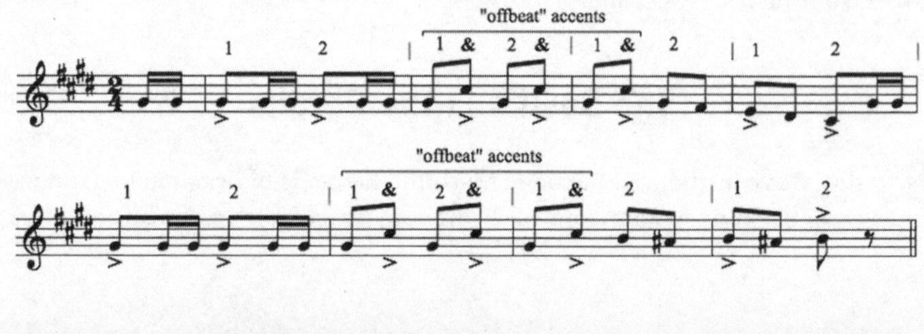

**Figure 5.16: Jerry Bock, "Sunrise, Sunset" from *Fiddler on the Roof* (chorus)—unexpected rhythmic accent**

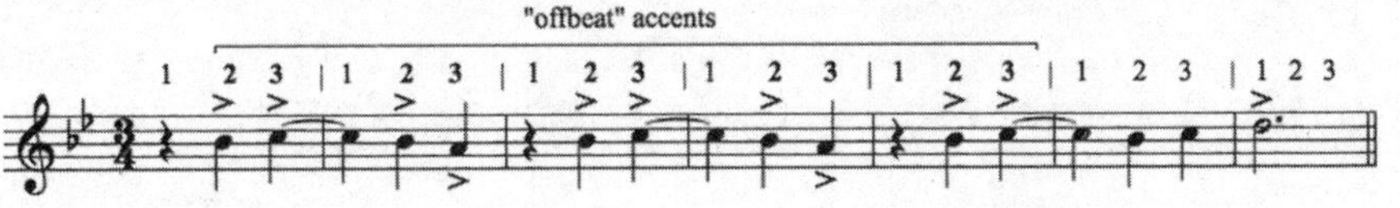


In these excerpts, the music introduces slight emphatic accents (>) that go against the expectations of the meter: on the "&s" of 1 and 2 in 2/4 meter (Rossini); on beats 2 and 3 in 3/4 (*Fiddler*)—with weaker emphasis on the meter's normally "strong" beats. This in turn creates a faintly jagged, interest-grabbing deviation in the flow of the music, like swerving periodically while bike riding down that same smooth path. The accents and less-predictable rhythms give a level of "life" to the music, and are often the parts that we remember or appreciate best. Indeed, it is the interaction between predictable and unpredictable rhythms that patently helps to define a song or work—and further, it is often the mark of a "successful" piece of music that it artfully manages to mix these two qualities in unexpected yet natural ways.

The accents placed on nonstrong beats—sometimes called **offbeats**—in the examples above are admittedly rather tame in their effect, certainly compared to the level of unpredictability that rhythm is capable of generating. The technical term for a prevailing conflict against metric expectation is **syncopation**. The term in fact has a few specific rhythmic definitions, beyond the general one just provided. Most notable of these specific definitions is "a regular shifting of each beat in a measured pattern by the *same amount* ahead of or behind its normal position in that pattern."[152] This technique, sometimes called "offbeat syncopation," has been used in the West going back to the Middle Ages and Renaissance (in a contrapuntal context), and actively embraced by classical composers ever since; here are two examples:

**Figure 5.17: Josquin des Prés, "Ave Maria . . . virgo serena" (late 15th c.)—"offbeat syncopation"**

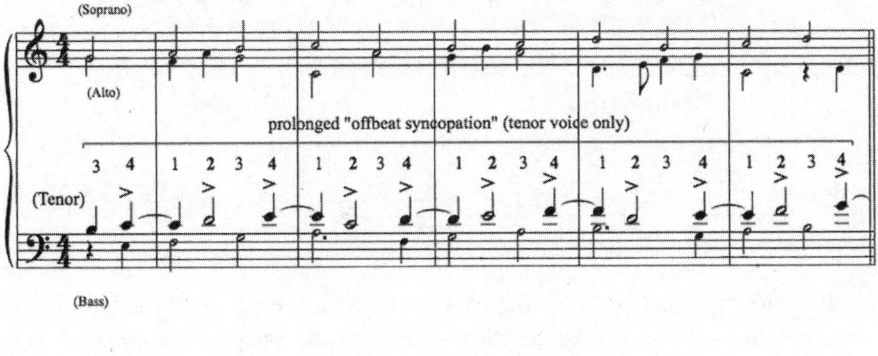

Figure 5.18: J. S. Bach, Invention no. 6 in E, BWV 777—"offbeat syncopation"

The use of steady offbeat syncopation has likewise become a common feature of jazz, pop/rock, bluegrass, and many other "pop" styles. Indeed, the consistent use of offbeat syncopation was *the* defining element in the proto-jazz style of ragtime when it first appeared in the 1880s, with the very name referring to the "ragged," or syncopated, rhythm that dominates most works in this style. Here are a few jazz and pop/rock examples:

Figure 5.19: Scott Joplin, "Maple Leaf Rag"—steady syncopation in ragtime (early jazz)

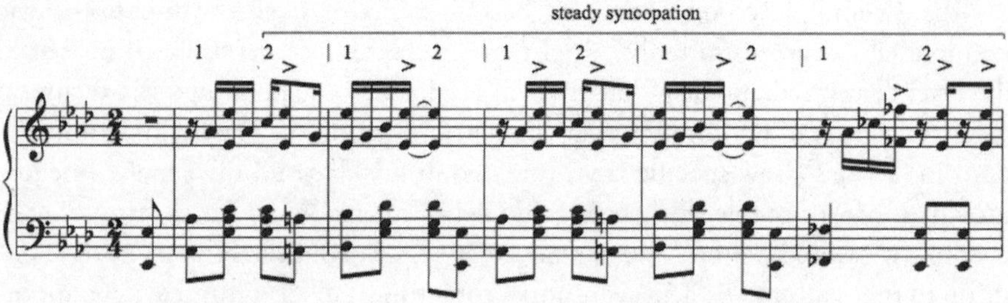

Figure 5.20: Glenn Miller Orchestra, "In the Mood"—steady syncopation in swing (jazz)

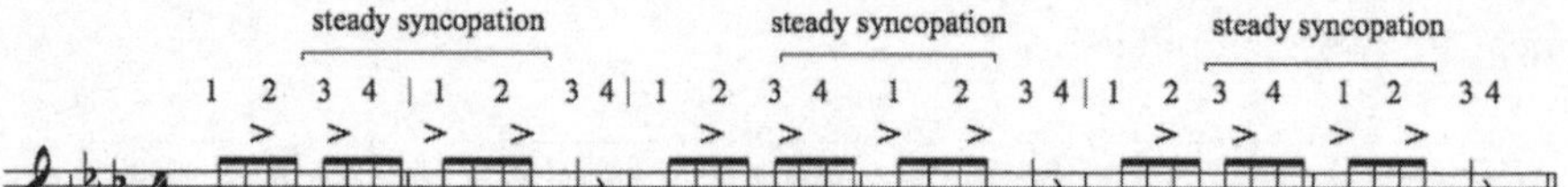


Figure 5.21: War, "Low Rider" (bass riff)—steady syncopation in rock

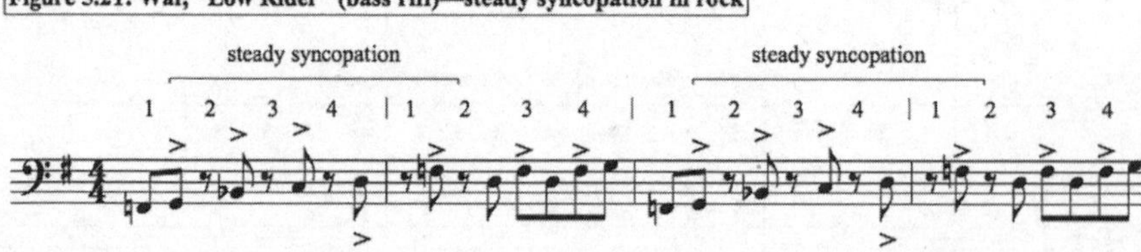


But more germane to our discussion of musical taste is that broader sense of syncopation—as a prevailing conflict against metric expectations, or more generally as the marked use of rhythmic accents placed "against" regular or strong beats. This then allows for the myriad ways in which "on-the-beat" activity can be replaced by accents "off the beat," whether in ways simple or complex, consistent or seemingly random, danceable or utterly confounding. And if one were to analyze the rhythmic identity of all the songs and works written over the past century, those lacking any kind of syncopation would be in the vast minority. Indeed, as a society, we are all but addicted to syncopated music.

Syncopation gets us moving in funk and hip hop, brings us to the dance floor in disco and electronica, and locks in our mental attention in jazz and bluegrass—among much else. We may all like different music, but much of what brings us closer or drives us further apart in our taste stems from the way in which syncopation is employed in the music. Collectively, however, we seem to be saying that defying strong beat expectations, from time to time at least, is a good thing.

Here is a sample of "typical" syncopation used in various "popular" styles:

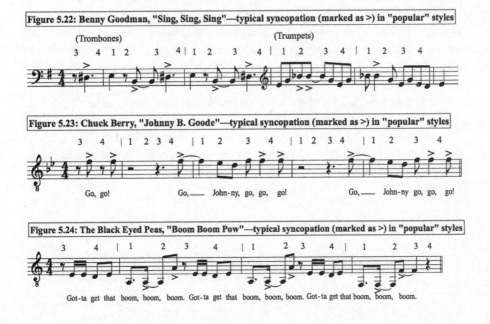

**Figure 5.22: Benny Goodman, "Sing, Sing, Sing"—typical syncopation (marked as >) in "popular" styles**

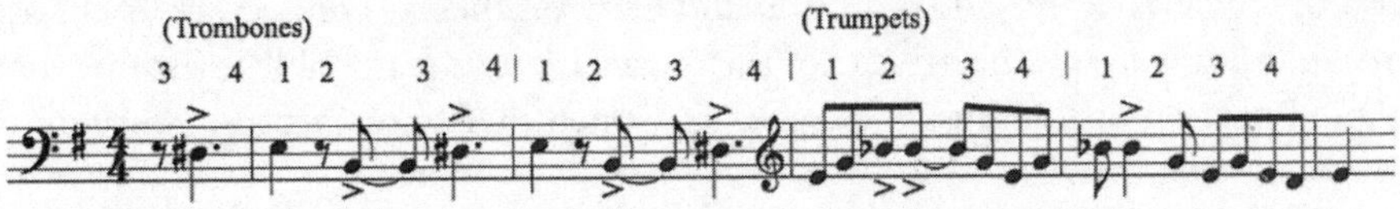


**Figure 5.23: Chuck Berry, "Johnny B. Goode"—typical syncopation (marked as >) in "popular" styles**

**Figure 5.24: The Black Eyed Peas, "Boom Boom Pow"—typical syncopation (marked as >) in "popular" styles**

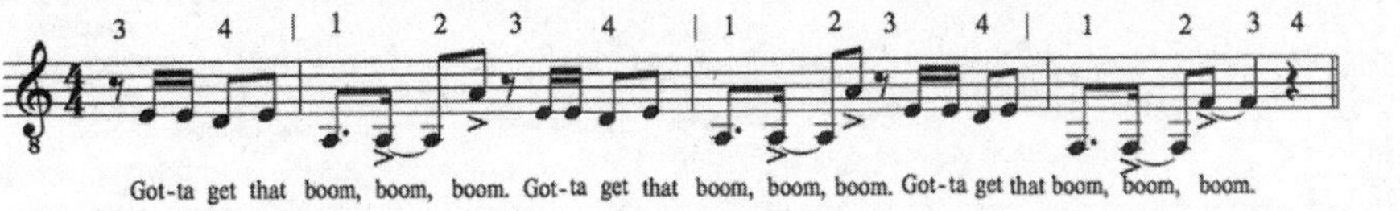


In many ways, the notated versions used above do a great disservice to the actual use of syncopation and rhythmic vitality in these songs, such as occurs in their actual performance. This is especially true given the flexible and multilayered rhythmic interplay of the instruments involved. Indeed, the syncopation produced in the drums and percussion in all of these songs (as recorded by the artists listed) is integral to our listening experience of them, and highly correlated to why you do or don't like them.

In this context, we'll highlight another key term of our rhythmic lexicon: "**groove**." The word is widely used and, like many complex human experiences, is easier to talk around than to cleanly define. Most attempts are rather tepid or apologetic, such as that offered "cautiously" by ethnomusicologist Steven Feld:

> An unspecifiable but ordered sense of something that is sustained in a distinctive, regular and attractive way, working to draw the listener in.[153]

What is present, whatever the definition, is the existence in the music of a steady and relatively consistent rhythmic identity that we can lock into, tapping into our inherent capacity for entrainment—and that likely contains at least some degree of syncopation and natural flexibility. Groove is that rhythmic quality that captures us, like being propelled through the groove of a smooth, steady canal. When we are truly *feeling* it, there is something intoxicating about the rhythm, something that, as Dan Levitin notes, "invites us into a sonic world that we don't want to leave."[154] It's not just the beats that we feel, moreover, but also the full "wave" that rides around and between them—connecting us almost metaphysically to the "heartbeat" of the music. It's thus reasonable to assume that a good portion of the music you like has earned that status because, for you, it grooves in just the right way.

This is not to say, however, that groove is the sole provenance of popular music written over the past century. Indeed, many of the "masterpieces" of the classical repertoire have earned that moniker by virtue of the way their creators succeeded in establishing an intoxicating "groove" at some point or another in the work—or at least as deemed so by their fans. To wit, two of my personal favorites:

**Figure 5.25: J. S. Bach, *Brandenburg* Concerto no. 3, 3. Allegro (mm. 15–16)—"groove" in classical**

**Figure 5.26: Franz Schubert, Symphony no. 9, 4. Allegro vivace (mm. 158–73)—"groove" in classical music**

## It Don't Mean a Thing . . . Straight, Swing, and Shuffle

Beyond the interplay between metric expectation and defiance—between "on-" and "off-the-beat" activity—there is another basic rhythmic dimension that affects a good majority of the music you listen to. At Savage Beast/Pandora we called it "rhythmic feel," and there are three main varieties: **straight**, **swing**, and **shuffle**. From a technical standpoint, the distinction normally concerns the disposition of eighth notes within a 4/4 or 3/4 meter.

The straight version, as you can guess, is the division of a quarter note into two equal eighth notes. This is the default disposition or "feel" for music in the Western classical tradition. It is, moreover, the "feel" in a majority of pop, rock, R&B, country, folk, Broadway, and related styles produced since the mid-1960s or so. Mozart's *Eine kleine Nachtmusik*, Diana Ross and the Supremes' "Stop! In the Name of Love," *The Lion King*'s "Can You Feel the Love Tonight," and Queens of the Stone Age's "Go with the Flow," to name a few random examples, all employ the "straight" feel.

The second "feel," swing, by contrast, is a rather different animal: although it is very familiar to modern ears, and easy to understand aurally, it is not so easy to get one's mind around conceptually. Even the actual rhythmic disposition is hard to quantify. Two "swung eighths" still combine in length to equal one quarter note, and yet are not performed with equal duration, as are "straight eighths"; instead, the first eighth is a bit elongated, "stealing" some time from the second. Underscoring the elusive disposition of the rhythm is the fact that when notated, the eighths are written as if they were straight—with an expectation that the performer will not play them as such, but instead simply know to "swing" them. Sometimes a directive is given in the written music, such as 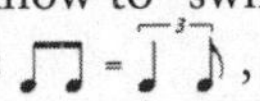, but this is just an approximation. So elusive, in fact, is swing rhythm to grasp intellectually, that most attempts to formally define it spend much of their entries emphasizing its intangible quality.[155]

And yet, despite this conceptual elusiveness, musicians and audiences totally and intuitively "get it"—particularly those acquainted with the jazz species, for which it is rather the default disposition. Every time you sway or groove to songs like Louis Armstrong's "St. James Infirmary," Glenn Miller's "In the Mood," Frank Sinatra's "I've Got You under My Skin," or Miles Davis' "So What," to again cite random examples, you are experiencing the swing feel—whether you know it or not.

As noted, swing rhythm is a staple of jazz, as it is also the name of an actual subgenre of the species—the "swing era"—during the 1930s and '40s. But again, "swing" is near synonymous with the whole of the jazz species, from New Orleans/Dixieland in the 1920s through today—though there are exceptions, notably Latin jazz and smooth jazz, where the eighths are generally straight.

This inevitably raises a question as to the origins and evolution of swing rhythm, which is likewise complex—and warrants a slight historical digression. I provide this in part because of its general interest, especially to jazz fans, but also because I have been struck by a seeming lack of any reasonable account in the literature.

Without a doubt, a vital source of development of the swing feel is the rhythmic traditions of West Africa, carried to the United States by those who would become slaves; in particular, the often complex, triple-based rhythms of West Africa were brought over and variably incorporated into the duple meter songs of the nineteenth-century American South, giving rise to changes in performance style.

Of course, the African influence on American music extends well beyond the disposition of eighth notes to broader elements of performance style, spirit, and energy, including the improvisatory approach that came to define jazz. But the move from straight to swung eighths had other sources as well, including the reels and jigs brought to America by Scottish and Irish immigrants, generally written in the compound duple 6/8 meter. In particular, popular (simple duple) American tunes played on the fiddle and the banjo, such as "Turkey and the Straw" (Figure 5.27), were often subjected to a triple-like feel:[156]

**Figure 5.27: Traditional, "Turkey in the Straw"—proto-swing rhythm**

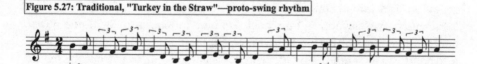

Undoubtedly, both traditions played a role in the rise of swing, and of jazz in general—as did other styles such as the African-influenced blues, spiritual, and field holler.[157] The so-called "banjo style" in particular has been associated with the roots of ragtime and its "ragged" beat. But in such discussions the expression "swing rhythm" is often confounded with syncopation. In fact, ragtime features the latter but not the former—at least based on piano rolls of Scott Joplin and other progenitors of the style. That is, ragtime did not swing.

By contrast, the earliest jazz recordings—such as those by the Original Dixieland Jazz Band (1917)—do include swung eighths, and from that time forward, swing became the default feel for jazz, as indeed for much American music over the next forty years. Almost all styles of popular music, whether created for the urban dancehall, the country barn dance, or the Broadway stage, were largely under the influence of the swing feel. Of course, the straight-eighth feel did not completely disappear from the popular hit parade—most notably with torch ballads and dramatic Broadway songs, like those of Rodgers and Hammerstein; but if you were to randomly select ten American hit songs written between 1920 and 1960, chances are good that eight or nine of them would be in the swing feel.

It was thus no surprise that when a new, youth-centric musical craze began in the mid-1950s—eventually called rock and roll—it too adopted the swung-eighth approach as its default. This is particularly so since the origins of rock and roll are directly traced to the rhythm and blues and "jump blues" performers of the 1940s and early '50s, such as Louis Jordan and Big Joe Turner—who themselves cut their teeth during the swing era. As such, the earliest rock and roll hits, such as "Shake, Rattle and Roll," "Rock Around the Clock," and "Hound Dog," featured a swing feel.

At the same time, a straight-eighth feel made an occasional appearance in the first generation of rock and roll. In both Little Richard's "Lucille" and Jerry Lee Lewis' "Great Balls of Fire," for example, the repeated straight-eighth note chords in the piano orient the entire song to that feel. Other straight-eighth examples include Buddy Holly's "Peggy Sue" and "Maybe Baby" and the Everly Brothers' "All I Have to Do Is Dream." These same artists, however, likewise produced hit songs in the swing feel—e.g., Little Richard's "Tutti Frutti," Jerry Lee Lewis' "Whole Lotta Shakin' Goin' On," Buddy Holly's "That'll Be the Day," and the Everly Brothers' "Wake Up Little Susie"—showing that by 1960 both options were equally viable for "pop" (as opposed to jazz) songs.

This flexible approach to rhythmic feel continued in the early years of the British Invasion. For example, the Beatles' early output includes a number of swing-feel songs, such as their cover of Little Richard's "Long Tall Sally" and their originals "Love Me Do," "All My Loving," and "Can't Buy Me Love." Yet they likewise produced straight-eighth feel songs such as "Please Please Me," "I Want to Hold Your Hand," and "I Saw Her Standing There"—as well as songs that fit somewhere in between, like "She Loves You."

While not an absolute rule, however, by 1964 and especially 1965, the swing-based rock and roll song became rarer and more specialized, such that by the mid-1960s the "default" feel in pop and rock had reverted back to straight eighths, and has remained so ever since. One stylistic exception to this was "classic country"—artists like Patsy Cline, George Jones, Hank Williams, and Dolly Parton—where the swung-eighth approach was maintained as the traditional rhythmic feel through the end of the 1970s or so; indeed, it was the adoption of the straight-eighth feel that was a prominent feature of the "modern country" movement in the 1980s and '90s, with artists like Vince Gill, Garth Brooks, and Tim McGraw.

The "history of swing" is certainly much richer than the pithy account just given. But it is fascinating to contemplate the firm grip that the swung-eighth feel has had on popular music over the past century or so. Indeed, it is hard to imagine how poor the American musical catalogue would be without it.

Finally, there is a third rhythmic feel: "shuffle." The term too has a variety of meanings, and admittedly a bit of ambiguity. Technically, I here define it as a strict and rhvthmically precise division of the quarter note into a dotted-eighth and sixteenth ♪. ♬. The most direct genre associations to the shuffle feel are boogie-woogie, honky-tonk, rockabilly, and "shuffle blues." In all of these the left hand of the piano, a rhythm guitar, and/or a bass line produce a bouncy dotted rhythm that propels the song forward (Figure 5.28).

**Figure 5.28: Shuffle rhythm—boogie-woogie piano left hand**

This approach—heard, for example, in Meade Lux Lewis' "Honky Tonk Train Blues," the Beatles' "Revolution 1," Steely Dan's "Reelin' in the Years," Boz Scaggs' "Lido Shuffle" (of course), and Flo Rida's "Right Round"—can indeed be finely articulated. But in many cases, it can be hard to distinguish a shuffle from a swing feel; indeed in musical discussions the two terms are often used interchangeably. As described in the Music Genome Project Manual, I acknowledge this point:

> It may be noted that between the two, shuffle is the more "difficult" to produce in the sense that it requires a consistency in the "dotted" or "bent" 8ths, in contrast to the more "relaxed" swing feel. . . . All this being said, it is also true that in some cases it may be difficult to make a determination between swing and shuffle. . . .

While all this may border on the technically arcane, I would argue that the rhythmic feel of a song can have a very significant impact on your listening experience, and perhaps on broader aspects of your musical taste—whether or not you recognize it. It is thus perhaps worth taking a few moments during your next music-listening session to see if you can determine which feel—straight, swing, or shuffle—each song utilizes, and how those rhythms affect you.

## The Tricky Side of Rhythm

Distinguishing swing from shuffle might be a bit challenging, but the parameter of rhythm—like harmony—is capable of engendering even more complex qualities that can greatly impact whether or not you like a piece of music. Given the vitality of rhythm in our everyday experience and in the musical language of so many cultures, it is not surprising that we humans have devised innumerable ways to create intricate meters, rhythms, and beats.

Indeed, the music of many cultures—especially in Africa, the Middle East, India, Indonesia, and Eastern Europe—is largely defined by its frequent use of complex rhythm. To those of us raised on a steady diet of Western commercial music, such complexities may be intriguing, but they also may be disorienting or unpleasant. Increasing our awareness and understanding of these complexities, in turn, can alter our perception and perhaps our appreciation of more "adventurous" approaches. Moreover, a complex approach to rhythm is by no means limited to musical approaches outside the West—with various "tricky" techniques going back to the Middle Ages, and especially gaining favor among some musicians over the past century or so.

As a warning, this section becomes gradually denser and more esoteric as it goes—so grab your popcorn and your concentration.

One common approach to rhythmic complexity is via an **irregular** (or "**odd**") **meter**—where the grouping of beats is something other than the "normal" two, three, or four. A classic example is Paul Desmond's "Take Five," from the 1959 Dave Brubeck Quartet album, *Time Out*. The song is written in 5/4, where each measure contains five beats, generally organized as 3+2 (Figure 5.29):

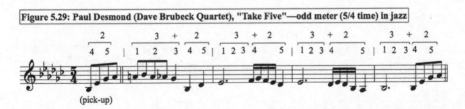

**Figure 5.29: Paul Desmond (Dave Brubeck Quartet), "Take Five"—odd meter (5/4 time) in jazz**

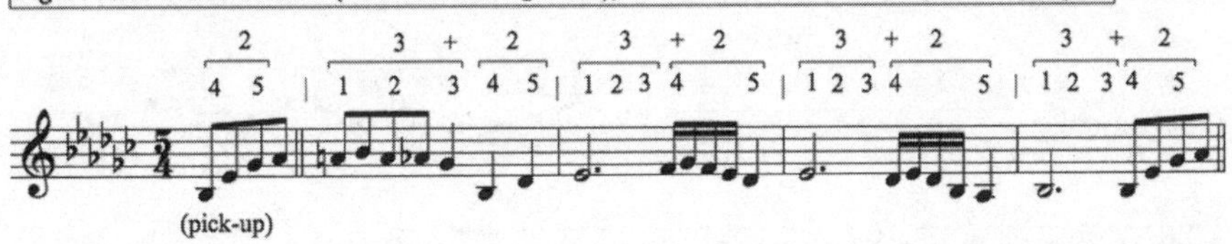


Despite its odd metric grouping, the song is able to create a steady and intoxicating groove, not least through the consistency and flow of the accompanying piano part.

The opening track from the same album, Brubeck's "Blue Rondo à la Turk," begins and ends with a section in 9/8 meter—generally organized as 2+2+2+3

| 2+2+2+3 | 2+2+2+3 | 3+3+3, each measure adding up to nine eighth notes (Figure 5.30):

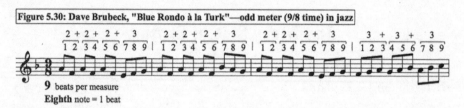

**Figure 5.30: Dave Brubeck, "Blue Rondo à la Turk"—odd meter (9/8 time) in jazz**

While the title might seem to be a play on Mozart's "Rondo alla turca," it actually stems from the complex metric pattern used in a song that Brubeck heard performed by street musicians during a concert tour to Turkey in 1958; when he asked them about the rhythm, they replied, "This rhythm is to us what the blues is to you"[158]—in turn inspiring the name "Blue Rondo," as well as perhaps the actual blues progression that makes up the extended, improvisatory middle section of the song.

Both "Take Five" and "Blue Rondo à la Turk" employ irregular meters, but do so in a way that easily elicits comfort even to those unaccustomed to rhythmic complexity. They accomplish this in large part by virtue of their use of repetition—that is, employing odd meters, but creating predictability via regularly repeating patterns of twos and threes. This is sometimes referred to as an "additive" approach to rhythm, where irregular beat groupings are joined successively to form larger patterns.[159]

Indeed, this is the case in most "world" cultures that commonly use a wide array of irregular meters—such as in Turkey, Bulgaria, and India: through routine exposure and consistent repetition of various patterns of twos, threes, and fours, even if complex, the meters eventually become familiar and comfortable. Here are two examples:

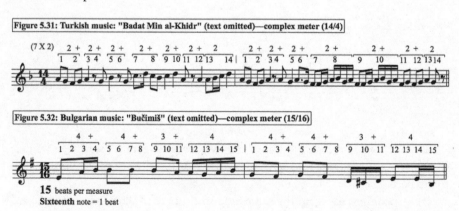

**Figure 5.31: Turkish music: "Badat Min al-Khidr" (text omitted)—complex meter (14/4)**

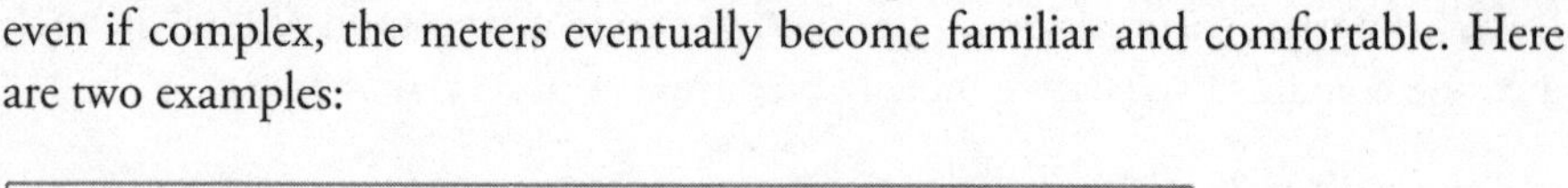


**Figure 5.32: Bulgarian music: "Bučimiš" (text omitted)—complex meter (15/16)**

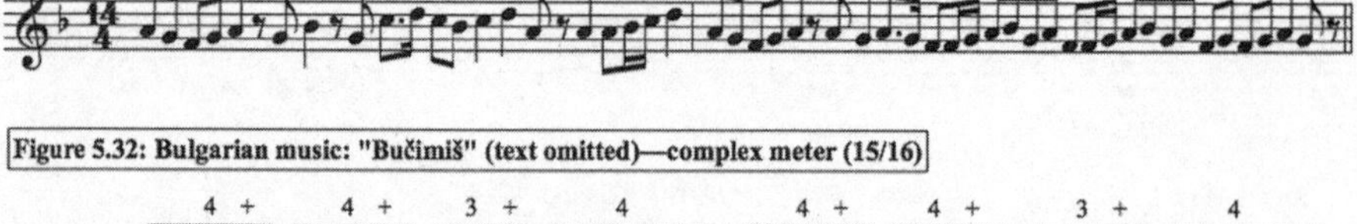

In practice, of course, elements of variety and flexibility are introduced into these rhythmic patterns. But as an accustomed audience has internalized their "normal" structure, such variety poses little challenge—much as a good dose of syncopation within 4/4 does little to unhinge our rhythmic center of gravity. On the contrary, it is the very variety inserted into an otherwise familiar rhythmic flow that *grabs* our attention, and perhaps enables us—as them—to dig into the groove a little deeper.

Jazz, by the way, isn't the only Western style capable of creating "groove" via an irregular meter; here are examples within the classical and rock arenas:

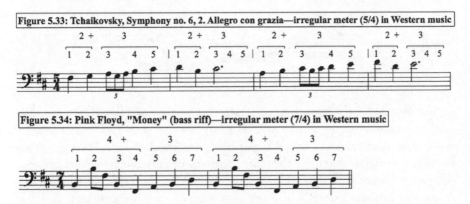

**Figure 5.33: Tchaikovsky, Symphony no. 6, 2. Allegro con grazia—irregular meter (5/4) in Western music**

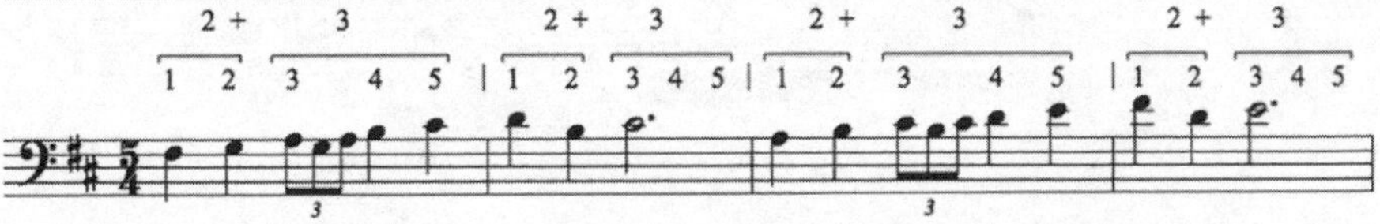


**Figure 5.34: Pink Floyd, "Money" (bass riff)—irregular meter (7/4) in Western music**

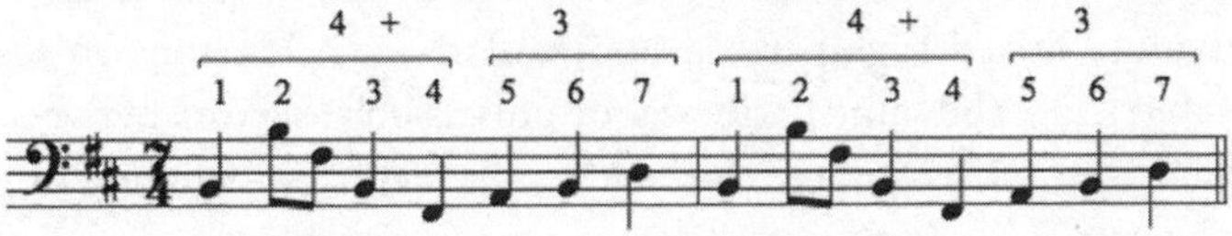


However, irregular meter can also be employed in ways that defy familiarity or that seem to intentionally thwart a rhythmic center of gravity. This is the case especially when irregular meters—such as 5/4, 7/4, 7/8, 11/8, etc.—are combined with a high level of syncopation and/or the use of **tuplets**. These latter include not only triplets (e.g., three eighth notes in the time of two), but any number of notes above or below the standard subdivisions of a beat—such as five or seven or eleven sixteenth notes in the time of one quarter note, etc. (Figure 5.35):

**Figure 5.35: Examples of various tuplets**

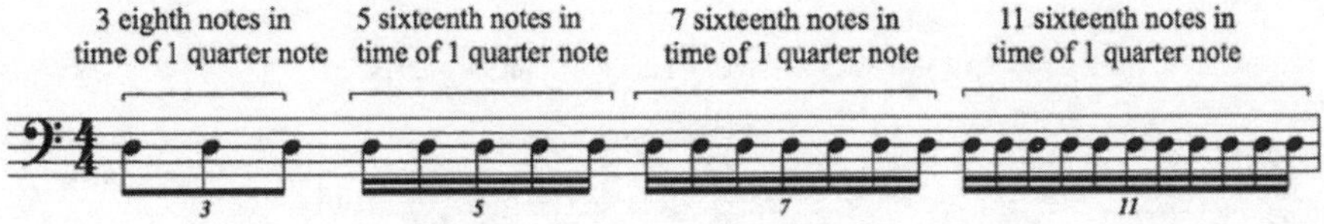


This uncentered approach to irregular meter is particularly common among Modern and Contemporary classical composers—as well as adventurous jazz and rock musicians. In such cases, the composers have elected to liberate themselves from the confines of a steady and predictable pulse, which indeed may be impossible to find. Here are two such examples:

Figure 5.36: Anton Webern, Variations for Piano, Op. 27 (mm. 19–21)—unpredictable/obscured pulse

Figure 5.37: Karlheinz Stockhausen, *Kontra-Punkte* (flute, mm. 23–24)—unpredictable/obscured pulse

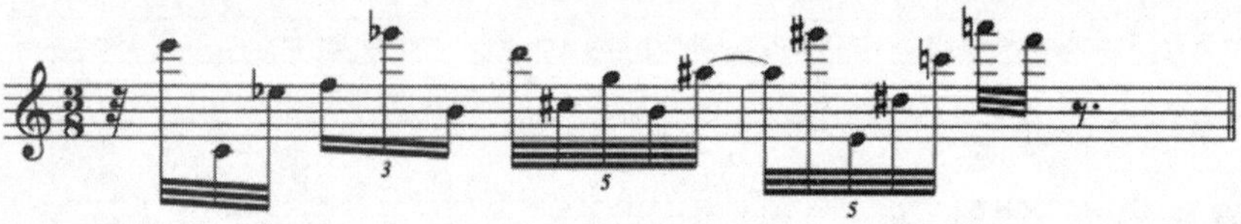

An approach related to irregular meters is known as **mixed meters**—that is, the combining of more than one meter within a song or a section of a larger work. The meters that are mixed together can be "regular"—when a song mixes two or more meters that share the same basic beat or pulse, such as a mix between 4/4 and 3/4 (both with the quarter note as the beat); or "irregular"—when a song mixes two or more meters where the beat differs between them, such as a mix between 4/4 (quarter note as the beat) with 3/8 (eighth note as the beat).

As crazy as all of this *can* get, in many cases the application of mixed meters is subtle and smooth—e.g., an occasional insertion of a 2/4 bar into an otherwise steady 4/4 meter song (creating a temporary count of six beats per "measure"). This does little to offset the basic rhythm or groove, and happens more often than you might guess. Yet even in these subtle cases, the metric shift does catch our attention to some degree, and is often that element of the song we most strongly remember or enjoy.

Here is a sample of a few cases using mixed meters, progressing from relatively simple and nonconfounding to complex and deliberately disorienting:

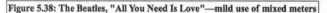

Figure 5.38: The Beatles, "All You Need Is Love"—mild use of mixed meters

Figure 5.39: Burt Bacharach, "Promises, Promises"—moderate use of mixed meters

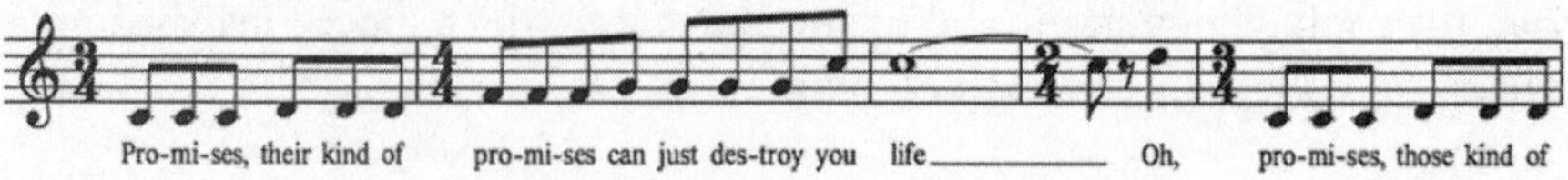

**Figure 5.40: György Ligeti, String Quartet no. 2, 4. Presto furioso—highly complex use of mixed meters**

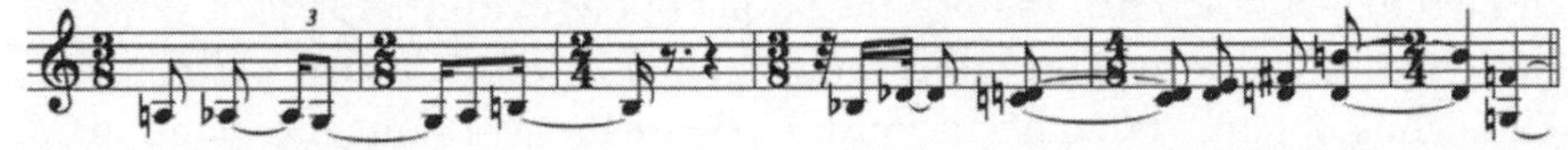

And if perchance you thought that this was the extent to which composers and musicians created rhythmic complexity in songs and works, you would be sadly mistaken—though by now you probably know better. Two more common techniques are:

**Hemiola**, literally, the ratio of 3:2—this refers especially to a common technique used in instrumental music of the Baroque era (early 18th c.) composed in 3/4 meter, especially at cadences. I admit that seems pretty rarified—and yet it is not only a staple of the Baroque, but also found in later classical, jazz, and rock styles, and so worth mentioning. It occurs when three successive groupings of two beats (1-2, 1-2, 1-2) occur across two measures of three beats each (1-2-3, 1-2-3); both sets equal six beats, yet the effect is as if the meter momentarily changed from 3/4 to 2/4—and sounds quite cool, if you ask me. Here is an example of hemiola, along with a hemiola-like usage in rock:

**Figure 5.41: G. F. Handel, Minuet in G minor—hemiola (3 against 2)**

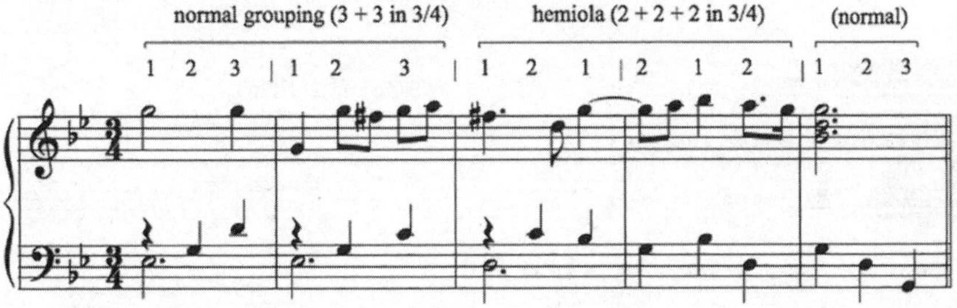


**Figure 5.42: Led Zeppelin, "Kashmir"—hemiola-like usage (3 against 4)**

**Polyrhythm** (sometimes called "**cross-rhythm**")—"is the superimposition of different rhythms or meters."[160] The appearance of two rhythms at once is found occasionally in musical works of various styles, both Western and non-Western. Hemiola, described above, is the most common example, but there are innumerable other examples: 4 against 3; 7 against 2; 4/4 against 3/4, etc. It's the musical equivalent of patting your head while rubbing your stomach, though it can get a lot more difficult than that. Justin London, a musicologist specializing in rhythm, has noted that in our perception of polyrhythm we actually don't hear both rhythms at once, "but rather an integrated rhythmic/metric pattern, either by singling out one strand of the musical texture for attention (and ignoring others) or by constructing a composite rhythm from the various strands."[161]

For some non-Western musical cultures, polyrhythm is actually the default approach to rhythm in general—notably in sub-Saharan Africa and Indonesia, especially gamelan music.[162]

Here are two examples from a Western and non-Western perspective:

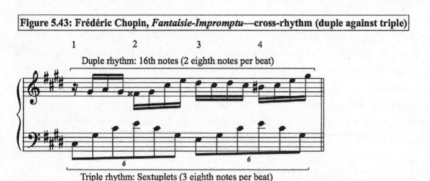

**Figure 5.43: Frédéric Chopin, *Fantaisie-Impromptu*—cross-rhythm (duple against triple)**

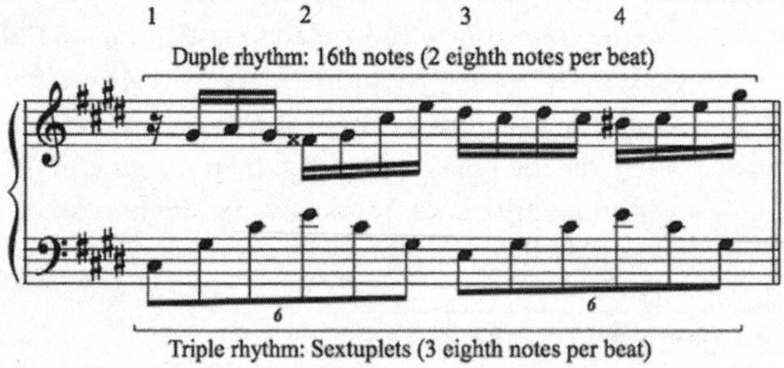


**Figure 5.44: African music: "Nyayito" dance (text omitted)—complex cross-rhythms**

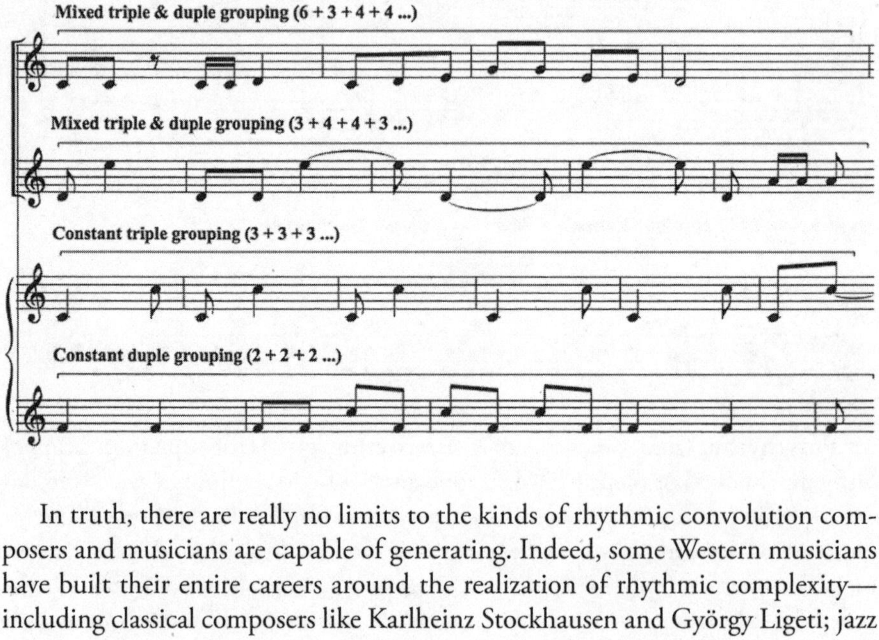


In truth, there are really no limits to the kinds of rhythmic convolution composers and musicians are capable of generating. Indeed, some Western musicians have built their entire careers around the realization of rhythmic complexity—including classical composers like Karlheinz Stockhausen and György Ligeti; jazz composers like Don Ellis and Stan Kenton; and rock musicians like Björk and Frank Zappa.

Here's an example of what this last-named iconoclast produced in the mid-1970s:

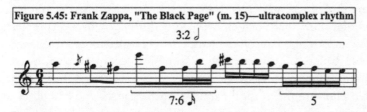

**Figure 5.45: Frank Zappa, "The Black Page" (m. 15)—ultracomplex rhythm**

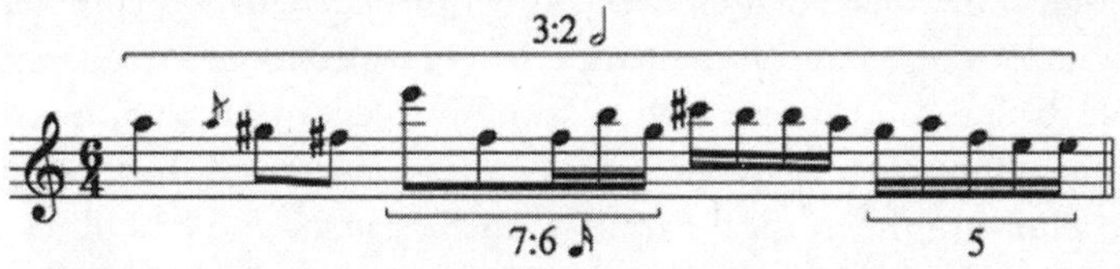


What is this—tuplets within tuplets (the 7:6 and 5 within the overall 3:2)? Where are beats 2, 3, or 4? Zappa's aim here is clearly not to make you want to dance or tap your fingers. Instead, it is to "tickle" your mind with a sophisticated and intellectual division of time. As philosopher Susanne Langer put it, rhythm is the "musical flow of sound through time," and Zappa is exercising his right to flow in a complex and unpredictable manner. You are very likely among the vast majority of listeners who would hear this rhythmic display and say, à la Homer Simpson, "I don't get it." But somewhere in the shadows are music fans who eat this stuff up for breakfast—and who are we to say that their taste in rhythms is any less valid than ours? Wait, maybe that's you who loves it!

On that note, here's what Zappa had to say about composing such a measure:

> Any piece of time can be subdivided any old way you like. And that's what happens when people talk, because people don't talk in 4/4 or 3/4 or 2/4—they talk *all over the place*. And if the rhythm of what you play follows along with the natural scan of human speech, it's going to have a different feel to it. In a way, it sounds weird; in another way, it sounds totally natural. It just depends on what you expect to hear from a piece of music.[163]

## Flexed, Borrowed, and Stolen Time

Zappa's comment linking musical rhythm to "what happens when people talk" also invokes that broader connection between music and speech—as we discussed in Interlude A. It is indeed true that unless presented as a kind of choral refrain—e.g., at a political rally or a football game—spoken language is generally atemporal (nonmetric), at least in any strict sense. It is thus somewhat remarkable that a strict, metric approach to rhythm is so common, indeed predominant, throughout the world, and not least in the West. That this is so speaks to the power of entrainment, the synchronization of organisms to an external rhythm, as a defining human and musical process. It also points to the inherent, even primal link between forms of refined speech—i.e., poetry—and music as a key source of metric rhythm.[164]

And yet, given our equally innate tendency to communicate in an atemporal manner, it is not surprising that much music making is presented without strict rhythm, to some degree or another. Indeed, even in "strictly" metric contexts, experimental studies show that rarely, if ever, do performers deliver a complete absence of durational variety—unless the tempo is set by electronic means (e.g., a drum machine). Reciprocally, listeners will naturally expect this type of metric variety, and will likely not even notice if slight, expression-derived fluctuations occur at expected points in the musical narrative, such as at the end of a phrase.

As Bruno Repp, a music-perception researcher, has suggested, "Listeners expect to hear music *expressively* timed . . . [that is], the almost continuous modulation of the local tempo . . . where the performer's (often subconscious) intention seems to be to 'act out' the music's hierarchical grouping structure and thereby to communicate it to listeners." Indeed, the absence of such natural fluctuation will have, as Repp puts it, "not only aesthetic but also perceptual consequences."[165] As such, that you like or don't like a given song or artist may stem in part from the degree to which you hear the music as "expressively timed," even if such perception is outside your awareness.

In the case of most "popular" genres—and especially dance-oriented ones like swing, disco, electronica, etc.—the expected "modulations of the local tempo" may indeed be slight, or even nonexistent if a drum machine is used. However, in other styles and genres, performers will adopt not so much a slight, unconscious metric fluctuation but rather one that is more pronounced and intentional. These genres include pop and jazz ballads, as well as a fair bit of classical music—especially during the Romantic era. The technical term for this pronounced temporal variation within an otherwise metric context is **rubato**—literally Italian for "stolen." The expression "tempo rubato" goes back to the early eighteenth century, and is generally applied in written music as a global directive to the performer (usually at the beginning of a section), without providing any actual notated rhythmic changes.[166]

The idea behind rubato is to follow the natural flow and demands of the music, with the performer "acting out" each *accelerando* (speeding up) and *ritardando* (slowing down) in accordance with the music's inherent melodic and harmonic structures. During the nineteenth century, composers found rubato an effective complement to their broader aesthetic drive for increasing expressive power, alongside an increasing chromatic approach to harmony, as we discussed in Chapter 4.

The "poster boy" of rubato is certainly Chopin, who used the term fourteen times in his piano works,[167] and whose music is generally performed with pronounced temporal fluctuation as a matter of course—and not just in works explicitly marked as rubato by the composer. How the approach taken comports with Chopin's own expectations, on the other hand, is a matter of considerable uncertainty, with Richard Hudson—an expert in rubato—noting that the results are often "utterly different from what he had in mind."[168]

A classic example is Chopin's famous Prelude in E Minor, Op. 28, no. 4. Due no doubt to its popularity, this work has been the subject of several perception and performance research studies, as well as a stimulating TED Talk given in 2008 by Benjamin Zander.[169] The figure below shows the opening four bars with arrows and lines illustrating a typical approach to rubato. As seen here, a common tendency is for the performer to stretch time at the beginning of each measure, followed by an acceleration to a midpoint in the measure, and then a ritardando toward the end—forming a kind of rhythmic counterpart to the tension-release dynamic at a harmonic cadence. It should be noted too that even more detailed tempo fluctuation measurements are possible via computer analysis—as has been carried out on performances by top-tier musicians like pianist Martha Argerich.[170]

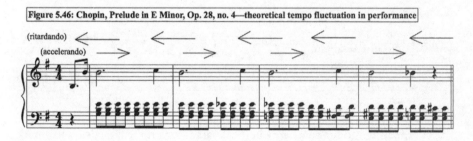

**Figure 5.46: Chopin, Prelude in E Minor, Op. 28, no. 4—theoretical tempo fluctuation in performance**

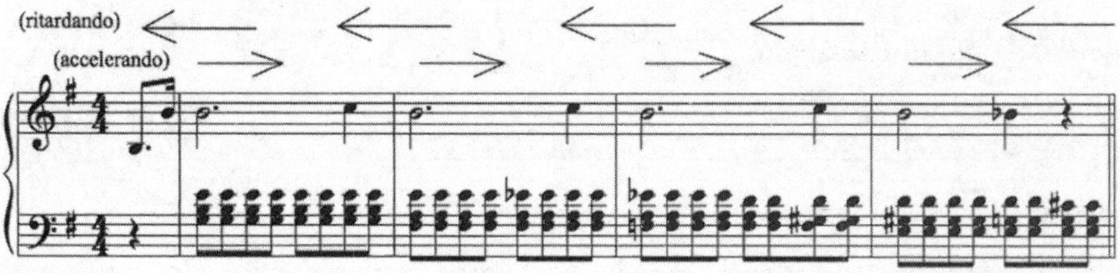


Of course, Chopin is not alone as a fertile inspirer of rubato performance within the classical repertoire. The music of J. S. Bach, his eldest son C. P. E. Bach, Mozart, Beethoven, Schumann, Liszt, and most mid- to late nineteenth-century composers are also common recipients, especially in their slower, more expressive works. Such is likewise the case with the music of twentieth-century composers such as Debussy, Stravinsky, and Bartók, who not infrequently marked sections of their music as rubato, as well as American composers like Aaron Copland and Virgil Thomson, among many others.

Rubato tempo, by definition, cannot be explicitly specified in notation. There is always a degree of subjective decision-making on the part of the performers—with some composers inspiring what music-perception specialist David Epstein calls a higher "ambiguity quotient" than others.[171] Mozart, for example, falls into this category. It is this variety, moreover, that helps account for the great number of recordings by different artists of the same classical works: every performer can hear a distinct way in which to realize rubato. And whether you prefer Martha Argerich or Claudio Arrau's performance of Chopin's Preludes, Op. 28, for example, will undoubtedly depend in part on how you respond to their rubato decisions.

And yet this doesn't mean it's "anything goes" when it comes to performing a passage in a rubato manner. In fact, studies have shown that there is a certain optimal range of *accelerandos* and *ritardandos* within a particular passage that is "effective" to a listener, beyond which emotional potency morphs into an experience that is somehow "less musical."[172] Perhaps the word "sappy" or "maudlin" is how you'd describe it.

Beyond rubato, there are other, more explicit ways a composer (or an editor) can indicate tempo fluctuations within the midst of a musical work or section. Most commonly, one of many speed-related expressions is applied, notably the Italian terms *ritardando* (*rit.*), *accelerando* (*accel.*), *più mosso* (faster), *meno mosso* (slower), *rallentando* (*rall.*, slowing down or "relaxing"), *stringendo* (*string.*, speeding up or "tightening"), *doppio movimento* (twice as fast), *a tempo* (back to original tempo), etc.

Here's an example from a sonata by Brahms:

**Figure 5.47: Johannes Brahms, Piano Sonata no. 1, 2. Andante (mm. 67–69)—explicit tempo fluctuation**

As noted, tempo fluctuation, whether marked or implied, is also a hallmark of nonclassical genres. The phrasing of jazz vocalists and instrumentalists, as well as rock and other pop styles, is often rubato by default. This generally entails the so-called "earlier" type of rubato, where the accompaniment stays in tempo while the melody shifts timing freely.[173] Frank Sinatra is commonly cited as a model of this "jazz phrasing" approach—called the "master of rubato" by celebrated vocal teacher Gary Catona[174]—but he is by no means alone, with Ella Fitzgerald, Mel Tormé, Billie Holiday, and Kurt Elling being a few of the many great singers who know how to "bend" rhythm in just the right way.

Similarly, a more general rubato approach—the so-called "later" type, where the overall tempo fluctuates—can be heard frequently in jazz, pop, and Broadway ballads, as well as in the verses of "standards," whether sung or performed instrumentally.

So, what is the effect of rubato performance on the listening experience, and to what degree does it impact musical taste? Like so many aspects of musical identity, the answer is not "one size fits all." The experience can be a kind of "floating" of musical time, disrupting the tempo without destroying it, and moving the listener more emphatically between states of "tension" and "release." Various theories have been posited as to how this takes place, aligning rubato with either an underlying "ground beat" or to the laws of physical motion—the so-called "kinematic" approach, akin to a person starting and stopping during a run.[175] Ultimately, however, the details and effects of rubato seem to be too individually based to draw any universal conclusions; these include the nuances of the melodic-harmonic structure, the performer's intuition, and the listener's personal response, among others. To be sure, the impact and variability of rubato is a testament to the overall power that rhythm has in defining the listening experience, and our musical taste.

## Free Rhythm

Rubato may provide a floating, quasi-free temporal experience, and yet it is still grounded on the existence of a steady meter and tempo—even if heavily subjugated. But as noted above, our innately atemporal manner of speaking is also reflected in music that is similarly atemporal—that is, without any sense of steady pulse or fixed tempo whatsoever. This is sometimes called "**free rhythm**"—a bit of an oxymoron, perhaps, but one that has gained currency in scholarly literature, even if a uniform definition is hard to find.[176]

A key question is whether or not a rhythm can be deemed "free," and yet can still have some kind of periodic pulse. According to ethnomusicologist Martin Clayton, who has studied this question in detail, the answer is yes—provided that the pulse is perceived without "periodic organization."[177] This is because most music we experience as "free" or "nonmetric" is still perceived cognitively as having some kind of discernible pulse, at least from time to time; what distinguishes it from "nonfree" rhythm, then, is the absence of consistency, or any kind of underlying meter.

In the West, free rhythm is fairly limited in its usage. The most demonstrable case is the present-day approach to singing Gregorian chant—the vast and largely anonymous repertory of single-lined "plainchant" (or plainsong) collated between roughly the eighth and eleventh centuries to accompany the liturgy of the Catholic Church.[178] That Gregorian chant may have originally been sung with some degree of metric rhythm—e.g., with each note receiving the same length or a proportional relation (e.g., 1:2, 1:3, etc.) based on the word accents—is actually a topic of some scholarly dissent, with various theories in play.[179] The most common performance approach today, however, is that advocated by the scholarly Benedictine monks of Solesmes in northern France, whose *Liber Usualis*, or *Book of Common Practice*, is the most practical and widespread compendium of the Gregorian repertory. In its introduction, the editors refer to the rhythm of plainsong as:

> . . . a movement of the voice wherein it rises and falls in orderly fashion. It is

a free interlacing of binary and ternary groups of notes so well balanced as to convey to, and produce in the mind a sense of order in the midst of variety. We constantly meet with this order in variety in all forms of art, indeed in nature itself. It is the mind's delight. Rhythm of every kind moves stepwise, but not necessarily with fixed mechanical regularity. All that is essential to it is proportion, balanced movement and repose, rise and fall, the due correlation and interdependence of parts producing a harmonious whole. Such is free rhythm, the rhythm of Plainsong.[180]

In many ways it is this lack of "fixed mechanical regularity" that gives Gregorian chant its meditative, spiritual quality—toward which a listener is apt to gravitate or not—above and beyond its religious significance. Again, this description does not suggest a complete lack of perceptible pulse at any point in a chant performance, but rather where such a pulse would appear within a broader "midst of variety."

In a unique bit of marketing genius, a recording simply called *Chant*—recorded in 1973 by the Benedictine monks of Santo Domingo de Silos in Spain, but released on Angel Records in 1994—became a commercial sensation, reaching the No. 3 position on *Billboard*, selling six million copies worldwide. Clearly the free rhythmic nature of the Gregorian repertory (sung in the Solesmes tradition) had the potential to resonate with modern audiences in 1994, as it very well may still today.[181] Here's a typical example:

**Figure 5.48: Gregorian chant, "Puer natus est nobis" (Christmas chant)—free rhythm**

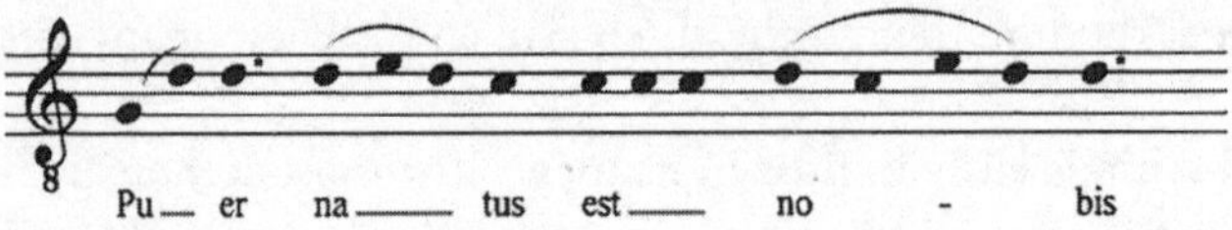


Free rhythm continued to have prevalence in the West well into the thirteenth century, at which point a fully "mensural" (measured or pulsed) approach began to take over—largely through the advent of polyphony (multiple parts at once). The explanation is obvious: with monophony (one single melody), it is easy to proceed without a strict pulse, but once you have two or more melodies moving simultaneously, rhythmic precision—a strict beat—becomes increasingly necessary.[182] And indeed, from the fourteenth through the nineteenth centuries, nearly *all* of Western music was conceived in metric orientation—even if subject to rubato treatment in performance.

There is, however, one important exception to the metric orientation in these same centuries: the **cadenza**—a generally improvised or improv-like written passage inserted usually near the end of a movement within a concerto (a work for soloist and ensemble), during which the soloist can display his or her virtuosity.

Cadenza passages are generally performed without strict meter, even if written out as individual measures.

Here's an example of a written-out cadenza from a work by Mozart:

**Figure 5.49: W. A. Mozart, Six Variations on "Salve tu, Domine," K. 398., 1. Allegro—solo cadenza realization (free rhythm)**

Cadenzas—and a few distinct musical forms such as the opera recitative and some Baroque "improvisational" keyboard forms (Fantasia, etc.)—aside, however, the vast majority of Western music from the fourteenth to the early twentieth centuries was conceived fundamentally as metric or "in tempo," even if the metric definition might frequently change within a given song or work. Yet, as with so many aspects of the musical status quo, the mid-twentieth century saw a rhythmic revolution, as some composers began experimenting with time—not just through the metric complexities discussed above, but also by reintroducing free or **nonmetric rhythm**. Like those "tricky" rhythmic techniques, these nonmetric experiments usually reflect an intellectual mind-set, and support a musical discourse that is inaccessible to many listeners. This is especially true of avant-garde classical composers like Witold Lutoslawski and John Cage—and the heady techniques they devised, such as aleatoric or "chance" music, graphic notation, etc.

But modern nonmetric music is not always conceived in such overtly intellectual terms. On the contrary, within several contemporary Western genres—notably new age and the electronica subgenre of ambient music—a nonmetric approach is more associated with emotional, sensual, meditative, and trancelike states where the intellect is deliberately placed at bay. In the new age realm, composers like Yanni, Enya, Mike Oldfield, and Steven Halpern utilize free-floating nonmetric music—usually with limited diatonic harmonies and sustained melodies—to evoke nonmusical themes of inner harmony, the cosmos, nature, and dreams. This is the genre of music you likely heard the last time you got a massage. Ambient music is similarly meditative or "chill"-inducing, although aimed at a decidedly edgier cultural demographic, as we'll explore in greater detail in Chapter 13.

If free rhythm occupies a somewhat marginal place in the Western canon, however, it is rather commonplace in many non-Western musical cultures. In his study on the subject, Martin Clayton identified around seventy genres distributed over all continents (especially Asia) that regularly employ free rhythm. These genres transcend all musical contexts—religious ritual (within the Christian, Jewish, Islamic, Hindu, Buddhist, and Shinto, etc., traditions); art music (e.g., Indian, Chinese, Japanese, and especially across the Arab and Arab-influenced world, from North Africa to the Middle East to Turkey and Central Asia, etc.); and folk music (e.g., in Romania, Mongolia, Java, etc.).[183] Not surprisingly, the diversity of free rhythmic approaches extends beyond region and context to actual style and form, including in the degree to which any kind of occasional pulse is identifiable in the music.

Most of this music is vocal, but there are also numerous examples of instrumental nonmetered music, most famously perhaps the quasi-improvised alap (opening section) within the North Indian classical raga tradition—as seen here:

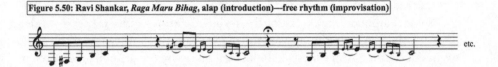

**Figure 5.50: Ravi Shankar, *Raga Maru Bihag*, alap (introduction)—free rhythm (improvisation)**

## Rhythm: Final Thoughts

If nothing else, the above discussion has suggested the near boundless ways in which rhythm manifests itself in musical works, as well as the sweeping impact it has on our experience of any piece of music. Rhythm is a bit like time itself, stamping every object by its presence, even if we hardly notice it passing: rhythm impacts the notes of a melody, the pacing of chords, the sway of sound and motion, the structure of musical form, etc. Musicians speak of melodic rhythm, harmonic rhythm, and just plain rhythm, but also of the philosophical and psychological implications of rhythm as it operates simultaneously on multiple levels.

Indeed, rhythm may be deemed the overriding parameter wherein the listener gains an intuitive understanding of the music as a whole. Rhythm's multidimensional, hierarchical, and interactive properties help inform the entire musical discourse—from the level of the phrase, to the theme, to the section, to the song or work. Rhythm is the context in which musical ideas are articulated. Thus, your experience of—and taste in—music cannot be separate from its rhythm.[184] So pay attention!

To test your awareness of rhythm in the music you hear, here are a few suggested exercises:

1. Next time you hear a rhythmic pop or rock song: Think about where you would naturally clap your hands to the beat; now try clapping at

a different metric level. What does that do to your experience of the song? How many different levels can you easily clap to?

2. Next time you hear a fast, rhythmic classical piece: Can you tell whether it is duple (two or four beats per measure) or triple (three or six beats per measure)? Now compare it to a slower, less rhythmic classical piece: What differences can you detect in how the strong beats (quarter notes) are subdivided (into eighth and sixteenth notes)?
3. Next time you hear a rhythmic jazz, R&B, or hip hop song: Can you clearly identify elements of syncopation? Is it being used in a consistent or ever-changing manner—or both? In what way does the syncopation impact the song's groove? Is the "feel" in the song straight, swing, or shuffle?
4. Next time you hear a rhythmically complex jazz, rock, or classical work: Can you consistently count three or four beats per measure, or is an "odd" beat count at play? Regardless, how does the rhythmic complexity impact your experience? Do you like the piece? How does rhythm play a part in your answer?
5. Next time you hear either an expressive classical or a new age piece: Can you detect the existence of a rubato or free rhythmic orientation? How does that impact your experience of the music, and your own mood? Can you still clearly count the beats as they pass or not?

We'll soon continue our musical primer with the overarching parameter of form, in Chapter 5. But first let's shift our mental focus with the next extramusical chapter, one that in fact follows upon lessons learned in the preceding musical discussion. Specifically, Interlude B explores the origins of our collective musical taste through the prism of mathematics and physics—with its direct application to the principles underlying harmony, intervals, and chords.

# Interlude B

## *It's the Overtones, Stupid: Music, Math, and Physics*

### Musical Hammers

For most collegiate music students in the Western world, the history portion of their program begins with a colorful story, which goes something like this:

> One day around 550 BCE, on the sunny Greek isle of Samos, the great philosopher-mathematician Pythagoras was taking a stroll when he heard some distinct clanging coming from the local blacksmith shop. As he peered in to investigate, he noticed something fascinating: two burly smithies were hitting their hammers on a pair of anvils, whereby their strokes produced two pitches an exact octave apart. Now some say he'd been drinking, but Pythagoras was in fact a musician: he played the lyre, a strummed harp popular in ancient Greece; as such, he knew an octave when he heard one. Upon further investigation, he discovered that the hammer producing the lower octave was exactly twice the weight of that producing the upper octave—12 minae (about 12 pounds) and 6 minae, respectively. But wait: he then heard two other familiar musical intervals—the (perfect) 5th and the (perfect) 4th—arising from the anvil strikes of two adjacent burly smithies. The 5th, he discovered, sounded when the 6 minae hammer was struck in concert with a hammer weighing 9 minae, while the 4th sounded when the 6-minae hammer was paired with one weighing 8 minae. Okay, he'd had a few glasses of Lemnian wine, but something was going on. . . . [185]

Let's explore a bit what all these numbers are saying. Indeed, let me first admit that grasping such math- and physics-based concepts in this interlude may well require some concentration. Yet given the fascinating grounding of our musical taste in fundamental principles of math and physics, and the impact of their historical unveiling to the very evolution of musical output, it may well be worth dusting off those painful memories of high school algebra—at least a bit. Okay, back to explaining Pythagoras' musical hammers.

The octave that Pythagoras allegedly heard in the striking of the two hammers was reflected in a *numerical* relationship of their weight, between a hammer of

12 minae and another of 6 minae—12 to 6, or 2 to 1 (2:1); the 5th was similarly reflected by a simple numerical weight relationship, in this case of 9 to 6 minae—or 3 to 2 (3:2); the 4th, then, was reflected by a relationship of 8 to 6 minae—or 4 to 3 (4:3). In other words, each of these strong musical intervals revealed an exact correspondence to a simple numerical ratio—or proportion—that was in turn reflected in the weight of different hammers striking an anvil: the octave (e.g., C to C) corresponded to a ratio of 2:1; the perfect 5th (e.g., C to G) corresponded to a ratio of 3:2; and the perfect 4th (e.g., C to F) corresponded to a ratio of 4:3. Now, that wasn't too bad, right?

But wait, we have a problem: as science now informs us, these intervals cannot be produced by virtue of ratios arising from relationships based on the weight or mass of objects like hammers. Instead, they only work when it comes to the relationships of string lengths—say on a guitar or violin. As noted, though, Pythagoras did play the lyre, likely the seven-string variety; he also purportedly invented a single-string instrument, the kanon, used primarily for theoretical experimentation.[186] As such, he would have been in a good position to make these observations without even leaving his house. Let me explain. . . .

Using his kanon, he could have plucked the open string and heard a note—call it C; if he stopped the string with his finger exactly halfway down the length (between the nut and the bridge, the two ends where the stings are attached)—the pitch would rise an exact octave to the higher C; thus the ratio of the full length (2) to half the length (1) equals an octave (Figure B.1a). Similarly, if Pythagoras had divided his kanon string in three equal parts and stopped it with his finger at two-thirds the length, the pitch would rise a 5th above the open string, to G—thus the ratio of the full length (3) to two-thirds the length (2) equals a 5th (Figure B.1b). Finally, if he saw fit to divide his kanon string into four equal parts and stopped it three-quarters of the way up, the pitch would rise a 4th above the open string, to F—thus the ratio of the full length (4) to three-quarters the length (3) equals a 4th (Figure B.1c). In this case, as with the apocryphal blacksmith tale, we in fact get the *same* result: the three key musical intervals arise from simple numerical ratios: the octave as 2:1; the 5th as 3:2; the 4th as 4:3.

**Figure B.1: Simple numerical ratios of key musical intervals**

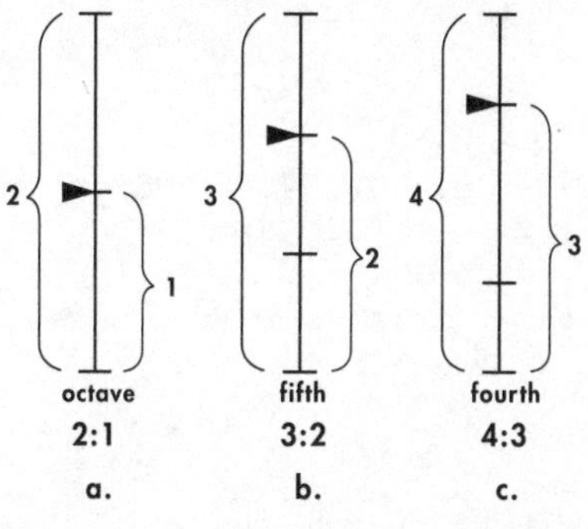

I'm sure you're agape with wonder at this story. If not, give it some time—as it does in fact reveal an astonishing correlation between simple mathematical truths and the principal intervals used in virtually every musical culture. Before getting to that, though, let's back up and say a bit more about this kanon-plucking fellow.

Pythagoras (c. 570–c. 495 BCE)—whom the reader may recall from my failed attempt to replace the name "Pandora"—was a quasi-mythical figure credited with great triumphs in the realms of mathematics, philosophy, and music. Born on the Greek island of Samos, he traveled widely before settling in Magna Graecia in Southern Italy. He is most famous of course, for the geometric theorem bearing his name, stating that the sum of the squares on the sides of a right-angle triangle equals the square of the diagonal (hypotenuse)—that is, $a^2 + b^2 = c^2$. Given the late documentation of his life (no original writings survive), however, we can't be entirely certain which ideas came from him, and which came from his contemporaries or followers—known as the Pythagorean school.

Regardless, Pythagorean thought centers largely on the belief that the entire physical world has numerical underpinnings—and indeed may be fully explained by virtue of numerical truths. Music was so vital to the Pythagoreans in part because it offered an immediate (if partial) means to validate this perspective, specifically by virtue of the link between mathematical ratios and the musical consonances (pleasing sounds) just noted. The octave, 5th, and 4th were already well recognized—and utilized—as pivotal and fundamental intervals in music making, but their grounding in these "perfect" proportions gave them a truly cosmic significance in the minds of the Pythagoreans.

Particularly significant was the correlation between these "perfect" intervals and the "tetractys," a triangular figure also supposedly invented by Pythagoras. This mystic symbol—upon which Pythagoreans swore oaths—consists of four rows of one, two, three, and four points, respectively (Figure B.2):

**Figure B.2: Pythagorean tetractys—symbolizing perfect intervals**

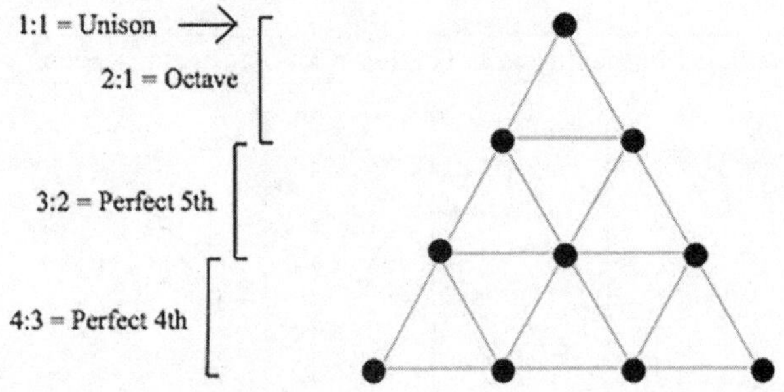

The rows were commonly linked to the four classical elements (fire, air, water, and earth) and collectively add up to 10, itself considered a number of higher order unity. But most symbolic was the tetractys' embodiment of the "perfect" musical intervals, whose ratios were obtained from just these numbers: the unison (1:1), the octave (2:1), the 5th (3:2), and the 4th (4:3). We explained a bit what these intervals mean and how they're used, melodically and harmonically, in Chapters 3 and 4.

It was this mystical, cosmic correlation, moreover, that informed a broader dimension of Pythagorean thought: the "Harmony of the Spheres." Simply put, the mathematical ratios or proportions that generate the "perfect" musical intervals are the same ones that define the distances between the earth and the celestial bodies (the sun, planets, and visible stars), as well as the speeds with which they orbit the earth. In *Timaeus*, for example, Plato describes, in allegorical terms, the "Creation of the Soul World"—that is, the soul or intelligence that "God" (the "cause" of the universe) placed into the living world:

> God, accordingly, set air and water betwixt fire and earth, and making them as far as possible exactly proportional, so that fire is to air as air to water, and as air is to water, water is to earth, thus he compacted and constructed a universe visible and tangible. For these reasons and out of elements of this kind, four in number, the body of the universe was created, being brought into concord [harmony] by proportion.[187]

In this same work, Plato offers other prescriptions on the origins of the cosmos—aligning, for example, the orbit of the heavenly bodies, and their speeds and directions, to the precise "musical" proportions of 2:1 (octave), 3:2 (5th), and 4:3 (4th)—as well as to other aspects of Pythagorean ratios that we'll soon encounter.[188]

Happily, the details of Plato's cosmic descriptions, and their exact relationship to Pythagoras' "Harmony of the Spheres," are not vital to grasp—if indeed they can be fully grasped at all.[189] What is important, rather, is simply knowing that according to Plato, the universe—and thus all of nature—is a very real extension of the "perfection" found in musical intervals, especially the three "perfect" intervals derived from Pythagoras' tetractys: the octave, the 5th, and the 4th. But why would that be? Why would perhaps the ancient world's greatest thinker—the father of Western philosophy—embrace such a notion? Is this just mystical hocus-pocus arising from a drunken story about musical hammers, or is something else going on?

## The Universal, Sonic Strength of Small-Integer Ratio Intervals

In the previous interlude (A), we touched upon the subject of "musical universals"—the notion that aspects of musical discourse, structure, and/or perception might be shared by peoples all over the world. As we saw, however, the notion of universals in music can be controversial, and there has long been skepticism among musicologists in even proposing such a thing—smacking as it does of "biological determinism" and ethnocentrism. However, a more forgiving and broad-minded approach to musical universals has recently emerged, bringing with it new insights into our shared musicality. Among the most noncontroversial of these "universals," in fact, is our collective embrace of these Pythagorean "perfect" intervals—the octave, 5th, and 4th—in both music making and music perception.

In a landmark 1962 survey of musical practices around the world, for example, famed ethnomusicologist Curt Sachs noted the universality of "octave equivalency." That is, whether in China, Africa, the Middle East, Micronesia, India, or Europe, one can find groups of people singing a melody at one pitch level and *simultaneously* at the same pitch level an *exact* octave higher. Sachs explains this universal practice as resulting "in the East as in the West from the natural distances of men's, women's, and children's voices."[190] In other words, when men and women sing the *same* melody, their very physiology inherently promotes (though does not dictate) that the notes be sung an octave apart. This may seem a bit unremarkable, perhaps, but let us recall that this universal, physiologically inspired interval, the octave, is also the smallest—and simplest—of our Pythagorean integer ratios: 2:1.*

And it doesn't stop there. Our remaining two Pythagorean intervals, the 5th and 4th, are likewise found as fundamental to music making around the world. Sachs, in fact, went so far as to assert in the same study: "Fifth and fourth parallels are almost as frequent as octaves." While this is a bit of an exaggeration, it has indeed been documented time and again that cultures around the world—from broad regions like China and India to small tribes like those of Melanesia (Oceania), not to mention the entirety of the Western world—utilize the 5th, and to a lesser degree the 4th, as *pillars* of both their music theory and practice.[191] We unveiled a bit of the theoretical basis of this claim as pertains to Western music in Chapters 3 and 4.

The preeminence that Pythagoras and Plato gave to the octave, 5th, and 4th thus appears to reflect a musical reality that extends far beyond the Hellenic world:

* 2:1 is the smallest ratio, that is, after the unison (same note)—whose ratio, of course, is 1:1.

in virtually *every* musical culture, those intervals that arise from "small-integer ratios"—2:1, 3:2, 4:3—assert a sort of universal sonic strength, hitting both the ear and the mind as vital. It is not surprising, then, that both ancient Greek and medieval theorists referred to them as "*perfect*" consonances, as we still do today.

Since the early seventeenth century, science has tried to explain empirically this "perfect" association—why we respond so favorably and universally to these simple, small-integer ratio intervals. Galileo, in 1638, first proposed a physiological rationale: that these "agreeable consonances . . . strike the ear with a certain regularity." He continues: "The pulses delivered by the two tones [i.e., those an octave, fifth, or fourth apart] . . . shall be commensurable in number, so as not to keep the ear drum in perpetual torment."[192] Galileo is here referring to the then recently discovered link between musical pitch on the one hand and the frequency (or speed) of sound waves on the other. In short, he is saying that those intervals formed by a simple ratio of their frequencies (2:1, 3:2, 4:3) provide a welcome stability or repose to the ear and thus sound strong; more on musical frequency in the pages ahead.

And, indeed, Galileo's intuitions about our physiological attraction to small-integer intervals have since been confirmed by modern science—including via neuroscience, studies on animal perception,[193] and studies on infant perception. For example, Sandra Trehub has demonstrated that infants retain melodies based on the 5th and 4th better than those based on the tritone. To Trehub, this preference implies that our aesthetic response to these intervals isn't merely a product of exposure, but instead reveals a "processing bias for tones related by small-integer ratios." She even goes so far as to call these three intervals "perceptual anchors" that in turn facilitate various fundamental tasks of music processing.[194]

In sum, science reveals that our love of octaves, 5ths, and 4ths is grounded in basic auditory-processing mechanisms that extend deep into our evolutionary past—and are not merely a product of "general-purpose learning" or cultural exposure. Who knew that your musical taste had such a strong mathematical basis?

## Bar Bands in Andromeda

Okay, so what is the point of all this? We've spent a good amount of time discussing what ancient Greeks, ethnomusicologists, and modern scientists have said about three common—indeed, universal—musical intervals. Why does it matter? Remember that these three intervals represent a sonic manifestation of simple or fundamental mathematical principles, based upon ratios, or logarithmic scales, that in turn are grounded on the most basic numerical relationships. The octave, 5th, and 4th sound strong to our ears, and act as pillars in musical practices all over the world, because they *are* strong in nature—built upon these simple or "pure" mathematical constructs. Our aural neurophysiology has evolved to respond favorably to the "perfection" of small-integer proportional relationships that nature had already—and automatically—bequeathed to sound. To a degree, nature was simply waiting for a life form with the neurological capability not only to recognize the strength of these three intervals but also to utilize them as the basis upon which to build a musical language.

Put another way: imagine some moment in the distant future, when we humans have invented the means to travel deep into the heart of the Andromeda galaxy 2.5 million light-years away. We navigate our way to a "Goldilocks" planet, where clear signals of intelligent life have been detected. We land on a sandy beach and are welcomed with friendly curiosity by the native life form. Using interstellar, nonverbal communication, the polite aliens provide us with a tour of their beautiful planet—including a visit to a recreational venue that resembles a bar. As we enter the establishment, above the din of an odd language, we hear something familiar yet exotic: music! Although the instruments, melodies, and vocal techniques are strange, perhaps a bit ugly to our ears, the musicologist in the group takes note: underlying the musical exoticism are three very familiar intervals: the octave, the 5th, and the 4th. Such, I would argue, is inevitable: even on a planet in far-flung Andromeda, the basis for most music making would *have* to be these "perfect" consonances; this is the case since the laws of math and physics are the same throughout the universe—and thus the ears (or hearing apparatus) of the Andromedans would have evolved to hear these "perfect" consonances as primary or fundamental, just as we have.[195]

We may never be able to prove such a hypothesis, of course; sadly, we may never hear an extraterrestrial bar band rock the night away. But regardless, we have established an important point here: our musical taste—for all of us—is at some fundamental level grounded on the three "perfect" consonances that some 2,500 years ago sparked a spurious tale of blacksmiths and hammer weights. And whether you prefer a three-minute song by the latest pop idol, a dirty 12-bar blues, a refined classical symphony, a spiritual Indian raga, or most any music that is commonly heard, you have felt the power—and gained the pleasure—from structural harmonic and melodic uses of the octave, the 5th, and the 4th. As such, we can *at last* begin to answer that pesky question of "why you like it": because, at least in part, the small-integer intervals told us to!

## Tuning, Temperament, and Taste

As suggested at the top of this interlude, tackling the math- and physics-based concepts of music requires concentration—and not infrequently leads to bouts of head-scratching by all but the most mathematically inclined (of which I'm assuredly not one). This is no truer than when dealing with the topics of tuning and temperament. To reduce the risk of overload, we'll here provide just the CliffsNotes version—along with a tad more detail in the endnotes (and WYLI website) for those wanting a challenge. This extrapolated understanding will be important, however, as it will help explain our inherent love of triads, as well as the evolution of modal and tonal harmony.

First, some basic definitions: By "tuning," I am *not* referring to the process of making your guitar sound "in tune" via an electric tuner, or hiring a piano tuner to fix the "out-of-tune" notes before your next dinner party. Instead, "tuning" here refers to the *process of defining the size and sound of simultaneous intervals* (3rds, 4ths, 5ths, etc.) by virtue of their precise ratios or proportions. For example, a major 3rd is not an absolutely fixed interval, but can be "tuned" differently—wider or narrower—depending on the *system* used to produce it; each system (e.g., Pythagorean, just, equal temperament, etc.) will have its own "recipe" for defining the ratios by which the individual intervals are tuned, as we'll soon see. In other words, using different tunings will make the *same* music sound *different*, even if only subtly so. By "temperament," then, is meant the *overall system by which the ratios for the full set of intervals are defined*, often developed as a process of experimentation.

Importantly, these shifts in tuning and temperament reflect not the mere abstract tinkering of mathematicians and physicists. As will be revealed in the pages ahead, alterations in these systems have literally changed the way music sounds—and thus is written and performed—over the past five hundred years or so. As such, the evolving tuning "recipes" of the major 3rd, and of the temperament systems broadly, have had a profound impact on your musical taste, beyond what can be easily quantified—and thus far more than that last-minute piano tuning before your next dinner party.

Okay, so with these definitions and caveats under our belt, onward we go . . .

The first tuning system we'll explore returns us to Pythagoras and his three "perfect" intervals: the octave (2:1), 5th (3:2), and 4th (4:3). As it turns out, the system that he and his followers devised to determine the "perfect" intervals likewise enabled them to define the other, "imperfect" intervals of the musical scale as well—via a system known as *Pythagorean tuning*. Basically, by relating the already determined interval ratios to those not yet determined, one can deduce the Pythagorean ratios for all twelve notes of the chromatic scale (i.e., all the white and black notes of the piano from C to the C an octave higher)—as follows (Figure B.3):[196]

**Figure B.3: Pythagorean tuning—ratios of all intervals**

| | | | |
|---|---|---|---|
| Minor 2nd (C–D♭) | 256:243 | Perfect 5th (C–G) | 3:2 |
| Major 2nd (C–D) | 9:8 | Minor 6th (C–A♭) | 128:81 |
| Minor 3rd (C–E♭) | 32:27 | Major 6th (C–A) | 27:16 |
| Major 3rd (C–E) | 81:64 | Minor 7th (C–B♭) | 16:9 |
| Perfect 4th (C–F) | 4:3 | Major 7th (C–B) | 243:128 |
| Augmented 4th (C–F♯) | 729:512 | Octave (C–C) | 2:1 |

Ignoring how these ratios are derived, though, you will still immediately notice something troublesome in the listing above: most of these "imperfect" intervals yield rather "irrational" ratios—far from the simple elegance of 2:1, 3:2, and 4:3. For example, the ratio for the major 3rd—81:64—is a far cry from those "pure" small-integer ratios. The one, partial exception is that for the major 2nd—9:8—which, like the "perfect" intervals, involves two consecutive smallish integers.

More importantly, Pythagorean tuning has an inherent flaw if one were to try to play (or sing) a song using all, or even several, of its twelve notes, since some of the pitches sound terribly out of tune. That major 3rd, for example, will sound rather "sour" compared to how it sounds on a modern piano. The exact reasons relate to how the "imperfect" intervals were mathematically devised in the first place.[197]

You're probably wondering by now what this has to do with musical taste—I get it. Well, let me first surprise you by noting that despite its sour notes and irrational ratios, the Pythagorean system endured as the basic means by which musicians in the West tuned their instruments and regulated their voices through to nearly the end of the fourteenth century. This includes not only single-line (monophonic) chants but also early polyphonic works by major composers like Perotin and Guillaume de Machaut. And that's where it relates to musical taste—especially back then: because of those "irrational" ratios and sour tunings, intervals like 3rds and 6ths were considered "dissonant." Composers thus avoided writing music that lingered on simultaneous 3rds and 6ths, and instead allowed them to sound *only in passing*; by contrast, the "perfect" intervals of the octave, 5th, and 4th were the "true" consonances, which composers could emphasize, sustain, and use to bring their works to a strong close.

One's musical taste in the Middle Ages was thus shaped in part by the peculiarities of Pythagorean tuning: you were inclined to love simultaneous 5ths and 4ths, and perhaps like other intervals in passing—so long as you didn't stray too far from the basic scale or mode from which you began. You were then inclined to *not* love music that was dominated by simultaneous 3rd or 6ths—because they were likely to be harsh and unpleasant. Indeed, for these same reasons, you'd have a hard time hearing such music in the first place: composers of the Middle Ages didn't like harsh-sounding music any more than listeners did. The rub: tuning limited taste; or, in plainer language, a music lover in the mid-twelfth century, for example, would have been as much influenced in his favorites by ratios of Pythagorean tuning as he was by the specific notes and rhythms written by the various composers of the day.

But that's not the end of the story, of course. And revealing my historian's bias, what follows is a rapid-fire, CliffsNotes summary of Western music from the late Middle Ages through the nineteenth century told from the standpoint of tuning systems. These ever-changing systems acted much like a sonic playing field on which composers and listeners operated, and forged their collective musical taste; more importantly, perhaps, they affected the actual musical output throughout these centuries.

By the mid-fourteenth century, especially in England, musicians began to question the bias against 3rds and 6ths. They realized that by tweaking or *tempering* the tuning of these intervals—that is, making them all a tad flatter (narrower) or sharper (wider) than their default Pythagorean disposition—they could actually sound quite lovely, not sour at all. Composers like John Dunstaple (c. 1390–1453) began indulging in these new tunings of 3rds and 6ths, and in the process *inadvertently* formed what we *today* call major and minor triads. This is because—as we learned in Chapter 4—major and minor triads are formed as stacked 3rds, which become 6ths when inverted, as shown with an F major triad in Figure B.4:

**Figure B.4: F major chord in root position and inversions—inverted 3rds become 6ths**

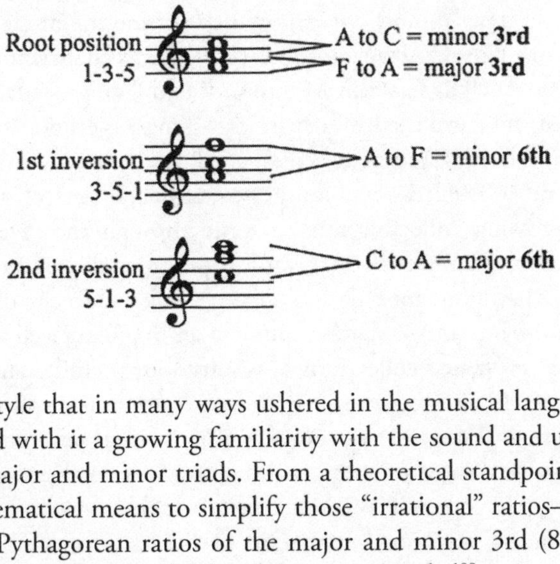


It was this English style that in many ways ushered in the musical language of the Renaissance—and with it a growing familiarity with the sound and usage of what we today call major and minor triads. From a theoretical standpoint, it entailed finding a mathematical means to simplify those "irrational" ratios—for example, tweaking the Pythagorean ratios of the major and minor 3rd (81:64 and 32:27) to the small-integer ratios of 5:4 and 6:5, respectively.[198]

In time, this informal tweaking was codified into a new formal system—one deemed pure or "just" by virtue of these more rational interval ratios. It was thus called "just intonation" (that is, "pure tuning")—which came to be the dominant tuning system during the Renaissance. It generated simpler ratios for all intervals, and especially for the newly labeled "imperfect" consonances of 3rds and 6ths (Figure B.5):

**Figure B.5: Just intonation—ratios of "imperfect" consonances**

| | | | |
|---|---|---|---|
| Minor 3rd (C–E♭) | 6:5 | Minor 6th (C–A♭) | 8:5 |
| Major 3rd (C–E) | 5:4 | Major 6th (C–A) | 5:3 |

The influential theorist Gioseffo Zarlino (d. 1590) even endorsed the just intonation system as embodying mystical powers—whereby the numbers 1 to 6 were deemed uniquely "sonorous," given that they could be used to generate "all" the consonances.[199] Once again, therefore, musical taste was influenced by a tuning system: with 3rds and 6ths now sanctioned by practice *and* theory, composers and audiences were free to collectively indulge in their "sweet blends"—as heard in the masterworks by Josquin des Prés, Palestrina, and others. These "imperfect" consonances indeed became the most prominent harmonic sonorities of the age, with the "perfect" intervals of the octave, 5th, and 4th now relegated to more structural roles. The seeds of tonality—the harmonic language of most music today—were planted by the resulting steady flow of major and minor triads.

And yet—as you might have guessed—the just intonation system, while solving some problems, created new ones, not least by exposing further limitations in how "remote" or chromatic (outside the mode) composers could go. A growing tension, from around 1600, between harmonically progressive composers—such as Claudio Monteverdi and Carlo Gesualdo—and the limitations of just intonation led to a spate of tuning experiments and new systems. These include various "temperaments": small yet deliberate tweaks in the tuning of any interval, as needed—including the sacrosanct "perfect" 5th.[200] As a consequence, the growing collective musical taste through the seventeenth and eighteenth centuries steadily evolved toward "experimental" instrumental music and adventurous harmonic modulation (changes in key). To cite one famous "experiment": none other than J. S. Bach promoted an irregular "well-tempered" tuning system in his two famed collections of twenty-four preludes and fugues—enabling him to progress across all twenty-four keys, both major and minor, in a single work.

The final stage in this complex story is **equal temperament**. This is the tuning system used most prevalently today (such as on the modern piano), where each half step (e.g., C to C♯) is sized the *exact same proportional distance* as every other. Put another way, equal temperament divides the octave into twelve equal parts—each half step being the 12th root of 2, yielding a ratio somewhere between 18:17

and 107:101. As a result, this tuning system blows up the older Pythagorean ratios for every interval except the unison (1:1) and the octave (2:1)—for example, the 5th is now a tiny bit wider than the 3:2 distance of the Pythagorean perfect 5th.[201] So what's the advantage? Well, if every interval is a product of an even twelve-part division of the octave, one can readily shift from one key to *any* other—even remote ends on the Circle of 5ths, like from C major to F♯ major—without fear of hearing "sour" notes.

The idea of equal temperament slowly gained momentum from the seventeenth century, becoming standard only around 1750—the year of J. S. Bach's death. Importantly, it also had its detractors, who lamented the loss of the "natural" beauty generated by pure Pythagorean and just intervals. By the mid-nineteenth century, however, equal temperament was all but ubiquitous, especially in the West, and not least via the influential writings of physicist-physician Hermann von Helmholtz (1863). Given the free rein it would now grant composers to shift from one chord or key to any other without fear of harsh or sour notes, it is no accident that the pronounced "chromaticism" (harmonic complexity) that began especially after 1850—in the music of Johannes Brahms and Richard Wagner, for example—coincided with the full blossom of equal temperament. Without equal temperament, such harmonic "revolutions" as the opening of Wagner's *Tristan und Isolde* would be unbearably out of tune. Once again, we see, changes in tuning dramatically influenced changes in musical taste among both musicians and audiences.

At the same time, the removal of any harmonic constraints enabled by equal temperament has had other, unforeseen consequences on both musical practice and musical taste. The unbridled ability to combine any note with any other has given license, in the twentieth and twenty-first centuries, to the "emancipation" of dissonance—as we discussed in Chapter 4. When composers no longer have to worry about their harmonic decisions based on the limits of a tuning system, they are free to let their imaginations run wild, including to exploit dissonance for its own sake—as exercised by musicians ranging from Schoenberg and Boulez to Coltrane and Zorn to Zappa and the Jesus Lizard, to name but a few. No longer, that is, do musicians *have* to rely on the "perfect" octave, 5th, and 4th—nor even the "imperfect consonances" of 3rds and 6ths in their music. To some, this is liberation; to others . . . not so much.

## The Scientific Revolution of Sound: The Quest for Frequency

It was in the course of this evolution in tuning systems that other fundamental truths were revealed about the nature of musical sound and our perception of it. These include, especially, a more accurate understanding of musical pitch and the curious phenomenon of the harmonic (or overtone) series. As with tuning and temperament, these discoveries unfolded in earnest starting around 1600, a manifestation of the broader shifts in the pursuit of knowledge subsumed under the Scientific Revolution (c. 1550–1700). More specifically, they arose as a gradual shift from explaining pitch and intervals via arithmetic (Pythagorean) dogmatism or scholastic metaphysics and toward using experimental, physically determined observation—that is, toward what we today call physics.

Even more than with Pythagorean intervals or shifting tuning systems, explaining physics-based observations on pitch or overtones can quickly get overwhelming. And yet, as much as any other line of scientific inquiry, they demonstrate the remarkable human capacity to build steadily upon incremental progress in order to unravel the opaque mysteries of nature. More narrowly for our purposes, their high-level conclusions reveal some striking relevance to our musical taste.

The notion that the source of sound—including musical pitch—extends beyond mere string lengths and proportional ratios was intuited at least as far back as Aristotle, who wrote in his treatise *On the Soul* that "sound is a particular movement of air."[202] This movement- or wave-based conception of sound was expanded in the first century BCE by the Roman architect Vitruvius, who speculated that sound travels "in circles like the ripples set up by a pebble thrown into a pond."[203] Even Boethius (d. 524), the authoritative disseminator of Pythagorean music theory to the West, echoed this water-wave analogy. However, it was only in the latter sixteenth century that a serious investigation into the true nature of sound began to unfold—something that would take nearly three centuries to fully explicate.

Among the earliest insights came from the mathematician Gianbattista Benedetti, when in 1563 he suggested to the progressive composer Cipriano de Rore that sound was propagated to the ear by a series of rapid "pulses" traveling from a given source of "vibrational disturbance," like a bowed string to the ear—the faster the disturbance, or frequency, the higher the pitch. He even put a mathematical formula to it—correctly deducing that the length of a string was inversely proportional to its frequency: a pitch producing two hundred vibrations per second, for example, would sound an octave higher than one producing a hundred vibrations per second. In the 1590s, Vincenzo Galilei then successfully demonstrated that any given interval could be generated by multiple ratios, depending on what property was measured.

Yet as with so many scientific disruptions in the early seventeenth century, it was Vincenzo's son Galileo who broke the sound query wide-open. Unaware of Benedetti's observations, he undertook a variety of relatively crude experiments to explain his father's findings. Among these was an "accidental" experiment conducted in 1638 with a brass plate scraped by a sharp iron chisel—which if run rapidly enough produced a whistling sound; moreover, Galileo observed that the scraping left on the plate "a long row of fine streaks parallel and equidistant from one another."[204] Upon further examination, he found that two whistles a 5th apart left forty-five and thirty streaks, respectively—equal to the Pythagorean ratio of 3:2.

From such experiments, Galileo made a series of remarkable inferences—starting with an enhanced echo of Benedetti's 1563 summary: "Sounds are produced and heard by us when . . . a frequent vibration of air shaken in tiny waves moves a certain cartilage of the tympanum in our ear. . . . [T]he more frequent the vibration, the higher the pitch; the less frequent, the lower."[205] It is notable here that Galileo not only presciently describes the link between pitch and sound waves, but also recognizes the requisite interaction of the vibrating eardrum in perceiving it. He continues: "I assert that the ratio of a musical interval is not immediately determined either by the length, size, or tension of the strings but rather by the ratio of their frequencies, that is, by the number of pulses of air waves which strike the tympanum of the ear, causing it also to vibrate with the same frequency." These observations in turn led to the novel theory of consonance cited above—why "some pairs of notes produce a pleasing sensation, others a less pleasant effect, and still others a disagreeable sensation"; due, that is, to whether the frequencies of the two tones possess either a "certain regularity," are "out of time," or are "incommensurable" (a ratio that cannot be expressed as a fraction of two integers), respectively.[206]

The quest to experimentally prove Galileo's assertions, and to discern the precise or absolute frequency of a given pitch, would then preoccupy generations of brilliant scientists. Minds no less than Descartes and Isaac Newton put themselves to the challenge, with the latter's (slightly flawed) formulation of the velocity of sound in 1676 playing a key role.[207] Chief among the next round of innovators was Galileo's disciple Marin Mersenne, who was the first to generate a mathematic law describing the rate of vibration or frequency of an individual pitch.[208] Although "Mersenne's Law" (proposed in 1637) was limited to determining the frequency of a stretched string, it laid the foundation for later experiments—by figures such as Robert Hooke, Joseph Sauveur, Johann Bernoulli, and Leonhard Euler—that would culminate in Johann Scheibler's "tonometer."[209] This was an array of forty-five tuning forks, whereby Scheibler, in 1834, was able to pinpoint the exact frequency of each pitch between the A below middle C and the A above it—which, incidentally, led to the fixing of the latter at 440 Hz (cycles per second), the "tuning" of A that is standard today.

By this time, of course, the propagation of sound was understood not to be pulses of air, as Benedetti and Galileo had surmised, but rather as waves that move in a four-part pattern: from a starting point (0) to an end point in one direction (1), back to the starting point (2), then to the parallel end point in the other direction (3), and back again to the starting point (4), before continuing on with the same pattern (Figure B.6):

**Figure B.6: The pattern of a sound wave**

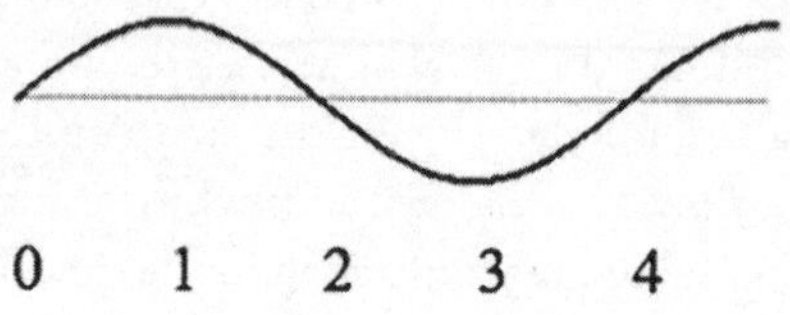


As Benedetti and Galileo noted correctly, however, the faster the speed of this propagation, the higher the pitch: the exact frequency being the inverse of the time it takes to complete the cycle defined above—measured as cycles per second or hertz (Hz), named after physicist Heinrich Hertz. That is, if it takes 1/100 of a second to complete the cycle, the frequency is 100 Hz.

It has been in more recent years, of course, that the "modern" sciences—acoustics, mechanics, physiology, computer science, etc.—have fleshed out the fine details of musical pitch. These include Charles Wheatstone's use of wooden sliders and bead wires to visualize sound waves in motion in the 1840s; Rudolph Koenig's 1876 expanded tonometer using 670 tuning forks to define the "full" range of human hearing from 20 Hz (F♯ below the bottom of a piano) to 4096 Hz (the top C of the piano)—since revised to 20,000 Hz or higher; the computer-based use of a "fast Fourier transform" (FFT) algorithm to convert any sound signal to representation in the frequency domain (devised in 1965), among many others whose details will here be mercifully omitted.[210]

## It's the Overtones, Stupid!

Collectively, these developments from Benedetti on down have empirically corroborated what Pythagoras revealed to us about "perfect" intervals 2,500 years ago—and then some, of course. As interesting as this unfolding may be, however, the actual discernment that musical pitch constitutes an absolute frequency of sound waves does little by itself to enlighten the disposition of our musical taste—sorry. Yet an offshoot of that line of inquiry most certainly does: the harmonic or **overtone series**. Indeed, I can almost hear the musical counterpart to political strategist James Carville yelling at me, "It's the overtones, stupid!" I could argue that explaining overtones without likewise explaining the true nature of musical pitch would be difficult or confusing . . . but he'd still be yelling!

As with intervals, any serious attempt to explain overtones inevitably involves some historical accounting and math-based explications—there's simply no way to avoid that. I've tried hard to make the following discussion clear and relatively pain-free, though complexity is, sadly, in the nature of the beast. Happily, the overtones phenomenon is not only fascinating, but also helps explain—on a scientific basis—why it is that we so love the sound of major, minor, and dominant 7th chords.

An awareness that a sounding pitch seems to generate other, softer pitches above it was recognized going back to Aristotle's day, but it was, yet again, only in the seventeenth century that the phenomenon was studied empirically. Mersenne—who we'll recall devised the first law of musical frequency—made the opening salvo; while carrying out his pitch-based research in the 1630s, he too noted this strange phenomenon: when he plucked a string, he heard faint notes—he called them "*petits sons*"—above the most audible or "**fundamental**" one. In fact, he apparently heard up to six higher pitches at once. He accomplished this through determined experimentation, noting: "It is necessary to find complete silence to perceive them, although this is not necessary when one has a trained ear."[211]

Importantly, these six *petits sons* that Mersenne heard were not random, but ascended consistently in a pattern of intervals that aligned with Pythagorean and other "just" intervals: an octave above the sounding pitch, or fundamental (e.g., C–C), a 5th above that (G), a 4th above that (C), a major 3rd above that (E), a minor 3rd above that (G), and finally, a slightly out-of-tune minor 3rd above that (a bit below B♭). What in the devil was going on? To seek answers, Mersenne communicated with several esteemed scientific minds of his day—including Descartes—none of whom could provide him with a satisfactory answer.[212] Mersenne at one point actually deduced the correct answer—that these *petits sons* might in fact be naturally occurring artifacts of the principal sounding pitch; however, noting a contrasting behavior in instruments like bells or organ pipes, he rejected it as "impossible to imagine."

The matter saw little movement until the latter part of the seventeenth century, when the English mathematician John Wallis recognized that a vibrating string has "nodes" or points along it that *do not* vibrate—which he identified by attaching small paper strips all up and down the string. Wallis recognized the arithmetic-based loci of these nodes above the fundamental—1/2, 1/3, 1/4, 1/5, etc., the length of the string—and yet he failed to link these to the *petits sons* Mersenne had heard. That was left, around 1700, to Joseph Sauveur, considered to be the "father" of acoustics, who likewise contributed to the pitch-frequency saga. Sauveur too identified the nodes, but this time recognized that each corresponded to one of those "*sons harmonique*," as he dubbed them: "Each half, each third, each fourth part of a string has its own special vibration, while at the same time the string vibrates as a whole."[213]

From there, the quest was to more accurately understand the relationship between the fundamental and the "harmonic" tones above it, and thus to understand what precisely nature was up to in this curious dynamic. Critical, for example, were the observations of Euler and Bernoulli, in the mid-eighteenth century, that the fundamental tone was a simple sine wave, a single, "smooth" oscillation, or repetitive pattern, of sound—as already shown in Figure B.6—upon which the upper "harmonics" are *overlapped* via the principle of "superposition" following an arithmetic pattern of 1X, 2X, 3X, 4X, etc. That is to say: an individual "harmonic" pitch produces a *superposition* of multiple waveforms *all at once* arising from a single, fundamental tone—where each successive overlapping waveform is two, three, four, etc., times the speed of the fundamental (see Figure B.7):

**Figure B.7: The "superpositioning" of a harmonic pitch via multiple waveforms (1X, 2X, 3X)**

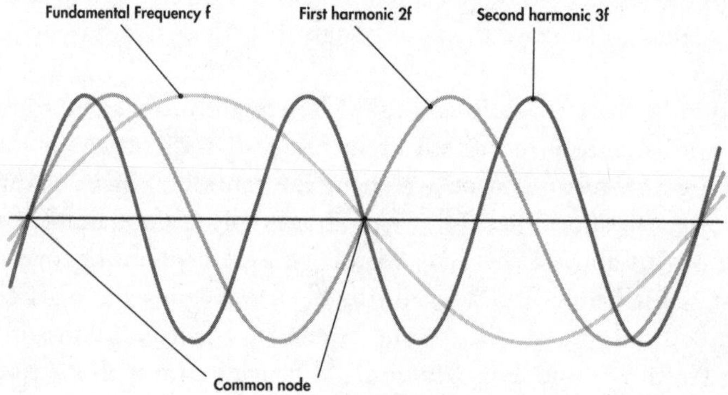


This "superposition," they noted, occurs whether the fundamental is produced on a vibrating string or via a column of air, as with a flute or trumpet. At the same time, they recognized that not all musical sounds (let alone nonmusical sounds) produce arithmetic or "harmonic" tones above a single fundamental. These include bells, drums, and other percussion instruments that fail to produce a single fundamental across the entire "resonant body"—as does, for example, a violin string or flute tone—and instead produce "inharmonic" overtones generated from multiple fundamentals at once.[214]

Okay, okay, I sense your eyes glazing, so we'll here stop our chronology, and cut to the chase of what all of this is getting at: What exactly are **overtones**?*

* The term, in fact, is an English mistranslation of the original German word "*Obertöne*" (upper tone), introduced by Hermann von Helmholtz in 1863 to identify the phenomenon of "upper partials."

In short, here is what happens: whenever a musical instrument or the human voice produces a "pitch," nature dictates that it oscillates, or repeats a wave pattern, at numerous frequencies—that is, pitches—at once. When you strike middle C on the piano, for example, your mind may perceive only one frequency (pitch). But accompanying it at a much softer volume are dozens of other, higher pitches likewise sounding at the same time. The dominant or perceived pitch, generally the lowest, is called the "fundamental," and is the frequency upon which the higher pitches are generated. Those higher pitches, in turn, are called "upper partials."

What is perhaps most significant for our purposes is that in "musical" cases—that is, when a musical instrument or voice produces a single, consistent fundamental—the upper partials are "harmonic." By that we mean that they proceed, from bottom to top, according to a pattern of (more or less) *integer multiples* of the fundamental frequency (*f*): 1X*f*, 2X*f*, 3X*f*, 4X*f*, 5X*f*, 6X*f*, 7X*f*, etc. This is the superposition that Euler and Bernoulli discovered in the mid-eighteenth century—as was shown in Figure B.7.

Let's say, for example, that you play the A below "low" C on the piano—which creates a fundamental (*f*) oscillating at 110 Hz (1X*f*). Simultaneously, "upper partials" or overtones will sound at 220 Hz (2X*f*), 330 Hz (3X*f*), 440 Hz (4X*f*), 550 Hz (5X*f*), 660 Hz (6X*f*), and 770 Hz (7X*f*). These frequencies in turn correspond to the steadily higher notes of A, E, A, C♯, E, and a slightly out-of-tune G, respectively.

Importantly, these same seven "harmonic" partials correspond to the *consonant intervals* we've been discussing throughout this interlude—the octave, perfect 5th, perfect 4th, major 3rd, and minor 3rd. This is by virtue of the simple arithmetic relationships or ratios created as we move from one "upper partial" to the next: 2:1 (e.g., 220 Hz to 110 Hz), 3:2 (e.g., 330 Hz to 220 Hz), 4:3 (e.g., 440 Hz to 330 Hz), 5:4 (e.g., 550 Hz to 440 Hz), 6:5 (660 Hz to 550 Hz), 7:6 (770 Hz to 660 Hz), etc.

What do I mean by this? Well, take a look at those arithmetic ratios just listed: 2:1, 3:2, 4:3, 5:4, 6:5, and 7:6. It will hopefully be recognized that, except for 7:6, they are the Pythagorean and "just" ratios discussed above. Now we're getting somewhere. The most common way to visualize these relationships is as a vibrating string and its "harmonic" nodes—as in Figure B.8:

**Figure B.8: The overtone series—demonstrated as nodes on a vibrating string**

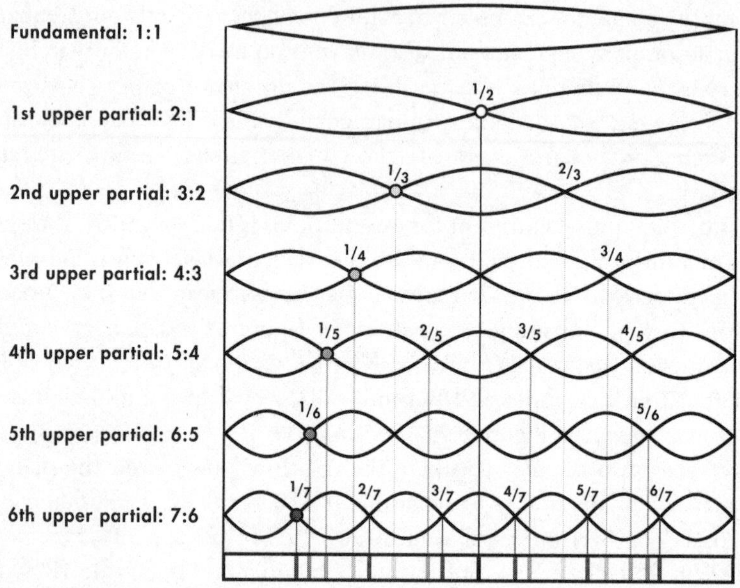


As the overtone series continues up—2:1, 3:2, 4:3, 5:4, 6:5, 7:6, 8:7, 9:8, 10:9, 11:10, etc.—a whole slew of intervals, both consonant and dissonant, appear above the preceding partial, and in turn above the fundamental. The first three (2:1, 3:2, 4:3) are, of course, the octave, 5th, and 4th of Pythagorean fame—which in turn produce notes an octave, 5th, and 4th above the fundamental. The next two, 5:4 and 6:5, we'll recall, are the "just" ratios first intuited by English composers like Dunstaple and later advocated by theorists like Zarlino for the major and minor 3rd, respectively—producing in turn the major 3rd and 5th above the fundamental. The next partial (7:6) produces that slightly "out-of-tune" (flat) minor 3rd—which is close to a minor 7th above the fundamental. And so forth . . .

Below, finally, is a more tangible example of the overtone phenomenon, such as produced on a piano by playing, as the fundamental, the C two octaves below middle C (C2)—extending up to the fifteenth overtone above the fundamental (Figure B.9)*:

* By virtue of their generation as integer multiples of the fundamental frequency (7:6, 8:7, 9:8, etc.), some of these initial fifteen overtones are "out of tune" as compared to the notes sounding on a well-tuned modern piano, for example. Specifically, the seventh, eleventh, and fourteenth overtones are a tad flat; the thirteenth overtone a tad sharp. In this book's illustrations, this is commonly shown with up or down arrows (for sharp and flat, respectively) above the notes—removed here and in Figure B.10 to avoid confusion.

**Figure B.9: The overtone series—overtones generated from C2**

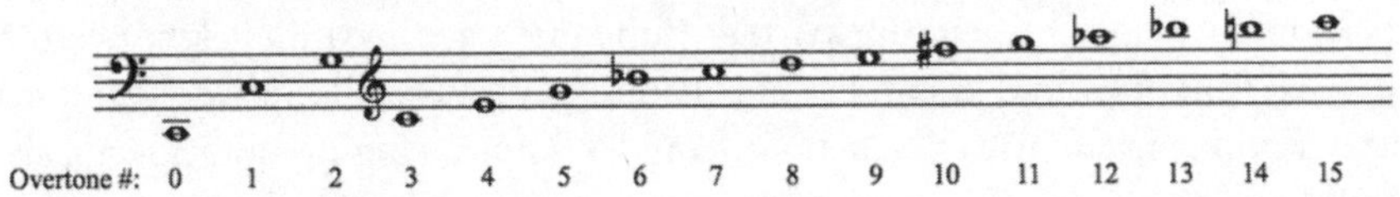


## And God Said: "Let There Be Triads!"

Okay, congratulations: you now understand the harmonic or overtone series—to some degree at least; so, why is it important, and what does it have to do with our musical taste? Well, first keep in mind that although Figure B.9 depicts each partial as a successive pitch, they in fact all sound *simultaneously*. That is, when you press the second lowest C on the piano (C2), your ears and brain perceive not only that fundamental, but all of its upper partials as well—though the latter at much softer volumes.

Indeed, neurobiological experiments have validated that each partial is interpreted by "finely tuned neurons throughout the auditory system," as musical neurologist Mark Tramo put it.[215] That is, the pitch frequency of each partial is matched by a neural firing in the auditory cortex at the *exact same rate* or frequency: for example, the frequency of middle C—the fourth partial (third overtone) of C2—both produces a sound wave oscillating at 261.6 Hz *and* triggers a neural firing in the brain at the identical rate; of course, the same is true for every partial, the fundamental (65.4 Hz) at the greatest intensity. These collective neural firings are then "synchronized," whereby we perceive the entire assembly as a single unified pitch.

The neurological perception of upper partials is also neatly demonstrated by what is called the "restoration of the missing fundamental" first confirmed by psychologist J. C. R. Licklider in 1954—whereby the brain can "hear" a fundamental even if only the upper partials are sounding. So if a pitch is manipulated such that the only sounding partials are 200 Hz, 300 Hz, 400 Hz, 500 Hz, etc., the brain will nonetheless "restore" the missing fundamental at 100 Hz—since those upper partials dictate that the fundamental can *only* be at that level.[216]

It is this mutual reality of the physical sound properties of the overtone series and the parallel response of each partial in the brain, then, that undergirds our musical taste. The universal perception of the strength of the octave, 5th, and 4th stems not only from small-integer proportional ratios, but also from their prominence in the overtone series. In turn, this leads to the remarkable fact that another type of musical construct is endemic to musical sound as well: triads—namely, the major and minor triad. As suggested in Chapter 4, these are perhaps the most ubiquitous musical entities that most of us hear on a regular basis—

regardless, practically, of what musical styles or approaches we love best.

How are triads endemic to musical sound? Well, if we were to simultaneously play on the piano the first nine partials (fundamental plus initial eight overtones) derived from *any* fundamental as one giant chord, we would in fact hear a major and a minor triad, as well as a dominant 7th chord, ringing out. Specifically, if we played this "chord" as derived from a fundamental on C2, we would hear a C major triad sounding from all the partials up through partial 6, and explicitly via partial 4, 5, and 6 (C–E–G); we'd hear a G minor triad, then, by virtue of the simultaneous sounding of partials 6, 7, and 9 (G–B♭–D); and we'd hear a C7 chord by virtue of a simultaneous sounding of partials 4, 5, 6, and 7 (C–E–G–B♭). This can be clearly seen in Figure B.10:

**Figure B.10: The overtone series—major, minor, and dominant 7th chords generated by overtones from C2**

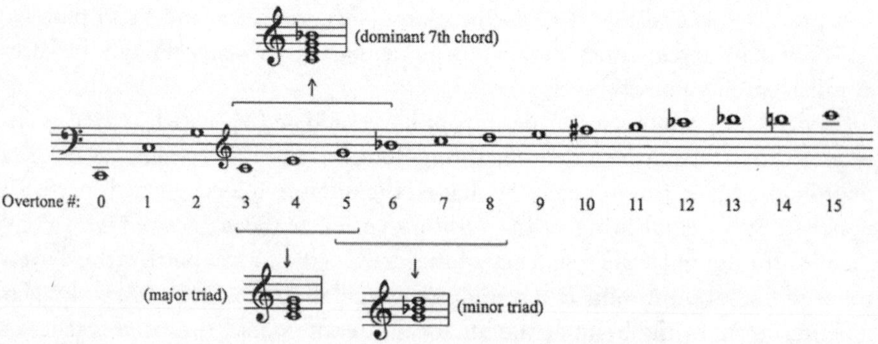


When combined with the fact that the constituent intervals that comprise major and minor triads—the 5th, the major 3rd, the minor 3rd—are themselves consonances perceived positively in the auditory cortex, without the roughness associated with dissonances, we discern something *inevitable* about our preference for them. Put another way, we humans didn't "invent" major and minor triads; God—or nature—did. They sound pleasing and proper to our ears because they are themselves built into the fabric of sound via the overtone series, which in turn we have evolved to perceive and eventually utilize in musical works.

What's more, by virtue of the overtone series, I can hereby assert the following mystical truth: God loves jazz! As noted in Chapter 4, the dominant 7th chord is a structural pillar not only of tonal harmony—the predominant language of Western music since the eighteenth century—but also of blues, jazz, and rock. That this chord is built into the very fabric of sound suggests that, in some mystical way, a musical species like jazz that is largely built on its exploitation is all but inevitable. Thus, let me repeat: God loves jazz—and blues, rock, and tonality—and so do we.

At the same time, this recognition of our "inevitable" preference for triads and dominant 7th chords can be subject to misuse and exaggeration. Most notably, the overtone series has been used as a "rationale" for both the Western system of tonal harmony as well as for the "primacy" of Western scales. A case in point is the elaborate, though faulty, theory proposed by the influential French composer-theorist Jean-Philippe Rameau in the early eighteenth century—in which overtones were seen as the means to understand every "natural" aspect of music. Although Rameau was wrong in many of his claims, he did rightly recognize the overtone series as a valid means to underscore the titanic shift then taking place in the West: from a contrapuntal (modal) orientation of composition to one based on keys, chords, and chordal relationship—that is, tonal harmony, as we unwound in Chapter 4.

Compared to Rameau, my assertion is much less lofty: it is simply that nature's overtone series helped provide the scaffolding upon which our taste—indeed obsession—for major and minor triads, as well as dominant 7th chords, could be built. It was, for example, their "inevitable" appeal that led English musicians in the fourteenth century to experiment with the tuning of 3rds that would enable these constructs to sound in the first place. How we've come to use them functionally says as much about our cultural identity and evolution as anything else, as we'll discuss in Interlude E. But the fact that we have become so fond of them—for *that*, I say, we can blame Mother Nature! As such, if we do ever succeed in hearing a tune or two from that bar band in Andromeda, we'd very likely hear not only the structural use of octaves, 5ths, and 4ths, but also a smattering of major triads, minor triads, and even dominant 7th chords. Certainly, if we want to know why we humans like "Louie Louie," "Music of the Night," or Schubert's "Ave Maria," to name but three, we have at least a partial answer: the overtones told us to.

Two final points: First, we should remember that not all sounds produce harmonic (integer-multiple-based) partials; instead, most sounds we hear produce inharmonic partials, whereby no single pitch can be discerned. At the same time, it is not only musical instruments that produce harmonic partials—think of birdsong, or the distinct pitch one hears when a steady wind passes through tree branches; as such, the basis for our auditory perception of triads far preceded our musical use of them.

Secondly, and very importantly: Upper partials play a role not only in harmony but also in the actual sound, or timbre, of the instruments that generate the music we hear—including the human voice: the relative strength or volume of those partials is what distinguishes the sound of a piano from a bassoon, for example. We'll continue that exploration in Chapter 7 on music and the brain!

Indeed, let's take a break from the extramusical musings and return to the practical matters of the music itself, with our last two parameters: form and sound.

part three

# UNITY AND HETEROGENEITY

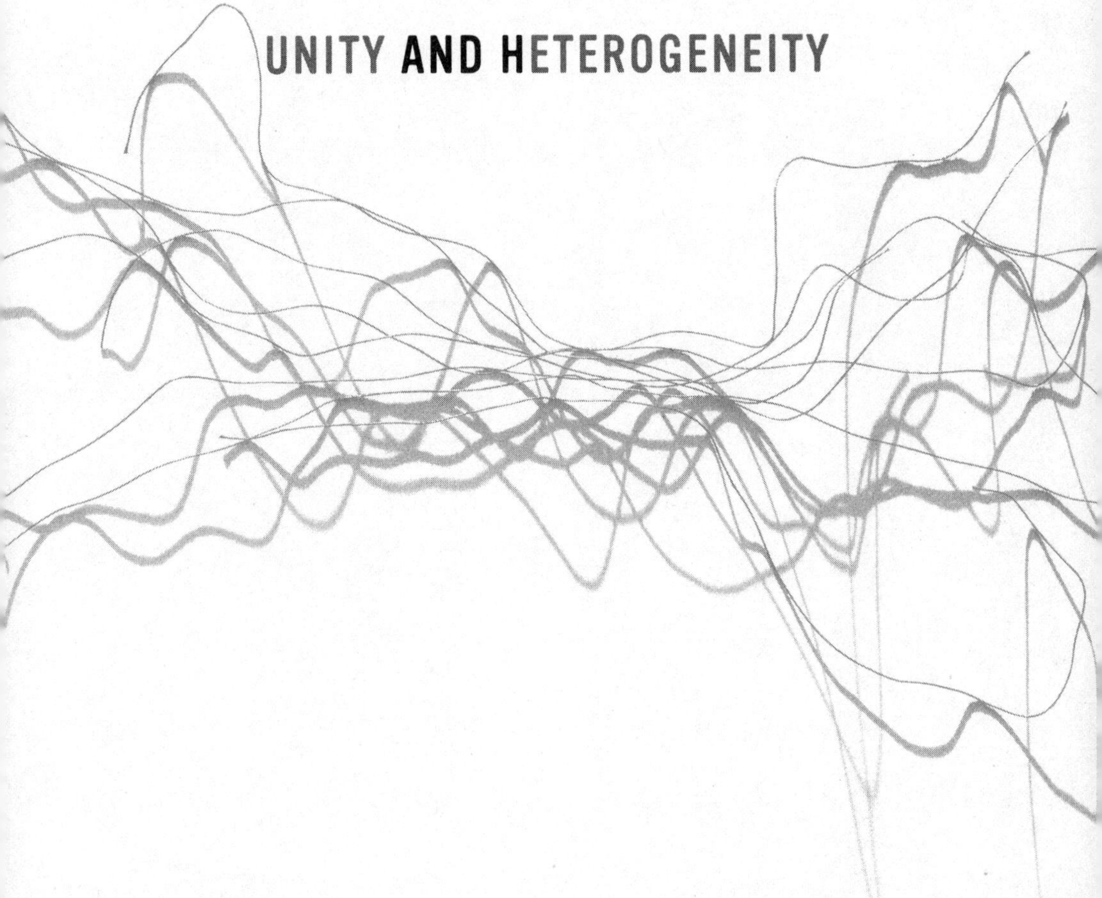

*six*

# FORM: THE SHAPE OF MUSIC

In "The Critic as Artist," Oscar Wilde's 1891 dialogic essay extolling critical contemplation, he writes:

> Form is everything. It is the secret of life. Find expression for a sorrow, and it will become dear to you. Find expression for a joy, and you intensify its ecstasy. . . . [I]t is Form that creates not merely the critical temperament, but also the aesthetic instinct, that unerring instinct that reveals to one all things under their conditions of beauty. Start with the worship of form, and there is no secret in art that will not be revealed to you. . . . [217]

For Wilde, our ability to access the "secrets" held within a work of art—whether a meaningful emotion, a precious image, or an aesthetic insight—requires that we first appreciate its form. **Form** is the vessel that holds the shape of the artwork, but is also the means whereby we discern its structure, design, and discourse. As poet Robert Hass has similarly expressed, the form of a poem is where we find "the shape of its understanding . . . not tone, not imagery, however deep or subtle, not particular qualities of content."[218] From this perspective, form is our window into the truth that resides in an artwork; it is the vehicle by which it succeeds or fails; and it is the reigning source to which all mere content is subordinate. And if this is the case, any true experience we might have listening to a song or musical work—and thus as impacting our musical taste—requires us to encounter its form.

Be prepared, though: musical form is a big and rather abstract topic. Unlike melody, harmony, and rhythm, you don't *hear* form; instead you experience it. As such, musicologists talk about it in a very different manner than they do the other, "tangible" parameters: more philosophical, more methodological, and more historically grounded. And so shall we here.

Okay, so what is musical form? The word "form" itself has multiple definitions, in and out of the arts, starting in *Merriam-Webster*'s dictionary with "the shape and structure of something as distinguished from its material."[219] Indeed, this notion of form as being "distinguished from" other things seems to be part of its very essence: form versus function, form versus matter, form versus content, etc. And yet, while the distinction is often highlighted, so too is the integration. As Frank Lloyd Wright famously said, "Form follows function—that has been misunderstood. Form and function should be one, joined in a spiritual union."[220] In musical works too, form cannot be wholly separated from the materials or content contained therein, although it can—and must, so it seems—be acknowledged in its own right. The key, though, is to do so with an awareness that form without actual content is but an abstraction. Wilde says, "Start with the worship of form," but the pursuit doesn't end there. Reverence of form must be accompanied by an appreciation of the limitless variety of detail that composers can bring to enliven it.

By way of anthropomorphic simile, it is a rather simple leap to align form with bodily shape. When we encounter someone, the "shape and structure" of their body—height, weight, girth, build, etc.—provide us with a valuable first impression. So much of who they are emanates from their external form, and yet it by no means tells the whole story. Indeed, their bodily shape can be a poor indicator of their potential—artistically, intellectually, spiritually, and even physically. At the same time, without their external bodily form, there can be no internal achievements in the first place; the two are indeed joined in "spiritual union."

## Unity and Heterogeneity

Beyond such philosophical and aesthetic abstractions, musical form is understood as the "constructive or organizing element in music," the basic plan or "architecture" it follows.[221] A song or work's musical form is, in essence, the sequence of its divisible sections, and the ways in which these sections relate to one another from beginning to end. In this context, a key strategy in discerning form is to determine the existence of repetition, contrast, and/or variation from one section to another. These are not the only terms used to describe the relationship between sections of a song or work, as we'll see, but they subsume much of the interaction. Indeed, musical form is in many ways a sort of balancing act between strict repetition on the one hand and unending contrast on the other, with each individual work falling somewhere on this continuum.

From this dynamic arises the question of unity or cohesion within a song or work, the documenting of which is often a principal task of music analysis. Rare indeed are works that provide absolutely no coherent link of material between any one section and another. A principal dimension of form, therefore, is the manner and degree to which this coherence is manifest—whether significant and obvious (e.g., a repeated chorus with identical melody and lyrics), or limited and subtle (e.g., the varied repetition of a short melodic motive in a symphony). The focus on unity within musicology, not to mention the ample manifestations of coherence within musical works, especially from the Renaissance, has given rise to postulations of not just coherent organization but "organicism"—that the unity exhibited is akin to that which exists in living organisms. The analogy between artworks and living entities has its roots in Plato and Aristotle, such as articulated in the latter's *Poetics*, written around 350 BCE with regard to drama:

> Tragedy is a representation of an action that is whole and complete and of a certain magnitude, since a thing may be a whole and yet have no magnitude. A whole is what has a beginning and middle and end. . . . In everything that is beautiful, whether it be a living creature or any organism composed of parts, these parts must not only be orderly arranged but must also have a certain magnitude of their own; for beauty consists in magnitude and ordered arrangement.[222]

The exaltation of organic unity as the measure of artistic success was subsequently adopted for other arts as well, especially during the late eighteenth and nineteenth centuries.[223] Among influential articulations of organicism with regard to music is that by the twentieth-century music theorist Heinrich Schenker, who in his 1935 treatise *Free Composition* wrote—in his typically overwrought style:

> Every linear progression shows the eternal shape of life-birth to death. The progression begins, lives its own existence in the passing tones, and ceases when it has reached its goal—all as organic as life itself.[224]

Translation: Every musical masterpiece, when distilled down to its analytical essence—namely, a single melodic-line summary of the entire work—can be likened to an organic being: from birth, through life's ups and downs, to its end.

But the bandwagon of musical organicism also has its critics, especially of the way it tends to downplay the variety, uniqueness, and "inorganic" heterogeneity that an individual work can apply through its materials and techniques.[225] This is particularly true with regard to classical works written since 1950, but is also worth bearing in mind when considering—and listening to—works of any period or style. Form is not formula, and though many songs and works can readily be attributed to an established formal template, as we'll see, it is equally important to acknowledge the ways in which each individual work deviates, or not, from the generic norms of that form. Careful reflection on the "whole" may indeed yield discoveries of organic unity, but likewise a wealth of heterogeneity, on both the compositional and performance fronts. As another theorist, A. B. Marx (who, incidentally, coined the term "sonata form"), wrote:

> The number of forms is unlimited, and there are ultimately no laws dictating what form a particular composition should take. . . . [Form is] the way in which the content of a work—the composer's conception, feeling, idea—outwardly acquires shape. . . . There are as many forms as works of art.[226]

## The Basics of Form

Before addressing the principal ways to define and delineate formal sections of a song or musical work, it is probably wise to define exactly what we mean by "section." In truth, this may be easier said than done. While in some cases there is little ambiguity on where a distinct section begins and ends, in many other cases it is not so simple. Much like the aural identification of the placement of the principal "beat" discussed in Chapter 5, what one person identifies as a distinct section may be deemed as two sections (or half a section, etc.) by another, and in fact they may both be right. One's individual perception, as well as perhaps a particular analytical "agenda," may influence one assessment versus another—as indeed a single observer may recognize the simultaneous validity of two or more orientations. From a listening experience and musical-taste perspective, moreover, the actual breakdown of formal sections is far less important than the overall impression of formal clarity or obtuseness, of simplicity or complexity, etc.

Let's begin to wrap our minds around form—and the identification of formal sections—by using our trusted standby, "Old MacDonald" (Figure 6.1):

**Figure 6.1: "Old MacDonald"—broad formal structure**

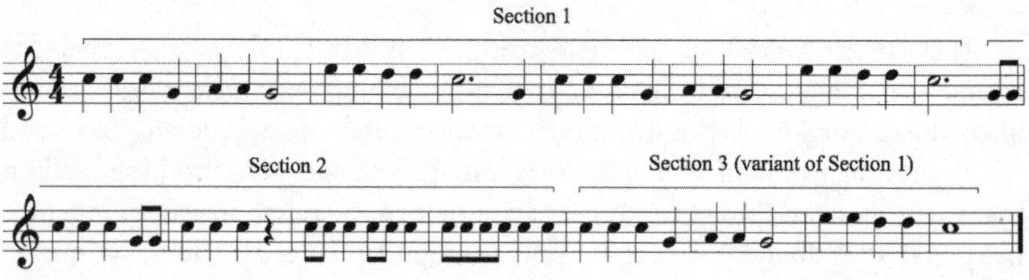


As shown in the above, this simple nursery rhyme can be divided into three distinct sections, where the third is a partial repeat of the first.

Drilling down, we can articulate a few additional levels of formal delineation. The primary, "intrasectional" subdivision is at the level of the phrase, as has been discussed in the context of a melody in Chapter 3, where it was likened to a sentence. The musical phrase is a coherent "remark," perhaps articulated or delimited with a weak or partial cadence, but it is not yet a complete "statement," not yet a full paragraph. In musicological terms, a phrase is somewhere between a "motive" (like a clause) and a "section" (like a paragraph). A phrase may itself contain elements of internal repetition, much as a single line of poetry can contain an internal rhyme, but again is not normally a fully articulated argument.

Here again is "Old MacDonald," now defined at the level of the phrase (Figure 6.2):

**Figure 6.2: "Old MacDonald"—formal structure at the level of the phrase**

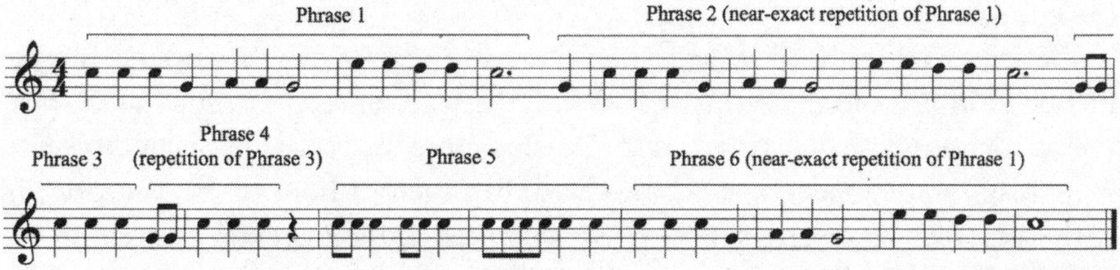


When two or more phrases are joined together to make a complete argument or musical statement, however, we enter the realm of a true formal subdivision. As just noted, we will use the word "**section**" to describe this higher level of organization, although the term "period" is sometimes used in formal musicological settings.[227] One defining notion of a section is that it "extends until its harmonic action has come to a close"—that is, ending with a strong and well-articulated cadence.[228] The length of a "complete" melodic-harmonic statement can vary, of course, but typical are passages of eight, twelve, sixteen, or thirty-two measures—each divided into two, three, or four phrases.

Common too is the presence of symmetry, where a section is divided into two relatively equal halves. In such simple cases, the first phrase is usually "open" (called the **antecedent**), while the second phrase is "closed" (called the **consequent**).[229] This can also be likened to a question and an answer—with the latter typically concluding with a strongly articulated cadence. Of course, composers have found innumerable ways to expand the disposition and length of their sections well beyond this simple orientation, as we'll see.

But first, here is another familiar nursery rhyme—"Mary Had a Little Lamb"—seen from the standpoint of antecedent and consequent (Figure 6.3):

**Figure 6.3: "Mary Had a Little Lamb"—antecedent-consequent structure**

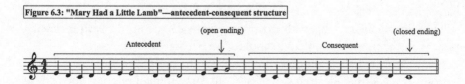

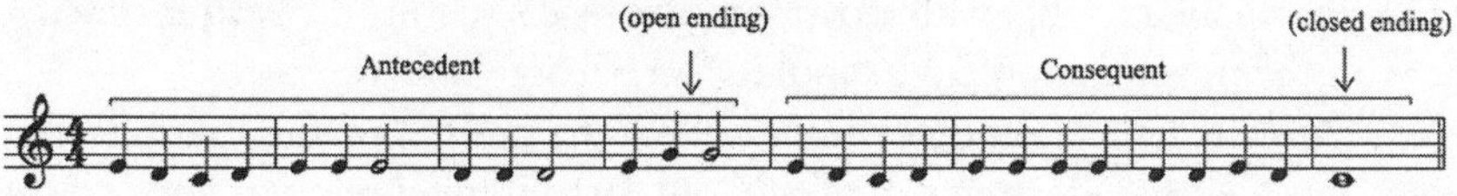

As seen already in "Old MacDonald," it is common—in folk, popular, and classical settings—for two distinct sections to be grouped together to comprise a full song or work, or the principal parts therein. The two sections can each appear once or, more commonly, alternate back and forth—as in "Old MacDonald." In addition, the two sections can be either contrasting or complementary to one another by virtue of their musical content, or some point in between. Especially when complementary, the two sections often display their own symmetry, even as symmetry exists internally within each section. Such is often the case, for example, in pop and rock songs, where the **verse** becomes a sort of "antecedent" to the **chorus**.

When analytically labeling sections, varying conventions are used. One approach is to use specific terms that define the roles of sections, such as "intro," "verse," "chorus," "exposition," "coda," etc. A more universal approach, however, is to assign uppercase letters (A, B, C, etc.) to each distinct musical section; in such cases, lowercase letters (a, b, c, etc.) are used to designate the content of the individual phrases (or subsections) within each section. The two levels (section/phrase) can then be put together to identify collectively which section and which phrase is being discussed, such A-a, A-b, B-c, etc. *Exact* musical repetitions are given the same letters; contrasting musical sections and phrases are given different letters; *varied* repetitions (involving some notable change) of the music are given "primed" letters (e.g., A', A"—meaning two distinct variations); here are a few examples:

**A-A** = exact repetition of the same musical section
**A-A'** = the second musical section is a varied repetition of the first
**A-B** = two distinct musical sections in succession
**A-a—A-b** = one musical section (A), divided into two distinct phrases (a and b)
**A-a—A-b—B-c—A'-b'** = three successive musical sections: the first (A) is divided into two distinct phrases (a and b); the second (B) is a contrasting section, consisting of a single phrase (c); and the third (A') is a varied repetition of the first, consisting of only a variation of the original second phrase (b')

I here provide this level of explanation since below and in subsequent music-based chapters I will be making use of this letter-based convention. Fear not that it will turn into alphabet soup: with repetition, and by comparing the written descriptions with the music examples, it should soon become quite intuitive.

As a test case, here is another simple song—the traditional English folk song "Greensleeves"—that illustrates all of the concepts and methods described above:

Figure 6.4: "Greensleeves"—formal design

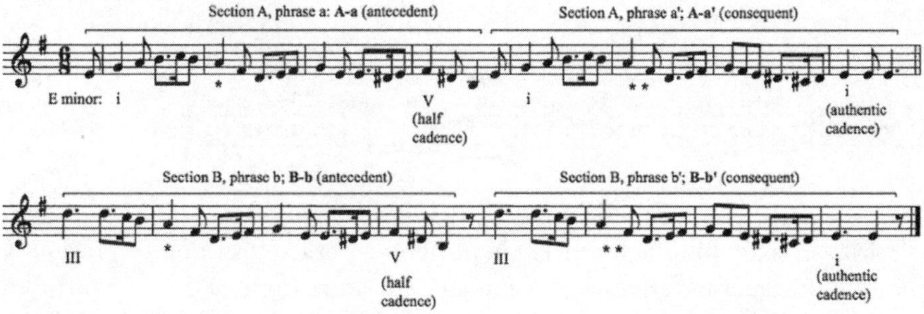


As seen, the song is in two sections, labeled A and B. The A section is divided into two phrases, with the second a varied repetition of the first—thus labeled A-a and A-a', respectively. It will be noted too that the first phrase, A-a, ends with a half cadence (to B major in the key of E minor), while the second phrase, A-a', starts the same but ends on a strong authentic cadence (to E minor). Similarly, the B section is divided into two phrases, where once again the second is a varied repetition of the first—thus labeled B-b and B-b', respectively. Likewise, the two phrases progress from a half cadence at the end of B-b to an authentic cadence at the end of B-b'.

The full diagram would thus be: A-a—A-a'—B-b—B-b'.

This example also partakes of symmetry, where each individual section (A and B) is divided into two even halves that balance each other as a predictable antecedent (question) and consequent (answer). Further, the two sections display their own overall symmetry: the final three measures of the antecedent and consequent of both sections are identical, harmonically and melodically (that is, measures 2 to 4 and 10 to 12 are the same as measures 6 to 8 and 14 to 16—marked * and **, respectively, in Figure 6.4).

## The Principal Functions: Repetition, Contrast, and Variation

Our review of "Greensleeves" underscores the role of three principal functions of formal distinction: repetition, contrast, and variation. Let's now clarify these further.

At one extreme of the formal spectrum is **strict repetition**—repeating a section of music exactly, either in immediate succession or subsequently. In written notation an immediate repetition is often indicated with a double line and vertical dots marking the start and end points, as on the next page (Figure 6.5):

**Figure 6.5: J. S. Bach, Polonaise in G Minor (from *Anna Magdalena Notebook*)—strict repetition**

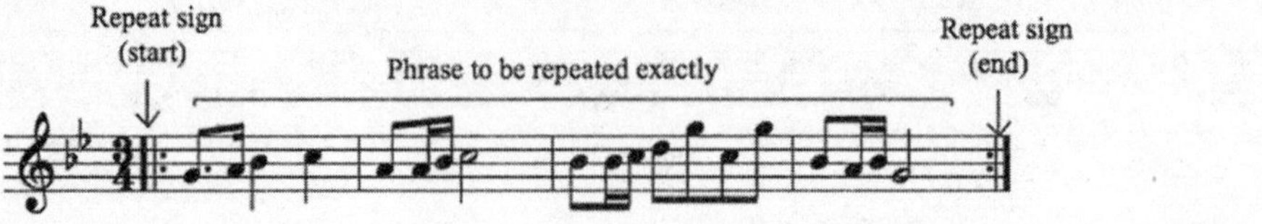


Many classical music forms are built upon an exact repetition of previously heard music later in the work—including both sonata form and rondo form. In popular music too, a subsequent exact repetition of a previous section is quite common—most notably via a recurring "chorus" or **refrain** containing the same music and text. We'll discuss many such cases in both realms below.

Of course, repetitions are not always exact, but can be varied in some regard—new vocal ornaments, an added instrument, and so forth. Indeed, we call this technique **varied repetition**. So long as the basic material—melody, chords, rhythms, etc.—are maintained, we'll generally still hear it as a repetition, even while acknowledging that something has changed.

This is what takes place, for example, in a pop song when the singer presents some ornamental melodic variation in the second, third, and fourth chorus; or when the melody of the second verse is altered subtly to accommodate different lyrics. Here is an example of varied repetition in subsequent verses of a song by Adele (Figure 6.6):

**Figure 6.6: Adele, "Hello" (start of verses 1 and 3)—varied repetition**

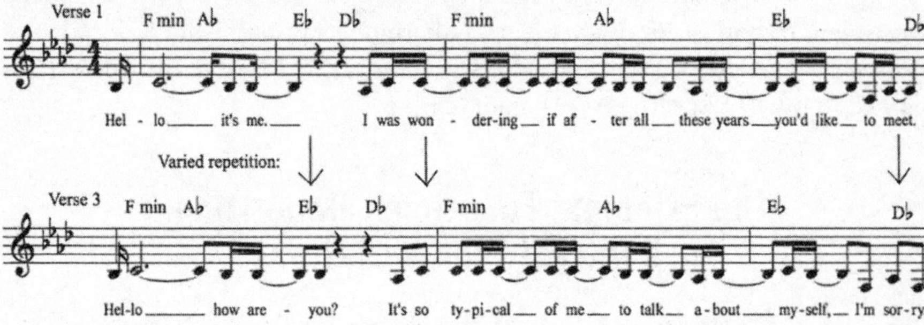


Varied repetition is a staple of music making in all styles and approaches. It simultaneously satisfies our desire for unity and heterogeneity. It is regularly employed, for example, in rock, jazz, and world music contexts by virtue of the focus in these realms on melodic ornamentation and improvisation.

In classical music, varied repetition can give new life and narrative momentum to subsequent occurrences of a principal theme. A famous example is that used on the theme (A section) of Chopin's Nocturne in E♭, which returns twice. In diagramming this approach, the three repeated sections would be labeled A, A', and A" (Figure 6.7).

**Figure 6.7: Frédéric Chopin, Nocturne in E♭, Op. 9, no. 2 (three passes at primary theme)—varied repetition**

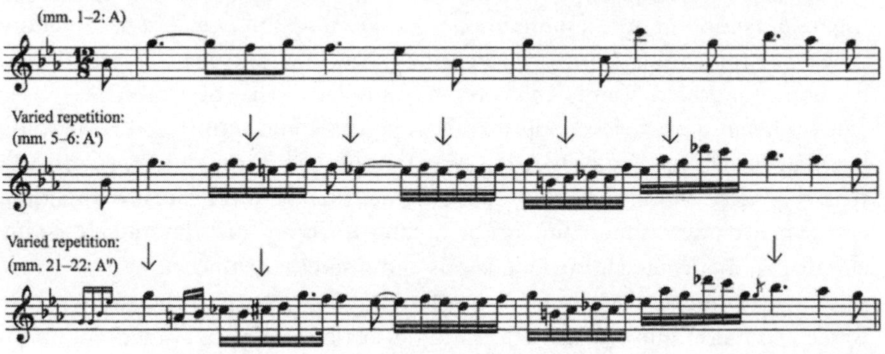
(mm. 1–2: A)
Varied repetition:
(mm. 5–6: A')
Varied repetition:
(mm. 21–22: A")

At times varied repetition can itself create considerable aural contrast, if the elements that are varied are significantly dramatic—for example, drastic increases in dynamics (volume), register (pitch placement), and/or instrumentation. An example of all three is the opening movement of Carl Orff's *Carmina Burana*—which we'll review in detail in connection to Chapter 15; here contrast is seen between the passage at "*semper crescis*" (measure 5) and its repetition at "*Sors salutis*" (measure 61):

**Figure 6.8: Carl Orff, "O Fortuna" (from *Carmina Burana*), soprano part—varied repetition via aural contrast**

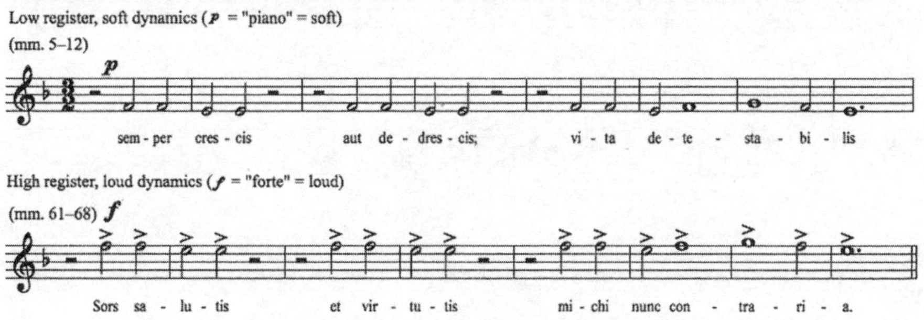
Low register, soft dynamics (p = "piano" = soft)
(mm. 5–12)
p
sem - per cres - cis aut de - dres - cis; vi - ta de - te - sta - bi - lis
High register, loud dynamics (f = "forte" = loud)
(mm. 61–68) f
Sors sa - lu - tis et vir - tu - tis mi - chi nunc con - tra - ri - a.

We next turn to the opposite side of the formal spectrum: **contrast**. Given the instinctive tendency to generate some level of organic cohesion within a song or musical work, one can plausibly argue the existence of some level of "relatedness" even in the most seemingly contrasting passages. Yet on a surface and especially experiential level, contrast is as essential to the musical arts as is repetition. Without the introduction of contrast to a repeating musical passage, no matter how beautiful, one eventually gets bored. Of course, one similarly loses interest without an eventual return of familiar material. Indeed, it is the interplay of repetition and contrast that in many ways defines the musical form of most songs and works.

Contrast, of course, comes in many shades, from slight to complete. From a listening standpoint, it can sometimes be hard to pinpoint exactly *why* something is heard as contrasting, even if we are certain it is. A chorus may have a melodic, harmonic, and/or rhythmic character very similar to that of a preceding verse, and yet it can nonetheless appear to us as palpably and unmistakably new. The fact that the chorus has a repeating lyric (as opposed to the different lyrics of a repeating verse melody) certainly plays a role. But there is generally something else at play as well, some "hooky" or notable quality about the melody and/or chords that marks the chorus in our ears and minds as distinct.

Not every musical contrast involves leading into a "hooky" chorus, of course. Rather, contrast concerns any delineation into a new section. Sometimes, moreover, the contrast is anything but subtle, and will instead involve dramatic changes within one or more musical parameters. Composers and performers make use of dramatic contrast to grab the listener's attention as well as to generally heighten the aural impact of the music. Dramatic contrasts most commonly occur between significant structural subdivisions, or sections, of a song or work. Here are two well-known examples (Figure 6.9 and 6.10):

**Figure 6.9: Chick Corea, "Spain"—dramatic constrast in subsequent sections**

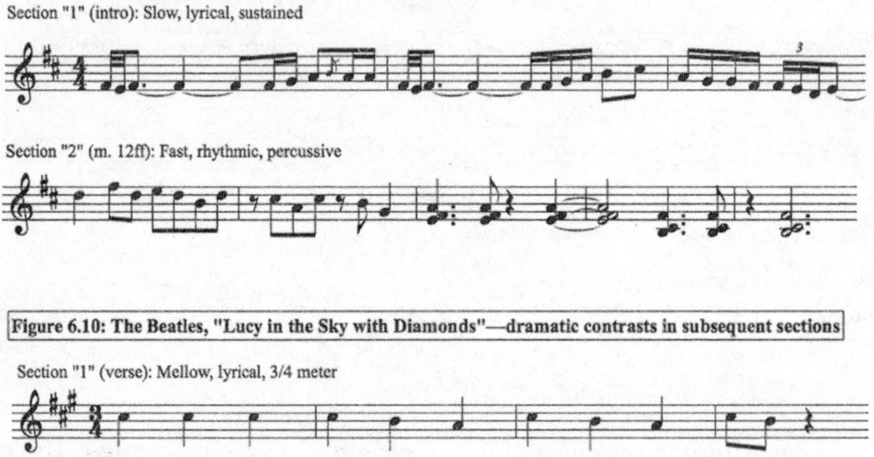
Section "1" (intro): Slow, lyrical, sustained
Section "2" (m. 12ff): Fast, rhythmic, percussive

**Figure 6.10: The Beatles, "Lucy in the Sky with Diamonds"—dramatic contrasts in subsequent sections**

Section "1" (verse): Mellow, lyrical, 3/4 meter
Pic - ture your - self in a boat on a ri - ver
Section "2" (chorus): Rhythmic, anthemic, 4/4 meter
Lu - cy - in the sky— with dia - monds, Lu - cy in the sky— with dia - monds

More common, though, are contrasts that fall somewhere in between the extremes just described: a subsequent section that presents content that is new and distinct, though not radically so. The trick from a compositional standpoint is to introduce material that provides sonic freshness and yet is heard as coming inevitably, organically out of what preceded it—carrying forth the musical narrative in a way that a listener finds reasonable and compelling. Here are some random examples, ranging from near varied repetition to near dramatic contrast—the latter using a work highlighted in Chapter 3:

**Figure 6.11: Kenny Rogers, "The Gambler"—near-varied repetition in subsequent sections**

**Figure 6.12: Collective Soul, "December"—slightly varied contrast in subsequent sections**

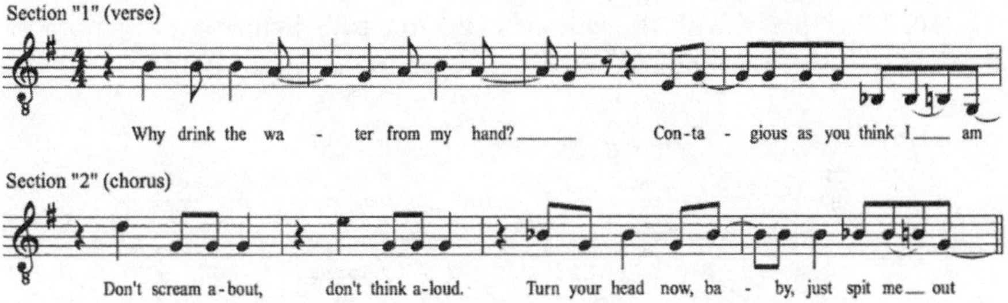


**Figure 6.13: Kurt Weill, "September Song"—moderate contrast in subsequent sections**

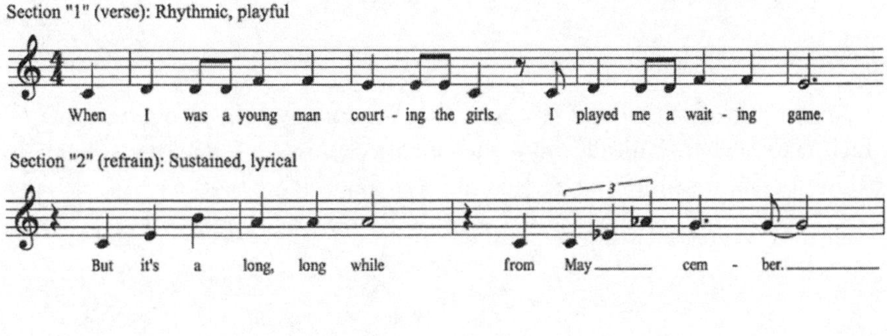

**Figure 6.14: Maurice Ravel, String Quartet, 2. Assez vif—near dramatic contrast in subsequent sections**

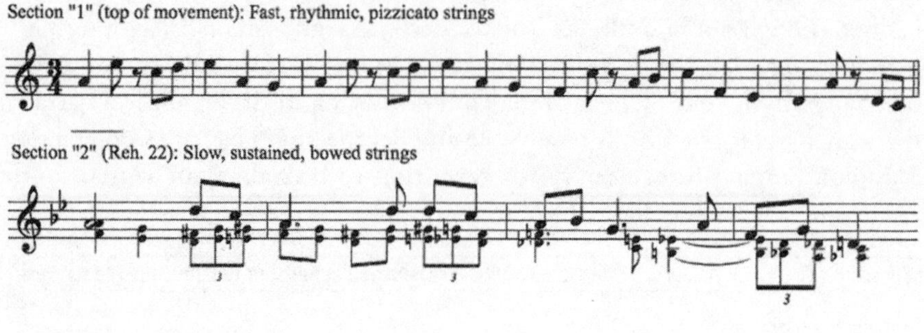


Okay, with all that as preparation, we are now ready to undertake a more involved exercise in formal analysis! For our next case study, we'll use a staple of early piano lessons, Beethoven's "Für Elise"—which I'm sure many of you played as a kid. This piece allows for a nice review of strict repetition, varied repetition, and various degrees of contrast. It also enables us to witness the multiple levels at which formal subdivision can take place. And yet, while some of you may be a ball of enthusiasm, others may be less so. As such, we'll present only the first main section of the piece (measures 1–24), along with some overall comments, in the body of the text. The remainder of the analysis, including notational excerpts, will be presented on the WYLI website—whereby you can indulge or bypass as you see fit.

"Für Elise" opens with the famous main "theme," divided into two phrases (A-a—A-a'), which is repeated exactly via repeat signs (Figure 6.15):

**Figure 6.15: Beethoven, "Für Elise" (mm. 1–9)—formal schema of opening section**

At the end of the second repeat of the A theme, we move to a new section, which takes us harmonically from the key of A minor to C major—the relative major—before transitioning back to the A theme (Figure 6.16):

Figure 6.16: Beethoven, "Für Elise" (mm. 10–24)—formal schema of subsequent section

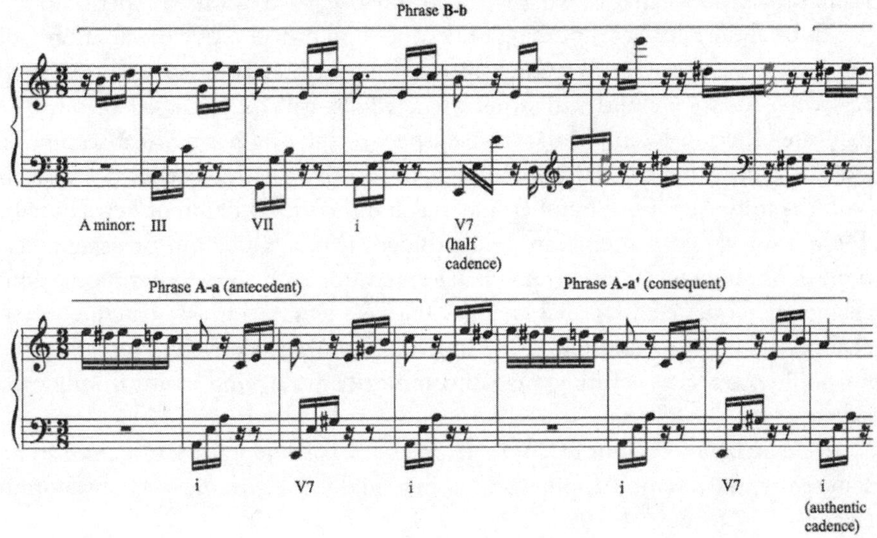


The passage starting in measure 10 is rather similar to material of the A theme in terms of melodic rhythm and accompaniment pattern, and yet by virtue of its harmonic shift and distinctive melodic contour is heard as new—a new B section, so it seems. It's unusually short, however, containing only one phrase (B-b) that leads to a half cadence (to E7) in the "home key" of A minor (measure 13). At that point we hear an exact repetition of the A section (both phrases, A-a—A-a'). The entire B section along with the following A are then repeated together.

Thus, so far it would seem that the form follows this layout: A-A-B-A-B-A.

As it turns out, however, this is *not* the best interpretation of the musical proceedings—at least as follows upon a careful review of the piece in its entirety. Instead, these opening twenty-four measures collectively represent only the first, large-scale A section (as A-a—A-a'—A-b—A-a—A-b—A-a') in what is in fact an overall formal schema of A-B-A-C-A, which is the classical structure of a rondo form. Again, for those so inclined, the remaining analysis of "Für Elise"—wherein the rondo form is revealed—can be found on the WYLI website (supplement to Chapter 6).

The third principal function of formal distinction is **variation**, which holds a kind of middle ground between repetition and contrast. Variation as a concept is common to a multiplicity of disciplines in the sciences as well as the arts, defined broadly by *Merriam-Webster*'s as "something that is similar to something else but different in some way." As a general musical tendency, variation is certainly archetypal, and must have arisen among primitive musicians to maintain the listener's (and musician's) interest while repeating an established melody or rhythm via improvisation—that is, what we've already discussed as varied repetition.[230]

To be clear, I am here speaking of the function or technique of variation—of varying musical content in some way—and not of the actual *formal template of variations* (or theme and variations, etc.), which will be discussed below. The requisite criterion is simply that some aspect of the original musical section be altered, while other aspects are maintained. In this way, the listener can discern both the reappearance of familiar material and the introduction of new content. The new or varied content can be anything: melodic alteration or ornamentation; rhythmic, metric, or tempo changes; harmonic changes (reharmonization, change of mode, etc.); formal changes (passage length, phrase structure, etc.); changes in instrumentation, etc.—individually or collectively. Naturally, the possibilities are vast, as is the range of complexity in carrying it out, from low to extreme.

Here are a few famous examples from the classical repertory to demonstrate some common variation approaches, from a mild to an extreme level of variation (Figures 6.17 through 6.19):

**Figure 6.17: W. A. Mozart, *Variations on "Ah, vous dirai-je Maman"* (Theme, Var. 2)—mild variation**

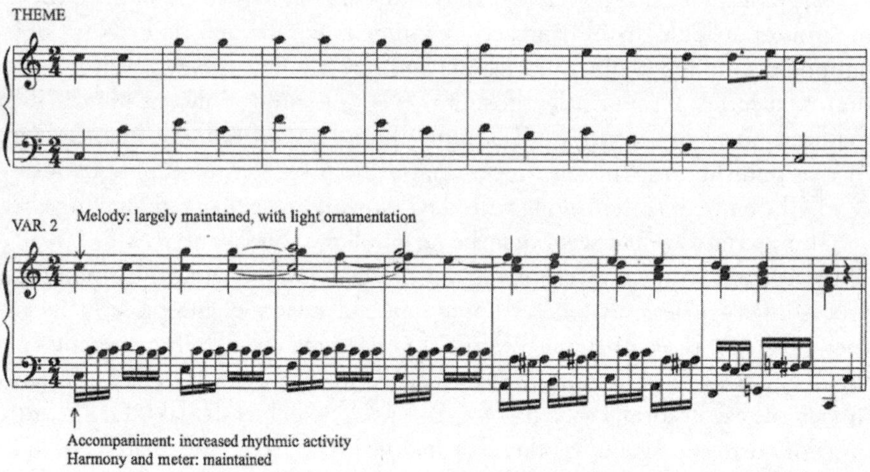

**Figure 6.18: Johannes Brahms, *Variations on a Theme by Haydn* (Theme, Var. 1)—moderate variation**

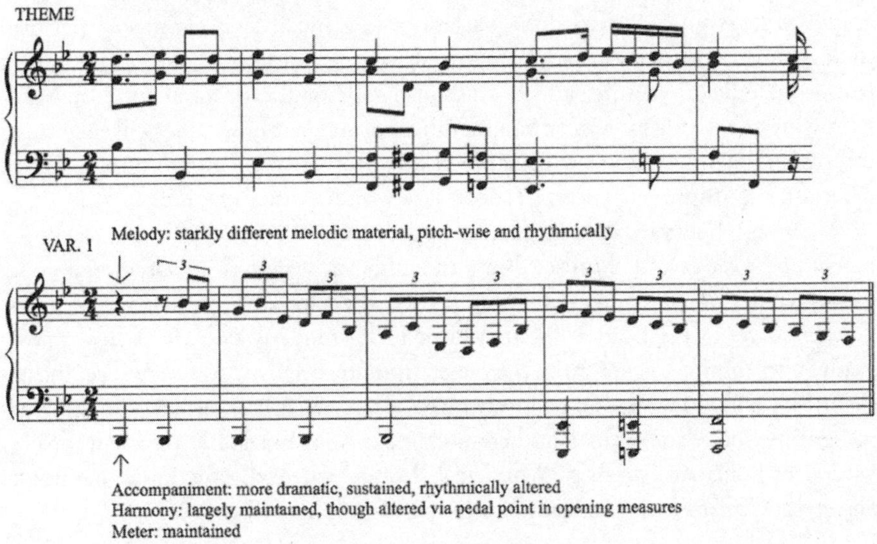


**Figure 6.19: Sergei Rachmaninov, *Rhapsody on a Theme of Paganini* (Theme, Var. 18)—extreme variation**

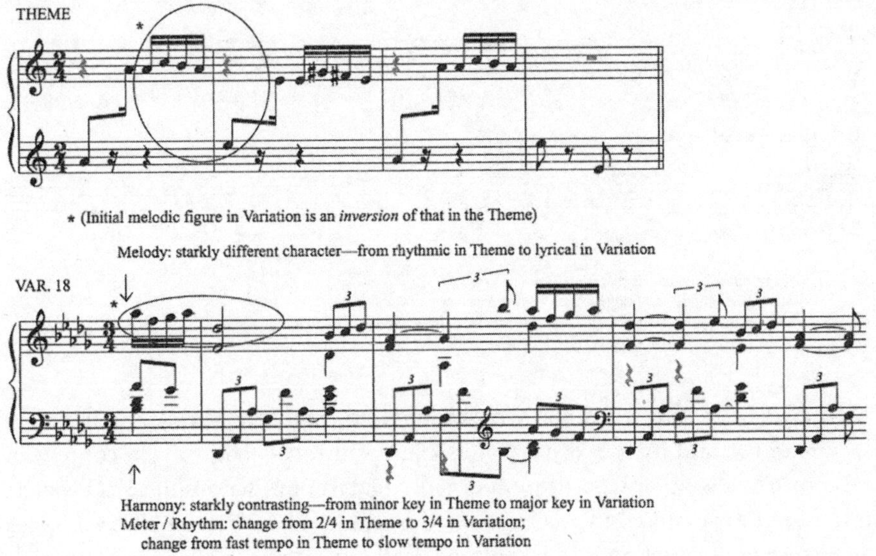


These examples illustrate how variation has amply enabled classical composers to flex their technical muscles—or "chops," as we musicians like to say. Indeed, as the example from Rachmaninov alone reveals, variation can so stretch the original material as to render it virtually unrecognizable except through rigorous analysis.

Again, variation is an archetypal compositional practice, and thus by no means limited to the notated repertoire of Western classical music. Jazz, for example, is largely predicated upon variation: jazz musicians commonly perform their own (varied) version of a recognized song or **standard**, applying variation to the melodic, rhythmic, and harmonic details of the original tune or **head**. Following the head, moreover, the members of the jazz ensemble will take turns improvising a solo based on its same chord progression—a common variation technique. Without variation, in short, jazz would cease to be jazz.

We've seen how variation is a staple of pop and rock music as well—e.g., via varied repetition in verses and choruses. But a more holistic approach to variation also occurs whenever one artist "covers" a tune by another. One well-known example is Joe Cocker's cover of the Beatles' "With a Little Help from My Friends," where among many other things, Cocker varies the meter, from the original's 4/4 to 3/4, yet the basic melody and lyrics are kept relatively intact. Thus, we as listeners have no difficulty recognizing the relationship. Another famed example is Israel "Iz" Kamakawiwo'ole's version of Louis Armstrong's "Wonderful World," where the rhythmic, harmonic, and stylistic nature is dramatically altered—as shown here (Figure 6.20):

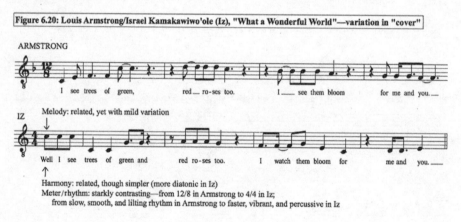

**Figure 6.20: Louis Armstrong/Israel Kamakawiwo'ole (Iz), "What a Wonderful World"—variation in "cover"**

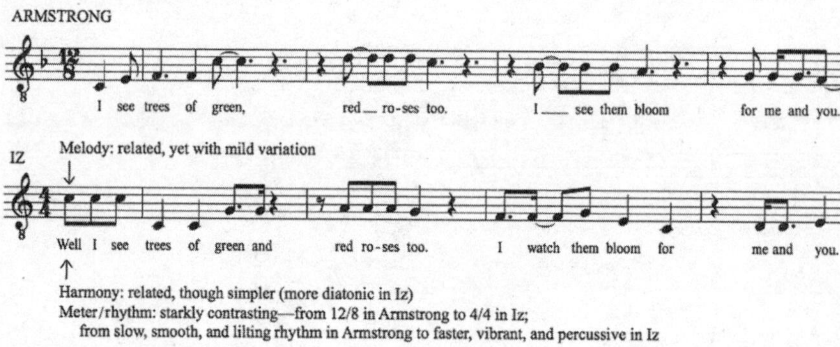


The impulse that Iz or Joe Cocker—not to mention Mozart, Brahms, or Rachmaninov, and most every jazz musician in history—had to vary content in the course of a song or work is undoubtedly tied to our own impulse as listeners to want to hear material that is at once fresh and familiar. One might even go so far as to say that variation is the "mother" of all music, since only by varying what already exists do new musical insights reveal themselves, including to us and our musical taste.

## Common Formal Templates

Before providing a rundown of several specific and commonly used musical forms, it will be useful to articulate a few of the principal types or *templates* that underlie them. Most of these formal templates, in fact, have already been described to some degree or another, even if not explicitly labeled.

The principal formal templates are strophic, binary, ternary, rondo, variations, and through-composed. We'll name and/or provide examples for each as we go.

### STROPHIC

**Strophic** is a musical form in which a single section (A) is repeated two or more times with little or no deviation among repetitions, thus carrying a diagrammatic plan of A-A-A-A, etc. Traditionally, strophic works are vocal, where each poetic stanza or verse is sung to the same basic melody, rhythm, and harmony—with melodic changes merely accommodating variation in syllabic count. Where a more marked change occurs between subsequent sections, the form may be labeled as "modified strophic" or something similar—with a plan something like A-A'-A", etc. Modification can also take place by virtue of a contrasting introduction or some kind of contrasting transition between stanzas.

Well-known strophic songs include "Amazing Grace," Bob Dylan's "Blowin' in the Wind," and such traditional Christmas carols as "Deck the Halls" and "Silent Night."

Common strophic vocal forms include the hymn, ode, ballad, lieder, and various types of art, popular, and folk songs from multiple cultures. Strophic form is likewise fertile ground for instrumental music, especially in popular and jazz settings; this famously includes the 12-bar blues, but also jazz "standards"—where outside of an intro and "outro" (or **tag**), each section is based on the same chord progression.

### BINARY

A **binary** form, as the name suggests, has two alternating sections—that is, A-B or, when repeating, A-B-A-B, etc. The two sections need not be of equal length or structural importance, but they are both fundamental to the identity of the work, and in some way are dependent on each other. This is in contrast to a strophic song with an introductory section that appears only once, for example.

Some familiar examples include "Home on the Range," the Beatles' "Yellow Submarine," and the modern Christmas songs "Silver Bells" and "Jingle Bells."

In classical music, it is not uncommon for each section of a binary form to be repeated twice—that is, A-A-B-B. This is especially true for those forms associated with various dance styles (minuets, gavottes, galliards, etc.), as well as early instrumental sonatas. In classical binary forms, there is often a deliberate harmonic trajectory established between the two sections. The first will begin in the "home" or tonic key and then modulate to a "related" key—typically the dominant for a major key, the relative major for a minor key; the second section will then complete the journey, modulating back to the tonic. Other key, or modal, relationships are just as possible—as seen, for example, in "Greensleeves."

Another common trend in classical binary works is that material from the A section returns at the conclusion of the B section, though often only partially—much as we saw in the opening (A) section of Beethoven's "Für Elise." This approach is called **rounded binary**, since the B section is "rounded off" to include a return of some A material; for this reason, the B sections are generally longer. By contrast, a lack of any return of the A material results in a **simple binary** form. The rounded binary form is common in classical dance forms (and indeed often called "minuet form"), but also in nineteenth-century popular songs, such as those by Stephen Foster—as here (Figure 6.21):

**Figure 6.21: Stephen Foster, "My Old Kentucky Home" (lyrics omitted)—design of rounded binary form (A-BA)**

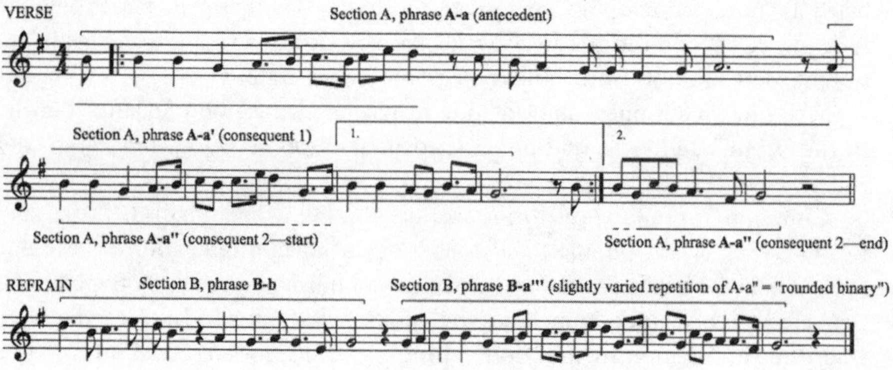


Binary form, or a modified version thereof, is also a default for contemporary pop and rock songs—that is, an alternation of verses (A) and choruses (B). In contrast to classical dance styles, however, it is more typical that both verse and chorus of a pop/rock song remain in the same key.

## TERNARY

**Ternary** form bears a resemblance to rounded binary form in that here too the A material returns at the end. However, unlike rounded binary, the B section is entirely contrasting and self-contained, followed by a complete return of the A section—that is, A-B-A. As musicologist W. Dean Sutcliffe notes, ternary form is "perhaps the most fundamental of musical forms, based on the natural principles of departure and return, and of thematic contrast then repetition."[231] This means too that both sections are generally "complete" (or "closed") harmonically, since the song or work will end with the conclusion of the A section, not the B.

Two examples include the nursery rhyme "Shoo Fly, Don't Bother Me" and John Williams' main theme to *Star Wars*.

Ternary form became popular among composers of the nineteenth-century "**character piece**" (generally for piano), including Chopin, Schumann, Brahms, and Grieg—where increasingly the second A section was subjected to some adaptation, that is A-B-A'. By contrast, the form was not strictly adopted into pop and rock music as a matter of course. However, examples suggesting ternary form do exist, such as the Beatles' "A Day in the Life"—which in truth is more like one long song ("I read the news today . . .") dissected by another, shorter one ("Woke up, fell out of bed . . .").

## RONDO

As can be seen through a full analysis—via the WYLI website—of "Für Elise," the **rondo** form follows a symmetrical plan of repetition and contrast, where an initial section (A) comes back in the middle as well as the end, broken up by two or more distinct and contrasting sections—such as A-B-A-C-A. The A section is sometimes referred to as the refrain and is generally in the tonic; the contrasting sections are called **episodes** and are generally in related keys. The notion of a steadily recurring theme or section is, like variations, rather archetypal—providing both familiarity and variety in a predictable and balanced pattern.

Perhaps the most famous example of a rondo is Mozart's "Rondo alla turca," or "Turkish Rondo," from his Piano Sonata in A Major, K. 331, whereas a somewhat unusual example in pop/rock music is "Every Breath You Take" by the Police.*

During the Baroque era, the rondo template was a popular device used in both vocal and instrumental music—where it is known as **ritornello** (little return) form. Ritornello form was used especially in the fast movements of concertos—works for soloist(s) and ensemble—such as in the famed *Brandenburg* Concertos of J. S. Bach. Here the full ensemble presents each returning refrain or ritornello, while the soloist(s) present the intervening episodes; the internal ritornelli, however, are generally performed as fragments, in various keys, thus only complete and in the tonic key at the beginning and end of the movement. In this way it is different from the later rondo form, wherein each refrain is complete and in the tonic.

The "classic" rondo form itself dates to seventeenth-century France in both

---

* Specifically, the form structure is: Chorus (A)—Verse (B)—Chorus (A)—Bridge (C)—Instrumental over Chorus (A)—Verse (B)—Chorus (A). This pattern is actually close to what is called a "symmetrical rondo," where the B section likewise returns: A-B-A-C-A-B-A.

vocal, especially opera, and instrumental music. It gained wide international adoption in the eighteenth and nineteenth centuries, especially as an instrumental movement within a larger form—such as Mozart's "Rondo alla turca." The popularity of the rondo naturally led to expansion. This includes the creation of internal binary or ternary patterns within each main section, as well as experimentation via thematic interplay between the sections, etc. Chief among these adaptions was the rondo's incorporation into sonata form, to create the sonata-rondo (see below), favored by composers like Mozart, Beethoven, and Brahms.

We should also note that the rondo template is also found commonly in various ethnic music styles, including in folk and dance songs of Nigeria, Bulgaria, Palestine, etc.—where the "episodes" are often improvisatory in nature.

## VARIATIONS/THEME AND VARIATIONS

We've discussed the technique and aesthetic of **variations** and its near-universal adoption as a musical archetype. It is then a small creative leap to turn this technique into an actual formal approach. As a template, variations is a kind of strophic form—that is, one section (A) that repeats several times, each iteration with one or more musical elements altered in some way (A-A'-A''-A''', etc.).

In the West, the template has its roots in the art of rhetoric or persuasion, for example, the Medieval *ars praedicandi*, or the art of giving a sermon, from the twelfth century—where a preacher is urged to first present an argument from Scripture (A), then reinforce it by amplification, elaboration, and rephrasing (A'-A''-A''').[232] Musically, such an approach can well "persuade" and please us through an artful combination of familiarity and contrast; at the same time, a simplistic or merely ornamental sequence of variations can create a hollow, disjointed listening experience if it lacks a quality of forward or narrative drive.

Musical works that display elements of variation—as a mix of technique and form—extend back to the Middle Ages and Renaissance, in both sacred and secular music. For example, the many "cantus firmus" (based on a Gregorian chant) or "parody" (based on a chanson or motet) Masses of the Renaissance present varied repetitions of the same music in each of their five movements. A stricter application of the variations template, however, originates in instrumental music, especially for dance. Initially, subsequent "variations" of a section were either improvised or presented as specifically rhythmic variations of the original—for example, twice as fast or slow.

Among the first formal "sets" of composed variations are Spanish diferencias from the early sixteenth century, instrumental works usually based on well-known songs, melodies, or bass/chordal patterns—such as the romanesca, which is the progression used in the second half of "Greensleeves." In the years that followed, various other terms were adopted to imply either a small set of one or two variations on an original theme or larger variation sets: "double," "partita," "division," "*mutanza*," and "*Veränderung*" (change), among many others. Bach adopted the latter term, in fact, for his famous *Goldberg Variations*—titling them *Aria mit verschiedenen Veränderungen* (Air with various changes). Of course, the expressions "variations" and "theme with variations" are also used.

Beginning in the seventeenth century, instrumental variation sets—especially for keyboard—became widespread, written in large numbers by composers such as Sweelinck, Scheidt, Frescobaldi, and Purcell. The variations themselves were often compositionally complex, stylistically varied, and virtuosic. Clearly, the variation form provided an inspiring vehicle whereby a composer could exercise his creativity while likewise gain popular enthusiasm.

This trend only increased into the Baroque and Classical periods, notably with the variations sets of Couperin, J. S. Bach, Handel, C. P. E. Bach, Haydn, Mozart, and Beethoven—who found increasingly sophisticated ways to incorporate variations into larger forms, including his symphonies. By the early nineteenth century, the variation set had increasingly become merely a shallow set of showpieces (e.g., those of Czerny and Moscheles), which in turn drew the disdain of more "serious" composers like Schumann (who nonetheless wrote several of his own variations sets). Brahms, by contrast, firmly embraced the variation set as a medium of serious and profound compositional activity (e.g., his *Variations on a Theme by Haydn*), a trend continued by composers like Elgar, Rachmaninov (e.g., the *Rhapsody on a Theme by Paganini*), and Britten. Despite its assumed tonal associations—that is, all variations would be in the same or at least related key—they were even popular among more "adventurous" twentieth-century composers like Schoenberg, Webern, Boulez, and Cage.[233]

In sum, few formal templates have proven more fertile than variations for classical composers, reinforcing both its archetypal nature and its potential to capture the interest and taste of listeners.

Beyond its archetypal presence as a musical technique, variation as a formal template, as a variation set, is fairly uncommon outside of Western classical music. "Theme and variation" is sometimes casually referenced in descriptive commentary of world music—e.g., in discussing the rhythmic (tabla) and melodic (sitar, sarod) parts of Indian ragas[234]—but to call these works variation sets would be incorrect. The same can be said for jazz and rock, where variation as a technique is ubiquitous, but the formal template is virtually nonexistent—Andrew Lloyd Webber's *Variations* for cello and rock band being the exception that proves the rule.

## THROUGH-COMPOSED

Our final formal template, **through-composed**, is in fact rather oxymoronic in this capacity: by definition, the term signifies a form that does not follow any set pattern or formula—so how can it be a template? The expression has several connotations, but principally implies a nonrepetitive, or at least nonformulaic, flow of continuous musical inspiration, where most if not all successive sections contain new musical material. The classic example is the through-composed setting of a strophic poem—e.g., Schubert's famous setting of "Der Erlkönig"—where each poetic verse is set to partly or entirely new music, as opposed to an actual strophic musical setting where each verse is set to the same music.

The expression, however, can also be used to describe any multipart work within classical music—such as a song cycle, a Mass cycle, a **sonata**, a **symphony**, a symphonic poem, an opera, etc. Somewhat confusedly, the term is often meant to imply that these distinct movements or parts have something that connects them, whereby the work as a whole is more unified—as in Berlioz' *Symphonie fantastique* (via a recurring melodic theme, called an "idée fixe") or Wagner's music dramas, via **leitmotifs** ("leading motives") where a single theme recurs across multiple movements or sections. Finally, the term can also refer to theatrical works that contain music throughout, with *no* spoken dialogue: this, for example, separates "through-sung" works like *Jesus Christ Superstar* and *Les Misérables* from the vast majority of Broadway shows that alternate songs with dialogue.

For our purposes, though, by "through-composed" we primarily mean the multisectional song or work noted above: where the flow of musical material is, for the most part, *continually new and nonrepetitive* from one section to the next—or at least to a degree outside of what might be expected given the "normal" flow of the musical species concerned.

Beyond the occasional through-composed song like "Der Erlkönig," this form template became common in classical music only in the twentieth century. This is especially the case among the postwar "avant-garde" composers like Messiaen, Xenakis, Boulez, and Stockhausen, though it also occurs in the "episodic" works of modernists like Stravinsky (e.g., *Symphonies of Wind Instruments*) and Schoenberg (e.g., Chamber Symphony, Op. 9). A through-composed approach then becomes rather a default among composers of the minimalist school, starting with Terry Riley's groundbreaking *In C.* As we'll discuss more in Chapter 13, through-composed minimalist music gradually unwinds and develops one or more musical ideas without truly "recapitulating" any previous musical section.[235]

In the realms of jazz and rock, through-composed form is largely synonymous with an experimental and/or uncommonly sophisticated approach—since the vast majority of songs in these genres conform to traditional, repeating structures (see below). Examples in jazz include expansive works by innovators like Charles Mingus (e.g., *Epitaph*), Weather Report (e.g., "Birdland"), and numerous compositions by Chick Corea, including a piano set called *Six Through-Composed Originals*, Pat Metheny, and Wynton Marsalis, among many others.

In rock music, some initial experiments in through-composed form came, not surprisingly, from the Beatles—famously in "Happiness Is a Warm Gun," which unfolds a formal scheme of A-B-C-C'-D-E-F-E'-E''. This admittedly shows a level of repetition and even recapitulation—E represents the section "Happiness is a warm gun"; F represents "When I hold you in my arms"—and yet, the overall form is clearly forward-driving, without reliance on any kind of recurring **verse-chorus** structure or a return of the opening material at the end.

As rock matured through the late 1960s and early 1970s, a number of other "progressive" rock artists likewise sought ways to expand the formal constraints of verse-chorus form, including with quasi- or fully through-composed structures. Celebrated examples include Queen's "Bohemian Rhapsody" and Genesis' "Me and Sarah Jane," as well as more decidedly experimental songs such as Frank Zappa's collage-like "Brown Shoes Don't Make It."[236] It should be noted, however, that a single through-composed song is distinct from a **medley** of connected songs or song sections, such as the Who's "A Quick One, While He's Away," Crosby, Stills & Nash's "Suite: Judy Blue Eyes," or the string of songs on side two of the Beatles' *Abbey Road*, from "You Never Give Me Your Money" to "The End."

In more recent, postmillennial years, rock artists aligned with various experimental subgenres—such as post-rock, math metal, neo-prog, etc.—have revealed their progressive aspirations in part by adopting a through-composed formal orientation. In an in-depth study of this trend, Brad Osborn traces the through-composed impulse of artists such as Radiohead, Sleepy Eyes of Death, and Emery, identifying several distinct approaches—one-part monothematic, multipart polythematic, etc.—that in turn show alignment to the rock subgenre in which the artists reside. Osborn notes too that in each case, the embrace of a through-composed approach corresponds to the artists' conscious decision to distance themselves from the commercial "pop" music market.[237]

Within world music traditions too, a continually evolving, through-composed approach is fairly rare, given the desired community involvement inherent in so much global music making. Exceptions occasionally appear within more sophisticated or "art"-oriented genres and approaches, such as within the Chinese "silk and bamboo" and Balinese gamelan traditions.[238] Yet even in such cases, the musical discourse tends to be unified by virtue of a recurring, or developing, rhythmic or melodic idea throughout the work, thus mitigating its "through-composed" nature.

From a musical taste perspective, therefore, formal complexity—and not just through-composed forms, but any complex, multipart structure—yields a particular kind of listening experience. The musical discourse in these cases is generally extensive, unwinding, and challenging in its demands on the listener's attention. The degree to which you are drawn to such songs and works thus says a great deal about your overall palate for "sophisticated" musical practice—whether or not you are aware of the particular formal approach taken within any given one.

## Four Common Form Types

We conclude our form primer with a discussion of four common form types—blues; the jazz standard with a 32-bar refrain; the sectional pop/rock song; and the sonata—that dominate the musical landscape within the species of jazz, pop/rock (and by extension hip hop and electronica), and classical.* Admittedly, these represent but a handful of the many forms that one could discern from a broad survey of music in these realms—not to mention bypassing entirely the realm of world music. Yet as an addendum to the discussions of formal templates above, they round out the formal dimensions that underlie a majority of the world's most "popular" music.

At the same time, it is important to bear in mind that form is *not* the same thing as genre—though the two are often confused. As we've seen, form involves issues of structure and the "architectural" treatment of material. By contrast, "genre" is a term of classification, grouping works together based on common conventions that may or may not comport with any formal design or strategy. More generally, "genre" suggests conventional qualities of scope, material, forces, social circumstances, function, etc., of past and future works within a given medium.[239] It is because of this limiting potential that some writers, notably the French philosopher Jacques Derrida, have criticized the very concept of genre:

> As soon as the word "genre" is sounded, as soon as it is heard, as soon as one attempts to conceive it, a limit is drawn. And when a limit is established, norms and interdictions are not far behind.[240]

This limiting potential of genre, moreover, was a driving factor behind the design of the Music Genome Project at Pandora—as we consciously sought to avoid the straitjacket that genre can potentially instill in the minds and expectations of listeners, as well as music analysts. This is not to dismiss the utility of genre labels in providing context or clues as to how the music might sound, but rather to recognize that labeling a song "Neo-Soul" or "Grunge" or "Alternative Country" is not a substitute for understanding either its specific musical character or the experience it can yield to a given listener. Rather than providing music recommendations by "bucketing" songs into a set of nuanced genre labels—as many of our competitors did, and still do—we aimed to base them on what was going on "under the hood" of the music, above and beyond genre; more on the genre bias in Chapters 8 and 13.

---

* We are here making an admittedly subtle distinction between a "formal template"—an established pattern or formula of sectional flow (e.g., ternary as A-B-A); and a "formal type"—an actual or specific formal designation adopted and adapted by composers, which may or may not be linked to a specific formal template (e.g., blues: commonly, though not always, a 12-bar strophic form, as will be seen).

This is not to say, however, that genre and form have no valid connection. In some cases—such as the Baroque-era **fugue**—the genre name of a work practically predefines its use of a single specific form. In other cases, a genre suggests a formal template that is true in many or even most cases—e.g., a hymn is usually strophic; a Classical-era minuet and a modern pop ballad are both generally binary; a Romantic-era nocturne is often ternary, etc. Even still, the genre of a song or work is not the same thing as its form, and exceptions to the convention are inevitable. We'll be exploring genre a bit more in the subsequent parts of this book, when we carry out holistic analyses of various individual works within a wide variety of music styles—relating the music to broader issues of individual musical taste.

In the meantime, here are overviews of the four formal types noted above—including their typical structures and common deviations. In addition, and to an even greater degree than was the case with the formal templates, these overviews dive a fair bit into the historical backstory and evolution of each form. If you're a fan of music history, therefore, this is your lucky day!

## BLUES

The first type, the **blues**, is one we've already traced through multiple musical dimensions: melodic, harmonic, and rhythmic. As a form, it is fairly simple and generally strophic. Significantly, it transcends the realms (and subrealms) of jazz, rock, rhythm and blues, and beyond. Blues, of course, is not only a form, but also a manner of performance, a state of mind, and a harmonic orientation. In all of these ways, it sprang from a variety of musical expressions of African-American slaves in the nineteenth century, such as the shout, the moan, and the field holler—so called for being sung while its singers toiled in the fields. Other key sources include the African-American minstrel song from the same period, as well as the call-and-response spiritual and its various West African antecedents.

The earliest blues, stemming from around 1900, came in a variety of formal arrangements. Among these was a pattern of twelve measures, made up of three phrases of four measures each, where the first two phrases are melodically and lyrically identical ("call-response"). Typically, this 12-bar pattern pursues a particular harmonic scheme, marked by the consistent use of a dominant 7th chord—as noted in Interlude B—even for the tonic (I). This harmonic pattern is so widespread, it is worth spelling out; using the Roman numeral system discussed in Chapter 4, it proceeds as follows: I7–IV7–I7–V7–I7. Here's an early example to make that clear (Figure 6.22):

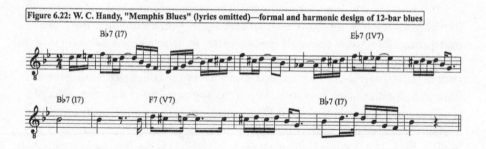

Figure 6.22: W. C. Handy, "Memphis Blues" (lyrics omitted)—formal and harmonic design of 12-bar blues

There were, and still are, myriad variations and elaborations in this harmonic pattern,[241] though once one pattern is established—in the first "chorus"—it is generally adhered to for the remainder of the song. The 12-bar structure became widely emulated, especially following the success of exemplars like "Memphis Blues" (1912), "St. Louis Blues" (1914), and "Livery Stable Blues" (1917).

The flexibility of the form enabled its adoption into a whole slew of distinct styles and genres of American music: ragtime (e.g., "One o' Them Things: Ragtime Two-Step" by James Chapman); early jazz (e.g., "West End Blues" by Louis Armstrong); boogie-woogie (e.g., "Pinetop's Boogie Woogie" by Clarence "Pinetop" Smith); swing (e.g., "One o'Clock Jump" by Count Basie); bebop (e.g., "Billie's Bounce" by Charlie Parker); hard bop (e.g., "Doodlin'" by Horace Silver); bluegrass (e.g., "Bluegrass Special" by Bill Monroe); country (e.g., "Folsom Prison Blues" by Johnny Cash); rock and roll (e.g., "Johnny B. Goode" by Chuck Berry); blues rock (e.g., "Crossroads" by Cream); soul (e.g., "Papa's Got a Brand New Bag" by James Brown), etc.

Of course, the 12-bar structure has likewise been the staple of the blues as a stand-alone genre, guided by such leading singers and composers as Blind Lemon Jefferson, Robert Johnson, and Charley Patton in the 1920s and '30s; Muddy Waters, Howlin' Wolf, and Little Walter in the 1940s and '50s; Memphis Slim, John Lee Hooker, and B. B. King in the 1960s and '70s; and Robert Cray, Stevie Ray Vaughan, and Bobby Rush since the 1980s—to name but a few.[242]

At the same time, however, the 12-bar arrangement is not the only version of the blues. The three most common deviations are the 8-bar blues (e.g., "Heartbreak Hotel" by Elvis Presley), the 16-bar blues (e.g., "I'm Your Hoochie Coochie Man" by Muddy Waters), and the 24-bar blues (e.g., "Slow Down" by Larry Williams, recorded by the Beatles). Each deviation in turn has its own set of harmonic variations and embellishments.

Regardless, though, all of these blues structures display a common *harmonic trajectory*, one that is best embodied in the 12-bar version: a reliable progression from I7 (tonic) to IV7 (subdominant) to V7 (dominant) and back "home" to I7—or, using actual chords in the key of C: C7–F7–G7–C7. Any additional and intervening chords merely add variety to this trajectory, without changing its nature.

The blues is often extolled as "America's music," and much of that stems from the universality and flexibility of the blues form.[243] It is a miniature form type that via repetition allows for a uniquely satisfying narrative musical experience—one that is most concretely defined by an initial harmonic movement from I7 to IV7. A key feature here is what we might call the "dominantization" of the tonic—that is, turning the tonic chord (I) into a dominant 7th chord (I7). To clarify a bit, remember from Chapter 4 that in traditional tonal harmony, a tonic (I) is a simple triad (e.g., C–E–G), whereas the dominant 7th chord is usually limited to the V chord; but in the blues, the tonic is itself a dominant 7th chord (e.g., C–E–G–B♭)—thus labeled I7.

This phenomenon too seems to have roots in the nineteenth-century African-American musical dialect. Moreover, this harmonic inclination is likewise found in much jazz, rock, country, and related genres that owe their inception and/or character to the blues. It is thus worth pondering that a defining and revolutionary characteristic of American music—the dominantization of the tonic—began life as an involuntary artistic expression of people originally brought to this country as slaves.

## THE JAZZ STANDARD: THE 32-BAR SONG REFRAIN

Jazz owes its origins and character in part to the blues, though likewise to a number of other African-American, European, and Caribbean musical influences—including ragtime, cakewalks, marches, European dance music (polkas, quadrilles, etc.), Creole songs, hymns, spirituals, minstrel songs, habaneras, etc.—that were all "in play" in New Orleans around 1900.[244] The first jazz songs (1910–1920) came in a variety of forms. Some were straight or modified blues songs—e.g., "Memphis Blues" (1912) and "St. Louis Blues" (1914). Others were march or ragtime songs written in a variety of multisectional forms—e.g., "Royal Garden Blues" (1917) and "Tiger Rag" (1917). These songs gained popularity via their recordings by artists such as the Original Dixieland Jazz Band, Louis Armstrong, and vocalist Bessie Smith.

Still others were songs that came out of "Tin Pan Alley"—a thriving source of "mainstream" song production between roughly 1890 and 1940, named after a district in lower Manhattan (West 28th Street between 5th and 6th Avenues) where "song pluggers" would play on pianos situated outside music publishers to sell sheet music. The songs these pianists "plugged" came from a variety of sources: vaudeville and Broadway, as well as ragtime, cakewalks, and early jazz songs. One early Tin Pan Alley triumph was "(Back Home Again in) Indiana" (1917) by Ballard MacDonald and James Hanley. After being recorded by the Original Dixieland Jazz Band in 1917, "Indiana" became a huge national hit, among the first jazz songs to achieve this status.

The success of "Indiana" also helped to solidify for jazz songs a formal type that had first appeared in the 1890s, but became especially prevailing after 1920: the **32-bar refrain** (or chorus).[245] In the case of "Indiana," the specific sectional scheme is A-B-A-C, where each section is eight measures, as shown here (Figure 6.23):

**Figure 6.23: James Hanley, "Indiana" (lyrics omitted)—32-bar Tin Pan Alley form (A-B-A-C)**

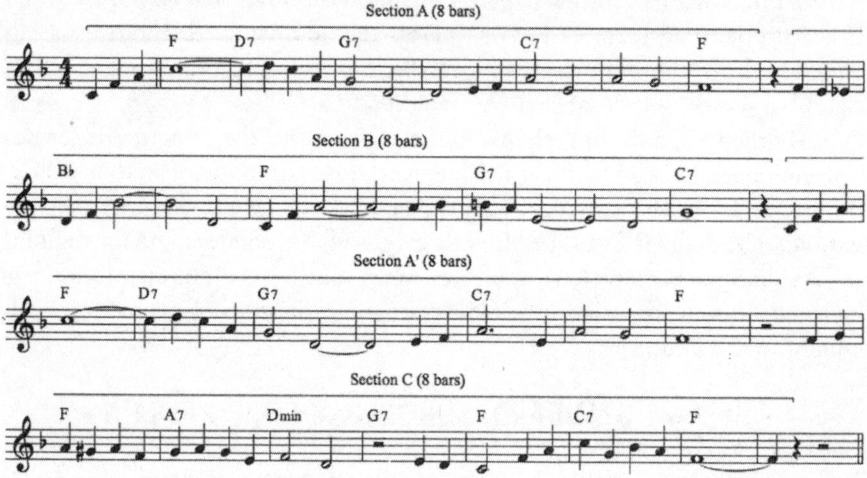


Another, even more common scheme for the 32-bar jazz refrain is that used, for example, by George Gershwin in his 1924 song "Oh, Lady Be Good": A-A-B-A, again with each section being eight measures.[246] In this form, the B section provides much-needed contrast (melodically, harmonically, etc.); it is often called the "bridge," but likewise the "middle eight," the "release," and others; the form is shown here (Figure 6.24):

**Figure 6.24: George Gershwin, "Oh, Lady Be Good" (lyrics omitted)—32-bar Tin Pan Alley form (A-A-B-A)**

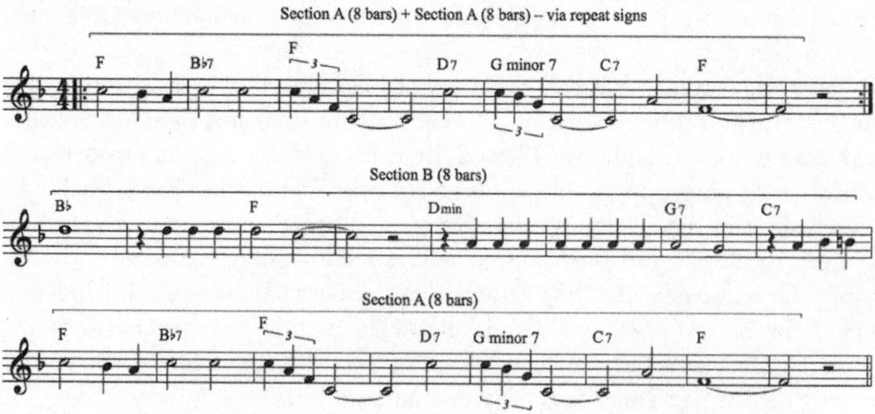

Indeed, the A-A-B-A scheme may be seen as a kind of default arrangement for the 32-bar refrain, particularly after around 1925. This is the disposition of such well-trotted songs as Irving Berlin's "Blue Skies," Jerome Kern's "Can't Help Lovin' That Man of Mine," Fats Waller's "Ain't Misbehavin'," Richard Rodgers' "My Funny Valentine," Cole Porter's "What Is This Thing Called Love," Hoagy Carmichael's "Georgia on My Mind," Duke Ellington's "In a Sentimental Mood," and Harry Warren's "I Only Have Eyes for You," to name but a few.

To be sure, there are all kinds of variants to the 32-bar default found among the gems of the Tin Pan Alley repertoire—all of which would have been conceived, and likely perceived, as creative "deviations" from the norm. These include such celebrated standards as "Autumn Leaves" (A-A-B-C); Jerome Kern's "Yesterdays" (A-B-C-D) and "All the Things You Are" (a 36-measure A-A'-B-A"); Gershwin's "I Got Rhythm" (a 34-bar A-A-B-A, by virtue of a two-bar tag at the end of the last A, usually omitted by jazz soloists); plus elongated songs such as Kurt Weill's "Speak Low" (56 measures), and Cole Porter's "Begin the Beguine" (108 measures). The nitty-gritty details for these latter songs, as well as a few others discussed in this chapter, are provided on the WYLI website (supplement to Chapter 6), for those keeping score.

And yet, like the 8-, 16-, and 24-bar blues, the formal identity of these jazz song variants is best understood in relationship to the "default" arrangement. The truth is that a solid majority of popular/jazz songs written in the period from 1920 to 1950 were of the 32-bar, A-A-B-A variety. This type, and its variants, served as the inspirational foundation for hundreds of popular songs by the most creative songwriters of the day. Such is the enduring legacy of this repertoire that the songs are casually labeled as "standards." They are the "bread and butter" of jazz recordings over the past eighty years by both vocalists and instrumentalists, including many "classic" jazz recordings.[247] A glance at recent jazz and jazz-pop recordings—such as albums by Michael Bublé, Keith Jarrett, Avishai Cohen, and Tom Rainey—suggest that the trend shows no sign of dissipating. Indeed, chances are pretty good that among these "standards" are some of your favorite songs.

One significant point worth noting here, however, is that there is generally more to these "standards" than just their refrains. From their earliest Tin Pan Alley and Broadway roots, these songs invariably had a verse, generally just one, preceding the refrain. In contrast to the repeating constructs of the refrain, the verse was generally through-composed and usually sung or played in a rubato manner, thus aesthetically setting up the arrival of the rhythmic refrain. Lyrically too the verse was rather utilitarian in nature, providing context for the sentiment to be expressed in the refrain. Given this, it's not surprising that these verses are generally performed only once—or, quite commonly, dispensed with altogether in recording or performance, at least following their original release or theatrical production. There are a few exceptions that one hears regularly, especially by Gershwin (e.g., "Someone to Watch Over Me": "There's a saying old, saying love is blind . . .") and Cole Porter (e.g., "Night and Day": "Like the beat, beat, beat of the tom-tom . . ."), beyond which only a few hardcore aficionados can recall by heart today.

In either event, it was the 32-bar refrain that defined this "golden" era of songwriting. The influence of this formal type was then extended into later musical styles and genres. These include the more "progressive" styles of jazz: bebop—e.g., "Donna Lee" (based on the same chord progression as "Indiana," a common tack for bebop musicians) by Charlie Parker and "Well, You Needn't" by Thelonious Monk; cool jazz—e.g., "So What" by Miles Davis and "The Duke" by Dave Brubeck; hard bop—such as "Moanin'" by Bobby Timmons; and Latin jazz—e.g., "Tin Tin Deo" by Dizzy Gillespie and Chano Pozo, and "Girl from Ipanema" by Antônio Carlos Jobim, to name but a few. All of these tunes are composed with 32-bar A-A-B-A refrains.

All of these are likewise examples of latter-day "standards"—which, along with their Tin Pan Alley forebears, are still performed by jazz musicians in clubs, jam sessions, and private parties any night of the week, anywhere in the world. The beauty of this repertoire is that musicians who have never before met can join forces on the bandstand and simply "call out a tune," which everyone is expected to know by heart. A simple count-off, and everyone would also be expected to know the basic "road map": Head (tune)—Solos—Head, sometimes preceded by a short intro and/or followed by a short tag. A *specific* manifestation of this basic "road map" of Head—Solos—Head is found in the 1956 recording by the Miles Davis Quintet (with tenor saxophonist John Coltrane, pianist Red Garland, bassist Paul Chambers, and drummer Philly Joe Jones) of Duke Ellington's A-A-B-A tune "Just Squeeze Me":

**Intro**—Eight measures: rhythm section (piano, bass, drums) only, on V7
**Head** (tune)—Miles plus rhythm section
**Solo Chorus 1**—Miles plus rhythm section (A-A-B-A)
**Solo Chorus 2**—Coltrane plus rhythm section (A-A-B-A)
**Solo Chorus 3**—Garland, plus bass and drums (A-A-B-A | A-A)
**Head** (second half of tune)—Miles, with Coltrane and rhythm section (B-A)
**Tag**—Repeat of last four bars, with standard ending

The solos, of course, are improvised using the same chord progression as the head; it is likewise common for soloists to take two or more solo choruses, especially for fast songs ("Just Squeeze Me" is a medium swing ballad). Naturally, both the original melody and chords are adapted and made "hipper" by the musicians—as is the case here, where Miles takes considerable liberty with Duke's melody.

After 1950 or so, another popular musical idiom—rock and roll—began to challenge jazz' hegemony, and with it arose a new formal type, as we'll soon see. But the 32-bar refrain form did not suddenly vanish. Alongside blues and other forms, the 32-bar A-A-B-A scheme continued strongly in the 1950s, for example, in the doo-wop subgenre—e.g., Frankie Lymon's "Why Do Fools Fall in Love" and the Platters' "The Great Pretender," both from 1956. Examples also appear in pre-Beatles pop/rock songs—such as Gerry Goffin and Carole King's "Will You Still Love Me Tomorrow" (1961, recorded by the Shirelles). The scheme, and its variants, likewise stayed popular among country music artists well into the 1970s, such as in Willie Nelson's "Crazy" (1961, recorded by Patsy Cline).

The post-1950 songs just listed reveal a direct aesthetic debt to the Tin Pan Alley tradition, and demonstrate the degree to which the 32-bar refrain, and especially its A-A-B-A variant, had become ingrained within American songwriting. But as a new kind of youth-oriented pop music exploded from the mid-1950s, a different formal type emerged, even as it revealed a debt to the one it displaced: the sectional song.

## SECTIONAL POP/ROCK SONG FORM: VERSE, CHORUS, BRIDGE, AND PRE-CHORUS

Like jazz before it, rock and roll was initially an amalgam of diverse musical streams that only gradually coalesced into a distinct musical idiom. Among these streams are blues, rhythm and blues, country, gospel, boogie-woogie, and the songs of Tin Pan Alley.[248] The immediate precursor was the repertoire of so-called "race records"—jump blues, country boogie, etc.—from black artists in the late 1940s and early 1950s, such as Louis Jordan. Eventually this offensive term gave way to the expression "rhythm and blues." And indeed, most rock and roll prototypes—such as Wild Bill Moore's "We're Gonna Rock, We're Gonna Roll" (1947), Jimmy Preston's "Rock the Joint" (1949), and Ike Turner's "Rocket 88" (1951)—are 12-bar blues.

It is thus not surprising that the blues format—12-bar and its variants—was firmly embraced by early rock and roll pioneers such as Chuck Berry (e.g., "Johnny B. Goode," "Roll Over Beethoven"), Bill Haley ("Rock Around the Clock"), Little Richard ("Long Tall Sally"), and Elvis Presley ("Hound Dog"). But these pioneers also embraced other established song forms, including the A-A-B-A scheme—32-bar and its variants—used for the Everly Brothers' "All I Have to Do Is Dream," Buddy Holly's "True Love Ways," and numerous doo-wop examples, as noted above.

At the same time, artists and songwriters—notably the songwriting duo Jerry Leiber and Mike Stoller, who wrote "Hound Dog," for example—began to explore other formal techniques and approaches.[249] Chief among the new formal developments was the growing reliance on a **hook** within the song—a catchy and pronounced melody/lyric that was repeated several times, and which usually bequeathed the song its title. Initially, this "refrain" was limited to a single line—e.g., at the end of an A section within an A-A-B-A song (e.g., Elvis Presley's "Treat Me Nice"), or in each phrase of a 12-bar blues (e.g., Gene Vincent's "Be-Bop-A-Lula"), or some combination (e.g., Buddy Holly's "Oh, Boy!"). The first two examples are shown here (Figures 6.25 and 6.26):

**Figure 6.25: Elvis Presley, "Treat Me Nice"—use of a single-line "hook" in early rock songs**

**Figure 6.26: Gene Vincent, "Be-Bop-A-Lula"—use of a single-line "hook" in early rock songs**

In some cases, the hook was extended to an entire section of the song, such as in the seminal rock and roll blues "Shake, Rattle and Roll"—recorded by Big Joe Turner (1954), Bill Haley and the Comets (1955), and Elvis Presley (1957). Although the song is a strophic blues, the same melody/lyrics periodically punctuate the form ("Shake, rattle and roll")—establishing the repeating section as a chorus and the nonrepeating sections as verses. Among rock music theorists, this is called a *simple* verse-chorus form, where both sections utilize the same formal and harmonic structure.

Soon this tendency to mark off a distinct formal section as a repeating chorus was extended beyond the 12-bar blues into other harmonic and formal orientations. Among the earliest exemplars was the Leiber and Stoller song "Poison Ivy" (recorded by the Coasters in 1959). The song is technically structured in an A-A-B-A configuration, with the "refrain" occurring at the end of each A. But rather than just being the closing portion of a single discrete section, as in "Treat Me Nice," the hook is a distinct eight-bar section of its own. Moreover, the hook section contrasts harmonically (vi) with the preceding eight-bar nonhook music, further establishing the two sections as distinct. As we saw with complex classical forms, such as in Beethoven's "Fur Elise," large-scale sections can often themselves be clearly divided into smaller subsections: in the case of "Poison Ivy," the "A" is really A-a—A-b, where the a is the verse, and the b is the chorus, thus a *contrasting* verse-chorus form (Figure 6.27):

**Figure 6.27: Leiber & Stoller, "Poison Ivy" (verse-chorus, partial lyrics)—layout of verse-chorus form: part A**

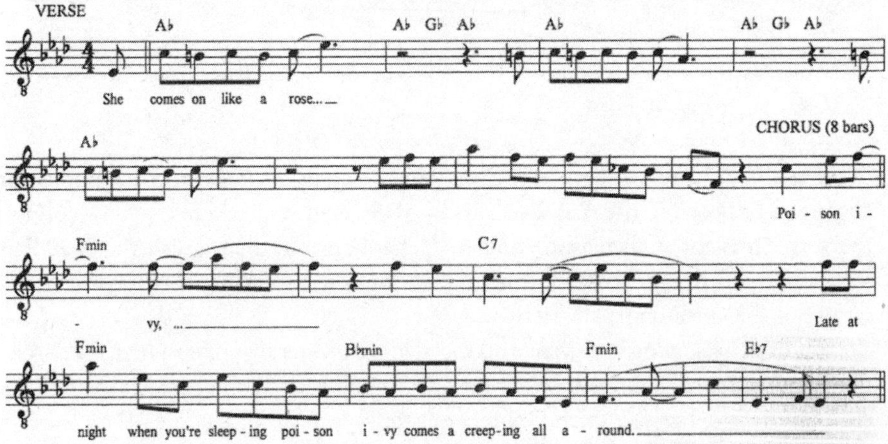


In keeping with the large-scale A-A-B-A scheme, this verse-chorus pairing (A) is then repeated (A), followed by an eight-measure contrasting section—the B—which likewise moves to a different harmonic area (IV). Following upon the nomenclature of the 32-bar Tin Pan Alley song, this section is commonly called the **bridge** (though likewise called the "middle eight," especially in England) (Figure 6.28):

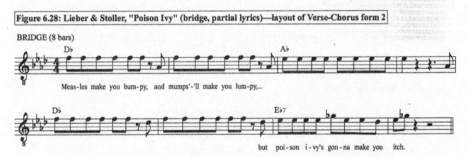

**Figure 6.28: Lieber & Stoller, "Poison Ivy" (bridge, partial lyrics)—layout of Verse-Chorus form 2**

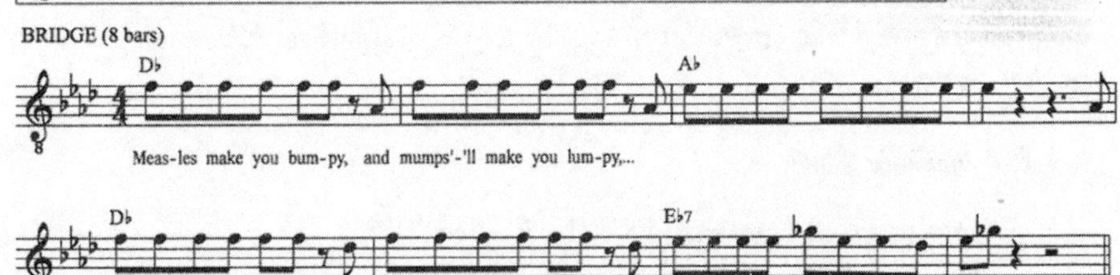


This is then followed by a return of the A supersection, again comprising the verse and chorus pairing. Yet while the overall form shows a debt to the older A-A-B-A scheme, the actual listening experience is rather different—namely a flow of discrete sections:

(Intro)—Verse—Chorus—Verse—Chorus—Bridge—Verse—Chorus

An alternate song form configuration that arose in the early years of rock and roll was one in which the verse and the chorus take on even more distinct identities, by dispensing entirely with a contrasting bridge section. In essence, these are simple binary forms, alternating A and B sections—in contrast to the A-A-B-A variety, which is ternary A-B-A, with the first A repeated. An early example of this verse-chorus form is Buddy Holly's "That'll Be the Day," which proceeds as follows:

(Intro)—Chorus—Verse—Chorus—Verse—Solo (Blues)—Chorus—Verse—Chorus—Chorus

One key distinction here as well is that the song begins with the "hook," or chorus, as opposed to the A-A-B-A variety of "Poison Ivy," where the hook follows the verse. It is for such reasons that rock theorists will distinguish the A-A-B-A song variety as being "verse-dominated," as opposed to the "chorus-dominated" nature of the verse-chorus variety.

But from a listening experience perspective the greater distinction here is between the new "sectional" approach of the post-1950 pop/rock song (verse-chorus-bridge, etc.) on the one hand, and the more "holistic" approach of the pre-1950 Tin Pan Alley jazz song (A-A-B-A, etc., within a single "chorus") on the other. A key source of this development was simply the gradual extension in length and profile of the individual sections. It also involved establishing ever-greater contrast between the sections via shifts in harmony, rhythmic identity, and/or mood.

In point of fact, both the A-A-B-A and verse-chorus-bridge pop/rock formats have continued to define pop and rock music through to the present day, and both have contributed their share of hit songs. At the same time, the dominant historic trend within these species has definitely been away from the A-A-B-A and toward the verse-chorus format.[250] Here is a small sample—ten each—of both varieties:

### A-A-B-A Pop/Rock Songs

"I Want to Hold Your Hand"—The Beatles (1963)
"(Sittin' on) The Dock of the Bay"—Otis Redding (1968)
"Raindrops Keep Fallin' on My Head"—Burt Bacharach (1969)
"Whole Lotta Love"—Led Zeppelin (1969)
"You've Got a Friend"—Carole King (1971)
"More Than a Feeling"—Boston (1976)
"New Amsterdam"—Elvis Costello (1979)
"Crazy Little Thing Called Love"—Queen (1979)
"Smells Like Teen Spirit"—Nirvana (1991)
"My Happy Ending"—Avril Lavigne (2004)

**Verse-Chorus Pop/Rock Songs (with and without a Bridge section)**

"Mr. Tambourine Man"—Bob Dylan (1965)
"Happy Together"—The Turtles (1967)
"Penny Lane"—The Beatles (1967)
"Daniel"—Elton John (1973)
"Can't Get Enough"—Bad Company (1974)
"God Save the Queen"—The Sex Pistols (1977)
"Little Red Corvette"—Prince (1983)
"Material Girl"—Madonna (1985)
"Tears in Heaven"—Eric Clapton (1992)
"Just the Way You Are"—Bruno Mars (2010)

While these two lists could certainly be lengthened considerably, there are many pop/rock songs whose formal design falls in neither category, or is disposed to ambiguity: Is this section a separate chorus or merely an extension of the verse? Do altered harmonies and lyrics turn this later chorus into a second bridge? How exactly do we formally divide these ambiguous sixteen measures? And so forth.[251] As stated earlier, two individuals may perceive the formal divisions of a passage differently—as is not uncommon among rock theorists—and both may have a good argument. And yet knowing some common approaches to the sectional pop/rock song type will undoubtedly inform our listening experience, even if we can't articulate a precise structure without producing a technical analysis.

Adding to the richness and complexity of the pop/rock song form type are various other sectional entities that have developed, or in some cases taken on extensive formal definition, since the 1960s. These include, most especially, the **pre-chorus**—a transitional, stand-alone section that leads into the chorus, generally following the verse. The viability of the term, its definition, and the frequency with which it occurs in pop/rock songs is a matter of some theoretical debate.[252] For example, some would prefer to conceive of this section more as a bridge, by virtue of lyric usage, etc. At the same time, there are a number of rock songs, particularly from the mid-1960s, that include a distinct section that can demonstrably be called a pre-chorus. In such cases, these sections carry an important aesthetic purpose: to create for the listener a measured transition from the particular nature of the verse (often of a lower intensity) to that of the chorus (generally of a higher intensity). The transitional quality of the pre-chorus can be manifested in various ways—generally via harmonic contrast, but also via melodic range, rhythmic, instrumentation, etc.—but in each case the effect is to generate a more impactful arrival to the chorus.

A clear example of a pre-chorus is "Piece of My Heart," recorded by Big Brother and the Holding Company (with Janis Joplin, 1967). As is not uncommon with the use of a pre-chorus, both the verse and chorus in this song use largely the same chord progression: E–A–B–A (I–IV–V–IV); the pre-chorus thus enables a more dramatic connection between the two sections by moving to a different harmonic area—in this case, the relative minor (C♯ minor, or vi); see Figure 6.29:

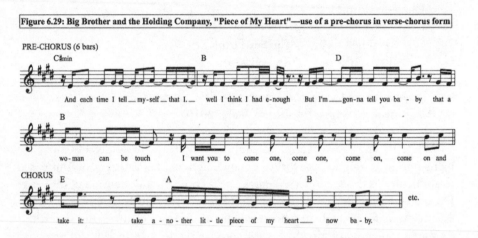

**Figure 6.29: Big Brother and the Holding Company, "Piece of My Heart"—use of a pre-chorus in verse-chorus form**

Other clear examples include David Bowie's "Life on Mars" (1971, from "But the film is a saddening bore"); Bon Jovi's "You Give Love a Bad Name" (1986, from "Oh, oh, you're a loaded gun"); Muse's "Time Is Running Out" (2003, from "Bury it, I won't let you bury it"); Taylor Swift's "You Belong With Me" (2008, from "But she wears short skirts"), as we'll discuss in Chapter 9; and Adele's "Someone Like You" (2011, from "I hate to turn up out of the blue uninvited").

Further, many adventurous rock songs will include elaborate and noteworthy intros, codas (concluding sections), riff structures, instrumental interludes, improvised "jams," and/or other internal sections that simply defy any clear label as verse, chorus, pre-chorus, or bridge. Such songs tend to be ambitious in scope, perhaps revealing a nod to classical or jazz traditions/techniques and thus eschewing commercial success—though not always. Examples with varying degrees of complexity and formal ambiguity include the Beatles' "I Want You (She's So Heavy)," King Crimson's "The Court of the Crimson King," the Doors' "The End," Led Zeppelin's "Stairway to Heaven," Queen's "Bohemian Rhapsody," Paul McCartney's "Band on the Run," Elton John's "Someone Saved My Life Tonight," Rush's "2112," the Grateful Dead's "Dark Star" (live concerts), Phish's "Reba," and Radiohead's "Lotus Flower," to name but a few.

Not surprisingly, songs that display formal complexity often display other types of musical complexity as well—notably in their harmonic and rhythmic orientations. Conversely, songs that follow a more well-defined and traditional formal structure (e.g., Short Intro—Verse—Chorus—Verse—Chorus—Bridge—Chorus) tend to embrace simpler and more predictable harmonic progressions and patterns, deliberately "catchy" melodic hooks, straightforward meters and rhythms, etc. This, of course, is likewise the approach found in most hit songs over the past fifty years or so, as it will likely be for the next fifty. Recognizing the formal profile of your favorite pop/rock songs—how specifically they manifest the sectional pop/rock song form type—can thus provide a valuable means to understanding the broader dimensions of your musical taste.

## SONATA FORM

If the sectional pop/rock song is the quintessential formal type among "popular" composers over the past fifty years, among "classical" composers (notably of instrumental works) from the mid-eighteenth through early twentieth centuries it was undoubtedly **sonata form**. No other classical form has received a comparable level of attention by music theorists and historians over the past 150 years. Undoubtedly, this is due to the fact that many of the most famous instrumental works by the most esteemed composers are written in sonata form—or in forms influenced by it. If you are a fan of classical music, chances are high that many of your personal favorites are in sonata form. As such, it is worth taking time to explore the basics and historical evolution of this formal type.

The term "sonata" stems from the Italian verb "*suonare*," "to sound," and was first applied in the late sixteenth century as a generic term for instrumental works—in contrast to music meant to be sung, or "cantata," from the verb "*cantare*," "to sing." As a genre designation, the sonata became popular during the Baroque era, especially for works written for one or two solo instruments (especially the violin) with keyboard accompaniment, as a series of dance-like or contrapuntal movements—and thus akin to the common Baroque genre of the dance **suite**.

As a formal type, by contrast, sonata form is a product of the **Classical era** (1750–1800), first gaining a semblance of formal consistency and enduring definition in the music of Franz Joseph Haydn, from the 1760s and '70s.[253] In many ways, sonata form signals the ultimate triumph of tonality as a harmonic system, where periodic shifts in key areas provide not only narrative articulation but also fundamental and clarifying architectural structure.

The sonata form likewise epitomizes the burgeoning spirit of the Enlightenment that infused the aesthetic of Classical-era composition as well: to communicate to the listener through musical discourse and structure in a clear and affecting manner. As the music theorist Johann Heinichen presaged in 1728, the highest aim of the composer was less to use his intellectual reason and more his skill and "good taste" to "make music pleasing to and beloved by the general, educated public."[254] Sonata form, with its elaborate and flexible plan of statement-departure-return—via both melodic and harmonic means—gave composers and audiences an excellent vehicle by which to forge the ideal relationship that Heinichen envisioned.

Naturally, the road to Haydn's codified sonata form scheme was varied and circuitous. The initial seeds were planted in the Baroque era—such as in the binary (A-B) dance movements (minuets, gavottes, etc.) of the French suites and partitas of J. S. Bach. As with the codified sonata form, these suite movements featured a broad harmonic trajectory: from the tonic to the dominant in the A section, followed by a return—via more "remote" harmonic areas—to the tonic in the B section. Further traits that later become standard in sonata form—including the use of clear and succinct primary and secondary themes, and a return of a secondary theme in the tonic—occur occasionally in works by various composers in various idioms through the early eighteenth century, most especially Domenico Scarlatti in his 555 keyboard sonatas, and C. P. E. Bach in his keyboard sonatas as well as his symphonies.

But it was Haydn who established the enduring principles and practices of sonata form. By his prolific example, sonata form became standard for first movements of the "major" instrumental genres of the eighteenth and nineteenth centuries: sonatas, string quartets, and symphonies, among several others. This practice was embraced and solidified by Mozart as well as Beethoven, who likewise revealed the great flexibility and rhetorical potential of the form. It is worth noting, however, that although composers after 1770 inevitably adopted the framework of sonata form for the opening movements of their instrumental works, actual prescribed definitions came only in the second quarter of the nineteenth century—and officially in 1845 by the theorist Adolf Bernhard Marx—by which time its normative practices were being regularly challenged or violated by the top composers of the day.[255]

A full review of the musicological elements and tendencies of sonata form is beyond the scope of this book, but we can provide a reasonable sense of it by referring to its high-level subdivisions and typical behavior. In essence, there are three distinct subdivisions of sonata form: exposition, development, and recapitulation. In reading this description, you might think of it like an adventure novel, where the themes discussed are like the exploits of the main protagonist. Our account addresses a textbook-like case in a major key, such as the first movement of Mozart's simple Sonata in C Major, K. 545, to be used as a specific illustration below.

In the **exposition**, a *primary theme* is presented in the *home (tonic) key*. The melodic material here is well articulated, with a memorable or "catchy" quality, whereby its subsequent return will be easily recognized. A transition follows where the music modulates harmonically from the *tonic to the dominant*. Upon arriving in the new key, a *secondary theme* is presented. The melodic material here is generally of a *contrasting* nature to the primary theme—e.g., lyrical if the primary theme is rhythmic, etc. Upon completion of the secondary theme, the exposition will conclude with a strong, authentic cadence in the dominant.* This is often supported by a *closing theme*, generally less substantive, more "concluding" in nature. Before about 1800, most expositions were repeated before continuing on to the development section, thereby increasing the familiarity of its thematic material (and harmonic movement) in the ears of the listener. After 1800, the ever-increasing length of the exposition made such repetition less practical.

The **development** section, as the name suggests, is often dedicated to "developing" previous material—that is, from the primary, secondary, and perhaps closing themes of the exposition. But a larger purpose is simply to provide *contrast* from the "expository" nature of the exposition, and many development sections do very little actual developing (variation, manipulation, etc.) of previous themes—though many do. Whether developed or not, however, most development sections will *revisit those earlier-heard themes*, while occasionally introducing new ones. More universal is that the development section is *relatively unstable harmonically*, often moving quickly from one key area to another, and rarely resting in any single one for long. The length of the development section can vary from fairly short (especially before 1800—e.g., 65 measures, or 60 percent of the length of the exposition, in Mozart's Symphony no. 40 in G Minor, K. 555) to substantial (especially after 1800—e.g., 241 measures, or 160 percent of the length of the exposition, in Beethoven's Symphony no. 3, Op. 55), but in either event will *announce its end by setting up harmonically a return to the tonic*, often with a sustained pedal point on the dominant.

The *return to the tonic*, and specifically the return of the *primary theme* in the tonic, marks the beginning of the **recapitulation**. The verb "to recapitulate" means "to summarize or restate briefly," which in fact belies its use in sonata form, since what transpires in this section is not merely restatement, but also *resolution*. To be sure, the recapitulation begins with a restatement of the primary theme in the tonic, and then follows with basically the same transitional material as in the exposition. However, instead of modulating to the dominant as in the exposition, the transitional material now alters its trajectory to *remain in the tonic*—whereby the *secondary theme*, as well as the *closing theme*, is no longer in the dominant but in the tonic. In so doing, there will likely be some adjustments in the melodic content of the secondary and closing themes, to accommodate the lack of modulation. In any event, the recapitulation succeeds in *resolving the "tension"* created in the exposition by now presenting *all thematic material in the tonic*, thus bringing the work to an aesthetically satisfying conclusion.

The full "generic" form can be represented schematically in the following diagram (Figure 6.30):

---

* This is the standard shift for sonata movements in a major key; for those in a minor key, the exposition will generally end in the relative major—e.g., if it starts in A minor, it will end in C major.

**Figure 6.30: Sonata form schema (for major key)**

| Section: | Exposition | Development | Recapitulation |
|---|---|---|---|
| Theme: | Primary *transition* Secondary [Closing] | New & Previous Material Developed | Primary *transition* Secondary [Closing] |
| Key: | ‖: Tonic (I) *modulation* Dominant (V) -------- :‖ | *(unstable / frequent key shifts)* ⟶ | Tonic (I) Tonic (I) ----------- |

To illustrate this formal type and its narrative thrust more substantively, below is a simplified scheme of the opening movement (Allegro) of Mozart's Sonata in C, K. 545 (Figures 6.31a–c). Even in this simple sonata, however, the flexibility of the formal type is demonstrated by virtue of Mozart's return of the primary theme within the recapitulation section not in the tonic (I), but rather in the subdominant (IV) key:

**Figure 6.31a: W. A. Mozart, Piano Sonata in C, K. 545, 1. Allegro—sonata schema: exposition**

**Figure 6.31b: W. A. Mozart, Piano Sonata in C, K. 545, 1.Allegro—sonata schema: development**

DEVELOPMENT OF CLOSING THEME—harmonic instability

DEVELOPMENT OF TRANSITION, ETC.

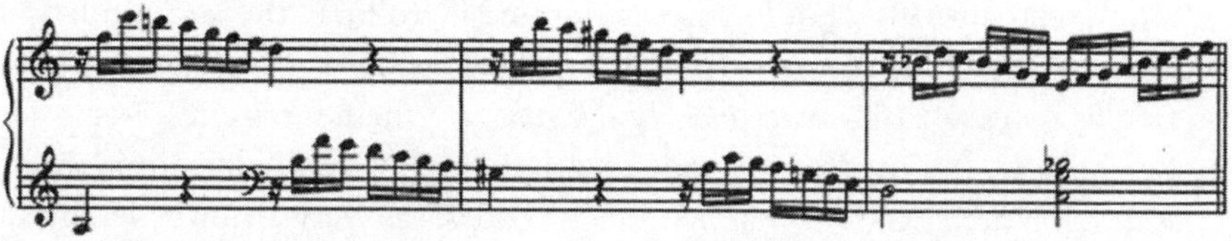


**Figure 6.31c: W. A. Mozart, Piano Sonata in C, K. 545, 1.Allegro—sonata schema: recapitulation**

PRIMARY THEME—subdominant (IV) key = break from norm

SECONDARY THEME—tonic key

CLOSING THEME—tonic key

In the interest of completeness, two other sections common to movements in sonata form should also be mentioned: the *introduction* and the **coda**.

Introductions, if they appear at all, are usually short and slow—contrasting with the generally bright—allegro—tempo of the movement itself. Their main purpose is to provide a level of gravitas to the movement as a whole, particularly when the primary theme of the exposition is lighthearted. Notable examples are found in Haydn's Symphony no. 104, Beethoven's Symphony no. 7, and Brahms' Symphony no. 1.

The coda (literally "tail"), likewise optional, follows the recapitulation to provide an even more substantive close to the movement. They commonly focus on one or two earlier ideas, especially the primary theme, at times—as in works by Beethoven—in order to carry out a level of development left unfinished prior. Like development sections, the lengths of codas can vary from generally quite short in Haydn and Mozart to often quite extensive in Beethoven (e.g., Symphony no. 5) and later composers (e.g., in the finale of Schumann's Symphony no. 2).

Some music theorists like to argue about whether sonata form is most closely descended from a binary (A-B), rounded binary (A-BA), or ternary (A-B-A) template. In truth, it synthesizes all three—or, as musicologist James Webster put it, "the power and sophistication of sonata form lie in this synthesis of a three-part design and a two-part tonal structure."[256] The schema is indeed in three parts, where the third is largely based on the first, and yet the large-scale harmonic motion—from the tonic to dominant and back again—is the traditional trajectory of binary form.

For our purposes, however, an even bigger question is how sonata form impacts the listening experience. To a large extent, the answer lies in the rich and unusual dialectic fostered by sonata form between composer, performer, and listener. Sonata form can be understood as a kind of blueprint—not a fixed scheme, but rather, as musicologist James Hepokoski calls it, "a constellation of normative and optional procedures that are flexible in their realization."[257] The large-scale framework of Exposition—Development—Recapitulation, and the harmonic expectations it implies, provide vital guideposts, and yet its specific realization demands individualized solutions. This transcends not only composers from decade to decade but also the same composer from work to work.

The relationship between the expectations of the "blueprint" and its realization is what gives the sonata-form-based work its unique expressive quality. It is also what informs the aesthetic decisions of the performer(s), and ultimately a listener's experience: how exactly the primary theme shifts harmonically toward the secondary theme; whether and how a closing theme is utilized; which themes of the exposition are treated in the development, and in what ways; and how the composer successfully navigates the harmonic resolution in the recapitulation, etc., are questions a well-prepared listener can hear as the music unfolds. It is a bit like a "whodunit" novel: you know the detective will eventually solve the case; the thrill is seeing how exactly he does it.

Sonata form carries such importance in classical music history by virtue of the flexibility and inspiration it provided composers, but also for its broader aesthetic and philosophical implications that are still being explored today. Sonata form, and its three-stage trajectory, is often used as a metaphor for extramusical qualities, including human action and even life itself. At any rate, its grip on instrumental compositional output for some 150 years was palpable. It was the "blueprint" for piano sonatas, chamber music, symphonies, overtures, **concertos**, serenades, and numerous other genres—not only for first movements, but in many cases for slow movements and finales (where it was at times combined with elements of rondo form to create a "sonata rondo") as well.

From Haydn's time onward, however, exceptions and modifications were a common part of the routine—expositions without a secondary theme; expositions with three thematic groups; recapitulations of the primary and/or secondary themes in keys other than the tonic; or recapitulations that dispense with the primary theme entirely, etc., etc. It is for such reasons that Charles Rosen referred to "sonata forms" in the plural.[258] The modifications only increased through the nineteenth century—e.g., in works by Berlioz, Chopin, Brahms, Mahler, and Sibelius—as in many ways the symmetrical and "abstract" structures of the form conflicted with the more emotional and literary inclinations of Romanticism.

Although the form waned in use from the twentieth century onward, and especially after World War II—not least due to the decline of tonality itself—the echoes of its compositional strategies are rarely far from any instrumental composer's efforts. And though you may not have known it, if your musical taste runs to such classical warhorses as Mozart's *Jupiter* Symphony, Beethoven's *Pathétique* Sonata, Schubert's *Trout* Quintet, Berlioz' *Symphonie fantastique*, or Richard Strauss' *Ein Heldenleben*, to name but a very few, you've experienced the flexibility and the inherent drama that is sonata form.

## Form: Some Final Thoughts

It is admittedly unlikely that the details of formal structure and flow are front and center in your perception as you listen to your favorite songs and works, regardless of your musical training. In many cases, form is something you experience only indirectly, without conscious recognition. And yet, as the discussion in this chapter has demonstrated, form is fundamental to musical identity. As such, increasing your conscious awareness of its elements, and its flow within individual works, can only enhance your musical appreciation and heighten your *engaged* listening.

We may not need to follow old Mr. Wilde's advice and "start with the worship of form," but our listening experience and enhancement will be well served if we at least include it within our daily musical devotion.

Here are a few suggested exercises to test your knowledge of form:

1. Next time you hear a blues, follow the form: Do you count twelve bars? Does the song use a refrain, and if so, does it appear toward the end of a verse or as a complete chorus?
2. Next time you hear a jazz "standard" sung by Frank Sinatra or Ella Fitzgerald, etc.: Can you hear an A-A-B-A structure, or another of the Tin Pan Alley schemes? If it's an instrumental version of a standard, how many choruses do the soloists take over the full form?
3. Next time you hear a rock, pop, country, R&B, or hip hop song: How is the sectional subdivision defined? Does it follow standard conventions of, for example, Verse—Chorus—Verse—Chorus—Bridge—Chorus, or something less obvious?
4. Next time you hear a symphony or sonata by Haydn, Mozart, or Beethoven (especially the first movement): Can you hear when the exposition ends? What parts of the exposition are "developed" in the development section, and how? Can you identify the return of the primary theme at the start of the recapitulation? What about the secondary theme?
5. Next time you hear *any* piece of music, try listening just for the formal structure: How does the music create contrast? Do you hear variation? What about strict repetition, or varied repetition? Is the form straightforward or complex?

seven

# SOUND: THE PERSONALITY OF MUSIC

• • •

We conclude our crash course in music theory with the first of Jan LaRue's acronym-based parameters: sound. As I explained in Chapter 2, my decision to place it last instead of first was motivated by a desire *not* to start with the thorny issues of sound waves and frequencies. That is true, but there's another reason for this decision that is as much dramatic as pedagogical.

The previously discussed parameters—melody, harmony, rhythm, and form—are in essence abstractions *until* they are made concrete through sound. These first four are like a detailed movie script: all the characters, their lines and attitudes, the settings, actions, and special effects may be vividly described on the page, but only when the film is shot and shown do we truly experience them; indeed, we often experience things that go beyond the confines or expectations of the script, especially in terms of our emotional reaction. Similarly, it is the sonic realization of musicological elements that brings them to life. Reading, or conceiving of, an extended melodic sequence, a cyclic harmonic pattern, a richly syncopated groove, or an unusual pop song sectional structure can intrigue us, but the actual music—and magic—happens when they sound!

As such, I have assigned to sound the anthropological simile of personality. Each of us has a wide range of intellectual, psychological, and physiological attributes and capabilities, but it is only when we reveal them through our personality—our "spirit"—that others get to experience them. As the old adage goes, it's not so much *what* you say, but *how* you say it. You may be wickedly smart and as kind in your heart as Mother Teresa, but if your tone is snarky or cold, you will likely gain few followers (except perhaps on Twitter). Likewise, a melody may be inherently sweet and lyrical, but if performed on a distorted electric guitar or placed within a dense sound bed, it will likely have little soothing effect.

Of course, we don't evaluate someone's behavioral traits in isolation, based on some objective criteria, before deciding if we like him or not; instead, we evaluate these traits as they are made manifest within his personality as a whole in rendering this judgment. So too with sound: it is not so much a matter of objectively evaluating this or that melody or rhythm in isolation that determines whether we like a piece of music or not; instead, it is how those elements are made manifest within a particular musical rendering—via Adele's voice, Stan Getz' tenor sax, Zakir Hussain's tabla drum, or the London Symphony's string section, etc.—that helps determine if a song or work matches our musical taste or not.

It is, moreover, for such reasons that we have a hard time using our "universal" song, "Old MacDonald," for the parameter of sound. For one, sound is hard to notate. But more importantly, how you hear this nursery rhyme—and whether or not you like it—will depend on any number of factors: what instrument(s) or voice(s) are performing it, how many, how loud or soft, how smooth or detached, how high or low, as a single melody or with other parts accompanying it, among much else. If it's being sung by a child you know, even if out of tune, you may love it; played densely by the London Symphony or loudly by a heavy metal band, perhaps not so much. . . .

At any rate, in this chapter we will address some key issues related to the sound and sonic elements of the music you hear. These include the nature of sound itself defined via pitch, dynamics, timbre, etc.; musical instruments; and texture.

## The Nature of Sound

We begin with that toughest of questions: What is sound? As you'll recall, we already had a fair bit to say about the topic in Interlude B—including on pitch, frequency, and overtones. As such, we'll here but briefly summarize/expand on the nature of sound and pitch, explicitly from a music theory and listening-experience standpoint.

Sound is a vibration propagating through a medium—most consequentially the medium of air, as few of us listen to music underwater.[259] The vibration originates from a kinetic source—a stick hitting a cymbal, a buzzing column of air passing through a trumpet, a felt hammer striking a piano string, etc.—that creates a disturbance in the air immediately around it: the air molecules literally collide with one another, going back and forth around their original position. This change of air pressure, albeit slight, travels away from the source not as actual air molecules (mass), but rather as energy, and specifically moves as a spherical wave—a **sound wave**. As the wave moves—in all directions at the speed of sound (340 meters per second)—it similarly disturbs all the air molecules in its path, thereby propelling (propagating) the sound itself forward.

Want a real-life example of sound waves disturbing air molecules in all directions? Okay, just think of the last time you pulled up to a red light, and the car stopped next to you was emanating a booming bass line you could feel in your bones—despite your windows being rolled up! Clearly, something other than matter is moving the sound from those blaring speakers, through metal and glass, to your ear.

## Pitch

When a sound wave is generated, the air molecules are caused to vibrate at a particular rate of speed. Again, this rate is called **frequency**, and it is what gives sound its pitch—the note we hear played or sung. As noted in Interlude B, frequency refers to the rate of a single *cycle* of the sound wave, from positive to negative and back to positive again—as was shown, via a sine wave, in Figure B.6.

Indeed, frequency is generally measured by the number of times the wave completes this cycle in one second—"cycles per second," or Hertz (Hz), again, named after Heinrich Hertz, the nineteenth-century German physicist who was the first to conclusively prove the existence of electromagnetic waves initially theorized by James Clerk Maxwell (1865). Of course, not all sound waves produce a discernible pitch—a slamming door, applause, an animated speaker, etc., produce no single pitch. This is due to their lack of regularity or consistency in the vibration and the resulting changes in air pressure. A musical pitch, by contrast, is produced when the air pressure is changing in a regular, repeating sequence—that is, consistently at the same frequency, such as 261.6 Hz, or middle C on the piano. By contrast, the slamming car door or the animated speaker produces a complex vibration, with rapidly changing frequencies that the ear cannot process as one individual pitch—the sound becomes, in a word, "noise," even if not unpleasant. But you already knew that!

Further, the human ear is limited in the range of frequencies it can actually hear—from roughly 20 Hz (a perfect 4th lower than the lowest note of the piano) to at most 15,000 Hz (two octaves above the highest note on the piano).* An interesting experiment in 2003 suggests that humans can "perceive"—although to disquieting ends—frequencies lower than 20 Hz, so-called infrasonics, even if we can't hear them.[260] In practical terms, however, the range of our musical hearing is considerably more limited: pitches much below the lowest G of the piano (49 Hz) are rather "muddy," while pitches much higher than the highest G of

* The upper limit of human perception may extend to 20,000 Hz. As experience teaches us, however, access to those higher frequencies dims as we age.

the piano (3136 Hz) are "tinny"—and thus hard to discern. This is basically the range of all the instruments of the orchestra, and thus the range within which most of us discern musical pitch—roughly 40 to 3000 Hz. Dogs famously can hear upwards to 45,000 Hz, while elephants apparently can hear as low as 12 Hz. Just imagine how a dog-elephant jam session would sound if they could, in fact, jam!

It should be quickly noted that we have thus far neglected the tricky but vital question of how exactly our ears and brains come to *hear* these vibrations, waves, and molecular disturbances as sounds and pitches. The truth is that sound waves don't actually make sound. As Dan Levitin puts it, "Sound is a mental image created by the brain in response to vibrating molecules": as the waves hit our ears, they may—if consistent in frequency within the limited range discussed above—trigger a neurochemical chain reaction that results in "an internal mental image we call pitch."[261] We'll happily have more to say about all that in Interlude C.

## Dynamics

Pitch, of course, is not the only quality we can discern from a musical sound wave. Critical as well are **dynamics**, or volume. The loudness or softness of a pitch has a great deal of impact on its character. So too do dynamic shifts—**crescendo** (getting louder) and **decrescendo** (getting softer). Indeed, dynamics play a huge role in our emotional reaction to music—particularly within the context of a performance.

Again, the sound wave is formed when air molecules collide with one another. It is the speed or frequency at which they bounce back and forth around their original position—their "equilibrium"—that determines the pitch. But it is their distance or displacement from that original position that determines the volume: the wider the displacement, the louder the pitch. When a piano key is pressed, or a guitar string is plucked, the molecules propagated by the wave begin with a relatively wide displacement, which gets smaller and smaller until there is no displacement at all. This process corresponds to the sound getting softer and softer until there is silence. What is important to note, however, is that although the displacement—also called the displacement amplitude—changes as the sound gets softer or louder, the *speed* at which the molecules bounce into one another remains constant. Striking a middle C on the piano leads to an ever-shrinking distance over which the air molecules bounce, but the frequency of that bounce remains constant at 261.6 Hz.

As noted, dynamics are an element not just of sound production, but also of musical performance—which we will take into account especially when discussing complete songs and works in Chapters 9–15.

## Timbre

A third pivotal aspect we can discern from a sound wave is known as **timbre** (pronounced "*tam*-burr," the *a* as in "apple")—which in short determines *how* the pitch sounds.[262] "Timbre" refers to the "color" or "tonal quality" of the pitch, and is that aspect of the sound that allows us, for example, to distinguish a piano from a violin or a trumpet—even if all three are playing the same pitch at the same dynamic; or that enables us to distinguish Tony Bennett from Nat King Cole when both sing "Fly Me to the Moon." Explaining how this happens, you might have guessed, requires us to dive back into the physics of sound—though, happily, to a topic you now already understand: overtones.

To remind you a bit, when that kinetic action—e.g., the striking of middle C on the piano—causes a musical sound wave to propagate, it generates not only its most audible *fundamental* pitch, but also a slew of harmonic (that is, integer-multiple) *overtones* or upper partials above it, all sounding simultaneously. It is this complete, complex wave form we hear when we strike middle C: not just the fundamental (in this case, at 261.6 Hz) but likewise *all* of the Pythagorean and "just" intervals above it, outlining the triads, dominant 7th chord, and other intervals noted in Interlude B, and as displayed in Figure B.9. To be sure, it is rare that one will actually hear any of those upper partials, as they generally sound with considerably less intensity than the fundamental. That is why we seem to unambiguously hear *one single pitch*, as middle C, and not a chord or cluster of pitches.[263]

But overtones don't just provide the physics-based origins of our love of major and minor triads and dominant 7th chords; they also provide instruments and voices with their own distinctive timbres. How? Well, it turns out that even though we rarely hear those upper partials as distinct notes, they have a huge impact on the *sound* emanating beyond the fundamental pitch we do hear. This is because each instrument produces a somewhat distinct *distribution* of its upper partials in terms of the *varied intensity* of each one. In other words, although every musical—that is, harmonic—wave form produces its array of upper partials, and always in the same integer-multiple distribution (as in Figure B.9), some partials are louder and more intense than others—and that's what gives each instrument its unique sound.

Clarinets, for example, generate strong molecular vibrations at every *other* partial starting with the first (i.e., the fundamental)—thus, the first, third, fifth, etc. Trumpets, by contrast, are more evenly distributed in the intensity of their partials, though they generally increase from the first through the sixth or seventh partial before tapering off. A bowed violin string typically has a peak of intensity at the first and second partials, with a gradual tapering off from there, and so forth.[264] It is a bit astounding that we know such nuanced distinctions of one instrument versus another—but that's the miracle of digital technology; below are the overtone distributions of the clarinet, trumpet, and bowed violin, using the fast Fourier transform (FFT) technique (Figure 7.1):

**Figure 7.1: Timbre distinctions via overtone distribution—a. clarinet; b. trumpet; c. bowed violin**

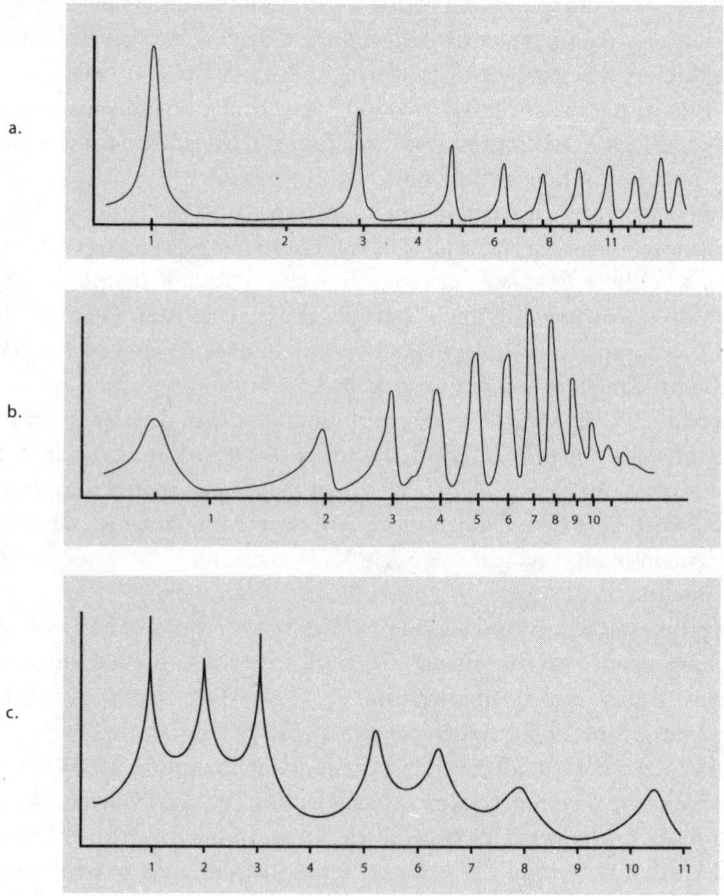


The bottom line is that each instrument has its own harmonic profile (or sets of harmonic profiles)—and this is one of the main reasons why you can easily tell a clarinet from a trumpet, and both from a violin or a flute, etc. How different instruments come to possess their own unique harmonic distribution is a complex amalgam of factors—including the shape and density of the materials used, the construction design, and the manner in which the sound itself is generated.

For example, a bowed violin gets its harmonic profile by virtue of the distinct shapes and materials of its body, bridge, tailpiece, pegs, sound bar, and bow; the metallic strands of the strings; the horsehair of the bow; the placement of the sound holes; and the gradual manner in which a bow sets a string to vibrate, among other things.

A modern flute gets its harmonic distribution from the gold, silver, and/or brass of its head joint, body, and foot joint; the placement and disposition of its keys and pads; the dimensions of its cylindrical bore; the "traverse" way in which in air is blown in to set up a vibration, among many other things.

A singing voice is affected by the muscle, bone, and tissue of the throat and face; the specific construction design of the trachea, larynx, vocal folds, etc.; and the means by which air from the lungs is constricted at the larynx, causing the vocal folds to vibrate and produce a pitch (a strong fundamental with generally harmonic partials), among much else.

Finally, we should add two additional factors that affect the timbre of an instrument: attack and decay. Since no instrument, including our voice, sets those molecules bouncing to and fro instantaneously, there is invariably a period *before* the so-called "steady state"—when the full, complex sound wave takes on its characteristic distribution. This introductory phase is called the "attack phase"—which generates an initial set of "inharmonic" (non-integer-multiple) partials that is unique to each instrument. Then, as the pitch falls away in volume, it creates another set of "inharmonic" partials, likewise unique to each instrument: the decay. This complete trajectory—from attack to steady state to decay—is called the sound "envelope," and its rich and complex disposition is what gives each instrument its distinct sonic identity.

Since the late 1940s, musically minded scientists have made productive use of all of this intricate and "run-for-cover" information: constructing "synthetic" versions of acoustic instruments by emulating their attack phase, harmonic distribution, decay parameters, etc. Processes such as additive synthesis, subtractive synthesis, FM synthesis, physical-modeling synthesis, and the like have led to the creation of myriad types of *synthesizers*—capable of not only emulating acoustic instruments but also devising new and often exotic sounds.[265] Synthesizers and related "instruments" have played an active part in music making since their inception—initially used by "avant-garde" classical composers such as Milton Babbitt and Otto Luening in the 1950s. From the 1960s onward, synthesized sounds—acoustic-instrument-oriented and not—have permeated, and in some cases dominated, the realm of popular music, especially in rock and electronica.

All of this underscores the infinite flexibility of timbre and its grand aesthetic influence on sound, and thus upon our listening experience. The subtle complexity of sound wave formation is stamped on the different instruments we hear by virtue of their inherent design and means of sounding—just as it is affected by the actual ways in which musicians play them. Our ears and brains, amazingly, can capture this tremendous subtlety, such that we can not only recognize the difference between a violin and a piano, but also distinguish one violinist from another.

Why one listener prefers Hilary Hahn's performance of the Mendelssohn Violin Concerto while another prefers that by Anne-Sophie Mutter likely has as much to do with the *sound* of their violin playing—its timbre—as with the particular phrasing and interpretative decisions they make. This in part stems from the material and construction distinctions between the two instruments they use—Hahn plays on an 1864 violin by French luthier J. B. Vuillaume, while Mutter plays the 1710 Lord Dunn-Raven by Antonio Stradivari, surely the most famous violin maker. But differences are certainly also due to untold nuances of how each violinist interprets the music, such as its famous opening theme (Figure 7.2):

**Figure 7.2: Felix Mendelssohn, Violin Concerto, 1. Allegro (mm. 2–8)—opening violin theme**

How much bow is applied to the individual notes of the theme? How much vibrato? How do they approach **articulation**—that is, are the individual notes played *legato* (connected) or *staccato* (detached), etc.? Where do the accents lie, and how strong are they? How are changes in dynamics (softer and louder) expressed? These are just some of the factors that influence the timbre of the violin as the theme is played. It is as if each violinist is painting the sound wave as she plays: raising this partial here, lowering that one there, tweaking this note to activate occasional inharmonic partials even during "steady state," etc. As such, our reaction to the music is akin to viewing a canvas while it is being painted in real time: the violinists surprise and move us as the colors and patterns of the notes and phrases take shape before our ears. Each timbral "canvas" is thus unique, which partly explains why new recordings of the same works keep appearing, even if the underlying melodies, harmonies, rhythms, and form don't change.

Timbre is also a major reason why we like or don't like certain singers. In the Music Genome Project, analysts "code" a singer's timbre on each song by identifying the degree to which certain dimensions are present—such as "smooth," "breathy," "nasal," "gritty," etc. Indeed this was taught as an exercise much like painting: Sade's voice is defined by a dominance of "smooth," Björk by "breathy," Bob Dylan by "nasal," and Tom Waits by "gritty." And yet each of these singers will have "dabs" and "drops" of many of the other timbral shades as well. Collectively, these shades defined the "color" of the singer's voice, at least in that song. This has become an excellent way to match singers together, and to more broadly assess the complexion of a listener's taste with regard to vocal sound. What timbral shades do you prefer?

As I've just demonstrated, the metaphoric link between musical timbre and visual color is often made. It forms a convenient way to conceptually characterize the great variety of tonal qualities that different instruments and voices can make. This connection has been embraced and exploited, especially in the past century or so, as composers and songwriters have experimented with different instrument combinations, usages, and techniques. One example is "*Klangfarbenmelodie*" (sound-color-melody), a term coined by Arnold Schoenberg in the early 1900s.[266] The technique involves dividing the notes of a single melody between different instruments, thereby adding a multidimensional aspect of timbre, or tone color, to the melodic line. The device is at times compared to pointillism in painting.[267]

The tonal-visual link also appears directly in the title of works where timbre is on display, as in Debussy's *Images* and Messiaen's *Couleurs de la cité céleste* (Colors of the Celestial City). Indeed, since World War II, composers have increasingly focused on timbre as a means of heightening the effect of their music—in contrast to the more commanding priority in earlier centuries on melody, harmony, and rhythm. The influential musicologist and philosopher Leonard B. Meyer saw this tendency—which he labeled as a shift from "primary parameters" (melody, harmony, rhythm) to "secondary parameters" (tempo, dynamics, timbre)—as the most defining trend in postwar music.[268]

But there's a deeper truth here: timbre is in many ways the summary manifestation of sound in a work or performance. When we hear a recording of the Dead Kennedys' "Holiday in Cambodia" or Charles Mingus' "Goodbye Pork Pie Hat" or "All That Jazz" from *Chicago* or "E lucevan le stelle" from Puccini's *Tosca*, the first thing we encounter is the overall "sound" of the music: its collective timbre. The distorted electric guitar, the unison tenor saxophones, the tinny piano, the high and smooth tenor voice heard in these respective recordings form musical colors that meld into the other colors on the track to form a full-palette canvas that evolves as the music continues. Of course, our ears can—and should—dive deeper into the music to pick out the varied and wonderful musicological details we've been reviewing. Yet each recording, each album, indeed each musical genre, has its own distinct timbral identity—which to some degree or another impacts whether you like it or not.

So ends our foray into the prickly nature of sound and its constituent elements. Hopefully you'll agree with my decision to delay this until after we'd introduced the other musical parameters. Regardless, you've happily made it through, and we can now move on to the less technically demanding topic of musical instruments.

## Instruments, Part 1: A Brief Historical Account

The discussion on timbre has naturally brought to bear a number of instruments, instrument combinations, and synthetic sounds. By virtue of timbre, we can distinguish one instrument from another, as well as make sense of them in combination—at least to some degree. Amazingly, our ears and brains can process the complex array of varying frequencies, fundamentals, harmonic and inharmonic partials, fluctuating dynamics, etc., to the point of being able to distinguish a guitar riff behind a rock singer, the chordal stabs of a piano within a jazz combo, or a solo cello in counterpoint with a full orchestra. Instruments and voices play a critical role in defining our listening experience—whether or not we can correctly identify them in the context of a recording or performance. It is thus important to gain a general understanding of how instruments came to be, are classified, and help breathe (or bow or pluck or strike) life into the music we love.

A musical instrument can be defined broadly as any device or tool capable of intentionally producing a musical sound.[269] Taken literally, this must certainly include the human voice, whether singing, scatting, rapping, or whistling. In fact, the influential medieval philosopher–music theorist Boethius (d. 524) regarded the human voice as the *only* meaningful application of "instrumental music" (*musica instrumentis*) in his influential tripartite classification of music (see Epilogue). The more common sense of the term today, however, involves the use of an external object of some kind—and thus likewise omits such "body percussion" as clapping and cheek slapping.

What follows next is a brief historical account of the rise of instruments through the centuries, and especially in the West. Putting instruments into an historical context is, to my mind, the best to way to understand their identity today.

As noted in Interlude A, we humans have made use of musical instruments from very early in our development, likely even before the dawn of *Homo sapiens* some 200,000 years ago. To quickly remind you, the earliest archeological evidence dates back only to around 60,000 years ago: the Divje Babe "flute," made from a bear femur and found in a cave in northwestern Slovenia—long before the Agricultural Revolution (14,000 years ago), but just shortly after the so-called "Cognitive Revolution" (70,000 years ago) and the rise of our ability to create "fiction."

Undoubtedly, the Divje Babe "flute" and other early archeological finds were preceded by untold numbers of less durable instruments made of "found" objects (shells, bones, animal horns, sticks, etc.). Indeed, a more consistent archeological and descriptive record of musical instruments only begins with the dawn of Neolithic civilizations (e.g., Akkadian, Babylonian, and Sumerian empires, etc.) in the third millennia BCE.

Above all, the history of musical instruments reveals the high impact of intercultural exchange between peoples across vast distances, as human migration was inevitably accompanied by the sharing of instrument technology and usage.[270] The earliest common instrument types, beyond a variety of pitched and nonpitched percussion, include harps, flutes, zithers, and trumpetlike instruments. Precursors to bowed fiddles, lutes, and oboes also appear in ancient Mesopotamian, Egyptian, and Israeli artifacts and depictions—as in the Old Testament.

Despite the great innovations made in music theory in ancient Greece, the era's most notable instruments—the lyre (a strummed string instrument), the kithara (the more sophisticated, "professional" version of the simpler, folk-oriented lyre), the aulos (a double reed wind instrument), and the syrinx (pan pipes)—were all originally imported from other regions. Yet to philosophers like Plato and Aristotle, the power of these instruments went beyond their purely musical attributes to their profound influence on human character. The ability of music to stir emotions meant that certain purely "professional" instruments, notably the aulos and kithara, were to be used sparingly and only in certain contexts; otherwise, the ecstatic emotions elicited by a virtuoso instrumental performance could well distract young listeners, and lead them down a morally compromising path. As Aristotle notes in his *Politics*, the aulos "must not be introduced into education, nor any other professional instrument, such as the kithara." Instead, he argues, it is the stolid lyre that "will make them attentive pupils."[271]

Division of instruments by the social class of their performers—mere entertaining musicians versus virtuous teachers of future citizens, for example—was by no means original to ancient Greece. Aristotle was here echoing the time-honored proscriptions by sages going back to ancient Mesopotamia. In Sumer, for example, professional musicians were identified as common laborers, alongside canal workers, brick makers, and basket weavers—what an outrage![272] Indeed, professional musicians were objects of suspicion by the learned well into the Middle Ages and beyond. This happily forms a contrast to the reverence generally granted to these professional performers in our own day.

In Europe before 1400, the most commonly used instruments were nearly all imports from India, Byzantium, Persia, and Arabia. Naturally, they underwent modification as they adapted to local musical customs and demands—via such medieval genres as the sequence, motet, troubadour chanson, and *estampie*. Key instruments depicted in illuminated manuscripts and described in narrative accounts include fiddles (vielles, rebecs, etc.), harps, portable organs, dulcimers, lutes, flutes, oboes, bagpipes, the hurdy-gurdy (a mechanical stringed instrument with both drone and melodic capability), and various bells and drums. Instrumental use, however, was generally limited to dance music and to the accompaniment of vocal music. In fact, written sources of the time give little or no indication as to which, if any, instruments are to be used in these capacities. This in turn explains the great variety and flexibility in instrumental use in modern-day performances and recordings of medieval music, whether accompanying voices or not.

Given the enduring influence of theorists like Boethius—and especially the commanding sway of the Christian Church and its liturgy—over artistic production, the dominant "instrument" during the Renaissance (15th–16th c.) continued to be the human voice. The spirit of humanism inspired a period of exquisite musical production using sophisticated techniques of polyphony (see below) in choral genres such as the sacred Mass and motet, and secular genres such as the chanson and madrigal. And yet this polyphonic choral output likewise inspired greater flexibility and expressiveness, as well as a heightened social profile, in instrumental usage as well. Initially, instrumental music amounted merely to **transcriptions** of vocal music—both for solo instruments like the lute, organ, and harpsichord (and other keyboards); and for various *consorts*—that is, ensembles—of strings like viols, or wind instruments like recorders. Specific instrumentation, however, was still generally left undesignated, especially for the consorts.

But from the mid-sixteenth century, composers adjusted their thinking, and began writing explicitly for instruments—such as Adrian Willaert did in his *Ricercar da musica nova* (1540). The musical style here was still largely vocal in nature, and the instrumentation was generally left unspecified, and yet the trend toward a more "liberated" use of instruments was becoming unstoppable. Composers and publishers increasingly focused on instrumental music, and especially dance music—where the performance capabilities and idiosyncrasies of instruments could be highlighted.[273] By 1600, many of the instruments we know today—the violin, cello, oboe, bassoon, and trumpet—began to take their present form and construction.

This liberating trend only accelerated through the Baroque era (c. 1600–1750), during which time instrumental music at first rivaled and then overtook the stature of vocal music. Composers now specifically designated which instruments were needed, and increasingly highlighted their unique performance attributes. This led to the rise of purely instrumental genres such as the concerto, suite, and sonata. Instruments began to be grouped together more regularly in ensembles or orchestras, subdivided in turn into sections of strings, winds, brass, and percussion. New instruments such as the horn and trombone took their modern form, as established instruments such as the violin, cello, oboe, flute, trumpet, and guitar attained new heights in sound quality and aesthetic design. Indeed, the string instruments built in Italy during the late seventeenth and early eighteenth centuries—by Stradivari, Amati, and Guarneri, especially—are the most sought after (and expensive) one can find even today.

Over the next two centuries—during the Classical and Romantic eras—several new instruments came into being, including the clarinet, tuba, and saxophone, as well as folk instruments like the accordion, harmonica, and banjo. Importantly, the piano (initially "pianoforte") replaced the harpsichord as the principal domestic keyboard instrument; it was initially designed around 1700 by Bartolomeo Cristofori as the "*arpicembalo che fa' il pian, e il forte*" (harpsichord that plays both soft and loud), but came into prominence only after 1760. The piano continued to evolve in construction and sonic power over the next century, reaching its present-day form in the 1870s.[274] The growing interest in timbre through the nineteenth century, moreover, led to a huge expansion in the size of the orchestra (reaching a hundred or more players), as well as the embrace of "alternate" instruments. These include the piccolo, cornet, English horn, and contrabassoon, as well as rarely used instruments such as the "Wagner tuba," which sounds like a mix between a trombone and a French horn.

By 1900, most of the acoustic instruments we hear in the West today had reached their current form. American "popular" styles such as ragtime, blues, and early jazz initially relied on instruments—the piano, guitar, harmonica, drums, tuba, trumpet, clarinet, trombone, etc.—already well established in other styles.

A dramatic revolution, however, was launched when electrical means were applied to amplify and later alter the sound of acoustic instruments, most notably the guitar. When, in 1931, George Beauchamp and Adolph Rickenbacker managed to amplify string vibrations of a lap steel guitar (by placing an electromagnetic pickup in which a current passed through a wire coil wrapped around a magnet), the initial application was merely to allow the guitar sound to penetrate the large ensemble of horns, piano, and drums around it. But as electric guitar technology evolved, the applications soon extended beyond amplification to an array of new sounds and effects, especially from the 1960s: feedback, distortion, chorus, delay, reverb, etc. Similar approaches were applied to keyboard instruments such as the organ and piano to create a variety of new instruments and sounds, adopted especially by jazz and rock musicians. Finally, as noted earlier, the past several decades have seen the rise of a whole host of commercial synthesizers, using analog and digital circuits and microchips, that have come to dominate a number of pop and rock styles.

When it comes to folk and traditional music outside Western Europe and North America, the number and variety of instruments quickly becomes dizzying.[275] As with language, dress, dance, and other forms of cultural expression, musical instruments reflect inherent qualities of the people and the land from which they stem—not to mention the musical style and language developed over centuries and millennia. Some instruments, indeed, become so intimately tied to regional or national identity that they become near symbols of the cultures themselves—such as the Irish harp, the Japanese koto (zither), the Chinese pipa (lute), the Indian sitar (lute), and the Aboriginal Australian didgeridoo (a wooden "trumpet"), etc. Given the cross-cultural exchanges noted above, many ethnic instruments are "cousins" of sorts to those used in the West—with a wide variety of fiddles, harps, flutes, reeds, horns, dulcimers, zithers, lutes, bagpipes, and especially percussion. We'll touch more upon several of these instruments in Chapter 14 and elsewhere.

## Instruments, Part 2: Types and Classifications

The broad range of materials and sound-production techniques used in music making over the years and across the world has bequeathed to us an amazing variety of instruments. These materials and techniques have in turn brought rich and varied "colors" to how the very musical parameters of melody, harmony, rhythm, and sound have been devised over time, and from place to place.

More pragmatically, the wide variety of instruments and instrument types has led to various attempts to create a universal system of classification. Many such systems have been proposed and adapted, but here we will briefly mention three:

The most basic is simply based on register, following upon designations used with vocal range. These are, from highest to lowest: **soprano**, **alto**, **tenor**, **baritone**, and **bass**. In some cases these terms are tagged onto the instruments themselves, especially when in a class or family of related instruments—as with the saxophone family, or the bass guitar. Indeed, the French word for the viola (the middle-range string instrument) is "*alto*." As many instruments have wide ranges (larger, for example, than a human voice), this classification system has limited utility.

Another common approach are the four divisions already mentioned with regard to the rise of the orchestra established in the Baroque era: *strings* (violins, violas, cellos, basses), *woodwinds* (flute, clarinet, oboe, bassoon, etc.), *brass* (trumpet, trombone, French horn, tuba, etc.), and *percussion* (drums, cymbals, gongs, marimbas, etc.). To this is usually added a fifth category: *keyboards* (piano, organ, accordion, etc.). Within the traditional four-category system, the piano is deemed a percussion instrument by virtue of the hammers that strike the strings. The mere presence of strings, however, makes this problematic.

At any rate, this four- (or five-) category system is the one that will be most resonant with practicing musicians—whether speaking of a classical orchestra, a jazz band, or even a rock group. Naturally, there are many further subdivisions, as between bowed strings and plucked or strummed strings—including the guitar. Shopping for instruments online will lead to still other subdivisions, as between guitars and bass guitars, between drums and other percussion, or between pianos and synthesizers.

In response to the limitations and potential contradictions of these two common approaches, scholars have sought a more "scientific" method of classification. The most widely embraced today is known as Hornbostel-Sachs, named after two German ethnomusicologists, Erich Moritz von Hornbostel and Curt Sachs, for their 1914 catalogue, which has been continually refined ever since. The system owes its origins to several previous systems, going back even to an ancient Indian treatise, the *Natya Shastra* (c. 200 CE). It is organized not unlike the

Dewey Decimal System into various categories, subcategories, sub-subcategories, etc., each with a multipart number code.[276] The five principal levels are:

1. *Idiophones*: the sound is produced by the vibration of the full body of the instrument (not by a membrane, string, or column of air) whether struck (directly or indirectly), plucked, rubbed, or blown
   Examples: cymbals, xylophone, thumb piano, musical saw, glass harmonica
2. *Membranophones*: the sound is produced by the vibration of a tightly stretched membrane, whether struck (directly or indirectly), shaken, plucked, rubbed, or blown
   Examples: timpani, snare drum, frame drum, tambourine, kazoo
3. *Chordophones*: the sound is produced by the vibration of one or more strings stretched between fixed points, whether simple or composite (where the resonating body is a necessary and integral part of the instrument)
   Examples: zither, piano, harpsichord, violin, acoustic guitar, harp, lyre
4. *Aerophones*: the sound is produced by a vibrating column of air, whether free (air not continually contained in instrument) or nonfree (most wind instruments)
   Examples: siren, accordion, flute, clarinet, oboe, trumpet, trombone, bassoon
5. *Electrophone*: the sound is produced in a manner involving electricity, whether by having electronic action or electronic amplification, or by using electronic means to directly produce the sound
   Examples: electric piano or organ, electric guitar, theremin, synthesizer

While nicely structured and well accepted by ethnomusicologists and "organologists" (the unfortunate term for those who study musical instruments), use of this system among rank-and-file musicians is practically nonexistent. That is, I've never heard a conductor, composer, performer, or avid music lover say, "The chordophones were too loud," or "That work made creative use of idiophones," etc.

As such, you'll be fine to organize and better understand the role that instruments play in defining your musical taste by simply adhering to the simple division of strings, brass, winds, percussion, and keyboards. Of course, the more you can aurally recognize one "exemplar" from another—a violin from a viola, a trumpet from a French horn, an oboe from a clarinet, a cymbal from a tambourine, a piano from a harpsichord, a lute from a guitar, even a sitar from a pipa—the better off you'll be.

## Texture

In our musical discussion thus far, we have made occasional passing reference to a key element of sound without actually defining it: **texture**. The delay is fitting, as the term represents a kind of summation of what constitutes musical sound—a constellation of melody, harmony, rhythm, timbre, and instrumentation—or, as the *Grove Dictionary* puts it, "a term used when referring to the sound aspects of a musical structure." An interesting fact is that unlike most every other musical term, there is not really a clear equivalent to "texture" in other European languages; the cognate in Italian, "tessitura," refers to something else entirely, namely a particular range or **register** of a voice. Perhaps the most akin is the German word "*Klangstruktur*" (sound structure), which, however, is rarely used. No doubt, all this is due to the diversity of factors subsumed by the English word "texture," as well as its relatively recent adoption.[277] And yet the texture of the music you hear plays such a pivotal role in your experience of it that it is worth gaining an understanding.

In the broad sense, texture embraces several qualities of a piece of music: the density of the sound; the range from the highest to the lowest notes; the number and distinct functions of the instruments and/or voices; the disposition of vertical and/or horizontal features; the relationship between foreground and background material; the "thickness" of the chords; the density of the rhythms; and the nature of the instrumental timbres, among others. With such an amalgamation of factors, it's little wonder that not every language has a direct equivalent. And yet, given the generic English definition of "texture"—as "the structure, feel, and appearance of something"—it seems an appropriate musical choice.

Fortunately, however, there is a more singular model by which texture is commonly understood by musicians—namely, as a set of distinct ways in which the individual musical parts or lines are put together. By common convention, there are four: monophony, heterophony, polyphony, and homophony. Be prepared, moreover, as a proper explanation of each of these textures requires some historical backstory.

### MONOPHONY

**Monophony** ("sounding alone") is music for a single voice or melodic line. Jennifer Hudson singing "The Star-Spangled Banner" at a Yankees game is an example of monophony: no accompaniment, no chords, no additional melodies. Yet so is the Michigan State Glee Club singing "The Victors" in octave unison, as well as the opening six bars of Tchaikovsky's Symphony no. 4 in F Minor (Figure 7.3):

**Figure 7.3: Pyotr Tchaikovsky, Symphony no. 4 in F Minor, 1. Andante sostenuto—opening monophonic melody**

Historically, monophony is the texture associated with the very roots of the Western classical canon, commonly referred to as Gregorian chant. As noted previously, this was the original liturgical repertoire of the Christian church, more properly called "plainchant," a term distinguishing it from measured or polyphonic music—with roots back to the eighth century and beyond. Indeed, the concept of "harmony"—in terms of chords or contrapuntal lines—was seemingly unknown prior to its development in Europe in the ninth and tenth centuries.

Monophony continued as the dominant texture in Europe through the twelfth century or so—for example, in the chansons of the troubadours and trouvères (Figure 7.4):

**Figure 7.4: Raimbaut de Vaqueiras, "Kalenda maya" (late 12th c.; lyrics omitted) —monophonic troubadour melody (potential rhythmic realization)**

By this time, however, the allure of polyphony was starting to gain the attention of the more adventurous composers, such as those at the new Notre-Dame Cathedral in Paris. Still, the ubiquity of Gregorian chant within liturgical practice kept the sound of monophony familiar to most Western listeners well into the seventeenth century. In more recent centuries, however, the dominance of chordal harmony has made us less and less accustomed to the practice of purely unaccompanied melody—aside from a few occasion-specific pieces like "Happy Birthday," "Taps," and "The Star-Spangled Banner." There are more elaborate exceptions, of course, such as J. S. Bach's unaccompanied suites and sonatas for violin and for cello (Figure 7.5):

**Figure 7.5: J. S., Bach, Cello Suite no. 1 in G, 1. Prelude—monophonic classical composition**

But in general, monophony is so seldom heard in the West—the success of the *Chant* album notwithstanding—that it can often sound odd or hollow to us today. This is too bad, as a single unaccompanied melody can indeed give rise to a subtle and deeply spiritual listening experience.

This power, moreover, is not lost on the many non-Western cultures for which monophony is still the dominant musical texture—as with the Chinese, Ghanaian, and Indian folk melodies shown in Figures 3.41–43.

In many cases, however, the pure "monophony" of monophonic music may be more theoretical than practical. In both Western and non-Western traditions, the single-voiced melody is often accompanied not with a chord or another countermelody, but instead with a sustained low tone, or drone, as we've discussed in Chapter 4. As noted there, the drone is an ancient, archetypal musical phenomenon, and was likely long improvised in ways and circumstances we can only presume today. Many non-Western song traditions are marked by their common use of drones below the established melodies. It's hard to say how commonly drones were used with monophonic melodies in the West during the Middle Ages—perhaps even chant—though the frequent depictions of drone instruments suggests that it was not unheard of. To be sure, modern interpreters of medieval music are quite fond of adding drones below melodies that only survive to us in a monophonic form, such as in the "ecstatic" sequences by Hildegard von Bingen (Figure 7.6):

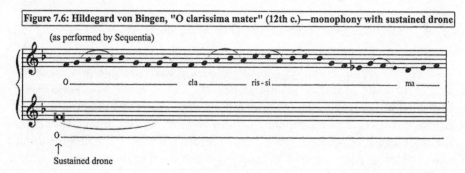

**Figure 7.6: Hildegard von Bingen, "O clarissima mater" (12th c.)—monophony with sustained drone**

(as performed by Sequentia)

O
cla
ris - si
ma
O
Sustained drone

Further, the drone need not be sustained to achieve its "effect," but could also be realized as a steady flow of repeated notes, often in the same rhythm as the actual melody—as in this rendition of another sequence by Hildegard von Bingen (Figure 7.7):

**Figure 7.7: Hildegard von Bingen, "O virga ac diadema" (12th c.)—monophony with rhythmic drone**

(as performed by Sequentia)

O vir - ga ac di - a - de - ma pur - pu - re re - gis
O vir - ga ac di - a - de - ma pur - pu - re re - gis
Repeated drone

This monophony-plus-drone texture is occasionally referred to as "biphonic," though more often it is simply identified as a commonplace (often improvised) facet of monophonic music. Regardless, it provides to many a moving, spiritual listening experience that helps explain its endurance, and its continued use in numerous musical styles found around the world.

## HETEROPHONY

The second texture, **heterophony**, is even less commonly heard, or at least differentiated, today, especially in the West. The term literally means "sounding apart" (or "a divergence of sound"), but this is somewhat misleading. It is not so much a separate sound—as in another, countermelody—but rather a simultaneous variation of the *same* melody. For example, if Jennifer Hudson and Beyoncé were to both sing "The Star-Spangled Banner" in unison without accompaniment, but each was told to freely embellish, the result would be one melody sung simultaneously in two variations. Your ear would most certainly process it as a single melody, though more multidimensional than if the two had sung it with the exact same notes and rhythms. The term "heterophony" dates back to at least Plato—who described it as a common though "unsuitable" practice of lyre players, taking liberties while accompanying the "pure" version being sung simultaneously by a singer.[278]

Heterophony was undoubtedly common throughout the ancient world in Plato's day, just as it is still commonplace in many musical cultures in our own. Indeed, whenever sophisticated monophony is the dominant texture, heterophony is likely common as well. Musical cultures that are celebrated for their sophisticated approach to heterophony include Arabic, Persian, Eastern European, gamelan, Japanese, Thai, Philippine, and Chinese traditions. At times, the variation between the different, simultaneous versions can be quite dramatic, and yet their alignment on key structural notes suggests that they are indeed renditions of the same melody—and not two different melodies. Here is an example of a heterophonic texture in instrumental music from China (Figures 7.8):

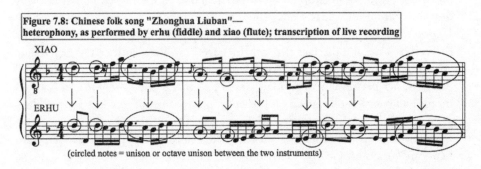

**Figure 7.8: Chinese folk song "Zhonghua Liuban"—heterophony, as performed by erhu (fiddle) and xiao (flute); transcription of live recording**

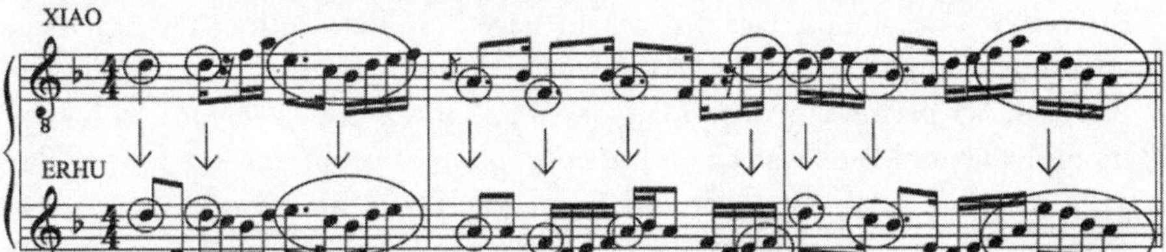


(circled notes = unison or octave unison between the two instruments)

Although perhaps arising from quasi-composed or traditional templates, even such elaborate versions of heterophony as this are largely improvised. And in fact heterophony can be primarily considered an improvised texture. It is for this reason, moreover, that heterophony is little known in the Western classical canon. With the rise of music notation in the ninth century, improvised practice took an historical backseat to explicit part writing. Of course, musicians continued to improvise—as it is a natural musical tendency, and the means by which musical styles rise and evolve in the first place. But as a result, cultivation of heterophony gave way to other textures, beginning with polyphony. As such, few examples of heterophony are found in the classical repertory before the twentieth century. A rare earlier example of a heterophonic approach occurs in Adagio of Beethoven's Ninth Symphony, where a slow melody in the woodwinds is simultaneously varied in florid ornamentation in the strings (Figure 7.9):

**Figure 7.9: Beethoven, Symphony no. 9, 3. Adagio (mm. 98–101)—heterophony between winds and violins**

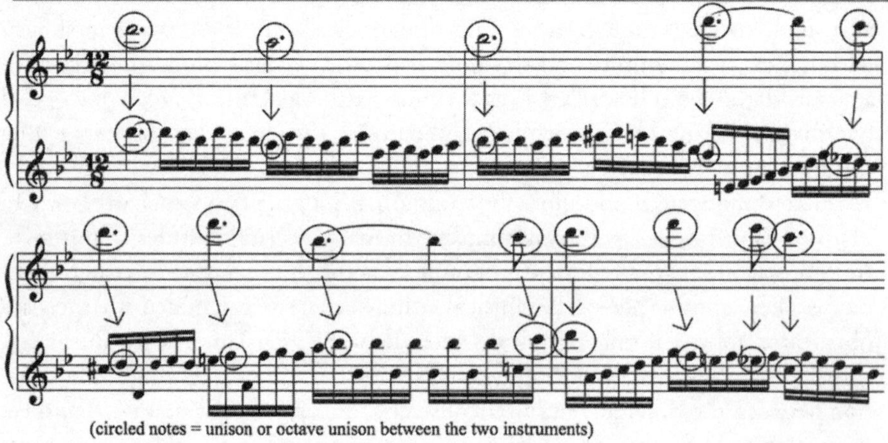

(circled notes = unison or octave unison between the two instruments)

While written examples in the West are rare, the advent of recordings has raised the profile of heterophony somewhat. For example, when you attentively hear a recording of Maria Callas singing "O mio babbino caro" from Puccini's *Gianni Schicchi*, you'll hear that her sung melody is varied from that played by the violins—despite the fact that on the page they are identical; the differences are subtle, and yet they are to a considerable degree what drives the emotion and power of her performance. Similarly, heterophony is at play when Earl Scruggs on his banjo and Paul Warren on his violin play a "unison" melody on the bluegrass classic "Cripple Creek"; or when Charlie Parker and Dizzy Gillespie race through "Be-bop"; or when we carefully listen to the relationship between John Lennon's vocal and George Harrison's sitar on "Norwegian Wood." Of course, none of these, including the Beethoven, are literal examples of heterophony, since these "simultaneously varied" melodies take place within the context of a fuller homophonic texture. Still, it is worth acquainting our ears to this textural approach, as it can be a substantial part of the identity, and thus experience, of the music we hear.

In contrast to monophony and heterophony, the next two textures are considerably more germane to the Western listening experience. They also point to the general evolution of musical composition from the Middle Ages through the Classical period in the eighteenth century.

## POLYPHONY

**Polyphony** literally means "many voiced" and implies that each such voice, or part, has a degree of independence. To continue our earlier example, if Jennifer Hudson's vocal rendition of "The Star-Spangled Banner" was accompanied by an improvised countermelody by trumpeter Wynton Marsalis, the result would be two-voiced polyphony or counterpoint. It is worth taking note of the remarkable fact that our ears and brain can process two (and more) distinct melodies at once, making sense of them separately and together—that we could follow Marsalis' melodic flow of notes and rhythms without losing stock of Hudson's rendition of the national anthem. This contrasts with the cognitive chaos that would ensue if Hudson and Marsalis were to speak different texts simultaneously, whereby "sense" would largely be lost.

Another simple way of thinking about polyphony is the round or canon, such as "Row, Row, Row Your Boat." With each new entrance among a group of three singers, we hear multiple, "independent" lines proceeding harmoniously at once—despite the fact that they're all the same (Figure 7.10):

**Figure 7.10: "Row, Row, Row Your Boat"—counterpoint created via a canon or "round"**

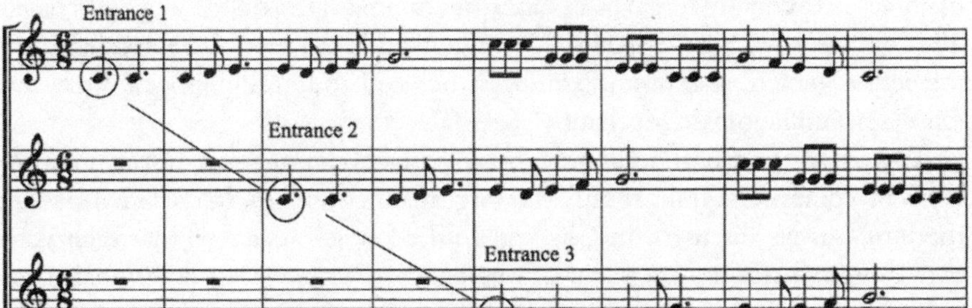


The development of polyphony or multivoiced writing is largely the history of Western music from the ninth through seventeenth centuries. It likely arose organically in the monasteries and cathedrals of the early Middle Ages as singers improvised simple accompanying lines to the liturgical chants they sang each day—perhaps as extensions of static and shifting drones. At any rate, by the mid-ninth century, the practice was widespread enough in northern France for an anonymous music theorist to document and codify it—giving the practice the name "organum." The examples cited in his *Musica enchiriadis* (Musical Handbook) were illustrative and not "composed" pieces, describing instead the "proper" ways to improvise a new melody (*vox organum*) against a Gregorian chant (*vox principalis*) in a note-against-note manner.[279]

While these "rules" would continually change over the centuries, the treatise introduces the three basic types of contrapuntal motion for two simultaneous lines: **parallel**—both lines moving in the same direction, often at the same interval distance; **contrary**—the two lines moving in opposite direction; and **oblique**—where one of the voices stays stationary, like a drone, while the other moves. These are shown in Figure 7.11:

**Figure 7.11: Principal types of two-part contrapuntal motion**

Over the next few centuries, these simple contrapuntal techniques would blossom into artful displays of composing simultaneous yet independent lines—that is, into true polyphony. Through the latter Middle Ages, distinct polyphonic genres would emerge—notably organum (which blossomed into a rich polyphonic practice in the eleventh and twelfth centuries at Notre-Dame in Paris), the motet, and the chanson. Works in these genres were largely for two or three, occasionally four voices, and predominantly vocal, as we've discussed. The composers who developed these styles include the most esteemed figures of the period, including Léonin, Perotin, Francesco Landini, Philippe de Vitry, and especially Guillaume de Machaut.

Critical in the evolution of polyphony were developments in music notation, whereby composers could specify not only distinct pitches, but also contrasting rhythms—as we discussed in Chapter 5. The key point here is that each voice part is more or less independent of one another, with at least occasional divergence in rhythm and melodic intervals. But this does not mean that each voice is of equal importance, nor even that each line can properly be called a "melody." Many internal contrapuntal lines, in fact, have little distinct musical identity of their own—as we discussed in Chapter 3. It is the top voice, not surprisingly, that is often the most distinct and "composed" of the set, with the others providing support and variety.

Theorists of the period in fact rarely speak of how the voices relate compositionally to one other, outside of then-current rules of "harmony"—meaning the accepted flow of consonance and dissonance. Further, the main focus of harmonic awareness was not so much the middle of phrases, but instead their beginnings and ends—that is, at cadences (see Chapter 5). This means that within phrases, clashes of passing dissonance are not uncommon—which is partly why medieval polyphony can sound odd or even "wrong" to us today.

Remember that this is long before the advent of chords and tonal harmony. The concern of composers in the eleventh to fourteenth centuries was not to move from one triad to another, or from one key to another. Instead, it was to follow the established rules of counterpoint at that moment, while likewise creating elegant individual lines and a rich mix of variety and repetition. The results can sound exotic or strange to our modern ears, but are worth testing against your current musical taste. Here are two examples of polyphony in the Middle Ages (Figures 7.12 and 7.13):

**Figure 7.12: Anon., "De rupta rupecula" (13th c. conductus; text omitted)—early medieval polyphony**

**Figure 7.13: Guillaume de Machaut, "Quant en moy" (14th c. motet; text omitted)—late medieval polyphony**

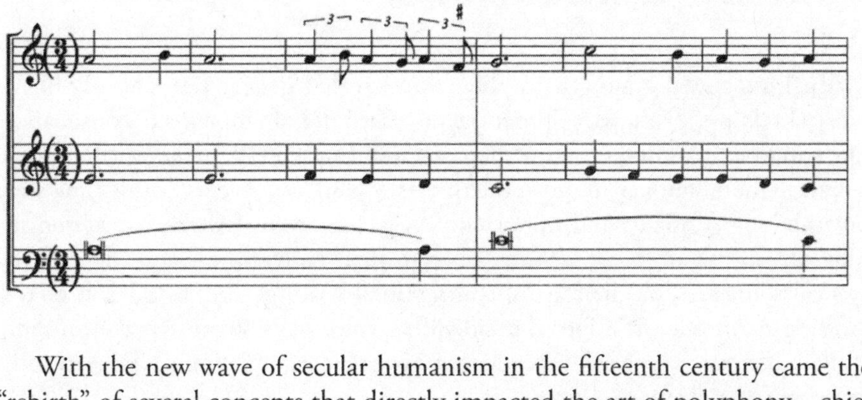

With the new wave of secular humanism in the fifteenth century came the "rebirth" of several concepts that directly impacted the art of polyphony—chief among them balance and symmetry.[280] The result was a new cognizance of how the individual voice parts can and should relate to one another. In contrast to medieval polyphony, where the voice parts rarely shared or integrated the same melodic material, composers of the Renaissance developed an increasingly conscious approach to contrapuntal integration.

This began with the motets, Masses, and chansons of Dufay and Ockeghem in the fifteenth century and reached its apogee in the works of Josquin des Prés and his contemporaries in the early sixteenth century. The term used today for this integrated approach is "**imitation**" or "imitative counterpoint," where each voice shares a relatively equal role in the musical discourse, passing phrases or phrase segments from one to another—like a conversation among equal partners. Here's an example of this approach (Figure 7.14):

**Figure 7.14: Josquin des Prés, "Stabat Mater" (early 15th c. motet)—early Renaissance (imitative) polyphony**

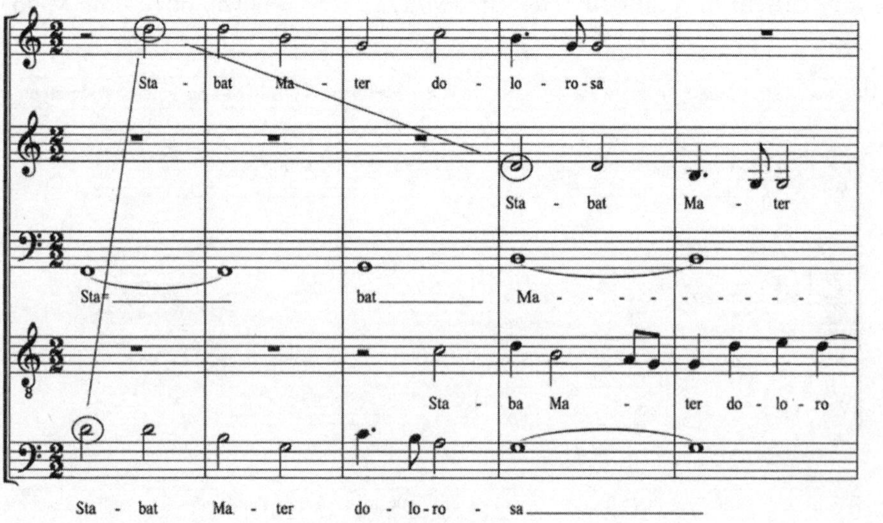


(circled notes = start of imitative contrapuntal phrases)

This integrated approach to polyphony created greater transparency in the musical texture. At the same time, the increased use of "imperfect" consonances (3rds and 6ths), as discussed in Chapter 4 and Interlude B, makes the harmonic language more familiar to our modern ears. Again, composers at this time were not thinking of major and minor chords, per se, even if we can anachronistically identify them in the texture. Instead, their concern was creating pleasing vertical sonorities via their artful contrapuntal writing. Still, as a result of this growing harmonic intuition, the individual voice parts began to take on more "functional" roles, especially at cadences. Here's an example from a late sixteenth-century motet (Figure 7.15):

**Figure 7.15: Palestrina, "Veni Creator Spiritus" (late 16th c. motet)—late Renaissance polyphony**

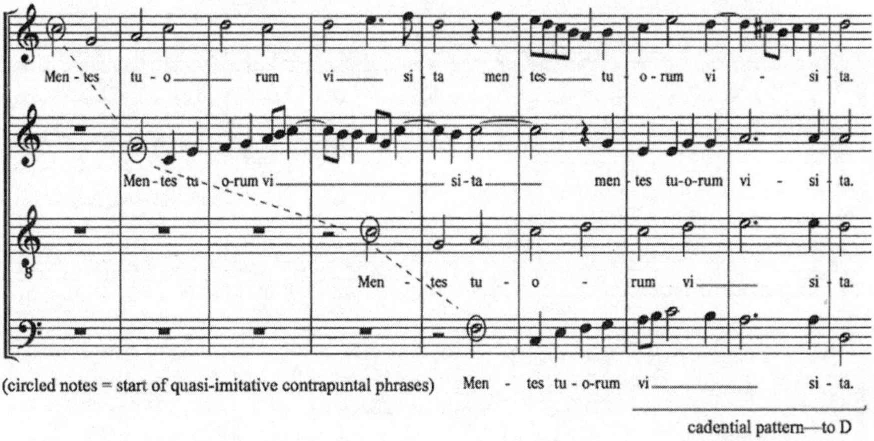
Men - tes tu - o rum vi si ta men tes tu o - rum vi - si ta.
Men - tes tu - o-rum vi si - ta men tes tu-o-rum vi - si ta.
Men - tes tu - o - rum vi si ta.
Men - tes tu - o-rum vi si - ta.
(circled notes = start of quasi-imitative contrapuntal phrases)
cadential pattern—to D

From the mid-sixteenth century, strict imitation gave way to a freer polyphonic approach. Imitation became just one of several viable contrapuntal approaches. This versatile polyphonic texture is found especially in the sacred choral works of the great masters of the "High Renaissance": William Byrd, Roland de Lassus, and Palestrina—the latter becoming the paradigm of what was later dubbed the "*stile antico*" (ancient style).

After 1600, however, other textural approaches began to challenge the hegemony of this polyphonic *stile antico*—thinner textures of one or two melodic lines with simple, subservient accompaniment. This trend went hand in hand with an increasingly conscious use of vertical "chords" and "chord progressions" that would later define tonality. The seeds of this so-called "*stile moderno*" (modern style) were planted by madrigal composers of the late sixteenth century, such as Cipriano de Rore, Giaches de Wert, and Luca Marenzio. They were then more forcefully launched in the secular works of Claudio Monteverdi—who labeled it the "*seconda pratica*" (second practice), in part defined by a more liberal use of dissonance brought on by adherence to the emotion of the texts. Here's an example, from a madrigal by Monteverdi from the 1630s (Figure 7.16):

**Figure 7.16: Claudio Monteverdi, "Ardo e scoprir" (mm. 32–40; from *Madrigals Book 8,* c. 1630)—early Baroque polyphony**

Polyphony at various levels of strictness—"*antico*," "*moderno*," and "*misto*" (mixed)—continued to play a commanding role in the output of music during the Baroque era. The flagship polyphonic genre/form during the latter Baroque was the instrumental fugue, which reached its apex in the music of J. S. Bach.[281] Here, sections of strict imitation alternate with "episodes" of freer polyphony, as in this example (Figure 7.17):

**Figure 7.17: J. S. Bach, Fugue in D minor (from *The Well-Tempered Clavier*, Book 1)—late Baroque polyphony**

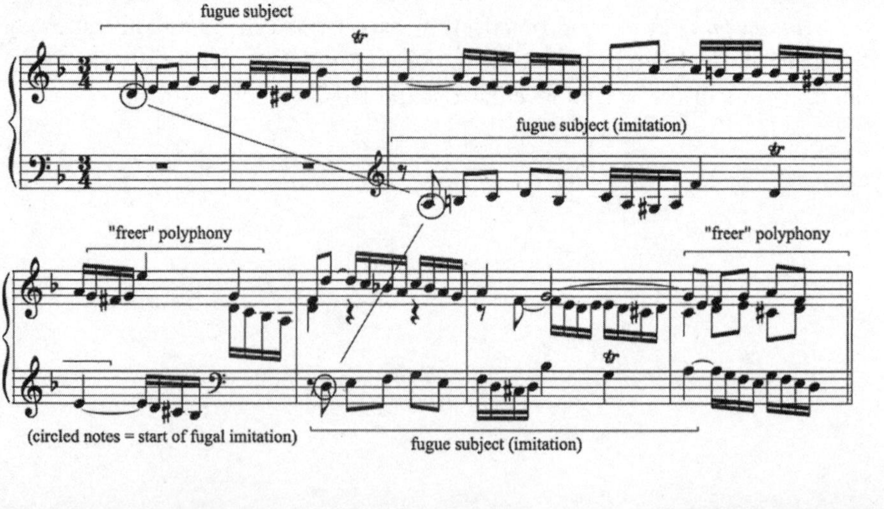

By this time, of course, tonal harmony was in full swing. Contrapuntal activity was now carried out with a particular mandate: to establish the "home key"; modulate to other, related key areas; and then return "home" again. The fugues of J. S. Bach—as well as those by Handel, Buxtehude, and others—are masterful exemplars of the ornate, polyphonic art of the late Baroque. And yet this same complexity began to invite a backlash in the early to mid-eighteenth century—in favor of a simpler, more pleasing style. The term used for this simpler approach was "galant," which C. P. E. Bach (son of J. S.) contrasted, and preferred, to the "learned"—that is, polyphonic—style of his father's generation. The result was the rise of the Classical style and a move toward a dominant use of the homophonic texture, as we'll soon see.

To be sure, the use of polyphony has continued vibrantly within the classical repertory through the ensuing centuries, as indeed it still does today. This includes especially fugues and contrapuntal sections in works by Mozart, Beethoven, Mendelssohn, Brahms, Verdi, Shostakovich, Stravinsky, Messiaen, Ligeti, and Elliott Carter, among many others. But a strictly and exclusively polyphonic texture became rather exceptional after 1750 or so—a single movement within a larger sonata or string quartet, for example. Beethoven's *Great Fugue*, Op. 133 and Shostakovich's *24 Prelude and Fugues*, Op. 87, are two well-known examples.

Beyond the Western classical tradition, "true" polyphony—where each voice part acts *independently*, and not merely in an accompanying role vis-à-vis a "principal" melody—is comparatively rare. Most such cases, moreover, are based on a purely oral tradition. Examples among indigenous world music traditions include those of the San people in southwestern Africa, the Mbuti people of the Congo region, and the famed gamelan tradition of Bali. Such polyphony is generally based on a principal melody with drones or heterophonic accompaniment, or via a set of short patterns that repeat and overlap in various, often rhythmically complex, ways—such as we saw in the African example given in Figure 5.44.

"True" polyphony is likewise fairly uncommon in nonclassical styles in the West, such as jazz and rock. The only jazz style to embrace polyphony in a concerted way, in fact, was the first: New Orleans jazz. In this style, the trumpet generally plays the main melody at the beginning and end of a performance, while the clarinet and trombone improvise around it. Undoubtedly this came out of the light counterpoint often used in marches of the period, such as the famous piccolo solo against the main theme in John Philip Sousa's "Stars and Stripes Forever" (Figure 7.18):

**Figure 7.18: John Philip Sousa, "Stars and Stripes Forever" (mm. 110–117)—polyphony in late 19th c. march**

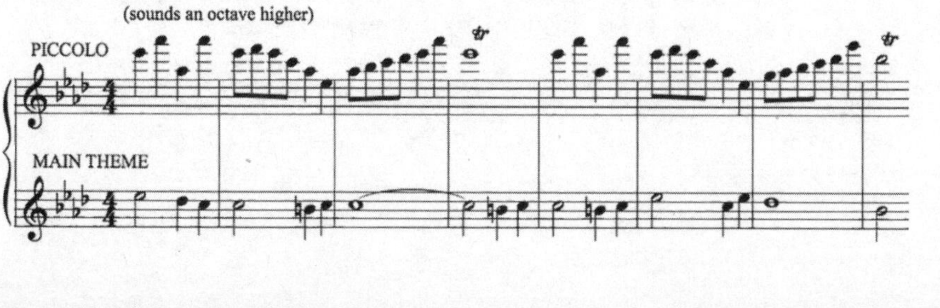

At the same time, the focus in these moments in New Orleans jazz is clearly on the main trumpet melody, with the clarinet and trombone providing simple, rather formulaic support. Once the swing era began in the 1930s, moreover, the simpler homophonic texture assumed priority within jazz, with only occasional exceptions in the more adventurous works by composers like Duke Ellington, Stan Kenton, Dave Brubeck, and Wynton Marsalis.

Similarly, polyphony is rare in rock music, and generally occurs in only brief passages, such as in the Beatles' "Eleanor Rigby" (Figure 7.19), or the closing section of "Black Water" by the Doobie Brothers (Figure 7.20):

**Figure 7.19: The Beatles, "Eleanor Rigby" (closing section)—rare polyphony in rock music**

**Figure 7.20: The Doobie Brothers, "Black Water" (a cappella coda)—rare polyphony in rock music**

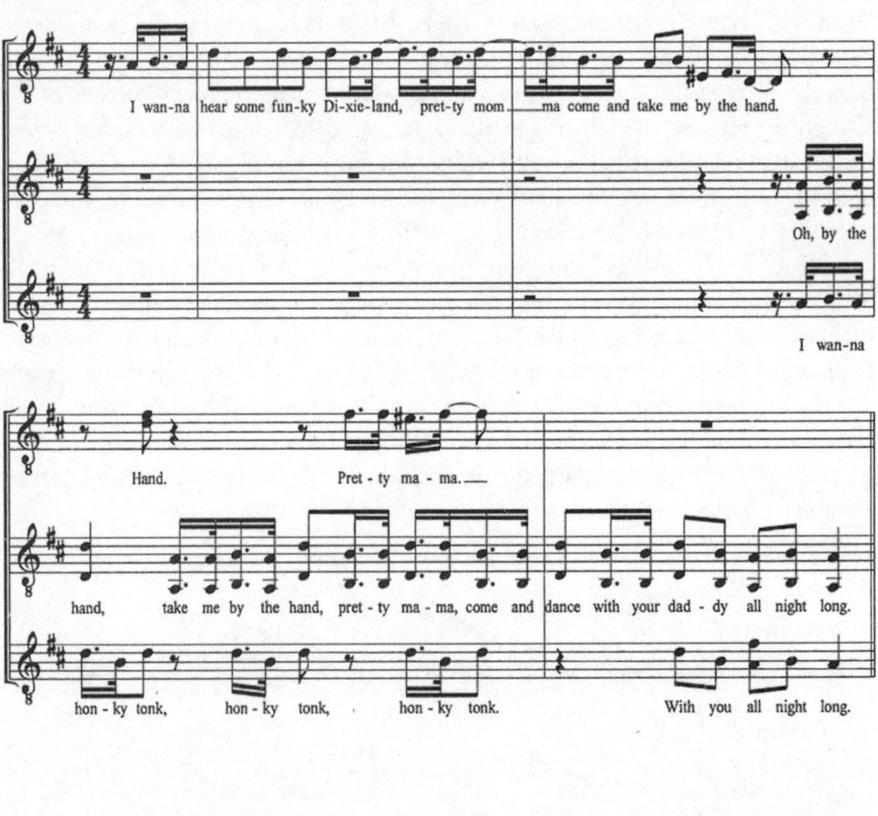

As noted above, however, making a clean distinction between a supporting line and a "truly" independent one can be tough and subject to debate from one listener to another. The prevalence of riffs or ostinatos in rock music demonstrates the complexity of drawing too fine a line. Indeed, most pop and rock indulges at least somewhat in multiple parts at once, whereby the energy and interest of the music is found: a lead vocal melody, a well-defined bass line, an active guitar ostinato, a horn or synth **obbligato** (independent line), a background vocal countermelody, etc. In most such cases, these latter parts are clearly supportive of the lead melody and thus not in line with our definition of polyphony—despite how infectious they are, or how critical they are to our experience of the music.

## HOMOPHONY

It is just this type of texture—a lead melody with one or more accompanying parts—that is subsumed under the term "**homophony**." Admittedly, this may generate some confusion, as the expression "homophony" literally means "sounding the same." What exactly is "the same" about a lead melody and different accompanying parts? In the case of most Western music written over the past 250 years or so, the answer is harmony. Once tonality was firmly established and composers began focusing on a simpler texture of melody and accompaniment, all parts were now functioning in support of the *same* underlying succession of chords and chord progressions.

In fact, however, this is but one of two textures subsumed under the term "homophony." The other, which we'll discuss more below, is considerably more intuitive, as it involves all parts moving in the same rhythm. For this reason, the latter is often called "chordal homophony" (or "homo-rhythm"), while the former is at times called **melody-dominated homophony**. This, incidentally, is how we differentiate between them in the Music Genome Project.

As unsatisfying as all that may be, it is tradition in musicology to refer to the texture of melody with accompaniment as homophony. Here are two examples from the classical repertory (Figures 7.21 and 7.22):

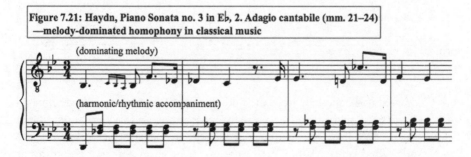

**Figure 7.21: Haydn, Piano Sonata no. 3 in E♭, 2. Adagio cantabile (mm. 21–24) —melody-dominated homophony in classical music**

**Figure 7.22: Modest Mussorgsky, "The Old Castle" (from *Pictures at an Exhibition*)—melody-dominated homophony in classical music**

This type of homophony, moreover, was not created out of whole cloth with the advent of tonality or with the move to a "galant" style in the early eighteenth century. Many works from the Middle Ages, Renaissance, and early Baroque demonstrate a texture comprising a single dominant melody with one, two, or three "accompanying" lines—less interesting melodically and/or rhythmically and clearly supporting a top line.

An early catalyst for this harmonically driven homophony was the repertory of monodic works from the early seventeenth century, especially in Italy. "*Monody*" (not to be confused with monophony) refers to a style of vocal music consisting of a melody with a single, accompanying bass line.[282] This repertory, found especially in madrigals by composers such as Monteverdi and Vincenzo Galilei (father of Galileo), was extremely influential. Not only did it help in developing the texture of homophony, but it also assisted in the rise of both tonality and the musical form of opera.[283] Here is an example of this texture in a motet by Monteverdi (Figure 7.23):

**Figure 7.23: Monteverdi, "Pulchra es, amica mea" (mm. 30–35, from *1610 Vespers*)—early melody-dominated homophony**

(large notes = written basso continuo line; small notes = "realized" harmony notes)

Once solidified, especially from the mid-eighteenth century, melody-dominated homophony became the default texture for most genres and styles that developed in the West. This includes, as noted above, the popular music realms of jazz, rock, and related genres. While each instrument or vocal part in a recording or performance may well have great interest and a degree of independence melodically and/or rhythmically, its "purpose" is to support the main melody and the harmonies that underlie it. Here is an example of a typical rock homophonic texture (Figure 7.24):

**Figure 7.24: Coldplay, "Yellow"—melody-dominated homophony in pop/rock music**

In many ways, the distinction between this type of multipart homophony and "true" polyphony is a matter of perception as much as any empirical reality of function or independence of individual parts: Is there one principal melody governing the musical discourse, or is that principal narrative role shared by two or more separate lines? As Leonard Meyer put it, "Texture has to do with the ways in which the mind groups concurrent musical stimuli into simultaneous figures."[284] Some "simultaneous figures" may be perceived as mutually sharing the primary discourse, while others might be perceived as merely supporting that discourse—or both at the same time. Nor is it likely that all will agree with the same verdict in a good many cases.

But this debate represents one of the most vital tools you can use in exercising your musical taste. Follow the music you hear and see how you categorize the various parts at any given moment—which are primary, which supportive, and why? The human ability to make sense of multiple simultaneous musical lines is one of the most astonishing aspects of the art form and our perception of it—all the more so when our ears are trained and engaged in the experience.

Finally, before leaving homophony, we must quickly discuss that other, distinct texture associated with the term—where all parts move in the exact (or near-exact) *same* rhythm, thus sometimes called "homo-rhythm." The archetype of this chordal approach to homophony are the 371 four-part chorale harmonizations by J. S. Bach, used by most every music-major undergraduate to master his or her understanding of tonal harmony (Figure 7.25):

**Figure 7.25: J. S. Bach, "Ermuntre dich" (chorale), BWV 43—chordal homophony in Baroque**

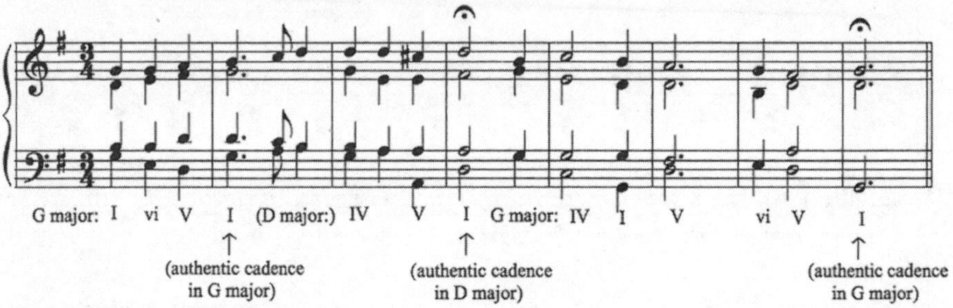


Chordal or "homo-rhythmic" homophony, however, long precedes the advent of tonality—indeed it dates back to the earliest polyphonic genres of the Middle Ages, such as organum. Among many famous pre-Bach examples include sections of the *Messe de Nostre Dame* by Machaut—notably at the sustained settings of "Jesu Christe" and "ex Maria Virgine," thereby enhancing the devotional import of these two sacred names (Figure 7.26):

**Figure 7.26: Guillaume de Machaut, *Messe de Nostre Dame* (mid-14th c.)—early use of chordal homophony**

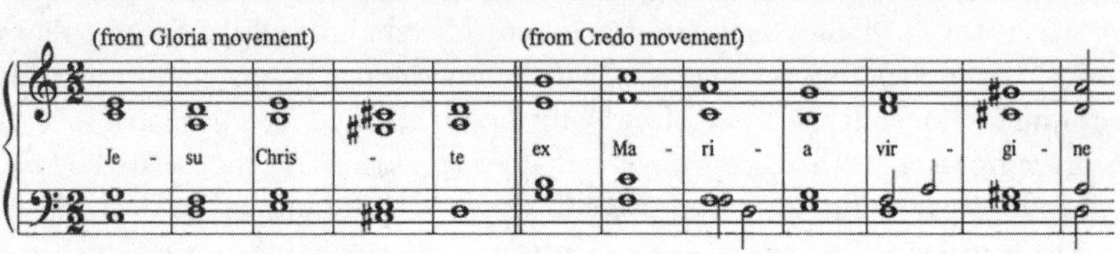


But examples of chordal homophony are manifold in every period of classical music, and likely every composer. Here is one famous example, from the end of Stravinsky's *Firebird* ballet (Figure 7.27):

**Figure 7.27: Igor Stravinsky, *Firebird* Suite, Finale (Reh. 206)—chordal homophony in 20th c. classical music**

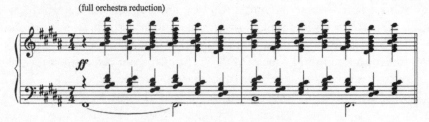

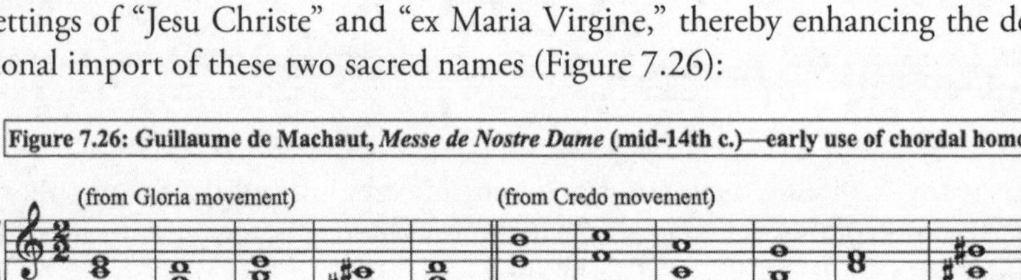

Similarly, this texture appears commonly in jazz and rock—such as in the opening of Queen's "Bohemian Rhapsody" (Figure 7.28):

**Figure 7.28: Queen, "Bohemian Rhapsody" (Intro)—chordal homophony in rock music**

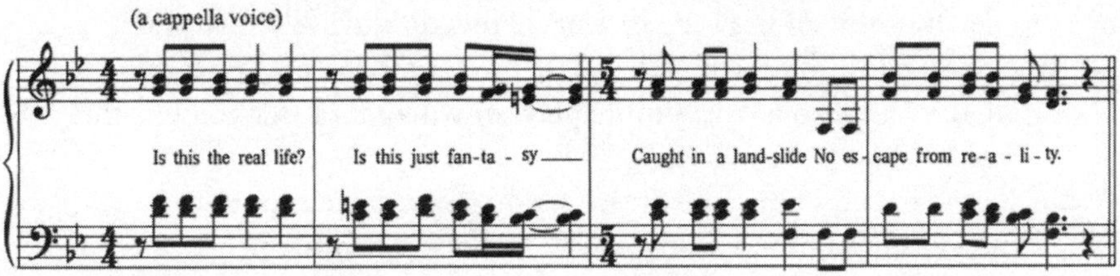


Examples of strict homophony—especially in two or three parts—are also occasionally found in non-Western indigenous music, such as in Africa, Indonesia, and China, as seen in this transcription of a two-part vocal piece from Tanzania (Figure 7.29):

**Figure 7.29: Tanzanian folk song: "Kitandoli matala" (lyrics omitted) —rare use of chordal homophony (two-part) in world music**

Texture has warranted such a comprehensive discussion, in my view, as it offers a valuable prism through which to evaluate the totality of musical proceedings in the song or work you are hearing. Establishing in your mind the texture at play in the music at any given moment—first monophony or heterophony, then chordal homophony, then polyphony, now melody-dominated homophony, etc.—provides a framework in which to more clearly evaluate the other musicological parameters. Through texture, the music becomes a picture in our minds, as a kind of metaphor for everyday life: here is foreground, there is background, there is collaboration, etc. It is then *how* these relations are manifest—through a particular melodic shape, harmonic progression, rhythmic pattern, formal structure, instrumental timbre, etc.—that fully defines the music, and our experience of it. The goal, let us remember, is not just to listen to music but also and principally to *engage* with it. Recognizing and experiencing the texture is a good means to this end.

Here are a few suggested exercises to test your awareness of sound:

1. Next time you hear a classical work: Listen for the sound (timbre) of the instruments. How clearly can you distinguish one from another? Can you hear how the timbre changes as instruments combine,

especially from different "families" (strings, winds, brass, etc.)? How do different instrumental timbres affect your appreciation of the music itself?

2. Next time you hear a work from any genre or style: Listen to the overall timbre of the song or work. How do the individual and combined timbres define that style for you? Can you gain a sense of what role the collective timbre plays in whether or not you like the music?
3. Next time you hear a medieval period work: Listen for the integration of monophony and polyphony. How frequently is each used? How does the polyphony strike you—pleasant or unpleasant?
4. Next time you hear a piece by Haydn, Mozart, or Beethoven: Can you clearly hear the homophonic (melody-dominated) texture? What are the other instruments doing to support the main melody (and the harmony)? Can you clearly distinguish each part and its function?
5. Next time you hear a pop or rock song: Listen just for the texture. Do you hear examples of polyphony? What about heterophony (e.g., between a voice and an instrument)? How many distinct parts do you hear, and what is their "function" in relationship to the main vocal melody?

We have admittedly covered a lot of terrain in these past five music theory chapters. This is dense stuff, admittedly, and you will be forgiven if some of the concepts are still a bit fuzzy. We'll have plenty more opportunities to fine-tune them in the chapters ahead. Plus you can always go back.

If you're so inclined, you can test your knowledge of the principles of music theory presented in these chapters via a test on the WYLI website; you can even take it several times, as there are multiple versions. If tests are not your thing, however, that's cool too. The truth is that our musical taste—as indeed the very power of music—resides not in theoretical explanations nor in carefully selected excerpts, but rather in the full flow and experience of complete musical performances, whether live or recorded. To wit, we'll soon turn to exploring complete songs and works—placed within the context of an individual listener's musical taste.

But first, we'll cleanse the mind a bit, so to speak, by shifting to our next interlude—on the fascinating relationship between music and the brain.

# Interlude C

## *The Singing Cerebrum: Music and the Brain*

### A Music-Processing Machine

It goes without saying that any insights we may derive about our musical taste from math, or music theory physics, are meaningless if we have no ability to perceive and make sense of music in the first place. Happily for us, our ears and especially our brains are veritable music-processing machines—organs whose very actions delimit key parameters of our collective and individual musical taste. Research in the realm of musical neuroscience has been on a tear over the past two decades, yielding ever new revelations as to how and where music is processed in the brain, and how our musical perception/response interacts with other aspects of our cognition.

Musical neuroscience is a subfield of cognitive neuroscience, which in turn is an amalgam of diverse disciplines: physiology, neurology, experimental psychology, and computer science, among others.[285] Cognitive neuroscience as an academic field began in the early 1960s, following pioneering research by Roger Sperry, Joseph Bogen, and Michael Gazzaniga at Cal Tech on the cognitive behavior of so-called "split-brain" patients—whose corpus callosum, the neural fibers that connect the two hemispheres of the brain, had been severed. The new field naturally benefited from innumerable prior insights regarding human cognition, behavioral psychology, and neuroanatomy—such as the detailed mapping of the brain carried out by Paul Broca and Korbinian Brodmann in the 1860s and '70s. The goal of cognitive neuroscience is nothing short of understanding "how the brain works," in Gazzaniga's words.[286]

Musical neuroscience (or the "cognitive neuroscience of music," as it's formally named) is thus dedicated to explaining the diverse functions of human cognition and their underlying brain mechanisms when we listen to, or perform, music. Thanks to brain-scanning technology developed since the 1990s, notably fMRI, or functional magnetic resonance imaging—which enables researchers to nearly directly observe brain activity via blood-oxygen-level dependent (or BOLD) contrasts during music processing—the field has come a long way in unveiling exactly how the musical brain works. Many mysteries persist, of course, keeping researchers and grad students busy at prominent neuroscience labs around the world. Indeed, cognitive science in general, and music cognition in particular, are two of the fastest growing majors at universities worldwide. The brain, it seems, is hot!

We've already had occasion to cite a few findings from musical neuroscience research in Interlude A. These include the sources of congenital amusia (impairments to the frontal lobe or auditory cortex) and the use of neurobiological evidence to both support and negate the adaptationist position of music in evolution—which introduced us to such fun concepts as domain specificity, localization, and modules. We likewise touched upon the "chill" effect elicited by music—and its vibrant intersection of emotion, neurotransmitters, and the sympathetic nervous system. In this interlude, we'll expand on these points to provide a high-level overview of how music processing and cognition interact with musical taste—along with some descriptive background for context.

## The Brain: Form and Function

Any detailed discussion of music processing inevitably entails enumeration of this or that region of the brain—lobes, cortices, gyri, membranes, and other anatomical thirty-five-cent words that can quickly become gobbledygook to the nonspecialist. While a thorough review of the anatomy and functionality of the brain, as well as related parts of the sensory and central nervous systems, is well beyond the scope of this book—not to mention my pay grade—some rudimentary orientation will provide valuable clarity and context.

One of the trickiest aspects of neuroanatomy is the multilevel hierarchies and subdivisions whereby the individual regions of the brain may be defined. For example, the region known as the planum temporale is associated with a rare skill among musicians, known as absolute or perfect pitch—being able to tell what note is being played or sung without an instrument—and especially when the portion of it located in the right hemisphere is congenitally smaller than normal;[287] the planum temporale is located partially in the auditory cortex, which in turn is located within the superior temporal gyrus (ridge), located on the cortical (surface) area of the temporal lobe, which is part of the cerebral cortex, itself the largest part of the cerebrum—which in turn is one of the principal parts of the brain. Got it?

Backing up a bit, the human brain (the only one we're discussing, by the way) as a whole is generally divided into three primary parts:

Cerebrum—the largest part of the brain, where higher brain processing, and the integration of sensory and cognitive functions, takes place

Cerebellum (little brain)—a small, separate structure tucked underneath the cerebrum, dedicated especially to motor and coordination control

Brain stem—the lowest portion of the brain, connecting it to the spinal cord, and involved in basic life functions such as breathing and heart rate

Our musical taste interests will intersect primarily with the cerebrum, so let's dive a bit deeper, so to speak, into its structure and function—using the illustration below as a relative "localization" map (Figure C.1):

**Figure C.1: Map of the brain**

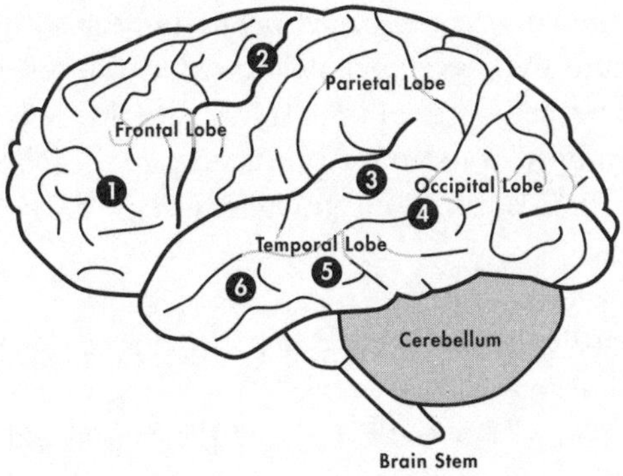


The cerebrum is the anterior (front) portion of the brain, located just under the skull, and makes up two-thirds of the brain's overall weight. It is divided into two halves, or hemispheres—right and left. Although the two hemispheres are roughly mirror images of each other, there is pronounced size asymmetry between them—as with the planum temporale.[288] This asymmetry is indeed associated with some differing functions, most notably the larger left hemisphere revealing a specialization for language—though the stereotype of the left hemisphere being logical and the right hemisphere being creative is as reliable as a Facebook poll. Both sides participate in most cognitive and motor processing, including music-related. Vital connection between the two hemispheres takes place via the corpus callosum, a set of neural fibers located beneath the cerebrum's surface.

The surface—cortex (plural "cortices")—of the cerebrum, extending two to four millimeters, is where much of the "higher-level" cognitive processing takes place. Most of the cortex—roughly 90 percent—evolved relatively recently, thus called the "neocortex," and is that very wrinkled gray matter that makes many of us squirm when looking at a real brain. As shown in Figure C.1, the cerebral cortex is divided into four lobes (areas):

Frontal lobe—associated with problem solving, speech, movement, social interaction, and various aspects of our "personality"
Temporal lobe—associated with hearing, language comprehension, memory, and emotion
Parietal lobe—associated with the processing of taste and touch, as well as language processing and spatial awareness
Occipital lobe—associated with visual processing

The brain's cerebral cortex, of course, is famously wrinkled, and it is in its wrinkled *ridges* and *grooves*—called gyri (singular "gyrus") and sulci (singular "sulcus"), respectively—that much specific neurological processing takes place. So, when, for example, you see the term "superior temporal gyrus," it indicates a ridge (gyrus) located on the top (superior) part of the temporal lobe. Easy, right?

Moreover, there are several regions located *within* one of the four lobes that, given their size and neurological importance, are themselves identified as "cortices." Especially important for music processing are the following (the numbers in parentheses refer to their locations in Figure C.1):

Frontal lobe:
Prefrontal cortex (1)—associated with our personality, planning, problem solving
Motor cortex (2)—associated with the control and execution of the body's voluntary motion
Temporal lobe:
Auditory cortex (3)—associated with the processing of sound, including speech sounds and musical pitch

Finally, there are a few "subcortical" regions, located deep within the four lobes of the cerebral cortex, that figure prominently in music processing. They include especially the hippocampus (4) and amygdala (5)—both within the temporal lobe—and the ventral striatum (6), a subregion of the basal ganglia, located at the base of the cerebrum. These three—the hippocampus, amygdala, and ventral striatum—in turn form part of the *limbic system*, a set of pan-lobe structures associated especially with emotion, as well as its profound link with memory and reward. Without the limbic system, that is, there would be no musical taste!

How music processing, or any type of processing, takes place in the brain involves a level of complexity we'll mercifully oversimplify here: it involves the functioning of brain cells—neurons—of which the brain possesses some 86 billion.[289] Each neuron can connect to thousands of others via synapses—gaps over which they send and receive electrical or chemical signals—in myriad and complex ways. Dan Levitin provides a useful metaphor: neuronal processing is like a telephone conversation with thousands of friends at once, each with a different mood or point of view.[290] Together, sets of connected neurons form neural networks, or pathways, that become active during cognitive processing. When sufficiently "excited," a neuron fires its signal across a synapse and in the process releases a neurotransmitter—a "brain chemical" such as dopamine—that activates adjoining neurons in a chain-reaction-like fashion; on the other hand, other types of neurotransmitters (like serotonin) inhibit the firing of connected neurons and bring the brain to rest. As we'll see, both "exciting" and "inhibiting" types are relevant to music processing—and to the predilections of your musical taste.

We, of course, have only scratched the surface (no pun intended) of brain form and function, but the above should be sufficient to move on to some specifics of music processing.[291] Well, almost. . . . We did forget one thing that's kind of important: the ear.

## The Ear and the Protoprocessing of Music

A miracle of anatomical architecture a billion years (give or take) in the making, the ear evolved for one primary purpose: to detect changes in molecular pressure—that is, vibration—occurring in the outside world, and to map the details of those changes onto the brain.[292] Without this awareness, for example, we'd be sitting ducks to any predator clever enough to waltz up behind us. It is this sensitivity to molecular pressure that enables our ears both to map sound and to maintain the balance required to remain upright, via a complex assemblage of flesh, bone, membranes, and fluid. To discuss this structure, moreover, is to likewise define the ear's role in sound processing, including music, of course—so let the games begin!

Like the brain, the ear can be divided into three parts. The outer ear—comprising principally the pinna (or auricle, the visible part of the ear), the concha (the deep cavity at the entrance to the auditory canal), and the eardrum or tympanic membrane—is that fleshy cone on each side of your head. The outer ear often gets short shrift in auditory discussions, but it is a wiz—with its many ridges and valleys—at collecting, localizing, and filtering incoming sound further into the ear. It is able to capture not only low-frequency sounds but also high-frequency ones (from 6000 Hz, about a 5th above the highest note on the piano, and above) that otherwise could be lost by virtue of their short wavelengths; we may not be able to discern pitches at such high frequencies, but by virtue of the upper partials of the overtone series, they make a profound difference in the music we hear.

The role of the middle ear, an air-filled cavity on the opposite side of the eardrum, is to receive the sound waves captured by the outer ear and to transmit them to the inner ear, where they can be transformed into electric signals the brain can read. The problem, though, is that the inner ear is filled with fluid, which is a terrible conductor of sound—just try yelling to a friend while underwater. To solve this dilemma, the middle ear contains three tiny bones, or ossicles—the malleus (hammer), incus (anvil), and stapes (stirrup)—connected to the eardrum and then to each other: much as a lever-and-piston system, the three bones in turn receive, transmit, and then amplify the sound waves some twenty times! Without this ingenious decibel-boosting bit of engineering, we'd perceive only 10 percent of the sound coming from the world outside—like hearing music with our heads in a bathtub.[293]

Happily avoiding this sad state of affairs, the inner ear is now ready to take on the first real bit of protoprocessing. So complex is its shape and structure that the inner ear is technically referred to as a "bony labyrinth"; its curious mix of dense bone and fluid vestibules does wonders to protect our hearing from the dangers of the outside world—which doesn't mean we can't mess it up with loud music and machinery. Within this bony cavity lies the cochlea, connected to the middle ear by a small oval window. Encased in the cochlea's twisty, snaillike shape, then, is the organ of Corti—literally named after the guy, physiologist Alfonso Corti, who discovered it in 1851: this is where hearing actually takes place.

The organ of Corti extends up the full shape of the cochlea and is situated between two stiff membranes: the basilar (bottom) and tectorial (top). The sound wave is further amplified by the organ of Corti, like a microphone, whereby it enables the basilar and tectorial membranes to respond to the motion now generated within three fluid-filled cavities or ducts—the vestibular, tympanic, and cochlear—that conduct the sound.

But here is where it gets good: sitting atop the basilar membrane is a steady line of "hair cells" (cilia), numbering 3,500 in all. When a now-amplified sound wave passes through the oval window, it causes the basilar membrane to vibrate, and with it the attached hair cells. However, the membrane—and corresponding hair cells—vibrates *only* at locations along it that correspond to the specific frequencies of that sound wave. This is possible since the basilar membrane varies in its width and stiffness: from narrow and stiff at the base to gradually wider and more flexible at the apex. It is much like the strings of a guitar: the low E string is rather loose and pliable, while the high E string is tight and stiff; similarly, the stiff base of the membrane picks up high frequencies (closest to the middle ear so as to minimize loss) with ever-lower frequencies captured as it moves toward the apex. You can thus think of it as a kind of curvy inverted piano, with high notes at the bottom and low notes at the top, where the keys are struck in the corresponding places on the keyboard by the "fingers" of the moving sound waves. Cool, right?

But wait, there's more: each of the 3,500 hair cells on the basilar membrane has a subset of smaller hairs, called stereocilia, located at the top—from 80 to 300 each, totaling around 20,000 across the entire organ of Corti. When a given hair cell is "displaced" by the sound wave, the stereocilia bend and deflect against the tectorial membrane, in turn releasing neurotransmitters that convert that specific frequency (as well as its specific amplitude, or volume) of the sound wave to an electric signal—via a process called "transduction."[294] This electric signal can then travel from the inner ear, along the cochlear (or auditory) nerve, to the brain stem, and then to the auditory cortex, where it can be truly processed. That is, these stereocilia act as a kind of supercharged analog-digital converter such as those found in expensive recording studios. That's right, folks: what top studios pay tens of thousands of dollars for, your head comes with free of charge at birth!

The full story of the ear's role in music processing, of course, is much more nuanced, but that's a good start. You can just imagine how busy those little cochleae are at any given moment, with every frequency—including upper partials—of speech or music displacing just the right hair cells on the basilar membrane to stimulate just the right stereocilia to properly represent the sound emanating from the outside world; and what if a whole symphony orchestra is playing? It should give us pause about taking undue risks with our hearing—as those 3,500 hair cells do not regenerate once damaged. That's why the elderly hear less well than the young: they've lost some of their hair cells (along with their actual hair), especially near the base of the cochlea—where high frequencies are processed; sadly, young people today are too often reckless with their earbuds and loud music, unaware of the damage they may be inflicting on their inner ears, and the future of their music appreciation.[295]

And this gets us to the first takeaway regarding music processing and our musical taste. Again, we possess 3,500 hair cells and 20,000 stereocilia (in each ear, that is), tracking and converting frequencies across the entire human audio range, between 20 Hz and 20,000 Hz or so. Not surprisingly, the extremes of this range don't fare as well as those in the middle, even for teenagers. Frequencies below 30 Hz and above 6000 Hz are difficult to resolve: too low they rattle our bodies uncomfortably (even to the point of nausea), too high they can be painful whistles; indeed, below 500 Hz and above 2000 Hz, humans tend to prefer octaves slightly smaller and larger than 2:1, respectively, showing a neuroperceptive compensation for the "extremes" of our hearing range.[296] Most of the music we hear resides between 50 Hz (the lowest G on a piano) and 4000 Hz (the top note of the piano)—not counting upper partials: roughly from the range of a tuba to that of a piccolo. For reference, an average male speaks between 85 Hz and 180 Hz, an average female between 165 Hz and 255 Hz.

Yet all these ranges are a trifle compared to those flying about planet Earth: from around 3 Hz, caused by disturbances in Earth's magnetic field to 3,000,000 Hz (3 MHz) and higher from extraterrestrial radio waves hitting our atmosphere. Even other animals fare better: as you may have gathered from your dog's inexplicable barking when you hear nothing, canines can perceive frequencies to 45,000 Hz, while cats can hear to 65,000 Hz, bats to 110,000 Hz, and porpoises to 150,000 Hz; on the other end, elephants are audio proficient at 14 Hz, and even goldfish can handily discern 16 Hz. In all, we humans have, as audiocentric neuroscientist Seth Horowitz notes, but "fair-to-middlin' ears" compared to our co-vertebrates.[297]

At the onset, therefore, our ears put limits on what constitutes a frequency "safe zone" for our musical taste—roughly 50 Hz to 4000 Hz, beyond which we tend to lose interest (and perception). But imagine what music we might dig if our cochleae had 35,000 hair cells instead of 3,500, capable of resolving pitches to 40,000 Hz or higher; or if we had only 350, perhaps limiting our range to between 1000 Hz and 2000 Hz: say good-bye to your Barry White records, not to mention most every hip hop album ever made. At the same time, thanks to the 3,500 hair cells and 20,000 stereocilia we do have, we are capable of discerning differences in musical pitch far greater than any piano—indeed as many as seventy "microtones" between a whole step (e.g., C and D), totaling some 1,400 distinct pitches up and down our hearing range! This in turn helps explain how we humans have so many different musical scales to choose from. One can only wonder what range of frequencies our Andromeda-based bar musicians might call their own. . . .

## The Brain and Music: Lower-Level Processing

Safely through the bony labyrinth, the collective data gathered from our sonic encounter with the outside world—now "digitally" encoded—can trace its way down the auditory nerve toward our audio command center: the brain. Of course, this data includes not only the harmonic (integer-multiple) frequencies of musical pitch, but also the inharmonic frequencies of speech, rustling leaves, freeway hum, and noises of every kind. Importantly, this data also includes another key aural input: rhythm—whether regular and "pulsed," as in most of the music we hear, or irregular and random, and everything in between. The processing of frequency and rhythm yields the building blocks of our music perception, and thus the raw materials of what ultimately defines our musical taste.

There are many ways to approach an overview of music processing in the brain—a topic easily overwhelming to a nonspecialist. One fairly clean model that has gained traction over the past decade is that first proposed in 2005 by German music neuroscientists Stefan Koelsch and Walter Siebel: their "neurocognitive model of music perception."[298] While by no means exhaustive, it provides us with a useful framework to carry out our own overview, supplemented via a modest sampling from the tens of thousands of writings under the rubric of "musical neuroscience."

Koelsch and Siebel's (henceforth Koelsch's) model is built upon the concept of musical "modules." As you'll recall from Interlude A, this term was used by

Isabelle Peretz to describe a process whereby distinct regions of the brain work *together* to carry out a particular cognitive function. In all, Koelsch's music-processing model includes ten "modules," which we'll here divide into two broad phases.

Phase 1—sometimes called "lower-level processing"—sets up the building blocks of music processing, and subsumes three of Koelsch's modules: "auditory feature extraction," "Gestalt formation," and "analysis of intervals." Let's get started:

## AUDITORY FEATURE EXTRACTION

When sound enters the ear, it is translated in the cochlea into electric or "neural" signals. These signals travel up the auditory nerve into the auditory portions of the brain stem and then to an area smack-dab in the middle of the brain—called the thalamus. The thalamus is also a member of the limbic system, connected directly to the amygdala, whereby we have an emotional response to music before we even know what we're listening to. From the thalamus, neural information is "projected" directly into the cerebrum's auditory cortex. It is here that the detailed information on pitch frequency encoded by the stereocilia is mapped and processed—as a kind of relay station whereby the "inverted piano" of the cochlea's basilar membrane is replayed and its frequency data registered.

Music psychologists refer to musical pitch in two ways that musicians often take for granted: pitch chroma and pitch height. "Chroma" is the general pitch level—whether corresponding to a note we can locate on a piano, or one seeming to reside "between" the keys; "height" is the specific register or octave in which the note occurs—whether at the low, middle, or high range of the piano, for example. Each aspect, in fact, is processed in a different part of the auditory cortex.[299] Coming together, though, they not only tell us how to find a given note on a piano—or trombone or violin, etc.—but they also play a key role in segregating one sound source from another. Technically, this is known as "auditory scene analysis," the neural means by which we can hear five sounds at once—a ticking clock, the wind blowing, a car driving past our house, our chair creaking, and a song playing on the radio—and distinguish them both physically and spatially.[300] It is also the means by which we can hear a rock song and clearly distinguish the bass line from the singer's melody, especially when paying attention. This ability begins with—and would not exist without—the auditory cortex's ability to distinguish pitch chroma from height.

It is astonishing, further, to contemplate, that this has to happen with *every single* note that sounds in a musical rendering, live or recorded: so the next time you hear Eddie Van Halen, Oscar Peterson, or Lang Lang lay down a torrential cascade of rapid-fire notes (as they are wont to do), you have your auditory cortex to thank for documenting each and every one—assuming you like that sort of thing. It is not only pitch chroma and height data that needs to be extracted, moreover, but also the intensity and timbre of each note. Both concepts are complex and multidimensional, and not surprisingly involve different parts of the brain merely to extract them.

Intensity is particularly tough to grasp—it is not simply loudness, though that is part of it.[301] Your perception of musical loudness, in fact, is decidedly subjective and a product of multiple factors: the frequency and density of notes, the timbre of the instruments sounding them, the level of dissonance incurred, and the sensitivity of your own ears, etc. The most germane way to understand intensity, by contrast, is the *amplitude* of the sound wave—that is, its *height* per oscillation or cycle, as opposed to the *speed* of the oscillation, which determines its frequency or pitch (see Figure C.2). The bottom line, generally speaking, is that the more intense a sound is, the greater its amplitude—and the louder it will appear to us (assuming we are similarly positioned in relationship to the sound source): middle C played by a hundred bagpipes in a small room will have a markedly higher amplitude, and thus seem louder, than when sung by a boy soprano in an open field; don't try this at home.

**Figure C.2: The amplitude (intensity) of a sound wave (low and high)**

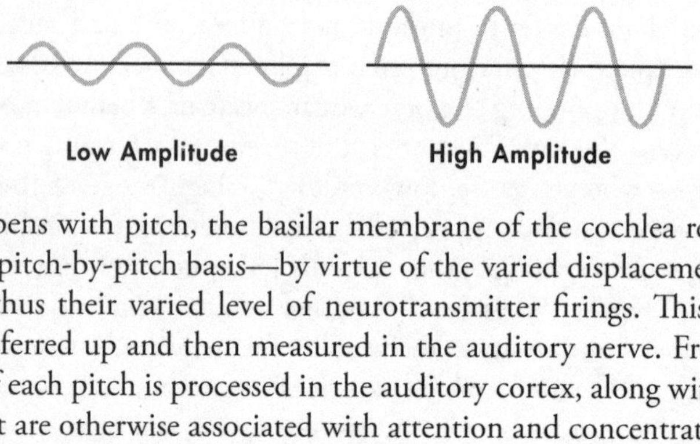


As happens with pitch, the basilar membrane of the cochlea registers intensity—on a pitch-by-pitch basis—by virtue of the varied displacement of the hair cells, and thus their varied level of neurotransmitter firings. This information too is transferred up and then measured in the auditory nerve. From there, the intensity of each pitch is processed in the auditory cortex, along with a few other regions that are otherwise associated with attention and concentration.[302]

Likewise decoded during "auditory feature extraction" is timbre, or the "color" of the sound. As you'll recall from Chapter 7, timbre is largely a product of the overtone series, based on the varying intensities or amplitudes of their upper partials—which collectively create a unique "spectrum" for each sound. It is by virtue of these varying spectra, again, that we can tell a violin from a trumpet playing the same note. As discussed in Chapter 7 as well, however, timbre is also affected by how the sound starts (attack), how it dies out (decay), and how the individual partials change over time as a natural product of sound production, called spectral flux.

All of this timbral information is initially processed in the same areas of the auditory cortex as pitch and intensity, since the hair cells in the cochlea register the frequencies and amplitudes of not only the fundamentals of each pitch but also their upper partials—and thus establish the neural basis of defining a trombone versus a tuba, for example. Yet, as just mentioned, extracting a sound's timbre also requires processing those other timbral elements: attack, decay, spectral flux, fullness and brightness of tone, etc., as well as its overall complexity.[303] Not surprisingly, therefore, dozens of individual brain regions—in both hemispheres—are associated with extracting timbral information.[304]*

Further, being able to identify a sound as being a trombone or a tuba involves the retrieval of memories based on previous experience you may have had with that sound—even unhappy ones dating back to your summers at band camp. In this way, the hippocampus (the memory indexing center) is triggered, which in turn taps your emotion-centric limbic system. Not surprisingly, there is some degree of lag, by single-digits to low tens of microseconds, between these various timbre-processing tasks—each occurring in its "separate channel" of the brain before integrating via memory. And all this just to identify the sound of a trombone!

Rounding out the extraction process, there is the rhythmic data. When utilized in music, rhythm is indeed a complex parameter, involving not just the presence or absence of a steady beat (tactus), but also its speed (tempo), organization into groups and subgroups (meter), regularity or lack thereof (syncopation, odd meters, etc.), overall rhythmic feel (groove), and much more (see Chapter 5). It is easy to take for granted our inherent ability to follow a beat—to clap our hands, tap our foot, snap our fingers, or dance to rhythmically vibrant music; and yet even such basic tasks require tremendous cognitive, motor, and predictive capabilities. How is it that we are able to hear individual pitches or percussive sounds and accurately predict when the next one will occur, not to mention organize them into patterns or follow them as they speed up or slow down? Pitch, intensity, and timbre at least have *objective* physical properties (frequencies, sound wave amplitudes, overtones) that the brain can directly translate and interpret. Rhythmic pulse, by contrast, is a "neural phenomenon"—meaning that its perception is *subjective* and occurs *within* the brain, sometimes with little actual basis in the raw acoustic data; in other words, your ability to perceive a steady beat doesn't necessarily mean that the sound wave itself is clearly defined by regular, pulsed spikes in amplitude (volume) as it proceeds. So where does this ability come from?

Technically, the ability to lock into a steady, consistent beat is called entrainment; as discussed in Interlude A, entrainment may have been targeted as an adaptive trait among our human ancestors for its ability to improve our capacity

---

* The specific brain regions involved in music processing, as discussed throughout this Interlude, are generally excluded from the text; the interested reader, however, can find them detailed on the WYLI website (supplement to Interlude C).

for collaboration and social bonding. Although still an open question, entrainment appears to be a uniquely human skill—lending further credence to the adaptationist position.

In any event, when your ear "captures" a song with a steady beat (say "Twist and Shout"), the neural signals fired by the hair cells in your cochlea relay data on not only the varied frequencies and overtones of each pitched and percussive instrument, but also the relative *timing and intensity* of each one. When this data reaches the brain, it triggers a complex and temporally precise communication between the auditory cortex and various motor-processing regions of the brain—notably the cerebellum, the premotor and supplemental motor cortices, and the subcortical basal ganglia. By virtue of this "conversation," all of these oscillations somehow synchronize—entrain—to those varied frequencies and overtones. And with that—voilà: a steady beat is created in the mind. How *exactly* that shift takes place, though, is matter of some debate. According to a theory developed by Anirrudh Patel and John Iversen—the Action Simulation for Auditory Prediction hypothesis (ASAP)—entrainment involves a temporal planning process in the motor regions of the brain via a *simulation* of periodic movement whereby the neural signals can *predict* the timing of the next beat, or recognize if such a prediction is foiled.[305]

Complexities aside, with the encoding of beat info, we have now accounted for the extraction of *all the individual raw materials* of music processing: pitch, intensity, timbre, and rhythm. This is amazing, but incomplete. For if our brains stopped there, we'd hear merely a bunch of well-articulated sounds: individual notes, specific instruments, steady beats, etc. We wouldn't hear, by contrast, any actual *music* with meaning or clarity. If our brains stopped there, we'd be unable to distinguish between any two songs or styles. It would be like trying to judge between two entries at a chili cook-off by tasting only their *individual ingredients*: you'd taste the beans, the onions, and the spices, but you'd have a hard time saying what the *chili* tasted like—or how the two bowls compared to one another.

## GESTALT FORMATION

Happily, though, it does not stop there. Phase 1, Step 2 of Koelsch's model involves creating a "Gestalt formation," which entails grouping or segregating the individual, extracted data points into a coherent yet discrete "whole" (*Gestalt*): pitches into melodies, scales, and contours; intensities into categories of loud and soft dynamics; timbres into instrument groups or families; and rhythms into meters and ostinatos or patterns, etc. Gestalt theory is itself a prominent strand of psychology, dating back to the writings of Christian von Ehrenfels in the late nineteenth century, with development by Max Wertheimer, Kurt Koffka, and Wolfgang Köhler. It is dedicated to the notion that we make sense of the world less as a series of distinct entities and more as a global, collective construct—

whether in trying to understand a visible object like a house or a face, or an aural object like a friend's voice or a familiar song. It thus follows upon our natural inclination to organize the world into groups and patterns. To Koelsch and others, musical Gestalt formation follows the same key principles as vision-based Gestalt: proximity, similarity, symmetry, and continuity—principles that likewise inform our everyday lives.[306]

We all experience Gestalt formation in music quite readily when we hear and recognize a familiar melody, regardless of the instrument it is played on, or the key or tempo in which it is performed. Think of "For He's a Jolly Good Fellow," or any familiar song sung at a piano bar, a wedding reception, or around a campfire. We may take note of the differences between one rendering or another (and formulate taste opinions accordingly), but we won't need to carry out a detailed pitch-sequence analysis to identify it as a song we already know—assuming it sticks close enough to the "original." Instead, we say, "Hey, I know that song," and maybe start to sing along. It is these same cognitive skills—via Gestalt formation—that give us the ability to recognize as familiar, and distinctly identifiable, other musical constructs as well: a melodic scale (contour), the sound of a string quartet (timbre), the use of waltz time (meter), or a Bo Diddley guitar rhythm (ostinato), etc.

In the brain, Gestalt formation relies on a kind of low-level auditory memory known as "echoic memory" that takes place in the auditory cortex and related areas of the temporal lobe. It also involves several areas of the frontal cortex that are predominantly linked with language processing. In general, though, these frontal cortex areas are associated with attention and working memory, which in turn points to Gestalt formation's key role in auditory scene analysis. I once attended an outdoor music festival, where within earshot I could hear three distinct and simultaneous musical performances—a solo piano playing Debussy's "Clair de lune," a rockabilly band playing Jerry Lee Lewis, and a vocal solo from *Les Misérables*; by simply shifting my focus, I could distinctly follow the musical discourse of each one in turn, somehow blocking out the others. For this remarkable ability, we have Gestalt formation, at least in part, to thank.

## INTERVAL ANALYSIS

According to Koelsch, our lower-level processing concludes with a rather specific musicological task: carrying out "fine-grained analysis" of musical intervals and chords—identified, moreover, as "closely linked" with Gestalt formation. It is acknowledged that neuroscience today has a rather limited understanding of the exact neural networks involved in processing intervals, and especially chords. Koelsch is specifically referring to tasks such as our ability to identify the "flavor" of a chord—as major, minor, dominant 7th, etc.; as well as its "position"—whether its "root," the named primary note, is on the bottom as is most basic, in the middle, or at the top of the chord. The best available evidence suggests that these functions likely require participation of both the temporal lobe and the prefrontal cortex—in regions otherwise associated with vowel processing and attention.

And yet, as Horowitz notes, one vital source of this processing—the perception of consonant and dissonant intervals—seems to lie as much in the machinery of the cochlea as in the regions of the brain. Specifically, those twenty thousand or so stereocilia protruding atop the hair cells that wind up the basilar membrane are divided up linearly into distinct groupings or "bands." Each grouping that is activated at the same general frequency range, or bandwidth, is called a "critical band"; that is, we perceive 440 Hz and 450 Hz as roughly the same pitch (A above middle C) because both of those frequencies lie within the same bandwidth. That is important, first of all, by virtue of the absolute widths of each critical band—the numerical distance between its lowest and highest frequency—which varies as the bands move along the basilar membrane: from narrow in the low frequencies (toward the apex) to wide in the high frequencies (toward the base). This enables us to yield very good pitch resolution in the normal range of music and speech (up to 4000 Hz), but increasingly poor resolution as we move toward 20,000 Hz—the extreme of human hearing; it's why we can clearly identify the pitch of middle C on the piano (261 Hz), but have a harder time doing so for the highest C (4186 Hz).

But it is the relative width of critical bands across the cochlea that impacts how we perceive the quality of intervals in our brains. In a famous experiment by Plomp and Levelt, music listeners were asked to rate various intervals as being either consonant or dissonant. The intervals in turn were measured by where along the critical bands their individual notes appeared—whether, for example, around 125 Hz (the C below middle C), or around 1000 Hz (the C two octaves above middle C). Importantly, the relative width of each critical band—the interval generated between its lowest and highest frequency—likewise varies as you move along the basilar membrane: in this case, from wide in low frequencies (a perfect 5th at 125 Hz) to narrow in higher frequencies (a minor 3rd at 1000 Hz). In the Plomp-Levelt experiment, when the two notes of an interval were separated by *less* than the width of a full critical band, the listeners overwhelmingly defined it as a dissonance; at greater than a full bandwidth, they more consistently rated it as a consonance.[307] In practice, this means that our perception of a major 3rd (e.g., from C to E) will vary: rough at 125 Hz—less than a full bandwidth at that frequency level (a perfect 5th), smooth at 1000 Hz—greater than a full bandwidth at that frequency level (a minor 3rd); this is why a C major triad played two octaves below middle C sounds "muddier" than two octaves above middle C.

In turn, this differential is reflected in our neurological processing: a separation of less than a full critical band generates smaller levels of neural firings—in turn creating a perception of dissonance; while a separation more than a full bandwidth will generate greater neural activity—in turn creating a perception of consonance.

All this admitted complexity is to say that the brain's ability to identify a pitch, detect a major or minor triad, or gauge consonance versus dissonance in general, takes a strong lead from the workings of the inner ear—how's that for teamwork! Of course, it must also be remembered that consonance and dissonance are ultimately subjective measurements, a fact that led Descartes to abandon its scientific study altogether in the early seventeenth century—it being a mere and unreliable matter of "taste," he lamented.[308]

We've documented no shortage of sophisticated music-processing tasks down at these "lower levels," to be sure. And yet, the skills underlying our real understanding and discrimination of music, not to mention our individual preferences, passions, and tastes, would not be possible if our brains were not likewise equipped to go into those "higher levels" of music processing, to which we now turn.

## The Brain and Music: Higher-Level Processing

I grew up, not surprisingly, in a music-loving family. As far as I know, no relatives before me had been drawn to a career in music, although my uncle Jerry (my mom's brother) held piano recitals as a teenager, and even played organ in a rock band in his early twenties. It was from Jerry, certainly, that I first developed my interest in the depth and breadth of the classical music repertoire. He owned over a thousand classical LPs, and could name the composers, orchestras, conductors, and soloists featured on any one I picked randomly off the shelves with only the smallest clue. At home, we had an old spinet piano that my mom, Marian, played occasionally, and upon which my older brother and I practiced our lessons. My brother Howard skipped from instrument to instrument (piano, trumpet, bass) before abandoning performance in his midtwenties. Only I was crazy enough to pursue music professionally.

On this account, moreover, I had no choice. Indeed, I have no memory of life before music was my main obsession. According to family lore, one day my mom was visiting with a friend in our kitchen, when they both heard "Three Blind Mice" coming from the living room; my mom assumed it was Howard practicing his weekly lesson, but when her friend peeked in, she exclaimed, "That's not Howard, it's Nolan!" Startled and enthused, my mom took me along with Howard to his next lesson with Norman Crane—the only piano teacher in my hometown of La Mirada, California. But instead of being excited, Mr. Crane dryly said, "Bring him back when he's six." This might seem lamentable (as it certainly stands in contrast to common practice today), and yet I actually think it may have been a blessing: for two full years, until I began receiving my own lessons, I was forced to develop my ear if I wanted to play music. Happily, I seemed to have had a natural inclination in that direction, since within a short time I had a reasonably large—and eclectic—repertoire of songs learned "by ear." As I'll explain more at the start of Interlude F, that skill and eclectic bent would soon serve me well in my budding music career.

And yet the most musically unusual member of my family was my dad, Jack. He may have had a mild case of amusia in that he was completely incapable of carrying a tune. Although this condition, if he had it, did nothing to limit his passion for music, it may have been tied to his rather atypical approach to music appreciation: playing the same recording over and over and over again without a need or desire for variety. Over the decades, he indeed shifted his obsession from one musical target to another, and yet each installment could last months or years. When I was growing up, they included pop albums like *The Nat King Cole Story*, Herb Alpert and the Tijuana Brass' *The Lonely Bull*, and Johnny Mathis' *All-Time Greatest Hits*, but also a number of classical works, including some pretty adventurous "warhorses" like Stravinsky's *Rite of Spring* and Copland's *Appalachian Spring*. During the last decade of his life, he was fixated on my own World Concerto—seems that I finally passed the audition.

But my dad's obsession du jour that had the greatest impact on me personally was Beethoven's Ninth Symphony. From age eleven to thirteen or so, this colossus of the classical repertory would relentlessly emanate from the cheap sound system in my parents' bedroom—located just next to mine. Like everyone else in the family, I sometimes was driven mad by the ceaseless repetition of the symphony's four movements, but there was no getting around it—it was his house, and this was his therapy after a long day working as a school psychologist. Never would he use the Ninth as a springboard to discover the wonders of Beethoven's other eight symphonies, or those of Schubert or Brahms: it was the Ninth Symphony (performed by the Berlin Philharmonic conducted by Herbert von Karajan) that received sole billing in my dad's jukebox.

There were undoubtedly many points within the four lengthy movements of Beethoven's Ninth Symphony that would momentarily catch my ear and attention as I otherwise focused on baseball cards or comic books in my room; there are certainly worse musical exemplars to be seeping into the unconscious mind of a young musician than this one. But the one moment that always grabbed me was not, as might be expected, the fiery opening or second movements, nor in the famed "choral" finale, but rather in the generally serene and abstractly lyrical third movement, Adagio molto e cantabile; this is an expansive and complex set of variations featuring long, ornate (melismatic) lines especially in the violins. In the final and most expansive variation, however, Beethoven interrupts the erstwhile serenity with two loud, martial fanfares featuring rhythmic trumpets in octaves that dramatically stick out from the surrounding lyrical material.

In order to properly understand the neuroscientific significance of this moment, we'll need to return briefly to some concepts discussed in Chapter 4, on harmony and cadences. Ready? Okay, so both fanfares here feature a *half cadence* in the key of B♭; again, a half cadence is a punctuating move to the V chord (F major in B♭) that results in a *temporary* feeling of repose, but one that ultimately should resolve to an authentic cadence to the I chord. To remind you, here are the conventional forms of these two cadence types—the half cadence and authentic cadence (Figure C.3):

**Figure C.3: Half and authentic cadences (in B♭ major)**

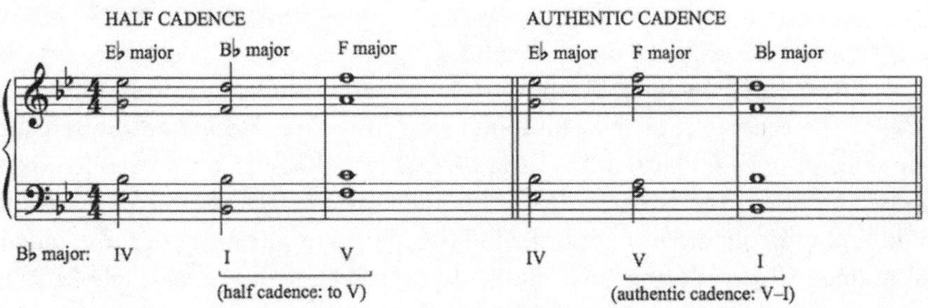


In his first fanfare, Beethoven follows the pattern of the half cadence shown above, but he then deviates a bit by moving from the F major chord (V) to an F minor chord. This shift from major to minor is a bit of a shock to the ears. Of course, Beethoven does it in an artful way—using octave Fs and changes in dynamics to make that shift to an F minor chord a bit smoother, as shown here (Figure C.4):

**Figure C.4: Beethoven, Symphony no. 9, 3. Adagio—Fanfare 1 (half cadence)**

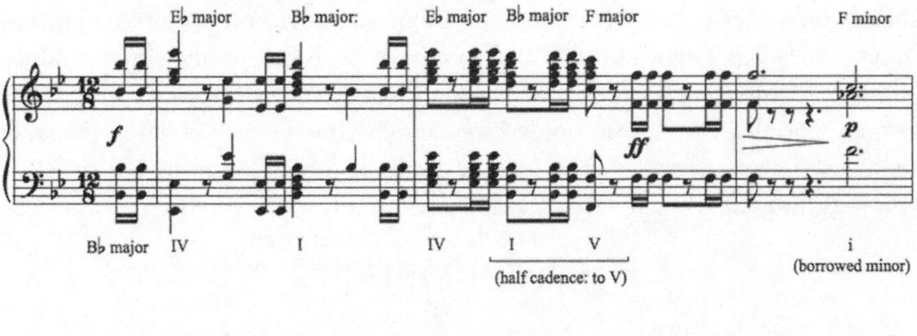


In the second fanfare, however, Beethoven starts with the same three chords (E♭–B♭–F), but then forcefully and *suddenly* concludes with a strong—**fortissimo**—chord on D♭ (the ♭III chord) on the downbeat. That is, where we here might expect resolution via an authentic cadence to B♭ (I), we instead get a "deceptive" cadence—as it is called—whose impact cannot be misconstrued, or ignored (Figure C.5):

**Figure C.5: Beethoven, Symphony No.9, 3. Adagio—Fanfare 2 (deceptive cadence)**

I present this review of Beethoven's cadential writing not simply to convey a curious anecdote from my childhood, but also to demonstrate the remarkable skills of our "higher-level" music processing—Phase 2 of our reduction of Koelsch's music-processing model. Although my twelve- or thirteen-year-old mind undoubtedly did not grasp the full theoretical implications of those cadential moments from Beethoven's Ninth, that second cadence *always* grabbed my attention as something both surprising and stirring—just as it still does today. How is that?

Our lower-level music processing goes a long way to detect and define the raw materials of the music we hear—pitches, scales, melodies, intervals, chords, instruments, rhythmic patterns, steady beats, and meters, among others. But it is the stunning sophistication of our higher-level processing that gives context and meaning to those raw materials and, perhaps more importantly, can infuse them with powerful memories and emotions.

In Koelsch's model, the higher levels of music processing (our Phase 2) are broken into no fewer than six modules, though we'll focus on just three: "musical syntax," "meaning and emotion," and "memory." A fourth higher-level module, "bodily reactions," we'll largely save for the Epilogue of this book. It is by virtue of these modules that music holds such tremendous esteem in our lives, and, some would argue, enables music to play such a palpable role in our development—as individuals, as societies, and indeed as a species.

## MUSICAL SYNTAX

The first of these, "musical syntax," is the module by which the musical cadences described above can be understood and distinguished in the first place. When most of us hear the word "syntax," of course, we immediately think of language. Syntax is the rules, conventions, and hierarchies that define the *structure* of a language, providing guidance as to how words and phrases may be properly combined into sentences. Syntax tells us where the noun, verb, or preposition should go, and thus allows us to recognize when a rule is violated. As defined by

Noam Chomsky, the father of modern linguistics, syntax is but one component of a language's grammar—along with semantics, or meaning, and phonology, or the rules by which sounds are combined.[309] Syntactic prowess develops in us as infants, where by means of *learned cues*, we are able to statistically track which structural patterns of language are typical and which ones are not.[310]

Music too has a vibrant syntactic identity. As with spoken language, infants will absorb the utterances of their "native" musical language and by similarly statistical learned cues will gradually develop rules, conventions, and hierarchies regarding how musical structures "should" and "should not" proceed. Indeed, studies by Sandra Trehub and others have shown that musical syntax develops no more slowly or comprehensively than does linguistic syntax—with basic competence by age two to three and adult-level mastery by age ten to twelve in both realms.[311] Mastery of musical syntax, moreover, develops *regardless* of whether or not a child receives formal music training—though training can naturally affect the speed or level of this mastery.

So what are the rules, conventions, and hierarchies of musical syntax? We've already provided the theoretical details in Chapters 3 through 7, but to quickly summarize: they involve the myriad ways in which those extracted "low-level" musical elements discussed previously—pitch, timbre, rhythm—are likely or unlikely to be *arranged* in musical songs and works. Importantly, though, this assessment of a likely or unlikely arrangement is based on the *expectations* of our "native" musical language. Pitches form into "viable" scales, chords, keys, or modes; timbres into "viable" instruments and instrument families; rhythms into "viable" meters and patterns, etc.

Most neuroscience studies, not surprisingly, have focused on the syntactic expectations associated with Western tonal (post–18th c.) music: major and minor scales, duple and triple meters, Western instrument groupings, etc. And yet, just as a child raised in the rural North Indian village of Uttar Pradesh will acquire syntactic proficiency in the Hindi language, so too will she acquire syntactic proficiency in North Indian music: the microtones (notes between the keys of the piano) of its scales, the timbre of the sitar and tabla, the asymmetrical meters—in groups of five, seven, eleven, etc.—of its rhythms, etc. Far from seeming exotic, these will all appear to her as "viable" and normal, and will form the syntax upon which expectations and violations can be detected and defined.

And so it was for me with the fanfares of Beethoven's Adagio molto e cantabile: by age twelve or thirteen, I had heard enough Western music—including classical—that my syntactic module "knew" the sounds and expectations of standard cadences, including half and authentic cadences. I may not yet have been able to identify the second fanfare (Figure C.5) as a "deceptive cadence going to the ♭III chord," but I knew that somehow it violated the expected syntactic rules.

To be sure, this wasn't necessarily a bad thing—indeed, quite the opposite. It's like turning a noun into a verb, as in "You should Google that": it may have first struck our ears as a violation, but now it sounds kind of cool. For those of us raised in the West, musical syntax means that we expect our songs to be defined in a single key throughout, or to change keys smoothly via authentic and half cadences, and to flow in consistent rhythmic groupings of twos or threes—and not in groupings of fives or sevens. If we hear a blues, for example, we'll expect it to have twelve measures per "chorus," and a dominant 7th (I7) chord as "home," and so forth. Again, violations of these rules of musical syntax don't make us scream or tear out our earbuds in disgust, but they do register in our minds, perk up our ears, and in some fashion or another impact the degree to which the "offending" song jibes with our musical taste, or doesn't.

To address the neurological side of things: violations in music syntax will elicit a response in our brain only *after* the constituent musical raw materials have been extracted and coalesced—via the "low-level" processing of Phase 1 described above. Getting nerdy, this happens between 180 and 350 milliseconds after Phase 1 is done. Based on brain-imaging studies by Koelsch, Patel, and Levitin, the regions activated in musical syntax include especially those in the frontal cortex—in areas otherwise recruited in the processing of language, comprehension, and decision-making (e.g., the inferior frontal gyrus). Most of these studies have measured the brain when processing violations in melodic and harmonic syntax—e.g., an "irregular" chord.

You may be struck by the fact that the brain regions aligned with tracking musical syntax, in the frontal cortex, are also those aligned with processing linguistic syntax. As touched upon in Interlude A (discussing music and evolution), the interplay between music and language is a prominent, and at times controversial, topic in neuroscience scholarship—and nowhere more so than with regard to syntax; indeed "music and language" is a separate (and final) module in Koelsch's model. Indisputable is the fact that both types of syntactic processing utilize overlapping neural resources—regardless of which takes precedence in development, if in fact either does. And indeed, just as we will *speak* with an accent any language we don't learn as a child, so too will we *hear* with an accent any music whose distinctive sounds and syntactic rules differ from those of our "native" musical language.

## MEANING AND EMOTION IN MUSIC, PART 1: MUSICOLOGY

Registering syntactic violations is cognitively significant, no doubt, but where music processing really gets "higher" is when those violations—or any musical stimuli—garner not just recognition but also Meaning, especially when Emotion is involved. The topics of meaning and emotion in music—individually and together—loom large in the literature not only of musical neuroscience but also of traditional musicology. And, indeed, given the insights that this latter discipline can bring to any discussion of meaning and emotion in music, it's worth spending at the outset a bit of time on these topics from a purely musicological perspective.

In considering this task, I am quickly reminded of a term paper I once wrote while a doctoral student at Stanford. It was for a seminar on the piano music of Frédéric Chopin, the poster boy of the Romantic-era composer—writing at a time when music was increasingly deemed to have "meaning" beyond the notes, not to mention lots of emotional content. The seminar was taught by my brilliant, if intimidating, professor Karol Berger, and involved a heavy load of philosophical readings by the likes of Jacques Derrida, Carolyn Abbate, and Susanne Langer; tough stuff, let me tell you. For this paper, we were asked to apply the study of *narratology* to a Chopin work of our choosing—meaning we were supposed to construct a "literary" narrative to the work, based just on the music and related writings (letters, etc.). I chose Chopin's *Ballade* No. 3 in A♭, Op. 47—and gave it the following narrative: Chopin escapes from his war-torn Polish homeland and makes his way to the enticements of Paris, before at last (though only in his imagination) returning "home" to Poland. Again, this story was not "told" in words, but only in notes. Although I managed to receive an A for the paper, Professor Berger warned me on the last page: "There is always a fine line between under- and over-interpreting"—by which, no doubt, he meant I'd committed the latter offense.

As with syntax, there is an obvious relationship between linguistic and musical semantics, though also some striking distinctions. Musical meaning can never be declared "true" or "false," or yield a "yes" or "no" response, as can language; that is, one cannot "translate" a passage of instrumental music as "The rowdy student aced the math test, to the astonishment of his teacher"—or at least not expect it to gain consensus with other listeners of the same passage. But this does not mean that music can yield no semantic meaning. The question in fact has animated musical discussions for a long time, famously in the latter nineteenth century during the so-called "War of the Romantics." This was an often heated schism between, on the one hand, those musicians (e.g., composers Johannes Brahms and Clara Schumann, violinist Joseph Joachim, critic Eduard Hanslick, etc.) who advocated a position of "absolute music"—where, as Hanslick noted, "musical form is its own content, it means itself"; and, on the other hand, those of the "program music" camp (composers Franz Liszt and Richard Wagner, journalists of the "New German School," etc.), who fully embraced music as capable of carrying extramusical significance—such as via the leitmotifs of Wagner's operas or the tone poems of Liszt. In the early twentieth century, the composer Igor Stravinsky—despite composing a series of successful ballets—revealed his support of the "absolute" position in declaring, "If music appears to express something, this is only an illusion and not a reality."[312]

A shift to a more flexible stance toward the issue of musical semantics arose in the mid-twentieth century, notably in the writings of theorists versed in psychology, such as Susanne Langer—writing in her influential 1942 book, *Philosophy in a New Key*:

> The assignment of [musical] meanings is a shifting, kaleidoscopic play, probably below the threshold of consciousness, certainly outside the pale of discursive thinking. The imagination that responds to music is personal and associative and logical, tinged with affect, tinged with bodily rhythm, tinged with dream, but *concerned* with a wealth of formulations for its wealth of wordless knowledge, its whole knowledge of emotional and organic experience, of vital impulse, balance, conflict, the *ways* of living and dying and feeling.[313]

This position was further solidified in musicological circles via the writings of Leonard Meyer, notably in his 1956 *Emotion and Meaning in Music*, combining notions of Gestalt psychology with the groundbreaking writings on semiotics—the study of signs—by Charles Sanders Peirce. Meyer's synthesis led him to dispel earlier notions, going back to Plato, of a sharp dichotomy between meaning and emotion, arguing that *both* rely on our perception: "Thinking and feeling need not be viewed as polar opposites, but as different manifestations of a single psychological process."[314] Foreshadowing later discoveries in cognition, Meyer thus understood that meaning and emotion are not separate in the mind, but interconnected. Meyer, incidentally, does not deny the prospect of music carrying extramusical meaning as well, although it is secondary to his interest in the intramusical sources of musical meaning.[315] In the ensuing years, however, the broader perspective has become standard: music *can* indeed provide a wealth of meaning and emotion, derived from both internal and external reference points—a perspective, moreover, increasingly informed by empirical insights from neuroscience, as we'll see.

From an experiential standpoint, this suggests that music can strike the listener in several ways. Most natural, and perhaps uncontroversial, are the semantic inferences that derive directly from the musical discourse itself—those "intramusical" gestures, effects, progressions, shifts, and transitions from one musical moment to another. These, indeed, are the syntactic details described above—the cadences, chord progressions, melodic contours, rhythmic configurations, timbral uses, etc., that define the discourse of a piece of music. These are the moments that provide the music with tension, resolution, continuity, lyricism, harshness, or—as in the second Beethoven fanfare—change. Such moments are no longer merely *recognized* as meeting or violating syntactic expectations, but are now given *meaning and significance* that shape and define the aesthetic listening experience. To be sure, however, they require an element of interpretation—recognition of what that "irregular" chord, or change in tempo, etc., might "signify." As such, they are inherently subjective, and may vary from listener to listener, even if they fall within some limited range of potential meanings—such as, "the tension in this passage is palpable," or "this passage is suddenly quite meditative," etc. Never, that is, can they ever claim to be a "translation" of the musical syntax that would possess the precision of a literary translation, say from English to Spanish.

This is even more the case as we shift from purely "syntactical meaning" toward the kinds of extramusical or "referential" meaning Meyer was wary of. From the 1980s, as semiotics gained currency in musicology, a set of three sign types first introduced by Peirce in 1903 as part of his "theory of signs" made their way into musical commentaries, such as in Robert Hatten's influential *Musical Meaning in Beethoven*. These sign types are indexical, iconic, and symbolic—which have likewise made their way into musical neuroscience, including within Koelsch's model.

Indexical signs are those that *point* toward something else, and thus might not actually resemble that which is signified; for example: smoke *points* to fire. Indexical meaning in music, therefore, is when a change in the music's syntax or activity *points* to a change in its mood or psychological state. An example is that second Beethoven fanfare: the change in syntax via the deceptive cadence points to a change in mood—namely, toward an increase in drama, even an arrival of triumph. Indexical moments are often based on an aspect of the music's movement, energy, or sound; they are also the ones wherein commentators frequently indulge in frilly or poetic language: a Haydn theme is "joyful" or "regal"; a Leonard Cohen chord progression is "haunting" or "mystical"; a Charlie Parker solo is "nervous" or "transcendental," etc. Of course, there is nothing actually "joyful" or "haunting" or "nervous" in any series of frequencies and rhythms. And yet these moods can be readily elicited in our minds as a natural means to *define* a given song or passage, whether to ourselves or to someone else. This is not to say that we will necessarily *feel* those emotions (short-lived) or moods (longer lasting), much as we don't necessarily feel joyful when we see a happy person.

Iconic signs are those that actually *stand for* or *resemble* something else, by seemingly possessing some of the same qualities, physically or otherwise; for example: a photograph *resembles* the person. As such, iconic meaning in music takes us more explicitly into the referential or extramusical realm. Iconic moments are those where a melodic contour or gesture, a rhythmic articulation, a harmonic progression, etc., appears to *resemble* something in the outside world: the melodic contour of Handel's "Ev'ry Valley Shall Be Exalted" from the *Messiah* resembles that of a mountain range; the opening of "Over the Rainbow" resembles a leap skyward; the staccato violins in Bernard Herrmann's *Psycho* score sound frighteningly like stabbings, and so forth. The first two are examples of "word painting," the latter a kind of "musical onomatopoeia"—both categories of iconic gestures. The most famous object of iconic meaning in the classical repertoire, surely, is the thunderstorm—found in Vivaldi's *Four Seasons* ("Summer"), Beethoven's *Pastoral* Symphony, Berlioz' *Symphonie fantastique*, Rossini's *William*

*Tell* Overture, among others, and is invariably set in a minor key with loud, rapid-fire rhythms in the strings.

It must be noted, however, that even in cases that seem obvious to us, the discerning of meaning from a musical moment—whether indexical or iconic—is ultimately subjective. Again, there is no "true" or "false" in music, and semantic descriptions are not "translations." Context always matters, and some level of cultural or historical reference is usually involved. Few first-time listeners, that is, would unequivocally hear "thunder" in Vivaldi's *Four Seasons* or Beethoven's *Pastoral* if they were not also given the names of the movements, or at least primed with other examples of classical music "storms." This is certainly the case with "tone poems" or operatic leitmotifs: without knowing the libretto of Wagner's *Die Walküre*, for example, the "Magic Fire Music" would simply sound bright and chromatic, and not like magical fire. Even more subjective are meanings we ascribe arbitrarily or via idiosyncratic association—where a particular musical gesture seems at the moment to resemble in the mind a waterfall, a walk on the beach, or the streets of Paris.

Finally, there are symbolic signs—which in music, as in language, are the most arbitrary of all; they are based purely on convention or culture, and must be learned; for example, "&" is the symbol for "and." The most obvious examples in music are national anthems—which do not palpably "sound" like the countries they symbolize any more than do other indigenous songs. So, when an American stands up at "The Star-Spangled Banner," it is not because the music has a uniquely "upright" quality to it, but rather that by convention the song means, "Be a patriot, stand up."* Similarly, religious music may have a generally spiritual quality, but "Silent Night" only makes you think of Christmas because it musically symbolizes that holiday.

It is all a bit like the movie *Fantasia*—the original 1940 film with Leopold Stokowski, not the paler 2000 remake. The opening work of the film is J. S. Bach's Toccata and Fugue in D Minor; the Baroque fugue is arguably the definitive genre of "absolute music," and indeed the animators render semantic meaning based purely on the intramusical discourse: contrapuntal melodic lines, dramatic chord progressions, deceptive cadences, etc., are depicted with abstract lines, shapes, and cloud formations that echo the "syntactic drama" of the music. The film's third number, and Disney's original inspiration for the film, then represents the opposite pole in the "Romantic War" debate, Paul Dukas' *The Sorcerer's Apprentice*; this is a tone poem (program music) based on a Goethe poem, "Der Zauberlehrling," where the composer himself devised specific, iconic musical gestures to depict the apprentice's naïve enchanting of a broom to do his labors, portrayed brilliantly in the film by Mickey Mouse. Finally, the film closes

* Or, as with the recent "take a knee" movement among American football players, that same song may also symbolize a call for a patriotic form of protest, as against police brutality.

with Modest Mussorgsky's *Night on Bald Mountain*, which elicits an indexical, extramusical rendering based on its dark and foreboding mood—which the animators creatively mold into a fantastic tale of demons and evil spirits. There is no specific symbolic exemplar in *Fantasia*, but you get the point: musical meaning comes in many (and subjective) varieties.

Okay, we've established that semantic meaning can be gleaned from music—so what about emotion? As you can imagine, the link of music and emotion is a heavily trodden topic in scholarship, not least as relates to musical taste. Langer, again, challenged the "absolutist" position espoused by Hanslick and Stravinsky—calling it a "silly fiction," and noting that music yields to the imagination not only associative logic but also affect or "emotional experience." Meyer then raised the bar by arguing that disentangling meaning from emotion is near impossible, as both are part of a "single psychological process."

For Meyer, as for most neuroscientists today, a prime source of emotion in music listening is the element of surprise: deviations from the normal tendency of musical discourse based on custom and tradition—that is, of learned syntactic expectations. Forging syntactical meaning from a deceptive cadence, for example, is reinforced via an emotional response, whereby we'll be even more alert for another such "surprise" in the future. Another commonly cited source of intramusical emotion is "tension-release," an almost clichéd trope referring to the way that a musical passage—a cadence, a melodic contour, or chord progression—can seem to build tension, like a coiled spring, which when "released" (through arrival of a cadential, harmonic, or melodic "resolution") can produce a wave of positive emotion, again reinforcing our attention to such syntactic unwindings in the future. It is in this context that we may experience the "thrills and chills" associated with the "reward" of resolving a previously tense musical experience.

I would emphasize, though, that intramusical or syntactic sources of emotional reaction, including "thrills and chills," should not *only* be associated with moments of surprise or in the resolution of perceived musical tension. Many of the most emotionally palpable music-listening experiences, for me anyway, take hold simply upon the arrival—or sustained flow—of a musically striking moment: call it a "beautiful arrival." There may well be nothing that is deceptive or violating or tense or surprising in the musical discourse at this moment, other than perhaps how utterly beautiful its arrival strikes us: a distinct melodic phrase, a flowing harmonic sequence, an enchanting use of counterpoint, a potent pedal point, an intoxicating groove, etc. The term "apotheosis" is sometimes used in musical analysis to indicate a moment—often three-quarters or so into a work—of aesthetic climax; these arrivals will certainly be a product of syntactic discourse (not to mention compositional skill), but not necessarily one where "rules" are violated or tension is generated, though they may. At any rate, such moments will likely play a major role in defining our musical taste. To cite two cases for myself: the cascade of harmonic sequences in the development section from the opening movement of Mozart's Piano Concerto no. 21 in C, K. 467, and the groove-filled bass line toward the end of Crosby, Stills, Nash & Young's "Carry On"—neither of which involves violations or musical tension in any traditional sense, and yet each gives me "chills" every time.

Emotion can likewise come via moments of extramusical meaning. Most obvious are indexical cases, when a mood or psychological state is perceived as emanating from the music. Again, hearing a musical passage as triumphant or melancholy or angry will not necessarily *induce* those emotions in a listener; rather, they may simply be *perceived* as representing the affective intention of the composer or performer—much like watching a good actor portray a triumphant, melancholy, or angry character in a play, following upon the author's intention. And yet, in part by virtue of our capacity for empathy, perceiving this *intended* emotion in the music may well trigger it in ourselves: "joyful" music can indeed instill in us a feeling of joy (particularly when we also move or dance), while "sad" or "melancholy" music can put us in a funk, and perhaps even make us cry; certainly, "frightening" music in a horror film score can by itself arouse fear in us—especially when the camera moves down a dark corridor.

It is a bit harder to quantify how exactly emotion is triggered from an iconic musical moment—a mountain silhouette, a thunderstorm, or a spellbound broom—without also factoring in some personal memory or self-generating association. This is what Koelsch refers to as "musicogenic" meaning (though not in its common association to epileptic seizures triggered by music), where we hear something and via memory or association, or both, we become nostalgic, melancholy, or otherwise moved. This is the phenomenon of getting teary-eyed when you hear your grandmother's favorite song, or the one playing on the radio when your college girlfriend dumped you. Not long ago, I heard the powerful finale from Beethoven's Ninth Symphony in a documentary about the 1989 fall of the Berlin Wall; the association of the movement (musically more than textually) with freedom was enough to bring me to tears, becoming a potent symbol in my mind for human struggle against oppression. This indeed is the source of emotion aligned with symbolic extramusical meaning: an Olympic gold medalist begins to sob when his or her national anthem plays at the medal ceremony not because the music is particularly emotive syntactically, but because of its personal—learned—associations to country, honor, and pride.

We'll return in more depth to the links between music and emotion in Interlude G, but let's now get back to the main theme of this interlude: the brain.

## MEANING AND EMOTION IN MUSIC, PART 2: NEUROSCIENCE

It was not merely in philosophical circles that meaning and emotion were once deemed separate domains, but also in neuropsychological ones—namely, under the rubric of cognition and affect, respectively. This dichotomy is seen most readily in the famed "mere exposure affect" or "familiarity principle," developed by psychologist Robert Zajonc—stating that our preference or liking for something is stimulated by mere (and precognitive) exposure to it.[316]

This "principle" has been proven in numerous experiments—using words, shapes, faces, and sounds—and has been a boon for the advertising industry ever since. Our ability to express preference automatically, without prior cognition, led Zajonc to propose: "Affect and cognition are under the control of separate and partially independent systems."[317] Zajonc's claim—under the adage "Preferences need no inferences"—was initially embraced in strict neuroscience circles, but through a series of brain-imaging studies in the early 2000s, a countering claim began to emerge, that "both semantic and affective features are represented in a *single* . . . network, and that semantic information has a necessary priority."[318]

The view of cognition and emotion as neurologically separate but equal was originally embraced in part due to their distinctive processes and networks. Cognition involves concepts such as attention, planning, language, and memory; it is widely understood as involving the cortical regions of the brain, that is the four lobes of the cerebrum. Emotion, by contrast, involves the murkier concepts of motivation, drive, reward, and punishment; as such, it is largely seen as an evolutionary adaptation—a kind of neurochemical feedback loop to actions and perceptions that long ago enhanced or threatened our survival: love toward an offspring, fear toward a predator, etc. The dominant view is that emotion is primarily processed in the subcortical regions—notably the more "primitive" limbic system: the amygdala, the ventral striatum, and the hypothalamus. By virtue of recent studies, as noted, cognition and emotion are no longer viewed as neurologically separate but rather interconnected. The main driver is the amygdala—the "emotional center of the brain"—whose neural networks are linked directly to the frontal and parietal lobes. In this way, our emotional responses—joy at hearing a loved one's voice, alarm at hearing it turn angry—provide guidance to our attention and planning. In short, garnering meaning via our senses triggers emotion, which in turn triggers further and refined cognitive processing.

This symbiosis takes place too when we listen to music, of course. Through research conducted by musical neuroscientists—not least Stefan Koelsch and his colleagues—we now know that semantic processing takes place some 100 to 150 milliseconds *after* syntactic processing. Koelsch has traced intramusical processing to both sides of the brain, and on the frontal as well as temporal lobe—e.g., the superior temporal sulcus, an area specifically tied to our ability to process meaning in language. Koelsch likewise found that our ability to draw extramusical or referential meaning—e.g., via an indexical or "mood" sign—is correlated to our processing of language, triggering the same brain regions and signals.

Things get more interesting when we look at the processing of emotion triggered by music listening. In the immediacy of an emotional response (as opposed to the broader psychological mood taking place over time), the "jackpot" to be garnered from music is the famed "thrills and chills," or "frisson." These blessed moments are associated with the amygdala, and notably when the neurotransmitter dopamine is released. To get a bit technical, "chills" are triggered in a region deep in the brain—the ventral striatum, which, as noted earlier, is located at the base of the cerebrum, and along with the amygdala forms part of the limbic system; more specifically, chills are activated in a subregion of the ventral striatum called the nucleus accumbens (NAc). Not coincidentally, this is also the area of the brain recruited in sex, as well as in drug addiction. It is by virtue of such sensational abilities that Dan Levitin calls the NAc the "center of the brain's reward system."[319]

By contrast, a sustained mood or feeling generated via "indexical" musical moments—either arousing or soothing—seems to involve multiple cortical regions, especially in the intersection of the frontal and parietal lobes, as well as in the frontal cortex, in areas involved not only in language processing but also in lower-level music processing (Gestalt formation). In addition, our ability to perceive a sustained mood from music has been identified with the so-called "mirror neuron" system of the frontal lobe and cerebellum. These are sensory-motor interactions, with origins dating back to early in our evolution, which underlie our ability to connect, imitate, and empathize with others. In essence, as researchers like Istvan Molnar-Szakacs and Katie Overy suggest, we internalize and *imitate* the mood of the music we perceive as emanating from the *intent* of the composer or performer.[320]

It is the likely involvement of motor coordination in experiencing musical emotion, moreover, that fascinates Levitin—as he describes in detail in *This Is Your Brain on Music*. Curious about the role of the cerebellum in the processing of musical emotion, he traces its connection not only to the musical parameters of rhythm and meter, but also to the brain's emotional and attentional epicenters: the amygdala and the frontal lobe. Movement and emotion, he notes, have an evolutionary link, since an involuntary emotional motor response (e.g., running in fear from a bear) enhanced our chances of survival. As Levitin writes, "Those of our ancestors who were endowed with an emotional system that was directly connected to their motor system could react more quickly, and thus live to reproduce and pass on those genes to another generation."[321] Further, as he and Vinod Menon revealed, this primitive link of music, movement, and emotion in the cerebellum provides a kind of steady, constant undercurrent to the *entire* cycle of music processing: from (1) lower-level extraction of the musical parameters in the auditory cortex to (2) higher-level processing of musical syntax and semantics in the frontal lobe to (3) the experience of emotion in the amygdala and—if potent enough to produce "chills"—the NAc.[322] Music, in other words, has an uncanny way of lighting up nearly the entire brain.

## MEMORY AND MUSIC, PART 1: GENERAL INTRODUCTION

The cerebellum, of course, isn't the only item operating nonstop during music processing; there is also our final—and most complex—"module": memory.

In a celebrated passage from Proust's *In Search of Lost Time*, the protagonist Charles Swann hears for the *second* time a sonata for violin and piano by the fictional composer Vinteuil. Swann had first encountered the sonata at a dinner party a year prior; already then Swann was captivated by the music, not least by the "little phrase" of the piano accompaniment, but was rather at a loss to comprehend what exactly he was hearing, appreciating "only the material quality of the sound which those instruments secreted . . . without being able to distinguish any clear outline, or to give a name to what was pleasing him." On that second hearing, however, everything changed—and not just because the sonata helped seed his growing infatuation with the ill-suited Odette. As Proust's narrator explains, it was the power of memory that now gave the music clarity: "This [initial] impression would continue to envelop in its liquidity, its ceaseless overlapping, the motives which from time to time emerge, barely discernible. . . . [D]id not our memory, like a laborer who toils at the laying down of firm foundations beneath the tumult of waves . . . enable us to compare and to contrast them with those that follow . . . so that, when the same impression suddenly returned, it was no longer impossible to grasp."[323]

Memory, indeed, is the overarching theme, the sine qua non, of Proust's epic novel—as much exemplified in Swann's newfound obsession for Vinteuil's "little phrase" (echoing his unhealthy obsession for Odette) as anything else. And as it was for Swann, so too is memory for all of us the sine qua non of any potential musical awareness we may have, let alone of any long-lasting appreciation or taste we may acquire for this or that piece of music. We'll discuss a possible real-life inspiration for Vinteuil and his violin sonata, incidentally, in Chapter 15.

Each of us experiences the essential role of memory in music processing on a daily basis: hearing that song you love on the radio and singing along with every lyric; admiring that hip "cover" of a well-known song in a completely different style from the original, without the slightest confusion as to its identity; being driven mad by that insipid TV commercial jingle that gets stuck, as an "earworm," in your head; getting teary-eyed when you hear Grandma's favorite song as you relive the last time you saw her, among countless others. The power and mystery of musical memory has gained currency in recent years through the fascinating tales by Oliver Sacks: of profound amnesiacs who yet maintain full musical fluency; or the heartwarming stories of Alzheimer's patients briefly escaping their frozen minds upon hearing a song from their youth, as in the 2014 documentary *Alive Inside*, etc. But where exactly does this powerful, mysterious ability come from, and how is it manifested?

Trying to grasp current thinking on how memory works when we listen to music is no mean feat for a nonspecialist, not least given the many ways in which the topic can be tackled. Indeed, the main prerequisite I've found to understanding musical memory is to first grasp exactly what memory is, and how it works. Too many discussions on music and memory presume a working knowledge of the general mechanisms of human memory, which can make them fuzzy and frustrating. As such, I've adopted a different approach: to preface our discussion on musical memory with a summary overview of how memory in general is understood—introducing its various theories, models, types, subtypes, and processes. In so doing, I've done my best to streamline this overview, relegating technical details to the endnotes (and occasionally on the WYLI website, supplement to Interlude C).

We begin with a brief scan of how memory has been conceived through the ages—including a few intriguing asides from the purview of musicology.

Attempts to systematically define memory date back at least to Plato—who referred to memory as a "block of wax" in our souls: the duration as well as veracity of any given memory, Plato explains, depends on the strength of the experience and the depth and consistency of the "wax block"—that is, of the individual soul itself.[324] Aristotle too embraced the wax metaphor, emphasizing the prime role of the senses in initiating memories as "pictures" or "sense-images." As we'll see, this wax or "storehouse" metaphor, as it is often called, was prescient—2,400 years ago—in its claim that memories leave something of a "trace" behind for later retrieval.[325] In later antiquity, a distinction was made between "natural" and "artificial" memory—the latter "strengthened by a kind of training and system of discipline."[326] Artificial memory would blossom into a full-fledged *ars memorativa* or "mnemonic art," which held sway through the Middle Ages. Indeed, the philosophers of the scholastic tradition (13th–14th c.), such as Saint Thomas Aquinas, looked upon the diligent cultivation of a proficient memory as a moral obligation: as memory scholar Mary Carruthers has noted, demonstrating proficient memorization was not a mere display of personal skill, but rather a sign of moral virtue and good character.[327]

This mind-set of "memory as virtue" in turn had profound ramifications for music during the Middle Ages and the Renaissance—not only from a pedagogical standpoint, but from a creative one as well. As noted, the foundational repertoire of Western music is the enormous corpus of religious song—Gregorian chant—created largely from the fifth to ninth centuries. Importantly, it was only in the ninth century that a system of music notation—via a class of symbols called neumes—was developed, meaning that prior to 800, oral transmission and memorization were the *only* means of generating and preserving this huge repertoire. Neumes, however, were never intended to replace memory, but only to act as a mnemonic tool: according to the influential eleventh-century music theorist Guido d'Arezzo, it took ten years for a monk to gain "only an imperfect knowledge of singing" (i.e., the chant repertoire)—something he hoped his new innovation, the staff, might cut down to one or two years.[328]

Indeed, the *ars memorativa* mentality was fully ingrained into the broader musical culture throughout the medieval period. For example, despite a few surviving names today—Léonin, Perotin, Guillaume de Machaut—music in this era was conceived of *not* as the inspired musings of an individual genius so much as a well-crafted "paraphrase" or "recomposition" of existing formulae *assiduously memorized* via a "memorial archive," as musicologist Anna Maria Busse Berger calls it. It was only in the Renaissance that one saw a gradual shift from collective to individual musical genius—and only in the early nineteenth century, notably with Beethoven, that the latter had decidedly trumped collective memory.[329]

The intense focus on memorization during the early modern era initially resulted in minimal effort to understand *how* the mechanism of memory actually works. That began to change in the seventeenth century, when philosophers like Descartes and Locke tepidly—and inaccurately—attempted to align the functioning of memory with our ideas, emotions, imagination, personal identity, and nervous system.[330] It is in fact only in the late nineteenth century, heralded by empirical research by psychologists and philosophers like William James and Ludwig Wittgenstein, when we start to see memory being discussed in terms that resemble our own understanding.

We can gain a quick sense of that current understanding by briefly mentioning two prominent theories of how memory works: the causal theory of memory and the multiple trace theory.

The causal theory of memory (CTM)—introduced by C. B. Martin and Max Deutscher in 1966—in essence states the following: to have an experience in life is to be in a particular "mental state"; that state in turn produces a set of "traces"—individual and collective aspects of the experience—that persist in the brain even after the experience has passed. When we subsequently remember the experience, or aspects of it, those traces are retrieved—which stand in a *causal* relationship to the original experience, hence the theory's name. Although the broad theory is widely accepted, CTM has a problem: it ignores the distinction between *concrete* facts (e.g., where exactly you were on 9/11) and more *abstract* conditions (e.g., the general mood of that day, what it meant historically, etc.), among other things.[331]

The multiple trace theory (MTT)—introduced into cognitive psychology in 1986 by Douglas Hintzman, and separately into neuroscience in 1997 by Lynn Nadel and Morris Moscovitch—fills in these gaps by addressing how we are able to simultaneously store both *abstract* knowledge and *concrete* details surrounding particular memories. Specifically, MTT suggests that the stored traces themselves contain both types of attributes: factual details, context (time and space), emotions, etc. Importantly, however, traces are not simply stored in a single location in the brain; instead *each* trace gets placed in multiple "categories," or mental constructs, at once. Each category in turn contains *all* the traces that *share* common attributes (e.g., "tragic events," "9/11," "New York," "tall buildings," etc.). Since each trace comprises multiple attributes, each will reside in multiple categories, hence the theory's name. And since each new experience creates new traces, no category is ever "fixed."[332]

Okay, let's break from such general theories of memory and apply them to a specific, musical example. Imagine that you are hearing for the first time a recording of Miles Davis' "Someday My Prince Will Come" (1961). As you listen, a multiattribute memory trace will be encoded, including the musical aspects of the track, the context in which you heard it, the emotion you felt, etc. Assuming previous experience with jazz, that trace—in all its multiattribute glory—will go into multiple existing categories of various types and dimensions: "music," "jazz," "Miles Davis," "Harmon mute," "waltz time," "Disney songs," "early 1960s," "John Coltrane," "Wynton Kelly," etc.; perhaps also contextual categories like "wintertime," "rainy days," "melancholy mood," etc. When, sometime later, a memory is triggered or "cued"—for example, you hear another Harmon mute track by Miles, you see a drawing of Snow White (the film for which the song was written), it starts to rain, you feel melancholy, etc.—the *abstract* quality of the new memory will be informed in part by that earlier listening experience of "Someday My Prince Will Come," just as any *concrete* details will be derived from it and/or from other, previously formed memory traces.

CTM and MTT are but two of many theories of memory in current circulation—and are here described but partially. And yet their descriptions should provide a useful and intuitive sense of what, conceptually, is believed to happen when a memory is triggered.[333] To more fully understand how we actually remember a piece of music, however, we'll need to dive a bit deeper—beyond theory, and into some of the *practical* ways in which memory has been shown to operate.

The first practical dimension concerns the "stores" in which memory is housed in the brain—following upon the "multistore" model developed in 1968 by Richard Atkinson and Richard Shiffrin. Each store is defined by virtue of the *length of time* that the memories are held within the brain, as well as the role that each store plays in the overall memory process.[334] Human memory "stores" are somewhat analogous to a computer's "memory banks," a mix of RAM (random-access memory) and long-term storage, working together to retrieve saved data for later use.

In our case, every song or symphony, every melody, riff, chord progression, rhythmic pattern, or exotic instrument timbre we hold in our memory is there because at *some point or another* it entered into *each* of our memory stores.

The process begins in the shortest and most immediate store, known as "sensory memory" (SM). Here, actual "memory" is only loosely at play, in that SM mainly involves the *unconscious* processing of incoming raw data from our senses.

Once extracted by our brains, this raw perceptual data does indeed remain there *beyond* the actual experience—but only for a few seconds, after which it will decay and disappear forever *unless it is otherwise captured*—or "rehearsed"—by our consciousness. Each sense (hearing, sight, touch, etc.) has its own "modality" of SM—with music processed via "echoic" memory—so called because it acts like an echo in the brain. At this point there are no memory traces or categories involved.

The next, intermediate memory "store" is in fact the topic of robust debate. On one side, following the conventional Atkinson-Shiffrin model, are those who support the existence of a "short-term memory" (STM) store—as a kind of "way station" between sensory memory and long-term memory. In this view, the raw data stored from SM, if sufficiently rehearsed, gets organized into "chunks"—up to nine at any one time—that in turn enter an "activated" state of consciousness. On the other side are those who see short- and long-term memory as a single, continuous store. In this scenario, the "way station" function is better understood as "working memory" (WM)—where the raw data chunks are not just stored, but actively manipulated, thereby helping us perform complex tasks: carrying out reasoning problems, learning new material, or analyzing and internalizing a piece of music.[335]

Whether held in STM or—as is increasingly more accepted—WM, those memory chunks are not yet placed into mental categories for later retrieval. That process, instead, is the purview of the final store, long-term memory (LTM). The process of *organizing* memory traces into categories can take weeks or months, but once in place, these traces can theoretically endure forever—and in potentially unlimited capacity. As suggested previously, you can think of your LTM like a computer's hard drive (with unlimited storage), and your WM like the RAM you have available for immediate use. Like the saved files on your hard drive, memory traces stored in your LTM will reside in a passive, unconscious state unless "opened" via a strong sensory or cognitive stimulus—a distinct smell, a humorous story, a familiar melody, etc. Of course, not every chunk becomes a memory trace stored in multiple categories: it must either be sufficiently rehearsed or possess a notably striking, novel, or emotional quality. In the end, though, LTM is where our memories are stored, and where they come to possess for us rich and complex meaning.

To return to our Miles Davis example: that first time you heard "Someday My Prince Will Come," its raw materials—notes, timbres, rhythms, etc.—were unconsciously processed by the "echoic" modality of your sensory memory. As you listened intently to its parts and dimensions—solos, harmonies, sounds, etc.—the song was temporarily stored in your working memory, whereby you could learn its properties and reflect on its relationship to other jazz songs you knew. If you never heard the song again, and especially if jazz was not part of your regular musical diet, chances are its traces would never enter your long-term memory. If, on the other hand, you heard the song frequently—even if during a single phase of your life—its traces, stored into various categories, might reside permanently in your LTM, to be retrieved into consciousness by any number of sensory or cognitive stimuli.

Next, LTM can be further broken down into two distinct types: explicit and implicit. Explicit—or declarative—memories are what most of us think of as "memories"; they are the facts and events that we intentionally and consciously recall whenever a potent stimulus triggers them out of their passive, unconscious state: "I remember meeting her last year," "Ringo Starr plays drums," etc. Explicit memories are thus often referred to as "knowing what" memories. Implicit—or procedural—memories, by contrast, are the "knowing how" memories, or "habit memories"; these are not facts that can be recalled, but rather *skills* one possesses, usually harbored in the body—such as riding a bike, tying one's shoes, or playing the piano.

In turn, explicit memories are delineated into two major subtypes: episodic and semantic; the distinction was made, and terms coined, by Endel Tulving in 1972. These subtypes, indeed, are where the rubber often hits the road whenever memory processing, musical or otherwise, is discussed. Episodic memories are those "of autobiographical events," as Sacks puts it: they connect our present selves to past events and experiences in all their multivariate dimensions, drawn from myriad categories—the "who," "what," and "where" of their proceedings, causes, and ramifications. Semantic—or "schematic"—memories, on the other hand, entail the general knowledge behind the events: these are the collective, cultural, historical, and contextual memories that provide meaning (semantics) to the autobiographical events. Using yet again our Miles Davis example: episodic memory enables you to recall that rainy, melancholy day you first heard "Someday My Prince Will Come"; semantic memory enables you to recall that Miles is among jazz' most esteemed trumpeters, and that the 1961 track was made *between* his "first classic quintet" (1955–58) and his second (1964–68) (see Chapter 11)—among much else.

And finally, to round out our introductory tour of memory, we note the two main processes that specialists identify as being involved in triggering our LTM—that is, in transferring those memory traces and categories from an unconscious to a conscious state: recognition and recall. Recognition involves, as it sounds, recognizing something within a stimulus that is familiar to us—whether a concrete or an abstract element, and whether of an episodic or semantic nature. Generally, therefore, recognition involves a triggering "cue" of some kind (seeing a face, hearing a song, etc.); the stronger the cue, the more likely and vivid the memory. Recall, by contrast, involves our ability to "recirculate" data that we once already knew—and can vary in quality from complete to sketchy. To use our Miles example one last time: recognition is when you can identify "Someday My Prince Will Come" simply by hearing the middle of Miles' solo; recall is the ability to cite it when someone asks you to name your favorite jazz rendition of a Disney song.

And with all that as background, we are ready to tackle music and memory head-on.

## MEMORY AND MUSIC, PART 2: REMEMBERING MUSIC

Music, of course, relies on memory to an extreme, given its identity as a temporal art: one that unfolds over time. At its most basic level, our music cognition relies on memory to make sense of what we're hearing, allowing each new musical stimulus "to be maintained on-line to be able to relate one element in a sequence to another that occurs later," as Isabelle Peretz and her colleague Robert Zatorre put it.[336] In memory-speak, this is our WM in action—keeping active an ever-running tally of four to nine distinct musical elements across various parameters: melody, harmony, rhythm, timbre, etc. It is in this context that Leonard Meyer states emphatically, "Without thought and memory there could be no musical experience."[337]

Backing up, we've already touched upon how musical memory operates within the models of causal theory and multiple trace theory, using our "Someday Our Prince Will Come" example. To flesh out the theories a bit more: imagine listening to one of your favorite Tom Waits tracks, "Jersey Girl," right after you break up with your own girlfriend; or hearing a string quartet play an arrangement of Jimi Hendrix's "Purple Haze" at the opening of an art exhibit. In both cases, it is reasonable to imagine that the experiences will leave memory traces of various varieties in your LTM, each placed into several categories—some old, some new. "Jersey Girl," already quite familiar, would come to reside alongside such earlier memories of the song, in categories like "Tom Waits songs," "gritty male vocalists," "rock ballads," and—with sufficient harmonic awareness—"I–IV–V songs," etc.; in the future, however, the song will likely evoke sadness as well, as the present trace comes to hold a prominent spot in the newly formed "my recent breakup" category. The "Purple Haze" arrangement, then, would not only join other traces in preexisting categories like "'Purple Haze' covers" and "string quartet pieces," etc., but also in new ones like "classical arrangements of rock songs" and "museum-exhibit songs."

What these theories are saying, in effect, is that every time we hear a piece of music that via rehearsal or novelty gains sufficient attentional presence to enter our LTM, its multivariate elements—the musicological details, the accompanying contexts and emotions, etc.—get encoded as *concrete* memory traces within the *abstract* dimensions of the mental categories in which they reside. This is how we are able to carry out the everyday miracles of musical memory: hearing one song while recalling others that are sonically similar; recognizing a familiar song despite its unfamiliar instrumentation; associating music with times, places, and moods of our past, etc. To Levitin, the organization of distinct musical traces into distinct music-oriented categories solves the mystery of how we can recognize a song despite its varied guises: "Our memory system extracts out some formula or computational description that allows us to recognize songs in spite of these transformations."[338] That is, for example, our memory system allows us to "extract out" the Hendrix quartet arrangement as a *concrete* iteration—"'Purple Haze': the quartet version"—by recognizing it within the broader, *abstract* category of "'Purple Haze': the song."

These theories, by the way, also help to explain the rich and many-splendored memories I myself experience whenever I hear the third movement of Beethoven's Ninth Symphony, and especially those fiery fanfares toward the end. They arise as memory traces formed via the many hundreds of times I've heard the work (live and in recording) as a musician and composer; in this way, they are stored in any number of purely musical categories: "the Ninth Symphony," "Beethoven," "the Romantic era," "deceptive cadences," "variations form," etc. But they also find place in context-oriented categories of a very personal nature—like "Dad," "my childhood," "my room," etc. Little wonder, then, that recognition of this music stirs up not only a wealth of *concrete* and *abstract* memories, but a burst of emotion as well.

The trace-category relationship, moreover, suggests that located within our brain too is a category dedicated to our "hit parade," where, in spite of their musicological, stylistic, cultural, historical, and autobiographical distinctions, a group of songs and works are united in their role as "gems" of our individual musical taste—at least for the moment. This means that whenever we hear a new song or work that in some way or another "resembles" the collective identity of that category's constituent traces, our cognitive attention centers perk up, which in turn enhances its chances of someday joining its ranks. In a way, this is what the Music Genome Project is all about: trying to identify those musicological traits that resemble the collective definition of your "hit parade" category. To be sure, of course, no man-made algorithm could ever match the sophistication of our brain and its memory processing—where not only sound, but also context, emotion, and biography are embedded into each candidate's trace.

Turning again from theory to practice, let's consider further how music interacts with the various "stores" of memory, from sensory to long-term. As noted, the SM modality devoted to music is called "echoic" memory—raw perceptual data that usually remains but an instant. It is by virtue of this raw, unformed state of memory perception, for example, that Proust's protagonist heard in Vinteuil's sonata "only the material quality of the sound . . . barely discernible." Echoic memory, moreover, proceeds near seamlessly into the lower-level processing modules of extraction and Gestalt formation—sometimes called "chunking." These chunks, of course, are then poised for use by our WM—to enable music processing to continue.

When it does transpire that those raw pitches and rhythms, formed into chunks, *endure* in our minds, they enter into our LTM—likened by Proust to "a laborer who toils at the laying down of firm foundations beneath the tumult of waves." According to Peretz and Zatorre, these auditory chunks in turn become memory traces, whereby a song's *concrete* or "surface" dimensions—its specific melodies and rhythms—may be stored in our LTM. This is what enables, for example, even a nonmusician to sing a familiar song in the correct key and tempo, as Levitin has shown.[339] At the same time, a listener is able to "follow the piece by a process of abstraction and organization," to get its "gist"—such that he can recognize a song even if he hears it in a *different* key and/or tempo.[340] This in turn provides neuroscientific support for the multiple trace theory: that both *concrete* (surface) and *abstract* musical elements are simultaneously stored in our LTM.

To be sure, the various memory stores never work in isolation, but continually in concert, in a kind of giant feedback loop. In the process, the stored musical traces themselves—containing both *concrete* and *abstract* elements—are at any given moment either fully unconscious, or at some level of semiconscious or conscious awareness. Whether a given musical memory trace stored in your LTM will rise up from the sea of unconsciousness into conscious awareness—via recognition or recall—will depend to a large extent on the cueing strength of the stimulus at hand: its similarity to the music you're hearing now, its comparability to the extramusical experience you're having now (the people, place, food, mood, etc., involved), and so forth. In all, it's some pretty impressive memory work our brains carry out each time we turn on the radio, get together with friends, or push play on our iPhones!

With regard to the types of LTM, music listening is almost exclusively the domain of explicit ("know what") memory, whereas music performance involves both explicit and implicit ("know how") memory—at least if a performer hopes to render music that is intentional and expressive. In our earlier summary, explicit memory was divided into episodic (autobiographical events) and semantic (general knowledge) memory, but these subtypes likewise extend to purely intramusical distinctions as well. In this context, episodic memory allows you to remember the names of individual songs, their specific melodies, rhythms, and sounds—including those nuanced details of a particular performance: Frank Sinatra's vocal inflections on "The Lady Is a Tramp," Michael Jackson's exclamations on "Billie Jean," Glenn Gould's humming on the *Goldberg Variations*, etc. Semantic memory, also called "collective" memory, provides the broader musical context that listeners as well as performers need in order to understand what they are hearing—including the formal and harmonic conventions shared among similar songs and works, and thus relies on musical syntax. Semantic memory, for example, allows us to guess the way a pop song might continue if it were suddenly cut off; it also explains why it is hard even for professional musicians to memorize atonal music, since by definition this approach is less reliant on convention—not to mention harder to sing.

Closing out on the *processes* of musical memory: recognition assuredly dominates in music listening, manifesting itself whenever the music you are hearing now seems "familiar" or "similar" to some previously heard trace stored in your LTM. The ability to recognize previously heard music begins in infancy, even in utero—Freud's so-called "infantile amnesia"—whereby newborns will respond to music they heard in the womb; indeed, infants as young as seven months can recognize complex music, such as themes of Mozart piano sonatas, after a two-week delay.[341] Again, recognition includes not only the *concrete* details of a particular recording or work, but also its *abstract* dimensions—enabling you to identify, for example, an experimental dance mix of a familiar song based on only its broad elements: the timbre of a singer's voice, the contour of a melody, a striking chord progression, etc. Classical and jazz composers often exploit this ability by deliberately reintroducing familiar material in a modified form—via variation, inversion, retrograde (backwards), etc.—thus turning recognition into a kind of aesthetic reward. Further, as Levitin observes, *abstract* musical recognition can extend to the overall "sound" of genres (e.g., heavy metal, Dixieland jazz, reggae) and historical periods (e.g., the harpsichord-based music of the Baroque era, the reverb-drenched guitar of 1960s surf rock). As noted, recognition can at times lead to identification, though not in every case, and especially with instrumental music: How many times have you asked a friend, "What is that piece I just heard? It goes, *Laaa-ti-da-da-deeee-daaah*?"*

While recognition is firmly tied to music listening, the other memory process—recall—is most directly aligned with performance, where a performer must re-create previously known music "by heart," even if partly improvised. Of course, many musicians rely on sheet music to properly recall what to play; studies, however, demonstrate that musicians rarely read every note, but instead use it periodically as a mnemonic aid, much like their medieval forebears—in turn showing the power of *abstract* knowledge in recalling *concrete* details. Music listening too makes use of recall, however, when we "rehearse" a song in our minds to remember how it goes, or whenever that damn TV jingle earworm gets stuck in our heads. Both recognition and recall, moreover, respond with greater acuity when the original memory trace is aligned with a strong emotional trigger—whether via association to an emotive extramusical experience, or given one's emotional response, positive or negative, to the music itself. I imagine that my uncle Jerry's uncanny memory for the particular conductors and soloists featured on his many classical recordings was in no small part impelled by his profound love for the many works—the symphonies of Sibelius, the concertos of Bartók, the piano sonatas of Scriabin—inscribed on the albums that lined shelf after shelf of his apartment.

* For those keeping score, this is the opening of the theme used by Johannes Brahms in his *Variations on a Theme by Haydn*.

Jerry's prodigious album-based recall, as impressive as it was, is rather mundane compared to the miraculous musical memory illustrated in the severe cases described by researchers like Oliver Sacks. There is the woman, "grossly forgetful and disabled" with Alzheimer's, who nevertheless plays piano by memory for hours each day; or the severe amnesiac Woody, who "has no idea what he did for a living, where he is living now, or what he did ten minutes ago," and yet can still sing by memory the a cappella baritone parts he sang forty years ago; or the esteemed English musicologist Clive Wearing suffering from herpes encephalitis (a rare brain infection), who despite having an episodic memory lasting only a few seconds retains a large piano repertory.[342] Such cases may bolster claims of neuroscientists like Peretz and Zatorre, who argue for music cognition modules distinct from those dedicated to language, or to other types of memory recall. At the same time, it might be argued that playing the piano or singing a choral part from memory, especially when other explicit memory skills are gone, would simply represent implicit/procedural ("knowing how") memory in action, like recalling how to shave; and yet witnesses have observed the striking presence of expressive phrasing and even improvisation in their performances—"infused with intelligence and feeling," as Sacks puts it—revealing the active use of explicit/declarative memory as well.

And finally, the mysteries of musical memory have in recent years been revealed as triggering tangible and *specific* neural activity in the brain. It is fascinating to imagine how exactly the brain conjures up memories—bringing something into conscious thought via indirect sensory stimulus, or even no stimulus at all. As noted early in this chapter, cognition happens when neurons connect to one another by firing chemical signals across synapses, releasing neurotransmitters that link them together. When memories occur, that chemical charge *endures beyond* the perception stimulus—and every neuron is capable of this. Some have argued that the memory is stored in the same neural network that processed the experience in the first place,[343] but such a notion has been challenged as evidence mounts that memory processing actually involves multiple regions of the brain at once.

This notion, that memory involves multiple regions of the brain at once, in fact comports nicely with the MTT theory—which, again, argues that memory traces are placed in multiple categories in the brain. MTT has argued, for example, that episodic/autobiographical memory traces are stored in both the hippocampus (part of the subcortical limbic system) and various areas of the cerebrum. Getting more specific, research shows that music-based "echoic" memory (part of the sensory memory store) is processed in the auditory cortex, as well as in various regions of the frontal lobe. Working memory (WM), for its part, involves *multiple* cortical as well as subcortical regions—which collectively are associated with language, spatial, attentional, and movement processing; this is not surprising, given the intense amount of control, planning, and sensorimotor coding involved in WM.

The precise neural processing of long-term memory, on the other hand, is still little understood—though we do know that the left hemisphere of the temporal lobe, the prefrontal cortex, and the planum temporale (associated, as you may recall, with perfect pitch) are heavily involved. This makes sense given that these same regions are also heavily involved with language, including our ability to attach words to the things we perceive. In addition, LTM involves the subcortical region of the hippocampus, especially in memory retrieval and recall. Not surprisingly, the amygdala has also been implicated in LTM, especially when memories are imbued with an emotional dimension. Lastly, those "implicit" or skills-based memories (tying your shoe, playing the piano, etc.) have been aligned to the more "primitive" and robust regions of the brain, the basal ganglia and cerebellum. This in turn explains why even patients with advanced dementia, amnesia, or Alzheimer's can still play the piano or violin, or sing baritone parts, as Oliver Sacks has shown.

## Music on Your Mind

I trust that, despite its admitted complexity, this discussion has granted you an overall appreciation for the wonder that is music processing—conceding my initial statement that our brains are veritable music-processing machines. And while there are some slight differences in neural functioning or structure between musicians and nonmusicians, it should be clear too that each of us is armed at birth with the same rich capacity to process music. To be sure, musical training can help "modulate" or heighten one's ability to carry out various tasks: to recognize timbral distinctions among instruments, syntactic regularities and irregularities, intramusical semantic meaning, altered iterations of songs held in your memory, etc. But that's why you're reading this book, right?

This book, of course, is mainly about musical taste, and so it is worth asking what all this info on music and the brain reveals about why we like the music we do. At a minimum, the music-brain connection underscores what we already learned in Interlude A: we are a musical species, and have evolved in no small way to love and benefit from music. Each module of music processing corroborates the role of music in our evolution: feature extraction in acquiring language and improving social integration (via pitch encoding and rhythmic entrainment); Gestalt formation in discriminating safe from dangerous sounds (via auditory scene analysis); syntax in anticipating future outcomes (via regular and deceptive cadences, etc.); semantic meaning in increasing abstract thinking (via indexical interpretations of tension-release, etc.); emotion in eliciting positive moods, personally and collectively; and memory in preserving knowledge, identity, and emotion. To writers like Cross, Huron, and Levitin, the palpable resources that our modern brains devote to music processing not only substantiate music's role in our evolution, but in fact reveal it as a deciding factor in *how* we have evolved—as Levitin writes, "Music gives the brain opportunities to explore, exercise, play with and train those mental, physical, and social muscles necessary for the maintenance and formation of society as we know it."[344] In essence, we love music because our very survival depends on it.

Okay, but what about our *personal* musical taste? In fact, I would argue that the nature of our music processing in and of itself does little to dictate our individual musical taste. To be sure, there are some specific *collective* taste parameters that are circumscribed by how our ears and brains process music: the particular range of frequencies (50–4000 Hz) we humans can adequately resolve limits the range of pitches and kinds of instruments we can possibly like; the speed parameters of our audio processing limit the velocity of notes and tempos we can possibly comprehend; our neural firing response to perfect and imperfect intervals impacts the broad confines of our harmonic sensibility, among a few others.

And yet the cognitive neuroscience of music won't tell us precisely why we as individuals like Hank Williams more than Merle Haggard, or the Lumineers more than Blink-182, or Lin-Manuel Miranda more than any of them. Instead, our brains set the boundaries, the conditions, and the options whereby our personal musical taste can be formed in the first place. Our neurocognitive capacity defines the range of musical elements that can (and cannot) be extracted and organized; it establishes the manner in which musical expectations can be set and denied; it allows for a delimited way in which music can (and cannot) carry meaning; it grants music the ability to yield powerful emotions and "chemical" rewards; and it enables a good many musical instances, along with their many-splendored contexts, to be embedded in our memory for later recognition and recall. In short, our brains set before us a smorgasbord of musical options from which to choose. It is then up to each individual brain—unique, moreover, in its structure, size, and synaptic potential—to make that choice based on its owner's particular cultural, subcultural, and psychological identity.

We'll begin to make our way toward that next-level inquiry in a bit, but first let's shift our newly defined brains back to the purely musical realm—with our first foray into the revealing world of musical genotypes.

part four

# MUSICAL METAPHORS

*eight*

# THE MUSICAL GENOTYPE

## Getting to Know Your Musical Genotype

Having now "conquered" the previous five music-parameter chapters, you need no longer sheepishly confess to the next musician you meet, "I love music; I just know nothing about it." You may not be quite ready to take the AP Music Theory exam, but you should certainly be able to discern, and competently discuss, quite a bit about the musicological proceedings taking place "under the hood" of the music you love—or hate. All the more so as you reinforce your newly acquired knowledge with review and further *engaged* listening. And lucky you, we'll adopt both of these tactics in subsequent sections of the book—across multiple musical realms.

Even better, we'll now move beyond isolated theoretical concepts, which by nature promote a dissection of songs or works into one or two musical parameters. Instead, we'll look at a good number of such songs and works in a holistic fashion, aiming to understand their overall "genomic" identity.[345]

At Pandora, we used the term "focus traits" to signify the coalescing or "clustering" of individual genes into larger musical profiles. These are utilized in part to share some high-level musicological qualities with users—with expressions like "modal harmony," "demanding instrumental part writing," "leisurely tempo," etc. But more so, they're used by the MGP database to identify prominent facets of a song or work. In short, "focus traits" are the assembly of key "activated" genes across the various musicological parameters that work in concert, and that make the song or work "tick" from a musical and experiential standpoint. As users provide feedback via a "thumbs-up" or "thumbs-down," they "train" the database as to which profiles resonate or conflict with their musical taste with regard to a given playlist. In this way, songs are identified as good or bad fits on your Pandora stations.

And on a broader level, each song or work may be defined as an assembly of its "focus traits"—its musical profiles along each of the key musicological parameters we've now reviewed. In turn, your response, positive and negative, to these collective profiles across the entire musical universe makes up what we may call your **musical genotype**. Enabling you to understand and *empower* your musical genotype—your musical taste—is indeed the main goal of this book.

In those five music theory chapters, I cited as musical examples over four hundred individual songs or works across all species—and a good number of "subspecies" within them. These do not include, moreover, scores of artists and genres to which no specific music was ascribed. To be sure, this represents but a tiny fraction of the music that readers of this book will hold in high—not to mention low—esteem. This is especially so given my desire, as noted, to focus largely on well-known music. Still, the substantial variety offered in these examples provides a fair frame of reference to even the most esoteric of individual musical tastes. That is, if you didn't recognize your musical favorites in the examples provided, you likely saw a good number of their "cousins"—music that presents traits akin to your musical genotype. And if not, hats off, as you have pretty a distinct musical taste!

## A Musical "Day in the Life"

To wit, the following seven music-focused chapters will offer a thought exercise using some of these examples as touchstones to define a set of fictional musical genotypes. Although none of these will be *your* genotype, of course, they should collectively help you to gain an increased appreciation of how yours may be defined—in terms of how your musical taste intersects with various profiles and "focus traits." If nothing else, we'll get to continue talking shop about some interesting music.

Specifically, my tack is to create a set of seven hypothetical music lovers who each enjoy a musically rich "day in the life." Each subject will be identified in these chapters by a set of four beloved songs and/or works in a mix of styles that at once represent their personal "hit parade" and also reflect the musical species to which they are aligned—at least to some degree; for those so interested, a fifth song has also been added to the definition of each subject's genotype—though consigned to the WYLI website, via discussions in the supplements to Chapters 9–15, respectively. In the book's chapters, all subjects will have their day broken up into four—out of a possible five—segments, wherein a given favorite is heard: (1) during morning exercise at the gym or outdoors; (2) on the way to work; (3) on the way home from work; (4) at a restaurant, club, or concert that evening; and (5) at home before bedtime; the missing segment in book's chapters, then, is the segment addressed in the website's chapter supplements.

Each genotype will begin with a brief historical and musicological overview of the species in question, along with a set of ten "touchstone" songs or works that typify it in the broadest sense—as stereotypes, if you will. With those formalities out of the way, we'll proceed with the hit parade songs. In generating each subject's hit parade, I used one of the selections—undifferentiated in the discussion—as a "seed," or at least a baseline of sorts, for the overall set; the remaining four songs or works were then either drawn from the pool of remaining examples or from elsewhere in the musical universe—depending on what was deemed suitable to round out the set. I have relied on a variety of criteria to select the songs and works for each set—ranging from purely musicological aspects to demonstrated preferences of actual listeners on Pandora and other personalized services.

The goal, again, is to begin defining the elements of an individual's musical genotype, the profile of one's overall musical taste. Of course, five songs a musical genotype do not make—especially given that these are fictional people. But in truth, fully defining anyone's musical genotype is always going to prove elusive: all we can really hope to gain is a robust set of factors and insights whereby we can begin to understand, encounter, and then more adeptly empower our musical taste. It is my hope that by observing the "conclusions" to be drawn about these seven fictional music lovers, you'll recognize yourself to some degree, and as a result begin to draw some personal insights.

As we proceed through the "hits" of the seven music lovers, we will present for each song or work both some historic background and a detailed musicological analysis. The discussions will start off fairly short, with minimal historical overview and limited depth of analysis, and gradually become longer and more detailed—such that by the time we reach the final music lover (a classical fan), both sections will be quite detailed and lengthy. This trajectory is partly due to the analytical "muscles" you will gradually build up over these chapters, and partly due to the greater degree of explication that these latter songs or works will "require," given their more pronounced sophistication and/or presumed unfamiliarity. Although I will at every turn endeavor to make even the most nuanced musicological discussions discernible to a nontrained reader, there will likely be moments where your eyes will glaze over. When that happens, do not fret: remember that you are gradually improving your musical cognizance—in turn enabling you to leap from simply listening to music to *critically* listening to it, especially to music that you love.

A potential strategy to employ as you go through these discussions is as follows:

1. Read the discussion, both "Background" and "Analysis"—playing the audio excerpts as you read.
2. Put the book down and simply listen to the song or work in its entirety, trying to identify some of the specific analytical points you just read.
3. Reread just the "Analysis" as you listen to the entire song/work,

trying to "engage" with the noted musicological elements as they appear.

This admittedly may be difficult to do in every case, but even periodically it'll pay off.

In all, twenty-eight works in seven species will be discussed in detail over the next seven music chapters—interrupted regularly by extramusical interludes, as has been the case previously. It is understandable that you will not be a current fan of each song discussed, or certainly not to the same degree. As such, you might be inclined to skip, or at least skim, over Pop or Hip Hop or Classical if those do not capture your fancy. You have my permission to do so—though not surprisingly, I would strongly counsel against it. Indeed, you are heartily invited, after completing the discussion of the fourth song, to steal away to the WYLI website to read through the background and analysis of that genotype's fifth exemplar. Knowledge is power, and the more you can open your mind to a currently unfamiliar or unpreferred species—such as afforded in part by the discussions here—the more you might encounter a future "hit" of your own. That, or at least you'll better understand the story behind the music you hate.

In sum, this section will certainly take you further down the path of understanding why you like the music that you do. To be precise, however, it will focus more directly on *what* you like than *why* you like it. By defining the "genotype" of the individual works that collectively inform a listener's overall musical genotype, we'll be able to draw some conclusions as to *why* one or another new work might be liked or disliked by that listener. But what we're *really* able to do is identify *what* elements—syncopated rhythm, diatonic harmony, repetitive forms, etc.—are especially in keeping with the profile of that listener's taste, or not. We'll dive more explicitly into the complex alchemy of *why* that might be the case in the four interludes ahead. But remember that you can't say *why* something happens until you understand *what* exactly is happening in the first place, right?

## A Side Trip: The Quagmire of Genre

Before we introduce our fabulous set of music lovers, it may be useful to linger a bit upon a musical topic referenced numerous times in the previous chapters: genre. As noted in the discussion on form in Chapter 6, genre is a tricky topic, and one that holds a somewhat mixed status in the Music Genome Project. Again, genre is not form, but rather a system of classifying songs or works into categories according to common conventions of style, sound, instrumentation, scope, social function, etc. It is not internal musicological data (though such may be implied), but rather external metadata. As the *Grove Dictionary* puts it, genre is "a class, type, or category sanctioned by convention."[346]

Genre classifications unquestionably serve a valuable purpose in our understanding of and interaction with music, as with all art forms. When we encounter a term like "polonaise" or "smooth jazz" or "punk" or "West Coast rap" or "calypso" or "trance," we immediately have a more meaningful frame of reference than if we simply heard "classical" or "jazz" or "rock or "hip hop" or "world music" or "electronica," respectively. Assuming some familiarity, these former terms suggest elements of both musical content and our likely aesthetic experience, beyond what we'd gain merely from the latter terms. Without genre labels, most of us would have a hard time deciding whether or not to attend a concert or, for that matter, knowing how to discuss our musical taste.

The potential function and utility of genre classifications have been hotly discussed and debated by musicologists and aestheticians. To some degree or another, genre labels distinguish and classify works, suggest and reinforce musical content, distinguish between "norms" and "deviations," intimate a social function, and elicit reception expectations, among other things. A key concept in recent discussions of musical genre is the social "contract" or "dialectic" that genre provides between composer and listener: here's what you might expect to hear, but don't be surprised if you get something entirely different. Indeed, some theorists consider it an obligation of an artwork to extend beyond the musical and experiential expectations of a genre label. As the influential German philosopher-musicologist Theodor Adorno wrote, for example, "The individual work that simply subordinates itself to a genre does not do justice to it. It is more fruitful if there is conflict between them."[347]

Indeed, as we've seen in our various historical reviews thus far, it is the natural tendency for composers and musicians to periodically deviate from expectations and established practices—genre-based and otherwise. Such is the natural evolution of art. At times, such deviations merely stretch the bounds of existing genres, while at other times they lead to the establishment of new ones. The increasing trend of classical composers from the nineteenth century onward to forge a "conflict" with established genres, to create unique works worthy of distinctive analysis, has ushered in, according to theorists such as Adorno and Carl Dahlhaus, the demise of artistic genres.[348] Given the "dialectic" tools they offer, however, classical composers will undoubtedly find them useful for many generations to come.

Within popular and jazz music, moreover, genres have yielded tremendous force and attraction—for artists, fans, and the music industry itself. Playing into our innate penchant for classification, genre labels are a handy way of marking commonalities and establishing distinctions between various musical approaches—in terms of musicological, lyrical, social, and aesthetic elements. Hearing a genre label not only produces an instant impression about how a song or artist might sound; it also provides a code whereby artists and fans can build solidarity or division. The labels "modern country," "death metal," "jam rock," or "Dixieland" can quickly segregate musicians and fans into factions before even a note has sounded.

But there's an inherent danger: genre labels are often subjective, vague, esoteric, and even contradictory. While genre labels may say something "true" about the music that subsumes them, they inevitably don't tell the whole story, and at times are downright misleading. Take the term "indie" (short for "independent"), for example: Are all songs assigned to this label by fans, labels, concert promoters, and DJs really raw, cheaply produced, hard-hitting, and aimed at low-income kids?[349]

Such risks and rewards were acutely in our minds when assessing the role of genre in the Music Genome Project. Relying too much on genres to define a song or work, we felt, would bring about a bevy of generic and bland matches. More troubling, it would assuredly foster plenty of matches that fundamentally conflicted with the musical language of the source: a contrasting rhythmic language, an opposing vocal and instrumental style, an unrelated harmonic approach, etc.

At the same time, to dispense with them entirely introduced other potential problems. Remember, genre labels can say something "true"—and to some degree inexplicable—about a song or work. That is, two songs labeled "psychedelic rock" or "rockabilly" or "Tex-Mex" or "acid jazz" will share a kinship that in some way transcends purely musicological data.

This is especially the case when dealing with what we at Pandora call "stylistic influence"—where a song dominantly in one genre, say rock, will incorporate elements of one or more others, say jazz or country. To state that this happens often is a gross understatement. Few indeed are the songs or works that reside pristinely within the musical, experiential, and aesthetic expectations of one genre alone. As such, "painting" a song with various stylistic influences—each to its appropriate degree—helps to support and supplement the overall genomic analysis. Again, not as a substitute for capturing the musicological details, but by fleshing out those qualities that somehow lie between or outside the raw data—much as our consciousness in some way transcends the details of our neural activity.

One of the aspects of genre that makes it complex is its ability to operate on multiple levels at once. A genre's ability to classify and validate musical content enables one overarching genre to have its own **subgenres**—or "constituent genres," as they're sometimes called. That is, pop/rock, hip hop, electronica (sometimes called electronic dance music or EDM), jazz, classical, and world are all in fact genres, just as each contains a myriad of subgenres, which in turn may have their own subgenres. Each level contributes to the range of expectations and definers that may or may not be realized in the actual music. Genre labels can even be defined in ways that transcend otherwise discrete genre categories—such as "instrumental," "vocal music," "**chamber music**," "orchestral music," "piano music," "choral music," "avant-garde," "holiday," etc. Just look online at various music-related sites—retail, concert, streaming—and you'll see the huge diversity and overlap of genre labels and markers.

All this is to say that genre is a challenging yet likewise powerful tool that we as music fans and consumers must take into account. It is impractical to list every named genre and subgenre here—though a few "comprehensive" web-based lists are provided on the WYLI website (supplement to Chapter 8).[350]

To cite one example, Wikipedia's "List of Music Styles" (a common alternative for "genre") lists 1,198 terms, broken into nineteen categories, including "other." A partial review of this and related lists will be useful in heightening our awareness of the subject. We've here dissected and divided the list into four practical tiers:

## TIER 1

First, Wikipedia's list includes each of the overarching species we'll use in this book: Pop, Rock, Jazz, Hip Hop, Electronica, World, and Classical.

## TIER 2

It also lists most of the "high-level" subgenres that have likewise been used in previous chapters—and which collectively subsume a good percentage of the music we hear:

**Pop/Rock**: Pop, Rock, Blues, Country, Folk, R&B/Soul, Easy Listening, New Age, Singer-Songwriter, Broadway, Gospel

**Jazz**: Ragtime, Dixieland/New Orleans, Swing/Big Band, Bebop, Cool Jazz, Hard Bop, Latin Jazz, Fusion, Smooth Jazz, Acid Jazz, Avant-Garde/Free Jazz

**Hip Hop**: Hip Hop, Rap, Old-School Rap, Hardcore Rap, West Coast Rap, East Coast Rap, Gangsta Rap

**Electronica (EDM)**: Techno, House, Trance, Drum and Bass, Trip Hop, Disco

**World** (partial): Reggae, Calypso, Celtic, Worldbeat, Afro-Beat, Soca, Raï, Cajun, Zydeco, Flamenco, Tex-Mex, Mariachi, Tango, Samba, Klezmer, Indian Classical, Bollywood/Filmi, Gamelan, Chinese Classical, Hawaiian Slack Key, Native American Song, (Other) Traditional/Folk Song, K-Pop, (Other International) Popular Song, etc.

**Classical** (partial): Gregorian Chant, Sequence, Organum, Chanson, Motet, Mass, Madrigal, Oratorio, Opera, Cantata, Ballet, Overture, Sonata, Symphony, String Quartet, Serenade, Concerto, Tone/Symphonic Poem, Variations, Song Cycle, Suite, Fugue, Nocturne, Prelude, Impromptu, Electronic, Film Music, etc.

## TIER 3

Next, diving further down, the list also includes scores of lesser-known subgenres and sub-subgenres—at least to those not well versed in the nuanced trends and subdivisions of the broader genre in question. For brevity sake, these are all partial lists:

**Pop/Rock**: Soft Rock, Adult Contemporary, Rockabilly, Folk Rock, Psychedelic Rock, Heavy Metal, Alternative Rock, Indie Rock, Punk Rock, New Wave, Grunge, Progressive Rock, Southern Rock, Glam Rock, Jam Rock, Bluegrass, Modern Country, Alternative Country, Doo-Wop, Funk, Modern Soul, Delta Blues, etc.
**Jazz**: Gypsy Jazz, Modal Jazz, Bossa Nova, Neo-Bop, Third Stream, West Coast Jazz, Jump Blues, etc.
**Hip Hop**: Jazz Rap, Lyrical Hip Hop, New Jack Swing, Turntablism, etc.
**Electronica**: Ambient, Dubstep, Hardcore, Hi-NRG, Downtempo, Industrial, etc.
**World**: Highlife, Csárdás, Contradanza, Celtic Rock, Tuvan Throat Singing, Jota, Norteño, Merengue, Danzón, etc.
**Classical**: Antiphon, Gradual, Conductus, Virelai, Ballade, Frottola, Lamentation, Ricercar, Lute Song, Passion, Chorale, Fantasia, Chaconne, Toccata, Opera Buffa, Opera Seria, Singspiel, Operetta, Divertimento, Bel Canto, Impromptu, Etude, etc.

## TIER 4

And finally, there are a whole host of sub-subgenres, or sub-sub-subgenres, that are likely known *only* to a handful of devotees. I've included these largely for grins and giggles given the creativity of some of these names, and just two per species:

**Pop/Rock**: Cowpunk, Stoner Rock, etc.
**Jazz**: Indo Jazz, Mushroom Jazz, etc.
**Hip Hop**: Comedy Rap, Bounce, etc.
**Electronica**: Chiptune, Ragga Jungle, etc.
**World**: Falak, Shidaiqu, etc.
**Classical**: Lauda, Danger Music, etc.

Do not be surprised if you came across terms that are unfamiliar to you—and especially with regard to the last two tiers. In fact, props to you if you were aware of any of those in Tier 4! Remember that it's in the nature of subgenres to delimit and specialize. Awareness and understanding of these deeper-layer genres are predicated on one's being "initiated" into the nuances, trends, cross-fertilizations, etc., of the broader musical realm. Yet, just for fun, I've included definitions for each of these terms on the WYLI website—so you need not endlessly wonder what exactly "Mushroom Jazz" or "Danger Music" is.

The topic of genre is useful not only as a general factor in quantifying our musical taste. It is also an aid in our forthcoming exercise: to unwind the musical "days in the life" of our seven fictional music lovers. That is, the songs of each subject will be identified by their musicological materials, of course, but also with genre definitions.

A few last-minute points before we get started:

First, each of our seven subjects will be, to some degree, taste-aligned with one of the seven Tier 1 genres: Pop, Rock, Jazz, Hip Hop, Electronica, World, or Classical—in that order. Not all favorites of a given subject will fall into that one species, though it will anchor his/her musical genotype to a notable degree.

Next, remember that these subjects are not real people, but fictional music lovers—and so the actual "logic" of how an individual's musical taste could encircle all five items may be questionable. In turn, I ask that you not be offended if you happen to like one song of a particular subject but hate another in the same genotype. The theory presented here is *not* that there is some intrinsic taste link between any two songs or works for all listeners—that if one likes *x*, one will necessarily like *y*. Indeed the book is dedicated to the opposite premise: if you like *x*, you may very well hate *y*, and that is okay. That is, by understanding the underlying musicological dimensions of the songs and works you love *as a collective whole*, you can open the window onto your own musical genotype.

Finally, I am intentionally being quite vague as to who these fictional music lovers are. Each will be listed only as Subject 1, Subject 2, etc. I will not indicate their gender, age, geography, occupation, socioeconomic status, educational level, or other such indicators of "cultural capital"—to use Pierre Bourdieu's expression. As we'll see when we explore this and related notions of musical sociology in Interlude F, it is quite common to observe conclusions being drawn as to one's musical taste and "personality" simply by virtue of these social and cultural trappings. In this way, stereotypes are drawn between one's financial or educational level and the likelihood that they'll prefer Pearl Jam to Arvo Pärt, or vice versa. Of course, stereotypes exist because there is usually an element of truth behind them. But when it comes to musical taste, no one need be a stereotype. Much more on this later, but suffice it to say here that we will not foster or counter this prospect by attaching a personal profile to the subjects. You may have your own sense (or bias) of whom these music lovers might be, but all I'll provide is their musical profile.

Okay, here we go!

*nine*

# THE POP GENOTYPE

## Introducing Subject 1

Subject 1 wakes up early and heads out for a run. Earbuds on, a playlist song is heard that particularly hits a sweet spot: **Taylor Swift's "You Belong With Me."** On the way to work, the car radio adds a somewhat recent personal gem, **Elle King's "Ex's & Oh's."** After work, a night of drinks with friends yields a beloved "oldie" classic on the jukebox, **Creedence Clearwater Revival's "Proud Mary."** Finally, winding down for bed, Subject 1 puts on a "mellow classical music" CD to bring the day to a quiet close, hearing a beloved work, **Lin-Manuel Miranda's "It's Quiet Uptown" from *Hamilton*.***

As a general assessment, the above hit parade suggests that Subject 1 is inclined toward well-known songs and works that likewise meet fairly straightforward musicological expectations for the realms they inhabit. At the same time, these hits reveal a pop orientation that is more eclectic, at times more raw, and decidedly less "bubblegum" than is sometimes the case among fans of this species.

Before diving deeper into these "pop" selections, here is a brief overview of this species—including a list of touchstones that are reasonably noncontroversial:

## The Pop Species: A Brief Review

Of all the species terms, "pop" is certainly the most imprecise. The word, of course, is short for "popular," by which definition Tchaikovsky's *Nutcracker*, Benny Goodman's "Sing, Sing, Sing," and the Gipsy Kings' "Bamboléo" could all be labeled pop—as each is well-known, frequently performed, and a big commercial seller. In our orientation, naturally, these are not "pop" tunes, but instead

---

* Subject 1's fifth song, heard on the way home from work, is Michael Bublé's 2009 rendition of "Georgia on My Mind." For its discussion, see the WYLI website, supplement to Chapter 9.

are exemplars of classical, jazz, and world music, respectively. More common, then, is the distinction between popular (pop, rock, country, R&B, etc.) and "serious" (classical, jazz, etc.) music. But this too is problematic, since much "popular" music is rather serious, just as much "serious" music is light and frivolous—a quandary we'll revisit in Chapter 15. Thus, we already sense the potential quagmire of genre, and we haven't even analyzed a single song!

Before we continue, let's consider a list of ten songs that we may comfortably label as touchstones or standard-bearers of the pop species. They are as follows:

Bruno Mars, "That's What I Like" (2017)
Katy Perry, "Roar" (2013)
Justin Bieber, "Baby" (2010)
'N Sync, "Bye Bye Bye" (2000)
Britney Spears, ". . . Baby One More Time" (1998)
Michael Jackson, "The Way You Make Me Feel" (1987)
Madonna, "Like a Virgin" (1984)
Abba, "Dancing Queen" (1976)
The Archies, "Sugar, Sugar" (1969)
Paul Anka, "Put Your Head on My Shoulder" (1959)

While the styles of these songs vary from one to the next, they all share qualities that epitomize and typify "pop" music: for one, they were all quite popular in their day. Musically, they are all modest in length (two to four minutes) and scope; they all feature predictable forms (verse-chorus); they all utilize catchy, repetitive melodies or hooks; they all rely on diatonic, simple harmonies; they are all moderately up-tempo; and they all feature glossy sound production and accessible voices/instruments. Other than these generalities, though, what exactly is pop music?

Critics and scholars have in fact been lamenting for decades the challenges of defining "popular" music. A typical observation was that articulated by musicologist Howard Mayer Brown in 1950: "'Popular' music is admittedly a difficult word. Everyone knows what it means and yet no one can define it quite precisely."[351] On the other hand, the influential British rock critic and music sociologist Simon Frith has noted the outrage the British Parliament caused when it actually attempted to define the term in 1990, as "all kinds of music characterized by a strong rhythmic element and a reliance on electronic amplification for their performance."[352] To a great degree, the definition of pop or popular music depends on who is doing the defining, and often has as much to do with what is *not* meant by the terms as with what *is* meant. Our definition, for example, is framed in part by our use of "pop" instead of "popular," but also by labeling it in contradistinction to the six other major musical species delineated in Chapters 10–15—most notably rock.

Historically, the term "popular music" came into use in the 1920s, spurred by the arrival of recordings—where it signified music that had "popular appeal," but also music that was grounded on folk (country, blues, jazz) as opposed to art (classical, theater) musical stock. The term "pop" gained distinct currency in the wake of rock and roll's appearance in the 1950s, and especially via the cultural dominance of the "pop charts," especially *Billboard*, based on singles sales and radio play. Further clarification of "pop" then came as rock itself matured in the mid-1960s—when more explicitly aesthetic, commercial, and stylistic elements were brought into the mix.[353] This latter orientation of pop, versus nonpop, is by and large the one used today: it thus explains why the British Parliament's definition was found so objectionable to fans and the industry alike, as it failed to distinguish between "bubblegum" singles for teens and album-based rock for adults, among much else.

So what then do *we* mean to say exactly by pop music? Our criteria can be divided into two categories: sociological/aesthetic and musicological. Starting with the former, pop music is created primarily for commercial purposes—or, as Frith put it, "as a matter of enterprise not art."[354] It is not intended, as are many other genres within the broader "popular" mantle, to tap into a deep and distinct level of personal or subcultural identity, but instead is aimed at immediate, broad, and disparate public appeal: to make a "hit." Given its commercial objectives, it is not surprising that major industry forces stand squarely and influentially behind its output and trajectory: entertainment companies like Universal and Disney, and network TV ventures like *American Idol* and *The Voice*, guided by industry-insider judges and coaches like Simon Cowell, Blake Shelton, and producer Jimmy Iovine, etc.

From such a sociological recipe, the musicological ingredients aren't too hard to figure out: scope and compositional orientation are conventional and conservative. Above all, pop music rewards previous models of success. This translates to short, predictable song forms—usually three-minute verse-chorus structures with simple "hooky" melodies and "explosive," repetitive choruses. The harmonic approach tends to be simple, diatonic, consonant, and primarily based on repeating patterns or two- or three-chord "pivot-based" progressions.[355] Rhythm is steady, driving, symmetrical, and frequently oriented toward a dance groove. Production quality is slick and professional. And yet there is a parameter where such uniformity is absent, and that is—ironically—in the realm of style or genre. Pop music is, within reason, agnostic when it comes to style: rock, country, hip hop, rap, R&B, EDM, even Latin and jazz, are all viable sources for a pop song—individually or collectively. *Success breeds success*, and a hit combining hip hop and rock in January will undoubtedly be "duplicated" in February. In our own time, EDM and hip hop hold sway as primary forces and/or influencers in pop music generation.

As can be imagined, the dividing line between a predictable, formulaic pop song and an authentic, original nonpop song is often blurry. One person's frivolous pop is another's "pure" R&B or rock or country, etc. This is indeed why the collective expression "pop/rock" is so widely embraced in the music industry—and why Pandora used it as its genome label to cover everything from pop to rock to folk to country to R&B to punk, etc. Moreover, a pop orientation, or genotype, can be readily applied to a wide diversity of genres and styles—including even jazz, classical, and world—by virtue of its sociological and musicological approach and listening experience. This explains, for example, the relatively eclectic mix of songs and works found in Subject 1's hit list, to which we now turn.

## The Morning Run: Swift's "You Belong With Me"

**Taylor Swift's "You Belong With Me"** gets us started with a fairly uncontroversial example of pop music, quite in line with the touchstones cited above. In this case, the stylistic foundation is country, with a moderate rock influence. Few artists represent pop music success in the early twenty-first century better than Taylor Swift, who has engendered a huge following of fans (called "Swifties"): predominantly female, white, and young. Like few others of her generation, Swift has tapped into the pop music ethos of the day and has the record sales to prove it. Her success, however, raises another important point about pop music: just because a song is a pop hit doesn't mean it isn't also creative and well crafted. At the end of the day, it is never *easy* to write a hit song! Swift's hits, like "You Belong With Me," may well possess a level of predictability and convention, but they still have much to commend them.

### SWIFT: BACKGROUND

Taylor Swift was born in 1989 in the small borough of Wyomissing, Pennsylvania. She early showed a talent for storytelling and singing, learning guitar from age twelve. Her first prominent influences were country artists, particularly strong female singer-songwriters like Shania Twain, Faith Hill, and the Dixie Chicks. But alongside staunch country artists, Swift was also drawn to pop singers like Britney Spears and Hanson. At age fourteen, she moved to Nashville and, through a mix of talent, tenacity, and good fortune, gained a record contract with Big Machine Records and a publishing deal. Her debut, self-titled album was released in 2006, and launched her career to popular and critical acclaim—including a No. 1 song, "Our Song," on the *Billboard* Hot Country Singles, alongside several major country music awards. And yet the pop inflection in her music was felt from the get-go, such as when *Rolling Stone* magazine labeled the album "as Britney [Spears] as it is Patsy [Cline]."[356]

From there, Swift's fame skyrocketed. Her second release, *Fearless* (2008), won four Grammy Awards and contained two chart hits, including "You Belong With Me"—which not only topped the country charts, but also reached No. 2 on the *Billboard* Hot 100. Her next two albums, *Speak Now* in 2010 and *Red* in 2012, were likewise big sellers in both the pop and country markets—the latter eliciting her first No. 1 *Billboard* Hot 100 song, "We Are Never Ever Getting Back Together." If the pop influence was somewhat tempered in her first four releases, however, it is on full display on her two most recent albums, *1989* (2014) and *Reputation* (2017)—the latter of which "cuts all ties with her Nashville roots in favor of the blare and honk of EDM-influenced pop," as the *Guardian* put it.[357] On both these albums, synths and drum machines replace the occasional fiddles and banjos of her earlier albums. Indeed, two recent hits—"Bad Blood" from *1989* and "End Game" from *Reputation*—feature guest rappers, Kendrick Lamar and Future, respectively. Her writing skills and stylistic instincts seem to be serving her well, moreover, as both releases easily topped the *Billboard* 200. Not yet thirty years old, Swift is a potent force in the music industry—even taking on, and beating, industry giants like Spotify and Apple.[358]

## SWIFT: ANALYSIS

"You Belong With Me" marked a turning point in Swift's career. In addition to its chart and radio achievements, the 2008 song also buoyed her career by virtue of its music video, and through a now infamous TV moment: while in the midst of her acceptance speech for the 2009 MTV Video Music Award for Best Female Video, Swift was dramatically interrupted by rapper Kanye West—in a bizarre tirade claiming that Beyoncé should have won the award.[359] This episode, which received tremendous media coverage, helped raise her profile as a national and international celebrity.

The song is generally labeled as falling in the "country pop" genre in print and online music sources.[360] The "country" part of this designation, as suggested above, is warranted as much for the song's inclusion of a banjo and pedal steel guitar, as well as the slight twang in Swift's vocal, as for anything intrinsic to the composition itself. In many ways, "You Belong With Me" fits a rather typical pop/rock schema. The form follows a verse-chorus formal structure (as opposed to the A-A-B-A pop song template), lacking as it does a bridge section. Further, as noted in Chapter 6, the song inserts a pre-chorus between the verse and chorus; these latter two sections, moreover, share the same simple chord progression, which, as will be recalled, was also the case with Janis Joplin's "Piece of My Heart."

The repeating chord progression in question follows the pattern of I–V–ii–IV (in F♯ major: F♯–C♯–G♯ minor–B)—a diatonic and common progression (Figure 9.1).

**Figure 9.1: Taylor Swift, "You Belong With Me"—chord progression used in both verse and chorus sections**

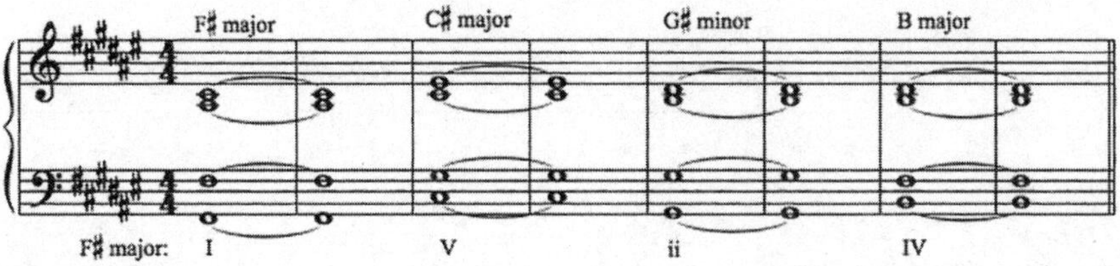


The pre-chorus too is quite simple harmonically, using the same chords, though in a different order (ii–IV–I–V), and changing every measure, whereas in the verse and chorus each chord is maintained for two measures. Rhythmically the song flows in a medium-tempo 4/4 meter, with very little syncopation, and with each section divided neatly into conventional eight-measure phrases. Dominating the listening experience as well is the song's melodic identity: each section, from verse to pre-chorus to chorus, rises in register whereby the chorus hook lands strongly (on "If you could see") at the highest part of the range. Swift then applies some appealing melodic variation throughout—such as between the first and third verses (especially from "laughing on a park bench"), and dramatically so between the first and second pre-choruses (Figures 9.2 and 9.3):

**Figure 9.2: Swift, "You Belong With Me"—minor and major melodic variation between 1st and 3rd verses**

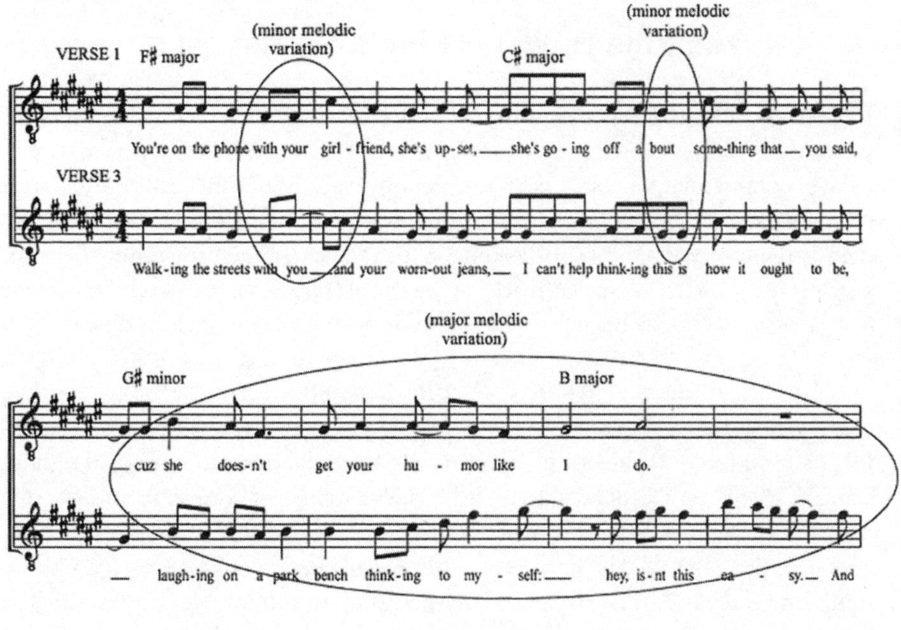

**Figure 9.3: Swift, "You Belong With Me"—dramatic melodic variation between 1st and 2nd pre-choruses**

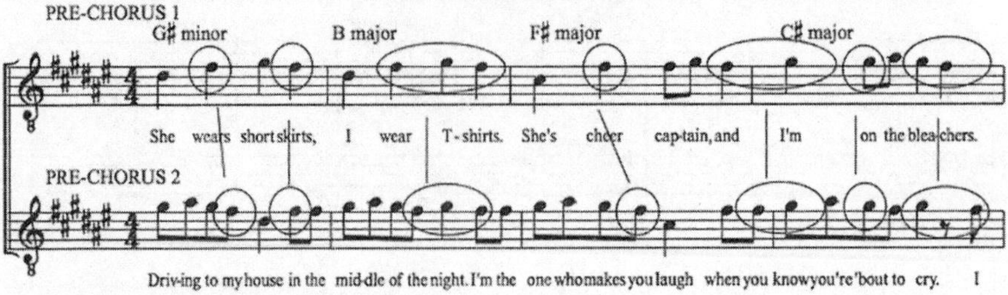


(circled notes = related melodic anchors)

Sonically, the song features a typical pop/rock assembly of electric and acoustic guitars, bass, and drums. Collectively, they carry out a melody-dominated homophonic accompaniment to support Swift's smooth and breathy vocal—in harmony on the chorus. And yet, as noted, the use of rhythmic banjo strumming and occasional slide guitar riffs gives the song its distinct "country" designation. It should be noted, incidentally, that part of the song's country designation (as indeed most of Swift's output, and a key source of her success) is the narrative or storytelling nature of her lyrics, consummately constructed, and invariably arising from her own personal love life—whereby she connects so forcefully to her fans.

## The Ride to Work: King's "Ex's & Oh's"

**Elle King's "Ex's & Oh's"** continues Subject 1's preference for accessible, straightforward pop songs—including those that have achieved the realm's primary objective: commercial success. Like "You Belong With Me," "Ex's & Oh's" conveys both a rock and country influence—though more explicitly in the edgy rock vein than is the case with Swift's song. Indeed, the secondary stylistic whiffs here appear more "Western" than "country," as we'll see. It is thus a bit too early to know just how agnostic is Subject 1's pop genotype with regard to style and genre.

### KING: BACKGROUND

Elle King was, like Taylor Swift, born in 1989—though she cannot claim to have achieved the latter's level of success. Still, this daughter of comedian and ex-*SNL* regular Rob Schneider and model London King has planted a foot in the pop music market over the last few years. After her parents' divorce, King grew up in southern Ohio, and by age thirteen had picked up the guitar. Her earliest musical influences would not immediately suggest the conventional constraints of pop music: the female punk band the Donnas, the edgy new wave band Blondie, and the heavy metal pioneers AC/DC. And yet her models also extended deep into soul (Aretha Franklin, Otis Redding) and country (Hank Williams, Johnny Cash, Earl Scruggs) music. This last artist, moreover, inspired King to pick up the banjo, which she has incorporated readily into her songwriting and performances. The result of this gumbo of influences is a style that is sometimes called alt-rock or retro rock, but also indie pop or pop/rock.

A debut, self-titled EP on RCA from 2012 included no commercial hit but gained some industry notoriety—as one of its songs, "Playing for Keeps," became the theme for the VH1 reality series *Mob Wives Chicago*. A decidedly higher profile came with her first full album, *Love Stuff* (2015) and especially its single, "Ex's & Oh's"—reaching No. 10 on the *Billboard* Hot 100 and garnering two Grammy nominations. In its wake, King gained a wider media and public platform, with appearances on the *Late Show with David Letterman* and *Austin City Limits*. With her bravura style and sassy appearance (lots of tattoos), King carries the trappings of a hardcore rocker, but in her music bears largely the restrained aesthetic of a pop star.

## KING: ANALYSIS

"Ex's & Oh's" is undeniably the song that put Elle King on the map as a national—indeed international—musical figure. It was released in September 2014, five months prior to the release of her debut album *Love Stuff*. It scored big on multiple *Billboard* charts—reaching No. 1 on both the Hot Rock Songs and Alternative Songs charts, beyond its No. 10 position on the Hot 100. With such a pedigree it might seem odd to consider this a pop song, as opposed to a pure rock song. As suggested above, it can be both, not only by virtue of its popularity but also by its musicological content. This pluralistic identity comes already by the various genre labels attached to it by music-industry sources: blues pop, retro rock, country rock, pop/rock, etc.

The song immediately announces its playful identity with a vibrant and insistent ostinato (repeating pattern) in the bass. The rhythm used is itself a convention, called the **tresillo**: a triplet-like figure linked to the Cuban habanera.[361] It was first introduced to the US, and especially to New Orleans, via the African and Caribbean slave trade. The bass-oriented, swinging rhythm was later adopted into a variety of twentieth-century popular music styles, most notably R&B and rockabilly, such as in Elvis Presley's "Hound Dog." This in part gives the song its retro quality (Figure 9.4).

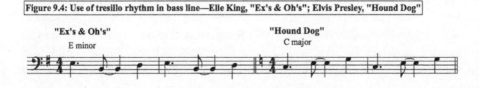

**Figure 9.4: Use of tresillo rhythm in bass line—Elle King, "Ex's & Oh's"; Elvis Presley, "Hound Dog"**

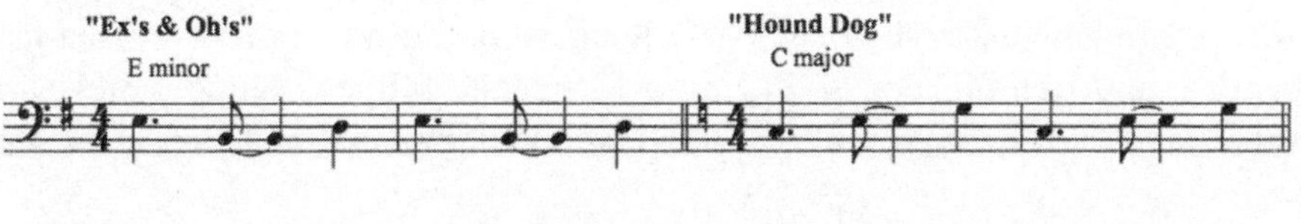

In King's song, the tresillo bass rhythm alternates predictably between the tonic (E minor) and the dominant (B major) chords throughout the verse, creating a driving, insistent groove. Like Swift's song, "Ex's & Oh's" has a pre-chorus, but rather than providing harmonic contrast between the verse and chorus, King's pre-chorus provides a lower-energy "breakdown"—drums and vocals only—with an implied continuation of the E minor "pedal." The melody of the pre-chorus is likewise similar to that of the verse (largely an arpeggio outlining the E minor triad), yet even more monotonic (on E).

This stasis then sets up the more "explosive" chorus—again, a common technique in pop/rock songs, especially over the past decade or so. The chorus presents a new chord progression in the relative major (G major), which initially suggests a common pattern (as used, for example in Pachelbel's famous Canon)—I–V–vi–III—before breaking it with a contrasting and somewhat unexpected I–V–ii–IV progression that via modulation leads nicely back to the original E minor (Figure 9.5).

**Figure 9.5: Elle King, "Ex's & Oh's"—chorus melody and harmony**

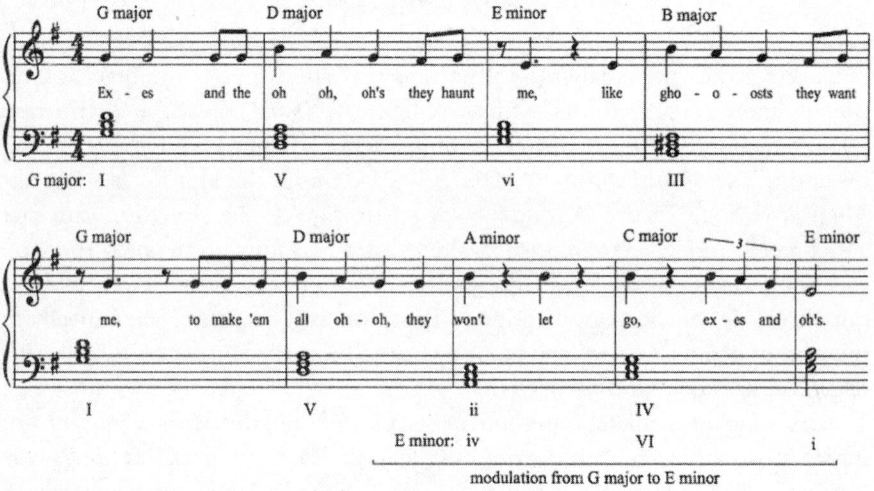


The form then proceeds conventionally using these three formal sections, inserting an electric guitar solo over the chords of the verse before the final double chorus.

The most striking experiential aspect of the song, and likely the parameter that most drives Subject 1 (and others) to it, however, is its "sound." The song begins with the dark, distorted, and reverb-laden tones of the bass guitar ostinato, combined with bouncy, Gene Krupa–esque drum toms, a whistle-like synth sound (reminiscent of an Ennio Morricone Western music score), and other rhythmic elements. But the sound is soon dominated by King's raspy and slightly nasal vocal timbre. Her bold vocal performance, in combination with the accompanying musical materials, bring to mind other assertive female songs like Peggy Lee's "Fever" and Nancy Sinatra's "These Boots Were Made for Walking." The distortion level increases as the electric guitar gradually gains prominence, but it never undermines the song's overall light, fun, and infectious groove.

In short, "Ex's & Oh's" has the attitude of a rock song, but in its predictable, straightforward, and accessible content lands a pretty direct pop punch.

## Drinks with Friends: CCR's "Proud Mary"

**Creedence Clearwater Revival's "Proud Mary"** may be considered a pop song "after the fact," as it was more definitively in the rock genre when it first came out in 1969. Since then, however, "Proud Mary" has become a kind of "pop star" within the realm of classic rock, a near ubiquitous presence on this format of radio—not to mention wedding cover bands everywhere—for decades. Its simple, straightforward, and catchy materials grant it, moreover, the accessible appeal to which every pop song aspires. At the same time, the song's style and sound confirm that Subject 1 has a particular penchant for country and/or Southern musical influences.

### CCR: BACKGROUND

The four kids who would become Creedence Clearwater Revival (CCR) met while in junior high school in El Cerrito, California, near San Francisco in the late 1950s. It is not for nothing, however, that the only member most folks—even fans of CCR—could name today is John Fogerty. As the band's lead singer, lead guitarist, and primary songwriter, Fogerty *was* CCR, for all intents and purposes. It is this lopsidedness, moreover, that would eventually drive the band apart.[362]

In 1967, CCR was signed to Fantasy Records, an independent jazz label under the direction of legendary music and film producer Saul Zaentz; they had earlier scored big with local jazz artists like Dave Brubeck and Vince Guaraldi.[363] CCR released its first, self-titled album in 1968—in turn landing a minor hit (No. 11 on *Billboard*'s Top 40), a remake of Dale Hawkins' 1956 rockabilly song "Susie Q." Armed with this success, the band headed to Los Angeles to record its sophomore album at RCA Studios—where the Rolling Stones had recorded "Satisfaction" three years earlier. The album, *Bayou Country*, reached No. 7 on the *Billboard* Top 200, while its double-sided single, "Proud Mary" and "Born on the Bayou," went to No. 2.

On this, and its two follow-up albums released in 1969 (*Green River* and *Willy and the Poor Boys*), CCR established its distinctive sound: raw, country- and blues-based, and Southern in affect and sonority—sometimes referred to as roots rock or even "swamp rock" by virtue of the frequent lyrical references to the bayou, Cajun country, and the Mississippi River. This is surprising, of course, given the band's Northern California origins. Still, CCR joins late 1960s rock artists like Canned Heat and the Band in laying down the foundation for what would become Southern rock in the 1970s, with acts like the Allman Brothers and Lynyrd Skynyrd. CCR produced several more Top 10 hits (though never a No. 1)—such as "Green River," "Down on the Corner," and "Have You Ever Seen the Rain" before breaking up in 1972. They mildly participated in the countercultural spirit of the times (e.g., with the 1969 antiwar song "Fortunate Son"); they even played at Woodstock, though few would know it today, as their performance was excluded on both the soundtrack and film.

## CCR: ANALYSIS

"Proud Mary," according to Fogerty, was written in celebration of his release from the US Army Reserve in 1968. As with many CCR hits, it was compiled from fragments of several previous songs and live jams, both musically and lyrically. The song's commercial success in turn inspired numerous covers (over a hundred to date), most famously that of Ike & Tina Turner in 1971—which itself reached No. 4 on the *Billboard* Top 40. As suggested above, the appeal of CCR's version rests in its artful fusion of various stylistic influences, including blues, rock, country, gospel, and soul. The result is a comfortable and "down-home" groove—in a medium tempo 4/4 meter—that has served the song well for nearly fifty years.

A key element of the song's identity is its initial riff—as noted in Chapter 5, a rather syncopated rhythmic figure based on a descending progression by 3rds, from C major to A major (Figure 9.6a). As Fogerty has noted, this riff was inspired by the opening motive of Beethoven's Symphony no. 5 in C Minor—though technically the latter is an octave unison descent of both a major and minor 3rd (Figure 9.6b), whereas the former is a chordal descent of only a minor 3rd.

**Figure 9.6a: Creedence Clearwater Revival, "Proud Mary" (intro)—chordal descent of 3rds**

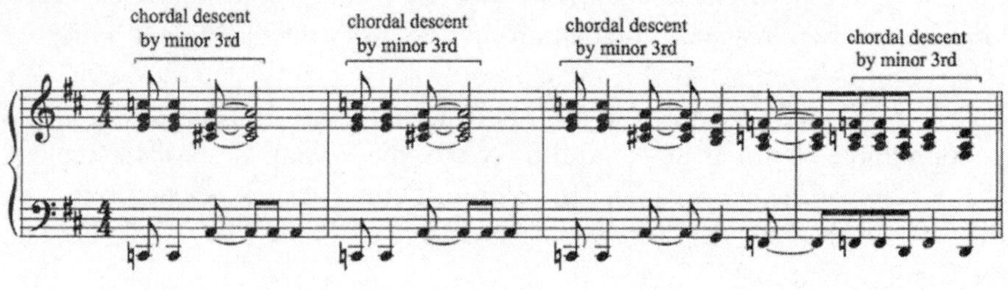

**Figure 9.6b: Beethoven, Symphony no. 5, 1. Allegro con brio—octave unison descent of 3rds**

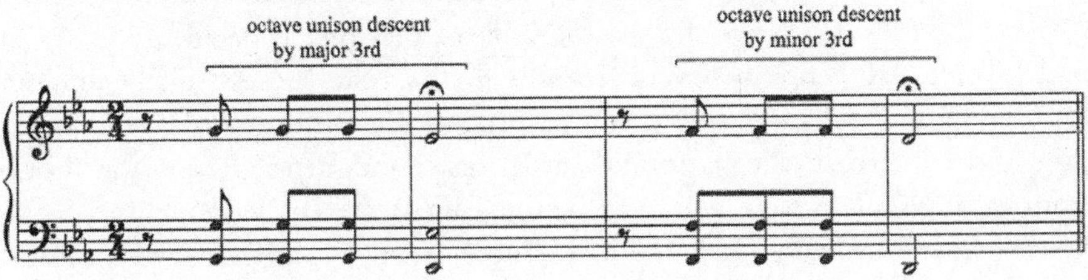


Despite the rhythmic and harmonic activity of the opening riff, though, the song soon settles into a more static mode—with a sustained chordal pedal on the tonic of D major. This harmonic stasis in turn dominates the musicological experience of the song, imparting to it the relaxed, down-home groove mentioned earlier. A two-bar **vamp** on D leads into an eight-bar verse that never abandons the tonic chord. The verse leads directly to a short pre-chorus that provides a bit of harmonic relief: to the V (A major) and then the vi chord (B minor). But the four-bar chorus ("Rollin', rollin', rollin' on the river") returns to the tonic, where it remains (Figure 9.7).

**Figure 9.7: Creedence Clearwater Revival, "Proud Mary"—melodic and harmonic motion of pre-chorus to chorus**

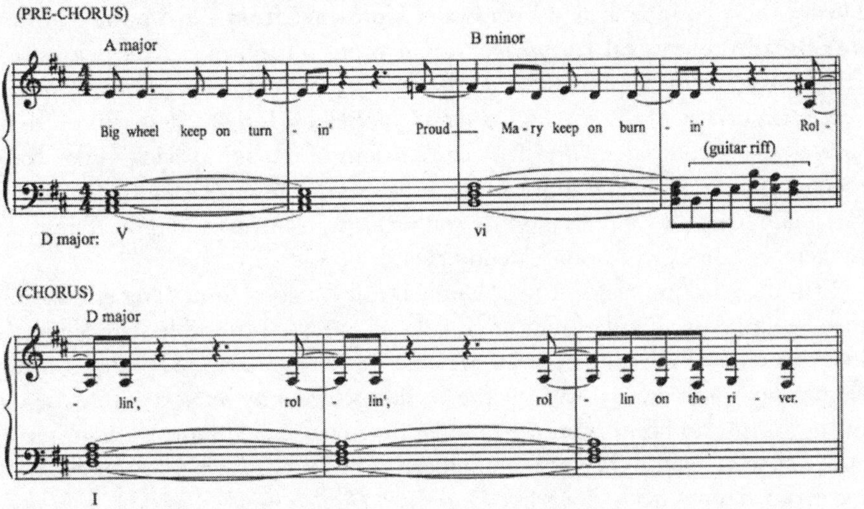


The form then continues as expected, with another verse, pre-chorus, and chorus. At that point, the opening riff returns, providing both architectural definition and continued balance between harmonic stasis and harmonic motion. The song concludes via a continued, if conventional, mix of the four formal elements: Guitar solo (over the verse and pre-chorus)—Chorus—Riff—Verse—Pre-chorus—Repeated chorus (4X, with fade). This last element, four repeats of the chorus, amounts to a steady sixteen bars on the tonic!

It is worth pondering how a song that spends so much time on one chord could meet the musical taste of so many people. Further, aside from the opening riff and the melody of the chorus, the bulk of the song is decidedly unsyncopated. There are certainly several reasons for its taste success, likely different for each listener. Chief among them, perhaps, is the artful way that the riff and pre-chorus interrupt the harmonic stasis, just enough to prevent the groove from getting stale. Key as well must be the song's well-chiseled melody. Despite possessing an unusually small ambitus (range)—only a 5th (B–F♯), with most of it limited to the top 3rd (D–F♯)—the melody is always well articulated, and is especially "hooky" on the chorus, with its repeated, syncopated F♯s. The chorus too provides the only section to use vocal harmony, reinforcing its "hooky" quality. Sonically, the song is conventional: guitar, bass, drums, and Fogerty's twangy, folksy vocals—all of which supports its down-home quality. In the end, however, there may just be something about that simple, bayou groove that keeps its fans—like Subject 1—coming back again and again.

## A Gentle Close to the Day: *Hamilton*'s "It's Quiet Uptown"

Finally, the emotional ballad **"It's Quiet Uptown," from Lin-Manuel Miranda's Broadway musical *Hamilton***, would seem to confirm our suspicions that Subject 1's taste in "pop" music is decidedly eclectic—embracing a broader, more aesthetic purview of the species than that implied by Top 40 charts alone. To be sure, the song comports with many conventions of the pop species—huge commercial appeal, accessible musical discourse, simple use of harmony, etc.—and yet, it also reveals an appreciation for sophisticated elements and procedures that, by stereotypical expectations, extend beyond "pop."

But the selection of "It's Quiet Uptown" may suggest something else as well: that Subject 1 is an ardent fan of Broadway. Sure, it is possible that Subject 1 first encountered the song in its 2016 remake by Kelly Clarkson—a singer firmly aligned with pop music. And yet the version selected by Subject 1 to close out the day is instead taken from the original Broadway cast album. Without seeing another ten or twenty choices from Subject 1's hit parade—whether, for example, it contained songs from shows like *Dear Evan Hansen*, *Wicked*, or even *The Sound of Music*—drawing such a conclusion is premature. Certainly, the 2015 *Hamilton* cast album was a "pop" sensation in its own right, reaching No. 3 on the *Billboard* Top 200. And yet, by choosing this particular song, at least some awareness of the musical seems likely.

At any rate, the selection of "It's Quiet Uptown" affords us an opportunity to not only examine the musicological proceedings of this "bedtime" song, but also to discuss its epoch-making source, *Hamilton*—as well as the latter's place in the broader history of the musical theater genre. Admittedly, these last two items could quickly take us beyond the scope of this book, and not least at this stage in the proceedings. As such, the following will be a somewhat modest account of these background contexts, certainly sufficient to thoroughly analyze Subject 1's hit ballad.

## MIRANDA: BACKGROUND

Lin-Manuel Miranda was born in 1980 in Inwood, New York, a largely Hispanic neighborhood at the northern tip of Manhattan.[364] Of predominantly Puerto Rican stock, his early musical exposure was defined by Latin-based styles: salsa, merengue, and the Latin pop music of Shakira, Marc Anthony, and Ricky Martin. As he got older, New York–based hip hop—artists like KRS-One, Fat Boys, Digable Planets, and Biggie Smalls (the Notorious B.I.G.)—became another influential soundtrack, and an inspiration for young Lin-Manuel to try his own hand at freestyle rap. And yet to this eclectic mix was also added another type of "soundtrack": the Broadway cast album, which his parents used as "clean-up music" after their salsa-infused parties. Beyond family recordings of "golden age" shows like *Man of La Mancha*, *Camelot*, and *The Unsinkable Molly Brown*, young Lin-Manuel saw three live productions on Broadway that made a big impression: *Phantom of the Opera*, *Cats*, and especially *Les Misérables*. As Miranda later told the *New Yorker*, these musical styles—Latin, pop, hip hop, Broadway—were all "in the same music folder in my brain."[365]

The mutual "theatricality" of Broadway and virtuosic rap clearly brought out Miranda's innate creative and showmanship proclivities. He began acting in high school—for example, starring in Gilbert and Sullivan's *The Pirates of Penzance*; and by his freshman year at Wesleyan University was regularly freestyling with his own hip hop group. At Wesleyan too he began writing and performing his own musicals, including the seeds for what would become his first smash hit, *In the Heights*. The original draft—which incorporated rap and hip hop into an otherwise Latin-based and traditional Broadway score—caught the attention of director Thomas Kail, himself a recent Wesleyan grad. Shortly after Miranda's own graduation in 2002, he and Kail joined forces to rework the show, incorporating a new book (script) by Quiara Alegría Hudes. Thus retooled, *In the Heights* would go on to open on Broadway in March 2008, earn three Tony Awards (including one for Best Musical), win the Grammy for Best Musical Show Album, and run at the sizable Richard Rodgers Theatre for a whopping 1,184 shows.[366]

It was while on vacation in 2008, in the midst of the run of *In the Heights*, that Miranda began to envision what would become his follow-up show; the inspiration: a leisure reading of Ron Chernow's 2004 biography of Alexander Hamilton. The realization of that vision, of course, is *Hamilton: An American Musical*—undoubtedly the most successful show to hit Broadway in a generation.[367] With a record-setting sixteen Tony nominations, eleven wins (including, again, for Best Musical), a Grammy for Best Musical Theater Album, a Pulitzer Prize for Drama, multiple regional runs and national tours, myriad box office sales records, and a continually sold-out run since its August 2015 opening, with no signs of slowing down, *Hamilton* has set a bar for Broadway success that will be hard, if not impossible, to beat. As its composer, lyricist, book writer, and title-role actor (through July 2016), Miranda is today a veritable pop culture celebrity in his own right. His additional activities in recent years include multiple acting stints—including on *Saturday Night Live*, *Curb Your Enthusiasm*, and the 2018 film *Mary Poppins Returns*; producing duties for several TV and film projects; and various composer-lyricist projects—notably for the 2016 Disney animated film *Moana*. Safe to say, the world awaits his next big theater piece.

With all that as background, the question naturally arises: What makes *Hamilton* such a rare and stunning phenomenon? And then: What does "It's Quiet Uptown," its tearjerker Act II ballad, reveal about the musical prowess behind its success?

## MIRANDA: ANALYSIS

Initially, *Hamilton* was conceived not as a theater piece, but as a stand-alone recording project: *The Hamilton Mixtape*. It was in this guise that Miranda performed an early version of the rap song "Alexander Hamilton"—now the show opener—at the Obama White House in May 2009. Such was the enthusiasm elicited by the song and its unlikely subject matter, however, that Miranda soon began to forge a grander vision for his "mixtape": a full-length musical about the life and death of one of America's most articulate Founding Fathers, the coauthor of the Federalist Papers, and the first secretary of the treasury.[368] And yet, importantly, Miranda's initial impulse to uncompromisingly write lyrically complex songs that a listener could play and replay to gain ever-greater clarity would remain, even as he widened the show's musical palette beyond hip hop. The rap-based songs in particular would take Miranda to daunting levels of lyric-writing prowess—like modern-day rebuttals to Meredith Willson's "(Ya Got) Trouble" from *The Music Man*—whereby he could emulate the rhyming and rhythmic acrobatics of his rap heroes: Big Pun, Tupac Shakur, Jay-Z, Rakim, Eminem, and Biggie, among others.[369]

And yet the impact of Miranda's studious embrace of rap would extend beyond the lyrical domain and into a driving component of the overall *Hamilton* score: the use of harmonic loops. In the *New Yorker* interview, Miranda describes his lyric writing process: "I will write 8 or 16 bars of music I think is exciting, or interesting . . . and put on my headphones and walk my dog and talk to myself." Given the harmonic form of a good many of *Hamilton*'s forty-six numbers, it seems likely that those "8 or 16 bars of music" were themselves composed of repeating loops of two or four chords.[370] Repeating chordal patterns, of course, are a staple of most every species and era, as noted in Chapter 4; and yet Miranda's approach is closely aligned with that used in the hip hop songs he grew up on—as found, for example, in Tupac's "Brenda's Got a Baby," a song Miranda specifically cites as reflecting a "Hamiltonian" kind of rhetorical skill.[371] These cycling loops help give the score its hypnotic momentum, and importantly enable Miranda to devise all kinds of variation in rhythm and—for the sung songs—melody. An example is the loop used in the opener, "Alexander Hamilton," which is then repurposed in several other songs as well (Figure 9.8):*

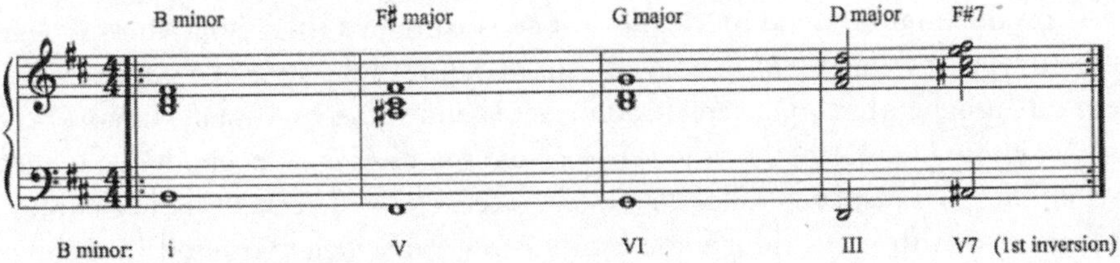

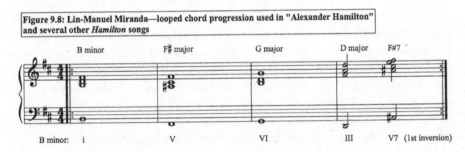

**Figure 9.8: Lin-Manuel Miranda—looped chord progression used in "Alexander Hamilton" and several other *Hamilton* songs**

As noted, however, the score of *Hamilton* is by no means limited to the language of rap and hip hop: it extends as well into jazz ("The Room Where It Happens"), R&B ("Helpless"), and Britpop ("You'll Be Back"), among others. Yet even when incorporating these other styles, Miranda will often maintain the "loop" approach to harmony/form, as we'll see—although in several songs he does adopt a more expansive formula.† Indeed, a good part of *Hamilton*'s success lies in its fluid and eclectic aesthetic, and not least in its embrace of elements drawn from the rich traditions of Broadway. This is manifest, for example, via explicit quotations of past shows—including from *South Pacific* and *1776*; but more profoundly by adopting several common Broadway "tropes"—notably the reintroduction of melodic or lyrical fragments from earlier songs to create narrative cohesion and heightened emotion. This leitmotif-like technique is common throughout Broadway's history—in shows such as *Show Boat*, *West Side Story*, *Sweeney Todd*, *Phantom of the Opera*, *Wicked*, and *Fun Home*, among many others. For Miranda, though, the most direct inspiration was surely *Les Misérables*—or as he put it: "I really got my 'Les Miz' on in this score, like being really smart about where to reintroduce a theme."[372]

This byzantine juxtaposition of hip hop, jazz, R&B, pop, and Broadway

---

* Other songs using the "Alexander Hamilton" chord progression are "A Winter's Ball," "Guns and Ships," "What'd I Miss," "The Adams Administration," and "Burn."

† Among the non-loop-based songs are "The Story of Tonight," "The Schuyler Sisters," "You'll Be Back" (and its later incarnations, all sung by King George III), "Hurricane," and "Blow Us All Away."

in turn raises that question of *Hamilton*'s place in the larger Broadway canon. While, again, a full assessment is beyond our purposes here, it does bring to mind what Leonard Bernstein said in his 1956 lecture on the history of musical theater: in comparing an "operetta"-like show (e.g., *Carousel*) and a "musical comedy" (e.g., *Guys & Dolls*), Bernstein delimited the latter by its substantial use of the "vernacular" musical language of the day.[373] In the 1950s that meant jazz, just as from the late 1960s it meant rock—embraced tepidly by Broadway with *Hair* in 1968, and becoming standard by the 1990s (e.g., *Rent*). Today, of course, our vernacular music is hip hop.

While certainly revolutionary, that is, *Hamilton* is in many ways simply updating the esteemed musical theater art form by demonstrating, once and for all, that if done right, the vernacular of rap and hip hop are "fair game" in a Broadway production—though maybe not for *every* song in a three-hour show.

To wit, "It's Quiet Uptown" is not hip hop, but in the style of a pop ballad. It appears roughly three-quarters through Act II and is the emotional climax of the show: Philip Hamilton, the nineteen-year-old son of Alexander and his estranged wife, Eliza, has just been killed in a duel—accepted to defend his father's honor. Consumed with grief, the couple escapes to a quiet neighborhood in uptown Manhattan, as Alexander, a shell of his former self, seeks forgiveness from Eliza for his past indiscretions.

Lin-Manuel Miranda's solution to this brutal emotional moment is not to explicitly discuss the boy's death or the parents' overwhelming grief. Instead he unveils the weight of the moment by clothing the song largely in narrative form—with verses that describe their newly solitary life exchanged between Eliza's sister Angelica and a chorus of men or women townsfolk, along with direct petitions to Eliza by Alexander himself. Musically, the composer then adopts three principal devices to support the drama, and thereby guide our listening experience.

The first device—one that begins the song as an evocative two-bar intro—is merely a descending arpeggiated figure in the solo piano (Figure 9.9):

**Figure 9.9: Lin-Manuel Miranda, "It's Quiet Uptown"—arpeggiated obbligato (intro, etc.)**

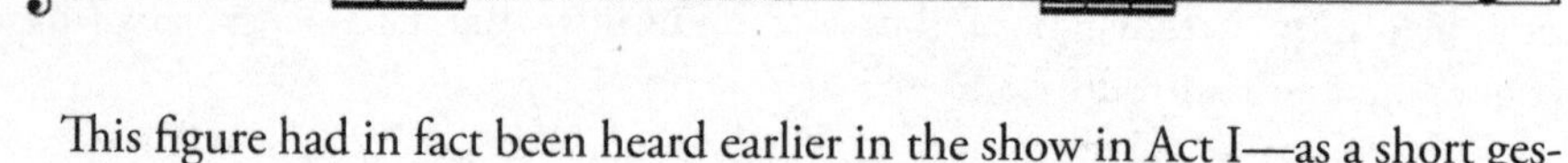


This figure had in fact been heard earlier in the show in Act I—as a short gesture to close "That Would Be Enough," Eliza's solo plea to Alexander to lessen his ambition and spend more time at home with his family. In "It's Quiet Uptown," however, the figure becomes an insistent accompanying obbligato—appearing periodically throughout the song: in the piano, a hammered dulcimer, a harp, and a violin. Accompanying obbligatos, to be sure, are common in Broadway, used for example in Sondheim's "Finishing the Hat" from *Sunday in the Park with George*—and here may be seen to symbolize Eliza's insistent presence in Alexander's mind.

The second device stems from Miranda's decision to set the song almost exclusively using, once again, a repeating four-bar harmonic loop. This loop too follows the same chordal-rhythmic disposition as that found in "Alexander Hamilton," among many other songs in the show: one chord for each of the first three measures, and two chords dividing the fourth measure, the last being the dominant (V). Here the progression is in the key of F major, and proceeds as I–iii6–IV–vi–V* (Figure 9.10):

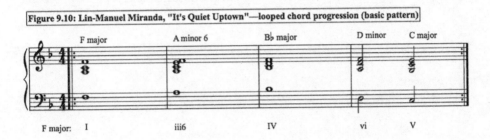

**Figure 9.10: Lin-Manuel Miranda, "It's Quiet Uptown"—looped chord progression (basic pattern)**

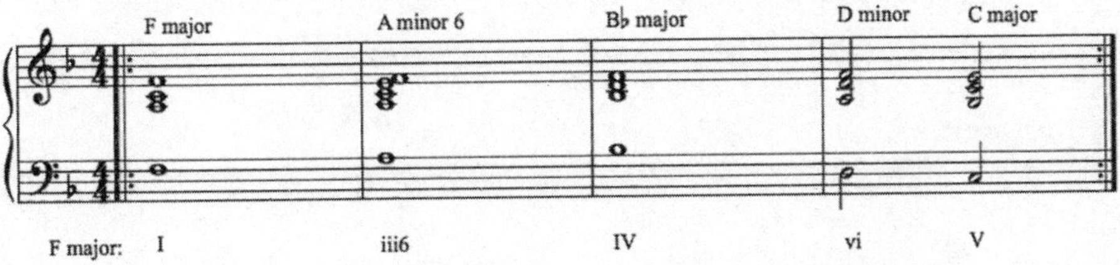


It is this chordal loop, moreover, that gives the song its pop sensibility: a "mellow" progression used in dozens of pop/rock and R&B songs since the 1970s—including Paul McCartney's "Live and Let Die," Berlin's "Take My Breath Away," and All-4-One's "I Can Love You Like That." As with *Hamilton*'s other chordal loops, the one found here becomes a foundation upon which Miranda generates near-constant variety. That is, "It's Quiet Uptown" does *not* employ a single melody for each verse, as a simple strophic song; instead it presents five distinct "themes" spread over the fifteen cycles of the loop. Each "theme" is varied by virtue of its distinct contour, rhythms, vocal assignment, and by means of periodic quotations from previous songs—namely, the lines "You knock me out, I fall apart" (cycle 6) from "Dear Theodosia"; "That would be enough" (cycles 7, 8, 10); and "Look around," initially from "The Schuyler Sisters" (cycle 12). Here is an overlay of these five melodic "themes" placed above the consistent chordal loop (Figure 9.11):

* A degree of harmonic variety is created throughout the song by periodically altering the second chord (A minor 6) of the main loop—e.g., to F/A or C/E, etc.—which, however, is less a deliberate harmonic shift and more a product of the instrumental arrangement.

**Figure 9.11: Lin-Manuel Miranda, "It's Quiet Uptown"—multiple melodic "themes" above consistent harmonic loop**

Miranda introduces further variety by inserting one contrasting harmonic pattern into the mix. It appears after the eighth cycle of the main loop and supports Alexander's penultimate solo verse—in the midst of his emotional plea for Eliza's forgiveness. This pattern and its dramatically ascending melody—an octave and a fourth—are likewise taken from "That Would Be Enough," though here altered to end on a chromatic shift from B♭ major to B♭ minor, from where it returns to the main loop. Here is that distinct progression and its melody (Figure 9.12):

Figure 9.12: Lin-Manuel Miranda, "It's Quiet Uptown"—contrasting harmonic pattern (Verse 9)

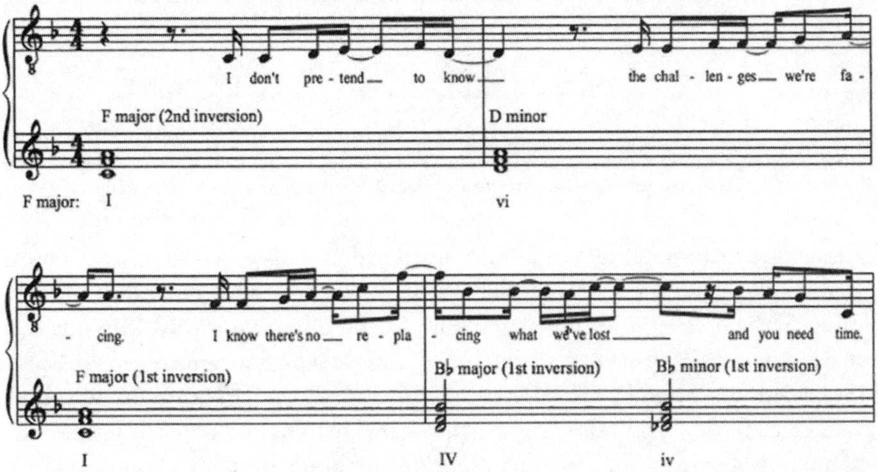

The third compositional device, then, is quite different. It involves the setting of a single lyric—one that Miranda uses to encapsulate the tragedy of what Alexander and Eliza are experiencing: "unimaginable." The word appears in seven of the sixteen total verses in the song, at the close of both the A and C themes (see Table 9.1). What makes this a "device" is Miranda's unique rhythmic setting of the word: a highly syncopated pattern that crosses over into the downbeat of the next cycle, whereby it creates great aural distinction: that is, you notice it. While it's too much to say that only a composer steeped in hip hop would set this word in quite this way, there's little doubt that Miranda's "virtuosic" rhythmic sensibility had something to do with it (Figure 9.13):

Figure 9.13: Lin-Manuel Miranda, "It's Quiet Uptown"—highly syncopated rhythm on hook ("unimaginable")

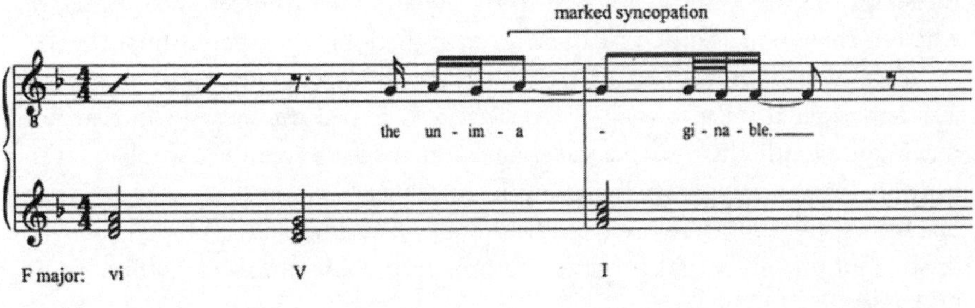


Taken together, the architectural assembly of these three devices—along with their thematic and vocal distributions—turns what could be a simple strophic song into a rich and complex structure. The overall arc-like form can be diagrammed as follows (Table 9.1):

**Table 9.1: Lin-Manuel Miranda, "It's Quiet Uptown"—diagram of overall and use of three main devices**

| Verse # | 1 | 2 | 3 | 4 | 5 | 6 | 7 | 8 | 9 | 10 | 11 | 12 | 13 | 14 | 15 | 16 |
|---|---|---|---|---|---|---|---|---|---|---|---|---|---|---|---|---|
| Harmonic Loop | 1 | 1 | 1 | 1 | 1 | 1 | 1 | 1 | 2 | 1 | 1 | 1 | 1 | 1 | 1 | 1 |
| Melodic Theme | A | A | B | B | C | C | D | D | E | D | C | C | A | B | F | C |
| Vocal Scoring | AS | AS | AH | AH | W | M | AH | AH | AH | AH | B | B | AS | AS | B | B |
| Obbligato | X | X | | | | X | | | | | | X | | X | | X |
| "Unimaginable" | X | X | | | X | | | | | | X | X | X | | | X |

AS = Angelica Schuyler (Eliza's sister); AH = Alexander Hamilton; W = women; M = men; B = both women + men

Finally, we cannot close this admittedly detailed analysis without mentioning one final element that forcefully defines the listening experience of "It's Quiet Uptown": the orchestration. As is standard for Broadway musicals, Miranda did not do this himself, but instead turned to a professional arranger—in this case Alex Lacamoire, who likewise orchestrated *In the Heights*.[374] Lacamoire is indeed often referred to as Miranda's "right-hand man," helping the latter to realize and heighten his ideas, not just via orchestration but also through harmonic embellishment, formal definition, etc. Such is often the relationship between Broadway composer and arranger—at times making it hard to distinguish the "song" from its arrangement.[375]

For "It's Quiet Uptown"—which Lacamoire has called "one of Lin-Manuel's most perfect songs"—he utilizes a palette of soft orchestral timbres: piano, strings, harp, guitar, and the exotic percussiveness of the hammered dulcimer. He employs these with constant variety and transparency—as when the violin and cello alone accompany Alexander's solitary moments in the garden (verse 3). Lacamoire's orchestration then helps set up the climax of the song (verse 14): moving from a full, rather rhythmic scoring, he pulls back to two quiet, sustained piano chords from D minor to C major, the second a sort of diatonic "cluster" (with third, fourth, and fifth degrees at once). At that point, Eliza sings her only line in the song, "It's quiet uptown"—indirectly signaling her forgiveness of Alexander, which is then made explicit by the chorus in the following, penultimate verse.

It's hard to say how many of these intricate details would be registered by Subject 1, particularly if the song elicits sleepiness as bedtime nears. On that note, one might wonder how such a sad song can make for a suitable complement to a bedtime ritual—a topic we'll pick up in Interlude G when discussing "the paradox of negative emotions." Certainly, though, its calm pacing, looped yet varied verses, and soft orchestral timbres offer much to commend it to Subject 1's pop hit parade.

## Insights Gained about Subject 1's Musical Taste

And speaking of Subject 1's musical genotype, what conclusions can be drawn from the songs/works that have marked this musical "day in the life"—the four discussed here plus the fifth (Michael Bublé's "Georgia") discussed on the WYLI website? At a high level, Subject 1 appears most attracted to straightforward and conventional modes of musical discourse within a broad "pop" mode: well-established, symmetrical forms (verse-chorus, A-A-B-A, quasi-strophic), use of predominantly diatonic harmony and simple rhythmic orientations (4/4 meter, only moderate syncopation), and traditional modes of sound and texture. Diving a bit deeper, however, a few more idiosyncratic preferences appear: a penchant for a country/Southern music genre influence; a desire for strongly identifiable hooks and ostinatos (whether vocal or instrumental); a fondness for steady, intoxicating grooves—across genres; and looping chord progressions. Further, some unconventionality occasionally manifests itself in the mix: use of unusual sonorities or instruments (banjo, distorted guitar, orchestral instruments, raspy vocals) and even moderately complex elements (counterpoint, mild chromaticism, accompanying obbligatos).

A logical follow-up question, then, involves divining what other songs/works might be good candidates for Subject 1's hit parade—here addressing only the four songs discussed in the chapter. This too can proceed on multiple levels. Most obviously, Subject 1 would likely enjoy songs that reside in close proximity to the "seeds" provided by this initial list. This would include, of course, related output by the artists and composers involved: "Love Story" (Swift), "Under the Influence" (King), "Bad Moon Rising" (CCR), "That Would Be Enough" (Miranda). Next would be songs written or recorded by other artists or for shows inhabiting similar musicological spaces as the seeds in question: "Fallin' for You" by Colbie Caillat or "Breakaway" by Kelly Clarkson (Swift); "365 Days" by ZZ Ward or "Written in the Water" by Gin Wigmore (King); "Time Was" by Canned Heat or "The Weight" by the Band (CCR); and "Bring Him Home" from *Les Misérables* or "Left Behind" from *Spring Awakening* (Miranda).

Diving a bit deeper would entail exploring songs/works by influencers on, and/or "heirs" to, the artists and composers involved: Dolly Parton and Hailee Steinfeld (Swift); Amy Winehouse and Adele (King); Bob Dylan and the Fabulous Thunderbirds (CCR); and Stephen Sondheim and Robert Lopez (Miranda). Finally, individual musicological elements suggest the prospect for even more remote artist/song candidates: Hank Williams or Earl Scruggs (country influence); Dr. John or Fats Domino (tresillo-based syncopation); "Superstition" by Stevie Wonder or "Birdland" by Weather Report (extended pedal points); or "Brenda's Got a Baby" by Tupac Shakur or Canon in D by Johannes Pachelbel (chordal loops), to name but a few. To be sure, there are many factors (musical and otherwise) that could explain why such candidates would be rejected or embraced by Subject 1, but such is the journey of exploring one's musical taste: your next hit could be where you least expect it.

# Interlude D

• • •

*At the Cellular Level: Music and Cell Biology*

## A Daunting Request

In late 2009, I received an unexpected invitation from Dr. Robert Mahley to speak at a public-outreach gathering at the Gladstone Institutes in San Francisco. The Gladstone Institutes is an independent biomedical research organization affiliated with the University of California, San Francisco, and dedicated to a translational model of medicine—going *directly* from research into practice. Gladstone's medical focus is on four areas: cardiovascular disease; virology and immunology; neurological disease, especially Alzheimer's disease; and stem cell technology. It is in the latter field that Gladstone has gained the most international acclaim, especially by virtue of the work of Shinya Yamanaka, who developed "induced pluripotent stem cells" technology. This fifty-cent expression refers to the technology whereby an adult skin cell can be "reprogrammed" to act in a pluripotent (all-powerful) manner—thereby acting like an embryonic stem cell, though without the latter's ethical challenges. For his revolutionary work, Dr. Yamanaka would receive the Nobel Prize in Physiology for Medicine in 2012.

At the gathering in November, called "Science4Life," Bob Mahley—director of Gladstone from its founding in 1979 until his retirement in 2010—asked me to join a small lineup of their team to give a twenty-minute lecture to the community. Of course, that lineup included Dr. Yamanaka, who would share with the crowd some of his new work on induced pluripotent stem cells. And I was there because . . . ?

I thought a lot about what I might say in my lecture. I could keep it broad, discussing my role at Pandora, as well as my work as a composer of science-themed works—including two commissioned by NASA: the *GLAST Prelude for Brass Quintet* (for the launch of the Fermi gamma-ray space telescope) and *Cosmic Reflection: A Narrated Symphony* (on the full history of the universe!). But something inspired me to consider how music might actually relate to cell biology. I had never considered such a topic before, and indeed had not really thought too deeply about the overriding link of music and science—beyond general connections of music, math, and physics that come with a PhD in musicology. As I told the crowd at the start of my talk, my background in biology consisted mainly of faithfully watching episodes of *Grey's Anatomy* over the past few seasons. And yet, with the incipient conclusions I drew in preparing my lecture at Gladstone, the seeds of my ensuing obsession for the music-science link—and thus this book—were planted, so to speak.

In the Preface, I likened this book to a mystery novel, a whodunit of our musical taste. It was my modest foray into cell biology in 2009, in fact, that unearthed an early clue in my mind as to the extramusical forces that—in a mystical way—lie behind the origins of our musical preferences, not so much for us as individuals but on a broader, human level. Specifically, I here propose a correlation between some overarching principles of cell biology and four universal principles of musical organization: repetition, development, variation, and symmetry.

With these proposed correlations, however, I am not claiming a direct causative link, but rather an abstract, metaphorical one. That is, I am not proposing that music possesses certain organizational qualities *by virtue* of their organic precedence in nature—no cause and effect is being argued here. Instead, I'm suggesting that fundamental principles found in our biology are an instructive and provocative *reflection* of the very way we, as humans, tend to organize music. In some mystical way, I submit, both cellular and musical tendencies derive from a common impulse, somehow intrinsic to "life," whether organic or artistic—such that it is no mere accident that music is rife with repetition, development, variation, and symmetry.

To make this argument, as I have in many talks over the years, I'll necessarily need to dive a bit into the source material of this metaphor: cell biology. I understand this is probably *not* why you bought this book, and that picturing me giving a lecture on mitosis is making you a bit queasy. Rest assured, however, that I have limited the purely biological details to those deemed necessary for my musical explications—with the more scientific minutiae relegated to the endnotes (and WYLI website) for those so inclined.

Finally, I would add that in attempting this interlude, I am inspired by the writings of architect and design theorist Christopher Alexander, who, in his four-volume "essay" *The Nature of Order*, made a somewhat related argument for how human structures in architecture often—though not always—reflect "living" structures in nature; more pointedly, he argued that far too much twentieth-century architecture *fails* aesthetically by ignoring those "living" principles in favor of "nonliving" ones—thereby producing works "outside the class of living structures"—or, as he calls them, "monsters."[376] While it is similarly true that much music from the twentieth century onward eschews, to some degree, the organizing principles found in cell biology, I am *not* suggesting, like Alexander, that they thereby fail on aesthetic grounds; instead, I'd simply say that such works reflect the human capacity, and occasional impulse, to bypass common and otherwise "universal" musical traits. Whether an individual one "succeeds" or "fails," then, is a matter of personal musical taste.

At the same time, this interlude, like Alexander's essays on architecture, does focus substantially on the abstract, theoretical underpinnings of music—specifically, again, the organizing principles of repetition, development, variation, and symmetry. At first glance, you might think that such a discussion bears little relevance to *your* musical taste. I would, however, vociferously disagree: instead I assert that whatever music you like—from the most conventional to the most esoteric—it relies, likely to a predominant extent, on these principles. Indeed, one could argue that I've employed this extramusical metaphor, as compelling as I find it, largely as an excuse to talk about them. At any rate, I contend that you simply cannot hope to understand or "empower" your musical taste without at least some awareness of these music-organizing principles. Hopefully you'll come to agree with me.

## Cell Biology for Dummies

As you may recall, cells are the "building blocks of life," those tiniest units of a living organism that make up each and every inch of your body—as well as those of all animals, plants, fungi, slime, bacteria, and archaea, dating back to the first living cell some 3.5 billion years ago. Cells carry out a whole host of processes, including those related to metabolism, protein synthesis, communication, and repair, but the most vital for the maintenance of life is *cell division*—whereby an organism grows and passes its hereditary material to the next generation. That hereditary material, of course, is DNA, or deoxyribonucleic acid, wherein all biological information is stored. DNA is tightly coiled within elongated structures called chromosomes: most human cells contain forty-six chromosomes, grouped as twenty-two "homologous" (similar) pairs and one pair of "sex chromosomes"—in all twenty-three pairs, one set from each parent.

The primary process of cell division is called mitosis. Its basic progression is that a single "mother" cell divides into two "daughter" cells—both then possessing the same, complete set of forty-six chromosomes. The full process contains seven steps, of which the first and final are outside the strict mitotic process. The first, interphase, however, is critical: this is the state of the cell *between* divisions, in the midst of which—during the so-called "S-phase"—each of the forty-six chromosomes "unzips" and replicates into two sister "chromatids," as the chromosomes are temporarily called.[377]

The full process of mitotic division is carried out constantly in our bodies, for both growth and regeneration. But cells can only divide after there is an "original" one to get the whole process started—what is called the zygote. In turn, a zygote can only be produced by virtue of a second cellular process: meiosis. Meiosis is how gametes—male sperm and female egg—are produced, each with only twenty-three chromosomes. It is similar to mitosis (with the same seven steps), yet goes through the series twice: a single "mother" cell divides into four "daughter" cells, each with twenty-three chromosomes.[378] Of course, when egg meets sperm, voilà: a zygote is created!

Armed with the requisite DNA instructions from both sets of twenty-three chromosomes, this single-celled zygote is now preprogrammed to successfully and aggressively increase its cell count via mitotic division. But it also is preprogrammed for something else: to enable some of these early mitotic divisions to *differentiate* into all the various types of cells we humans need to grow and develop.

Cells capable of differentiation are called stem cells. At first, these stem cells are "totipotent"—meaning that they can form into any cell type either within or external to the growing embryo. Those within the embryo are called embryonic stem cells and are "pluripotent"—meaning that they can morph into *many* kinds of cells. It is these pluripotent stem cells, finally, that over the ensuing weeks and months will differentiate into the numerous "specialized" cell types we possess: cardiac muscle, red blood cells, skeletal muscle, brain neurons, etc. Eventually they form into our forty trillion or so cells—all, again, derived from a single cell zygote.[379]

Okay, lecture's over! Hopefully it didn't stir up too many bad memories of high school bio class. So, now what again does this have to do with musical taste?

In essence, the processes found embedded in human cell division and embryonic stem cells' "potency," I argue, echo fundamental and universal ways in which music is put together structurally and formally. More specifically, I would suggest that two archetypal musical techniques—repetition and motivic development, along with the derivative principles of theme and variation and symmetry—are aesthetic embodiments of these biological mechanisms. Clearly, musicians have not been consciously emulating cell behavior in their songs and works over the millennia—especially since we've only understood the nuances of cell biology for about a century. And yet our natural gravitation toward its musical "counterparts" must be a kind of metaphysical reflection or recognition: that is, these musical techniques and approaches seem natural to us because they are literally encoded into our DNA.

## Stasis and Change

In his *Elements of Harmony*, the ancient Greek music theorist-philosopher, and pupil of Aristotle, Aristoxenus (4th c. BCE) drafted perhaps the first work of musicology by relating the art form not merely to metaphysics, but also to practical experience and perception. Indeed, he boldly deviated from Pythagorean norms by stating that the nature of intervals was "best discovered by the senses," above and beyond the mathematical rules that may underlie them. His discussions of melody, intervals, scales, and rhythms in fact provide us with the most vivid account of ancient Greek music theory and practice. In summarizing the key role of perception in "discovering" music, moreover, Aristoxenus made this keen observation:

> But for the student of musical science, accuracy of sense perception is a fundamental requirement; for if his sense perception is deficient, it is impossible for him to deal successfully with those questions that lie outside the sphere of sense perception altogether. . . . And we must bear in mind that musical cognition implies the *simultaneous cognition of a permanent and of a changeable element*, and that this applies without limitation or qualification to every branch [parameter] of music.[380]

Even among the earliest observers of "musical science," that is, was recognition of the dual phenomena of repetition and development in both musical discourse and perception—some things are "permanent"; others are "changeable." Indeed, the two techniques are intimately linked, as we'll see. Here we'll first focus on repetition, as a metaphoric reflection of the "repetition" that takes place during the S-phase of interphase, wherein our chromosomes "unzip" and replicate in preparation for mitosis proper—whereby we are able to grow and develop as human beings.

## Musical S-Phase: Repetition

Repetition: it is everywhere in music. Without it, your hit parade would undoubtedly look very different. Imagine no repeated choruses in Neil Diamond's "Sweet Caroline," or no repeated guitar riffs in the Rolling Stones' "Satisfaction"—the songs and the experiences they engender would be dramatically altered. It is, indeed, hard to think of a single pop or rock song that does not rely substantially on the repetition of its melodic, harmonic, rhythmic, and/or formal material as a defining quality of the music. The same likewise extends to a good portion of jazz, hip hop, classical, and world music of all types and varieties. And electronica? Fuhgettaboutit—the species wouldn't even exist without repetition.

"Intelligibility in music seems to be impossible without repetition," wrote composer and theorist Arnold Schoenberg—one of dozens of such statements by prominent musical thinkers I could cite.[381] Repetition is so common in the music you hear, in fact, that you're probably oblivious to just how often it occurs. So common—and vital—is repetition in music, moreover, that it is worth diving into more formally.

First, to orient you, let's revisit the children's song "Twinkle, Twinkle, Little Star," partially quoted in Figure 6.17—using the French name of the melody, "Ah, vous dirai-je Maman"—to demonstrate variations form (Figure D.1):

Figure D.1: "Twinkle, Twinkle, Little Star"—extreme use of repetition

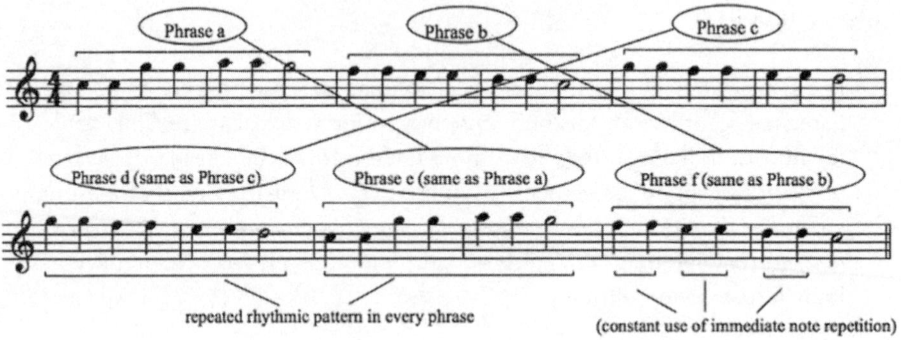


As the diagram demonstrates, repetition takes place constantly in the song, and on multiple levels. This short verse can be divided into six phrases, of which the last two (e–f) are an exact repetition of the first two (a–b); the third and fourth phrases (c and d) are likewise an exact repetition of one another. Beyond these exact repetitions, then, are several "partial" repetitions: all six phrases repeat the exact same rhythm (six quarter notes followed by a half note); the third and fourth phrases (c and d) also use the same stepwise descending shape (contour) as the second and sixth (b and f). There is even the immediate repetition of each note in each phrase, except for the final note. Without repetition, that is, the song practically disappears.

Repetition, as seen in "Twinkle, Twinkle," can be manifest on various levels: melodic, harmonic, rhythmic, and formal. Perhaps our most obvious encounter with musical repetition, however, is at the level of form—such as when a chorus or refrain is repeated exactly after each verse within a pop/rock or folk song.

Many classical musical forms too are all but defined by their regular use of repetition; common examples include binary (A-A-B-B), ternary and the **da capo aria** (A-B-A), and rondo (A-B-A-C-A) forms (see Chapter 6). Standardized formal repetition was less rampant during the medieval and Renaissance eras, though it was surely common in performance. By the Baroque era, however, sectional repetition was nearly a universal practice, with repeated sections often used as a basis for improvised or composed variation. Strict formal repetition in classical music began to wane in the nineteenth century, in favor of more through-composed techniques.

But sectional repetition came back with a vengeance in jazz and popular music in the twentieth century. Indeed, the essence of jazz is to copiously repeat a song's refrain—harmonically and formally—over which the performers can display their prowess by improvising a melody; pop music of all varieties since the 1950s is likewise substantially built upon the power of the repeated refrain or chorus.

And yet, as noted, formal repetition is but one type of repetition: another prominent kind is harmonic—that is, a cycle of repeating chords. Without musical training (or at least reading this book), much of this type may be hard to discern at first pass. As we discussed in Chapters 4 and 9, however, chordal repetition is a constant of many musical styles—especially pop and jazz, though by no means only those. To cite just one case, for argument's sake: one of those "looped" songs in the musical *Hamilton*—"My Shot"—features five and a half minutes of essentially a single repeated chord progression: G minor–B♭–C minor–E♭–D; go ahead, give it a listen.

A more readily audible form of musical repetition is melodic—where a discrete theme, motive, or phrase is repeated sporadically, if not incessantly, within a single formal section, as we saw with "Twinkle, Twinkle." There is virtually no style or genre of music that does not indulge in melodic repetition of some kind or another—or at least no genre that can claim a substantial following of listeners.

We will not spend much time corroborating the point here, but we can briefly remind you of the substantial prominence of melodic repetition in jazz and pop/rock music since its origins. The most blatant use, as noted many times, is the "riff"—a short melodic idea repeated extensively throughout a song, vocally and/or instrumentally, to help establish a vibrant, intoxicating rhythmic propulsion or "groove." Riffs appear early in jazz history, in Tin Pan Alley songs such as in the melody of Irving Berlin's "Alexander's Ragtime Band" (1911), and really take off during the swing era (1930s and '40s), where they are often used as accompanying figures—such as in Tommy Dorsey's recording of "Opus No. 1" (1944). They then come to dominate in rhythm and blues, rock and roll, and later rock styles—such as the guitar and bass riff in the Beatles' "Day Tripper," to name one of countless examples; here are the examples just cited (Figures D.2–4):

**Figure D.2: Irving Berlin, "Alexander's Ragtime Band"—repeating riff in melody**

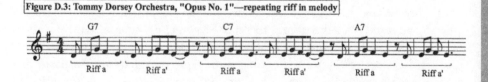

**Figure D.3: Tommy Dorsey Orchestra, "Opus No. 1"—repeating riff in melody**

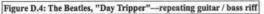

Figure D.4: The Beatles, "Day Tripper"—repeating guitar / bass riff

According to ethnomusicologists like John Chernoff and Ingrid Monson, the extensive use of riffs and melodic repetition in jazz and pop/rock music reveal the pervasive influence of the African diaspora on these American-born species. That is, the ubiquity of riffs in jazz, blues, and rock echo the extensive use of melodic repetition within the call-and-response traditions found among the various peoples of sub-Saharan Africa—where melodic phrases are repeated as they pass from one group of singers to another, a tradition alive and well in gospel music.[382] Social theorists such as Henry Louis Gates Jr. have then aligned the repetition found in hip hop culture to constructive social bonds within African-American culture via techniques like "signifyin'"—where slang phrases or musical "loops" with collective meaning are continually repeated, to either praise or tease the intended receiver.[383]

Again, riffs and formal sections are not the only means by which repetition marks musical discourse. The most comprehensive account of the technique, not surprisingly, can be found coming from the field of music theory—that opaque corner of music scholarship where the incurably analytical musicians go to play. Most prominent music theorists over the past century have remarked on the prevalence of repetition, though usually focusing on only one or two dimensions—such as form, melody/pitch, or rhythm.[384]

Perhaps no music theorist has been more ambitious, if idiosyncratic, in his quest to document the prevalence of repetition in music than Adam Ockelford—via his so-called "zygonic theory," based on the Greek word "*zygon*," meaning "yoke": that which binds or connects two things.[385] Imitation is the essence of Ockelford's theory, as he came to recognize its ubiquity in *all* music, and its profound impact on our cognitive processing of it—whether consciously so or not. In short, Ockelford argues that we humans operate in a universe "founded on the similarity and sameness of things."[386] What is key here—as this quote suggests—is that imitation need not mean exact repetition, but also the many, varying degrees of similarity or approximation, including development and variation.

To express his theory, Ockelford developed a complex notation system whereby he could trace the various forms of "zygonicity"—that is, types of imitation (pitch, melody, contour, harmony, rhythm, timbre, among others)—that undergird a piece of music. In notating these types of imitation, Ockelford is especially interested in the "zygonic relationship" by which they define the overall structure of a work. The theoretical details of Ockelford's theory, though, are less important to us than is his forceful and intricate recognition of the commanding role that imitation plays in music of all styles and at all levels—from individual notes and phrases (foreground) to a work's overarching form and structure (background). Most importantly, Ockelford defines zygonicity as essential to our *experience* as music listeners—whether from a "populist" (casual, nonexpert) perspective, in which many imitations might be missed, or from a "progressive" (intent, expert) one. Due, no doubt, to the complexity of its notational approach, Ockelford's "zygonic theory" has exerted little influence in academic music circles; and yet his observations on the prevalence and impact of repetition/imitation are provocative food for thought.

In sum, even from the arcane and hardcore depths of analytical music theory, repetition can be seen as part and parcel of music's DNA, so to speak. But why is this the case, and what does repetition have to do with our musical taste? Before turning to these questions, it should be pointed out that not everyone has seen our universal obsession with musical repetition in a positive light.

The most cited critic is the philosopher Theodor Adorno—notably in his essays "On Jazz" (1936) and "On Popular Music" (1941). Adorno was also a composer, having briefly studied with Alban Berg, and he blasted the reliance of repetition in popular "hit music" (that is, jazz) in scathing terms—both that taking place within songs (sectional and melodic), and by virtue of the incessant radio-play hits received by song "pluggers." Specifically, he saw rampant musical repetition as reflecting our loss of individuality as well as mindless standardization and consumerism in the industrial age—indeed as reflecting childish, primitive, and hysterical behavior: "Listening to popular music is manipulated not only by its promoters, but as it were, by the inherent nature of this music itself, into a system of response-mechanisms wholly antagonistic to the ideal of individuality in a free, liberal society."[387] But don't feel bad, pop music fans: Adorno also attacked the multimodal repetition found in the music of Mozart, of Debussy, and especially of Stravinsky—whose melodic and rhythmic repetitions (as in the *Rite of Spring*) he cast as infantile, psychotic, and even resembling "schema of catatonic conditions."[388]

Adorno's disdain for musical repetition is in part grounded on high-minded philosophical precepts—given its seeming antithesis to "organic" growth and development, such as is inherent in literature. In this way, Adorno was expanding upon a common aesthetic concern expressed in the latter nineteenth century—such as when the Wagner devotee Ferdinand Praeger asked (in 1882): "Would ever a poet think of repeating half of his poem; a dramatist a whole act; a novelist a whole chapter? Such a proposition would be at once rejected as childish. Why should it be otherwise with music? . . . Since any whole [sectional] repetition in poetry would be rejected as childish or as the emanation of a disordered brain."[389]

The adverse philosophical and aesthetic implications of music's "repetition compulsion" is explored in even greater detail in musicologist Peter Kivy's influential essay, "The Fine Art of Repetition." The title is actually ironic, since it is by virtue of its heavy reliance on repetition that Kivy provocatively refutes music's status as a "fine art."[390] Channeling the earlier arguments of Praeger, Kivy points out that no play would repeat Act 1 after Act 2; nor do we continually repeat the same stories or arguments when we speak: "Folks don't do that sort of thing. They don't repeat verbatim what they just said a minute after they said it." Similarly, Kivy argues, life (e.g., an embryo) does indeed evolve and develop, even in ways resembling the developing motive of a Beethoven sonata, but it doesn't repeat itself: we don't live two childhoods. For this reason, Kivy redefines music not as a fine art based on "organic" principles, but as a "decorative" one—like a mosaic—where artful use of repetition is common. Indeed, Kivy goes so far as to refer to music as "tonal wallpaper"—though he quickly adds that in the hands of a genius like Beethoven, it can be *great* wallpaper.

Apart from the provocative nature of Kivy's aesthetic categorizations, his basic impulse derives from an attempt to better explain music's distinctive reliance on repetition. And, we should note, he's primarily talking about sonatas and symphonies from the eighteenth and nineteenth centuries: imagine how he'd characterize the obsessive sectional and melodic repetition of today's pop music, let alone EDM.

In light of the metaphor used in this interlude, however, a forceful rebuttal may here be offered to a key premise in Kivy's argument: that ample repetition negates music's candidacy within his "organism" model. While it may be true that living organisms don't repeat temporal phases of their life cycle, it is also true—as we've seen—that repetition is an *essential*, indeed inceptive process for every living organism. The complete and continual replication of an organism's chromosomes, wherein its DNA is stored, is the basis by which *all* life comes into being, grows, and develops. In short, no replication of genetic material, no life. As such, it would be wholly inaccurate to say that music's pervasive use of repetition disqualifies it from Kivy's "organism" model, whereby Kivy relegates it to "wallpaper." By contrast, I would argue, the "fine art of repetition" strongly bolsters the argument that music is in fact "organic," and thus (in Kivy's theory) a proper and unique representative of the fine arts.

In recent decades, such dismissive (even hostile) attitudes toward musical repetition have given way to a growing recognition of its inherent aesthetic value—as well as the key role repetition plays in our overall musical perception and tastes, as noted in our review of Ockelford's zygonic theory. To be sure, many music critics still attack an overuse of sectional or melodic repetition in pop songs as "childish" or "primitive"—and indeed we all have our taste threshold for repetition of various sorts in various contexts. And yet, as pop/rock musicologists like Richard Middleton argue, repetition in "hit songs" cannot simply be reduced to "the political economy of popular music production," as he terms it; in his view, it likewise reflects other, more positive social functions, including the so-called "psychic economy"—where the persistent melodic riffs in pop and rock songs can result in a sort of collective "hypnotic abandon" among the audiences hearing them, leading in turn to the blissful loss of one's individual conscious self.[391] Pop musicologist Luis-Manuel Garcia goes even further, finding in the nonstop, looping repetition within EDM (as well as minimalism) a means of gaining pleasure—via the actual *process* of discerning and tracking the gradual shifts of layered repetitive patterns, above and beyond the sound of the music itself, or the associated dancing.[392]

While admittedly not all of you will find pleasure in the hyperlooping stasis of EDM or minimalism, it certainly must be the case that active, multimodal musical repetition imparts pleasure within us—otherwise it wouldn't be so universal in both style and geography. This universality is further supported via a number of studies involving young children and nonmusicians. In one, John Kratus invited eighty musically untrained children aged five to thirteen to create their own melodies on a keyboard using only two rules: the melodies had to begin with the three notes C–D–E, and only the white notes of the keyboard could be used.[393] Although age-related variety was displayed in the construction of the melodies, Kratus found that melodic repetition was "quite common in songs from all age groups."

For music to be perceived as music, so it seems, it must involve a degree of repetition. As Elizabeth Margulis notes, we even perceive as "musical" nonmusical sounds—a spoken phrase, for example—when repeated in a loop.[394] Margulis, indeed, has in recent years become an influential—and popular—expert on musical repetition, focusing especially on how it impacts our listening, perception, and preference. She cites, for example, the "mere exposure effect" as a partial explanation for why musical repetition pleases us: where our preference increases after hearing the same melody, rhythm, or chord progression three or four times; with each repetition, she rightly observes, we have the opportunity to hear something we missed the previous time.

The observations and postulations just cited are but a tiny number contained in Margulis' 2014 monograph on the subject, entitled *On Repeat*—the most well known of her many writings on the phenomenon of musical repetition.[395] They are drawn from her career as a musicologist and cognitive scientist, and over a decade of innovative experiments on the perceptions and effects of the technique. Not unlike the summary here, Margulis calls upon diverse disciplines to explore the topic: musicology, music theory, ethnomusicology, and cultural studies—adding a good dose of cognitive studies to query our psychological response. Indeed, she couches the ubiquity of musical repetition—what she calls a "handprint of human intention"—in deep-seated, universal terms, arguing that our "basic psychological . . . and perceptual tendencies," consistent across cultures, help to constrain and define how we make music.[396] That is, our "appetite for repetition" arises from an innate perceptual impulse that makes it desirable in music even if unwelcome in other realms, notably literature—as we've seen discussed by others.

Critical too, Margulis points out, is the importance of context in how repetition strikes us. As Ockelford notes as well, we will never consciously observe every manifestation of repetition in a musical work, and those we do observe will depend not only on the level of musical knowledge we possess, and the degree to which we're paying attention, but also on how many times we've heard a piece—repeated listens, as Adorno pointed out, being another striking manifestation of our obsession with repetition. And yet, regardless, for Margulis the impact of repetition cannot be overstated: it is, as she calls it, a "quasi-magical agent of musicalization," whereby simply hearing a phrase, rhythm, or section repeated, we are invited to participate "imaginatively" with the music in ways not possible with a single utterance; via repetition, that is, we do not merely listen to the music, but listen along with it—whether in our heads or outwardly by tapping, swaying, or singing along—by virtue of the fact that on some level, at least, we know what's coming next.

As to why we humans have this obsession in the first place, Margulis offers several rationales—most notably the "embodiment thesis": the notion that our cognition is directly tied to the aspects and capacities of our body. That is, listening to repeated music—especially repeating rhythms and rhythmic patterns—manifests itself in the hands and feet, where via the basal ganglia and motor cortex, for example, it can register pleasurable emotion in the brain: "Its appreciation might lie in the body as much as in the mind, and . . . the idea that we 'feel' music may be nearer to the truth than the idea that we 'think' it."[397] This, in turn, helps to explain the universal role of music in human rituals (see Interlude E), where repetition-infused music helps focus the mind on the formalized actions of ceremonies and liturgies.[398]

Much as with the question of why we love music, the question of why we love repetition in music can perpetually slide backwards: we love music that we hear repeatedly due to the "mere exposure effect," which in turn stems from an innate "psychological tendency" within the human mind, which in turn is manifest in the capacities of the human body, which in turn suggests a link to a broader "organism model" of the musical arts, which in turn . . . Cannot we therefore source the ubiquity and universality of musical repetition to something fundamental within us: where the repetition that initiates *each cellular division*, in some mysterious and metaphysical sense, informs the way we make, perceive, and appreciate music?

Maybe, but my proposed link between S-phase chromosomal replication during mitosis and musical repetition is far less important than is the key takeaway from this discussion: regardless of the nuances of your musical taste—whether you like West African call-and-response, Tin Pan Alley, Brahms symphonies, EDM, or none of the above—chances are high that your favorites are literally replete with repetition.

## Musical Mitosis: Motives and Development

If repetition is a sine qua non of musical discourse, then so too is its ontological counterpart: **development**. This, of course, is the "changeable" element that, according to Aristoxenus, simultaneously occupies our musical cognition alongside the "permanent," or repetitive, one. Both, indeed, are necessary techniques for musical viability: most of us would soon lose interest if either repetition or development were the exclusive state of the musical proceedings—even fans of EDM on the one hand or avant-garde classical on the other. The two, moreover, are by no means mutually exclusive, but often interact in myriad and interesting ways.

From a theoretical as well as perception standpoint, musical development is not as straightforward as repetition. While in most cases one can forge an objective judgment about whether or not a musical element is exactly repeated, development is often more subjective: what is considered a development of a previous idea to one listener may be heard as an entirely "new" idea to another. Still, there are some well-established things we can say about it.

To begin, when musicians talk about development, they are often thinking in terms of a motive or "motif." As we noted in Chapter 3, the *Grove Dictionary* defines a motive simply as "a short musical idea." Its most common application is as a *melodic* element, namely "the shortest subdivision of a theme or phrase that still maintains its identity as an idea."[399] It is thus a sort of fundamental unit of a melody—and in fact the term "cell" is sometimes used to describe it, or at least aspects of it.[400]

Before continuing, let's remind ourselves what melodic motives look and sound like: here are six annotated motives that underscore the technique's broad and diverse manifestations across the musical universe (Figures D.5a–f).

**Figure D.5a–f: Six melodic motives and common types of motivic develpment (diverse musical sources)**

Within these six examples are found several common means of rendering **motivic development**—including "classic" motivic expansion (Figures D.5a and D.5e); melodic sequence (that is, repeating a melodic contour at a different pitch level, Figure D.5b); and "varied repetition" (Figures D.5c, D.5d, and D.5f). This latter technique—repeating an idea with only minor variation—is very common indeed, perhaps as close as music can get at capturing the "gist" of an earlier stated idea. Of course, this brand of musical paraphrase still needs to *repeat* some *exact* elements of the original (notes, rhythms, contour, etc.) to clarify the connection to the ear, unlike in spoken or written language. Thus, while in music there can be repetition without development, there can be no development without at least some repetition—just as there can be no mitotic cellular division without DNA replication. . . .

Regardless of how a motive may be defined musically, the assumption is that it plays some kind of significant or structural role in the composition as a whole.

Given this, it is not uncommon that a principal motive appears at or very near the beginning of the work, thereby establishing itself as a defining, even generative entity. Obviously, the motive may be exactly repeated, but implied in the term, again, is that it is also developed. This means that some element of it is changed—or manipulated, or varied, etc. Clearly, though, not every aspect of the motive can be markedly developed, lest it cease to reveal itself as related to the original. Thus, already we see an intersection of our Aristoxenian principles of permanence and change. What is required, therefore, is that the developed motive appear "similar" to the original to some degree or another.

It also goes without saying that musical development—generating similarity to material that came before—is not limited to a single motive within a composition. Many works, particularly of the Western classical tradition, have several defining "motivic" ideas sprinkled throughout. Similarly, a melodic theme, or portion thereof, can be varied once or many times in a work without being an actual "motive"—for example, as a varied or ornamented rendering of a melody or phrase. Likewise, a localized rhythmic or harmonic pattern—even a song's overall chord progression—can be "developed" via discernible shifts, changes, modifications, or alterations in a way that is simply similar to an earlier iteration. In short, musical development is a many-splendored thing, which we'll encounter many times as this book proceeds.

Defined broadly, musical development is an appearance of one or more iterations of a musical idea that are similar, but not identical, to an earlier version. And so defined, development is as universal and ubiquitous as repetition. Almost every pop/rock song with a verse-chorus structure will feature melodic and rhythmic variation from verse to verse to accommodate the differing lyrics; and unless the singer is oddly consistent (or the original version is simply "pasted" later in the track), subsequent choruses too will include some "development." In jazz and blues, then, creating variation on initial melodies, rhythms, and harmonies is all but mandatory for both singers and instrumentalists: each "repetition" of the same phrase will inevitably display an element of improvised variation, lest the performer gets booed off the bandstand! This propensity for development in Anglo-American rock, jazz, and blues, as with repetition, finds root in the African diaspora, emanating out of a "culture of improvisation, extemporization, and imagination in the aesthetic universe of the enslaved," as cultural anthropologist Clinton Hutton put it.[401] Call-and-response, for example, often involves the "song leader" improvising melodic variations upon the traditional melody while the group repeats it back more faithfully.[402]

Of course, it is within classical music that variation in general, and motivic development in particular, is especially cultivated. Starting in the Renaissance era, composers began utilizing short melodic "motives" that would be temporarily passed from one voice part to another (via the technique of imitation), whereby subsequent versions would be *varied* in details of pitch and/or rhythm.

In the Baroque era, one popular genre, the fugue, was entirely built around a single motive—or "subject," announced at the beginning—being reintroduced throughout in *varied* iterations, such as in different keys. Sonata form, then, the commanding blueprint of the eighteenth and nineteenth centuries, was likewise defined largely by motivic and thematic development—where from Beethoven onward, the process took on increasingly philosophical dimensions. These are but a fraction of the innumerable ways in which development is manifest within the overall classical species.

As with repetition, musical development has been a common source of rumination among classical music theorists and musically inclined philosophers, who generally emphasize a distinct aspect of motivic development: melodic intervals, contour, timbre, etc.[403] Among a good many writers, moreover, a key implication of musical development is its ability to impart unity or coherence upon the work as a whole—and especially during the Romantic era (c. 1800–1900).

To quickly cite three such ruminations: there is first Arnold Schoenberg's notion of *Grundgestalt* (basic shape)—the amalgam of intervals, rhythms, and harmonies introduced near the start of a composition that in the hands of a great composer form its unifying "germ."[404] Second, there is Leonard Meyer's well-cited discussion on musical coherence—where motivic development, above all other techniques, can best foster an intellectually and emotionally satisfying experience for the listener.

And third, there are the forceful words of Theodor Adorno—that harsh critic of repetition. Indeed, his contempt for musical repetition, as the embodiment of commodification and the loss of the individual in modern society, finds its antipode in his esteem for *development* in the works of the old masters. Adorno couches its use not only in sociological terms, but also in philosophical and organic ones. Specifically, he draws a stark distinction between the static state of *Sein* (being) and the organic state of *Werden* (becoming). As expected, mere "being" is manifest in repetition, whereas transcendent "becoming" is found in the "working out" of musical material. Yet here too Adorno passes rather stern judgment: while acknowledging that J. S. Bach achieved this "working out" with proficiency, it was only Beethoven, Adorno asserts, who achieved the "true realization" of the technique. Little wonder, then, that Adorno disliked jazz and popular music.

The point of all this highfalutin theory, of course, is not just to relay a few academic opinions on the glory that was the motivic practices of nineteenth-century classical music, as interesting as that may be. Instead, it is to drive home the point that musical development—change derived out of prior material—is not only a cornerstone of musical practice, but is also an element that speaks to the higher aesthetic essence of music. And although articulated in complex terms by theorists and philosophers, it is nevertheless something that speaks to all of us on a basic, instinctual level, as a pillar of our overall musical taste: development is good, just as is repetition. That popular music scholars are relatively quiet on motivic development is simply due to the fact that pop, rock, and jazz are in general more informally (improvisationally) constructed, and built upon less expansive and architecturally "worked-out" structures than is usually the case with Western classical; and indeed a few writers have traced motivic development in the more "worked-out" songs of progressive rock groups like Genesis, Yes, Pink Floyd, and Jethro Tull.[405] Yet, as we've seen, melodic development—via sequence, varied repetition, fragmentation, etc.—is just as common in nonclassical styles, maybe even more so.

Development, that is, is both a natural part of music making and also a quality that resonates within us as something natural and organic. Undoubtedly, our ability to mentally track both the static and changing elements in music goes back to our origins as a species, and likely proved an adaptive aid—a "safe forum"—in which we could hone our skills at recognizing subtle *changes* within an otherwise *static* environment, as David Huron and Dan Levitin might say.

As we've seen, some writers have hit upon those natural, organic qualities of musical development—with terms like "seed" and "germ"; one writer, musical phenomenologist Alfred Pike, went ever further in his biological reference, noting that motivic development is "a dynamic process of genetic growth."[406] By paying close attention and "grasping" a composition's motivic structures, Pike argues, the listener can increasingly take into mind its overall form—the "Gestalt"; what was opaque becomes increasingly transparent.

More recently, Alexandra Lamont and Nicola Dibben brought the perspectives of cognitive psychology to the question of how we *perceive* musical development. Their study tested the ability of both musicians and nonmusicians to recognize "similarity relations" in piano works by Beethoven (tonal/less complex) and Schoenberg (atonal/more complex).[407] The surprising upshot of their study was that in *all* cases recognition of musical development was most strongly influenced by the "surface" features of the music—accents, tempo, instrumentation, dynamics, etc.; and yet, as predicted, those "deeper" relations of development were better observed by listeners with greater musical expertise and/or familiarity with the music.

In many ways, these findings corroborate a truth that runs throughout this book: listening to music is not a homogenous or consistent exercise; depending on our musical experience, level of listening focus, and familiarity with a style or work, we hear different things—at both a surface and a "deeper" layer. We may not consciously recognize at first listen the extent to which a melodic phrase is the result of motivic development or variation, but we likely *will* recognize at least some degree of similarity—in many ways laying the seeds for a potentially deeper, more "analytical" listen the next time. And indeed, the Lamont and Dibben study does reveal that upon further hearings, both the musicians and nonmusicians in the study recognized those "deeper" (melodic, harmonic, rhythmic) motivic similarities.

Thus, as with so much of our cognitive perception of music, detection of musical development draws upon both our innate and learned abilities. Our musical taste too is reliant on and fostered by the various ways in which we hear similarity—whether in "listening" or "analytical" mode, or somewhere in between, and even varying from listen to listen of the same music: at a concert with friends versus at home with headphones, for example. It is, if you will, not unlike the way in which we may appreciate our cellular composition: on a surface level, brain neurons, cardiac muscle cells, bone cells, and red blood cells appear related to themselves but distinct from one another; and yet, with further examination, we recognize the "deeper" way in which they all are related—having the same twenty-six pairs of chromosomes. In a more general way, moreover, motivic/musical development can be seen to reflect the continual change and development that our cells carry out, via mitosis, as the means by which our bodies form and mature.

Before you pass final judgment on the worthiness of my metaphorical link between cell biology and musical taste, allow me to close with very brief reference to two additional "universals" of musical taste: the formal principles of theme and variations and of symmetry. Although both are significant, stand-alone functions in all types of music, and thus worthy of deep examination in their own right, they are also fundamental products of repetition and development. As such, we can do with brief summaries here, enlivened with further discussion and examples later in the book.

## Pluripotent Music: Theme and Variations

We, of course, have already referenced the use of variation as an inherent function of musical development—as in the "varied repetition" of a melodic phrase seen above in Figure D.5 (page 342), and below in Figures D.6 and D.8 (page 350). More broadly, variation may be cited as a root element of every instance of musical development, since by definition it involves varying some aspects of a "prototype" while maintaining others. And yet this universal element—as an intrinsic process of musical creation, performance, and perception—can also be more *explicitly* incorporated into musical practice in various ways.

At one extreme are the fully formalized, notated compositions falling under the rubric of "theme and variations" (or merely "variations," "chaconne," "ground bass," etc., all forms defined by initial material followed by a set of variations) within the Western classical tradition—with roots in medieval rhetoric (see Chapter 6). In such cases, an initial formal section (A) is treated to variation in subsequent iterations (A', A'', A''', etc.) by introducing new melodies or rhythms to a repeating bass line or chord progression; sometimes the original melody is clearly audible in the variation; at times it is not. An example in the formal case is the famous variations by Mozart on "Ah, vous dirai-je Maman" ("Twinkle, Twinkle," Figure D.1)—shown more fully in Figure 6.17.

But the expression "theme and variation" can also be applied to myriad less formal structures, particularly within an improvised or quasi-improvised setting. This is seen, for example, in the dance song "Agbekor" of the Ewe people of West Africa (Figure D.5f), where a fixed melody ("theme") is intentionally subjected to new variations each time it comes back around, likely with a degree of improvisation. This process no doubt lies at the root of the structural discourse of jazz, as well as the improvised solos of blues and rock, etc. As noted in Chapter 6, and discussed in more detail in Chapter 11, jazz is in large part predicated on a formal schema where a fixed melody and chord progression (A) is followed by repeated iterations of the same chords over which the soloist improvises a new melody (A', A'', A''', etc.); every new "chorus," that is, is a kind of "variation" on the original theme—even if the actual "theme" is nowhere to be heard.

Similar traditions are found around the world—famously within Indian classical music, where quasi-improvised variations on fixed rhythmic patterns (talas) are a mainstay of tabla drum performance; or within Indonesian gamelan music, where performers improvise simultaneous variations on an established theme. In such cases, the fixed element becomes what Bruno Nettl calls a "model," or what music psychologist Jeff Pressing calls a "referent": an "underlying formal scheme or guiding image specific to a given piece, used by the improviser to facilitate the generation and editing of improvised behavior."[408]

Theme and variations holds a dear spot in this chapter, since it was the original spark in my mind for a metaphoric link between musical taste and cell biology. Remember that Dr. Yamanaka's expertise was in reprogramming adult skin cells to behave like embryonic stem cells—those early phase cells that are "pluripotent": able to shift into any kind of cell. Given my anxiety at speaking alongside the future Nobel laureate, I naturally started my preparation there. As I thought about the matter, it occurred to me that each of those resultant cell types are different from the original stem cells, and yet are directly *based* upon them, containing the same DNA; they are, in essence, variations on the same theme. Aha, I exclaimed (using my inside voice): this is just like the common musical form. Perhaps, I wondered, the conceptual link between pluripotent stem cells and theme and variations suggests a broader association between how we commonly structure music and how our cells function. This was, at any rate, the epiphany that launched a ton of research, and ultimately the interlude you're reading now.

## Musical Cytokinesis: Symmetry in Music

Finally, we touch briefly upon yet another universal of music, as indeed of all art and science: symmetry. This is a commonplace concept of philosophy, mathematics, physics, biology, chemistry, and aesthetics, among much else—and undoubtedly has been held in high esteem, as an ideal, since early in our evolution. To the ancient Greeks, symmetry was an essential ingredient of beauty, or as Aristotle wrote in the *Metaphysics*: "The chief forms of beauty are order and symmetry and definiteness."[409] In *Timaeus*, Plato gave priority to the four elements due to their symmetrical shapes: fire (tetrahedron), earth (cube), air (octahedron), and water (icosahedron).[410] Not surprisingly, the ancients saw symmetry most manifestly expressed in mathematics, whether as a specific formula (e.g., the golden mean) or in geometric shapes (e.g., Euclidean isometries). In our own time, physics has revealed the prevalence of symmetry in the natural world as well as in the laws of physics—such as the laws of conservation;[411] however, perfect symmetry rarely, if ever, exists in nature: even archetypically symmetrical snow crystals reveal slight "distortions."

More practically, symmetry is a staple of the biological life we see all around us: in the "radial" symmetry (looking the same no matter how you rotate it) of plants, and the "bilateral" symmetry (identical if split down the middle, along the sagittal plane) of most animals—including ourselves. As with most physical objects, biological symmetry is inevitably imperfect to some degree—mercifully so in our case, as photographer Alex Beck revealed in his eerie mirror portraits of several human faces, entitled *Both Sides Of*.[412] It is a curious question as to why nature abounds in *near-perfect* or partial symmetry, even within its laws; as physicist Richard Feynman noted at the close of his lecture "Symmetry in Physical Law," perhaps "the true explanation of the near symmetry of nature is this: that God made the laws only nearly symmetrical so that we should not be jealous of His perfection!"[413]

Such partial imperfections, however, are readily ignored or missed when considered at a surface level, for indeed we humans are fascinated by symmetry; everyone, Feynman notes in that same lecture, "likes objects or patterns that are in some way symmetrical." This fascination is reflected too in our psychology, suggested already by Aristotle's definition of beauty. In Gestalt psychology, symmetry is the basis for one of its many laws or principles of "grouping"; these laws account for the way in which we humans perceive form or structure—how we organize separate parts and patterns into whole objects. The "law of symmetry" states that we prefer symmetrical forms to asymmetrical ones, and that we naturally gravitate toward perceiving objects as symmetrical out from a central point, if possible. Symmetrical perception enables us to integrate elements into a unified whole, whereby we may associate them with positive attributes like stability and balance—and where the symmetrical elements are conceived of as sharing similar functions.

It is thus no surprise that symmetry has figured prominently within aesthetics, not to mention within the arts themselves. The art most immediately associated with symmetry is architecture, in concert with the concepts of beauty, order, and proportion. As the Roman architect Vitruvius wrote in *De architectura*, "Symmetry . . . is the appropriate harmony arising out of the details of the work itself: the correspondence of each given detail to the form of the design as a whole. As in the human body, from cubit, foot, palm, inch and other small parts come the symmetric quality of eurhythmy [harmony of proportion]."[414] We see this ideal realized not only in untold works of architecture from throughout the ages and around the world, but also copiously in paintings of every era, and in decorative arts like mosaics and carpets; it can even be found within literature, by means of poetic forms, or via large-scale structures based on themes or characters—including classics like Shakespeare's *Hamlet*, Hemingway's *Old Man and the Sea*, and Dante's *Divine Comedy*.[415]

In music, symmetry is manifest in various ways—both theoretical and practical. The former includes scales (e.g., the whole tone scale), chords (e.g., the augmented triad—a symmetrical stack of major 3rds), and harmonic constructs like the Circle of 5ths. On a practical level, musical symmetry—occasionally perfect, more often imperfect—is nearly as ubiquitous as repetition and development. Indeed, symmetry can be seen as a particular variety of repetition, since without at least some element repeating (and some changing), there can be no symmetry.

As an organizing principle, there are, in essence, two types of musical symmetry—on the level of the phrase and on the level of overall form.

Adjacent phrases can create symmetry by starting the same, but ending differently (e.g., antecedent-consequent); or by starting and ending the same, but varying in the middle (a type of "bookend symmetry"). Other, more complex symmetrical patterns utilize time-honored musical techniques: inversion (the intervals of a first melody or part are inverted in the second), retrograde (where the intervals of a first melody or part are reversed in the second), and palindrome (the same exact melodic line played backwards and forwards), among others. These latter three are almost exclusively found within the classical repertory, particularly within the medieval (e.g., isorhythmic motets), Baroque (e.g., canons and fugues), and modern (e.g., serial or 12-tone works) eras—as part of generally complex contrapuntal structures. By contrast the first two types, especially antecedent-consequent, are common within most styles of music: in its conventional form, the antecedent phrase is "counterbalanced" by the consequent, as a kind of call-and-response or varied repetition. Examples of all five types of phrase symmetry are found here (Figures D.6–D.10):[416]

**Figure D.6: Traditional, "Home on the Range"—symmetry via antecedent-consequent balanced phrases**

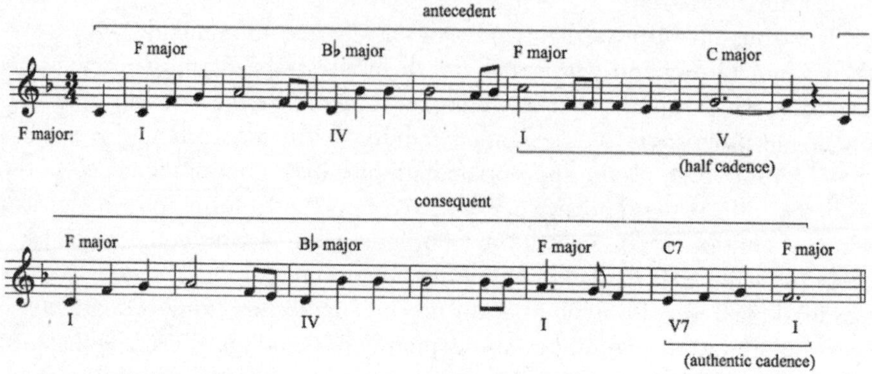


**Figure D.7: The Beatles, "Something"—symmetry via "bookends" (same music at beginning and end)**

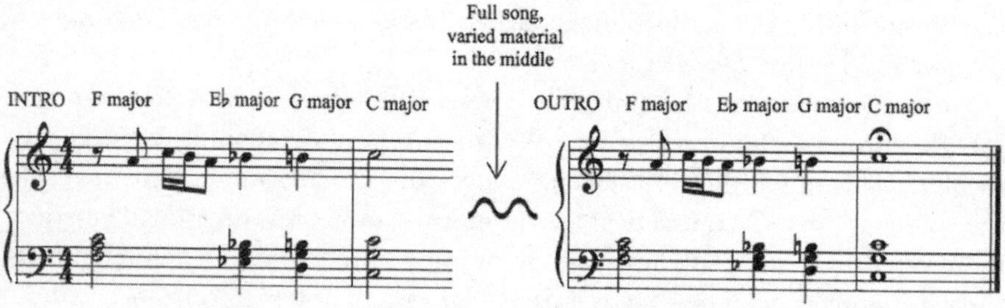


**Figure D.8: J. S. Bach, *Art of the Fugue*, Fugue (contrapunctus) 13—symmetry via inversion**

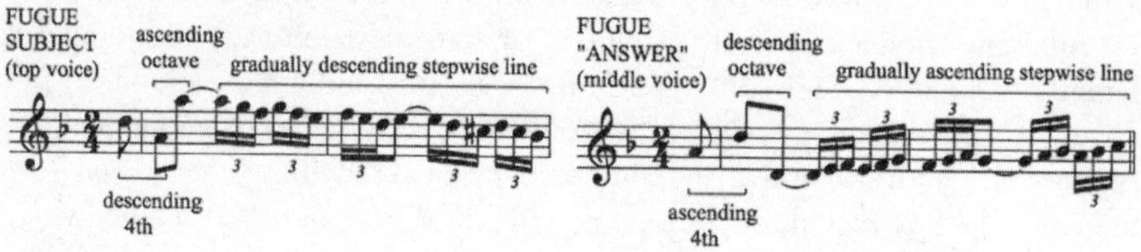


**Figure D.9: Guillaume de Machaut, "Ma fin est mon commencement"*—symmetry via retrograde**

* Machaut broadcasts his symmetrical approach in this chanson via its very title (and text): "My end is my beginning."

**Figure D.10: Haydn, Symphony no. 47, 3. Minuet and Trio (Minuet section)—symmetry via strict palindrome**

Where musical symmetry is usually more readily discernible, and certainly more impactful, is at the level of form. The archetypal symmetrical form in music is "ternary," with the schematic structure of A-B-A. A vast amount of music in every style around the world utilizes a direct or emended version of this formal layout: to begin with a particular musical discourse, depart from it, and conclude with a return of the opening material. As a general strategy, this corresponds to what Meyer calls the "law of return" (a variant of the Gestalt "law of symmetry"), which he expresses as: "Other things being equal, it is better to return to any starting point whatsoever than not to return."[417]

Examples within the classical repertory—many of which we saw in Chapter 6—include the minuet and trio of an eighteenth-century symphony; the da capo aria of Baroque operas; the piano "miniature" of the nineteenth century (e.g., many Chopin preludes, nocturnes, and waltzes; Schumann "character pieces"); as well as older forms like the Mass cycle, in the Kyrie and Sanctus, to cite but a few. In many such cases, the returning A is varied to some degree—whether via improvisation (as in the da capo aria) or written out. More complex forms of symmetry include sonata form, whose tripartite structure generates an overall ternary form via a dialectic (thesis-antithesis-synthesis) process, as well as the rondo form, both in a five-part (A-B-A-C-A) and seven-part (A-B-A-C-A-B-A) schema, among many others.

Though less formalized, ternary form is likewise a staple of popular and jazz styles—generally carried out via an "imperfect" symmetry, where the "return" is altered via improvisation or intentional variation. This includes the Tin Pan Alley form of jazz "standards," with the schema A-A-B-A; although an asymmetrical kind of symmetry, it still obeys the "law of return." More broadly, then, the default format of jazz performance follows a ternary orientation of Tune—Solos—Tune. Likewise is this type of "imperfect" symmetry common in the pop/rock realm: such as Verse/Chorus—Bridge—Verse/Chorus, as we chronicled in Chapter 6. Finally, ternary and rondo-like "cyclic" forms are commonplace in various world music styles, such as in the Zulu tradition of South Africa, the instrumental (raga) and vocal music of India, and Indonesian (gamelan) music—where an opening section or refrain repeatedly returns after each contrasting section.

We will, again, have further opportunities to reveal the manifold incarnations of musical symmetry in the pages ahead, but the above hopefully drives home the point that the "laws" of symmetry and return have been intuitively adopted by musicians of all varieties as a natural and welcome technique. And just as nature rarely delights in perfect symmetry, so too do musicians frequently indulge in some level of "distortion" by varying the return with fresh material—so that they might, in David Huron's words, "allow expectations to be aroused and manipulated."[418]

Not surprisingly, our attraction to symmetry appears biologically grounded—as displays of symmetry are demonstrated in the everyday behavior of species ranging from earwigs (pincer bugs) to humans; it is manifest in mating as well as nonmating behavior, such as honeybees' preference for symmetrical flowers. Explanations range from the way symmetry reflects seemingly positive qualities in the object observed (a more fitting mate, a sweeter flower, etc.) to symmetry as a by-product of our general recognition systems—reflecting our global visual-encoding strategy, for example.[419] Indeed, neuroscience studies have shown that infants can recognize symmetry after only a short-term glance,[420] while aesthetic judgments of beauty via symmetry observations are shown to trigger activity in the frontal cortex as well as the parietal lobe—specifically in regions otherwise aligned with social and moral cues.[421]

All this is to say that our love and embrace of musical symmetry is grounded deep in our identity as humans, reflecting an innate tendency, which again is expanded and fine-tuned through learning and experience. Symmetry, in other words, is in our bones—and in our blood, our brain, our heart, and our skin. It is found throughout our body via the mitotic divisions of our cells, initiated upon formation of our original zygote. More specifically, the five-part process of mitosis proper concludes with one called telophase, by which point the original, single cell has divided into two symmetrical halves, each with its own complete set of forty-six chromosomes, around which new membranes now form; overlapping with the end of telophase is the final (post-mitotic) cytokinesis phase, in which the two halves fully separate—each a near-perfect, *symmetrical* "varied repetition"—of the other.

Could it be that the symmetry that populates so much music we hear, and that comports so innately with our musical taste, is a type of metaphysical reflection of this biological process? If so, it would join our other musico-cellular connections: *repetition* as a reflection of S-phase chromosome replication; *motivic development* as a reflection of our overall mitotic processes; and *theme and variations* as a reflection of the behavior of pluripotent stem cells.

## The Good News

And with that: so ends my best efforts to convince you of a connection—nonlinear, metaphorical, and metaphysical though it may be—between the processes and techniques of our cell biology and the processes and techniques aligned with our musical taste. But the good news is that it doesn't really matter. Whether you found my argument compelling, sketchy, or downright ridiculous, we've accomplished something far more important by defining some innate, universal pillars of your musical taste: repetition, development, variation, and symmetry.

In all, our foray into the dense intersection between music and science over these past four interludes has posited the overall claim that *before* we hear even a note of music, we are to a large extent prewired with some powerful forces guiding our musical taste: (1) an intense, intrinsic love for music as a fundamental dimension of our individual and collective identity (evolution); (2) a natural gravitation toward perfect consonances (octaves, fifths, fourths) and consonant chords (major, minor, dominant 7th) as strong, attractive pillars of harmonic sound (math and physics); (3) an impressive ability to process complex sonic content into concrete syntactic and semantic constructs laden with emotion and embedded in memory (neuroscience); and (4) a propensity to embrace a distinct arsenal of organizing techniques (repetition, development, variation, and symmetry) to drive musical narrative (cell biology).

Where our musical taste goes from there—how it goes from a collective to a more individualistic quality—requires us moving into our next extramusical topic: culture. But first, let us return to the expressly musical realm as we continue with our fictional music lovers and their respective genotypes: rock and jazz.

part five

# PARLEZ-VOUS GAMELAN?

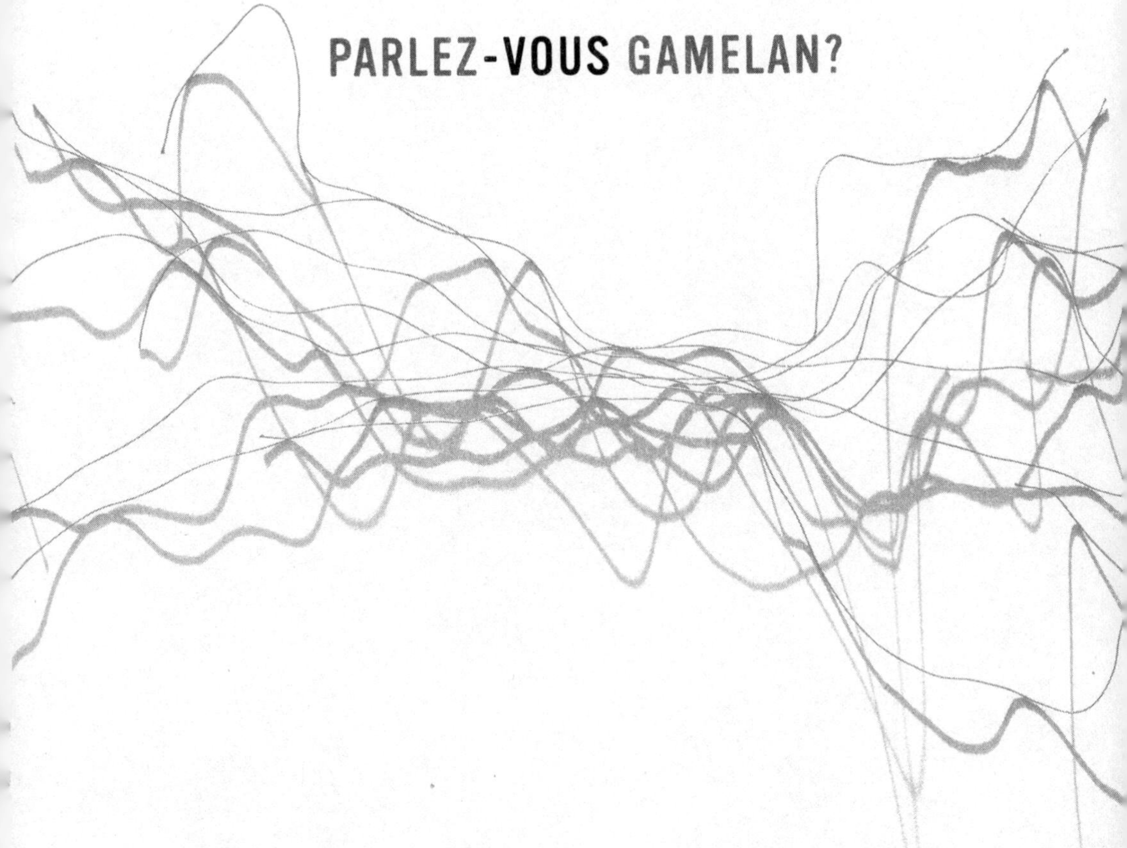

ten

# THE ROCK GENOTYPE

## Introducing Subject 2

Let's meet our next music lover: Subject 2 begins the day needing a jolt of energy while at the gym, and finds it with an old classic: **Led Zeppelin's "Ramble On."** Heading to work, a relative newcomer to the hit list is cranked up over the car speakers: **Alabama Shakes' "Don't Wanna Fight."** Driving home, a playlist staple helps clear the mind after a long day, **Muse's "Butterflies and Hurricanes."** Finally, a small dinner party at home that night hits a high point when the sound system plays a jazzy favorite, **Louis Prima's "Just a Gigolo/I Ain't Got Nobody."***

On the surface, this hit parade suggests that Subject 2 is a dedicated rock fan, with a moderately eclectic orientation that embraces a degree of musicological sophistication—though consistently within a framework of a driving groove.

Before getting into these selections, however, a brief overview of the rock species:

## The Rock Species: A Brief Review

We've already had several occasions to discuss aspects of rock's origins and evolution, in fact, as well as key musicological hallmarks of the species—especially in Chapter 6. A full historical survey, moreover, is well beyond the scope of this book. As such, we'll provide but a high-level overview of some key trends, as well as a bit more on what distinguishes this fascinating and culturally dominant genre from an aesthetic and artistic standpoint.

Let's first provide a broad framework of rock music by considering a list of ten touchstone songs that typify the species:

---

* Subject 2's fifth song, heard as a relaxing way to wind down the day, is Lucinda Williams' 2007 song "Are You Alright?" For its discussion, see the WYLI website, supplement to Chapter 10.

Arctic Monkeys, "Do I Wanna Know?" (2013)
Green Day, "American Idiot" (2004)
Nirvana, "Smells Like Teen Spirit" (1991)
Guns N' Roses, "Sweet Child o' Mine" (1988)
The Clash, "Should I Stay or Should I Go?" (1982)
Aerosmith, "Walk This Way" (1975)
Lynyrd Skynyrd, "Sweet Home Alabama" (1974)
Jimi Hendrix, "Purple Haze" (1967)
The Kinks, "You Really Got Me" (1964)
Chuck Berry, "Johnny B. Goode" (1958)

Many of you will no doubt take issue with my having listed these particular ten songs, and not some other classic or stereotypical rock anthem—as is to be expected in a species with such impassioned cultural attachment, as we'll explore in Interlude F. And yet I trust that most rock fans would concede that these songs reasonably epitomize the realm: all feature a driving and up-tempo intensity, fueled by aggressive electric guitars and heavy drums; they are all propelled via short, infective guitar riffs; they all use diatonic blues-based harmonies, marked by short cyclic chord patterns; their melodies feature short, anthem-like motives, particularly for the chorus; their forms are largely verse-chorus conventions; and they all feature assertive vocals by strong-personality singers. Okay, but clearly there is more to defining the rock species than just these musicological components.

In the previous chapter, we discussed pop music as an aesthetic orientation built on accessibility, predictability, and adherence to convention, a species whose prime motivation is popular and commercial success. Such does not preclude the exercise of impressive craft and creativity, of course—so long as they don't stand in the way of making a hit record. By contrast, rock music is motivated by "authenticity" and originality—which economist Joseph Schumpeter called "an act of creative destruction," and which Adam Grant recently defined as "rejecting the default and exploring whether a better option exists."[422] Starting with originality, therefore, can be a risky way to make a buck. This doesn't mean it won't—as many highly original rock songs have become big hits and made lots of money. It is thus more a matter of attitude and intent: pop intends to please; rock intends to shake its fist and say, "I don't give a shit if you like me or not!" In theory, anyway; in reality the line is often considerably less rigid—hence the common hybrid term "pop/rock."

A good part of what motivates the authenticity of rock music is its perennial drive back to "the roots"—the almost mythological purity of those raw and rebellious early days of rock and roll: reckless teens playing simple, hard-driving songs in an old, beat-up garage. This "ur-rock" ushered forth a fresh mantra "about disturbance, race, sex, and a new youthful power," as Mikal Gilmore put it in his farewell tribute to David Bowie.[423] Get too far from it, some will always say, and it's not *true* rock and roll. And yet innate to this music as well is an uncanny potential and flexibility. You can throw any musical idiom onto the rock canvas, and like a shape-shifter, it produces a style and sound that is new, and yet is still rock. No other species seems to have quite this ability—nor as many hybrid names, and not just Tier 4 obscure ones known only to a handful of devotees.

There's *blues rock* (John Mayall and the Bluesbreakers, Cream, Blues Traveler, etc.), *folk rock* (Bob Dylan, the Byrds, Simon & Garfunkel, etc.), *psychedelic rock* (Jefferson Airplane, the Doors, the Grateful Dead, etc.), *glam rock* (T. Rex, David Bowie, New York Dolls, etc.), *art rock* (Pink Floyd; Emerson, Lake, and Palmer; Genesis, etc.), *jazz rock* (Steely Dan; Blood, Sweat & Tears; Chicago, etc.), *country rock* (the Eagles, Emmylou Harris, the Band, etc.), *heartland rock* (Bruce Springsteen, Tom Petty, John Hiatt, etc.), *punk rock* (the Stooges, the Sex Pistols, Green Day, etc.), *rap rock* (Linkin Park, Rage Against the Machine, Kid Rock, etc.), *electronic rock* (Kraftwerk, Nine Inch Nails, Radiohead, etc.), among others—not to mention dozens of rock subgenres that dispense with the word, but which still imply the integration of some external musical and/or aesthetic identity: *heavy metal* (Black Sabbath, AC/DC, Korn, etc.), *grunge* (Nirvana, Pearl Jam, Stone Temple Pilots, etc.), *new wave* (Devo, Talking Heads, Tears for Fears, etc.), *emo* (Panic! at the Disco, Dashboard Confessional, My Chemical Romance), etc. And this doesn't even consider all the neo-, post-, and revival rock genres.

Above all, rock has shown an impressive ability to continually reinvent itself. Each new generation of youth finds within the rock species a musical/aesthetic means to claim an original sound—indeed, usually multiple original sounds per generation. Through it, and the cultural trappings that accompany it, rock has thus become the social context par excellence through which youth have forged their distinct subcultural identities over the past sixty years—though it's been getting a run for its money in recent decades from hip hop. And when two rock identities have come into conflict—as between the mods and rockers (mid-'60s) or between the punks and teds (late '70s)—things could get pretty explosive; more on this in Interlude F.

But as noted, each subgenre variation likewise takes on its own distinct musicological approach. This can be broadly simple (e.g., garage rock in the mid-'60s, punk rock in the late '70s) or complex (e.g., progressive and jazz rock in the late '60s to mid-'70s); it can emphasize dense and distorted electronic sounds (e.g., heavy metal and grunge in the '80s, industrial rock in the 2000s) or light and transparent acoustic sounds (e.g., folk rock in the '60s, "Americana" in the '90s); it can embrace complex harmonic progressions, atypical forms, and orchestral instruments (e.g., glam rock in the '70s, symphonic metal in the '90s) or relish three-chord verse-chorus songs and stark guitar-drum sonorities (e.g., surf rock in the '60s, post-punk revival in the 2000s), amid much more. Often multiple such tendencies will appear within the same subgenre, as indeed within songs by the same artist (e.g., the Beatles, Pink Floyd, Led Zeppelin, Elton John, Elvis Costello, Muse, Coldplay, etc.), though generally with slants toward one or two of them. How you, the listener, responds to these various musicological tendencies, and how wide or narrow the range you embrace, is then what defines your rock genotype.

All this, of course, does not negate the importance of nonmusical attributes to the appeal of, or disdain for, distinct rock subgenres and artists. Because rock, going back to its origins as "rock and roll" in the mid-'50s, has been music primarily made by and for youth, lyrical themes and social images have always been vital. Whether addressing teenage dating dressed in tailored suits (British Invasion in the early '60s), social injustice and drugs in tie-dyes and beads (folk and psychedelic rock in the mid- to late '60s), mysticism and mythology in robes or tight trousers (hard and progressive rock in the '70s), sex and anarchy with piercings and combat boots (punk in the late '70s), romance and partying in spandex and big hair (new wave in the '80s), social alienation and apathy in T-shirts and ripped jeans (grunge in the '90s), or a critique of modern suburban life in polo shirts and jelly shoes (post-Britpop in the 2000s), the extramusical element has always mattered to why kids would like this or that rock act. However, they certainly *wouldn't* like it if they also didn't like the way the music actually sounds.

"Rock and roll," as rock historian James Miller notes, was originally a "classifying device by people in business . . . a euphemism for black music, for rhythm and blues."[424*] It morphed into "rock" in the mid-1960s, a sign of its social acceptance and aesthetic coming of age: it was tough, boisterous, and here to stay. Unlike other major species, notably classical but also jazz, however, it is difficult to point to any single, overarching evolutionary trajectory over these past sixty years. Yes, there is the initial maturation of musicological, technological, and virtuosic possibilities, especially from the mid-'60s to the mid-'70s—which, indeed, is a "golden age" for many rock fans. But otherwise, rock history has consisted largely of simultaneous, often contradictory trends that rise and overlap in classical patterns of experimentation, maturity, and declining mannerism. What distinguishes them often comes down to their relationship to "the roots," as well as to the external styles—blues, soul, folk, country, classical, jazz, hip hop, electronica, etc.—that inform them. These same things, of course, help inform whether you like them or not.

* The term likely evolved from the expression "rocking and rolling"—initially describing the movement of a ship, but was likewise a common euphemism for sex among African American musicians in the early twentieth century.

## At the Gym: Led Zeppelin's "Ramble On"

**Led Zeppelin's "Ramble On"** immediately establishes Subject 2 as a serious, card-carrying devotee of classic hard rock—one aware, if not downright fond, of the touchstones listed above. The band's tremendous critical and commercial success notwithstanding, being a fan of Led Zeppelin—and especially of a slightly hidden gem like "Ramble On," as opposed to evergreens like "Stairway to Heaven" or "Whole Lotta Love," for example—means possessing a genuine, as opposed to casual, rock genotype. It suggests that howling and blues-based vocals, distorted guitar, and aggressive drumming are sonorities to embrace, not avoid. At the same time, the nuances of this song point to a complementary taste for subtle tones and acoustic timbres—not to mention a mesmerizing, syncopated groove.

### LED ZEPPELIN: BACKGROUND

Next to the Beatles, and perhaps the Rolling Stones, Led Zeppelin is arguably the most influential act in rock music history—whose music "changed things far more than anybody ever expected, or might have wanted," as Mikal Gilmore put it.[425] A now rich academic record on the band has dispelled naïve summaries that it was but a champion of musical testosterone or merely the "progenitors of heavy metal."[426] To be sure, its guitar-heavy, blues-infused sound helped fulfill an inevitable trajectory of rock music in the 1970s as loud, aggressive, and hedonistic. And yet its embrace of folk, world music, and even classical elements—increasing with each album—likewise helped confirm the eclectic and progressive promise of the species in a post-Beatles world. More impactful, perhaps, was its influence on the music industry as a whole, and especially its emphasis on live performance as a sine qua non of rock success. Its tours were legendary not only for their unprecedented scope—four-hour shows before stadium crowds of fifty thousand plus—but also for their self-indulgent escapades backstage, in hotel rooms, and on their "party plane."[427] On many levels, Led Zeppelin provided a template for rock success that no subsequent rock act could ignore.

In contrast to Creedence Clearwater Revival, most fans (and many nonfans) of Led Zeppelin know each band member by name. Virtuoso guitarist Jimmy Page was among the three future guitar legends to join the prominent mid-'60s blues rock band the Yardbirds—along with Eric Clapton and Jeff Beck. After Beck's departure in late 1966, Page set out to form his own band, and eventually teamed up with fellow blues devotee Robert Plant, then singing in the little-known group Band of Joy. Plant brought on his bandmate John Bonham on drums; bassist and keyboardist John Paul Jones, then a London-based studio musician and friend of Page, rounded out the band.

At first calling themselves the New Yardbirds, they changed their name to Led Zeppelin (originally suggested by Who drummer Keith Moon) just as they were signed to Atlantic Records in October 1968.[428] Like Fantasy, Atlantic had begun as a jazz label, but later expanded to soul, R&B, and eventually rock—through the eclectic and visionary taste of its Turkish-American founder, Ahmet Ertegun.[429] Atlantic offered Led Zeppelin (via their manager Peter Grant) a $200,000 advance, plus full artistic freedom, after hearing a tape of their self-funded debut album. This offer was rather unprecedented for a new rock band, but given their eventual two-hundred-million-plus albums sold, it clearly paid off.

In all, Led Zeppelin produced eight studio albums, plus a post-breakup collection of previously unreleased tracks (*Coda*, 1982). Each reached the Top 10 on the *Billboard* Top 200 charts, with six of them—*Led Zeppelin II* (1969), *III* (1970), *IV* (1971), *Houses of the Holy* (1973), *Physical Graffiti* (1975), *Presence* (1976), and *In Through the Out Door* (1979)—reaching the No. 1 spot. Led Zeppelin epitomizes the "AOR" (album-oriented rock) aesthetic of rock recording and radio format; indeed the band generally eschewed the release of singles. Despite this, many of their songs—even epic eight-minute offerings like "Stairway to Heaven" from *Led Zeppelin IV* and "Kashmir" from *Physical Graffiti*—received steady FM radio play at the time, just as they still do today. The band's excesses, musical and otherwise, extend even to its demise in December 1980—following the tragic alcohol-induced death of John Bonham. It is these excesses that undoubtedly repel many music lovers, just as they attract the many folks who call themselves fans and admirers, such as Subject 2.

## LED ZEPPELIN: ANALYSIS

"Ramble On" stems from the band's sophomore album, *Led Zeppelin II*, which was released in fall 1969, and was recorded at various studios in America and the UK while the band was on tour. As is typical for Led Zeppelin songs, especially up through *Physical Graffiti*, Page wrote the music and Plant penned the lyrics. The latter displays a direct reference to J. R. R. Tolkien's *The Lord of the Rings*, a favorite literary source of his used in other Zeppelin songs as well.* As Plant noted about the album as a whole, "It was still blues-based but it was a much more carnal approach to the music and quite flamboyant."

Indeed, the song is variably labeled as residing in the hard rock, folk rock, and blues rock subgenres—each of which is warranted as the 4:23 song proceeds. The latter two subgenres are immediately corroborated by virtue of the acoustic guitar riff and the repeating I–IV chord progression of the song's intro, respectively—remembering that this harmonic shift is emblematic of blues harmony (Figure 10.1):

* Notably "Misty Mountain Hop" and "The Battle of Evermore," possibly also "Stairway to Heaven."

Figure 10.1: Led Zeppelin, "Ramble On"—guitar intro

The hard rock label, then, is confirmed about one minute in, as Page's distorted electric guitar and John Bonham's heavy drumming enter the soundscape, buoyed by Plant's ever more explosive delivery.

Although Led Zeppelin, as suggested above, was not alien to complex harmony—as heard in songs like "The Rain Song" from *Houses of the Holy* and "Ten Years Gone" from *Physical Graffiti*—a good number of their songs do indulge in either extended pedal points or oft-repeating, blues-inflected chord patterns. "Ramble On" is one such case, and sits rather on the extreme side: almost the entire song maintains the two-chord progression from the intro, with one chord per measure rocking back and forth in an easygoing 4/4 bluesy groove (Figure 10.2):

Figure 10.2: Led Zeppelin, "Ramble On"—start of Verse 1

The only exception is a four-bar instrumental interlude (the second of two) about halfway through the song, which moreover rests on the IV chord. One might imagine the potential for tedium by virtue of this harmonic stasis, but such is avoided by virtue of the contrast created between the relatively mellow verses and the more explosive choruses. Such stark contrasts—or "terraced dynamics," in the words of heavy metal musicologist Robert Walser—are indeed a common trait of Led Zeppelin. As we've seen with regard to Carl Orff's *Carmina Burana*, moreover, the narrative power of dynamic contrasts is by no means limited to rock (see also Chapter 15). Helping too is the infectious groove laid down in the verses by the rhythmic strumming of the acoustic guitar, a sparse, high-register bass ostinato, and sixteenth note hand percussion played by Bonham on a closed guitar case.[430]

Plant's distinctive vocal delivery likewise plays a role in propelling the song's narrative, alternating between a generally low register and breathy timbre in the verses and a higher tessitura (centered on high B) and loud, raspy tone in the choruses. The melody itself is often monotonic and fairly improvisatory in nature, especially in the verses, by virtue of the varied prose of the lyrics. At times this leads to some interesting rhythmic play, such as the syncopated hemiola-like (3 against 2) figure in the third verse—on "How years ago in days of old when magic filled the air"; the chorus melody, by contrast, is rhythmically more defined and "on the beat," via the hook on "Ramble on" (Figures 10.3a–b):

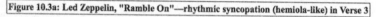

**Figure 10.3a: Led Zeppelin, "Ramble On"—rhythmic syncopation (hemiola-like) in Verse 3**

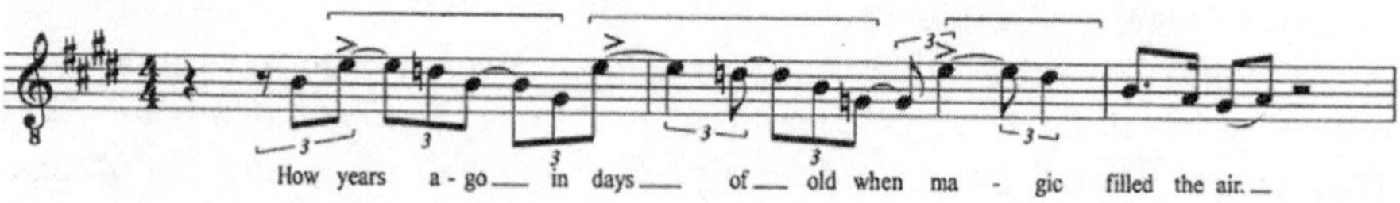


**Figure 10.3b: Led Zeppelin, "Ramble On"—rhythmic clarity ("on the beat") in chorus**

Finally, formal interest is generated by a short, syncopated pre-chorus after the first and third verses, and especially by two instrumental interludes (after Verse 2 and Chorus 2, respectively) featuring harmonized electric guitars panned left and right; the first in particular, harmonized at the tenth, brings to mind some earlier "psychedelic" folk rock songs, such as Buffalo Springfield's "Bluebird."

In all, there is much to engage Subject 2 with this song, with the driving—and at times explosive—groove a likely key source of that jolt needed at the gym.

## Heading to Work: Alabama Shakes' "Don't Wanna Fight"

**Alabama Shakes' "Don't Wanna Fight"** shares a fair bit in common with Subject's 2's first hit of the day, "Ramble On"—more than one might think at first glance. Like its British companion on the list, "Don't Wanna Fight" is hard-hitting, blues-based, and features a larger-than-life vocalist in Brittany Howard. That two songs recorded forty-six years apart could traverse so much of the same terrain demonstrates that "back to the roots" strain noted above. At the same time, "Don't Wanna Fight" reveals other stylistic influences, as well as its own unique attributes. We'll thus have to see just how narrow Subject 2's rock genotype turns out to be.

## ALABAMA SHAKES: BACKGROUND

Alabama Shakes, the alt-rock or neo-soul quintet from Athens, Alabama, arose to national prominence in a rather archetypal manner: a collection of school friends forms a band, plays for years in bars, make a self-produced EP, gets recognized by a radio DJ, gets signed by a label, and quickly jumps into the limelight.[431] Indeed, with their 2015 sophomore album, *Sound & Color*, the band went beyond cult status to broad commercial fame: the album reached No. 1 on the *Billboard* Top 200 chart and won the 2016 Grammy Award for Best Alternative Music Album; likewise, its single "Don't Wanna Fight" won the Grammy for Best Rock Song. Not bad for a small-town bar band!

At first simply called the Shakes, the band had its debut gig at a bar in Decatur, Alabama, in May 2009. Their set that night—a mix of James Brown, Aretha Franklin, Otis Redding, AC/DC, and Led Zeppelin—largely defined who they would become musically. The set shows a confluence of two powerful Tier 2 genres: hard rock and R&B/soul. The latter, moreover, reveals a "hometown" association—namely, to the so-called "Muscle Shoals school." This small town in northwest Alabama is celebrated among music aficionados for the wealth of great music recorded there in the mid-1960s and '70s. At the iconic FAME Studios, among others, soul artists like Franklin, Redding, Etta James, Wilson Pickett, and Percy Sledge recorded hard-driving hits—e.g., Pickett's "Mustang Sally" and Sledge's "When a Man Loves a Woman." This success would then inspire soul-friendly rock artists such as the Rolling Stones (e.g., "Brown Sugar") and Paul Simon (e.g., "Loves Me Like a Rock") to make the trek to Alabama and soak up that magic Southern spirit.

This attraction was then even more natural for the Athens-based quintet, moving from covers to tentative originals over the next few years. Guitarist Heath Fogg, in particular, has cited his affection for the sound: "Just about everything that's ever come out of Muscle Shoals we're fans of—you name it."[432] Other influences include more contemporary, hard-edged alternative bands such as the Red Hot Chili Peppers, Nine Inch Nails, and the Mars Volta.

Following the release of their EP and sudden radio play, the band received a slew of offers from record companies—as well as a claim of "dibs" on the name Shakes, leading to the addition of the state qualifier. By all accounts, a good measure of Alabama Shakes' success stems from the dynamic and colorful persona of their lead singer, Brittany Howard—who to varying degrees reveals the influence of singers like Janis Joplin, Bobby Womack, James Brown, Bon Scott (of

AC/DC), and—indeed—Robert Plant, whom Howard cites as a direct and powerful influence; the admiration, in fact, is mutual: Plant is a big fan of the band, and once invited them to stay at his home in Austin, Texas, during the 2012 South by Southwest music festival.[433]

## ALABAMA SHAKES: ANALYSIS

"Don't Wanna Fight," again, is the lead single from the band's 2015 sophomore release, *Sound & Color*. It peaked at No. 13 on the *Billboard* Hot Rock Songs.

Its musicological proceedings make it apparent why the song would join "Ramble On" on Subject 2's hit parade, despite the forty-six years that separate them. Most strikingly, the former is likewise defined via a two-chord "vamp"—that in this case dominates the song in its entirety! The chords here are E♭ minor 7–B♭ minor 7, a minor mode variant of the traditional I–V progression—though more a modal (Dorian) than either a tonal (e.g., i–V) or blues (e.g., i–IV) progression (Figure 10.4):

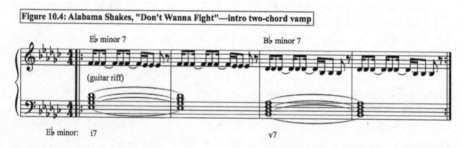

**Figure 10.4: Alabama Shakes, "Don't Wanna Fight"—intro two-chord vamp**

Two-chord vamps are, to be sure, quite common in post-1960s pop/rock, but seem to be particularly emblematic of the soul and funk styles that "Don't Wanna Fight" emulates—particularly the branch arising from Muscle Shoals. A cursory review of the output of such early 1970s soul artists as Curtis Mayfield, Bobby Womack, Donny Hathaway, Isaac Hayes, and the Isley Brothers reveals dozens of songs based on two-chord patterns, mostly of the blues variety (I–IV, i–IV, or i–iv), but occasionally—as in Womack's "Across 110th Street," Hathaway's "I Love You More Than You'll Ever Know," and the Isley Brothers' "That Lady"—using the same i7–v7 vamp as "Don't Wanna Fight."[434]

This distinct yet rather hypnotic chordal vamp (two measures per chord), in tandem with the syncopated medium-tempo 4/4 funky groove, gives the song much of its energy and appeal. And yet a driving force is, again, Howard's impassioned vocal. With her gritty tone and fiery articulation—initiated by a full-measure primordial scream that recalls James Brown (a fitting gesture to begin a diatribe against domestic strife)—Howard shows her debt not only to soul figures like Womack and Mayfield but also to rockers like Joplin and Plant.

The melodic material of the verse is built on varied repetition and resides in the lower part of Howard's range. It then becomes more distinct and "hooky" in the chorus, as it ascends ever higher. This chorus melody also aligns with a harmonic shift from the tonic E♭ minor 9 of the intro and verse to a more distinctive E♭ minor 13 (melody on C) on "*Don't wanna fight* no more," before then ascending to a screechy high F (Figure 10.5):

**Figure 10.5: Alabama Shakes, "Don't Wanna Fight"—chorus melody and harmony**

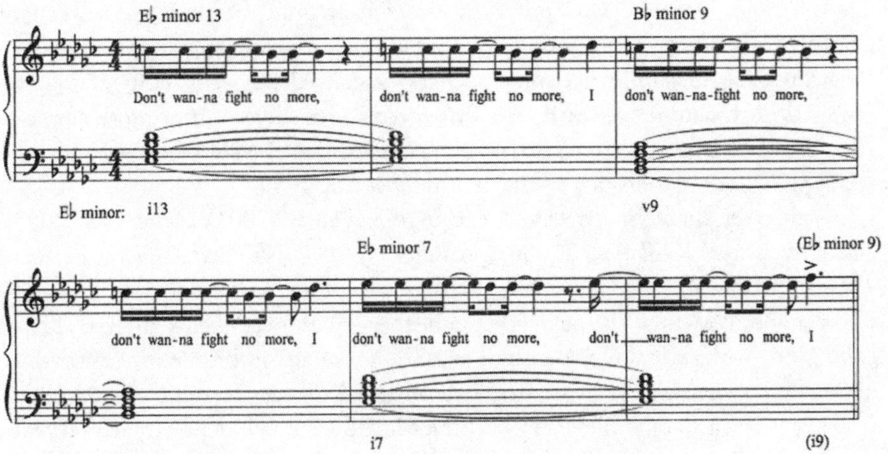


Throughout the song, sparse, syncopated ostinatos and reverb-laden chords in the guitars gently accompany Howard's tense vocal; these guitar lines likewise form the song's intro and then morph into a more atmospheric interlude midway through—that to some degree recalls some instrumental passages by Pink Floyd. In all, one can hear a variety of rock, soul, and funk attributes that understandably could have elevated "Don't Wanna Fight" to hit status for Subject 2.

## Driving Home: Muse's "Butterflies and Hurricanes"

**Muse's "Butterflies and Hurricanes"** demonstrates the risks of presuming too much about one's musical taste based on only one or two songs. While the Muse song is similar to Subject 2's earlier hits in its embrace of an edgy and aggressive rock landscape, it is also considerably more eclectic and ambitious in its musicological proceedings. Indeed, as we'll see, the song even wanders into the realm of late nineteenth-century classical music—including the use of some fairly chromatic harmony. Evidently, Subject 2 doesn't require an incessant two-chord vamp to find musical satisfaction. At the same time, if the members of Alabama Shakes themselves can find affinity between hard rock, Southern soul, and a 1990s progressive alt-rock band like the Nine Inch Nails, it is entirely reasonable that their fans can too.

## MUSE: BACKGROUND

As with CCR and Alabama Shakes, the members of the alt/progressive rock trio Muse met as youth in a small town—in their case, the English hamlet of Teignmouth, in the southwest county of Devon. And like those American bands, Muse too is by and large dominated, creatively and image-wise, by one member: singer, guitarist, pianist, and lead songwriter Matthew Bellamy—supported by bassist Chris Wolstenholme and drummer Dominic Howard.[435] By his own account, Bellamy was self-taught (starting piano from age six, guitar from age eleven), which is quite impressive given the frequent classical influence and references—e.g., to Beethoven, Saint-Saëns, Chopin, and Rachmaninov, as we'll see—evidenced in his songs.* After producing two EPs, the band landed a contract with the American label Maverick (cofounded by Madonna), leading to its first studio album, *Showbiz*, in 1999.

With every subsequent release—*Origin of Symmetry* (2001), *Absolution* (2003), *Black Holes and Revelations* (2006), *Resistance* (2009), *The 2nd Law* (2012), and *Drones* (2015)—the band has steadily expanded its profile to become one of the most popular and influential alt-rock bands in history—with over twenty million albums sold. Along with several No. 1 albums and Top 10 singles in Britain, their past three albums have earned slots in the top five on the *Billboard* Top 200—with *Drones* peaking at No. 1. Not unlike Led Zeppelin, Muse owes much of its success and reputation to its live concerts—including headlining the dominant popular music venue type of our day, the modern rock festival: Glastonbury, Lollapalooza, Outside Lands, Austin City Limits, BottleRock, etc. They've released four live albums, and have been called "probably the best live act in the world today" by no less than the drummer of Queen, Roger Taylor.[436]

Fueling Muse's success as well has been a steady expansion of its artistic and musicological horizons. Bellamy's ambitious compositional style took off from glam and progressive bands like Queen and 1990s alt-rock pioneers Radiohead, but has continued to develop via other eclectic influences with each new release—not only late-Romantic classical, but also jazz, electronica, film scores, funk, Arabic music, hard rock, and cabaret, among others. Not surprisingly, this occasionally involves the use of nonrock instruments—both orchestral, especially strings, and synthetic—though most of their songs limit the proceedings to the traditional rock template of distorted guitars, piano, bass, and drums. With their often theatrical, expansive (e.g., the three-part, thirteen-minute "Exogenesis: Symphony" on *Resistance*), and harmonically sophisticated approach, Muse may not be every traditional rock fan's cup of tea, but sometimes those same fans—such as Subject 2—need a little variety in their day.

* For example: "Space Dementia" (Rachmaninov) and "United States of Eurasia" (Chopin).

## MUSE: ANALYSIS

"Butterflies and Hurricanes," from *Absolution*, is one such ambitious and expansive song. It features chromatic harmony, prominent use of a string orchestra, and a complex form.† The song title refers to the so-called "butterfly effect" of chaos theory—where the fluttering of the insect's wings can, nonlinearly, give rise to something as grand and seemingly unrelated as a hurricane weeks later. While the theory bears only remote connection to the song's lyrical theme of "change," it does comport to its lofty ambition—especially to its fairly usual form.

At a surface level, the song might seem to conform to a traditional verse-chorus alternation, without a vocal bridge, but in many ways this is misleading. A more reliable formal construct can be seen with the use of letters, where it proceeds:

(Intro)-A-A'-B-C-A''-A''-B'-C-D-A'-B'-C

In this schema, A can be labeled the verse (A-A' being a "double verse"), B the chorus, C a short instrumental riff, and D an extended instrumental interlude. As the B section ("Best, you've got to be the best . . .") repeats the same lyrics three times, it seemingly warrants a chorus designation, and yet the first two sets of As likewise repeat the same lyric ("Change everything you are . . ."), varying only on the final, half-length A ("Don't let yourself down").

Adding to the ambiguity is the wholesale shift in vocal register—up an octave—between the melody of the first A-B pairing and the next, accompanied by a fuller orchestration. Further complexity, then, is accrued by virtue of the instrumental interludes, harmonically dominated by a polychord: G diminished 7th over A major in the bass. The first interlude—C—is a short, two-measure syncopated riff in the piano, bass, and drums (Figure 10.6):

**Figure 10.6: Muse, "Butterflies and Hurricanes"—first Section C interlude**

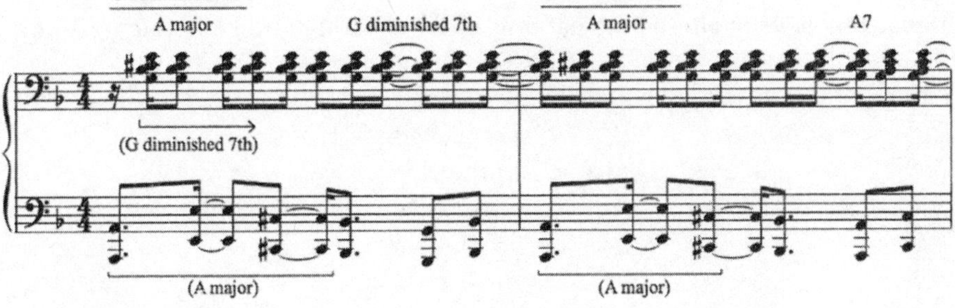


† There are in fact multiple versions of "Butterflies and Hurricanes" released, including one with guitar instead of piano, and a shorter radio edit. This analysis is based on the standard CD version.

Section D, then, is a considerably extended (1:20) instrumental interlude—that in turn can be broken into three distinct sections. Strikingly, it utilizes virtually no material from elsewhere in the song. As noted in Chapter 6, the definition of musical form and subdivision can take place on multiple levels at once—particularly when, as here, the discourse is complex.

From an experiential perspective, a driving force of "Butterflies" is its harmonic language, as noted above. The song begins (A sections) in D minor, shifting to the relative major, B♭, in the B sections, and then to D major during the extended instrumental interlude (D section). Each section, moreover, partakes in a degree of chromaticism: the A sections begin with a chromatic stepwise descent of D–C♯–C♮–B–B♭, against a D minor chord pedal, at which point a rapid and syncopated descent from D to G♯ moves us to an E7 (♭9) and then a half cadence on A7 (Figure 10.7).

**Figure 10.7: Muse, "Butterflies and Hurricanes"—Section A harmonic progression**

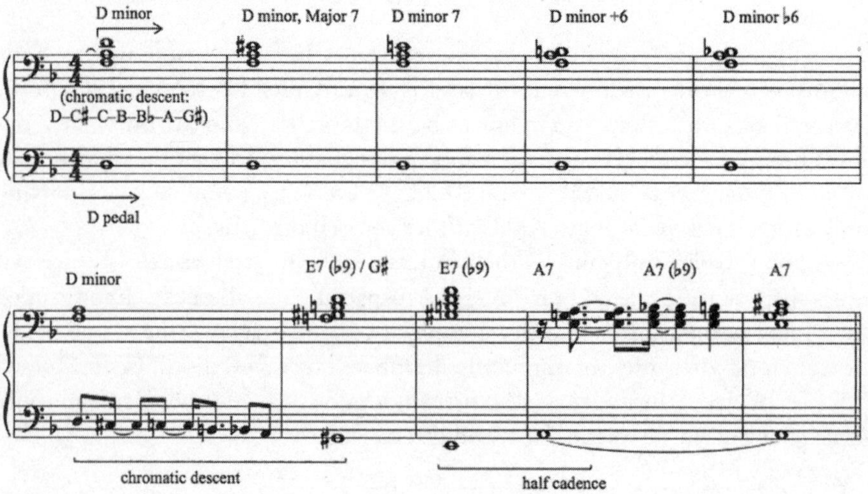


The B section similarly includes a chromatic ascent: F–D/F♯–G minor, flanked by pairs of alternating patterns of B♭–D minor and B♭–F (Figure 10.8):

**Figure 10.8: Muse, "Butterflies and Hurricanes"—Section B harmonic progression**

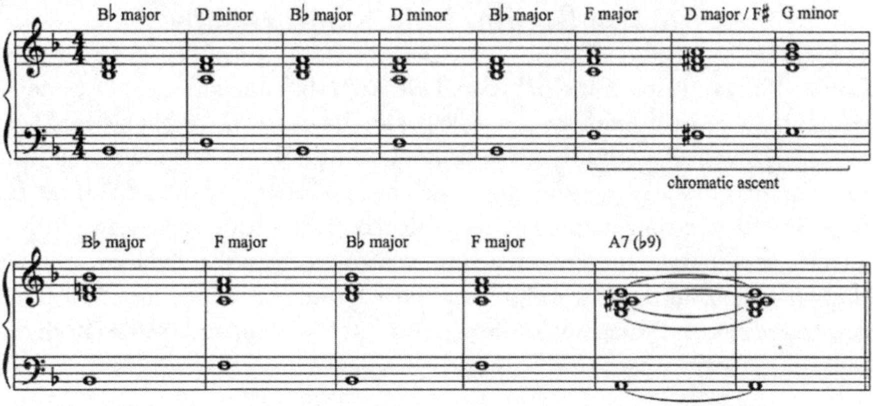


The extended interlude (D) section is likewise rather chromatic. In media accounts of the song, this is inevitably referred to as a "piano solo," with a vague reference to Rachmaninov. Specifically, the second part of the interlude (starting at 3:19) makes an oblique reference—stylistically, harmonically, and a bit thematically—to the latter's Piano Concerto no. 2 in C Minor, Op. 18, third movement, second theme. Bellamy, despite his lack of training, is able to deliver Rachmaninov-esque arpeggios and chromatic octave scales convincingly; here he indulges in the richly expressive shift from D to C minor/E♭—technically a "borrowed" Neapolitan 6th chord, a progression likewise used by Rachmaninov.[437] In its quasi-improvised, bravura manner, actively accompanied by strings, this rubato interlude dramatically breaks from the mold of most rock songs, and is certainly one of the elements that gives the song its unique listening identity.

Otherwise, "Butterflies and Hurricanes" proceeds along fairly traditional rock lines. Apart from the extended interlude, the song is in an aggressively rhythmic 4/4 medium groove—marked by the drumlike "paradiddle" pattern, as Bellamy calls it, in the electric piano. Inserted throughout, however, is a lively syncopated figure—a fairly common pattern, in fact: ♩. ♩. ♩. ♩. ♩ ♩ —used, for example, at the end of the interlude in Bruce Springsteen's "Born to Run." This figure is used in the rapid chromatic descent in the A section noted above, as well as in the C section interlude; it thus acts as a kind of unifying compositional motive for the song.

Finally, Bellamy's voice carries with it a great deal of presence and emotive identity, though is considerably less gritty than either Plant's or Howard's; in general, Bellamy's rather mannered vocal delivery perfectly matches the "gothic" and melancholy tone of the song as a whole—from the sultry low register of the first A and B sections to the breathy falsetto (up to a high B♭) of the latter B sections. In all, Subject 2 had much to musically process on that mind-clearing drive home after work.

## Dinner-Party Time: Prima's "Just a Gigolo/I Ain't Got Nobody"

**Louis Prima's "Just a Gigolo/I Ain't Got Nobody"** provides further evidence that Subject 2's rock genotype is not limited to hard-driving or blues-based hard rock songs; indeed, with this jazzy, jump-blues-type shuffle it doesn't even seem to be limited to rock, let alone of the touchstone variety. At the same time, the popular and accessible nature of this particular track—with rock associations of its own, as we'll note shortly—does not necessarily suggest that Subject 2's taste is thrown wide-open to the world of jazz. Indeed, it may better be seen to reaffirm a strong penchant for medium tempo songs with a vibrant and consistent rhythmic groove—which this tune possesses in spades.

### PRIMA: BACKGROUND

To many casual fans, singer and trumpeter Louis Prima is known only for his role in the 1967 Disney animated film *The Jungle Book*, where he voiced the sly orangutan King Louie—who aimed to steal the secrets of fire making from the boy Mowgli while singing the Sherman brothers' classic "I Wan'na Be Like You (The Monkey Song)." In many ways, the film adjusts King Louis' character to Prima's own larger-than-life personality; certainly, the iconic scene of the ape leading a musical procession through the jungle was inspired directly by a mainstay of Prima's long-standing Las Vegas act—when he and his band would march wildly through the crowd.

But Prima (1910–78) was by then near the end of a long, eclectic, and fairly prominent career.[438] His overall musical trajectory in some ways mirrors that of American popular music more broadly—from the dawn of the jazz age to the advent of rock and roll. A native of New Orleans, Prima started playing Dixieland in the '20s, led his own swing-era big band in the '30s and '40s, and transitioned to a proto-rock-and-roll jump swing combo in the mid-'50s. This latter took shape in the showbiz frontier of Las Vegas, starting at the Casbar Lounge at the Sahara hotel in November 1954: with his fourth wife, singer Keely Smith, and a sextet backup band, christened the Witnesses, and featuring arranger and tenor saxophonist Sam Butera, Prima created a sensation. Their music—about which *DownBeat* magazine stated, "No, this isn't jazz; in fact, it's down right rock 'n roll"[439]—drew huge crowds, including stars like Frank Sinatra and others of the Rat Pack. By virtue of his successful live show, Prima signed with Capitol Records, and released the first of several hit records, *The Wildest!* (1956)—and its smash single, "Gigolo/Nobody."

Underlying Prima's success was certainly his impressive and high-ranging trumpet playing, but it was his eccentric, comical, and Italian-inflected vocal style that made him a star. Prima's colorful persona and witty composing skills had been serving him well for decades prior to the Vegas gig. His early hits were generally quasi-comical numbers that highlighted his informal, often semispoken vocal antics—such as "Angelina" (1944), "Bell-Bottom Trousers" (1945), and "Chop Suey, Chow Mein" (1951). On the other hand, it was a straightforward swing tune, "Sing, Sing, Sing" (1936), that became immortalized when Jimmy Mundy arranged it for the Benny Goodman Orchestra in 1937; this latter, of course, would go on to become one of the most popular jazz recordings of all time. And yet—his role as King Louie notwithstanding—it is Prima's mid-'50s "rock and roll" material with Smith and Butera—hits like "Gigolo/Nobody," "Oh Marie," and "Old Black Magic"—for which he is most celebrated today, not least by rock fans like Subject 2.

## PRIMA: ANALYSIS

"Gigolo/Nobody" is, as the slash suggests, a medley of two distinct songs. However, by virtue of the success of Prima's paired version—and that of its later covers by the Village People (1978) and especially former Van Halen frontman David Lee Roth (1985)—it is deemed a single tune in the minds of many. Both parts date from the early twentieth century: the former is an English adaptation of a 1929 Austrian cabaret song entitled "Schöner Gigolo, armer Gigolo" that was made famous as "Just a Gigolo" by Bing Crosby in 1931; the latter is an A-A-B-A ragtime song from 1915 that became a standard after recordings made by Bessie Smith and Louis Armstrong, among others. Prima first started pairing them in the mid-1940s with his big band, and then revised it—using a dazzling arrangement by Butera—for the Las Vegas lounge act, re-created for his debut album on Capitol.

Several things give this recording its distinct and infectious listening identity. Chief among them, not surprisingly, is Prima's colorful vocal personality. Like fellow New Orleans native Louis Armstrong, Prima was a consummate **scat** (improvised vocalization) singer—something on display throughout this medley, as it was in "The Monkey Song." The most striking example here takes place during the "Nobody" section, as a fiery monotonic, triplet-rhythm vocal break just after the horn riff section (Figure 10.9):

**Figure 10.9: Louis Prima, "Just a Gigolo/I Ain't Got Nobody"—Prima scat break (lyrics approximate)**

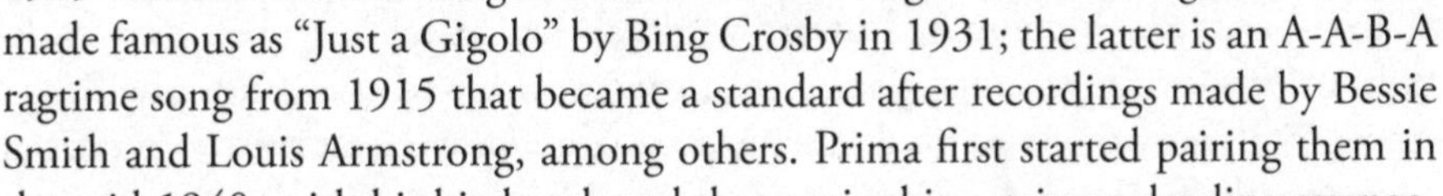

Another chief experiential factor in the medley is the bouncy "Prima shuffle" groove. This is, in fact, just one of several of his recordings that begin with a characteristic shuffle intro: a two-bar pattern in the piano, bass, and drums that outlines the harmonic progression of I–ii–V (Figure 10.10):

**Figure 10.10: Louis Prima, "Just a Gigolo/I Ain't Got Nobody"—intro shuffle pattern**

This intro pattern appears in a variety of Prima tunes, including "Pennies from Heaven," "Basin Street Blues," and "Oh Marie"—at different tempos and intensities. The version in "Gigolo/Nobody" is set in a relaxed yet driving medium-slow tempo, maintained throughout the medley. A defining element of the "Prima shuffle," not surprisingly, is the rhythmic feel provided by the drummer, Bobby Morris, an infectious groove falling somewhere between a pure shuffle and pure swing that is undoubtedly a key part of the song's—and Prima's mid-1950s—identity.

Following the intro, the medley continues with two choruses of "Gigolo"—a sixteen-bar through-composed melody. Prima's lead vocal is echoed by a background chorus on "Gigolo, gigolo," featuring Smith and the band. The song's harmony is fairly diatonic (in A♭ major), but contains a characteristic descent in its second half: A♭-G♭-F7. While not remarkable in itself, this I-to-VI progression ties "Gigolo" directly to "Nobody"—which begins with a similar chordal descent: A♭-G-G♭-F7 (Figures 10.11a–b):

**Figure 10.11a: Louis Prima, "Just a Gigolo/I Ain't Got Nobody"—I-to-VI harmonic progression in "Gigolo"**

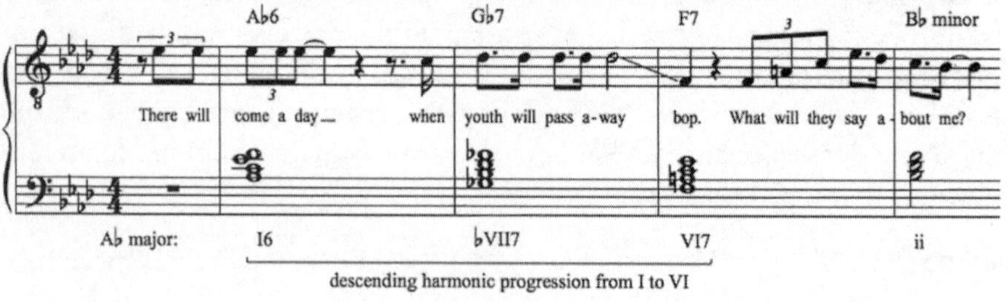

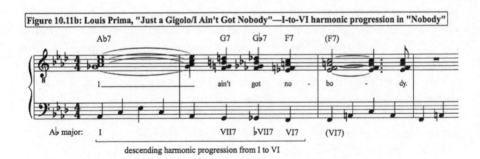

Figure 10.11b: Louis Prima, "Just a Gigolo/I Ain't Got Nobody"—I-to-VI harmonic progression in "Nobody"

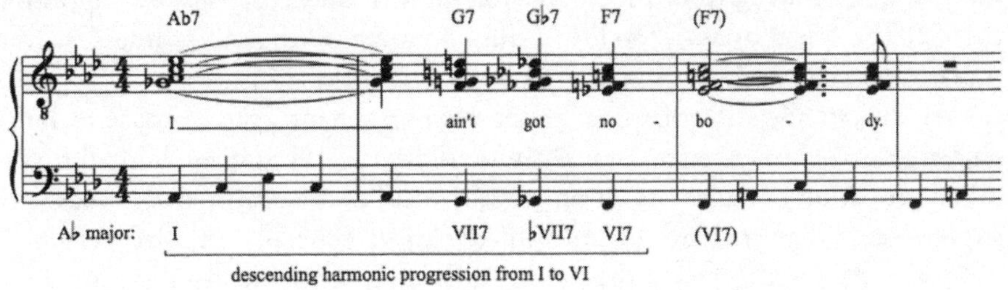


How impactful was this in Prima's decision to merge the two songs? Hard to say, but it does help explain their aural compatibility. In any event, "Nobody" is certainly the prime focus of the medley—receiving three full choruses plus an extended coda. Here, Prima's horn section steps into the fore, not only with a pair of solos in the second chorus (tenor saxophone, trombone), but also with a rhythmic riff or "shout chorus" behind Prima's vocal in the B sections. Such is typical of the jump blues (proto-rock-and-roll) style that Prima's band embraced in these years. With an ample dose of scatting and an animated vocal call-and-response during the coda (reminiscent of Cab Calloway's style thirty years earlier), the medley continually ramps up its energy before closing with Prima's signature tag (Figure 10.12):

Figure 10.12: Louis Prima, "Just a Gigolo/I Ain't Got Nobody"—signature tag ending

In point of fact, this really isn't rock and roll, despite *DownBeat*'s pronouncement to the contrary—there isn't even an electric guitar solo! But the raw energy and driving (dare we say "rockin'") groove of "Gigolo/Nobody" make its attraction to Subject 2 easy to understand.

## Insights Gained about Subject 2's Musical Taste

Seeking conclusions about the overall musical taste of our second fictional music lover, what can we say based on these five songs—the four discussed here plus the fifth (Lucinda Williams' "Are You Alright?") discussed on the WYLI website? Clearly, Subject 2 gravitates to the broad template of "rock" music, though seemingly embracing a wider circumference than is perhaps typical: from classic rock to neo-soul to progressive alternative to Americana; the preference for Louis Prima's 1956 jump swing/proto-rock-and-roll hit then only confirms the impression that Subject 2 does not put too firm a limit on genre boundaries—at least within the broader view of the rock species.

Yet we can also discern some conservative penchants: the embrace of long-repeating two-chord patterns, consistent and driving 4/4 grooves, limited rhythmic syncopation or harmonic chromaticism, etc. Likewise favored are songs with strong vocals delivered by singers with dynamic, generally emotive personalities—as is the case in each of these hits. At the same time, the complex form and harmonic sophistication of "Butterflies and Hurricanes" and the jazz inflections of "Gigolo/Nobody" reveals that Subject 2's musical sweet spot may be wider than one might think from only the first two tracks.

As we attempt to divine other songs (or works) that might appeal to Subject 2, once again we can begin with songs closely aligned to the "seeds" of the hit list—here, again, only the four songs discussed in the chapter. We thus get groove-based songs by the same artists—such as "When the Levee Breaks" (Led Zeppelin), "Hold On" (Alabama Shakes), "Uprising" (Muse), or "Jump, Jive, an' Wail" (Prima). Next up would be songs by artists residing in the same musicological space: "I'd Love to Change the World" by Ten Years After or "You Can't Always Get What You Want" by the Rolling Stones (Led Zeppelin); "They Told Me" by Sallie Ford and the Sound Outside or "Fever" by the Black Keys (Alabama Shakes); "Paradise" by Coldplay or "Warriors" by Imagine Dragons (Muse); or "Caldonia" by Louis Jordan or "It Don't Mean a Thing" by Louis Armstrong (Prima; that's a lot of Louies).

Moving to the next layer would, again, involve exploring songs by influencers on and/or "heirs" to the artists involved: the Yardbirds and Guns N' Roses (Led Zeppelin); Curtis Mayfield and James Brown (Alabama Shakes); Queen and Radiohead (Muse); and Cab Calloway and Brian Setzer (Prima). Finally, the individual musicological elements suggest yet other, more remote prospects: Muddy Waters or Woody Guthrie (harmonic patterning); the Grateful Dead or Miles Davis (modal harmony); King Crimson or Sergei Rachmaninov (complex forms and chromatic harmony); or Ella Fitzgerald or Kurt Elling (jazz scatting), to name but a few. It would remain to be seen whether any of these "outliers" would be embraced by Subject 2, but given the eclecticism we already see in these five hits, we shouldn't be surprised if they were.

*eleven*

# THE JAZZ GENOTYPE

## Introducing Subject 3

We next meet Subject 3, who begins the day on a stationary bike and a fiery workout playlist that peaks with a breakneck favorite, **Dizzy Gillespie's "Bebop."** On the way to work, something a bit mellower is needed to prepare the workday, with success coming via **Wayne Shorter's "Footprints."** After a hectic eight hours, a quiet dinner party with close friends hits a groove with **Antônio Carlos Jobim's "Águas de Março."** At last, preparing for bed, a precious favorite provides a much-needed calm: **Bill Evans' "Peace Piece."***

Subject 3's identity as a jazz fan is rather undeniable by this hit parade, and yet a level of eclecticism is strongly suggested by the inclusion of some styles and musical approaches that extend beyond the stereotypes of the realm.

Before diving into these selections, however, some words on the jazz species:

## The Jazz Species: A Brief Review

Jazz, with its complex hundred-year history, naturally defies any brief summation. Much beyond that, however, would quickly exceed the scope of this book.[440] A good bit about the origins, development, and musicology of jazz, moreover, is seeded throughout previous chapters. Thus, I'll here simply offer some overriding thoughts on this rich and hard-to-define species, focusing specifically on instrumental jazz,[†] in order to set the stage for our discussion of Subject 3's day-in-the-life picks.

---

* Subject 3's fifth song, heard on the drive home from work, is Bela Fleck and Abigail Washburn's 2014 song "Railroad." For its discussion, see the WYLI website, supplement to Chapter 11.

† This is by no means intended as a slight against vocal jazz, but simply an acknowledgment of the weightier place of instrumental jazz in the historical thrust of the species.

First, however, let's consider my proposed candidates for ten touchstone songs that typify the jazz species, as challenging as such an exercise may be:

The Bad Plus/Joshua Redman, "As This Moment Slips Away" (2015)
Wynton Marsalis, "Black Codes" (1985)
Chick Corea, "My One and Only Love" (1968)
John Coltrane, "My Favorite Things" (1961)
The Dave Brubeck Quartet, "Take Five" (1959)
Miles Davis, "So What" (1959)
Charlie Parker, "Yardbird Suite" (1946)
The Glenn Miller Orchestra, "In the Mood" (1939)
Coleman Hawkins, "Body and Soul" (1939)
Louis Armstrong, "West End Blues" (1928)

Given its ever-changing, century-long history, formulating a single list of jazz touchstones is a bit of a fool's errand; this one, though, is perhaps as good as any other in calling to mind those elements that epitomize or stereotype the species. More specifically, they all utilize acoustic instruments only, with prime focus on the trumpet, saxophone, and piano; they are all dominated by improvisation, where the soloist's technique and sophisticated approach to melody and harmony are on firm display; they all adopt a complex approach to harmony, with near constant use of altered chords; and they are all defined by swing rhythm, at least predominantly, along with a decidedly sophisticated approach to rhythm via heavy syncopation and/or odd meter. While these songs and traits epitomize one dominant strain of jazz, however, they by no means tell the whole story. Let's take a closer look.

As suggested in Chapter 10, jazz has undergone a rather more rational and traceable evolutionary trajectory than has rock—its comparatively unruly stepchild. By "evolutionary trajectory," I certainly do not mean progress. Nor do I mean any unidirectional development based on this or that musical parameter (e.g., harmony or rhythm)—although such can be traced at times. As Thelonious Monk famously said in 1957, "I don't know where jazz is going. Maybe it's going to hell."[441] There are always conservative and progressive impulses in the unfolding of art, jazz included. And, of course, one listener's "progress" is another's "going to hell." In short, art evolves, which is not to say that it improves.

Yet compared to the markedly pluralistic flow of rock history, with multiple and ever-changing styles and subgenres vibrant at any given moment, jazz has evolved with more consistency and uniformity. In this way, it resembles European classical music: a slow, steady flow from movement to movement, with gradual introductions of new techniques, forms, and subgenres (see Chapter 15). Indeed, jazz is often termed "America's classical music"—a declaration promoted by the fervent embrace of jazz education at high schools and universities around the world.

However, there are problems with this simple analogy. As *New York Times* music critic Jon Pareles put it, "Far from having to borrow status from classical music, jazz should get respect on its own very different terms." We need not review all those many differences here, but it should be remembered that at its heart, jazz is folk music, not "art" music—initially a confluence of unschooled African-American impulse with the grit and informality of ragtime, marches, and Tin Pan Alley songs.* Further, whereas the tendencies of classical styles generally endured throughout most of an individual musician's lifetime, the transitions in jazz have been considerably more frequent—in most cases, no more than a decade apart. This is a far cry from the parallel trends in rock, where most subgenres last a few years at most, but still!

Of course, this intermediate status between rock and classical seems logical. As practiced by its luminaries over the past century, jazz is in many ways the "genetic" link between these two species: a greasy, from-the-streets music that nonetheless has shown an uncanny ability to easily embrace musical elements otherwise associated with the academy: mind-bending musicological sophistication, jaw-dropping virtuosity, and a haughty demand for reverence from its listening audience.

To be sure, jazz has seen periods of vibrant stylistic diversity in its past. Most notably, the decade 1955–65 saw several simultaneously thriving styles (see below)—each with its distinct aesthetic impulses, musicological emphases, and devoted fan base. Many, in fact, look upon this fragmented period as jazz' "golden age"—when figures like Miles Davis, John Coltrane, Charles Mingus, Sonny Rollins, Bill Evans, Horace Silver, Ornette Coleman, Eric Dolphy, Dave Brubeck, and the Modern Jazz Quartet, to name but a few, were at their most prolific and creative.

By contrast, however, the active lanes in the realm's opening three decades were decidedly more uniform and sequential. The entire period of the 1920s–'50s saw a gradual, overlapping shift between only three key subgenres: Dixieland (c. 1917–29—e.g., Louis Armstrong, Fats Waller, Jelly Roll Morton, etc.), swing (c. 1930–45—e.g., Benny Goodman, Duke Ellington, Glenn Miller, etc.), and bebop (c. 1943–50—e.g., Charlie Parker, Dizzy Gillespie, Bud Powell, etc.).

Importantly, these chronological shifts corresponded to an arc in the public's conception of jazz: from endearing curiosity (1920s) to beloved mainstay (1930s) to unintelligible self-indulgence (post-1945). Bebop, by intention and sociohistorical happenstance—a declining demand for big bands, a disruptive recording ban, increased drug use by progressive musicians, growing racial friction,

---

* The word "jazz" was first used in 1912 in association with baseball to mean "lively"—a meaning it still carries today, as in "Let's jazz things up." Its association with music supposedly began when white New Orleans bandleader Tom Brown took his band to Chicago: Brown's band played so loud that the crowd angrily called the music "jazz"—meaning "too loud." The name stuck. Like "rock and roll," "jazz" also came to hold association with sex (e.g., the 1921 song "Jazz Me Blues").

etc.—took jazz from ubiquitous entertainment to underground experimentation: "Outsiders even within the jazz world, the [bebop] players had the dubious distinction of belonging to an underclass within an underclass," notes jazz historian Ted Gioia.[442] Ironically, their "outsider" innovations brought an inevitable sophistication, indeed maturation, to jazz just as the wider audience began to shift its attention to the far simpler language of jump swing—the precursor to rock and roll.

Despite its sophistication, however, bebop now became the foundation—the new "roots" if you will—of modern jazz, from which most subsequent subgenres would evolve. The techniques, influences, and aesthetics of these new styles would differ in palpable ways, but most would adopt bebop's mantle of harmonic complexity, melodic virtuosity, and a solemn reverence for the poetic musings of the improvising soloist. Bebop took jazz from being mere entertainment to becoming an experience of veneration and transcendence, at least by those "in the know."

This is no better seen than in the poetry and prose of the Beat generation—whose protagonists, like Jack Kerouac, Allen Ginsberg, and Gregory Corso, regularly attended jam sessions at the cutting-edge New York jazz clubs on 52nd Street and up in Harlem that featured Parker, Monk, and Gillespie. The writers befriended the musicians and deliberately adopted their lingo, attitude, and prosodic style into their literary works—from the quasi-improvised lines and beat-like breaths of Ginsberg's "Howl" to the hipster prose of Kerouac's classic *On the Road*. In the latter, Kerouac makes his and his peers' adoration of bebop readily apparent:

> Dean [Moriarty, a stand-in for Kerouac's friend Neal Cassady] stood bowed and jumping before the big phonograph listening to a wild bop record I had just bought called "The Hunt," with [tenor saxophonists] Dexter Gordon and Wardell Gray blowing their tops before a screaming audience that gave the record fantastic frenzied volume.[443]

Kerouac would later compose a poem to mark the untimely passing of Charlie Parker in 1955, at the age of thirty-four, noting then when Parker took a solo, he told the crowd, "All is well / You had the feeling of early-in-the-morning, like a hermit's joy . . ." The Beat writers thus helped to evangelize "modern" jazz and demand reverence for its masters. In so doing, they helped to formulate the mystical and mysterious relation—as still exists today—between jazz music and jazz lover.

Among the key post-bebop styles of jazz include: *cool jazz*, utilizing a more relaxed discourse (c. 1950–60—e.g., Davis, Chet Baker, Gerry Mulligan); *hard bop*, marked by the incorporation of soul/R&B and gospel (c. 1955–65—e.g., Silver, Mingus, Art Blakey, etc.); *bossa nova*, a fusion of jazz and Brazilian music (c. late 1950s to mid-1960s—e.g., Antônio Carlos Jobim, Stan Getz, João Gilberto, etc.); *free* or *avant-garde jazz*, embracing wildly experimental approaches akin to those taking place in classical music at the time (c. 1955–65—e.g., Coltrane, Coleman, and Dolphy, etc.); *third stream*, incorporating broader elements of classical music (e.g., Brubeck, Gil Evans, Modern Jazz Quartet, etc.); and *fusion*, a hybrid of jazz and rock (c. late 1960s to the present—e.g., Herbie Hancock, Chick Corea, John McLaughlin, etc.).

In more recent years, jazz has admittedly become a truly pluralistic species, nearly as prone to generating new hybrid styles as rock—there's smooth jazz, acid jazz, jazz rap, nu-jazz, punk jazz, etc. At the same time, the output of "mainstream" jazz (post-bebop) continues undiminished, with an endless stream of talented young musicians signing up for its rigorous technical and musicological demands—including my own son, Preston. The crossover between mainstream jazz and other styles (rock, hip hop, metal, etc.), moreover, is so ubiquitous and varied these days that subgenre labels are pointless.

And yet, in the wake of all this creative evolution, the species has seen its market share steadily decline over the years—representing only 2 percent of all record sales today. This despite the reverence paid to its icons of the past, as well as to the occasional superstar—Wynton Marsalis, Kenny G, Diana Krall, etc.—who manage to break through the pop/rock glass ceiling. All the while, the Kerouacian "in-crowd" reverence is maintained: jazz devotees—such as Subject 3—are content to listen instead of dance (preferably with a drink in their hands); they are pleased to hear their heroes play live in small clubs instead of huge arenas. And they are likely as not to echo the response Louis Armstrong purportedly gave when asked, "What is jazz?" "If you still have to ask," Louis exclaimed, "shame on you!"

## A Fiery Workout: Dizzy Gillespie's "Be-bop"

**Dizzy Gillespie's "Be-bop"** suggests off the bat that Subject 3 is a serious "jazzer" or devotee. Few music lovers would think to start their day with a tune like this except someone steeped in—and dedicated to—the species. Indeed, compared with many other staples by Gillespie, "Be-bop" is fairly obscure, even if able to qualify as a touchstone along with those cited above. By declaring this tune a hit, Subject 3 seems to announce a jazz genotype marked by a love for complex harmony and diabolical speed. We'll see how this assessment holds up.

### GILLESPIE: BACKGROUND

John Birks "Dizzy" Gillespie (1919–93) was born in rural South Carolina, the son of an amateur pianist—who housed an array of instruments on which young John could experiment. By age thirteen, he had settled on the trumpet and began sitting in with local bands. That same year, he heard a broadcast of a concert at the Savoy Ballroom in New York by Teddy Hill and His Orchestra with trumpeter Roy Eldridge—among the most progressive players of the day. Gillespie was hooked, and now dedicated himself to becoming a professional jazz musician in the mold of Eldridge: virtuosic, rhythmically fierce, and with a huge range. After much intense practicing—"woodshedding" in musician-speak—like learning Eldridge's solos note for note, Gillespie moved to New York, in 1937. Almost immediately, at that same Savoy Ballroom, Gillespie had a chance encounter with Hill, who invited him to fill in for his hero on a European tour. By then, Gillespie had acquired the nickname "Dizzy," by virtue of his odd and clown-like antics—such as carrying his trumpet around in a paper bag.[444]

Gillespie followed his stint in Hill's band with gigs in other high-profile, New York–based groups—most notably those of singer Cab Calloway (1939), pianist Earl Hines (1943), and singer Billy Eckstine (1944). All were vital to the young musician's growth, both on and off the stage. From Calloway (famed for the theatrical scat tune "Minnie the Moocher"), Gillespie picked up a taste for eccentric attire and a kooky stage presence—which would distinguish him from his fellow, otherwise stone-faced beboppers. More importantly, he began to expand his musical vocabulary, harmonically and technically. Gillespie also met other young musicians who shared his progressive vision—notably drummer Kenny Clarke and alto saxophonist Charlie Parker. "I was astounded by what the guy could do," Gillespie said of first hearing Parker in his native Kansas City in 1940. "Charlie Parker and I were moving in practically the same direction too, but neither of us knew it."[445]

The Gillespie-Parker partnership didn't begin to develop, though, until 1942, when Parker joined Hines' band. Particularly significant were the late-night jam sessions at Harlem nightclubs like Minton's Playhouse on 118th Street—whose "house band" included Clarke on drums, Thelonious Monk on piano, and Charlie Christian on guitar. These near-mythical jam sessions gestated a new post-swing language built upon fast tempos, altered chords, complex syncopations, and overlapping phrases. Yet, as Gillespie himself noted, the intention was not a revolution: "It was just trying to get a new image of the music—not necessarily revolutionary, but evolutionary."[446] The term "bebop" (or "rebop"), by the way, can be credited to the '40s musicians themselves, scatting nonsense syllables to their as-yet-unnamed tunes.* Due to a prolonged recording ban (1942–44), there is sadly little direct evidence of this fertile period of experimentation. Indeed, only a handful of small-label studio and live concert recordings of Gillespie and Parker between 1945 and 1953 exist at all.[447]

---

* As Gillespie explained (in the same 1972 interview): "We'd be on the stand on 52nd Street—I'd say 'Max Is Makin' Wax,' the title of the tune. They wouldn't even know what I was talking about! So I'd say: be-op-a-dop-a-doo-doo-de-be-bop, and they knew exactly what I'm gonna play. Most of the things we played ended on bebop or something like that when you hum it. So the people started coming up asking: 'Hey, play that song!'—'What song?'—'That song that goes bebop?' And they just picked it up from there, and then the writers started saying that we're playing 'be-bop music.'"

By the early 1950s, moreover, the musical winds were blowing in new directions. Gillespie had already turned his attention back to the big band format in 1946, now under his own direction. While continuing to play and promote bebop, he also began experimenting in Afro-Cuban jazz—fusing bebop with the rhythms of Cuban music—notably in collaboration with conga player Chano Pozo (e.g., the seminal hit "Manteca"). Until his death in 1993, Gillespie maintained a high profile as a virtuosic player, a generous teacher—especially to trumpet players like Miles Davis, Jon Faddis, and Arturo Sandoval—and a potent ambassador of jazz around the world.

## GILLESPIE: ANALYSIS

The tune "Be-bop" was written by Gillespie in 1944 or '45, and first recorded by the trumpeter, along with tenor saxophonist Don Byas, on January 9, 1945—on a session that likewise first captured his classic "Salt Peanuts."[448] "Be-bop" never achieved the currency of other Gillespie tunes like "A Night in Tunisia" or "Groovin' High," but it has been recorded by many great jazz players, including Charlie Parker, Milt Jackson & John Coltrane, Bud Powell, and Stan Getz & Sonny Stitt, among others—as well as several times by Gillespie himself. Subject 2's version stems from a 1963 studio recording under Gillespie's leadership, called *Something Old, Something New*, featuring tenor saxophonist James Moody and pianist Kenny Barron.

True to its name, "Be-bop" is a barn burner, clocking in at around 320 beats per minute, making the tempo itself a defining factor of the listening experience—and surely a speed motivator for Subject 2 on the stationary bike. Like many Gillespie tunes, "Be-bop" includes a distinct and well-defined intro that is inevitably included in any recording or performance: a ten-bar unison passage whose triplet pickup establishes the tune's key of F minor; in its "undulating" (ascending *and* descending) contour, a mix of scale and arpeggio, this syncopated intro melody is a microcosm of the bebop melodic language, and immediately establishes to the listener that the musicians mean business (Figure 11.1):

**Figure 11.1: Dizzy Gillespie, "Be-bop"—unison intro melody**

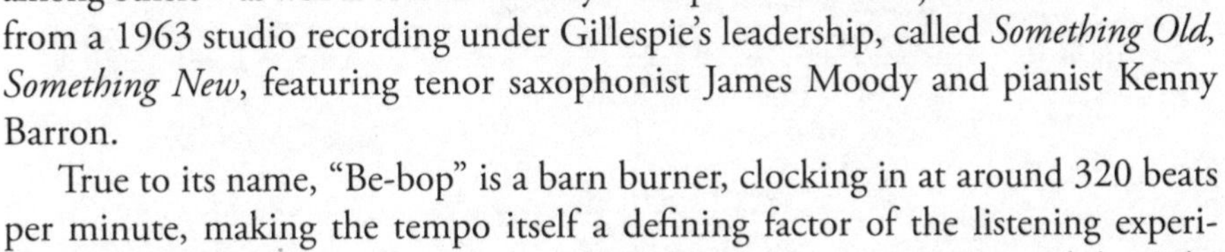

The main body of the song itself is fairly conventional. Like most "bop" tunes, "Be-bop" resides in a 32-bar A-A-B-A form, and is relatively diatonic. The A section remains on F minor, with auxiliary ii–V chords, as it supports an ascending melody composed largely of skipping 3rds. The B section provides contrast: harmonically, it proceeds as a pair of quickly modulating ii–V–I chords, in E♭, then D♭, progressing as it does through the Circle of 5ths (in reverse actually, thus better labeled the Circle of 4ths)—F–B♭–E♭–A♭–D♭—before a ii–V in F minor returns us to the final A section; melodically, it proceeds as a two-part sequence that in many ways is an archetype of a bebop solo: a rapid, near-steady descent of eighth notes, creatively mixing half steps, whole steps, and leaps (Figure 11.2):

**Figure 11.2: Dizzy Gillespie, "Be-bop"—melody and phrase structure of "head" (Sections A and B)**

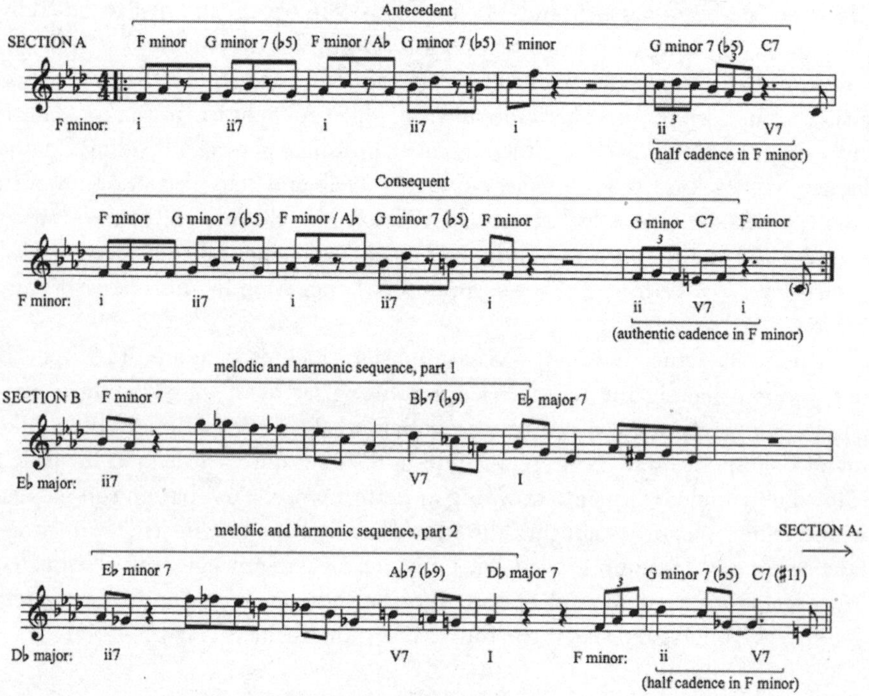


Of course, the main experiential thrust of "Be-bop," as with most jazz recordings, is the solo (improvisational) section. The solo order proceeds: Moody (four choruses), Gillespie (six choruses), and Barron (three choruses)—demonstrating their respective billing on the record. Given the high velocity of the tune, a major consideration is the degree to which each soloist can artfully and fluidly articulate steady streams of eighth notes (each proceeding at the rate 10.7 per second!). Not surprisingly, all three rise to the occasion, each warranting that esteemed jazz moniker: "shredder."

Gillespie, in particular, dazzles with at times highly extended passages of nonstop eighth notes: in one case for twenty-two straight measures (starting at 2:53)! This is the kind of electric energy that must have floored the early fans of bebop. More common, though, are shorter bursts of eighth notes, alternating with rhythmic or sustained phrases, often built out of sequences or metric syncopations (as Moody does at around 1:36). Barron, only twenty years old at the time, struggles a tad more than his counterparts at the rapid-fire challenge, but still delivers a "tasty" solo, and presages the great career he'd forge for himself over the next five decades.

Following Barron's solo, the song reprises the head, followed by a return of the intro melody, concluding this time with a quirky, prolonged tag, emphasizing the tritone—at last allowing Subject 3 to take a needed breath (Figure 11.3):

**Figure 11.3: Dizzy Gillespie, "Be-bop"—concluding "quirky" tag**

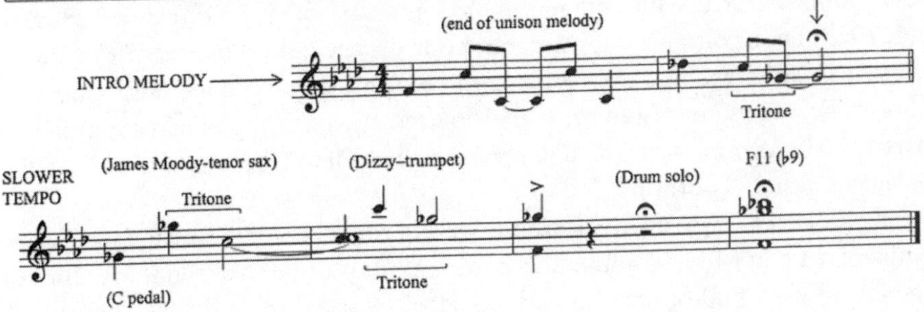


## On the Way to Work: Wayne Shorter's "Footprints"

**Wayne Shorter's "Footprints"** maintains our impression of Subject 3 as a serious and devoted jazz fan. "Footprints," it is true, has become a somewhat rare commodity for this species—a post–Tin Pan Alley "standard"—and yet it is one that is little known outside circles of jazz cognoscenti. This recording likewise builds up a picture of a jazz genotype that resides squarely within the realm's "mainstream."

### SHORTER: BACKGROUND

Wayne Shorter may not be the seismic jazz "evolutionary" Gillespie was, but few others have helped to define so many distinct styles in jazz: hard bop, post-bop/ "mainstream," modal jazz, free jazz, and jazz fusion. Perhaps only Miles Davis, Shorter's one-time boss, can claim greater influence in this regard. Born in 1933 in Newark, New Jersey, Shorter was initially attracted to the visual and cinematic arts. That changed in 1947, in ways strangely parallel to Gillespie's experience fifteen years earlier: while listening to a radio broadcast with his family, the thirteen-year-old Shorter heard music that was new and intoxicating: bebop—recordings by Monk, Parker, and Bud Powell. He later recalled, "My ears perked up when I heard it, and something must have clicked, 'cause I wasn't into music at all."[449] Soon, however, he picked up the clarinet, switching to tenor saxophone in high school. By graduation, he had committed to a life in music—determined to emulate his bebop idols.

Shorter landed his first big break in 1959, playing with drummer Art Blakey's Jazz Messengers—the archetypal hard bop combo, and a famed breeding ground for young jazz players for decades.[450] There he established a reputation as a gifted tenor player, but also as an imaginative composer, with songs like "Lester Left Town." Among his admirers, particularly of his composing work, was Miles Davis—whose "first classic quintet" (with John Coltrane, Bill Evans, etc.) had helped define cool jazz in the late 1950s. So when Coltrane left to pursue his own group in 1961, Miles offered Shorter the post; he turned it down. But by late 1963, after going through several tenor players, Miles increased the courtship—just as he was assembling his hard bop/post-bop "second classic quintet." Shorter now consented, and through 1968 recorded a string of classic albums as part of Miles' group—for which he wrote such modern jazz standards as "E.S.P.," "Nefertiti," and "Footprints."

But Shorter's legacy would extend well beyond his role as a sideman. Even while playing in Miles' quintet, he recorded albums under his own leadership for the famed hard-bop-oriented Blue Note label. Shorter's style likewise continued to evolve—moving into modal jazz, free jazz (e.g., his 1969 album *Super Nova*), and jazz fusion. This latter style took form not least under Miles' leadership, with two albums from 1969: *In a Silent Way* and *Bitches Brew*;[451] Shorter, now playing soprano sax, was a guest on both. In 1971, he went further: leading the influential fusion band Weather Report, along with pianist-composer Joe Zawinul, until 1986. In the years since, Shorter has produced a steady flow of recordings in multiple jazz styles—including as a guest with rockers like Joni Mitchell and Carlos Santana. Considering Shorter's eleven Grammys and untold honors, his fans—like Subject 3—would likely concur with the *New York Times*' "standard line" on Shorter (in 2013): "The greatest living composer in jazz, and one of its greatest saxophonists."[452]

## SHORTER: ANALYSIS

In Shorter's words, "Footprints" was initially written "when Miles asked me for something to play at gigs."[453] Trying to emulate the cool tone of tunes on the latter's famed *Kind of Blue* album (1959), Shorter took the template of a triple-rhythm-feel blues (as in "All Blues"), but then went someplace entirely new. Shorter actually recorded two quite distinct versions of the song in close proximity—one with a quartet under his own leadership and another with Davis' quintet, for the album *Miles Smiles*, released in February 1967.* The latter version is the more well-known, and indeed the one embraced by Subject 3. It features, beyond Davis and Shorter, the famed rhythm section of the "second classic quintet": pianist Herbie Hancock (also appearing on Shorter's quartet version), bassist Ron Carter, and drummer Tony Williams. The 9:46 recording is a serious and progressive embodiment of late 1960s jazz, variably labeled post-bop, modal jazz, and even "experimental" jazz.

"Footprints" is based on a blues—a minor blues, to be specific—and indeed the head is twelve bars long, as one would expect of the form. Yet it takes this musical template, and the listener, to quite different terrain. "Footprints" follows harmonic expectations in its opening eight bars—moving from C minor to F minor and back to C minor, thus i–iv–i. But whereas a "traditional" minor blues would then make its way to G7 (V7), Shorter's tune instead uses the following complex progression (bars 9–10): F♯ minor 11(♭5)–B7(♯9)–E7(♯9, ♯11)–A7 alt (Figure 11.4):

**Figure 11.4: Wayne Shorter, "Footprints"—chords used in head**

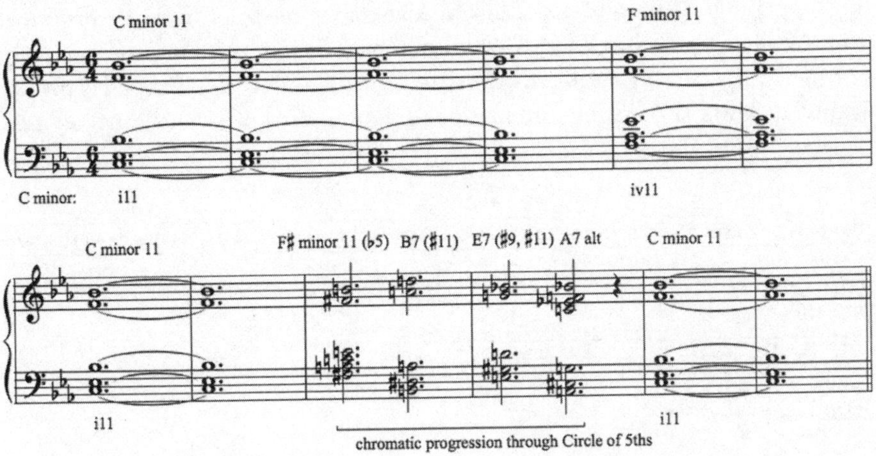


This progression, like the B section in "Be-bop," moves through the Circle of 5ths (in reverse), but nowhere is the expected G7 chord; instead "Footprints" goes straight from the A7 alt back to C minor for its final two bars. This combination of traditional blues harmony (measures 1–8, 11–12) with unexpected and dramatic chromaticism at the "turnaround" (measures 9–10) is a major source of the song's distinct identity and, undoubtedly, its strong appeal among jazz musicians.

---

* Shorter first recorded the song for his own solo album *Adam's Apple* in February 1967, and only then in October with Miles' quintet for the album *Miles Smiles*, yet the Miles album was released ten months before Shorter's—which in part may explain its greater celebrity.

Likewise distinct—and complex—is the rhythmic language of "Footprints." Again, like "All Blues," "Footprints" utilizes a triple feel. But whereas the Davis tune is written in a fairly conventional compound duple (6/8), "Footprints" is explicitly written in 6/4 meter. Technically, 6/4 (six quarter notes per measure) is an "odd" meter, as opposed to 6/8, which is divided into two beats of three eighth notes each (see Chapter 5). This is established in the opening bass figure (Figure 11.5):

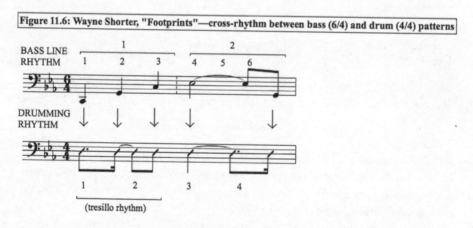

**Figure 11.5: Wayne Shorter, "Footprints"—bass line intro**

And yet, in these opening bars of the recording, a triple feel is clearly heard, revealing not an unsubdivided six-count, but rather a triple-count broken into two "beats": *1*-2-3, *4*-5-6—that is, compound duple. But wait, there's more! As the song progresses—and especially during the long solo section—drummer Tony Williams introduces a cross-rhythm that calls into question the bass line's 6/4 meter. Specifically, Williams turns that bass line into a syncopated pattern against a slower 4/4 meter (often felt in "double time"), via his fancy cymbal playing (Figure 11.6):

**Figure 11.6: Wayne Shorter, "Footprints"—cross-rhythm between bass (6/4) and drum (4/4) patterns**

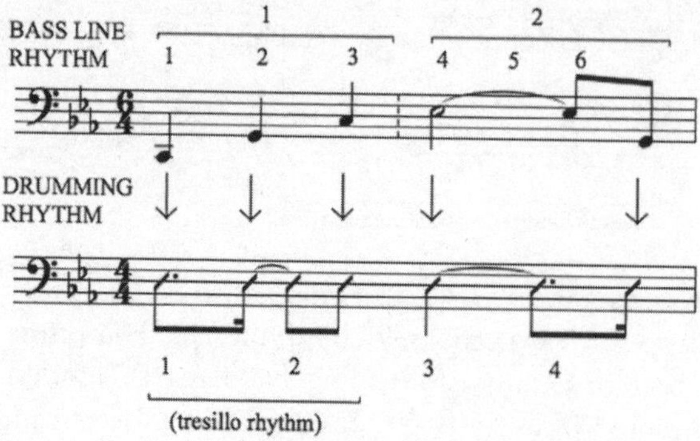


Those paying rapt attention will note that the first part of this syncopation is none other than the tresillo rhythm we encountered in Elle King's "Ex's & Oh's." In various permutations throughout the recording, Williams reinforces or obfuscates this 4/4 meter superimposition against the steady six-beat bass pattern played by Carter. So, which is the correct meter of the song: 6/4 compound-duple or syncopated 4/4? The answer, of course, is both—at times in alternation, at times in combination. To add to the fun, the actual melody of "Footprints" introduces its own complexity and syncopation—e.g., with a quintuplet (5:3) in measure 2 (Figure 11.7):

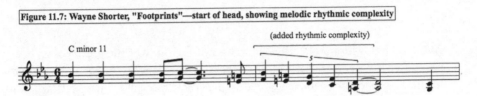

**Figure 11.7: Wayne Shorter, "Footprints"—start of head, showing melodic rhythmic complexity**

The combined richness of its harmonic, rhythmic, and melodic language is certainly a big part of the appeal of "Footprints." But no less so is its power as a template for improvisation—which begins following a double chorus of the head. Most prominently, the song enables Davis to showcase his unique style, melodic inventiveness, and trademark "mystical" trumpet tone (pinched notes and all): through eight choruses, Davis runs the gamut from short, jagged fragments to sustained repeated figures to intricate, often chromatic scale patterns, etc. This is not the dazzle of Gillespie on "Be-bop," but rather a musical "storyteller," floating above the ever-shifting sands of the song's harmony and rhythm. Shorter himself is next, with five choruses. *Miles Smiles* was Shorter's second album with the Davis Quintet, again filling the chair once held by Coltrane (1955–60); he was thus still finding himself as a soloist, and his performance at times lacks a bit of focus—though a fire begins brewing in the middle of the fourth chorus (at around 5:30) that is sustained through to the end. Hancock then takes a three-chorus solo that is predominantly chordal—indeed, quite dissonant and rhythmically angular, recalling Thelonious Monk a bit. "Footprints" concludes with a returned double chorus of the head, followed by an interlude-like drum solo by Williams, another head chorus, and a fading vamp.

It is interesting to contemplate how much of these musicological intricacies were discerned by Subject 3 while listening to "Footprints." But regardless, they all played a role in the listening experience—and in it obtaining the coveted hit status. With the broad fame of this recording among jazz fans, and the song itself among jazz musicians (recorded by over sixty different artists), Subject 3 is clearly not alone.

## A Quiet Dinner Party: Jobim's "Águas de Março"

**Antônio Carlos Jobim's "Águas de Março"** continues to expand Subject 3's eclectic embrace of jazz, with a foray into international influences. A new picture is thus emerging with this recording—of a jazz fan who seeks out distinctive works both within and without the conventional mainstream of the species. At the same time, nothing yet stretches too far into the avant-garde or sonically extreme, thus suggesting that Subject 3 has limits to what is deemed musicologically "acceptable." We'll see if this holds up through the rest of this musical day.

## JOBIM: BACKGROUND

Antônio Carlos Jobim (1927–94) has been called "one of the greatest pop composers of his time," if not of the entire twentieth century.[454] His fame lies chiefly in the dozens of bossa nova standards that took root in his native Brazil, and then internationally. Jobim (known affectionately as "Tom") was born into a middle-class family in Rio de Janeiro, near the beach districts of Copacabana and Ipanema. This city—known for its natural beauty, seductive samba music, and desperately poor slums, or "favelas"—would play a dominant role in informing Jobim's unique output: "I was a beach boy, and I believe I learned my songs from the birds of the Brazilian forest."[455] As with the preceding artists in Subject 3's hit parade, Jobim was first drawn to music in his teens, after his stepfather bought him a piano. His initial passions were Brazilian popular music and jazz (e.g., Miles Davis and Gil Evans), and yet he received formal lessons in classical composition, orchestration, and harmony—including from Hans Koellreutter, a German-born 12-tone composer who immigrated to Brazil in the 1930s!

After briefly studying architecture, Jobim committed to a life in music in his early twenties, playing piano in bars (called *inferninhos*, or "little hells") and nightclubs in Rio, and working as an arranger for local record labels. In so doing, he absorbed a variety of musical influences—from Pixinguinha (the "father" of Brazilian pop music) to cool jazz to the Impressionist composers Debussy and Ravel—and began forging his unique take on the *bossa nova*, or "new trend," stirring in Rio in the 1950s. His first big break came in 1959, when a few of his songs—cowritten with poet Vinicius de Moraes—appeared in the Academy Award–winning Brazilian film *Black Orpheus*. Most consequential, though, was the international sensation created when tenor saxophonist Stan Getz recorded several of his songs in the early 1960s: the album *Getz/Gilberto* (1963), featuring vocalists João and Astrud Gilberto, became a popular and critical blockbuster—winning five Grammys, including Album of the Year (rare for a jazz album) and Record of the Year for the hit single "Girl from Ipanema."[456]

Since *Getz/Gilberto*, Jobim's songs have been recorded by scores of the most celebrated vocalists and instrumentalists across virtually all genres: Frank Sinatra, Queen Latifah, Oscar Peterson, Kenny G, Amy Winehouse, James Galway, the Vienna Boys' Choir, to name a few. Among the most popular songs are "Wave," "Corcovado," "Chega de Saudade," "Desafinado," and especially "Girl from Ipanema"—recorded over 240 times! Jobim himself also enjoyed a successful career as a recording artist, primarily as an accompanist (including three albums with Sinatra), but also as a vocalist—as in "Águas de Março." By his death at the age of sixty-seven, Jobim was a true living legend, and the recipient of countless awards and accolades. The world, indeed, seems to have fallen in love with the mellow, harmonically rich, and intoxicating grooves of bossa nova—and most especially as rendered by Jobim.

## JOBIM: ANALYSIS

Bossa nova, again, grew out of various forms of Brazilian popular music in the late 1950s—the first commercial hit being "Bim-Bom" (1958) by vocalist-guitarist João Gilberto. Specifically, the style developed as a more mellow and "refined" version of samba—the vibrant, percussive musical/dance style that for many symbolizes Brazilian culture. Like samba, bossa nova features a multilayered and syncopated rhythmic pattern in the accompaniment, with a general emphasis on beat 2—such as this (Figure 11.8):

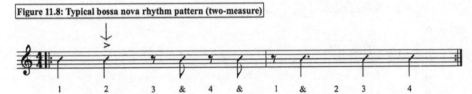

**Figure 11.8: Typical bossa nova rhythm pattern (two-measure)**

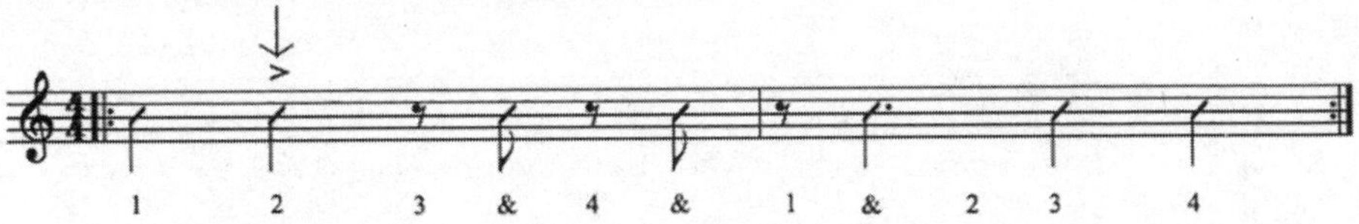


Unlike samba, however, bossa nova tends to feature a slower tempo, a toned-down percussion regimen, a simple strumming acoustic guitar, light vocal delivery, and—especially in the hands of a composer like Jobim—more sophisticated and jazz-inflected harmonies. As noted above, Jobim's take drew upon earlier Brazilian popular composers like Pixinguinha, as well as modern jazz and the Impressionist harmonies of Debussy and Ravel. Few of his compositions display this wealth of stylistic alchemy better than "Águas de Março," written in 1972.

"Águas de Março," or "Waters of March," never had the widespread fame of some other Jobim songs, but it is by no means obscure. It has been recorded dozens of times by artists ranging from Art Garfunkel to David Byrne to Al Jarreau to Cassandra Wilson. Arguably the "definitive" recording is a 1974 vocal duet by the composer and female singer Elis Regina—among the most celebrated Brazilian vocalists of her time; this, moreover, is the recording beloved by Subject 3. This 3:35 version features a simple arrangement of two guitars, piano, rhythm section, and a small orchestra of unison strings, flute, and horns.

The most striking musicological element of "Águas de Março," as revealed in this recording, is its combined harmonic structure and melodic character. The former instantly draws our attention with an unusual voicing in the four-bar guitar intro: a B♭ major triad with an A♭ in the bass—that is, a B♭7 chord with the seventh on the bottom. This establishes a level of harmonic ambiguity while also setting up a descending trajectory in the bass in the following eight bars. Indeed, a "trajectory of descent" underlies the composition as a whole—inspired by its lyrics (also by Jobim): a series of poetic images of the continual fall and flow of rain, as well as items both natural and man-made (wood, stone, slivers of glass, etc.), during the perennial storms of March in Rio de Janeiro. As the vocals enter, the bass initiates its descent—A♭–G–G♭–F–E–E♭—below chords in both root position and inversion, before circling back to B♭ via A♭7, creating a cadential chord progression worthy of Debussy.

In contrast to the descending nature of the harmony—almost as a foil—is the song's static melody: a perpetual, rhythmic ostinato built out of a motive of a falling major 3rd, from D to B♭. This acts as a kind of pedal point (on B♭) over which the harmony carries out its stepwise descent—reminiscent of what happens in the A section of Jobim's famed "One Note Samba." Here is this combined harmonic-melodic interaction from measures 5 through 12 of "Águas de Março" (Figure 11.9):

**Figure 11.9: Antônio Carlos Jobim, "Águas de Março" (mm. 5–12)—Section A melody and harmony**

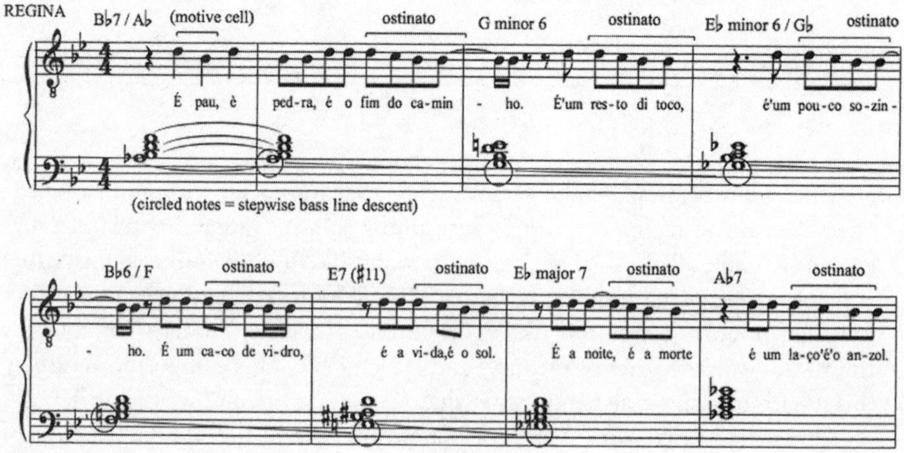


The overall song form eschews traditional A-A-B-A or related schema, as are generally adopted by Jobim, and instead proceeds as a sort of "stream of consciousness" alternation between two complementary sections: the one described above (Section A), and one where the melody jumps to the upper B♭ before descending to G and then G♭ (Section B; see Figure 11.10):

**Figure 11.10: Antônio Carlos Jobim, "Águas de Março" (mm. 17–20)—Section B melody and harmony**

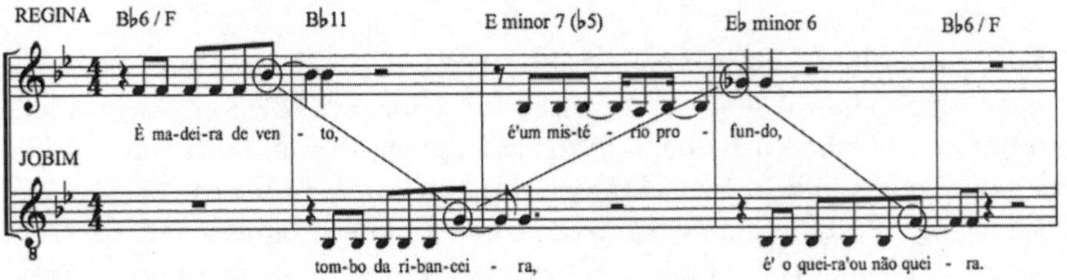


(circled notes = descending melodic line)

As the song continues, harmonic and melodic variation are introduced, to be sure, especially in its second half. Most palpable is the repeated use of a B♭ pedal below descending triads (D♭/B♭–C/B♭–B/B♭–B♭) accompanying a minor variant of the melodic ostinato (D♭–B♭)—starting at 2:20 (Figure 11.11):

**Figure 11.11: Antônio Carlos Jobim, "Águas de Março" (mm. 96–100)—closing section with B♭ pedal**

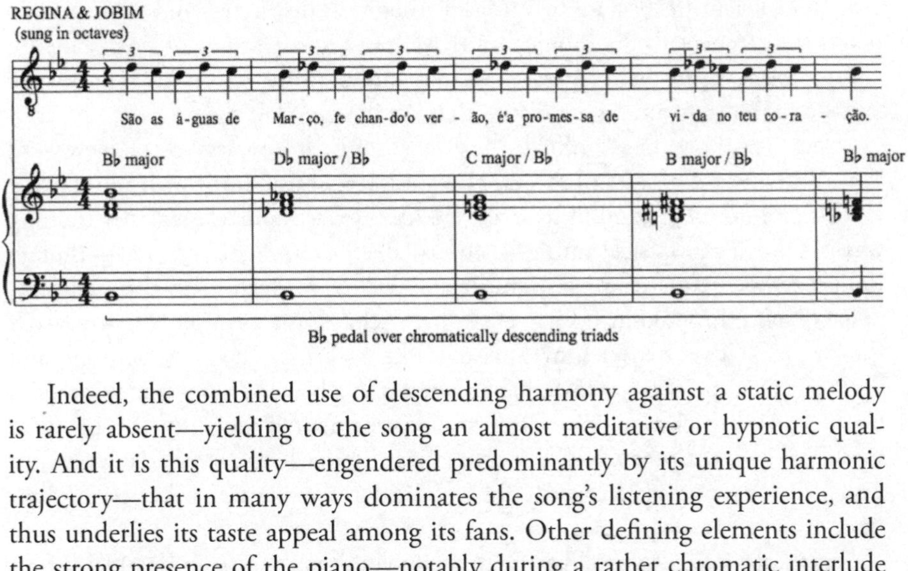


Indeed, the combined use of descending harmony against a static melody is rarely absent—yielding to the song an almost meditative or hypnotic quality. And it is this quality—engendered predominantly by its unique harmonic trajectory—that in many ways dominates the song's listening experience, and thus underlies its taste appeal among its fans. Other defining elements include the strong presence of the piano—notably during a rather chromatic interlude (at 1:48), made strangely "out of tune" by accompanying whistling. Striking too is the playful back-and-forth between Jobim and Regina on vocals—at times alternating phases, at times in unison, and at times dividing phrases in an almost *Klangfarbenmelodie* fashion (see Chapter 7). All of this combines to form a fun and quite original recording, one that understandably contributed to the vibe of Subject 3's dinner party.

## Calm Before Bedtime: Evans' "Peace Piece"

**Bill Evans' "Peace Piece"** brings Subject 3's day to a close in near total sonic opposition to how it so intensely began with Gillespie's "Be-bop"—with a level of meditative calm rarely found in the jazz canon. This, in other words, is not a typical touchstone of jazz. However, this selection *is* a beloved "hidden gem" among devotees of its highly esteemed pianist-composer, Bill Evans. As such, the tune solidifies our conception of Subject 3 as possessing a jazz genotype largely grounded in the mainstream of the species, and yet also one that embraces a rather broad-scoped notion of its viable styles and modes of execution.

### EVANS: BACKGROUND

As Miles Davis is on the trumpet and John Coltrane is on the tenor saxophone, so is Bill Evans (1929–80), in the minds of many jazz fans and musicians, the quintessence of mastery on the piano—and especially during those "golden years" of the late 1950s and early '60s. Through his distinctive and sophisticated piano style, especially harmonically, as well as a small group of now-standard compositions, Evans has bequeathed a tremendous influence on the trajectory of jazz—and not only among pianists—that is still being felt today.[457]

Evans was born in Plainfield, New Jersey, a bedroom suburb of New York City. Both he and his older brother, Harry, took to music early, with Bill starting lessons on both piano and flute, from age six. As was standard, his early training was grounded in classical music—Mozart, Beethoven, Schubert, etc.—though unlike many "mainstream" jazz musicians, Evans' dedication to this realm remained solid throughout his career. In high school, for example, he discovered the music of twentieth-century masters like Debussy, Ravel, Stravinsky, and Darius Milhaud—thereby fostering an interest in advanced harmonic techniques like polytonality, chromaticism, Impressionism-oriented modality, etc. Likewise significant was the music of J. S. Bach, especially the *Well-Tempered Clavier*—to which Evans returned frequently for technical assistance and coloristic inspiration.

Evans' attraction to jazz likewise began in childhood, initially via older genres like Dixieland and big band, then gradually via progressive pianists like George Shearing, Nat King Cole, and most significantly bebop pioneer Bud Powell, who became a huge influence.[458] Although he studied classical piano and flute at Southeastern Louisiana University, by 1950, at age twenty-two, Evans had made a commitment to a career in jazz and moved to New York City. Over the next six years, which included a three-year stint in the army, he perfected his craft and developed a unique approach to harmony, improvisation, and emotional expression. Initially his style was harshly attacked—to which he responded with deep insecurity and reclusiveness, in turn feeding a destructive vulnerability to drug abuse that would plague him the rest of his life.

Gradually, though, musicians took notice. One significant break came in 1956 when the experimental composer-theorist George Russell hired Evans for an ambitious recording project—*Jazz Workshop*—putting into practice the ideas he had set forth in his 1953 treatise, *Lydian Chromatic Concept of Tonal Organization*. In short, Russell's theory helped solidify a shift in jazz harmony from a tonal to a modal orientation, which in turn had a major impact on figures like Evans, Davis, and Coltrane—reminiscent of the impact an earlier theoretical orientation had on progressive French composers in the late nineteenth century, as we'll discuss in Chapter 15.

In the wake of the Russell project, Evans entered into his most fruitful period. He gained a contract with Riverside Records, working with acclaimed jazz producer Orrin Keepnews; their first album, *New Jazz Conceptions* (1957), featured Evans within the construct of the piano trio, with bass and drums, which would largely define his legacy. Critical too was his association with Davis, whose classic sextet included Coltrane and alto saxophonist Cannonball Adderley, from April 1958: his official association was short-lived—only eight months—and yet it is immortalized by virtue of Davis' subsequent invitation for Evans to join in the recording project that became *Kind of Blue* (1959)—the best-selling jazz album in history.[459] In Evans, Davis found a kindred spirit with which to explore the new implications of a modal approach to jazz—such as in their collaborative track on the album, "Blue in Green."

After leaving Davis, Evans produced a string of significant recordings, starting with *Everybody Digs Bill Evans* (1958)—which contains "Peace Piece." Most significant, though, were the studio and live recordings made with a trio consisting of bassist Scott LaFaro and drummer Paul Motian—e.g., the live recordings *Sunday at the Village Vanguard* and *Waltz for Debby* (both 1961). The latter features the Evans standard of the same name, composed eight years earlier. Following LaFaro's tragic death in 1961, Evans carried forth with a variety of trios through the end of his life, most notably with bassist Eddie Gomez from 1966 to '77. He also produced a number of other interesting projects—including two albums where he overdubbed himself (e.g., *Conversations with Myself*, 1963) and an album featuring jazz arrangements of classical works (*Bill Evans Trio with Symphony Orchestra*, 1966), among many others. In all of these, Evans perfected a style of reflective lyricism, rhythmic and harmonic complexity, block chords, sequential melodic improvisation, subtle pedaling, among much else—elements embraced and furthered by younger pianists like Chick Corea, Herbie Hancock, and Eliane Elias, to name a few.

Evans' emotional frailty and drug abuse eventually caught up with him, leading to his death from cirrhosis of the liver at the age of fifty-two. As jazz critic Gene Lees put it, "Bill Evans committed the longest and slowest suicide in music history."[460] Tragedy aside, Evans accrued much critical acclaim during his lifetime, including seven Grammy Awards—and not least the enthusiastic adoration by hardcore jazz fans around the world, for his near unparalleled influence on jazz piano and the species as a whole.

## EVANS: ANALYSIS

As noted, "Peace Piece" appears on Evans' second trio album, *Everybody Digs Bill Evans*, released in December 1958. It followed two years of pleading by Riverside executives—during which time, Evans noted, he had "nothing new to say."[461] After working with Davis' group, however, he felt ready and hired two Davis regulars, bassist Sam Jones and drummer Philly Joe Jones (who by most accounts introduced Evans to heroin) for the session. One of the tracks from the session was a solo piano recording of Leonard Bernstein's "Some Other Time" from the musical *On the Town*. Ironically, the latter track wasn't released on the original album (it was reissued as a bonus track in 1987), but another, related solo track was: "Peace Piece."

The track arose as a complete improvisation at the end of the session—using the same accompanying one-bar intro Evans had devised for "Some Other Time": a simple I–V progression voiced as C major 7–G11 (Figure 11.12a):

**Figure 11.12a: Bill Evans, "Peace Piece"—intro**

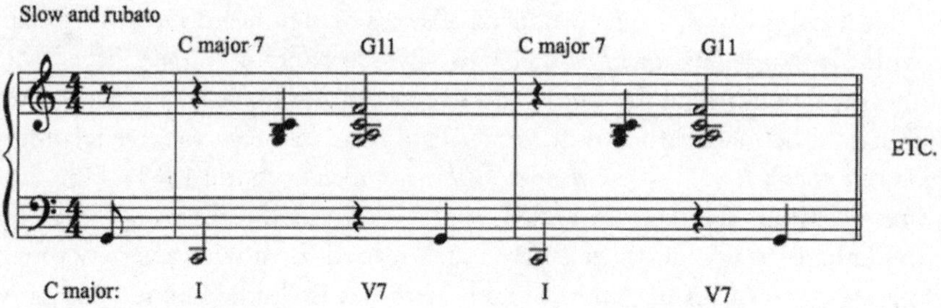


Although much happens in the right hand through the 6:31 recording, Evans' left hand sticks fundamentally to this same one-bar pattern until a final, sustained V11 precedes the I chord at the very end. According to Evans, "What happened was that I started to play the introduction, and it started to get so much of its own feeling and identity that I just figured, well, I'll keep going."[462] Some other accounts suggest that the performance was perhaps not as unpreconceived as all that—including Evans' apparent awareness of the similarly near-incessant I–V accompaniment of Chopin's Berceuse in D♭, Op. 57 (Figure 11.12b):[463]

**Figure 11.12b: Frédéric Chopin, Berceuse in D♭, Op. 57—intro**

At any rate, "Peace Piece" has become a bit of a cult hit among Evans fans, despite its anomalistic relationship to most of his output. It is jazz, sort of, but also something else; through the first calm, consonant, and ethereal three and a half minutes, the piano music of Erik Satie comes to mind (particularly its reliance on a I major 7)—even presaging later minimalist composers like Philip Glass. As it proceeds, however, notably between 3:34 and 5:34, Evans introduces varying degrees of dissonance and atonality above the steady consonance of the accompanying ostinato. Parallel major 7ths and angular chords alternate with highly chromatic and discordant figuration, seemingly revealing Evans' fondness for modern classical composers like Stravinsky and Alexander Scriabin. Here is a transcription of one such passage (Figure 11.13):

**Figure 11.13: Bill Evans, "Peace Piece" (at 4:58)—particularly dissonant passage**

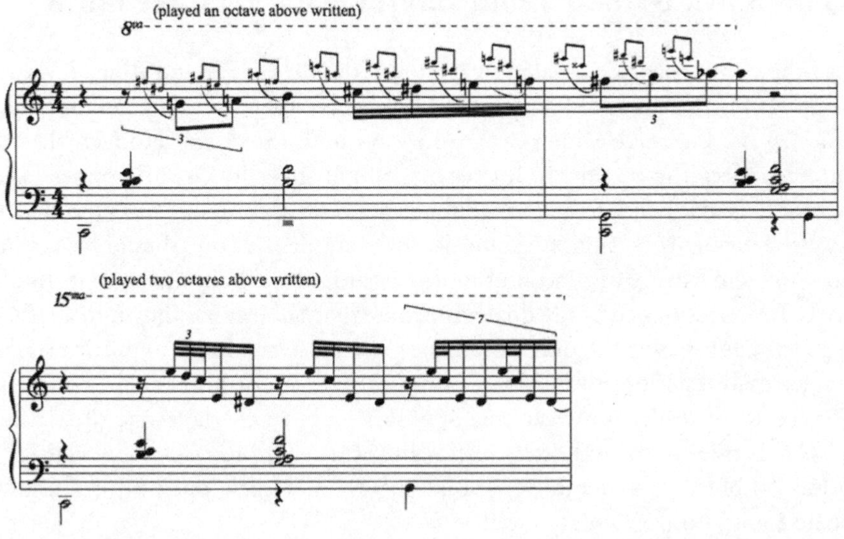

At 5:42, Evans returns to consonance—interestingly by quoting the opening phrase of Bernstein's "Some Other Time" (Figure 11.14)—and remains there to the end.

**Figure 11.14: Bill Evans, "Peace Piece" (at 5:46)—quote of Bernstein's "Some Other Time"**

The recording thus produces a balanced arc of repose-tension-repose. Yet even in its most dissonant moments, the overall pacing and piano touch retain an air of calm—enabled via the reassuring consonance of the left-hand accompaniment.

Surprisingly, "Peace Piece" has been reproduced by other artists, notably classical pianist Jean-Yves Thibaudet, though at times (as in new age pianist Liz Story's version) avoiding the dissonant elements. The intro figure also famously begins "Flamenco Sketches," one of the tracks from *Kind of Blue*. Like Chopin's Berceuse (meaning "lullaby"), "Peace Piece" brings forth a meditative yet probing narrative that is a bit unusual for Evans, but makes for a fitting bedtime track for Subject 3.

## Insights Gained about Subject 3's Musical Taste

With these four selections—along with the fifth (Bela Fleck and Abigail Washburn's "Railroad") discussed on the WYLI website—there is little ambiguity that Subject 3 is a knowledgeable jazz fan. In ways both direct and indirect, the recordings reflect the broad history, aesthetic, and diversity of this species. The impression is made that Subject 3 would rather be at an intimate jazz club than a concert featuring rock or classical music, for example. But one should be careful to not draw too many assumptions in this regard, as we'll discuss more in Interlude F. The selections certainly do demonstrate that Subject 3 is drawn to a rather progressive musicological orientation, not shying away from sophisticated or complex manifestations of melody, harmony, rhythm, form, or sound—though not necessarily to the most extreme approaches. Further, the range of stylistic interplay between jazz and other realms in these recordings—notably classical, world, and bluegrass—demonstrate that Subject 3 is likely open to, if not passionate about, nonjazz styles as well.

As to what other specific songs or works Subject 3 might be open to, if not passionate about, we again can start with those by the same artists residing in close sonic proximity to the hit parade "seeds"—here addressing only the four songs discussed in the chapter. These might include "Dizzy Atmosphere," e.g., as recorded with Parker at Carnegie Hall in 1947 (Gillespie); "Nefertiti," as recorded with Davis in 1967 (Shorter); "Corcovado," as recorded with tenor saxophonist Stan Getz (Jobim); or "Reflections in D" (Evans).

Next up are songs by other artists occupying the same musicological space—or indeed by the same artists in different "incarnations" of their careers: "Move (Take A)" by trumpeter Fats Navarro, as recorded in 1948 with tenor saxophonist Don Lanphere and drummer Max Roach, or "Manteca" by Dizzy Gillespie and His Orchestra, as recorded in 1957 (Gillespie); "Maiden Voyage" by Herbie Hancock, as recorded in 1965 with trumpeter Freddie Hubbard, or "Tears" by Weather Report (Shorter); "Menina Flor" by Luiz Bonfa, as recorded in 1963 with Stan Getz, or "Bim-Bom" by João Gilberto, as recorded in 1958 (Jobim); or "Blue in Green" by the Miles Davis Sextet, as recorded in 1959, or "Gloria's Step" by the Bill Evans Trio, as recorded in 1961 with bassist Scott LaFaro (Evans).

Our dive into the deeper levels of Subject 3's potential genotype then involves an exploration of influencers on and/or "heirs" to the artists and composers involved: Roy Eldridge and Arturo Sandoval (Gillespie); John Coltrane and Branford Marsalis (Shorter); Radamés Gnattali and Eliane Elias (Jobim); and Nat King Cole and Keith Jarrett (Evans). Finally, the musicological nuances of the five "seeds" can help suggest even more remote candidates: Eric Clapton or Gabriela Montero (prodigious improvisation); Busta Rhymes or Slayer (fast tempos); Béla Bartók or Frank Zappa (polyrhythm); Stephen Foster or Lead Belly (traditional American); Astor Piazzolla or Buena Vista Social Club (Latin music influences); Igor Stravinsky or Cream (ostinato usage); or Erik Satie or Hildegard von Bingen (meditative feel), to name but a few. Admittedly, we've gone a bit far afield on some of these suggestions, but such is the journey of musical taste: you never know where it might lead you.

# Interlude E

## *Listening with an Accent: Culture and Musical Taste*

### Composing with an Accent

Long before I harnessed my penchant for musical eclecticism on behalf of a music technology start-up, I applied it to the more conventional musical tasks of performance and composition. The former, indeed, is how my eclecticism took root: from age eleven to sixteen, I played piano every weekend afternoon in the food court of the La Mirada Mall—a few blocks from the house where I grew up in this working-class suburb of Los Angeles. I got the job thanks to the chutzpah of my best friend, Rich Gelbart, as one Saturday we made our way to Noah's Arcade—our weekend ritual. Spotting a newly installed black-and-white checkered stage with an upright piano atop, Richie elbowed me and said, "I dare you to go play it." By age eleven, I had been playing for six years, and had a decent repertoire for a kid of my years. Rarely wimping out on one of Richie's dares, I stepped onto the stage and began playing Scott Joplin's "Maple Leaf Rag," or maybe Elton John's "Bennie and the Jets" (I don't remember); the next thing I knew there was a crowd around me, with several people placing dollar bills into the large brandy snifter that Richie had managed to nab from the confectionary just opposite the stage. Unbeknownst to me, Richie then took off looking for a mall manager, and by sheer luck found one—who hired me on the spot.

As I look back at it now, my steady gig at the La Mirada Mall had a profound impact on my overall musical sensibilities—including, undoubtedly, my sensitivity to the varied musical tastes of the listening public. On any given day, I'd get a request for "The Entertainer," the theme from *Doctor Zhivago*, "Take Five," anything by Mozart or the Beatles or Rodgers and Hammerstein, and—invariably—Led Zeppelin's "Stairway to Heaven." The gig instilled in me not only an understanding that playing requests is a surefire way to get tips, but a sense that if you want to be a professional musician, you have to "play it all." Of course, my sense of "it all" was rather limited in those days, but my five years in the food court enabled me to build up a pretty sizable repertoire and, importantly, trained my ears (and fingers) to render a multitude of musical styles—classical, ragtime, show tunes, jazz, rock and roll, etc.

In short order, I began applying my budding eclecticism to composition, writing pop/rock songs, rags, "movie themes," jazz tunes, and short classical pieces, etc., while still in high school. To be sure, some were better and more "natural" than others, but the inclination to compose in a wide variety of American and pan-European styles is something that remains with me to this day. Indeed, my compositional eclecticism has served me well, as I often receive commissions that require the use of rather disparate styles—gospel, Weimar-era cabaret, Baroque-era classical, and so forth.

Occasionally, moreover, these requests have taken me even further afield, pushing my boundaries of musical assimilation. My variable challenges in realizing them, in turn, can provide an instructive window into how our native culture frames our collective musical taste. Allow me, therefore, to indulge in a tad more autobiography as I cite three original works whose contents lay outside my cultural comfort zone.

The first, mildly challenging case, from 2003, was a Celtic-style work entitled "Irish Easy Pieces"—composed as a thank-you gift to Mr. Declan Ganley of county Galway for his commission of a large orchestral work. "Irish Easy Pieces" is a setting for voice and Irish band of a poem by my friend (and famed golf architect) Robert Trent Jones Jr. In preparation, I spent weeks listening to one of Declan's favorite Irish folk bands, Planxty—with mandolin, bodhrán (Irish frame drum), Irish whistle, and especially the sweet, plaintive sound of uilleann pipes, played by Liam O'Flynn. I'd heard my fair share of Irish sing-alongs, but this was something different, with "unpredictable" modal chord progressions, frequent irregular metric groupings, and a melodic language that was—to my ears—wildly labyrinthine, rich in ornaments, and exotic in its harmonic inflections. After a few weeks of near-incessant listening, I completed a seven-minute work, including an extended instrumental interlude—doing my best to emulate, but not copy, the melancholy motifs of "The Cliffs of Dooneen" and the animated reels of "The Jolly Beggar." The work was performed and recorded with the help of some Irish and Irish-American friends, was well received by Mr. Ganley, and manages an occasional reprise at St. Patrick's Day celebrations even today.*

Feeling buoyed by my experience in the Celtic arena, I boldly accepted a considerably more ambitious, cross-cultural commission a few years later, in 2007. The request came from an Oakland-based insurance executive, Mr. Jim Bell, who desired to commission a bold and global artistic statement to reflect the increasingly global outlook of his business. Together, Mr. Bell and I devised an elaborate scheme to incorporate influences from around the world: the West, China, India, and the Middle East. The programmatic conceit of the work was a cello concerto where this decidedly Western instrument would embark on a kind of global

* The recording features singer Dennis McNeil and uilleann piper Todd Denman.

trek, meeting and "dialoguing" with instruments from each of these regions: the Chinese erhu (a two-string bowed fiddle), the Indian sarangi (a voice-like bowed string with a drone), and an Arabic oud (a lute-like plucked instrument).

I quickly wondered what I had gotten myself into: What did I know about Chinese, Indian, and Arabic music? I had heard a fair bit of music from these realms while designing the World Music Genome for Pandora, but listening in order to define and code analytical "genes" is not the same as having the skills to articulate *original and idiomatic* musical ideas. I thus embarked upon yet another intense study of "foreign" musical languages. My goal was to assimilate the practical and theoretical constructs of these ethnic styles and instruments to the point where I could somewhat intuitively *create* in Chinese, Indian, and Arabic musical dialects.[464] The resulting *World Concerto* was premiered by the Oakland Symphony and conductor Michael Morgan, and featured the renowned Israeli cellist Maya Beiser, along with a trio of celebrated virtuosos on their instruments: Jiebing Chen (erhu), Aruna Narayan (sarangi), and Bassam Saba (oud). The performances happily met with some nice critical praise;[465] even more gratifying, as noted in Interlude C, this concerto came to occupy a longstanding "place of honor" in my dad's monocular playlist.

And yet, as good as I may feel about my attempts to assimilate these culturally remote musical idioms into my original works, I must admit that they were just that: attempts. Having lived exclusively in California until age twenty-four (when I left to study in Paris), my musical identity—my *enculturation*, as we'll discuss below—is decidedly American and Western; the best I can hope to accomplish, therefore, is to have absorbed enough of these non-native musical idioms to have reasonably *masked* my musical "accent." That is, regardless of how much I had studied the musical parlance of the Celtic, Chinese, Hindustani, and North African traditions prior to embarking on my projects, I would inevitably be "composing with an accent"—one that any true native of these traditions would quickly recognize, much as with a late-learned spoken language. In so doing, I was—in the techno-speak of music psychologists Steven Morrison and Steven Demorest—"accommodating" these remote styles via my own, innate "organizational strategies," even if my extensive music education enabled me to fare better than many others charged with the same task.

Before we actually dive into the "science" behind the cultural constraints that underlie our musical taste, let me share one last compositional anecdote. In the summer of 2009, not long after the premiere of the *World Concerto*, I received a call from Rabbi George Gittleman of Congregation Shomrei Torah in Santa Rosa, California—requesting from me a short chamber work to commemorate the arrival of a new Torah to the synagogue, where my family and I had been longstanding members. I scored the work, entitled *V'Samachta* (Celebration), for clarinet, violin, cello, and piano—and devised for it a simple narrative: the clarinet would "embody" the newly arriving Torah, while the cello would "embody" the older Czech Torah already there; a musical dialogue between clarinet and cello in the work would thus symbolically reflect the kind of exchange or *imut* (debate) that one might have heard between two village rabbis—one long-established, the other newly arrived.

For preparation, I embarked on a bit of self-study, particularly of the traditional Jewish chant, or cantillation formulas—called *ta'amim*—given my intention to quote the actual cantillation for one of Rabbi George's favorite scriptural passages, Leviticus 19:18: "Do not seek revenge or bear a grudge against anyone among your people, but love your neighbor as yourself. I am the Lord." This quote, "sung" by the clarinet, would come near the end of the piece, signifying that the young rabbi had indeed "earned" his rightful place in the congregation. Beyond this traditional passage, I blended contemporary classical with more decidedly Jewish passages, including both a hora-like dance and a klezmer-like lament featuring the violin.

For these latter, however, I needed scant review: this was music I knew in my bones. I grew up in a (Reform) Jewish home and have maintained a fairly steady religious practice to this day; I have thus been hearing Jewish and Eastern European/klezmer-infused music since I was a young child and understand its distinctive scales, rhythms, ornaments, and melodic inclinations well beyond a theoretical or academic level—rather on a visceral, familiar one. In other words, I am "bimusical" in both the Euro-American and Jewish musical idioms—and as we'll discuss below, this is an actual thing. There are certainly musicians who know the klezmer genre better than I do, but to a deep and encultured degree, I "speak" Jewish as a composer and listener. In passages reflecting this tradition, I could write in a way that I knew would resonate with other congregants who, like me, were steeped in Jewish (or at least Jewish-American) music. The commemoration that November was an emotional affair, and it was beyond gratifying that at the conclusion of *V'Samachta*, I saw a few tears shed (including from Rabbi George), suggesting that I had successfully conveyed this distinctly Jewish musical message.

## Back to Universals

The above, admittedly indulgent foray into my personal history touches upon several points relevant to the role that culture plays in defining and delimiting our musical taste. On the one hand is the notion that we each possess a native or familiar music culture in which we are raised and assimilated; on the other hand is the suggestion that by virtue of this distinct assimilation we will be limited in the degree to which we can fully comprehend a remote, unfamiliar musical culture. And yet underlying this relationship too is another pivotal point: the existence of "universals" that transcend any individual musical culture. Were it not for these musical universals, we would be hard-pressed to gain *any* comprehension of a non-native or unfamiliar musical culture once we have reached adulthood, for example—except through intense study. But clearly that is not the case: while being able to compose like a native may require an abundance of musical "enculturation," merely gaining some comprehension of it—not to mention enjoyment—does not. "Musics," as we again quote Bruno Nettl, "are not as mutually unintelligible as languages."

A key assumption of musical universals, of course, is that they exist in every musical culture. We touched lightly on this topic in Interlude A, in part to explore our universal love of music and its potential roots in our evolution. On a broader level, Interludes B, C, and D have also suggested the existence of musical universals—namely those that undergird our collective musical taste, regardless of our cultural background: a seemingly inherent predilection for perfect consonances, consonant chords, the musical techniques of repetition, variation, and symmetry, etc. Given our focus in this chapter on distinct and varied musical cultures around the world and their interplay with our cognition and taste, however, we can now return to this topic in a more explicit way, as informed via ethnomusicology and music psychology.

In Interlude A, we exposed the naïveté of Longfellow's claim that music is a single "universal language"—noting the wide diversity in which music is actually "spoken" around the world, as well as the shortfalls of employing an overtly Western ethnocentrism in defining musical discourse. Yet we also noted how a refutation of Longfellow's claim does not negate the existence of certain universal dimensions of music making among us humans. To begin, there is the very presence of music within every culture on earth; indeed, as Ian Cross notes, music appears "integral to the human capacity for culture," whereby it may have played a significant role in our evolution.[466] Pioneering ethnomusicologist John Blacking goes even further—highlighting our innate musical skills as individuals. In noting that "the almost universal distribution of musical competence in African societies," he suggests that "musical ability is a general characteristic of the human species, rather than a rare talent."[467] As such, music appears to sit alongside other human universals: the use of abstraction in human language, a cultural belief in a supernatural power, an ability to recognize basic emotions in facial expressions, a cultural taboo against incest, a fear of snakes, and the use of culturally defined rites of passage, to name but a few.[468]

Musical universals contribute two vital insights to our musical taste "mystery novel," whereby a small review of their details seems warranted: first, they reveal those elements that our shared—pan-geographic—culture yields to our collective musical identity; and second, they delimit those elements from which individual cultures can and do deviate to forge unique, cultural distinctions.

There are in turn three types of musical universals: (1) the *properties* that derive from the music itself; (2) the *perceptions* we all share when encountering music; and (3) the *functions* that music serves across cultures.

Starting with universal properties, Table E.1 lists some broadly accepted elements:

**TABLE E.1: UNIVERSAL MUSICAL PROPERTIES**

**Pitch/Tone/Melody**

- The octave as a 2:1 ratio (octave equivalence between men and women, etc.)
- Melodies composed of discrete/fixed pitches
- Predominant use in melodies of an interval resembling a major 2nd (e.g. C–D)
- Predominant use in melodies of small intervals (less than a 5th)
- Distinct repertoire that features only three or four notes in individual melodies
- Melodic contours that alternate large intervals up and small intervals down
- Predominant use in melodies of descending melodic contours
- Scales/modes of seven notes or fewer per octave
- Scales/modes comprising unequal intervals (major and minor 2nds, 3rds)
- Natural ability to transpose melodies to start on any note

**Harmony**

- Use of drone or pedal point (sustained pitch below or above melody)

**Rhythm**

- Use of steady (isochronous) rhythms (beats)
- Use of repeating rhythmic patterns
- Organization of steady rhythms into set meters or "rhythmic modes"
- Predominant use of meters based on multiples of two or three beats—especially two
- Limited repertoire of rhythmic patterns/meters per genre or style

**Form**

- Organization of melodies/music into short, distinct phrases
- Use of repetition and variation within and between phrases

**Sound/Performance/Expression**

- Use of vocal music
- Use of instrumental music, including as imitation of vocal style
- Use of ornamentation/embellishment in vocal melodies
- Predominant use of chest voice in singing
- Predominant use of singing words (not vocables)
- Predominance of group singing—especially by men
- Association of distinct modes, styles, tempos, etc., with distinct emotions

To be sure, not all of the musical *properties* in Table E.1 are as "universal" as others. A handful—octave equivalence (the fact that when men and women sing the same melody, they often will naturally sing it an octave apart), use of discrete pitches, a dominant melodic interval resembling a 2nd, transposable melodies, use of vocal music, organization into phrases—can be said to be truly, or nearly, universal; a few others—use of drones, limited repertoire of rhythmic patterns per genre—are more common than universal, while the others fall somewhere in the middle. An influential 2015 study led by Peter Savage and Steven Brown proposed an even stricter division: between absolute universal properties, with no exceptions, and "statistical" universal properties, where exceptions are possible, but which appeared "significantly above chance."[469] In their examination of thirty-two candidates, they applied their methodology across a broad spectrum of 304 global recordings and identified eighteen properties that met their criteria for "statistical universals," including some that are rarely cited; these are all included within Table E.1.

Although one can take issue with this or that item on the list, we can confidently assert that all of these musicological properties possess a kind of *inevitability* or at least unremarkability whenever and wherever music is made. That is, if you were to be dropped without warning into any remote musical milieu—downtown Istanbul, a rural village in Indonesia, the jungles of the Congo, etc.—you could confidently expect to hear most if not all of these musical properties in the course of a few days. You might not particularly like the music you heard there, of course, but given their confirmed universality, all of us—regardless of our cultural origins—would find those specific properties appropriate, satisfying, and indeed to our musical taste.

While scholars at times debate whether the universal *properties* arise via nature or our collective practices of nurture, it is unequivocal that our universal musical *perceptions* have biological origins, grounded specifically in our cognitive processes; in other words, we are neurologically preprogrammed to perceive—recognize, register, etc.—a number of musical properties regardless of our cultural identity. Some of the most pronounced of these *perceptions* are listed in Table E.2:

**TABLE E.2: UNIVERSAL MUSICAL PERCEPTIONS**

**Pitch/Tone Melody**

- The octave as a 2:1 ratio (octave equivalence between men and women, etc.)
- Scales/modes composed of unequal intervals (major and minor 2nds, 3rds)
- Perception of "tonal hierarchy": scales have "stable" and "unstable" notes
- Reception to the "statistical properties" of tonal and melodic tendencies

**Harmony**

- Statistical preference for consonance over dissonance

**Rhythm**

- Ability to "entrain" (lock in) to steady (isometric) rhythms
- Preference for simple (proportional) rhythms over arbitrarily complex ones
- Reception to the "statistical properties" of rhythmic and metric tendencies

**Form**

- Ability to categorize/group patterns of pitches, phrases, etc. (e.g., repetition)
- Ability to perceive beginnings/ends of phrases ("boundaries")

**Sound/Performance/Expression**

- Ability to group tone sequences on basis of pitch, loudness, timbre
- Ability to perceive performer's "intended" emotion via cues
- Association of basic emotions with music attributes (tempo, density)

As can be seen, some of these universal perceptions corroborate and/or underlie the observed universal properties listed in Table E.1. For example, our innate cognitive ability to entrain—technically defined by Catherine Stevens as "a process where two rhythmic processes interact with each other, eventually locking in to a common phase and/or periodicity"[470]—corroborates our ability (*virtually* unique in the animal world[471]) to lock into and prominently use steady rhythms, and underlies our universal tendency to organize rhythmic patterns into fixed meters.

A key point underscored by scholars who consider musical universals is our innate ability to process "statistical properties" of both tonal/pitch and rhythmic tendencies in musical practice. In layman's terms, this means that from shortly after birth, our infant brains (specifically in the prefrontal cortex) begin acting much like a supercomputer, calculating the statistical tendencies of pitch and rhythm relationships, identifying some as dominant and hierarchically significant, others as secondary, and still others as violations of those tendencies. This "statistical learning" is carried out implicitly, without our conscious awareness, and establishes to our ears the inductive "rules" that govern the musical discourses we encounter, especially in our early years. It is true, as we'll see, that this implicit process will quickly set in motion certain biases that vary from one musical culture to another. And yet we all possess the ability to carry out this remarkable statistical learning, including to embrace those universal properties—like octave equivalence, scales of unequal intervals, regular rhythms, etc.—that transcend cultures; this includes too, as David Huron emphasizes, our ability to draw an emotional response from the realizations and/or violations of those statistical tendencies.

Interesting likewise are the universal perceptions that don't necessarily garner scholarly consensus as universal properties, as well as the opposite: universal properties that seem not to show up as universal perceptions. Key among the former is the "robust" preference that researchers like Laurel Trainor and Nobuo Masataka have observed among infants for consonance—both the perfect (octave, 5th, and 4th) and "imperfect" (3rds, 6ths) varieties—over dissonance (e.g., 2nds, tritones, 7ths).[472] While indeed some scholars would include the predominance of consonance over dissonance as a universal property, others would hedge that bet given the existence in some music cultures—Hungarian, Balkan, West African, Baltic, among others—of rich traditions that embrace parallel 2nds and other dissonant indulgences.[473] As suggested in Interludes B and C, our "statisticial" preference for consonance may find root in the physics of sound (small-integer proportions, the overtone series) and more immediately in the mechanisms of our auditory system (e.g., the frequency resolution of the basilar membrane); this does not mean, however, that as adults we cannot indulge in the rougher side of the harmonic palette, as these cultures—and many in our own—are clearly wont to do at times.

Those dimensions identified as universal *properties* but not *perceptions*—predominant use of the major 2nd, genres featuring three to four notes per melody, scales with seven or fewer notes, use of a drone, vocal ornamentation, etc.—would then seem to suggest either the commanding role of cultural diffusion in establishing their universality, or a need to carry out future experiments to corroborate an original cognitive impetus for this status. In any event, all of these universal perceptions help to further define our collective, cross-cultural musical taste: that is, we are undoubtedly more prone to like—or at least judge with aesthetic clarity—those musical qualities that we innately recognize (consonances, stable scale tones, steady rhythms, melodic and rhythmic patterns, intended performer emotions, etc.) than those we don't.

The third and final type of musical universality relates to *function*—that is, the uses, purposes, and behaviors aligned with music making that appear to cut across cultures and thereby represent a sort of archetypal quality. A list of commonly accepted universal musical *functions*—broken into distinct cultural categories in which music is utilized—is shown in Table E.3:

**TABLE E.3: UNIVERSAL MUSICAL FUNCTIONS**

**Overall Cultural Identity**
- Reflects society's broad values
- Supports integrity of collective and individual social groups
- Maintains cultural identity during times of diaspora

**Social Cohesion**
- Assists in conflict resolution/social uncertainty
- Supports social bonding, as between parents and children (e.g., lullabies)
- Supports/chronicles romantic love/courting
- Supports patriotism and cultural loyalty

**Religion/Ritual**
- Directs or accompanies communication with the supernatural
- Accompanies/supports religious rituals
- Accompanies/supports rites of passage

**Work/Productivity**
- Supports work via synchronous/coordinated movement (e.g., work songs)
- Accompanies hunting

**Defense**
- Supports defense preparation (march songs)
- Supports battle (war songs)

**Knowledge/Education**
- Supports childhood pedagogy (childhood songs)
- Encodes cultural/social history (epics, ballads)
- Provides clues/warnings on survival

**Entertainment/Aesthetics/Spirituality/Wellness**
- Provides entertainment/enjoyment
- Enables shift in individual consciousness
- Provides therapy/healing
- Provides comfort/eases tension/regulates mood
- Triggers trance state
- Affirms value and joy of life

At first glance, it might seem that the function of music would have little bearing on our musical taste: Why should we care why or where a song was originally performed or composed so long as we like it? In some sense this is true—and especially in our own day, when we can hear practically any song or work in the comfort of our own home regardless of what function it may have served initially.

On the other hand, many distinctly musicological and experiential dimensions of a song or work—its tempo, mode, melodic style, etc.—are explicit reflections of its original function; as such, it will often share those musicological dimensions with other songs/works aligned with that same function, even those found in other musical cultures. Indeed, a dismissal of the functional importance of music is very much a Western ethnocentric stance, where the dynamic is often a *passive* one—moving unidirectionally from a performer or a recording to an inactive listener seeking entertainment or an aesthetic experience. This, however, contrasts with the predominantly *interactive* approach to music making in many other parts of the world, as we'll discuss. At any rate, I would caution against such a dismissal, and argue that awareness of music's function—initially and/or subsequently—is an invaluable asset in understanding and empowering our musical taste.[474]

A vital aspect of musical function concerns its dual involvement with collective society on the one hand and an individual member of that society on the other. But there is then a vibrant interaction between the two as well—what Clayton calls the "middle ground," or Marina Roseman the "socio-centric self"—where the boundaries between the personal and the social are fuzzy and porous.[475] For Cross, this reflects music's unique ability to act as an "interactive participatory medium," enabling individuals to "communicate" or interact with one another in a manner less threatening than language. Specifically, this is enabled through our ability to entrain to music, and through what Cross calls music's "floating intentionality"—its variable meaning, where each individual can draw his or her personal interpretation or motivation from the music without raising tensions between individuals in the way language is prone to do; as such, music functions particularly well in those "socially uncertain" cultural moments, like weddings and rites of passages: the group maintains cohesion despite an often high variability in individual response.[476]

Table E.3 shows that many of these functions explicitly target *societal* uses and behaviors—such as those related to defining cultural identity, group bonding, religious rituals, work and hunting activities, going to war, pedagogy, and the preservation and dissemination of cultural history. In such cases, the utilization of music helps us to coordinate our actions as well as our emotions and mentalities, enabling us—despite our individuality—to feel connected to one another as a single, collective whole. At its most profound level, music-based functions help to produce a kind of "emergent behavior" within society. "Emergence" is an oft-cited phenomenon aligned with various disciplines (biology, economics, philosophy, art) where simple, independent actions add up to complex systems without coordinated, causal intention. For example, this is the behavior observed in the symmetry of a snowflake, formed by discrete patterns recurring at different, local scales; or in the behavior of an ant colony, where despite a lack of centralized direction, individual ants somehow "know" how to carry out highly complicated actions like building an anthill.[477] Similarly, then, the codification of cultural and social histories, religious rituals, children's pedagogy, and the like may well have begun as individual music-based expressions that unconsciously "emerge" as collective cultural products.

Other functions more directly target *individuals*, or pairs of individuals—such as those related to conflict resolution, rites of passage, healing, trance states, regulation of mood, entertainment, and of course romantic love. Yet as you may well sense from the items in this list—entertainment, for example—it would be wrong to say that music serves either an individual or a societal function exclusively; instead, music can *and often does* serve both targets simultaneously. Indeed, many scholars highlight the ambiguous, "polysemic"—multiple meaning—nature of musical function as compared to language, as a primary source of its wide functional adoption. This is doubtless a product of music's "floating intentionality" as discussed above. But it also speaks, as noted in Interlude C, to music's extraordinary power to trigger emotion, and to train and enhance memory. It is no accident that so many major religious and cultural histories—the Homeric epics, the Jewish Torah, the *Epic of Sundiata* (Mandinka people of West Africa), the ancient Vedic (Indian) *Ramayana*, among countless others—were wholly or partially created and disseminated in song; music enables the mind to remember what words alone cannot.

It is this "floating" and flexible power of music—its "indeterminacy" as Clayton calls it—that stands behind one of the more unique discussions I've read on musical function: that found in my friend Dan Levitin's *The World in Six Songs*. Levitin selects six song types—those of friendship, joy, comfort, knowledge, religion, and love—that to him have helped shape human nature from an evolutionary, neurological, and cultural perspective. This creative premise gives him an opportunity to indulge in an engaging, wide-ranging discussion touching on myriad topics: science, culture, history, psychology—though notably, with far more attention to the lyrics of songs, predominantly pop/rock, than to their musical content. Several of the functions cited above stem from his discussion.

Two song types especially appear important to Levitin in forging human history. The first is knowledge songs, to which he traces everything from our epics, to children's alphabet songs, to societal warnings about eating poisonous foods. As he puts it: "Knowledge songs are perhaps the crowning triumph of art, science, culture, and mind, encoding important life lessons in an artistic form that is ideally adapted to the structure and function of the human brain." The second type is love songs—not only of the romantic variety (which music amply chronicles in all its phases), but also those directed to our children, parents, friends, and country; by virtue of music's ability to form an "honest signal" (that is, one harder to fake than language), music pairs emotion with *trust*, granting to us the decidedly human ability to care for someone else more than ourselves. In Levitin's words: "Love songs imprint themselves in our brains like no others; they speak of our greatest human aspirations and loftiest qualities. . . . [W]ithout the innate ability to have such thoughts, societies could not be built."[478]

Finally, one point just noted about Levitin's book—his predominant, though by no means exclusive, citation of Anglo-American pop/rock songs to substantiate his claims—hints at an important question: How do the musical functions listed above fall on the "gradient of universality"? Although the issue is not as thoroughly vetted as with universal properties and perceptions, it does seem safe to presume that music *does not* fulfill each of these functions with an equal degree of universality. For example, not every culture has experienced a veritable diaspora; many cultures, moreover, have no musical repertoire to accompany an established tradition of hunting, or its collective cultural history, or one that deliberately triggers a trance state, etc. Indeed, many traditional (non-Western) cultures shun the notion of music as mere entertainment—notably within many African, Middle Eastern, and Southeast Asian societies.[479] At the same time, one could likely count as fully or "statistically" universal the use of music for rites of passage and religious rituals—which are themselves as universal as music. Many others as well—those supporting or chronicling romantic love, patriotism, war, childhood pedagogy, healing, etc.—are likely found in most cultures around the world in some capacity or another.

Regardless, the use of music to support and heighten these functions does appear universal in at least its *potential* application—provided that a culture's other facets enable and sanction it. From a musical taste standpoint, this suggests that we would likely find it entirely reasonable and satisfying if, within our own native culture, music would find an essential place in association with any of the functions/behaviors listed above. Similarly, this suggests that our taste would respond with a degree of knowing awareness—whether positive or negative—to the "universal" musicological traits associated with at least some of these functions: the steadily rhythmic, drum-accompanied style of war songs; the rousing tempo of a hunting song; the simple singing style of children's pedagogic songs; the harmonically sustained style of trance music; the likely serious, ornate, and aesthetically potent style accompanying communication with the supernatural, and so forth. Of course, awareness doesn't necessarily mean preference, but it does suggest that if you dislike one war song, you may also dislike others, whereas if you fall in love with one song to the all-powerful, you may well dig the next one you hear as well.

## Cultural Distinctions

It might seem strange that we have devoted so much space to the topic of universals in a chapter ostensibly dedicated to cultural distinctions and constraints. Well, aside from the sheer interest the topic holds in its own right, and its importance to the formation of musical taste, the truth is you can't really understand the latter without explaining the former. Such, at any rate, is the case in the scholarly literature dedicated to the constraining effects of enculturation on music perception and cognition. We'll dive directly into those matters shortly, but first we should make at least some reference to the purely musical dimensions of culture.

As an aside, you should note that a more dedicated discussion of "world music" will take place in Chapter 14, where again we will present five distinct works in detail. Here, by contrast, we'll merely point out a few basic ethnomusicological distinctions to better set up the following section on enculturation and cultural constraint.

To begin, it is worth pointing out that some ethnomusicologists have attempted to set up an historical lineage of musical growth and "diffusion," including points of origin and branches of division—based on musicological as well as migration data. As Nettl notes, for example, several scholars going back to Carl Stumpf and Curt Sachs in the early twentieth century, and followed up by more recent writers like Victor Grauer, have attempted to identify a kind of "first layer" or "ur-music" in a particular "stratum of songs" found in the African Bushman and Pygmy traditions—"as a kind of baseline for the development of the rest of human music."[480] The musical style in these songs is fairly simple, consisting of rhythmically vibrant repeating melodies of only three to four notes, dominated by something close to a major 2nd, and used in social gatherings and rituals, etc. According to this theory, as our early ancestors migrated out of Africa, they took this style with them; this would explain the similar styles found as at least a minority repertory in all ("statistically" speaking) societies around the world—with especially robust repertoires in regions as disparate as Sri Lanka, Micronesia, and the indigenous peoples of North and South America.

In this case, musical practice would have begun simply and gained in complexity as it evolved and disseminated. By contrast, others scholars, such as Joseph Jordania, have considered the idea that an initially complex form of counterpoint in 2nds (as found in the Baltic styles noted above) was in most cases later abandoned in favor of a simpler, single-voice (monophonic) style; this, indeed, would parallel a common trend in spoken language, from more to less complex—think of the shift from Greek to Latin to French.[481] Yet another theory is that posed by Alan Lomax in his *Cantometrics* (1976), in which he compared four thousand songs from 148 regions, reducing them to ten families that in turn could be traced to two original roots: the "Arctic style," a monophonic unison song set in a coordinated but free rhythm, and sung by male hunter-gatherers in Siberia; and the "African Gatherer style," a vibrant, steady rhythmic approach using short repeating melodies, sung by both sexes in African hunter-gatherer tribes—and thus similar to the style posed by Sachs and Grauer.[482]

Of course, we'll never know which if any of these theories are accurate, but they do paint a conceivable scenario where initial similarity in musical practice across all parts of the inhabited globe gradually evolved to greater and greater individuation within distinct cultures. Don't worry: we'll bypass the potential nuances of how that story might have gone down over the past hundred thousand years or so.

Instead, we'll break down a sampling of that individuation based on the key musical parameters we discussed in Chapters 3 to 7—following the order used to list the universal musical properties above:

Starting with *pitch/tone/melody considerations*, we have noted the universal property whereby most functioning scales contain seven or fewer notes per octave; we also indicated that the distribution of these notes generally comprise "unequal intervals"—meaning a mix of differing intervals as the notes ascend and descend, those being more or less the minor 2nd (e.g., C–D♭), major 2nd (e.g., C–D), and minor 3rd (e.g., C–E♭). Further, a number of scholars have pointed to the predominance of five-note or "pentatonic" scales. While a few intervals—notably the perfect 5th and octave above the ground or "root" note—are themselves fairly universal, the specific distribution of the "internal" notes within a given scale reveals an incredible variety from one culture to another, indeed often within a single culture. We demonstrated a tiny bit of this variety in Chapter 3, with more to come in Chapter 14—though a full taxonomy would require a book of its own.[483]

Importantly, the principal scales used in Western music—major and minor, as well as pentatonic, the eight church modes, etc. (see Chapter 3)—are understood today as grounded on equal temperament, as on a modern piano (see Interlude B). This, however, is not the case among most scales used in traditional societies, such as those in sub-Saharan Africa, Southeast Asia, Aboriginal Australia, etc.—where the specific tuning system used is often a product of the inherent tuning found on various instruments (mallets, pipes, etc.); as such, scales can vary subtly from one neighboring tribe to another even if the approximate intervals are the same. In Africa alone, there are dozens of distinct pentatonic scales in common use, as well as numerous tribes/groups that use distinct six- (hexatonic) and seven-note (heptatonic) scales.[484] Some scales, for example the five-note "*slendro*" and seven-note "*pelog*" used in Indonesian gamelan music, are decidedly "exotic," even odd-sounding, to uninitiated Western ears, by virtue of their distinct distribution of 2nds and 3rds, combined with tunings quite apart from the piano. In other cases—such as in Arabic lands (maqam) and India (ragas)—a single culture will possess numerous distinct modes, each with its own distribution of intervals, usually heptatonic, and tuning, along with its associated affects and melodic tendencies.

In most cases, the scales in common use by a culture will reveal the influence of **tonal hierarchies**—where one or more notes will hold a position of primacy and/or greater "stability" than others. This in turn impacts the way melodies are constructed and oriented, including the kinds of interval relations favored or suppressed in one culture versus another. In a few cases, as in gamelan music, no perceivable tonal hierarchies are in effect—instead a more cyclic approach is used, where all the notes of a scale hold equal import. Naturally, such an approach would influence the kinds of melodies created. On a more nuanced level, even cultures within the same broad tradition (Western Europe, China, West Africa, etc.) and using the same repertory of scales will adopt differing approaches to melodic construction: emphasizing different intervals, melodic patterns, and rhythmic scansions; this latter is often a reflection of traits found within the distinct spoken languages of the region, such as vowel lengths and accent patterns. It is these nuanced traits, for example, that enable those of us steeped in Western music to distinguish an English folk melody from a German, Italian, or French one.

As regards the parameter of *harmony*, it will here be recalled that most traditional cultures around the world do not utilize sophisticated vertical harmony—that is chords—in their music. To be sure, many utilize two pitches simultaneously, as well as counterpoint of two or more voices, but such is different from a conscientious use of harmonic vertical structures. Indeed, as we detailed in Chapter 4, the conscious use of chords and a defined system of vertical harmony (tonality) came into effect in Europe only in the seventeenth century. It should be added, however, that over the past fifty years, the influence of Western pop music has made itself felt in nearly every corner of the globe, such that a good majority of cultures incorporate vertical harmony in at least some of their musical output. Not surprisingly, individual cultures will utilize the harmonic idiom—chord progressions, levels of chromaticism, tonal or modal propensities, etc.—in distinct ways, such that the harmonic language used in West Africa is sonically and theoretically different from that found in Japan, Malaysia, or North Africa. The specific use of chords, moreover, is in no small part a product of each culture's native tonal and melodic tendencies, among other musical qualities.

We turn next to another realm of vibrant musical distinction: *rhythm* (see Chapter 5). We've mentioned on several occasions the vital role of entrainment—locking into rhythm—in seeding our collective appreciation for and cultivation of music. This presupposes, obviously, that the music has a pulse—or a beat or "tactus"—that is steady and vibrant enough for people to lock into in the first place. And yet we've also adopted Clayton's broad definition of music as requiring only vocal/instrumental utterance and "rhythmic coordination"; this latter does not necessarily mean that a steady pulse is discernible, but only that rhythmic flow is in some ways "coordinated"—even if only by a single performer. While, indeed, most cultures of the world employ a steady pulse within a substantial part of their musical output, other cultures—e.g., Tibetan, Japanese, Indian, Western (Europe, etc.)—make at least occasional use of a nonpulsed or nonmetric approach. When pulse is adopted, moreover, it most commonly proceeds as a single, steady and predictable—"isometric" or equal timing—flow, whereby entrainment can take place. Yet rhythm can also flow in a more complex—polymetric—manner, where two or more pulses operate simultaneously in more or less coordinated ways, as found in many West African traditions, as well as in gamelan music, among others.

Saying that the music has a steady pulse, however, doesn't quite tell the whole story, and indeed, we'll need to get a bit technical for a spell. Pulses, or beats, can be organized—via patterns of stress on particular beats within a defined cycle—in myriad ways. These cycles, moreover, commonly occur at multiple levels simultaneously: at a primary level (the full cycle), but also at one or more sublevels and sub-sublevels. As we discussed and illustrated more explicitly in Chapter 5, this kind of organization is called "meter," and most cultures prefer some metric structures over others—even if, as in the West, they adopt a great many.

Throughout much of the world (including the West), primary-level patterns commonly flow in steady, regular groupings of twos, threes, or fours—though likewise six, eight, nine, or twelve—beats per cycle. It is common as well that sublevel patterns divide the full cycle into steady, regular groupings of twos, threes, or fours. Such situations are termed "isochronous" (regularly timed), suggesting both a regular grouping of beats per cycle at the primary level, but especially a regular grouping (mainly twos and threes) at the sublevel. However, in other areas—notably the Balkan regions, including Bulgaria and Turkey—a "non-isochronous" approach is more the norm. This means not only that primary groupings include an "irregular" grouping (five, seven, nine, eleven, etc.) of beats per cycle, but also that the sublevel proceeds in inconsistent or *uneven* patterns—such as 2+3 (for five beats per cycle), 2+2+2+3 (for nine beats per cycle), or 2+3+3 (for eight beats per cycle), etc. Naturally, this engenders a level of rhythmic complexity to the overall musical proceedings that a noninitiated listener might find disorienting—unable, for example, to find the beginning—or "downbeat"—of the cycle. To a native Turk, however, such would be commonplace.

There are, of course, many other ways in which pulsed rhythm is utilized in music, and thus which can distinguish one culture from another. For example, in many West African cultures, the steady pulse employed is not so much organized into metric cycles, but instead flows in a steady, nonhierarchical manner; this style—which Blacking calls "pulsations"—proceeds without structural, cyclic accentuation, yet does vibrantly invite free play *against* that steady beat. Technically, of course, this is called "syncopation," and its African provenance and subsequent impact on American genres like ragtime, jazz, R&B, and hip hop is something we've already documented to a sizable degree. Yet another prominent type of pulsed rhythmic organization is the Tal system of North Indian music (see Chapter 14), which is less a meter and more a temporal "framework"—cyclic and hierarchical, yet often involving the complex interaction of different rhythmic structures.

It may be mentioned, finally, that the rhythmic component of music is intimately linked to another human universal: dance. For one thing, there can be no dance without music—although the opposite is clearly not true. Many writers emphasize this intimate link—Levitin, for example, often uses the expression "music-dance." The link surely goes back to the origins of our species, and ever since has played a role in promoting group bonding and cohesion.[485] As such, the rhythmic language of a given culture's music will inevitably reflect distinct ways in which that culture approaches movement in general, as well as the role that dance plays within it. Among some Aboriginal tribes of Australia, for example, each genre of music is associated with a specific dance and a particular set of rhythmic patterns—such that it would be unthinkable to use that same rhythmic pattern in a different genre.

As noted above, the purpose of this section was to give enough tangible examples of musical distinctions among cultures to set up the following discussion of enculturation and constraint. Naturally, of course, we only scratched the surface of the many, varied ways in which those distinctions are manifest. We bypassed, for example, the tremendous variety in instrumental sonorities used by different musical cultures—from the didgeridoo of Aboriginal Australia to the talking drum of West Africa to the many pitched gongs used in gamelan orchestras (see Chapter 7)—as well as the tremendous variety of vocal techniques/sonorities used by singers around the world—from yodeling in Central Africa to virtuosic ornamentation in Pakistan to pronounced vibrato in the Middle East and North Africa, among much else. The overriding point, however, should be clear: depending on where you were born and raised, what constitutes "normal" music will vary widely—with profound ramifications not only on *what* you'll hear, but *how* you'll hear it.

## Enculturation and Cultural Constraint

Born and raised in Southern California, the cultural *what* I heard growing up in the late 1960s and '70s was decidedly Euro-American in its musicological distinctions. This means that I—like many of you, I suppose—consistently heard, in my formative years, music that comports to the *sound and structure* of "Western" music. Technically speaking, this translates into music that features: (1) equal-tempered scales, such as those played on a modern piano; (2) tonal "hierarchies" emphasizing the first (tonic) and fifth (dominant) degrees of the scale;

(3) vertical sonorities or chords that can be organized hierarchically into keys or modes; (4) predominantly steady (isometric) rhythm organized into steady (isochronous) meters, such as 4/4 and 3/4, spiced up with regular use of syncopation; (5) timbres of both acoustic and electric Western instruments—such as guitars, pianos, drums, trumpets, flutes, and violins; (6) relatively mild use of vocal ornamentation; (7) song forms defined by symmetry, balanced phrases, repetition, and variation; and (8) an aesthetic stance that sees music largely serving as entertainment and informal self-regulation.

The near-exclusive diet I heard of these Euro-American musical traits during the first decade plus of my existence in turn impacted, to a decisive degree, the *how* of my musical perception. I may have begun to expand my musical awareness to other cultures in my late teens (and especially from my late twenties), but by then it was too late: the circuitry of my musical cognition was largely fixed and ingrained.

As we've noted several times, this process is known as "enculturation." If musical culture is, to quote Patel, "the degree to which informal musical experiences are shared by people growing up in a similar time and place," then musical enculturation is the process whereby we gain knowledge about those experiences. What is key here is that this knowledge comes not by explicit or formal education, although that doesn't hurt. Instead it is gained implicitly, by informal, everyday listening—in our homes, on the radio, at the supermarket, etc. If we hear music with any regularity at all during our developing years, we automatically become encultured to it. Implied in the process, to be sure, are those universal, "culture-general" perceptions discussed above, and notably the computerlike "statistical learning" from which we form "rules" governing tonal and rhythmic hierarchies. To complete the process, however, "culture-specific" learning is needed. This, again, arrives implicitly, merely by listening to the music of our native culture—tracking the cues that will come to concretely define those "rules." These cues define the specific intervals and hierarchies of the scales used, common harmonic relationships, rhythmic/metric constructs, standard tunings and temperaments of vocal pitches and instruments, common timbres, and so forth.

Musical enculturation has become a big topic over the past ten-plus years, not unrelated to the simultaneous push to better understand musical universals. Indeed, many of the same scholars are involved in both inquiries, often discussed in the same studies, especially from the perception side of things. Through studies in music psychology and neuroscience, we're learning some fascinating things about the effects and limitations of enculturation.[486]

Common to enculturation studies, as with universals, is the challenge of Western ethnocentrism. It comes in various forms: using only Western listeners to gauge cultural response, having non-Westerners listen only to Western music, etc. Recent studies increasingly use both Western and non-Western participants—the latter primarily from India, Turkey, China, and Africa, but also Japan and Indonesia, etc. Far too few to date, however, are what Patel calls "fully comparative"—where, for example, listeners of two cultures respond to music from both cultures. This is all complicated, moreover, by what Huron calls the "irreversible loss of cultural diversity"[487] via globalization, and especially the increasingly ubiquitous presence of Western music, especially pop, throughout the world. Such a bias, in fact, has led some scholars to argue against using Western music at all in enculturation studies.

At any rate, we have certainly learned much about the enculturation process—including the astounding rate at which it takes root. Through numerous infant studies, Erin Hannon and Sandra Trehub, for example, have shown that prior to six months or so, we have virtually no cultural boundaries in our music listening—unable, for example, to recognize violations in any culture-specific manifestation of pitch or rhythm hierarchies.[488] Such "boundary-less" hearing continues even through ten months, although the implicit learning of our native music has by then already forged some "culture-specific brain structures and representations."[489] A watershed moment seems to be at around twelve months. By this time, infants demonstrate considerable sensitivity to musical tendencies of their own native music, yet far less sensitivity to those of a foreign culture. In essence, from the age of one we start to hear music outside of our own culture "with an accent." This aligns with our culture-specific development in other realms, such as with speech and face perception. Interestingly, though, Hannon and Trehub have shown in experiments that after a brief (e.g., two-week) exposure, a twelve-month infant can indeed learn "foreign rules"—such as those tied to rhythm. The enculturation process, to be sure, continues to develop and becomes more complex and sophisticated throughout childhood, but even before most of us can walk, we already can recognize what makes our native music tick.

This then begs the question of what impact enculturation has on how we listen to native versus non-native music—what Morrison and Demorest call the "enculturation effect."[490] To what degree do we recognize the hierarchical rules of a non-native system? What is the impact of prolonged exposure to non-native music in children? Which musical parameters/experiences are more or less impacted by our "hearing accent"? And especially, how might all of this impact our musical taste? To help answer these questions, we'll once again target key parameters (pitch/harmony and rhythm) and cognitive processes (emotion and memory) to see what enculturation experiments reveal about the cultural constraints of our listening.

## PITCH AND HARMONY

To begin, it is studies on pitch and harmony that confirm that for several months after birth, infants are relatively "boundary-less" in their music perceptions—that

is, no culture-specific musical *properties* dominate their *perception*. For example, a Western-raised adult can detect a single-note violation in an unfamiliar tonal melody that alters its scale or its implied harmony; by contrast, an eight-month-old will detect any such single-note violation equally as well—whether or not it alters its scale or its implied harmony.[491] As Hannon and Trainor put it, "Enculturation to pitch structures follows a clear developmental trajectory in which universal aspects are grasped during or before infancy and system-specific aspects are acquired during childhood."[492] To be specific, by age five, a child is encultured to her culture's scales, while from age six or seven she also becomes encultured to the culture's more complex systems—chords, implied harmony, tunings, etc.[493]

At play too in pitch-related cultural constraints, incidentally, is the distinction around the world between tonal and nontonal languages. A tonal language is one in which the pitch (frequency) or pitch-shift of a word influences its meaning—such that the same raw sound will signify something different if sounded at a higher or lower pitch, or if the pitch rises or falls, or both. A classic example is the Mandarin Chinese word "*ma*," which can mean either "mother" (high pitch), "hemp" (rising), "horse" (falling, then rising), or "to scold" (falling). Surprisingly, perhaps, 70 percent of the world's languages are tonal—most notably in Southeast Asia (Vietnamese, Thai, etc.), East Asia (Chinese, Japanese), and Africa (dozens of languages), but also among many indigenous American and Australian tribes, and even in Europe (e.g., Norwegian). Several studies have shown a correlation between being a native tonal language speaker and having a higher propensity to possess "perfect" or absolute pitch (AP)—that is, the ability to identify a pitch without reference to an instrument, which as Trehub and others suggest, may have a genetic basis.[494] The impact of being raised in a tonal-language culture, however, is not only a greater propensity for AP, but also a heightened general sensitivity to pitch and tonal relations—with ramifications on music listening as well as memory.

## RHYTHM

As with studies on pitch, those on rhythm have confirmed an initial period of boundary-less music perception. Interestingly, Hannon and Trainor have suggested that our universal, statistical learning of rhythm-based norms precedes even that of pitch. For example, at six months, Western infants can detect violations in *both* isochronous (even, regular) and non-isochronous (uneven, irregular) meters. That is, at this stage, no culture-specific enculturation has yet taken root. Instead these six-month-old infants have seemingly already mastered the basic "rules" of both simple and complex rhythmic behavior. This "pluripotency," however, soon begins to wane, and by twelve months the Western infants generally fail to detect violations in the Balkan rhythms; that they can regain this ability after a mere two-week period of regular exposure, though, shows that the enculturation process initially grants us a flexible window. Alas, this flexibility is not limitless. Western adults, for example, continuously fail to detect violations in Balkan rhythms even with prolonged and repeated exposure. In fact, in most cases they can't even correctly find the downbeat or tap along with these non-native rhythms.[495]

This is not to suggest that adult nonmusicians are incapable of correctly tapping along with complex syncopations or odd meters, etc. Rather, it suggests that success is far more assured when it concerns one's own native rhythm than when it does a non-native rhythm. This is confirmed in several perception studies—including by musicologists Petri Toiviainen and Tuomas Eerola—where Finnish nonmusician adults largely failed to correctly clap along with typical African rhythms, unlike study participants from South Africa, who had no such problem.[496]

An ability to more easily synchronize or detect violations with respect to our native rhythmic language in turn suggests a more general conclusion: by virtue of our musical enculturation—where we grow up—adults are not all on equal footing in their broad abilities and tendencies of musical perception. Native Bulgarians and Senegalese, for example, are more likely to be proficient in processing and comprehending complex rhythms than those born and raised in Japan or Korea, where rhythmic complexity is largely de-emphasized. Similarly, though for reciprocal reasons, natives of India and Iraq are more likely to possess acute sensitivity to melodic and pitch-related complexity—such as microtones—than those raised in Germany or Canada. It is of course dangerous and silly to make blanket generalities about musical culture—and certainly there is no value judgment implied by these random examples. My point is simply that each of us will perceive the various musical parameters in a distinct and differentiated way—one that reflects and reinforces the common propensities of our native musical language.

Beyond tracking individual parameters like pitch and rhythm, a good many studies approach musical enculturation from a more holistic, experiential perspective—via the topics of emotion and memory. As we discussed in Interlude C, these are the highest and most complex "modules" of our neurobiological music processing, acting much as grand summations of all parameter-based perception: auditory feature extraction, Gestalt formation, music syntax, etc. We've seen that culture impacts how you perceive the musical "rules" of pitch and rhythmic behavior. Is the same true with regard to how you perceive and feel music-based emotions? Could a piece of music sound sad to one culture, but angry or happy in another? Do we remember elements from a native song differently than from a non-native one?

## EMOTION

Emotion, of course, is a human universal, with deep adaptive roots in our evolution. The perception of emotion arising from music listening is likewise universal. Yet research demonstrates that the emotion we derive from music taps into culture-specific dimensions as well. We'll explore the psychological link of music and emotion more fully in Interlude G, but we may here note the vital role that enculturation plays.

First, the research reveals a strong universal dimension to our emotional response to music with regard to the most basic of "basic emotions": happy and sad. With these two at least, there seems to be what music psychologist Heike Argstatter calls a "pan-cultural emotional lexicon," where two listeners of even remote cultures will hear the same musical passage as eliciting or representing a happy or a sad affect—or, in the parlance of psychology: positive or negative valence. An oft-cited case in point is a 2009 experiment by Thomas Fritz in which distinct groups of Western and Mafa (a small, remote ethnic group from Cameroon) listeners were asked to recognize the expression of either a happy, sad, or scared emotion within a group of Western-styled melodies.[497] Each melody was specifically designed to align with one of these three emotions, based on aspects of mode (major or minor), tempo, pitch range, tone density, and rhythmic regularity. The study results revealed that both groups identified all three emotions correctly, by pointing to universal facial expressions from the Ekman archive, "above chance level," that is, not randomly—though showing higher success with happy than with both sad and fearful.

The Fritz study, to be sure, has its problems[498]—and yet it does substantiate the claim that recognition of happy and sad (less so scared) in music transcends culture. The most common explanation for this comes back to those universal perceptions listed above—and specifically to our innate preference for consonance on the one hand and simple rhythm on the other. That is, music that is predominantly consonant and set in a simple, steady rhythmic flow will universally be recognized as holding positive valence, while music that is largely dissonant and/or set in an uneven, disjointed rhythm will hold the opposite.

Diving deeper, the recognition of happy or sad in music—as with any emotion—arrives via the aural "cues" heard within it, as interpreted via our innate perception as well as our culture-based statistical learning. In the Fritz study, it was especially the cues based on the mode, tempo, tonal density (consonance versus dissonance), and rhythmic regularity of the piano excerpts that triggered the recognition of an emotion in the Western and Mafa listeners. These types of cues—along with those based on contour, timbre, sound level, and energy—are labeled "psychophysical" by music psychologists Laura-Lee Balkwill and William Forde Thompson.[499] Our ability to recognize positive or negative valence based on these cues appears indeed to be universal, and thus independent from the experiences we gain from the music in our own culture. In other words, you could be dropped tomorrow on a remote island in the middle of the Pacific Ocean, and based on its "psychophysical" cues, whatever music the locals recognize as happy or sad, you likely would as well.

So, happy and sad music transcends culture: What about the other emotions? Not surprisingly, recognition within music of subtler emotions—surprise, anger, humor, spirituality, etc.—is decidedly more culture-specific. While tempo, density, rhythmic pulse, and other "psychophysical" cues carry with them *universal* triggers for basic emotions, a whole battery of other musical cues trigger emotions on a more encultured level—things like instrumental tuning, scale disposition, vocal and instrumental intonation, use of ornamentation, harmonic behavior, and so forth. These, of course, are many of the same culture-specific parameters that help constrain our perception of pitch and harmony within non-native music. This makes sense: if you can't recognize how a scale should properly proceed, what "normal" tuning sounds like, what makes for a logical chord progression, which vocal ornaments are typically used, etc., how could you possibly recognize when the music is meant to represent an emotion as nuanced as anger, surprise, or humor?

And so it shakes out in enculturation studies targeting emotion. In an elaborate study by Argstatter, for example, four cultural groups—German, Norwegian, Korean, and Indonesian—were asked to map a set of targeted melodies improvised by Western musicians to one of six emotional categories: happiness, sadness, surprise, fear, disgust, and anger.[500] As expected, the happy and sad melodies were recognized at the highest rates for all cultures—although the two Western groups performed better than did the two non-Western ones (63.5 percent to 46.5 percent). The worst performing group was the Indonesians—especially for melodies representing surprise (19.4 percent; compared to 56.2 percent for Germans, 31.1 percent for Koreans) and disgust (22.1 percent; compared to 42 percent for Norwegians, 40 percent for Koreans); this makes sense given the hegemony in Indonesia of gamelan and Arabic music, whereas in Korea there is a prevalence of Western pop and classical music. Indeed, as Argstatter notes, the Indonesian language has no distinct word for "disgust," which instead is aligned to the category of anger. Little wonder finding cultural disparity in recognizing musical emotion, then, if the very emotions themselves are culturally distinct.

## MEMORY

As detailed in Interlude C, listening to music also involves the continual and multilayered processing of memory; without memory, the art of music would simply not exist. Emotion may be critical to our experience of music, but memory reveals the degree to which we *understand* what we are hearing. By quantifying memory performance, therefore, we can gain valuable insight into how well we understand the music of our native culture, as opposed to that of a non-native one. Cross-cultural musical memory studies have taken off in the past decade, most notably by the musicologists Morrison and Demorest.[501] Critical in their studies, especially, is tracking the degree to which listeners remember events from unfamiliar or novel music. Their findings, as with so many other enculturation studies, reveal the importance of statistical hierarchies, and especially that of pitch.

In one study, for example, a group of adults from the US and Turkey (musicians and non-) listened to novel music from both the Western and Turkish classical traditions, as well as from Chinese classical music. As may be guessed, the American and Turkish participants most accurately remembered material from their own culture—including those Turkish musicians trained in Western classical.[502] Similar results were found even when a group of American fifth graders were given an eight-week curriculum on Turkish music: they fared no better than adults in remembering Turkish musical elements compared to elements within novel Western music. In short, these studies suggest that when it comes to memory—and thus to musical understanding in general—once encultured, beginning at age one or so, we not only hear non-native music but also remember and understand it "with an accent."

The bottom line from *all* these cognition studies, despite the complexities of the details just reviewed, is in fact rather simple: we process, experience, and remember music of our own culture considerably better than we do music of an unfamiliar or non-native culture. It is, admittedly, a rather obvious conclusion. But at least now you see it borne out in evidence. We can thus state confidently: the "enculturation effect" in music is real and makes a concrete difference in how music strikes us.

Okay, so what exactly happens, cognitively and perceptually, when we hear music from a non-native culture? Much as I did when trying to write music in a Celtic or Indian or Chinese style: we "accommodate" to the best of our abilities. We first tune in to those universal, psychophysical, culture-general elements—tempo, pulse, mode, sonic density, consonance level, energy, etc.—to get our bearings about what we're hearing. Instinctively wanting to go deeper, however, we then fall into a trap by imposing our own culture-specific "rules" onto music that very likely follows a different path. This implicit process invariably leads to what Patel calls "style-inappropriate expectancies." For example, a Western listener "statistically" familiar with the major pentatonic scale (as in "Amazing Grace") will apply its expectancies onto the pentatonic scales they hear in an African or a Chinese melody—which very likely will defy those expectations in myriad ways. We are, in essence, hearing the music "falsely" without being aware that we are doing so. It is this dissonance (no pun intended) between our "inappropriate" expectations and the empirical behavior of the non-native music that generates a heavier, less fluid "cognitive load," meaning that our brains work harder. Our inability to hear the music on its own terms in turn helps explain why our memory falters when we confront non-native music.

## Parlez-vous Gamelan?

Innate enculturation—via the implicit processing of statistical learning—is not the only factor at play when we confront non-native music. It is true that an eight-week curriculum on Turkish music had no real impact on the memory performance of fifth graders; it is also true that the many enculturation studies that tested professional musicians showed that they did *not* perform demonstrably better than nonmusicians in processing or recalling culturally unfamiliar music. Our "hearing with an accent," in other words, appears to run deep and across levels of musical literacy.

This does not mean, however, that acquiring musical knowledge and training will have no impact on how we hear non-native music. Without at least some knowledge about a given non-native musical style, that is, your ability to objectively judge it will be severely limited. True, you may never hear it the way a native listener does, but with acquired knowledge you can at least know what to listen for: whether the style is generally simple or complex; what types of rhythms are common; what scale tones are normally used, etc. Indeed, while an eight-week course may not change your perception or processing, perhaps an eighteen-week—or two-year—course would. At some point, certainly, you'd start to hear the non-native style with something approaching an innately encultured ear. Western musicians such as saxophonist Stan Getz (Brazilian bossa nova) or guitarist John McLaughlin (Indian classical) demonstrate the potential of late-stage enculturation—where through intensive study and natural facility, both musicians were able to approach near bicultural proficiency in a musical language outside their native style.

Who knows: with enough time spent with an initially unfamiliar music culture, you might eventually become somewhat "bimusical." As noted above, this is an actual academic designation, introduced by musicologists Patrick Wong, Elizabeth Margulis, and Anil Roy in a well-cited study from 2009.[503] The team took three groups of nonmusician adults: American, rural Indian, and bicultural Indian-Westerners living in the US. The monocultural groups had no previous exposure to the musical style of the other, while the bicultural group had ongoing exposure to both styles since birth. All three groups first listened to excerpts from both Western and Indian classical music and were then tested on memory recall, following procedures used by Morrison and Demorest. The results, as you might guess, showed a clear memory bias (higher recall) for the monocultural groups with regard to their own native style, and yet—significantly—the bicultural group successfully recalled both styles equally. That is, just as members of the third group were *bilingual* in English and Hindi (or another Indian language), so too did they appear *bimusical* in Western and Indian music processing, perception, and recognition. The groups, admittedly, were not tested on purely musicological perception challenges; however, a second—emotion-based—finding of the study supports this broader conclusion: whereas the monocultural groups rated the other culture's music as *more tense* than their own, the bicultural group found neither style to be particularly tense.

A key assumption in the Wong study is that just as enculturation to a single native music happens implicitly, so too does bimusical native enculturation. Explicit training in a second musical culture, in other words, is not required—just steady exposure, and especially from early infancy. But implied in this notion too is another parallelism with language: just as we can grow up with partial levels of bilingualism ("I spoke a bit of French as a kid," "My grandparents taught me some Chinese," etc.), so too can we grow up acquiring varying degrees of bimusicalism. Such would explain, for example, my natural affinity with Jewish music—I "spoke" it somewhat growing up. Indeed, more so than with actual spoken language, this partial bimusicalism is based on not just what we hear as a child, but also the degree to which any two musical languages are "related"—based on their "cultural distance," in Morrison and Demorest's phrase.[504] English and Irish music, for example, are certainly not identical, but they are "cousins," so to speak, in their statistical hierarchies, etc. As such, a native Brit will by default be quasi-fluent in Celtic music, and vice versa. This in turn suggests that many of us are to some degree not only bimusical but "polymusical," whether we know it or not—particularly if we grew up in a culture with common properties to several others that surround it. This, moreover, is distinct from the levels of partial bimusicalism, or polymusicalism, we can hope to gain post-infancy via intense exposure and explicit study/training.

## Enculturation and Musical Taste

Finally, this leads us to the crux of the matter: What is the impact of the enculturation effect on our musical taste? For example, can you like a non-native music that you don't understand? In a word—yes. This indeed is one of the miracles of music: comprehension is not a prerequisite for preference. In spoken language, a lack of comprehension makes for uselessness. True, an English speaker may appreciate the tonal nature of Vietnamese or the exotic percussive qualities of an African Khoisan ("click") language, but after thirty seconds or so, you'd quickly get bored and walk away. With music, of course, it is different: we actually *can* gain sustained pleasure and even garner profound meaning and emotion from music that, in truth, we are hearing with "inappropriate expectancies." There are many non-native styles I quite enjoy hearing—Javanese gamelan, Hungarian csárdás, Pakistani qawwali, etc.—despite having little understanding of what's going on musicologically. My own history as a musician, in fact, is in large part a result of having "fallen in love," in my early twenties, with a musical culture I didn't understand. Admittedly, this music—sacred polyphony of the Renaissance—is non-native only from an "intracultural" perspective (see Interlude F)—and yet from a statistical standpoint, especially pitch- and harmony-wise, it may as well have been written on a small island in Micronesia. Okay, perhaps not, but you get my point. . . .

Incidentally, the musical taste of listeners is occasionally addressed in music enculturation studies.[505] Although there are some mixed results, the most prominent conclusion, as in the Morrison and Demorest studies, is that preference has *no* impact on cognitive performance with non-native music. That is, we may like the sound of a particular non-native song or work, but our ability to "correctly" perceive its pitch or rhythmic elements, recognize specific emotions within it, or remember what we've heard will be no better than for someone who hates it. The only circumstance in which preference does appear to aid memory, in fact, is with native music.

All right, so we can like music we don't understand. And our personal taste plays little role in how we cognitively perceive music from another culture. But these are not to say that enculturation has no impact on our musical taste—of course it does. As is fairly intuitive—and will be explored more in Interlude G—we tend to like things we know and dislike things we don't. This innate bias against the unfamiliar, with evolutionary roots, leads us to close our minds to stimuli that are different from what we're used to. Without an open mind, and at least some preparatory exposure, many of us will simply shut down our preference radar when we encounter unfamiliar, non-native music: "That instrument sounds weird," "I don't understand that melody," "Where's the beat," and so forth. In some cases, of course, the perceived beauty or sheer interest of the music—perhaps aligning to those universal traits we innately prefer—will enable us to overcome this bias. But in general, we are little prone to welcome non-native music to our hit parade.

Given what we've learned in this interlude, these conclusions should not be surprising: If you can't accurately predict where a song's melody is going, or you can't comfortably find the downbeat or feel its groove, how much can you really get into the music, ride its narrative wave, and feel its discursive power? If the music is trying to emulate a very specific emotion that you can't recognize, how emotionally bonded can you become? And to what degree can you love a work that cognitively and neurologically you are unlikely to remember next time you hear it? Well, to some degree, perhaps, but not like with music from your own native culture—music whose statistical properties have been ingrained into you since before you could walk, and that have steadily accompanied you in your life ever since; music you understand not just from a hierarchical standpoint, but also by means of the nuanced "idioms" and "colloquialisms"—the riffs, patterns, progressions, motives, etc.—that only one raised in the milieu would recognize as native.

As members of the cultures to which our native music is aligned, our musical taste gets tethered to the statistical and culture-specific templates of the various musical discourses we hear—like an anchor set upon a vast seafloor of musical possibilities. Encultured during infancy, made more complex during childhood, and fully ingrained as "norms abstracted over a lifetime," as Margulis puts it, this becomes "our" musical language. In ways beyond our conscious control, our musical taste is a product of this native language, even as we may strive to enrich and expand it.

And yet, while what sounds normal and what sounds weird to us is seeded by our broad, native culture, our musical taste is *fine-tuned* by the subcultures and socioeconomic classes in which we live—the increasingly idiosyncratic ways that music is received from one neighborhood or clique or social class to another. We'll explore this topic shortly, but first let's return to the purely musical realm with two more genotypes—both largely defined by their subcultures: hip hop and electronica.

*twelve*

# THE HIP HOP GENOTYPE

• • •

## Introducing Subject 4

Next up is Subject 4, who starts the day at the gym doing some weight training with the perfect laid-back track, **Snoop Dogg's "Gin & Juice."** A more recent favorite, **Kendrick Lamar's "i,"** then forms an upbeat companion for the trek to work. Rather tense after a long workday, a standby—**Eminem's "Lose Yourself"**—brings forth a regroup on the way home. Feeling better, a night on the town hits a high point with an old classic, **Earth, Wind & Fire's "Shining Star."***

Based on this hit parade, Subject 4's musical genotype clearly resonates with hip hop, though it is seemingly not as "hardcore" or exclusively focused on that as other fans out there.

Before diving into these hits, however, some words on the hip hop species:

## The Hip Hop Species: A Brief Review

Of the six musical species that undergird Pandora's Music Genome Project, and that animate the days in the lives of our seven music lovers, a full three of them—jazz, rock, and hip hop—arose directly out of the African-American cultural experience. Of these, however, only hip hop maintains an existential connection to that same culture to this day. Indeed, although one can speak of a "jazz culture," a "rock culture," and even an "EDM culture," hip hop actually *is* a culture—of which music is but one seminal component. With thirty-plus years of history behind it now, hip hop culture—its language, dance, dress, street art, and music—is a topic of academic inquiry, debate, and preservation, the Hiphop Archive & Research Institute at Harvard University's Hutchins Center being one manifestation.[506]

---

* Subject 4's fifth song, heard as a winding down before bedtime, is Common and John Legend's 2014 soundtrack song "Glory." For its discussion, see the WYLI website, supplement to Chapter 12.

At ground zero in any effort to understand hip hop culture, of course, are its songs. Let's thus get our bearing with a list of ten touchstone tracks that may be seen to typify the hip hop musical species:

DJ Khaled, "I'm the One" (2017)
Lil Wayne, "6 Foot 7 Foot" (2010)
Jay-Z, "99 Problems" (2004)
OutKast, "B.O.B" (2000)
Lauryn Hill, "Lost Ones" (1998)
The Notorious B.I.G., "Juicy" (1994)
Public Enemy, "Fight the Power" (1989)
N.W.A, "Straight Outta Compton" (1988)
Grandmaster Flash and the Furious Five, "The Message" (1982)
The Sugarhill Gang, "Rapper's Delight" (1979)

These ten songs—all historically significant and/or chart-topping—feature an array of musicological elements that typify hip hop. They are all, it must be said, oriented predominantly around their lyrics—focused on sociopolitical issues reflecting African-American youth culture and lifestyle, often via explicit language; the lyrics are mainly, though not always, presented as rapped rhymes—often with displays of rhythmic virtuosity; in many of the songs, however, rapping is interspersed with sung melody, especially as chorus hooks—or even, as in the DJ Khaled song, replaced entirely by singing; they all feature a vibrant, multilayered, and highly syncopated rhythmic language, always in 4/4 meter; all employ a harmonic language that is simple and largely static, often via a single chord, or a short cycle of two or three chords; all songs are punctuated by short and oft-repeated instrumental riffs—performed by both synthetic and electric instruments; and all utilize a rich production style that relies heavily on sampling, scratching, and a sonic focus on the low, booming side of the frequency spectrum.

At heart, hip hop and rap music reflect the experience of young, urban, working-class African-Americans, and more explicitly "the systems of subjugation that have created class discrepancies in the United States," as sociologist Becky Blanchard put it.[507] These two musical genres, by the way, are not synonymous; rap is a subset of hip hop, which in turn need not include the use of spoken word or rapping. And yet rap is what most readily defines hip hop music in the minds of many listeners, as well as what most directly reflects the anger and despair of the otherwise underrepresented populations that hip hop culture embodies.

The origins of rap, however, go considerably deeper: to the ancient African practice of the griot—the traveling minstrel who transmitted tribal histories and tales of war and peace, as well as to the West African concept of *nommo* ("the creative word"), where poetic words were infused with a power to alter the physical world.[508] This latter, for example, is echoed by rapper Jay-Z when he defines the mission of the poet "to make words do more work than they normally do, to make them work on more than one level."[509] Roots lying closer to home include the practice of New World slaves to conceal the meaning of their communications by means of clever, coded rhymes, and more recently in the Jamaican tradition of "toasting" during the 1960s—where an MC would praise and entertain by improvising spoken word while a DJ spun reggae records, among much else.

Hip hop proper arose in the 1970s in the Bronx, a borough hard-hit by debilitating civic policies—where gangs, drugs, graffiti, and poverty were the stuff of daily life for the largely African-American and Hispanic residents. It began as Jamaican-influenced experiments, such as those by DJ Kool Herc: MC'ing entertaining "raps" over extended percussion "breaks" within reggae, funk, soul, or disco tunes while kids performed novel dance moves—hence "breakdancing." By the mid-'70s it had morphed into a stand-alone approach. The poetry was simple and innocuous, with funky beats and looped "samples"—melodic riffs or other parts borrowed from funk and R&B recordings. Initially, the songs were performed live at block parties, often as competitions for the best rapping "skillz" among neighboring "crews." Things started to change, however, when the first recordings were made at the end of the decade—most notably "Rapper's Delight" by the Sugarhill Gang (1979), whose lyric "Da hip da hop, da hippity da hip hip hop" is often credited for term's adoption.* Local DJs caught on, the song entered *Billboard*'s Top 40, and a species was born.

With broader exposure, and hence a wider gamut of practitioners, hip hop was primed to move forward in typical artistic evolution as the 1980s began: toward greater sophistication, aesthetic definition, and stylistic interplay. Critical too was the advent of new, cheaper technology—notably drum machines and samplers—especially the Roland TR-808 and AKAI S900, respectively. In the songs of "old-school" rappers like Kurtis Blow and Grandmaster Flash, music and lyrics became more complex—including occasional use of social commentary (e.g., Flash's "The Message," 1982), multilayered instrumental parts, and incorporation of nonfunk genres like electronic music. From 1983, a "new-school" approach then pushed the stylistic bounds further by embracing hard-edged rock—notably Run-D.M.C. and the Beastie Boys, whose "She's Crafty" (1986), for example, samples the opening riff of Led Zeppelin's "The Ocean." It is worth noting here that in subtle distinction to the conventional notion of a composer and lyricist found in most other species, hip hop songs are generally defined as a collaboration between a music producer who assembles the beats and instrumen-

* More likely, the term's origins extend back to the mid-1970s: two famous stories are early rapper Keef Cowboy's tease of a military friend by faux-marching with "hip-hop-hip-hop," and community leader and pioneering DJ Afrika Bambaataa's promotion of Bronx block parties as "Hip Hop Beeny Bop"—in both cases leading to the incorporation of "hip hop" into raps. Initially, the term was pejorative, especially by members of the disco community, but by 1982 it took on a more positive connotation. See Steven Hager, "Afrika Bambaataa's Hip Hop," *Village Voice*, September 21, 1982.

tal/vocal track and a rapper who writes and performs the lyrics—a practice that spans the full history of hip hop.

As often happens with artistic trajectories, historians have identified a "golden age" of hip hop—from the mid-'80s to early '90s: a period of a great diversity, musical and poetic innovation, social consciousness, and broader commercial visibility. It is also one where the nexus of creativity shifted from the hegemony of New York to other parts of the US—especially Los Angeles. Decisively, the tame social commentary of "old-school" rap gave way to explicit and confrontational approaches: songs like "Fight the Power" (1989) by New York "political rap" group Public Enemy and especially "Fuck tha Police" by LA (Compton) "gangsta rap" group N.W.A (1988) led to a heightened awareness of rap by the broader public—not to mention an outcry of condemnation, censorship, parental advisory labels, etc. To many socially minded observers of hip hop, however, such approaches are part of the realm's essence, and reflect, as oppose to instigate, the despair, anger, and hopelessness black youth face in the inner city—where "thug life," as Cornel West notes, is celebrated for "the opportunity it may provide for economic and social power in neighborhoods where hope has been lost."[510] Not surprisingly, the musical accompaniment of these songs is most often sonically dense, up-tempo, and based on hard-edged funk and rock samples—often with dozens of distinct sources.

Since the mid-'90s, hip hop has seen its share of new trends, innovative highs, and mannered lows—all of which may be seen, to some degree, in relation to the feats and challenges laid down by the hard-edged, socially minded songs of the "golden age." Particularly significant is the degree to which the realm became embraced by the mainstream: three of the ten best-selling albums in 2000, for example, were by hip hop artists. The tremendous commercial success of rappers—those representing the rival styles of *West Coast G-Funk* (Dr. Dre, Snoop Dogg, Tupac Shakur) and *East Coast Hardcore* (Jay-Z, Nas, Notorious B.I.G) in the 1990s,[511] megastars like Nelly, OutKast, Eminem, and 50 Cent in the early 2000s, the "pop rap" of Kanye West today, to name but a few—demonstrates the degree to which hip hop has moved from marginal entertainment to cultural mainstay.

Some have questioned whether this mainstream embrace of hip hop is a good thing for the music itself: as rap historian and consultant for Pandora's Hip Hop Genome Davey D put it, "The business of music has bastardized rap."[512] Small, local, African-American owned labels have largely given way to major international ones—many owned by upper-class whites—in fostering new hip hop artists. For the genre to thrive, Davey D has argued, rappers must "learn their history," and not ignore the raw racial and social factors that spawned it in the first place.

This commercial embrace, however, has hardly dampened the use of "objectionable" language in rap songs—the ubiquitous N-word, rampant vulgarity, themes of violence, misogyny, and homophobia, etc. As importantly, the past twenty years have greatly expanded the hip hop musicological landscape: *"alternative rap"* artists like A Tribe Called Quest and the Roots have embraced everything from jazz to country to punk, as well as the latest R&B styles. To this can then be added a huge array of regional hip hop styles in the US (Southern, Midwest, etc.) and around the world (Cuba, Pakistan, etc.), usually as a vehicle of social resistance. Indeed, contemporary American artists like Kendrick Lamar reveal that social consciousness in American hip hop is today alive and well—a factor, no doubt, that helped him earn a Pulitzer Prize in 2018. And if you're still looking for proof that the species has entered the American mainstream, just recall our discussion of Lin-Manuel Miranda's musical *Hamilton*: still today a very desirable—and expensive—ticket on Broadway.

## Morning Weight Training: Snoop Dogg's "Gin & Juice"

**Snoop Dogg's "Gin & Juice"** is among the classic, touchstone songs of early 1990s West Coast rap, specifically of the subgenre known as "G-Funk" or gangsta funk. It thus establishes Subject 4 as harboring a soft spot—at the least—for a well-established and comparatively low-intensity branch of hip hop's "golden age." We'll have to see how much deeper into the species we get by the end of the day.

### SNOOP DOGG: BACKGROUND

Snoop Dogg in many ways epitomizes the mainstream embrace of hip hop artists from the early 1990s onward, as well as the larger-than-life persona that fuels much of their public success. Born in Long Beach, California, in 1971, Calvin Cordozar Broadus Jr. earned the nickname "Snoopy" when his mom spotted a resemblance to the cute *Peanuts* character. His upbringing, however, was not so innocent: the Eastside of Long Beach, like Compton ten miles to the north, was rife with gangs, drugs, and poverty. By his teens, Broadus was getting into legal trouble for drugs and illicit activity, associating, for example, with the notorious Rollin' 20 Crips gang. A love of music, however, was also part of Broadus' childhood, fostered initially while singing in a local church choir. By his teens, he had become a devotee of hip hop, and began rapping under the moniker Snoop Doggy Dogg—part of a "crew" of friends called 213—the local area code. In 1992, Warren G, a member of 213, passed their "mixtape" (a noncommercial promo) to his stepbrother Dr. Dre, then preparing to record his first solo album, *The Chronic*; Dre was impressed.[513]

Snoop's resulting work with Dr. Dre—the producing force behind N.W.A—provided the young rapper with an extraordinary opportunity for apprenticeship and exposure. Snoop became Dre's "right-hand man," as *Rolling Stone* put it, appearing on numerous tracks on the latter's influential *The Chronic* album. In its wake, the two collaborated on Snoop's own debut album, *Doggystyle* (1993), which shot up to No. 1 on *Billboard*'s Top 200, and went on to become the biggest-selling rap album to date. Both albums typify the G-Funk style—featuring a laid-back musical affect, yet plenty of provocative lyrics glorifying the gangsta life of drugs, sex, and violence. Given his profile, Snoop became the public face of everything "wrong" with rap, and the imperative for stricter censorship. An example was the Senate Judiciary Committee hearing convened in February 1994 by Illinois senator Carol Moseley-Braun to discuss "violent and demeaning imagery in popular music"—where Snoop, in absentia, was "made to appear like hip-hop's Mephistopheles, seducing black children to trade their souls for the corrupt delights of G-Funk," in Michael Eric Dyson's words.[514] This, of course, was only good for Snoop's brand, as he continued his rise to international celebrity status.

In the ensuing years, Snoop has produced over a dozen albums, mainly in the orbit of G-Funk—though more recently extending into reggae, under the name Snoop Lion; traditional R&B, with his 2015 album *Bush*, featuring Stevie Wonder and Gwen Stefani; and even gospel, with his 2018 release *Bible of Love*. Most of his albums have sold quite well, though only the first three—*Doggystyle*, *Tha Doggfather* (1996), and *Da Game Is to Be Sold* (1998)—reached the No. 1 spot on the Top 200. In all of these recordings, Snoop Dogg (he dropped the "Doggy" in 1996) delivers his raps with a characteristic lazy "drawl." The gangsta references, moreover, are not mere facade: his life has been peppered with arrests and legal confrontations for drugs and arms possession; he even spent time working as a pimp and producing pornographic films. In hip hop, as much as in any entertainment arena, however, all publicity is good publicity: Snoop has parlayed his decadent notoriety into regular appearances in films and on TV, even his own "reality" show. As much as anyone, Snoop Dogg demonstrates that hip hop artists can take their difficult, volatile lifestyles all the way to the bank—and into the hearts of millions of fans.

Indeed, the prevalent "misbehavior" of prominent rappers and hip hop moguls is a potent source of the realm's cultural and commercial success. For at least some hardcore fans, that is, the rough-and-tumble lives and attitudes of its artists is a source of pride and affinity; as African-American studies scholar Jayna Brown put it, they love hip hop "for its irreverence and misbehavior . . . for its bad manners and its immorality, its lack of respectability or restraint, for its illicit embrace of overabundance and excess."[515] This may simply be a manifestation of our irresistible worship of celebrities and their foibles, a kind of catharsis that helps us transcend the relative mediocrity of our everyday lives—and as such is a facet of rock culture as much as hip hop. Of course, not all serious hip hop fans embrace the "bad boy" image of the species, as many prefer artists—like Talib Kweli, A Tribe Called Quest, or Common—who adopt a positive, socially

conscious stance. Still, for some fans, the "irreverent" antics of artists like Snoop Dogg only add to the appeal.

## SNOOP DOGG: ANALYSIS

"Gin & Juice" was one of two hit singles from Snoop's debut album, *Dogg style*, the other being "What's My Name?" It exemplifies the G-Funk style ar its trademark slow, laid-back tempo, female backup voices, and layered synth sizers—including the use of a distinct '70s-era "saw-wave" synth lead. The pression "G-Funk" is a play on "P-Funk," the 1970s funk style associated w George Clinton and his Parliament-Funkadelic collective—many of whose sc were sampled by Dr. Dre and other G-Funk producers. Specifically, "Gi Juice" samples the drum part (not the bass as often claimed) used in George McC 1975 soul song "I Get Lifted."

Before diving into the music, however, a small point: an observant r may well have noted a potential contradiction arising from a comment mad back in Chapter 3—that this book won't focus much on lyrics. Clearly, tl not been the case in the above review of hip hop, where lyric topics have center stage. Indeed, the history and essence of hip hop, and especially ra but impossible without a deep consideration of lyrical themes and perfo styles. The same is true, admittedly, when considering musical taste—as no doubt that rap lyrics are a significant factor in driving fans toward, from, the songs they hear. This is due, of course, to the complex and ofte not to mention explicit, nature of the lyrics, and to the high stock p artists' rapping "skillz," as noted earlier. This explains, moreover, why Hip Hop Genome contains literally dozens of genes detailing rap ly language, topic, etc.

Still, I would argue that a rap song's purely musical discourse is n in eliciting a response from a prospective fan than is the case with genre. That said, I'll here note that the lyrics of "Gin & Juice" emb called "cruising" lifestyle and its hedonistic mix of drugs, alcohol, and misogynistically described, presaging Snoop's actual pimping activit later.

True to its G-Funk lineage, "Gin & Juice" quickly initiates a d bed" (often improperly termed the "beat") in a laid-back tempo of once fully loaded contains at least five separate synth parts, each either a two- or four-bar ostinato cycle. Most of these are simple an consisting of only a single note or an octave (usually on C) place on a particular offbeat. The synth parts float in syncopated pa two-measure drum and bass loop. As noted, the drum loop is a sa Lifted," whereas the bass part is original. Undoubtedly, the bass much of what gives the song its unique musical groove, which is h

copated and a bit chromatic (F–A♭–G♭–C). The resulting harmony is likewise chromatic, a two-bar progression of F minor–E♭ minor 11/G♭, where the Cs act as a kind of pedal point. Technically, this progression can be labeled as a kind of diatonic variant of the "minor Phrygian" mode (i–♭II), normally moving as F minor–G♭ major, as shown in Figures 12.1a–b:

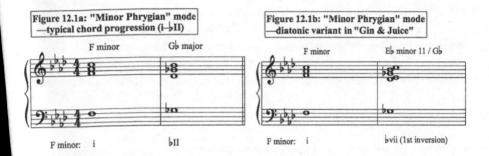

**Figure 12.1a: "Minor Phrygian" mode —typical chord progression (i–♭II)**

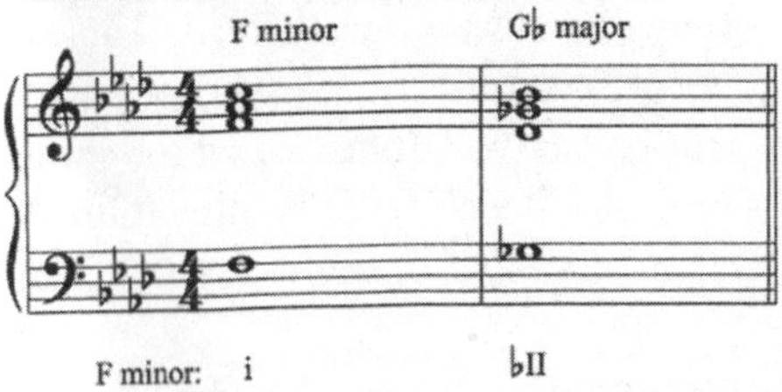


**Figure 12.1b: "Minor Phrygian" mode —diatonic variant in "Gin & Juice"**

Whether consciously understood as Phrygian or not, this was and continues to be a popular progression in hip hop and rap—such as in Tupac Shakur's "Ambitionz Az a Ridah," 50 Cent's "Candy Shop," and Nicki Minaj's "Anaconda"—probably due to its simultaneously dark and exotic quality.

Two of the synth parts in particular are pivotal: one is a two-bar chordal pattern buried in the "bed"; the other is more overt—a syncopated four-bar ostinato in that space-age "saw-wave" synth sound noted above. This full bed—surely a result of Dr. Dre's producer's handiwork—is shown here (Figure 12.2):

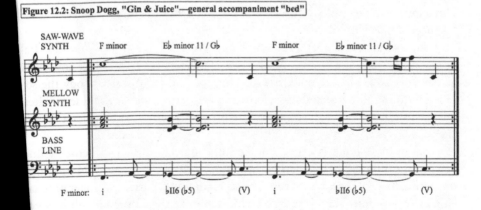

**Figure 12.2: Snoop Dogg, "Gin & Juice"—general accompaniment "bed"**

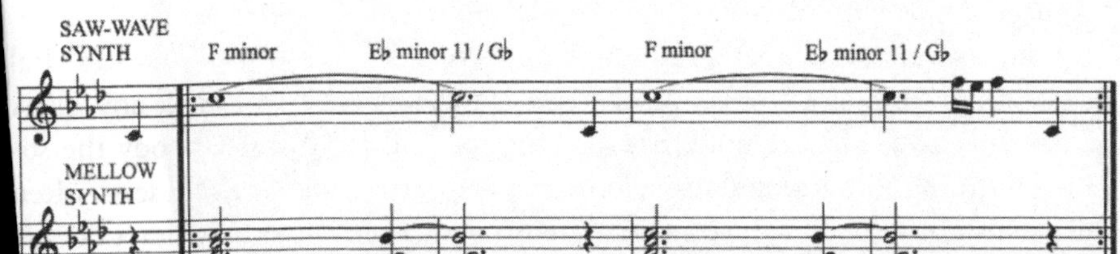


This being a rap song, however, the defining element of the song is its rap erformance—delivered by Snoop in his characteristically laid-back, "behind-e-beat" manner. During the verses, he produces a generally pitchless rap that ten centers near F or G♭ (tonics of the chords), but frequently inflects up and

down, as speech is wont to do. Interest is generated by the continually varied rhythmic patterns he creates—generally a mix of eighth and sixteenth notes. At times, indeed, he introduces a fair degree of rhythmic complexity—including a hemiola (on "*Turn* off the lights and *close* the door/*but* but what . . .") and even a three-part canon (on "six in the mornin'"). And yet, the patterns seem to be largely based on a fairly simple "metric template" presented at the very beginning of the song (Figure 12.3):

**Figure 12.3: Snoop Dogg, "Gin & Juice"—opening rap rhythm (approximate, "behind the beat")**

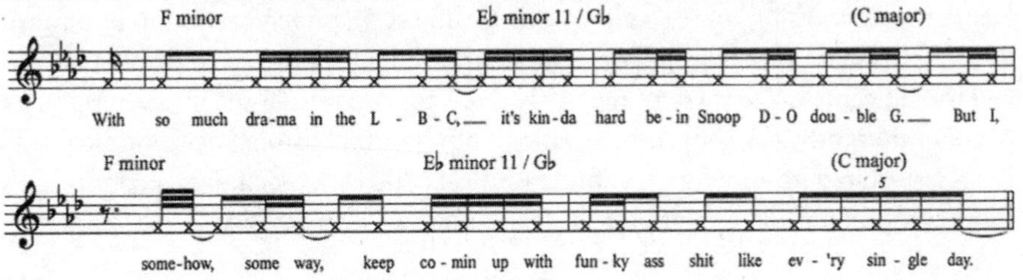


As impressive as Snoop's rapping is, however, the element that undoubtedly made the song such a big commercial hit is its catchy, sung hook (harmonized in 5ths and 4ths). The melody is actually a variation on the chorus hook used in the 1980 R&B song "Watching You" by Slave; specifically, it adopts the same basic rhythm as its source, though is varied melodically and harmonically (Figures 12.4a–b):

**Figure 12.4a: Slave, "Watching You"—chorus "hook"**

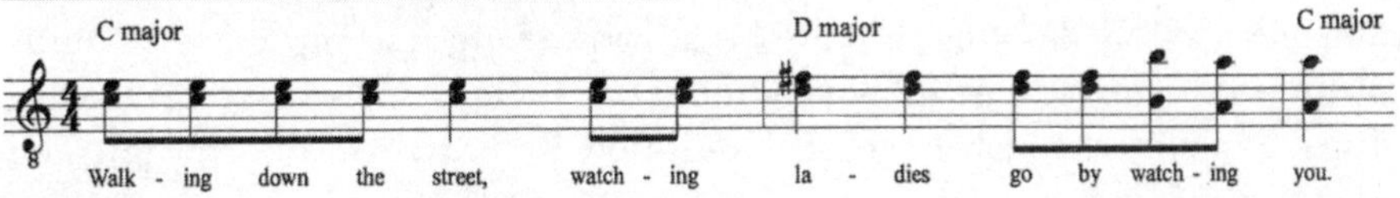


**Figure 12.4b: Snoop Dogg, "Gin & Juice"—chorus "hook"**

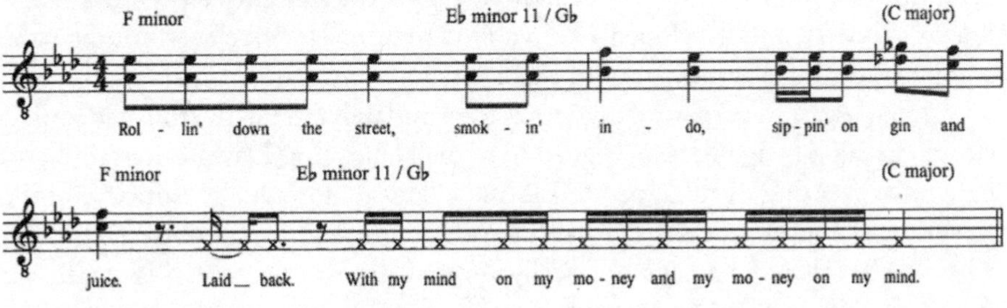


This just reinforces a basic aesthetic of hip hop—quite distinct from pop and rock: borrowing and adapting an existing musical element is far from a weakness, but rather a badge of honor and a symbol of creative interplay with the past. Snoop intersects the hook by rapping the mantra "laid-back," as well as the antimetabole (wordplay) "With my mind on my money and my money on my mind." Although an odd thematic choice for a morning workout, the collective ingredients of "Gin & Juice" add up to a three-and-a-half-minute rap song that keeps its fans coming back for more.

## The Trek to Work: Kendrick Lamar's "i"

**Kendrick Lamar's "i"** offers a glimpse into Subject 4's preference in hip hop music twenty-plus years after Snoop Dogg's breakout hit. It also suggests how the species—and the subgenre of West Coast rap—has changed, and not, in the intervening years. More importantly, the song, a modern-day hip hop touchstone, demonstrates Subject 4's kinship with more sophisticated musical constructs, including a considerably more complex rap-delivery approach, than found in "Gin & Juice."

### LAMAR: BACKGROUND

Kendrick Lamar has risen to become one of the hottest hip hop artists of the past few years, suggesting that reports, starting from around 2005, of rap's creative decline have been greatly exaggerated.[516] Lamar (full name Kendrick Lamar Duckworth) was born in Compton, the epicenter of West Coast rap, in 1987, and experienced the kind of rough-and-tumble youth so common among rap artists. Growing up on welfare, Lamar witnessed two fatal shootings by the time he was eight, in a neighborhood replete with gangs and crack addicts. It was a different kind of shooting, however, that had the greatest impact on his future plans: a 1995 music video shoot for the song "California Love" by Dr. Dre and Tupac Shakur—then labelmates at Death Row Records, owned by the infamous Suge Knight; watching the video shoot on his dad's shoulders, Lamar saw his future calling. His teen years, like those of Snoop Dogg, were surrounded by gang violence and run-ins with the police, and yet the straight-A student was also drawn to poetry, and developed a keen ability to unravel with clever wordplay the complexities and contradictions of inner-city life.

Lamar began to earn a reputation as a formidable rap talent from his earliest efforts, in 2003 at age sixteen. Signed to a small label, Top Dawg Entertainment, he released a string of mixtapes and music videos that gradually earned him the attention of hip hop celebrities like Lil Wayne. Among these too was Dr. Dre, who in 2011 heard Lamar's politically infused gangsta rap song "Ignorance Is Bliss": as with Snoop Dogg twenty years earlier, Dre was so impressed that he signed Lamar to his own label, Aftermath, and coproduced his debut album, *good kid, m.A.A.d city*, in 2012. The album shot up to No. 2 on *Billboard*'s Top 200, and gained several Top 40 singles, including "Poetic Justice." Critical accolades likewise came pouring in, such as when *GQ* magazine named Lamar "Rapper of the Year" in 2013, or when *Rolling Stone* called him "hip hop's most exciting rapper."[517] His second album, *To Pimp a Butterfly* (2015)—including the song "i"—garnered him even greater success, debuting at No. 1 on the Top 200, and winning Best Rap Album at the 2016 Grammy Awards.

It was at this Grammy show, moreover, that Lamar gave a live performance that became a subject of considerable discussion, controversy, and acclaim—and that underscored his identity as today's most provocative rap artist.[518] Dressed in prison garb and chains, Lamar combined two songs from *To Pimp a Butterfly*—"The Blacker the Berry," inspired in part by the Trayvon Martin case, and "Alright," an unofficial anthem of the Black Lives Matter movement—along with another highly charged song, "Untitled 3," that again references Martin (a day that "set us back four hundred years"). The medley then closed with a plea that seemed to underlie his overall intent: "Conversation for the entire nation, this is bigger than us"—which, as Spencer Kornhaber of the *Atlantic* notes, is "illuminated by a fire that has been roaring for longer than America has existed." In so doing, Lamar provided us with yet another reminder of the West African *nommo* tradition, and hip hop's potential for poetic words to change the world.

And indeed, since that catalytic 2016 Grammy performance, Lamar has continued to change the world with his poetry—most notably via his 2017 album, *DAMN.* Not only did the album sail to No. 1 on the Top 200, become the biggest-selling hip hop album of 2017, and score Lamar his first No. 1 song, "Humble," on the *Billboard* Hot 100; the album also earned him, as noted earlier, the 2018 Pulitzer Prize for Music. The drama of this is hard to overstate: as the first Pulitzer given outside the realms of classical or jazz music, the 2018 award has been called a "vindication of hip hop," and yet more than that, it corroborates the potential of the species—in the hands of an artist like Lamar—to achieve both commercial and cultural glory.[519]

In his work, Lamar displays the influence of rappers like Eminem, Jay-Z, and especially Tupac Shakur, and draws on musical references ranging from funk to rock to free jazz—he especially cites his love for Miles Davis. Yet from these and other sources, Lamar has revealed his as a unique musical and poetic voice who is decisively writing the next chapter of hip hop history.

## LAMAR: ANALYSIS

As noted above, "i" stems from *To Pimp a Butterfly*, and itself won two Grammy Awards, including Best Rap Song in 2015. Lyrically, the song presents a largely self-affirming message—the refrain is "I love myself"—though set amid articulations of myriad dark forces, personal and cultural—written specifically to ward off dark thoughts and to raise the spirits of "friends in the penitentiary," as Lamar told *Rolling Stone*.[520]

Musically, "i" shares with "Gin & Juice" a primary hip hop characteristic in its use of a 1970s-era source, and indeed goes far beyond the latter in its level of borrowing. The source here is the 1973 R&B hit "That Lady" by the Isley Brothers—itself a remake of their own song, "Who's That Lady," from 1964. But rather than directly sampling (lifting from an existing recording), Lamar decided to rerecord the "sampled" elements. The reliance on the source is indeed palpable, but only for the first half of the track, after which it deviates fully. Specifically, Lamar borrows the "jangling" rhythm guitar, the drum pattern, bass line, and main guitar riff of the intro of "That Lady" to undergird both the principal verse and chorus of "i." The resulting chord progression, interestingly, is C minor 7–F minor 7 (i7–iv7), the same one used at the start of Wayne Shorter's "Footprints" (Figure 12.5):

**Figure 12.5: Kendrick Lamar, "i"—intro "jangling" guitar riff**

Initially, "i" seems to be setting up the same verse-chorus form as "Gin & Juice," but it instead forges a distinct structure. To explain, note that "That Lady" alternates its C minor 7–G minor 7 chorus with a four-bar "bridge," using the progression A♭ major 7–G minor/B♭–A♭ major 7–G minor (starting at "Here me callin' after you"); "i" adopts this four-bar section to support a pre-chorus, but only prior to the second and third choruses. Things get even more complex after the varied (sung) fourth verse, as Lamar introduces an entirely different "bed," based on a descending bass line: C–B♭–A–A♭–G—the same line used in Chicago's "25 or 6 to 4"—to support the fourth chorus material (with the hook "tuned" down a 4th), and then maintains it for three more sections (Figure 12.6):

**Figure 12.6: Kendrick Lamar, "i"—Chorus 4, with descending bass line**

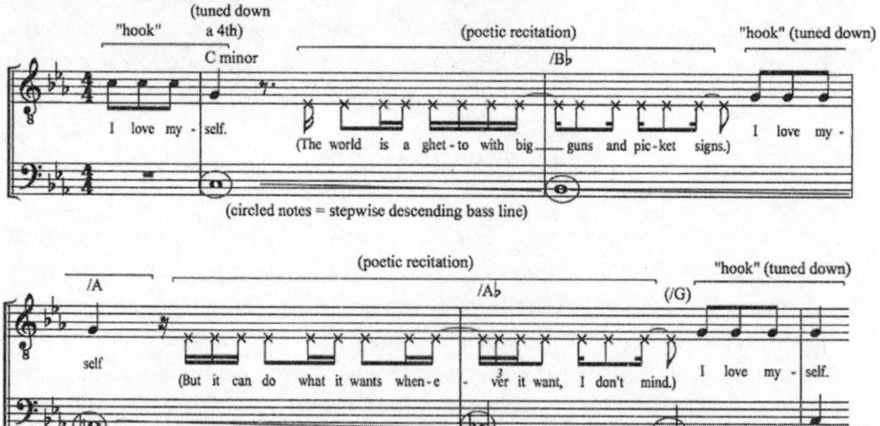

As such, "i" as a whole produces a rather complex form of A-B-A'-C-B'-A''-C'-B''-A'''-D-D'-D''-D'''.

As with "Gin & Juice," the dominant experiential element of "i" is, of course, Lamar's vocal delivery. The two songs, however, feature notably different approaches. Far more than Snoop Dogg, Lamar is a singer as well as a rapper, and thus able to fluidly alternate between the two approaches. In the first verse (A), for example, he begins with monotone spoken rap (focused a bit on G) for the first three bars, then shifts to a sung monotone on C. These pedal-like Cs then continue directly as the sung chorus hook ("I love myself"), repeated four times, with a syncopated leap to a jazzy E♭ on the final "self"—except when tuned down, as in Chorus 4 (D). As displayed in part in Figure 12.6, each sung hook is echoed by a third kind of delivery: less a strictly rhythmic rap and more an inflected poetic recitation; the full sung chorus hook (at the normal pitch, without inserted poetic recitation) is shown in Figure 12.7.

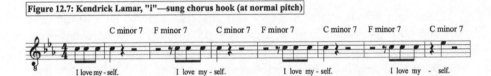

**Figure 12.7: Kendrick Lamar, "i"—sung chorus hook (at normal pitch)**

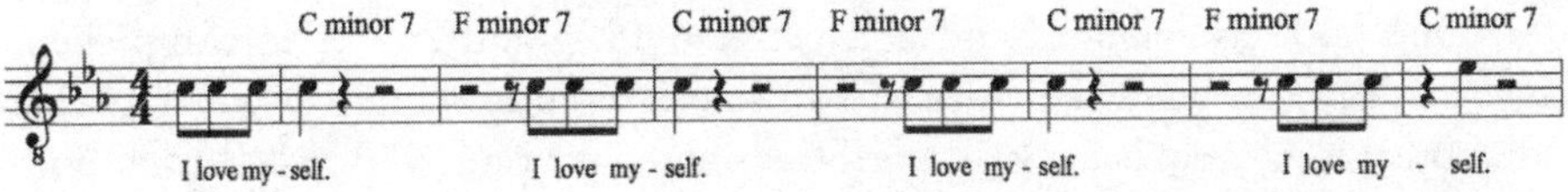


Indeed, this multistyle vocal approach all but defines "i." Additional techniques include: in Verse 3 (A''), a set of two-pitch alternations, first spoken, then sung ("These days of frustration") on G–E♭, rhythmically emulating the children's "name game" song; in Verse 4 (A'''), a sung alternation of C and E♭ on successive quarter notes ("Walk my bare feet"); in D' (following "I went to war last night"), a decidedly more aggressive and percussive rap style, akin to predecessors like Eminem and Tupac; and in D'' ("I lost my head"), where Lamar sings a syncopated, offbeat descending octave. It is this impressive variety of material and techniques—coupled with an equally varied and often quite complex approach to rhythm—that has surely helped propel Lamar to superstardom (Figures 12.8a–d):

**Figure 12.8a: Kendrick Lamar, "i"—vocal delivery style in Verse A''**

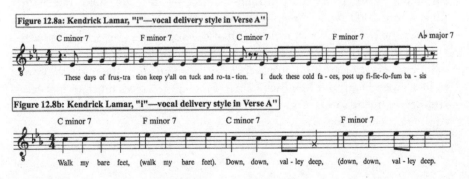

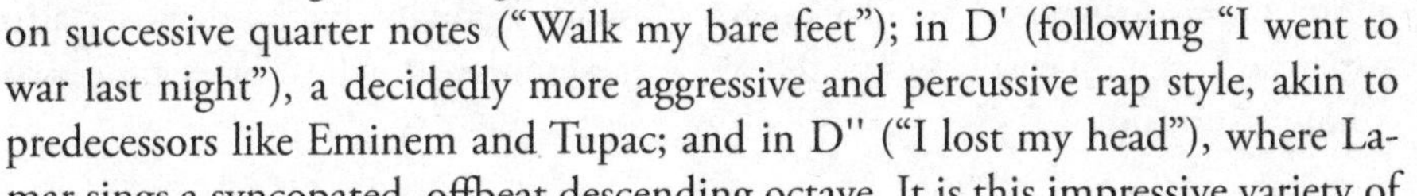


**Figure 12.8b: Kendrick Lamar, "i"—vocal delivery style in Verse A''**

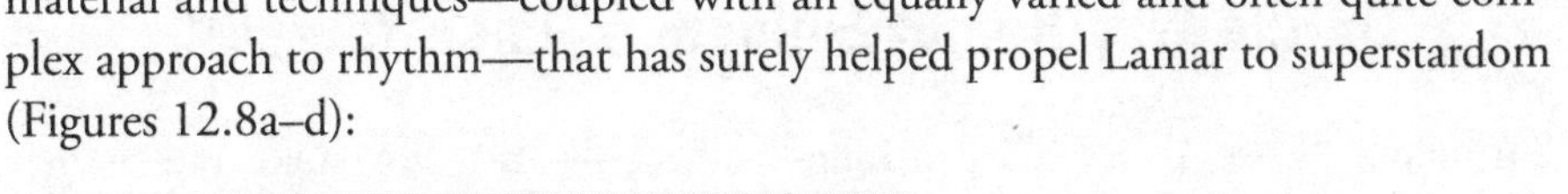

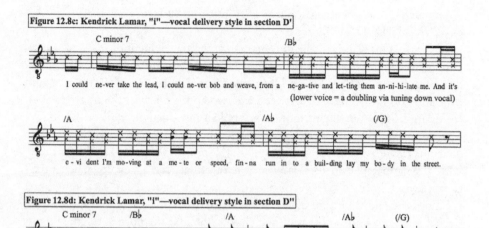

Figure 12.8c: Kendrick Lamar, "i"—vocal delivery style in section D'

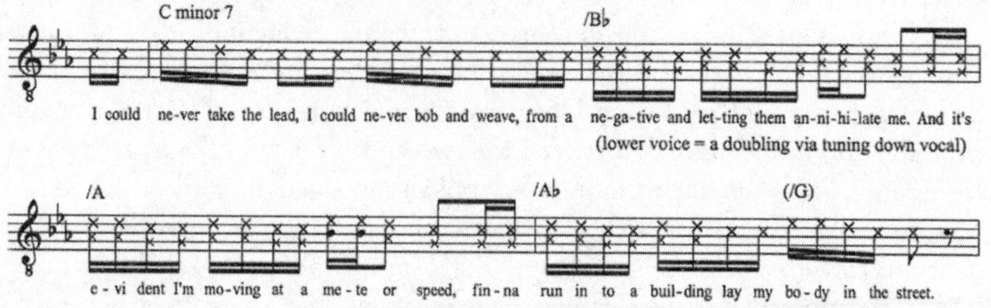
C minor 7
/B♭
I could ne-ver take the lead, I could ne-ver bob and weave, from a ne-ga-tive and let-ting them an-ni-hi-late me. And it's
(lower voice = a doubling via tuning down vocal)
/A
/A♭
(/G)
e - vi dent I'm mo-ving at a me - te or speed, fin - na run in to a buil-ding lay my bo - dy in the street.

Figure 12.8d: Kendrick Lamar, "i"—vocal delivery style in section D"

C minor 7
/B♭
/A
/A♭
(/G)
I lost my head, I must've - mis - read what the Good Book said, Oh, woes

Discussing Lamar's vocal diversity also enables, as noted above, a look at how hip hop has changed, and not, between 1993 and 2015. No comprehensive account can be made with just two songs, of course, but it is worth noting that both songs rely heavily on borrowed material from 1970s R&B/soul, both alternate rapping and singing, both feature lots of additional vocal interpolation (echoes, unison doubling, etc.), and both reflect the experience of black youth in their lyrics—Lamar's, again, being an account of self-affirmation amid the tribulations of inner-city life. And yet, whereas "Gin & Juice" undergirds the vocals with rather simplistic synth parts, "i" utilizes no synth work, but rather an active and at times quasi-virtuosic instrumental "bed" of guitars, piano, drums, Latin percussion, and especially bass—the work of Thundercat, whose jazzy funk solo dominates section D'''.

## On the Way Home: Eminem's "Lose Yourself"

**Eminem's "Lose Yourself"** continues Subject 4's taste for spiky rap, with a song—from 2002—that exemplifies popular hip hop at near the halfway point between the two "faves" just reviewed. It also demonstrates the sizable impact—whether known or not—that Dr. Dre has had on Subject 4's preferences, not to mention a good bit of hip hop's overall development since the mid-1980s; that is, like Snoop Dogg and Kendrick Lamar, Eminem too owes much of his success and development to Dr. Dre—the rapper, producer, and business mogul born Andre Romelle Young.[521]

## EMINEM: BACKGROUND

Whatever success Snoop Dogg or even Kendrick Lamar—and thus most any other rap artist—can claim, however, it would seem to pale in comparison to that accrued by Eminem over the past seventeen years: fifteen Grammy Awards, ten No. 1 albums, and an astounding 172 million albums sold, among much else. It is for such data-based feats that *Rolling Stone* bestowed upon him the title "King of Hip Hop" in 2011, beating out the likes of Drake, Kanye West, Jay-Z, and Lil Wayne.[522] To some, however, this exalted title offered to a white rapper from Detroit, by a mainstream publication, smacks of racial microaggression—and thus lacks legitimacy, if not worse.

Marshall Mathers III was born in 1972 in St. Joseph, Missouri, but spent his formative years in a gritty, low-income, and largely African-American neighborhood of Warren, Michigan—a suburb of Detroit. Raised by a troubled, at times erratic single mother, Mathers certainly had no idyllic childhood—though arguably not as challenging as that of Snoop or Lamar, or indeed many other prominent rappers. As one of only a few white kids in an otherwise black neighborhood, and being rather a loner, he was frequently bullied—once to the point of being hospitalized in a near coma. Hip hop thus became an outlet for his frustrations, insecurities, and anger—starting from age eleven, when his uncle first played him Ice-T's "Reckless" (1984). Using the stage name M&M, he began to create his own idiosyncratic approach to MC'ing at age fourteen. Always a poor student, Mathers dropped out of high school at age seventeen and set his sights on earning respect in the rough "8 Mile" rap scene of Detroit. Despite the bigotry he received being a white rapper, Eminem managed to earn respect via the "freestyle rap battles" that took place each weekend at the popular Hip-Hop Shop—enough, anyway, to enable a local label to release his debut album, *Infinite*. Detroit radio DJs, however, were unimpressed, and the album flopped.

Back in Warren, Eminem struggled to support his combative wife, Kim, and their young daughter, Hailie—both of whom would become frequent, and controversial, subjects of his lyrics.[523] At his darkest moment, following a suicide attempt, Eminem had a life-altering inspiration: to create an alter ego, Slim Shady, whom *Rolling Stone* defined as "a vengeful gremlin . . . with a taste for a bit of the ultra-violent."[524] By all accounts, Mathers was fairly mild-mannered: not saintly to be sure, but not pathological either. With Slim Shady, however, Eminem could lash out cruelly at all of his enemies and "take revenge on the world." To this biting commentary, moreover, was added another element: humor. He had now found a winning formula for his provocative rap lyrics—which had also matured compositionally to include virtuosic layers of internal rhyme and syncopation. Ever the kingmaker, Dr. Dre heard some tracks from Eminem's *Slim Shady EP* in 1998, and quickly signed him to Aftermath; Dre in fact caught a lot of flak for signing a white rapper, to which he famously retorted, "I don't give a fuck if he's purple; if you can kick it, I'm working with you."[525] Given the unbridled success of their first collaboration, *The Slim Shady LP* (1999), the gamble clearly paid off.

With its funny yet vile, violent, and blatantly misogynistic songs—such as "My Name Is"; "'97 Bonnie & Clyde," depicting his now ex-wife's fictitious murder; and "Brain Damage," in which he fantasizes revenge on the bully who put him in a coma—*The Slim Shady LP* set up a model of potent shock rap that has proven enormously successful. Each successive album—*The Marshall Mathers LP* (2000), *The Eminem Show* (2002), *Encore* (2004), *Relapse* (2009), *Recovery* (2010), *The Marshall Mathers LP 2* (2013), *Revival* (2017)—has topped the charts and sold astronomically well. This despite innumerable lawsuits, weapons charges, condemnations, and controversies—many arising from his vicious attacks on other celebrities, such as Michael Jackson and Christina Aguilera, not to mention on his own mom and ex-wife! What ultimately endears him to his fans, of course, are the compositional and performance dimensions of his songs: virtuosic rap lyrics, a theatrical delivery, and a hard-hitting, rock-based musical style that is not above sampling from unusual sources—e.g., Dido's "Thank You" in "Stan" (2000), about a deranged fan. And with *Revival* (2017) debuting atop the *Billboard* Top 200—his eighth consecutive to achieve this, a record—Eminem shows little signs of slowing down.

## EMINEM: ANALYSIS

"Lose Yourself" is not from one of the aforementioned albums, but was specifically recorded for Eminem's 2002 semiautobiographical film, *8 Mile*, for which it won the Academy Award for Best Original Song, the first hip hop song to do so. The song also won two Grammy Awards in 2003 and held the No. 1 spot on the *Billboard* Hot 100 for twenty-three weeks, a record for a rap song. Clearly, it did something right!

Interestingly, given its tremendous commercial and critical success, the song is actually fairly simple in its structure and musicological discourse. The form follows a consistent verse-chorus alternation. The harmonic language is likewise simple: it remains throughout on a D minor pedal, with a verse built on a two-bar alternation of D minor–D minor 6 (one bar each), and the chorus a related two-bar pattern of D minor–D minor 6–C/D (Figure 12.9):

**Figure 12.9: Eminem, "Lose Yourself"—chord progressions of verse and chorus**

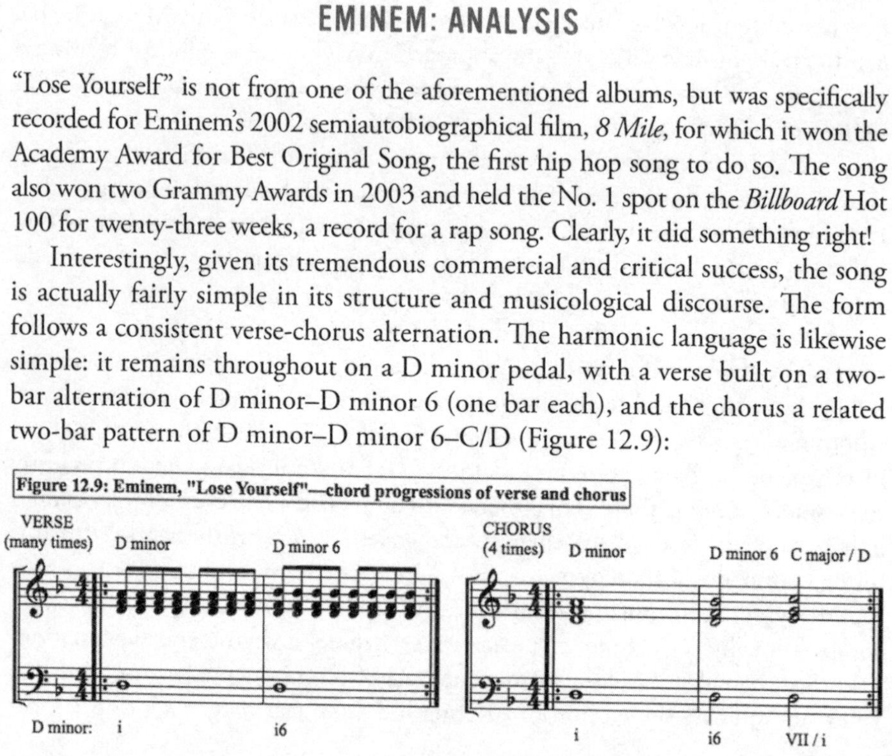

Similarly, the song utilizes straightforward instrumentation: a steady rhythm guitar riff, utilitarian bass and drum parts, simple piano figuration, and an occasional sustained string pedal (on D). Noteworthy, in contrast to the previous two songs, "Lose Yourself" dispenses with any musical borrowing whatsoever.[526] The song, further, is set in an unremarkable medium tempo in 4/4 meter (86 bpm).

So what accounts for the song's unbridled success? To a great degree, of course, it is by virtue of Eminem's very accomplished rapping "skillz" and his uncanny ability to capitalize on the power of repeating rhythmic patterns. Again, Eminem is celebrated for the humor in his lyrics (e.g., on "My Name Is" and "The Real Slim Shady"), but in this intense exhortation to seize opportunity despite all odds that is the theme of "Lose Yourself," humor is uncharacteristically absent. Instead, the song's impact is derived from the cleverly infectious—and often quite syncopated—rhythmic patterns whereby the rapper accentuates multiple internal rhyme structures.

An example is in the second half of the first verse (from "Snap back to reality"), where he produces a two-beat pattern or ostinato that, with occasional variation, is repeated no fewer than fourteen times—producing a potent level of momentum that drives the musical narrative headlong into the first chorus (in part, Figure 12.10):

**Figure 12.10: Eminem, "Lose Yourself"—rap rhythmic pattern in verse 1, second half**

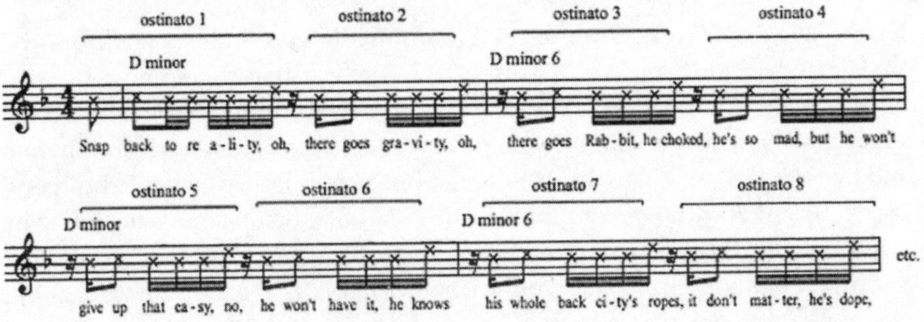


The chorus then employs Eminem's nominal singing chops to produce another compelling rhythmic structure. Specifically, it alternates F and D (the 3rd and root above the pedal) in a pattern that is especially syncopated in the first half of its two-part phrase (repeated twice). It is undoubtedly this catchy pattern—combined with the subtly changed harmonic movement and simple riffs in the piano and guitar—that helped propel "Lose Yourself" to the top of the charts (Figure 12.11):

Figure 12.11: Eminem, "Lose Yourself"—rap rhythmic pattern in chorus

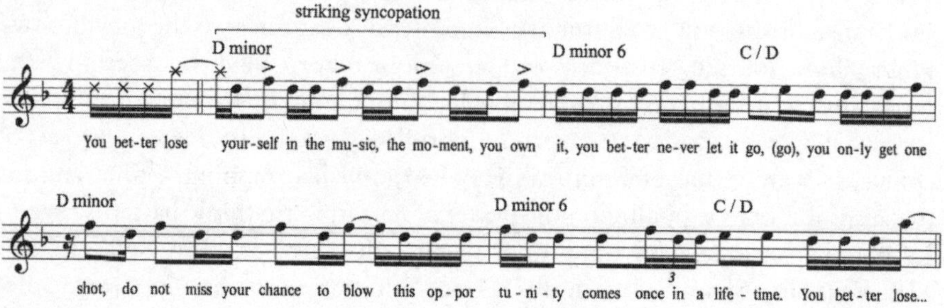

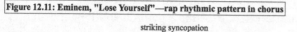

No one song, of course, can explain the appeal—or lack thereof—of an individual artist, especially one as impactful as Eminem. That said, the song "Lose Yourself" does seem to suggest that when it comes to this particular rapper, the "traditional" musicological parameters of melody, harmony, form, and instrumentation seem to take a backseat to that of rhythm and rap delivery in dictating "why we like it"—or at least, anyway, why Subject 4 would give it the nod for the commute home.

## Night on the Town: Earth, Wind & Fire's "Shining Star"

**Earth, Wind & Fire's "Shining Star"** admittedly constitutes a stark musical change of pace for Subject 4, but not necessarily one that should raise any eyebrows. Earth, Wind & Fire (EWF) is part of that select roster of key 1970s R&B/soul/funk artists whose songs have time and again been "plundered" for hip hop and rap samples. In all, over four hundred hip hop songs have sampled riffs and "beds" by EWF, with twenty-four sampling "Shining Star" alone—including by Public Enemy, Busta Rhymes, and Snoop Dogg.[527] As such, the song reveals Subject 4 as a hip hop fan who not only acknowledges the roots of the species, but also embraces them as part of a hip everyday playlist.

### EARTH, WIND & FIRE: BACKGROUND

EWF is among the most successful popular music acts of the past forty years, having sold over a hundred million albums and won countless awards and honors—including six Grammys and an induction into the Rock & Roll, Grammy, and NAACP Halls of Fame, among others. More specifically, EWF had an outsized impact on African-American music making in the pre–hip hop era: their unique interplay of R&B, soul, funk, jazz, and disco helped "change the sound of black pop in the 1970s," according to *Rolling Stone* magazine.[528]

As with many long-lived musical collectives, EWF's success arose largely through the talent and efforts of one individual—singer, songwriter, producer, and kalimba (African thumb-piano) player Maurice White. Born in Memphis in 1941, White spent his formative years in Chicago, surrounded by music; his grandfather had been a honky-tonk pianist. After studying percussion at the Chicago Conservatory, he worked as a session drummer for Chess Records—a pivotal label in the birth of rock and roll, having recorded proto-rock songs like "Rocket 88" and countless records by seminal electric blues artists like Howlin' Wolf, Muddy Waters, Buddy Guy, and even Chuck Berry.[529] While at Chess (1963–66), White recorded not only with blues artists but also with soul groups like the Impressions, before joining pianist Ramsey Lewis' trio in 1967—for example, playing on his hit "Wade in the Water."

In 1969, White decided to form his own soul band, initially called the Salty Peppers, soon changed to Earth, Wind & Fire—after the three symbols of White's astrological sign, Sagittarius. He relocated to LA, and experimented with various styles and personnel configurations (e.g., with soul singer Donny Hathaway). Critical hires came in 1971 with vocalist Philip Bailey, whose distinctive falsetto became a signature sound of the band, as well as funk guitarist Al McKay, and a four-member horn section—later dubbed the Phenix Horns. White only began singing lead with the band in 1973, just as White and Bailey initiated a vibrant songwriting partnership. EWF's first five albums brought critical attention and a few Top 40 songs on the R&B and pop charts (e.g., "Mighty Mighty," 1974), but their breakout came with their 1975 studio album, *That's the Way of the World*. With its megahit, "Shining Star," the album rose to No. 1 on the *Billboard* Top 200, and established EWF as a uniquely powerful group in the pop, rock, and R&B sphere.

Through the end of the 1970s, EWF scored a string of successful albums and singles—notably the albums *Spirit* (1976), *All 'n All* (1977), and *I Am* (1979), and the songs "Getaway," "Fantasy," "Got to Get You into My Life," and "September," among others. They also developed an extravagant live show complete with magic, pyrotechnics, lasers, etc. But what defined their identity as much as anything was the positive messaging of their lyrics, embodying a "spiritual transcendence" that in social historian James B. Stewart's words reflected "disillusionment with the failure of political advocacy and Civil Rights–Black Movement to overcome structural inequalities"—as found in the lyrics of songs like "Shining Star":[530]

*You're a shining star*
*No matter who you are*
*Shining bright to see*
*What you can truly be*

It was this positivity—along with the appeal of their music, of course—that drew future hip hop artists like Questlove of the Roots and Q-Tip of A Tribe Called Quest to EWF: upon White's passing in 2016, for example, Q-Tip called EWF "the blueprint for Tribe."[531] EWF's chart success and musical evolution continued through the 1980s and beyond—embracing styles like disco and even electronica; indeed the band continues to this day. But it is their classics of the 1970s that most inspired hip hop artists of the '90s and beyond, as it does current hip hop fans like Subject 4.

## EARTH, WIND & FIRE: ANALYSIS

"Shining Star," as noted, stems from EWF's 1975 breakout album, *That's the Way of the World*. Cowritten by White, Bailey, and EWF keyboardist Larry Dunn, it is one of the group's biggest hits—reaching No. 1 on both the *Billboard* R&B and Hot 100 charts, and winning a Grammy for Best R&B Performance. It has appeared in dozens of films and TV shows, including *Seinfeld*, *Scandal*, and *Glee*.

In many ways, "Shining Star" is a textbook example of the funk subgenre, most palpably during its two extended verses of twelve and twenty-four bars, respectively. These sections are harmonically defined but by a single chord—E7(♯9)—set in a medium tempo (104 bpm) 4/4 meter with a syncopated groove. The dominant 7th chord with the ♯9 (combining the major *and* minor 3rd above the root, in this case, G♯ against G♮) is perhaps the very embodiment of the funk sound (Figure 12.12):

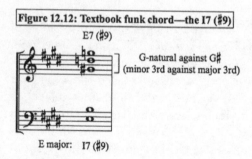

**Figure 12.12: Textbook funk chord—the I7 (♯9)**

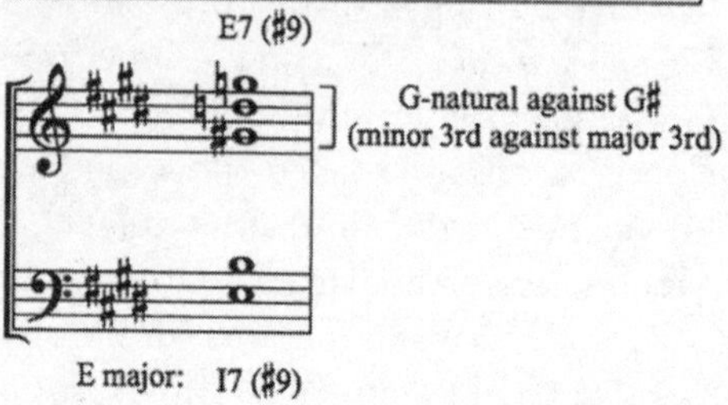


This chordal "pedal" is embodied by a "jangling" rhythm guitar, steady drums and percussion, a rhythmic Rhodes piano, "phased" electric guitar riffs, occasional horn "hits," and especially a percussive "slapped" electric bass line. The vocal melody of the verse, emphasizing G♮, further reinforces the infectious funk vibe (Figure 12.13):

more remote candidates: Ray Charles or Mahalia Jackson (early soul and gospel influence); Philip Glass or Fatboy Slim (heavy ostinato/repetitive rhythms); Stanley Clarke or Steely Dan (chromatic bass and jazz-influenced harmony); "White Rabbit" by Jefferson Airplane or the Gregorian hymn "Pange lingua" (Phrygian mode); Indian ragas or the *Farewell* Symphony by Franz Joseph Haydn (complex or unique formal approaches); or the Moody Blues or Howard Shore film scores (orchestral writing), to name but a few. If nothing else, it would be interesting to see how Subject 4 would respond to these suggestions—perhaps more favorably than one might think at first glance.



**Figure 12.13: Earth, Wind & Fire, "Shining Star"—Verse 1 melody**

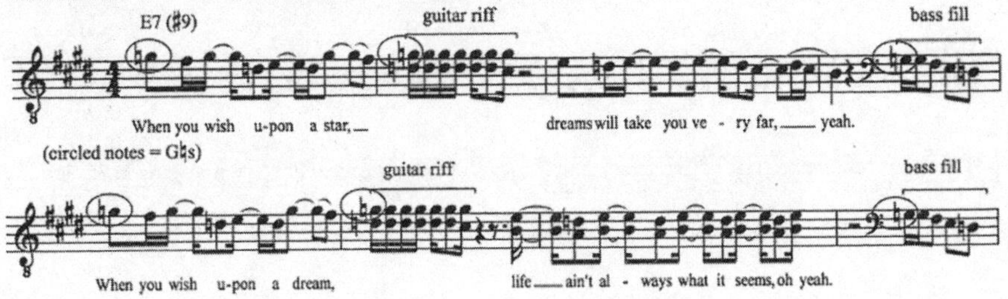


The "hooky" four-bar chorus dividing, and following, the two verses is then rather a contrast to these funky verses. Harmonically it utilizes a relatively swift-moving progression of two chords per measure following the Circle of 4ths: A7–D7–G7–C7, repeated twice. Melodically it is less improvisatory in style than the verses, much more "chiseled," and presented in octave unison between Maurice White and vocalist Philip Bailey—whose distinctive falsetto timbre is again one of the signature traits of EWF. Sonically too the chorus is more "refined," with unison horn lines and a mellow rhythm section (Figure 12.14):

**Figure 12.14: Earth, Wind & Fire, "Shining Star"—chorus**

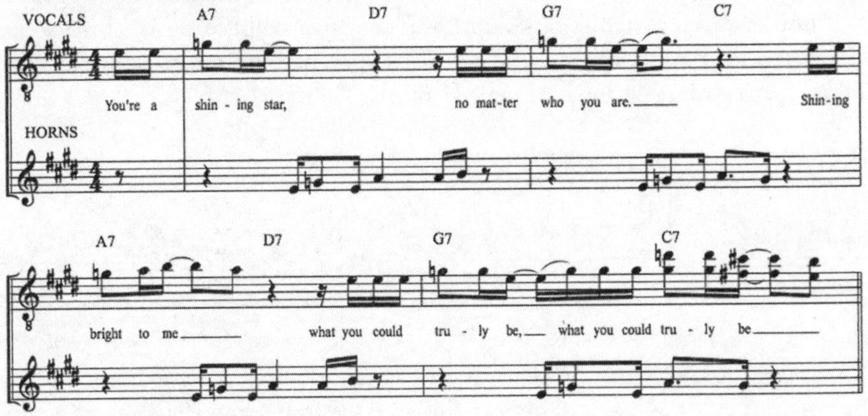


Even more contrast, however, is generated by the short but very chromatic solo interlude that follows the first chorus. Harmonically it proceeds, after two bars on E7(♯9), as a very syncopated and fully chromatic chord progression—from G13 to E♭13—driven by horn hits and underscoring a wild almost Hendrix-like guitar solo by Johnny Graham (Figure 12.15):

**Figure 12.15: Earth, Wind & Fire, "Shining Star"—syncopated, chromatic horn hits in instrumental interlude**

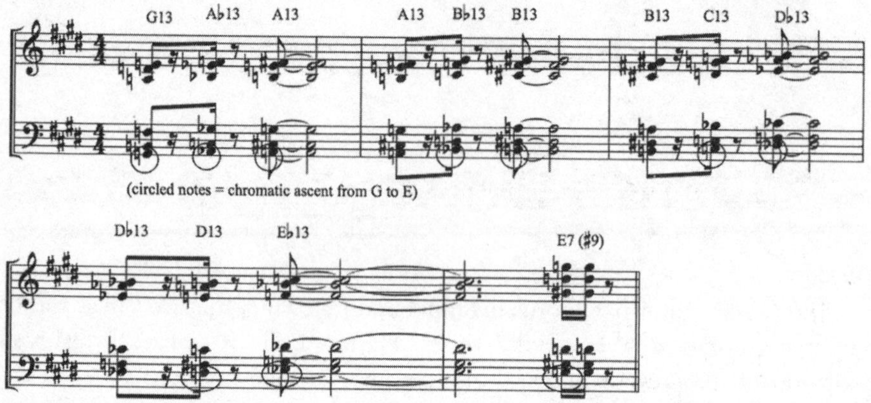


All of this demonstrates a quite sophisticated and well-designed formal architecture, providing "Shining Star" with a clear balance of continuity and contrast that drives the listening experience. One also hears a solid command of the various styles associated with EWF: funk, R&B, soul, and jazz—particularly in the solo interlude. The graceful integration between these stylistic strains is no doubt a key reason why EWF is among the best-selling bands of all time, in any genre.

Another striking manifestation of EWF's creative skill is the end of the song, where after the repeat of the second chorus, it launches into a coda dominated by offbeat syncopations in the harmonized vocals (Figure 12.16):

**Figure 12.16: Earth, Wind & Fire, "Shining Star"—a cappella coda**

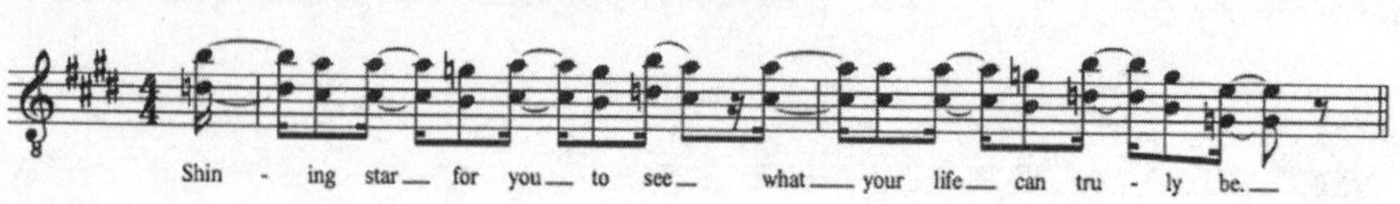
Shin - ing star— for you— to see— what— your life— can tru - ly be.—

Supporting the vocals, however, is a slowly subtracting accompaniment: first the guitars, keys, and horns disappear, followed by drums, then bass—leaving the final two bars a cappella. Such a narrative brings to mind (for those so inclined) the end of the final movement of Haydn's *Farewell* Symphony. It is unlikely, of course, that either Maurice White or Subject 4 rendered any such connection, but regardless, the vibrant and funky groove of "Shining Star" has plenty to offer the latter while enjoying a night on the town.



## Insights Gained about Subject 4's Musical Taste

Given the five favorites tracing this musical day in the life—the four discussed here plus the fifth (Common & John Legend's "Glory")—what conclusions can we draw regarding Subject 4's musical taste? We identify a hip hop fan, to be sure, but one open to the broad dimensions of the species—from its roots in funk and R&B through nearly its full historic trajectory. At the same time, we also can discern a fan who seems to gravitate toward a fairly conventional—or at least commercially viable—subset of the realm. Each song in the hit parade attained blockbuster and/or award success, which traditionally eschews avant-garde or ultracomplex discourse. Although there is no shortage of sophisticated, even edgy material, Subject 4 here evades the more aggressive, "hardcore," or underground side of hip hop, as represented by artists such as Public Enemy, DMX, Onyx, and Blackalicious, to name but a few.

Musicologically, the songs selected are generally straightforward if not simple with regard to broad melodic, harmonic, formal, and sonic (instrumentation, texture, etc.) elements—with some exceptions, of course: form in "i," harmony in "Shining Star," etc. On the other hand, the songs reinforce the notion that Subject 4 is attracted to a vibrant rhythmic orientation, whether rapped, sung, or played instrumentally. In all, the tunes might suggest that Subject 4 is a relatively older hip hop fan, perhaps coming of age in the late 1980s or early '90s, while still continuing to follow fresh trends. It is just as likely, however, that Subject 4 is a hip hop newbie, now in the process of discovering—as all "young" music lovers should—the gems of the past. Both trends, indeed, are healthy and laudable.

When considering what other songs Subject 4 might enjoy, we once again can start with those by the same artists in close musicological proximity to the "seeds"—here addressing only the four songs discussed in the chapter. Candidates include "Snoop Bounce" (Snoop Dogg), "Duckworth" (Lamar), "The Way I Am" (Eminem), and "Getaway" (EWF).

Moving on, we can seek out songs by other artists who reside in similar musicological terrain: "Nuthin' but a 'G' Thang" by Dr. Dre or "California Love by Tupac Shakur (Snoop Dogg); "No Role Modelz" by J. Cole or "Till the End by Logic (Lamar); "In the End" by Linkin Park or "Remember the Name" b Fort Minor (Eminem); or "Superstition" by Stevie Wonder or "Play That Fun Music" by Wild Cherry (EWF).

Diving yet deeper into Subject 4's genotype takes us to influencers on ar or "heirs" to the artists and composers involved: N.W.A and Bow Wow (Sno Dogg); Rakim and Gil Scott-Heron (Lamar); the Beastie Boys and 50 Cent (E inem); and Sly and the Family Stone and the Brand New Heavies (EWF). Fin although one runs the risk of getting a bit far-flung when the general musico cal breadth is fairly narrow, as is the case here, these "seeds" can still suggest *thirteen*

# THE ELECTRONICA (EDM) GENOTYPE

• • •

## Introducing Subject 5

Subject 5 heads to a high-energy dance class to start the day, "shuffling" to an old favorite in **the Chemical Brothers' "Hey Boy Hey Girl."** On the way to work, something fresher is taking hold as a keeper: **Armin van Buuren's "Embrace."** But after a workday requiring way too much concentration, a welcome mind-cleansing arrives from the opening movement of **Steve Reich's *Music for 18 Musicians*.** Exhausted after a long day, a necessary "chill" is found with a classic track, **Brian Eno's "Always Returning."***

The dedication that Subject 5 has to the broad realm of dance music—or electronica, or EDM—is clear. Yet it is likewise the case that Subject 5 seems to generally shun the ultramainstream side of the species, instead casting a fairly wide, somewhat esoteric musicological net.

Before diving into these hits, however, some words on the electronica species:

## The Electronica Species: A Brief Review

As noted briefly in Chapter 7, "electronic music," including that generated by synthesizers, can be heard within pop music as early as the 1960s. Its use as the underlying *essence* of a distinct species of pop music, on the other hand, is a more recent reality—blossoming in the early 1980s, with roots back to the late '70s. Electronica thus echoes hip hop in its chronological trajectory, and like the latter has evolved to become a dominant force within the music industry over the

---

* Subject 5's fifth song, heard at a vibrant dance club, is Messinian's 2011 dubstep song "Holy Ghost." For its discussion, see the WYLI website, supplement to Chapter 13.

past two decades. And though hip hop has in recent decades expanded vibrantly outside the US, not least as a mode of social commentary, electronica is by definition an international phenomenon—perhaps more dynamic outside the US than within it.

Here, before we continue, is a sample set of ten touchstone tracks of the electronica or EDM (electronic dance music) species:

Martin Garrix, "Animals" (2013)
Skrillex, "Scary Monsters and Nice Sprites" (2010)
deadmau5, "I Remember" (2008)
Daft Punk, "One More Time" (2001)
Fatboy Slim, "Right Here, Right Now" (1999)
Moby, "Go" (1991)
Orbital, "Chime" (1989)
Rhythim Is Rhythim, "Strings of Life" (1987)
Cybotron, "Clear" (1983)
Kraftwerk, "Computer Love" (1981)

These tracks, of varying styles and EDM subgenres (house, trance, dubstep, etc.), feature musicological elements that typify the species. The predominant sonic impetus here, unlike in hip hop, is instrumental—with vocals, often manipulated, being used largely as secondary components. Beyond the prominence of drums, the instrumentation is synthesizer-dominant, yielding a mix of timbres ranging from airy to metallic. The tracks are defined by vibrant, pulsating, and multilayered rhythm—inevitably in 4/4 meter—with minimal syncopation; all feature melodic material built on short, heavily repeating ostinatos—often fragmented, manipulated, and overlapping; all utilize a simple harmonic language comprising drones and/or short cyclic patterns of two to four chords; all employ a formal approach that is sectional yet abstract: shifting between established material in an unpredictable manner; and most rely on a degree of sampling—especially voices, both spoken and sung.

A more proper understanding of electronica, however, requires a cursory review of the underlying musico-technological roots behind it. This in turn takes us into the arcane worlds of both physics and avant-garde classical music—lucky you.

From at least the 1860s, when German physicist Hermann von Helmholtz published his *On the Sensations of Tone* (1863), Western musicians have pondered the prospects of tone creation beyond the confines of the equal-tempered scale played upon acoustic instruments. A steady stream of early experiments, starting famously with Thaddeus Cahill's "Telharmonium" (1895)—which converted electronic signals to sound over telephone lines—proved that new and unusual timbres could be produced using electrical means. Through the first half of the twentieth century, musically inclined physicists developed tools to produce, manipulate, and project electronic sounds: oscillators to generate the basic wave forms (sine, square, saw tooth) that undergird all musical tones, microphones to capture acoustic sounds, tape recorders to manipulate those sounds, and amplifiers to "broadcast" them, among much else. At the same time, adventurous composers—Edgard Varèse, Luigi Russolo, George Antheil, Olivier Messiaen, John Cage, Pierre Boulez, Karlheinz Stockhausen, Milton Babbitt, Otto Luening, and Morton Subotnick, to name but a few—utilized these tools to construct experimental, avant-garde classical works, with and without use of acoustic instruments. Not surprisingly, the ranks of music fans devoted to these experimental endeavors have never been sizable.[532]

Given the complexity and huge expense of the technologies involved, most electronic music creation from the 1920s to the 1960s took place within large studios associated with state-run broadcast centers or universities—such as Radiodiffusion–Télévision Française (Paris), Nord-West Deutsche Rundfunk (Cologne, Germany), Columbia and Princeton Universities, etc. Among the principal developments after 1950 was the synthesizer—where the sound or timbre could be manipulated at the point of input, not just output; the first such experiments were huge, clunky, and cumbersome, but through the 1960s and '70s, innovators like Robert Moog made synthesizer technology (e.g., the Minimoog, released in 1970) available in a compact and reasonable format. Suddenly, an average musician could own one of these synthesizers—to create simultaneous waveforms or white noise, manipulate the attack and decay of each tone, alter the overall sound through filters and modulators, and even create repeating patterns or sequences.[533]

The ensuing decades saw computers and user-friendly digital software take over the more technically rigorous demands of manipulating analog sound sources, such that today one often speaks of "computer music" rather than "electronic music." From the 1980s especially, the level of "democratization" of music technology has exploded: from algorithm-based polyphonic synthesizers and the institution of universal digital protocols in the 1980s, to the digitization of analog instruments and the creation of "digital audio workstations" to record and manipulate sounds in the 1990s, to the creation of complex sound design/sequencing software and digital turntables in the 2000s, etc.[534] Today, anyone with a few thousand bucks and a limited musical or technological background can create "electronic" music tracks that would stupefy the most progressive minds from even thirty years ago.

It was in Europe that pop/rock musicians first began to catch wind of the sonic potential of "electronic music" for their songs, beginning in the late 1960s. German avant-garde pop bands like Can, Kraftwerk, and Faust, and English "progressive rock" groups like King Crimson, Yes, and Emerson, Lake, and Palmer (ELP) took rather idiosyncratic approaches to their electronic sound creations—initially with experimental techniques like tape manipulation (especially Kraftwerk), and later with synths like the Minimoog and the ARP Odyssey, released in 1972. Their concert use is often visually embodied in the "sea" of keyboards (electric and synthetic) encircling Rick Wakeman of Yes or Keith Emerson of ELP during live shows.

In the mid-1970s, "Euro-disco" producers like Giorgio Moroder in Munich created full "beds" of synthesized sounds, including primitive drum machines, to support the vocals—as in Donna Summer's 1977 hit "I Feel Love." The impact of this particular track was noted even at the time: Brian Eno, for example, said upon its release, "This single is going to change the sound of club music for the next 15 years."[535] He was right. Then, in the early 1980s, the "new wave" rock movement was defined in part by the prevalent use of synthesizers (polyphonic ones like the Yamaha DX7 and Oberheim OB-X) and drum machines, via English artists like Pet Shop Boys and Eurythmics. In all such approaches, however, the electronic sources were used primarily to support vocal-dominated songs within the confines of established pop/rock genres: rock, disco, pop, etc.

A different approach, however, took root back in the US—in Chicago in the early 1980s—that would establish a new musical paradigm: electronica. Initially desiring long-playing disco records to spin at dance clubs, Chicago DJs like Frankie Knuckles, Ron Hardy, and Farley "Jackmaster" Funk edited together disco songs, at times adding a drum machine. Soon, original songs were produced along this aesthetic—notably Jesse Saunders' "On and On" (1984), and the subgenre of *house music* was born—the name stemming from the Ware*house*, the Chicago dance club where Knuckles was DJ.[536] As house took form, several elements became normative: the use of the Roland 303 bass synthesizer and Roland 808 drum machine—the same one used in early hip hop; polyphonic synths (e.g., the Korg Poly-61) for harmony; samples of early disco and R&B songs; and, most importantly, little or no vocals. The songs were also quite minimalistic musically, often with only one or a few patterned chords and endlessly repeating instrumental or vocal ostinatos. All of this, of course, to encourage the music's prime objective: nonstop dancing.

The success of songs like "On and On" spread the nascent electronica species and its creative potential beyond Chicago. A key development took place in nearby Detroit, where DJs Juan Atkins, Kevin Saunderson, and Derrick May broadened the influences beyond disco to include funk and the synth pop of Kraftwerk, etc. The result was *techno*—an even more "abstract" approach to dance music, featuring slightly faster tempos and insistent, multilayered ostinatos. The next big hub was the UK, which took up the electronica mantle with a vengeance: from the late 1980s and throughout the '90s, new electronica genres arose fast and furious—such as *jungle/drum and bass*, *big beat*, *trance*, *progressive house*, *hardcore*, etc.—several of which are defined more specifically in the musical discussion below. These styles differ not just in compositional design and tempo, but especially by virtue of the external genre influences they adopt—most notably hip hop, rock, and Jamaican styles like *dancehall* and *dub-reggae*.

The spinning by DJs of house and techno tracks had thus far mainly taken place in small dance clubs filled with avid devotees, but as the music caught on, the experience at those clubs began to intensify—not least by virtue of illicit drugs like MDMA, better known as "ecstasy." Music and drugs had long been companions, of course (see Chapter 11), but in this case the psychoactive, euphoric drugs accentuated the hypnotic nature of the distorted bass lines and steady "four-on-the-floor" bass drum created by the Roland 303 and 808 synths, respectively. Dance shows thus turned into "raves"—taking place increasingly in large club spaces or abandoned warehouses, especially in London at the famed Shoom club, but also in Chicago, Berlin, and elsewhere—while the names "acid house" and "acid techno" were applied to the music.[537] Indeed, from the late 1980s to today, a self-indulgent element has remained a common component of the EDM realm—where "raves" become "assemblages of individual and collective actions that materialize hedonistic pursuits; that is, they are the outcomes of the 'lust for explosive exhilaration' that drives EDM music forwards," as sociologist Alistair Fraser put it.[538]

At any rate, the popularity, and ever-increasing notoriety, of the rave scene helped disseminate the music even further, including to the attention of leading pop stars, who from the mid-1990s began to incorporate EDM elements into their songs—such as in Madonna's 1998 hit "Ray of Light." This success in turn helped bring some mainstream commercial success to British electronica acts such as the Prodigy, Fatboy Slim, and the Chemical Brothers. By 2005, the overall species had become a huge business: today, it brings in over $7 billion globally through record sales and live shows. Top-draw DJs and artists like Tiësto, Skrillex, and Armin van Buuren—active within subgenres like dubstep and progressive trance—can fill stadiums of a hundred thousand or more. No longer confined to clubs, the music is now a huge draw at rock festivals like Coachella and Lollapalooza, as well as at dedicated EDM festivals like Electric Daisy Carnival, Tomorrowland, and Ultra Music Festival. Indeed, electronica and EDM are thriving around the world, with active scenes in nearly every region—most notably in North America, Europe, Southeast Asia, and Latin America.

Today, moreover, electronica is broken into a dizzying number of subgenres and sub-subgenres.[539] As noted in Chapter 8, these subdivisions (especially Tiers 3 and 4) can quickly become mumbo-jumbo to those not "in the know." Things are particularly complex in this realm given the frequent overlap of subgenre names—for example, electro-house is synonymous, or at least closely aligned, with tech house, tech pop, electro-clash, neo-electro, among several others. The distinctions between subgenres are, again, usually quite nuanced: the specific tempo (bpm) used; the orientation of the kick drum; the use of syncopated drum patterns or "breaks"; the presence or absence of vocal or instrumental forces; the use or not of a big "build" (crescendo) leading to a full-textured "drop"; the presence of extended drumrolls; the use of samples; and especially the influence of other genres, such as funk, soul, hip hop, rock, punk, metal, classical, etc.

New or slightly varied dance subgenres seem to be developed and christened constantly, like fresh compounds manufactured in a chemical plant. This, indeed, seems to be intrinsic to the very aesthetic of the genre. Even the overarching label is in flux: "electronica" was the catchall term for both dance and nondance synthesizer-based music from the late 1980s to the late 2000s. It is still in currency today in this broad context. But from around 2010, the acronym "EDM" began being pushed by the US music industry, and especially for the commercial dance subgenres—in part to "rebrand" the music in the wake of the bad publicity engendered by the drug-filled rave scene. In the UK, however, the term "dance music" is more commonly embraced as an alternative to "EDM."

And all this for a species that admittedly can sound rather narrowly conceived for those with limited exposure—something surely not the case, though, for a connoisseur like Subject 5. And with that, let's turn to the music.

## A High-Energy Dance Class: The Chemical Brothers' "Hey Boy Hey Girl"

**The Chemical Brothers' "Hey Boy Hey Girl,"** from 1999 (not to be confused with "Hey Boy! Hey Girl!" by Louis Prima and Keely Smith), well exemplifies the state of dance music at the end of the twentieth century. It reveals both the musicological developments whereby the realm had matured and diversified over the preceding two decades, and also the mainstream acceptance that dance music was then starting to garner around the world. In short, an EDM touchstone to get things started.

### THE CHEMICAL BROTHERS: BACKGROUND

Tom Rowlands (born 1970) and Ed Simons (born 1971) are not, in fact, brothers, but they have been nearly inseparable creative partners since their late teens. Each raised in London, the two met while studying medieval history and literature at the University of Manchester. This suggests already an intriguing distinction from what we've seen with hip hop, pop, rock, and jazz—namely, that a commercially explosive outfit would have roots in esoteric academia rather than in the rough-and-tumble of urban street life. At the same time, urban music—specifically hip hop acts like Public Enemy—was a key childhood passion for both, along with interest in other musical realms, including rock, new wave, and, in Rowlands' case, the electronic sounds of Kraftwerk and Cabaret Voltaire.[540]

In the early 1990s, Manchester had a thriving underground rave scene—

earning the city the nickname "Madchester." Rowlands and Simons adopted the name the Dust Brothers, after the production team behind the Beastie Boys, and started DJ'ing at local clubs. They quickly transitioned from doing remixes of popular house and techno songs to creating their own original tracks. In so doing, however, they took an "antipurist" approach—mixing in up-tempo hip hop "breaks" with distorted bass riffs and a highly syncopated rock drum sound: think of Ringo Starr's iconic syncopated groove on "Tomorrow Never Knows." Among these post-techno experiments was a track entitled "Chemical Beats" (1994), and with it was born a new dance subgenre: big beat. The duo began to tour, and as their fame spread, the original Dust Brothers caught wind and demanded a name change—to wit, the Chemical Brothers.

Their first two albums—*Exit Planet Dust* (1995) and *Dig Your Own Hole* (1997)—earned the Brothers a huge following in the UK, including two No. 1 songs, "Setting Sun" and "Block Rockin' Beats." In the US as well the duo gained a sizable audience, winning a Grammy Award for the latter track. Moreover, this marks the rise of the industry term "electronica" in the US, spawned largely from big beat hits by the Brothers, as well as by their countrymen the Prodigy and Fatboy Slim. Yet, sensing oversaturation with this "heavy" dance style, on their third album, *Surrender* (1999), the Brothers changed direction in part by reviving the older house style: "lifting you up instead of blasting you out of a cannon," in Rowlands' words.[541] Although the album—including "Hey Boy Hey Girl"—went to No. 1 in the UK, it received a mixed response in the US. Indeed, in the years since, the Brothers have maintained a far greater profile in the UK than elsewhere, at least among casual EDM fans.

Among music critics and electronica aficionados, on the other hand, the Brothers have maintained a high prestige in the ensuing years, becoming rather mythical in the realm's history. Through their five subsequent, often experimental studio albums and flamboyant live shows, the Brothers have often collaborated with other marquee artists—ranging from Noel Gallagher, singer of the band Oasis; to folk singer Beth Orton; to rapper Q-Tip, from A Tribe Called Quest. Their latest album, *Born in the Echoes* (2015), for example, includes a collaboration with singer Beck, and has been praised by *Billboard* as "electrifying . . . integrating the abrasive tone-bending and mesmeric repetition of EDM into the context of hooks and melodies."[542] Presumably, Subject 5 would agree.

## THE CHEMICAL BROTHERS: ANALYSIS

"Hey Boy Hey Girl," as noted, stems from the Chemical Brothers' third album, *Surrender* (1999), and represents a stylistic shift away from the big beat style to a sort of neo-house sound—defined by a continuous four-on-the-floor kick drum, other disco elements, and generally a lot of musicological repetition. At the same time, the track does maintain some vestige of the big beat style, notably a strong level of syncopation and hip hop influence, as we'll see. The combination proved fairly successful commercially, as the track rose to the No. 3 spot in the UK Top 20.

"Hey Boy" also indulges in a key feature of so much electronica: the technique of layering—where different rhythms, ostinatos, and sounds, mostly synth-generated, are stacked one on top of the other, and then removed or mixed-and-matched as the song proceeds. In this way, the music can continue for long periods without actually changing its discourse. "Hey Boy" begins with a metallic synth sound held on a D pedal, as a syncopated, tresillo-like groove is gradually assembled, at 127 bpm. As this big-beat-like groove is stacked, a repeating vocal hook is introduced: "Hey girl, B-boys, superstar DJs, here we go"—sampled and sped up from the old-school hip hop song, "The Roof Is on Fire" by Rock Master Scott and the Dynamic Three (1984). Next, a two-beat ostinato (D–E♭–D) is heard above the D pedal that establishes the Phrygian-mode sonority that underlies most of the song (Figure 13.1):

**Figure 13.1: Chemical Brothers, "Hey Boy Hey Girl"—sonic layering in opening (A) section**

At around 0:50, a second rhythmic template is then introduced above these stacked elements: a stereotypical "house groove" with a four-on-the floor kick drum and offbeat, disco-like hi-hat hits. It is this groove that now dominates the track, establishing it as principally in the house style, with a big beat influence. Again, "Hey Boy Hey Girl" thus contrasts with earlier songs by the Brothers, such as "Chemical Beats" and "Block Rockin' Beats," which are more decidedly in the big beat style.

The Phrygian ostinato continues above a D pedal for a spell, but is then interrupted by a four-bar shift to a G pedal (accompanied by the vocal hook) and back again. This generates a I–IV–I harmonic trajectory that recurs several times (Figure 13.2):

**Figure 13.2: Chemical Brothers, "Hey Boy Hey Girl"—layering in B section (to G)**

By a considerable degree, though, the song is harmonically defined by a D pedal.

As the song continues, numerous other layered elements are periodically introduced—including an oft-repeating ostinato on A–G–A in a distorted guitar patch (e.g., at 1:53); a rapid, Arabic-sounding D–E♭–D synth pattern (at 2:48); and a sixteenth note synthesized vocal ascent on a "da-da" sound (e.g., at 1:34), along with numerous other subtler elements (Figure 13.3):

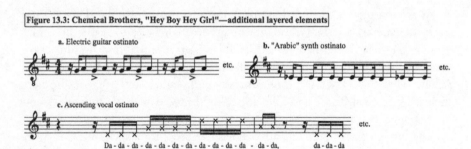

Figure 13.3: Chemical Brothers, "Hey Boy Hey Girl"—additional layered elements

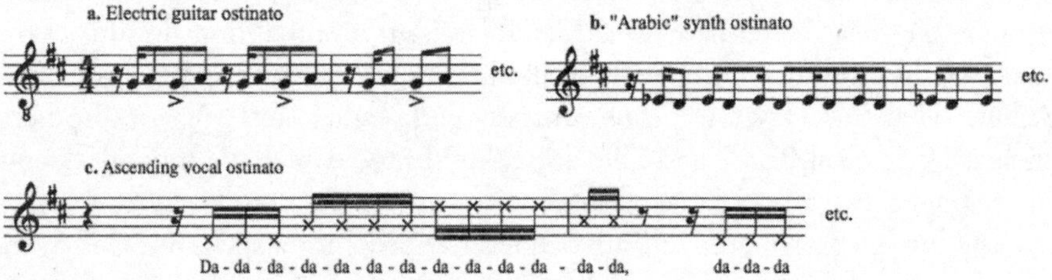


By this admittedly prosaic description, it should be clear that making strict formal delineations in the electronica/EDM realm can be rather challenging. And yet it is just this insistent, disparately layered, and stream-of-consciousness approach that makes songs like "Hey Boy Hey Girl" so infectious to fans like Subject 5.

## On the Way to Work: Van Buuren's "Embrace"

**Armin van Buuren's "Embrace"** represents a creative strain of contemporary dance music by a prominent figure in today's EDM world. It further suggests that Subject 5 may well possess a rather eclectic electronica palette, given its insider remoteness from "Hey Boy." At a minimum, "Embrace" shows that Subject 5 is plugged into among the hottest trends in EDM today: progressive trance.

### VAN BUUREN: BACKGROUND

Dutch DJ and producer—remixer, composer—Armin van Buuren was born in Leiden, Netherlands, in 1976. At age ten, he discovered the wonders of the computer and within a few years was combining his fascination with technology with a love of dance music to create his own mixes. Soon thereafter he was providing DJ duties at school parties, from where he quickly transitioned to the local club scene in Leiden. By this time too he had begun law school at Leiden University, eventually earning his law degree—thus continuing an intriguing intersection between electronica success and higher education. At venues like Club Nexus in Leiden he gained a reputation for putting on a great DJ show, sometimes lasting six to seven hours; he would gradually parlay that into an ability to hold an audience for twelve hours at a time!

Van Buuren began to augment his DJ'ing with the creation of original trance remixes and tracks, scoring a minor UK dance chart success with the song "Communication" in 2000. Prior to putting out studio albums, he released a series of "compilation" albums of his remixes—the first entitled *A State of Trance*

(2000). The next year he co-opted that name for a two-hour radio show, playing the latest popular trance tracks. The show has since exploded: van Buuren has thus far produced over 650 episodes of the *State of Trance* radio show, reaching over thirty-seven million listeners in eighty-four countries each week. His first studio album, *76* (2003), further bolstered his reputation, and helped him secure ever-larger DJ'ing gigs. His "dance parties" have likewise skyrocketed in profile in the ensuing years, as van Buuren now travels the globe with his *State of Trance* and *Armin Only* tours, drawing crowds of a hundred thousand or more at each show for hours of music, lasers, psychedelic videos, and fireworks—rave parties on an epic scale.

Musically, a pivotal influence has been French composer Jean-Michel Jarre, an electronica and ambient music pioneer. Van Buuren's tracks are thus often compositionally sophisticated—whether purely digital or in collaboration with vocalists and instrumentalists. His collaboration with Canadian singer Trevor Guthrie on "This Is What It Feels Like" from his fifth studio album, *Intense* (2013), for example, earned van Buuren a Grammy nomination—quite rare for a trance track. Creative collaborations continue as well on his most recent album, *Embrace* (2015), including the title track, as we'll see. All of this has established van Buuren as perhaps the most successful artist in trance—regularly earning him the moniker of "king," or "overlord," or "top ambassador" of trance.[543] If you'd never before heard of van Buuren or trance music, now you know that there are literally millions around the world who have. As van Buuren put it in a recent interview with *Billboard*, "I know that trance was not always going to be the most popular sound out there; but I'm not just doing it for the sake of popularity, I do it because I love the sound. . . . [I]t's more than just music, it's a lifestyle for a lot of people."[544]

So what is trance? It is one of the mainline (Tier 2) subgenres of electronica, with origins in Germany in the mid-1990s, such as by the duo Jam & Spoon. It features 4/4 tempos between 125 and 145 bpm, with prominence placed on oft-repeating—that is, trancelike—rhythmic and melodic figures, often generated via arpeggiated chords. Like house—from which it largely evolved—trance uses a four-on-the-floor kick drum, but is especially marked by the use of one or more "builds" (usually articulated by extended drumrolls) leading to full-texture "drops" followed by a "break," or dissipation of the texture. It is such moments that trance fans live for!

## VAN BUUREN: ANALYSIS

"Embrace," the title track from van Buuren's 2015 album, includes all of the above-noted features of trance, but likewise shows the composer's eclectic and experimental tendencies—including the use of some rather sophisticated formal and rhythmic devices. Like a good percentage of EDM, "Embrace" involves collaboration between the producer (van Buuren) and another performer. But instead of working with a vocalist, as is most common, van Buuren here joins forces with Dutch jazz trumpeter Eric Vloeimans. The intersection of synth-based electronica with jazz trumpet exemplifies the flexibility that is inherent in EDM, and embodies van Buuren's own expressed aim on this album "to 'embrace' several different instruments and sounds, and incorporate them into my sound."[545]

Van Buuren uses Vloeimans' trumpet improvisation to set up a striking form: an interesting interplay of three distinct sections. The A section begins rubato (out of tempo), and is set for piano, atmospheric synth pads, and solo trumpet. Supporting the proceedings is a looping modal chord progression in B minor, colored by diatonic nonchord tones in the improvising trumpet. The resulting sonority may be defined as the track's "ambient" section—another primary influence on trance. A clear theme arrives in the trumpet (at 0:57), leading to the introduction of a new, tonal chord progression that will soon come to dominate the track: a sixteen-bar progression divided into two varied repetition phrases of eight bars each (a-a'), each ending on a kind of "half cadence"—to the VII and II chord, respectively. The progression itself begins rather typically, based on the Circle of 4ths—starting B–E–A–D—and found, for example, in the jazz standard "Autumn Leaves" (Figure 13.4):

**Figure 13.4: Armin van Buuren, "Embrace"—(tonal) harmonic progression of Section A**

After a dramatic and ascending trumpet flurry, the main "trance" thrust of the song takes off: the B section (at 2:01). An arpeggiated synth line defines the above chord progression in strict tempo—first without drums, then (at 2:30) with the expected four-on-the-floor kick: we are now in familiar trance territory. The B section is again repeated via a typical drumroll build over an extended V chord (at 3:00), followed by a return of the "ambient" A section and Vloeimans' trumpet. The back-and-forth continues with yet another B section, though now transposed from the original B minor to E minor (at 4:03)—likewise via a drumroll build and subsequent "drop."

One might assume that the track would simply conclude using this alternation between the "ambient" A and "trance" B sections. But instead, at 5:07, the texture changes entirely with a surprising shift in meter—from the standard 4/4 to 6/8, played in a manner akin to a children's song on a Rhodes electric piano. The trumpet soon joins with a variation of its earlier theme to mark this C section (Figure 13.5):

**Figure 13.5: Armin van Buuren, "Embrace"—contrasting triple-based (compound duple) meter in Section C**

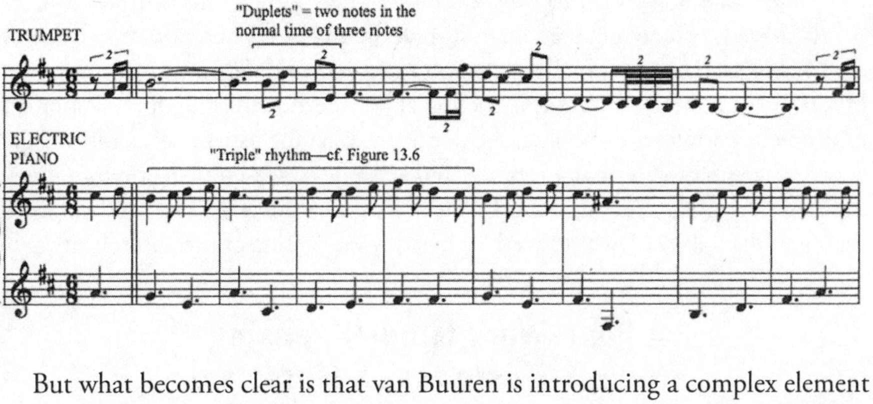


But what becomes clear is that van Buuren is introducing a complex element of polyrhythm, not unlike what Wayne Shorter used in "Footprints." What sounds like 6/8 meter is in fact a superimposition above the steady 4/4 trance beat, though with the latter initially absent. Specifically, this is a hemiola (3 against 2) relationship of quarter note triplets against the 4/4 flow of the trance beat—suggested already in "duplets" in the trumpet melody in Figure 13.5. When the 4/4 trance beat is removed, all we hear is the triple (6/8) feel. Van Buuren reveals his intentions clearly, however, when steady eighth notes appear in a synth bass toward the end of this unexpected C section (Figure 13.6):

**Figure 13.6: Armin van Buuren, "Embrace"—realization of cross-rhythm: 6/8 against 4/4 trance beat**

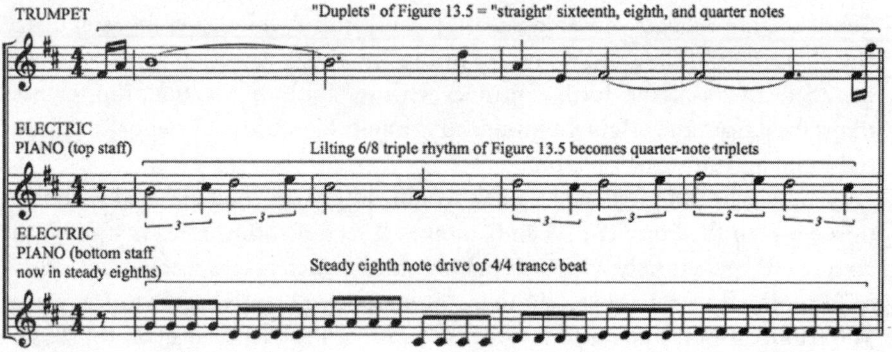


Following a very long drumroll build on the V, we return with a "drop" and a final B section. A final "ambient" section then ends the song—a typical EDM technique that allows a DJ to transition to another song in any tempo.

As this admittedly detailed analysis reveals, EDM is a realm that plays by its own rules and requires some level setting to understand. In contrast to "Hey Boy Hey Girl," "Embrace" utilizes less layering and more a contrasting formal approach to define its narrative. To be sure, the dominant listening experience is this contrast between a tempo-free ambient sonority and a steady, trance-inducing rhythm. But as the above discussion reveals, there's a lot more going on in the process, and much that fans like Subject 5 would seemingly enjoy navigating and want to hear again.

## A Post-Work Mind-Cleansing: Reich's *Music for 18 Musicians*

**Steve Reich's *Music for 18 Musicians*** throws light on Subject 5's musical taste as one who truly embraces the aesthetic and sonic elements that underlie the musicology of electronica, and not just the EDM lifestyle. Indeed, it suggests a level of historic awareness and appreciation regarding the technical and experiential precedence to electronica that likely exceeds that of many devotees of the species.

### REICH: BACKGROUND

Steve Reich, to be sure, is not directly associated with the electronica or EDM realm, but rather is a classical composer—specifically, one of the progenitors of the minimalist school in the mid-1960s. Yet Reich's significance, at least to some, far exceeds the confines of a single, esoteric subgenre of contemporary classical—with such exalted sources as the *New York Times* and *Guardian* newspaper praising him as "our greatest living composer" and among "a handful of living composers who can legitimately claim to have altered the direction of musical history," respectively.[546] Not all will agree with these lofty accolades, as well it should be, and yet Reich's influence on various musical realms—including electronica—is well-founded.

Reich was born in New York City in 1936 into a home well acquainted with music—his mother was a songwriter and his uncle an established Broadway producer.[547] He began conventional classical piano lessons as a young child, but by age fourteen was being stimulated by more adventurous sounds—most notably Bach, Stravinsky, and bebop: "three musics," Reich would later recall, "that basically form who I am."[548] After receiving his BA in philosophy at Cornell, he jumped headlong into music, studying composition at Juilliard with Vincent Persichetti and then at Mills College with both Darius Milhaud (who had earlier taught Dave Brubeck) and avant-garde Italian composer Luciano Berio. Yet rather than embracing the ultramodernist—that is, serial or 12-tone—techniques sanctioned by the "classical establishment" in the mid-1960s, Reich gravitated toward a radically different approach: minimalism. Significantly, Reich was involved in the premiere in San Francisco of Terry Riley's *In C*—often cited as the first influential minimalist musical work.

Minimalism is grounded on several musical concepts and techniques, most of which consciously spurn the highly complex, dissonant, and rhythmically abstract approaches being pursued by postwar composers like Boulez and Stockhausen, then all the rage in the American classical "academy." By contrast, minimalist works—pioneered mainly in New York through the 1960s and '70s, and especially by Riley, Reich, La Monte Young, and Philip Glass—embrace a consistently consonant approach to harmony, a continuously steady pulse, and a musical discourse generally devoid of obvious narrative or teleological direction.[549]

Reich initially followed Riley's lead via works using tape collage and manipulation (e.g., *It's Gonna Rain*, 1965) that created a "phasing" technique, whereby two or more parts would gradually "slip" in and out of sync. With determined experimentation, he devised how to translate this technique to live instruments, with works such as *Piano Phase* (1967), *Clapping Music* (1972), and *Drumming* (1971). The latter, in fact, followed Reich's trip to Ghana to study African drumming—the desire for which dated back at least to his infatuation with John Coltrane's 1961 album *Africa/Brass*: sixteen minutes on one chord, yet for Reich never boring. His trip to Africa in turn confirmed his commitment to the universality of repeating rhythmic patterns and consonant harmonies, and his own belief that he was on the right path.

From there, however, Reich began to take a new tack on the minimalist approach—moving from phasing to "pulsing," where the instruments or voices play or sing pulsating notes within each slow-shifting chord. Among the prototypes of this pulsing style was *Four Organs* (1973), built on a single "polychord" of

D major over E major, with a pulse of steady eighth notes provided by nonstop maracas. The resulting harmonic and rhythmic stasis was clearly novel and caused, as Alex Ross put it, "the last great scandal concert of the [twentieth] century" when it was performed at Carnegie Hall.[550] But the pinnacle of this technique, and probably Reich's most famous work, was *Music for 18 Musicians* (1974), which we'll discuss below.

Since the mid-1970s, Reich has continued to evolve his technical arsenal while staying true to the minimalist aesthetic. Most notable has been his increased use of the human voice, stemming in part from his intense study of Jewish chanting or cantillation techniques. Key among these works is *Different Trains* (1988), dedicated to the dark theme of the Holocaust, which won the 1990 Grammy for Best Contemporary Classical Composition, and which noted musicologist Richard Taruskin praised as "the only adequate musical response—one of the few adequate artistic responses in any medium—to the Holocaust."[551] Indeed, Reich can boast a dazzling list of awards and accolades, including a Pulitzer for the 2008 work *Double Sextet*. His influence has been profound on later generations of classical composers, including John Adams and David Lang. Yet while many have credited Reich for transforming the landscape of contemporary classical music, he himself is more measured—saying in 2013, "What my generation did wasn't a revolution, it was a restoration of harmony and rhythm in a whole new way, but it did bring back those essentials that people wanted, that people craved, but in a way they hadn't heard."[552]

A similar and, for our purpose, more fundamental question is what influence Reich may have had on popular music, and especially electronica. Many are quick to acclaim Reich's direct sway on a range of "pop" realms, from rock to hip hop to EDM. His experimental use of tape sampling in the mid-1960s led *Rolling Stone* to call him the "father of sampling" in 1999; several critics have chronicled the admiration gained by mid-1970s British rockers, such as Brian Eno (Roxy Music), Robert Fripp (King Crimson), and David Bowie upon hearing Reich's works, especially *Music for 18 Musicians*. Regarding dance music, some have noted that disco—with its similar imperative of a steady pulse—emerged in the mid-1970s just as Reich's mature works were gaining wider attention, and more empirically, many are the electronica and EDM artists who have sampled Reich's works over the past twenty-five years, including the Orb, DJ Spooky, and Blu Mar Ten, as well as on two "Reich Remix" compilations (1999 and 2006). Ironically, Reich was never much moved by pop or rock music—having noted even his relative lack of interest in the Beatles during their mid-'60s creative burst, despite living in San Francisco and being friends with Grateful Dead bassist Phil Lesh.[553] In all, therefore, rather than ascribe any direct lineage between Reich's minimalism and the advent or evolution of electronica, we might better adopt the view espoused by writer Tim Rutherford-Johnson: "Both [styles] were attuned to the similar musical and technological currents: Afro-diasporic beats;

the technology of the turntable, tape loop and cross-fader; and the possibilities of accumulative and layered musical forms."[554] Subject 5 would no doubt concur.

## REICH: ANALYSIS

*Music for 18 Musicians* (1974–76) is, as noted, Reich's most well-known composition, and follows a decade of tape-based and solo instrument works wherein he developed many of the techniques now synonymous with minimalism. Again, these include "phase shifting"—where two voices start in sync and gradually "shift" apart as one increases the tempo over the other; and "augmentation"—where a melodic, harmonic, or rhythmic element is gradually and subtly expanded; among others. *Music for 18 Musicians* combines these and other techniques with the minimalist imperatives of a steady pulse and fully consonant/diatonic harmony to construct an hour-long hypnotic discourse. As much as any other work, it helped propel Reich and minimalism to the near-celebrity status he has enjoyed now for decades.

As the title states, the work is scored for eighteen musicians, though Reich himself recommends using more players to double the several dual-instrument parts. In all, the work calls for four pianos, three marimbas, two xylophones, one metallophone (a vibraphone without the motor), two clarinets/bass clarinets, one violin, one cello, and four female voices. Together they make for a surprisingly uniform sonic palette, where the percussive nature of the piano and mallet instruments blend into a kind of multipart "super" instrument. The strings, clarinets, and vocalizing female singers stab out of the palette somewhat, though it is striking to hear just how much they too blend into a collective soundscape. This is due in large part to the pure saturation and incessantness of the musical discourse: continuously active rhythms produced by a boisterous ensemble of instruments, especially the pianos and marimbas. Indeed, the music-listening experience is all but dominated by the pure density of the sonic-rhythmic propulsion. This in turn is what generates that hypnotic trancelike experience that beguiles the devoted fans, such as Subject 5, of this music.

Structurally, the hour-long work is divided into thirteen contiguous movements: an opening and closing "summary"—both titled "Pulses"—and eleven intervening "sections." Overall cohesion for the work is provided by a cycle of eleven "chords"—presented in their entirety in both bookend movements, and then individually, in sequence, in the eleven intervening sections. These are not traditional chords, such as major or minor triads, but rather diatonic "constructs" built out of between seven and eleven tones. Each construct comprises a set of strong 4ths or 5ths in the lowest and highest registers (with one exception) and a mix of 3rds and 2nds (often in a cluster formation) in the middle register. All "chords" are diatonic to a key signature of 3 sharps (F♯, C♯, G♯), though to say that there is a functional reference to A major, F♯ minor, or any particular mode would be wrong: the harmony is instead a kind of "pan-modality" based on a scale of 3 sharps (Figure 13.7):

**Figure 13.7: Steve Reich, *Music for 18 Musicians*—11 chords (diatonic clusters) underlying the work's 11 sections**

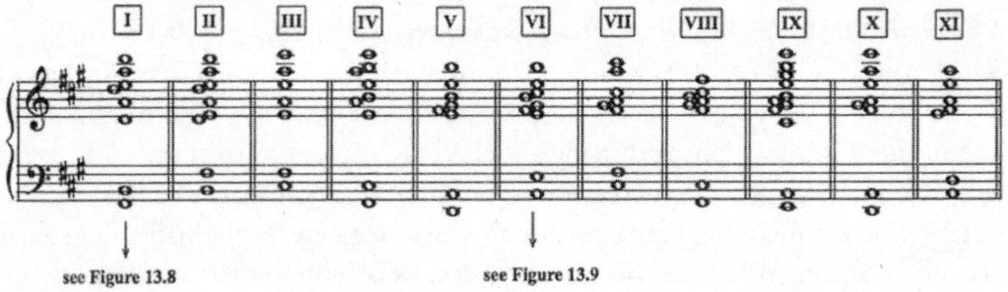


In the opening and closing movements ("Pulses"), the eleven-chord cycle unfolds in its entirety, but not in any cleanly articulated way. Instead, two gradual crescendo-decrescendo cycles completed over two full breaths of the clarinets and vocals trigger a subtle shift (every twenty seconds or so) from one "chord" to the next—much as a slow dissolve fades one photo into another in a computer slideshow. The ambiguity of the "chords" is heightened through the staggered arrival of the highest and lowest tones of the construct. The result is an abstract yet hypnotic set of energetic "pulses," ebbing and flowing without any real sense of direction. The internal, individual "sections," by contrast, are more "composed," though still experientially dominated by the insistent pulsations of the pianos and mallets. With each section based—predominantly, though not exclusively—on the notes of just one of the eleven "chords," the harmonic landscape is more static, and thus focus is placed on the rhythmic figuration in the other instruments. This figuration is generally built upon short, syncopated patterns that gradually expand or contract. Multiple patterns are layered one upon another at different intervals, keeping the discourse fluid and unpredictable. Here is an example from Section I (Figure 13.8):

**Figure 13.8: Steve Reich, *Music for 18 Musicians*, Section I (mm. 103–105)—sample of layered rhythmic patterns**

Reich maintains interest throughout the work by virtue of the varied and often infectious character of the individual rhythmic patterns that float above the static harmonies of each section. The patterns are introduced, repeated near endlessly, subtly augmented or diminished, and layered over by others. Some of these patterns (as in Section VI), moreover, have a decidedly jazzy—that is, syncopated and groove-based—quality; this is not surprising given Reich's own love of jazz, especially Miles Davis and John Coltrane, as noted in Figure 13.9:

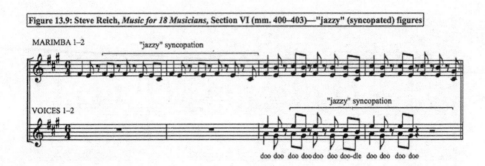

Figure 13.9: Steve Reich, *Music for 18 Musicians*, Section VI (mm. 400–403)—"jazzy" (syncopated) figures

The discourse in each section is guided by a formal construct—essentially an "arch" form (A-B-C-D-C-B-A)—and broader unity is rendered by the varied repetition of some patterns from one section to another (e.g., Sections I and XI). And yet, again, the overall experience here is one of stasis and quasi-meditative trance. This is not music for everyone, as some will find the incessant repetition maddening. But for fans like Subject 5, *Music for 18 Musicians*—even if there's only time for the opening movement on the way home from work—offers the goods that keep on coming.

## "Chill" Before Bedtime: Eno's "Always Returning"

**Brian Eno's "Always Returning,"** of all the subjects' closing hits thus far, is the most manifestly appropriate for a "bedtime" track—an ambient track that indeed befits the composer's own dictate that the style "be as ignorable as it is interesting."[555] "Always Returning" also corroborates our impression that Subject 5 takes a broad and historically minded approach to the electronica species, well beyond the imperative of spinning the latest adrenaline-inducing dance track.

### ENO: BACKGROUND

In a manner not unlike Steve Reich, Brian Eno is one of those rare artists over whom music critics and commentators often fall over themselves in praise. The AllMusic Guide, for example, claims that Eno "forever altered the ways in which music is approached, composed, performed, and perceived," while *Rolling Stone* similarly credits him with "an entirely new way of thinking about music." More pointedly for our purposes, Paul Morley of the *Guardian* believes he "helped determine what the history of electronic music was between the avant-garde 1950s and the pop 21st century." Not bad for a man who once called himself a non-musician, who can't read or write music, nor play an instrument with anything approaching virtuosity.

Eno was born in Suffolk, England, in 1948, near a US Air Force base, where as a kid he heard Armed Forces Radio—and a steady diet of American doo-wop and rock and roll. His childhood talents, however, gravitated to the visual arts, and like fellow Brits John Lennon and Pete Townshend he attended art school before making the shift to music. Indeed, it was at the Winchester School of Art in 1968 that Townshend himself gave a guest lecture on the use of tape machines for nonmusicians; the experience for Eno, near graduation, was transformative. He actually had owned a tape recorder since age fifteen, after begging his parents for it the way most teens do for an electric guitar. As Eno told famed rock critic Lester Bangs in 1979, "I'm very good with technology; I always have been."[556] Eno's initial efforts in tape manipulation followed the model set out by progressive classical composers like Cage and Reich (notably his *It's Gonna Rain*), but when he heard the Velvet Underground's "Loop" in 1966—which signaled for him an ability to straddle the "process" of classical and the "results" of pop music—he knew his path forward was not as a visual artist.[557]

The unwinding of Eno's musical accomplishments is traced as much through his restlessly eclectic interests as by his chronology. A common refrain throughout his chameleonlike career is the notion of chance: relying on random criteria to determine notes, rhythms, or sounds—something he may have picked up from his study of John Cage. It manifests itself not only in how he constructs his own compositions (or "treatments," as he calls them), but also in how he's worked as the producer for dozens of seminal pop/rock artists since the mid-'70s: Devo, Genesis, Talking Heads, David Bowie, Laurie Anderson, U2, and Coldplay, to name but a few. As Eno told the *New Yorker* in 2014, for example, "Musicians do their best work when they have no idea what they're doing."[558] Peppered in there as well is Eno the public-facing artist, though largely limited to the early 1970s, first as vocalist–synth player–"mixer" for the glam rock band Roxy Music, then as an esoteric solo artist—releasing a set of experimental "electro-pop" albums that at times presaged later rock trends, such as the proto-punk track "Seven Deadly Finns" (1974). His restless curiosity even led him to explore African rhythm in the early 1980s, much as Reich had done a decade earlier; in Eno's case, the results planted seeds for worldbeat music (see Chapter 14), such as in the Talking Heads' "Once in a Lifetime" (1980). Throughout his career too has been a bevy of creative collaborations, with artists such as Robert Fripp, David Byrne, and avant-garde composer Harold Budd.

Most prized by hardcore Eno fans, however, are his efforts in the ambient realm—a genre he helped create in the early 1970s. His experimental 1973 collaboration with Fripp (*No Pussyfooting*) saw Eno perfect his tape-based skill set (delays, loops, etc.), and featured a rugged, atmospheric proto-ambient style. Then in early 1975, Eno was struck by a taxi while walking and was laid up for months; one day a visiting friend brought an album of eighteenth-century harp music—which remained on even after he left, although it played so softly as to blend with the rain falling outside his window. What Eno experienced was not music but sound, or rather a sonic atmosphere—and with that epiphany, ambient music was born. Eno developed the genre through a series of albums in the '70s and '80s—such as *Discreet Music* (1975), *Music for Airports* (1978), and *Apollo: Atmospheres & Soundtracks* (1983), which includes "Always Returning." Several of his ambient albums are collaborations—notably with Budd and Daniel Lanois—though many are solo efforts, including his most recent release, *The Ship* (2016). In either case, Eno's contributions are less as composer or performer and more as "sonic landscaper," as he now describes himself. Much as Duke Ellington used his orchestra as an "instrument" during the jazz age, Eno uses the studio as his "compositional tool," whether or not he has input the sounds themselves onto the tape.

"Ambient," according to Eno—who seems to have christened the term—stems from the Latin verb "*ambire*" meaning, "to surround." The sense here is that the music bypasses traditional modes of musical discourse—based on forward-driving melodies, harmonies, and rhythms—in favor of a timeless, unobtrusive, and "atmospheric" flow that "surrounds" the listener without demanding anything. The key parameters explored are sound and texture. Harmony is inevitably simple and diatonic, and the rhythm is often "free" and lacking a steady pulse. With roots going back to Erik Satie's aesthetic of *musique d'ameublement* (furniture music) and John Cage's aleatoric (chance) music, ambient had its main heyday in the 1970s with Eno, Mike Oldfield, and Jean-Michel Jarre (again, an influence to van Buuren); it then enjoyed a healthy revival in the 1990s with bands like the Orb and Aphex Twin.

It is, in truth, a bit anachronistic to call ambient a subgenre of electronica, given that it began nearly a decade before the first house track was produced in Chicago. And yet, by virtue of its similar reliance on synths and electronics, manipulation of "tape" (today digital) content, and an Eno-esque adherence to the notion of the studio as a "compositional tool," electronica/EDM has embraced the ambient genre as one of its own. Today, ambient (and its "cousins" dark ambient, dub ambient, and psybient, among many others) is indeed an active part of the EDM repertoire and lifestyle—often used as a meditative "chill-out" between house and trance tracks or, as is the case now for Subject 5, a welcome respite to close out a busy day.

## ENO: ANALYSIS

"Always Returning," again, stems from Eno's 1983 album, *Apollo: Atmospheres & Soundtracks*, originally recorded as the soundtrack of Al Reinart's documentary *Apollo*—using original 35mm footage of the Apollo moon missions. The title is an apt description of the track's musical proceedings: it does, in fact, always return to where it has been before. This is "cyclic music" without beginning or end, an endless loop of which the listener hears only a four-minute sliver, fading both in and out.

At the same time, the music traces a quasi-tonal progression in B♭ major that never quite resolves. A stepwise descending line in the electric bass is the principal formal element of the cycle: one "complete revolution" is sixteen measures long, comprising two passes of an eight-measure half cycle with a change only on the final bar of each half—D the first time, F the second. This latter shift, from F back to B♭, is what defines the cycle as tonal (V–I), though the effect of the work is as much modal (B♭ Ionian) as tonal (Figure 13.10):

**Figure 13.10: Brian Eno, "Always Returning"—harmonic progression (full cycle)**

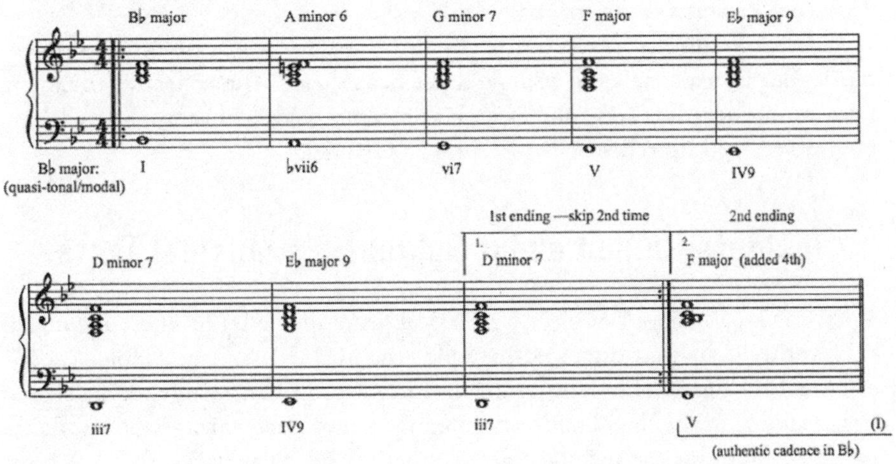


The other structural element of the cycle is a repeating two-bar ostinato—C–F–G–F—in the electric guitar (performed by the album's coproducer, Daniel Lanois) that reinforces the track's ambiguous harmony (Figure 13.11):

**Figure 13.11: Brian Eno, "Always Returning"—electric guitar ostinato**

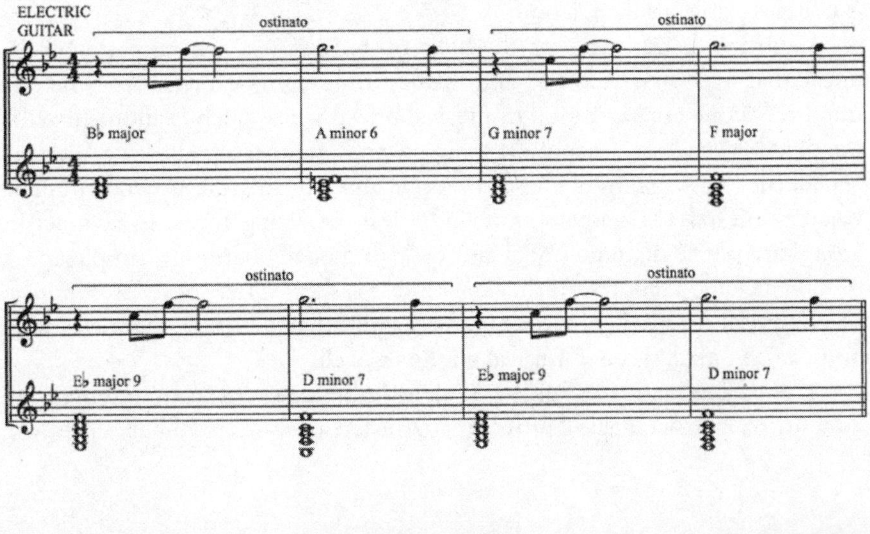

The ambient identity of "Always Returning" is embodied in the soft, heavily reverberant sonic texture and overall meditative flow of the cycle. Beyond the bass and guitar, the soundscape consists of sparse and "floating" piano fills (played by Brian's brother, Roger), periodic backwards tape snippets that sound vaguely like a pedal steel guitar, and an airy synth background "pad." The accompanying instruments dispense with any narrative discourse—e.g., the piano figures avoid anything that could resemble development or repetition—thus keeping them abstract and atmospheric. They do, however, color the harmonic palette with extended or nonchord diatonic tones—which, like in *Music for 18 Musicians*, creates a degree of "pan-modality."

"Always Returning" is not in free rhythm (rubato), as is common for ambient music, but instead moves at a languid yet steady pace. The collective result is a four-minute relaxing and mind-wander-prompting track that might well have put Subject 5 to sleep before completing its final fade.

## Insights Gained about Subject 5's Musical Taste

What can we say about Subject 5's musical genotype based on these five musical favorites—the four discussed here plus the fifth (Messinian's "Holy Ghost") discussed on the WYLI website? To be sure, we can define a genotype that is well-rounded in the broad and variegated terrain of electronica—not just dance or EDM, but also the technical and aesthetic span of a species that has roots dating back to at least the mid-1960s. Subject 5's musical taste is seemingly most charged by the parameter of rhythm—and especially when propulsive and dynamic. Whether syncopated ("Hey Boy Hey Girl," "Holy Ghost") or steady-pulsed ("Embrace," *Music for 18 Musicians*), a robust and dominating rhythmic identity is primary to Subject 5's musical happy place. Of course, the gentle rhythmic flow of "Always Returning" and portions of "Embrace" show that such is not necessarily a sine qua non.

Aligned with this taste for rhythmic propulsion is a general preference for music that instills an absorbed and meditative listening experience—where the mind can "zone out" in a kind of musical brown study. Such is afforded well by the dense, layered, and nebulous sonic palette—synthesizer and/or acoustically generated—of so many of these tracks. It also explains the general simplicity whereby the other parameters unwind: clear, repeating forms in symmetrical groupings; purely diatonic (tonal and/or "pan-modal") harmony; simple and repeating melodic ideas, etc. At the same time, the sheer variety of styles, sonorities, and technical approaches in these tracks suggests that Subject 5 might well feel at home in a myriad of other musical terrains as well.

As to what other tracks Subject 5 might embrace, we first turn to those by the same artists in musicological proximity to the favorites—here addressing only the four songs discussed in the chapter. These might include "Under the Influence" (Chemical Brothers), "Intense" (van Buuren), *Music for a Large Ensemble* (Reich), or "Emerald and Stone" (Eno).

Extending out a bit, we look to tracks by other artists operating in similar arenas: "Right Here, Right Now" by Fatboy Slim or "Climbatize" by the Prodigy (Chemical Brothers); "The Only Way Is Up" by Tiësto or "When It Ends It Starts Again" (original instrumental version) by ATB (van Buuren); *Music in Twelve Parts* by Philip Glass or *In C* by Terry Riley (Reich); or "Wanderer" by Harold Budd or "First Approach" by Vangelis (Eno).

Diving yet deeper into Subject 5's prospective music picks, we can look at influencers on and/or "heirs" to the artists and composers involved: Kraftwerk and Cabaret Voltaire (Chemical Brothers); Jean-Michel Jarre and the KLF (van Buuren); John Cage and John Adams (Reich); or Erik Satie and Aphex Twin (Eno).

Finally, a potentially wide array of nonelectronica sources may be offered as potential candidates for Subject 5's musical predilection: Balinese gamelan music or the orchestral music by Witold Lutoslawski (dense sonic layering); Dr. John or Igor Stravinsky (rhythmic propulsion); Paul Winter or Perotin (pan-modality); Arvo Pärt or Tibetan flute music (meditative flow); Edgard Varèse or Nine Inch Nails (raw "bass drop" sonorities); or Mozart or Irish folk music (symmetrical formal structures). At a minimum, such a wide-ranging list demonstrates the kinds of disparate and interesting trajectories that one can chart when trying to expand upon a narrow list of known favorites.

# Interlude F

## *Staking Your Claim: Intraculture and Musical Taste*

### A Tale of Two Bands

Rich Gelbart, my enterprising young friend who booked me my first steady gig at the La Mirada Mall at the age of eleven, was part of a quartet of best buddies—the "four musketeers" of Temple Beth Ohr's Saturday afternoon religious school. Beyond Rich and myself, there were Kenny Mandler and Mitch Fadem. If Rich was my arcade partner, Mitch was my music mate: like me, he played the piano quite well, and he had a great, if off-color, sense of humor—that more than once got us in trouble for laughing uncontrollably during Shabbat services. Whenever it was just the two of us, we'd talk nonstop about music, usually in terms that can only be described as obsessive. Talking obsessively about music, of course, is nothing unusual for twelve- and thirteen-year-olds, as we were then: at this age, the music you listen to isn't just important—it's everything.[559] As noted in Interlude C, by age eleven or twelve our neural processing is reaching maturity, and we begin to see the world as something we can forge for ourselves, distinct from our parents; music becomes the soundtrack of our nascent independence, and the bonds of friendship we claim are built firmly out of the newly autonomous decisions we make: the clothes we wear, the activities we prefer, and the music we listen to. Clear lines of "us and them" can be drawn between those who share our musical likes and dislikes and those who don't. That Mitch and I were budding musicians only raised these stakes higher.

We both loved the Beatles and Scott Joplin, and listened religiously each Sunday night to Dr. Demento's radio show—featuring novelty recordings such as "Shaving Cream" and Allan Sherman's "Hello Muddah, Hello Faddah." But in one fundamental area we disagreed, and vehemently. For me, the best "modern" rock band in the world was Queen; for Mitch it was Kiss. Our debates would last hours, each of us spinning our favorite songs from the stack of albums we lugged from one house to another to illustrate our point of view. For me, the music of Kiss was noisy, repetitive, self-indulgent, and simplistic—revealing a basic lack of musical inventiveness and technical chops; by contrast, Queen's music was creative, sophisticated, technically dazzling, and endlessly engaging. Mitch, of course, was unconvinced: to him, Kiss songs were fun, anthemic, filled with intoxicating riffs and memorable melodies; Queen songs, on the other hand, were prissy, melodramatic, meandering, and kitsch. When gathered in larger groups, Mitch and I would attempt to bolster our respective arguments by conscripting allies to our side, forcing schoolmates to take sides in the Temple Beth Ohr episode of "the battle of mid-'70s glam rock bands." As the months passed, we began to seek aesthetic kinship beyond our immediate circle of religious school friends, and before we knew it our differing positions on the matter took on a level of import we could hardly have predicted.

The battle lines that Mitch and I formed between Queen and Kiss are indicative of the impassioned allegiances that music can foster, particularly among youth. It is a bit the interpersonal equivalent of Sayre's law of academia—"The disputes are so bitter because the stakes are so small"—or, perhaps better, Freud's formulation of why culturally similar nations are so touchy about the details of their distinction: the "narcissism of small differences." Western music history is in fact replete with such "narcissisms," where factions that arise in literally the same milieu go to war over differences that to an outsider might seem imaginary: Monteverdi vs. Artusi, Wagner vs. Brahms, Stravinsky vs. Schoenberg (classical eras), the Beatles vs. the Rolling Stones, Nirvana vs. Guns N' Roses (rock eras), the Notorious B.I.G. vs. 2Pac (1990s hip hop), etc., etc. More than once have such factions erupted into actual brawls and riots—as in Paris at the premiere of Stravinsky's *Rite of Spring* (1913), or between the "mods" and "rockers" in early 1960s England. While it never rose to quite that fevered a pitch, Mitch and I did get into some pretty good shouting matches. At some point, our Kiss-Queen feud went beyond the music, into aspects of dress, language, attitude, and ultimately larger issues of identity.[560]

## Identity and Intracultural Loyalty

Through the preceding chapters of our "mystery novel," we have been pursuing the ever-narrowing foundations of our musical taste: from the physics of our universe and rocky planet to the evolution and biology of our species to our dominant and defining culture. As we steadily home in on what makes our musical taste uniquely our own, we likewise home in on what grants us our distinct identity as individuals. These paired queries now kick into high gear in the present chapter as we here seek to unravel the byzantine ways in which our musical taste entwines with the many and varied identities we adopt as members of that dominant culture.

As detailed in the previous interlude (E), one's dominant culture places several key constraints upon an individual's musical taste—from both a musicological and functional perspective. No culture, however, is a monolith. By birth and by deed, members of any culture will proceed to fragment, parse, divide, and splinter it into any number of subdivisions, based on any number of factors: wealth, occupation, education, ethnicity, faith, politics, temperament, hobby, curiosity, among countless others—singularly and in untold combinations. At the same time, each of us maintains, by definition, a relationship to the dominant or overarching culture within which those subdivisions reside.

The typical term used to identify these social subdivisions, as you may have guessed, is "subculture." It is, however, not the only term used—with common alternatives being "group," "community," "scene," and "tribe," among others. As we'll see in this interlude, however, each of these terms has been subject to vigorous scholarly debate by virtue of some perceived flaw or lack of definitional clarity. So substantial, in fact, are the holes poked in each of them that I have been tempted to introduce my own neutral term: "intraculture"—meaning a social division taking place "within" (intra-) as opposed to "under" (sub-) the dominant culture.[561] In so doing, though, I must accept the risk of trying to introduce a new term into an already crowded academic and pop culture space: that it too will be subject to dispute and objection.

Far more important than nomenclature, of course, are the actual qualities and functions that these social subdivisions hold within the broader culture, and especially for our purposes, how they relate to the development of our musical taste. These are the issues we'll dive into below, but it may first be useful to present a quick, if imperfect, metaphor to illustrate how these "intracultures" provide us with opportunities to formulate our musical taste: the shopping center metaphor.

Picture yourself hanging out at your local major shopping center—whether enclosed, like the La Mirada Mall of my youth, or one of those outdoor, unenclosed types. The shopping center as a whole—its retail stores, restaurants, administrative and security offices, landscaping, pathways, etc.—may be thought of as your broad culture. When you park in its parking lots, travel down its pathways, or eat in its common "food court" areas, you are participating collectively as members of your overarching culture—the "mainstream," as it is often called. The shopping center, however, has a whole slew of distinct, individual stores of varying dimensions and types, ranging from big retail chains (Macy's, Nordstrom's, Target, etc.) to more specialized chains (Pottery Barn, Gap, Apple Store, etc.) to any number of individual, nonchain shops; they run the gamut—selling clothes, electronics, housewares, stationery, food, entertainment, you name it.

As a "member" of your shopping center culture, you will undoubtedly have varying types of relationships with a good number—likely dozens and dozens—of individual stores. In our metaphor, each store is an intraculture, and your relationship to each will be somewhat distinct: at some—especially the large, crowded retailers—you will regularly spend a good deal of time and money browsing and shopping; at others—perhaps smaller, independent stores—you will shop obsessively, knowing the salesclerks, and perhaps other customers, by subcultures—the intracultural collectives—to which you in some way "belong": the stores at which you shop, so to speak. It is to this often prickly topic that we now turn.

## Intraculture at a Glance

Academics have addressed the intersection of music and intraculture (subcultures, communities, etc.) from a wide variety of perspectives and trajectories—that not infrequently intersect or contradict one another. Sociology, cultural studies, ethnography, ethnomusicology, traditional musicology, consumer behavior, and marketing are among the disciplines brought to bear on this confluence, such that it can be easy to miss the forest for the trees—something we'll try to prevent here.

In essence, these theories and arguments aim to answer a single question: How does one's intraculture influence the music one consumes? Or in our parlance: How does intraculture influence musical taste? It is not surprising that many of these theories, based as they are on a mix of chronologically stamped surveys and tightly held philosophical precepts, in time come to be revised, challenged, or rejected outright. They are worth reviewing in some depth here, however, since they collectively get us closer to the "truth" regarding the above question than would be possible otherwise—and for *you* personally: How does *your* identity as a member of various intracultures affect the way you listen to music? Indeed, it is by exploring the various theories devised over the years that I am able to offer my own take on the matter: that our many-splendored intracultural identities grant us *access* to and *ownership* of a wealth of music that we would otherwise never know. Intracultures, that is, are the very gateway to our own, personal musical taste.

To get us started, it will be helpful to first note the typical parameters by which "intracultures"—labeled as social groups, classes, subcultures, etc.—have historically been defined. Useful, for example, is the notion that such groups are composed of individuals who are unified to some degree at least by one or more "markers." The most commonly cited include class, education status, race/ethnicity, age, gender, and region; beyond these "structural" (identity-oriented) markers are those aligned with "behavior"—such as dress/fashion, consumer patterns, and performance venues. Fashion, in fact, holds historic resonance in "intraculture" studies; in 1905, the pioneering sociologist Georg Simmel, friend of Max Weber, cited it as a key indicator of both class identity and "intracultural" distinction: "Fashion signifies union with those in the same class, . . . [and yet] provides the best arena for people . . . whose self-awareness requires that they be recognized as distinct and as particular kinds of beings."[566] As we'll see, later writers will attribute these same powers of association and distinction to music.



name; at still others you will merely browse occasionally or even just window-shop, only rarely moved to make an actual purchase. On the other hand, there will also be a good many stores in the center that hold absolutely no interest to you—where you wouldn't be caught dead shopping, whether for reasons of content, style, age-appropriateness, etc. By contrast, those stores at which you *do* shop, even occasionally, may be said to be part of your "intracultural" shopping makeup. By simply showing up, you are in essence given access, indeed permission, to consume the wares these stores offer. You will not purchase everything available, of course, but by virtue of being displayed at a store in your intracultural orbit, the items there are more likely to attract your serious consideration.

As suggested, it is an imperfect metaphor—for example, we aren't exactly linked to some stores by birth (unless your parents own one). Still, it may be helpful to you as we explore in detail the often complex nature of subcultures, communities, intracultures, etc., and how they might or might not intersect with the music you love. The principal point offered here is that just as we shop at many different stores, with distinct degrees of "loyalty" to each, so too do we belong to many different intracultures—some large, some small, and to each with a distinct degree of allegiance, affiliation, passion, etc. And yet, just as each individual store is by default aligned with its broader shopping center, so too is each intraculture by default aligned with its broader culture.

## Culture Deconstructed

As in the previous interlude, where we introduced the topic of cultural distinction by first revisiting universals, so too will it be useful here to return briefly to the topic of culture as a prelude to a fuller discussion of subcultures—as we'll call these subdivisions for the moment. In so doing, though, we'll rely less on ethnomusicology and music psychology than on sociology and cultural anthropology.

An important caveat first, however: the discussion of culture and intraculture in this interlude will focus exclusively on the Western experience—indeed, more narrowly on the experience of the Anglo-American orbit, with some reference to France. This assuredly does not reflect any bias or cultural superiority on my part, but simply the limited scope of my knowledge and resources enlisted. Every culture, of course, will have its own complex system and interrelations of intracultures—you'll just have to go elsewhere to learn about most of them.[562] Okay, onward.

As with its subdivisions, one's broad, overarching culture is commonly identified by several different terms. Among the most common include "mainstream," "popular culture," "commercialism," "dominant culture," "status quo," and "hegemony." The first three underscore the prominence of economic forces within a society: culture is defined by the most common and popular targets of business investment and consumer behavior. The last three terms, by contrast, place greater emphasis on societal divisions of political and cultural authority.

The concept of cultural hegemony in particular arose out of Marxist philosophy—such as that developed by Antonio Gramsci in his prison notebooks of the early 1930s.[563] The basic premise is that in the modern, capitalist state, the "ruling class" (the bourgeoisie, business elites, politicians, etc.) maintains control over society by establishing prevailing norms, values, institutions, and ideologies—as opposed to compelling conformity by brute force or economic coercion. Implicit in this idea, however, is the notion that culture is inherently complex and fragmented, indeed often oppositional and disharmonious: society may well be guided by a "dominant," overarching, hegemonic culture, but it is also constantly being provoked—and thereby altered—by the many alternative, oppositional, and otherwise "dominated" forces in its midst. At the same time, the dominant culture can employ tools to reinforce its hegemonic control—whether relatively benign like intense media exposure or more questionable like censorship.

The modern, "post-structuralist" school of sociology has then looked to forces beyond economics and class to explain "culture," turning especially to aspects of everyday life. Two prominent examples include Roland Barthes' focus on the "myth" of red wine within modern French society—as a status quo social "equalizer"; and Michel Foucault's emphasis on the many ways in which the state maintains control over its citizens, as a kind of "panoptic" (watchman) machine—whether via prisons, increased surveillance, or subtler forms of arbitrating what is "normal" versus "abnormal" behavior in speech, dress, achievement, etc.[564] As with the hegemonic view, though, the picture created with these models is of an overarching, dominant, or mainstream culture seeking to exert influence and/or control over a wide and potentially unruly number of alternative, non-mainstream groups.

In approaching the topic of culture, most *music* scholars have adopted these common terms without issue—especially "mainstream" and "dominant culture." The ethnomusicologist Mark Slobin, however, took a deep look at the complex interrelations of culture and subculture and devised a few original concepts that I've found useful for our discussion here. The first is his use of the term "superculture," rather than "hegemony" or "mainstream," to aptly describe the "overarching structure" that exerts influence over members of a society—whether via ideology or practice.[565]

The second is his division of culture into five distinct "landscapes" that collectively shape the superculture and its constituent subcultures: the "ethnoscape"—our varied ethnicities and religions; the "mediascape"—the media channels all around us; the "technoscape"—the technologies that affect our lives; the "financescape"—the economic channels that impact us; and the "ideoscape"—the myriad ideas, identities, and political viewpoints, etc., of society members. To be sure, these forces operate in myriad overlapping ways—even at times coalescing



in a single, communal, supercultural moment, such as a Super Bowl halftime show featuring the likes of a Beyoncé or Lady Gaga.

One last element of Slobin's discussion worth noting is his cogent delineation of how musical life is made manifest at the supercultural level. He specifically articulates three components at play, at least in the West. The first is the music "industry"—the amalgam of major record labels and executives, media outlets (iHeartMedia, SiriusXM, Pandora, etc.), charts and award shows (*Billboard*, the Grammys), etc.; together, these forces promote and celebrate the highest-profile—that is, mainstream—artists, recordings, and genres to the collective superculture, while also acting as the "guardian" whereby the many music subcultures are granted a seat at the table, so to speak, or not. A second pillar of the music superculture is the state itself (federal, regional, local)—where via laws, grants, and institutions (copyright laws, school music programs, art-based agencies, etc.), a collective musical consciousness is framed and endorsed; through its varied instruments, the state can even pick "winners" and "losers"—by sponsoring an official song (e.g., John Denver's "Rocky Mountain High" as the "official" song of Colorado) or by targeting censorship explicitly at certain genres (rap, heavy metal), respectively. Finally, in a more decentralized manner, the musical superculture is circumscribed via the widespread and collective channels of musical practice and experience: the sanctioned careers, high-profile performance venues, and collective events (e.g., the national anthem at sporting events, carols during Christmastime, etc.) that inform music making.

In short, much as we are "forced" to walk along the shopping center's communal pathways if we want to move from one store to another, or eat in the communal food court if we're hungry, the superculture imposes on us a collective or "mainstream" orientation of which songs, works, artists, recordings, and genres are deemed most highly celebrated and sanctioned just by being members of it. Our superculture, our broad culture, thus not only provides us with the raw musicological material that defines our "native" music (scales, meters, instruments, etc.) and the main functions it fulfills (child pedagogy, religious ritual, social bonding, etc.), it also tells us what music we as a "people" venerate and profile. Through our superculture, we know and admire Michael Jackson as the "king of pop," Bruce Springsteen as "the boss," Beyoncé as "Queen B," and James Brown as the "godfather of soul"; it is why we know the melody and words of "Americ the Beautiful" and "Rudolph the Red-Nosed Reindeer." It is also why we are u likely to know the string quartets of Charles Ives or the songs from Frank Zapp first album, *Freak Out!*

To be sure, just because a song is embraced as part of your supercultu mainstream does not mean that you as an individual will like it, but it suggest that you probably know it, and will recognize it as something "pop and well loved by many, if not most, of your fellow citizens. Where your does get more individually and narrowly framed, by contrast, is at the level

Intraculture groups vary not only by the unifying "markers" of their members, but also by their size and makeup—ranging from intimate groups of family, friends, or "cliques" (as with those that Mitch and I assembled for Kiss and Queen) to neighborhoods, communities, and "clubs" to much larger collectives that traverse local settings—as in ethnic groups separated in the diaspora. At root, of course, are the individuals within these groups, and their unique "biographies," as John Clarke and colleagues at the Centre for Contemporary Cultural Studies (CCCS) labeled it in their influential work on British youth subcultures: "the means by which individual identities are constructed out of collective experiences."[567] The complex dynamic between the individual and the intraculture—including the question of one's opportunity, or lack thereof, to participate in the first place—is critical; indeed, as we'll see, acknowledging the individual can be a bulwark against oversimplifying the very idea of what an intraculture can be. More positively, it can help inform useful and broad-based definitions, such as when cultural sociologist Emre Ulusoy defends the role of subculture in our lives as "combining the urge for individual identity and self-expression with perspectives of communality and collectivity."[568]

To be sure, there are many other factors that go into defining and delimiting intracultures, especially as relates to music. But let's first back up a bit to review a few of the chief scholarly contexts in which this pairing has been scrutinized.

## The Many Distinctions of Cultural Capital

In a manner reminiscent of the adaptationist versus nonadaptationist debate on the role of music in human evolution, the link of music and intraculture has spawned a number of vibrant scholarly disputes of its own. The most high profile, even today, is the debate extending from Pierre Bourdieu's theory of "cultural capital" and Richard Peterson's theory of the "omnivore"—along with their supporters and detractors. Bourdieu, indeed, is a sine qua non figure in any discussion on taste, musical or otherwise, despite the now-questionable tenor of his categorizing terminology.

A friend and colleague of Michel Foucault at the Collège de France (though the two were by no means always aligned intellectually[569]), Bourdieu came to prominence in the rigorous environment of French structuralism and postmodernism during the 1960s. The bulk of Bourdieu's ideas were compiled in his monumental book *Distinction: A Social Critique of the Judgment of Taste* (1979, tr. 1984)—praised vociferously in sociological circles, as when Loïc Wacquant called it a "Copernican revolution in the study of taste."[570]

Bourdieu's basic theory is that we live in a status-based society, divided hierarchically into a "dominant" class at the top and two "dominated" classes—a middle class (petite bourgeoisie) and working class—underneath. The status distinctions or "social place" of each class is undeniably influenced by the economic status of its members, and yet is substantially reflected in the degree to which individuals hold "mastery" over art and culture. Bourdieu labels the power granted by this arts-based mastery as "cultural capital"—and identifies art consumption as the principal marker of class distinction: "Art and cultural consumption are predisposed, consciously and deliberately or not, to fulfill a social function of legitimating social differences."[571] Bourdieu specifically divides the objects or "artifacts" of cultural capital into three "zones" of taste: "legitimate," "middlebrow," and "popular"—each of which he associates with particular artists and artworks.

A quick editorial interruption: admittedly, terms such as "legitimate" and "middlebrow"—and their logical counterparts, "illegitimate" and "lowbrow"—are, on the surface, judgmental and potentially offensive if one's taste were said to align with the latter designations rather than with the former. By utilizing these terms in this discussion, therefore, one *could* get the impression that this book—and its author—are passing judgment on music that falls within Bourdieu's "legitimate" bucket as being better, or displaying more creativity, than music that does not. But such is by no means accurate. As noted many times in this book, no one's taste can be labeled as more "legitimate" than another's, and an artwork aligned with one Bourdieu "brow" cannot be deemed *better* or *worse* than an artwork aligned with another. A hip hop song by Erik B. & Rakim is every bit as "valuable" or "creative" as a symphony by Brahms in any objective sense—even if they possess varying degrees of complexity or scope. Yet while it might be socially expedient to bypass or alter Bourdieu's terminology, to do so, in my view, would be historically inaccurate and intellectually dishonest. For one, in labeling and defining these "brows," Bourdieu was not aiming to declare his personal opinion, but rather was relaying his studied academic assessment of how society and its institutions at the time viewed and responded to those taste distinctions; that he and other academics might have likewise shared those biases—as some still do today—is beside the point. And for that matter, if loving Led Zeppelin's "Ramble On," Kendrick Lamar's "i," and the Chemical Brothers' "Hey Girl Hey Boy" makes my taste "illegitimate" in the eyes of some in today's society—then amen to having "illegitimate taste."

Okay, so where were we?

The identification of Bourdieu's "artifacts" comes by way of his methodology: a massive quantitative survey of 1,217 French citizens between 1963 and '68—querying both demographic and aesthetic factors. The latter included leisure activities, tastes in singers, fashion, films, and books, and knowledge of "legitimate" forms of painting and music—even asking respondents to identify the composers of sixteen classical works.[572] The massive data set was then used by Bourdieu to draw conclusions on the relationship between class, demographics, and taste. It reveals, for example, the importance of "educational capital" (highest diploma, etc.) in determining how well one aligns with the legitimate forms of cultural capital—even more than one's "social origin" (family wealth, etc.). Importantly, Bourdieu recognized that not all aesthetic forms are equally revealing: although not a musician, Bourdieu touted the potency of music as a symbol of social place—as in his oft-cited remark "Nothing more clearly affirms one's 'class,' nothing more infallibly classifies, than tastes in music."[573]

Delineating class by taste and knowledge of classical music was not original to Bourdieu, of course. In early nineteenth-century Vienna, for example, a distinction was made between those members of the bourgeoisie who preferred the "demanding" music of Beethoven and those who favored the "lighter" music of Rossini.[574] A split between "heavy" and "light" classical music, indeed, is still very much in play in our own day—as seen in the contrast between "serious" as opposed to "pops" or "light classical" concerts and radio stations. Bourdieu follows suit in his survey to distinguish between the three taste zones on the basis of respondents' knowledge of/preference for the sixteen classical works—which, he notes, "roughly correspond to educational levels and social classes": (1) "legitimate taste" (e.g., J. S. Bach's *Art of the Fugue* and *Well-Tempered Clavier*, Maurice Ravel's Concerto for the Left Hand, and Pierre Boulez' *Le Marteau sans maître*); (2) "middlebrow taste" (e.g., George Gershwin's *Rhapsody in Blue* and Franz Liszt's Hungarian Rhapsody no. 2 in C♯ Minor); and (3) "popular taste" (e.g., Johann Strauss Jr.'s "Blue Danube" Waltz, Giuseppe Verdi's *La Traviata*, and Georges Bizet's *L'Arlésienne*).[575] This was France, after all.

Importantly, however, Bourdieu does not limit the taste zones to classical music. Jazz is defined almost legalistically as "the most legitimate of the arts that are still in the process of legitimization," and is elsewhere labeled a "middle ground art"; however, he weakens his argument considerably by making no reference to any specific jazz artists or works. French chanson, by contrast, is rather narrowly delineated—namely, between major singer-songwriters like Jacques Brel as "middlebrow" and cabaret performers like Charles Aznavour as "popular." The bias of Bourdieu's schema against the broad species of rock music is evident in his description of "popular" works as "songs totally devoid of artistic ambition or pretension."[576]

Bourdieu's main point in aligning taste in music, and other signals of cultural capital, with one's status or place in society is to explain his notion of "habitus." This refers to the inclinations one holds that act as a sort of road map for what is socially acceptable for one's class, or as Bourdieu terms it, "the dispositions characteristic of the different classes."[577] At root is one's "distance from necessity" or, alternately, from a "life at ease," whereby one will be more or less prone to gain a taste for "forms over function, of manner over matter," as he puts it. That is, one with a "cultivated" habitus will possess the leisure of capital to pursue complex, aesthetic, or abstract objects of culture, as in Bach's *Art of the Fugue*; by contrast, one with a noncultivated habitus, constrained by necessity, is bound by a taste for the simple, functional, or practical—objects "devoid of artistic ambition," as in rock music.

## The Highbrow's Musical Buffet

The acclaim of Bourdieu's *Distinction*, and its emphasis on the "infallible" reveal of musical taste, made it an object of great interest to musically inclined sociologists. Here was a highly structured and pristine means of relating musical knowledge/preference to large intracultural groups marked by class and social status. Yet, by the early 1990s, interest had given way to skepticism, as writers, particularly in the US, began to question via their own research whether the link between cultural capital and social status was as pronounced as Bourdieu had suggested. The most impactful critique came via a pair of articles by sociologist Richard Peterson from 1992 and 1996 (with Albert Simkus and Roger Kern, respectively).[578] Using data from the 1982 and 1992 Surveys of Public Participation in the Arts (conducted by the US Census Bureau for the NEA), Peterson examined the relationship between musical taste and social status—tiered as "highbrow," "middlebrow," and "lowbrow," and based mainly on income and education. Like Bourdieu's questionnaire, the NEA survey captured demographic data, but limited its queries on musical taste/knowledge to genres: a varying list including classical, opera, Broadway musicals, jazz, rap, soul, blues, bluegrass, country, rock, folk, gospel, etc.

Most striking to Peterson and his colleagues was that "highbrow" Americans did not, as Bourdieu asserted, limit their musical preferences to the "legitimate" genres of classical and opera—although they generally ranked these as "best-liked." Instead they extended their taste to genres that are themselves labeled, in studies of the period anyway, as "middlebrow"—especially Broadway musicals and jazz; and "lowbrow"—including rock, soul, and blues. In turn, Peterson argued that Bourdieu's notion of the highbrow "snob" was outdated—a vestige of nineteenth-century Anglo-Saxon values, where immigrant-spawned "popular" music was judged a corrupting influence.[579] To wit, he offered his own perspective: the theory of the "omnivore." In using this term, Peterson acknowledged it does not suggest someone who *likes* everything indiscriminately; instead, omnivorousness "signifies an openness to *appreciating* everything"; as such it is "antithetical to snobbishness, which is based fundamentally on rigid rules of exclusion." The omnivore, Peterson argues, embraces a tolerant, liberal attitude—which "commands status by displaying any of a range of tastes as the situation may require."[580]

Significantly, Peterson also found that "highbrows of all ages are becoming more omnivorous," between the 1982 and '92 surveys—mainly by virtue of a growing interest in at least some "lowbrow" genres. And while the "middlebrow" class also increased its genre-based omnivorousness, though to a lesser degree, the "lowbrow" class remained consistently enamored of only one or two of the "lowbrow" genres—either rap or country in these surveys; these, interestingly, in a single, communal, supercultural moment, such as a Super Bowl halftime show featuring the likes of a Beyoncé or Lady Gaga.

One last element of Slobin's discussion worth noting is his cogent delineation of how musical life is made manifest at the supercultural level. He specifically articulates three components at play, at least in the West. The first is the music "industry"—the amalgam of major record labels and executives, media outlets (iHeartMedia, SiriusXM, Pandora, etc.), charts and award shows (*Billboard*, the Grammys), etc.; together, these forces promote and celebrate the highest-profile—that is, mainstream—artists, recordings, and genres to the collective superculture, while also acting as the "guardian" whereby the many music subcultures are granted a seat at the table, so to speak, or not. A second pillar of the music superculture is the state itself (federal, regional, local)—where via laws, grants, and institutions (copyright laws, school music programs, art-based agencies, etc.), a collective musical consciousness is framed and endorsed; through its varied instruments, the state can even pick "winners" and "losers"—by sponsoring an official song (e.g., John Denver's "Rocky Mountain High" as the "official" song of Colorado) or by targeting censorship explicitly at certain genres (rap, heavy metal), respectively. Finally, in a more decentralized manner, the musical superculture is circumscribed via the widespread and collective channels of musical practice and experience: the sanctioned careers, high-profile performance venues, and collective events (e.g., the national anthem at sporting events, carols during Christmastime, etc.) that inform music making.

In short, much as we are "forced" to walk along the shopping center's communal pathways if we want to move from one store to another, or eat in the communal food court if we're hungry, the superculture imposes on us a collective or "mainstream" orientation of which songs, works, artists, recordings, and genres are deemed most highly celebrated and sanctioned just by being members of it. Our superculture, our broad culture, thus not only provides us with the raw musicological material that defines our "native" music (scales, meters, instruments, etc.) and the main functions it fulfills (child pedagogy, religious ritual, social bonding, etc.), it also tells us what music we as a "people" venerate and profile. Through our superculture, we know and admire Michael Jackson as the "king of pop," Bruce Springsteen as "the boss," Beyoncé as "Queen B," and James Brown as the "godfather of soul"; it is why we know the melody and words of "America the Beautiful" and "Rudolph the Red-Nosed Reindeer." It is also why we are unlikely to know the string quartets of Charles Ives or the songs from Frank Zappa's first album, *Freak Out!*

To be sure, just because a song is embraced as part of your superculture's mainstream does not mean that you as an individual will like it, but it does suggest that you probably know it, and will recognize it as something "popular" and well loved by many, if not most, of your fellow citizens. Where your taste does get more individually and narrowly framed, by contrast, is at the level of the subcultures—the intracultural collectives—to which you in some way "belong": the stores at which you shop, so to speak. It is to this often prickly topic that we now turn.

## Intraculture at a Glance

Academics have addressed the intersection of music and intraculture (subcultures, communities, etc.) from a wide variety of perspectives and trajectories—that not infrequently intersect or contradict one another. Sociology, cultural studies, ethnography, ethnomusicology, traditional musicology, consumer behavior, and marketing are among the disciplines brought to bear on this confluence, such that it can be easy to miss the forest for the trees—something we'll try to prevent here.

In essence, these theories and arguments aim to answer a single question: How does one's intraculture influence the music one consumes? Or in our parlance: How does intraculture influence musical taste? It is not surprising that many of these theories, based as they are on a mix of chronologically stamped surveys and tightly held philosophical precepts, in time come to be revised, challenged, or rejected outright. They are worth reviewing in some depth here, however, since they collectively get us closer to the "truth" regarding the above question than would be possible otherwise—and for *you* personally: How does *your* identity as a member of various intracultures affect the way you listen to music? Indeed, it is by exploring the various theories devised over the years that I am able to offer my own take on the matter: that our many-splendored intracultural identities grant us *access* to and *ownership* of a wealth of music that we would otherwise never know. Intracultures, that is, are the very gateway to our own, personal musical taste.

To get us started, it will be helpful to first note the typical parameters by which "intracultures"—labeled as social groups, classes, subcultures, etc.—have historically been defined. Useful, for example, is the notion that such groups are composed of individuals who are unified to some degree at least by one or more "markers." The most commonly cited include class, education status, race/ethnicity, age, gender, and region; beyond these "structural" (identity-oriented) markers are those aligned with "behavior"—such as dress/fashion, consumer patterns, and performance venues. Fashion, in fact, holds historic resonance in "intraculture" studies; in 1905, the pioneering sociologist Georg Simmel, friend of Max Weber, cited it as a key indicator of both class identity and "intracultural" distinction: "Fashion signifies union with those in the same class, . . . [and yet] provides the best arena for people . . . whose self-awareness requires that they be recognized as distinct and as particular kinds of beings."[566] As we'll see, later writers will attribute these same powers of association and distinction to music.

name; at still others you will merely browse occasionally or even just window-shop, only rarely moved to make an actual purchase. On the other hand, there will also be a good many stores in the center that hold absolutely no interest to you—where you wouldn't be caught dead shopping, whether for reasons of content, style, age-appropriateness, etc. By contrast, those stores at which you *do* shop, even occasionally, may be said to be part of your "intracultural" shopping makeup. By simply showing up, you are in essence given access, indeed permission, to consume the wares these stores offer. You will not purchase everything available, of course, but by virtue of being displayed at a store in your intracultural orbit, the items there are more likely to attract your serious consideration.

As suggested, it is an imperfect metaphor—for example, we aren't exactly linked to some stores by birth (unless your parents own one). Still, it may be helpful to you as we explore in detail the often complex nature of subcultures, communities, intracultures, etc., and how they might or might not intersect with the music you love. The principal point offered here is that just as we shop at many different stores, with distinct degrees of "loyalty" to each, so too do we belong to many different intracultures—some large, some small, and to each with a distinct degree of allegiance, affiliation, passion, etc. And yet, just as each individual store is by default aligned with its broader shopping center, so too is each intraculture by default aligned with its broader culture.

## Culture Deconstructed

As in the previous interlude, where we introduced the topic of cultural distinction by first revisiting universals, so too will it be useful here to return briefly to the topic of culture as a prelude to a fuller discussion of subcultures—as we'll call these subdivisions for the moment. In so doing, though, we'll rely less on ethnomusicology and music psychology than on sociology and cultural anthropology.

An important caveat first, however: the discussion of culture and intraculture in this interlude will focus exclusively on the Western experience—indeed, more narrowly on the experience of the Anglo-American orbit, with some reference to France. This assuredly does not reflect any bias or cultural superiority on my part, but simply the limited scope of my knowledge and resources enlisted. Every culture, of course, will have its own complex system and interrelations of intracultures—you'll just have to go elsewhere to learn about most of them.[562] Okay, onward.

As with its subdivisions, one's broad, overarching culture is commonly identified by several different terms. Among the most common include "mainstream," "popular culture," "commercialism," "dominant culture," "status quo," and "hegemony." The first three underscore the prominence of economic forces within a society: culture is defined by the most common and popular targets of business investment and consumer behavior. The last three terms, by contrast, place greater emphasis on societal divisions of political and cultural authority.

The concept of cultural hegemony in particular arose out of Marxist philosophy—such as that developed by Antonio Gramsci in his prison notebooks of the early 1930s.[563] The basic premise is that in the modern, capitalist state, the "ruling class" (the bourgeoisie, business elites, politicians, etc.) maintains control over society by establishing prevailing norms, values, institutions, and ideologies—as opposed to compelling conformity by brute force or economic coercion. Implicit in this idea, however, is the notion that culture is inherently complex and fragmented, indeed often oppositional and disharmonious: society may well be guided by a "dominant," overarching, hegemonic culture, but it is also constantly being provoked—and thereby altered—by the many alternative, oppositional, and otherwise "dominated" forces in its midst. At the same time, the dominant culture can employ tools to reinforce its hegemonic control—whether relatively benign like intense media exposure or more questionable like censorship.

The modern, "post-structuralist" school of sociology has then looked to forces beyond economics and class to explain "culture," turning especially to aspects of everyday life. Two prominent examples include Roland Barthes' focus on the "myth" of red wine within modern French society—as a status quo social "equalizer"; and Michel Foucault's emphasis on the many ways in which the state maintains control over its citizens, as a kind of "panoptic" (watchman) machine—whether via prisons, increased surveillance, or subtler forms of arbitrating what is "normal" versus "abnormal" behavior in speech, dress, achievement, etc.[564] As with the hegemonic view, though, the picture created with these models is of an overarching, dominant, or mainstream culture seeking to exert influence and/or control over a wide and potentially unruly number of alternative, non-mainstream groups.

In approaching the topic of culture, most *music* scholars have adopted these common terms without issue—especially "mainstream" and "dominant culture." The ethnomusicologist Mark Slobin, however, took a deep look at the complex interrelations of culture and subculture and devised a few original concepts that I've found useful for our discussion here. The first is his use of the term "superculture," rather than "hegemony" or "mainstream," to aptly describe the "overarching structure" that exerts influence over members of a society—whether via ideology or practice.[565]

The second is his division of culture into five distinct "landscapes" that collectively shape the superculture and its constituent subcultures: the "ethnoscape"—our varied ethnicities and religions; the "mediascape"—the media channels all around us; the "technoscape"—the technologies that affect our lives; the "financescape"—the economic channels that impact us; and the "ideoscape"—the myriad ideas, identities, and political viewpoints, etc., of society members. To be sure, these forces operate in myriad overlapping ways—even at times coalescing were identified as the only "lowbrow" genres that were disliked by the "highbrow" class. In turn, this lack of aesthetic adventurousness led Peterson to coin a companion term to the omnivore for the "lowbrow" or working-class taste: the "univore."

Peterson's conclusion is that while cultural "snobbishness" worked to define the taste of "highbrow" individuals in times past, it did so no more. A tolerant, open-minded approach to musical taste was now the norm, "the new embodiment of contemporary middle class domination," as sociologist Mike Savage put it.[581] It was, in essence, no longer cool to be a snob; instead, to demonstrate cultural sophistication was now to expand taste beyond the "legitimate" genres to "middlebrow" and "popular" genres once thought beneath them. Again, this does not mean that anything goes, for as noted, "highbrows" consistently rebuked some decidedly "lowbrow" (and otherwise "mainstream") genres like rap and country. Taste still signaled "habitus"—one's behavioral inclinations—to individuals of varying social classes, but those in the upper echelons now sought out greater self-realization as opposed to snobbish exclusivity. Peterson explained the shift from snob to omnivore as arising from a number of broad societal trends: structural change (rising income, greater education); easier social mobility for those in lower classes; ubiquitous mass media; general rise in social tolerance; new art marketplace realities; sustained loyalty to popular music among younger generations; and an increasing "gentrification" of popular culture into dominant status culture.

So, let's take a small breather from our historical survey of intraculture theories and ask what this means—so far—for you and your musical taste.

At a minimum, both Bourdieu and Peterson seem to suggest that the music you know and love—whether "legitimately" sophisticated works like a Bach fugue or Ravel concerto, "moderately" involved works like a Miles Davis tune or a Frank Loesser musical, or "popular" songs like those by Keith Urban or Chance the Rapper—depends *first and foremost* on the social class to which your income, occupation, and education status ascribe you. If you are a "highbrow," for example, Bourdieu suggests that you'll likely love the classical works and dismiss the popular ones; Peterson, by contrast, believes that you'll like both sides of the spectrum—though with caveats on the lower end. Now, if your skeptical radar is aroused by such broad pronouncements, you aren't alone—I'm right there with you. Happily, though, scores of scholars over the past two decades have taken up both theories—and in the process have added considerable clarity as to what is going on between your intracultural status and your musical taste.

For a good many scholars—such as sociologists Alan Warde, Andrew Cheyne, Amy Binder, Modesto Gayo, David Cutts, and Paul Widdop, etc.—the two theories are seen as largely compatible, with Peterson's cultural omnivorousness deemed an update to Bourdieu's delineations of cultural capital. Just as Bourdieu revised premodern precepts of taste, such as Immanuel Kant's stark distinctions between "aesthetic" and "ordinary" consumption, so too did Peterson update Bourdieu's postwar distinctions of the "highbrow," to now cross the chasm between "legitimate" and "popular" music. That is, as pop and rock music became more diverse and sophisticated through the 1960s and '70s, Peterson argued, the "highbrow" likewise became more open-minded and eclectic—achieving, as Cheyne and Binder put it, a more "cosmopolitan" habitus.[582]

To supporters of both theories, then, what was called for was yet further updates and expansions on cultural omnivorousness—to dive deeper via new surveys into how exactly highbrows consume across all musical "brows" and how univorism is manifest, especially as times and "goods offered" change.

Among these updates was the realization that there are in fact different kinds of omnivores. There is the "voracious" omnivore, who consumes across "zones" of taste, but with an insatiable appetite beyond that of his "general" counterpart. The latter may embrace a wider array of popular and "legitimate" genres, but the voracious omnivore—more apt to reside in an urban setting, alongside similarly voracious folks—consumes them more *intensely* and in quicker successions: perhaps "bingeing" on a box set of Otis Redding over a long weekend. In keeping with our ever-harried and multitasking times, the voracious omnivore is easily bored, and yet is one whose "wants are seemingly endless," as Cutts and Widdop put it.[583]

On the other side, not all univores go for rap and country; some, it turns out, are equally narrow-minded, but with "legitimate" genres like classical, opera, or jazz. They are, in effect, "highbrow snobs": possessing higher levels of income and education, but no longer yielding the highest levels of cultural capital. Further, not all omnivores even like classical music, while some previously "illegitimate" genres can be updated as "legitimate" based on consumption habits. As Cheyne and Binder have shown, for example, rap now has its "elite critics": high-status individuals who seek out hip hop that is produced in local—"authentic"—venues as opposed to the sanitized environment of a commercial or corporate recording studio.[584] In short, for supporters of the Bourdieu-Peterson trajectory, the specific definitions of "high-," "middle-," and "lowbrow" taste may change over time and place—and yet their underlying intracultural roots continue to be based on class and social status.

## Questioning the Omnivore

A good many writers, however, have taken a more directly critical view of Peterson's omnivore theory—while in some cases defending Bourdieu's basic model. On the tame side, some question whether omnivorousness is unique to Western industrial nations like the US, Great Britain, Australia, etc.; or else whether it is applicable to income and education but less relevant to issues of age or gender.

Far more serious, however, have been attacks along two other main lines: Peterson's quantitative (mass survey) methodology and his overreliance on genre as the gauge of musical taste. While US Census Bureau surveys get you lots of data, they gloss over the details, including the varied rationales/contexts in which folks actually consume cultural activities. This doesn't by itself negate the validity of the omnivore theory—as Cutts and Widdop's qualitative (interviews) study shows—but it does raise questions about what information may be missing. Musical genres are even more problematic. As Mike Savage, among many others, has argued: if you really want to understand the musical taste of large, intracultural groups, you'll ultimately need a "more nuanced understanding of genre categories."[585]

We've already addressed this topic in Chapter 8, as the prelude to introducing our seven "musical genotypes," but a few points are worth revisiting here. Genres are not static; instead, each constantly evolves in its actual musical content, and in the perceptions it generates in listeners' minds—on its own and in relation to other genres. There is something almost organic in the fluid, ever-changing identities of genres. As cultural sociologist Mark Rimmer puts it, genres constantly "blossom or wane in their popularity, fall out of usage, become institutionalized or else hybridize and 'crossover.'"[586] As such, making assumptions about their meaning at any given moment is risky—especially for broad, high-level (Tier 1) genres like classical, jazz, rock, and hip hop. Undoubtedly, these labels suggest very different types of music depending on whom you ask, and when. Adding to the challenge is the increasing "hyper-commodification of popular cultural forms," using sociologist Barry Sandywell's expression—meaning that in our digital/Internet age, even a "narrow" subgenre like heavy metal (Tier 2) gets split and commoditized into a plethora of nuanced sub- and sub-sub-subgenres (Tiers 3 and 4): death metal, metalcore, nu-metal, speed metal, math metal, rap metal, etc., etc. Genre labels are not meaningless, to be sure, but their utility in defining the tastes of intraculture groups as consequential as "social class" is questionable at best.

In response, some writers have proposed using other criteria to draw aesthetic distinction between those of differing social classes. Savage and Gayo, for example, have proposed replacing the omnivore-univore dichotomy with a more practical one: "expert" versus "nonexpert." In a recent survey (the Cultural Capital and Social Exclusion project), they queried two thousand British citizens on their awareness/attitude toward eight individual works—including Gustav Mahler's Symphony no. 5, Miles Davis' *Kind of Blue*, Oasis' "Wonderwall," Eminem's "Stan," and Britney Spears' "Oops! . . . I Did It Again"—as well as genre labels. From the data, Savage and Gayo concluded that what really matters is *not* one's tolerance or liberal attitude toward different musical styles, as Peterson had proposed, but simply one's level of musical knowledge. Specifically, they found that those with some level of musical training (e.g., piano lessons as a child) were more prone to like the classical (Mahler), jazz (Davis), and rock (Oasis) examples and dislike the rap (Eminem) and pop (Spears) ones. The latter point is critical: taste is not just articulating what you like, but also what you *don't*—it is not, as they put it, mere "undiscriminating pluralism."[587]

Importantly, moreover, these conclusions still conform to Bourdieu's link between social class and "cultural capital": it is precisely those with high social status who are most likely to be "experts." As sociologist Will Atkinson similarly observed from his interviews of residents of Bristol, England, those in the "privileged" classes are more likely to have had parents willing to "invest" in piano lessons or other forms of early music education. In turn, this yields a more positive attitude toward a more diverse, eclectic set of genres and artists. They may well prefer rock to classical, but are likely to have at least a "detached interest" in the latter, occasionally attending concerts or listening to it while studying, etc. By contrast, those in the "dominated" classes in both the Savage and Gayo and Atkinson studies were less inclined to such "cerebral" or "civilized" music, preferring genres/artists within the mainstream, hip hop, or hard rock spheres—music aligned by the authors with having fun and gaining "physical release." In the Savage and Gayo study, for example, those deemed "nonexperts" preferred the rap and pop examples, and showed either ignorance or aversion toward the others.

Okay, so where are we *now* in our quest to understand how intraculture impacts our musical taste? According to these updates to the Bourdieu-Peterson debate, the prime source continues to be the social class in which we are raised. The resulting educational opportunities grant us more or less access to cultural capital, such as music lessons as a child—in turn granting us greater or lesser degrees of musical expertise. This distinction then frames our mind-set and opportunities as we interpret the musical universe around us: with expertise comes access to and desire for those "legitimate" styles of music—classical, jazz, *or* popular—that stimulate us intellectually and that speak to our "artistic" sensibilities; lacking such expertise, we are limited to those "noncerebral" forms of popular music that offer us more physical release than mental stimulation. Those with expertise may well gravitate toward a wider array of musical styles than nonexperts, though the stance can be poorly understood if we gauge it only through the fuzzy labels of genre or subgenre. Experts are likewise more apt to articulate precisely what music they *dislike*, as well as to locate themselves in places (e.g., big cities) where they can be surrounded by similarly expert, eclectic, and "voracious" people.

While I embrace several of these updates—notably the importance of one's musical education and geographic place in helping to frame one's taste, and the limits of genre as a useful measure—problems still exist. First, there is the lingering bias in these class- and style-based labels. Apart from the continued use of "legitimate" to tag some musical realms but not others—notably hip hop, country, and hard rock—there is also the unfortunate tendency to align those latter styles with seemingly baser effects: merely "having fun" or gaining "physical release" as opposed to "stimulating us intellectually," etc. Such value judgments are dangerous, potentially offensive, and limiting in all kinds of ways—including placing constraints on our own taste, as we'll discuss below. Plus, like all stereotypes, they're often wrong: a classical or jazz work can be merely "fun" just as readily as a hard rock or hip hop song can be "mentally stimulating"—depending on the specific music and the individual listener. Indeed, the best listening experiences are those that elicit *both* types of effect. As noted earlier, however, such biases are still out there, and not only in academic assessments—and thus we would be ill advised to ignore them.

Happily, though, that is not the end of our survey. Indeed, one recent constructive trend is something just suggested: an effort to take into account the great *variety* of taste held by different members of any given class-based group.

One scholar who has addressed just this issue is French sociologist Bernard Lahire, a student of Bourdieu at the Collège de France—in turn challenging some widely held assumptions on the class-taste dynamic. Lahire does not dispute that class distinctions and social inequities exist—nor that a "highbrow" social status gives rise to the existence of dominant and "legitimate" forms of culture. Yet he has strongly cautioned against assigning too much weight to class/social status as the arbiter of taste distinctions. In a 2008 study, for example, he analyzed the results of a survey he conducted of three thousand French citizens; in it he used a questionnaire that was specifically designed to generate a differentiated cultural profile for each respondent: not just what they knew or liked, but which music, books, films, etc., they consumed *more and less frequently*.[588] One weakness in his survey was the limiting use of genre labels—divided again into three "zones": "very legitimate" (classical, opera); "moderately legitimate" (jazz); and "not quite legitimate" (rap, hard rock, punk, etc.). Still, Lahire was able to draw some keen insights.

First, he acknowledges that social class does indeed provide a prevailing framework for one's cultural taste: highbrows gravitate toward the "very legitimate" zone, lowbrows toward the "not quite legitimate" zone. But far more striking is that in *every* class the prevailing mode was both heterogeneity (lots of different genres) and, notably, "dissonance"—that is, transcending more than one taste zone; again, this was the case not just among "highbrows," but among "middle-" and "lowbrows" as well. Indeed, 75 percent of all respondents across the three class levels embraced cultural dissonance. Lahire calls this phenomenon "intra-individual variation"—stating, "Individual portraits are the only way of describing how cultural practices and preferences vary in relation to the domains, sub-domains, contexts or circumstances of cultural activity or practice."[589] Most individuals, he notes, behave on the whole like others in their class, but they likewise act in atypical ways—thus "both typical and marginal at the same time." The potential sources of this shift are many—increased social mobility, the Internet, declining faith in "artistic" culture, the rise of personal consumption, etc.—but regardless, to understand cultural hierarchies today is to embrace the "dissonance" of individuals.

Okay, now we are getting somewhere: although social class—and the conforming (or conflicting) level of musical expertise we grow up with—influences the formation of our musical taste, it only gets us so far. Instead, we fall into traps if we draw too fine a corollary between our class/level of expertise and the "zones" of taste we gravitate toward—not to mention the actual artists, composers, works, and songs we like. Increasingly, in fact, there is no single domain of cultural "legitimacy" in modern society—it may be classical to one music fan, but jazz, rock, hip hop, or punk to another. The "intra-individual variation" we find across the spectrum is a symptom, as Lahire notes, of the "plurality" that exists in both the cultural offerings we encounter every day and the *varied* social groups to which we belong. Cultural consumption is thus not a fundamental indicator of our social/class status, but more a product of our *individual* circumstances—where the pull of our taste may be strong or weak. Consumption may reflect intellectual aspirations of creativity, or social activism, or physical release, or mere curiosity, or none of the above.

Indeed, Lahire's "cultural dissonance" has only magnified over the past decade or so—and not least with respect to music. Thanks to Internet-based services like Pandora, Spotify, and Apple Music, barriers of access have become all but neutralized. The only thing stopping a socioeconomic "lowbrow" from spending an hour listening to Mahler's Fifth Symphony is knowing how to spell "Mahler"—and with autocorrect, not even that. Media and marketing trends constantly blur the boundaries between "zones"—as when rap becomes "legitimate" history via the film *Straight Outta Compton* or the Netflix series *The Get Down*. Ripped jeans are no longer a signal of poverty, and a Facebook "check-in" at the opera house tells no one you're wealthy. As Tom Vanderbilt puts it, "Traditional taste signifiers have gotten a bit slippery and, in theory, more democratized."[590] Increasingly, everyone is an omnivore and no one is a univore. It now comes down to far more nuanced and decisive acts of individual cultural practice.

In short, as Dutch sociologist Koen van Eijck put it, "Prevailing dichotomies like highbrow–lowbrow or omnivore–univore do not suffice if we want to understand what kind of people we are actually dealing with."[591] We don't need to abandon class, cultural capital, and expertise as actors in the intraculture–musical taste dynamic, of course, but we'll need to go a bit deeper if we want to truly understand it.

## The Birth of "Subculture"

Wonky intraculture terms like "cultural capital" and "omnivorousness" aren't the only ones to have been put through the academic wringer. As noted, even mundane labels like "subculture" and "community" have undergone scholarly scrutiny. And as with the former, a brief trip through these latter and yet other terms will prove useful in our quest to understand how our position *within* culture impacts our musical taste.

It was our discussion of those first two terms, of course, that introduced us to a primary type or category of intraculture: social class—divided by theorists like Bourdieu into tiers of upper ("dominant") class, middle class, and working class. As with all intracultures, class comprises "markers," in this case based on collective definitions of income, occupation, education, and cultural capital. Each class is generally deemed mutually exclusive from the other two—that is, you can't be both "dominant" and middle class at the same time; this can raise challenges, of course, when the individual markers are at odds—a poorly educated millionaire, a doctor living in poverty, etc.—though in such cases, income will likely carry the verdict. In any event, to supporters of the Bourdieu-Peterson trajectory, social class can be embraced as a useful prism through which to understand one's musical taste—even if the relationship between the two keeps changing.

But we've also seen that class is not a foolproof way to trace the intracultural origins of musical taste and behavior. Lahire and others have shown that as individuals we are highly prone to deviate from the "mean" taste expectations of our class—in turn making it risky to assume too close a correlation between one's class and one's taste. This is ever more the case as culture fragments, and as social classes loosen their impact on personal identity.

Indeed, we as individuals increasingly define our relationship to the broad culture in ways beyond class—and instead herald our "memberships" in the many other intracultural groups we subscribe to, whether we can define them or not. As noted, these can be oriented via all sorts of markers: ethnicity, faith, age, consumption, fashion, hobby, social cause, etc.—that is, by Slobin's five "landscapes" cited earlier in this interlude. In many intracultures, of course, music serves a vital auxiliary function of engendering identity and cohesion among members, and as a vehicle to support its various activities and causes. But in many others, music is more than an accessory; it is a *core* component. We can call them "*music intracultures.*" They are the groups that provide an explicit vehicle to collectively celebrate and promote a given musical approach and the lifestyle it begets—wherein individuals assemble, as musicologist Gilbert Chase put it, "according to their own needs and musical taste."[592]

Colloquially and in the academic literature, the taxonomical term most often used for these music-focused assemblies is "subculture." Not surprisingly, the term was first used with direct reference to social and economic status—under the rubric of "subculture theory."[593] It sprang from a group of sociologists at the University of Chicago in the 1920s and '30s with a focus on youth gangs—and with the specific aim of identifying the values, attitudes, and life conditions which would lead teenagers into a life of crime and violence.[594] The association of subculture and working-class youth gangs was embraced by British sociologists in the 1950s, but then underwent a significant transformation at the Centre for Contemporary Cultural Studies (CCCS) at the University of Birmingham in the 1970s.

## Teddys, Skinheads, and Mods, Oh My!

Phil Cohen was a community activist working in London's gritty East End in the late 1960s; he went by the nickname of Dr. John—after the New Orleans singer-pianist. Cohen was spokesman for the London Street Commune—a movement highlighting the issue of homelessness in London that famously occupied, as a "hippy squat," a mansion on Piccadilly Road in 1969; he was also a member of the more radical "King Mob" group, promoting awareness of cultural anarchy and social alienation then mounting in Britain. In these capacities, Cohen interacted with various groups of working-class youth—notably mods and skinheads (not the present-day racist group, but a 1960s working-class subculture of the same name). In an influential 1972 article, "Subcultural Conflict and Working-Class Community," Cohen described the effect of urban redevelopment of the East End slums and working-class neighborhoods on youth culture—and especially the subcultures that arose, as he put it, to "retrieve the solidarities of the traditional neighborhoods." As continuity and predictability were lost, youth invested in *identities*—as "magical resolutions"—aimed at regaining the "socially cohesive elements destroyed in their parent culture."[595] The distinguishing tools they used were dress, slang, and above all music: British R&B/rock bands like the Who and Small Faces for the mods; Jamaican ska, reggae, and rude boys (Desmond Dekker, Supersonics, etc.) for the skinheads.

By highlighting the social conditions and frustrations of these groups, Cohen had potently shifted the focus of subculture studies from youth gangs to youth *style*—with music now posited as a primary element. His article was published in an early collection of the CCCS—whose most famous publication was a 1975 book entitled *Resistance through Rituals: Youth Subcultures in Post-War Britain*—with essays by Dick Hebdige, John Clarke, and Tony Jefferson, among others. Like Cohen, the authors in *Resistance* credit the rise of youth subcultures to working-class destabilization via redevelopment and community/family breakdown. And they too underscored music as a catalyzing factor.

In his study on mods, for example, Hebdige notes how the youths' flamboyant nightlife guise—the close crops, exquisitely tailored parker coats, and sleek scooters—belied the mundane and servile quality of their daily realities: working in low-wage office or merchant jobs, if at all. At night, however, they donned their sharply cut jackets, popped a handful of amphetamines, and crammed into all-night R&B clubs in the Soho district. As Hebdige notes, "mod was pure, unadulterated style, the essence of style" by which a youth could "compensate for his relatively low position in the daytime status-stakes over which he had no control." Music, as much as anything, was the glue that held the scene together, both through dancing and songs—like the Rolling Stones' "Mother's Little Helper" ("What a drag it is getting old") and the Who's "My Generation"—that acted as unifying anthems. The mods, incidentally, had their roots in the "teddy boys" of the early to mid-1950s; the teds too had attempted to "resolve" their working-class insecurities by wearing secondhand Edwardian suits and blue suede shoes, while listening to early rock-and-rollers like Bill Haley, Elvis Presley, and Eddie Cochran.

By contrast, the 1960s skinheads, products of the even more dislocated and oppressive neighborhoods of South London, adopted a harsher response. With their bovver boots, stained jeans, motorcycles, and menacing bald scalps, skinhead style represented, in Clarke's words, "an attempt to re-create through the 'mob' the traditional working class community, as a substitute for the real decline of the latter."[596] Rejecting mainstream rock, skinheads forged their solidarity through the marginalized, protest musical style of West Indian immigrants—reggae and ska, such as Dandy Livingstone's 1967 rocksteady song, "A Message to You, Rudy."

The CCCS school thus introduces to us a useful concept in our quest to understand how intracultures—musical intracultures in particular—shape our musical taste: under challenging social circumstances, music can become an indispensable tool to help us cope, to carry out a "magical resolution" of the broader struggles we face in our daily lives. Music becomes the driving force, or certainly a vital one, within an overall social *style* that we as individuals employ in this struggle. If we are caught up in those challenging circumstances—e.g., living in a depressed neighborhood, subject to uninspiring routines, victims of social upheaval, etc.—we will inevitably be made aware of the specific music embraced by our cohorts to "resolve" those challenges. We'll instinctively feel the pull of this music as something we "ought" to like—music that speaks to our plight, our cause, and our struggle. It is like being led into a store, in that metaphoric shopping center, by one of your most trusted friends when he or she says, "Trust me, you're going to love their stuff." As you enter, you are practically reaching for your wallet.

## An Expanding Intracultural Taxonomy

The CCCS take on mods and skinheads, however, still leaves us with an unsatisfying understanding of musical intracultures: in this case, narrowly associating a specific musical taste "genotype" with working-class youth resistance. One prominent critic is Australian sociologist Andy Bennett. As Lahire might have done,

Bennett questions CCCS' rigid focus on structuralist markers—that is, class—as the prime source of the youths' cultural behavior. Indeed, Bennett is skeptical even with the assertion that mod, skinhead, and teddy "styles" were aimed at confronting their social challenges in the first place. He likewise criticizes the limited focus in CCCS studies on the youth groups' external "street life" experiences, ignoring their behavior at home, with family, etc., and thus their likely "dissonant" individual biographies. In fact, Bennett goes even further: to him the very word used to describe these movements—"subcultures"—has become overused, now a mere "catch-all used to describe a range of disparate collective practices whose only obvious relation is that they all involve young people."[597]

Noting the changing societal and musical trends since 1980 that warrant this rethinking, therefore, Bennett sought a revised taxonomical approach—one that would reflect his view that the most vibrant force underlying musical behavior is not class but *consumerism* based on *individual decisions*. Such decision-making, he argues, is not fixed and ideological, but rather fleeting and fluid, if not arbitrary and contradictory—as Lahire noted. Bennett cites an increased desire by individuals to *belong*, as part of a "community of feeling" consisting of like-minded companions.

Bennett supports his take on musical intracultures—under the rather awkward name of "neo-tribes"—via a set of interviews with forty young activists in the urban dance (EDM) scene in Newcastle upon Tyne, England. In their interview responses, the youth confirmed to Bennett their fragmented, fluid affiliation with the experience: moving impulsively from floor to floor of a single dance club, each floor featuring its own EDM style—techno, dub, ambient, etc. As one respondent noted: "I think dance-music culture has allowed people to be quite open about the fact that they actually like a lot of different stuff." Although each "activist" has an individual experience, together they enjoy a collective affiliation to the broader Newcastle EDM scene—whereby they gain a tangible kind of shared "cultural capital."

Bennett, moreover, is not alone in proposing new and insightful takes on intraculture. One worth citing is political scientist Benedict Anderson's "imagined communities"—referring to any group-based entity whose cohesion is based on imagined (whether true or not) shared beliefs, interests, passions, etc.[598] Though initially applied to nation-states, Anderson's concept of "imagined communities" has been adopted within ethnomusicology, musicology, and music sociology as well.

Further, the term "community" has itself been utilized by a number of writers to clarify the intraculture–musical taste dynamic. One example is ethnomusicologist Kay Kaufman Shelemay, who embraced the term in support of her study on the Ethiopian-American diaspora. Beyond the details of her own study, Shelemay finds "community" a quite suitable term to identify any collective formed around a particular cultural behavior—such as musical practice and consumption. Indeed, she provides the following useful definition of a "musical community":

> A musical community is, whatever its location in time or space, a collectivity constructed through and sustained by musical processes and/or performances. A musical community can be socially and/or symbolically constituted. . . . A musical community does not require the presence of conventional structural elements nor must it be anchored in a single place. . . . Rather, a musical community is a social entity, an outcome of a combination of social and musical processes, rendering those who participate in making or listening to music aware of a connection among themselves.[599]

She further delineates three "processes" animating musical communities: *descent*—those built on national, ethnic, or religious elements; *dissent*—those built on social and/or political opposition, resistance, or conflict with the mainstream; and *affinity*—those built on individual preference and the desire, in Shelemay's words, for "social proximity or association with others equally enamored."[600]

To be sure, these three processes often commingle in myriad ways; for example, an ethnically based community (descent) can also be grounded in political resistance (dissent), such as in numerous African-American musical communities over the past century or more—from Congo Square to spirituals to soul to hip hop, via artists like Bessie Smith, Nina Simone, Charles Mingus, Abbey Lincoln, James Brown, Marvin Gaye, N.W.A, Kendrick Lamar, etc. Similarly, musical communities may evolve from one process to another—such as the progression of the reggae-based musical "community" from one based on dissent to one grounded in affinity.

When it comes to musical taste, the most palpable of the three processes enumerated by Shelemay is assuredly affinity. Indeed, in my view this is the *prime source* of "membership" for most of the musical intracultures to which you "belong." Consciously or not, you come to them ultimately by *choice*, on behalf of some imagined or intuited benefit—aesthetic, experiential, developmental, emotional—that this membership will offer you. What is key, though, is that there is no single membership level but rather a wide continuum: from tepid "toe-dipper" to avid participant to cutting-edge definer as performer, creator, critic, etc.—and everywhere in between. Indeed, your membership status in affinity-based intracultures is rarely static—commonly progressing from toe-dipper as you discover a potential candidate to avid participant as you fully commit.

And with this review of the second batch of intraculture-taste theories, we are ready to dive into my own formulation—and especially what it all means to you.

## What's in It for You?

Whatever term you prefer ("subculture," "community," "neo-tribe," "scene," "world," etc.), the intraculture to which you belong provides an invaluable ser-

vice to your musical taste, and to your lifestyle—one you'd miss out on otherwise. If you're an Italian-American, for example, you can take proud ownership of the rich body of Neapolitan songs rendered by Perry Como, Tony Bennett, and Mario Lanza; as an activist in the feminist movement, you'll be invited to sing loudly to anthems by No Doubt ("I'm Just a Girl"), Katy Perry ("Roar"), Queen Latifah ("U.N.I.T.Y."), and Aretha Franklin ("Respect"); as a junkie of urban "fitness culture," you'll be encouraged to embrace Mark Ronson featuring Bruno Mars' "Uptown Funk," Van Halen's "Jump," or Beyoncé's "Get Me Bodied."

On a broader level, if you're a committed subscriber to the mainstream, you'll get your musical ticket punched on a near daily basis via the dominant media- and financescapes all around you. You'll likewise find ritual validation through recurring events like the Grammy Awards, Super Bowl halftime shows, and stadium world tours of marquee artists. If, by contrast, you eschew the mainstream in favor of more esoteric or rarified intracultures, you may be less saturated with daily options, but you'll be amply rewarded in other ways: hearing expert or "legit" performers rendering certified and fresh "gems" in lavish venues like symphony halls, opera houses, Broadway theaters, dimly lit jazz or dance clubs, and hidden bars—all while hobnobbing with similarly esoteric or rarified co-members. Of course, the actual benefits you receive will depend on the nuanced details of the intraculture in question—both in terms of their "audible entanglements" (in ethnomusicologist Jocelyne Guilbault's clever phrase) and the lifestyle dimensions they support.

Not long ago, for example, I enjoyed an evening in my capacity as a card-carrying, if hypercritical, member of the wider "classic rock" music intraculture. It was during a trip visiting my mom in La Mirada, when my immediate family ventured out for dinner on a Saturday night. As we drove down Beach Boulevard in nearby Buena Park, my wife, Lynn, spotted a colorful guitar-shaped sign up the road: Rock & Brews! A pathway lined with classic rock album discs—Pink Floyd's *Dark Side of the Moon*, *Led Zeppelin IV*, etc.—gave way to the ambiance of an Aerosmith concert as we entered the rock-themed restaurant. The place was packed with middle-aged white folks and their kids, with a contingent of black-leathered twenty somethings playing a version of Tinder Live at the adjacent bar. Strewn upon the walls and ceilings was a canopy of rock flags and posters representing all the big icons: the Beatles, the Stones, the Who, Rush, Queen, the Police, David Bowie, U2, the Grateful Dead, Kiss, Blondie, you name it. A half a dozen video screens and surround-sound speakers blared classic rock videos as diners like us scarfed down high-end pub food—artisan cheeseburgers with Angus beef, microbrew IPAs, and the like.

Rock & Brews thus provided my fellow "classic rockers" and me with a musical and lifestyle experience expressly catered to our intraculture—aesthetically defined by this specific musical preference, and dominated by a handful of "structural" markers: white, affluent, twenty to sixty years old, family-friendly, etc.[601]

While no one likely enjoyed every song that played over the course of dinner, we were all unified in our mutual appreciation for the overall experience it offered: a culinary-based ritual of a classic rock collectivity. Those inspired to repeat the experience now have eighteen other Rock & Brews locations in the US and Mexico to choose from—not to mention hundreds of similarly themed Hard Rock Cafes around the world. My only slight chagrin came in learning that Rock & Brews was cofounded in 2010 by Gene Simmons and Paul Stanley—the two frontmen of Kiss! Score one for Mitch.

Intracultures, musical and otherwise, are by definition communal. They come into being, in theory at least, whenever two or more people hold an identity—heritage, faith, gender, cause, affinity, etc.—to which they collectively claim ownership. As such, intracultures offer members the perks and trappings of this mutual ownership, and the experiences and lifestyles they yield.

One intriguing manifestation of this group identity is the phenomenon of the "superfan." Examples abound, especially for the modern-day pop and rock intracultures: the Grateful Dead's "Deadheads," Kiss' "Kiss Army," Jimmy Buffett's "Parrotheads," Aerosmith's "Blue Army," Barry Manilow's "Fanilows," Justin Bieber's "True Beliebers," Beyoncé's "Beyhive," Lady Gaga's "Little Monsters," Katy Perry's "KatyCats," Clay Aiken's "Claymates," and Taylor Swift's "Swifties"—to name just a few. These are the most passionate consumers and advocates of individual bands and artists—those "fan armies" who are increasingly recognized as a prime source of revenue by the music industry: they attend more concerts, consume more music, and buy more merchandise than an average "fan," as much as twelve times more.[602] Their dedication (and dollars) gives them access to more immersive and intense experiences—such as prerelease gifts or events, exclusive social media access, etc. But it also gives them solidarity with like-minded souls who share an intense passion for the music as well as its surrounding "lifestyle."

Recently, my wife, Lynn, and I got to participate in a "superfan" intracultural experience, when we saw the Rolling Stones at the brand-new U Arena in Paris. Thanks to my friend Tim Ries, the band's tenor saxophonist since 2003, we were able to enjoy a preconcert gathering in the "VIP Lounge" and then see the terrific three-hour concert from "the pit," right next to the stage and adjoining catwalk. But perhaps even more memorable was the time we spent before, during, and after the concert with a small group of Rolling Stones "superfans" (I call them "Rollingistas," but no official name exists). These were folks in their forties to sixties who had each seen dozens, if not hundreds of Stones concerts—including most others on this *same* tour. They knew where to stand, special song highlights, the set list, and—critically it turned out—when exactly to leave so as to avoid the mass crowd exodus.

More profoundly, though, they shared something intangible: a collective affinity for the Rolling Stones and the ethos, aesthetic, and history the band has built up over its incredible fifty-six-year career. Our dozen mini-intraculture attendees that night hailed from six countries across three continents, from varying socioeconomic status, both genders, and undoubtedly a wide array of careers, education levels, and other affinities musical and otherwise. However, as they (and we) shared the concert, and then drinks afterwards until 3 a.m., they were one body: sharing insiders' stories of Stones shows in '67 or '75 or a week earlier in Stockholm, as well as any number of personality traits and/or life perspectives that unified them in ways no one could articulate. This was their musical intraculture, and they were damn proud of it.

And yet, as Lahire, Bennett, and others have underscored, critical to intracultures as well are the specific benefits and opportunities they grant to individuals—apart from their shared aesthetics and practices with other members. For membership also subsumes more *personal* influences: on behavior, growth, and identity—becoming a "scaffolding for self-construction," as music sociologist Tia DeNora put it.[603] Paradoxically, that is, despite its communal identity, a musical intraculture can enable quite profound opportunities for individuation.

Most obvious are the external influences offered: dress, hairstyle, modes of speech, social behavior, etc. This is especially apparent with the more "extraordinary" of the music intracultures—heavy metal, punk, grunge, etc.—where fashion becomes a uniform. Active members of heavy-metal-based intracultures, for example, show up to concerts and festivals adhering to a strict dress code: black leather, combat boots, spikes, studded belts, jewelry, piercings, tattoos, spiked hair, garish makeup, etc.—appropriating "signs and commodities as a sort of semiotic guerrilla warfare," in cultural sociologist Cotton Seiler's words.[604] In this way, the intraculture creates a status leveling among members, where distinctions of social class and education are obliterated in favor of fashion homogeny—an irony considering the generally rebellious stance of the intraculture. In other cases, as in hip hop, external influence is more varied and ever changing—baggy pants giving way to tight-fitting jeans, gold jewelry giving way to wooden beads—with influence stemming directly from intracultural leaders: top-selling rappers, singers, and producers. As "hip hop culture" gains in broader "capital," moreover, fashion becomes an ever-finer delineator of power and stature (leaders versus followers) within the intraculture itself.[605]

Interestingly, individual behavior can also be influenced by how a given music stands *in opposition to* the identity of an intraculture. Infamous examples include the use of rap (e.g., Eminem), heavy metal (e.g., AC/DC), or children's songs (e.g., the *Barney* theme) on prisoners at Guantanamo Bay as part of the CIA's "no-touch" torture program.[606] Less inflammatory has been the "weaponizing" of classical music to deter teens from trespassing and committing crimes, as has been employed in commercial sites and public squares around the world. While the music of Mozart may act as a source of pride and edification for members of a fine arts intraculture, it can be anathema to intracultures aligned with the more aggressive forms of rock or urban music. As musicologist Lily Hirsch notes,

"Classical music is successful not in elevating or rehabilitating hooligans, but in chasing them away."[607] This suggests how music can function not only positively to build solidarity among intraculture members, but also negatively to delimit their behavior and social space.

While not as readily discernible as spiked hair or tattoos, our membership in intracultures can yield palpable effects on our internal life as well—on our thinking, attitudes, and self-perceptions. This was the case, for example, with the British working-class youth in the 1960s (mods, skinheads), who employed their intraculture to help offset feelings of socioeconomic alienation and marginalization.

This technique no doubt continues today within contemporary rock-, EDM-, and hip hop–based intracultures. One subtle example is the use of sampling in hip hop: according to ethnomusicologist Peter Manuel, rap artists can sample snippets of existing music or speech in part to "negate" the oppressions of their social reality. For example, in the track "News Break," rapper Redman sampled and manipulated news feeds of the 1992 LA riots—not, in Manuel's view, to trivialize the event, but "to comment on the artificiality of bourgeois media discourse and contrast it with the rage and desperation of black street culture."[608] Through this slice of hip hop intraculture, in other words, Redman and his fans could confront their internal frustrations and anxieties in an *aesthetic* manner not possible otherwise.

Of course, the inner-life effects of membership extend well beyond class-based issues. In a 2016 study, for example, Emre Ulusoy extensively interviewed fifteen members of what he calls "Dionysian music subcultures"—based around "ecstatic" rock genres like heavy metal, hardcore, death metal, grunge, punk, post-punk, etc. His goal was to detail the experiences of active consumers within these intracultures in order to identify the key values that membership afforded them. The culminating experience, according to Ulusoy, is an opportunity to realize one's "extraordinary self": through Dionysian intracultures, members are able to (1) carry out social resistance without confrontation (through dress or dancing), (2) escape from feelings of isolation and alienation, and (3) feel safe despite violent physical contact (thrashing around a heavy metal "mosh pit," for example) by virtue of well-defined codes of conduct. As one of Ulusoy's interviewees put it, "moshing" is far better than mixing it up "with some complete stranger on a shooting spree."[609]

To be sure, music is not the only impactful force within Dionysian intracultures, but it is clearly a catalytic one. Further, it is not only "ecstatic" music intracultures that yield inner-life effects on its members, but refined, traditional, and "mellow" ones as well. Among the many inner-life benefits one can imagine stemming from membership in musical intracultures include a heightened sense of purpose, greater connectedness to the world and to others, personal growth and edification, and increased self-confidence. Hopefully, future studies will grant a more specific notion of how distinct intracultures become distinct "scaffolds for self-construction."

One final benefit of intracultural membership is here worth noting: the ability to grant us as individuals a better understanding of our place within the broader superculture. Every intraculture forges some kind of relationship with the "mother" culture or mainstream. It may be complementary—supporting the superculture's general flow and evolution; or its very essence may be one of opposition and rebellion to the mainstream. Indeed, Ulusoy's very use of the term "Dionysian" refers to the classic dichotomy of the Greek gods Dionysus and Apollo: Dionysus, the god of wine, theater, and religious ecstasy, representing passion, irrationality, unpredictability, and chaos stands in contrast to Apollo, the god of the sun, truth, and music, representing order, reason, logic, and comfort. In most cases, of course, the intraculture-mainstream interrelationship is both complementary and oppositional at any given moment, not to mention over time. For one, most intracultures would be entirely unknown were they not to some degree acknowledged, if not fêted, by the broader superculture.

As members of intracultures, we thus weave in and out of our superculture like threads through a tapestry—matching colors here, contrasting them there. Between our lives at home, work, play, and purpose, we move frequently from one intraculture to another, as between our intracultures and the mainstream and back again. The composite gives us a sense of our overall sociocultural identity, with clues to where we fit in, how well, with whom, and how we might maintain or improve our standing. Not uncommonly, the interrelation is complex and paradoxical—as when a huge mainstream star like Beyoncé presents an extravagant performance at the 2017 Grammy Awards that in fact was largely targeted at an intraculture centered on African-American women. The Grammy for 2017 Album of the Year did not go to Beyoncé's highly successful album *Lemonade* (No. 1 on *Billboard* Top 200), but to Adele's *25*. As Myles Johnson wrote in a *New York Times* op-ed: "Perhaps [Beyoncé] knew the win was in the fact that when all eyes were on her, she didn't decide to make herself more palatable to white viewers. Instead, she let her imagination serve her goals, her child and her community."[610]

Sociologists borrow the linguistic notion of "code-switching" (alternating between languages or varieties in conversation, developed by William Labov in the 1970s), to refer to our ability to shift—easily or not—between group boundaries or, as anthropologist Susan Gal put it, "to create, evoke, or change interpersonal relations."[611] And as we transcend intracultural boundaries, our musical taste follows suit, enabling us to sing church hymns in the morning, protest songs in the afternoon, and trance EDM hits in the evening—among much else. Through our intracultures—each informed and defined by the ethno-, finance-, techno-, media-, and ideoscapes we encounter every day—our musical taste takes root.

With that let's return to our shopping center metaphor. As noted, the overall property represents our broad culture: the common areas the mainstream, each store an intraculture. As no one shops in every store, no one belongs to every intraculture; indeed, given our hectic lives, we probably only have time for a small number. And just as there's no escaping the common areas, we can't but participate in the mainstream—even if just in passing. But shopping in a store doesn't mean you'd want to buy everything in it, even if you had the money. Stores you regularly frequent, that resonate strongly with you, are like intracultures where you're an active member—much of what's offered will appeal, and little will offend. Thus, the biggest benefit is *access*. You walk into a favorite store, and you have easy access to a narrow or wide variety of products you just might love—products probably not available at other stores. Again, you won't love everything they have, but when a new item appears, your impulse is to check it out with positive expectations.

And so it is with intracultures—especially musical intracultures—and your musical taste: if you're an active member of an intraculture centered on Baroque opera or contemporary Broadway or bebop or classic soul or bluegrass or zydeco or death metal or dubstep, there will be a whole host of "established" works, artists, and composers that you'll be expected to know and like—with ready access to the more "obscure" portions of its repertoire. When a new work, recording, or artist enters the fold, you'll have access to those too, with reasonable chances for a positive assessment—maybe even if it challenges the intraculture's traditional boundaries. Access and expectations are naturally lessened with a more modest commitment—as when you're new to an intraculture, or only "shop" there occasionally. Class-, education-, ethnic-, political-, and other "structure"-based intracultures likewise provide access to various musical styles and orientations, as we've seen, but in the end it is *affinity*—whether structure-derived or not—that gets you inside the store.

Access, I repeat, is the power that intracultures provide your musical taste. Each musical intraculture to which you belong by definition cordons off a distinct chunk of the broader musical culture. The chunk can be small or large in size, narrow or wide in its musicological scope, scarcely or widely known by other citizens, etc. But regardless, the intraculture helps *you* to organize and understand its musical content: what is classic, what is fringe, who are the heroes, who the revolutionaries, and where can you go to hear more. But access is not prescriptive: no one forces you to like a song, work, or artist, even if they are sacrosanct to the intraculture. You can be Italian-American and hate "That's Amore"; you can be an activist feminist and hate Helen Reddy's "I Am Woman"; and you can be a card-carrying member of the classic rock infrastructure and hate Kiss—or Queen for that matter. What drives that final mile of your musical taste is, in essence, what Lahire was talking about: you as an individual, and more specifically your psychology and the way that individual musical work reflects or not your psychological identity. We'll explore that final leg of our "mystery novel" in the next section.

## Heuristics and Stereotypes

Before we move on toward that next bit of traveling, however, we need to readdress a critical point made in passing above—one with major ramifications for you and your musical taste. It concerns the biases that arise from terms like "legitimate," "highbrow," "mentally stimulating," and "physical release," along with other trappings commonly used to valuate songs, works, genres, and genotypes. As we noted, value-laden judgments not only are offensive and wrong, but they also can put unintended constraints on how you view others—or even yourself.

We've seen in Lahire's work, for example, that most of us, regardless of our socioeconomic or educational standing, reveal a level of "dissonance" in our musical taste. In short, we tend to know and consume not only music that is traditionally associated with our "class"-based intracultures, but also music that is predictably at odds with them—perhaps even more than music that *is* predictable. Knowing intellectually that we're all to some degree eclectic and pluralistic, however, will not prevent us from letting our biases get the better of us. It is thus worth broaching the topic of heuristics, and how those biases turn intraculture membership—including our own—into limiting and potentially pernicious stereotypes.

Daniel Kahneman, the reigning guru of the field, defines "heuristics" as "a simple procedure that helps find adequate, though often imperfect, answers to difficult questions." He adds that the word "comes from the same root as 'eureka.'" Kahneman and his longtime friend and fellow Israeli psychology colleague Amos Tversky pioneered the field of heuristics; the two, indeed, are frequently labeled the "Lennon and McCartney" of psychology or social science—though never saying which is which.[612] In his book *Thinking, Fast and Slow,* Kahneman presents to a lay audience the many dimensions of heuristics and how they reveal "a puzzling limitation of our mind: our excessive confidence in what we believe we know, and our apparent inability to acknowledge the full extent of our ignorance."[613]

To help unravel this puzzle, Kahneman creates a two-part system of cognition or "thinking." System 1 is our fast, "automatic" system, and draws upon our intuitions, impressions, and feelings; you use it to make quick decisions about which cereal to buy or which security line to stand in at the airport, for example. System 2, by contrast, is our slow, "effortful" system, and comes into play when more conscious and calculating thought is required than what System 1 can offer—such as solving a math problem, deciding which college to attend, or analyzing a piece of music. The problem is that while we'd like to believe that our judgments about the world are products of careful System 2 deliberation, the truth is rather different. As Kahneman puts it, "System 1 is more influential than your experience tells you, and it is the secret author of many of the choices and judgments you make."[614]

The ways in which System 1 can "get us into trouble" are many and varied; and, of course, the two systems interact in all kinds of complex ways. To be sure, System 2 kicks in whenever things get truly complicated, or when we have good reason to be suspicious, or when our expectations are discernibly violated. And yet our System 1 is always "on," and thus our unconscious intuitions and hunches leave their mark on our decision-making *and* our judgments. As Kahneman puts it, System 2 is rather lazy, and will often endorse the beliefs of System 1—despite the flat-out errors it is frequently prone to make. In turn, this enables us to accept things based on unchallenged assumptions, biases, and stereotypes—or, in his favorite acronym, on WYSIATI: what you see is all there is.

The point here is that when we learn that someone is wealthy or holds an advanced college degree, we might well assume that they like classical music and dislike punk or EDM; or alternately, if we know that someone skipped college or is lower middle class, we might assume they love pop music and hate jazz. Or, perhaps, we see someone dressed in a heavy metal "uniform" of black leather and spikes, or pull up next to a car with a hip hop bass line blaring from twelve-inch subwoofers, and our intuition suggests that they couldn't possibly also be fans of opera, or even classic rock. Or, by contrast, we see a couple emerge from an opera house, and we assume they also love symphonic music, etc., etc. That is to say, we *imagine* we see a classical, jazz, heavy metal, or hip hop fan, and our System 1 thinks, "What you see is all there is": we know this person's musical taste, and by extension what kind of person they are.

And while you might often be correct, from a statistical standpoint, you are just as likely, if not more so, to be wrong. As music psychologists Adrian North and Adam Lonsdale have discussed, this tendency to judge the musical taste of people based on a *perceived* similarity to others in the same group is known as the "representativeness heuristic."[615] And it not only impacts the musical taste we project onto others, but also other characteristics we project onto them as well: their values, views, class status, etc. Indeed, as North and Lonsdale show, we tend to treat others better if we *think* they share our musical taste. The problem, again, is that these perceptions can be wrong, or at least incomplete—as when one of Ulusoy's Dionysian interviewees expressed his passion for heavy metal, while also expressing great affection for jazz, ambient, and new age music.

By giving in to our System 1 biases, therefore, we not only risk leveling unfair, inaccurate, or even offensive stereotypes onto others, but we also risk losing out on adding potential new friends or co-members to our various musical intracultures.

And even more risky, by virtue of our heuristic blinders, we can impose unnecessary and unfortunate limits on our *own* musical taste. Don't assume, for example, that because you are a huge fan of hip hop, you couldn't possibly also like segments of classical or jazz or world music—or vice versa. Your membership in one musical intraculture is a gateway to a whole host of music you will discover and hopefully love, but it should not at the same time shut the door on any other intraculture just because tradition, expectation, assumptions, or biases say it should.

Next up: the seventh and penultimate part of our musical journey—starting with the final two genotypes: world and classical music.

part seven

# WHO ARE YOU, ANYWAY?

*fourteen*

# THE WORLD MUSIC GENOTYPE

• • •

## Introducing Subject 6

Subject 6 joins a "worldbeat" dance class and locks into an inspired groove with **Cheb Mami's "Youm Wara Youm."** The congested drive to work is then sweetened a bit with **Youssou N'Dour's "Birima."** After a mind-numbing day of meetings, welcome relief is found with an old favorite, **Hamza El Din's "Assaramessuga."** Finally, Subject 6 enters a meditative pre-bedtime ritual with **Ravi Shankar's *Morning Love*.***

By these hits, Subject 6 seems to embrace an eclectic array of world music styles. A particularly sweet spot appears concentrated in the Arabic and West African milieus, especially when an embrace of Western pop music is evident. The El Din and Shankar choices, however, reveal that such restrictions are not mandatory.

## The World Music Species: A Brief Intro

As noted in Chapter 1, the expression "world music" is used to denote the huge array of music created by musicians beyond North America and England—or in styles outside the traditional Western genres subsumed by pop, jazz, and art music.

This amorphous and vague definition notwithstanding, we'll get started with a list of tracks that can be reasonably labeled touchstones of the species—or at least that a broad population in the West might consider suitable exemplars of "world music":

---

* Subject 6's fifth song, heard with friends at a city nightclub, is Afro Celt Sound System's 1999 song "Release." For its discussion, see the WYLI website, supplement to Chapter 14.

Yo-Yo Ma and the Silk Road Ensemble, "Briel" (2013)
A. R. Rahman, "Jai Ho" (from *Slumdog Millionaire*, 2008)
Ladysmith Black Mambazo, "Inkanyezi Nezazi" (1999)
Buena Vista Social Club, "Chan Chan" (1997)
The Chieftains and Sting, "Mo Ghile Mear" (1995)
Nusrat Fateh Ali Khan, "Mustt Mustt" (1990)
The Gipsy Kings, "Bamboléo" (1987)
Astor Piazzolla, "Libertango" (1974)
Sérgio Mendes and Brasil '66, "Mas, que Nada" (1966)
Edith Piaf, "La vie en rose" (1947)

The range of styles and sounds represented in these ten tracks—all hits by world music stars from across five continents—makes detailing a short set of musicological traits a bit of a challenge; in fact, these hits typify more the Western-influenced, accessible wing of the species than its full, eclectic breadth. That said, all but one here ("Libertango") is vocal, at least in part—sung in languages other than English (except portions of "Mo Ghile Mear"). Melodies are generally florid and ornamented, often improvisational in nature; rhythm is mostly vibrant and highly syncopated, often in 4/4 meter, with rock or jazz influence—though frequently organized into odd-number phrase groupings; harmony in these tracks is commonly static via drones, based on non-Western modal scales—though not uncommon too is the use of Western (tonal) chord progressions, especially via repeating patterns; form in most tracks is clear and sectional, especially binary-based, where improvisation is a staple; and—most overtly—the timbres used comprise a rich mix of "exotic" ethnic instruments with the familiar ones of Western classical, jazz, and rock.

Using the term "world music" to label these ten touchstone tracks, let alone the wider non-touchstone repertoire associated with the species, is admittedly rather arrogant—if not offensive: lumping together an immense and incredibly diverse array of musical identities into a single non-Anglo-American bucket. Indeed, a good many musicians and writers have expressed umbrage at the expression, perhaps most pointedly David Byrne of the band Talking Heads, who in a 1999 *New York Times* editorial entitled "I Hate World Music" called it "a way of dismissing artists or their music as irrelevant to one's own life . . . something exotic and therefore cute . . . by definition, not like us."[616] Others have noted its implied cultural superiority or even its coarse echoes of Western colonialism.[617]

So why is it used? The expression dates back initially to the early 1960s within an academic environment, as a user-friendly spur for students to take courses in ethnomusicology. Its use as a commercial label then dates to the mid-1980s, ostensibly from a 1987 meeting among reps of UK indie record labels specializing in various kinds of "ethnic" music.[618] Seeking a term to better enable record stores to assemble and sell their products, they rejected things like "worldbeat" or "international" and settled on "world music" as the least problematic. Thus, as with "EDM," the music industry manufactured a term for commercial expediency that some thirty years later is still in vogue—for better or worse.

For most Anglo-American music fans, the expression "world music" implies a degree of *cross-fertilization* between a non-Anglo-American musical style and a broad Western "pop music" mode—pop, rock, R&B, hip hop, electronica. In this way it is somewhat synonymous with commercial terms like "worldbeat" and "global tracks." Indeed, this hybrid approach is the one most highly promoted and embraced in the marketplace—well beyond the more purely indigenous folk, religious, or classical music practices from around the world. At the same time, the musicological elements found in the "hybrid" styles will often point directly to those found in the more "indigenous" practices, suggesting that fans of the former could well become fans of the latter with a little encouragement.

Our use of "world music" is thus not meant to denote any particular approach, but rather *any* music that to *at least a discernible degree* reflects the traditional practices of regions outside the Anglo-American or Western jazz or art music spheres. It need not display any reference to Western pop, jazz, or art music, but it can. Thus, given the incredibly broad array of musical styles, techniques, and aesthetics that can be subsumed by this species—from Argentinian tango to Celtic pipe tunes to Chinese opera to Jewish klezmer to South African Zulu music to Tuvan throat singing, to name but a tiny percentage—this brief intro was not intended to provide anything resembling a comprehensive summary of world music. Hopefully, though, the discussion below will provide a reasonable and tantalizing entrée to a rich and endlessly fascinating realm of music making.

## A Worldbeat Dance Class: Cheb Mami's "Youm Wara Youm"

**Cheb Mami's "Youm Wara Youm"** is a clear example of the kind of pop-derived world music hybrid discussed above. It also reveals the commercial taming that its traditional Algerian genre, raï, has witnessed over the past several decades. Subject 6 is here staking a claim to the fun and exotic—though touchstone—side of the world music species that lies behind its global success over the past few decades.

### CHEB MAMI: BACKGROUND

Cheb Mami (born Mohamed Khelifati in 1966)—the name means "young mourner"—is an Algerian-born composer-singer living in Paris; he is among the most well-known raï artists today, with a modest but vibrant international following. After selling homemade cassettes in his native Saïda, typical for raï musicians in the 1980s, Mami's career took off following a concert with Cheb Khaled, the "king of raï," at a festival in Oran, especially after he moved to France toward the end of the decade. Mami became a favorite in the club scene of the French communities of North African immigrants, gaining the nickname "prince of raï." Success with UK and American audiences then followed upon his duet with Sting, on the latter's song "Desert Rose," in 1999—leading to a set of American appearances, including at the Super Bowl in 2001.[619]

"Raï" literally means "opinion" or "advice," which underscores the social dimension of this Algerian music genre, with roots going back to the 1920s. Musical cross-influence has always defined the genre: initially between traditional bedouin shepherd songs and Spanish/Andalusian genres such as flamenco—with some input from the cabaret tradition of France, the colonial power that governed Algeria from the 1830s. Raï lyrics often touched on the social injustice of life under colonial rule, but also on the "hedonistic" escapes of sex, alcohol, and dancing.

After Algeria achieved independence in 1962, the genre emerged as a symbol of Algerian national identity, though likewise as a vehicle to protest inequities now under local governance. From the 1970s onward, raï musicians began incorporating influences from Western popular music: reggae, funk, pop, rock, and hip hop—including their associated instruments of electric guitars, synthesizers, and drum machines. The subgenres of "pop raï" and "love raï" emerged, gaining a wider audience—especially after stars like Khaled and Mami moved to France. Such was precipitated through the increasing censorship or worse by government and Islamist authorities; they complained about the overt sexuality and consumerism of the lyrics and the genre's "bawdy" musical style. Indeed, even today, Paris is the capital of the raï music scene.[620]

## CHEB MAMI: ANALYSIS

"Youm Wara Youm" (Day after Day) is a "love raï" duet between Cheb Mami and Samira Said, a famed Moroccan pop singer. In fact, the song, written by Mami, first appeared on an album of the same name released by Said—for which she won Best Middle Eastern Artist at the 2002 BBC World Music Awards. In the song, the two singers continually bat the melody back and forth, somewhat reminiscent of Jobim's "Águas de Março"—although the two melodies could not be more different. Melody, to be sure, is the most pronounced parameter in the listening experience of "Youm," and the one most "exotic" to ears steeped in Western music.

As noted in Chapter 4, melodic attributes and performance techniques—in concert with rhythm—are critical to the definition of most non-Western musical practices. Given the absence of an indigenous system of vertical harmony—as is the case in most non-Western societies—the nuanced definition of scale, intonation, and especially ornamentation becomes a principal means by which a local musical culture defines itself. In the case of music in the broader Middle East, a highly ornamented approach to melody is commonplace. Specifically, an ancient monophonic tradition there celebrates a virtuosic vocal style: long, melismatic melodies with a wide array of trills, slides, rapid repeated notes, bent notes, microtones, and other ornaments. In pre-Islamic (before the seventh century) times, quasi-improvised chants often featured female singers, aimed at bringing the listener into a state of ecstasy.

In "Youm" this highly ornamented melodic approach is on display from the get-go. After a short intro, Said performs an opening (A) section consisting of a four-bar phrase repeated four times. The basic melodic shape (hook) is relatively simple, although the flurry of virtuosic ornamentation—varied each time—creates a rich aural experience. To demonstrate, below is a comparative view of a hypothetical unornamented version of Said's second phrase as might be sung by a Western pop singer (Figure 14.1a) above the phrase actually sung by Said (Figure 14.1b):

**Figure 14.1a–b: Cheb Mami, "Youm Wara Youm"—Section A, phrase a', hypothetical "Western" and actual**

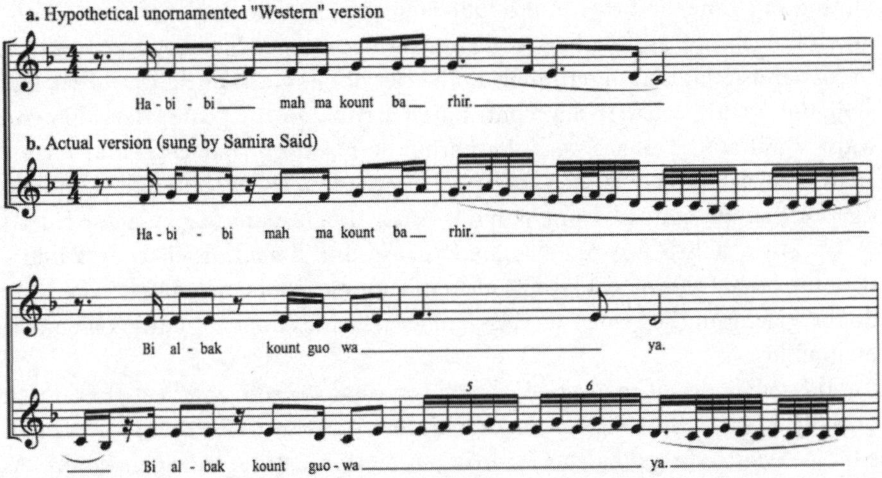
a. Hypothetical unornamented "Western" version
Ha - bi - bi mah ma kount ba rhir.
b. Actual version (sung by Samira Said)
Ha - bi - bi mah ma kount ba rhir.
Bi al - bak kount guo wa ya.
5
6
Bi al - bak kount guo - wa ya.

The actual melody is sung atop a descending chord progression in D minor: D minor–C–B♭–C–D minor. This schema (i–VII–VI–VII–i) is standard to flamenco and related Spanish/Andalusian musical styles; indeed, it is called the "Andalusian cadence"—where it typically continues down to the V chord (i–VII–VI–V); such, in fact, occurs in the bridge (D) section (at 2:44) of "Youm" (Figures 14.2a–b):

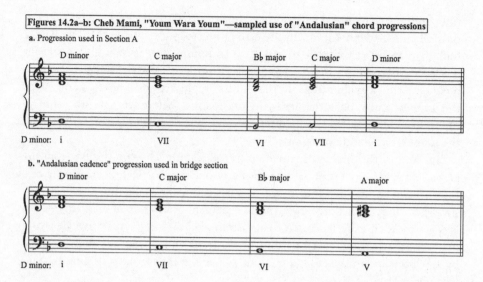

Figures 14.2a–b: Cheb Mami, "Youm Wara Youm"—sampled use of "Andalusian" chord progressions

a. Progression used in Section A

b. "Andalusian cadence" progression used in bridge section

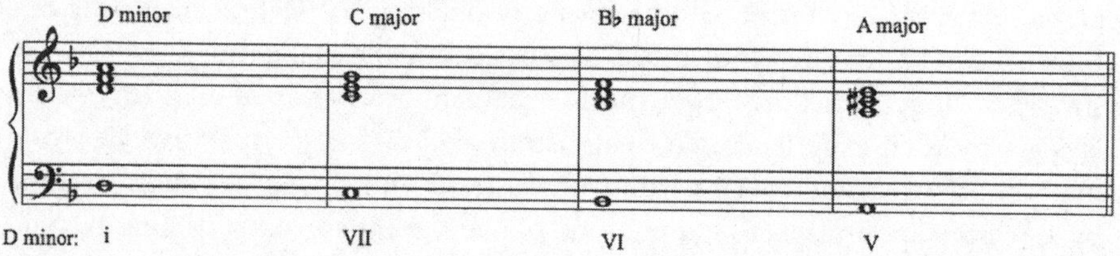


This juxtaposition is not at all surprising. Recall that the Maghreb (Northwest Africa) was, from 711 to 1492, aligned with al-Andalus, or Muslim Spain. During this time, and even more following the "Reconquista" by the Catholic queen Isabella of Castile, when scores of Muslims escaped Spain to North Africa, the two musical idioms intermingled. The city of Oran, the birthplace of raï, had a vibrant Spanish quarter that contributed actively to the genre's development. Most significant, perhaps, was the harmonic palette of flamenco and related genres—which explains why a good percentage of raï songs feature the "Andalusian cadence" or similarly simple minor-mode progressions (e.g., Cheb Khaled's "Hiya Hiya," Cheb Nasro's "Nargoud Ala Wadnia," etc.). Their compatibility with the ornate and modal aspects of Arabic monophonic melodic practice is no doubt a factor in the genre's success—and a salient example of music's linguistic malleability.

The remainder of the track in many ways follows conventionally upon that opening section. The song continues with four other sections, each four or eight bars in length—revealing the recurring A section as the principal refrain. As noted, the two singers continually exchange the spotlight, equally virtuosic in their delivery. The exchanges are both intersectional and frequently intrasectional—the latter taking place especially during the unusually monotonic Section C (from 1:07), where at times the singers go back and forth between rapidly repeating notes (Figure 14.3). While single-line vocal exchanges predominate, the two vocalists sing occasionally in unison, in harmony (in 3rds), and even a bit contrapuntally, toward the end.

**Figure 14.3: Cheb Mami, "Youm Wara Youm"—vocal melodic exchanges in Section C**

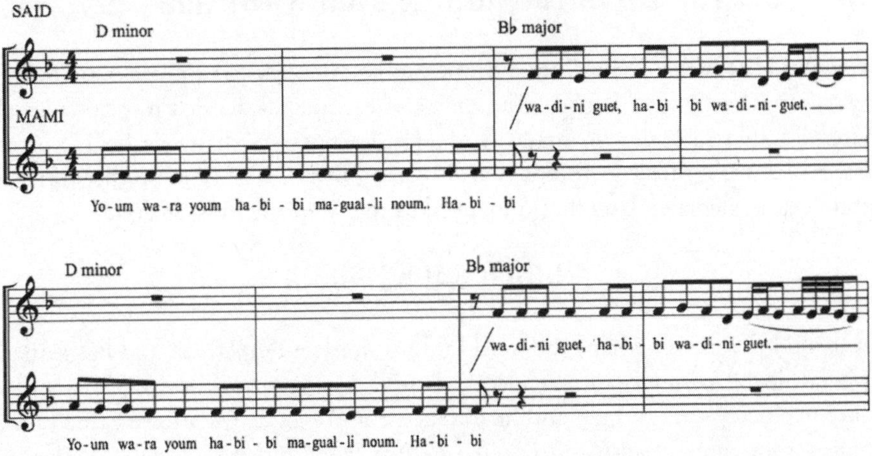


Little else warrants explication. The harmonic language maintains the "Andalusian" progression to one degree or another throughout the song. The rhythmic approach too is straightforward: a vibrant, medium-tempo dance/pop feel in 4/4, with only one moment of notable syncopation (at 1:17). Similarly, the instrumentation is conventional: largely synthesized, including drum machines and synth violins on periodic rhythmic obbligatos. It is this instrumental approach, moreover, that gives these songs a rather "cheesy" sonority to those unaccustomed to the style.

In short, it really is the melodic language that most palpably distinguishes the listening experience of "Youm Wara Youm," especially from an insular Western perspective. The mix of catchy hooks and dazzling ornamentation, set in a snappy rhythmic framework, is likely what attracts Subject 6 to the song. In one striking example, Mami sings fourteen notes within three beats, including both a chromatic F♯ and a diatonic F♮ against the D minor mode (at 1:45)—similar to a gesture he sang in Sting's "Desert Rose" (Figure 14.4):

With a song like this, we aren't in Kansas anymore.

**Figure 14.4: Cheb Mami, "Youm Wara Youm"—melismatic singing by Mami in Section A'**

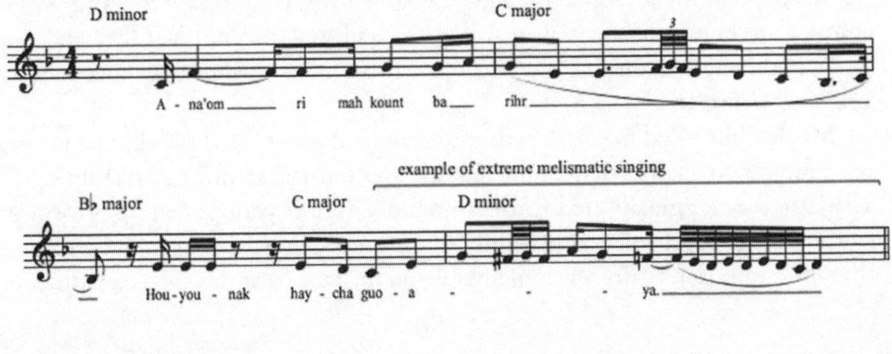

## The Drive to Work: N'Dour's "Birima"

**Youssou N'Dour's "Birima"** extends the profile of Subject 6's musical taste to the West African nation of Senegal. The song also exemplifies the rich musico-cultural interplay that underlies so many world music styles. With it, we begin to see traces of a world music genotype that craves not just the fun but also the spiritual and deep-seeded elements that undergird so many ethnic musical styles.

### N'DOUR: BACKGROUND

Youssou N'Dour is perhaps the most famous musician in Africa, and has gained a good degree of international success as well. His vocal prowess (an extraordinary five-octave-plus range) and heightened emotional delivery have earned him praise from elite Western sources like *Rolling Stone* and the *New York Times*—which hails his "kindly clarion of a voice, which is equally sweet, lithe and resolute."[621] In his music, N'Dour blends and reconciles multiple traditions from within and beyond Senegalese society.

N'Dour was born in Dakar, Senegal, in 1959, and began singing publicly before reaching his teens. On his mother's side, he stems from the ancient caste of the griots—the "troubadours" of Africa, who in song and story pass down the history, myths, and wisdom of the ancients from generation to generation.[622] Through the 1970s and '80s, with groups such as Étoile de Dakar, N'Dour forged a neo-griot identity by creating a new genre: mbalax—mixing Senegalese traditions with various pop/rock and Latin elements. His vocal extemporization in Peter Gabriel's 1986 hit "In Your Eyes" helped introduce N'Dour to audiences beyond Africa, as have later collaborations with Sting, Paul Simon, and Branford Marsalis, among many others. As a soloist, N'Dour received the Grammy Award for Best World Music Album in 2005.

Senegal, like Algeria, was a French colony from the mid-nineteenth century—gaining independence in 1960. Similarly, Senegal is predominantly Muslim, having been converted by Moroccan invaders in the eleventh century. In this way too, some Arabic musical elements would have undoubtedly been assimilated into the local practices. At the same time, the ethnic Serer and Wolof cultures are hugely influential in Senegalese cultural and musical life, and not only via the griot tradition. N'Dour himself is a Sufi Muslim with mixed Serer and Wolof ethnicity.

Mbalax (the word means "rhythmic accompaniment" in the Wolof language) is an outgrowth of an ancient and religious Serer musical genre known as njuup.[623] The latter was originally tied to the initiation rites of young men, as a form of spiritual focus prior to circumcision! Njuup features a particular style and active rhythmic approach to drumming, notably on the sabar drums—played with both the hand and a stick. Each of three different sabar drums (high-medium-low) has a distinct function and rhythmic profile within any given chant. In contrast to the severe style of njuup, however, the mbalax style developed by N'Dour and his compatriots is decidedly more "party" in spirit. The musical palette is expanded with influence from various external sources: blues, rock, R&B, salsa, and Caribbean styles such as zouk. Instrumentally, mbalax introduced electric guitars, synthesizers, as well as other traditional African drums, including the tama or "talking drum." The songs are sung not in French, the official language of Senegal, but in the Wolof, as by N'Dour, or Serer languages—thereby augmenting the genre's "Africanized" quality.

## N'DOUR: ANALYSIS

"Birima" is from N'Dour's 2000 album *Joko*, meaning "the link." And indeed, the song's lyrics make explicit N'Dour's personal link to the ancient griot tradition: they tell the story of the sixteenth-century kingdom of Cayor (modern Senegal) and the benevolent King Birima, who patronized griots and promoted a culture of harmony and cooperation among all the classes. Extolling this theme is undoubtedly a reflection of N'Dour's own progressive social activism in Senegal, for which he has been duly celebrated—e.g., he was appointed minister of culture in 2012.

As is true with a good number of songs reviewed thus far, "Birima" establishes material of keen interest in its intro section. We immediately hear an exotic-sounding string instrument playing a lively rhythmic melody. For those so familiar, it sounds rather like a kora or a xalam, both traditional West African instruments used to accompany the songs of the griots. But in fact, it is the archetypal rock and roll electric guitar, the Fender Stratocaster—whose tone and performance style have been modified by Jimi Mbaye, a renowned African guitarist and longtime associate of N'Dour. Beyond the sound, moreover, this melody is striking for its complex syncopation, whereby the listener is "thrown off" as to where the downbeat resides—something we truly discern only when N'Dour's vocal melody begins. With this intro, we are immediately aware that rhythm is going to play a key role in the listening experience of "Birima" (Figure 14.5):

**Figure 14.5: Youssou N'Dour, "Birima"—ambiguous (highly syncopated) rhythmic pulse in guitar intro**

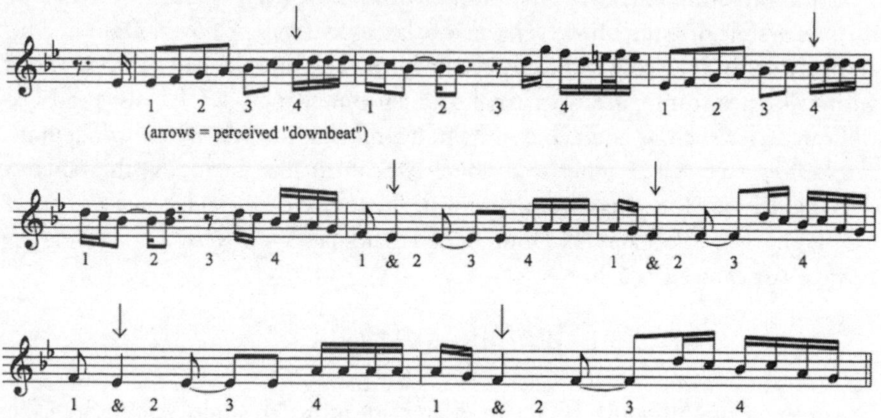


As soon as N'Dour's vocal enters, so too does the rest of the ensemble: drums, percussion, electric bass, synth, and additional guitars. We now clearly feel the beat in this medium 4/4 groove. The style is a hybrid: we hear bits of pop/rock and R&B, but also the Caribbean styles of zouk and reggae, plus something distinctly African—this is mbalax. From the intro, we already were able to identify a two-chord vamping progression, which now continues in the verse: E♭ major–F major, one bar each. N'Dour's verse melody, a quick stepwise descent followed by a more sustained rejoinder, is a varied repetition of the guitar intro line. After its third repetition, the F major chord is extended a bar leading into the refrain. Thus far, N'Dour's sweet vocal timbre is in a consistently low register, down to a low C (Figure 14.6):

**Figure 14.6: Youssou N'Dour, "Birima"—melody and harmony in verse**

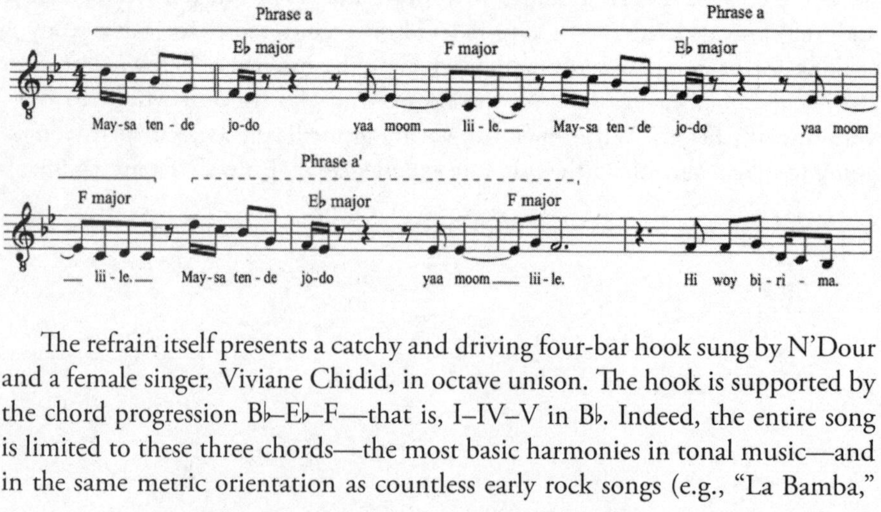


The refrain itself presents a catchy and driving four-bar hook sung by N'Dour and a female singer, Viviane Chidid, in octave unison. The hook is supported by the chord progression B♭–E♭–F—that is, I–IV–V in B♭. Indeed, the entire song is limited to these three chords—the most basic harmonies in tonal music—and in the same metric orientation as countless early rock songs (e.g., "La Bamba,"

"Lucy in the Sky with Diamonds," "Sweet Home Alabama," etc.). The hook is repeated four times, with choral echoes and harmonies reminiscent of mbube, the South African style made famous by Ladysmith Black Mambazo. N'Dour maintains the low register, but his delivery features a soulful behind-the-beat phrasing—one with clear spiritual kinship to jazz and soul, as indeed to all African-American music (Figure 14.7):

**Figure 14.7: Youssou N'Dour, "Birima"—refrain melody/harmony (1st phrase)**

The verse and refrain repeat, but it is in the midst of the second refrain that the real focus of the track arrives: N'Dour's rich vocal extemporization (Figure 14.8). With it we hear a considerably more vibrant melodic approach, more ornamented and in a higher register—a full octave above that of previous material. The second refrain is then followed by an extended interlude that features a rapid-fire solo by the tama (talking drum), its pitch gradually rising as it proceeds. After eight bars of this, however, N'Dour returns with his most explosive and virtuosic solo: his timbre is dynamically more potent as he soars to the highest points of the tenor voice range, to a high C'' and D''. With such a performance, we hear not only what grants N'Dour high praise among his fans, but also the distinct nature of West African melody. There are traces of Arabic ornamentation (trills, rapid repeated notes, etc.), as heard in "Youm Wara Youm"—though admittedly less virtuosic. Yet there is also a soulful, relaxed quality that is quite different from raï. It is in such a moment that we can further sense the infinite pliability of cross-cultural musical interaction.

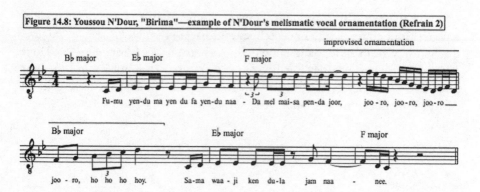

**Figure 14.8: Youssou N'Dour, "Birima"—example of N'Dour's melismatic vocal ornamentation (Refrain 2)**

N'Dour's vocal extemporization continues in the final refrain, taking him yet further into the stratosphere, to a high E♭''. As such, his total ambitus (range) in this song is two octaves and a third—quite remarkable for any singer! The power and emotional impact of N'Dour's vocal delivery is thus a likely prime source of Subject 6's ardor for "Birima." But so too is the infectious and syncopated rhythmic groove that propels the song—as indeed it does for so much sub-Saharan African music. That and the song's overall "exotic" sonority—instrumentally and chorally—help explain the growing taste for mbalax, by Subject 6 and increasingly by the rest of the world.

## Post-Work Relief: El Din's "Assaramessuga"

**Hamza El Din's "Assaramessuga" (Childhood)** points us back to the early years of the world music phenomenon, and reveals Subject 6's interest in the species as extending beyond mere pop/rock-infused hybrids. By contrast, here emerges a genotype likewise drawn to the timeless force of ancient, indigenous folk music—even if, as in El Din's case, it arose largely from the innovative vision of one musician.

### EL DIN: BACKGROUND

Hamza El Din (1929–2006) was a composer, vocalist, oud player, and percussionist from the Nubian region of modern Egypt. After studying classical Arabic music in Cairo, as well as Western classical music at the Accademia Nazionale di Santa Cecilia in Rome, El Din returned to his Nubian homeland. In the early 1960s, traditional Nubian culture was under threat by virtue of the Aswan High Dam project (1960–70): in an effort to control the risky and unpredictable flooding of the Nile River, a plan was devised to build a huge dam and reservoir (Lake Nasser) near the city of Aswan, resulting in the forced displacement of scores of small Nubian villages—including Toshka, El Din's birthplace.

Sensing the impending loss, El Din traveled by donkey from village to village, learning folk songs from local musicians in the hopes of preserving a practice that otherwise may well have perished—akin to what Bartók and Kodály did decades earlier in their native Hungary. El Din likewise introduced the sound of the oud. This pear-shaped string instrument is, in fact, not indigenous to Nubia, but instead is primary to Persian, Arabic, Greek, and Turkish music; its origins go back perhaps five thousand years, and it is the ancestor to both the European lute and guitar. Although El Din admitted that the oud sounded with a "Nubian accent," he loved it, as did the villagers who were mesmerized by his performances.[624] Such was enough to inspire El Din to abandon his pursuit of Arabic classical music and to begin composing new songs that fused Nubian folk music with traditional oud practice—along with an awareness of Western formal and harmonic practice for good measure. The result of El Din's unique cultural and musicological mélange is a recorded output that has earned him the moniker "founder of modern Nubian music."

In 1964, George Wein, the cofounder of the Newport Folk Festival, invited El Din to perform at the festival—alongside the likes of Bob Dylan and Joan Baez. His success there led to a recording contract with Vanguard Records (Baez' label) and two solo albums, including *Al Oud* (The Oud) in 1965, which opens with "Assaramessuga." These, and especially his 1971 release *Escalay: The Water Wheel*, may be considered the earliest "world music" albums to gain a broad audience in the West. Their appeal and influence on American musicians has been notable—including on minimalist composers Steve Reich and Terry Riley, and most especially on Grateful Dead drummer Mickey Hart. El Din performed several times with the Grateful Dead—including, famously, at the pyramids in Egypt—and Hart produced his 1978 album, *Eclipse*. Indeed, Hart's own fierce commitment to "global drumming" can be much traced to his connection with El Din—from whom he learned the tar, a traditional Nubian single-skinned frame drum. El Din spent much of his career in the US, and died in Oakland in 2006.

Traditional Nubian music is itself an amalgam of various influences: Arabic, Sudanese, and Eastern Christian (Greek and Coptic), among others. Nubian culture dates back to around 4000 BCE, gaining importance as a trading center more than a millennium before the Old Kingdom of ancient Egypt. From the fourth through thirteenth centuries, the region was under Christian control, though with constant threat by Muslim invaders—who finally gained the upper hand from the fourteenth century onward. The importance of rhythm in Nubian music is attested by the primacy of the tar frame drum and the complex tradition of ollin aragiid, or hand clapping. What we know of traditional Nubian folk melody, on the other hand, comes as much from El Din's original compositions as from any extant examples. He thus established the path forward for Nubian folk song, even as he sought to preserve a threatened tradition. In so doing, that is, he inevitably incorporated his own personal style, while interpolating it with the Arabic oud tradition, and even the subtle imprint of Western form and harmony.

As such, El Din stands in a long line of composers who, while indebted to the slow churn of musical culture and the incremental evolution by musicians from generation to generation, helped define a new musical discourse for their contemporaries and heirs—much as Dufay, Monteverdi, Haydn, Wagner, Stravinsky, Reich, Armstrong, Parker, Davis, Presley, Dylan, Lennon and McCartney, Dre, Eno, and Jackson, to name but a few, did in their own times and musical milieus.

## EL DIN: ANALYSIS

"Assaramessuga," as noted above, stems from El Din's second release, *Al Oud* (1965), and remains one of his most well-known songs. The vibrancy of the oud playing, the driving strength of the melody, and El Din's warm, "reedy" voice together create a recording that is exotic but not terribly remote to Western ears. From the onset, one is struck by the rhythmic and highly articulated sound of the oud, accompanied subtly by the tar, the Nubian frame drum—overdubbed by El Din himself. The oud performance is technically dazzling, with the steady eighth notes of the melody often embellished by repeated sixteenth notes plucked by a hard plectrum (pick)—creating a vivid, energetic momentum. We have to take El Din's word for it that the oud sounds "with a Nubian accent," though it certainly seems to suit his melodic and vocal style.

The opening oud melody also establishes two other musicological issues that define the song. First is its harmonic language: with little exception, the song alternates between E and B major (I and V in E). There are no vertical chords defining this relationship or accompanying the vocal melody; instead it is defined by the frequent repetitions of either E or B as recurring pedal points (at times with the 5th above), as well as by the actual melodic tones that reinforce the harmonic primacy of those two pitches. And yet, the melodies and countermelodies are not presented as a single mode, but indeed as a deliberate alternation between "tonic" and "dominant" harmonies (Figure 14.9):

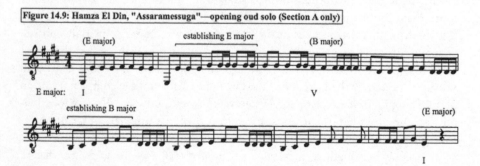

**Figure 14.9: Hamza El Din, "Assaramessuga"—opening oud solo (Section A only)**

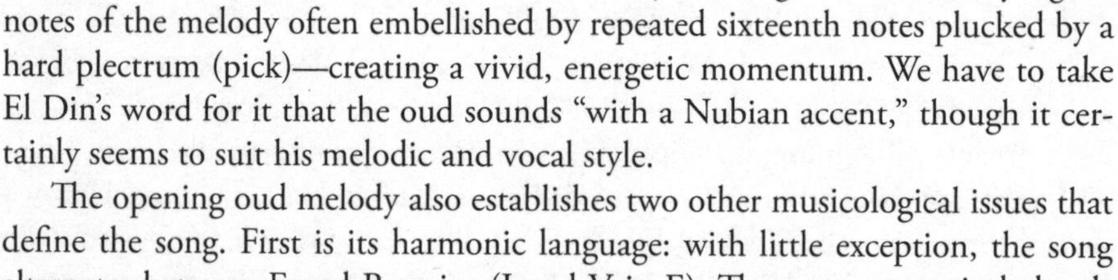

The one exception to this is a brief alternation between roots on E and F♯ (at 2:50), first in the oud (Section H), then in the vocal melody (Section H'—Figure 14.10):

**Figure 14.10: Hamza El Din, "Assaramessuga"—melodic-harmonic shift between E and F♯minor (Section H')**

The second issue is the formal orientation of the song. In the opening oud solo, El Din presents several distinct melodic phrases/sections/ideas. Recalling Oscar Wilde's counsel to "start with the worship of form," "Assaramessuga" does seem to reveal much of its essence in its rather ornate formal design. Indeed, this four-and-a-half-minute song presents in all a quasi-through-composed template with at least eight distinct divisions, with several recurring. The intro specifically presents three ideas: Sections A, B, and C. Each is a symmetrical eight bars in length—though in what appears an improvisatory hiccup, the opening section is only seven bars long. All three maintain harmonic focus on E major, with slight "half cadences" on B within. The third idea (Section C) in particular sets up the arrival of the vocal melody.

That vocal melody arrives using the oud part of Section C as accompaniment—with its short descending 5th (B–E) motives acting as intertext echoes. Setting as it does the title "Assaramessuga," or "our childhood," on a repeating E, this feels like a refrain, and it does repeat twice more. After this six-bar Section C, El Din introduces a longer Section D: a B major pedal, accompanying a forward-driving melody that anchors on melodic B, with leaps up to a high E before slowly meandering back down to low E. Many fans of El Din marvel at the "meditative" quality of his music, and this section gives good reason; there is indeed something meditative about the steady B pedal supporting this repetitive and driving melody—enabling those receptive to it to enter into a groove-inflected brown study. A return to the "refrain" (Section C) closes this opening vocal section (Figure 14.11):

**Figure 14.11: Hamza El Din, "Assaramessuga"—Sections C (refrain) and D melody & harmonic definition**

A twelve-bar interlude by the oud reprises Section B, though now extended and more virtuosic. The vocals continue with a new four-bar folklike, sequence-oriented melody (Section E), which concludes with a one-bar oud tag of a rapidly descending 5th (B–E). This "tag motive" will recur numerous times throughout the remainder of the song, like a unifying thread; in this way it is reminiscent of Machaut's fourteenth-century *Messe de Nostre Dame*, which similarly uses a short "interlude" to link the Gloria and the Credo.[625] A nine-bar Section F (1:49) then follows, including two ascending phrases and a meandering, syncopated descent leading to a slow trill (E–F♯), which likewise becomes a recurring motive. As should be clear by now, this is no simple verse-refrain structure (Figure 14.12):

Figure 14.12: Hamza El Din, "Assaramessuga"—Sections E and F

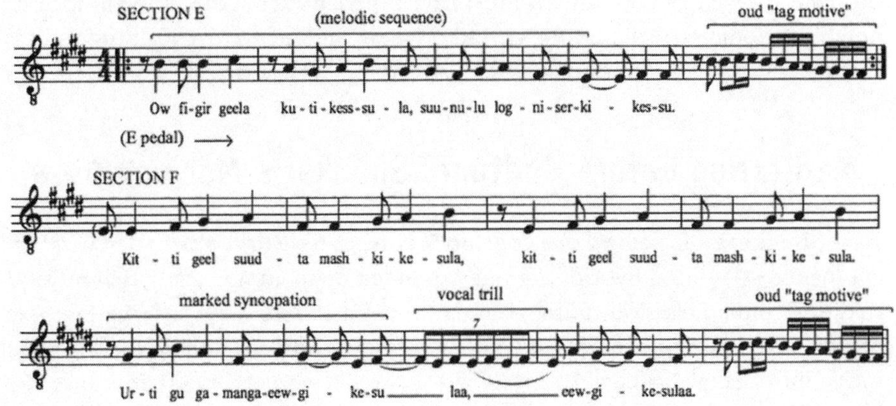


Finally, we'll note two other sections: the first is Section G (2:24): a twelve-bar passage with a B pedal which begins with an extended monotonic melody on B—quite striking in comparison to the generally stepwise contour of the other sections; the second is Section I (3:14), featuring a delightfully folklike contour followed by a striking syncopation—displayed in Figure 14.13:

Figure 14.13: Hamza El Din, "Assaramessuga"—Section I

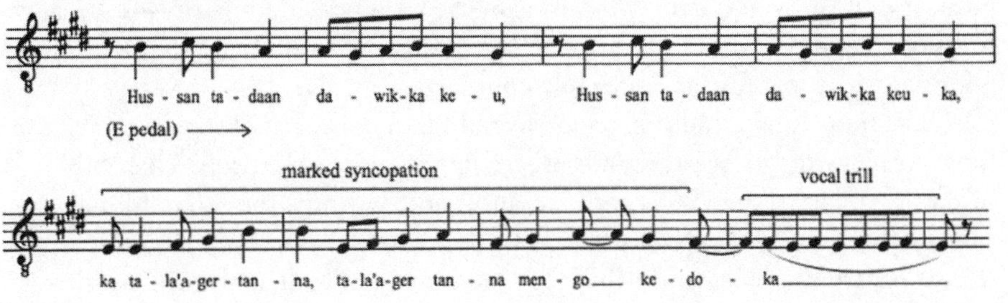


Following a recurrence of the fourteen-bar Section D' over a B pedal (3:30), the song concludes with an extended (twenty-four bars) return of Section G, staying consistently on the monotone B melody, as El Din sings a lengthy, steady **diminuendo** to the end. The complete form may thus be diagrammed as: A-A'-B-C-C'-D-C'-B'-E-E-F-D'-G-C'-H-H'-I-D'-G'; again, this is no simple ditty. The character of the vocal melody, however, is never overly ornamented, as were the Cheb Mami and Youssou N'Dour songs. Moreover, the only notes used are those of the E major scale, though without any seventh. Again, this melody is entirely original by El Din, even as it is strikingly folklike in nature. How much specifically was "lifted" from sources he heard on his donkey travels would be fascinating to know. At any rate, the folk quality is quite fitting for this song, as its lyrics recount various childhood memories—like those of gathering dates for the harvest—that El Din himself must have experienced in Nubia. In all, with its notable melodic variety, impressive oud prowess, and meditative propulsion, it is easy to see how "Assaramessuga" made Subject 6's hit parade.

## Meditation before Bedtime: Shankar's *Morning Love*

**Ravi Shankar's** ***Morning Love*** concludes Subject 6's world music day with yet another cross-cultural hybrid, but one grounded upon an unusually rich musical tradition: Indian classical music. As such, this track becomes a striking example of the naïveté—if not the hubris—of trying to bundle all non-Euro-American music into a single catchall species. With it we likewise observe that Subject 6's interest in the more "authentic" and "exotic"—less overtly touchstone—side of world music gleaned from the El Din track was, apparently, not a fluke.

### SHANKAR: BACKGROUND

Indian music is one of several broad traditions—along with Arabic, Persian, Turkish, and Chinese, to name the most dominant—that are steeped in dense history, theory, and repertoire relatively on par with Western classical. All of these, and not least Indian classical music, are complex and weighty topics that require a great deal of study and dedication to gain even a modest familiarity—especially for those raised on Western pop/rock. The rewards, of course, are well worth the effort, as with great history inevitably comes great music.

Of all those broad traditions, moreover, Indian music has probably gained the most currency in the West, thanks especially to George Harrison's championing of Ravi Shankar in the 1960s and '70s and, more recently, the international success of "Bollywood" composers like A. R. Rahman. Thus, as futile as it might be, it is worth trying to provide a thumbnail summary of Indian classical music—if nothing else, as a means to better discuss the work beloved by Subject 6.

The Indian classical music tradition extends back to the dawn of Indian culture, as a vital complement to the sacred Sanskrit texts, the four Vedas (knowledge) that form the basis of Hindu spirituality and philosophy. Much as Gregorian chant became a key vehicle to transmit Christian theology to the faithful, so too were Indian chants essential to preserving and disseminating the sacred *śruti* (revealed) literature—dating back to the second millennium BCE. Specific notated melodies appear, for example, in the *Samaveda* (song knowledge), from c. 1700 BCE, while more detailed music theory is provided in the *Natya Shastra*—an elaborate treatise on the arts written between 200 BCE and 200 CE. In the latter are various theory discussions such as the division of an octave into twenty-two tones/microtones, principles of consonance, and distinct definitions of the individual notes of the scale (*sargam*). The raga—a key melodic dimension of Indian classical music—is suggested from the third century CE in a music treatise called *Dattilam*, where they are called *jati* (musical structures).

With the introduction of Islamic rule in northern India in the thirteenth century, a decisive division was made between the Hindustani (northern) and the more insular Carnatic (southern) traditions—akin to the split in Europe between Protestant and Catholic musical practice three centuries later. The influence of Arabic practice upon Indian classical music led to the introduction of new forms (e.g., qawwali and khyal), but also to greater musical systematization of the raga tradition and the introduction of new instruments such as the sitar and the tabla. As Ravi Shankar, the composer-performer of *Morning Love*, is from the Hindustani tradition—as is most Indian music heard in the West—we will limit further musicological discussion to the Hindustani branch.

The theory/practice of Hindustani music is quite dense, but we can outline a few key principles. First among them is the raga—a system and concept of melody documented from the fifth century. The Sanskrit term means "color" or "dye," but is often aligned with mood or emotion, especially love. It is common to equate a raga with a scale in Western music, but this is not quite accurate; a better equivalence is with the ancient Greek modes as discussed by Plato and Aristotle: they are indeed a set of pitches set within an octave, but are also a prescribed manner of composition and improvisation.[626] Like the names of Greek modes, the names of many ancient ragas are derived from particular regions, and must have originated from idiomatic practices in those areas. Each raga is associated with a different emotion or affect, and even with a particular time of day and season: for instance, Raga Bhairav is associated with "awesome grandeur," and intended for performance in the morning during autumn. Musicologically, each raga is defined by a distinct set of notes (from five to nine per octave), often with different inflections (flat, natural, or sharp) depending on whether ascending or descending. But each is perhaps better defined by its first- and second-most prominent notes—*vadi* and *samavadi*, respectively—defined by (1) repetition or sustain, (2) a characteristic melodic phrase, and (3) a specific approach to microtonal inflection. There are eighty-four common ragas, with six considered "primary."

A second fundamental element of Hindustani music is the rhythmic concept of tala. The Sanskrit term means "clap" and refers to the rhythmic cycles that underlie a composition. It is common to align tala with Western meter, but a better analogy is to the medieval rhythmic modes: distinct patterns of grouped rhythms that form a larger, repeating cycle.[627] In the case of the tala, these cycles consist of individual beats that are grouped into a small number of phrases that each consist of two, three, four, or five beats, proceeding in a generally inconsistent pattern. For example, the Jhaptal tala comprises ten beats divided into four phrases of 2+3+2+3 beats. This rhythmic construct of the tala is repeated throughout a composition, or section thereof, with the "downbeat" (*sam*) emphasized to ensure clarity for the melodic performers. However, much as the ragas do not prescribe the specific ways in which the defined notes and phrases can be performed, the talas allow for nearly limitless variety in how the individual beats or phrases may be expressed or subdivided, especially during fast, virtuosic solo sections. There are some 350 talas in Hindustani music, of which only ten are common.

Actual performance details then reveal other key elements of Hindustani music. Given its aesthetic ties to sacred and spiritual texts, the original and "purest" mode of performance of Indian classical music is vocal. As such, the key melodic instruments featured in Hindustani music—the sitar (plucked string), sarod (Indian lute), and sarangi (bowed string)—were developed and are celebrated by virtue of their ability to emulate the human voice.

Most large-scale performances, such as of the popular dhrupad genre, are divided into two principal parts: the first, called the alap, is itself generally divided into three sections: (1) alap—a long improvisatory, rubato section; (2) jor (instrumental) or nomtom (vocal)—a section with a slow, simple rhythm; and (3) jhala—a fast, concluding section, where an active rhythmic accompaniment often overwhelms the melodic material. Not surprisingly, this last is where the percussion—especially the tabla (Indian "bongos")—is featured. The alap is then followed by the gat, a fixed, sectional composition—usually defined by a repeated refrain separated by improvisational passages. The ragas and talas to be used are predetermined, whereby key structural and performance expectations are set. They establish not only the mood and character of the work, but also the parameters by which both fixed and improvised elements may be introduced—including the use of microtonal inflections, slides and ornaments, and opportunities for soloing.

As cursory and incomplete as the above summary may be, it does allow us to review Shankar's composition *Morning Love* with a degree of grounding that would have been impossible had we just "jumped in." But first, an admittedly brief word about its extraordinary composer-performer:

Ravi Shankar (1920–2012) grew up in the holy city of Varanasi, along the river Ganges. He studied dance as a child, but turned his attention to the sitar after hearing the great sarodist Allauddin Khan. He was invited by Khan to study with him in Maihar, in central India, thereby becoming part of the latter's esteemed *gharana* (musical "school" or community); in this way, Shankar participated in a system of musical apprenticeship dating back to the Mughal invasion in the sixteenth century, where a local prince would patronize each "school"—not unlike the noble cappella (chapel) system in the West.[628] In so doing, he was obliged to follow a highly intensive, ten-year regimen likewise undertaken by Khan's son, the celebrated sarodist Ali Akbar Khan; Shankar and the younger Khan became lifelong friends, and performed and recorded together often. Shankar's success from the early 1950s was marked by his placement as music director

at All India Radio, and by increasing invitations to concertize in the West. As noted, Shankar went on to become a pivotal figure in introducing Indian classical music to Western audiences. His impact goes back to a set of US and European tours in the late 1950s, and especially via his collaborations with such Western artists as George Harrison, violinist Yehudi Menuhin, and flutist Jean-Pierre Rampal. A testament to Shankar's embrace in the West was his appearance at both the Monterey Pop (1967) and Woodstock (1969) festivals.

## SHANKAR: ANALYSIS

*Morning Love* is one of several works written by Shankar that reveal his own interest in fusing Indian classical with Western practices—including two concertos for sitar and orchestra and even a "symphony." Shankar never formally studied European classical music (as Hamza El Din did, for example), but his many interactions with Western musicians—ranging from Harrison to Menuhin to Philip Glass to John Coltrane—had certainly exposed him to non-Indian concepts of harmony, rhythm, instrumentation, and performance. *Morning Love* is one of two collaborations with French classical flutist Jean-Pierre Rampal, both of which stem from 1976.[629] Interestingly, Shankar's introduction of *Morning Love* to Rampal was not, as might be expected, with sheet music, but the old-fashioned way: by ear!

The twelve-minute recording of *Morning Love* features sitar, flute, tabla, and tanpura—a long-necked plucked string instrument that, as is typical, sustains a drone throughout. Although predominantly grounded in Hindustani tradition, *Morning Love* also makes several interesting accommodations to Western practice. Beyond the obvious inclusion of the Western flute, these include especially the ragas and talas chosen for the work, as well as aspects of its formal identity.

Beginning with its form, *Morning Love* comprises both an alap and a gat. The alap, however, contains only two subsections, the alap and the jor, dispensing with the lively—and often rhythmically complex—jhala section. The initial, rubato alap subsection is itself divided into two distinct parts: first featuring the sitar, then the flute, thereby announcing their rather juxtaposed partnership. The jor, however, features only the sitar, in what is likely an improvised section by Shankar; Rampal does not improvise at all in the work. Throughout the opening alap supersection, the tabla is silent, somewhat unusual for a jor—wherein a steady (duple) beat may be heard.

Following the conclusion of the jor, however, is an extended passage f tabla alone, performed by Alla Rakha, a frequent collaborator of Shankar' demonstrating a fair degree of virtuosity. While this might seem unremark to Western ears—like a drum solo in a jazz performance—it is in fact highl characteristic of Indian classical music, where the tabla is expected to maint accompanying role. Despite the backlash Shankar received for this breach

conservative Hindustani musicians, he frequently allotted solos to his tabla players even in India, to the crowd's delight—resulting in the subsequent fame of tabla players like Zakir Hussain. It was perhaps Shankar's interaction with jazz musicians like Coltrane in the early 1960s that alerted him to such performance possibilities.

The gat that follows is considerably longer, and is in a form known as *raga-mala* (garland of ragas), a juxtaposition of related ragas in a manner that resembles theme and variations—affirming the universality of this musical archetype. More specifically, the form here is a kind of rondo or, even better, a ritornello (such as used in a Baroque concerto grosso)—where the ritornello "refrain" returns frequently but often not in its complete form. Between returns of the refrain are no fewer than sixteen "episodes" that occasionally shift away from the original (dominant) raga of the composition. The episodes build in intensity toward the end—both in the speed of notes played by the sitar and flute and by their ever-quickening exchange. Helping to heighten the intensity here as well is a second tabla solo prior to the final episode-refrain (at 10:26), wherein a second tala is introduced. For the more diligent listeners among you, the WYLI website (supplement to Chapter 14) includes a detailed table with timings of each subdivision noted above—including the many exchanges between gat "refrains" and "episodes."

The lengths of the gat episodes vary widely, from two seconds (Episodes 11–15, 8:46 to 9:08) to considerably longer (e.g., thirty-five seconds for Episode 3, 5:35 to 6:10; and one minute, five seconds, for Episode 16a, prior to the second tabla solo). The refrains too vary from two complete cycles (Refrain 1, 4:24 to 4:42) to two-second fragments of one cycle (Refrains 11–15, 8:44 to 9:02). These latter, and especially with equally short episodes, are what build tension toward the end. Identifying the main theme of the gat, therefore, is critical to an informed listening experience, and to understanding the form and performance flow of the work as a whole. Before discussing that, however, a brief word about the ragas and talas used in the work:

The principal raga used in *Morning Love*, as indeed the track title announces, is Raga Nata Bhairav (or Natabhairavi). This is already something unusual, as it is not a Hindustani raga, but a Carnatic (southern Indian) one. Shankar had become acquainted with the Carnatic practice somewhat, but was by no means an expert. It is thus not surprising that he bypassed some musicological aspects normally aligned with this Carnatic raga—such as the emphasized notes (*vadi*, *samavadi*), rules of ascending or descending notes, or traditional phrases. So why would he choose this raga? Its basic notes are as follows (Figure 14.14):

**Figure 14.14: Raga Nata Bhairav (Carnatic scale)—primary melodic basis of *Morning Love***

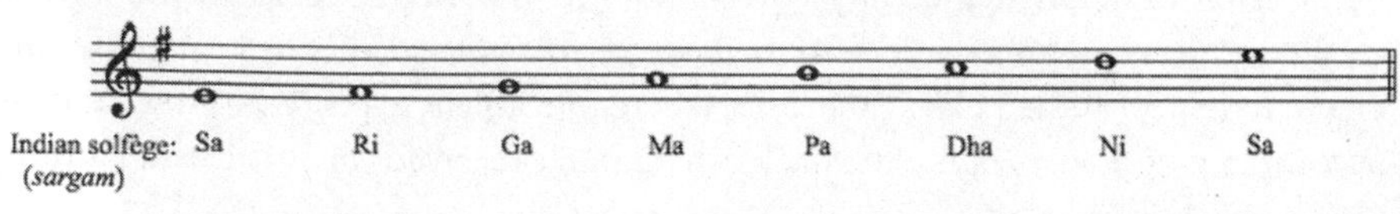

As may be obvious, these notes are the same ones as in a Western minor scale, or more specifically the Aeolian mode—in this case, starting on E: E–F♯–G–A–B–C–D–E'. By centering his composition on this raga, Shankar ensured that Rampal would be interacting with a modal language he and Western listeners knew well—as opposed to some ragas that involve unusual or "exotic" intervals.* This does not mean, however, that Shankar is at all limited to those seven notes, much as a Western composer is not limited to the notes of the major or minor scale to which his or her composition's key is aligned. Some level of chromaticism does indeed appear throughout *Morning Love*, even pronounced at times, but inevitably the melodies return to those of the principal raga. Further, as suggested by the *ragamala* form, the gat introduces several other ragas as it proceeds. These shifts in ragas are very much akin to modulation in Western music—changing from one key to another, and just as a good modulation requires preparation, so too is Shankar careful to prepare the change from one raga to another—generally by repeating a "pivoting" note prior to the shift. Specifically, the gat introduces three other ragas, as follows (Figures 14.15a–c):

**Figures 14.15a–c: Secondary ragas used as melodic basis of *Morning Love***

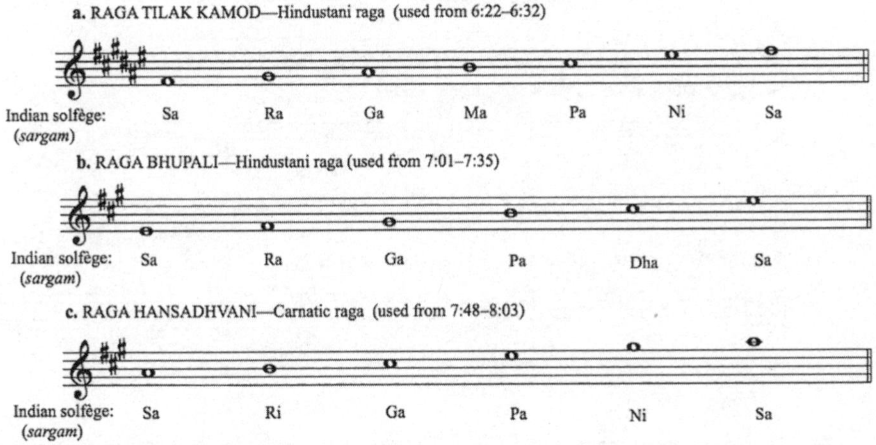


Not surprisingly, these ragas too have a direct frame of reference to Western music: the Raga Tilak Kamod (from 6:22, Episode 4) is like a major scale without the sixth degree; the Raga Bhupali (from 7:01, within Episode 5) is the familiar major pentatonic scale; and the Raga Hansadhvani (from 7:48, Episode 6) is likewise similar to a major scale, without the fourth and sixth degrees. The modal affinity between East and West in these ragas thus allowed for a natural and seamless interaction between the sitar and flute as they continuously bat the melodic spotlight back and forth.

---

* An example of an "exotic" raga is the Raga Bhupal Todi, whose notes—starting on C—are: C–D♭–E♭–G–A♭–C♭.

Moving now to rhythm, the talas used in *Morning Love* likewise reflect an accommodating stance to an East-West interchange. While, as noted above, many Hindustani talas are metrically complex, Shankar here utilizes two simple talas that are correlated directly to common Western meters. The principal tala, used through most of the gat, is the Dadra tala, whose metric identity is 3+3—corresponding to the Western meter of 6/8, a "compound duple" meter, with two strong beats each divided into three subbeats. As will be discussed below, however, the dominant meter actually heard once the gat refrain melody begins is not 6/8, but rather its metric cognate 3/4. The Dadra tala is then interrupted briefly by the Kaharwa tala: an eight-beat cycle divided into two subcycles of 4+4—corresponding to the common Western meter of 4/4. The Kaharwa tala begins with the second tabla solo (10:16) and continues until the final refrain returns with the original Dadra tala (11:36) to conclude the work. It is important to note, though, that Shankar's use of "simple" talas should not be seen to suggest that the rhythmic language of *Morning Love* is itself simple. Although the listener can clearly hear the equivalent Western meters of 6/8, 3/4, and 4/4 throughout the gat, there is no shortage of intricate syncopation, and especially hemiolas (3 against 2) in the musical discourse (Figures 14.16a–b):

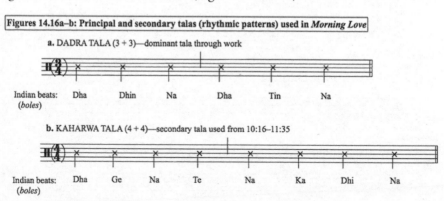

**Figures 14.16a–b: Principal and secondary talas (rhythmic patterns) used in *Morning Love***

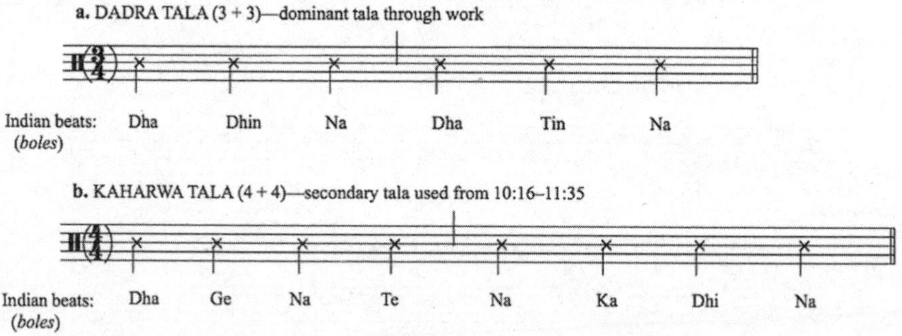


A fourth key element to detail here is the actual refrain melody that defines the gat. The complete refrain is eight "measures" long—each measure corresponding to one full cycle of the Dadra tala. As seen in the figure below, the most practical way to transcribe the theme is not in 6/8 but rather 3/4—with three strong beats of two subbeats each; since both 6/8 and 3/4 consist of six eighth notes per measure, alternating between them does not alter the disposition of the notes themselves. Indeed, this marks a defining element of the work—a **polymetric** interplay of a 6/8 rhythm in the tabla against a 3/4 melody in the sitar and flute, somewhat akin to what we saw in Wayne Shorter's "Footprints" or Armin van Buuren's "Embrace." Here is the complete refrain (Figure 14.17):

**Figure 14.17: Ravi Shankar, *Morning Love*—complete refrain of the gat section**

As noted in the formal discussion above, the entire gat is composed of an elaborate alternation between this eight-bar refrain melody and contrasting episodes, each of varying length. The refrain is initially repeated twice in its entirety, and is thereafter presented in lengths shorter than that—though always from the beginning. As the gat progresses, and especially from Refrain 8 (8:19), the length of the refrain becomes in fact quite short—first four "measures" long, and then, from Refrain 11 (8:44), only two "measures." Shankar, however, maintains clarity for the listener in this exchange by virtue of the strong character of the refrain's opening—much as J. S. Bach does in the ritornelli of his *Brandenburg* Concertos, for example. From section to section, the sitar and flute perform either together or as alternating soloists. In defining this narrative, Shankar introduces tremendous variety and unpredictability in terms of which formal element is presented, its length, and its level of virtuosity.

Naturally, much more detail could be provided in analyzing *Morning Love*, though you're likely reaching a capacity point by now. Before finishing up, however, it is worth elaborating on how all of this interplays with Indian classical as opposed to Western practices. We've already noted Shankar's use of the European flute and his choices of "Western-friendly" ragas and talas. One other Western element, however, is actually at odds with Indian classical practice: the simultaneous sounding of both the sitar and flute. Traditionally, such simultaneous playing would occur only "by accident" at the transition points between two solo passages (e.g., from sitar to sarod), since Hindustani music—like so many non-Western practices—is fundamentally monophonic. In *Morning Love*, however, Shankar introduces the gat refrain straightaway in octave unison and then intersperses this texture in numerous subsequent refrains and episodes (e.g., from 4:42 in Episode 1; from 6:10 in Refrain 4). Further, he places the two instruments in other simultaneous textures as well: in oblique (nonmoving against moving, e.g., from 6:22 in Episode 4), contrary (from 9:41 in Episode 16a), and even parallel (e.g., from 9:49 and from 10:06 in Episode 16a) motion. Figures 14.18a–c show a few of these examples:

**Figures 14.18a–c: Ravi Shankar, *Morning Love*—examples of simultaneous counterpoint between flute and sitar**

a. Oblique motion (from 6:22)

b. Contrary motion (from 9:41)

c. Parallel motion (from 9:49)

At the same time, Shankar does not dispense with elements that are fundamentally based on Hindustani practice—quite the contrary. Traditional Indian elements include—beyond the basic instrumentation, formal construct, and use of traditional ragas and talas—the specific manner in which melodic chromaticism (e.g., from 5:39 in Episode 3) and complex or hemiola-based syncopation (in the jor section, e.g., from 7:01 in Episode 5) is expressed. These syncopations often occur within the contexts of melodic sequences (repeating patterns at different pitch levels), a technique indeed as intrinsic to Indian as it is to Western musical practice. It is not for nothing, moreover, that these complex Hindustani elements generally, though not exclusively, take place during Shankar's sitar solo sections, many of which were likely improvised. Yet another traditional aspect is the use of the tihai—a thrice-repeated rhythmic cadence often placed just prior to gat refrains (e.g., from 7:32, just prior to Refrain 6). Figures 14.19a–c show a few such examples:

**Figures 14.19a–c: Ravi Shankar, *Morning Love*—examples of melodic material in episodes**

**a.** Mild chromaticism in Episode 3 (from 5:39)

**b.** Rhythmic complexity in Episode 5 (from 7:01)

**c.** Elaborate melodic material, including use of "tihai" (concluding cadence) in Episode 5 (from 7:27)

With this decidedly involved analysis, the reader will recognize the richness and complexity of this final world music track. For a listener inclined to this music, such as Subject 6, there is much to commend it and to draw the ear's attention: a variety of instrumental sounds and textures, impressive displays of virtuosity, modal definition and variety, melodic chromaticism, rhythmic dynamism and syncopation, a well-articulated formal plan, strong thematic material and manipulation, etc., etc. Beyond that, moreover, is the palpable spiritual component inherent in this kind of musical discourse, whereby Subject 6 would indeed have a fulfilling pre-bedtime listening experience.

## Insights Gained about Subject 6's Musical Taste

With these five diverse tracks—the four discussed here plus the fifth (Afro Celt Sound System's "Release")—what conclusions can be drawn about the musical genotype of Subject 6? To a degree, the mere fact that Subject 6 (presumably raised in the West) is drawn to "world music" suggests a degree of open-mindedness and adventurousness toward musical style and discourse that is rather outside the norm. This does not mean that Subject 6 would be unmoved by more "traditional" Western music, whether popular or art, but simply that the more "exotic" approaches to music making are particularly appreciated. At the same time, by these five tracks alone a certain limit to Subject 6's taste spectrum can be discerned. Although there are ample demonstrations of indigenous musical elements from non-Euro-American traditions, all five examples to one degree or another reveal a connection to Western music—ranging from more demonstrative in "Release" and "Birima" to subtler in *Morning Love* and "Assaramessuga." Absent, for example, are fully uninfluenced tracks, such as might come from the Tuvan throat singing, Pakistani qawwali, or Chinese opera traditions. Indeed, the breadth of global music represented here is fairly circumscribed: with musical practices limited to the Middle East, West Africa, and North India, plus a dash of Celtic in "Release."

Musicologically, Subject 6 seems particularly motivated by songs or works with a strong and consistent rhythmic drive—indeed, music that one can dance to, as is the case with a great deal of "world fusion." Likewise apparent is a fondness for sophisticated and idiosyncratic melodic construction, including the use of unusual modes, heavy ornamentation, and even microtones. Not particularly required, on the other hand, is a sophisticated approach to harmony, as chromatic chordal or even melodic harmony is limited—notably in *Morning Love*. Formal complexity is by no means obligatory (e.g., the simple forms of "Youm Wara Youm" and "Birima"), though neither is it out-of-bounds (e.g., the complexity of "Assaramessuga" and *Morning Love*). Finally, as is obvious, a broad affection for "exotic" sonorities—both vocal and instrumental—seems to be at play in defining Subject 6's musical taste.

If we think about other tracks Subject 6 might appreciate, we can safely start with related works by the same artists—here addressing only the four songs discussed in the chapter. We might list "Haoulou" (Mami); "Sagal ko" (N'Dour); "Shortunga" (El Din); and *Raga Piloo*, for sitar and violin (Shankar).

Moving to the next level, we can imagine a favorable response to tracks by other artists occupying a similar musical space: "C'est la vie" by Cheb Khaled or "Abdel Kader" by Rachid Taha (Mami); "Taar Doucey" by Ismaël Lô or "Salmanimmo" by Baaba Maal (N'Dour); "Umri ma bansa—Soudan" by Abdel Gadir Salim or "Nouba" by Ali Hassan Kuban (El Din); or *Raga Hemant* by Paul Livingstone or "Taaruf" by Tabla Beat Science (Shankar). In truth, identifying actual parallels to several of these artists/tracks is no mean feat, as in most cases (except perhaps Cheb Mami) the hybrid approach taken is rather idiosyncratically rendered. But such is the joy—and rewarding challenge—of exercising your musical taste!

Extending yet further into Subject 6's taste potential, we turn to influences on and/or "heirs" to the artists and composers involved: Bellemou Messaoud and Cheb Houssem (Mami); Raam Daan and Wally Ballago Seck (N'Dour); Khedr El-Attar and Alsarah and the Nubatones (El Din); and Allauddin Khan and Shakti with John McLaughlin (Shankar).

Finally, a much wider range of music may be suggested if we extend the musicological references to realms beyond world music: Mariah Carey or Handel oratorios (heavy vocal ornamentation); Bobby McFerrin or Verdi operas (vocal virtuosity); Joe Satriani or Andrés Segovia (string instrument virtuosity); Hubert Laws or Jethro Tull (flute solo); Woody Guthrie or Aaron Copland (folk-influenced song); troubadour songs or La Monte Young (drone-based music); or Claude Bolling or Emerson, Lake, and Palmer (stylistic cross-intersection). The list could certainly go on, and no small amount of trial and error would be required to identify which remote musicological connections might find resonance. Chances are, though, that given Subject 6's hit parade, a potentially wide musical net may be confidently cast.

World music has warranted such a detailed discussion by virtue of both its broad-ranging traditions and its general unfamiliarity to most Western music lovers. As noted throughout this book, musical appreciation can only increase as one becomes better acquainted with the "backstory" and internal workings of a given song or work—and especially if one is previously unfamiliar with the underlying style or approach. It is worth taking note of the minor miracle that we humans can gain appreciation and indeed pleasure from a completely foreign musical discourse even with no prior experience. Contrast this with the lack of appreciation that would come from purely spoken discourse in a foreign language—as discussed in Interlude E, for example. That said, there can be no doubt that the more we understand and the more we dive "under the hood" of the music we are enjoying, the greater that potential appreciation and pleasure can be.

*fifteen*

# THE CLASSICAL GENOTYPE

## Introducing Subject 7

Subject 7 finishes breakfast and heads to work with earbuds on, arriving in a state of confidence with the **opening Allegro from Antonio Vivaldi's Concerto for Four Violins, Op. 3, no. 10**. After a more exhausting day than usual, the travel home requires the uplifting grandeur of the second movement, **Allegretto, from Ludwig van Beethoven's Symphony no. 7 in A, Op. 92**. A pair of tickets to the symphony pays off especially with the programming of a longtime favorite, the **Overture to Leonard Bernstein's *Candide***. Finally, unwinding for bed, Subject 7 puts on a soothing gem, the third movement, **Sicilienne, from Gabriel Fauré's *Pelléas et Mélisande*, Op. 80**.*

Based on these hits, Subject 7 may be revealed as a well-seasoned fan of classical music. At the same time, the selections display Subject 7 as embracing a fairly well-heeled slice of this species. While mainly remote from "light" or "pop" classical, all can be considered "warhorses," or close. Further, a preference for instrumental, indeed orchestral, music can be gleaned, as none of the four works cited above is vocal.[630]

Before diving deeper into these works, a brief review of this species:

## The Classical Species: A Brief Review

As with pop, rock, and jazz, we've already touched upon several historical and descriptive elements of classical music in previous chapters. Moreover, with a thousand-plus years of history, providing a short summary is a near-impossible endeavor, as it was with Indian classical music. Indeed, Western classical has a

---

* Subject 7's fifth work, heard during a pre-breakfast jog, is the opening movement, "O Fortuna" from Carl Orff's *Carmina Burana*. For its discussion, see the WYLI website, supplement to Chapter 15.

dimensional scope even beyond that of non-Western traditions, by virtue of the massive extant written repertoire going back to at least the tenth century—that and an unparalleled amount of academic scholarship going back centuries, and growing by the day. As noted above, it is this massive scope that in part makes classical music so intimidating to those with little or no background with it. Let us work to undo that intimidation!

First up, of course, is my attempt—inevitably imperfect—to list ten touchstone works that can be argued to typify the classical music species; at a minimum, these are works that a casual listener might recognize as exemplifying "classical music":

Samuel Barber, *Adagio for Strings* (1936)
Sergei Rachmaninov, *Rhapsody on a Theme of Paganini*, Variation 18 (1934)
Edvard Grieg, "In the Hall of the Mountain King" (from *Peer Gynt* Suite, 1876)
Richard Wagner, "Ride of the Valkyries" (from *Die Walküre*, 1870)
Frédéric Chopin, Nocturne in E♭, Op. 9 (1832)
Franz Schubert, *Unfinished Symphony*, 1. Allegro moderato (1822)
Ludwig van Beethoven, *Moonlight* Sonata (1801)
Wolfgang Amadeus Mozart, *Eine kleine Nachtmusik*, 1. Allegro (1787)
George Frideric Handel, "Hallelujah" Chorus (from *Messiah*, 1741)
Johannes Pachelbel, Canon and Gigue in D ("Pachelbel's Canon," c. 1700)

All of these works—or, in most cases, movements of larger works—are classical "warhorses"—meaning they are critically respected, yet also hugely popular, even among nonclassical fans. At the same time, these ten are decidedly limited in scope vis-à-vis the broader classical repertoire, not unlike what we saw with the world music touchstones. For example, neither modality nor atonality is represented, since all were written in the more "accessible" harmonic language of tonality—even the two works composed *after* the so-called "common practice" period (1650–1900). Despite such limitations, however, these works are as good as any to prompt a general or "casual" summary of the musicological aspects of the classical species.

As noted, the harmony—the scales, chords, modulation, etc.—in all of these works is grounded in the functional language of tonality. At the same time, they may be seen as undergoing a steady evolution through their 230-year span: from fairly diatonic (Pachelbel, Handel, Mozart) to quite chromatic (Wagner, Rachmaninov, Barber); as with EDM, the primary sonority in these selections is instrumental, except the Handel, showcasing especially a string-based orchestra and/or a solo piano; melodic material, though quite varied in character, is often lyrical and sustained, though at times vibrant and energetic—as in the Mozart, Wagner, and Grieg; rhythm in these works is mostly fluid and straightforward, with only occasional use of syncopation—primarily in support of dramatic moments, as in the Schubert; all of these works, moreover, are consistently in 3/4 or 4/4 meter—except for the quasi-rubato Barber;* and although the formal designs vary considerably among these ten works (canon, sonata, theme and variations, ternary, etc.), all adopt an ambitious scope in service of an aesthetic grounded in drama and emotional expression.

Much as occurred with the Indian "classical" music tradition, we can trace a broad trend in the underlying foundation of Western classical production and patronage: from sacred to princely to bourgeoisie. During the **Medieval era** (5th–14th c.), the Catholic Church was the principal source of both patronage and musical subject matter via vocal settings of sacred texts: chant, organum, motets, Mass movements, etc. Secular music under princely patronage, however, was by no means absent in this period—in genres such as the chanson and secular motet. During the Renaissance and Baroque eras (15th–early 18th c.), the tide shifted gradually from sacred to secular, and from church to princely support, though all dimensions thrived—via genres such as the motet, Mass cycle, chanson, opera, oratorio, fugue, concerto, and sonata. As these latter few genres demonstrate as well, this period saw a gradual shift in emphasis from vocal to instrumental music.

During the Classical and Romantic eras (late 18th–19th c.), the trend toward secular music escalated, as patronage shifted from the princely court to the middle-class citizenry—via "popular" genres such as the symphony, concerto, sonata, opera, and song cycle. Finally, during the **Modern** and **Contemporary eras** (20th c.–today) the increasingly complex and variegated discourse of classical music (primarily secular) resulted in a steady decrease in its popular support, relegating it more and more to a marginal—if not "museum"—realm, much as may be said of post-1960s jazz.

These same historical periods/genres also witnessed a number of broad musicological trends. Key among them was a gradual shift from a monophonic to a polyphonic texture—from single-line chant and song to two-, three-, and four-part vocal genres—between the eleventh and fourteenth centuries. Initially, the relationship between the simultaneous polyphonic voices was governed purely by rules of consonance and dissonance, as the prevailing orientation was still horizontal (melodic) rather than vertical. This began to change, slowly, from the later fifteenth century, finally becoming codified in the seventeenth century as a system of vertical harmony, or chords. In turn, the structural and theoretical relationship between these chords became standardized in a shift away from the

* Technically, Wagner's "Ride of the Valkyries" is written in 9/8 meter—which to most ears is indistinguishable from 3/4 meter with eighth-note triplets.

older—horizontal—modal system to the newer—vertical—tonal system, and a set of twenty-four major and minor keys.

Through the eighteenth and especially nineteenth centuries, this vertical tonal system became increasingly complex via a chromatic, as opposed to diatonic, approach to harmony. Such, moreover, was accompanied—and inspired—by an ever more potent emotive and extramusical orientation, complemented in part by creative orchestration. This intensifying chromaticism eventually led, from the early twentieth century, to the demise of the tonal system—at least for many composers in the classical tradition. The result was the rise of various atonal, often dissonant approaches, to the chagrin of many music lovers. In turn, "secondary" or sound-based parameters—e.g., instrumental and vocal timbre, dynamics, tempo, etc.—often came to the fore as the main focus of musical discourse. Today, a many-splendored palette of musical and aesthetic possibilities lies open to the classical composer—and fan—including via intersection with *any* other music style or approach: popular, jazz, or world.

Finally, a word about the actual word "classical" to describe this species: many (myself included) bemoan its use to subsume everything from a hymn by Hildegard van Bingen to a symphony by Mahler to an electronic piece by Morton Subotnick—much as David Byrne complained about using "world music" to embrace every brand of non-Euro-American music. Leonard Bernstein famously vetted the various options to supplant "classical" in his "What Is Classical Music?" lecture (1959)—in turn rejecting "good," "serious," "high-brow," "art," "symphony," and even "long-hair" as equally unsatisfying.[631] For Bernstein, what distinguished the realm was not the name, but the fastidiousness with which a composer notates every conceivable element of the music's performance, but that too is easily debunked. The use of "classical" to represent the entire Western tradition from medieval to contemporary can be traced back to the 1880s, as music that had "withstood the test of time" (this, by the way, is distinct from the word "Classical" to delineate the era of Haydn and Mozart, which dates to the 1830s).[632] I personally tend to prefer "art music," while likewise recognizing the inherent bias the term implies: Is not much jazz or rock, etc., also artful? Thus, alas, it's probably best for us to stick with the word "classical."

## The Ride to Work: Vivaldi's Concerto for Four Violins, Op. 3, no. 10

**The opening Allegro from Antonio Vivaldi's Concerto for Four Violins in B Minor, Op. 3, no. 10,** firmly suggests that Subject 7's musical genotype extends beyond the "pop" side of classical music—as might have been reasonably argued solely from Subject 7's morning jog "hit," Carl Orff's "O Fortuna" (see the WYLI website, supplement to Chapter 15). That latter argument would have become stronger had Subject 7 chosen to enhance the morning commute with the "Spring" concerto from Vivaldi's *Four Seasons*—one of the most ubiquitous works in the classical repertory. But the twelve concertos of Opus 3 may be considered "well-known" only to those fairly steeped in the repertoire of Vivaldi and the Baroque era in general. Indeed, they are widely regarded as being of great historical significance to the evolution of the Baroque concerto, as we'll discuss below, yet it is relatively unlikely (not impossible, of course) that Subject 7 would have come to favor this particular concerto without at least a bit of time spent in the late-Baroque corner of "classical land."

## VIVALDI: BACKGROUND

Antonio Vivaldi (1678–1741) is among the most frequently performed and recorded of all classical composers. He likewise holds sway with the "experts" as among the most influential composers in Western music history, especially in the Baroque era.[633] His appeal, moreover, speaks to the broad enthusiasm for music of the latter third of the Baroque (c. 1700–1750) among classical music fans—even those who otherwise keep their distance from the species. The reasons for this enthusiasm, of course, are complex and subjective, but may include factors such as the era's rich, evolved state of tonal harmony, its pervasive yet accessible employment of counterpoint, and its florid yet graceful approach to string writing. As much as anyone, Vivaldi may be credited with cultivating these and related developments—and with writing a good deal of cherished music in the process.

Vivaldi spent most of his career in Venice, which had been a nexus of musical innovation and flowering since the late sixteenth century. Indeed, the seismic shift from the musical Renaissance to the Baroque era was to a large degree exercised in "La Serenissima," as was the wealthy Republic of Venice commonly referred.

In particular, the city's main cathedral, St. Mark's Basilica, employed a string of composers—Giovanni Gabrieli and Claudio Monteverdi chief among them—who played decisive roles in ushering in those dramatic musical changes of the early seventeenth century: a shift from a modal, predominantly polyphonic orientation to an incipient tonal one built on vertical harmony. Over the ensuing decades, composers, especially from Italy, indulged in a flurry of experimentation on a variety of musical fronts—harmony, form, instrumentation, and genre. Among the most impactful, certainly, was the rise of the purely instrumental forms of the sonata and concerto, by composers such as Alessandro Stradella, Giuseppe Torelli, and Arcangelo Corelli. It was these developments that in turn laid the foundation for Vivaldi's innovations and acute originality in the early eighteenth century.

From age twenty-four to a year before his death at age sixty-three, Vivaldi worked—in fits and starts—for the Pio Ospedale della Pietà (Devout Orphanage of Mercy). This was one of four major orphanages in Venice that thrived under aristocratic support, and that specifically cultivated the musical talent of orphaned girls. Vivaldi provided musical instruction as the *maestro di violino* (violin teacher) and later as *maestro di coro* (music director). As part of his duties, he also wrote a steady stream of sonatas and concertos for the Ospedale's weekly musical services, which were a social highlight for the Venetian nobility. Vivaldi likewise cultivated relationships with patrons outside Venice—including with Grand Prince Ferdinand of Tuscany, who likewise patronized Handel and Alessandro Scarlatti, to whom he dedicated the Opus 3 concertos. Their publication in 1711 catapulted Vivaldi's fame throughout Italy and into Northern Europe—even influencing J. S. Bach, as we'll see—and helped establish a new template for the concerto. Other prominent publications followed—including *Il cimento dell'armonia e dell'inventione* (The Contest Between Harmony and Invention, 1725), the first four concertos of which are those of *The Four Seasons.*

Beyond his impressive instrumental output—five hundred concertos and one hundred sonatas—Vivaldi was also a prolific composer of vocal music, including many sacred Masses, motets, and cantatas. He was, in fact, an ordained priest—famously nicknamed "*il prete rosso*" (the red priest), a reference to his crimson hair. Yet he rarely performed any priestly duties, mainly on account of his demanding composing schedule; allegations of a decades-long romantic affair with soprano Anna Girò, on other hand, have never been proven. Vivaldi's worldly predilections are better revealed by his zealous efforts as an opera composer and impresario—writing around fifty operas and producing another forty by other composers. His success in the theater was mixed at best, and by his final years few of his operas were receiving extended or repeat performance, in Venice or elsewhere. It is worth noting, moreover, that none of Vivaldi's operas can be said to be part of today's standard repertoire.

By the time of his death in 1741, not only Vivaldi's operas but also his instrumental music had fallen out of favor. Within a few decades, his music was all but forgotten. Even the *Four Seasons* concertos were unknown by the 1760s. It was only in the wake of the rediscovery of J. S. Bach's music in the 1830s that musicologists and composers began to investigate Vivaldi's output—and initially only by virtue of his influence on Bach. That changed in the 1920s and '30s, when more and more of Vivaldi's manuscripts were rediscovered and concerts of his music promoted—such as the famed "Vivaldi Week" concerts produced in 1939 by Italian composer Alfredo Casella, with help by poet Ezra Pound. The rest, as they say, is history.

## VIVALDI: ANALYSIS

The Concerto in B Minor stems, as has been noted, from Vivaldi's collection of twelve concertos, Opus 3, entitled *L'estro armonico*, or "Harmonic Fancy."[634] Granting such colorful names to published musical collections was typical of the era, and of Vivaldi in particular—who commonly named even individual concertos after performers, moods, musical techniques, etc. Publisher Estienne

Roger issued *L'estro armonico* not in Venice but in Amsterdam in 1711. It was a resounding international success, so much so that it was reprinted twice: in London (1715) and again in Amsterdam (by Roger in 1717). Following its publication, composers from across Italy, as well as from Germany, streamed into Venice to study with Vivaldi. Soon the techniques he employed in Opus 3 became "normal practice" for concertos across Europe. Significantly, J. S. Bach was so taken with the collection as to transcribe five of the concertos for either solo keyboard (harpsichord or organ) or, in the case of No. 10 in B minor (Subject 7's pick), for four harpsichords and strings.

To be sure, Vivaldi did not realize the new standards of the concerto out of whole cloth. As suggested above, a great deal of experimentation preceded the "perfection" he achieved in Opus 3, as is nearly always the case in art. Indeed, most of the elements employed in Vivaldi's Opus 3 concertos had precedent in works by earlier composers. The concerto genre is built out of the principle of contrast or "benign rivalry" between distinct groups of musicians. It finds precedent, for example, in the antiphonal (back-and-forth) polychoral works written at St. Mark's Basilica by Andrea Gabrieli and his more famous nephew, Giovanni, in the late sixteenth century.

By the 1670s, Alessandro Stradella was specifying instrumentation for a small group of soloists—*concertino*—in contrast to an accompanying ensemble—*concerto grosso* (large consort)—from which the new genre name arose. More consequential were the innovations of Giuseppe Torelli, notably in his Concerti Grossi, Op. 8. There, two key elements are introduced: the use of the ritornello technique—a recurring, multitheme tutti (full-ensemble) "refrain" interrupted by solo episodes—and a three-movement structure alternating fast-slow-fast. Vivaldi adopted and standardized both elements, yet also added other innovations that would make his Opus 3, to quote biographer Michael Talbot, "perhaps the most influential collection of instrumental music to appear during the whole eighteenth century."[635]

Subject 7's "fave" among the twelve concertos of *L'estro armonico*, No. 10 in B minor, is certainly a fine and distinguished representative—not least the opening Allegro, on which we'll focus. The concerto as a whole is often singled out in modern discussions of the collection, as it was even in Vivaldi's own day.[636] And as noted above, it served as the model for Bach's Concerto for Four Harpsichords, BWV 1065[637] *—the only harpsichord concerto not adapted from Bach's own original music.

Vivaldi's Concerto No. 10 in B Minor is scored for four solo violins (the "concertina," or soloists), a less prominent "concertante" cello, and a larger ("ripieno," or full) ensemble of strings and harpsichord. It follows the newly normative formal plan of three movements, proceeding Allegro (fast)—Larghetto (rather

* "BWV" is the abbreviation for *Bach-Werke-Verzeichnis* (Bach-Works-Catalogue), the standard cataloguing system for J. S. Bach's complete works—introduced in 1950 (see also Endnote 637).

slow)—Allegro. Likewise normative is its adoption of the ritornello structure in the opening Allegro, as we'll soon unwind. The manner in which Vivaldi implements this latter technique, however, is by no means formulaic or predictable. In fact, Vivaldi routinely avoids falling into ready-made molds in his concerto writing—belying the old saw of him constantly rewriting the same music.[638]

From an experiential standpoint, a list of the most salient aspects of the Allegro must certainly include the overall sonority of the music. Early eighteenth-century Italy was the very apex of string construction, especially the violin—on which Vivaldi was a virtuoso, as were most leading composers of the era. With four solo violins playing in "rivalry" with a larger string ensemble, there is a pure density of texture here that in many ways defines the overall musical experience. Indeed, it is not uncommon that all four violins play distinct lines and rhythms against the accompanying ensemble, creating a kind of bowed "wall of sound," mitigated only by the metallic chords of the harpsichord, as in this passage from the opening ritornello (Figure 15.1—where the circled notes highlight the echo-like interaction of the violins):

**Figure 15.1: Antonio Vivaldi, Op. 3, no. 10, 1. Allegro (mm. 5–9)—opening (full) ritornello**

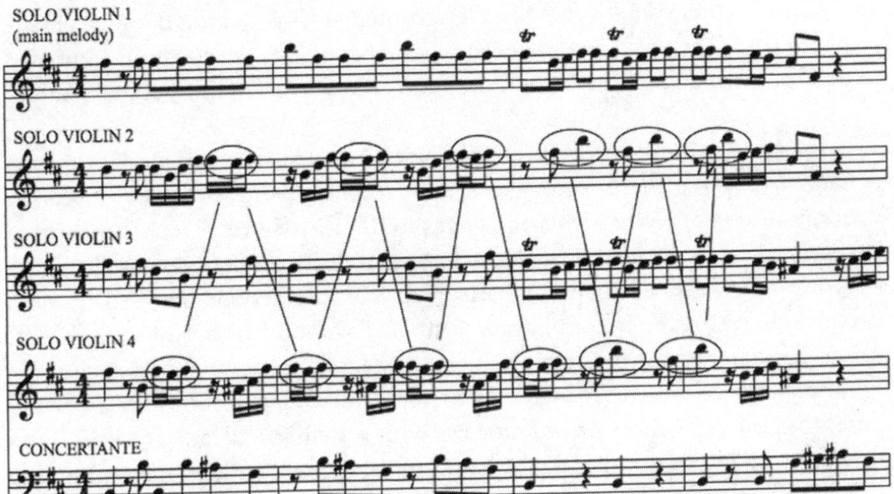


Adding to this density is the propulsive and often overlapping rhythms that bustle along in both the ritornello and solo episode sections. The meter here is a simple 4/4, and yet Vivaldi provides a level of dynamism and unpredictability by frequently displacing the "downbeat" from the top of the bar to the middle (beat 3). In essence, this amounts to frequent insertions of bars of 6/4, though not notated as such—where a new ritornello or episode starts in the middle of a bar (Figure 15.2):

**Figure 15.2: Antonio Vivaldi, Op. 3, no. 10, 1. Allegro (mm. 11–13)—rhythmic displacement**

The combined use of lively overlapping rhythms and metric displacement results in a great deal of rhythmic vibrancy, despite the general absence here of syncopation. In a way, the overall sound of this music—dense, homogenous, and rhythmically vibrant—has affinity with some of the works we discussed with regard to electronica in Chapter 13, such as "Hey Boy Hey Girl" and *Music for 18 Musicians*. Increasingly, moreover, instrumental works of the Baroque era are recorded using "period" instruments—whose distinctive, exotic sound compared to their modern counterparts might be a factor in why a fan like Subject 7 might like it.

Moving to a level of greater musicological nuance, we find another key experiential factor in the Allegro: the heavy use of melodic sequences (repeating patterns at a successively higher or lower pitch). The degree of sequence writing encountered thus far in this book, including even its pronounced use in Shankar's *Morning Love*, pales in comparison to Vivaldi's actions here. To be sure, the melodic sequence is commonplace to all styles and historical periods, but it is a true cornerstone of the Baroque era. It plays a substantial role in the very sonic identity of this repertoire, and as such must help account for its broad public appeal. Sequences provide the ear with a well-articulated, trackable, and narrative-driving device that in the hands of a good composer can also intensify the emotional trajectory of the music. Few composers have used sequences as frequently or with as much variety as Vivaldi: perhaps to a fault, as too much sequence writing can quickly become cliché (as some might argue happens a fair bit in Vivaldi's music).

Specifically, all but two of the seven solo episodes in the Allegro are defined by at least one set of sequences. Most of these sequential patterns are built out of a steady flow of sixteenth notes over two beats, though a few are longer—of four or even six beats. The sequence patterns generally ascend or descend by step, but in one case pass from one string part to another by descending 5ths. As a general rule, after three repetitions of a sequential pattern the ear starts to fatigue, but that doesn't stop Vivaldi from extending to four, five, or even six repetitions. Several episodes (the fifth, sixth, and seventh) string sets of sequences one after the other—with Episode 6 made up of four sets in a row followed by three quasi-sequential passages!

What keeps all this sequence writing from becoming mundane? Well, beyond the infectiousness inherent in the melodic sequence in general, it is the variety of contour in Vivaldi's patterns, as well as the presence or absence of internal repetition within the individual patterns, that collectively provides an element of unpredictability. In combination with the bright pace of the music, this parade of sequences gives the ear (or at least Subject 7's) much to feast upon.

Here are three of the fourteen distinct sequences used in the seven episodes (Figures 15.3a–c):

**Figures 15.3a–c: Antonio Vivaldi, Op. 3, no. 10, 1. Allegro—examples of melodic/harmonic sequences**

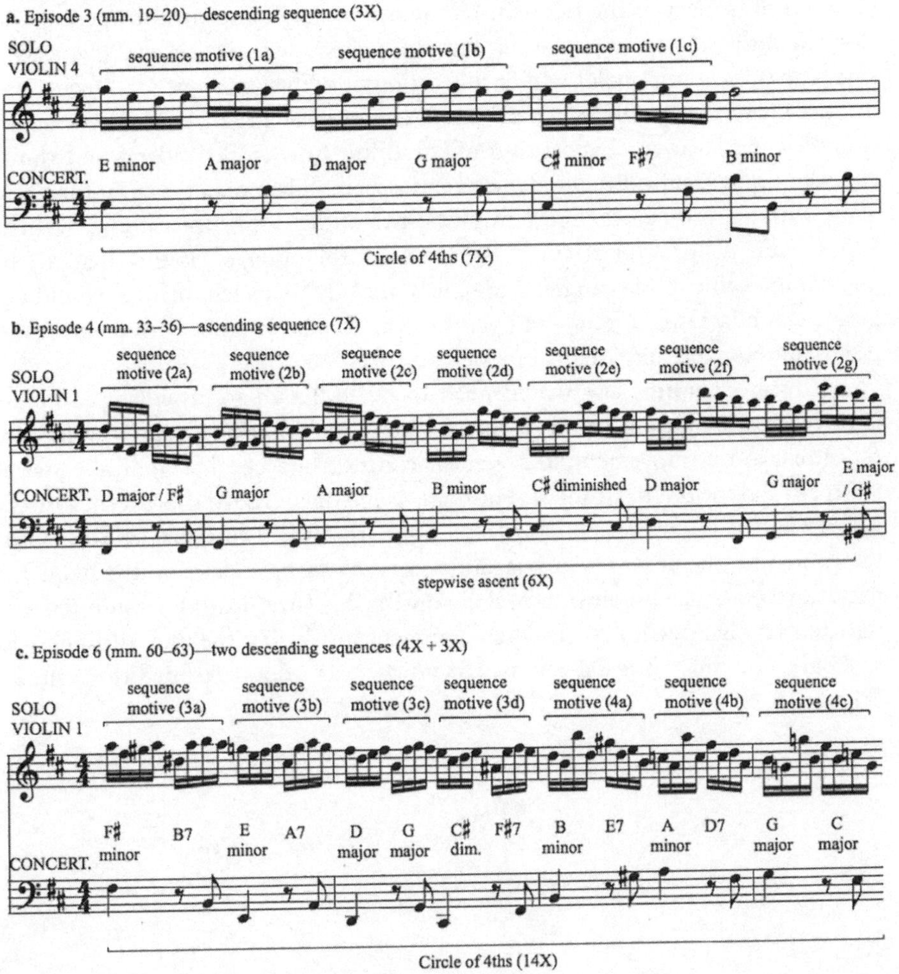

Getting a bit more technical, it may be noted in Figure 15.3 that these sequences have a harmonic component to them as well—that is, they each imply a chord progression. Most chordal patterns accompanying the sequences are one of two kinds: (1) by step (e.g., in Episode 3, from measure 33: D/F♯–G–A–B minor–A/C♯–D) or (2) via the Circle of 4ths (e.g., in Episode 3, from measure 19: E minor–A–D–G). In one extreme case, in Episode 6 (mm. 60–66), Vivaldi carries out a steady flow of a twenty-three-part continuous run along a "diatonic" version of the Circle of 4ths![639] These two approaches are demonstrated in Figure 15.3.

It is unlikely that Subject 7 would have grasped this kind of harmonic detail, and yet whether grasped or not, it does impact the listening experience—and thus helps to explain why this work made it into Subject 7's hit parade.

Similarly, an in-the-weeds account of the Allegro would want to take stock of Vivaldi's approach to the ritornello structure—including how ritornelli and solo episodes are formally and thematically defined. One of Vivaldi's most influential innovations, in fact, is the frequent recurrence of material from the opening ritornello in the solo episodes; he employs this technique here—though atypically, since the Allegro begins not with a ritornello but with a solo episode.[640] Moving on, the second ritornello is a near-exact repetition of the first, while the sixth ritornello is a near-exact repetition of the third; further, the second and third episodes begin identically, while the final ritornello mixes material from the first, along with a unison violin figure from the end of the third ritornello. . . . Okay, I know, this is not a dissertation—but you get the point of how formally rich and complex this music can be. Again, it is unlikely that such nuances would be gleaned from a casual listen—and yet the overall organic unity within this Allegro unquestionably impacts its experience.

And indeed, much else would need to be addressed to provide a comprehensive musicological account of this Allegro—including the overall harmonic trajectory of the movement; the general contrast between harmonically static ritornelli and the often chromatic episodes; the frequent use of short-term formal repetition; the importance of the descending 4th from B to F♯ in defining both the ritornello "theme," such as it is, and several of the episodes; and the frequent use of extended pedal points, especially on B. This latter includes a quintessential, and I'd say beautiful, "Vivaldian" moment just before the final ritornello: a sixteenth note high B pedal against ascending 3rds below, repeated three times (Figure 15.4):

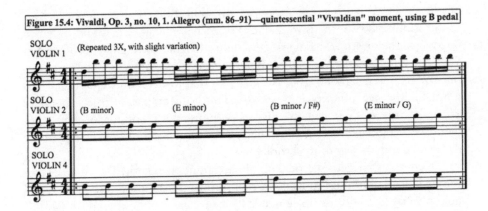

Figure 15.4: Vivaldi, Op. 3, no. 10, 1. Allegro (mm. 86–91)—quintessential "Vivaldian" moment, using B pedal

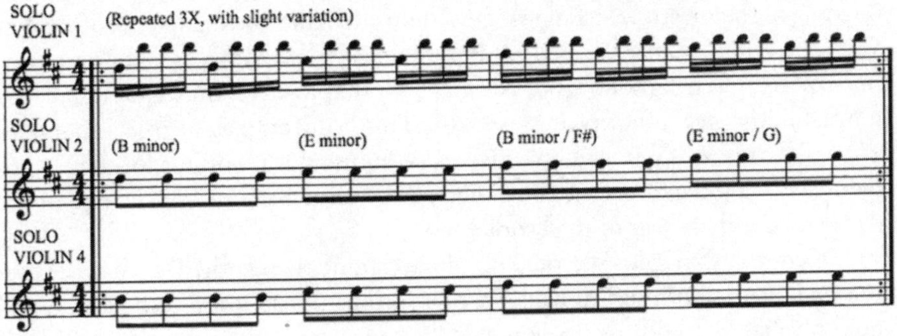


Our detailed discussion underscores the fact that even a four-minute Baroque concerto grosso movement invites a wealth of historical and musicological discussion just to scratch the surface. Now, it is absolutely true that great listening pleasure can be derived with little or even none of this background. Yet, I would argue, an awareness of some, not to mention lots, of this same background can only increase that potential pleasure—particularly if, like Subject 7, you are a fan of this music.

## The Ride Back Home: Beethoven's Allegretto

**The Allegretto from Ludwig van Beethoven's Symphony no. 7 in A, Op. 92,** provides further evidence that Subject 7 gravitates toward works that garner both critical and popular esteem among the well-heeled classical crowd. To Beethoven experts and aficionados, the Seventh Symphony is revered, a prominent representative of the composer's "middle period," as we'll discuss below. Moreover, the Allegretto, the symphony's second movement, is often singled out as a prime example of the composer's creative prowess, both technically and expressively. Yet the work—and movement—is also among the most popular of Beethoven's canon. As such, the choice stands apart from other touchstone options by Beethoven that Subject 7 might have "thumbed up"—as either esteemed but less well-known (e.g., the String Quartet in C♯ Minor, Op. 131) or highly popular but of limited scholarly import (e.g., "Für Elise" or the *Moonlight* Sonata).

### BEETHOVEN: BACKGROUND

Beethoven. The name alone conjures a near archetypal essence. As Einstein is to science and Shakespeare is to literature, so too—for many around the world—is Beethoven to music, as the epitome of genius and creative mastery. This does not mean, however, that you are under any obligation to love or even like his music: as discussed in the Introduction, many before you have found things to disparage. The prominent English critic John Ruskin, for example, confessed in 1881 (fifty-four years after the composer's death): "Beethoven always sounds to me like the upsettings of bags of nails. . . ."[641] That Mr. Ruskin would today find himself in the vast minority among classical music lovers may be true, but it does not make him wrong in any objective sense. I raise this point just for the record, by the way, lest we forget a basic premise of musical taste: that at the end of the day it resides in the ear of the beholder.

Of course, divergent personal opinions cannot change the fact that Beethoven had—and continues to have—a tremendous impact on music history, and not only classical. Almost single-handedly, he ushered in the consequential shift from the Classical to the Romantic eras at the turn of the nineteenth century; again, the whole notion of this dichotomy arose, around 1830, to articulate real aesthetic and technical changes before and after Beethoven—whereas, most agree, he resides forcibly in both eras. Classical music certainly has other titans of influence and prestige—Machaut, Dufay, Josquin, Palestrina, Monteverdi, Vivaldi, J. S. Bach, Haydn, Mozart, Schubert, Brahms, Wagner, Stravinsky, to list my candidates—but there is something unique about Beethoven. As Joseph Kerman put it, he is "probably the most admired composer in the history of Western music."[642] Chin up, John Ruskin.

This admiration, along with a massive amount of surviving material, both creative and personal, also means that Beethoven's story and legacy have been documented to a profound degree. We'll thus here provide only a cursory summary, sufficient to prepare our discussion of the Allegretto. Those of you desiring a more thorough account will have plenty of references to choose from, with in-print Beethoven biographies numbering in the many hundreds. A safe bet is the celebrated monograph by Maynard Solomon, who, among much else, provides compelling evidence as to the long-mysterious identity of Beethoven's "Immortal Beloved"—believed to be the Viennese art collector Antonie Brentano—the intended recipient of an impassioned letter written, but not sent, on July 6–7, 1812, three months after the completion of the Seventh Symphony.[643]

I raise the somewhat random detail of Beethoven's "Immortal Beloved" saga not only to chronologically situate the Allegretto, but also to underscore the fact that in many ways Beethoven's historical importance arose from two intertwining roots: (1) the revolutions in musical discourse ripe to spark around 1800 and (2) the melodramatic details of his personal biography that inspired him to realize them; that, of course, and a good dose of prodigious musical talent.

Ludwig van Beethoven (1770–1827) sprang from musical lineage in Bonn, Germany; both his father and grandfather were professional musicians. Although his early displays of talent failed to grant him the international "prodigy" status Mozart had gained fifteen years earlier, it was enough to attract the support of patrons in Bonn—whereby, at age twenty-one, Beethoven was able to move to Vienna, and study with Joseph Haydn—the veritable father of the Classical era. Given the latter's travels, alas, these lessons lasted but two years. Still, it is worth noting how Vienna played that same pivotal role in the shift from the Classical to the Romantic era as Venice had played from the Renaissance to the Baroque two hundred years earlier.

Initially, Beethoven's public success came through his activities as a virtuoso pianist and improviser. By 1800, however, he had issued several major publications—including two symphonies, three piano concertos, fifteen or so piano sonatas, and numerous chamber works, etc. Collectively, these earned him a good deal of fame and money in Vienna, and led to a general consensus that this young Beethoven was the true heir to Mozart and Haydn. At the same time, in works such as the *Pathétique* Sonata, Op. 13 (1798), a new and forward-thinking musical vision can be discerned—with a more adventurous approach to melody, harmony, form, scope, and expression.

By 1796, Beethoven began suffering from acute tinnitus, making it hard to hear music and especially conversations; the next twenty years were a steady march toward deafness, which was near total by age forty-four (1814). The despair that would have derailed most composers, however, Beethoven met with superhuman resolve—to carry on in service of his art: "I would have ended my life—it was only my art that held me back," he wrote in the famous "Heiligenstadt Testament" in 1802.[644] The musical upshot was nothing short of a revolution, launching—with the monumental Symphony no. 3 (*Eroica*)—Beethoven's "middle period" (1803–15) and the dawn of the Romantic era. The extensions in harmony, scope, and expression seen before 1803 were now blown wide-open, with the production of dozens of the most impactful works in classical music history: Symphonies 3–8, Piano Concertos 4–5, the Violin Concerto, the opera *Fidelio*, the *Waldstein* Piano Sonata, the Opus 59 String Quartets, etc., etc.

As if deafness were not enough, Beethoven was challenged and provoked by a whole host of other extramusical forces as well: a continually disappointing love life, frequent financial woes, the continual threat of war in and around Vienna by Napoleon's armies, recurring illness, and the broad aesthetic shifts taking place generally in Europe at that time—notably in literature (Goethe, Byron) and philosophy (Kant, Hegel), etc. The times they were a-changin', and Beethoven met them with a fierceness of spirit perhaps unequaled in music history. Now, it should be noted that the musical landscape itself was already ripe for this kind of transformation: periods of "classical" equilibrium, such as that achieved by Haydn and Mozart in the late eighteenth century, inevitably demand disruption and experimentation. But Beethoven went above and beyond the call of aesthetic duty, and heroically paved the way for nearly a century of thematic, harmonic, formal, and expressive development.

It was specifically in the midst of another potent mix of personal and musical stimuli that Beethoven entered his "late period," around 1816—namely, a bitter fight to obtain custody of his nephew on the one hand, and an intense study of the contrapuntal music of J. S. Bach on the other. In the final decade of his life, Beethoven's music became ever more introspective and ambitious—crowned by the epic Ninth Symphony, the late string quartets, and the *Missa Solemnis*, among others. Not everyone appreciated or even understood these "otherworldly" works; Rossini was certainly more popular at the time. But indeed, Beethoven was writing for the future more than for the present. Quite unlike Vivaldi, moreover, Beethoven's music was not forgotten following his death in 1827 (at age fifty-six). Instead it became the sine qua non of awareness and study for every composer who followed—as indeed is still the case in many circles today.

## BEETHOVEN: ANALYSIS

The Symphony no. 7 in A, Op. 92, as noted, falls toward the end of Beethoven's "middle" period. Indeed, some prefer to look at it, and the Eighth Symphony, completed shortly thereafter, as more of a transition between the "middle" and "late" periods.[645] Certainly, the Seventh continues to push formal and technical boundaries (e.g., the enormous slow introduction in the first movement), just as it maintains the aesthetic force and drama found in the Third, Fifth, and Sixth Symphonies. But there is also something effortless, indeed elegant, in its narrative—where those just prior were more feverish in the way they broke new ground. It is almost as if Beethoven were gearing up for the titanic struggle that would come five years later with the start of the Ninth. This mature elegance too may help explain the tremendous popularity of the Seventh—which always ranks among Beethoven's "most performed" symphonies—though in a tight race with the Fifth. But whereas concert programmers bank on the Fifth's famous opening movement to ensure "butts in seats," with the Seventh it's doubtless the Allegretto.

Before diving in, though, a brief summary of how Beethoven came to conceive his symphonies on such a grand scale. Like the concerto, the symphony (Greek for "sounding together") had a long, sinuous evolution starting in the early Baroque. The Italian label "sinfonia" was used generically for a suite of dance movements and, after 1650, as a stand-alone movement placed within an opera or sacred vocal work. By the late seventeenth century, the opera sinfonia—notably those by Alessandro Scarlatti—had developed, like the concerto and sonata, into a three-movement, fast-slow-fast genre. And indeed, the Classical era's embodiment of the symphony began as a kind of amalgam of these three key forms: sonata, concerto, and sinfonia. A host of experiments in Italy—by Giovanni Battista Sammartini and Luigi Boccherini, etc.—and Germany—by C. P. E. Bach and Johann Stamitz, etc.—during the first half of the eighteenth century then paved the way for the template to come after 1770.

That template was solidified especially in the 104 symphonies of Joseph

Haydn, most of which were written for his employers, the Hungarian princes of Esterházy. As with Vivaldi and his predecessors in the concerto form, many of the elements that Haydn standardized for the Classical symphony—a four-movement scheme, the use of sonata form in the first movement, the use of a minuet and trio in the third, etc.—were first implemented by others. But that's what happens when you write 104 of them! Haydn's younger contemporary, Wolfgang Amadeus Mozart, likewise embraced the symphony as a vital creative medium, completing forty-one in his short life. In their grandest examples—Haydn's London symphonies (Nos. 93–104) and Mozart's Nos. 39–41—a bold approach to technical, dimensional, and expressive elements does seem to point to a new paradigm. As a student of Haydn and a fierce admirer of Mozart, Beethoven would naturally take up that mantle in his early iterations. Yet few in 1802 could have imagined the quantum leap he would take with his Third Symphony, titled *Eroica* (Heroic), a work of unprecedented length and emotional weight.[646] With it, Beethoven invoked a new vision—a new "symphonic ideal," to again quote Joseph Kerman—embracing the genre as a transcendent and triumphant psychological journey, an epic aesthetic adventure.

The Seventh was composed in Vienna between winter 1811 and spring 1812, following a period of ill health and subsequent recovery at the Bavarian spa town of Teplitz. Feeling refreshed, Beethoven entered into a period of intense creativity, completing the Seventh and Eighth back to back, with initial intentions of moving on to a Ninth—which clearly did not yet materialize. The Seventh was premiered on December 8, 1813, at a benefit concert for soldiers wounded in the Battle of Hanau against Napoleon's army. And while the critics were occasionally left puzzled by the new symphony, as per usual, the crowd was unhesitant in its adoration for the Allegretto: so intense was the applause that it had to be repeated. The Allegretto remained a crowd favorite during the rest of Beethoven's life, as indeed it still does today.

Many are the musicological elements that drive the listening experience of the Allegretto. However, the one that tends to dominate the scholarly literature, including concert program notes, is that of rhythm. Specifically, much focus is placed on a rhythmic ostinato— ♩ ♫|♩ ♩ —found nearly ubiquitously throughout the movement. Indeed, it appears at the very start of the opening theme (Figure 15.5):

**Figure 15.5: Beethoven, Symphony no. 7, 2. Allegretto (mm. 3–10)—principal theme with rhythmic ostinato**

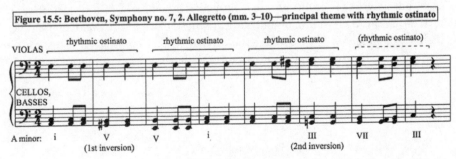

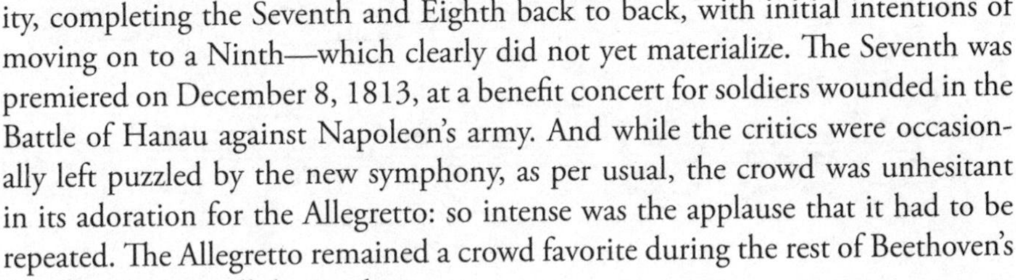

If anyone is famed for making hay out of a musical rhythm, it is Beethoven—just think of the famous opening of the Fifth Symphony. The marchlike ostinato—rhythmically comprising a dactyl (long-short-short) plus a spondee (long-long)—dominates the movement, both melodically and as an accompanying figure. Indeed, the entire Seventh Symphony is often described as being consumed by rhythm. This, for example, is what Richard Wagner was getting at when he famously labeled the Seventh as "the apotheosis of the dance"—demonstrating this by dancing nonstop as Liszt played his transcription on the piano![647]

Beethoven then creates even more rhythmic vitality as the work proceeds, by overlaying a number of cross-rhythms onto the steady flow of quarters and eighths in the ostinato. These include eighth note triplets (creating a hemiola) as well as steady sixteenth notes, etc. Here is a sample of the hemiola against the ostinato (Figure 15.6):

**Figure 15.6: Beethoven, Symphony no. 7, 2. Allegretto (mm. 75–78)—example of rhythmic layering**

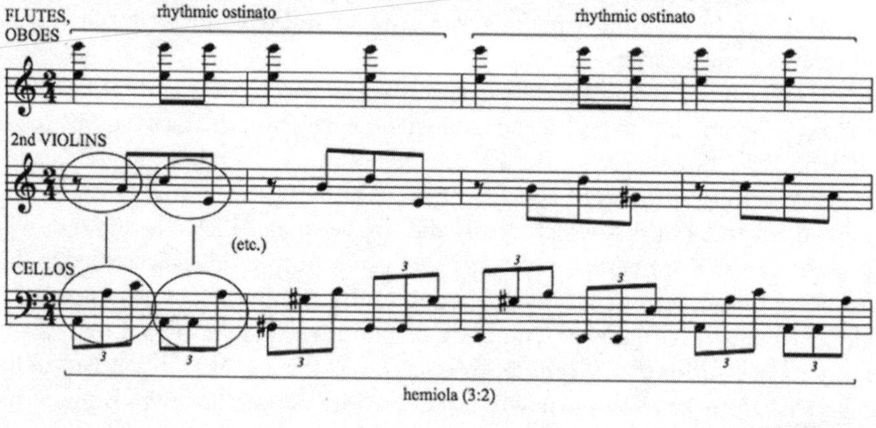


Beyond acknowledging its infectious and multilayered use of rhythm, any informed listening experience of the Allegretto also requires us to confront its form. Not surprisingly, knowing Beethoven, this is no straightforward proposition. At first glance, the form appears as a set of variations, based on a rather simple theme in A minor. The theme itself comprises two balanced phrases of eight bars each, but where the second phrase is immediately repeated (a-b-b). Three complete variations then follow. Significantly, though, in each case the main "simple" theme is augmented by a counter-theme that in fact commands of us greater attention by virtue of its stronger melodic and rhythmic definition (Figure 15.7):

**Figure 15.7: Beethoven, Allegretto (mm. 26–42)—principal theme + counter-theme (Section A, phrases a–b only)**

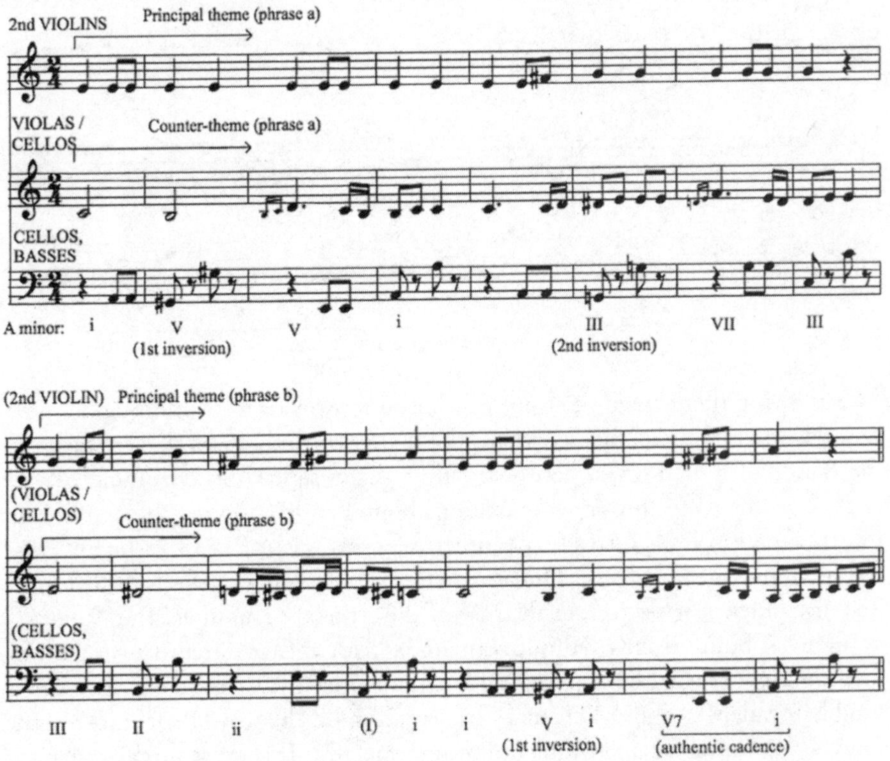


Even more palpable is the fact that in these three variations, Beethoven raises the stakes from one to the next: a steady increase in register (at a higher octave), textural density (more instruments and accompanying lines), and dynamics (from piano to fortissimo). This intensity starts to temper toward the end of the third variation, via a gradual decrescendo—but that's where Beethoven throws a wrench into our formal expectations. Following a brief tag, he gives us not only a new section, but also a new key: A major. So much for a simple theme and variations!

The new section itself comprises several phrases, which can be diagrammed as c-d-e-e'-d'-f. The melodic material here is considerably more lyrical, just as the texture and orchestration are more varied. The rhythmic ostinato (the dactyl portion) is relegated to an accompanying figure in the low strings. Harmonically too this section is fairly rich and contrasting: phrases d and d', for example, make use of a canonic melody over a striking pedal point; the result is a rustic or pastoral quality, reminiscent of Beethoven's Sixth Symphony, itself titled *Pastoral* (Figure 15.8):

**Figure 15.8: Beethoven, Allegretto (mm. 117–122)—use of pedal point in Section B (pastoral feel)**

Following the A major section, Beethoven returns us to A minor and a new variation on the main theme, where the countermelody takes center stage. In the hands of a traditional composer, this might signal the beginning of the end—but this is Beethoven we're talking about. An extension at the end of this fourth variation leads instead to another new section (m. 183)—a highly contrapuntal passage known as a "fugato," since it passes a fugue-like "subject" from one instrument (or section, in the case of the strings) to another. The "subject," naturally, is built on the rhythmic ostinato, at least at first. After this good bit of contrapuntal writing, Beethoven builds up the intensity yet again and drives to a loud half cadence. This ushers in a fifth variation on the main theme; its return, however, is truncated and omits the countermelody. This must surely signal the end, right? Sorry. Instead, we get a quick return (phrase c) of the A major section, followed, in quick succession, by a sixth—and rather dissected—variation on the main theme, with which Beethoven ends the movement.

There is a joke about Beethoven that he had a hard time ending a piece of music—most famously in the finale of the Fifth Symphony. One gets that same impression here too. But his formal meanderings are in fact part of a larger vision. The seemingly curious flow from section to section actually adds up to a graceful and emblematic form of the Classical era, as discussed in Chapter 6: the seven-part rondo (A-B-A-C-A-B-A). Specifically, it goes as follows: Theme with Variations (**A**)—A Major section (**B**)—Variation (**A**)—Fugato (**C**)—Variation (**A**)—A Major section (**B**)—Variation (**A**). The incarnation of each section may be unpredictable, but the resulting symmetry is, again, a definite part of the experience—whether you hear it or not.*

Regardless, it is through the epic and byzantine form of the Allegretto, a sort of "variations rondo," that we experience the flow of the actual musicological

* A more detailed musicological discussion, including claims of the movement as a "double variation" form, is found on the WYLI website (supplement to Chapter 15).

material. We've discussed many of its details above. One parameter, however, is worth fleshing out: harmony. The Allegretto makes use of an approach to chromaticism in various sections, notably in the A major section. But there is another usage that is distinct and overt. It occurs in the theme, and specifically in phrase b—with a descending series of chromatic and mode-shifting chords: C–B–B minor–A–A minor–E/G♯, resulting in an inner-descending melody of E–D♯-D♮–C♯–C♮–B. The passage was included in Figure 15.7, but is worth highlighting here (Figure 15.9):

**Figure 15.9: Beethoven, Allegretto, Section A, phrase b—use of harmonic "color" and chromaticism**

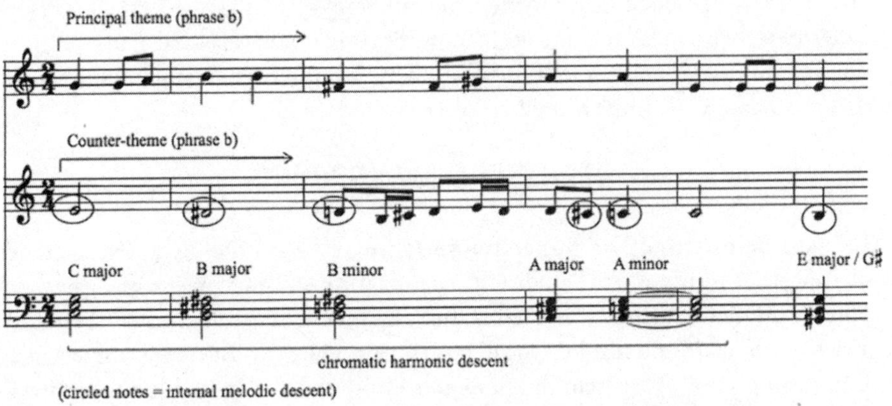


This may be seen as a fine example of what a former professor of mine, Leonard Ratner, termed "harmonic color."[648] There is nothing functional about this chord progression—notably the immediate shift from an A major to an A minor chord—and yet its "color" strikes the ear in a distinctive way. It thus stands apart from the "harmonic action" that underlies the flow of chords in the music of Haydn and Mozart, for example. Such "coloristic" use of harmony by Beethoven would later be picked up in the works of Schubert, Chopin, and Wagner, among others, and indeed may be viewed as an early seed of tonality's ultimate demise in the early twentieth century (see our discussion of Fauré's Sicilienne, later in the chapter). In any event, to my mind the "sound" of this progression is likely a key factor, subtle though it may be, behind the success of the Allegretto among its many fans.

Whatever the reason, however, the Allegretto seems to possess the "right stuff" to have made it a favorite from its debut in December 1813 until the present day. Few pieces of classical music can say that. Its magic ingredients—for those so inclined—have made it a continual mainstay of the concert repertoire, a favorite of Hollywood films from 1935 to at least 2013 (including *Mr. Holland's Opus* and *The King's Speech*), the source material of subsequent musical works (e.g., by John Corigliano and Jacques Loussier), and, of course, the short list of Subject 7.

## A Night Out: Bernstein's Overture to *Candide*

**Leonard Bernstein's Overture to *Candide*** reinforces our expectations that a hit for Subject 7 would also be a touchstone of the classical concert repertoire—and not an obscure outlier. Such, at any rate, is again the case with this operetta overture, among the most frequently performed orchestral works by any American composer. This hit, however, expands our concept of what a music lover like Subject 7 might deem worthy of garnering "staple status": not only works by European composers, but also American works infused with popular and/or theatrical elements. Indeed, the Overture ably symbolizes the ascendancy of American-created classical music in the minds of many classical fans—and, in the process, introduces us to a musician who, as much as anyone, helped make that ascendancy possible in the first place.

### BERNSTEIN: BACKGROUND

Leonard Bernstein (1918–90) epitomizes in many ways the disruptive presence of American music on the traditional classical music stage: a Jewish, gay composer, conductor, pianist, and educator embracing the full gamut of musical styles swirling around him: classical, jazz, theater. In contrast to the conventional European pattern, Bernstein did not enter into a clear, well-established compositional lineage—as had Vivaldi and Beethoven. Even the musical revolutionaries in Europe in the Modern era—Debussy, Schoenberg, Stravinsky, Bartók, etc.—had inherited and internalized their time-honored traditions before upending them with new practices. Things were not so neatly packaged in America. In the nineteenth century, American composers like Edward MacDowell and Louis Gottschalk had to study in Europe just to gain legitimacy. Their subsequent attempts to forge an American musical language were tepid, and often based on conservative, nostalgic, and/or stereotyped elements.[649]

Things began to change in the early twentieth century, perhaps most prominently through the efforts of Bernstein's friend and mentor Aaron Copland—another Jewish, gay composer, conductor, pianist, and educator.[650] In the early 1920s, Copland studied in Paris with famed pedagogue Nadia Boulanger. There he internalized the modernist trends of Stravinsky, Bartók, Berg, and others—offering an alternative to the Romantic conservatism back home. In such early works as his Piano Variations (1930), Copland embraced this progressive orientation: with often harsh dissonance and other aspects of compositional complexity. Likewise in Copland's early mix, however, was the incorporation of jazz elements, as in his Piano Concerto (1926)—even if not as naturally absorbed as in the "concert" music of Gershwin (*Rhapsody in Blue* and *An American in Paris*). However, from the late 1930s, Copland began to forge a more populist and distinctively "American" sound—devising an open, diatonic, and quasi-tonal harmonic language that evoked the spirit of the Western prairie. This is heard in works like *Billy the Kid* (1939), *Rodeo* (1942), and *Appalachian Spring* (1944), which remain among the most popular American works in the classical repertoire.

Such, therefore, was the new, if unspoken, "manifesto" adopted by Copland and his like-minded American contemporaries—Roy Harris, Roger Sessions, Walter Piston, and Virgil Thomson, who dubbed the group "Copland's commando unit": instead of a clear and singular tradition, American composers were invited to embrace a broad and eclectic vision, mixing and matching any and all musical inputs in service of aesthetic and/or commercial aims. Bernstein—who studied with Piston and first met Copland in 1938 after performing his Piano Variations (without yet knowing anything about the composer)—not only embodied this vision, but also, through his stellar conducting career, actively championed it like no other.

Bernstein's eclecticism was manifest early on: he studied conducting, composition, piano, and aesthetics while a student at Harvard and then the Curtis Institute of Music. But while most musicians would thereafter settle into one or at most two career paths, Bernstein did his best to maintain them all feverishly throughout his career. The resulting time demands were often personally painful to him, and were especially tough on his compositional output—which, in fact, is relatively modest.[651]

Arguably, Bernstein's most prominent identity is as a conductor—notably via his tenure as music director of the New York Philharmonic, from 1957 to 1969. While retaining an association with the NY Phil to the end of his life, as "laureate conductor," he also developed a close relationship with several other orchestras—especially the Vienna and Israel Philharmonics. His conducting style and thematic programming won him much public support and critical praise—though not all critics condoned his at times extreme expressiveness, notably regarding tempos. Amid an overall eclectic repertoire, from Baroque to Contemporary, Bernstein championed several composers in particular—including Beethoven, Mahler, Carl Nielsen, and especially the American composers Charles Ives, Marc Blitzstein, Copland, Gershwin, Harris, William Schuman, and, not surprisingly, himself. Many of his recordings of these and other composers are even today considered definitive.

Such a wide swath of classical music would naturally yield to any composer a sizable breadth of stylistic and technical influence. But from an early stage, Bernstein was also drawn to jazz and theater music. His thesis at Harvard was dedicated to the "absorption of race elements" in American music, and he supported himself in part by playing jazz gigs. After graduation, his earliest professional work was playing piano for a theater troupe in New York called the Revuers—which included the lyricist-playwrights Adolph Green and Betty Comden. Their collaboration, along with Broadway director-choreographer Jerome Robbins, led to

Bernstein's first big hit, the musical *On the Town* (1944)—itself an adaptation of his ballet *Fancy Free*.[652] With Comden and Green, he then wrote his next musical, *Wonderful Town*, in 1953; it too was a hit and like *On the Town* was adapted into a popular movie.

Bernstein's most enduring successes, however, came in 1956 and '57, with two works written near simultaneously: the jazz-inflected musical *West Side Story* and the eclectic operetta *Candide*. That these major compositional efforts would coincide with his appointment at the NY Philharmonic speaks to Bernstein's versatility as well as his prodigious talent. *West Side Story*, of course, has become one of the most successful Broadway shows in history. It reunited Bernstein with Jerome Robbins and introduced to the world a young lyricist-composer, Stephen Sondheim, who would go on to spark his own revolution in musical theater in the 1970s and '80s, with such shows as *Follies* (1971), *Sweeney Todd* (1979), and *Into the Woods* (1987). *West Side Story* ran for a resounding 732 performances on Broadway; the 1961 film adaptation won ten Academy Awards, including Best Picture.[653] Its evergreen Overture notwithstanding, *Candide* did not fare as well in its initial run; it has, however, become quite popular in recent years, as we'll see.

Beyond Bernstein's theater works, then, are a number of "serious" compositions—including three symphonies, the *Chichester Psalms* (1965) and other choral works, and a handful of chamber pieces. The symphonies—*Jeremiah* (1942), *Age of Anxiety* (1949), and *Kaddish* (1963)—enabled Bernstein to utilize a broader and more sophisticated musical palette, including occasional harsh dissonance, use of Jewish liturgical melodies, twelve-tone techniques, etc. Much as with Vivaldi's operas, however, Bernstein's symphonies have never become part of the standard orchestral repertoire; indeed, their general neglect in his own lifetime was a source of personal unhappiness to the composer—and perhaps points to the downside of being pulled in so many directions. Also rather neglected is Bernstein's ambitious *Mass* (1971)—a quasi-theater piece mixing classical, Broadway, and even rock styles;[654] it included lyrics by Stephen Schwartz, who would go on to make his own history on Broadway—notably with *Godspell* (1971), *Pippin* (1972), and *Wicked* (2003).[655]

Finally, Bernstein left an indelible impact as an educator—and especially as the affable guide to the broader public on various musical topics, classical and otherwise. His Young People's Concerts—a set of fifty-three broadcasts carried out between 1958 and 1972—introduced a whole generation of Americans to the wide classical repertoire with clear explanations, historical anecdotes, and humor.[656]

## BERNSTEIN: ANALYSIS

*Candide* is a "comic operetta" based on the 1759 satiric novella of the same name by the French philosopher-writer Voltaire. It premiered at the Martin Beck Theatre on Broadway in December 1956. It was a flop, running for only seventy-three performances. While the music was largely praised, the libretto—by Lillian Hellman—was attacked in *Time* magazine as "too serious" for Bernstein's "mocking lyricism."[657] Voltaire's novella uses comic allegory to lampoon what he saw as the unhealthy idealism in the writings of the German polymath Gottfried Wilhelm Leibniz. This so-called "optimism" is famed for the notion that an omnipotent God must have made ours "the best of all possible worlds," despite the imperfection we see in it. In the novella, Voltaire humorously upends the optimism of a Leibniz devotee, Candide, in order to insert some sober pragmatism and a new mantra: it is up to us to "cultivate our garden."[658] This would become the basis for Bernstein's heartfelt finale, "Make Our Garden Grow." In its original musical rendering, however, *Candide* was deemed too serious for Broadway—just as it was initially considered too glib for opera houses.

Yet while the premiere was a failure, a number of later revisions (e.g., a new libretto by Hugh Wheeler) would yield several successful revivals—including a 1974 production under Harold Prince that ran for a whopping 740 performances. Bernstein continued to retool the music even after this triumph, leading to a final revision and subsequent recording in 1989—the year before his death. Today, the work exists in several viable versions, and is produced with some regularity around the world, not least by high school and college companies in the US.

Part of the charm, as well as the challenge, of *Candide* is its indulgence in stylistic pastiche—that is, the use of distinct musical styles to depict particular times and/or places. In devising such a strategy, Bernstein was inspired in part by Voltaire's original episodic storyline, where Candide travels incessantly from country to country. The result—often contradicting stylistic and chronological expectations—is a near-dizzying array of styles among the operetta's thirty or so vocal and instrumental numbers: a Renaissance hymn, French cancan, Viennese waltz, Argentinian tango, Bach-like chorale, jazzy riffs, Broadway ballad, grand-opera bel canto, comic-opera vocal acrobatics, Mahler-esque lyricism, Berg-like 12-tone chromaticism, etc.

That a Broadway-bound theater piece could take on such an eclectic agenda is not only in line with Bernstein's versatile musical chops, but also comports well with his personal concept of American musical theater. As we touched upon in Chapter 9, he articulated this in an impressive lecture presentation on the subject, broadcast as part of the *Omnibus* TV series on October 7, 1956—two months before the premiere of *Candide*.[659] In words and excerpts, Bernstein unwinds the evolution of American musical theater from the nonintegrated variety show of the late nineteenth century to the quasi-integrated musical comedy of the 1920s and '30s (via the edifying influence of operetta on the one side and the vernacular language of jazz on the other) to the full "maturity" of the genre in the 1940s and early '50s. For the latter, he cites "recent" shows like *South Pacific* (1949) and *Guys & Dolls* (1950) as crowning gems.

He then concludes with an optimistic vision for the future:

> We're in a historical position now. . . . [A]ll we need is for our Mozart to come along. If and when he does, what we'll get will certainly not be any *Magic Flute*; we'll get a new form, and perhaps "opera" is not the word for it; there must be a more exciting word than "opera" for so exciting an event. But this event can happen any second; it's almost as if it's our moment in history, as if there were an historic necessity that gives us such a wealth of talent at this precise time. . . .[660]

By "wealth of talent," Bernstein was certainly referring to composers like Richard Rodgers, Frank Loesser, and Frederick Loewe. But he must also have been projecting hope for his own impending arrivals: the operetta *Candide* and the jazz-inflected musical *West Side Story* (opening nine months after *Candide*). To Bernstein, operettas and musicals were just two sides of the same coin—distinguished merely by the use (operetta) or lack thereof (musical) of a vernacular musical and spoken language.[661] Bernstein's disappointment at the initial failure of *Candide* must therefore have been acute. Happily for him, though, this failure was mitigated shortly thereafter by the stunning triumph of *West Side Story*.

And yet a few pieces from *Candide* caught the public's attention even from its 1956 premiere, and became embraced as stand-alone showpieces. These include especially the coloratura (virtuosic) soprano aria "Glitter and Be Gay," premiered by Barbara Cook, and, of course, the Overture. Following its concert debut by Bernstein and the New York Philharmonic in January 1957, the Overture was performed a hundred times by various orchestras in two years! It remains among the most frequently programmed work by Bernstein, indeed by any American composer.

The Overture, as much as any other single work by the composer, amply demonstrates Bernstein's eclectic, pastiche-like propensities. At once, it emulates the Broadway musical overture, the nineteenth-century operatic overture, and even the late seventeenth-century opera sinfonia, as we'll see. And it does all these things with a vibrant, nervous energy that is quintessentially Bernstein, and somehow endemically American. *Candide* is not a jazzy score—indeed it is a kind of homage to various European styles and periods—and yet, to an experienced listener, could not have been composed anywhere but in America, if not New York in particular.

As is typical of the 1950s-era Broadway musical, the Overture is a preview of themes and songs heard in the actual show. But whereas the overture to a show like *South Pacific* is a string of hits in a predictable medley format, the *Candide* Overture utilizes bits and pieces from several numbers as source material for a unified, classical-type composition. Their utilization, moreover, is anything but predictable. In some cases, the original material is short and/or manipulated, while in other cases it is kept largely intact. There is also new material. The result is an overture that comes off as being entirely fresh and self-contained, not to mention grand. It is worth noting too that the Overture was the only part of the original *Candide* production that Bernstein himself orchestrated; again following Broadway protocol, another arranger—Hershy Kay in this case—orchestrated the rest.

There are several musicological elements that dominate the listening experience of the Overture. Among them—not surprisingly to those familiar with Bernstein's music—is rhythm, particularly the use of syncopation and odd-beat phrase construction. But equally palpable is the dichotomous use of tonal harmony, the rich and diverse use of orchestral timbre, and the work's unique formal construction. As we've done before, let's utilize the last to explicate the others.

The Overture begins with a vibrant "fanfare" gesture: a leap of a minor 7th in the brass—repeated and expanded in a syncopated manner (Figure 15.10):

**Figure 15.10: Leonard Bernstein, *Candide* Overture—opening dramatic fanfare**

As the ascending tritone is in *West Side Story*, so too is the ascending minor 7th a kind of defining interval to the score of *Candide*—heard, for example, in the related arias, "Candide's Lament" and "Make Our Garden Grow," though indirectly via an octave leap.* More specifically, this gesture appears in a rather different guise in the comical aria "Words, Words, Words," sung by Martin, Candide's scholarly companion. It is very much a "laughing" gesture—reflecting Martin's mocking pessimism to Candide's naïve notion of ours being "the best of all possible worlds." With this dynamic (and quasi-jazzy) start, Bernstein thus announces to his listeners that we're in for a frolicking good time.

The next section is largely original, a restless and "jaunty" melody in E♭ major that arises out of an ascending arpeggiated gesture found in the operetta's "Battle Music"—the source of several other Overture elements as well. The melody

* Indeed, each show begins by demonstrably announcing their respective intervals: the ascending tritone in the "Prologue" of *West Side Story*, the ascending minor 7th in the Overture of *Candide*.

seems to meander nervously, as do the underlying harmonies, as if seeking shelter—invoking the frivolity of a Gilbert and Sullivan operetta (Figure 15.11):

**Figure 15.11: Leonard Bernstein, *Candide* Overture (mm. 10–16)—jaunty theme (Section B)**

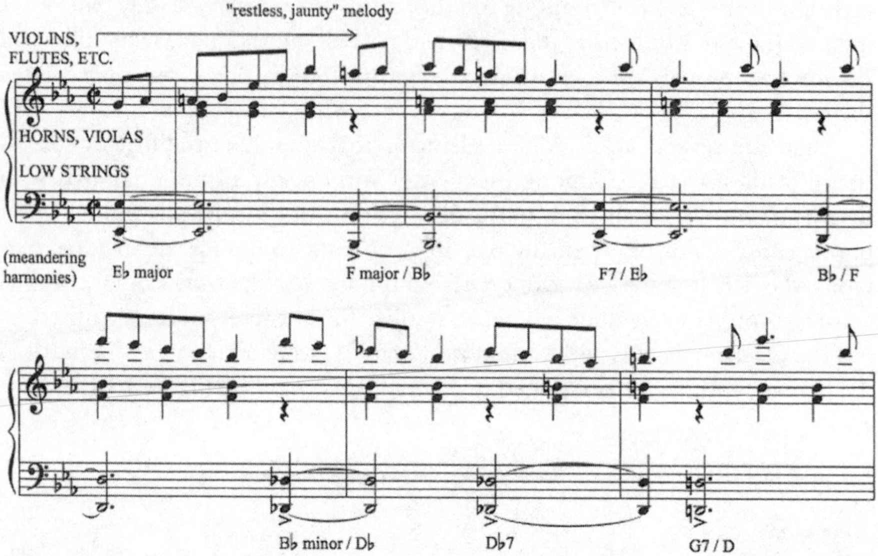


This first main theme is rather short (six bars) and rather syncopated in its fast-paced 2/2 (two beats per measure, half note gets the beat) meter. It quickly moves from chord to chord—including juxtaposed shifts from B♭ major to B♭ minor (reminiscent of what we saw in Beethoven's Allegretto), en route to C minor, the relative minor of E♭. We then arrive at what appears to be a new and contrasting section—a French cancan. Yet after two bars, we are back at the fanfare—now transposed from the original B♭ to our "home" key of E♭.

A slightly truncated version of the fanfare again leads to the "jaunty" theme. This time, however, we are then treated to a full, energetic rendering of the cancan: a two-part, nonsyncopated section that is as harmonically chromatic as it is humorous and playful—quickly shifting from C minor to A minor to E♭ minor to C minor to F♯ minor by means of the ever-flexible diminished 7th chord, before returning forcefully and confidently to C minor with a marked cadence (Figure 15.12):

**Figure 15.12: Bernstein, *Candide* Overture (mm. 32–46)—cancan theme and harmony (Section C)**

This then leads into the most direct and lengthy quote from within the operetta so far, again from "Battle Music": a march theme in B♭ (the dominant of E♭) followed by a "cute" rejoinder passage—both repeated via repeat signs. These two sections are harmonically quite stable and tonally simple compared with previous sections, such as the cancan theme—which by contrast has a chromatic, almost "pan-tonal" (all keys) harmonic orientation (Figure 15.13):

**Figure 15.13: Bernstein, *Candide* Overture (mm. 47–61)—march theme and "cute" rejoinder (Sections D & E)**

To take stock, we've thus far heard a swift and restless progression of sections that collectively give the listener an edge-of-your-seat nervous listening experience:

A (fanfare)—B ("jaunty")—C (cancan)—A'—B—C'—D (march)—E ("cute")

Beyond the rhythmic, thematic, and harmonic elements discussed above, Bernstein adds further listening focus by virtue of his creative orchestration. We can here imagine the insights gained from his years of conducting the symphonic and operatic standard repertoire: Offenbach-inspired brash horns, then pizzicato strings, xylophone, and muted trumpets for the cancan section; Rossini-esque grace-noted flutes and strings for the "cute" rejoinder of the march, etc.

As we come to observe, moreover, this marks the end of the first main section of the Overture, closing in the dominant key of B♭. Those taking notes will recall that an initial formal move from the tonic (e.g., E♭) to the dominant (e.g., B♭) is indicative of sonata and related forms. Typically in such cases, next to appear would be either a development section, utilizing material from the exposition, or perhaps a secondary theme in that same dominant key. At first blush, a mini-development seems at play, as we hear—in lighter, wind-based orchestration—fragments from the "jaunty" theme, a Stravinsky-esque ostinato passage (taken from the same "Battle Music" number), and a development of the cancan theme in the piccolo.

However, an extended F7 chord at the end of the cancan fragment leads to an entirely new theme in B♭—a lyrical melody in the strings, based on the Act 1 love duet, "Oh, Happy We" (Figure 15.14):

**Figure 15.14: Bernstein, *Candide* Overture (mm. 83–94)—lyrical theme (Section F)**

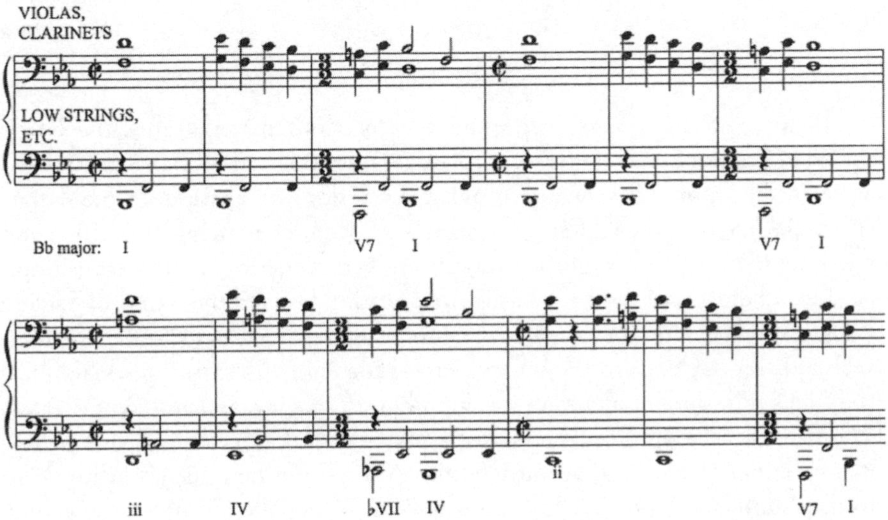


Contrasting frenetic and rhythmic material with lush and lyrical themes is a bit of a Bernstein trademark, and such is presented vividly here. In contrast to Section 1's unpredictable contrasts of short, restless subsections, here is a single, broad section of short- and long-term symmetry. Each subsection is built of four phrases, each of which is three measures long; in turn, each individual phrase is built of seven beats (presented 2+2+3), which is also vintage Bernstein. And yet the aural experience of these unsymmetrical phrases is somehow elegant and flowing—not unlike the swinging 5/4 (3+2) flow of Paul Desmond's "Take Five." The phrase structure of the "lyrical" section largely proceeds a-a'-b-a''; the primed designations are only by virtue of varied orchestration and added accompanying material—which at times is reminiscent of Mahler (a hero of Bernstein's) in its gestural figurations.

Disrupting slightly that symmetrical a-a-b-a schema is an inserted passage right after the b phrase—with a passage also taken from the vocal duet. Specifically, it is a mini-coda that repeats the concluding V–I cadence at stepwise intervals: D–E♭–E♮–D. This is in fact one of the most aurally striking gestures in the whole Overture, by virtue of its sweet yet unpredictable cadential patterns (Figure 15.15):

**Figure 15.15: Bernstein, *Candide* Overture (mm. 119–22)—chromatic string of cadences**

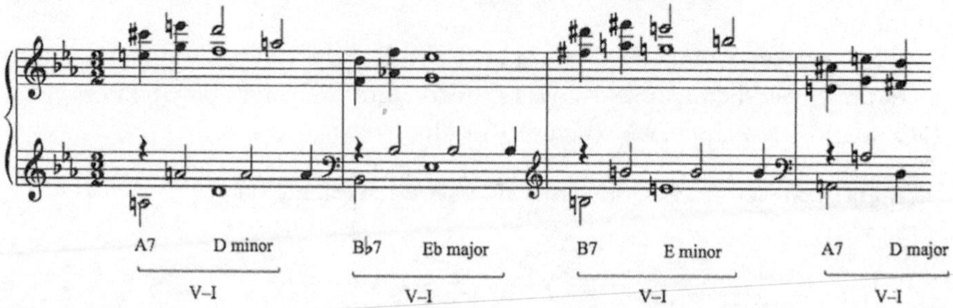


There is no additional development of previous material after the lyrical theme of Section 2, but rather a complete recapitulation of Section 1 material—again in the "home" key of E♭. In quick succession, we move from the fanfare (A) to the "jaunty" theme (B) to the cancan (C), to the march (D) to the "cute" rejoinder (E), with only slight variation from their renderings in the "exposition." At the end of the last, however, a slight truncation leads to the return of Section 2's lyrical theme (F)—but now in the "home" key of E♭. As such, Bernstein reveals a direct reference to the binary (large-scale A-A') precursor of sonata form (lacking a pure development), as was found in the late seventeenth-century opera sinfonia. To be more precise, the initial, A large-scale division consists of two main sections (1 and 2) that move harmonically from the tonic (I) in E♭ major to the dominant (V) of B♭ major; this tension is then "resolved" in the second, A' large-scale division, where Section 2 now remains in the tonic E♭—as shown in the following schema:

| Large-Scale Division | A | | A' | |
|---|---|---|---|---|
| Main Section | 1 | 2 | 1 | 2 |
| Subsection | A-B-C-A-B-C-D-E-D-E (transition) | F | A-B-C-D-E | F |
| Key Center | E♭ | B♭ | E♭ | E♭ |

The return of Section 2, moreover, is abridged: it uses only the main phrase (a) of subsection F, repeated twice. This is then followed by the same stepwise mini-coda used at the end of the phrase b, concluding with a "grand pause"—a dramatic gesture to get our attention.

What follows next is a distinct closing section that borrows one last number from the operetta: the famed coloratura vocalization from the aria "Glitter and Be Gay." This, incidentally, is among the most challenging arias in the entire operatic literature—with multiple high Cs and D♭s—and is modeled (theatrically more than musically) on the "Jewel Song" aria from Charles Gounod's *Faust*. For the Overture, Bernstein utilizes two passages from his aria: the vocalization passage noted above—complete with the original's canons at both the half note and whole note, and the driving concluding passage (Figure 15.16):

**Figure 15.16: Bernstein, *Candide* Overture (mm. 224–33)—closing section, based on "Glitter and Be Gay"**

This closing section, with a straightforwardly tonal harmonic language, provides the Overture with a fiery race to the end, akin to the best traditions of nineteenth-century grand opera. And yet Bernstein still isn't done: after the "Glitter" coda (G), we are treated to yet another quick pastiche of previous sections: a smattering of A, B, D, and F largely in guises heard before. It's almost as if Bernstein was reluctant to bring the work to a close. With a final, cute operetta-like V–I cadence, however, he does.

As this admittedly dense play-by-play analysis reveals, Bernstein employs his bag of tricks to deliver one of the most eclectic individual works we'll have discussed in this entire section—or certainly one rivaling that found in ACSS's "Release" or Shankar's *Morning Love*. And yet, the Overture seems to reflect not only Bernstein's personal eclecticism, but also the eclectic taste he expects from his listeners. He seems to be saying that the "modern" music lover has the opportunity—if not the obligation—to get acquainted with the wealth of diverse styles (classical, jazz, theater, etc.) out there, and thereby enjoy their appearance individually, as well as in combination. This message of "music without borders" is likewise something he echoed during his lifetime of lectures on an unusually wide array of musical topics. At a minimum, Subject 7, a confirmed devotee of the Overture, seems to have gotten the memo.

## Unwinding for Bed: Fauré's Sicilienne

**The Sicilienne, from Gabriel Fauré's *Pelléas et Mélisande*, Op. 80,** brings Subject 7's day to a close with a work that edges a bit closer to the obscure side of classical music, without actually getting there. The Sicilienne constitutes a good example—of which there are many in classical music—of the "I've heard that before but can't name it" phenomenon. Many classical works, by virtue of their periodic presence in media and the concert stage—not to mention the force and attraction of their musical materials—will be familiar to us even if we are at a complete loss to identify them. Indeed, there are hundreds of Internet sites dedicated to alleviating this head-scratching condition for music lovers—including sophisticated melody-input services like Musipedia.[662] In this particular case, Subject 7 has identified a familiar, if unnamable, movement from a composer, Gabriel Fauré, who for many is rather mysterious himself.

As such, the Sicilienne provides a great opportunity to explore the music of an historically significant, if little-known, composer. It may be noted too that with our discussion of this work, we reach the final detailed musical analysis in this book.

## FAURÉ: BACKGROUND

Gabriel Fauré (1845–1924), again, holds the somewhat unenviable distinction of being celebrated in academic circles yet little known among rank-and-file classical music fans—at least those outside the composer's native France.[663] In fact, his obscurity in America led a young Aaron Copland in 1924 to make Fauré the subject of his inaugural effort in music criticism, in an article entitled "Gabriel Fauré, a Neglected Master." Copland had just completed his studies in Paris with Nadia Boulanger, a former student of Fauré, and was keen to expose a "curious" reality: "Perhaps no other composer has ever been so generally ignored outside his own country, while at the same time enjoying an unquestionably eminent reputation at home."[664] Copland's esteem for Fauré was palpable: he called him "the Brahms of France," not due to imitation, but because "he possesses a genius as great, a style and a technique as perfect as that master." Such lavish praise no doubt helped raise Fauré's international reputation among music cognoscenti, even if his profile among average listeners has remained limited.

Limited, but not invisible: at least with regard to a few individual works. Those most frequently heard include the Pavane in F♯ Minor, Op. 50; "Berceuse" from the *Dolly Suite*, Op. 56; and the Requiem Mass, Op. 48—especially the movements "Pie Jesu" and "In Paradisum." The Pavane is especially well-known, not least by virtue of the plethora of arrangements available. This elegant, Spanish-tinged miniature was originally written for piano and chorus, but later adapted by the composer for orchestra and chorus; it has been used in dozens of films and TV shows. In that same small list of familiar "tunes" by Fauré, then, is Subject 7's pick: the Sicilienne from his orchestral suite *Pelléas et Mélisande*, which has likewise been the object of numerous adaptations.

But Fauré's historical contributions extend well beyond his creation of a few beloved musical gems. To better understand these contributions, it's worth presenting a brief overview of the broader musical evolution—following Beethoven's death in 1827—that could have given rise to a masterful yet underappreciated "Brahms of France" in the first place.

In the wake of Beethoven's groundbreaking innovations—alongside those of his contemporaries Schubert, Rossini, and Carl Maria von Weber—European classical music found itself, post-1830, fully ensconced in a new era: Romanticism. Its key musical attributes are those already found with Beethoven: an expanded view of tonality and chromaticism; greater organic cohesion through melodic and rhythmic "motives"; and a grander, less constrained approach to form. But increasingly, extramusical influences also gave vital impetus to the movement. These include a growing kinship with literature and poetry, giving rise to "program music"; a fascination with nature and spirituality; and a desire for intense subjective expression, among others.[665]

Leading exponents of this new style and aesthetic include especially Mendelssohn, Schumann, Chopin, Berlioz, and Liszt. While the symphony, concerto, and other grand forms continued to entice composers, it was the intimate genres of piano works, the art song, and chamber music that were particularly suited to the Romantic ideal. Much of their genesis arose not in the concert hall, but in private "salons"—gatherings of musicians, writers, artists, and intellectuals in aristocratic homes, notably in Paris. For example, much of the most beloved piano music today, such as the nocturnes and etudes of Chopin, was premiered in a private salon.

After 1850, two German musical titans—Johannes Brahms and Richard Wagner—led the Romantic era into a schism of sorts. Brahms began his career as a protégé of Schumann, who hailed him as "a genius . . . destined to give ideal expression to the times."[666] More forcibly than the earlier generation of Romantics, Brahms embraced the legacy of Beethoven and adopted a compositional approach that, while innovative on many levels (especially harmonically and via complex counterpoint), was fairly conservative with regard to form and extramusical affect. Brahms wrote a great deal of piano, art song, and chamber music, and yet his most impactful works were his four symphonies (the first labeled "Beethoven's Tenth"), branding him as the dedicated heir to tradition.

By contrast, Wagner was a revolutionary, embracing those extramusical aesthetics with a vengeance and using them as inspiration for his considerable musical innovations.[667] Rather than symphonies and piano sonatas, Wagner embraced the grandest of all musical genres, opera—later termed "music dramas"—as the vehicle by which to create an "Artwork of the Future": a "*Gesamtkunstwerk*" (total work of art), fully integrating music with every other element of theater.* In such works as *Tristan und Isolde* and the four operas of the *Ring* Cycle, Wagner realized this vision with a wildly advanced approach to harmony, motivic unity (via the leitmotif technique), orchestration, and especially emotional expression.[668]

As the fame of both composers grew, so too did their polemic, triggering an often bitter war between the Brahmsian "absolute music" and Wagnerian "programmatic music" schools. Other composers—especially in Germany, but spilling into France, Italy, and Eastern Europe—were to a degree forced to take sides. Wagner had Liszt and Bruckner as key allies, while Brahms had Clara Schumann—Robert's widow and a notable composer in her own right—and later Antonin Dvořák.

Such was the musical world into which Gabriel Fauré came of age. Initially, his own career path seemed destined toward that of a provincial church musician: at the age of nine, he was brought to Paris from his native Provence to study at

---

* Italy, to be sure, also made seminal contributions to music in the nineteenth century, though largely limited to the realm of opera: from the *bel canto* of Donizetti and Bellini (1830s) to Verdi's nationalism (1850s–'60s) to the *verismo* (realism) of Puccini (1890s), etc.

the École Niedermeyer, whose goal it was to produce church organists and choirmasters. In 1861, however, the sixteen-year-old Fauré came into contact with one of the more progressive composers in France, Camille Saint-Saëns—brought in briefly to replace the recently deceased school founder, Louis Niedermeyer. Saint-Saëns was an ardent admirer of Wagner and Liszt, even if his own works are more conservative, and he introduced these modern—indeed still scandalous—composers to his students' attention. This was enough to redirect Fauré's artistic ambitions, even if he was ill poised to make the transition career-wise.

Indeed, not unlike Bernstein, Fauré struggled throughout his life to find sufficient time to compose—and his overall output is relatively modest compared to many of his contemporaries. Until a degree of fame came his way after his fiftieth birthday, Fauré was forced to earn money as an organist in various Parisian churches and by teaching piano privately—neither of which he enjoyed much; curiously, while he produced a great deal of important piano music, he composed nothing for the organ. And yet his commitment to "progressive" music was steadfast: in 1871, he helped cofound the Société Nationale de Musique—together with Saint-Saëns and other leading French composers of the day, including Georges Bizet, César Franck, Vincent d'Indy, and Jules Massenet—specifically to promote new French music.

Fauré's own relationship to Wagner's revolutionary musical vision was complex. He certainly admired and knew the German's music well and, like so many young composers in the 1870s, traveled far and wide, including to Wagner's own Bayreuth Festspielhaus, to see performances of his operas and music dramas. But whereas most of his countrymen readily incorporated elements of Wagner's larger-than-life musical approach into their own works, Fauré resisted: the excesses in scope and sentiment were in direct contrast to his soberer, more natural aesthetic sensibilities.

This is not a trivial point, since it was the progressive mind-set, if not the materials he took from Wagner, that helped inspire Fauré to develop his own unique, progressive, and quintessentially French musical language. Most important were the barriers he broke in the realm of harmony—introducing a brand of chromaticism and fluid modulation, as well as extended chords (9ths and 11ths) and occasional dissonance, that would later inspire and inform Impressionist composers like Debussy and Ravel. Interestingly, Fauré was never interested in overt nationalism, and yet by his individual aesthetic he helped define a distinctly French style and sound. One thinks a bit of Charles Ives, who in an admittedly more radical and peculiar way did something similar for the United States in the early twentieth century.

Fauré's progressive style, not surprisingly, took a while to catch on with the French public—with few major successes before 1900. By contrast, he was greatly admired within the Parisian salon circuit, where many of his piano solo pieces, art songs, and chamber works were performed. It was in one of these salons—at the home of Princess Edmond de Polignac—that the composer met Marcel Proust, and the two became friends; Fauré was thus at least a partial inspiration for the novelist's fictional composer Vinteuil, in the first volume of *In Search of Lost Time*.[669]

Beyond these "intimate" genres, of course, Fauré wrote a number of larger works as well, including some—such as the Pavane (1887), the Requiem Mass (1888), the *Dolly Suite* (1897), and *Pelléas et Mélisande* (1898)—that earned him popular as well as monetary support. With growing fame came new professional opportunities, most notably his appointment, in 1905, as head of the Paris Conservatory—where his esteemed students included Boulanger, Maurice Ravel, George Enescu, and several other important composers of the Impressionist and 1920s generations. By his final years, Fauré was a hugely celebrated figure in France, and the recipient of many awards and concerts *d'hommage*. He eventually tried his hand at opera, such as *Pénélope* (1913), though none have entered the standard repertory. Most especially, however, Fauré was—and is—celebrated among his devotees for his often adventurous piano music (especially his thirteen nocturnes), his late chamber music (such as his two piano quartets), and above all his art songs, or "*mélodies*" as they are termed in French, such as "Après un rêve" and "Clair de lune."[670]

The power of Fauré's music, to those so inclined, is surely its delicate, airy, and coloristic French sensibility—with a kinship to predecessors like Rameau as well as successors like Debussy, Ravel, and Poulenc.[671] This "French-ness" in fact may help explain Fauré's limited appeal elsewhere, much to Copland's chagrin. There, is, by the way, a bit of irony in Copland's label of Fauré as the "the Brahms of France"—since by anecdotal evidence we learn that neither was a fan of the other.[672] Even geniuses, so we see, have a right to their own musical taste.

## FAURÉ: ANALYSIS

Fauré's *Pelléas et Mélisande* exemplifies one key dimension of the extramusical dynamic undergirding the romantic ideal: the symbiotic link between music and literature. The source here is the symbolist play of the same name by Belgian author Maurice Maeterlinck, written in 1893. Fauré's music was initially composed as incidental music (underscoring, between scenes, etc.) for a London production of the play in June 1898. He received the commission after Debussy—then at work on his own operatic adaptation, an idea apparently inspired by the iconoclastic composer Erik Satie—turned it down.[673] Having but a few months to complete the music, Fauré quickly sketched out a set of sixteen numbers of varying lengths, while likewise revisiting and adapting one earlier work: the Sicilienne. Given the limited time, as well as Fauré's general indifference to orchestration, as we'll see, he left that task to his student Charles Koechlin. Strikingly, the first critical reaction to Fauré's music, in the London *Times* on June 22, 1898, was anything but glowing:

> Judged by the ordinary standards of theatrical music . . . it is scarcely satisfactory, being wanting alike in charm and in dramatic power. It has, indeed, the vagueness of melodic and harmonious progression which may be held to suit best the character of the play, but its continued absence of tangible form, not to speak of its actual ugliness at many points, is such as to disturb rather than assist the illusion of the scene.[674]

One is reminded of the nasty 1907 *New York Post* reaction to Debussy's *La Mer* quoted in the Introduction. Again, critics often get it wrong, at least from history's vantage point. Indeed, within a few years, Fauré's music for *Pelléas* was widely celebrated even in London, with multiple performances of Maeterlinck's play accompanied by his incidental music over the next decade or so. More influential, though, was the abridged suite (Op. 80) consisting of four movements that Fauré reorchestrated himself and published in 1901—the object, again, of Subject 7's "hit parade" status. Before getting to that, however, a brief word on the musical influence of this symbolist play, and that of its immediate literary precursors.

During the nineteenth century, a good number of poets, novelists, and playwrights were embraced as perennial sources of musical inspiration. These include, especially, the German Romantic poets—such as Friedrich Schiller, Heinrich Heine, Friedrich Rückert, and Johann Wolfgang von Goethe—whose poems were set as lieder (German for "songs") by prominent composers like Schubert, Schumann, Brahms, Berlioz, Wolf, and Gounod. Arguably the century's most influential literary source on music, however, was Goethe's play version of the Faust legend—a fantastical tale of a scholar willing to offer his soul to the devil in exchange for transcendent knowledge—that inspired dozens of songs, orchestral "tone poems," and operas by composers such as Schubert, Liszt, Gounod, and Wagner to stretch the bounds of melodic, harmonic, formal, and instrumental norms.[675]

At the end of the century, another play became a notable catalyst for musical innovation: Maeterlinck's *Pelléas*. Admittedly, its embrace was not nearly so widespread or enduring as that of *Faust*, but it did inspire four significant works at the turn of the twentieth century—a particularly transformative period in classical music, as we've noted before. The first musical counterpart was Fauré's incidental music and suite (1898, 1901), followed by Debussy's opera (1902), a tone poem by Schoenberg (1903), and finally new incidental music by Jean Sibelius (1905).

The appeal of *Pelléas* among composers was less thematic and more stylistic and psychological. Maeterlinck followed upon the aesthetic of the French symbolist poets—such as Baudelaire, Mallarmé, and Verlaine, whose poems Fauré frequently set. Symbolist literature is dedicated to imagery rather than realism, to the world of dreams, mysticism, and the unconscious. The story of *Pelléas*—that of ill-fated lovers whose forbidden affair leads to tragedy—is not unique: a similar tale is told in Wagner's *Tristan und Isolde*, for example. But Maeterlinck's interest is less the actual love story than an exploration of the metaphysical duality of love and destruction, the mysticism behind coincidence, and the symbolic force of elements like water and dust. Little wonder that the play would go on to inspire both the Impressionist language of Fauré and Debussy, and the proto-expressionism of Schoenberg.[676]

As noted, the Sicilienne was not originally composed for *Pelléas*, but was written five years earlier, in March 1893, as a stand-alone work for cello and piano (Op. 78). This might suggest a superficial relationship to Maeterlinck's play. And yet it is worth noting that the four movements chosen by Fauré for the suite are not actually underscoring of particular scenes, but true "incidental" movements: the first (Quasi adagio) was the Prelude; the remaining three ("Fileuse" or "Spinning Song," the Sicilienne, and "Mort de Mélisande") were entr'actes, performed *between* acts. Still, scholars are quick to suggest direct connections between these movements and prominent symbols or emotions in the play—including the Sicilienne, said to depict a brief moment of joy shared by the two lovers, Pelléas and Mélisande. Indeed, as the Fauré scholar Jean-Michel Nectoux suggests, "If one did not know where the 'Sicilienne' came from, very few people would guess that it did not belong to *Pelléas*."[677] Rather than mere expediency, therefore, the Sicilienne seems to have been destined to find a new home in support of the play, and the ensuing suite.

Turning to the music itself, a decent degree of the listening experience is signaled right off the bat by the work's title: "sicilienne" is the French spelling of a popular Baroque-era Italian genre, the siciliana. As found in opera arias and scenes by Alessandro Scarlatti, as well as sonatas and concertos by Corelli and J. S. Bach, the siciliana is typically in a minor key, and invariably in a dotted triple-based rhythm—usually in the compound duple meter of 6/8 or 12/8. Likewise typical is a pastoral quality with a tinge of melancholy. All of these elements are on display in Fauré's Sicilienne, most of which are heard in the opening theme (see Figure 15.17 on the next page).

This, incidentally, is a useful reminder of the power of genre to shape not only the creativity of composers and artists, but likewise our listening expectations and experience. Before a composer or artist renders a note of a new blues or tango or waltz or fugue or siciliana, to name but a few, much of what we expect—and often hear—will emanate from rhythmic, harmonic, formal, melodic, and/or sonic conventions established through long-standing practice and well-known repertory. In what precise fashion those expectations are met or obfuscated—not to mention our reaction to it—is the magic and mystery of musical creativity and personal taste.

The experience of the Sicilienne begins with qualities aligned with its genre, but it certainly doesn't end there. As suggested above, a significant source of focus in this work—as in much of Fauré's music—is his unique and forward-looking approach to harmony. The opening theme shown below (following a characteristic one-measure arpeggiated intro in the harp) establishes the graceful dotted-triple rhythm of 6/8, as well as the sentimental tone of the key of G minor, but it likewise takes us to exotic harmonic terrain as the phrase unwinds. Specifically, the first full phrase starts and ends in G minor, but in its balanced eight-bar antecedent-consequent structure introduces chords and chord progressions quite atypical of a tonal phrase in G minor (Figure 15.17):

**Figure 15.17: Gabriel Fauré, *Pelléas et Mélisande*, 3. Sicilienne (mm. 2–9)—primary theme (Section A, phrase a)**

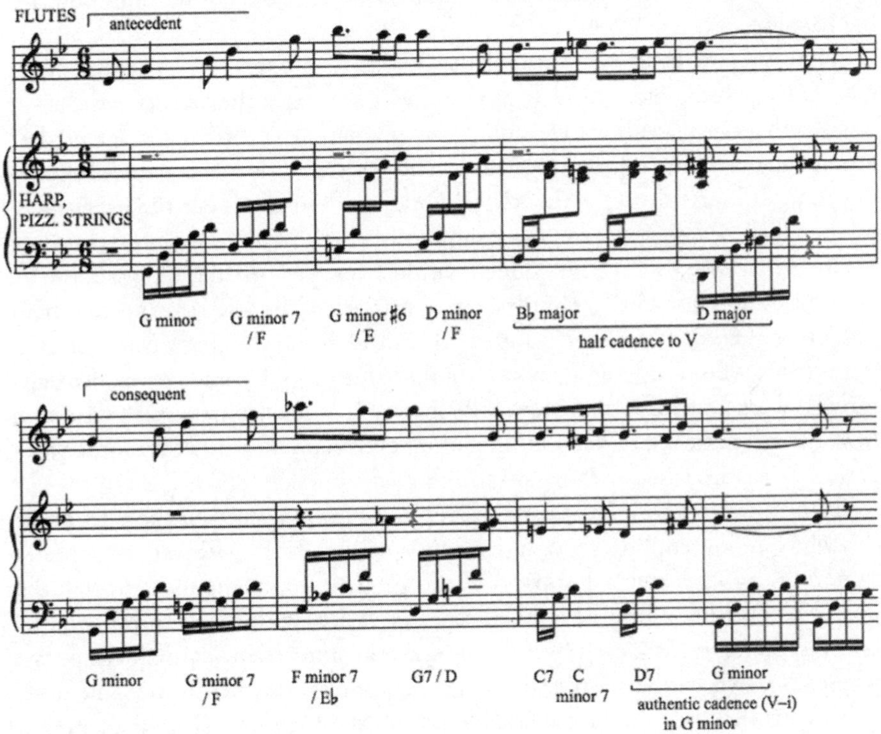


From a technical standpoint, Fauré introduces in this opening phrase (a) both a degree of tonal chromaticism and modal writing. The former, as we've seen, had been brewing and evolving since Beethoven's day, but the former was unusual for the times, and may have root in Fauré's youthful studies of Renaissance music—which, of course, is grounded on the church modes (see Chapter 3). The antecedent (mm. 2–5) quickly moves via a descending bass line to an inverted D minor (v)—instead of the "proper" major V chord. It then ends with an expected half cadence to D major, but via a progression from B♭ to C, with E♮ in the melody (instead of the expected E♭ as the sixth degree). The conclusion drawn from this "in-the-weeds" account is a kind of modal variant of the tonal key of G minor.*

(The discussion below indeed gets a bit detailed: take a look at the musical examples and listen to them with the commentary in mind. The main point is simply that Fauré is breaking some harmonic "rules" in order to get the unique sound we hear.)

The consequent (mm. 6–9) goes even further afield, quickly introducing an F minor 7 chord (with an A♭ in the melody), continuing on to an inverted G7 (I7) chord, followed by a parallel shift from C7 to C minor 7 (IV7 to iv7) before concluding with an expected V–i authentic cadence in G minor. While defying simple analysis, this phrase introduces an element of the Phrygian mode (via the ♭II degree of A♭) along with general chromaticism—enabled by a simple descending bass line.

How precise Fauré was in articulating these progressions as tonal versus modal, etc., in his own mind is hard to say, but clearly they struck his ear—as ours, perhaps—as fresh yet elegant. Some scholars have traced his flexible harmonic language, including the kinds of "modal suggestions," as James Sobaskie put it, just discussed, to the theoretical notions of Gustave Lefèvre, his harmony teacher at the École Niedermeyer, who published a *Traité d'harmonie* (Harmony Treatise) in 1889. In it, he sanctioned within a "proper" tonal framework the use of altered and "borrowed" chords (e.g., a minor 3rd instead of expected major 3rd, or vice versa), as well as expanded 9th and 11th chords, etc.[678] But regardless, it was Fauré who translated such new thinking into tangible and well-constructed musical works—whose influence made its way into the Impressionist writing of the next generation and beyond, including eventually into the harmonic world of jazz, as we discussed with regard to Bill Evans in Chapter 11.

Fauré's exotic harmonic palette is even more pronounced in the next phrase (b), which follows upon a repetition of the opening phrase with varied orchestration. In it, we also catch a glimpse of Fauré's inventive melodic style: an eight-bar phrase comprising a four-bar phrase repeated twice, with the slightest variation between them; in turn, each four-bar phrase is an antecedent-consequent phrase, where both two-bar halves repeat the same contour and many of the same notes. In all, this demonstrates a remarkable economy of means—a kind of musical equivalent to the internal rhyme structure favored by the symbolist poets (Figure 15.18):

* That is, G Dorian—in essence, a G minor scale with E♮, as a raised sixth degree.

**Figure 15.18: Gabriel Fauré, *Pelléas et Mélisande*, 3. Sicilienne (mm. 18–25)—Section A, phrase b**

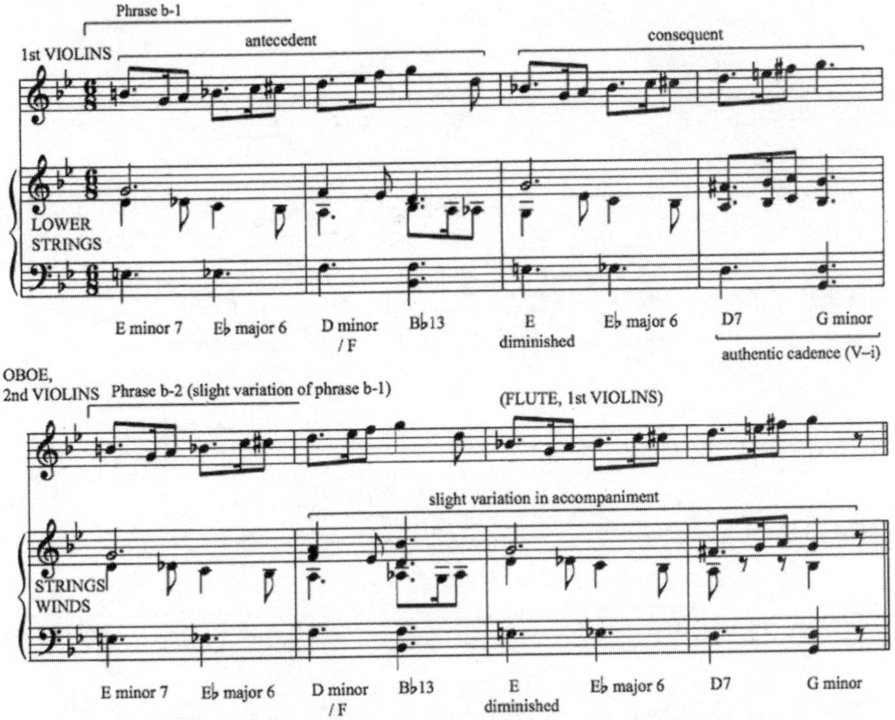


The melody here demonstrates Fauré's penchant to gracefully "unfold" a melody via varied repetitions and sequences. Combined with the subtle and chromatic shifts in harmony—particularly the unpredictable alternations of B♮ (within an E minor 7th chord) and B♭ (within an E♭6 chord)—the phrase rather tickles the ear.

A third phrase (c) then ensues with a sustained and dramatic contrast to the more lyrical opening phrases. Here too the harmony is classic Fauré, via a progression suggesting that for him mere triads alone often don't cut it. Specifically, it is another overall eight-bar antecedent-consequent phrase that, like phrase b, is composed of a two-bar subphrase repeated four times; distinctly, though, each begins with a striking and sustained chord progression: F9–G minor 6. The fourth of these (c-2') then winds down with an unexpected F minor 6 chord that heralds the return of the opening phrase in G minor (Figure 15.19):

**Figure 15.19: Gabriel Fauré, *Pelléas et Mélisande*, 3. Sicilienne (mm. 26–33)—Section A, phrase c**

A single pass of the opening (a) phrase signals the end of the first main section (A)—thus proceeding: a-a-b-b-c-c'-a. There then follows a comparatively short B section, which ably fulfills another expectation of the siciliana genre: a pastoral quality. As used frequently in the music of Beethoven, Wagner, and others, a bucolic mood is effectively conjured via use of a harmonic pedal. The B section is made up of four phrases, following the formal schema: d-e-d'-f: phrase d begins in E♭ major (the relative major to G minor), in a mildly chromatic progression over an E♭ pedal; in phrase e, it shifts to a similar passage over a B♭ pedal before returning to the E♭ pedal in phrase d'. Yet, the most interesting phrase of this section, at least harmonically, is phrase f, where the E♭ pedal supports an intriguing and quite chromatic two-bar chord progression: F7–C♭7–E♭, repeated twice. In this, we hear a faint hint of Debussy's *Prélude à l'après-midi d'un faune*—that groundbreaking Impressionist work written in 1894, a year after Fauré's original version of this Sicilienne (Figure 15.20):

**Figure 15.20: Gabriel Fauré, *Pelléas et Mélisande*, 3. Sicilienne (mm. 58–61)—Section B, phrase f**

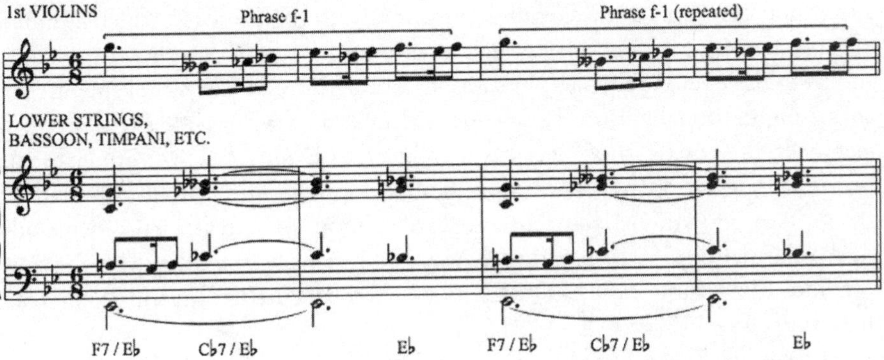


Apart from its pastoral affect, and the striking Impressionist harmony of its closing phrase (f), the B section is notable for two other musicological dimensions otherwise absent in the A section. The first is a level of rhythmic asymmetry, built out of a sequence of odd-numbered phrase lengths (5+3+3+3+4); this, in fact, is about the extent of Fauré's rhythmic convolution, as his approach to this parameter is generally conservative—in keeping with his overall penchant for narrative fluidity. The second element, more typical of Fauré, is the use of counterpoint. Here it appears mildly in the opening (d) phrase, as two balanced lines in contrary motion: one descending in the winds, the other ascending in the cellos (Figure 15.21):

**Figure 15.21: Gabriel Fauré, 3. Sicilienne (mm. 44–48)—Section B, phrase d (light counterpoint)**

The Impressionist harmony of that closing phrase (f) not only yields sonic focus of its own, but likewise acts as an effective transition back to the A section; specifically it returns to the equally Impressionist third phrase (c), which as noted also begins with an F7 chord, though now in root position. We then predictably return to the opening theme (phrase a), heralding the end of the movement. Not surprisingly, though, Fauré closes out with a coda that revisits a few previous elements: it begins with a "deceptive" cadence to E♭; it proceeds with elements of modal suggestion by virtue of its descending bass line through D♭ and A♮ (hinting at both the Mixolydian and Lydian modes). The arpeggiated melody in the clarinet echoes the opening theme, and its closing interplay with the flute provides a final hint of the G Dorian mode via the recurring E♮. And so ends our harmony lesson!

It may have been noted that our analysis made relatively little to-do about the formal structure of the Sicilienne—noting in passing the progression of large-scale sections and internal phrases. In part this reveals my confidence in your ability to process formal schema by this point in our discussion, but it also relates to the fact that for Fauré, form is generally a pretty conventional thing. Not unlike Brahms, Fauré's approach to form is by and large conservative, embracing well-trodden templates—such as the ternary (ABA) form favored in the piano and chamber works of Schumann and Chopin—both major influences on the Frenchman.

Similarly, this discussion has virtually bypassed the topic of instrumentation and "sound"—often deemed synonymous with French music, especially early Modern composers like Debussy and Ravel. In fact, Fauré was famously uninterested in orchestration; his decision to allow his student to orchestrate the original incidental version of *Pelléas* was not merely a matter of time management, but also a reflection of his creative aesthetic: he was notably disparaging of overly vivid orchestral effects (such as those found in Wagner), finding them a frequent disguise for a dearth of musical ideas.[679]

By contrast, Fauré's key concern seems to have been the "pure" musical idea and its proper and creative development. This led him above all to explore new and innovative approaches to harmonic and melodic writing, whose impacts are still being felt today. In short, Fauré seems to have understood what he was good at and focused his efforts on developing just those things. Happily too Subject 7 seems to have understood what Fauré was good at—at least in his Sicilienne: enough to embrace it as an ideal favorite with which to call it a day!

## Insights Gained about Subject 7's Musical Taste

Following our rather intensive discussion of these five classical works—the four discussed here plus the fifth (Carl Orff's "O Fortuna" from *Carmina Burana*) discussed on the WYLI website—what can we conclude about Subject 7's musical taste? First, as noted several times, the hits selected tend to be works that have earned a place of some currency and status within the broader classical music repertoire. From the composers and titles alone, they suggest that Subject 7 did not stumble upon these works casually—as from a set of CDs borrowed from the library or bought impulsively at a garage sale. Instead, they suggest that these favorites arose through a degree of scrutiny and dedication to the species—and that Subject 7 could readily add dozens (or hundreds) of other, similarly esteemed classical favorites. Of course, that may not be the case at all—for taste assumptions based on a small sample are always dangerous, as we noted in Interlude F. At the same time, it appears presumptuous to call Subject 7 a "classical expert" who lives and breathes the nuances and arcana of the species. Not only the composers, but also the works themselves, are relatively "well-heeled": commonly inserted into concert programs, radio playlists, and even "classical favorites" compilations. Absent, that is, are truly obscure composers or even obscure or "academic" works by well-known composers—a choral work by C. P. E. Bach or a chamber work by Alban Berg, for example. Again, one cannot confidently assert that Subject 7 dislikes C. P. E. Bach's Magnificat in D, Wq. 215, or Alban Berg's *Lyric Suite* for string quartet—though it might be a reasonable bet.

From a musicological standpoint, we can attempt a provisional taste profile of Subject 7, despite the variety of musical styles, techniques, and eras represented. For example, each work possesses, in its own way, an element of driving, pulse-based rhythm. Whether by steady ostinatos (Beethoven), perpetual sixteenth note motion (Vivaldi), near-constant syncopation (Bernstein), or lilting dotted rhythms (Fauré), each work moves with a level of propulsion that invites at least some toe tapping. By contrast, none of these works operates with either a pulseless rubato or an unusually complex metric language. The takeaway, therefore, might be a taste profile of Subject 7 for classical works with a strong metric drive.

Among other elements found frequently in this hit list include the use of pedal points (often with a pastoral affect), a degree of counterpoint (palpably in the Vivaldi and Beethoven), and a creative use of sonic contrasts via changes in dynamics and orchestration (notably in Beethoven). In still other areas, Subject 7 seems decidedly eclectic and open-minded: notably in the realm of harmony, where diatonic, chromatic, modal, and tonal discourses all find favor—sometimes in the same work (e.g., Bernstein and Fauré). This latter, indeed, suggests that Subject 7 has developed a fairly discerning ear for advanced harmony—not to mention sophisticated approaches in formal construction. Of course, there still remains some mystery as to Subject 7's genotype: for example, we'd be hard-pressed to say how welcome melodic sequences (Vivaldi) or stylistic pluralism (Bernstein) might be in other contexts, given their limited exposure here.

At any rate, we can already make some musical suggestions for Subject 7, starting with related works by the same composers—here addressing only the four works discussed in this chapter. Specifically, we might name "Allegro assai" from Concerto for Four Violins in E Minor, Op. 3, no. 4 (Vivaldi); "Marcia funebre" from Symphony no. 3 in E♭ (*Eroica*), Op. 55 (Beethoven); "Prologue" to *West Side Story* (Bernstein); and "Pastorale" from the *Masques et bergamasques* suite, Op. 112 (Fauré).

Stretching out beyond these composers, a positive opinion by Subject 7 seems plausible for works by other composers residing in similar historical/stylistic spaces: Allegro from Arcangelo Corelli's Concerto Grosso in C Minor, Op. 6, no. 3, or Allegro from Pietro Locatelli's Concerto Grosso in E Minor, Op. 1, no. 4 (Vivaldi); "Andante con moto" from Franz Schubert's Symphony no. 9 in C, D. 944, or "Andante con moto" from Felix Mendelssohn's Symphony no. 4 in A (*Italian*), Op. 90 (Beethoven); *El Salón México* by Aaron Copland or Overture to *The School for Scandal*, Op. 5, by Samuel Barber (Bernstein); or *Prélude à l'après-midi d'un faune* by Claude Debussy or *Menuet antique* by Maurice Ravel (Fauré).

We can then expand Subject 7's horizons further by considering influences on and/or "heirs" to the composers involved: Alessandro Stradella and J. S. Bach (Vivaldi); Joseph Haydn and Johannes Brahms (Beethoven); Charles Ives and Stephen Sondheim (Bernstein); and Camille Saint-Saëns and Francis Poulenc (Fauré).

Finally, extending Subject 7's musicological preferences beyond classical music would open yet a more remote repertoire: the Chieftains or Donna Summer (driving rhythm); Brad Mehldau or Dead Can Dance ("modal flavor"); David Bowie or Jerome Kern (complex tonal harmony); Nirvana or Stan Kenton (sonic contrasts); Frank Zappa or Stephen Schwartz (stylistic pluralism). Admittedly, going from Vivaldi and Beethoven to Nirvana and Donna Summer might be a bridge too far, but keeping an open mind and ear is the key to forming a vibrant musical genotype—so why not?

Classical music is clearly a species that invites a deeper layer of discourse than many others. The intricate weave between individual works, composer biographies, and broad historical trends is built into the fabric of classical music in a way generally not the case with jazz or rock, for example. This is certainly not to say that those other species don't also invite this vibrant intersection of music, musicians, and history, particularly to their devotees. Indeed, it is an assertion of this book that the more one understands the milieu—personal and historical—surrounding any piece of music, the more its musicological elements will come alive to a listener, positively or negatively. Yet classical music, with its thousand-plus years of history, where composers prominent and obscure unwind a lifetime of steady development and continuous output (to a degree beyond that in other species), is perhaps most susceptible to such unwinding. As a result, the in-depth discussions in this chapter will likely have been more expected to those already predisposed to classical music than those new to the party. Hopefully, though, the sheer wealth of history and nuance aligned with just these five works alone will entice those unfamiliar to open their minds—and ears—to uncover their own hit list of classical favorites, such as Subject 7 just did.

One final side note: You will likely have noticed that in all of our discussion of classical music, very little was said about a key constituency of the species: the performers. This is by no means meant to minimize the importance or appeal of classical artists, who are among the most impressive and accomplished musicians anywhere. The issue, however, is that your personal taste concerning a particular piece of classical music is by and large not contingent on *who* is performing it. That is, if you love or hate the Allegretto from Beethoven's Symphony no. 7, it is likely that this opinion has very little to do with whether it was conducted by Herbert von Karajan or Nikolaus Harnoncourt, or if the orchestra involved was the London Symphony or the Royal Concertgebouw Orchestra. Of course, a "bad" performance can turn you off to a work you'd otherwise love, just as a particularly inspired performance can open your heart to a work that you'd otherwise ignore. But assuming that the notes and rhythms are performed correctly, and that the interpretation is in keeping with the expectations of the composer and the era, the *real* criteria will be the music itself. This is the same rationale for why Pandora only provides one analysis per classical work, and doesn't code one performance versus another. The classical artist assuredly plays a role in gaining your attention, but it is the composer who ultimately determines whether you like it or you don't.

# Interlude G

*Mind Over Music: Psychology and Musical Taste*

## The Final Mile

Now that we've covered the musicological and sonic foundations of our musical taste—well, okay, not covered . . . introduced, perhaps—we may at last move into that final mile of our aesthetic whodunit: the interaction of music and psychology.

Of all the extramusical topics addressed in this book, in fact, this is the one I am most naturally predisposed to discuss. This is due especially to having grown up with a school psychologist as a father—who in later years became a hardcore Jungian. During practically every phone call or visit home, my dad would all but require a lengthy discussion on Carl Jung, the powers of the unconscious, and its profound influence on our everyday behavior. That my daughter, Camille, is now pursuing a career in cognitive neuroscience only reinforces this tendency. At any rate, I have in this interlude the vital task of unwinding the myriad connections between music and psychology, and their combined influence on our musical taste—or, as it is generally labeled in the field, our musical preferences. More specifically, this interlude will focus on the insights to be gained from a musical exploration of two specific subfields: behavioral and personality psychology.

Framed by these two subfields, music psychology has pursued a wide array of questions on how we experience music and what it means to us as individuals. Given its ubiquity in our daily lives—between 14 and 17 percent of waking hours—scholars have sought to quantify how music listening impacts our character and our personal and social identity—especially during youth—as well as its potential links to our physical, mental, and emotional well-being; these latter issues will be taken up more explicitly in the Epilogue. Other topics of interest include the varied ways in which we listen to music—cognitively, emotionally, socially, and aesthetically—as well as the psychological effects triggered by varied musical stimuli by virtue of aspects like tension-release, expectation, familiarity, motion, etc.

Most extensively, behavioral and personality psychology have in recent years tackled two broad topics: (1) the nature and experience of musical emotions, and (2) the complex dynamic between our personality, our listening behavior, and our musical preferences. By covering these two topics in detail, this interlude is perhaps the most intensive in the book. Such is warranted, in my view, not only because these two broad topics—and the various competing theories that underlie them—are in fierce development and debate at this very moment, but also and especially because it is here that we truly get to the heart of this book: why *you* like it.

## A Language of Emotion

Undoubtedly, the high esteem we humans have universally granted music derives in large part from its potent associations with emotion. Defining or quantifying that association, on the other hand, has never enjoyed universal consensus. Indeed, as we saw in Interlude C, the mere question of how concretely one can define this association divided musicians and music lovers into near warring factions in the nineteenth and early twentieth centuries (the "War of the Romantics")—between those claiming any concrete semantic or emotional link was "only an illusion," as Stravinsky put it, and those, like Wagner and Liszt, who saw the association as fundamental to music's very essence. In the wake of the more nuanced mid-twentieth-century reflections by philosophers and theorists like Susanne Langer and Leonard Meyer, we today have embraced a more empirical approach to explaining the link—not only neurobiologically, as we discussed in Interlude C, but also psychologically, as we'll discuss here. Although Deryck Cooke's original meaning has since been challenged—that melodic archetypes trigger concrete emotions—most today would agree with his 1959 description of music as a "language of emotion"[680]; but how?

Stepping back, the ancient Greeks staunchly promoted music's emotional force, as we've remarked previously. Aristotle's admonition against the use of professional instruments like the kithara in education reflects not so much an issue with the sound of the instrument, per se, but rather with the *style* of music—modes, rhythms, improvisatory approaches—that professional musicians routinely employed on it. That is, experience had clearly revealed to Aristotle the emotional sway that a good kithara performance could hold over an audience, who likely screamed for more—in turn compelling him to endorse constraints on its public use.[681]

Plato, in the *Republic*, went so far as to narrow music's emotional force to the level of particular modes: "The Mixolydian," he wrote, "and the intense Lydian, and others similar to them . . . we must do away with them," by virtue of their ability to arouse sadness, sloth, and softness in both women and men; by contrast, "there are certain Ionian and Lydian [modes] that are called relaxed," while there is also the Dorian, "that would fittingly imitate the utterances and the accents of a brave man who is engaged in warfare."[682] While, once again, Plato was undoubtedly referring to the *styles* of melodies and rhythms associated with these modes, his comments must also reflect his personal witness of music's potent emotional qualities—sadness, calm, bravery—and its associated influence on one's overall character and virtue.

With all the lofty pronouncements of music's emotional powers uttered by philosophers, writers, and musicians over the centuries, and not only in the West, but likewise in India, Persia, and Japan, etc.,[683] it was only in the twentieth century that efforts were made to delimit and quantify them via actual research. Early attempts, such as those by Harry Weld (1912), Kate Hevner (1936), Lage Wedin (1972), and Edward Asmus (1985), gradually yielded a taxonomical approach to identifying those specific emotions that could be empirically aligned with the experience of listening to music. Hevner, for example, proposed an eight-spoked "adjective circle," with each spoke comprising six to eleven "closely related and compatible" words ("merry," "joyous," "gay" . . . ; "pathetic," "doleful," "sad" . . .); listeners were asked to select from a list of sixty-six adjectives used to characterize various classical works, as well as distinct musicological elements: major versus minor mode, strict versus rubato rhythm, etc.[684] Asmus similarly asked participants to evaluate the appropriateness of ninety-nine words "indicative of musical affect" while listening to three rather random pieces of music, based on varying levels of intensity; using the statistical method of "factor analysis," he was then able to devise a nine-factor model of music-emotion dimensions—an odd mix of nouns and adjectives: evil, sensual, potency, humor, pastoral, longing, depression, sedative, and activity.[685]

As we'll see below, such taxonomical approaches to quantifying musical emotion are alive and well in music psychology today, with varying theories and methodologies at play. Yet, importantly, the use of statistically controlled studies to match music to specific emotions has become part of a much broader effort to empirically validate that ancient intuition that music is indeed a "language of emotion"—perhaps most concretely via the neurobiological findings we reviewed in Interlude C.

Before diving deeper into current thinking on the non-hard-science side of musical emotions, however, it will be good to first consider some of the things these researchers have considered so useful about them. If, as music psychologist John Sloboda writes, music's emotional effects are "why we love it," we may rightly wonder what exactly those effects might be.[686] Chief among the powers of music are its ability to influence our mood, regulate our emotional state, relieve stress, adjust our mind-set or behavior, impact our sexual arousal, alter our state of consciousness, increase or lessen our socialization, and affect our mental, physical, and psychological well-being. Not an insignificant list.

## To Feel or Not to Feel

When Hanslick and Stravinsky challenged the notion that music was capable of expressing emotion, they were in essence accusing their opponents of committing an "attribution error"—mistaking the *perception* of emotional affect in the music for the *induction* of an aroused emotion within the listener. In modern parlance, they were articulating the dichotomy of the "cognitivist" versus the "emotivist" position of musical emotions: the former, with roots in Meyer, poses that music is in fact incapable of inducing emotion within us, and that instead our perception of it stems from our cognitive appraisal of the affect we hear in the music; the latter, of course, argues that, no, music *is* capable of inducing emotion within us.[687] Complicating matters is the fact that, until recently, the two perspectives were often conflated in discussions of musical emotions—writers would often discuss them without clearly stating whether they were articulating perceived or felt emotions, or both.[688]

As was revealed in Interlude C, the evidence is now undisputed that music can elicit emotions within us, indeed powerful ones with strong psychophysical dimensions (e.g., thrills and chills)—and others akin to emotions we feel in everyday life in response to the events and people we encounter. And yet it is important to note that perceived and induced emotions are not the same thing, even if they at times overlap in the same musical experience. Happy-*sounding* music, it is true, can and often does make us *feel* happy. Think of the last time you heard Gene Kelly's "Singing in the Rain," or Beethoven's "Ode to Joy," or even Pharrell's "Happy"—did you not feel at least a bit more content? Perhaps you feel upbeat just thinking about them. Similarly, sorrowful-*sounding* music can make us *feel* sad—as perhaps happened to you when you last heard "Dido's Lament" (from Henry Purcell's *Dido and Aeneas*), Billie Holiday's "Gloomy Sunday," or Chris Isaak's "Wicked Game."

The six songs just listed, in fact, fit the musical stereotype of these opposing moods: happy music as upbeat and in a major mode, sad songs as slow and in a minor mode. But like all stereotypes, there are flaws in this simple characterization. Among the most consistently rated "sad songs" in online polls, for example, is Adele's "Someone Like You"—which is in a major mode, featuring two common chord cycles for its verse and chorus: I–iii–vi–IV and I–V–vi–IV, respectively. And would you label Elton John's "Your Song" or Debussy's "Clair de lune" as "happy-sounding," despite the fact both are in a major key and not particularly slow? Lyrics make a difference, of course, but affect is also grounded in the music—and "Your Song" *is* an upbeat lyric.

More to the point, these contrasting moods provide an occasion to confirm the distinction and potential mismatch between our perception and inducement of musical emotions—namely, via the so-called "paradox of negative emotions."

This is the expression used in modern aesthetics to refer to the fact that we often find pleasure in experiencing art that depicts decidedly negative emotions or scenarios, with direct origins in Aristotle's "paradox of tragic pleasure," or catharsis. The paradox or at least dissonance between depicted/perceived negative emotions in works of literature, art, and music and the positive emotions we experience/feel in encountering them has consistently piqued the interest of writers, philosophers, and scholars—including Saint Augustine, Hume, Kant, Schopenhauer, and legions of modern scholars in varying disciplines.[689] Their deliberations have yielded varied explanations for how the paradox is resolved, if not dissolved out right: that we find pleasure in experiencing negative situations of sorrow, fear, or pity in a decidedly safe environment; that art is able to portray negative emotions in a beautiful and aesthetic way; that the pain or negativity in art provides positive and intrinsically valuable life lessons; and that the felt pleasure comes via cognitive processes such as the fictive use of simile and metaphor, among others.

Music-oriented scholars have also sought to explain the paradox. David Huron, for example, proposed a "hedonic" (pleasurable) theory: in at least some cases, sad-sounding music—perhaps amplified by cognitive processes and/or subjective associations—triggers the release of the hormone prolactin, with the effect of calming and consoling the listener. Prolactin—best known for its role in enabling females to produce milk—is released during pregnancy and nursing, after sex, and notably during moments of psychic, as opposed to physical, pain. As such, the "state of sadness" conjured by the music in essence tricks the brain into releasing prolactin—in turn creating a sense of pleasure, particularly given the absence of an actual sad event. "At the end of the day," Huron writes, "the listener is (cognitively) aware that they are merely listening to music, and that the grief-like feelings do not warrant the negative appraisals of a true tragedy."[690]

The range of theories (of which there are many others) aside, the paradox of negative emotions is proof that there is indeed a distinction between perceived and felt emotions in music, at least on occasion. Yet this famed paradox is by no means the only instance of a "disconnect" between these two emotional reactions. To cite two obvious examples: First, the jingle for the Kars4Kids TV commercial is undeniably happy-sounding—major mode, jaunty tempo, positive message—and yet for many listeners, the emotion induced is anything but happy; in fact, it has been labeled the "most hated" and "most annoying jingle of all time" in online forums.[691] Second, the opening of Chopin's "funeral march"—from his Piano Sonata no. 2 in B♭ Minor—is, from a purely musicological standpoint, the epitome of sad-sounding music: minor mode, slow and plaintive pacing; and yet, its overuse in cartoons and comedy sketches—Looney Tunes, Monty Python, *Beetlejuice*, etc.—have made it so hopelessly cliché as to only arouse pleasurable laughter within us today.[692]

One more case is worth citing that bears on one's cognitive appraisal, musical experience, and subjective interpretation. Imagine you're invited to attend your niece's high school orchestra concert. First on the program is the opening movement of Mozart's *Eine kleine Nachtmusik*—assuredly among the most happy-sounding pieces in the entire classical repertoire: major mode, brisk tempo, simple arpeggiated melody, balanced antecedent-consequent phrases. The performance, on the one hand, has issues—remember, this is your niece's *high school* orchestra: the intonation or tuning of the strings is rather shaky (to be kind), rhythmic alignment among the players and voice parts frequently off, and expressive interpretation lacking. Your niece's best friend—raised, like Subject 1, on the pop genotype of Taylor Swift et al.—hears the movement's bouncy tempo, familiar melodies, and sweet harmonies, and is overcome with a *felt* happy emotion. You, on the other hand, are a classical aficionado: you've heard this work hundreds—maybe thousands—of times, performed by the greatest orchestras in the world. While you are proud of your niece for playing the violin, and glad you came to the concert, hearing this performance induces not a happy emotion, but rather one that vacillates between embarrassment, unease, and outright anger.

In short, music may be a language of emotion, but the emotions one perceives emanating from the music's sonic qualities may be distinct from, if not contrary to, those one feels inside one's own heart and mind. Further, one may perceive a particular emotion in a piece of music, and yet feel absolutely nothing; or, by contrast, may perceive no emotion in the music, or at least nothing concrete, and yet feel a powerful surge of concrete emotion welling up inside. Given the role that these emotional dynamics play in the music you like—or don't—they are worthy of careful attention. So, what emotions are these? Are perceived emotions different from induced ones? Which are more common in our music-listening experiences?

We'll address these and related questions shortly. But before we do, let's take a step back and consider how emotions are typically conceptualized and measured, as well as how music might be capable of expressing emotion in the first place.

## Dimensions and Categories

Psychologists—including of the music variety—talk about emotions in myriad ways. There is, first of all, the rather nuanced distinction between affect, emotion, and mood—terms often conflated by scholars, not to mention in everyday language. Through the efforts of psychologists like James Russell, Lisa Feldman Barrett, and Nico Frijda, however, these terms have increasingly gained more precise, technical meanings as distinct components of "emotion" writ large.[693] As we'll refer to these components many times below, their distinctions are worth noting:

*Affect* is the simple yet fundamental psychological *state* that underlies our moods and emotions—such as pleasure or displeasure, tension or relaxation, energy or inactivity.[694] *Emotion* is the fuller and more specific *feeling* we get in response to an event, a person, or thing we encounter, whether real or "in our head." At root, our emotions draw upon the general affects we experience (pleasure, displeasure, tension, relaxation, etc.), but they are more precise—bemusement, joy, melancholy, despair, nervousness, terror, etc.—and in turn incorporate other "co-occurring" components: behavior, attention, attribution of origin, etc. *Mood* is similar to emotion, but is *longer lasting* and less specific in its point of origin or object; indeed, moods can be disconnected from any particular stimuli in either time or space.[695]

Next, in studying the interplay of music and emotion, scholars have looked at these three components via two broad approaches: *dimensions* and *categories*.

The dimensional approach to organizing musical emotions applies only to affects, which it measures as falling into one of two binary dimensions. The most common of these is *valence*, whereby an affect is measured as being either *positive or negative*—for example, happy, excited, joyful, and humorous all have "positive valence"; sad, tense, sorrowful, and frightening all have "negative valence." Other common dimensional ways to organize musical emotions are *arousal* (*tense* or *relaxed*), *intensity* (*energetic* or *inactive*), *activation* (*high* or *low*), and *potency* (*dominant* or *submissive*).

In practice, however, only two of the dimensional measures are employed when discussing musical affect: valence and arousal; this is the approach used, for example, in James Russell's popular "circumplex model"—visually represented in circular space with arousal as the vertical axis and valence as the horizontal axis (see Figure G.1). To demonstrate this model using our previous musical examples: Pharrell's "Happy" would measure *high in arousal* (animated, energetic, thrilling) and *positive in valence* (joyful, happy, content); "Gloomy Sunday" would measure *low in arousal* (gentle, meditative, relaxed) and *low in valence* (sad, depressing, sorrowful); Debussy's "Clair de lune," by contrast, would likely measure *low in arousal* (slow, rubato tempo) yet *high in valence* (major, lyrical). This is illustrated more intuitively in Figure G.1.

**Figure G.1: Circumplex Model (for "Happy", "Gloomy Sunday", "Claire de lune")**

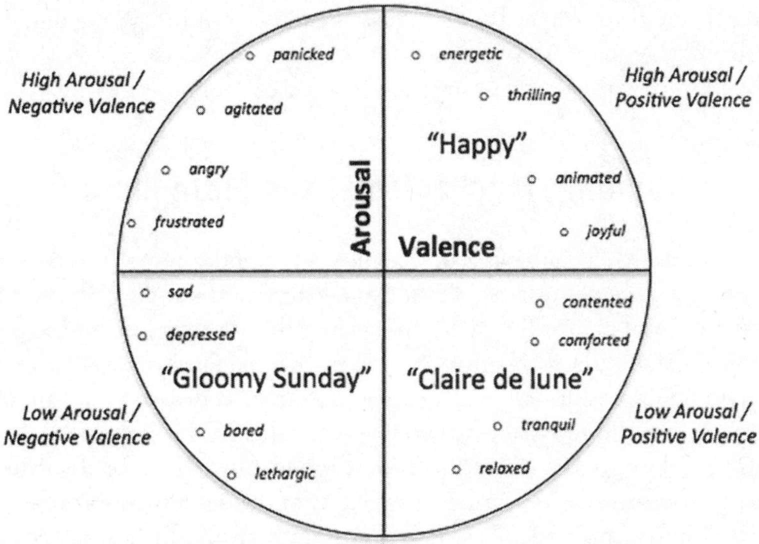


Measuring the impact—perceived or felt—of musical emotion using the dimensional approach, based on affect alone, has the advantage of simplicity and uniformity: a small set of dimensions with clear opposite poles: positive/negative; high/low. And yet, not surprisingly, some music-emotion researchers have criticized its limiting aspects, especially over the past decade. Marcel Zentner, for example, calls the two-tiered "circumplex" approach a "procrustean bed" that lacks the "qualitative differentiation required by the study of the emotional effects of music."[696] As such, Zentner and other leading music-emotion researchers today, such as Patrik Juslin, advocate moving *beyond* the broad, continuous, and dimensional nature of affect and into the more discrete, specific, and complex arena of emotions and moods. By definition, their discrete nature means that they are organized and measured as categories—with clear, distinct boundaries.

Juslin, for example, notes that while both the dimensional and categorical approaches have neurophysiological support, they are not equally equipped to measure the *concreteness* of emotional expression—such as that emanating from music: "People do not spontaneously report emotions as coordinates within an abstract, multi-dimensional emotional space."[697] Anger and fear, for example, are both *high in arousal* and *negative in valence*—and yet they are obviously rather different emotions; relying solely on dimensions, we could not tell them apart. To use a musical parallel: John Philip Sousa's "Stars and Stripes Forever" and Duke Ellington's "Take the A Train" are both *high in arousal* and *positive in valence*—up-tempo, rhythmically vibrant major mode, etc.—and yet few, I presume, would describe them as expressing, or inducing, the same emotion.

To wit, the discrete, categorical approach has become the one most favored by researchers to measure and describe musical emotions—though the dimensional approach has by no means disappeared, as we'll see. Which categories are deemed suitable, and how they are best organized, however, is another matter.

## Coding, Mechanisms, and Metaphors

Whether measured as categories or dimensions, or both, however, it is a separate question to ask *how* music is able to express an emotional identity that can in turn be perceived and/or felt by us. In tackling this thorny issue, music psychologists have followed a path similar to those—like Stefan Koelsch—who sought to explain how we code *semantic* meaning in music, as discussed in Interlude C. Perhaps the most influential, and prolific, researcher in this pursuit has been the Swedish psychologist Patrik Juslin. In laying out his defense of the categorical approach to measuring musical emotions, Juslin devises a three-pronged theory on how emotions are "coded" within music—and specifically how music conveys emotional, as opposed to semantic, meaning.[698]

The first, and by far most important, process for Juslin is *iconic coding*. Specifically, this states that emotional expression in music is directly "based on innate and universal 'affect programs' for vocal expression of emotion."[699] That is, our ability to perceive emotion in music is directly reflective of our involuntary and physiological reaction to the varied ways in which people *speak*—which in turn is grounded in our very evolution as a species.[700] Of course, we've already seen this presumed evolutionary link between musical expression and vocal sounds in Interlude A. At any rate, Juslin argues that this iconic coding—generated specifically via *performance* attributes such as tempo, timbre, volume, etc.—"will have the most *uniform* impact on musical expression."[701] A soft, lilting flute melody, for example, reflects a tender speech and thus is coded via positive emotions; a jagged, loud melody played on a distorted guitar, by contrast, codes rather the opposite.

The presumed uniformity in emotional coding—grounded in evolution, and based on the involuntary, physiological link between musical expression and vocal sounds—grants iconic coding its priority within Juslin's schema. More specifically, the priority inspires Juslin to forge a direct link between iconic coding and so-called "basic emotions"—categories of primary "everyday life" emotions: happiness, sadness, anger, fear, etc. Yet, Juslin admits, "basic emotions" are not the only categories of emotions that music is capable of expressing. For other, more "complex" emotions—surprise, tension, pride, etc.—Juslin attributes two other processes: *intrinsic coding*—the intramusical, syntactically grounded sources of meaning and emotion already noted by Meyer, and experienced, for example, when hearing a deceptive cadence; and *associative coding*—the arbitrary correlations enabled through cultural, contextual, and/or personal associations of music and meaning/emotion, such as experienced when hearing your national anthem or the music used in the religious services you attend regularly.

It is important to note here that Juslin's theory of the three coding processes refers only to how we *perceive* emotion in music, and not to how music can induce or arouse emotions within us. For that, Juslin—in collaboration with fellow Swedes Daniel Västfjäll, Simon Liljeström, and others—has iterated, via numerous studies, a well-cited theory of eight underlying *mechanisms* whereby music can induce emotions. These mechanisms address induction of both basic/everyday (utilitarian) emotions as well as the more complex, "aesthetic" emotions associated with intrinsic and associative coding.[702] As Juslin notes, the type of emotion induced is directly dependent on the underlying mechanism that caused it.

These eight emotion-inducing *mechanisms* may be briefly summarized as follows:

1. *Brain stem reflexes*—involving arousal of the autonomous nervous system (ANS), and spiking at the onset of loud, high, or low frequencies, rapidly changing sounds, etc. It results in typical ANS arousal responses like increased heart rate and shallow breathing—and is associated with stark emotional responses like *surprise.*
2. *Rhythmic entrainment*—relying on the mechanisms discussed in Interludes A and C, the mind individually and communally locks, in on a steady beat in the music, whereby we can "lock in" with it via our heart rate, breathing, etc., in turn triggering emotions of increased arousal and social connectedness.
3. *Evaluative conditioning*—involving emotion aroused due to an unconscious "pairing" of the music one hears and some external stimuli, positive or negative, such as when a song aligned with a sad personal event makes you sad in other circumstances.
4. *Emotional contagion*—involving the induction of emotion within a listener as a "mimicking" of the emotion perceived in the music—emotion that, as in iconic coding, relies on the intrinsic link of music and vocal expression. Juslin here follows Koelsch and others in suggesting the activity of "mirror neurons," whereby we feel connected to those delivering to us an emotional expression.
5. *Visual imagery*—involving the induction of emotion within a listener by "conjuring up inner images" that arise out of the music: a pretty landscape, forward movement, etc. As with Koelsch's iconic signs triggered via extramusical resemblances, emotions evoked by images—pleasure, deep relaxation, energy, etc.—are grounded in

the music's structural narrative and our ability to "map" from it *metaphors* of height, depth, direction, speed, etc.[703]

6. *Episodic memory*—involving the induction of emotion within a listener by virtue of a personal memory associated with the music, regardless of how the music might strike the listener absent the memory. This is related to what Koelsch called "musicogenic" meaning, where our experience triggers within us the meaning associated with the original memory—in turn triggering emotions such as nostalgia or pride, but also joy or sadness.
7. *Musical expectancy*—involving the induction of emotion within a listener by virtue of the fulfillment or violation of expectations based on the intramusical activity: melodic contour, harmonic cadence, use of dynamics or timbre, etc. This is where "thrills and chills" can arise, but also surprise, awe, or anxiety.
8. *Aesthetic judgment*—enabling induction of emotions stemming from more complex, if nebulous, aesthetic judgments on music. Aesthetic emotions are dependent on/aligned to the music's perceived value as "art," however subjective and fickle such judgments may be. When sufficiently strong, the aesthetic attitude will hit a "threshold," whereby it can trigger an aesthetic emotion—if, that is, the music is deemed sufficiently beautiful, original, expressive, skilled, etc. Aesthetic emotions are defined in terms of valence, positive or negative, and interact with the other seven mechanisms.

Juslin's multidimensional theory of musically induced emotions is thorough and admittedly complex—and given its partial reliance on conjecture is not without its critics. It is reminiscent of the collective, multidimensional, and highly interactive way in which the brain processes the myriad elements of music—as we discussed in Interlude C. Further, the order of the eight mechanisms represents for Juslin the sequence in which they appeared in our evolutionary development, as successive adaptive functions that assisted in our survival.[704]

While for Juslin the first seven mechanisms follow a "long evolutionary history," the final mechanism, aesthetic judgment, is a more modern development—one that relies on higher cognitive functions, along with a "fluid, individualized process that may change across time and context." That is, whereas the first seven processes are grounded in human "universals," aesthetic judgment is based on more *individualized criteria*: cultural, intracultural, and especially personal, subjective factors that reflect our individual personality. Importantly, music-based aesthetic judgments do not trigger particular emotions, but rather are manifest at the broad level of *affect,* via positive or negative valence whereby you like the music or you don't. Aesthetic judgments reflect notions of "artistic" merit that are granted or not, and at various degrees of intensity. They thus involve cognitive "inputs"—reasoning, comparison, etc.—which may be explicitly or implicitly triggered, and are aligned to varied notions of sublimity, beauty, originality, skill, etc.[705]

Aesthetic judgment is worth lingering over since, in my view, it provides a valuable window through which to consider our musical taste. To be sure, not every song or musical work we like or dislike is a product of our aesthetic judgment, as we've noted on countless occasions thus far. But it may indeed play a seminal role in determining those songs, works, artists, and composers that we *truly* love—particularly those that we would embrace and cultivate during the highest manifestation of our music listening, what I will call the "aesthetic mode" of listening. The other seven mechanisms may indeed be sufficient to induce music-based emotions of various sorts, and thereby manifestly influence our "musical genotype," but only when aesthetic "processing," as Juslin calls it, is triggered can we hope to identify music that rocks our world—or, when the judgment is sufficiently negative, that makes us want to scream, or at least change the station. When you talk about the music you truly love, that you could not live without, that in your view "everyone should know," chances are high that an aesthetic judgment is involved.

## Taxonomies of Musical Emotions

Before moving beyond the topic of musical emotions, let's drill down a bit further to explore the actual ones we might experience—as perceived, felt, or both. This is worthwhile, in my view, since our very experience of listening to music is so often defined by the emotions we perceive and/or feel as it proceeds—whether we love it, hate it, or somewhere in the middle. As such, it can only serve us well to better understand which discrete emotions experts have identified and presented, via their theories and statistical data sets, as well-defined taxonomies.

Following the experimental approaches of Hevner, Asmus, and others cited above, there was little attempt to devise a robust and methodical taxonomy of musical emotions—such that Marcel Zentner could exclaim in 2008: "There is at present no systematic, empirically derived taxonomy of musically induced emotions."[706] Indeed, to Zentner, this was part of a larger challenge of the time whereby music scholars were poorly distinguishing perceived from felt emotions. The result, he argued, was an overreliance on nonmusical theories, most notably the concept of "basic emotions," as the means to classify and measure music-based emotions. The concerns leveled by Zentner in turn touched upon some broader questions, some of which we've already broached. What is the source of these emotions: The brain? Evolution? Aesthetics? What is the relationship between musical and everyday emotions? Are certain emotions tied to specific properties in the music?

The notion of "basic" or "primary" emotions is an ancient one, dating back to the Confucian era (c. 500 BCE) of ancient China and the *Book of Rites* (*Liji*)—where seven "feelings of men" were identified: joy, anger, sadness, fear, love, disliking, and liking. The concept found prominent revival in the late twentieth century, notably via the work of psychologists Paul Ekman, who identified six basic emotions: anger, disgust, fear, happiness, sadness, and surprise; and Robert Plutchik, who identified eight emotions: anger, fear, sadness, disgust, surprise, anticipation, trust, and joy. For both Ekman and Plutchik, the innate, "hardwired" presence of these emotions reflects biologically primitive responses that evolved to increase reproductive fitness, to enable suitable fight or flight responses, and to promote cooperation and caring.[707]

The big question for music psychologists, therefore, is whether to classify music emotions using "basic emotions" or using other, more intrinsically "musical" emotions. Supporting the former argument has been Patrik Juslin—who sees the bond between music and basic emotions as rooted in our evolutionary link between music and vocal expression. Taking the alternate position have been several writers active over the past decade—including Zentner, Tuomas Eerola, Klaus Scherer, and Emmanuel Bigand—who have picked up upon earlier attempts by Hevner and Asmus in order to create taxonomies of intrinsically musical emotions.[708]

Perhaps the strongest argument for a distinct set of intrinsically musical emotions stems from a simple fact: many negatively valenced basic or everyday emotions—disgust, fear, as well as guilt, embarrassment, etc.—are rarely perceived or felt in music; fear, another negative basic emotion, is similarly almost never expressed in music—except when accompanying a scary film or some other extramusical narrative. By contrast, the emotions we do commonly perceive or feel when listening to music—nostalgia, sentimentality, peacefulness, amazement, etc.—*do not* neatly fall within the confines of the "basic emotions" model.

The most rigorous attempt to date at defining a so-called "music-specific" taxonomy of emotion is surely that by Zentner et al.—a multiyear study that ultimately yielded GEMS: the Geneva Emotional Music Scales.[709] Starting from an original list of 515 emotion-oriented terms, the team settled on eighty-nine of them; these terms were presented to two thousand attendees of a multigenre music festival (La Fête de la Musique in Geneva). This real-world study of music lovers—evaluating how they felt while listening to a variety of music—in turn gave way to a model of nine emotional factors: Wonder, Transcendence, Tenderness, Nostalgia, Peacefulness, Power, Joyful Activation, Tension, and Sadness. Each factor was then delineated into four or five subfactors—for example, Wonder was broken into happy, amazed, dazzled, allured, and moved; Nostalgia into sentimental, dreamy, nostalgic, and melancholic, etc.

In follow-up studies, Zentner then found that his GEMS model led to greater agreement among listeners—as well as offered more accurate descriptions of their felt emotions—than either "basic" emotions or the "circumplex" model, which again limits emotional classification to the affects of valence and arousal.

So why do music-specific emotions reflect the reality of music listening better than either basic emotions or broad affect dimensions? Zentner gives credit to the more nuanced, complex, and aesthetic—as opposed to biologically grounded—nature of the former. By virtue of their more "refined" nature, Zentner argues, music-specific emotions—amazement, nostalgia, melancholy, tension, etc.—are closer to actual, pragmatic mental states than are the vague physiological or neurobiological experiences aligned with basic emotions or affect dimensions. To be sure, the emotions we feel or perceive when listening to music may not be full or profound, but can be partial or "mixed"—as is the case with life in general; it will depend on an array of factors: the music itself, our personality, how we're listening, etc.

One particularly good and common example of an "intrinsically musical" felt emotion from Zentner's studies is melancholy—a sort of enjoyable sadness, where real physical or psychological distress is removed. It is not for nothing, indeed, that *melancholia* is a common trope within musicological literature, where it is often hailed as an ideal affect in the music of composers like Josquin, Bach, and Brahms—and, since the seventeenth century, deemed an antidote to actual sadness.[710] Musicologist Michael Steinberg even goes so far as to call melancholy "the condition of *all* music," borne out of the inevitable gap that exists between emotional music and semantic speech: "This is the melancholia of music itself, the predicament that gives music so much rhetorical and emotional importance for modern listeners."[711]

You might be wondering how exactly all this relates to you and your musical taste. It is not unlikely, for example, that you rarely register which, if any, specific emotions you perceive, let alone feel, when you hear music. Does the fact that a group of music fans in Geneva uniformly felt dazzled, sentimental, and impatient when listening to music—mainly classical—mean that you would too? Maybe. And which emotional approach would best reflect your perceptions and felt experiences when you hear your favorite Clifford Brown, Carly Simon, Aerosmith, or Lady Gaga song? Zentner's study seems to suggest that specific, intrinsically musical emotions would best do the trick, though Juslin is still not so sure—noting that the GEMS model itself includes basic emotions within it.[712]

Yet whether the designations arise from discrete basic emotions, music-specific emotions, or broad dimensional modes of affect or arousal—or a mix of all three—the evidence is irrefutable: we do *perceive* and *feel* a wide range of emotions when we listen to music. The nature and experience of those emotions in turn helps inform our musical taste, whether we know it or not. It thus behooves us all to acknowledge, register, and cultivate the emotional taxonomy that, for us, permeates the music we hear, and especially the music that defines our own genotype.

## Emotion, Musicology, and the Power of Surprise

The music emotion studies of Zentner, Juslin, and others collectively reveal the rich array of possible emotional categories/terms aligned to music—both as perceived within the music as it proceeds and felt within us as we listen to it. According to the literature, the emotions we most commonly *perceive within music* seem to include tenderness, peacefulness, happiness, power, and sadness; in turn, the emotions we most commonly *feel within us* as we hear music include nostalgia, melancholy, tenderness, happiness, and amazement. It may be worth spending a few minutes to review these lists and consider how they relate to you and the music you love.

As you carry out this exercise, though, another follow-up question comes to mind: How do these—or other—emotions correlate to the specific musicology found in the music? What kinds of melodies, chord progressions, rhythms, forms, or sounds trigger which emotions, and how?

These are great questions, but sadly, not ones to which the academic literature has all that much to offer the average, nonacademic music lover—despite an abundance of robust and methodologically sound studies. Most of the conclusions drawn, that is, are fairly obvious or not specific enough to be useful. They include, as we've seen, the common correlation of fast and major-mode music with happy, as opposed to slow and minor-mode music with sad; or similarly generic alignments of high register, loud volume, and rising melodic contour with both happy and angry, as opposed to low register, low volume, and falling melodic contour with sad and tender.[713] By this account, however, Green Day's "American Idiot" sounds as joyful as it does annoyed, while Erroll Garner's "Misty" sounds as sorrowful as it does tender. Even using complex computer analysis, the takeaways are minimal: increased sonic "roughness" aligned with perceptions of power and tension, as compared to low "spectral complexity" aligned with peacefulness.[714] Again, not terribly useful. . . .

In all, the research aligning musicological factors with the emotions you'll perceive and/or feel offers little more than "ground rules" for the average listener; they certainly do not tell the whole story of how emotion operates when we listen to the music we love or hate. Instead, the real-time narrative flow of music hits each of us with a far greater degree of subjectivity, as well as musicological and emotional nuance, than these summaries suggest. A rising melodic line may well sound or make you feel happy, but it could just as likely evoke tenderness, nostalgia, or power, or any of a dozen other emotional categories or dimensions. Included in the mix are your cultural and intracultural identity, your listening mode, your memories, and your personality—as we'll soon discuss.

If research tells us little as to exactly when or how music *objectively* sounds tender, angry, happy, or sad, there is one emotion about which it is quite revealing: surprise. Interestingly, this is not an emotion that listeners commonly register as one they perceive or feel from music, and yet surprise is an emotion that profoundly informs our overall music-listening experience—particularly when it comes to music we truly love. We already touched a bit on musical surprise in Interlude C, as a neurological source of emotion, following upon the fulfillment or denial of musical expectation, but given its impact on our musical taste, let's here dive a bit deeper.

So what precisely do we mean by musical surprise? There is, to be sure, the explicit kind of "oh my God" surprise that music is capable of producing, as through sudden shifts in volume—e.g., the unexpected fortissimo chord in the second movement of Haydn's *Surprise* Symphony or Roger Daltrey's vocal scream in the Who's "Won't Get Fooled Again." There are also the more nuanced instances found in complex, compositionally driven musical works, especially in the classical species—such as the surprising resolution of the "Tristan chord" at end of the "Liebestod" in Wagner's *Tristan und Isolde*.[715] But these are all quite rare, or require expert musical training to discern in the first place.

But while overt or expertly discerned musical surprise is rare, its impact on our overall musical experience is decidedly not. As noted in Interlude C, Leonard Meyer was the first to point to expectation as the "basis of the affective and the intellectual aesthetic response to music," crediting it to the composer's ability to "choreograph" the thwarting, delaying, or granting of what our ears expect to hear.[716] By far, the greatest attention in this regard has been placed on the most palpable manifestation of musical expectation, what we've called "thrills and chills." Other expressions for this psychophysical response include "shivers down your spine," "gooseflesh," the tantalizing label "skin orgasm," and the most academically embraced, "frisson."*

This latter term indeed points to the psychophysical origins and responses of frisson, as we too shall now call it. Our ability to react to music in such a demonstrably physical manner has been traced back to our prehuman origins: initially as a thermoregulatory response to cold—hence the accompanying "piloerection," or involuntary erection of hairs on our skin, as a means to insulate air on the skin. The cold response of piloerection in turn became an "artifact" to the emotional response of fear—perhaps, as William James and Carl Lange argued, through the association of "trembling" when crying in sorrow.[717] At any rate, when in an actual life-threatening situation, the fear response activates the sympathetic nervous system—piloerection, but also increased heart rate, deeper breathing, dopamine activation, along with sharper memory and attention. The intent is to prepare the body for action—fight, flight, or freeze. Importantly, frisson also responds sensitively to sound, including to "aversive" sound, such as fingernails on a chalkboard, as well as loud and high-frequency sounds.

---

* The word "frisson" stems from the French word for "shiver," in turn deriving from the Latin verb "*frigere*" (to be cold).

Of course, frisson not only arises through the onset of cold or truly fearful situations, but also through pleasurable moments of music listening. The sensations indeed arise via the same mechanisms and regions of the brain: the thalamus, amygdala, midbrain, neurotransmitters, etc. But why does music produce this effect, and how can this possibly relate to running in terror from a bear?

The most detailed explanation is certainly that by David Huron, via his ITPRA theory and related arguments. His full discussion is naturally well beyond our scope here, and readers interested in this fascinating dynamic are encouraged to read his monograph on the subject, *Sweet Anticipation.* In short, Huron identifies these evolutionary sources of frisson as the source of our adaptive ability, honed by natural selection, to predict the future. Surprise, he points out, is a bad thing, a "sign of adaptive failure"—one that in certain conditions could even cost us our lives. Nature thus devised myriad ways to "overreact" to potentially bad predictions, to conserve energy, and to attain the appropriate levels of arousal and attention needed to respond when the time is called for. Not every surprise, of course, leads to peril, and yet the underlying "biology of pessimism" is always at play—even when the actual experiential results of poor predicting are pleasant. Composers and musicians, he argues, are uniquely suited to "exploit" these biological predispositions.

Huron makes his case via the ITPRA theory—a five-part "comprehensive theory of expectation," wherein various "feeling states are first activated." First is *Imagination*, a stage that may last moments to years prior to an event, where we both think about and *feel* future possibilities, based in large part on previous learning schema. Next is *Tension*, as we prepare for an expected event that may well be negative; this stage is always unpleasant and can be highly stressful—even when what we anticipate is positive (what if it doesn't happen?). *Prediction* is where we use our previous learnings to hopefully circumvent danger or exploit positive opportunities—with rewards or punishments as a consequence. *Reaction* follows immediately from the outcome, as a "quick and dirty" response; it is usually unconscious and in some cases a mere reflex (as in jerking one's hand upon touching a hot stove). Finally, *Appraisal* is a far more leisurely assessment of the outcome, taking into account complex social and environmental responses via our conscious thought—whereby we can at times revise or augment our initial Reaction.

In essence, every time the Prediction is incorrect (as it often is), the resulting Reaction is decidedly negative. To be sure, that "quick and dirty" negative response can be quickly countered by a neutral or positive Appraisal—as quick as a fraction of a second later: as when you say "Boo" to a toddler or when a group of friends yells out "Surprise" as they present you with a birthday cake. When the actual outcome is not in fact negative, the result is a "contrast in valence"—between the negative Reaction (to any surprise) and the neutral or positive Ap-

praisal. The result in either case is pleasure: the greater the contrast in valence, the greater the pleasure we experience.

Music, as we know, affords untold opportunity to be surprised: an unexpected melodic leap or varied pattern (Chapter 3), a deceptive cadence or unexpected modulation (Chapter 4), a sudden shift in meter or clever syncopation (Chapter 5), a break in expected form or unusually complex structure (Chapter 6), a change in dynamics or unanticipated introduction of a new instrument (Chapter 7)—to name a few generic cases. In each case, no lives are placed at risk, survival isn't on the line, and thus the inherently negative Reaction will be met with a neutral and not infrequently with a positive Appraisal—thus yielding a pleasurable emotional experience. An admitted exception is when the actual outcome is sonically negative: an out-of-tune instrument, an "ugly" chord, an unexpectedly boring or incessant melodic repetition, etc.—in which case your Appraisal will align with your Reaction and actually yield a negative experience.

Such hopefully rare, unfortunate incidents aside, Huron points to three palpable manifestations of musical surprise, each of which he correlates to an aspect of our primordial biology of pessimism. The first is *laughter*—aligned with "flight": occasionally overt, this occurs when the actual musical outcome is wildly and cleverly surprising, such as when a well-prepared authentic cadence leads to a grossly chromatic "resolve"—think of the music of P. D. Q. Bach. The second is *awe*—aligned with "freeze": this occurs when the contrasting valence of Reaction to Appraisal is huge, yielding an overpowering emotional reaction, such as when a complex form culminates in a stunningly beautiful yet simple conclusion. The third, then, is *frisson*—aligned with "fight": that sweet spot of musical surprise, yielding the blessed "thrills and chills" that undergirds the music we love.

Importantly, what makes all these reactions possible is the kind of statistical/schematic learning we discussed in Interludes C and E, and which arise by virtue of the syntactic and culturally defined norms of melody, harmony, rhythm, form, and sound that we acquire through a lifetime of music listening. In the best of moments, these surprises produce sufficient contrasting valence—between our well-formed statistical learning and its "exploitation" by a clever musician—as to provide a moment that, as psychologist Luke Harrison put it, "resonates so deeply and viscerally as to elicit a physical, bodily response."[718] In truth, frisson is relatively rare: only 30 percent of people report having experienced it. Happily, though, it is far more common amid avid music lovers, particularly when they are engaged in focused listening. Context too plays a role—for example, frisson, as well as awe, occurs more often when we're alone, whereas musical laughter is generally a social phenomenon.[719]

This leads us back to the two topics with which we started this section: emotion and musicology. We know that frisson yields an emotional response, and we now know that this response arises from surprises based on intrinsic, syntactical violations in the musical proceedings. But which emotions, and which viola-

tions? The answer, again, depends—as in both cases there are untold subjective factors involved: your level of musical expertise, your cultural/intercultural background, the context of your listening experience, your personality, the genotype of your musical taste, etc.

Still, there are a few general things we can say, starting with some specific musicological elements associated with frisson/"thrills and chills." As discerned in studies by Juslin, Huron, John Sloboda, Oliver Grewe, and others, these include the onset of loud dynamics, extremely soft passages, slow music, descending melodic contours, harmonic progressions/sequences through the Circle of 5ths, abrupt modulations, and harmonic shifts by 3rds (e.g., C major to E♭ major).[720] Whether and when these musicological elements actually induce frisson will again depend on myriad subjective and contextual factors. And yet they are qualities worth registering in the music if and when you experience frisson—to the degree you can, of course. For me, for example, the "chills" I noted experiencing when listening to the development section of the first movement of Mozart's Piano Concerto no. 21 are indeed aligned to an extended string of harmonic sequences through the Circle of 5ths. A surprise? Perhaps not. . . . These may not be syntactical violations in the traditional sense (e.g., a deceptive cadence), but my unconscious mind is clearly responding to a pleasant chain of unfulfilled expectations. You might also want to try Huron's technique to increase "chills": turn up the volume!

As for the actual emotions felt, frisson seems to operate much as does Juslin's "aesthetic mechanism": not generating a distinct emotional category, per se, but rather "qualifying" positively the emotions already induced by other means. Huron specifically calls frisson and other surprise-based effects "emotion amplifiers"—with surprise worsening negative stimuli and heightening positive stimuli, and where the level of "boost" depends on the degree of contrasting valence between the Reaction and Appraisal responses. The net result is likely a rush of positive valence to accompany the more fine-grained emotional response—or simply positive valence alone if no other emotion is registered. In many cases too, the result will be an additional song or work added to your musical genotype—since any music that delivers you some "thrills and chills" is likely one that you'd want to hear again.

## Familiarity (and Prediction) Breeds Preference

With all this talk about surprises and failed predictions, you might be wondering what happens when we actually predict correctly. What if we expect an authentic cadence or the arrival of a new formal section or the use of a particular syncopated rhythm and they in fact happen? As it turns out, those too yield pleasure—lucky us. Importantly, moreover, successful predictions play a not insignificant

role in our musical taste—at least initially. Technically, this relates to a phenomenon we broached briefly in Interlude C—known as the "mere exposure effect." As we'll see, however, this correlates not only to exposure and familiarity, but also to successful prediction. It also begins to weave a tale fleshing out the subjective, multivariegated factors involved in linking our psychology to our musical taste—most notably via our personality, with which we'll soon close our mystery novel.

Testing the age-old adage "Familiarity breeds contempt," psychologists have, since the late nineteenth century, explored the relationship between repeated exposures and liking or preference. In many ways, researchers aimed to empirically test what advertisers apparently knew all along: repeated exposures increase one's liking. The first serious corroboration came via the work of Robert Zajonc in a 1968 paper, in which he exclaimed: "Mere repeated exposure of an individual to a stimulus object enhances his attitude toward it."[721] As he developed his "mere exposure effect" over the next few decades, Zajonc came to recognize that the effect was not dependent on extensive, prior conscious thought, but instead our affective judgments generally *precede* cognition, and "are less subject to control by the attentive process." That is, our attitude toward something—increased liking, for example—is formed even when a stimulus is presented subliminally, hence his famous motto: "Preferences need no inferences."[722] To wit, Zajonc proposed "some separation between affect and cognition" (feeling and thought)—with ramifications that extend beyond liking to the decisions we make every day: we decide on things often before we can formulate why we have done so. Affect is fast; thinking is slow—much as we've seen in Kahneman's two-system theory of heuristics, itself reliant on Zajonc's ideas.

Music psychologists have likewise taken up Zajonc's ideas to explore how exposure impacts musical preferences.[723] In the process, they have introduced some new ideas, including the so-called "perceptual fluency" theory, developed by Robert Bornstein and Paul D'Agostino in the 1990s. In short, this theory states that when, in the wake of repeated exposures, we register our preference for a song, we are in fact "misattributing" that preference for what is really just greater perceptual ease on our parts: that is, we like it more because it is easier to process, or as they put it: "An increase in perceptual fluency is induced by repeated exposure to a stimulus."[724]

Even more impactful was when David Huron merged Bornstein and D'Agostino's notion of "misattribution" into his own ITPRA theory. Huron argues that Mother Nature too utilizes misattribution, by assigning credit for our emotional reactions—whether positive or negative—to whatever is close at hand: "Misattribution is the price we pay for trying to draw conclusions from small amounts of information."[725] Huron similarly echoes Zajonc's notion that conscious awareness actually *stifles* the potential power of repeated exposures—which in turn has enormous consequences for our musical taste. It suggests that a mere *unconscious* awareness that we've heard a given harmonic chord progression, or cadential for-

mula, or melodic riff, or syncopated rhythm before may increase our chances of liking it within a song we're hearing—more, that is, than if we *knew* we'd heard it before.

But Huron goes even further. The misattribution we make via our increased perceptive fluency in music listening, he asserts, comes about more precisely thanks to our *predictive* abilities. That is, the pleasure or increased liking we gain when we hear a chord progression or rhythmic pattern we've heard before stems not from a mere increased ease in processing, but rather from our improved ability to *predict* what will happen next. The real source of our "pleasure," Huron notes, is the "mental circuit" that successfully—though unconsciously—made the prediction.

Indeed, for this reason Huron prefers the expression "predictive effect" to Zajonc's "exposure effect."[726] Thanks to a lifetime of exposure to the music of our native culture and preferred intracultures, along with the incredible level of repetition that underlies all musical styles—as discussed in Interludes D, E, and F—we continually hear the same songs, the same cadential patterns, the same melodic figures, the same chord progressions, etc., over and over again, whether we know it or not. As a result, we unconsciously build up statistical knowledge of these musical parameters. Our Prediction response is thus better able to predict how these parameters will proceed in the music we are hearing right now—which in turn grants us pleasure and increased liking. Familiarity breeds preference by way of prediction.

All this brings us back to a question referenced at the start of this section: Does familiarity ever in fact breed contempt? Put another way, if we continually gain pleasure and increased liking from multiple exposures and successful predictions, why would we ever dislike a song or work we've heard before? Zajonc and Huron in fact point to a trajectory of ever-increasing, linear function liking based on mere exposure and successful prediction, respectively—where, as Huron puts it, "each additional repetition tends to increase the preference, but the amount of increase gets progressively smaller." Experience, of course, tells us that we often do fall "out of love" with music—so what gives? Huron in fact has a clear answer: additional exposures endlessly increase liking as relates specifically to the predictive response, although, he notes, the increase becomes "very small" after about thirty repetitions. But, as we've seen, Prediction is not the end of the "expectation cycle"—there is also Reaction and especially Appraisal that follow. The pleasure garnered from successful Prediction may only increase, but it can be *overruled*, so to speak, by our follow-up Appraisal—where a "predictable" chord progression, "inelegant" melodic phrase, or "dorky" rhythmic element may, in retrospect, be deemed banal, obvious, unoriginal, etc. In a battle between Prediction and Appraisal, that is, the latter can readily carry the day at the expense of the former, turning liking into disliking.

Other researchers, however—notably Hargreaves, Szpunar, and Schellen-

berg—have offered an alternate perspective. All, in fact, have argued that exposure does not increase liking linearly, but at some point—after as few as three or eight, or as many as thirty or thirty-two repetitions—reverses course and produces a decrease in liking by the listener. Szpunar, for example, notes the existence of a "satiation effect," whereby "exposure generates increases in positive affect until boredom outweighs the benefits of learned safety, resulting in *satiation*, or decreases in liking." The pattern, each argues, follows that of an "inverted U"—rising for a while before falling back.

In developing their explanations, Schellenberg and Szpunar in particular have turned to another of the general theories of exposure: the "2-Factor" model developed in the 1970s by Daniel Berlyne.[727] This proposes that there are two oppositional forces underlying the relationship between exposure and liking; the first is "habituation" or cognitive fluency, which increases with repeated exposures, as we've seen; the second is tedium or boredom, whereby liking decreases. The determining factor, Berlyne contends, is the so-called "arousal potential" of the stimulus—based on its "psychological strength," and the degree to which it can shake us up and "take control" of our behavior.[728] In other words, it depends on how "interesting" the thing is—something generally equated with "complexity." So long as a stimulus, such as a chord progression or melodic line, is deemed sufficiently interesting—novel or complex—the pleasure from it will rise, whereas it will peak and fall once the arousal potential weakens.

In fact, I would argue, Schellenberg, Szpunar, and Huron are all saying the same thing. What determines whether something has exhausted its "arousal potential"—if it's still interesting—if not our Appraisal? Assumedly, something sufficiently cliché, obvious, unoriginal—think the Kars4Kids jingle—will for many listeners score extraordinarily high in Predictability, thereby generating immediate habituation, but then almost immediately, perhaps even by the end of the first listen, will return a poor Appraisal due to its unusually low arousal potential. The result will be tedium and dislike. Studies may show that it takes fifteen or thirty listens of a song before liking decreases, but it seems much more accurate to say that it all depends: if, unlike with Kars4Kids, a song is appraised perpetually interesting, whether via complexity or otherwise, it will continue to increase liking indefinitely—or at least until some other form of tedium arises that, as Berlyne states, "takes over control."

You will have noted that the "exposure/prediction effect" provides a direct link between our psychology and our musical taste—or at least our capacity to like music we've heard before. The preceding discussions show that our psychology—our ability to predict, react, and appraise—sets up a dynamic whereby we can add music to our genotype *whenever* it provides a satisfying fulfillment *or* surprise to our statistically grounded expectations. We are, in essence, psychologically and neurobiologically preprogrammed to like music that sounds similar to music we've heard before, and to like it more and more every time we hear it.

That we don't like *everything* we hear, that by contrast we all have discriminating and idiosyncratic taste, however, reaffirms that other factors are also at play. The notion that every song has an "arousal potential" based on its complexity or "interest" already suggests the role of individual traits and conditions: what is complex or interesting to one person may be simple or tedious to another. Thus far, therefore, our psychology—both our ability to perceive/feel emotion and our predilection to like things we've heard before—helps provide a growing set of *options* for our individual musical taste, fed in turn by the science-based, cultural, and intracultural factors that, as we've noted, make us musical. The final "half mile" of our mystery novel, if you will, requires more fine-tuned criteria—starting with our personality.

## The Factors of Music Preference

The belief that one's personality can contribute to an understanding of his or her musical taste began with a short-lived burst in the early 1950s, when the innovative and highly prolific behavioral psychologist Raymond Cattell turned his attention to music. Cattell was a firm, if at times controversial, proponent of empirically quantifying the distinct "traits" of personality that in turn impact our cognitive and motivational tendencies. To that end, he was an early champion and fine-tuner of factor analysis—the statistical procedure to define a small number of underlying factors out of a larger observable set of interrelated variables. In a set of studies, Cattell and colleagues devised a music preference inventory—or test—based on 120 classical and jazz excerpts, which were in turn related to personality traits drawn from his "16 Personality Factor Questionnaire," such as warmth, dominance, and self-reliance: "Our aim must be to see first whether consistent, common patterns of choice exist in a set of musical excerpts and thereafter to discover what features of personality or stimulus situation are responsible for each of these."[729] Using factor analysis, he devised twelve distinct, if nebulous, music preference dimensions—such as "surgency" (positivity), which he speculated might correspond to "rhythmical emphasis, fast tempo, individual interpretation, and discordant harmonies."[730] As with other manifestations of personality, Cattell believed that our music preferences satisfy unconscious needs, as "effective avenues to deeper aspects of personality."[731]

Cattell's work was largely ignored, not least due to its rather imprecise correlations of personality and music preferences. A few limited attempts were made in the ensuing decades to better bridge the gap—such as by Marvin Zuckerman and Patrick Litle in the mid-1980s, who, like Cattell, used factor analysis to align folks with varying manifestations of a "sensation-seeking" personality to a preference for either rock ("total sensation seeking") or folk and classical music ("thrill and adventure seeking"), etc.[732] It was only in 2003, however, that a truly

robust effort was begun to define music preferences as an extension of personality—starting with research led by personality psychologists Jason Rentfrow and Sam Gosling.[733]

## Who Are You, Anyway?

Before discussing Rentfrow and Gosling's work and the stones they upturned, let's briefly step back to ground ourselves on the mysteries of personality, and some common ways in which to categorize it. There are today a wide array of personality models and associated tests. Some of the most well-known include the Myers-Briggs model, the Rorschach inkblot, the HEXACO model, and the Minnesota Multiphasic Personality Inventory (MMPI), among many others. When it comes to the study of music preferences, however, the most popular model by far is the Big Five Personality Model—also known as the Five Factor Model (FFM).[734]

Like many popular personality models (especially Myers-Briggs), the Big Five is indebted to the innovative thinking of my dad's hero, Carl Jung. Chief among Jung's contributions to psychology are his writings on personality, especially *Psychological Types* (1921). Jung saw personality as a hierarchical *typology*. At root are two contrasting *attitude types*: extroverted and introverted. These two attitudes modify one of two broad *psychological functions*: a rational function and an irrational function. The rational function is in turn divided into two *psychological types*: thinking and feeling; and the irrational function is similarly divided into two contrasting psychological types: sensation (perception) and intuition (unconscious motivations). In short, it is our dominant *attitude* (extroverted or introverted) combined with our associated and variously dominant *functions* (thinking, feeling, sensation, and/or intuition) that largely inform our behavior and actions—via a complex interplay that exceeds our interest here.[735]

The Big Five Model is not a functional typology like Jung's, but rather a *trait-based* model, like Cattell's 16 Personality Factors. Trait-based theories hold that our behavior emerges out of a set of dominant personal traits or qualities, and not merely from the emotional states we experience in response to particular situations. In the early 1980s, Lewis Goldberg created his own word-based approach via factor analysis, yielding a five-factor-based trait model, dubbed the Big Five. These personality traits are: *Openness to Experience*, *Conscientiousness*, *Extroversion*, *Agreeableness*, and *Neuroticism*; this fifth term refers not to the common use of "neurotic," as in an unbalanced or emotionally ill person, but rather to frequent experiences of anger, anxiety, and depression.[736]

## And What's Your Music Preference Factor?

As noted, the Big Five model forms the basis of a good many, though not all, queries into the correlation of personality and music preference. The latter part of this equation thus also needs a theoretical framework or model—that is, a set of discrete "music preference factors" to which individual listeners will gravitate or not. The one formulated by Rentfrow and Gosling in 2003, as noted, was an important early step. These two scholars sought to answer that basic question: Why do people listen to music? Their view, as with Cattell fifty years earlier, was that our musical preferences reflect our personality—though not as unconscious motives or desires. Instead they were "manifestations of explicit psychological traits, possibly in interaction with specific situational experiences, needs, or constraints." Their goal, therefore, was to create an "interactionist" model, whereby specific musical choices reinforce and reflect personalities, attitudes, and emotional profiles.

Rentfrow and Gosling's approach to defining music preference factors was as follows: they began by assembling a group of sixty-six music genres and subgenres, designating these "how people naturally think about and express music." With a small panel of "music experts" and a set of undergrads to "ground-truth" the findings, they settled on a working list of fourteen genres: alternative, blues, classical, country, electronica, folk, heavy metal, rap/hip hop, jazz, pop, religious, rock, soul/funk, and soundtracks. Next, using factor analysis, the fourteen genres were grouped into four factors, whose main themes were captured by a small team of psychologists. To wit, their four-factor model of music preferences: *Reflective/Complex* = blues, jazz, classical; *Intense/Rebellious* = rock, alternative; *Upbeat/Conventional* = country, soundtracks, pop, religious; and *Energetic/Rhythmic* = rap/hip hop, soul/funk, electronica, dance, and pop. As seen here, each genre fits but one factor, with the exception of pop, which fits two. Finally, a team of "experts" tagged a set of ten "prototype" songs/works from each genre with a small set of both psychological affects and musical qualities (e.g., tempo, complexity, sonic density); from these, the authors were able to label each factor with a few descriptive "categories"—for example, *Reflective/Complex* was labeled as "complex, positive and negative valence, and low energy."[737]

Voilà—the first widely acknowledged set of music preference factors. The notion here is that an individual listener will gravitate in his or her musical preferences to only one of these four factors or profiles, while eschewing the others. Yet while some scholars embraced Rentfrow and Gosling's music preference model, others chose instead to devise their own—using similar methods—over the next eight years or so. These variants—by writers like Darren George, Marc Delsing, and Peter Dunn—generally draw from a smaller number of genres than Rentfrow and Gosling, only up to thirty or so, grouping them into a similarly

small number of factors, with generic names like Rebellious, Rock, Rhythm n' Blues, Bass Heavy, etc.[738]

Beyond the diversity of conclusions, you will likely have noticed something eerily familiar in all of these music preference models: the prominent use of genres. As we saw all too well in our discussion of subcultures and intracultures, genres may provide convenient musical markers and may indeed be, as Rentfrow and Gosling note, how most people "naturally think" about music. But they are, as we ourselves noted in Interlude F, fluid and ever changing, and thus highly questionable to use when making blanket statements—whether about one's social class or one's musical preference profile. Curiously, many of the music preference factors by the authors just listed are simply genre names themselves—such as Rock, Classical, Jazz & Blues, Easy Listening, etc., even if they encompass other genres beyond those labeled.

At last questioning the utility of using genres to exclusively define music preference factors, Jason Rentfrow, along with a team of collaborators, returned to the topic in 2011 with an entirely new model.[739] In justifying his reexamination, Rentfrow highlighted the need for a *pan-genre* approach, reflecting more broadly a listener's emotional—that is, affective—responses to the music. Noting, for example, how a single artist, such as Frank Sinatra, can be varyingly categorized in multiple genres (popular, vocal, swing, easy listening, jazz, etc.), a better approach, he argues, is to tie a music preference profile to an *integrated mix* of psychological, sonic, *and* genre attributes. Further, unlike models whose factors are all but mutually exclusive, a better approach is "orthogonal"—meaning that a listener's preference for one dimension does not preclude his or her preference for another as well; what matters is context—a point likewise emphasized by the music psychologists Adrian North and David Hargreaves.[740] However, in his new studies, Rentfrow argues that music preferences "are based on liking for certain combinations of musical attributes" more than on "social or other extra-musical connotations associated with a particular genre."[741] This, of course, is not unlike the conclusions drawn by our work at Pandora—though their conclusions are fairly distinct from the ones we drew via the Music Genome Project.

Rentfrow's new model, in fact, begins similarly to his first one: using listener preferences for various genre designations—each represented by rather obscure music—a factor analysis yields five music preference factors. These are designated *Mellow*, *Unpretentious*, *Sophisticated*, *Intense*, and *Contemporary*; not coincidentally, it seems clear, the five factors create the acronym "MUSIC."[742] Broadly speaking, the Mellow factor is aligned with pop, soft rock, soul, and R&B; Unpretentious with country, folk, and singer-songwriter; Sophisticated with classical, jazz, and world music; Intense with rock, punk, and heavy metal; and Contemporary with rap, EDM, acid jazz, and Euro-pop. But Rentfrow then addresses the need to go *beyond genre* by adjoining each factor with distinct psychological and musical attributes. He includes a total of thirty-eight psycho-

logical attributes, divided into four categories: positive valence (e.g., amusing, animated, enthusiastic), negative valence (e.g., abrasive, angry, depressing); energy level (e.g., calming, gentle, lively, manic); and perceived complexity (e.g., deep, reflective, sophisticated). He also includes fourteen musical attributes: dense, distorted, electric, fast, instrumental, loud, percussive, plus seven instrumental attributes (e.g., piano, brass, raspy voice). The result is indeed a pan-genre definition of each factor; for example, Mellow is defined as slow, quiet, not distorted, acoustic, largely positive, low energy, cerebral, reflective, thoughtful, deep, sophisticated, and intelligent.[743]

Rentfrow's new MUSIC model of music preferences has now been embraced as the basis for a number of very recent academic studies on music preference—including those led by Markus Schedl and David Greenberg. It may indeed be praised for diving beyond the limits of genre to define one's music preference profile through an amalgam of psychological, musical, and genre-related characteristics; likewise commendable is its acknowledgment that most of us are defined by more than one such profile, and thus a more variable, independent approach—where, in this case, a preference for "Mellow" music one moment may be supplanted for a preference for "Intense" music the next, depending on contextual factors—is sensible.

At the same time, there are a number of questionable aspects worth noting; these include the fact that the model still relies to a considerable degree on broad and "fuzzy" genres; this is then exacerbated by the fact that a number of song-genre associations are questionable at best—such as labeling Norah Jones as smooth jazz, the Red Hot Chili Peppers as heavy metal, Ornette Coleman as acid jazz, or Philip Glass as avant-garde classical. Similarly odd are some psychological alignments of examples used in the studies—such as labeling Charlie Parker's "Ko-Ko" (a bebop tune recorded at three-hundred-plus beats per minute) as "low intensity," or Led Zeppelin's "Black Mountain Side" (a modal song with North Indian influences) as "unpretentious." More problematic are the limited use of musical terms, such that some factors are given the most banal associations, such as Sophisticated aligned only with slow, acoustic, piano, woodwinds, nonvocal; or Intense with loud, fast, percussion, electric, and yelling voice. In large part this arises from the fact that although the terms used stem from "experts," the actual tagging of songs was done by nonmusicians—and only by using a fifteen-second clip of each song!

The point here is not to nitpick Rentfrow's model, but to underscore that any such attempt to "bucket" musical preference factors around a small number of attributes, including only fourteen musical ones, is hard—and especially when based on fifteen-second clips of a limited (and, as noted, rather esoteric) repertoire, whose attributes are "coded" by subjectively minded, untrained listeners. To argue that Rentfrow's MUSIC model of music preference factors represents a definitive, objective account of our musical taste profiles, therefore, is not some-

thing I can subscribe to. We'll have to see, however, what comes around next to give it a run for its money.

## Put Them Together and . . .

In the meantime, we can begin exploring what current research has to say about the link between personality and music preference factors. It should come as little surprise that the literature reveals no unequivocal basis to assert that a given personality trait (e.g., Openness from the Big Five Model) will consistently and demonstrably gravitate toward a distinct music preference factor (e.g., Mellow from the MUSIC model). Yet, as with the many proposed links between intraculture and musical taste, the often contradictory findings linking personality and preference can still yield some valuable insights.

The first such attempts, of course, followed upon Rentfrow and Gosling's formation of the four-factor music preference model in 2003. In tandem with that development, the authors surveyed 1,700 undergraduates on both their personalities and their music preference profiles. For the former, they used an inventory of the Big Five, along with seven supplemental tests gauging their self-views, cognitive abilities, etc. For the latter, they used the STOMP (short test of musical preferences) inventory developed by Gosling: participants indicated their preference level for each of the fourteen "working list" genres on a seven-point scale, whereby they could be aligned to one or more of the four music preference factors. The combined results showed, in their view, a "fascinating pattern of links" between Big Five personality traits on the one hand and the four-factor model of music preferences on the other. For example, they revealed a "positive correlation" between Openness to Experience and both the Reflective/Complex (blues, jazz, classical) and Intense/Rebellious (rock, alternative) profiles, as well as between Conscientiousness and Extroversion and both the Upbeat/Conventional (country, pop) and Energetic/Rhythmic (hip hop, R&B, EDM) profiles—among other correlations.[744] The statistical strength of their findings led them to conclude: "If music preferences are partially determined by personality, self-views, and cognitive abilities, then knowing what kind of music a person likes can serve as a clue to his or her personality, self-views, and cognitive abilities."[745]

Unfortunately, not all subsequent studies corroborated these findings. The study by Darren George, for example, found that the Openness personality trait was "negatively correlated" to his Rebellious (rock) profile; while Extroversion was only weakly correlated to the Rhythmic and Intense (hip hop, pop) profile—both in contrast to the related findings by Rentfrow and Gosling.[746] The study by Peter Dunn began by observing that the personality trait most aligned to classical music was not Openness but Neuroticism, leading him to question the very definition of the Reflective/Complex factor—and eventually inspiring

him to devise his own music preference model. Even then, however, the lack of statistical clarity led him to conclude that "relatively few reliable correlations exist between personality and music preference," and those that do exist are "relatively weak."[747] Adrian North, in a 2010 study, similarly questioned whether any of the Big Five traits could be more than weakly aligned to music preference—arguing that other individual differences, such as age, sex, and income (i.e., intracultural factors) were more revealing.[748]

At the heart of these inconsistencies, no doubt, was the overreliance on genres to define this first batch of music preference factors. This is observed, for example, in the often generic insights drawn by Rentfrow and Gosling, such as: "When a person high on the Reflective and Complex dimension is feeling cheerful, she may listen to jazz music that is lively, but when she is feeling sad she may choose the blues."[749] The suggestion that folks who like reflective and complex music would simply choose a lively jazz track when happy and a random blues track when sad is bland to the point of being meaningless. The obvious next question is: Does Rentfrow's MUSIC model provide the basis for a more convincing correlation of personality and preference?[750]

Among the most rigorous attempts to answer this question thus far is a 2016 study by David Greenberg and colleagues (including Rentfrow and Levitin). Here the Big Five personality traits (and subtraits) are mapped against a preference for the twenty-six subgenres and thirty-eight psychological attributes used by Rentfrow to inform his MUSIC model—even using the same rather obscure tracks. Greenberg's decision to exclude the fourteen strictly musical attributes is intentional, as he wants to correlate personality most explicitly to the psychological attributes *perceived* in the music. More precisely, Greenberg groups the thirty-eight psychological attributes into three aspects from the dimensional/affect gauge of emotion: valence, arousal, and cognitive depth—with acknowledged reliance on Russell's "circumplex" model of valence and arousal.[751]

In his study, Greenberg surveyed the personalities and music preference profiles of nearly eight hundred Facebook-recruited participants. In order to discern a link between personality and genre, Greenberg takes an indirect path—at first defining each genre by its corresponding levels of arousal, valence, and cognitive depth or sophistication. For example, heavy metal has high arousal; adult contemporary has low arousal; Latin music has positive valence; soft rock has negative valence; classical music has high cognitive depth; rap has low cognitive depth. Clearly, we see here echoes of the same unfortunate biases of "highbrow" and "lowbrow" genres as found when labeling various intracultures, as discussed in Interlude F. That shortcoming aside, Greenberg is then able to use these psychologically tagged genres to forge statistical correlations between the personalities of the participants and their music preference profiles. So, for example, he correlates Openness with low arousal, positive valence, and high cognitive depth; Neuroticism with both high and low arousal, negative valence, and high cognitive depth, etc.[752]

As just suggested, Greenberg's study has its limitations—a set of unfortunate genre biases, reliance on genre without specific musical attributes, measuring affect in a binary fashion, using obscure repertoire tagged via short clips, etc. Still, his study does seem to be pointing to a more substantive relationship between personality and music preferences. The dimensions of affect, for example, correspond to tangible aspects of our everyday life: our mood (valence), our preferred level of stimulation/relaxation (arousal), and our cognitive predispositions (depth). In particular, the level of cognitive or aesthetic depth one perceives in the music one likes—its complexity, poeticism, spirituality, etc.—seems a useful measure by which to correlate to one's personality. It makes sense, that is, that people who are markedly open, agreeable, and conscientious would gravitate toward music they perceive as rich in cognitive depth—as opposed to those who are markedly neurotic (anxious or depressed) or extroverted, who would not. Together with perceived levels of energy (arousal) and mood (valence), we may finally be getting somewhere.

But do the correlations between one's personality traits and the perceived affect of one's favorite music tell the whole story?

## A Bigger Basket of Factors

In the 2008 "exposure effect" study by Schellenberg and music neuroscientist Isabelle Peretz cited above (Endnote 723), the authors noted that in addition to repeated exposures, music preference was also gauged by the nature of the listening condition. Whether participants liked the music they heard, that is, was in no small way influenced by whether they were listening intently or experiencing the music as background. Listening focus is in turn but one of numerous factors beyond personality traits and music preference factors that researchers have begun to take into account over the past decade to more fully document the sources and influences of musical taste.

Other factors include cognitive styles, musical sophistication or expertise, listening function or context, and even substance use. To be sure, these do not represent every variable being investigated at the moment—and in truth many of the conclusions drawn on their behalf are a bit tenuous in explaining the source of our music preferences. Yet their discussion should prove useful in widening our vista on how our individuality might influence the music we love.[753]

Cognitive styles—also referred to as "brain types"—is a music preference factor explored by David Greenberg and colleagues. It refers to the somewhat controversial theory developed in 2009 by psychologist Simon Baron-Cohen whereby individuals may be defined by their measurement along a two-dimensional scale: *empathizing* (E) and *systemizing* (S). By the former is meant a cognitive tendency to identify, predict, and respond to the mental states or perspectives of others in an emotionally sensitive manner; by the latter is meant a tendency to analyze and explore the various "systems" we encounter in our daily lives—whether social, physical, classification-based, etc.—and to extract the underlying rules that govern their behavior. By means of their "Empathy Quotient," people can be labeled as Type E, Type S, Type B (balanced), or "extreme" E or S.[754]

In a 2015 joint study with Baron-Cohen, Greenberg attempted to correlate the cognitive style of listeners with the dimensions of their musical taste. Specifically, he embraced the MUSIC factors of Rentfrow et al., including the psychological (grouped into the same affect categories discussed above) and sonic (instrumentation and timbre) attributes associated with the factors. The study results are not surprising: those aligned with the Type E cognitive style were most positively correlated with Mellow music, though also with Unpretentious and Contemporary music; the affect states of low arousal, negative valence, and positive emotional depth; and the musical attribute of "strings." By contrast Type S folks were aligned with Intense music; high arousal, positive valence, and positive cognitive depth; and the musical attributes of dense, loud, percussive, fast, brass, and electric guitar. Undoubtedly, there is some level of correspondence between the cognitive styles of empathizing and systemizing on the one hand and the personality traits of the Big Five on the other—e.g., between high empathizing and Openness to Experience, and between high systemizing and Conscientiousness. Indeed, Greenberg concedes that both "play a significant role in predicting music preferences," but also suggests that one's empathy or systemizing "brain type" may account for unique variance.[755]

A second factor recently explored is a bit more intuitive: one's level of music sophistication or expertise. Here too David Greenberg has been an active researcher. Specifically, Greenberg has attempted to discern how one's personality type—one's dimension in the Big Five Model—predicted one's level of "musicality." In a large study, Greenberg assessed the musical sophistication of some eight thousand participants—for example, their ability to detect repetition or variation of a given melody—to draw his findings.[756] These include a "positive correlation" between musical sophistication and those participants identified with a high score in the Openness, Extroversion, and Agreeableness personality dimension. The inference here is that those who are naturally open, extroverted, or agreeable are more prone to seek out and achieve musical "expertise" than those who possess other personality traits; in turn, this might suggest a similar preference for more "sophisticated" music—though such conclusions are left to others to corroborate or refute.

Incidentally, this same Greenberg study included data on one other, somewhat curious variable: the use of recreational drugs, notably marijuana. The study revealed that those who acknowledged moderate to frequent drug use performed better than those who did not on the "active engagement" segment of the musicality inventory. They also performed particularly well on the rhythmic-perception assessment—pot smoking indeed being the "strongest predictor" of a high score on this test. Now, this should not necessarily be seen as advocating for the use of recreational drugs while listening to rhythmically vibrant music, but it may explain why the guy you saw rocking out so intricately on his "air drums" at the rock or jazz concert last night was also high as a kite!

Finally, several recent studies have explored the individual and individualistic nature of context—that is, the particular "factors" or "uses" wherein people may listen to this or that piece of music. This is related to the inventory of universal functions we discussed as relating to one's broad culture in Interlude E—and especially those aligned to social cohesion, work, and entertainment/aesthetics. In this case, though, we move from a collective function at the societal level to a personal function at the individual level. It thus relates to the specific question: What music do people listen to in different contexts or situations?

Rentfrow and Gosling made reference to the varying contexts in which people listened to music as a way to help orient their general notion of music preference: while driving, exercising, hanging out with friends, alone at home—not unlike the contexts we utilized with our fictitious subjects in the "genotype" chapters. A few studies have circumscribed their research to particular contexts—such as Dunn, whose participants were measured exclusively while at their desks at work. To say the least, chained to a desk is by no means the sole venue by which to measure one's musical taste. In North's 2010 study noted above, he correlates distinct music preferences by gender to differing music-listening uses: for females, these included pure enjoyment, relieving boredom, helping through difficult times, expressing emotions, and reducing loneliness; for males, they included to "be creative," using one's imagination, and pleasing friends.[757] Rentfrow et al. in their MUSIC studies highlight still other listening contexts, including mood regulation, enhancing concentration (e.g., during studying), increasing work productivity, and as a "badge of honor"—meaning as a means to promote and elevate their own self-identity.

Among the more interesting music psychology studies I've seen wherein music-listening contexts play a key role is one not by an American or European researcher but by a team of Indian music psychologists led by Durgesh Upadhyay.[758] As much as any study I know, the goal here seems to be to throw in as many dimensions as possible to help explain musical preferences—in this case, of a small population of seventy-seven Indian college students. The variables include participants' personality (via the Big Five Model), genre-based music preferences, degree of musical engagement (hours/week), listening focus, perceived emotions during listening, listening styles, and various listening contexts—or "functions of music." The last two are interrelated: listening style refers to the manner in which the experience takes place—whether as an emotional, analytical, somatic (bodily movement), or visual-imagination activity; function follows the more traditional understanding of the word, in this case based on an inventory presented in 1999 by John Sloboda—including things like to enhance or reinforce current mood, to calm or relieve stress, to remind of past events, to bring enjoyment, etc.

Although the small and demographically circumscribed study sample obliges us to consider Upadhyay's results with caution, a few are worth noting. These include an association between a preference for sad songs and the context of listening alone or desiring to improve a bad mood, a preference for rock and hip hop while in social settings (e.g., at a dance club), pop music while driving, and classical or world music to calm or relieve stress. Upadhyay et al. also notes a positive correlation between Openness and an "analytical" listening style, corroborating Greenberg, as well as between Neuroticism and an "emotional" listening style. Further, they found a correlation between focused listening and a preference for such listening functions as enhancing mood, bringing enjoyment (e.g., moving to tears), whereas passive or background listening was desired for functions tied to nostalgia and calming.

One final point of interest in this study is the manner in which perceived emotions are discussed—not via the conventional set of categories we've seen, as in the GEMS model. Instead, the study frames emotions using the ancient Indian construct of *rasas*. These are *aesthetic moods* attributed to Bharata Muni and compiled in the *Natya Shastra*—discussed in Chapter 14. To a degree, *rasas* function like emotional factors, each with a set of subfactors, and yet a *rasa* is more a cluster containing one of the basic emotions along with a related set of "transitory" (day-to-day) emotions and expressions. An example is *Śrngāra*, meaning love, but also arousal, longing, desire, naughtiness, and romance. The study details are not terribly important here, yet adopting this kind of broad, interactive approach to emotional states—partly fixed, party transitory—is instructive, especially when considering the kind of abstract emotional perceptions that music is capable of eliciting.

A stated aim of Upadhyay and his colleagues in this study is to develop an overall model of musical preferences and listening behavior, and especially to distinguish gender differences among young people. Their tentative "Music Engagement Model for Young Adults"—linking gender distinctions to personality factors, music preferences, listening styles, listening functions, listening focus, and *rasas*—may have a ways to go. But to my mind it points the way toward a smarter and more realistic approach to understanding individual musical taste: not merely a link of personality and musical preferences, but a rich amalgam of variables, a big basket of factors, that interact in myriad ways to help drive us toward the music we love.

## The Path Forward

You may rightly be wondering about now: What are we to make of all this? Put more pointedly: What does all this data about personality traits, music preference factors, psychological affect states, listening focus modes, musical expertise levels, listening contexts, demographics, and substance-use habits have to do with you and your musical taste? In a word (or two): it depends.

It depends first on how well you know yourself. Do you know where you fit within the Big Five Model, your dominant musical preference factor (genotype), the psychological affects you most desire in music, the distinct modes and functions in which you consume music, and your level of musical sophistication? (I assume you know your demographic identity, as well as your substance-use patterns.) It then depends on how well your identity within these areas maps onto the parameters currently studied by researchers, as well as how consistently and authentically you actually align to any of these dimensions, among other things.

In true Gestalt fashion, of course, the whole is greater than the sum of the parts. Just as our intracultural identity provides but the outlines or "stores" from which we may derive our musical taste, so too do individual psychology-based factors—our dominant personality trait, musical genotype, listening habits, or musical sophistication, etc.—provide but a window into how a given piece of music may or may not strike us. Even individually, though, these latter provide substantially more clarity. For example, simply knowing that you score high in the Openness to Experience trait, or that you are highly empathetic, will reveal that your musical interests will likely be fairly broad and eclectic, with a willingness to explore previously unknown songs, artists, and genres; and that you'll likely gravitate toward music that is uplifting, complex, and introspective. By contrast, knowing that you score high in the Extroversion trait suggests that you may have a penchant for a less broad array of music styles, predominantly rhythmic, energetic, less overtly uplifting, and not necessarily too complex—as well as aimed at social purposes.

But these are still fairly generalized, of course. With a clearer and more holistic sense of "who we are"—musically and otherwise—as well as how precisely we approach our music listening, we may begin to see how our individual identity truly and fully correlates to our musical taste.

For example, by Subject 1's love of Elle King's "Ex's & Oh's" we may presume someone who scores high in the Extroversion personality trait; possesses a "systemizing" brain type; subscribes to "Intense" and "Contemporary" music preference factors; prefers music with affects of high arousal, mixed valence, and negative depth; listens to music in social settings to relieve boredom and bring enjoyment; and possesses a modest level of music sophistication. By Subject 3's preference for Wayne Shorter's "Footprints," we may find someone who scores high in the Openness or possibly Neuroticism personality trait; possesses an "empathizing" brain type; subscribes to "Mellow" and "Sophisticated" music preference factors; prefers music with affects of low arousal, negative valence, and positive depth; listens to express emotions and reduce loneliness or stress; and possesses higher than average music sophistication. And by Subject 6's passion for Vivaldi's Concerto for Four Violins, Op. 3, no. 10, we may find someone who scores high in the Openness or Conscientiousness personality trait; possesses a mixed (Type B) "brain type"; subscribes to the "Sophisticated" music preference factor; prefers music with high arousal, negative valence, and positive depth; listens to music alone, to enhance concentration, and in an analytical listening style; and possesses a high level of musical sophistication. You get the idea.

Of course, these presumptions may well be wrong or incomplete—or they may reflect but one side of each subject's varied and complex musical genotype. In any event, this matrix of factors suggests that we would do well to heed that ancient Delphic maxim "Know thyself" if we want to properly understand our musical taste.

As the recent studies of Greenberg, Rentfrow, Schedl, and Upadhyay suggest, the trend in music psychology scholarship seems to be toward just such a multi-pronged approach to explaining music preferences. Interestingly, both Greenberg and Rentfrow propose the potential benefits of integrating their research into the functioning of music streaming and recommendation services, citing Pandora by name; in truth, however, their discussions reveal a limited understanding of how the Music Genome Project's coding operation actually works—something not surprising, given that Pandora has never publicly released its music analysis data.[759] At the same time, there is a steady stream of new services and technologies—such as Aivvy headphones, and Spotify's Echo Nest lab—that are attempting to match music playlists to user behavior.[760] To be sure, indeed, any recommendation or listening platform would do well to incorporate as much musical, personality, psychological, and contextual information as possible, to create not just the "best" playlist but the ideal playlist for that particular user at that particular moment.

I'm naturally biased, but I'd argue that Pandora would be in the best position to ultimately crack that code—given its comprehensive, standardized, and professional approach to musicological analysis or coding. At any rate, Pandora would do well to incorporate these other variables in a similarly rigorous way, to the degree possible. Who knows, with this book behind me, I might even have time to lend a hand in order to help Pandora build out the next generation of music recommendation. Indeed, Jason Rentfrow has noted to me my "extremely desirable position" in such an eventuality, by virtue of my greater proximity to Pandora user and analysis data.

On that note, I am in the midst of two studies of my own—to be uploaded to the WYLI website when complete—that, I hope, will carry forth the promise of recent studies. The first will take a close look at one particular music-listening mode: what I have called the "aesthetic mode" (see Interlude G). This mode involves giving focused attention to the music, likely while alone, with the aim of bringing intense enjoyment—perhaps even chills—and enhancing one's mood, fostering creativity, etc. As such, it involves the act of listening to songs and works that have a particularly profound impact on individual music lovers by virtue of the artistic merit, beauty, originality, and/or sublimity with which they strike them. The "aesthetic" listening mode by no means defines one's musical taste or genotype, but it does play a central role—and further can provide an important reflection of a listener's personality, musical and otherwise. As a fun bonus, the participants surveyed for the study will be some of the top musicians of our day, including ones whose music is featured in this book. Stay tuned for more.

The second study is broader in scope and population. It will involve a large number of general listeners—specifically drawn from Pandora's eighty-million-plus users a month. I'll thus be able to gain an immediate understanding of each participant's "music preference factors"—by virtue of the Pandora stations they've created, and the tracks they've thumbed up or down. Enhancing this will be a survey that discerns the personality of each participant, as well as the listening modes and contexts related to their consumption of individual Pandora stations. This should help provide a fuller picture of the musical genotypes of listeners and help expand our knowledge of how one's musical taste informs and relates to one's broader personality.[761]

As noted, it is an exciting time to be considering the links between our psychology, our personality, and our musical taste. Might as well hop along for the ride.

## The End of Our Mystery Novel

We have come a long way. In this final chapter of our mystery novel, the whodunit of our musical taste, we've explored that realm where the rubber meets the road. At the end of day, it is our psychology that explains why your favorite Beatles song is "Eleanor Rigby" while your best friend's is "I Want You (She's So Heavy)"—not to mention why your brother prefers the Rolling Stones or perhaps Herbie Hancock (as does my musician son, Preston). Given the prominence of psychology in defining and delimiting our musical taste, why, you may ask, did I not simply start there?

My response is that we tend to take too much of our musical taste for granted. But it is not to be taken for granted that the laws of physics and mathematics stipulate that steady frequencies produce overtones that align in perfect proportions, stacking up to produce intervals that comprise major, minor, and dominant 7th chords. It is not to be taken for granted that we humans evolved a capacity to hear individual tones across a wide bandwidth of frequencies, to discern octaves, fifths, and triads as pleasing entities, or to experience music as a viable means to communicate meaning, emotion, and social bonding. It is not to be taken for granted that our brains developed an ability to perceive, process, and remember complex patterns of pitch and rhythm, and to forge them into rich and distinct syntaxes marked by specific pitch distributions, rhythmic groupings, and repetitive schema. It is not to be taken for granted that based on where we are born and raised, we are given access to broad traditions of music that, whether we like them or not, are heard and experienced as "home," with rules and tendencies we can understand, explore, and cultivate. And it is not to be taken for granted that the classes, social circles, and intracultures we travel in seed in us the candidates of our individual musical taste.

Much, that is, had to happen before our psychology—our personality and individual identity—could ever be in a position to deliberate between two Beatles songs, or any other musical exemplars you can think of. They are all part of the miracle of music: why mere frequency and rhythm should carry such resonance within us, and why our individuality could shape on our behalf a unique and fully personal musical taste. It is something *not* to take for granted, but rather something to resoundingly celebrate, to explore, and to take as seriously—and joyfully—as we can.

part eight

# YOUR HIT PARADE

*sixteen*

# THE WHAT AND WHY OF MUSICAL TASTE

• • •

## The Road Just Traveled

In our travels through the sources and dimensions of our musical taste, we have navigated back and forth between musical and extramusical topics; the rationale, again, was to draw a complete picture while also minimizing overload on either one side or the other. It thus seems fitting that we likewise conclude our journey with one last back-and-forth—starting with a quick wrap-up of the seven musical "genotypes."

Through those "genotype" chapters (Chapters 9–15), we unwound the history and analysis of twenty-eight individual songs and works (not including the seven unwound on the WYLI website), covering a wide swath of musical terrain—from Taylor Swift to Led Zeppelin to Dizzy Gillespie to Eminem to the Chemical Brothers to Ravi Shankar to Beethoven, and then some. No doubt you found the discussion challenging at times, as prose on music theory is wont to be—even for trained musicians. My hope, however, is that you persevered through the musicological discourse—perhaps with reference to the previous chapters on the musical parameters to brush up on fuzzy concepts.

Admittedly, you might have wondered at times why I was diving into such technical detail when describing the musical proceedings of these hits, particularly as regards harmonic and formal discourse. Isn't this a book for nonmusicians? Am I really expecting an untrained reader to follow every musicological nuance—perhaps expecting you to be able now to carry out such an analysis on your own? Well, yes and no:

On the one hand, I look at the inclusion of detailed music analyses in a book written for nonmusicians much like a book for nonphysicists might include details on string theory or general relativity. No doubt much will get lost in translation. And yet, with patience and attention, the reader will come away better informed and more coherent on these previously mysterious matters than when the book was first cracked open. However, unless you decide to pursue that PhD in physics your grandmother always dreamed you'd earn, the only place you'll likely reencounter ten-dimensional space-time or gravitational lensing is the next time you pick up a lay account on string theory or general relativity.

By contrast, you listen to music all the time! You may not yet immediately recognize a harmonic modulation to the dominant or the use of binary form (though you may), but you are very likely hearing these elements regardless—just by putting on your favorite CD or loading up your go-to streaming radio service. You can of course enjoy the music without making such identifications, much as you can appreciate the beauty of a rainbow without understanding the science behind light refraction. Indeed, the research evidence is mixed as to whether increased knowledge alone improves musical appreciation.[762] But that is not the point: while theoretical knowledge alone may not affect what music you like or dislike, there can be no doubt that understanding—to at least some degree—the musical proceedings of the music you do love can enable a deeper and richer listening experience, while likewise opening your ears to new musical vistas. This, at any rate, is a key tenet of this book: that understanding the content—the *what*—of the music you love is essential to understanding *why* you like it.

## Your Hit Parade

This is especially the case when it comes to the complex relationship between that music you love—your hit parade—and the rich definition of your personality or psychology, as we've just reviewed. Beyond that, however, it is worth highlighting a few additional points stemming explicitly from the music genotype discussion:

First, it is worth remembering our previous adage: five songs a musical genotype do not make. As we saw with a good many of the music-loving subjects, our impressions after the first two or even three selections could be countered or recalibrated by those that followed. Similarly, the closing two or three hits could highlight as significant musicological elements that may have been missed or dismissed in the initial ones. Thus, drawing conclusions based on five—or even fifty or a hundred hits—can be a risky proposition; by five hundred, however, we'd probably have a pretty good idea of where your taste resides—maybe. Remember, though, we are focusing on songs and works you *truly like at this moment in time*, not just those you know, or would not turn off if they came on the radio, or that you used to love but now can't stand, etc.

A few years back, the now-defunct TidySongs tallied an average of 7,160 songs per iTunes library; Spotify currently enables up to ten thousand saved songs per subscriber library—though according to Spotify, fewer than 1 percent of users ever reach that limit. Yet any "total" numbers are misleading, as a good many tracks are simply residue from downloaded or saved albums, most of which would never rise to hit status for their purveyor. Pandora's thumbs-up count is perhaps more telling—accessible as a single "station" via "Thumbprint Radio": the average "highly active" Pandora listener, for example, has nearly five hundred thumbs-up'd songs.[763] But this too is an unreliable gauge, as at least a sampling of these upward thumbs were made for reasons divorced from actual preference—e.g., "I thought I liked it, but in fact, I don't." More importantly, the number of "liked" tracks an average Pandora user neglects to tag when they have the chance—or which never appear on their station at all—is undoubtedly significant.

So, how many songs do we actually love—or at least like, or want to hear again? No scientific study I know of has attempted to answer that question definitively. Indeed, it is hard to find consensus on how many songs/works the average person even knows—with estimates ranging from a few hundred to five thousand or more—depending on what is meant by "knows." One statistic I did find is the amount of time an average UK citizen spends listening to music over a lifetime—the answer, as compiled by Japanese headphone maker Audio-Technica in 2012: thirteen years![764] Interesting, and indicative of how much of our lives we devote to music, but not very useful in determining how many songs define a musical genotype. Considering first the songs we know, I would hasten a guess of around five hundred "beloved" songs per an average music lover—comporting in fact to Pandora's "thumbprint" average for active listeners. Your musical genotype, however, is by no means limited to songs/works you know, but also includes those you would love given the chance. In this scenario, the number could well rise into many thousands—even before we begin exploring new terrain.

A second important point worth remembering is that not all the songs or works "liked" by a listener would be "liked" to the same degree at all times or in all places: context matters—as we discussed in Interlude G. Among our music lovers, for example, it is doubtful that Subject 1 would have enjoyed Lin-Manuel Miranda's "It's Quiet Uptown" as much had it been served up during the morning run; or that Subject 5 would have grooved as hard to "Hey Boy Hey Girl" when getting ready for bed. The famed 2007 *Washington Post* experiment "Pearls before Breakfast"—featuring an incognito Joshua Bell playing his $3 million violin once owned by Fritz Kreisler in a Washington, DC, metro stop, as thousands of commuters walked past with utter disregard—is proof enough that context influences our listening experience.[765] This is but one example of an aesthetic framework known as "institutionalism," which suggests that we evaluate art (or nonart) in large part by the institution—museum, concert hall, subway station, etc.—in which it is presented.

At any rate, it is certainly true that we would not rate every song or work in the same way regardless of when or where we hear it. But that does not negate the fact that those songs or works we love—even within only a single context: a morning run, for example—do comport to our musical genotype. That is, it is *not* the case that we would love any old piece of music if it were just heard in the "right" time or place. Context matters, but content is king when it comes to defining our overall musical taste. Of course, our musical taste is not—and should not be—static: a song we love today could be irritating tomorrow, while one we'd "skip" this year could become one of our all-time favorites next year, etc. There are intracultural and psychological factors underlying why this might come to pass, though one key reason *should be* the continued and deliberate evolution of our musical genotype.

## In Defense of Sampling

I will readily acknowledge that the thirty-five songs and works reviewed here and on the WYLI website will not strike everyone as definitive for an exercise aimed at musicologically fleshing out the entire musical universe. I can hear the complaints already: How could you not include something by Michael Jackson or Nirvana or Duke Ellington or Jay-Z or Kraftwerk or Ladysmith Black Mambazo or J. S. Bach (though see the WYLI website, supplement to Chapter 16) or Tchaikovsky—or any of a thousand other equally or lesser-known artists or composers—in your fictional account? Believe me, I hear you. Few things have been as painful to me as denying so many talented musicians to this list, and then having to limit those selected to fewer than three dozen. Moreover, it is certainly unlikely that any actual person would induct those precise five songs into an official hit parade. Indeed, like most of you, a real "subject" would be hard-pressed to select just five favorite songs to punctuate a musical day. Further, a musical genotype is truly defined not just by the songs included in a list, but also by those to be assuredly excluded—or thumbed down, if you will—and we had only few things to say in that regard.

All that said, a couple of rebuttals. First, you will probably be glad that I did not follow up on my initial plan of selecting ten songs or works per music lover! Of course, some will have wished I'd only selected one or two per subject; you can't please everyone. Second, although I'd be willing to bet that you are not a fan of each and every one of those thirty-five selections, I'd be even more surprised if there were *none* that you substantially like at this moment of your life. As such, you will hopefully have learned a thing or two about your musical genotype by virtue of these discussions and analyses. And finally, as noted in Chapter 8, my purpose in this analytical section was not just to explicate those specific songs and works, but also to use them as markers within a larger musicological context—thus the attention made to place each work within a broader historical framework. It is, in short, my hope that this musical "sampling" served to elucidate the elements of musicological discourse generally while also providing some substantive grounding for the various "worlds" within which your musical genotype resides.

# Epilogue

## *Living with Music*

### The Unrivaled Power of Music

Sprinkled throughout our discussion on the origins and nature of our musical taste has been the occasional remark underscoring the overall positive value that music brings to us in our daily lives. We've noted, for example, the evolutionary power of music to help us better collaborate and socially bond with those around us—to woo a mate, or at least help us get to second base (Interlude A). We've also mentioned the broad ways in which music enhances aspects of our cognitive functioning—including engaging in reflective or abstract thought, empathizing with others, and improving our memory (Interlude C). In addition, we've noted how music enables us to better identify with our native culture, as well as to improve our social standing and sense of inclusion with the various intracultures to which we align ourselves (Interludes E and F). Finally, we noted in passing music's potent ability to improve our mood, reduce stress, positively adjust our mind-set or behavior, and regulate our emotions, among other psychological benefits (Interlude G).

In this concluding Epilogue, we will expand upon these perfunctory comments and unwind a bit the broader themes concerning the many benefits that music offers us in our lives—physically, psychologically, and spiritually. The goal here is certainly not to provide a comprehensive account on these points (a book in itself), but rather to lay down a clearer imperative for all of us to do more than merely recognize the sources of our music taste—but rather to "empower" it, and to develop a strategy whereby we may truly "live" with the music we love and *will* love. Making this leap may not always be easy, but as with all good things, it will be well worth the effort.

By contrast, it *is* easy to find written reference to the benefits and powers of music. A quick Internet search reveals a whole host of fascinating tidbits—that background music at the office increases worker productivity by 15 percent; that our eyesight improves by 25 percent when we listen to music; or that soldiers walk faster when moving to music, etc. Philosophers from Plato and Aristotle to Schopenhauer and Hegel to Jean-François Lyotard and Slavoj Žižek have spent sizable energy extolling music's great—"unrivaled," as Hegel calls it—power to influence our psyche, spirit, and character;[766] to many deep thinkers, music has a unique ability to engender civilizing and ethical traits within us, especially when properly administered. Neuroscience, as we've seen, has linked music engagement to higher executive functioning and improved brain plasticity, while psychology, as just noted, has aligned music listening with improved mood and heightened feelings of well-being.

Among the many benefits accorded music, however, the dimension that has received the greatest attention in recent years involves the physical body—especially when things go wrong. This is the realm of **music therapy**. We recall the striking stories of neurologist Oliver Sacks that led him to exclaim: "Our auditory systems, our nervous systems, are tuned for music."[767] In discussing the potential for people with dementia, for example, Sacks argued that music therapy can extend beyond an ability to improve motor or speech disorders, to also address "the emotions, cognitive powers, thoughts, and memories, the surviving 'self' of the patient, to stimulate these and bring them to the fore."[768] With this observation, Sacks was echoing an age-old intuition: that music has extraordinary power to connect the mind, body, and spirit—or, in the locution of Italian Renaissance philosopher Giovanni Pico della Mirandola: "Medicine heals the mind, soul, and spirit by the body, but music heals the body by the mind, soul, and spirit."[769] Again, this is an ancient notion, but one worth briefly tracing—as our final historical jaunt of this book.

## Musica Humana and the Path Toward Music Therapy

It seems reasonable to assume that music has been used as a healing agent from the very beginning. Perhaps, indeed, before instruments like the Divje Babe "flute" were ever imagined as sources of aesthetic entertainment, they were employed to rid a resident cave dweller of an evil spirit or debilitating illness. Depictions of harp-playing priests healing the sick in ancient Mesopotamia can be found dating back to 4000 BCE, with related depictions and accounts found in artifacts of ancient Assyria, Egypt, Babylonia, India, and China. The ancient Greeks expressed an understood link between music and medicine already in their mythology: Apollo was the god of both music and medicine, and his son Aesculapius became the god of healing within the medical arts after being instructed in archery, medicine, and music. Aesculapius became among the earliest music therapists when, according to tradition, he regularly "restored the spirits of 'frenetics' disturbed by the disease, to their natural state by means of the symphony [music]."[770] This indelible link of music and wellness was upheld in the school of Pythagoras, and later in the writings of Plato, Aristotle, and Ptolemy.[771]

Transmission of the music-body connection into the Middle Ages came primarily through the authoritative writings of Boethius, specifically his *De institutione musica* (On the Principles of Music). Boethius here expands upon the Pythagorean notion of the "Harmony of the Spheres," especially as relayed by Plato in *Timaeus*, by creating a tripartite classification of music: *musica mundana* (universal or cosmic music), *musica humana* (human music), and *musica instrumentis* (audible or instrumental music, produced by tension, wind, water, or percussion).[772] While the first and third kinds of music had clear origins in ancient writings, the second was fairly new. Boethius defines "human music" as the "joining together" of "the incorporeal nature of reason with the body," as well as the music that "unites the parts of the soul," and finally that which "holds together the parts of the body in an established order."[773] Put more succinctly, *musica humana* is the music that runs through our bodies, connecting the functions of the flesh with the actions of the soul and spirit. So where did this expression come from?

In a recent study, historian Donatella Restani casts Boethius' formulation of *musica humana* both as an example of his originality and as a reflection of contemporary thought in sixth-century Rome. Boethius is in fact renowned for his neologisms: he famously invented the term "quadrivium," referring to the four subjects—arithmetic, geometry, music, and astronomy—that underlay a medieval education.* Boethius' impulse to add "human music" to the two kinds established by the ancients, then, may have arisen from ideas already brewing at the time linking music to anatomy. Popular, for example, was a presumed link between the "perfect" musical intervals and the phases whereby an embryo develops into a baby.[774]

At any rate, once formulated, Boethius' *musica humana* became an underpinning for the rather "magical" correlations made, well into the eighteenth century, between music and wellness—notably that associated with "humoral theory." In short, this theory suggested that good health is a product of *balance* between the four primary fluids ("humors") of the body: black bile, yellow bile, blood, and phlegm; disease, that is, occurred when there was imbalance among any of the four humors. Most common was an excess of black bile that led to the condition of "melancholia"—whose treatment famously included music, or at least certain types of melodies and instruments, especially the harp and flute.[775]

Somewhat related to "humorism" is the theory known as "vitalism," which

* To this was later (in the eighth century) added the regimen of the "trivium"—grammar, logic, and rhetoric—thereby making up the "seven liberal arts."

took hold in Europe from the eighteenth century, not least among the aristocracy. As articulated by the musician and physician Franz Anton Mesmer, for example, vitalistic theory held that all organic processes were reliant on a "vital" fluid that permeated not just individual animate bodies, but the entire universe. Disease and bodily dysfunction arose when the proper, downward flow of this fluid was blocked, interrupted, or otherwise out of balance.[776] The term generally used for this improper flow was "excitability," caused by an excess or deficiency in vital fluid. Common treatments included such shiver-inducing procedures as bloodletting, leeches, and enemas; thankfully, though, other, more pleasurable approaches were also touted, notably music—given the "therapeutic property of sound," as one popular medical treatise put it, to heal an unbalanced soul.[777]

In the mid-nineteenth century, a new more "positivistic" approach—based on natural phenomena, experimentation, and evidence—took hold in medicine. Yet while this boded well for the healing arts, music now became relegated to supplementary status, no longer an active tool in the medical arsenal. This gradually began to change in the early twentieth century: in 1914, for example, Dr. Evan Kane began using music in his operating room; he published a report stating that patients exposed to music during surgery were less anxious and better able to handle anesthesia than those who were not. From there, empirical studies—especially tied to the military during World Wars I and II—increasingly found that, when used before, during, and after surgery, music decreased the need for painkillers. By the early 1950s, a new discipline was launched: music therapy.[778]

## Music Therapy: Activating the Therapeutic Properties of Sound

Over the ensuing decades, music therapy has become a thriving and respected discipline. Board-certified music therapists work in hospitals, nursing homes, hospice centers and other health settings, schools, prisons, community centers, etc. Undergraduate and graduate degrees in music therapy are offered in a good many universities in the US—with NYU, the University of Miami, and Arizona State University among the highest rated. At the same time, the field is still relatively small (only about six thousand practicing music therapists in the US; twenty thousand around the world), is occasionally dismissed by researchers in other health and music areas, and is little understood by the general public. These challenges are gradually dissipating, however, as the palpable benefits of music therapy become more and more demonstrated by empirical evidence and promoted via film, books, and articles.[779]

As the pioneering Helen Bonny, who developed the Guided Imagery and Music (GIM, or the Bonny Method) approach in the 1980s, defined it, music therapy is "a systematic application of music as directed by the music therapist to bring about changes in the emotional and/or physical health of the person."[780] As such, the field emphasizes the functional as opposed to entertainment or aesthetic properties of music—although both are undeniably at play in generating salutary effects.

The practical benefits of using music to bring about positive health outcomes are obvious: it is safe, relatively easy (requiring only a few musicians or recordings), cheap, and carries no side effects; it also ably complements and enhances traditional and pharmacological interventions. Among the ever-expanding list of physiological benefits of music therapy include its ability to treat and reduce pain, lessen anxiety, and counter fatigue; it can reduce blood pressure, heart rate, respiration, and body temperature; it can stimulate the immune system, change plasma stress hormone levels, and improve one's mood, among much else. Importantly, moreover, it entails a "rehumanization" of therapy, as Italian physician Donatella Lippi calls it—enabling a mix of biological, psychological, and social factors whereby health professionals can "care for" the patient, and not just cure.[781] All of these benefits are happily enabling hospitals and other facilities to use music therapy more consistently on behalf of patients in an array of circumstances.

Not surprisingly, given its now sixty-plus years in development, there are several distinct methods and theories used by music therapists to carry out their work. Among the most well-known is, indeed, GIM. This entails using music—exclusively classical, as we'll see—to elicit imagery in the minds of patients in order to put them into a relaxed, altered state whereby they may bring about a "mental synthesis or resolution" with therapeutic benefits. As such, it embraces one of the eight mechanisms—visual imagery—proposed by Juslin to explain how music can induce emotion (see Interlude G). Interestingly, Bonny developed her method while working at the Maryland Psychiatric Research Center, proposing it as an alternative to LSD-based psychotherapy. Today, it is used to treat depression and issues of low self-esteem, as well as to help cancer patients cope with the anxiety of treatment.

Other popular methods include two also associated with youth music education—the Kodály and Orff Music Therapy methods. Hungarian composer Zoltán Kodály developed a philosophy of musical pedagogy in the 1940s using rhythm, movement, and music notation that over the past twenty years has evolved into set of techniques to assist with perception, learning, and motor-skill development—especially for handicapped children and those with challenges of social integration. Orff Music Therapy is based on the Orff Schulwerk (schoolwork) approach, developed by composer Carl Orff in the 1920s, as discussed on the WYLI website (supplement to Chapter 15); it similarly focuses on musical rhythm and movement, as well as improvisation and performance, and is aimed at children with developmental rather than physical difficulties.[782]

More recently, as the application of music therapy has expanded more broadly into health care, there has been a shift away from practices based on psychology, social science, and education to those involving hard science and empirical research. Especially critical have been the recent advances in brain research and neuroimaging. Neurologic Music Therapy (NMT) first emerged in Colorado in the late 1990s and has since become a vibrant model that uses a wide array of techniques to train or retrain the injured or diseased brain. NMT embraces the insights gained from music neuroscience—including frisson—that have demonstrated music's profound ability to trigger complex perception, cognition, and motor-control processes. Certified Neurologic Music Therapists use myriad techniques—or "therapeutic music exercises"—of music perception and production to treat conditions such as stroke, Parkinson's disease, Alzheimer's disease, and physical injury. An example is using rhythm perception and our innate skill at entrainment to alter brain rhythm and thereby improve locomotion. Beneficiaries include Congresswoman Gabrielle Giffords, who greatly credits NMT for her success in recovering language and the ability to walk following her tragic gunshot wound to the head in 2011.[783]

Indeed, music therapy is today finding success and advocacy in a wide array of health care scenarios. A century after Dr. Kane's experiments, music continues to prove effective in pre- and postoperative care: to reduce the need for sedatives and pain medications, to lessen stress and anxiety, and to decrease recovery time. In one postoperative study, for example, music therapy was measured comparable to ten milligrams of morphine.[784] Cancer treatment has been another active arena of music therapy practice and research, notably at hospitals like Memorial Sloan Kettering and Mount Sinai Beth Israel in New York City. Three decades of randomized trials and meta-analyses have revealed music therapy's "statistically significant" ability to reduce distress (anxiety, pain, etc.) during radiation and lessen nausea while undergoing chemotherapy, among other benefits. In all such medical scenarios, therapists exploit music's ability to trigger neurochemical production, especially endorphins and oxytocin; lower cortisol levels; and more generally heighten emotion and arousal. Music thus functions as an "auditory analgesia," as Harvard-based surgeon Claudius Conrad put it, one whose powers are still being revealed.[785]

The discipline of music therapy is still in its formative years, and not least in defining *how* exactly the therapy should be administered: which music, how often it should be heard, how the patient should engage with it (passively, actively), etc. Such details are in fact generally lacking in academic studies on music therapy. When specific music is discussed, it is generally limited to broad genre categories—almost exclusively classical or new age. Occasionally, individual composers or musicians are mentioned—most especially J. S. Bach, but also Debussy, new age composer Steven Halpern, and jazz/world music guitarist John McLaughlin. Even more rare are accounts of specific songs/works or a detailed regimen for how to hear them.

An exception is the set of specific programs defined by Helen Bonny for her GIM method. She began by classifying musical works by the musicological parameters best suited to elicit the desired imagery: melodic contour, harmonic structure, rhythm, etc.; she then defined a set of distinct "programs" with specific emotional characteristics and benefits: Imaginative, Supportive, Creative, Positive, etc.; finally, she created a specific playlist of classical works that fit these criteria—such as Brahms' Third Symphony for the Imaginative program; Debussy's String Quartet for the Supportive program; Bizet's "Intermezzo" from *Carmen* for the Creative program, etc. This no doubt represents a progressive approach, utilizing specific music in a concrete therapeutic model. However, if classical music is not your thing, it is questionable that you would obtain the optimal outcome.

On that note, I would mention that I myself have begun working on an initiative in collaboration with Memorial Sloan Kettering Cancer Center to develop a model of personalized music therapy—one aimed at helping to reduce the distress associated with cancer treatment. The hope for a forthcoming study is to forge an "algorithm" that takes into account a patient's individual musical taste, the musicological parameters best associated with positive outcomes, and a well-defined regimen for listening and music engagement. A preparatory exercise involved my creating an original composition that explicitly utilized a few musicological elements identified in the literature as being positively associated with decreased pain and anxiety in cancer patients. Specifically, these include a stepwise descending bass line and a pedal point over changing harmonies (see Chapter 4)—elements revealed by analyzing two rare citations of individual works: J. S. Bach's "Air on the G String," from the Orchestral Suite in D Major and Debussy's *Prélude à l'après-midi d'un faune (Prelude to the Afternoon of a Faun).* In essence, this amounts to a kind of "reverse engineering" of the Music Genome Project: creating, as opposed to analyzing, music based on its intrinsic musicology. The work is entitled *The Wellness Suite*, and can be heard on YouTube.[786]

## The Mutual Adaptation of Music and Well-Being

Striking anecdotes and inspiring case studies demonstrating the distinct power of music therapy are not hard to find. There are the miraculous tales relayed by Oliver Sacks or filmmaker Michael Rossato-Bennett (*Alive Inside*) of nonresponsive patients with brain injury or Alzheimer's disease suddenly blossoming cognitively when singing or listening to music. Or the amazing story of musician-turned-therapist Andrew Schulman, brought back to health from an induced coma following complications from pancreatic cancer surgery—when his wife played J. S. Bach's *St. Matthew Passion* in his earbuds.[787] Or, more recently, the miraculous "escape" that music therapy gave to eleven-year-old Samantha Mc-

Carthy during the last year of her life while fighting the rare bone marrow disease Fanconi anemia; in the wake of her passing, her mother, Nikki, founded Sam's Fans, supporting music therapy programs in hospitals that treat seriously ill children.

In short, the verdict is in: musical engagement helps heal and succor the body when something goes wrong. But that is not all. Music also improves and enhances the well-being of even healthy humans. In this spirit, let us briefly return to Boethius. Although Boethian theory was co-opted to support such irrational theories as humorism and vitalism—whereby music could restore the body's lost equilibrium—Boethius' writings on music make no direct reference to illness or disease. Rather, his discussion on the three species of music is placed within a philosophical and moral context. He then precedes his classification of music by noting the inescapable role of music in our lives: "From all this it appears clear and certain that music is so much a part of our nature that we cannot do without it even if we wish to do so."[788] Thus, a millennium and a half before smartphones and Internet radio, Boethius could already articulate the necessity, and hence the ubiquity, of music in our lives.

And yet, unlike the declamatory way in which Boethius defines "*musica mundana*" and "*musica instrumentis,*" his definition of "*musica humana*" is posed largely in rhetorical form. Here is the original passage:

> What human music is, anyone may understand by examining his own nature. For what is that which unites the incorporeal activity of the reason with the body, unless it be a certain mutual adaptation and as it were a tempering of low and high sounds into a single consonance? What else joins together the parts of the soul itself, which in the opinion of Aristotle [*On the Soul*] is a union of the rational and the irrational? What causes the blending of the body's elements or holds its parts together in established adaptation?[789]

Boethius, in short, invites us to ponder this metaphysical notion of "human music"—the relationship of music and our bodies—for ourselves. Do not you too sense, Boethius asks, this deep, profound, and essential connection between music, our body, and our soul? Understanding its nature and origins, he adds, requires simply that we examine our own nature.

In our own time, researchers in various fields have scientifically corroborated this "mutual adaptation" between music and our everyday body and soul that Boethius long ago intuited. The validated benefits of music to our general health and well-being are many and varied—including several we've noted in previous discussions: reducing stress and anxiety; evoking positive feelings of joy, self-empowerment, and relaxation; helping us to cope with problems and challenges; facilitating positive social relations; providing us with a greater sense of belonging and purpose; counteracting loneliness, social isolation, and negative feelings; improving self-confidence and self-efficacy; providing calm, inspiration, comfort, and motivation; triggering memory and ease of cognition; stimulating greater wholeness of body and mind; and yielding a stronger sense of feeling alive and hopeful, among much else. In short, music has a proven ability to help with our general survival and heighten our capacity to achieve success in our lives.

One marker used by psychologists to articulate this ability is "subjective well-being," or SWB. In a 2016 study, Australian psychologist Melissa Weinberg utilized data gathered in a broad survey of the Australian Unity Wellbeing Index to try to quantify the relation between music engagement and SWB—which she defined as "an individual's perception of the quality of their own life," one that "is driven by an affective core." Her approach relies on the so-called "homeostasis theory," which simply notes that our SWB is affected not only by external factors (money, social relationships, etc.), but also by internal ones—and not least the cognitive strategies we employ in the face of life's challenges and opportunities.[790] Music, she notes, is one such key cognitive strategy, whether employed purposefully or not. Not surprisingly, the study revealed a direct correlation between music engagement and heightened SWB. While an increase was realized regardless of how music was consumed—whether actively or passively, alone or with others, via performance, dancing, or mere listening, etc.—the greatest results in the study came for those who engaged *actively* in music, and especially in the social contexts of choral singing and dancing.

As noted, a key factor articulated by Weinberg for how music is able to impact our SWB is through its role in shaping the very cognitive strategies we employ to regulate our moods or emotions—whereby we are able to gain greater or lesser "mastery" over the world. In another recent Australian study, psychologists TanChyuan Chin and Nikki Rickard go yet further to delineate the precise ways in which music affects SWB—namely, as "mediated" by one of two distinct emotional regulation strategies: reappraisal or suppression.[791]

In discussing the results of their study of more than six hundred participants, Chin and Rickard note that these two cognitive strategies each pursues a different goal: reappraisal is antecedent in nature, taking shape *before* the emotional response is registered in the mind and body; suppression, by contrast, is responsive, jumping into action only *after* the emotion has set in. Further, reappraisal—whereby the meaning of an event is preemptively changed in one's mind—is associated with higher SWB: positive affect, higher self-esteem, lower depression, improved mood, etc.; suppression, on the other hand—whereby emotions are simply *not* expressed—is associated with lower SWB: lower self-esteem, higher depression, mood disorders, as well as negative physical outcomes, such as increased sympathetic activation of the cardiovascular system. The results themselves are rather predictable: musical engagement is demonstrably shown to support the cognitive reappraisal that leads to higher SWB. As in the Weinberg study, this strategy is most especially associated with active and social music engagement—notably via improvisation and communal singing. It does so, they note, "because music facilitates one's ability to regulate the experience and expression of emotions"[792]—as we saw so palpably in Interlude G.

At the same time, however, the authors also reveal the cautionary results that in some contexts—involving *some* passive social or solitary listening—suppression *could* take hold instead of reappraisal, in turn leading to low SWB and its negative psychological and physiological effects. What, then, can we do to prevent this?

## Living with Music: Empower Your Musical Taste

Music, of course, is not a panacea. When serious illness or injury strikes, music alone will undoubtedly not enable full healing or recovery. And individuals who are psychologically prone to suppress rather than reappraise their emotions will not suddenly experience high subjective well-being simply because they turn on the radio or put on a CD they like. And yet, as we have underscored throughout this book, we are deeply and intrinsically wired to respond favorably to music—especially when we are actively engaged in its discourse.

Passive listening, to be sure, has its place, its powers, and its pleasures—the potential of reinforcing unhealthy emotional suppression notwithstanding. Even more impactful, then, is listening to enjoyable music with friends; or dancing to music you find fun and uplifting; or singing music you like in a community choir, etc. To reap the highest rewards that music has to offer—cognitively, physiologically, and psychologically—you are best off engaging actively with music you love.

And this is where your musical taste comes in. Again, you don't need to love the music you are hearing to enjoy or benefit from it, nor do you need to be paying constant, rapt attention. Yet to maximize the potential pleasure as well as benefits of music, to trigger the blessed release of neurochemicals that brings "chills" and other good things, you must *actively engage*—at least from time to time—in music that you *truly love*; this is how you *empower* your musical taste.

So what does this mean exactly?

First, it means taking steps to better understand the music you currently like—to know your "musical genotype." What styles, genres, species, and eras do you generally prefer? What approaches to melody, harmony, and rhythm? What musical instruments and timbres, types of forms, levels and modes of sophistication, and compositional techniques? Don't worry if you can't articulate any of these things in "proper" musicological language—though use the guides in this book (and other resources) to bolster what you do know. In fact, give yourself some credit: you were born musical, and you understand and "properly" hear more than you think you do. Indeed, regardless of how technically proficient you are, or how much you think you know about music, *never* stop learning and exploring. As my advisor at Stanford, William Mahrt, used to say, music is a "bottomless pit"—and in fact, he was just talking about Gregorian chant! No one ever knows it all.

As an aside, this can't help but evoke the fiery topic of music education, and our society's woeful abdication of the essential need to provide our children with a proper grounding in the musical arts and creativity—but that's another book.[793]

Next, use the music you *know* you like to continually expand your hit parade with *new* gems—much as we suggested could be possible with our seven music lovers. No song or work is an island, and similar or related music to your prized favorites is most certainly out there—waiting for you to discover it. It may be coy and take a while to enter your esteemed graces, or it may be love at first listen. It may come from within close proximity of the music you already love—similar composers, artists, genres, eras, etc. But do not sell yourself short by sticking too close to home: your next favorite may be lurking in a genre or species or era that you've rarely stepped foot in. Remember, your musical taste is in many ways a product of musicological techniques and approaches that cut across many, if not all, musical realms. Be bold and patient—keeping in mind that the "mere exposure" effect will likely make anything sound better the second time. Of course, that doesn't mean you'll want to hear it a third or tenth time around. And that's okay; thus be discriminating and picky as well. Make sure you are not seduced by an exotic sound or approach, but that the music truly "hits home" and is worthy of deep affection.

In this pursuit to expand the bounds and breadth of your musical taste, make use of every resource at your disposal—Internet radio services like Pandora, of course, but also friends, libraries, musicians; even your parents, kids, and siblings. Importantly, don't let yourself become a victim to your heuristics (see Interlude F); own your biases and challenge them—just because you're not "supposed" to like a style or artist doesn't mean you won't. An annoyed Pandora user once wrote us to complain that his Sarah McLachlan station was playing songs by Celine Dion—a singer, he said, he detested. After a few email exchanges, in which we explained the actual musicological connections, he finally wrote back—almost in disbelief: "Oh my God, I like Celine Dion!"[794] Undoubtedly, we all have a "Celine Dion" moment or two waiting to happen, and we owe it to ourselves to let them.

Finally, employ your hit parade in a dedicated and deliberate manner whenever you have the luxury to do so. You, of course, love different music for different occasions and circumstances, based on myriad practical, psychological, and intracultural factors. Some favorites are so identified for their exceptional ability to support studying and concentration, others for exceptionally enlivening a particular kind of social occasion, still others for best motivating your workout regimen or for especially pumping you up before a big presentation, etc., etc.

Take note of these varied scenarios and the musical jewels that best support them. In so doing, you can explicitly draw upon a rich, and ever-expanding, repertoire of your *personal* musical playlist for just the right occasion—like knowing which outfits are most guaranteed to bolster a given function.

In some moments, however, the function to be supported by music is not practical or social, but internal and personal; this is aesthetic listening. It is when the act of listening becomes an end in itself. Not as a duty or an obligation—as when you study for a test or aim to acquaint yourself with a style or artist you don't know. I'm referring instead to those moments when you *deliberately decide* to listen to music with the pure goal of pleasure, enrichment, and joy. To be sure, not all music will enable this mode of engagement, nor should it. These are the rare gems, the precious pearls of the musical canon that have *your* name written on them; in many cases, they took effort to locate and identify, but if so, the effort was well worth it. These are the musical works that yield a special power over you and, at least on occasion, have an extraordinary ability to transform your mind, body, and spirit into a blissful place they did not inhabit prior. These songs and works are fickle, and just because they held this power once does not mean they will the next time you give them a go. They are the rare fern flowers of music—blooming only rarely, and only to those lucky enough to find and cultivate them.

But simply identifying or "hearing" them will not reveal their full power. Realizing the potential of aesthetic listening requires full engagement on your part—attentive, effortful, sustained, active, and intentional. It requires you to follow the musical discourse in aesthetic time—following intently the melody, harmonies, rhythmic flow, the changing timbres of the voices or instruments, the shifting forms and techniques to the best of your abilities. When possible, choose those moments deliberately, select works high on your aesthetic playlist, put on quality headphones, turn up the volume, and trace the musical narrative as if internalizing an actor's speech or words of wisdom from a trusted counsel. If you're lucky, such aesthetic moments may arrive without warning, at a concert or during passive listening. If so, stop and engage as best you can, shut out the rest of the world. It may even be music you've never heard before, which yet possesses all the right ingredients to enrich your mind's ear—in turn triggering all the benefits we've been discussing. If so, write down the name of the music so that you might gain that experience again.

Again, finding music that successfully enables such profound and salubrious aesthetic listening is generally not easy. It is also not a once-and-done, but a continual process—a lifelong learning and living project. When I was in my early twenties, I would never have predicted that the sacred polyphony of Josquin des Prés would bring me to ecstatic aesthetic heights in my late twenties; nor that much of the glam rock by Queen that thrilled me as a teen would in later decades fill me more with nostalgia than bona fide joy; nor that in recent months

the compositions of Tunisian oud player Anouar Brahem would have granted m so many moments of joy and enrichment. A world of aesthetic richness awa you—so get out there!

To carry out all these tasks—whether to identify the best music to accomp tomorrow's workout, to pick music to best animate your next dinner part to sit down with a new group of songs to indulge your aesthetic listening— empower your musical taste. It is not always possible, admittedly, especia our rushed, overdigitalized, and socially fragmented world, but to do so tainly worth a try from time to time. Your ears, brain, cells, body, soul, an will thank you.

# ACKNOWLEDGMENTS

Writing a book, I quickly learned, is a marathon, not a sprint. This is especially true when you almost immediately start expanding upon your initial vision, and then—as in my case—you start expanding upon your expansion. To wit, the expression "when the book is done…" long ago became a meme in my house; I guess I had it coming in choosing a topic as bottomless as musical taste. Along the way, moreover, I learned another truth about writing: it is far less a solo effort than a team sport—and I have been blessed with a great team in writing this book.

It began with my initial book agent at WME, Kirby Kim, and my initial editor at Flatiron Books, Colin Dickerman, both of whom helped to shape the notion of what *Why You Like It* could and should be. Enabling me to get an early handle on the titanic amount of literature I'd need to encounter in researching the book was my "librarian" Jennifer Rodrigues. Rounding out the early team, then, were a couple of close friends—Steve Miller (not the rocker) and David Hall—who read through early drafts, providing welcome encouragement plus some valuable reader insights. I trust they'll be plenty surprised to see the final product.

For the latter phases of this process, I've been fortunate to have the sage guidance of Erin Malone and Jamie Carr at WME, and a spectacular team at Flatiron—most especially my brilliant editor Jasmine Faustino. More recently, I've benefitted from the impressive observation skills of my copy editor (also a trained musician), Mary Beth Constant, who saved me from more than a few embarrassing blunders.

Critical too has been the invaluable feedback I've received from a host of brilliant and generous academics and "expert" readers, most of whom are featured in the book. I am beyond grateful for the time and attention they gave in reading chapters and formulating thoughtful feedback—corrections, questions, and challenges—all of which, without question, has made the book better than it would have been otherwise. They include (in alphabetical order): Michael S.

Gazzaniga (an early champion), Will Glaser, John Hadja, Erin Hannon, David Huron, Donald Johanson, Daniel J. Levitin, Elizabeth Hellmuth Margulis, Steven Morrison, Bruno Nettl, Adam Ockelford, Jason Rentfrow, Mark Rimmer, William Sethares, and Mark Slobin. Needless to say, any remaining flaws in the book are entirely my own.

I'm also eternally grateful for the love, support, and encouragement of my parents, Jack and Marian Gasser—who not once told me to go out and get a real job, no matter how dire my career situation got. As was noted, my dad's rather peculiar musicality played a sizable role in shaping my musical identity, as did his deep insights into the human psyche gained through a lifetime in psychology. Sadly, my dad passed away in July 2017, as I was penning the first draft of the Epilogue; he was 90. It is painful for me that he did not live to see the book appear in print, though it is a bit comforting that he knew of its imminent completion; the many conversations we had about this or that passage played an invaluable role in helping me persevere when the going got tough. That my mom will witness the release of this book to the world, however, is a truly joyful thing.

Finally, this book would not have happened without the love and belief of my family: my son Preston, a future musician; my daughter Camille, the most talented writer in the family, now pursuing her own future in cognitive neuroscience; and my beloved wife Lynn, the rock of my world, without whose guidance, counsel, reassurance, and patience (did I say patience?) this book would certainly not exist. To them I lovingly say, "Can you believe it: the book is done!"

# GLOSSARY

**ACCENT** A performance-based or written articulation (notated as >) indicating that a note or chord is to be emphasized, whether on a strong beat or not.

**ALTO** The second highest of the four principal designations of vocal or instrumental register, below soprano.

**AMBITUS** The full range of a melody or melodic phrase, from the lowest to the highest pitch.

**ANTECEDENT** The first—"open" or "call"—phrase of a two-part symmetrical melody; typically followed by a related "consequent" phrase that concludes with a more strongly articulated cadence.

**ARTICULATION** A general term referring to the manner in which notes are played, individually and in sequence—e.g., *legato* (connected), *staccato* (detached), accented, etc.; notated with distinct symbols/signs.

**ATONAL** A harmonic orientation that eschews the system of tonality (post-1900), often associated with dissonant and/or complex vertical sonorities.

**AUTHENTIC CADENCE** A strong and commonly used cadence in tonal music, proceeding V–I (or V–i in minor), likewise called a "perfect cadence."

**BAR** See "measure."

**BARITONE** The vocal or instrumental register, outside of the four principal designations, between tenor and bass.

**BAROQUE ERA** The era of Western classical music from roughly 1600 to 1750, associated with the shift from modality to tonality and composers such as Monteverdi, Vivaldi, and J. S. Bach.

**BASS** The lowest of the four principal designations of vocal or instrumental register.

**BASS CLEF** In music notation, the symbol indicating the pitch of written notes where its two dots delimit the second line from the top, defining it as the note F below middle C—thus also called the "F clef."

**BEAT** See "pulse."

**BINARY** A formal template comprising two alternating sections, diagrammed as A-B, such as the successions or alternation of a verse (A) and chorus (B) in a pop/rock song.

**BLUES** A formal type and genre—commonly 12-bar and strophic—that arose around 1900 out of the African-American experience, and influenced jazz, rock, and other popular styles.

**BLUES SCALE** A distinct scale commonly used in blues, jazz, and rock styles—similar to a minor pentatonic scale, though with an extra note a tritone above the tonic.

**BPM** "Beats per minute"; a standard way to indicate the tempo (speed) of the music, commonly ranging from 60 to 150 bpm.

**BRIDGE** A formal section providing contrast (melodic, harmonic, etc.) to the otherwise dominant or regularly recurring sections of a song, such as the verse and chorus.

**CADENCE** A point of harmonic punctuation, as a partial or complete stop in melodic and/or chordal movement.

**CADENZA** A generally improvised or improv-like passage usually performed by a soloist, commonly placed near the end of a concerto wherein the performer displays virtuosic skills.

**CHAMBER MUSIC** A designation for generally instrumental—especially classical—music for "small" forces: solo piano, violin sonata, string quartet, small ensemble, etc.

**CHANSON** The French word for "song"; more specifically, solo vocal works of the classical species, especially in the medieval and Renaissance eras, as well as in the nineteenth and twentieth centuries.

**CHARACTER PIECE** A genre-based term used especially to designate short solo piano compositions, often in ternary form, by composers of the nineteenth century, such as Chopin, Schumann, Brahms, etc.

**CHORD** The vertical or simultaneous sounding of three or more notes, most commonly as stacked 3rds (and their inversions): major, minor, diminished, augmented, 7th chords, etc.

**CHORD PATTERN** Repeating patterns—or loops—of a sequence of chords, commonly in groups of two or four measures, but likewise as larger sequences.

**CHORD PROGRESSION** Any sequence, repeating or not, of chords within a song or work, or a section or passage thereof.

**CHORUS** See "refrain."

**CHROMATIC** A scale or sequence of intervals comprising consecutive half steps; or alternately, chords built upon pitches outside of a key's primary scale.

**CHROMATICISM** A general approach to harmony marked by sonorities (chords, intervals) beyond simple, diatonic principles, especially via chord progressions.

**CHURCH MODES** Generally refers to the eight modes used as the codifying framework for the repertoire of Gregorian chant; in all, four "tonics" or finals for the eight modes: D, E, F, and G.

**CIRCLE OF 5THS** A theoretical construct illustrating the relationship between keys within the tonal system; the twelve major/minor key pairs proceed by 5ths clockwise around the circle, whereby they are most closely related.

**CLASSICAL** One of the seven musical species highlighted in this book, referring principally to the Western tradition of "art" music from roughly 500 to the present.

**CLASSICAL ERA** The era of Western classical music from roughly 1750 to 1800, associated with the standardization of sonata form and composers such as Haydn, Mozart, and Beethoven (early output).

**CLUSTER** A group of adjacent half steps and/or whole steps sounding simultaneously, whether diatonic or chromatic.

**CODA** The Italian word for "tail"; a concluding section of a song or work.

**COMMON PRACTICE PERIOD** A term used to describe the period of Western classical music during which tonality was the prevailing harmonic system, roughly 1650 to 1900.

**COMPOUND METER** A metric orientation where each beat is divided into *three* equal parts, as opposed to the "simple" orientation of two; specific examples are compound duple (6/8), triple (9/8), and quadruple (12/8)—where dotted quarter notes (2, 3, and 4, respectively per measure) are each divided into three even eighth notes.

**CONCERTO** A common genre within the classical species written for a soloist (or group of soloists) in "contrast" with a larger ensemble.

**CONSEQUENT** See "antecedent"; the "closed" or "answer" phrase to the antecedent phrase.

**CONSONANCE** Literally a "pleasing sound"; today refers to intervals, divided between "perfect"

(4th, 5th, octave) and "imperfect" (3rds, 6ths) —as well as chords and sonorities that utilize these and related intervals.

**CONTEMPORARY ERA** The era of Western classical music from roughly 1950 to the present, associated with a pluralism of musical approaches and composers such as Boulez, Reich, Arvo Pärt, and John Adams, etc.

**CONTOUR** The overall shape of a melody.

**CONTRARY MOTION** One of the principal types of contrapuntal motion, where two melodic lines simultaneously move in opposite directions.

**CONTRAST** A formal approach where, to some degree or another, from partial to complete, music that follows is contrasted to what precedes it.

**COUNTERPOINT** Adjectival form: "contrapuntal"; a musical texture where two or more voice parts move simultaneously.

**CRESCENDO** The Italian word for "increasing"; a shift in dynamics by getting louder.

**CROSS-RHYTHM** See "polyrhythm."

**DA CAPO ARIA** A common genre used for arias (solos, duets) in operas during the Baroque and early Classical eras, in a ternary form (A-B-A); the term "da capo" is Italian for "from the top."

**DECEPTIVE CADENCE** A cadence that does not resolve in the expected way, but instead "deceives" the ear by going to another chord; also called an "interrupted cadence."

**DECLAMATORY** Also "monotonic"; an approach to text setting where, generally, each syllable is sung to one note.

**DECRESCENDO** The Italian word for "decreasing"; a shift in dynamics by getting softer.

**DEVELOPMENT** A general compositional technique where previous material—such as a melodic motive or theme—is varied to some degree, though likewise revealing similarity to its original presentation.

**DEVELOPMENT SECTION** The middle section of the sonata form—following the exposition—where earlier material is "developed" to some degree, often moving through numerous harmonic areas.

**DIATONIC** Greek for "proceeding by tones"; refers to the notes within the scale or mode of a given musical passage, as well as any intervals or chords generated from them.

**DIMINUENDO** See "decrescendo."

**DISSONANCE** Literally a "displeasing sound"; today refers to the major and minor 2nd, the tritone, and the major and minor 7th—as well as chords and sonorities that utilize these and related intervals.

**DOMINANT DEGREE** The fifth degree or step of the scale, usually symbolized with the Roman numeral V.

**DOMINANT 7TH CHORD** A chord built from a major triad plus a minor 3rd, most especially from the fifth (dominant) degree of the scale; also implying extended 7th chords (added 9ths, etc.) such as is common in jazz.

**DRONE** A sustained, "droning" pitch sounding throughout a work or section, while one or more other voices/melodies appear above (as is most common) or below it.

**DUPLE METER** A metric orientation where each measure, or rhythmic division, is divisible by two, such as 2/4 and 4/4; duple meters can be simple (each beat divided in two) or compound (each beat divided in three).

**DYNAMICS** The general dimension of musical sound related to volume, as fixed for a given section or as shifts—getting louder or softer.

**EDM** Acronym for "electronic dance music," alternately "electronica;" one of the seven musical species highlighted in this book, referring to music created explicitly for dancing, often featuring synthesizers, drum machines, etc., arising in the late 1970s.

**EIGHTH NOTE** The note value (in music notation, ♪) that is one-half of a beat where, as is common, each beat is articulated as a quarter note.

**ELECTRONICA** See "EDM."

**ENTRAINMENT** The rather uniquely human ability to lock into a regular, periodic pulse or beat in synchrony with others.

**EPISODE** A section within several classical music forms—rondo, fugue, concerto grosso, etc.—that forms a contrast to the principal musical section or material, often presented in new key areas.

**EQUAL TEMPERAMENT** The tuning system prevalent today, as on the modern piano, where each half step is sized the exact same proportional distance as every other—specifically measured as 100 "cents" per half step.

**EXPOSITION** The first section of sonata form, where the primary and secondary themes are presented, usually progressing from the tonic (I) to dominant (V) keys (or from i to III for minor keys).

**EXTENDED CHORD** The advanced harmonic practice of adding notes above simple triads or 7th chords, such as with 6ths, 9ths, 11ths, and 13ths.

**FLAT** The definition of a musical note, whether written (as ♭) or sounding, that is a half step lower than the note name to which it is attached.

**FORM** One of the five principal or primary parameters discussed in this book, referring to the structure or organizing dimension of music.

**FORTISSIMO** The Italian word for "very strong"; the dynamic (volume) level indicating the music is to sound very loud, notated as *ff*.

**FREE RHYTHM** Also "nonmetric rhythm"; any rhythmic orientation where there is no steady pulse or fixed tempo.

**FREQUENCY** The rate or speed of a single cycle of a sound wave, generally measured as cycles per second (Hertz), in turn corresponding to a particular pitch if sufficiently regular.

**FRISSON** The French word for "shiver"; a technical term for the "thrills and chills" associated with a strong, positive psychophysical response to music.

**FUGUE** A contrapuntal instrumental genre of the Baroque era involving an alternation of strict imitation with episodes of freer polyphony; or this contrapuntal technique utilized within discrete sections of other genres.

**FUNDAMENTAL** The lowest and generally dominant or perceived pitch/frequency when a note is sounded, upon which higher partials (overtones) are generated.

**GENRE** The somewhat elusive term whereby songs or works are classified into categories, large and small, according to conventions of sound, style, instrumentation, scope, function, etc.

**GROOVE** A colloquial term to indicate the steady, flowing rhythmic quality that underlies a work or section, and that captures a listener positively.

**HALF CADENCE** A commonly used cadence in tonal music ending on the dominant or V chord, whereby it brings a passage to a midpoint pause.

**HALF NOTE** The note value (in music notation 𝅗𝅥) that is two beats where, as is common, each beat is articulated as a quarter note.

**HALF STEP** The smallest interval—also labeled a minor 2nd—in the equal temperament system, such as the distance between C and D♭ on a modern piano.

**HARMONY** One of the five principal or primary parameters discussed in this book, referring to the vertical or simultaneous sounding of two or more pitches—as intervals, chords, and the systems governing them.

**HEAD** The colloquial term, particular in the jazz sphere, referring to the original tune (melody and chords), in distinction to the improvised solos over the chord changes.

**HEMIOLA** Greek for "the whole and a half"; generally indicating a rhythmic cross-relation of 3 against 2, as when two measures of 3/4 are presented as three measures of 2/4, or 3 notes in the time of 2, etc.

**HETEROPHONY** Literally "sounding apart"; one of the primary musical textures, where a single melody is performed by two or more voices and/or instruments with some level of variation between them.

**HIP HOP** One of the seven musical species highlighted in this book, referring to the music aligned with African-American-based hip hop culture, including rap, from the late 1970s to the present.

**HOME KEY** In the tonal system, the key center to which the song or work is most dominantly associated, such as where it begins and/or ends; notated as I (or i for minor keys).

**HOMOPHONY** Literally "sounding the same"; a term used for two distinct musical textures: (1) all voice parts moving in the same rhythm; and (2) a single dominant melody supported by subordinate accompaniment.

**HOOK** A colloquial term for a catchy and pronounced melodic and/or lyrical element in a song (especially in the "pop" realm) that is generally repeated numerous times throughout the song.

**IMITATION** Also "imitative counterpoint"; a strict approach to counterpoint or polyphony, common during the Renaissance era, where each voice part shares to some degree in the same melodic material in relative equality.

**IMPERFECT INTERVALS** In present-day music theory, a subset of consonant intervals identified as less "perfect" than the unison, 4th, 5th, and octave; specifically, the major 3rd, minor 3rd, major 6th, and minor 6th.

**IMPRESSIONISM** The movement in Western classical music from roughly 1890 to 1920, associated with exotic scales, extended chords, a "coloristic" approach to timbre, and composers such as Claude Debussy, Maurice Ravel, and Erik Satie.

**IMPROVISATION** Also "taking a solo"; the act of spontaneously creating music, melodic or otherwise, particularly germane to jazz, but likewise common to all musical species.

**INTERVAL** The distance between one pitch and another, whether as a melodic (horizontal) or harmonic (vertical) relationship—identified by both a number (2nd, 3rd, etc.) and a quality (major, minor, perfect).

**INVERSION** Any disposition of a chord where the root, or named chordal note, is *not* on the bottom—e.g., the third ("first inversion") or fifth ("second inversion") of the major or minor triad as the bottom note.

**IRREGULAR METER** Also "odd meter"; a broad metric orientation denoting a grouping of beats beyond the more "normal" two, three, or four beats per measure or rhythmic division.

**JAZZ** One of the seven musical species highlighted in this book, referring to the music forged around 1900 as a mix of Western and African-derived styles/techniques, with a focus on improvisation.

**KEY** In tonal music, the definition of a song or work, or section thereof, by virtue of its adherence to a particular major or minor scale.

**KEY SIGNATURE** In music notation, the display of one or more sharps (♯) or flats (♭)—or the absence of either in the case of C major and A minor—at the start of each staff to indicate the key of the song or passage.

**LEITMOTIF** The German word for "leading motive"; a recurring theme used to embody or suggest a character, object, or idea—most directly associated with the operas or music dramas of Richard Wagner.

**MAJOR CHORD** The quality or "flavor" of a triad (three-note chord) built from the simultaneous sounding of the first, third, and fifth degrees of a major scale, either in "root" position (1–3–5) or in inversion.

**MAJOR INTERVALS** A subset of intervals—melodic (horizontal) or harmonic (vertical)—built from a major scale: the major 2nd (e.g., C to D), major 3rd (e.g., C to E), major 6th (e.g., C to A), and major 7th (e.g., C to B).

**MAJOR PENTATONIC SCALE** A specific pentatonic scale orientation, such as formed when the black keys are played starting on G♭; common in numerous cultures around the world.

**MAJOR SCALE** In tonal music, a seven-note diatonic scale comprising an alternating pattern of whole and half steps such as forged when playing the white keys of a piano from C to C; the scale associated with a major key.

**MEASURE** Also "bar"; in music notation, the notes and rhythms circumscribed by vertical "bar lines" on either side, based on the grouping of beats dictated by the meter or rhythmic division of the work or passage.

**MEDIEVAL ERA** The era of Western classical music from roughly 500 to 1400, associated with the rise of modality, the flourishing of Gregorian chant, the rise of polyphony, and composers such as Machaut.

**MEDLEY** Also called "mash-up" in contemporary vernacular; a string of songs/works, or portions thereof, performed or recorded one after another.

**MELISMATIC** After the noun "melisma"; a florid approach to text setting where individual syllables are set to five or more notes.

**MELODY** One of the five principal or primary parameters discussed in this book, referring to a linear or horizontal set of pitches arranged in a particular order—defined as intervals and in some relation to scales or modes.

**MELODY-DOMINATED HOMOPHONY** See "homophony"; one of two textures of homophony, where a single dominant melody is supported by subordinate accompaniment.

**METER** The term used to define the pattern or grouping of strong (stressed) and weak (unstressed) beats—usually in groups of two, three, or four—whereby the rhythmic flow of the music is organized; examples: 4/4 and 6/8, etc.

**MICROTONE** Intervals smaller than a half step, or minor 2nd, common in numerous cultures outside the Western world.

**MINOR CHORD** The quality or "flavor" of a triad (three-note chord) built from the simultaneous sounding of the first, third, and fifth degrees of a minor scale, either in "root" position (1–3–5), or in inversion.

**MINOR INTERVALS** A subset of intervals—melodic (horizontal) or harmonic (vertical)—built from a minor scale: the minor 2nd (e.g., C to D♭), minor 3rd (e.g., C to E♭), minor 6th (e.g., C to A), and minor 7th (e.g., C to B♭).

**MINOR PENTATONIC SCALE** A specific pentatonic scale orientation, such as formed when the black keys are played starting on E♭; common in numerous cultures around the world.

**MINOR SCALE** In tonal music, a seven-note diatonic scale comprising an alternating pattern of whole and half steps such as forged when playing the white keys of a piano from A to A'; the scale associated with a minor key.

**MIXED METER** An approach of complex rhythm where two or more meters are combined within a song or work, or section thereof; e.g., 4/4 + 3/4 (regular), 4/4 + 3/8 (irregular), etc.

**MODALITY** Adjectival form: "modal"; the melodic/harmonic system used in the West prior to the advent of tonality, based on the church modes, and which governed chants and polyphonic music from roughly 500 to 1650.

**MODE** An alternate term to "scale"; a distinct sequence of half steps and/or whole steps, perhaps also skips—usually, though not always, extending a full octave—from which melodies are to some degree forged.

**MODERN ERA** The era of Western classical music from roughly 1900 to 1950, associated with the "decline" of tonality, the rise of atonality, the emancipation of rhythm, and composers such as Schoenberg, Stravinsky, and Bartók.

**MODULATION** The process of shifting from one key or harmonic area to another in the midst of a song or work, whether temporary or more structural; it may be harmonically adjacent or remote, achieved smoothly or suddenly.

**MONOPHONY** Literally "sounding alone"; one of the primary musical textures, where a single melody only is performed, whether by one voice/instrument, or by multiple voices at the exact same pitch level or exact octave.

**MOTIVE** Also "motif"; a common term used for a short musical idea, generally melodic, often used as a structural or compositional device in a song or work to generate cohesion.

**MOTIVIC DEVELOPMENT** The compositional process of developing an identifiable motive in some way as a song or work proceeds—via expansion, varied repetition, sequence, and/or other techniques.

**MUSIC THEORY** The study of the musical underpinnings, systems, parameters, and procedures of musical composition and performance.

**MUSIC THERAPY** The systematic application of music to bring about emotional and/or physical health to the listener.

**MUSICAL GENOTYPE** A metaphoric expression signifying the boundaries, characteristics, and content of one's musical taste—both positively and negatively—at any given moment.

**MUSICAL TASTE** As defined in this book: the full mix of musical and cultural dimensions—from the macro level of genre, style, and era to the micro level of distinct musicological attributes—that at any given moment and in any particular configuration correspond to an individual's liking and appreciation.

**MUSICOLOGY** The academic study of music from an historical, theoretical, philosophical, compositional, performance, and reception standpoint.

**NEUMATIC** After the noun "neume," the notational symbols of Gregorian chant; an approach to text setting between declamatory and melismatic—generally two to three notes per syllable.

**NONCHORD TONES** Notes outside the standard triads and 7th chords that sound simultaneous to the chord tones.

**NONMETRIC RHYTHM** See "free rhythm."

**NOTE** The constituent element of a melody or chord, whether written or sounding; also called "pitch" or "tone."

**OBBLIGATO** An independent, accompanying melodic figure, usually instrumental, appearing periodically through a song or work.

**OBLIQUE MOTION** One of the principal types of contrapuntal motion, where one voice remains stationary, like a drone, while the other moves.

**OCTAVE** The interval where the two notes sound at the same pitch level, though at two different registers; specifically, the interval eight notes away from the lower pitch in the diatonic scale.

**OCTAVE TREBLE CLEF** See "treble clef"; via the addition of an "8" at the bottom, the clef indicating that the notes sound an octave below the same pitch in treble clef; commonly used for male singers and guitars.

**ODD METER** See "irregular meter."

**OFFBEAT** A rhythmic accent placed on a nonstrong beat, often as part of a syncopated rhythm.

**ORNAMENTATION** An approach of embellishment, via effects or techniques, upon the basic notes of a melody, vocal or instrumental, common especially in non-Western vocal traditions.

**OSTINATO** The Italian word for "obstinate"; a melodic pattern, primary or accompanying, that repeats many times in succession, even as harmonic or other melodic elements change.

**OVERTONES** The harmonic "upper partials" produced whenever a steady pitch is produced by a voice or instrument, and that (softly) sound simultaneously to the "fundamental" in a particular sequence.

**OVERTONE SERIES** The specific sequence of overtones or upper partials that proceed by integer multiples (2:1, 3:2, 4:3, etc.) from a fundamental frequency, in turn producing a particular sequence of intervals.

**PARALLEL MOTION** One of the principal types of contrapuntal motion, where two melodic lines simultaneously move in the same direction.

**PASSING TONES** Notes outside the standard triads and 7th chords that sound "in passing" between two chord tones.

**PEDAL POINT** See "drone"; so called by virtue of the ability of an organist to sustain a drone pitch by holding down a foot keyboard pedal, as in various Baroque era genres like the fugue and fantasia.

**PENTATONIC SCALE** A scale of five notes per octave, as a mix of stepwise and skipped intervals, found commonly in indigenous musical cultures around the world in varying configurations.

**PERFECT INTERVALS** In present-day music theory, a subset of consonant intervals consisting of the unison, 4th, 5th, and octave, identified as more "perfect" than other (imperfect) consonances.

**PHRASE** A melodic "remark" of some notable substance and identity, perhaps articulated or delimited with a weak or partial cadence—more than a motive but less than a full sectional melody.

**PITCH** See "note."

**PLAGAL CADENCE** A fairly strong cadence in tonal music, proceeding IV–I (or iv–i in minor); sometimes called an "Amen cadence" due to its common use in hymns and gospel music.

**POLYCHORD** A type of complex harmony created by simultaneously sounding two or more simple chords—such as a D major triad above an E major triad.

**POLYMETRIC** A complex approach to rhythm, found in some non-Western styles, where two meters proceed simultaneously—such as one voice part in 4/4 moving against a second in 3/4.

**POLYPHONY** Adjectival form: "polyphonic," literally "multivoiced"; one of the primary musical textures, where two or more independent melodies proceed simultaneously.

**POLYRHYTHM** Also called "cross-rhythm"; a complex approach to music where two or more contrasting rhythmic constructs appear simultaneously, whether or not in distinct meters—such as a hemiola (3 beats against 2).

**POP** Short for "popular"; one of the seven musical species highlighted in this book, referring to music that is generally commercial in its orientation and simple/predictable in its musicological scope.

**POP/ROCK** A commonly used genre expression referring to rock music that is decidedly accessible in its scope and orientation and/or music that straddles the line between the pop and rock species.

**PRE-CHORUS** Within pop and rock songs, a transitional, stand-alone section that leads directly to the chorus, generally following the verse.

**PULSE** Also called "beat" or "tactus"; the most fundamental temporal or rhythmic unit of a song or work—the element to which one taps, claps, sways, etc., when the music has a pronounced rhythm.

**QUARTER NOTE** The note value (in music notation ♩) that is one full beat where, as is common, each beat is articulated as a quarter note.

**RANGE** See "ambitus."

**RECAPITULATION** The concluding section of sonata form—following the development—where the thematic material of the exposition returns, though now maintained in the tonic (I or i) key.

**REFRAIN** Also called "chorus"; a formal section of a song or work that recurs as the music proceeds, containing more or less the same music and text.

**REGISTER** The relative range, in terms of the "height" or octave(s) of the pitches involved, of a particular melody or a given instrument or instrument family.

**RELATIVE KEY** In tonal music, the pair of major and minor keys that have the exact same key signature, or number of sharps or flats—such as G major/E minor (1 sharp), F major/D minor (1 flat), etc.

**RIFF** An informal term for an "ostinato": an infectious repeating pattern used in various pop, rock, and jazz styles, such as a short recurring guitar pattern behind a vocal melody.

**RITORNELLO** Italian word for "little return"; in Baroque vocal and instrumental forms, a recurring refrain whose returns are separated by intervening episodes, often in contrasting harmonic areas.

**ROCK** One of the seven musical species highlighted in this book, referring to the music forged around 1950 from the roots of rhythm and blues, commonly aligned with high energy and youth culture.

**ROMANTIC ERA** The era of Western classical music from roughly 1800 to 1900, associated with heightened harmonic, formal, and expressive modes and composers such as Beethoven, Schubert, and Wagner.

**RONDO** A formal template that follows a symmetrical plan of repetition and contrast, where an initial section (A) returns in the middle and end, broken up by contrasting sections—such as A-B-A-C-A.

**ROOT** The named note within a chord, such as the note C in a C major chord.

**ROOT POSITION** The disposition of a chord where the root, or named chordal note, is the lowest written or sounding pitch.

**ROUNDED BINARY** A formal template that is a common variation of standard binary form (A-B), where the B section is "rounded off" to include a return of some A material.

**RUBATO** Italian word for "stolen"; an expressive term calling on the performer(s) to subjectively vary the tempo of the music—either the overall musical discourse or, in some cases, the melody only.

**SCALE** A distinct sequence of half steps and/or whole steps generally extending a full octave; in tonal music, related to a particular major or minor key, as well as a source from which melodies are forged.

**SCAT** A vocal technique of improvised vocalization common to jazz music, often using nonsense syllables and performed as an improvised solo.

**SECTION** A formal designation referring to a substantial division of a larger song or work, based on which subsequent sections will display an element of repetition, contrast, and/or variation.

**SEQUENCE** A melodic technique involving the immediate (or varied) repetition of a melodic phrase at a pitch degree higher or lower than the original—common to all species of music.

**SHARP** The definition of a musical note, whether written (as ♯) or sounding, that is a half step higher than the note name to which it is attached.

**SHMRF** An acronym for Sound-Harmony-Melody-Rhythm-Form, introduced by musicologist Jan LaRue and cited (in varied order) as a source for the key musical parameters discussed in this book.

**SHUFFLE** A rhythmic orientation or feel common to several blues-based genres—boogie-woogie, rockabilly, etc.—where each quarter note is divided as a dotted eighth and sixteenth note.

**SIMPLE BINARY** An alternate term for "binary" form (A-B); the standard orientation of this template, without a return of A material at the end of the B.

**SIMPLE METER** A metric orientation where each beat is divided into *two* equal parts, as opposed to the "compound" orientation of three; examples include 2/4, 3/4, and 4/4.

**SIXTEENTH NOTE** The note value (in music notation, 𝅘𝅥𝅯) that is one-quarter of a beat where, as is common, each beat is articulated as a quarter note.

**SOLO** An informal term used to signify when a performer improvises during a song or work, especially over established chord changes in jazz, rock, and related styles; alternately, any song or work performed by one person.

**SONATA** The Italian word for "sounded"; a solo/chamber instrumental genre with roots in the late Renaissance that flourished in the eighteenth and nineteenth centuries—generally adopting sonata form in at least the first movement.

**SONATA FORM** A formal type employed in several instrumental forms—sonata, symphony, concerto, etc.—from the eighteenth century, defined via the tripartite progression: Exposition—Development—Recapitulation.

**SONG** A common, if generic term for a short composition for voice with or without accompaniment; likewise an often inappropriate term to designate any piece of music, vocal or otherwise.

**SOPRANO** The highest of the four principal designations of vocal or instrumental register.

**SOUND WAVE** A change of air pressure, as energy moving as a spherical wave, that causes air molecules to vibrate at a particular speed (frequency), in turn yielding a pitch, volume, etc.; one complete cycle of this process.

**SPECIES** A term used in this book to designate one of seven broad realms of musical repertoire and music making: pop, rock, jazz, hip hop, EDM, world, and classical.

**STANDARD** A colloquial term to indicate a well-recognized and commonly performed song, particularly of the Tin Pan Alley repertoire—generally adopting the 32-bar refrain form type.

**STRAIGHT EIGHTHS** A rhythmic orientation or feel common to most musical styles, whereby consecutive eighth notes are performed with equal duration—as opposed to swung or shuffled eighths.

**STRICT REPETITION** An approach to repeating a musical idea (melody, chord progression, rhythm, formal section, etc.) where the repetition is exact, either in immediate succession or subsequently.

**STROPHIC** A formal template consisting of a single section (A) that repeats two or more times with little or no deviations among repetitions—thus with the schema A-A-A, etc.

**SUBDOMINANT** The fourth degree or step of the scale, usually symbolized with the Roman numeral IV or iv; alternately, a triad built from the fourth degree of the scale.

**SUBGENRE** The term used to label the constituent genres of broader genre realms, where the stylistic expectations and significations can become increasingly idiosyncratic.

**SUITE** A set of individual movements, usually instrumental, organized into a collective whole—common especially in the Baroque era.

**SWING EIGHTHS** A rhythmic orientation or feel common to jazz and other styles, whereby consecutive eighth notes are performed with unequal, partly "stolen" duration—as opposed to straight or shuffled eighths.

**SYLLABIC** See also "declamatory"; an approach to text setting where each individual note is aligned with a single syllable.

**SYMPHONY** The Greek word for "sounding together"; an ensemble-based genre with roots in the early Baroque that flourished as a multimovement orchestral medium in the eighteenth and nineteenth centuries.

**SYNCOPATION** A rhythmic orientation involving a prevailing conflict against metric expectations, most especially by virtue of a pronounced use of rhythmic accents placed against regular or strong beats.

**TACTUS** See "pulse."

**TAG** An informal term, used especially in jazz, to indicate a short concluding passage or section—"outro"—to a song performance or recording.

**TEMPO** The speed at which the music is performed, often defined as "beats per minute," or bpm.

**TENOR** The second lowest of the four principal designations of vocal or instrumental register, above bass.

**TERNARY** A formal template comprising three sections where two complete iterations of an opening (A) section are separated by a contrasting and self-contained (B) section—thus A-B-A.

**TEXTURE** A general term of musical sound, commonly understood as defining the distinct ways in which musical parts are put together: monophony, heterophony, polyphony, or homophony.

**THEME** A general term to indicate a principal melody or melodic idea of a song or work, or a section thereof—likewise used as a musical reference to a character or other extramusical entity.

**THEME AND VARIATIONS** As a formal template, see "variations"; also a genre where the variations template is employed, common in the classical species.

**32-BAR REFRAIN** A formal type commonly used in Tin Pan Alley/jazz-era songs ("standards") written between the 1920s and 1950s, often following the schema A-A-B-A.

**THROUGH-COMPOSED** A formal template signifying a form that does not follow any set pattern or formula.

**TIMBRE** A term referring to the "color" or "tonal quality" of a voice or instrument, and those sonic dimensions whereby we can distinguish one from another.

**TIME SIGNATURE** In music notation, the display of the meter (4/4, 3/4, etc.) of a song, work, or section thereof, displayed on the staff of each voice part at the beginning of the music and at moments of change.

**TONALITY** Adjectival form: "tonal"; the governing system of twenty-four major/minor keys—and their constituent scales, chords, and chord progressions—that has reigned over Western music since the mid-seventeenth century.

**TONAL HIERARCHY** Those scale or modal tones that hold a position of primacy or greater stability than others, whereby a particular ethnic or regional melodic language is defined or constrained.

**TONE** See "note."

**TONIC** The first and key-defining degree or step of the scale, usually symbolized with the Roman numeral I or i; alternately, a triad built from the first degree of the scale.

**TRANSCRIPTION** The output of arranging—"transcribing"—a composition for different forces, instrumental or vocal, than its original version, such as a piano transcription of an orchestral work.

**TREBLE CLEF** In music notation, the symbol indicating the pitch of written notes where its curl encircles the second line from the bottom, defining it as the note G above middle C—thus also called the "G clef."

**TRESILLO** A distinct triplet-like rhythm common to music of the Caribbean, such as the Cuban habanera, and subsequently incorporated into various twentieth-century popular styles, such as rockabilly.

**TRIAD** A three-note chord, most commonly arranged as two stacked 3rds; the common versions are the major, minor, diminished, and augmented triad.

**TRIPLE METER** A metric orientation where each measure, or rhythmic division, is divisible by three, such as 3/4 and 9/8; triple meters can be simple (each beat divided in two) or compound (each beat divided in three).

**TRIPLET** A "borrowed division," where three notes sound in the normal rhythmic space of two notes—notated with a small 3 above the notes and pedagogically pronounced "tri-po-let" or "tri-pa-let."

**TRITONE** The interval defined by three consecutive major 2nds (e.g., C to F♯), also called an augmented 4th or diminished 5th, and historically labeled "*diabolus in musica*" (the devil in music).

**TUNING** The systems by which the notes of scales and modes are defined, varying historically and across ethnic regions; more specifically, the process of defining the size and sound of specific intervals.

**TUPLET** Any "borrowed division" of note values, where a beat is divided by a number of notes above or below the standard subdivision—such as three, five, seven, or eleven notes in the time of one quarter note.

**UNISON** The interval defined by the simultaneous or consecutive sounding of the *same* note as that of another voice part.

**VAMP** Also "chordal vamp"; a repeating or cyclic chord progression, generally short (two or four measures), common in numerous species, not least in pop, rock, and related styles.

**VARIATION** See also "development"; a general compositional technique whereby subsequent iterations of a given musical idea are varied in details of pitch, harmony, rhythm, instrumentation, etc.

**VARIATION FORM** As a formal template, a varied strophic form, where a single section (A) is repeated several times, but with each iteration varied in some way; also the formal type employing this template.

**VARIED REPETITION** See also "variation"; a general compositional technique whereby an earlier idea is repeated, but where some element—pitch, rhythm, harmony, etc.—is varied to some degree.

**VERSE** A formal section of a song or work where the music is repeated, but where the text is different; generally occurring in alternation with a refrain or chorus.

**VERSE-CHORUS** The form type comprising a sectional alternation of verses and choruses—alongside other sections, e.g., bridge and pre-chorus—common to pop, rock, and related commercial forms.

**VOICE LEADING** The techniques and conventions used by composers/performers to yield smooth-sounding melodies within a multivoice or polyphonic texture

**WHOLE NOTE** The note value (in music notation, 𝅝) that is four beats where, as is common, each beat is articulated as a quarter note.

**WHOLE STEP** The second smallest interval—also labeled a major 2nd—in the equal temperament system, such as the distance between C and D on a modern piano.

**WORD PAINTING** The compositional technique of depicting the semantic meaning of a word or phrase—whether explicit via sung text or implicit in the work's title, etc.—with a targeted musical response.

**WORLD MUSIC** One of the seven musical species highlighted in this book, referring to the music arising from musical traditions outside of the Anglo-American tradition.

# NOTES

## INTRODUCTION: IN THE EAR OF THE BEHOLDER

1 See Nicolas Slonimsky, *Lexicon of Musical Invective: Critical Assaults on Composers Since Beethoven's Time* (New York: W. W. Norton, 2000); the quote on Debussy is on p. 94; attacks on Beethoven, pp. 42–52; on Brahms, pp. 68–79; on Mahler, pp. 120–24.

2 Plato, *Laws*, 679 d-e, tr. See also A. E. Taylor, *The Collected Dialogues of Plato*, eds. E. Hamilton and H. Cairns (New York: Pantheon, 1961), 1266.

3 The unsigned article, "George, Paul, Ringo, and John," was the cover story for the February 24, 1964, edition of *Newsweek*, "Bugs About Beatles"; see also Karl Shaw, "They Don't Love You, Yeah Yeah Yeah: Musical Geniuses, or 'Crowned Heads of Anti-Music'? Quotes from Beatles Critics over the Decades," *Wall Street Journal*, September 24, 2011.

4 In a footnote to his 1936 collected music reviews, under the pen name "Corno di Bassetto," Shaw apologized for his "hasty (not to say silly) description of Brahms' music"; see Eugene Gates, "The Music Criticism and Aesthetics of George Bernard Shaw," *Journal of Aesthetic Education* 35, no. 3 (2001): 67.

5 See Matthias R. Mehl and James W. Pennebaker, "The Sounds of Social Life: A Psychometric Analysis of Students' Daily Social Environments and Natural Conversations," *Journal of Personality and Social Psychology* 84, no. 4 (2003): 866. Some estimates are even higher: music psychologist Peter Rentfrow, for example, cites evidence for up to 17 percent of our waking lives spent listening to music; see "The Role of Music in Everyday Life: Current Directions in the Social Psychology of Music," *Social and Personality Psychology Compass* 6, no. 5 (2012): 402.

6 See David Hume, *Essays Moral, Political, Literary*, ed. Eugene Miller (Indianapolis: Liberty Fund, 1985), 241; see also Nick Zangwill, *Music and Aesthetic Reality: Formalism and the Limits of Description* (London: Routledge Studies in Contemporary Philosophy, 2015).

7 "On Musical Taste," *The Musical World*, September 27, 1838, 35.

8 "On Musical Taste," *The Musical World*.

9 "A Prosing About Music," *Spirit of the Times*, July 8, 1854, 242.

## CHAPTER 1: THE RISE AND REBIRTH OF THE SAVAGE BEAST

10 The story of Pandora has been traced, to some degree or another, in countless newspaper and journal articles, blog posts, dissertations, and books—several of which are cited below. See especially: Rob Walker, "The Song Decoders," *New York Times Magazine*, October 14, 2009; Matthew Lasar, "Digging into Pandora's Music Genome with Musicologist Nolan Gasser," *Ars Technica*, January 12, 2011; and Manuel Roig-Franzia, "Pandora and Internet Radio Royalty," *Washington Post*, April 3, 2013.

11 It should be noted that the account of Pandora's origins provided in this chapter attempts to clarify the one commonly given—namely, by highlighting the critical role that Will played in launching the company, and most especially in devising and directing the technological

and product solutions that enabled it to become a viable business, and ultimately a successful enterprise. In a word, Pandora would not have succeeded to become the company it is today without both Tim and Will.

12 See Michael Copeland, "Pandora Founder Tim Westergren Rocks the Music *Biz*," *Fortune*, June 29, 2010.
13 Jonathan Van Meter, "What's a Record Exec to Do with Aimee Mann?" *New York Times*, July 11, 1999.
14 Meter, "What's a Record Exec to Do."
15 See, for example, Bengt Carlsson and Rune Gustavsson, "The Rise and Fall of Napster: An Evolutionary Approach," *Proceedings of the 6th International Computer Science Conference on Active Media Technology*, Lecture Notes in Computer Science 2252 *(2001):* 347–54; and Raymond Shih Ray Ku, "The Creative Destruction of Copyright: Napster and the New Economics of Digital Technology," *University of Chicago Law Review*, 69 no. 1 (2001): 263–324.
16 For more on Donald A. Glaser, see his biography entry in Wikipedia.
17 Indeed, most corporate technologies are identified not by a public-facing name, per se, but simply by the programming languages they utilize—SQL and NoSQL (Instagram), Scala and FlockDB (Twitter), JavaScript and Python (Uber), etc.
18 See, for example, Hub Zwart, "Human Genome Project: History and Assessment," *International Encyclopedia of Social & Behavioral Sciences* (Oxford: Elsevier, 2015): 311–17.
19 For a discussion on the biological validity, or lack thereof, of Pandora's use of the expression "Music Genome Project," see the WYLI website (Chapter 1, suppl., n. 19).
20 Most of the technology behind how Pandora works has never been disclosed, but for a peek into one small aspect, see Pandora's patent, William Glaser et al., "Consumer Item Matching Method and System," US Patent 7,003,515 B1, filed February 21, 2006. See also the WYLI website (Chapter 1, suppl., n. 20).
21 Don Heckman, "Geller's German Gig Lasts a Lifetime,"All That Jazz, *Los Angeles Times*, June 15, 2001.
22 Interestingly, a prominent early consultant to MoodLogic was Daniel Levitin, author of *This Is Your Brain on Music*, and a frequent reference in this book. The company was bought by AllMusic Guide in 2006 and, like the other early competitors, is no longer in business. A journalistic summary of all these music recommendations services, including Savage Beast, is found in Don Clark, "New Web Sites Seek to Shape the Public's Taste in Music," *Wall Street Journal*, November 14, 2000.
23 Clark, "New Web Sites Seek to Shape the Public's Taste in Music."
24 Clark, "New Web Sites Seek to Shape the Public's Taste in Music."
25 Clark, "New Web Sites Seek to Shape the Public's Taste in Music."
26 Clark, "New Web Sites Seek to Shape the Public's Taste in Music." Microsoft bought Mongo-Music in 2000, merging it with its MSN Music, which operated through 2008.
27 Independently, Israeli computer scientist Dan Gang founded MusicGenome—attempting to mix artificial intelligence with musical taste via questionnaires, etc.; the company folded in 2007.
28 *New Media Music*, October 14, 2001; alas, I have only a copy of the text and the name of the source, not the name of the author or the title of the article.
29 For more on Classical Archives, see the WYLI website (Chapter 1, suppl., n. 29).
30 See Noam Wasserman and L. P. Maurice, "Savage Beast (A)," Harvard Business School Case 809-069, November 19, 2008 (rev. November 2012).
31 For a brief early history of Internet radio, see Franc Kozamernik and Michael Mullane, "An Introduction to Internet Radio," *EBU Technical Review*, October 2005.
32 See sources listed in Chapter 1, note 10, above.
33 The Charlie Rose interview can be seen at: https://charlierose.com/videos/15815.
34 See Chapter 1, note 12, above.
35 See, for example, Stephanie Clifford, "Pandora's Long Strange Trip," Inc.com, October 1, 2007.
36 See Ben Sisario, "Proposed Bill Could Change Royalty Rates for Internet Radio," *New York Times*, September 23, 2012.
37 A simple explanation of the debate is found in Ed Christman and Glenn Peoples, "Wait, What? The Copyright Royalty Board, Webcasting Rates, and Paying Artists, Explained," *Billboard*, December 16, 2015. A defensive argument from the songwriter's perspective is found in John Seabrook, "Will Streaming Music Kill Songwriting?" *New Yorker*, February 8, 2016; a detailed argument from the music streaming services was made admirably by Tim Westergren in a post, "Pandora and Royalties," on the company blog, June 26, 2013.
38 See, for example, Roger Waters, David Gilmore, and Nick Mason, "Pink Floyd: Pandora's Internet Radio Royalty Ripoff," *USA Today* op-ed, June 23, 2013, to which the company

responded—see Greg Sandoval, "Pandora to Pink Floyd: You've Been Misled about What We Pay Artists," *The Verge*, June 26, 2013.

39 See also John Brandon, "Pandora Uses Machine Learning to Make Sense of 80 Billion Thumb Votes," *VentureBeat*, July 12, 2017; and longtime Pandora engineer Eric Bieschke's interview with *Forbes* magazine in 2013: Amadou Diallo, "Pandora Radio's Dominance Built on Big Data Edge," *Forbes*, October 6, 2013.

## CHAPTER 2: UNDER THE MUSICAL HOOD: AN ORIENTATION

40 Jan LaRue, *Guidelines for Style Analysis* (Sterling Heights, MI: Harmonie Park Press, 1992), xv, etc. The acronym was initially "SHRMG," with the final letter standing for "growth"; LaRue himself changed the *G* to *F* (form) in "Style Analysis: An Approach That Works at Any Level, with Any Element, in Any Music," *Music Educators Journal* 59, no. 5 (1973): 62–64.

41 For example, see Jonathan Harnum, *Basic Music Theory: How to Read, Write, and Understand Written Music* (Createspace Independent Publishers, 2013); Nicolas Carter, *Music Theory: From Beginner to Expert* (Createspace Independent Publishers, 2013); and Michael Pilhofer and Holly Day, *Music Theory for Dummies* (Hoboken, NJ: John Wiley & Sons, 2015).

42 J. Peter Burkholder, "Music Theory and Musicology," *Journal of Musicology* 11, no. 1 (1993): 13—to which he dutifully adds: "And I am certain music history is better when it is theoretically informed."

## CHAPTER 3: MELODY: THE FACE OF MUSIC

43 See, for example, Francesca Simion and Elisa Di Giorgio, "Face Perception and Processing in Early Infancy: Inborn Predispositions and Developmental Changes," *Frontiers in Psychology* 6 (2015): 969.

44 See Judy Plantinga and Laurel J. Trainor, "Melody Recognition by Two-Month-Old Infants," *Journal of the Acoustical Society of America* 125, no. 2 (2009): EL58–EL62.

45 Valerie N. Stratton and Annette H. Zalanowski, "Affective Impact of Music vs. Lyrics," *Empirical Studies of the Arts* 12, no. 2 (1994): 173–84.

46 See Jeremy Day-O'Connell, "Pentatonic," *Grove Music Online* (*2001*).

47 For example, see Bruno Nettl, "Infant Musical Development and Primitive Music," *Southwestern Journal of Anthropology* 12, no. 1 (1956): 87–91; and Bruno Nettl, "North American Indian Musical Styles," *Journal of American Folklore* 67, no. 263 (1954): 44–56.

48 "Monotone," Grove Music Online.

49 William Drabkin, "Sequence (ii)," Grove Music Online.

50 Laure Schnapper, "Ostinato," Grove Music Online.

51 William Drabkin, "Motif," Grove Music Online.

52 See, for example, Alan Lomax et al., *Cantometrics: A Method in Musical Anthropology* (Berkeley: University of California, 1976; first published 1943).

53 Regina Randhofer, "Singing the Songs of Ancient Israel: taᶜame ʹemet and Oral Models as Criteria for Layers of Time in Jewish Psalmody," *Journal of Musicological Research* 24, nos. 3–4 (2005): 241–64; and Curt Sachs, *The Rise of Music in the Ancient World, East and West* (1943: Mineola, NY: Dover, 2008).

54 See Richard L. Crocker, "Melisma," Grove Music Online.

55 David Browne, "Trilling Songbirds Clip Their Wings," *New York Times*, December 24, 2010.

56 See, for example, Tim Carter, "Word-Painting," Grove Music Online.

## INTERLUDE A: THE EVOLUTION OF MUSICAL TASTE: MUSIC AND ANTHROPOLOGY

57 See, for example, Isabelle Peretz, Stéphanie Cummings, and Marie-Pierre Dubé, "The Genetics of Congenital Amusia (Tone Deafness): A Family-Aggregation Study," *American Journal of Human Genetics* 81, no. 3 (2007): 582–88.

58 Oliver Sacks, *Musicophilia: Tales of Music and the Brain* (London: Picador, 2012), 198–99.

59 You might assert that this statement ignores the deaf; in fact, research shows that deaf persons—

so long as other parts of their neurology are working well—do "hear" music, though via feeling and vibration perceived in the auditory cortex, etc. See, for example, Robert Cervin, "Deaf People Can 'Hear' Music," *NVRC eNews*, November 18, 2013. See also the TED Talk given by deaf percussionist Evelyn Glennie: "How to Truly Listen."

60 Henry Wadsworth Longfellow, *Outre-Mer: A Pilgrimage Beyond the Sea* (Boston: Houghton, Mifflin, and Co., 1883), 197.

61 See Dave Itzkoff, "Despite Protests, Alicia Keys Says She Will Perform in Tel Aviv," *New York Times*, May 31, 2013.

62 Kathleen Marie Higgins, *The Music between Us: Is Music a Universal Language?* (Chicago: University of Chicago Press, 2012), 12.

63 For more on the Western-centric limitations of defining music, see Bruno Nettl's valuable, yet little-known article: Nettl, Bruno. "Music" Grove Music Online. See also the WYLI website (Interlude A, suppl., n. 63).

64 The orchestras were from Manchester and Lancashire, respectively. See George Bernard Shaw, *Music in London: 1890–94*, rev. ed. vol. 1 (London: Constable and Company Limited, 1949), 90–91.

65 Leonard B. Meyer, *Emotion and Meaning in Music* (Chicago: University of Chicago Press, 1956), 62.

66 Bruno Nettl, *The Study of Ethnomusicology: Thirty-Three Discussions* (Urbana: University of Illinois Press, 2015), 32.

67 Joydeep Bhattacharya and Hellmuth Petsche, "Universality in the Brain while Listening to Music," *Proceedings of the Royal Society B: Biological Sciences* 268, no. 1484 (2001): 2423–33.

68 Alan P. Merriam, *The Anthropology of Music* (Evanston, IL: Northwestern University Press, 1964), 227.

69 Henkjan Honing et al., "Without It No Music: Cognition, Biology and Evolution of Musicality," *Philosophical Transactions of the Royal Society B: Biological Sciences* 370, no. 1664 (2015): 2.

70 The Haua Fteah "whistle" was dated between 80,000 and 100,000 years ago; its practical use as a playable instrument, however, is highly debatable. See Iain Morley, *The Prehistory of Music: Human Evolution, Archaeology, and the Origins of Musicality* (Oxford University Press, 2013), 37.

71 See Claudio Tuniz et al., "Did Neanderthals Play Music? X-Ray Computed Micro-Tomography of the Divje Babe 'Flute,'" *Archaeometry* 54, no. 3 (2012): 581–90.

72 See, for example, Adler, Daniel S. "Archaeology: The Earliest Musical Tradition," *Nature* 460, no. 7256 (2009): 695–96.

73 See, for example, Francisco J. Ayala and Camilo J. Cela-Conde, *Processes in Human Evolution: The Journey from Early Hominins to Neanderthals and Modern Humans* (Oxford University Press, 2017).

74 Steven Mithen, *The Singing Neanderthals: The Origins of Music, Language, Mind, and Body* (Cambridge, MA: Harvard University Press, 2006); see also Steven Mithen, "Singing in the Brain," *New Scientist* 197, no. 2644 (2008): 38–39.

75 Mithen, *The Singing Neanderthals*, 172.

76 Maggie Tallerman, "Abracadabra! Early Hominin for 'I Think My Humming's Out of Tune with the Rest of the World,'" review of *The Singing Neanderthals*, *Cambridge Archaeological Journal* 16, no. 1 (2006): 97–112.

77 Philip Lieberman, "Review of *The Singing Neanderthals*," *Language* 85, no. 3 (2009): 735.

78 Mithen, *The Singing Neanderthals*, 77–78.

79 Trân Quang Hai and Nicholas Bannan, "Vocal Traditions of the World: Towards an Evolutionary Account of Voice Production in Music," in *Music, Language, and Human Evolution*, ed. Nicholas Brennan (Oxford University Press, 2012): 142–72.

80 Cited in Daniel Albright, ed., *Modernism and Music: An Anthology of Sources* (University of Chicago Press, 2004), 23.

81 See Iain Morley, "Evolution of the Physiological and Neurological Capacities for Music," *Cambridge Archaeological Journal* 12, no. 2 (2002): 195–216.

82 Aniruddh D. Patel, *Music, Language, and the Brain* (Oxford University Press, 2008).

83 *Merriam-Webster's Collegiate Dictionary* (Springfield, MA: Merriam-Webster, 2004).

84 For these and other definitions, see "Definition of Music" in Wikipedia.

85 Bruno Nettl, *The Study of Ethnomusicology: Twenty-Nine Issues and Concepts* (Urbana: University of Illinois Press, 1983), 19. See also Nettl. "Music," which includes a good many more definitions of "music" from various sources.

86 Homer Garner Barnett, *Innovation: The Basis of Cultural Change* (New York: McGraw-Hill, 1973), 181.

87 R. Keith Sawyer, *Explaining Creativity: The Science of Human Innovation* (Oxford University Press, 2012), 253.
88 For more on the concepts of "cognitive fluidity" (combining different ways of processing knowledge) and "metacognition" (having an awareness of one's own thinking), see Steven Mithen, *The Prehistory of the Mind: The Cognitive Origins of Art, Religion, and Science* (London: Thames & Hudson, 1999).
89 Charles Darwin, *The Descent of Man, and Selection in Relation to Sex* (1871; Princeton, NJ: Princeton University Press, 1981), 51–52.
90 Darwin, *The Descent of Man*, 337.
91 See, for example, Nettl, *The Study of Ethnomusicology: Thirty-Three Discussions*, 31ff; and Maria Ujhelyi, "Social Organization as a Factor in the Origins of Language and Music," in *The Origins of Music*, ed. Nils L. Wallin et al. (Cambridge, MA: MIT Press, 2000), 125–34.
92 Darwin, *The Descent of Man*, 56.
93 William James, *The Principles of Psychology*, vol. 2 (New York: Henry Holt & Company, 1890), 484.
94 There were, naturally, a few exceptions in the intervening years, including by ethnomusicologist John Blacking, who in the mid-1970s argued for an adaptive role for music; see John Blacking, *How Musical Is Man?* (Seattle: University of Washington Press, 1976).
95 Steven Pinker, *How the Mind Works* (New York: W. W. Norton, 1999), 528.
96 Pinker, *How the Mind Works*, 534.
97 Pinker, *How the Mind Works*, 525.
98 Ian Cross, "Music, Cognition, Culture, and Evolution," *Annals of the New York Academy of Sciences* 930, no. 1 (2001): 35.
99 Mithen, *The Singing Neanderthals*, 273.
100 Geoffrey F. Miller, "Evolution of Human Music through Sexual Selection," in *The Origins of Music*, ed. Nils L. Wallin et al. (Cambridge, MA: MIT Press, 2000), 338.
101 Miller, "Evolution of Human Music," 348.
102 According to eye-popping estimates, Jagger has slept with four-thousand-plus women, while Simmons claims to have slept with nearly five thousand women. See Kiki Von Glinow, "Mick Jagger Sex Life: Rocker Has Slept with 4,000 Women, Biographer Says," *Huffington Post*, July 11, 2012.
103 Steven Brown, "Evolutionary Models of Music: From Sexual Selection to Group Selection," in *Perspectives in Ethology* (Boston: Springer, 2000), 257.
104 See Ian Cross, "The Evolutionary Nature of Musical Meaning," *Musicae Scientiae* 13, no. 2_suppl (2009): 182.
105 See, for example, Sandra E. Trehub, "Musical Predispositions in Infancy," *Annals of the New York Academy of Sciences* 930, no. 1 (2001): 1–16; and Sandra E. Trehub, "The Developmental Origins of Musicality," *Nature Neuroscience* 6, no. 7 (2003): 669–73.
106 Trehub, "Musical Predispositions," 7.
107 Trehub, "Musical Predispositions," 10.
108 Daniel J. Levitin, *This Is Your Brain on Music: The Science of a Human Obsession* (New York: Dutton, 2006), 241ff. See also the WYLI website (Interlude A, suppl., n. 108).
109 Peretz et al., "Without It No Music," 19ff.
110 Peretz et al., "Without It No Music," 11–12.
111 Patel, *Music, Language, and the Brain*.
112 Patel, *Music, Language, and the Brain*, 367.
113 Patel further notes that whereas one can provisionally identify a specific gene in our DNA (FOXP2) as directly related to language acquisition, no such "music gene" has yet been found. *Music, Language, and the Brain*, 404ff.
114 Patel, *Music, Language, and the Brain*, 400.
115 Patel, *Music, Language, and the Brain*, 401.
116 For example, in Aniruddh D. Patel, "Music, Biological Evolution, and the Brain," in *Emerging Disciplines: Shaping New Fields of Scholarly Inquiry in and Beyond the Humanities*, ed. Melissa Bailar (Houston: Rice University Press, 2010), 91–144; and Aniruddh D. Patel, "Music as a Transformative Technology of the Mind," paper presented at the Music: Its Evolution, Cognitive Basis, and Spiritual Dimensions symposium, Cambridge University, (2008), 340–42.
117 See Steven Robert Livingstone and William Forde Thompson, "The Emergence of Music from the Theory of Mind," *Musicae Scientiae* 13, no. 2_suppl (2009): 83–115.
118 See Eckart Altenmüller, Reinhard Kopiez, and Oliver Grewe, "A Contribution to the Evolutionary Basis of Music: Lessons from the Chill Response," in *Evolution of Emotional*

*Communication: From Sounds in Nonhuman Mammals to Speech and Music in Man*, eds. Eckart Altenmüller, Sabine Schmidt, and Elke Zimmermann (Oxford University Press, 2013), 313–35.
119 Michael S. Gazzaniga, *Human: The Science Behind What Makes Your Brain Unique* (New York: HarperCollins, 2009): 226, 244–45.
120 Yuval N. Harari, *Sapiens: A Brief History of Humankind* (New York: Random House, 2015), 33ff.
121 Daniel J. Levitin, *The World in Six Songs: How the Musical Brain Created Human Nature* (New York: Dutton, 2008), 27.
122 Peretz et al., "Without It No Music."

## CHAPTER 4: HARMONY: THE INTERNAL BODY OF MUSIC

123 See, for example, Francis MacDonald Cornford, *Plato's Cosmology: The "Timaeus" of Plato* (Oxford: Routledge, 2014), 66ff.
124 See Carl Dahlhaus et al., "Harmony," Grove Music Online.
125 For an influential pedagogical resource in this regard, see Walter Piston, *Harmony*, 5th ed. (New York: W. W. Norton, 1987).
126 Dalhaus et al., "Harmony."
127 See William S. Rockstro and George Dyson, "Cadence," Grove Music Online.
128 In minor keys, the subdominant chord is not major (IV) but minor, thus noted as iv; by contrast, the dominant chord is indeed major, thereby requiring a "borrowed" major 3rd.
129 Arnold Schoenberg, *Fundamentals of Musical Composition*, rev. ed. (London: Faber & Faber, 1999). We'll have much more to say about "organic" properties of music in Interlude D.
130 Indeed, some have traced the blues progression to such "ancient" harmonic cycles as the passamezzo moderno (Figure 4.19); see Manfred Schuler, "Vom Passamezzo Zum Blues," *Musica* 16 (1962): 65–66.
131 See, for example, George Dyson and William Drabkin, "Chromatic," Grove Music Online.
132 See, for example, Allen Forte, "Schoenberg's Creative Evolution: The Path to Atonality," *Musical Quarterly* 64, no. 2 (1978): 133–76.
133 See, for example, Stefan Kostka and Matthew Santa, *Materials and Techniques of Post-Tonal Music*, 5th ed. (1999; New York: Routledge, 2016).
134 Harold S. Powers and Frans Wiering, "Medieval Modal Theory," Grove Music Online.
135 James W. McKinnon, "Gregorian Chant," Grove Music Online.
136 For more on the byzantine road from modality to tonality, see, for example, Harold S. Powers, "Tonal Types and Modal Categories in Renaissance Polyphony," *Journal of the American Musicological Society* 34, no. 3 (1981): 428–70; and Gregory Barnett, "Modal Theory, Church Keys, and the Sonata at the End of the Seventeenth Century," *Journal of the American Musicological Society* 51, no. 2 (1998): 245–81.
137 See, for example, Peter Van der Merwe, *Roots of the Classical: The Popular Origins of Western Music* (Oxford University Press, 2004), 53–65.
138 Van der Merwe, *Roots of the Classical*, 62.
139 See Paul M. Walker, "Pedal Point," Grove Music Online.

## CHAPTER 5: RHYTHM: THE MOVEMENT OF MUSIC

140 Susanne Langer, "The Primary Illusions and the Great Orders of Art," *Hudson Review* 3, no. 2 (1950): 227.
141 See, for example, Gianfranco Cervellin and Giuseppe Lippi, "From Music-Beat to Heart-Beat: A Journey in the Complex Interactions between Music, Brain and Heart," *European Journal of Internal Medicine* 22, no. 4 (2011): 371–74; and H. Bettermann et al., "Musical Rhythms in Heart Period Dynamics: A Cross-Cultural and Interdisciplinary Approach to Cardiac Rhythms," *American Journal of Physiology: Heart and Circulatory Physiology* 277, no. 5 (1999): H1762–H1770.
142 See, for example, Kevin Laland et al., "The Evolution of Dance," *Current Biology* 26, no. 1 (2016): R5–R9.
143 For example, see Diane J. Urista, *The Moving Body in the Aural Skills Classroom: A Eurythmics Based Approach* (Oxford University Press, 2016).
144 For another broad overview, see Justin London, "Rhythm," Grove Music Online.

145 "Beat (i)," Grove Music Online.
146 Justin London, "Tempo (i)," *Grove Music Online* (2001).
147 See, for example, Aniruddh D. Patel and John R. Iversen, "The Evolutionary Neuroscience of Musical Beat Perception: The Action Simulation for Auditory Prediction (ASAP) Hypothesis," *Frontiers in Systems Neuroscience* 8 (2014): 57.
148 London, "Rhythm."
149 See, for example, Erin E. Hannon and Scott P. Johnson, "Infants Use Meter to Categorize Rhythms and Melodies: Implications for Musical Structure Learning," *Cognitive Psychology* 50, no. 4 (2005): 354–77; and Tonya R. Bergeson and Sandra E. Trehub, "Infants' Perception of Rhythmic Patterns," *Music Perception* 23, no. 4 (2006): 345–60.
150 One such claim of 90 percent is found in Dorothea E. Hast, ed. *Exploring the World of Music: An Introduction to Music from a World Music Perspective* (Dubuque, IA: Kendall Hunt, 1999), 99.
151 Joseph Kerman and Gary Tomlinson, *Listen*, 7th ed. (New York: Bedford St. Martin's, 2012), 9.
152 "Syncopation," Grove Music Online.
153 Steven Feld, "Aesthetics as Iconicity of Style, or 'Lift-up-over Sounding': Getting into the Kaluli Groove," *Yearbook for Traditional Music* 20 (1988): 76.
154 Levitin, *This Is Your Brain on Music*, 166.
155 See J. Bradford Robinson, "Swing (i)," Grove Music Online.
156 See the Library of Congress online article "History of Ragtime", https://loc.gov/item/ihas.200035811.
157 For a comprehensive history of jazz, including its roots in earlier styles and approaches, see, for example, Ted Gioia, *The History of Jazz* (Oxford University Press, 2011), especially "The Prehistory of Jazz," pp. 3–26.
158 Quoted in the PBS documentary *Rediscovering Dave Brubeck* (2001).
159 See Curt Sachs, *Rhythm and Tempo: A Study in Music History* (New York: W. W. Norton, 1953).
160 "Polyrhythm," Grove Music Online.
161 London, "Rhythm."
162 For a comprehensive study on polyrhythm in general and African practices specifically, see Simha Arom, *African Polyphony and Polyrhythm: Musical Structure and Methodology* (Cambridge: Cambridge University Press, 1991); see also Leslie Tilley, "Dialect, Diffusion, and Balinese Drumming: Using Sociolinguistic Models for the Analysis of Regional Variation in Kendang Arja," *Ethnomusicology* 58, no. 3 (2014): 481–505.
163 Interview with Frank Zappa, "Absolutely Frank: First Steps in Odd Meters," *Guitar Player* 16, no. 11 (November 1982): 116–21.
164 A comprehensive collection of essays on the interrelation of poetic meter and musical rhythm can be found in Paul Kiparsky and Gilbert Youmans, eds., *Phonetics and Phonology: Rhythm and Meter* (San Diego: Academic Press, 1989).
165 Bruno H. Repp, "Obligatory 'Expectations' of Expressive Timing Induced by Perception of Musical Structure," *Psychological Research* 61, no. 1 (1998): 33.
166 See Richard Hudson, "Rubato," Grove Music Online; and Richard Hudson, *Stolen Time: The History of Tempo Rubato* (Oxford: Clarendon Press, 1994).
167 Hudson, "Rubato." Most commonly, Chopin simply uses the word "*rubato*," but likewise "*poco rubato*" (a bit rubato), "*languido e rubato*" (languid and rubato), etc.
168 Hudson, *Stolen Time*, 196.
169 Benjamin Zander, "The Transformative Power of Classical Music," TED Talk, February 2008. See also Cosmo Buono, "The Chopin Prelude in E Minor Amplified," *Perspectives for Adult Piano Students* (blog), June 30, 2014.
170 Olivier Senn et al., "Expressive Timing: Martha Argerich Plays Chopin's Prelude Op. 28/4 in E Minor," in *Proceedings of the International Symposium on Performance Science* (2009): 107–12.
171 David Epstein, *Shaping Time: Music, the Brain, and Performance* (New York: Schirmer Books, 1995), 47ff.
172 See Christopher M. Johnson, "Effect of Rubato Magnitude on the Perception of Musicianship in Musical Performance," *Journal of Research in Music Education* 51, no. 2: 115–23.
173 Hudson, "Rubato."
174 For example, see Catona's blog post "Frank Sinatra: The Master of Rubato," February 13, 2013.
175 See, for example, Maarten Grachten and Gerhard Widmer, "The Kinematic Rubato Model as a Means of Studying Final Ritards across Pieces and Pianists," in *Proceedings of the Sixth Sound and Music Computing Conference* (2009): 173–78.

176 Martin R. L. Clayton, "Free Rhythm: Ethnomusicology and the Study of Music without Metre," *Bulletin of the School of Oriental and African Studies, University of London* 59, no. 2 (1996): 323–32.
177 Clayton, "Free Rhythm," 323.
178 McKinnon, "Gregorian Chant."
179 See Willi Apel, *Gregorian Chant* (Bloomington: Indiana University Press, 1958), 132; also David Hiley, *Western Plainchant: A Handbook* (Oxford University Press, 1993), 279–84, 378.
180 Benedictines of Solesmes, eds., *The Liber Usualis* (Tournai, Belgium: Desclée & Company, 1956), xxx.
181 See David Lister, "Plainsong Soars up the Charts," *Independent*, August 31, 2012.
182 For a concise summary of the path to strict rhythm, from the rhythmic modes of the "Notre-Dame school" to a flexible use of both duple and triple meters in the fourteenth century, see Alberto Gallo, *Music of the Middle Ages II*, trans. Karen Eales (Cambridge: Cambridge University Press, 1985), 1-48.
183 Clayton, "Free Rhythm." Specific genres/forms cited include the *taksim* in Turkey, the *avaz* in Persia, the *alap* in India, *qin* playing in China, and *shakuhachi* music in Japan.
184 For the zealous reader, there are several elaborate theories on the pervasiveness of rhythm in our experience of music. As an example, see Fred Lerdahl and Ray Jackendoff, *A Generative Theory of Tonal Music* (Cambridge, MA: MIT Press), 1983. See also the WYLI website (Chapter 4, suppl., n. 184).

## INTERLUDE B: IT'S THE OVERTONES, STUPID: MUSIC, MATH, AND PHYSICS

185 A more formal summary along with fuller discussion of the Pythagoras myth can be found, for example, in Kitty Ferguson, *The Music of Pythagoras: How an Ancient Brotherhood Cracked the Code of the Universe and Lit the Path from Antiquity to Outer Space* (New York: Walker & Company, 2008), 66ff.
186 Ferguson, *The Music of Pythagoras*, 64.
187 Plato, *Timaeus*, ed. R. D. Archer-Hind (London: Macmillan, 1888), 99.
188 Plato, *Timaeus*, 109.
189 For a full treatment, see Cornford, *Plato's Cosmology*, 57ff.
190 Curt Sachs, *The Wellsprings of Music* (The Hague: Martinus Nijhoff, 1962), 177.
191 For example, see Nazir Ali Jairazbhoy, *The Rāgs of North Indian Music: Their Structure and Evolution* (Bombay: Popular Prakashan, 1995), 8, 49–50; and Hugo Zemp, "Melanesian Solo Polyphonic Panpipe Music," *Ethnomusicology* 25, no. 3 (1981): 383–418. See also Patel, *Music, Language, and the Brain*, 88ff.
192 Cited in Reinier Plomp and Willem Johannes Maria Levelt, "Tonal Consonance and Critical Bandwidth," *Journal of the Acoustical Society of America* 38, no. 4 (1965): 549. See also Galileo Galilei, *Dialogues Concerning Two New Sciences*, trans. Henry Crew and Alfonso de Salvio (1638; Mineola, NY: Dover 1954), 97ff.
193 See Anthony Wright et al., "Music Perception and Octave Generalization in Rhesus Monkeys," *Journal of Experimental Psychology: General* 129, no. 3 (2000): 291–307; see also Arnaud J. Noreña et al., "Increasing Spectrotemporal Sound Density Reveals an Octave-Based Organization in Cat Primary Auditory Cortex," *Journal of Neuroscience* 28, no. 36 (2008): 8885–96.
194 Sandra Trehub, "Human Processing Predispositions and Musical Universals," in *The Origins of Music*, ed. Nils L. Wallin et al. (Cambridge, MA: MIT Press, 2000), 432.
195 For more on the academic pros and cons of my hypothetic extraterrestrial scenario, see the WYLI website (Interlude B, suppl., n. 195).
196 Two *relatively* digestible discussions of the Pythagorean (and other) tuning systems are James Murray Barbour, *Tuning and Temperament: A Historical Survey* (Mineola, NY: Dover, 2004); and William A. Sethares, *Tuning, Timbre, Spectrum, Scale* (Madison, WI: Springer, 2005), especially pp. 52–56; see also Mark Lindley, "Temperaments" (and related articles), Grove Music Online.
197 See Sethares, *Tuning*, 52ff.
198 See Barbour, *Tuning and Temperament*, 89–106; Sethares, *Tuning*, 60–63; and Mark Lindley, "Just Intonation," Grove Music Online. This English penchant for 3rds—termed "*la contenance anglois*" (the English countenance)—would soon influence composers on the Continent, notably Guillaume Dufay, the "father" of the musical Renaissance. See David Fallows, "The Contenance Angloise: English Influence on Continental Composers of the Fifteenth Century," *Renaissance Studies* 1, no. 2 (1987), 189–208.

199 See Robert W. Wienpahl, "Zarlino, the Senario, and Tonality," *Journal of the American Musicological Society* 12, no. 1 (1959): 27–41.
200 See Sethares, *Tuning*, 65ff.
201 Sethares, *Tuning*, 56–60.
202 Aristotle, *On the Soul (De anima)*, 420b, 10; cited in *Stanford Encyclopedia of Philosophy* (online).
203 Vitruvius, *On Architecture (De architectura)*, V.iii.6; cited in David Wiles, *Tragedy in Athens: Performance Space and Theatrical Meaning* (Cambridge: Cambridge University Press, 1997), 50.
204 For a rich discussion of the early scientific experiments of sound, see H. D. Cohen, *Quantifying Music: The Science of Music at the First Stage of the Scientific Revolution, 1580–1650* (Ontario: Springer Science, 1984).
205 Galileo, *The Assayer (Il Saggiatore)* (1623), trans. E. A. Burtt, in *The Metaphysical Foundations of Modern Physical Science* (New York: Doubleday Anchor Books, 1924), 75ff.
206 Galileo, *Dialogues Concerning Two New Sciences*, 103. The "disagreeable sensation" referred to by Galileo is technically called "beats" or "beating," meaning an audibly recognized interference pattern occurring when two sounds are of slightly different frequencies. See Cohen, *Quantifying Music*, 103ff.
207 For a technical discussion of Newton's proposal (in *Principia Mathematica*, Book II) and its flaw, see David T. Blackstock, *Fundamentals of Physical Acoustics* (Austin, TX: John Wiley & Sons, 2000), 35. See also Mike Bannon and Frank Kaputa, "The Newton-Laplace Equation & Speed of Sound," ThermaXX Jackets, December 12, 2014.
208 See Cohen, *Quantifying Music*, 101.
209 See, for example, Sigalia Dostrovsky et al., "Physics of Music," Grove Music Online.
210 For more on all these developments, see Dostrovsky et al., "Physics of Music"; also Peter Pesic, *Music and the Making of Modern Science* (Cambridge, MA: MIT Press, 2014).
211 Pesic, *Music and the Making*, 116.
212 Pesic, *Music and the Making*, 103ff.
213 Cited in John Augustine Zahm, *Sound and Music* (Chicago: A. C. McClurg & Company, 1892), 141.
214 See Murray Campbell, "Inharmonicity," Grove Music Online.
215 Mark Jude Tramo et al., "Neurobiological Foundations for the Theory of Harmony in Western Tonal Music," *Annals of the New York Academy of Sciences* 930, no. 1 (2001): 92.
216 Tramo et al., "Neurobiological Foundations." See also J. P. Rauschecker and R. V. Shannon, "Sending Sound to the Brain," *Science* 295, no. 5557 (2002): 1025–29.

## CHAPTER 6: FORM: THE SHAPE OF MUSIC

217 Oscar Wilde, *The Critic as Artist: Some Remarks Upon the Importance of Doing Nothing* (CreateSpace, 2014), 74.
218 Robert Hass, "One Body: Some Notes on Form (essay, 1978)," in *Claims for Poetry*, ed. Donald Hall (Ann Arbor: University of Michigan Press, 1982), 153.
219 "Form," *Merriam-Webster's Collegiate Dictionary* (2016).
220 Quoted in Ken Burns and Lynn Novick, *Frank Lloyd Wright* (documentary film), PBS Home Video, 1984.
221 Arnold Whittall, "Form," Grove Music Online.
222 Aristotle, *Poetics*, Book 7, trans. W. H. Fyfe (Cambridge, MA: Harvard University Press, 1932): 1450b.
223 Including figures like Goethe, Coleridge, and Kant. See, for example, Caroline Van Eck, "Goethe and Alberti: Organic Unity in Nature and Architecture," *The Structurist* 35–36 (1995): 20.
224 Heinrich Schenker, *Free Composition (Der freie Satz)*, vol. 3, *New Musical Theories and Fantasies*, trans. Ernst Oster (Hillsdale, NY: Pendragon Press, 1977), 44. See also William Drabkin, "Urlinie," Grove Music Online.
225 An influential call to look for "other kinds of aesthetic value in music besides organicism" is found in Joseph Kerman, "How We Got into Analysis, and How to Get Out," *Critical Inquiry* 7, no. 2 (1980): 311–31.
226 A. B. Marx, *Die Lehre von der musikalischen Komposition, praktisch-theoretisch* (1837–47); cited in Ian Bent and Anthony Pople, "Analysis," Grove Music Online.
227 For more on the changing usage of the terms "period" and "section," see Leonard Ratner,

"Period," Grove Music Online. It should be noted, though, that "period" is decidedly not a term in practical usage today; never, that is, have I heard a conductor or fellow musician say, "Let's take it from the beginning of the period."

228 Ratner, "Period."

229 "Antecedent and Consequent," Grove Music Online. A medieval precedent to this formal pair is the "*overt*" (open) and "*clos*" (closed) for repeated sections in French and Italian secular music; see "Ouvert," Grove Music Online.

230 See, for example, Van der Merwe, *Roots of the Classical*, 262.

231 W. Dean Sutcliffe and Michael Tilmouth, "Ternary Form," Grove Music Online.

232 See Gregory Kneidel, "Ars Praedicandi: Theories and Practice," Oxford Handbooks Online. For an extended historical and lexical discussion on "variation" in music, see Elaine Sisman, "Variations," Grove Music Online.

233 Sisman, "Variations," Part 10: The 20th Century.

234 For example, see Allyn Miner, *Sitar and Sarod in the 18th and 19th Centuries* (Delhi: Motilal Banarsidass Publishers, 1997), 187ff.

235 For a more nuanced look at the variants of through-composed form in minimalism, see Edward Strickland, *Minimalism: Origins* (Bloomington: Indiana University Press, 1993).

236 For an in-depth look at this latter song, see Martin Knakkergaard, "Zappa and Modernism: An Extended Study of 'Brown Shoes Don't Make It,'" in *Frank Zappa and the And*, ed. Paul Carr (Surrey, England: Ashgate Publishing 2013): 167–84.

237 Brad Osborn, "Understanding Through-Composition in Post-Rock, Math-Metal, and Other Post-Millennial Rock Genres," *Music Theory Online* 17, no. 3 (2011).

238 Terry E. Miller and Andrew Shahriari, *World Music: A Global Journey*, 3rd ed.(New York: Routledge, 2012), 83, 171, 199.

239 See Jim Samson, "Genre," Grove Music Online.

240 Jacques Derrida, "The Law of Genre," trans. Avital Ronell, *Critical Inquiry* 7, no. 1 (1980): 56.

241 For common variants, see Barry Kernfeld, "Blues Progression (Jazz)," Grove Music Online.

242 Among the many good books covering the history of the blues are Albert Murray and Paul Devlin's, *Stomping the Blues* (Minneapolis: University of Minnesota Press, 1976); and, for more recent figures, Jas Obrecht's *Rollin' and Tumblin': The Postwar Blues Guitarists* (Milwaukee, WI: Hal Leonard Corporation, 2000).

243 See, for example, the pronouncement on June 22, 2004, by Representative Elijah Cummings, cited in *United States of America Congressional Record* 150, part 10 (June 17–24, 2004): 13261.

244 As previously cited (Chapter 5, note 157), a good early account of jazz is Ted Gioia's *The History of Jazz*, 3–26. Among other good historical accounts of jazz, see Gary Giddins *Visions of Jazz: The First Century* (Oxford University Press, 1998); and Marc Myers, *Why Jazz Happened* (Berkeley: University of California Press, 2013).

245 See, for example, Ralf von Appen and Markus Frei-Hauenschild, "AABA, Refrain, Chorus, Bridge, Prechorus—Song Forms and Their Historical Development," *Samples: Online-Publikationen der Gesellschaft für Popularmusikforschung* (2015). See also the WYLI website (Chapter 6, suppl., n. 245).

246 See von Appen and Frei-Hauenschild, "AABA, Refrain," 14–16.

247 See, for example, Ted Gioia, *The Jazz Standards: A Guide to the Repertoire* (Oxford University Press, 2012).

248 Among the comprehensive books on the history of rock music are Charlie Gillett, *The Sound of the City: The Rise of Rock and Roll* (New York: Outerbridge & Dienstfrey, 1970); Ed Ward et al., *Rock of Ages: The Rolling Stone History of Rock & Roll* (Ontario: Summit Books, 1986); and Mark Paytress, *The History of Rock: The Definitive Guide to Rock, Punk, Metal, and Beyond* (New York: Parragon Books, 2011).

249 See Jerry Leiber and Mike Stoller, *Hound Dog: The Leiber & Stoller Autobiography* (New York: Simon & Schuster, 2010).

250 See Von Appen and Frei-Hauenschild, "AABA, Refrain."

251 Among the more exhaustive reviews of form in rock music, including on common variants of the typical rock formats and our perception thereof, see John Covach, "Form in Rock Music," in *Engaging Music: Essays in Music Analysis*, ed. Deborah Stein (Oxford University Press: 2005), 65–76; and Trevor Owen de Clercq, *Sections and Successions in Successful Songs: A Prototype Approach to Form in Rock Music* (dissertation, University of Rochester, 2012).

252 See, for example, de Clercq, *Sections and Successions*, 89–91.

253 Of particular note among broad discussions on sonata form during the Classical era is Charles Rosen, *Sonata Forms* (New York: W. W. Norton, 1988); see also Gordon Cameron Sly, ed., *Keys to*

*the Drama: Nine Perspectives on Sonata Forms* (Surrey, England: Ashgate Publishing, Ltd., 2009); and James Webster, "Sonata Form," Grove Music Online. One, incidentally, could argue that the sonata is both a formal type and a template—since, as we'll see, it is conventionally neither binary nor ternary, but something distinct.

254 From Johann David Heinichen, *Der General-Bass in der Composition* (1728); cited in Piero Weiss and Richard Taruskin, *Music in the Western World*, 2nd ed. (Belmont, CA: Thomson Learnin, 2007), 217.

255 Marx, *Die Lehre von der musikalischen Komposition*, vol. 3, 213. See also Scott Burnham, "The Role of Sonata Form in A. B. Marx's Theory of Form," *Journal of Music Theory* 33, no. 2 (1989): 259ff; and James Hepokoski and Warren Darcy, *Elements of Sonata Theory: Norms, Types, and Deformations in the Late-Eighteenth-Century Sonata* (Oxford University Press, 2006).

256 Webster, "Sonata Form."

257 Hepokoski and Darcy, *Elements of Sonata Theory*, 15.

258 Rosen, *Sonata Forms*, ix.

## CHAPTER 7: SOUND: THE PERSONALITY OF MUSIC

259 See Charles Taylor and Murray Campbell, "Sound," Grove Music Online. A broader technical discussion of sound can found, for example, in Thomas Rossing and Neville H. Fletcher, *Principles of Vibration and Sound* (New York: Springer, 2004).

260 The experiment, titled "Infrasonic," involved comparing two performances of an original composition by Sarah Angliss with and without infrasonics. See Sarah Angliss, "Infrasonic: Haunted Music?", January 23, 2009 Sarah Angliss, http://www.sarahangliss.com/portfolio/infrasound-the-pipe.

261 Levitin, *This Is Your Brain on Music*, 24.

262 See Murray Campbell, "Timbre (i)," Grove Music Online. A good discussion is likewise found in Levitin, *This Is Your Brain on Music*, 43ff.

263 Though as noted in Interlude B, some percussion instruments—snare drums, cymbals, etc.—produce "inharmonic" partials, and thus yield no discernible pitch.

264 For further clarification on this complex topic, see the WYLI website (Chapter 7, suppl., n. 264).

265 For a review of one key synthesizer development—the rise of digital synthesis at Stanford's CCRMA—see Julius O. Smith, "Viewpoints on the History of Digital Synthesis," *Proceedings of the International Computer Music Conference* (October 1991): 1–15. A more comprehensive review of how synthesizers work can be found, for example, in Mark Vail, *The Synthesizer: A Comprehensive Guide to Understanding, Programming, Playing, and Recording the Ultimate Electronic Music Instrument* (Oxford University Press, 2014).

266 See Christopher Lloyd Hamberger, *The Evolution of Schoenberg's Klangfarbenmelodie: The Importance of Timbre in Modern Music* (master's thesis, Pennsylvania State University, 2012). See also the WYLI website (Chapter 7, suppl., n. 266).

267 See, for example, Hamberger, *The Evolution*, 24, 45, etc.; see also Charles Hoffer and Darrell Bailey, *Music Listening Today* (Ontario: Nelson Education, 2015), 275.

268 Leonard B. Meyer, *Style and Music: Theory, History, and Ideology* (University of Chicago Press, 1989), 14ff.

269 See Klaus Wachsmann et al., "Instruments, Classification of," Grove Music Online.

270 Among the most comprehensive accounts of instruments, from prehistoric to modern times, is Curt Sachs, *The History of Musical Instruments* (1940; Mineola, NY: Dover, 2012).

271 Cited in Oliver Strunk, *Source Readings in Music History: Antiquity and the Middle Ages* (London: Faber & Faber, 1981), 20–21.

272 Joshua L. Mark, "Daily Life in Ancient Mesopotamia," *Ancient History Encyclopedia* (online, 2014).

273 See, for example, Howard Mayer Brown, *Music in the Renaissance* (Upper Saddle River, NJ: Prentice Hall, 1976), 257ff; see also Victor Coelho and Keith Polk, *Instrumentalists and Renaissance Culture, 1420–1600* (Cambridge: Cambridge University Press, 2016).

274 See, for example, Cyril Ehrlich, *The Piano: A History* (Oxford University Press, 1990).

275 See, for example, Max Wade-Matthews, *The World Encyclopedia of Musical Instruments* (London: Anness Publishing, 2000).

276 See Stéphanie Weisser and Maarten Quanten, "Rethinking Musical Instrument Classification: Towards a Modular Approach to the Hornbostel-Sachs System," *Yearbook for Traditional Music* 43 (2011): 122–46.

277 For example, "texture" was first included in the *Grove Dictionary of Music and Musicians* (dating to 1879) only in 1980. See also Jonathan Dunsby, "Considerations of Texture," *Music & Letters* 70, no. 1 (1989): 46–57.
278 Plato, *Laws*, 13.812.d–e.
279 See Raymond Erickson, "Musica Enchiriadis, Scolica Enchiriadis," Grove Music Online: 5. Theory and practice of organum.
280 As an example, see Rudolf Wittkower, *Architectural Principles in the Age of Humanism* (New York: W. W. Norton, 1971): 57ff.
281 See Paul M. Walker, "Fugue," Grove Music Online.
282 As displayed in Figure 7.23, the accompaniment to monodic music was generally notated as a single bass line with numbers atop the notes—referring to the intervals to be played above it by a chordal instrument like the harpsichord, organ, or lute; in this way it is not unlike a modern "fake book" for pop or jazz music.
283 See Nigel Fortune and Tim Carter, "Monody," Grove Music Online.
284 Meyer, *Emotion and Meaning in Music*, 185.

## INTERLUDE C: THE SINGING CEREBRUM: MUSIC AND THE BRAIN

285 See, for example, Richard Passingham, *Cognitive Neuroscience: A Very Short Introduction* (Oxford University Press, 2016); see also the authoritative textbook in the field: Michael Gazzaniga, Richard B. Ivry, and George R. Mangun, *Cognitive Neuroscience: The Biology of the Mind*, 4th ed. (New York: W. W. Norton, 2014).
286 Michael S. Gazzaniga, *Tales from Both Sides of the Brain: A Life in Neuroscience* (New York: Echo Press, 2015), 58.
287 Julian Paul Keenan et al., "Absolute Pitch and Planum Temporale," *NeuroImage* 14, no. 6 (2001): 1402–8.
288 Kate E. Watkins et al., "Structural Asymmetries in the Human Brain: A Voxel-Based Statistical Analysis of 142 MRI Scans," *Cerebral Cortex* 11, no. 9 (2001): 868–77.
289 See, for example, Azevedo, Frederico A. C. et al., "Equal numbers of neuronal and nonneuronal cells make the human brain an isometrically scaled-up primate brain," *Journal of Comparative Neurology* 513, no. 5 (2009): 532-541.
290 Levitin, *This Is Your Brain*, 89–90.
291 Among the many books available to the lay reader describing and/or depicting brain form and function, see, for example, Rita Carter, *The Human Brain Book* (New York: Penguin, 2014); and John Nolte, *The Human Brain in Photographs and Diagrams* (Amsterdam: Elsevier Health Sciences, 2013). For the more hardcore reader, see, for example, Stephen G. Waxman, *Form and Function in the Brain and Spinal Cord: Perspectives of a Neurologist* (Cambridge, MA: MIT Press, 2003).
292 For an overview of the ear and our sense of hearing, see Seth S. Horowitz, *The Universal Sense: How Hearing Shapes the Mind* (New York: Bloomsbury Publishing USA, 2012). For a clarification of my claim of a billion years of evolution leading to the rise of the human ear, see the WYLI website (Interlude C, suppl., n. 292).
293 See Peter W. Alberti, "The Anatomy and Physiology of the Ear and Hearing," in *Occupational Exposure to Noise: Evaluation, Prevention, and Control* (World Health Organization, 2001), 55ff.
294 See A. J. Hudspeth, "The Cellular Basis of Hearing: The Biophysics of Hair Cells," *Science* 230, no. 4727 (1985): 745–52.
295 As Oliver Sacks (*Musicophilia*, 141) notes, "It is said that more than fifteen percent of young people now have significant hearing impairments." See also Wen Jiang et al., "Daily Music Exposure Dose and Hearing Problems Using Personal Listening Devices in Adolescents and Young Adults: A Systematic Review," *International Journal of Audiology* 55, no. 4 (2016): 197–205.
296 Martin F. McKinney and Bertrand Delgutte, "A Possible Neurophysiological Basis of the Octave Enlargement Effect," *Journal of the Acoustical Society of America* 106, no. 5 (1999): 2679–92.
297 Horowitz, *The Universal Sense*, 5.
298 Stefan Koelsch and Walter A. Siebel, "Towards a Neural Basis of Music Perception," *Trends in Cognitive Sciences* 9, no. 12 (2005): P578–84; later revised in Stefan Koelsch, "Toward a Neural Basis of Music Perception—A Review and Updated Model," *Frontiers in Psychology* 2 (2011): 110–29.

299 See J. D. Warren et al., "Separating Pitch Chroma and Pitch Height in the Human Brain," *Proceedings of the National Academy of Sciences* 100, no. 17 (2003): 10038–42.
300 For a thorough and definitive discussion, see Bregman, Albert B. *Auditory Scene Analysis: The Perceptual Organization of Sound.* (Cambridge, MA: MIT Press, 1990).
301 Among the objective measurements of sound intensity are decibels (dB), sound pressure levels (SPL), and phons, etc. The definitive source on the subject is Frank Fahy, *Sound Intensity* (London: E. & F.N. Spon, 1995).
302 Pascal Belin et al., "The Functional Anatomy of Sound Intensity Discrimination," *Journal of Neuroscience* 18, no. 16 (1998): 6388–94.
303 For more, see Caclin, Anne, Stephen McAdams, et al. "Interactive Processing of Timbre Dimensions: An Exploration with Event-Related Potentials," *Journal of Cognitive Neuroscience* 20, no. 1 (2008): 49–64.
304 See, for example, the study by McAdams, Levitin, and others wherein the processing of timbre is mapped to specific parts of the brain: Menon, Vinod, D. J. Levitin, S. McAdams, et al. "Neural Correlates of Timbre Change in Harmonic Sounds," *Neuroimage* 17, no. 4 (2002): 1742–54.
305 Patel and Iversen, "The Evolutionary Neuroscience of Musical Beat Perception."
306 See also Bregman, *Auditory Scene Analysis*, 18–36 for a detailed discussion on how Gestalt principles of grouping provide ground rules for audio perception.
307 Reinier Plomp and Willem Johannes Maria Levelt, "Tonal Consonance and Critical Bandwidth," *Journal of the Acoustical Society of America* 38, no. 4 (1965): 548–60.
308 See Arthur W. Locke, "Descartes and Seventeenth-Century Music," *Musical Quarterly* 21, no. 4 (1935): 427–28.
309 See Noam Chomsky, *Syntactic Structures* (Berlin: Mouton de Gruyter, 2002), 15.
310 See Alexa R. Romberg and Jenny R. Saffran, "Statistical Learning and Language Acquisition," *Wiley Interdisciplinary Reviews: Cognitive Science* 1, no. 6 (2010): 906–14.
311 See, for example, Sandra E. Trehub et al., "Development of the Perception of Musical Relations: Semitone and Diatonic Structure," *Journal of Experimental Psychology: Human Perception and Performance* 12, no. 3 (1986): 295–301; and Anthony K. Brandt, Robert Slevc, and Molly Gebrian, "Music and Early Language Acquisition," *Frontiers in Psychology* 3 (2012): 327.
312 This phrase follows Stravinsky's more infamous line: "For I consider that music, by its very nature, is essentially powerless to express anything at all." From *Chronicle of My Life* (1935), cited in White, Eric Walter. *Stravinsky: The Composer and His Works*, 3rd ed. (Berkeley: University of California Press, 1979), 566.
313 Susanne K. Langer, *Philosophy in a New Key: A Study in the Symbolism of Reason, Rite, and Art* (Cambridge, MA: Harvard University Press, 1957), 244.
314 Meyer, *Emotion and Meaning in Music*, 39.
315 Meyer, *Emotion and Meaning in Music*, 2–3.
316 See, for example, Robert B. Zajonc, "Feeling and Thinking: Preferences Need No Inferences," *American Psychologist* 35, no. 2 (1980): 151–75; more on this topic in Interlude G.
317 Zajonc, "Feeling and Thinking," 151.
318 Justin Storbeck and Gerald L. Clore, "On the Interdependence of Cognition and Emotion," *Cognition and Emotion* 21, no. 6 (2007): 1218.
319 Levitin, *This Is Your Brain on Music*, 189.
320 Istvan Molnar-Szakacs and Katie Overy, "Music and Mirror Neurons: From Motion to 'E'motion," *Social Cognitive and Affective Neuroscience* 1, no. 3 (2006): 235–41.
321 Levitin, *This Is Your Brain on Music*, 183.
322 Vinod Menon and Daniel J. Levitin, "The Rewards of Music Listening: Response and Physiological Connectivity of the Mesolimbic System," *Neuroimage* 28, no. 1 (2005): 175–84.
323 Marcel Proust, *Swann's Way: In Search of Lost Time*, trans. C. K. Scott Moncrieff (New Haven, CT: Yale University Press, 2013), 238. See also Christie McDonald and François Proulx, eds., *Proust and the Arts* (Cambridge: Cambridge University Press, 2015), 96.
324 Plato, *Theaetetus*, XIII, 190e5–196c.3.
325 Aristotle, *De memoria et reminiscentia*, 450a, 29–32. Despite the association of the "storehouse" metaphor with Plato and Aristotle, that specific reference was first articulated by John Locke in "An Essay Concerning Human Understanding" (1689): "This is *Memory*, which is as it were the Store-house of our Ideas." Cited in Robert A. Wilson, *Boundaries of the Mind: The Individual in the Fragile Sciences—Cognition* (Cambridge: Cambridge University Press, 2004), 190.
326 From the oldest surviving treatise on rhetoric, *Ad Herennium*, written around 80 BCE—and formerly attributed to Cicero.

327 See Mary J. Carruthers, *The Book of Memory: A Study of Memory in Medieval Culture* (Cambridge: Cambridge University Press, 1992), 71ff.
328 For more on Guido and his many impactful musical innovations, see Claude V. Palisca and Dolores Pesce, "Guido of Arezzo," Grove Music Online.
329 See Anna Maria Busse Berger, *Medieval Music and the Art of Memory* (Berkeley: University of California Press, 2005), 45ff.
330 For more on Descartes' rather tortured theories of memory, see Desmond Clarke, *Descartes's Theory of Mind* (Oxford University Press, 2003), 93; see also the WYLI website (Interlude C, suppl., n. 330).
331 Charles B. Martin and Max Deutscher, "Remembering," *Philosophical Review* 75, no. 2 (1966): 161–96. For later revisions of their theory see, for example, Kourken Michaelian, "Generative Memory," *Philosophical Psychology* 24, no. 3 (2011), 323–42; and Sarah Robins, "Representing the Past: Memory Traces and the Causal Theory of Memory," *Philosophical Studies* 173, no. 11 (2016): 2993–3013.
332 See, for example, Douglas L. Hintzman, "'Schema Abstraction' in a Multiple-Trace Memory Model," *Psychological Review* 93, no. 4 (1986): 411; and Lynn Nadel et al., "Multiple Trace Theory of Human Memory: Computational, Neuroimaging, and Neuropsychological Results," *Hippocampus* 10, no. 4 (2000): 352–68.
333 For a deeper dive, see, for example, Michael Rossington and Anne Whitehead, eds., *Theories of Memory: A Reader* (Baltimore: Johns Hopkins University Press, 2007); and Alan F. Collins et al., eds., *Theories of Memory*, vol. 1 (Hove, England: Lawrence Erlbaum Associates, 1993). See also Levitin, *This Is Your Brain on Music*, 129ff.
334 Richard C. Atkinson and Richard M. Shiffrin, "Human Memory: A Proposed System and Its Control Processes," in *Psychology of Learning and Motivation*, vol. 2 (San Diego: Academic Press, 1968), 89–195.
335 For more on the notion and functioning of working memory, see Alan D. Baddeley and Graham Hitch, "Working Memory," in *Psychology of Learning and Motivation*, vol. 8 (San Diego: Academic Press, 1974), 47–89; and Alan Baddeley, "Working Memory," *Science* 255, no. 5044 (1992): 556–59.
336 Isabelle Peretz and Robert J. Zatorre, "Brain Organization for Music Processing," *Annual Review of Psychology* 56 (2005): 95.
337 Meyer, *Emotion and Meaning in Music*, 87.
338 Levitin, *This Is Your Brain on Music*, 145.
339 Daniel J. Levitin, "Absolute Memory for Musical Pitch: Evidence from the Production of Learned Melodies," *Perception & Psychophysics* 56, no. 4 (1994): 414–23.
340 Peretz and Zatorre, "Brain Organization for Music Processing," 96–97.
341 Jenny R. Saffran, Michelle M. Loman, and Rachel R. W. Robertson, "Infant Memory for Musical Experiences," *Cognition* 77, no. 1 (2000): B15–B23.
342 Sacks, *Musicophilia*, 201ff.
343 This theory is known as "proceduralism," introduced by Craik and Lockhart in 1972; see Fergus I. M. Craik and Robert S. Lockhart, "Levels of Processing: A Framework for Memory Research," *Journal of Verbal Learning and Verbal Behavior* 11, no. 6 (1972): 671–84.
344 Levitin, *The World in Six Songs*, 104. Here, in point of fact, Levitin is summarizing a core idea of David Huron's ITPRA theory, which we'll detail more in Interlude G.

## CHAPTER 8: THE MUSICAL GENOTYPE

345 For a more academic discussion and defense of my use of the term "genotype" to refer to musical taste, see the WYLI website (Chapter 8, suppl., n. 345).
346 Samson, "Genre."
347 Theodor Adorno, *Aesthetic Theory*, trans. Christian Lenhardt (Oxford: Routledge, 1984), 288.
348 Samson, "Genre."
349 David Hesmondhalgh, "Indie: The Institutional Politics and Aesthetics of a Popular Music Genre," *Cultural Studies* 13, no. 1 (1999): 34–61.
350 See, for example: www.musicgenreslist.com; https://www.allmusic.com/genres; https://gist.github.com/sampsyo/1241307; and https://en.wikipedia.org/wiki/List_of_music_styles, etc.

## CHAPTER 9: THE POP GENOTYPE

351 Howard Mayer Brown, "The Chanson Rustique: Popular Elements in the 15th- and 16th-Century Chanson," *Journal of the American Musicological Society* 12 (1959): 16–26.
352 Cited in Simon Frith, "Pop Music," in *The Cambridge Companion to Pop and Rock* (Cambridge: Cambridge University Press, 2001): 94–95.
353 See, for example, Jon Stratton, "Between Two Worlds: Art and Commercialism in the Record Industry," in *Popular Music: Critical Concepts in Media and Cultural Studies*, ed. Simon Frith (London: Routledge, 2004): 7–23.
354 Simon Frith, *Taking Popular Music Seriously: Selected Essays* (London: Routledge, 2007), 168.
355 For more on the common tendencies of pop harmony, see Peter Winkler, "Toward a Theory of Pop Harmony," *In Theory Only* 4, no. 2 (1978): 3–26.
356 *Rolling Stone*, Artists: Taylor Swift (2008); archived at http://archive.li/7Bfmg.
357 Alexis Petridis, "Taylor Swift: Reputation Review—Superb Songcraft Meets Extreme Drama," *Guardian*, November 10, 2017.
358 For a summary of Swift's public battles with streaming services, see Kaitlyn Tiffany, "A History of Taylor Swift's Odd, Conflicting Stances on Streaming Service," *Verge*, June 9, 2017.
359 For the history of the back-and-forth battle between Swift and West, see Keith Harris, "Taylor Swift vs. Kanye West: A Beef History," *Rolling Stone*, February 16, 2016; and Alice Vincent, "Why Taylor Swift and Kanye West Hate Each Other," *Telegraph*, August 28, 2017.
360 For example, on the AllMusic website.
361 See, for example, Christopher Washburne, "The Clave of Jazz: A Caribbean Contribution to the Rhythmic Foundation of an African-American Music," *Black Music Research Journal* 17, no. 1 (1997): 59–80. Moreover, Elle King released her sophomore album, *Shake the Spirit* (2018), which reached No. 68 in the *Billboard* 200.
362 For details on the band's rocky five-year history, see, for example, Hank Bordowitz, *Bad Moon Rising: The Unauthorized History of Creedence Clearwater Revival* (Chicago Review Press, 2007). Initially called the Golliwogs, the band assembled their admittedly "weird" three-part name somewhat randomly in late 1967 (pp. 39–40).
363 For the story of the contentious relationship between Fogerty and Zaentz, see *Bad Moon Rising*, 202ff.
364 For more on Miranda's background and activities, see his biography on the AllMusic and Wikipedia websites, as well as the opening portions of Rebecca Mead, "All About the Hamiltons," *New Yorker*, February 9, 2015; and Kat Harrison, *Lin-Manuel Miranda: Composer, Actor, and Creator of Hamilton* (New York: Enslow Publishing, 2017).
365 Mead, "All About the Hamiltons."
366 For more on the development of *In the Heights*, see, for example, David Low, "Scaling the Heights," *Wesleyan Magazine*, June 20, 2007.
367 For more on the development, content, and impact of the show, see, for example, Lin-Manuel Miranda and Jeremy McCarter, *Hamilton: The Revolution* (London: Hachette, 2016). See also Mead, "All About the Hamiltons," as well as Mark Binelli, "'Hamilton' Creator Lin-Manuel Miranda: The Rolling Stone Interview," *Rolling Stone*, June 1, 2016; Alisa Solomon, "How 'Hamilton' is Revolutionizing the Broadway Musical," *Nation*, August 27, 2015; and the Wikipedia entry on the musical.
368 See Ron Chernow, *Alexander Hamilton* (London: Head of Zeus, 2016).
369 A detailed and interesting review of Miranda's rap techniques in *Hamilton*, as relates to those used by other hip hop artists is found in Joel Eastwood and Erik Hinton, "How Does 'Hamilton', the Non-Stop, Hip Hop Broadway Sensation Tap Rap's Master Rhymes to Blur Musical Lines?" *Wall Street Journal*, June 6, 2016. Among the techniques discussed are consonance, assonance, rhyme weaving, and West Coast influence.
370 Miranda's quote about his process is cited in Mead, "All About the Hamiltons."
371 As noted in Mead, "All About the Hamiltons."
372 Cited in Mead, "All About the Hamiltons." See also "Use of Leitmotif in *Les Misérables*" (2004), originally published on the blog *Notes, Analysis & Essays for OCR A Level Music*, archived at https://www.yumpu.com.en/document/view/11525740.
373 For my personal deliberations on the validity of identifying a distinct musical species for Broadway music, see the WYLI website (Chapter 9, suppl., n. 373). These deliberations, it should be noted, are informed in part by my own involvement in the Broadway realm, via the musical

*Benny & Joon*, for which I am the composer—in collaboration with lyricist Mindi Dickstein, book writer Kirsten Guenther, director Jack Cummings III, and producer Larry Hirschhorn.

374 For more on Lacamoire, see his biography on the Wikipedia website; see also Tim Greiving, "He's Lin-Manuel's Right-Hand Man: The 'Hamilton' Arranger Who Hasn't Let Hearing Loss Derail the Dream," *Los Angeles Times*, August 10, 2017.

375 For more on the role and importance of Broadway arrangers, see, for example, Steven Suskin, *The Sound of Broadway Music: A Book of Orchestrators and Orchestrations* (Oxford University Press, 2011).

## INTERLUDE D: AT THE CELLULAR LEVEL: MUSIC AND CELL BIOLOGY

376 Christopher Alexander, *The Process of Creating Life*, vol. 2 of *The Nature of Order* (Berkeley, CA: Center for Environmental Structure, 2002), iv.

377 For more detail, see Bruce Alberts et al., "An Overview of the Cell Cycle," in *Molecular Biology of the Cell*, 4th ed. (New York: Garland, 1994).

378 The term "meiosis" is Greek for "a lessening." Alberts et al., "The Cell Cycle."

379 For more info on stem cells, see Jonathan Slack, *Stem Cells: A Very Short Introduction* (Oxford University Press, 2012). The details of Dr. Yamanaka's innovative work can be found in Shinya Yamanaka et al., "Induction of Pluripotent Stem Cells from Adult Human Fibroblasts by Defined Factors," *Cell* 131, no. 5 (2007): 861–72.

380 Cited in Strunk, *Source Readings*, 27.

381 See Schoenberg, *Fundamentals of Musical Composition*, 20. For related academic quotes on repetition, see the WYLI website (Interlude D, suppl., n. 381).

382 See John Miller Chernoff, *African Rhythm and African Sensibility* (University of Chicago, 1981), 111; Ingrid Monson, "Riffs, Repetition, and Theories of Globalization," *Ethnomusicology* 43, no. 1 (1999): 31–65.

383 Henry L. Gates, *The Signifying Monkey: A Theory of African-American Literary Criticism* (Oxford University Press: 1988).

384 For specific areas of focus aligned with leading scholars who address musical repetition, see the WYLI website (Interlude D, suppl., n. 384).

385 Ockelford developed his theory in 1991, and has updated it ever since. See especially Adam Ockelford, "Zygonic Theory: Introduction, Scope, Prospects," *Zeitschrift der Gesellschaft für Musiktheorie* 6, no. 1 (2009): 91–172. More recently (2017), Ockelford has incorporated his "zygonic theory" into a broader examination of how music works, and creates meaning, in Adam, Ockelford, *Comparing Notes: How We Make Sense of Music* (London: Profile Books, 2017).

386 After the conclusions drawn by music theorist Eugene Narmour; see Adam Ockelford, *Repetition in Music: Theoretical and Metatheoretical Perspectives* (London: Routledge, 2017), 120.

387 Theodor W. Adorno and Richard Leppert, *Essays on Music* (Berkeley: University of California Press, 2002), 442.

388 Cited in Theodor Adorno, *Philosophy of Modern Music*, trans. Anne G. Mitchell and Wesley V. Blomster (New York: Continuum, 1973), 178.

389 Cited in Elizabeth Hellmuth Margulis, *On Repeat: How Music Plays the Mind* (Oxford University Press, 2014), 4. See also Luis-Manuel Garcia, "On and On: Repetition as Process and Pleasure in Electronic Dance Music," *Music Theory Online* 11, no. 4 (2005): 2.

390 Peter Kivy, *The Fine Art of Repetition: Essays in the Philosophy of Music* (Cambridge: Cambridge University Press, 1993), 327–359. Kivy defines three potential models of defining music: "literal" (like a play or novel, etc.), "organism," and "wallpaper."

391 He calls this "musematic" repetition; see Richard Middleton, "'Play It Again Sam': Some Notes on the Productivity of Repetition in Popular Music," *Popular Music* 3 (1983): 261ff.

392 See Garcia, "On and On," 8.

393 John Kratus, "The Use of Melodic and Rhythmic Motives in the Original Songs of Children Aged 5 to 13," *Contributions to Music Education* 12 (1985): 1–8.

394 From Elizabeth Margulis' TED-Ed Talk, "Why We Love Repetition in Music." See also Deutsch, Diana, Trevor Henthorn, and Rachael Lapidis. "Illusory Transformation from Speech to Song," *Journal of the Acoustical Society of America* 129, no. 4 (2011): 2245–2252.

395 See Interlude D, note 389, above.

396 Margulis, *On Repeat*, 59, 78. See also, for example, Margulis, Elizabeth Hellmuth, "Musical repetition detection across multiple exposures." *Music Perception* 29, no. 4 (2012): 377–385;

Margulis and Elizabeth Hellmuth, "Aesthetic Responses to Repetition in Unfamiliar Music," *Empirical Studies of the Arts* 31, no. 1 (2013): 45–57; and, as a useful summary, Margulis' essay, "Why Repetition Can Turn Almost Anything into Music," https://aeon.co/essays/why-repetition-can-turn-almost-anything-into-music; my thanks to Professor Margulis for this latter reference.

397 Margulis, *On Repeat*, 115.

398 Margulis, *On Repeat*, 56–60.

399 Drabkin, "Motif."

400 For example, the *Encyclopédie de la Pléiade* regards it as a "melodic, rhythmic, or harmonic cell." Cited and expanded in Jean-Jacques Nattiez, *Music and Discourse: Toward a Semiology of Music* (Princeton University Press, 1990), 156–58.

401 Clinton Hutton, "The Creative Ethos of the African Diaspora: Performance Aesthetics and the Fight for Freedom and Identity," *Caribbean Quarterly* 53, nos. 1–2 (2007): 129.

402 See David Locke, "Improvisation in West African Musics," *Music Educators Journal* 66, no. 5 (1980): 125–33.

403 For specific areas of focus aligned with leading scholars who address musical development, see the WYLI website (Interlude D, suppl., n. 403).

404 For a fuller discussion, see Patricia Carpenter, "'Grundgestalt' as Tonal Function," *Music Theory Spectrum* 5, no. 1 (1983): 15–38.

405 See, for example, Nors S. Josephson, "Bach Meets Liszt: Traditional Formal Structures and Performance Practices in Progressive Rock," *Musical Quarterly* 76, no. 1 (1992): 67–92.

406 Alfred Pike, "The Perceptual Aspects of Motivic Structure in Music," *Journal of Aesthetics and Art Criticism*, 30, no. 1(1971): 80.

407 Alexandra Lamont and Nicola Dibben, "Motivic Structure and the Perception of Similarity," *Music Perception* 18, no. 3 (2001): 245–74.

408 Cited in Aaron L. Berkowitz, *The Improvising Mind: Cognition and Creativity in the Musical Moment* (Oxford University Press, 2010): 4–5.

409 Aristotle, *Metaphysics* 8, Book 13, Chapter 3, 1078b.

410 Plato, *Timaeus*, 55c4–6. These mysterious associations likely drew upon mathematical writings of Pythagoreans such as Timaeus of Locri. See Ferguson, *The Music of Pythagoras*, 134.

411 See, for example, Victor J. Stenger, *Timeless Reality: Symmetry, Simplicity and Multiple Universes* (Amherst, NY: Prometheus Books, 2000), 282ff.

412 See Alex Beck's website: http://alexjohnbeck.com/project/bothsidesof_versions/

413 Richard P. Feynman, Robert B. Leighton, and Matthew Sands, *Mainly Mechanics, Radiation, and Heat*, vol. 1 of *The Feynman Lectures on Physics* (New York: Basic Books, 2010), 52:12.

414 Vitruvius, *On Architecture*, trans. Frank Granger (Cambridge, MA: Harvard University Press, 1970), 26–27. See also Interlude B, note 203, for more on the historical impact of Vitruvius' emphasis on symmetry.

415 See, for example, Boro Pavlović and Nenad Trinajstić, "On Symmetry and Asymmetry in Literature," in *Computers & Mathematics with Applications* 12B, nos. 1–2 (1986), 197–227.

416 For a more technical discussion, see Davorin Kempf, "What Is Symmetry in Music?" *International Review of the Aesthetics and Sociology of Music*, 27, no. 2 (1996): 155–65.

417 Meyer, *Emotion and Meaning in Music*, 151.

418 From Huron's Ohio State lectures: David Huron, "Meyer and the Gestaltists," http://csml.seom.ohio-state.edu/Music829D/Notes/Meyer2.html. See also Meyer, *Emotion and Meaning in Music*, 91.

419 See Magnus Enquist and Rufus A. Johnstone, "Generalization and the Evolution of Symmetry Preferences," *Proceedings of the Royal Society B: Biological Sciences* 264, no. 1386 (1997): 1345–48.

420 Jennifer J. Stoecker et al., "Long- and Short-Looking Infants' Recognition of Symmetrical and Asymmetrical Forms," *Journal of Experimental Child Psychology* 71, no. 1 (1998): 63–78.

421 Specifically in the intraparietal sulcus; see C. J. Cela-Conde et al., "The Neural Foundations of Aesthetic Appreciation," *Progress in Neurobiology* 94, no. 1 (2011): 39–48.

## CHAPTER 10: THE ROCK GENOTYPE

422 Both quotations cited in Adam Grant, *Originals: How Non-Conformists Move the World* (New York: Penguin, 2017), 7, 13.

423 Mikal Gilmore, "David Bowie: How Rock's Greatest Outsider Continually Re-Created Himself, and Changed the World along the Way," *Rolling Stone*, February 11, 2016.

424 Marc Woodworth, Robert Boyers, and James Miller, "Rock Music & The Culture of Rock: An

Interview with James Miller," *Salmagundi* 118/119 (1998): 206–23. See Mark Spicer, ed., *Rock Music* (New York: Routledge, 2016), xviii.

425 Mikal Gilmore, *Stories Done: Writings on the 1960s and Its Discontents* (New York: Simon & Schuster, 2008), 314. For an in-depth look at Led Zeppelin's story, output, and influence, see, for example: Mick Wall, *When Giants Walked the Earth: A Biography of Led Zeppelin* (London: Macmillan, 2010); Keith Shadwick, *Led Zeppelin: The Story of a Band and Their Music, 1968–80* (Milwaukee, WI: Hal Leonard Corporation, 2005); and Hank Bordowitz, ed., *Led Zeppelin on Led Zeppelin: Interviews and Encounters* (Chicago Review Press, 2014).

426 As an example of an academic discussion of the band, see Susan Fast, *In the Houses of the Holy: Led Zeppelin and the Power of Rock Music* (Oxford University Press, 2001). For an alternate view of the "origins" of heavy metal—claimed instead for the little-known San Francisco band Blue Cheer (1967)—see Joe Queenan, "The Unlikely Fathers of Heavy Metal," *Guardian*, December 21, 2007.

427 See, for example, Richard Cole, "A Taste of Decadence," in *Whole Lotta Led Zeppelin: The Illustrated History of the Heaviest Band of All Time*, ed. Jon Bream (Minneapolis, MN: Voyageur, 2008), 72–75.

428 See "The 10 Wildest Led Zeppelin Legends, Fact-Checked," *Rolling Stone*, November 21, 2012.

429 For the story of Ertegun and Atlantic Records, see Dorothy Wade and Justine Picardie, *Music Man: Ahmet Ertegun, Atlantic Records, and the Triumph of Rock 'n' Roll* (New York: W. W. Norton, 1990).

430 Martin Popoff, *Led Zeppelin: All the Albums, All the Songs* (Minneapolis, MN: Voyageur, 2017), 55.

431 For further background on Alabama Shakes, see Joe Rhodes, "Alabama Shakes's Soul-Stirring, Shape-Shifting New Sound," *New York Times*, March 18, 2015; see also the list of articles in *Rolling Stone* on their website.

432 Russ Corey, "Athens' Alabama Shakes Channel Muscle Shoals Sound," *Florence (AL) Times Daily*, November 6, 2011. Bassist Zac Cockrell specifically cited the influence of "old-school" bassists Donald "Duck" Dunn (Booker T. & the M.G.'s), David Hood (Muscle Shoals), Rick Danko (the Band), and Tommy Cogbill (Aretha Franklin).

433 Cited in Howard's interview for the *Scotsman*, April 29, 2012. For more on the links between Plant and Alabama Shakes, see the WYLI website (Chapter 10, suppl., n. 433).

434 Among soul tunes that utilize the i–iv vamp are: Isaac Hayes' "Hung Up on My Baby"; Curtis Mayfield's "Little Child Runnin' Wild" and "Love Me (Right in the Pocket)"; and Bobby Womack's "Dayglo Reflection."

435 For more on the band's history and output, see, for example, Mark Beaumont, *Muse: Out of This World* (London: Omnibus Press, 2014). Moreover, Muse released its eighth studio album *Simulation Theory* (2018), which reached No. 12 on the *Billboard* 200.

436 Expressed as Taylor and Queen guitarist Brian May presented Muse with the O2 Sliver Clef Award; see "Rockers Muse Win Silver Clef Award," July 2, 2010. https://www.independent.ie/entertainment/music/rockers-music-win-silver-clef-award-26663519.html/.

437 The Neapolitan 6th chord is a major chord built on the ♭II degree of a minor key, generally presented in first inversion and typically proceeding to the V7 chord in an authentic cadence.

438 For more on Prima's career and music, see, for example, Garry Boulard, *Louis Prima* (Urbana: University of Illinois Press, 2002); and Tom Clavin, *That Old Black Magic: Louis Prima, Keely Smith, and the Golden Age of Las Vegas* (Chicago Review Press, 2010).

439 Boulard, *Louis Prima*, 111.

## CHAPTER 11: THE JAZZ GENOTYPE

440 See Chapter 6, note 244, for a few introductions to jazz music and history.

441 From an interview in 1957, cited in Scott DeVeaux, "Constructing the Jazz Tradition: Jazz Historiography," in *Black American Literature Forum* 25, no. 3 (1991): 525–60.

442 Gioia, *The History of Jazz*, 189.

443 Jack Kerouac, *On the Road* (1957; New York: Penguin, 2003), 112.

444 For a fuller account of Dizzy's career and music, see, for example, Alyn Shipton, *Groovin' High: The Life of Dizzy Gillespie* (Oxford University Press, 2001); and Raymond Horricks, *Dizzy Gillespie and the Be-Bop Revolution* (New York: Hippocrene, 1984). The nickname "Dizzy" was given to Gillespie by fellow trumpeter Palmer Davis when the two played in Frankie Fairfax's band in 1935 (Shipton, *Groovin' High*, 25).

445 Cited in Gioia, *The History of Jazz*, 209.
446 Mike Bourne, "Fat Cats at Lunch: An Interview with Dizzy Gillespie," *DownBeat*, May 11, 1972.
447 For a discussion on these recordings, see Fred Kaplan, "Bird Lives! The Birth of Bebop, Captured on Disc," *New York Times*, July 31, 2005.
448 See complete discography in Jan Evensmo, "The Trumpet of John Birks Gillespie," *Jazz Archeology*.
449 Cited in a good resource on Shorter's career and output: Michelle Mercer, *Footprints: The Life and Work of Wayne Shorter* (New York: Penguin, 2007), 27.
450 See, for example, Alan Goldsher, *Hard Bop Academy: The Sidemen of Art Blakey and the Jazz Messengers* (Milwaukee, WI: Hal Leonard Corporation, 2002).
451 See, for example, George Grella Jr., *Miles Davis' Bitches Brew* (New York: Bloomsbury Publishing USA, 2015). For more on Miles Davis' career overall, see, for example, John Szwed, *So What: The Life of Miles Davis* (New York: Simon & Schuster, 2004).
452 Nate Chinen, "Major Jazz Eminence, Little Grise: Wayne Shorter's New Album is 'Without a Net,'" *New York Times*, January 31, 2013.
453 Mercer, *Footprints*, 118.
454 Quoted in William Grimes, "Antonio Carlos Jobim, Composer, Dies at 67," *New York Times*, December 9, 1994. More on Jobim's career, music, and legacy can be found, for example, in Helena Jobim, *Antonio Carlos Jobim: An Illuminated Man* (Milwaukee, WI: Hal Leonard Corporation, 2011).
455 From Jobim's 1991 interview with the Associated Press.
456 For more on the Getz-Gilberto partnership, see, for example, Dave Gelly, *Stan Getz: Nobody Else but Me* (San Francisco: Backbeat Books, 2002), 117ff.
457 As famed jazz critic Leonard Feather put it, Evans was "the first genius of the piano since Art Tatum"; see Leonard Feather, "Bill Evans: The Gentle Giant," *Contemporary Keyboard*, December 1980. More on Evans' music and legacy can be found, for example, in Peter Pettinger, *Bill Evans: How My Heart Sings* (New Haven, CT: Yale University Press, 1998).
458 See, for example, Evans' high praise of Powell in the foreword of Francis Paudras, *Dance of the Infidels: A Portrait of Bud Powell* (Boston: Da Capo Press, 1998), ix.
459 Among several accounts on this historic album, see Eric Nisenson, *The Making of Kind of Blue: Miles Davis and His Masterpiece* (New York: St. Martin's Press, 2013).
460 Evans' drug abuse began with heroin, and continued to cocaine in later years; see Gene Lees, *Friends Along the Way: A Journey Through Jazz* (New Haven, CT: Yale University Press, 2003), 284.
461 Cited in Martin Gayford, "Bill Evans: Everybody Still Digs Him," *Telegraph*, September 22, 2007.
462 Pettinger, *Bill Evans*, 68.
463 Pettinger, *Bill Evans*, 69.

## INTERLUDE E: LISTENING WITH AN ACCENT: CULTURE AND MUSICAL TASTE

464 For more on my prepatory strategy for composing this concerto, see the WYLI website (Interlude E, suppl., n. 464).
465 See, for example, Sue Gilmore, "Oakland Symphony Delivers Global Triumph," *Oakland Tribune*, January 25, 2009.
466 Ian Cross, "Musicality and the Human Capacity for Culture," *Musicae Scientiae* 12, no. 1_suppl (2008): 147.
467 Cited in John Blacking, *Music, Culture, and Experience: Selected Papers of John Blacking* (University of Chicago Press, 1995), 236.
468 Cross and Blacking's statements notwithstanding, an overall scholarly embrace of musical universals has ebbed and flowed over the decades. See, for example, Bruno Nettl, "An Ethnomusicologist Contemplates Universals in Musical Sound and Musical Culture," in *The Origins of Music*, ed. Nils L. Wallin et al. (Cambridge, MA: MIT Press, 2000), 463–72; and Donald E. Brown, "Human Universals, Human Nature & Human Culture," *Daedalus* 133, no. 4 (2004): 47–54.
469 Savage, Patrick E., Steven Brown, Emi Sakai, and Thomas E. Currie, "Statistical Universals Reveal the Structures and Functions of Human Music" *Proceedings of the National Academy of Sciences* 112, no. 29 (2015): 8987–8992. The authors used a music-feature-based approach ("CantoCore") to assess 304 global recordings—including field, onsite, studio, etc., from the *Garland Encyclopedia of World Music*.

470 Catherine J. Stevens, "Music Perception and Cognition: A Review of Recent Cross-Cultural Research," *Topics in Cognitive Science* 4, no. 4 (2012): 658.

471 That is, a few animals—parrots, a sea lion, and (to some degree) chimpazees—have demonstrated the ability to entrain; more details on the WYLI website (Interlude E, suppl., n. 471).

472 See, for example, Trainor, Laurel J. et al. "Preference for Sensory Consonance in 2-and 4-month-old Infant," *Music Perception* 20, no. 2 (2002): 187–194; and Masataka, Nobuo "Preference for Consonance over Dissonance by Hearing Newborns of Deaf Parents and of Hearing Parents." *Developmental science* 9, no. 1 (2006): 46–50. For reference to some recent scholarly questioning of our innate preference of consonance over dissonance, see the WYLI website (Interlude E, suppl., n. 472).

473 See citations of such traditions, for example, in Joseph Jordania, *Who Asked the First Question?: The Origins of Human Choral Singing, Intelligence, Language and Speech* (West Beach, Australia: Logos, 2006), 69ff (Ukraine), 78ff (Georgia), 109 (Serbia), 110 (Bosnia), 119 (Lithuania), 175 (Melanesia), etc.; see also Peter Fletcher, *World Musics in Context: A Comprehensive Survey of the World's Major Musical Cultures* (Oxford University Press, 2004), 42ff.

474 Interest in detailing universal *functions* has seen a similar ebb and flow as *properties* and *perceptions*. A few key articulations of the various arguments include: Alan P. Merriam and Valerie Merriam, *The Anthropology of Music* (Chicago: Northwestern University Press, 1964); Steven Feld and Aaron A. Fox, "Music and Language," *Annual Review of Anthropology* 23, no. 1 (1994): 25–53; Martin Clayton, "The Social and Personal Functions of Music in Cross-Cultural Perspective," in *The Oxford Handbook of Music Psychology* (Oxford University Press, 2009), 35–44; Nettl, "An Ethnomusicologist Contemplates Universals"; Nettl. "Music": 5. The Function of Music; and Levitin. *The World in Six Songs*.

475 Clayton, "The Social and Personal Functions of Music," 46; Marina Roseman, *Healing Sounds from the Malaysian Rainforest: Temiar Music and Medicine* (Berkeley: University of California Press, 1991), 46ff.

476 See Ian Cross, "Music and Communication in Music Psychology," *Psychology of Music* 42, no. 6 (2014): 809–19.

477 See, for example, Steven Johnson, *Emergence: The Connected Lives of Ants, Brains, Cities, and Software* (New York: Simon & Schuster, 2002).

478 Levitin, *The World in Six Songs*, 279.

479 For example, in Bruno Nettl, *Music in Primitive Culture* (Cambridge, MA: Harvard University Press, 1956), 6.

480 Nettl, *The Study of Ethnomusicology: Thirty-Three Discussions*, 45.

481 Jordania, *Who Asked the First Question?*, 112, 114, 201, 209, etc.

482 Lomax et al., *Cantometrics*, 19, 36, etc.

483 For example, see Hugh Tracey, "Towards an Assessment of African Scales," *African Music* 2, no. 1 (1958): 15–20.

484 Tracey, "Towards an Assessment of African Scales," 19–20.

485 Levitin, *The World in Six Songs*: 53, 60, 83, 102, etc. For a specific hypothesis viewing the explicit cooperation of music and dance as an adaptive force in our evolution, see Edward H. Hagen and Gregory A. Bryant, "Music and Dance as a Coalition Signaling System," *Human Nature* 14, no. 1 (2003): 21–51.

486 For more on the leading scholars and their work in this regard, see, for example, Erin E. Hannon and Laurel J. Trainor, "Music Acquisition: Effects of Enculturation and Formal Training on Development," *Trends in Cognitive Sciences* 11, no. 11 (2007): 466–72; Steven J. Morrison, Steven M. Demorest, and Laura A. Stambaugh, "Enculturation Effects in Music Cognition: The Role of Age and Music Complexity," *Journal of Research in Music Education* 56, no. 2 (2008): 118–29; Heike Argstatter, "Perception of Basic Emotions in Music: Culture-Specific or Multicultural?" *Psychology of Music* 44, no. 4 (2016): 674–90; Thomas Hans Fritz, Paul Schmude, Sebastian Jentschke, Angela D. Friederici, and Stefan Koelsch, "From Understanding to Appreciating Music Cross-Culturally," *PloS one* 8, no. 9 (2013): e72500; and Laura-Lee Balkwill and William Forde Thompson, "A Cross-Cultural Investigation of the Perception of Emotion in Music: Psychophysical and Cultural Cues," *Music Perception* 17, no. 1 (1999): 43–64.

487 David Brian Huron, *Sweet Anticipation: Music and the Psychology of Expectation* (Cambridge, MA: MIT Press, 2006), 379.

488 Hannon, Erin E., and Sandra E. Trehub, "Tuning in to Musical Rhythms: Infants Learn More Readily than Adults" *Proceedings of the National Academy of Sciences* 102, no. 35 (2005): 12639–43.

489 Hannon and Trainor, "Music Acquisition," 466. For more on my use of the expression "boundary-less," see the WYLI website (Interlude E, suppl., n. 489).

490 Morrison and Demorest, "Enculturation Effects in Music Cognition." See also Steven M. Demorest, Steven J. Morrison, et al., "The Influence of Contextual Cues on Cultural Bias in Music Memory," *Music Perception* 33, no. 5 (2016): 590–600.
491 See Hannon and Trainor, "Musical Acquisition," 466–67; and Morrison and Demorest, "Enculturation Effects in Music Cognition," 68–69. For clarification on this scenario, and further academic references, see the WYLI website (Interlude E, suppl., n. 491).
492 Hannon and Trainor, "Musical Acquisition," 468.
493 See Christiane Neuhaus, "Perceiving Musical Scale Structures," *Annals of the New York Academy of Sciences* 999, no. 1 (2003): 184–88. See also Lynch and Eilers, "Children's Perception."
494 See, for example, E. Glenn Schellenberg and Sandra E. Trehub, "Good Pitch Memory Is Widespread," *Psychological Science* 14, no. 3 (2003): 262–66; and Siamak Baharloo, Paul A. Johnston, Susan K. Service, Jane Gitschier, and Nelson B. Freimer, "Absolute Pitch: An Approach for Identification of Genetic and Nongenetic Components," *American Journal of Human Genetics* 62, no. 2 (1998): 224–31.
495 Hannon and Trainor, "Musical Acquisition," 468.
496 See Tuomas Eerola et al., "Perceived Complexity of Western and African Folk Melodies by Western and African Listeners," *Psychology of Music* 34, no. 3 (2006): 337–71.
497 Thomas Fritz et al., "Universal Recognition of Three Basic Emotions in Music," *Current Biology* 19, no. 7 (2009): 573–76.
498 For a discussion of one key problem in the Fritz study—its identity as a "partially comparative" study—see the WYLI website (Interlude E, suppl., n. 498).
499 Balkwill and Thompson, "A Cross-Cultural Investigation."
500 Argstatter, "Perception of Basic Emotions in Music."
501 See, for example, Demorest and Morrison, "The Influence of Contextual Cues"; also Steven J. Morrison, Steven M. Demorest, et al., "Effect of Intensive Instruction on Elementary Students' Memory for Culturally Unfamiliar Music," *Journal of Research in Music Education* 60, no. 4 (2013): 363–74; and Steven M. Demorest, Steven J. Morrison, et al., "An fMRI Investigation of the Cultural Specificity of Music Memory," *Social Cognitive and Affective Neuroscience* 5, nos. 2–3 (2009): 282–91.
502 Morrison and Demorest, et al., "Effect of Intensive Instruction." The Turks, however, did remember the Western examples better than those from Chinese music—to which they had had no exposure.
503 Patrick C. M. Wong, Anil K. Roy, and Elizabeth Hellmuth Margulis, "Bimusicalism: The Implicit Dual Enculturation of Cognitive and Affective Systems," *Music Perception* 27, no. 2 (2009): 81–88.
504 Demorest and Morrison, "The influence of contextual cues."
505 For example, Morrison et al., "Effect of Intensive Instruction."

## CHAPTER 12: THE HIP HOP GENOTYPE

506 For a fuller survey of hip hop music, culture, and historical context, see, for example, Jeff Chang, *Can't Stop Won't Stop: A History of the Hip-Hop Generation* (New York: St. Martin's Press, 2007); Chuck D, *Chuck D Presents This Day in Rap and Hip-Hop History* (New York: Hachette, 2017); and Mark Anthony Neal, *That's the Joint!: The Hip-Hop Studies Reader* (London: Psychology Press, 2004).
507 Becky Blanchard, "The Social Significance of Rap and Hip-Hop Culture," *Journal of Poverty & Prejudice* (Spring 1999): 1–10.
508 See, for example, Ronald L. Jackson II and Elaine B. Richardson, eds., *Understanding African American Rhetoric: Classical Origins to Contemporary Innovations* (New York: Routledge, 2014), 8ff.
509 Jay-Z, *Decoded* (New York: Random House, 2010), 54.
510 Cited in Blanchard, "The Social Significance," 4.
511 For more on the East-West rivalry, see Jeff Weiss and Evan McGarvey, *2pac vs. Biggie: An Illustrated History of Rap's Greatest Battle* (Minneapolis, MN: Voyageur, 2013).
512 Davey D, "Why Rap Is So Powerful," https://www.daveyd.com/whyrapispowerart.html.
513 For more on Snoop Dogg's music and background, see, for example, Snoop Dogg with Davin Seay, *Tha Doggfather: The Times, Trials, and Hardcore Truths of Snoop Dogg* (New York: Harper

Collins, 2000). See also the biographies of Snoop Dogg on the AllMusic and Wikipedia websites. Moreover, Snoop Dogg released his seventeenth studio album, *I Wanna Thank Me* (February 2019).

514 Michael Eric Dyson, *The Michael Eric Dyson Reader* (London: Hachette, 2008), 419.

515 Jayna Brown, "Hip Hop, Pleasure, and Its Fulfillment," *Palimpsest: A Journal on Women, Gender, and the Black International* 2, no. 2 (2013): 147.

516 See Ta-Nehisi Coates, "Hip-Hop's Down Beat," *Time*, August 17, 2007. For background on Lamar's music and impact, see, for example, Josh Eells, "The Trials of Kendrick Lamar," *Rolling Stone*, June 22, 2015. See also the forthcoming cultural biography by Marcus Moore, to be titled *The Butterfly Effect: How Kendrick Lamar Ignited the Soul of Black America*.

517 Eells, "The Trials of Kendrick Lamar."

518 See, for example, Rob Sheffield, "Grammys 2016: King Kendrick Lamar Steals the Show," *Rolling Stone*, February 16, 2016.

519 For more on the interesting process of how hip hop in general and Lamar in particular came to the Pulitzer jury's attention, see Joe Coscarelli, "Kendrick Lamar Wins Pulitzer in 'Big Moment for Hip-Hop,'" *New York Times*, April 16, 2018.

520 Eells, "The Trials of Kendrick Lamar."

521 For more on Dr. Dre as a producer, see Jake Brown, *Dr. Dre in the Studio: From Compton, Death Row, Snoop Dogg, Eminem, 50 Cent, The Game & Mad Money* (New York: Colossus Books, 2006).

522 See Chris Molanphy, "Introducing the King of Hip-Hop," *Rolling Stone*, August 15, 2011.

523 The dysfunction between Eminem and Kim Scott Mathers is illustrated by such Eminem songs as "'97 Bonnie and Clyde" and "Kim," both of which portray fictionalized accounts of her murder by drowning. See, for example, Sam Patrick, "Strange Things about Eminem and Kim's Relationship," *Nicki Swift* https://www.nickiswift.com/42674/strange-things-eminem-kims-relationship/.

524 Anthony Bozza, "Eminem Blows Up," *Rolling Stone*, April 29, 1999.

525 Bozza, "Eminem Blows Up."

526 For more on Eminem's limited but interesting use of sampling or borrowing, see the WYLI website (Chapter 12, suppl., n. 526). Moreover, Eminem swiftly released his tenth studio album, *Kamikaze* (2018), which became his ninth in a row to reach No. 1 on the *Billboard* 200.

527 As indicated on the website www.whosampled.com.

528 Cited in the *Rolling Stone* online artist biography of "Earth, Wind & Fire." For more background on the group, their music, and legacy, see Maurice White and Herb Powell, *My Life with Earth, Wind & Fire* (New York: HarperCollins, 2016).

529 For more on Chess Records, see, for example, Rich Cohen, *The Record Men: The Chess Brothers and the Birth of Rock & Roll* (New York: W. W. Norton, 2005).

530 James B. Stewart, "Message in the Music: Political Commentary in Black Popular Music from Rhythm and Blues to Early Hip Hop," *Journal of African American History* 90, no. 3 (2005): 215.

531 Tweet cited in Kat Boehrer, "Earth, Wind & Fire Co-Founder Maurice White Has Passed Away," *Complex*, February 4, 2016. https://www.complex.com/music/2016/02/maurice-white-of-earth-wind-and-fire-has-passed-away.

## CHAPTER 13: THE ELECTRONICA (EDM) GENOTYPE

532 Among sources on the history and techniques of electronic, computer, and similarly experimental music, see, for example, Daniel Warner, *Live Wires: A History of Electronic Music* 4th ed.(London: Reaktion Books Limited, 2017); Peter Manning, *Electronic and Computer Music* (Oxford University Press, 2013); and Nick Collins and Julio d'Escriván, eds., *The Cambridge Companion to Electronic Music* (Cambridge: Cambridge University Press, 2017).

533 See citations in Chapter 7, note 265; see also Hugh Davies, "Synthesizer," Grove Music Online.

534 See, for example, Alan P. Kefauver and David Patschke, *Fundamentals of Digital Audio* (Middleton, WI: AR Editions, 2007).

535 Cited, for example, in Simon Reynolds, "Song from the Future: The Story of Donna Summer and Giorgio Moroder's 'I Feel Love,'" *Pitchfork*, June 29, 2017.

536 For an inside account of the rise of house music, see Jesse Saunders, *House Music* (Baltimore: PublishAmerica, 2007).

537 The result was a so-called "Second Summer of Love" in both 1988 and 1989. For more on the

acid house and rave phenomena, see Luke Bainbridge, *The True Story of Acid House: Britain's Last Youth Culture Revolution* (London: Omnibus Press, 2014); and Simon Reynolds, *Generation Ecstasy: Into the World of Techno and Rave Culture* (London: Routledge, 2013), 56–91.

538 Alastair Fraser, "The Spaces, Politics, and Cultural Economies of Electronic Dance Music," *Geography Compass* 6, no. 8 (2012): 501.

539 See, for example, the exhaustive "List of electronic music genres" on Wikipedia; and Androids, "An Idiot's Guide to EDM Genres," *Complex*, October 13, 2017.

540 For more on the story and music of the Chemical Brothers, see their biography on the AllMusic and Wikipedia websites.

541 Cited in Alexis Petridis, "'Drugs and Clubs? That's the Only Test People Have Now,'" *Guardian*, January 25, 2002.

542 Douglas Wolk, "The Chemical Brothers Make a Triumphant Return After Five Years with 'Born in the Echoes': Album Review," *Billboard*, July 20, 2015.

543 Called "king of trance," for example, in Kat Bein, "Armin van Buuren Finds a New Groove with Conrad Sewell, Scott Storch," *Billboard*, February 2, 2018; see also Sophie Lai, "Armin van Buuren x Phillips: The Trance Overlord," *Boom Online*, April 3, 2014.

544 "Armin van Buuren: 'Dance Music Is Investing in Their Own Future'" (video interview), *Billboard*, June 4, 2015 https://www.billboard.com/video/armin-van-buuren-dance-music-is-investing-in-their-own-future-6590065.

545 "Armin van Buuren Announces New Artist Album 'Embrace,'" *A State of Trance* (van Buuren's website), September 3, 2015.

546 Anne Midgette, "In a Mozart Year, Other Stars Blazed," *New York Times*, December 24, 2006; and cited, for example, on Reich's biography on the website of his publisher, Boosey & Hawkes.

547 For an in-depth review of Reich's music, aesthetic, and impact, see, for example, Paul Griffiths, "Reich, Steve," Grove Music Online; Steve Reich, *Writings on Music, 1965–2000* (Oxford University Press, 2002); and David J. Hoek, *Steve Reich: A Bio-Bibliography* (Santa Barbara, CA: Greenwood Press, 2002).

548 Alexis Petridis, "Steve Reich on Schoenberg, Coltrane and Radiohead," *Guardian*, March 1, 2013.

549 For more on the minimalist movement, see Keith Potter, "Minimalism," Grove Music Online; and Keith Potter, *Four Musical Minimalists: La Monte Young, Terry Riley, Steve Reich, Philip Glass* (Cambridge: Cambridge University Press, 2002). See also the WYLI website (Chapter 13, suppl., n. 549) for further references and discussion.

550 Alex Ross, *The Rest Is Noise: Listening to the Twentieth Century* (New York: Macmillan, 2007), 547.

551 See Richard Taruskin, *The Danger of Music and Other Anti-Utopian Essays* (Berkeley: University of California Press, 2008), 101.

552 Petridis, "Steve Reich on Schoenberg, Coltrane, and Radiohead."

553 Petridis, "Steve Reich on Schoenberg, Coltrane, and Radiohead."

554 Tim Rutherford-Johnson, "The Influence Engine: Steve Reich and Pop Music," *NewMusicBox*, March 27, 2013.

555 From Eno's liner notes for the album *Ambient 1: Music for Airports* (1978).

556 Lester Bangs, "Interview with Brian Eno," *Musician*, July 1979. For more on Eno's music and aesthetic, see David Buckley and Cecilia Sun, "Eno, Brian," Grove Music Online; Sean Albiez and David Pattie, eds., *Brian Eno: Oblique Music* (New York: Bloomsbury Publishing USA, 2016); and Brian Eno, *A Year with Swollen Appendices* (London: Faber & Faber, 1996).

557 Cited in Paul Morley, "On Gospel, Abba and the Death of the Record: An Audience with Brian Eno," *Guardian*, January 16, 2010.

558 Sasha Frere-Jones, "Ambient Genius: The Working Life of Brian Eno," *New Yorker*, July 7, 2014.

## INTERLUDE F: STAKING YOUR CLAIM: INTRACULTURE AND MUSICAL TASTE

559 The topic of how our musical taste becomes entangled with our identity in these early adolescent years is playfully discussed in Seth Stephens-Davidowitz, "The Songs That Bind," *New York Times*, February 10, 2018.

560 For scholarly references to some of these famous music-based rivalries, see the WYLI website (Interlude F, suppl., n. 560).

561 The adjectival form "intracultural" is found occasionally in scholarly literature—related to science, business, sociology, etc.—generally in the context of "intracultural variation"; for example, Linda

C. Garro, "Intracultural Variation in Folk Medical Knowledge: A Comparison between Curers and Noncurers," *American Anthropologist* 88, no. 2 (1986): 351–70. To my knowledge, however, the term "intraculture" has *not* been used in the context intended here.

562 For example, see Ian Biddle and Vanessa Knights, eds., *Music, National Identity and the Politics of Location: Between the Global and the Local* (London: Routledge, 2016).

563 See, for example, Chantal Mouffe, "Hegemony and Ideology in Gramsci," in *Gramsci and Marxist Theory*, Chantal Mouffe, ed. (London: Routledge, 2014), 178–214; and Bob Jessop, "From Karl Marx to Antonio Gramsci and Louis Althusser," in *The Routledge Handbook of Language and Politics*, eds. Ruth Wodak and Bernhard Forchtner (Oxford: Taylor & Francis, 2017).

564 See, for example, Roland Barthes, "Wine and Milk," in *Mythologies: The Complete Edition in a New Translation*, trans. Richard Howard and Annette Lavers (New York: Hill & Wang, 2012), 79–82; and Michel Foucault, *Discipline and Punish: The Birth of the Prison*, trans. Alan Sheridan (New York: Pantheon, 1977), 195ff; see also Dino Franco Felluga, *Critical Theory: The Key Concepts* (New York: Routledge, 2015), 204–6.

565 Mark Slobin, "Micromusics of the West: A Comparative Approach," *Ethnomusicology* 36, no. 1 (1992): 1–87.

566 Cited in John Storey, *From Popular Culture to Everyday Life* (New York: Routledge, 2014), 83.

567 Tony Jefferson and Stuart Hall, eds., *Resistance through Rituals: Youth Subcultures in Post-War Britain* (Oxford: Routledge, 2003), 57.

568 Emre Ulusoy, "Subcultural Escapades via Music Consumption: Identity Transformations and Extraordinary Experiences in Dionysian Music Subcultures," *Journal of Business Research* 69, no. 1 (2016): 246.

569 See, for example, Staf Callewaert, "Bourdieu, Critic of Foucault: The Case of Empirical Social Science against Double-Game-Philosophy," *Theory, Culture & Society* 23, no. 6 (2006): 73–98.

570 Pierre Bourdieu, *Distinction: A Social Critique of the Judgement of Taste*, trans. Richard Nice (Cambridge, MA: Harvard University Press, 1989). Wacquant's praise and further background on Bourdieu and his legacy is found in Simon Susen and Bryan S. Turner, eds., *The Legacy of Pierre Bourdieu: Critical Essays* (London: Anthem Press, 2011), 102, etc.

571 Bourdieu, *Distinction*, 7.

572 Bourdieu, *Distinction*, 516.

573 Bourdieu, *Distinction*, 19.

574 See Tia DeNora, "Musical Patronage and Social Change in Beethoven's Vienna," *American Journal of Sociology* 97, no. 2 (1991): 310–46.

575 Bourdieu, *Distinction*, 16.

576 Bourdieu, *Distinction*, 16. Beyond Aznavour, Bourdieu's exemplars of "popular" music include cabaret singer Georges Guétary and two quasi-rock performers—Johnny Hallyday (the "French Elvis") and English singer Petula Clark (who enjoyed a prominent career in France).

577 Bourdieu, *Distinction*, 6

578 Richard A. Peterson and Albert Simkus, "How Musical Tastes Mark Occupational Status Groups," in *Cultivating Differences: Symbolic Boundaries and the Making of Inequality*, eds. Michèle Lamont and Marcel Fournier (University of Chicago Press, 1992), 152; and Richard A. Peterson and Roger M. Kern, "Changing Highbrow Taste: From Snob to Omnivore," *American Sociological Review* 61, no. 5 (1996): 900–907.

579 See, for example, Henry Ford's anti-Semitic attacks on jazz and theater music in the early 1920s, cited in Walter Rimler, *George Gershwin: An Intimate Portrait* (Urbana: University of Illinois Press, 2011), 39.

580 Peterson and Simkus, "How Musical Tastes," 170.

581 Mike Savage and Modesto Gayo, "Unravelling the Omnivore: A Field Analysis of Contemporary Musical Taste in the United Kingdom," *Poetics* 39, no. 5 (2011): 338.

582 Andrew Cheyne and Amy Binder, "Cosmopolitan Preferences: The Constitutive Role of Place in American Elite Taste for Hip-Hop Music, 1991–2005," *Poetics* 38, no. 3 (2010): 336–64.

583 See David Cutts and Paul Widdop, "Reimagining Omnivorousness in the Context of Place," *Journal of Consumer Culture* 17, no. 3 (2017): 480–503.

584 See Cheyne and Binder, "Cosmopolitan Preferences," 358.

585 Savage and Gayo, "Unravelling the Omnivore," 342.

586 Mark Rimmer, "Beyond Omnivores and Univores: The Promise of a Concept of Musical Habitus," *Cultural Sociology* 6, no. 3 (2012): 302.

587 Savage and Gayo, "Unravelling the Omnivore," 345.

588 Bernard Lahire, "The Individual and the Mixing of Genres: Cultural Dissonance and Self-Distinction," *Poetics* 36, nos. 2–3 (2008), 166–188.

589 Lahire, "The Individual and the Mixing of Genres," 169.
590 Tom Vanderbilt, *You May Also Like: Taste in an Age of Endless Choice* (New York: Simon & Schuster, 2016), 87.
591 Koen van Eijck and John Lievens, "Cultural Omnivorousness as a Combination of Highbrow, Pop, and Folk Elements: The Relation between Taste Patterns and Attitudes Concerning Social Integration," *Poetics* 36, nos. 2–3 (2008): 241.
592 Gilbert Chase, *America's Music: From the Pilgrims to the Present*, 3rd ed. (Urbana: University of Illinois Press, 1992), xv.
593 See, for example, Shane Blackman, "Subculture Theory: An Historical and Contemporary Assessment of the Concept for Understanding Deviance," *Deviant Behavior* 35, no. 6 (2014): 496–512.
594 Key members of the Chicago school included Frederic Thrasher, Robert Merton, and later Albert Cohen; see Blackman, "Subculture Theory," 500.
595 Phil Cohen, "Subcultural Conflict and Working-Class Community," in *Rethinking the Youth Question* (London: Palgrave, 1997), 57.
596 John Clarke, "The Skinheads and the Magical Recovery of Community," in *Resistance through Rituals: Youth Subcultures in Post-War Britain*, 2nd ed., eds. Stuart Hall and Tony Jefferson (Oxford: Routledge, 2003), 80.
597 Andy Bennett, "Subcultures or Neo-Tribes? Rethinking the Relationship between Youth, Style and Musical Taste," *Sociology* 33, no. 3 (1999): 605.
598 See Benedict Anderson, *Imagined Communities: Reflections on the Origin and Spread of Nationalism* (London: Verso Books, 2006).
599 Kay Kaufman Shelemay, "Musical Communities: Rethinking the Collective in Music," *Journal of the American Musicological Society* 64, no. 2 (2011): 364.
600 Shelemay, "Musical Communities," 373.
601 See, for example, Courtney Jenkins, "5 Things You Didn't Know about Classic Rock Music Fans," *Houston Marketing Matters*, July 29, 2015.
602 See, for example, "Engaging with the 'Super-fan': A Growing Source of Incremental Revenue," report by PricewaterhouseCoopers, 2014.
603 Tia DeNora, "Music as a Technology of the Self," *Poetics* 27, no. 1 (1999): 31.
604 Cotton Seiler, "The Commodification of Rebellion: Rock Culture and Consumer Capitalism," in *New Forms of Consumption: Consumers, Culture, and Commodification*, ed. Mark Gottdiener (Lanham, MD: Rowman & Littlefield, 2000): 217.
605 For a related discussion of how UK dance club "intracultures" forge competitive internal hierarchies by virtue of the varying "subcultural capital" of their members ("hip" vs. "phony", etc.), see Thornton, Sarah. *Club Cultures: Music, Media and Subcultural Capital* (Hanover, NH: Wesleyan University Press, 1996).
606 See, for example, Andy Worthington, "A History of Music Torture in the 'War on Terror,'" *Huffington Post*, May 25, 2011.
607 Lily E. Hirsch, "Weaponizing Classical Music: Crime Prevention and Symbolic Power in the Age of Repetition," *Journal of Popular Music Studies* 19, no. 4 (2007): 348.
608 Peter Manuel, "Music as Symbol, Music as Simulacrum: Postmodern, Pre-modern, and Modern Aesthetics in Subcultural Popular Musics," *Popular Music* 14, no. 2 (1995): 234.
609 Ulusoy, "Subcultural Escapades," 250. Specifically, Ulusoy labels these three consumption experiences as "radical self-expression," "therapeutic praxis," and "controlled chaos," respectively.
610 Myles E. Johnson, "What Beyoncé Won Was Bigger Than a Grammy," *New York Times*, February 14, 2017.
611 Susan Gal, "The Political Economy of Code Choice," *Codeswitching: Anthropological and Sociolinguistic Perspectives*, ed. Monica Heller (Berlin: De Gruyter Mouton, 1988), 247.
612 Notably, Michael Lewis, *The Undoing Project: A Friendship That Changed Our Minds* (New York: W. W. Norton, 2016).
613 Daniel Kahneman, *Thinking, Fast and Slow* (New York: Macmillan, 2011), 13–14.
614 Kahneman, *Thinking, Fast and Slow*, 13.
615 See, for example, Adam J. Lonsdale and Adrian C. North, "Musical Taste and the Representativeness Heuristic," *Psychology of Music* 40, no. 2 (2012): 131–42.

## CHAPTER 14: THE WORLD MUSIC GENOTYPE

616 David Byrne, "Crossing Music's Borders: 'I Hate World Music,'" *New York Times*, October 3, 1999. For a more thorough introduction to world music as a broad musical genre—or "species" in our terminology—see, for example, Philip V. Bohlman, *World Music: A Very Short Introduction* (Oxford University Press, 2002); Philip V. Bohlman, ed., *The Cambridge History of World Music* (Cambridge: Cambridge University Press, 2013); and Simon Broughton, Mark Ellingham, and Richard Trillo, eds. *World Music*, vols. 1, *Africa, Europe and the Middle East*, and 2, *Latin and North America, Caribbean, India, Asia and Pacific* (London: Rough Guides, 1999).

617 See, for example, Ian Birrell, "The Term 'World Music' Is Outdated and Offensive," *Guardian*, March 22, 2012; and Anastasia Tsioulcas, "What Makes globalFEST So Interesting?" *All Things Considered*, January 16, 2014: "Let's get this out of the way: Even within the 'world music' community, *nobody* likes the term 'world music.' It smacks of all kinds of loaded issues, from cultural colonialism to questions about what's 'authentic' and what isn't. . . ."

618 See, for example, Ian Anderson, "International Pop Anyone?" *Guardian*, June 14, 2008.

619 For more on Cheb Mami, see his biographies on the AllMusic and Wikipedia websites; see also Andrew Hammond, *Pop Culture Arab World!: Media, Arts, and Lifestyle* (Santa Barbara, CA: ABC-CLIO, 2005), 148, 168.

620 For more on the rise and flowering of raï music, see Broughton, Ellingham, and Trillo, eds., *World Music*, vol. 1, 415ff; see also Hana Noor Al-Deen, "The Evolution of Rai Music," *Journal of Black Studies* 35, no. 5 (2005): 597–611.

621 Jon Pareles, "Youssou N'Dour Performs at the Brooklyn Academy of Music," *New York Times*, September 14, 2014. For more on the music and impact of Youssou N'Dour, see his biographies on the AllMusic and Wikipedia websites; see also Lucy Duran, "Key to N'Dour: Roots of the Senegalese Star," *Popular Music* 8, no. 3 (1989): 275–84.

622 For more on the griot tradition and its requisite demands of memorization, see for example, Thomas A. Hale, *Griots and Griottes: Masters of Words and Music* (Bloomington: Indiana University Press, 1998); and Jan Jansen, *The Griot's Craft: An Essay on Oral Tradition and Diplomacy*, vol. 8 of *Forschungen zu Sprachen und Kulturen Afrikas* (Hamburg: LIT Verlag, 2000). For griots in Senegal in particular, see Cornelia Panzacchi, "The Livelihoods of Traditional Griots in Modern Senegal," *Africa* 64, no. 2 (1994): 190–210.

623 For more on mbalax, see Broughton, Ellingham, and Trillo, eds., *World Music*, vol. 1, 617ff; see also Timothy Roark Mangin, *Mbalax: Cosmopolitanism in Senegalese Urban Popular Music* (dissertation, Columbia University, 2013).

624 Cited in Jon Pareles, "Hamza El Din, 76, Oud Player and Composer, Is Dead," *New York Times*, May 25, 2006. For more background on the life and music of Hamza El Din, see his biographies on the AllMusic and Wikipedia websites; see also Broughton, Ellingham, and Trillo, eds., *World Music*, vol. 1, 345–46.

625 See, for example, Richard H. Hoppin, *Medieval Music* (New York, W. W. Norton, 1978), 415–16.

626 For more on the theory and practice of the raga system, see, for example, Harold S. Powers and Richard Widdess, "Rāga," Grove Music Online; Broughton, Ellingham, and Trillo, eds., *World Music*, vol. 2, 65ff; and Reginald Massey and Jamila Massey, *The Music of India* (New Dehli: Abhinav Publications, 1996), 92–109.

627 For more on the concept and practice of tala, see Harold S. Powers and Richard Widdess, "Rhythm and Tāla," Grove Music Online; Broughton, Ellingham, and Trillo, eds., *World Music*, vol. 2, 65ff; and Massey and Massey, *The Music of India*, 110–14.

628 For more on the life and output of Ravi Shankar, see, for example, Stephen Slawek, "Shankar, Ravi," Grove Music Online; see also Ravi Shankar, *Raga Mala: The Autobiography of Ravi Shankar* (New York: HarperCollins, 1999). For more on the gharana sytem, see Massey, *The Music of India*, 69ff.

629 Rampal himself was no stranger to cross-cultural intersections, notably via his work with jazz composer-pianist Claude Bolling on his *Suite for Flute and Jazz Piano* (1975). A transcription and analysis of *Morning Love*, moreover, is the subject of a doctoral thesis: Bethany Padgett, *Transcription and Analysis of Ravi Shankar's Morning Love for Western Flute, Sitar, Tabla and Tanpura* (doctoral thesis, Louisiana State University, 2013).

## CHAPTER 15: THE CLASSICAL GENOTYPE

630 As will be seen via review of the WYLI supplement, however, the fifth work, Orff's "O Fortuna", utilizes dramatic choral forces.
631 A transcription of Bernstein's lecture "What Is Classical Music"—part of his New York Philharmonic Young People's Concert series, presented at Carnegie Hall on January 24, 1959—can be found on the www.leonardbernstein.com website; the video (in four parts) can be found on YouTube.
632 See, for example, Daniel Heartz and Bruce Alan Brown, "Classical," Grove Music Online; see also the "classical" entry on the Online Etymology Dictionary website.
633 For example, Vivaldi scholar Michael Talbot labels him "the most original and influential composer of his generation"; see Michael Talbot, "Vivaldi, Antonio," Grove Music Online. Among other broad overviews of Vivaldi's life and works, see H. C. Robbins Landon, *Vivaldi: Voice of the Baroque* (University of Chicago Press, 1996); Susan Adams, *Vivaldi: Red Priest of Venice* (Oxford: Lion Books, 2010); and the collection of scholarly essays: Michael Talbot, ed. *Vivaldi* (New York: Routledge, 2016).
634 For further background on the *L'estro armonico* (Opus 3) concertos, see Landon, *Vivaldi*, 42–48.
635 Michael Talbot, *Vivaldi*, Master Musicians Series (Oxford University Press, 2000), 40.
636 See, for example, Landon, *Vivaldi*, 44–45.
637 For more on BWV and other widely used catalogue abbreviations for prominent composers, see the WYLI website (Chapter 15, suppl., n. 637).
638 For caustic quips in this regard by the likes of Stravinsky and pianist Charles Rosen, see Joel Bixler, "On the Rating of Composers," Letter to the Editor, *New York Times*, April 26, 1987.
639 By a continuous "diatonic" run of the Circle of 4ths, I mean a "circle" that remains within the diatonic limitations of a single key—in this case B minor, with two sharps: F♯ and C♯. This means that rather than move from G to C, a sequence would move from G to C♯; as such there are only seven distinct chords/tones in a complete cycle of 4ths: B-E-A-D-G-C♯-F♯-(B). In measures 60 to 66, specifically, the twenty-three part "diatonic" Circle of 4ths proceeds: F#-B-E-A-D-G-C#-(3 times)-F#-B-E.
640 See, for example, Claude V. Palisca, *Baroque Music* (Englewood Cliffs, NJ: Prentice Hall, 1991), 168–69.
641 Slonimsky, *Lexicon of Musical Invective*, 52.
642 Douglas Johnson, Scott G. Burnham, William Drabkin, Joseph Kerman, and Alan Tyson, "Beethoven, Ludwig van," Grove Music Online. Among other useful introductory reviews of Beethoven's life, music, and legacy, see, for example, Maynard Solomon, *Beethoven* (London: Schirmer Trade Books, 2012); Lewis Lockwood, *Beethoven: The Music and the Life* (New York: W. W. Norton, 2005); and Jan Swafford, *Beethoven: Anguish and Triumph* (Boston: Houghton Mifflin Harcourt, 2014).
643 Solomon, *Beethoven*, 207–46.
644 For more on the "Heiligenstadt Testament" see Solomon, *Beethoven*, 145–63; see also Sean P. Harty et al., "The Psychology of Beethoven and The Eroica Symphony," *2017 Festschrift*, 1–9.
645 For more on the commonplace division of Beethoven's career into three stages—dating back to the 1840s by Anton Schindler, among the composer's earliest biographers—see, for example, Maynard Solomon, *Beethoven Essays* (Cambridge, MA: Harvard University Press, 1990), 116–25.
646 Instructive, for example, is the visual distinction—using "waveform graphics from audio recordings"—between Mozart's Symphony no. 40 (1788) and Beethoven's *Eroica* (1803) displayed by the BBC's *Discovering Music* website; as displayed, the extension took place especially via the striking length of the development and coda sections.
647 See, for example, Betsy Schwarm, "Symphony No. 7 in A Major, Op. 92." *Encyclopaedia Britannica* (website).
648 Leonard G. Ratner, *Romantic Music: Sound and Syntax* (New York: Simon & Schuster Books for Young Readers, 1992).
649 For a general review of classical music in the United States, see, for example, Richard Crawford et al., "United States of America," Grove Music Online; John Warthen Struble, *The History of American Classical Music: MacDowell through Minimalism* (New York: Facts on File, 1995); see also Kyle Gann, *American Music in the Twentieth Century* (San Francisco: Cengage Learning, 2005).

650 For a review of Copland's life, music, and legacy, see for example Howard Pollack, "Copland, Aaron," Grove Music Online; Aaron Copland and Vivian Perlis, *The Complete Copland* (Hillsdale, NY: Pendragon Press, 2013); and Howard Pollack, *Aaron Copland: The Life and Work of an Uncommon Man* (New York: Henry Holt & Company, 1999).
651 For a general review of Bernstein's life and multifaceted career, see, for example Paul R. Laird and David Schiff, "Bernstein, Leonard," Grove Music Online; Allen Shawn, *Leonard Bernstein: An American Musician* (New Haven, CT: Yale University Press, 2014); Meryle Secrest, *Leonard Bernstein: A Life* (Visalia, CA: Vintage, 1995); and Kenneth LaFave, *Experiencing Leonard Bernstein: A Listener's Companion* (Lanham, MD: Rowman & Littlefield, 2015).
652 See Carol J. Oja, *Bernstein Meets Broadway: Collaborative Art in a Time of War* (Oxford University Press, 2014).
653 See Nigel Simeone, *Leonard Bernstein: West Side Story* (New York: Routledge, 2017). For more on the music and legacy of Stephen Sondheim, see, for example, Joanne Gordon, ed. *Stephen Sondheim: A Casebook* (New York: Routledge, 2014); and Robert L. McLaughlin, *Stephen Sondheim and the Reinvention of the American Musical* (Jackson: University Press of Mississippi, 2016).
654 See LaFave, *Experiencing Leonard Bernstein*, 151ff. This unusual work also included acting, dancing, and left-leaning politics; sometimes, perhaps, eclecticism can go too far!
655 See, for example, Carol De Giere, *Defying Gravity: The Creative Career of Stephen Schwartz, from Godspell to Wicked* (New York: Applause Theatre & Cinema Books, 2008).
656 For Bernstein's most impactful educational and outreach efforts, see Leonard Bernstein, *Leonard Bernstein's Young People's Concerts* (Milwaukee, WI: Hal Leonard Corporation, 2005); and Leonard Bernstein, *The Unanswered Question: Six Talks at Harvard* (Cambridge, MA: Harvard University Press, 1976).
657 Louis Kronenberger, "New Operetta in Manhattan," *Time*, December 10, 1956. Similarly, Walter Kerr in the *New York Herald Tribune* (December 3, 1956) called her libretto "academic, blunt, and barefaced." By contrast, John Chapman of the *New York Daily News* (December 3, 1956) praised it as "strong, clear, and humorous." Cited in Elizabeth B. Crist, "The Best of All Possible Worlds: The Eldorado Episode in Leonard Bernstein's *Candide*," in *Opera after 1900*, ed. Margaret Notley (New York: Routledge, 2016), 435. For more on Bernstein's *Candide*, see, for example, Jon Alan Conrad, "Candide," Grove Music Online; and Helen Smith, *There's a Place for Us: The Musical Theatre Works of Leonard Bernstein* (New York: Routledge, 2017), 99–138.
658 For more on Voltaire's novella, see, for example, Voltaire, *Candide or Optimism*, trans. Theo Cuffe, with an introduction by Michael Wood (New York: Penguin, 2005).
659 For more on the Omnibus TV series and Bernstein's appearance, see the WYLI website (Chapter 15, suppl., n. 659).
660 Transcribed from Bernstein's *Omnibus* presentation "American Musical Comedy."
661 To wit, and as noted in Chapter 9, Bernstein calls Rodgers and Hammerstein's *Carousel* an operetta, but Loesser's *Guys & Dolls* a musical. Indeed, his own shows swapped material during their parallel creation: the music of "Gee, Officer Krupke," for example, was originally written for *Candide*, as was "One Hand, One Heart."
662 See www.musipedia.org
663 For a review of Fauré's life and music, see, for example, Jean-Michel Nectoux, "Fauré, Gabriel," Grove Music Online; Jean-Michel Nectoux, *Gabriel Fauré: A Musical Life*, trans. Roger Nichols (Cambridge: Cambridge University Press, 2004); and Gabriel Fauré, *Gabriel Fauré: His Life through His Letters*, ed. Jean-Michel Nectoux (London: Boyars, 1984).
664 Aaron Copland, "Gabriel Fauré, a Neglected Master," *Musical Quarterly* (1924): 573.
665 Such romantic impulses are often aligned with an overarching "longing for the infinite," articulated, for example, in the poetry and prose of German writers like Novalis and Schiller. See John C. Blankenagel, "The Dominant Characteristics of German Romanticism," *Publications of the Modern Language Association of America* 55, no. 1 (1940): 6. For more on musical romanticism in particular, see, for example, Walter Frisch, *Music in the Nineteenth Century* (New York: W. W. Norton, 2013); Leon Plantinga, *Romantic Music: A History of Musical Style in Nineteenth-Century Europe* (New York: W. W. Norton, 1984); and Carl Dahlhaus, *Nineteenth-Century Music* (Berkeley: University of California Press, 1989).
666 For this quote and more on the life and music of Brahms, see Jan Swafford, *Johannes Brahms: A Biography* (New York: Vintage, 2012), 80, etc.
667 Wagner too looked to Beethoven as inspiration—but more the revolutionary impulses of his later works, and especially the dramatic power of the Ninth Symphony. See, for example, Klaus Kropfinger, *Wagner and Beethoven: Richard Wagner's Reception of Beethoven* (Cambridge:

Cambridge University Press, 1991); see also, more explicitly, Richard Wagner, *Richard Wagner's Beethoven*, trans. Roger Allen (1870; Rochester, NY: Boydell & Brewer Ltd, 2014).

668 For a more general review of Wagner's music and legacy, see Barry Millington et al., "Wagner, (Wilhelm) Richard," Grove Music Online; and Thomas S. Grey, ed., *Richard Wagner and His World* (Princeton University Press, 2009).

669 For possible sources of Proust's "Sonate de Vinteuil," including by Fauré, see Jean-Jacques Nattiez, *Proust as Musician* (Cambridge: Cambridge University Press, 1989), 3–4.

670 By means of this repertoire, of course, Fauré helped pave the way for the more pronounced harmonic and formal musical revolution ushered in by his younger contemporaries, Debussy and Ravel. See also Jann Pasler, "Impressionism," Grove Music Online.

671 Poulenc, along with composers Darius Milhaud, Arthur Honegger, and others, formed a kind of composer collective called Les Six, which thrived in Paris in the 1920s—largely under the influence of that other early twentieth-century French revolutionary, Erik Satie. For more on Satie and Les Six, see, for example, Robert Shapiro, ed., *Les Six: The French Composers and Their Mentors Jean Cocteau and Erik Satie* (London: Peter Owen Publishers, 2014).

672 See Sigismond Stojowski, "Recollections of Brahms," *Musical Quarterly* 19, no. 2 (1933): 143–50.

673 Robert Orledge, "Fauré's 'Pelléas et Mélisande,'" *Music & Letters* (1975): 170–79.

674 Cited in Orledge, "Fauré's 'Pelléas et Mélisande,'" 172.

675 See, for example, Lorraine Byrne Bodley, ed., *Music in Goethe's Faust: Goethe's Faust in Music* (Woodbridge, England: Boydell & Brewer, 2017).

676 See, for example, David Fanning, "Expressionism," Grove Music Online.

677 Nectoux, *Gabriel Fauré*, 155–56.

678 For more on Lefèvre's novel (more modal) conception of harmony and its influence on Fauré, see Nectoux, *Gabriel Fauré*, 227ff; see also James Sobaskie, "The Emergence of Gabriel Faure's Late Musical Style and Technique," *Journal of Musicological Research* 22, no. 3 (2003): 223–76.

679 For more on Fauré's continued attacks on Debussy, and the rather quizzical "full circle" they make with the attacks lobbed at this much-beloved composer cited in Introduction, see the WYLI website (Chapter 15, suppl., n. 679).

## INTERLUDE G: MIND OVER MUSIC: PSYCHOLOGY AND MUSICAL TASTE

680 Deryck Cooke, *The Language of Music* (Oxford University Press, 1959), 25.

681 Aristotle, *Politics*, 341a. See also Sheramy Bundrick, *Music and Image in Classical Athens* (Cambridge: Cambridge University Press, 2005), 41–42.

682 Strunk, *Source Readings*, 5.

683 For example, the fifth-century BCE Indian treatise, the *Natya Shastra*, directly correlates certain modes (ragas) and musical forms with specific emotions and aesthetic states aroused in the listener. See Alessia Pannese et al., "Metaphor and Music Emotion: Ancient Views and Future Directions," *Consciousness and Cognition* 44 (2016): 61–71; we'll have more to say on insights gained from ancient Indian practice below.

684 Kate Hevner, "Experimental Studies of the Elements of Expression in Music," *American Journal of Psychology* 48, no. 2 (1936): 246–68.

685 Edward P. Asmus, "The Development of a Multidimensional Instrument for the Measurement of Affective Responses to Music," *Psychology of Music* 13, no. 1 (1985): 19–30.

686 See John Sloboda, *Exploring the Musical Mind: Cognition, Emotion, Ability, Function* (Oxford University Press, 2005), 203.

687 For a good review of these arguments, see Marcel Zentner, Didier Grandjean, and Klaus R. Scherer, "Emotions Evoked by the Sound of Music: Characterization, Classification, and Measurement," *Emotion* 8, no. 4 (2008): 494–521.

688 For direct articulation of this problem, as a common academic conflation between "emotion expression-perception, and emotion induction-experience," see Pannese et al., "Metaphor and Music Emotion," 62.

689 See Jerrold Levinson, *Suffering Art Gladly: The Paradox of Negative Emotion in Art* (London: Springer, 2013).

690 David Huron, "Why Is Sad Music Pleasurable? A Possible Role for Prolactin," *Musicae Scientiae* 15, no. 2 (2011): 153.

691 See, for example, the "Commercials I Hate" message board; see also Dan Ozzi, "1-877-KARS-4-KIDS: Behind the Most Hated (and Best) Jingle of All Time," *Noisey Vice* (website), November 11, 2015.

692 See Elizabeth Blair, "Chopin's Iconic Funeral March," *NPR Music* (website), March 1, 2010.
693 See, for example, James A. Russell, "A Circumplex Model of Affect," *Journal of Personality and Social Psychology* 39, no. 6 (1980): 1161–78; Lisa Barrett Feldman, "Solving the Emotion Paradox: Categorization and the Experience of Emotion," *Personality and Social Psychology Review* 10, no. 1 (2006): 20–46; and Nico H. Frijda, "Emotion Experience and Its Varieties," *Emotion Review* 1, no. 3 (2009): 264–71.
694 See James A. Russell, "Core Affect and the Psychological Construction of Emotion," *Psychological Review* 110, no. 1 (2003): 147; see also Panteleimon Ekkekakis, *The Measurement of Affect, Mood, and Emotion: A Guide for Health-Behavioral Research* (Cambridge: Cambridge University Press, 2013), 38–40.
695 See Ekkekakis, *The Measurement of Affect, Mood, and Emotion*, 33–51, for a fuller discussion of affect, emotion, and mood.
696 Zentner, Grandjean, and Scherer, "Emotions Evoked by the Sound of Music," 495.
697 Patrik N. Juslin, "What Does Music Express? Basic Emotions and Beyond," *Frontiers in Psychology* 4 (2013): 4.
698 See Juslin, "What Does Music Express?" For more on the relationship between Juslin's emotional coding types and Hatten and Koelsch's semantic coding types (Interlude C), see the WYLI website (Interlude G, suppl., n. 698).
699 Juslin, "What Does Music Express?" 4.
700 See Patrik N. Juslin and Petri Laukka, "Communication of Emotions in Vocal Expression and Music Performance: Different Channels, Same Code?" *Psychological Bulletin* 129, no. 5 (2003): 770.
701 Juslin, "What Does Music Express?," 4.
702 See Patrik N. Juslin, "From Everyday Emotions to Aesthetic Emotions: Towards a Unified Theory of Musical Emotions," *Physics of Life Reviews* 10, no. 3 (2013): 235–66.
703 For more on the role of metaphor as a "mediator" between music, language, emotion, and our aesthetic response, see Pannese et al., "Metaphor and Music Emotion."
704 See Juslin, "From Everyday Emotions to Aesthetic Emotions," 242–43.
705 Juslin, "From Everyday Emotions to Aesthetic Emotions," 247.
706 Zentner, Grandjean, and Scherer, "Emotions Evoked by the Sound of Music," 494.
707 See, for example, Paul Ekman, "An Argument for Basic Emotions," *Cognition and Emotion* 6, no. 3–4 (1992), 169–200; and Robert Plutchik, *The Emotions*, rev. ed. (Lanham, MD: University Press of America, 1991).
708 See, for example, Tuomas Eerola and Jonna K. Vuoskoski, "A Review of Music and Emotion Studies: Approaches, Emotion Models, and Stimuli," *Music Perception* 30, no. 3 (2013): 307–40.
709 Zentner, Grandjean, and Scherer, "Emotions Evoked by the Sound of Music."
710 For more on the relationship between music and melancholy, dating back at least to Robert Burton's *The Anatomy of Melancholy* (1621), see Stephanie Shirilan, *Robert Burton and the Transformative Powers of Melancholy* (London: Routledge, 2016); see also Michael P. Steinberg, "Music and Melancholy," *Critical Inquiry* 40, no. 2 (2014): 288–310.
711 Steinberg, "Music and Melancholy," 289, 310.
712 Juslin, "What Does Music Express?," 11.
713 See, for example, Juslin and Laukka, "Communication of Emotions"; and Emery Schubert, "Modeling Perceived Emotion with Continuous Musical Features," *Music Perception: An Interdisciplinary Journal* 21, no. 4 (2004): 561–85.
714 Those curious, however, can see Markus Schedl et al., "On the Interrelation between Listener Characteristics and the Perception of Emotions in Classical Orchestra Music," *IEEE Transactions on Affective Computing* (2017): 1–18.
715 See also Anthony Tommasini, "Bombshells Felt in the Balcony: Readers Name Some Favorite Musical Surprises of Their Own," *New York Times*, April 25, 2014.
716 Meyer, *Emotion and Meaning in Music*, 43.
717 Cited in Huron, *Sweet Anticipation*, 11.
718 Luke Harrison and Psyche Loui, "Thrills, Chills, Frissons, and Skin Orgasms: Toward an Integrative Model of Transcendent Psychophysiological Experiences in Music," *Frontiers in Psychology* 5 (2014): 790.
719 See Altenmüller et al., "A Contribution to the Evolutionary Basis of Music," 323.
720 See, for example, Patrik N. Juslin and John A. Sloboda, "Music and Emotion," in *The Psychology of Music*, 3rd ed., ed. Diana Deutsch (Oxford: Elsevier, 2013): 583–645; Oliver Grewe et al., "Listening to Music as a Re-Creative Process: Physiological, Psychological, and Psychoacoustical

Correlates of Chills and Strong Emotions," *Music Perception* 24, no. 3 (2007): 297–314; and Jaak Panksepp, "The Emotional Sources of 'Chills' Induced by Music," *Music Perception* 13, no. 2 (1995): 171–207.

721 Robert B. Zajonc, "Attitudinal Effects of Mere Exposure," *Journal of Personality and Social Psychology* 9, no. 2 (1968): 1–27.

722 Zajonc, "Feeling and Thinking."

723 Notably, David Hargreaves, Karl Szpunar, E. Glenn Schellenberg, and David Huron. Schellenberg and Isabelle Peretz, "Liking for Happy-and-Sad-Sounding Music: Effects of Exposure," *Cognition and Emotion* 22, no. 2 (2008): 218–37.

724 Robert F. Bornstein and Paul R. D'Agostino, "The Attribution and Discounting of Perceptual Fluency: Preliminary Tests of a Perceptual Fluency/Attributional Model of the Mere Exposure Effect," *Social Cognition* 12, no. 2 (1994): 103.

725 Huron, *Sweet Anticipation*, 137.

726 Huron, *Sweet Anticipation*, 138–39.

727 See Karl K. Szpunar, E. Glenn Schellenberg, and Patricia Pliner, "Liking and Memory for Musical Stimuli as a Function of Exposure," *Journal of Experimental Psychology: Learning, Memory, and Cognition* 30, no. 2 (2004): 370–81; see also Daniel E. Berlyne, *Aesthetics and Psychobiology* (New York: Appleton-Century-Crofts, 1971).

728 Berlyne, *Aesthetics and Psychobiology*, 70.

729 Raymond B. Cattell and David R. Saunders, "Musical Preferences and Personality Diagnosis: I. A Factorization of One Hundred and Twenty Themes," *Journal of Social Psychology* 39, no. 1 (1954): 6; see also Raymond B. Cattell, "A Shortened 'Basic English' Version (Form C) of the 16 PF Questionnaire," *Journal of Social Psychology* 44, no. 2 (1956): 257–78.

730 Cattell, "Musical Preferences and Personality Diagnosis," 17.

731 Raymond B. Cattell and Jean C. Anderson, "The Measurement of Personality and Behavior Disorders by the I.P.A.T. Music Preference Test," *Journal of Applied Psychology* 37, no. 6 (1953): 446–54.

732 Patrick Litle and Marvin Zuckerman, "Sensation Seeking and Music Preferences," *Personality and Individual Differences* 7, no. 4 (1986): 575–78.

733 See, especially, Peter J. Rentfrow and Samuel D. Gosling, "The Do Re Mi's of Everyday Life: The Structure and Personality Correlates of Music Preferences," *Journal of Personality and Social Psychology* 84, no. 6 (2003): 1236–56.

734 The Big Five/FFM (1989) has become the most widely used framework among researchers dealing with personality issues among health participants; its prominence in music research is thus aligned with its overall research popularity, and not due to any specifically musical orientation.

735 For more on Jung's theories of psychological types, including their relationship to his broader output, see, for example, Clare Crellin, *Jung's Theory of Personality: A Modern Reappraisal* (Sussex, England: Routledge, 2014). The more dedicated can also review Carl Jung, *Psychological Types*, ed. R. F. C. Hull, trans. H. G. Baynes (Oxford: Taylor & Francis, 2016).

736 In the order presented here, the five traits spell out the commonly used acronym "OCEAN." For a broad overview on the Big Five model, see, for example, Boele de Raad, *The Big Five Personality Factors: The Psycholexical Approach to Personality* (Ashland, OR: Hogrefe & Huber Publishers, 2000). For more info and background on the Big Five, see also the WYLI website (Interlude G, suppl., n. 736).

737 Rentfrow and Gosling, "The Do Re Mi's of Everyday Life."

738 See Darren George et al., "The Association between Types of Music Enjoyed and Cognitive, Behavioral, and Personality Factors of Those Who Listen," *Psychomusicology* 19, no. 2 (2007): 32–56; Marc J. M. H. Delsing et al., "Adolescents' Music Preferences and Personality Characteristics," *European Journal of Personality* 22, no. 2 (2008): 109–30; and Peter Gregory Dunn et al., "Toward a Better Understanding of the Relation between Music Preference, Listening Behavior, and Personality," *Psychology of Music* 40, no. 4 (2012): 411–28, respectively.

739 See Peter J. Rentfrow, Lewis R. Goldberg, and Daniel J. Levitin, "The Structure of Musical Preferences: A Five-Factor Model." *Journal of Personality and Social Psychology* 100, no. 6 (2011): 1139–75; and, importantly, the follow-up paper, Peter J. Rentfrow, Lewis R. Goldberg, David J. Stillwell, Michal Kosinski, Samuel D. Gosling, and Daniel J. Levitin, "The Song Remains the Same: A Replication and Extension of the MUSIC Model," *Music Perception* 30, no. 2 (2012): 161–85.

740 Adrian C. North and David J. Hargreaves, "Lifestyle Correlates of Musical Preference: 1.

Relationships, Living Arrangements, Beliefs, and Crime," *Psychology of Music* 35, no. 1 (2007): 58–87.

741 Rentfrow et al., "The Song Remains the Same," 166.

742 For discussion of a somewhat curious discrepency between Rentfrow's 2011 and 2102 studies, see the WYLI website (Interlude G, suppl., n. 742).

743 For the full list of attributes aligned with the pan-genre MUSIC factors, see Rentfrow et al., "The Song Remains the Same," Table 2.

744 Rentfrow and Gosling, "The Do Re Mi's of Everyday Life," Table 3.

745 Rentfrow and Gosling, "The Do Re Mi's of Everyday Life," 1251.

746 George et al., "The Association between Types of Music," 47–49.

747 Dunn et al., "Toward a Better Understanding," 15–16.

748 Adrian C. North, "Individual Differences in Musical Taste," *American Journal of Psychology* 123, no. 2 (2010): 199–208.

749 Rentfrow and Gosling, "The Do Re Mi's of Everyday Life," 1252.

750 As a kind of preview to the discussion that follows, for those interested: see my summary of a recent meta-analysis led by Thomas Schäfer—yielding a negative conclusion—on the WYLI website (Interlude G, suppl., n. 750). Or see the actual article: Schäfer, Thomas, and Claudia Mehlhorn. "Can personality traits predict musical style preferences? A meta-analysis." *Personality and Individual Differences* 116 (2017): 265–73.

751 David M. Greenberg, Daniel J. Levitin, and Peter J. Rentfrow et al., "The Song Is You: Preferences for Musical Attribute Dimensions Reflect Personality," *Social Psychological and Personality Science* 7, no. 6 (2016): 597–605.

752 For the full account of correlations between the personality and musical preference factors, see Greenberg et al., "The Song Is You," 601.

753 For my discussion of the curious disconnect I've found between music scholars working in the field of subculture/interculture and those working in the psychology space, as well as the related citation of demographic variables by the latter group, see the WYLI website (Interlude G, suppl., n. 753).

754 David M. Greenberg, Simon Baron-Cohen, Peter J. Rentfrow, et al., "Musical Preferences Are Linked to Cognitive Styles," *PloS one* 10, no. 7 (2015): 1–22. To understand some of the controversy surrounding this theory, see also Simon Baron-Cohen et al., "Sex Differences in the Brain: Implications for Explaining Autism," *Science* 310, no. 5749 (2005): 819–23; and Cordelia Fine, *Delusions of Gender: How Our Minds, Society, and Neurosexism Create Difference* (New York: W. W. Norton, 2010).

755 Greenberg et al., "Musical Preferences Are Linked to Cognitive Styles," 9.

756 David M. Greenberg et al., "Personality Predicts Musical Sophistication," *Journal of Research in Personality* 58 (2015): 154–58.

757 Adrian C. North, "Individual Differences in Musical Taste," 16–17.

758 Durgesh K. Upadhyay et al., "Exploring the Nature of Music Engagement and Its Relation to Personality among Young Adults," *International Journal of Adolescence and Youth* 22, no. 4 (2017): 484–96.

759 For example, Greenberg et al., "The Song Is You," 602: "One way of expanding the scope of musical attributes is to examine the sonic attributes in music (e.g., timbre and instrumentation). This is similar to how the Music Genome Project codes music for Pandora, the Internet radio, and streaming interface."

760 For some background on Echo Nest, for example, see Thierry Bertin-Mahieux et al., "The Million Song Dataset," Proceedings of the 12th International Society for Music Information Retrieval Conference (2011): 591–96.

761 Further, my approach to specifying personality in these studies will extend beyond the Big Five model alone. Instead, I will attempt to incorporate a fairly recent approach to personality definition known as "whole trait theory," developed principally by William Fleeson. For more on this theory, see, for example, William Fleeson and Eranda Jayawickreme, "Whole Trait Theory," *Journal of Research in Personality* 56 (2015): 82–92.

## CHAPTER 16: THE WHAT AND WHY OF MUSICAL TASTE

762 See, for example, the insignificant results in Warren Prince's classic 1974 study on the attitudes of junior high school students toward atonal music after a music appreciation class: Warren F. Prince, "Effects of Guided Listening on Musical Enjoyment of Junior High School Students," *Journal of Research in Music Education* 22, no. 1 (1974): 45–51; see also Leif Finnäs, "How Can Musical Preferences Be Modified? A Research Review," *Bulletin of the Council for Research in Music Education* 102 (1989): 1–58.

763 To be precise, the average number of thumbs-up for "highly active" Pandora users—the largest category of "active" listeners—is 482.7; averages for "medium" and "lightly" active users are 238.4 and 160.9, respectively. Those considered in these calculations have been Pandora subscribers for between one and six years; my thanks to Steve Hogan and Pandora data scientist Gordon Rios for providing these numbers.

764 Audio-Technica, "Official Study Reveals That the Average Person Will Spend 13 Years of Their Lives Listening to Music," *RealWire* press release, April 18, 2012.

765 Gene Weingarten, "Pearls Before Breakfast: Can One of the Nation's Great Musicians Cut through the Fog of a D.C. Rush Hour? Let's Find Out," *Washington Post*, April 8, 2007.

## EPILOGUE: LIVING WITH MUSIC

766 See Arthur Schopenhauer, *The World as Will and Idea*, trans. R. B. Haldane and J. Kemp, vol. 1 (London: Routledge, 1964), 134. See also Edward A. Lippman, *A History of Western Musical Aesthetics* (Lincoln: University of Nebraska Press, 1992), 233–36 (Hegel); and Martin Scherzinger, ed., *Music in Contemporary Philosophy* (Oxford: Routledge, 2016): 81–94 (Lyotard), 105–116 (Žižek).

767 Oliver Sacks, "The Power of Music," *Brain* 129, no. 10 (2006): 2532.

768 Sacks, *Musicophilia*, 373.

769 Cited in Andrew Schulman, *Waking the Spirit: A Musician's Journey Healing Body, Mind, and Soul* (New York: Macmillan, 2016), xi.

770 Jackie Pigeaud, "The Tradition of Ancient Music Therapy in the 18th Century," in *The Emotional Power of Music: Multidisciplinary Perspectives on Musical Arousal, Expression, and Social Control* (Oxford University Press, 2013): 315.

771 See Martin West, "Music Therapy in Antiquity," in *Music as Medicine: The History of Music Therapy Since Antiquity*, ed. Peregrine Horden (New York: Routledge, 2017), 51–68.

772 Strunk, *Source Readings*, 79–86. Today, the third type of music is commonly identified as "*musica instrumentalis*," not "*musica instrumentis*"—which is how Boethius indicated it. The alternate term seems to have been first used in a treatise, contained within a letter—an *Epistola cum tracta de musica*—written around 1026 by Adalbold, bishop of Utrecht: "*Sunt enim tres species musicae mundana, humana, instrumentalis.*" No explanation is given for his change from Boethius, if it was even noticed; yet from this period the latter form becomes standard. See Gabriela Ilnitchi, "Musica Mundana, Aristotelian Natural Philosophy and Ptolemaic Astronomy," *Early Music History* 21 (2002): 37–74.

773 Ilnitchi, "Musica Mundana," 85.

774 Donatella Restani, "Embryology as a Paradigm for Boethius' *Musica Humana*," *Greek and Ron Musical Studies* 4, no. 2 (2016): 161–90.

775 See Donatella Lippi et al., "Music and Medicine," *Journal of Multidisciplinary Healthcare* 3 (2010): 139.

776 Lippi et al., "Music and Medicine," 139. See also Elizabeth A. Williams, *A Cultural History o Medical Vitalism in Enlightenment Montpellier* (Oxford: Routledge, 2017).

777 J. L. Roger's *Traité des effets de la musique sur le corps humain* (1803); cited in Lippi et al., "M and Medicine," 139.

778 Lippi et al., "Music and Medicine," 139; see also Claudius Conrad, "Music for Healing: Fr Magic to Medicine," *Lancet* 376, no. 9757 (2010): 1980–81.

779 For an introduction to modern music therapy, see, for example, Leslie Bunt and Brynjulf S *Music Therapy: An Art beyond Words*, 2nd ed. (East Sussex, England: Routledge, 2014); see Penelope Gouk, ed., *Musical Healing in Cultural Contexts* (Oxford: Routledge, 2017).

780 Helen Lindquist Bonny, "Music and Healing," *Music Therapy* 6, no. 1 (1986): 4.

781 Lippi et al., "Music and Medicine," 137–38.
782 For more on the Orff approach to music therapy, see Cynthia M. Colwell et al., "The Orff Approach to Music Therapy," *Introduction to Approaches in Music Therapy*, 2nd ed., ed. Alice-Ann Darrow (Silver Spring, MD: American Music Therapy Association, 2008): 11–24; for a recent application of the Kodály approach to music therapy, see Natee Chiengchana and Somchai Trakarnrung,"The Effect of Kodály-Based Music Experiences on Joint Attention in Children with Autism Spectrum Disorders," *Asian Biomedicine* 8, no. 4 (2014): 547–55.
783 For a thorough review of NMT, see Michael H. Thaut and Volker Hoemberg, eds., *Handbook of Neurologic Music Therapy* (Oxford University Press, 2014).
784 Shih-Tzu Huang, Marion Good, and Jaclene A. Zauszniewski, "The Effectiveness of Music in Relieving Pain in Cancer Patients: A Randomized Controlled Trial," *International Journal of Nursing Studies* 47, no. 11 (2010): 1354–62.
785 Conrad, "Music for Healing," 1981.
786 See also the documentary surrounding its inception and performance: "The Collectors: Breaking Music Down To Its Genes" available on the FiveThirtyEight website.
787 Rossato-Bennett's film *Alive Inside: A Story of Music and Memory* chronicles, and now helps advocate for, the music therapy work done by the Music & Memory organization, led by Dan Cohen. *Alive Inside* illustrates the power of music to stir patients otherwise "shut down" by dementia and Alzheimer's disease. Schulman's inspiring story and subsequent music therapy work is detailed in Schulman, *Waking the Spirit*.
788 Strunk, *Source Readings*, 84.
789 Strunk, *Source Readings*, 85. Following this statement, Boethius adds: "This also I shall take up later." Yet, in fact, he never returns to the subject.
790 See Melissa K. Weinberg and Dawn Joseph, "If You're Happy and You Know It: Music Engagement and Subjective Wellbeing," *Psychology of Music* 45, no. 2 (2017): 257–67. For more on subjective well-being homeostasis theory, see Robert A. Cummins, "Subjective Wellbeing, Homeostatically Protected Mood and Depression: A Synthesis," *Journal of Happiness Studies* 11, no. 1 (2010): 1–17.
791 TanChyuan Chin and Nikki S. Rickard, "Emotion Regulation Strategy Mediates Both Positive and Negative Relationships between Music Uses and Well-Being," *Psychology of Music* 42, no. 5 (2014): 692–713.
792 Chin and Rickard, "Emotion Regulation Strategy," 695.
793 Aligned with the present "crisis" in music education, in the US at least, is the decline in liberal arts education generally for our youth—as discussed, for example, in Fareed Zakaria, *In Defense of a Liberal Education* (New York: W. W. Norton, 2015), 150.
794 Walker, "The Song Decoders."

# INDEX